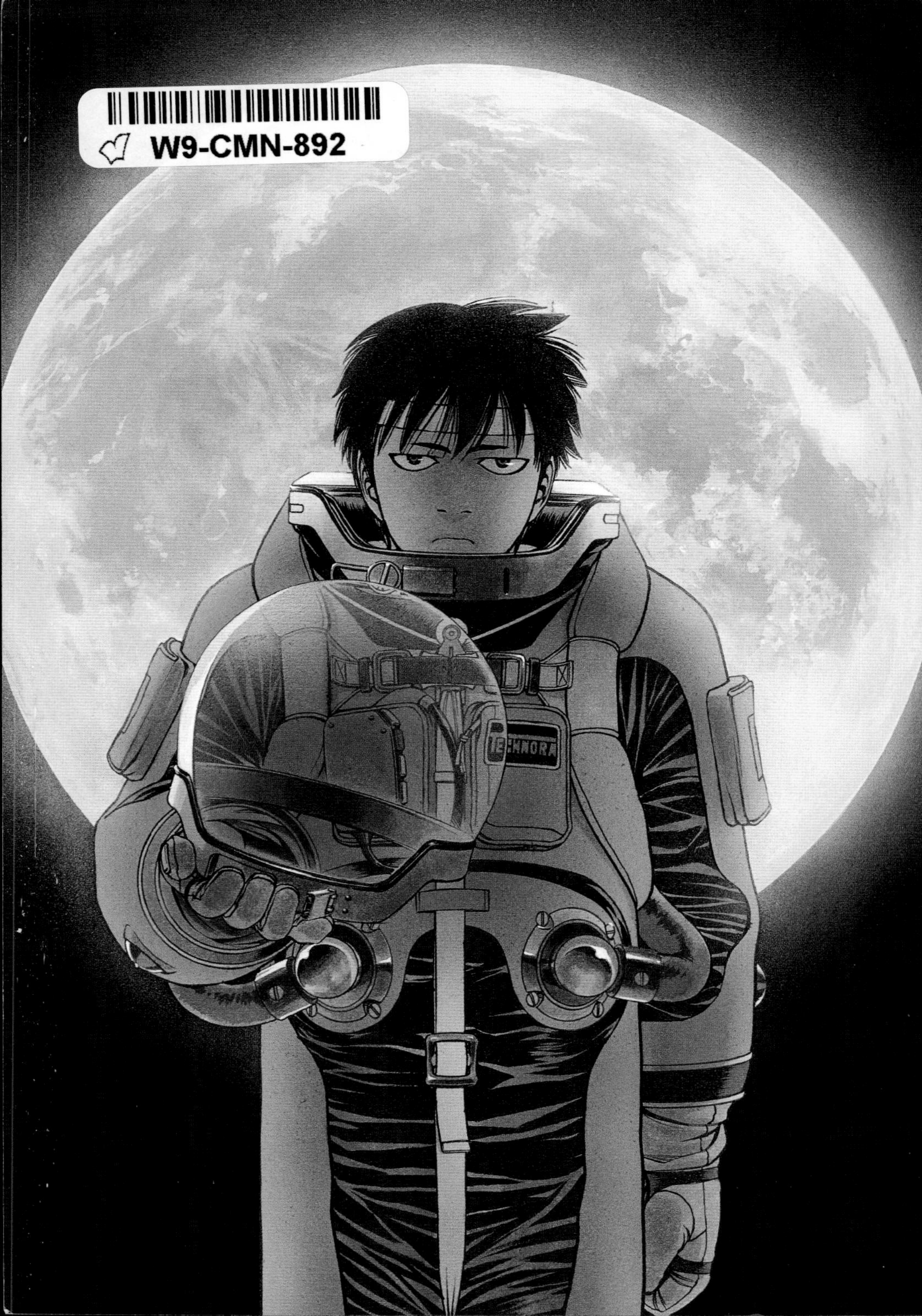

CONTENTS

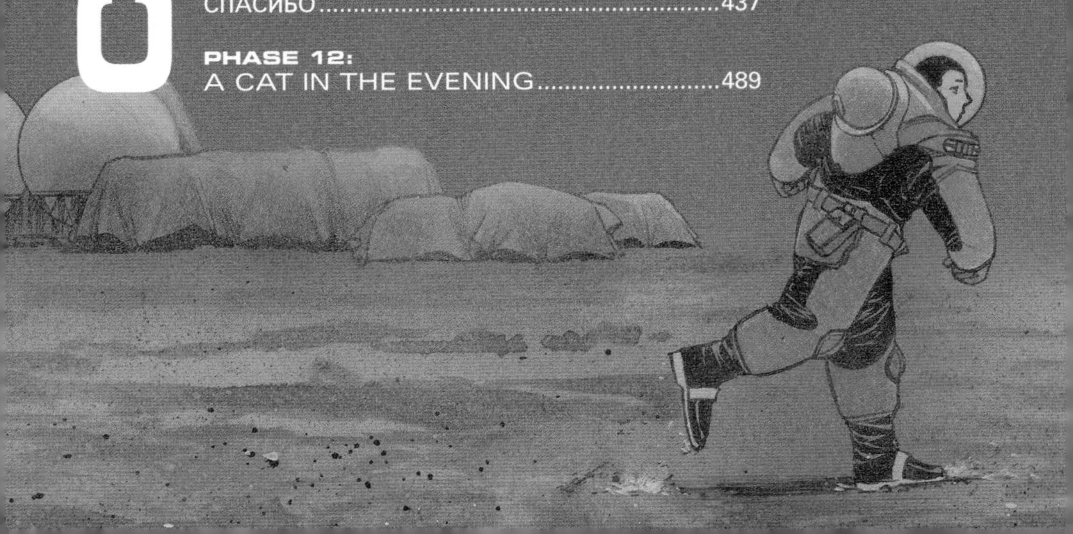

PLANETES

PLANETES

STORY AND ART
MAKOTO YUKIMURA

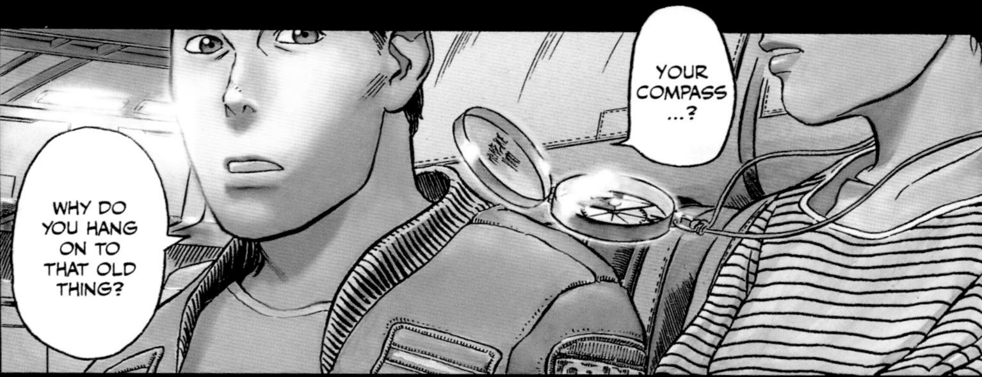
YOUR COMPASS ...?
WHY DO YOU HANG ON TO THAT OLD THING?

July 13, 2068.

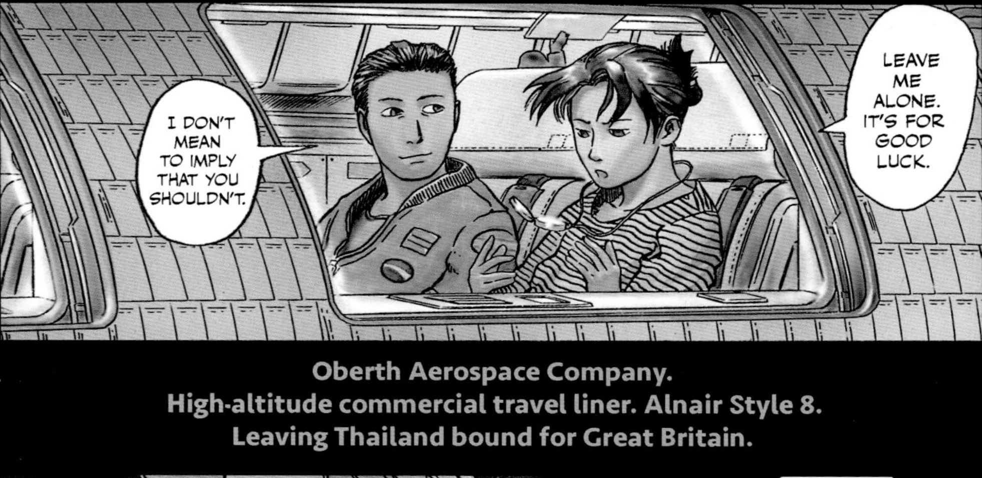
LEAVE ME ALONE. IT'S FOR GOOD LUCK.
I DON'T MEAN TO IMPLY THAT YOU SHOULDN'T.

Oberth Aerospace Company.
High-altitude commercial travel liner. Alnair Style 8.
Leaving Thailand bound for Great Britain.

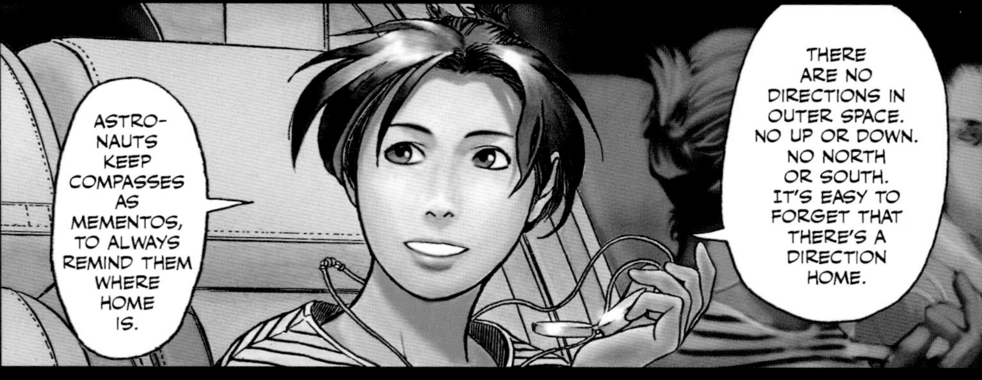
THERE ARE NO DIRECTIONS IN OUTER SPACE. NO UP OR DOWN. NO NORTH OR SOUTH. IT'S EASY TO FORGET THAT THERE'S A DIRECTION HOME.
ASTRO-NAUTS KEEP COMPASSES AS MEMENTOS, TO ALWAYS REMIND THEM WHERE HOME IS.

Altitude: 150 km.
Well into Earth's ionosphere.

PHASE 1
A STARDUST SKY

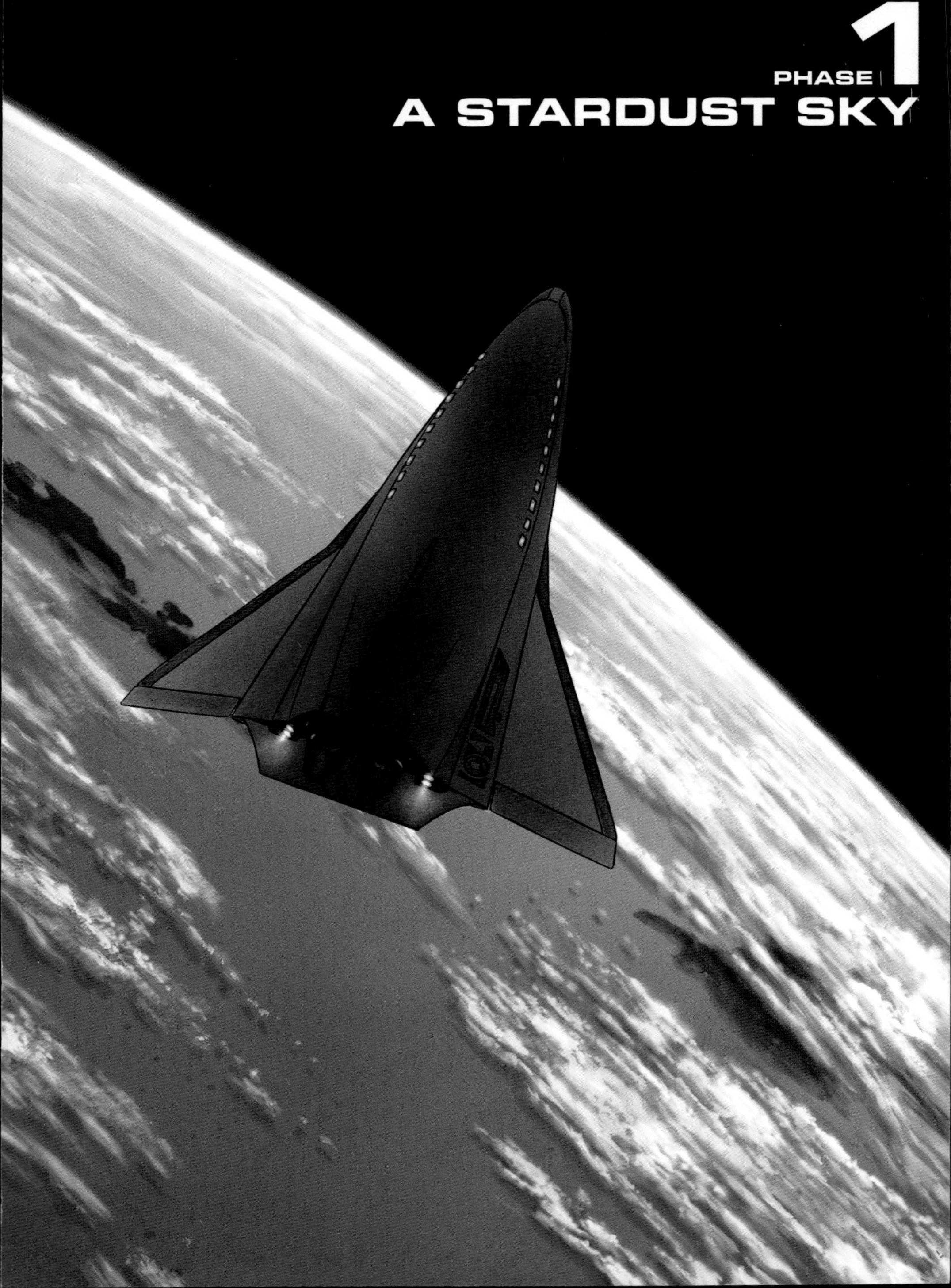

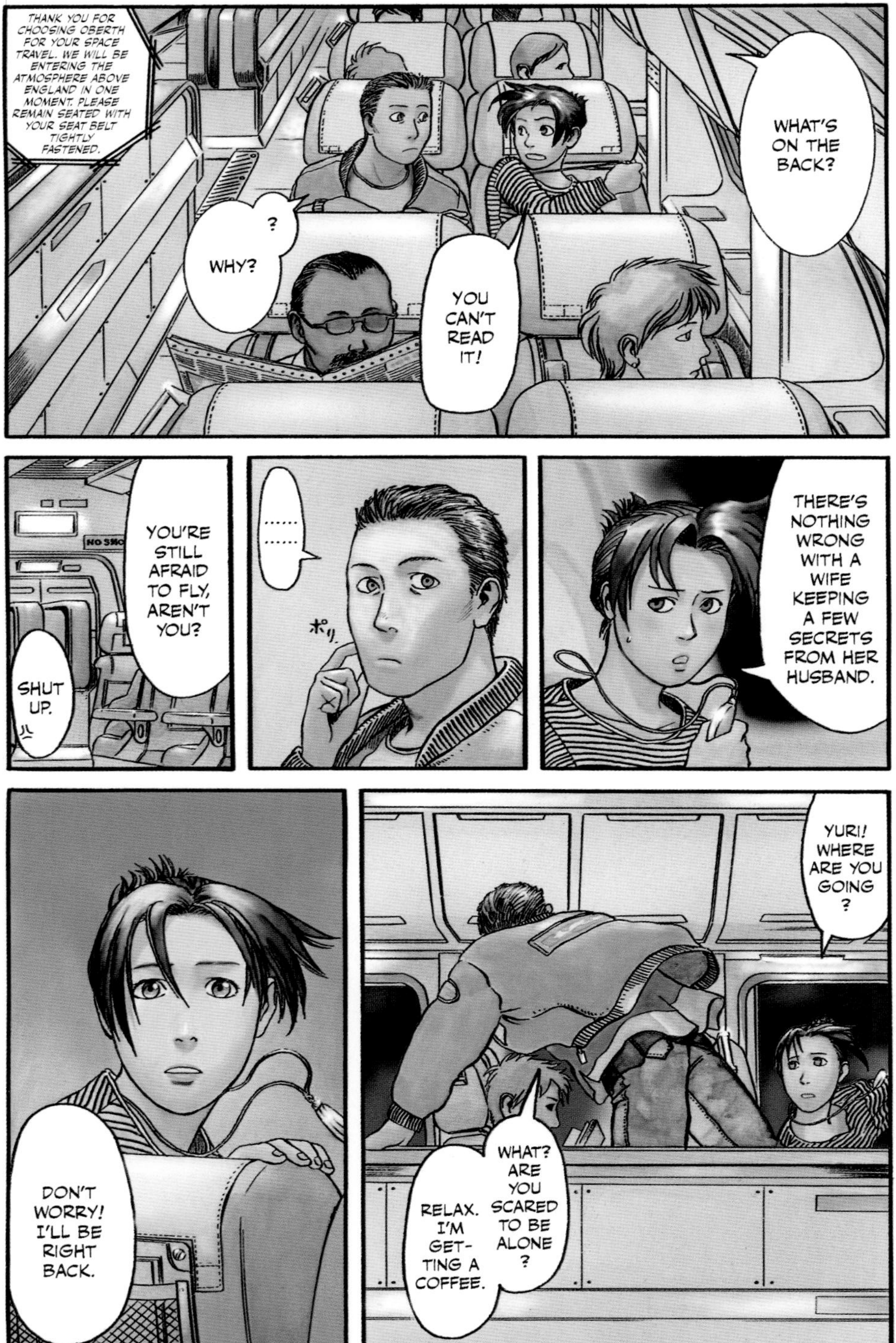
WHAT'S ON THE BACK?
?
WHY?
YOU CAN'T READ IT!
THANK YOU FOR CHOOSING OBERTH FOR YOUR SPACE TRAVEL. WE WILL BE ENTERING THE ATMOSPHERE ABOVE ENGLAND IN ONE MOMENT. PLEASE REMAIN SEATED WITH YOUR SEAT BELT TIGHTLY FASTENED.
THERE'S NOTHING WRONG WITH A WIFE KEEPING A FEW SECRETS FROM HER HUSBAND.
....
ポリ
YOU'RE STILL AFRAID TO FLY, AREN'T YOU?
SHUT UP.
YURI! WHERE ARE YOU GOING ?
WHAT? ARE YOU SCARED TO BE ALONE ?
RELAX. I'M GET-TING A COFFEE.
DON'T WORRY! I'LL BE RIGHT BACK.

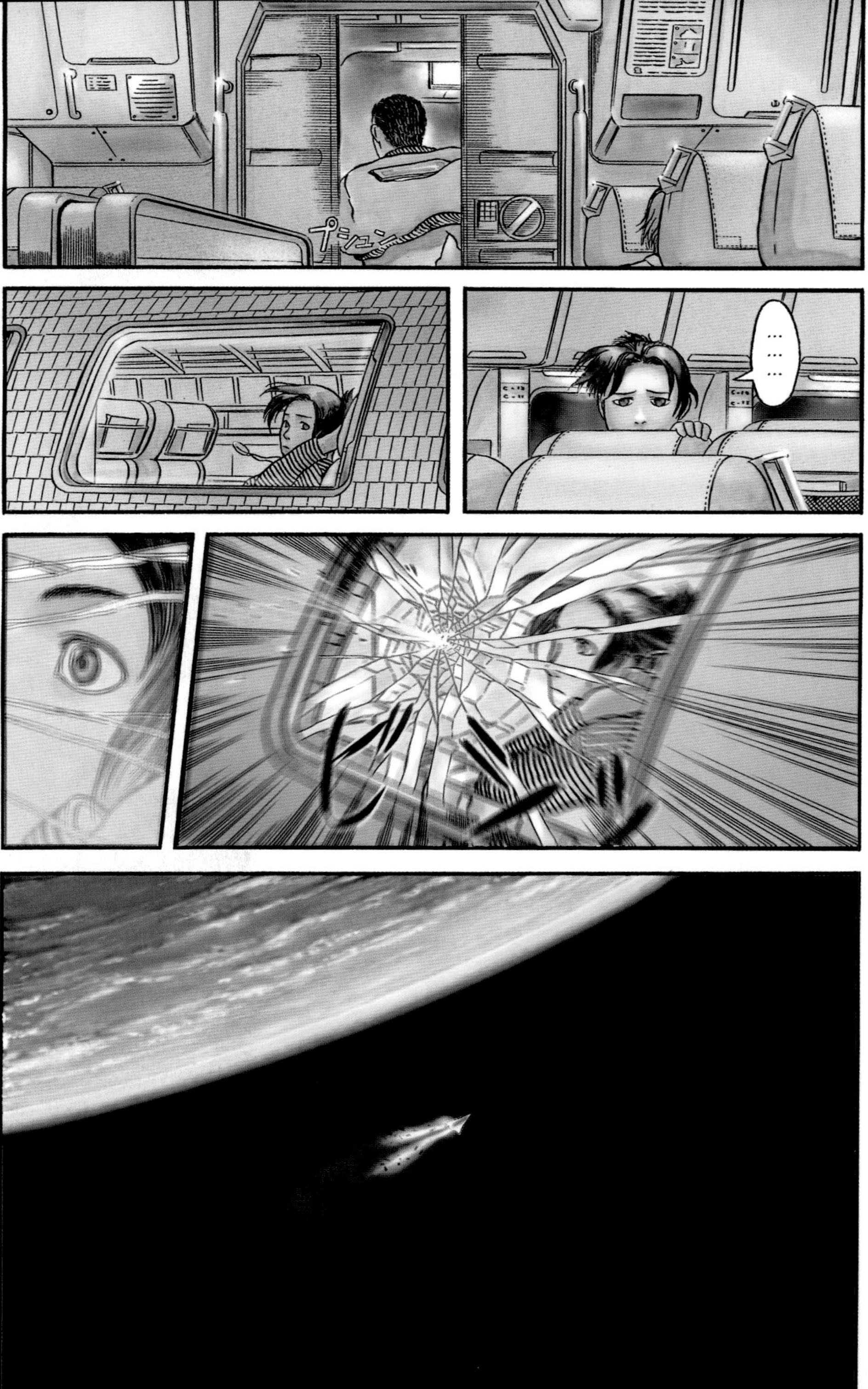
プシュー
………

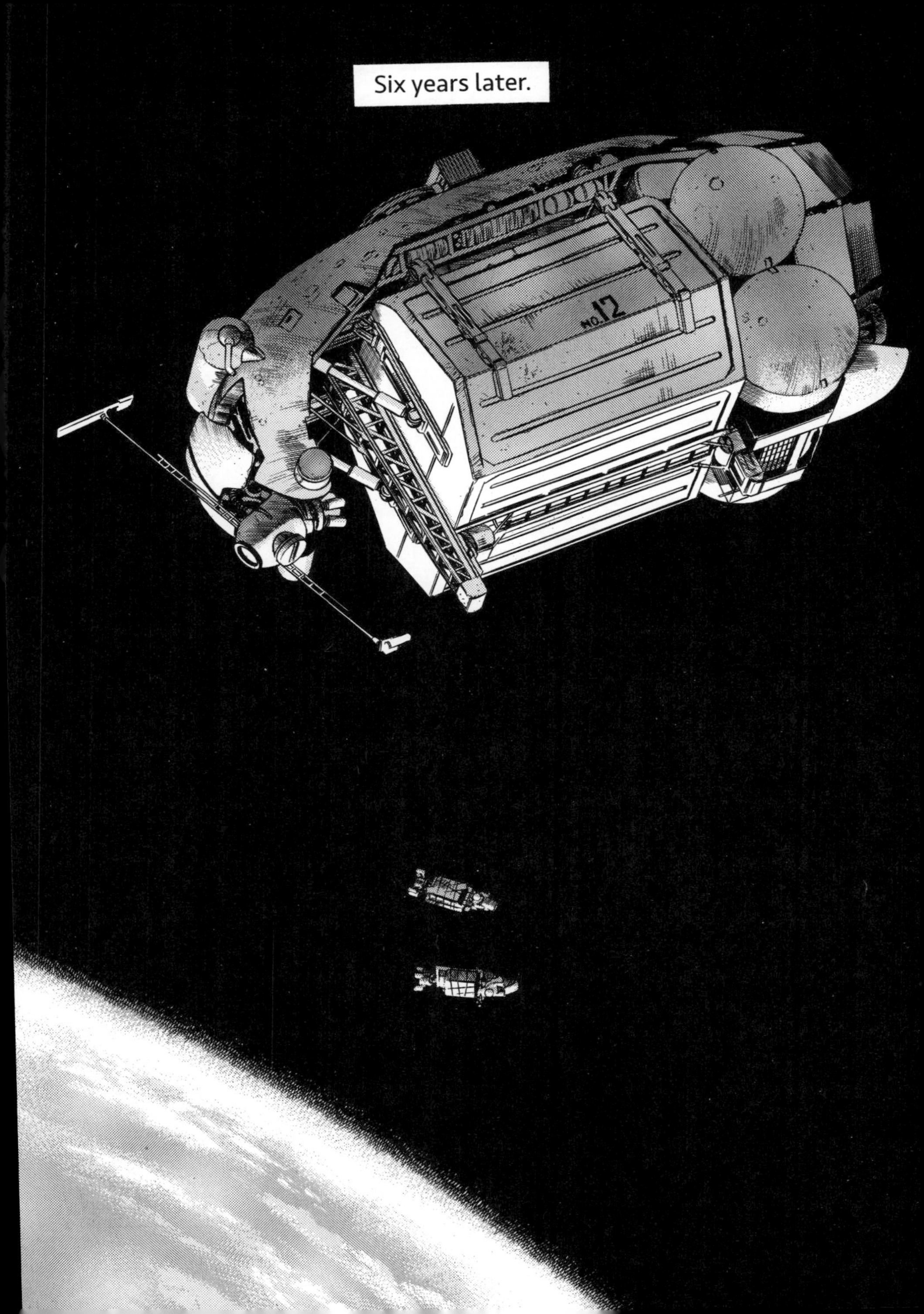
Six years later.
NO. 12

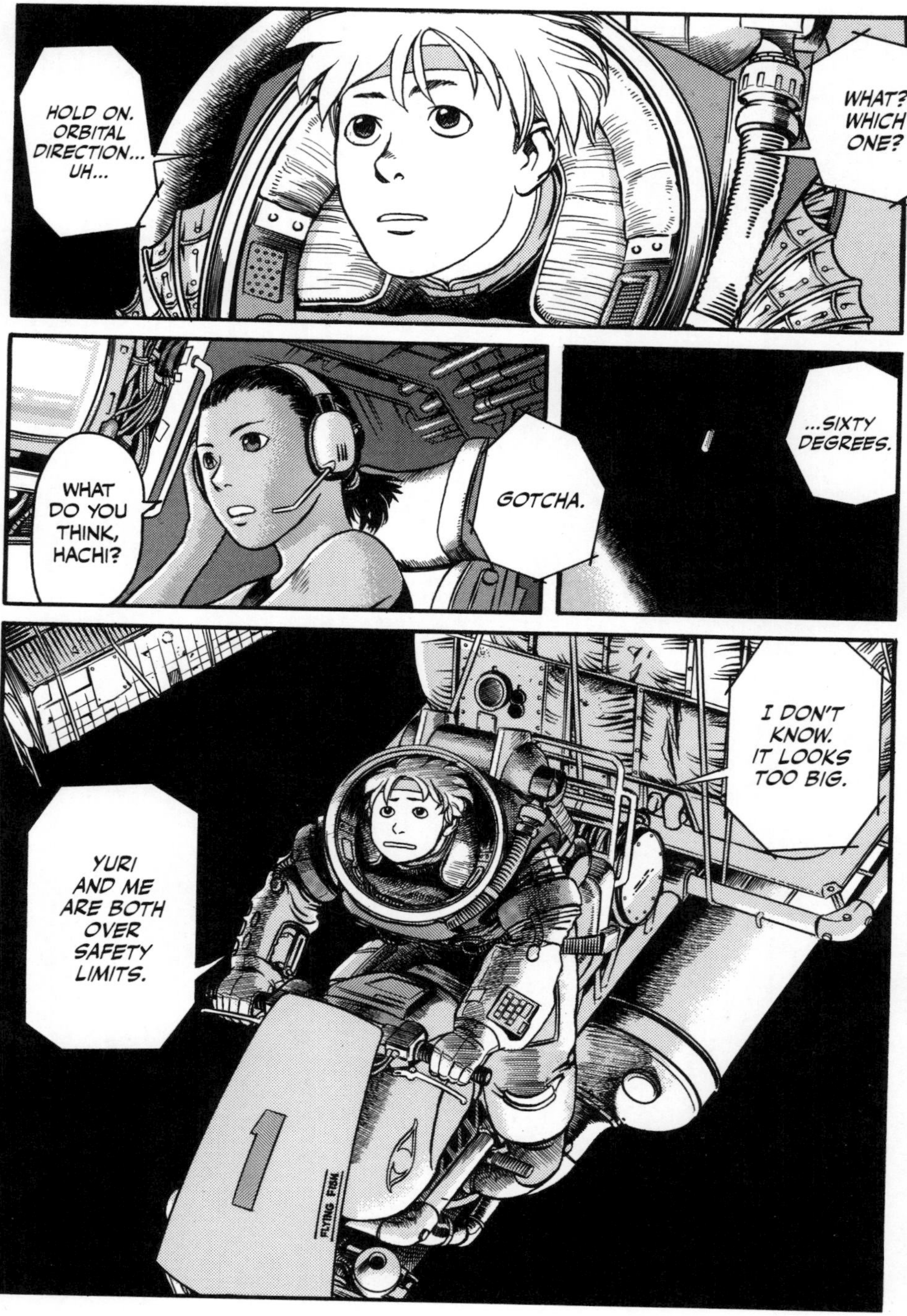
WHAT? WHICH ONE?
HOLD ON. ORBITAL DIRECTION... UH...
...SIXTY DEGREES.
GOTCHA.
WHAT DO YOU THINK, HACHI?
I DON'T KNOW. IT LOOKS TOO BIG.
YURI AND ME ARE BOTH OVER SAFETY LIMITS.
FLYING FISH

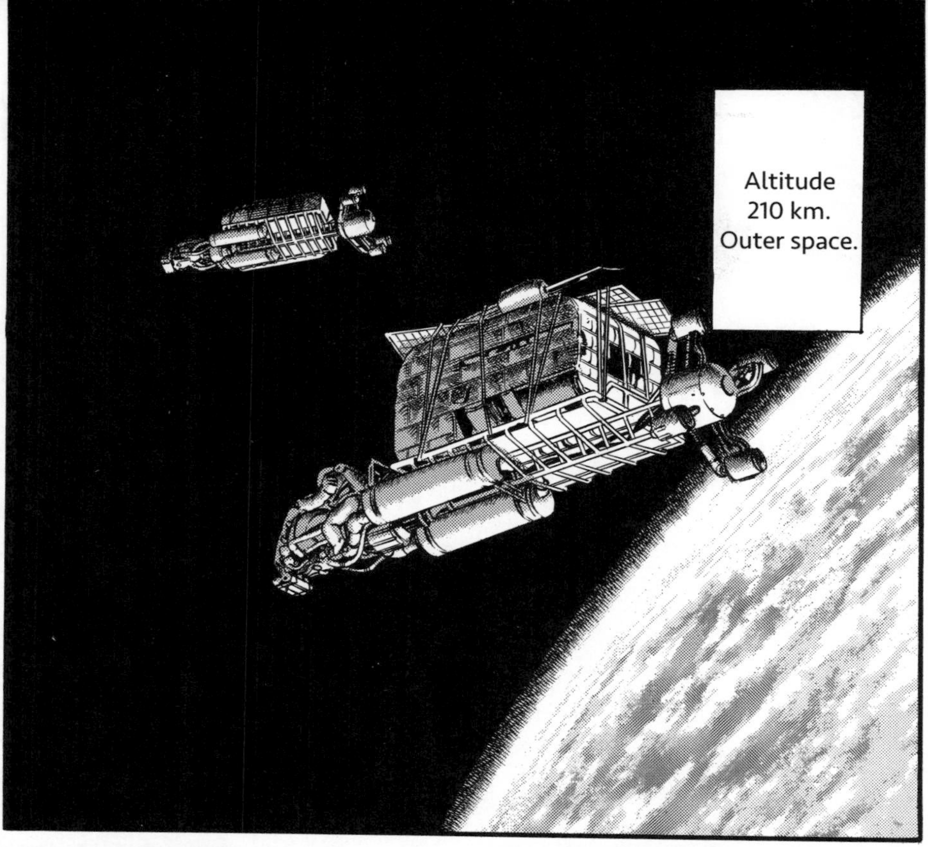
Altitude 210 km. Outer space.

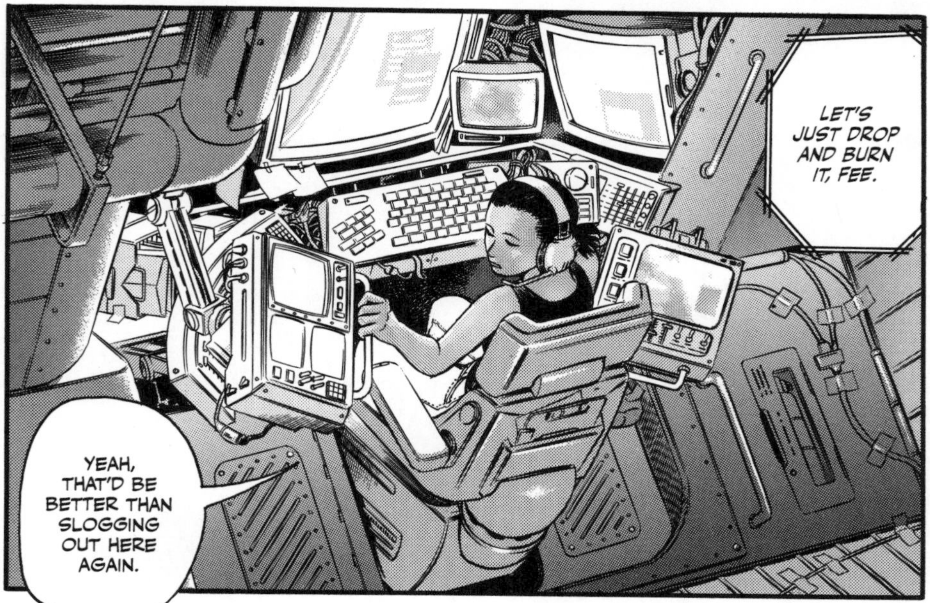
LET'S JUST DROP AND BURN IT, FEE.
YEAH, THAT'D BE BETTER THAN SLOGGING OUT HERE AGAIN.

THIS IS
WHERE
I WORK.

IT'S
UP TO
YOU.

OKAY.

IF YOU'RE
WONDERING
WHAT I'M
DOING UP
HERE IN THIS
CELESTIAL
SOLITUDE...
JUST WAIT.

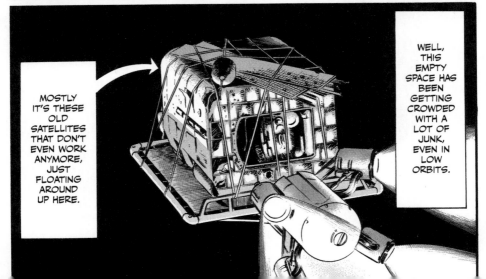

WELL,
THIS
EMPTY
SPACE HAS
BEEN
GETTING
CROWDED
WITH A
LOT OF
JUNK,
EVEN IN
LOW
ORBITS.

MOSTLY
IT'S THESE
OLD
SATELLITES
THAT DON'T
EVEN WORK
ANYMORE,
JUST
FLOATING
AROUND
UP HERE.

YURI, ARE YOU THERE, DUDE?

DO YOU READ ME? YURI!

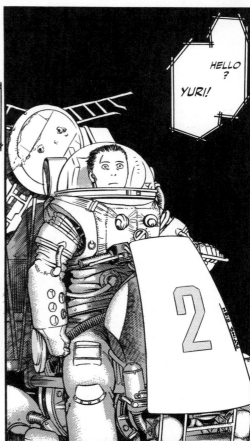

HELLO?

YURI!

YES, HERE. SORRY.

I'M COMING.

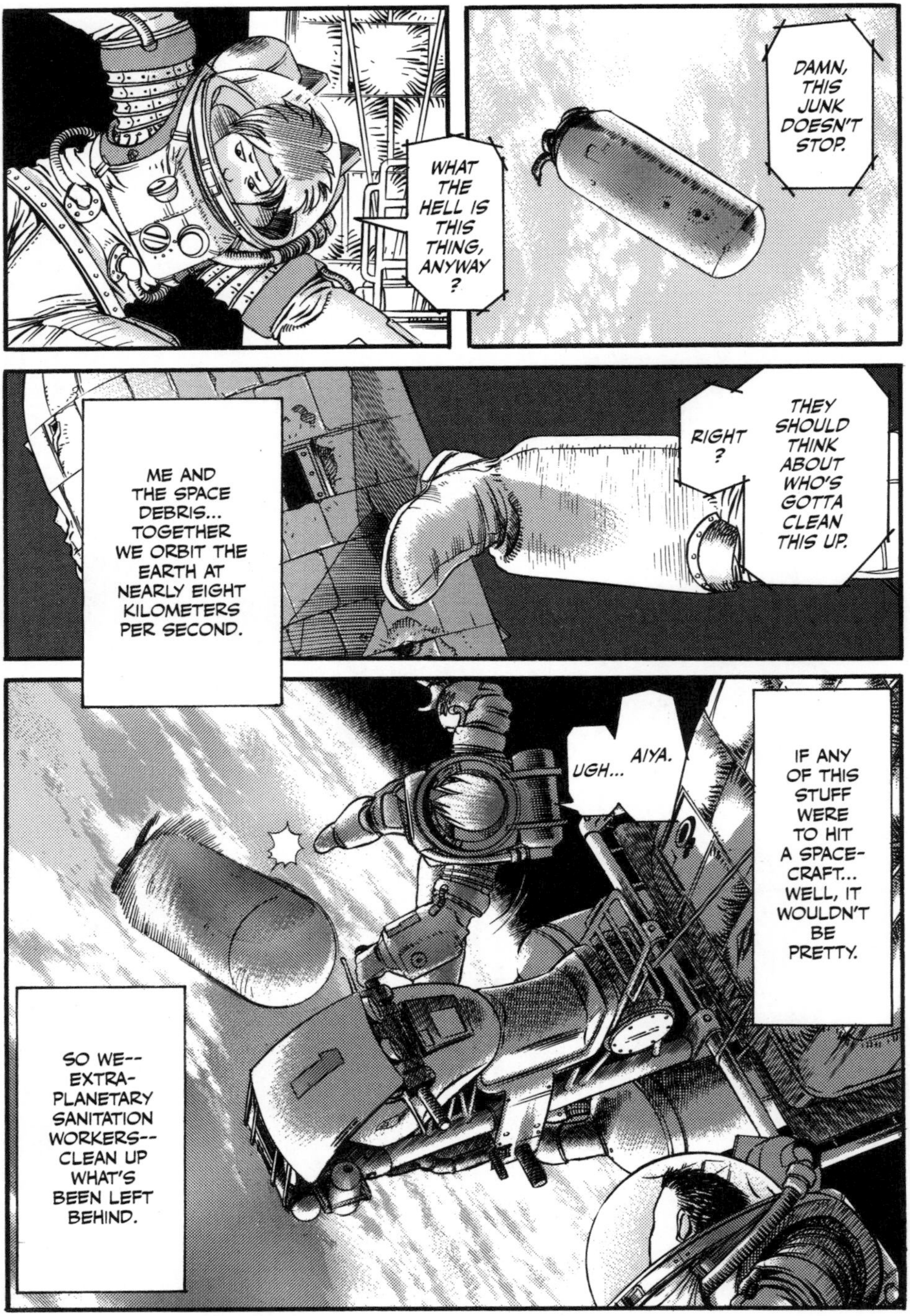
DAMN, THIS JUNK DOESN'T STOP.
WHAT THE HELL IS THIS THING, ANYWAY ?
THEY SHOULD THINK ABOUT WHO'S GOTTA CLEAN THIS UP.
RIGHT ?
ME AND THE SPACE DEBRIS... TOGETHER WE ORBIT THE EARTH AT NEARLY EIGHT KILOMETERS PER SECOND.
IF ANY OF THIS STUFF WERE TO HIT A SPACE-CRAFT... WELL, IT WOULDN'T BE PRETTY.
AIYA.
UGH...
SO WE-- EXTRA-PLANETARY SANITATION WORKERS-- CLEAN UP WHAT'S BEEN LEFT BEHIND.

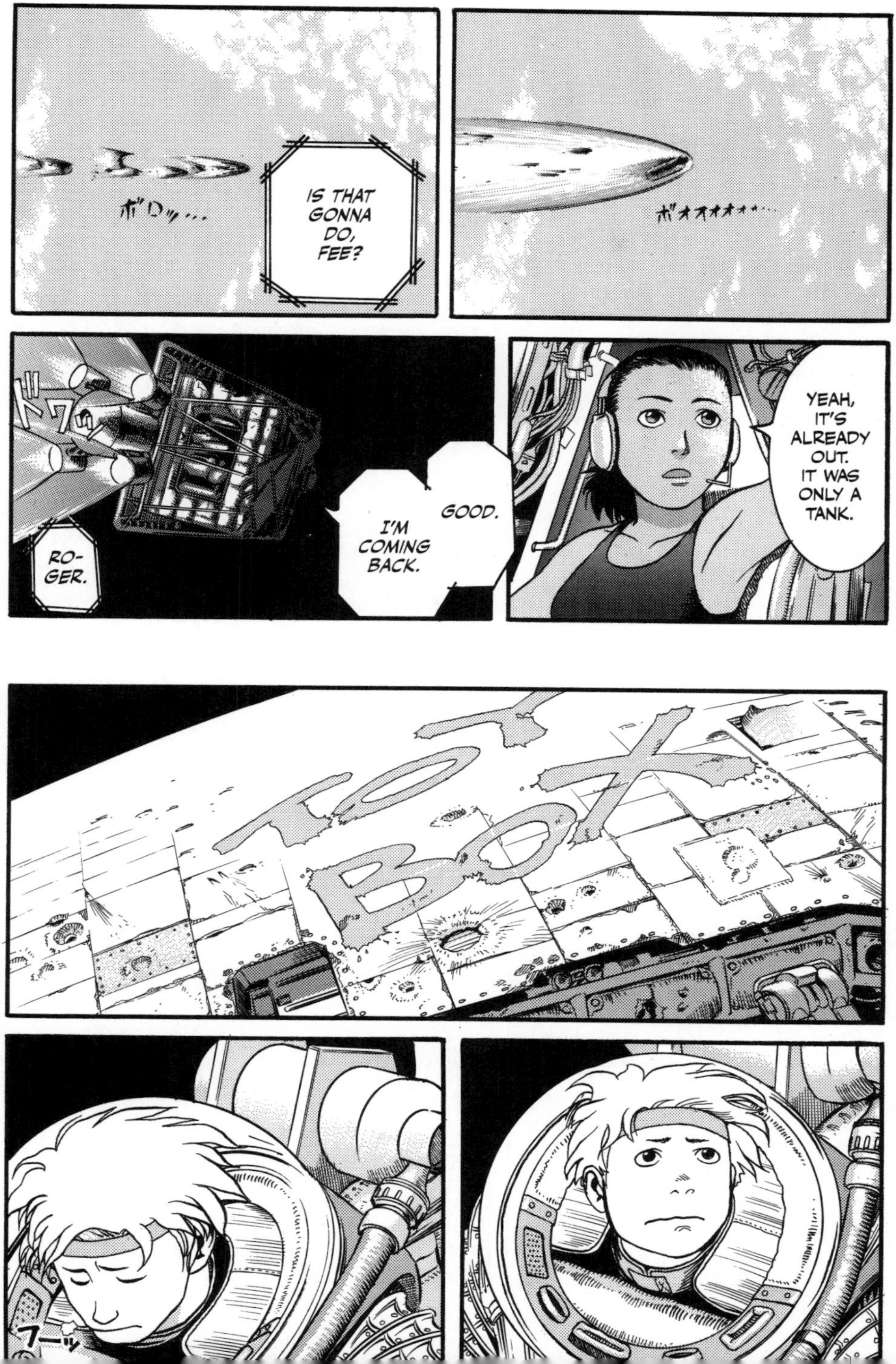
ボオオオオオ…
IS THAT GONNA DO, FEE?
ボロッ…
YEAH, IT'S ALREADY OUT. IT WAS ONLY A TANK.
GOOD. I'M COMING BACK.
ROGER.
ドワッ
TOY BOX
フーッ

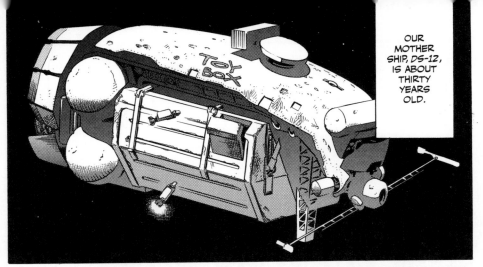

Toy Box
OUR MOTHER SHIP, DS-12, IS ABOUT THIRTY YEARS OLD.
IT'S A HUNK OF JUNK. WE KNOW.
ALL THE DEBRIS HAULERS ARE.
WELCOME BACK.
ポイ。
I WARMED IT UP FOR YA.

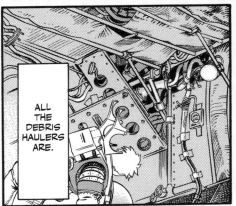

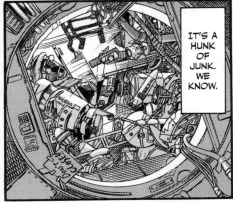

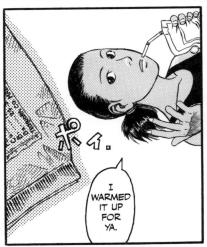

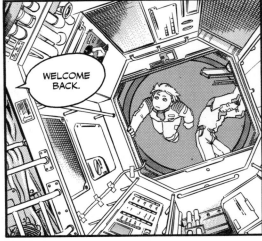

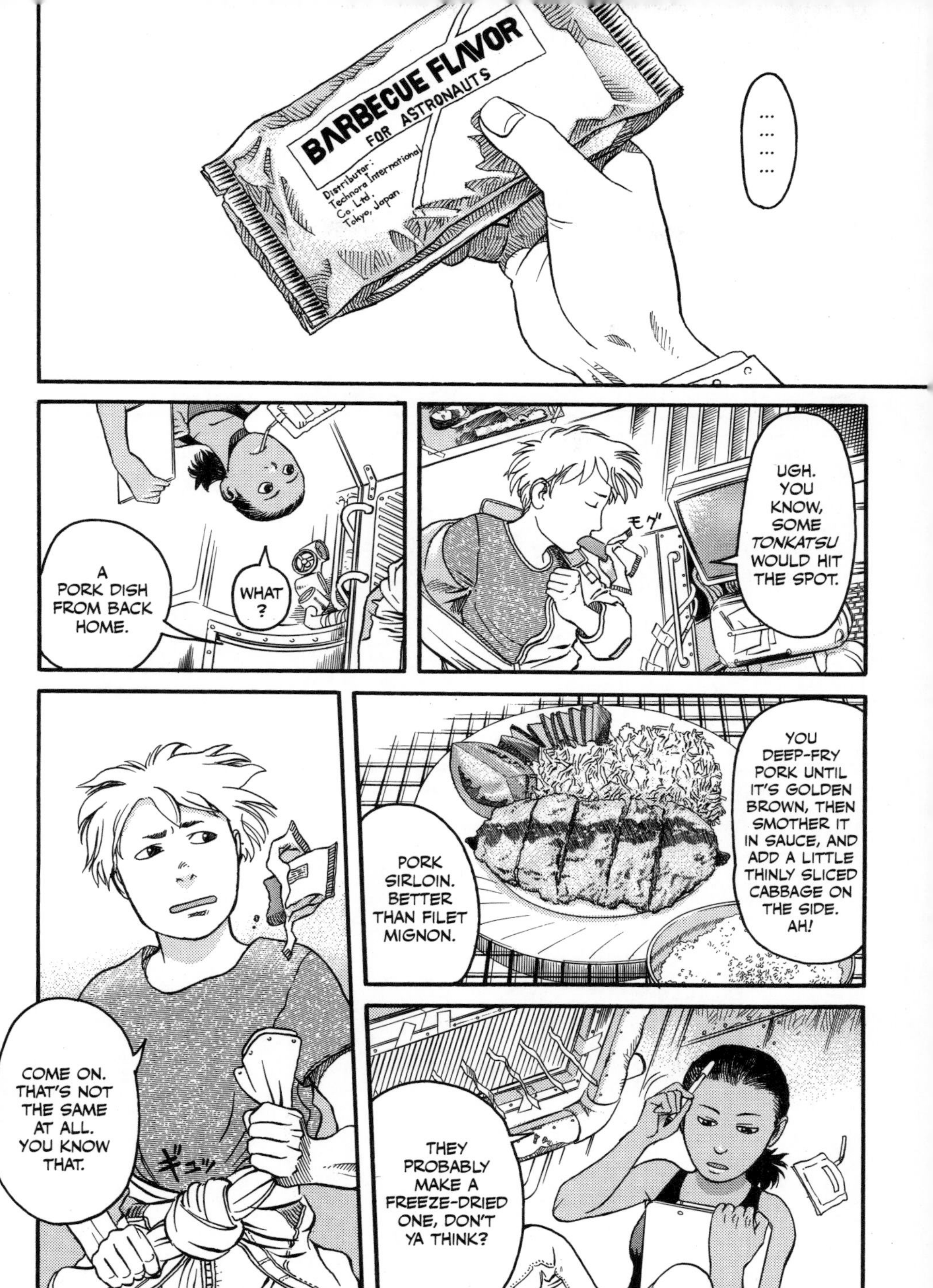
BARBECUE FLAVOR
FOR ASTRONAUTS
Distributor: Technora International Co. Ltd. Tokyo, Japan
....
UGH. YOU KNOW, SOME *TONKATSU* WOULD HIT THE SPOT.
モグ
WHAT?
A PORK DISH FROM BACK HOME.
YOU DEEP-FRY PORK UNTIL IT'S GOLDEN BROWN, THEN SMOTHER IT IN SAUCE, AND ADD A LITTLE THINLY SLICED CABBAGE ON THE SIDE. AH!
PORK SIRLOIN. BETTER THAN FILET MIGNON.
THEY PROBABLY MAKE A FREEZE-DRIED ONE, DON'T YA THINK?
COME ON. THAT'S NOT THE SAME AT ALL. YOU KNOW THAT.
ギュッ

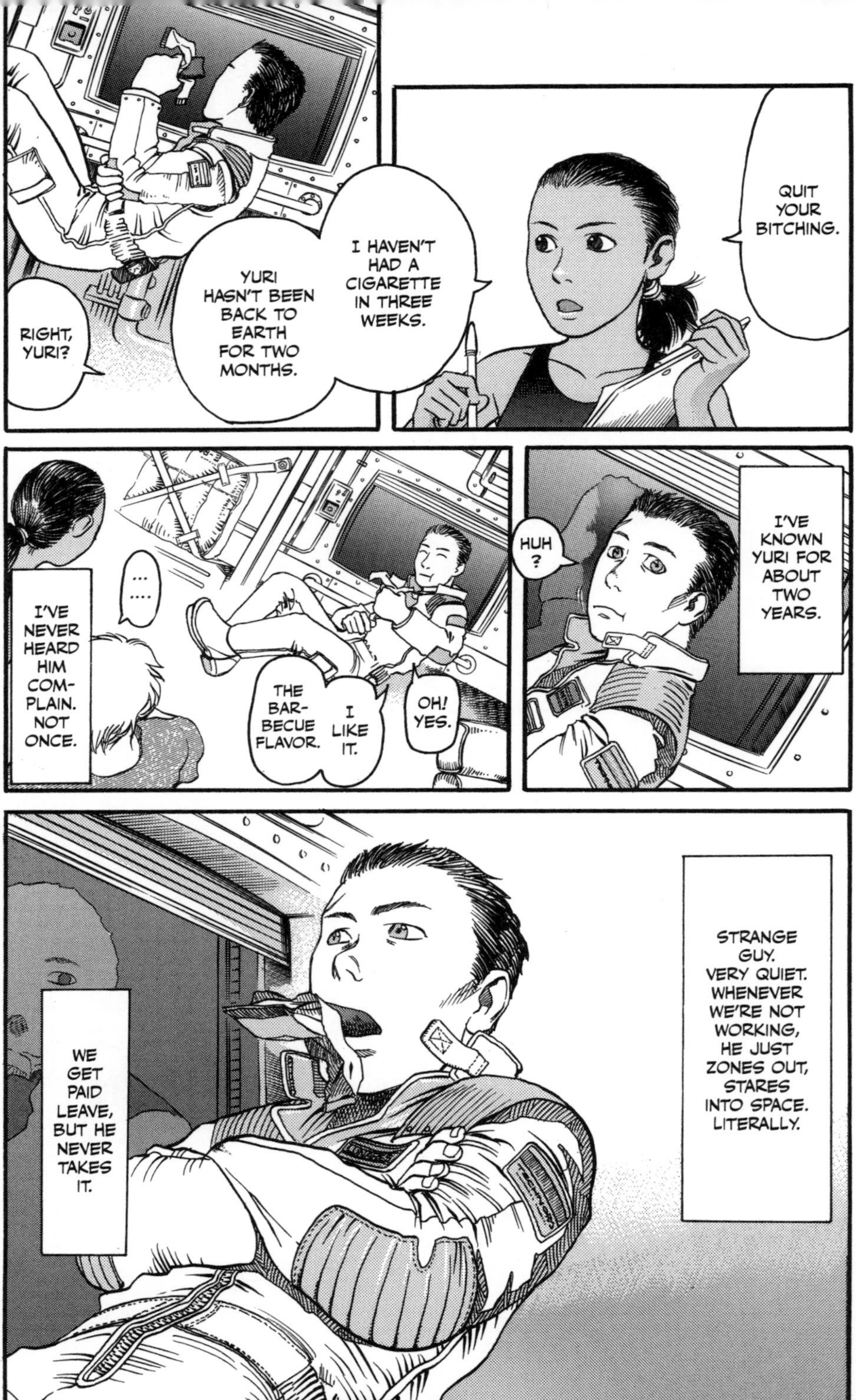
QUIT YOUR BITCHING.
I HAVEN'T HAD A CIGARETTE IN THREE WEEKS.
YURI HASN'T BEEN BACK TO EARTH FOR TWO MONTHS.
RIGHT, YURI?
I'VE KNOWN YURI FOR ABOUT TWO YEARS.
HUH?
OH! YES.
I LIKE IT.
THE BARBECUE FLAVOR.
... .
I'VE NEVER HEARD HIM COMPLAIN. NOT ONCE.
STRANGE GUY. VERY QUIET. WHENEVER WE'RE NOT WORKING, HE JUST ZONES OUT, STARES INTO SPACE. LITERALLY.
WE GET PAID LEAVE, BUT HE NEVER TAKES IT.

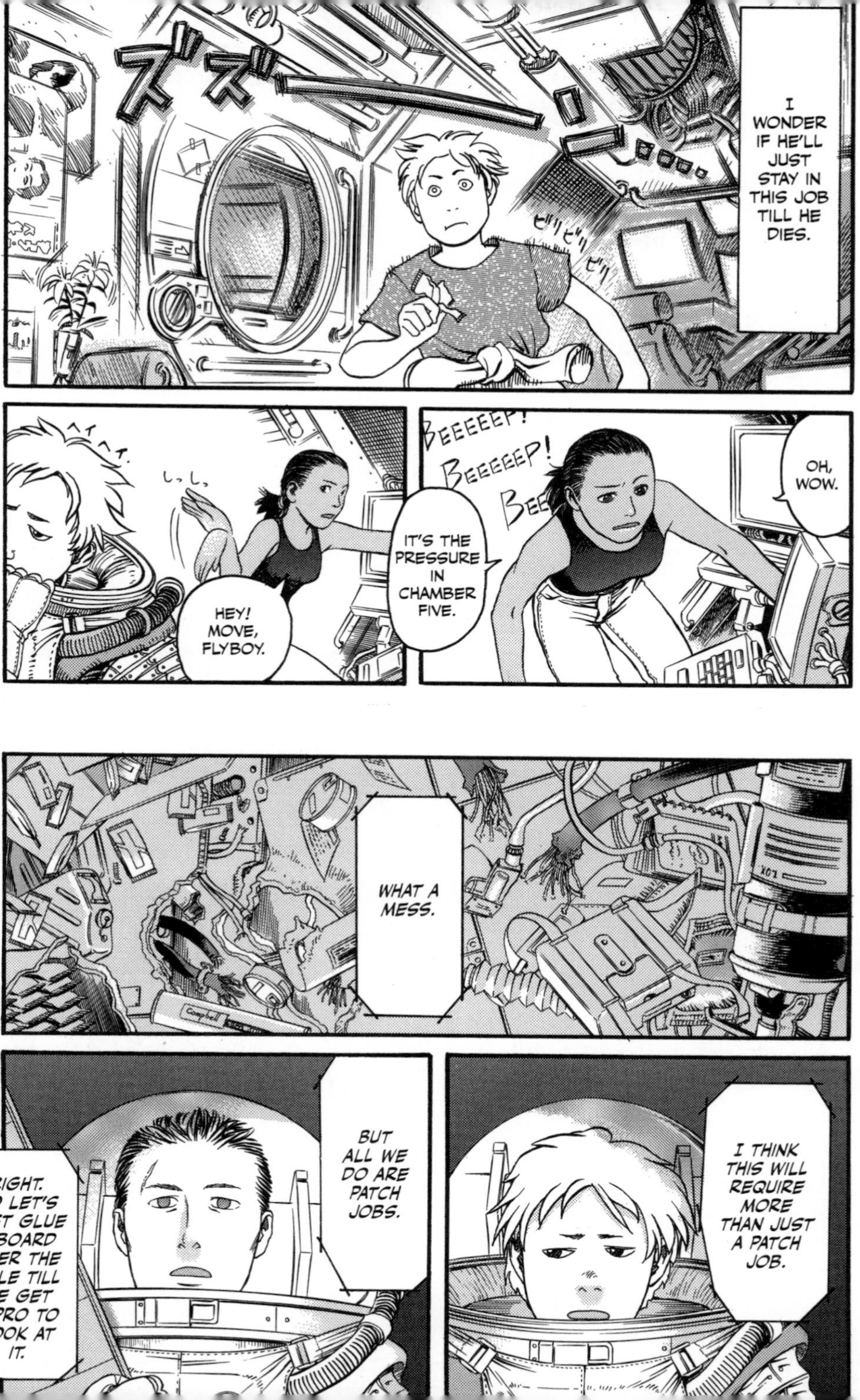
I WONDER IF HE'LL JUST STAY IN THIS JOB TILL HE DIES.
ビリビリビリ
OH, WOW.
BEEEEEP!
BEEEEEP!
IT'S THE PRESSURE IN CHAMBER FIVE.
HEY! MOVE, FLYBOY.
WHAT A MESS.
I THINK THIS WILL REQUIRE MORE THAN JUST A PATCH JOB.
BUT ALL WE DO ARE PATCH JOBS.
RIGHT. SO LET'S JUST GLUE A BOARD OVER THE HOLE TILL WE GET A PRO TO LOOK AT IT.

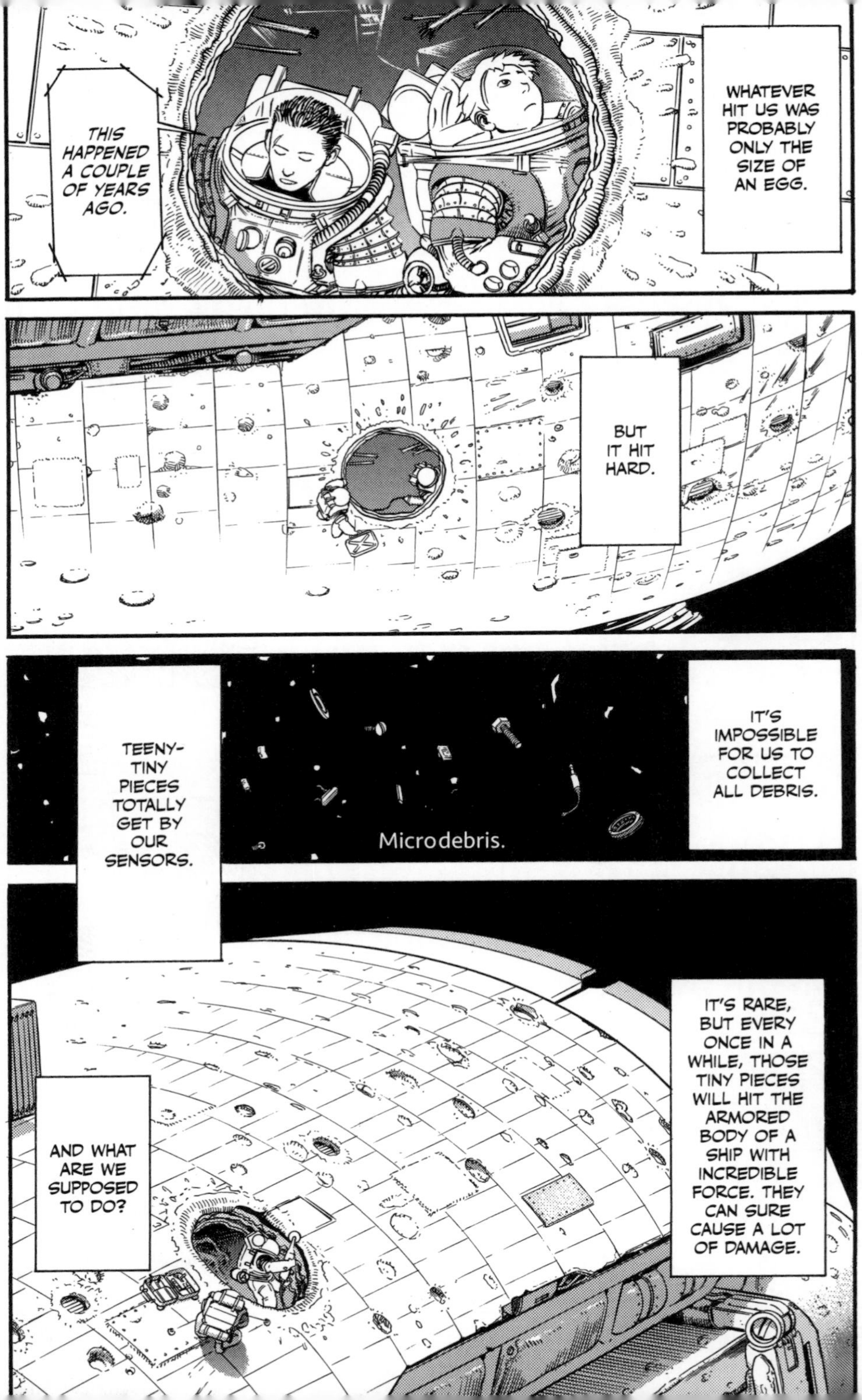
WHATEVER HIT US WAS PROBABLY ONLY THE SIZE OF AN EGG.
THIS HAPPENED A COUPLE OF YEARS AGO.
BUT IT HIT HARD.
IT'S IMPOSSIBLE FOR US TO COLLECT ALL DEBRIS.
Microdebris.
TEENY-TINY PIECES TOTALLY GET BY OUR SENSORS.
IT'S RARE, BUT EVERY ONCE IN A WHILE, THOSE TINY PIECES WILL HIT THE ARMORED BODY OF A SHIP WITH INCREDIBLE FORCE. THEY CAN SURE CAUSE A LOT OF DAMAGE.
AND WHAT ARE WE SUPPOSED TO DO?

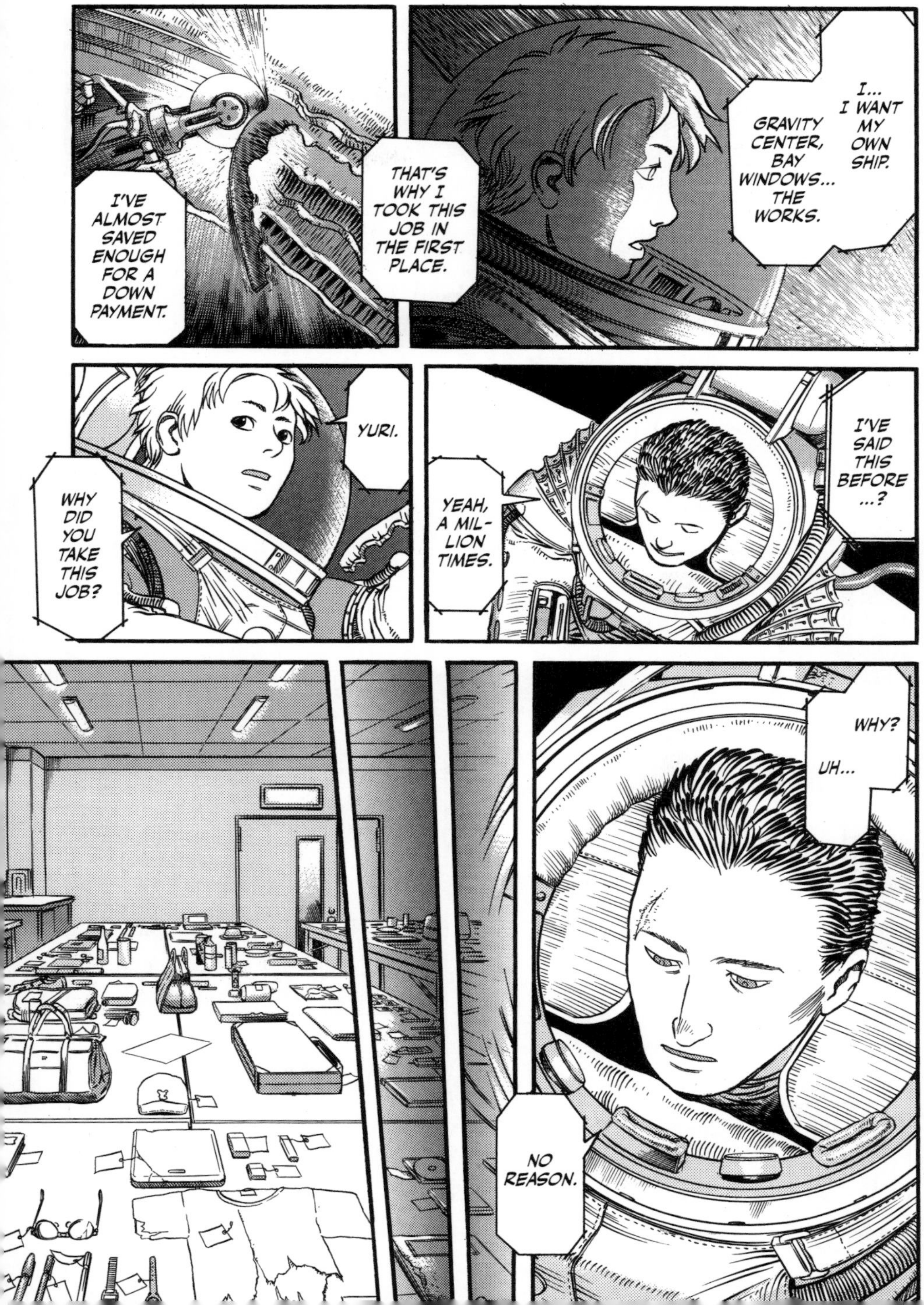
I... I WANT MY OWN SHIP.
GRAVITY CENTER, BAY WINDOWS... THE WORKS.
THAT'S WHY I TOOK THIS JOB IN THE FIRST PLACE.
I'VE ALMOST SAVED ENOUGH FOR A DOWN PAYMENT.
I'VE SAID THIS BEFORE ...?
YEAH, A MIL-LION TIMES.
YURI.
WHY DID YOU TAKE THIS JOB?
WHY?
UH...
NO REASON.

THIS IS ALL WE'VE FOUND FROM THE ACCIDENT.

IF YOU DON'T SEE IT HERE, THEN I'M SORRY, BUT IT'S PROBABLY LOST.

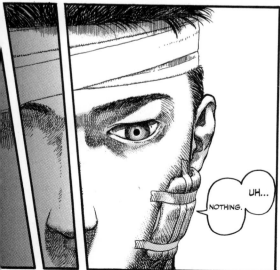

UH... NOTHING.

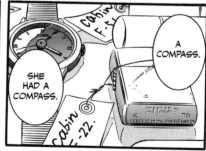

SHE HAD A COMPASS.

A COMPASS.

PARDON?

22

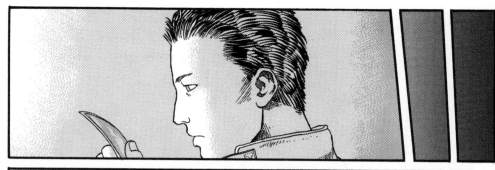

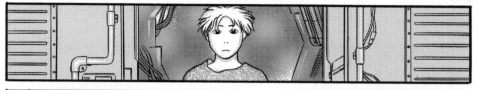

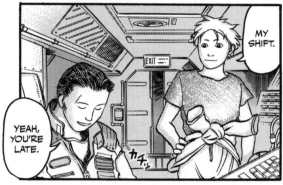

YURI ?
MY SHIFT.
YEAH, YOU'RE LATE.
カチッ
WHO'S THE CHICK ?
カチッ
LUCKY MAN...
HE DIDN'T SAY A WORD.
HUH?
WHAT DOESN'T HE WANT TO TALK ABOUT?

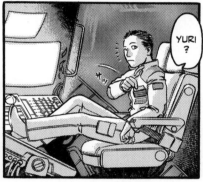

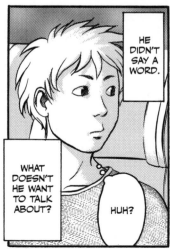

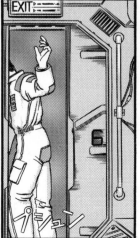

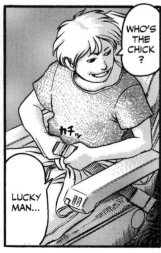

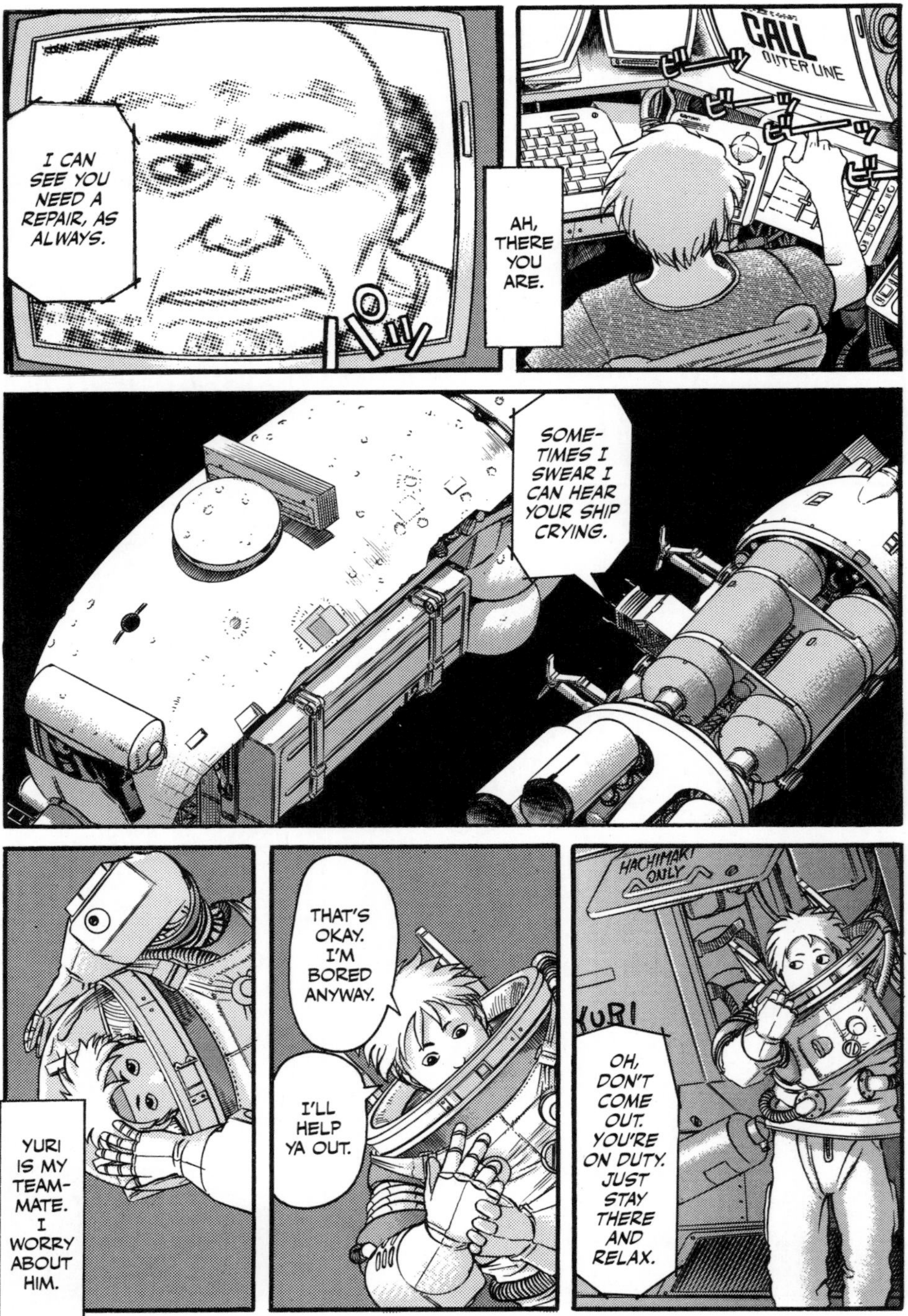
CALL
OUTER LINE
AH, THERE YOU ARE.
I CAN SEE YOU NEED A REPAIR, AS ALWAYS.
SOME-TIMES I SWEAR I CAN HEAR YOUR SHIP CRYING.
HACHIMAKI ONLY
YURI
OH, DON'T COME OUT. YOU'RE ON DUTY. JUST STAY THERE AND RELAX.
THAT'S OKAY. I'M BORED ANYWAY.
I'LL HELP YA OUT.
YURI IS MY TEAM-MATE. I WORRY ABOUT HIM.

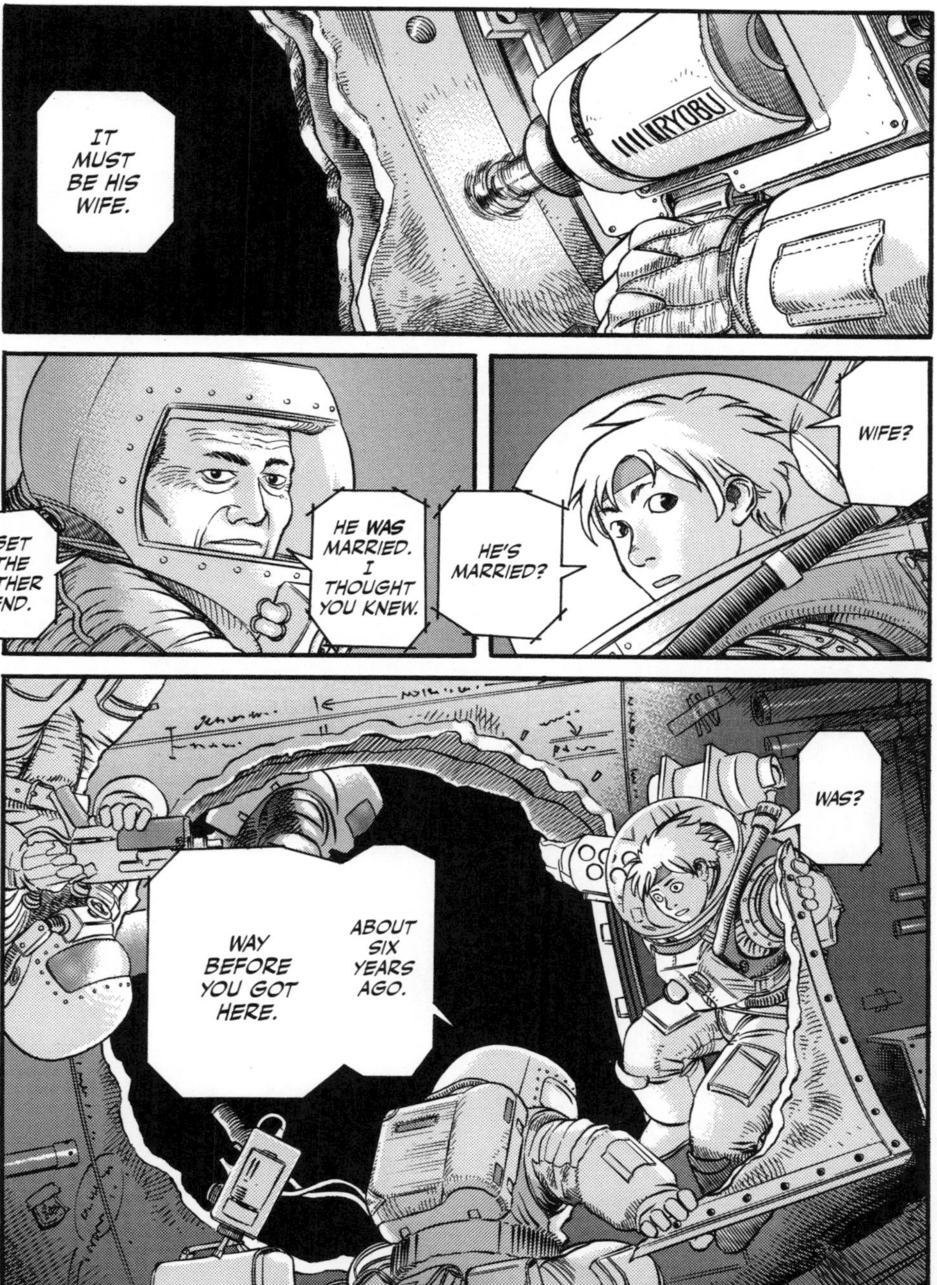
IT MUST BE HIS WIFE.
RYOBU
WIFE?
HE'S MARRIED?
HE WAS MARRIED. I THOUGHT YOU KNEW.
GET THE OTHER END.
WAS?
ABOUT SIX YEARS AGO.
WAY BEFORE YOU GOT HERE.

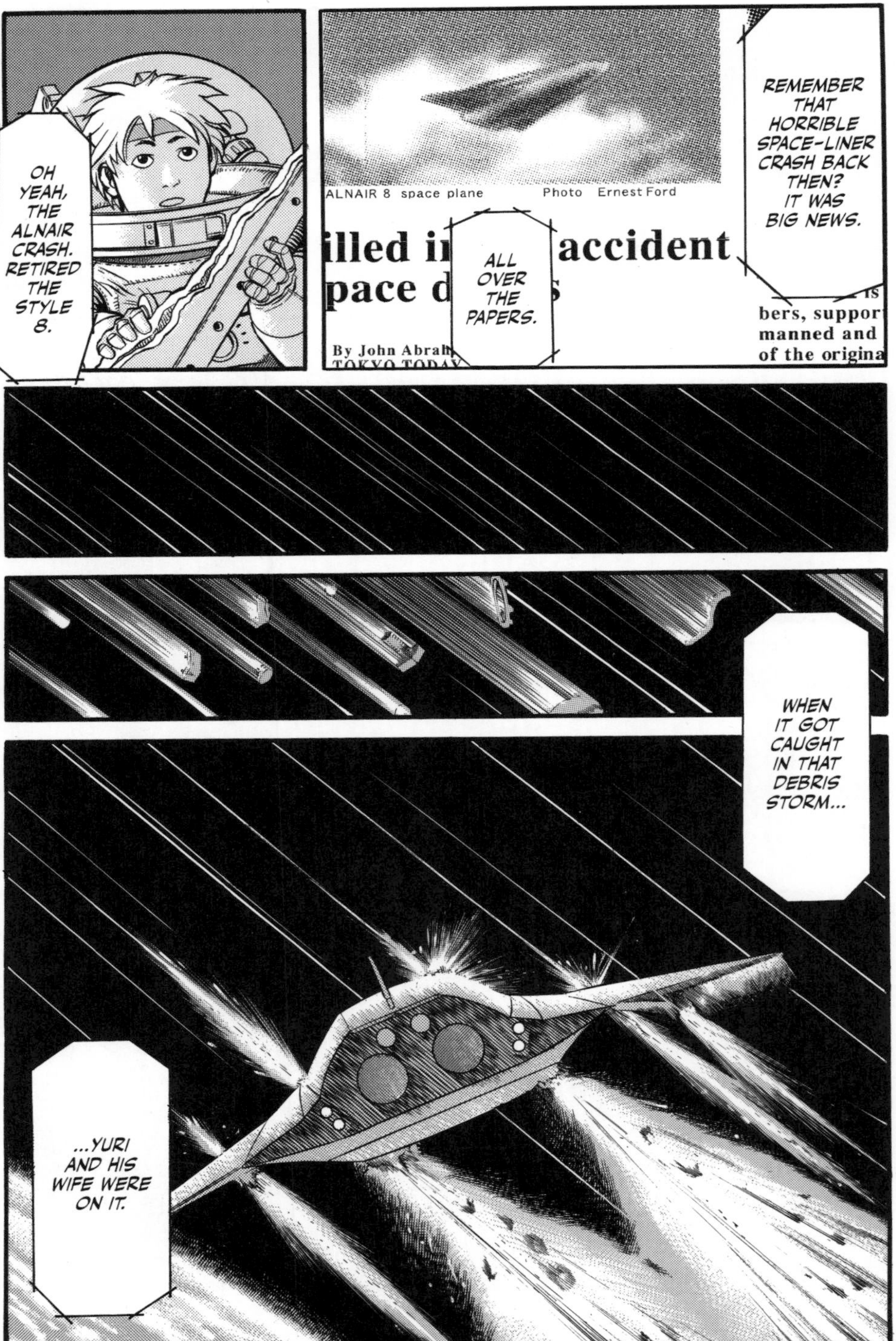
REMEMBER THAT HORRIBLE SPACE-LINER CRASH BACK THEN? IT WAS BIG NEWS.
ALNAIR 8 space plane
Photo Ernest Ford
illed ir accident
pace d s
By John Abrah
bers, support
manned and
of the origina
ALL OVER THE PAPERS.
OH YEAH, THE ALNAIR CRASH. RETIRED THE STYLE 8.
WHEN IT GOT CAUGHT IN THAT DEBRIS STORM...
...YURI AND HIS WIFE WERE ON IT.

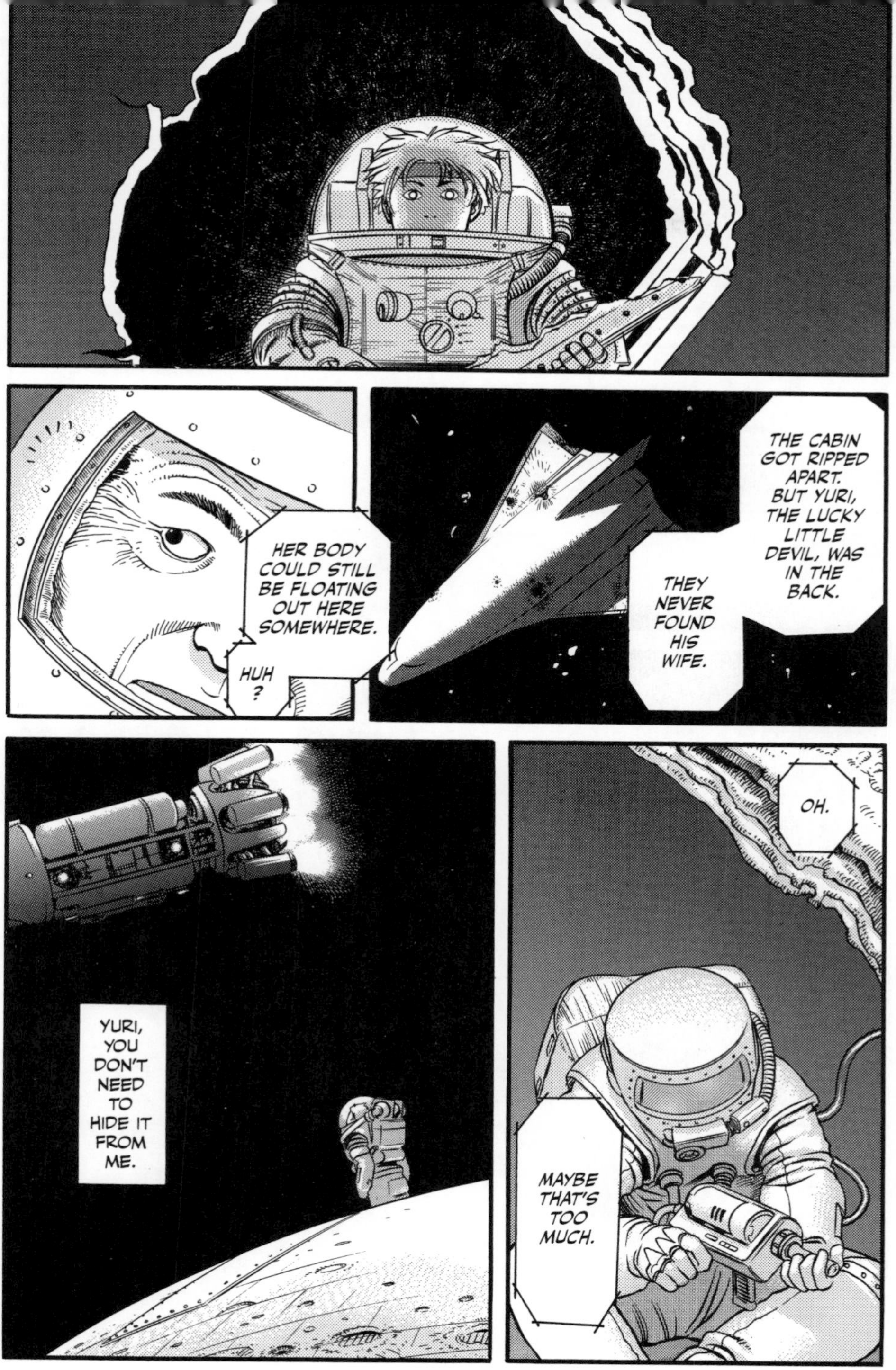
THE CABIN GOT RIPPED APART. BUT YURI, THE LUCKY LITTLE DEVIL, WAS IN THE BACK.
THEY NEVER FOUND HIS WIFE.
HER BODY COULD STILL BE FLOATING OUT HERE SOMEWHERE.
HUH?
OH.
MAYBE THAT'S TOO MUCH.
YURI, YOU DON'T NEED TO HIDE IT FROM ME.

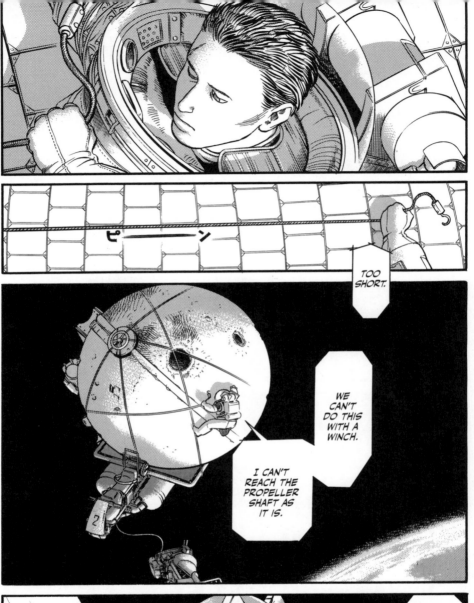

ピーーン

TOO SHORT.

WE CAN'T DO THIS WITH A WINCH.

I CAN'T REACH THE PROPELLER SHAFT AS IT IS.

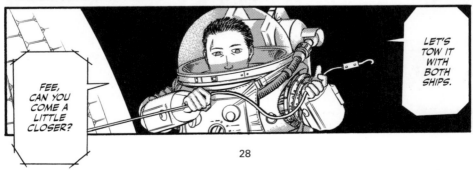

LET'S TOW IT WITH BOTH SHIPS.

FEE, CAN YOU COME A LITTLE CLOSER?

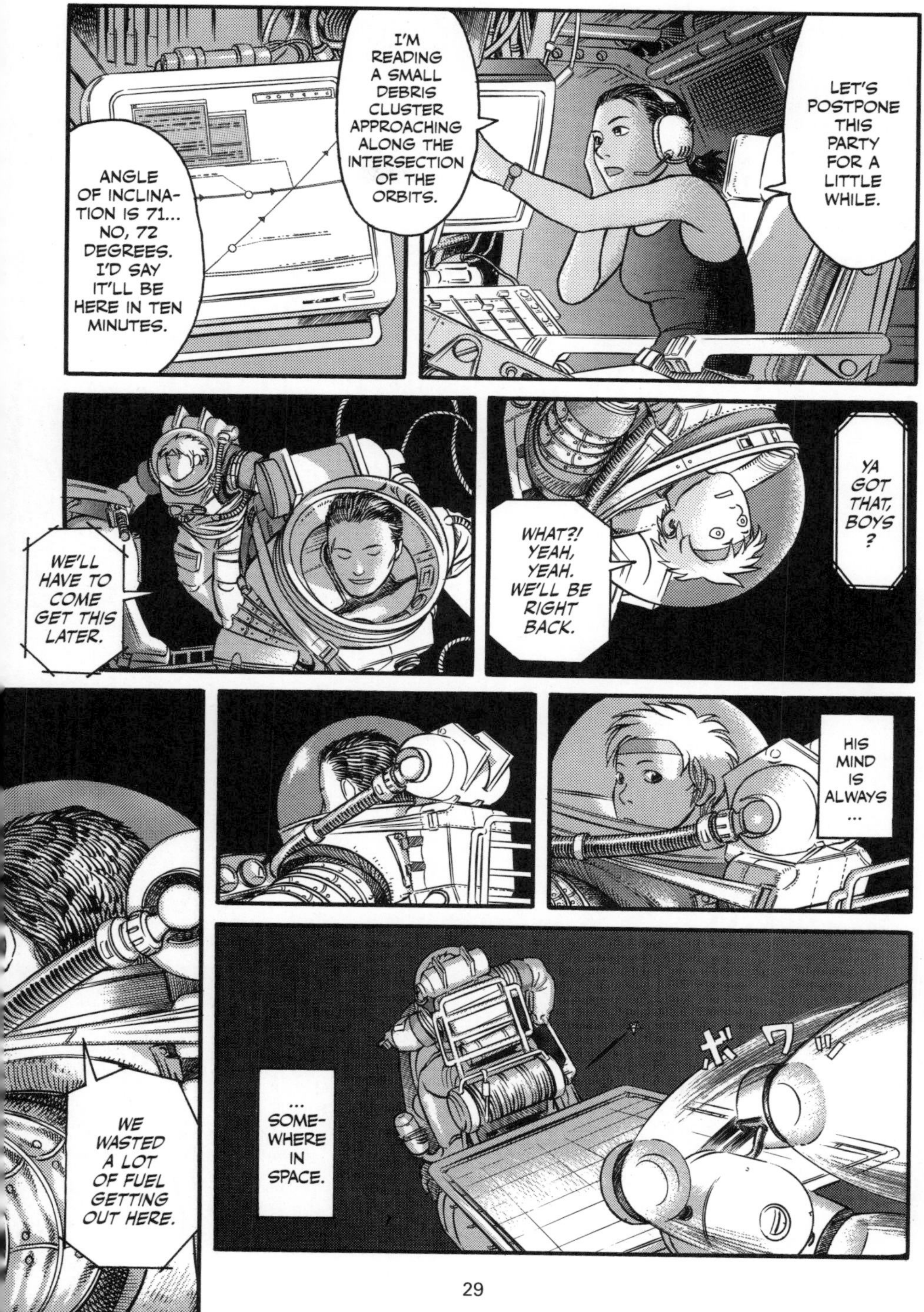
LET'S POSTPONE THIS PARTY FOR A LITTLE WHILE.
I'M READING A SMALL DEBRIS CLUSTER APPROACHING ALONG THE INTERSECTION OF THE ORBITS.
ANGLE OF INCLINATION IS 71... NO, 72 DEGREES. I'D SAY IT'LL BE HERE IN TEN MINUTES.
YA GOT THAT, BOYS?
WHAT?! YEAH, YEAH. WE'LL BE RIGHT BACK.
WE'LL HAVE TO COME GET THIS LATER.
HIS MIND IS ALWAYS ...
... SOME-WHERE IN SPACE.
WE WASTED A LOT OF FUEL GETTING OUT HERE.

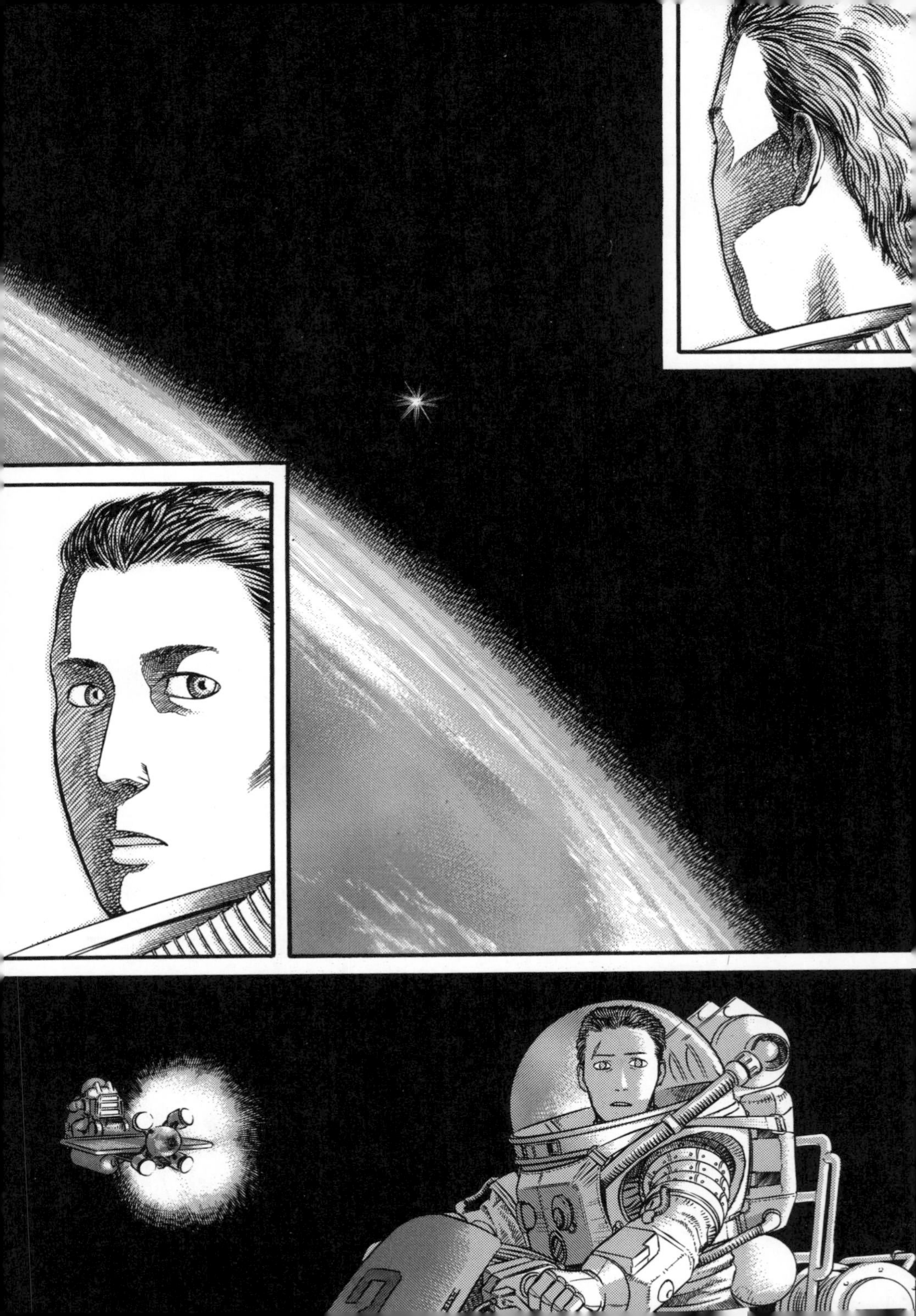

... ...
HEY, YURI...
...POPS TOLD ME ABOUT YOUR WIFE.
I HOPE THAT'S ALL RIGHT. HE JUST...
...I DON'T MEAN TO BUTT IN, BUT...
...WELL, IT MADE ME THINK...
...ABOUT WHY YOU'RE DOING THIS JOB, AND...
ピーッ
WHOA, WAIT A SEC.
ピッ ピッ ピッ ピッ
YURI
HACHIMAKI
YURI ?!

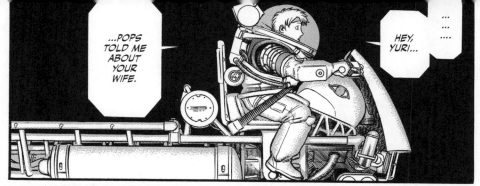

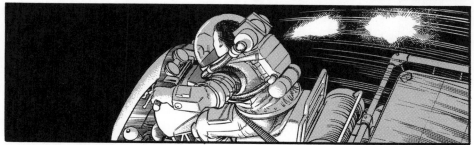

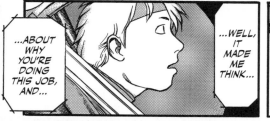

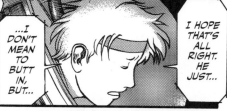

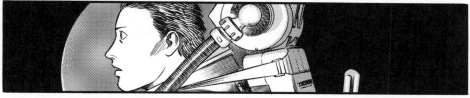

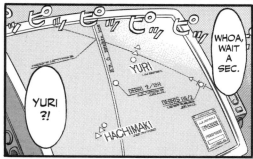

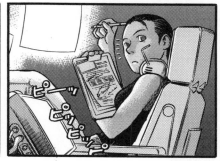

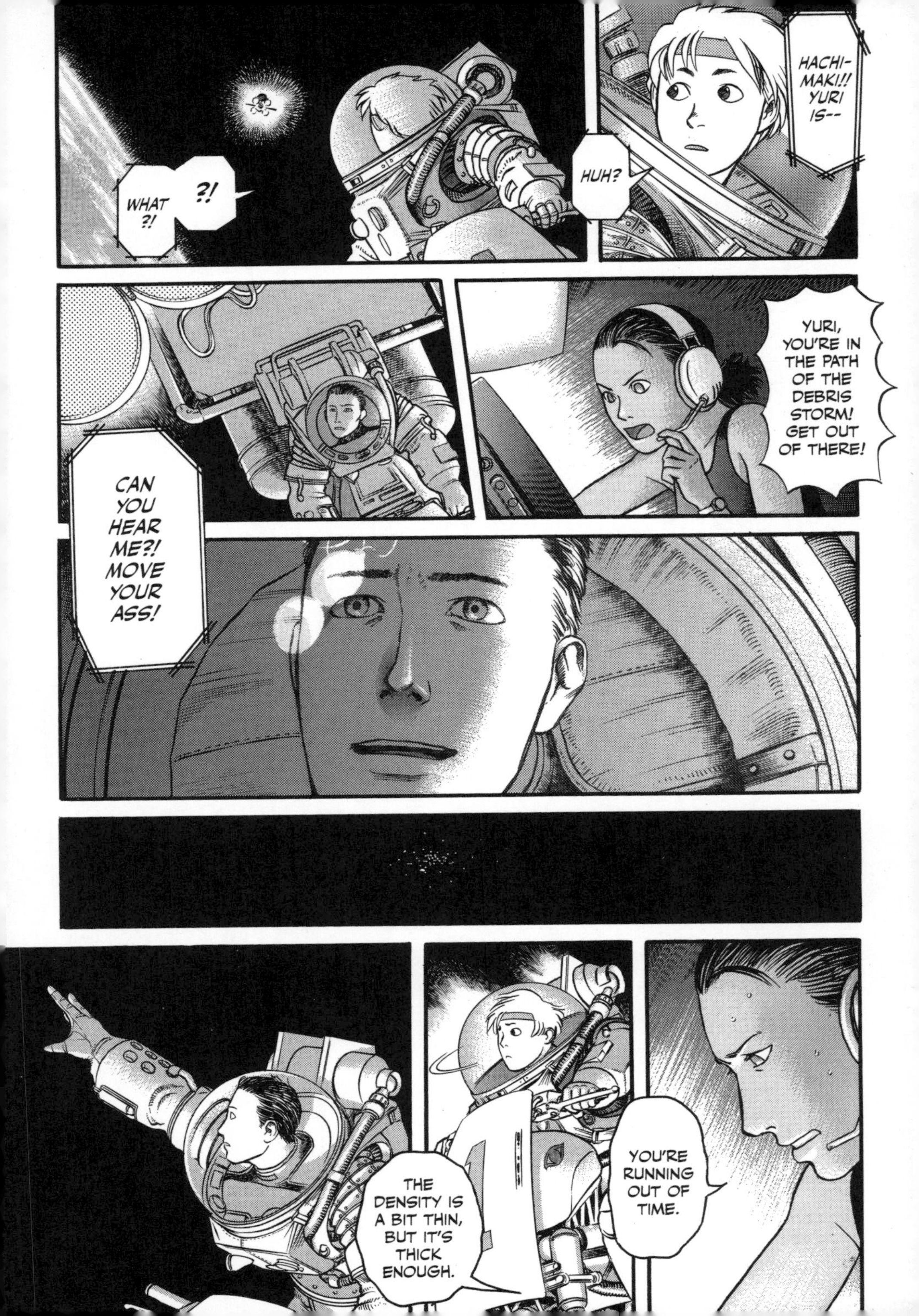
HACHI-MAKI!! YURI IS--
HUH?
?!
WHAT ?!
YURI, YOU'RE IN THE PATH OF THE DEBRIS STORM! GET OUT OF THERE!
CAN YOU HEAR ME?! MOVE YOUR ASS!
YOU'RE RUNNING OUT OF TIME.
THE DENSITY IS A BIT THIN, BUT IT'S THICK ENOUGH.

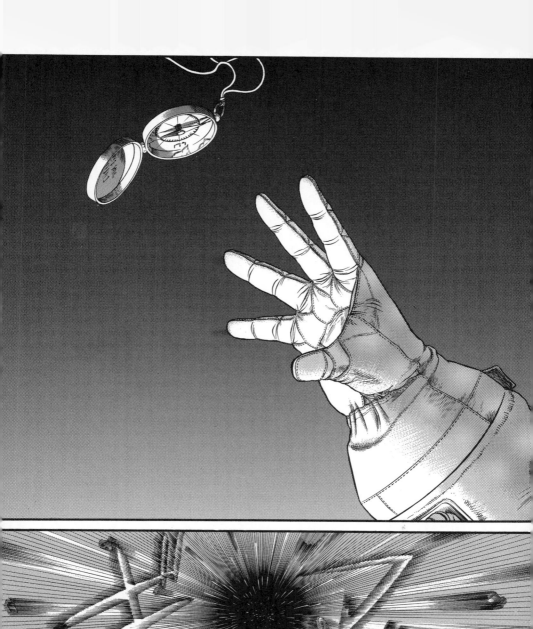

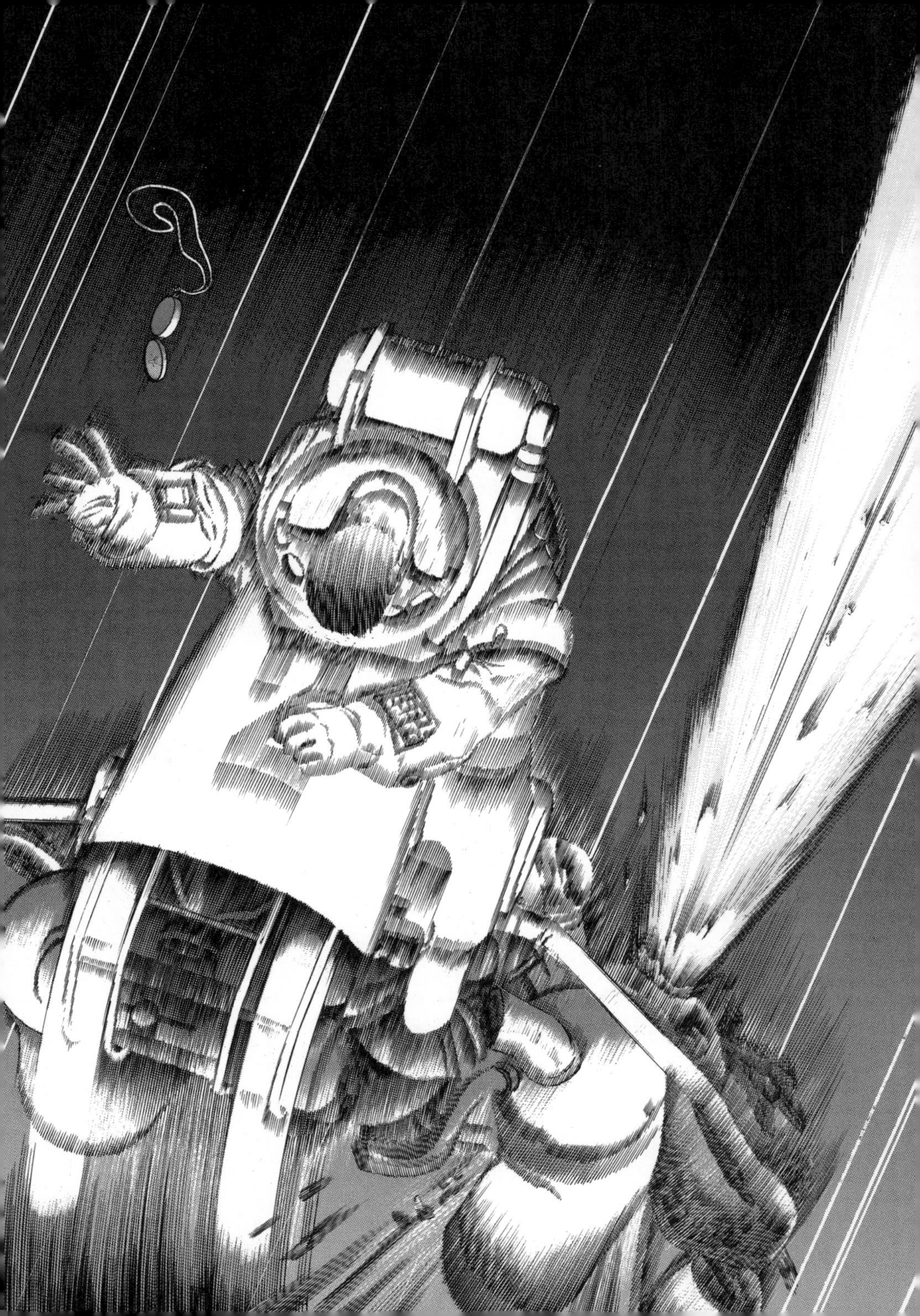

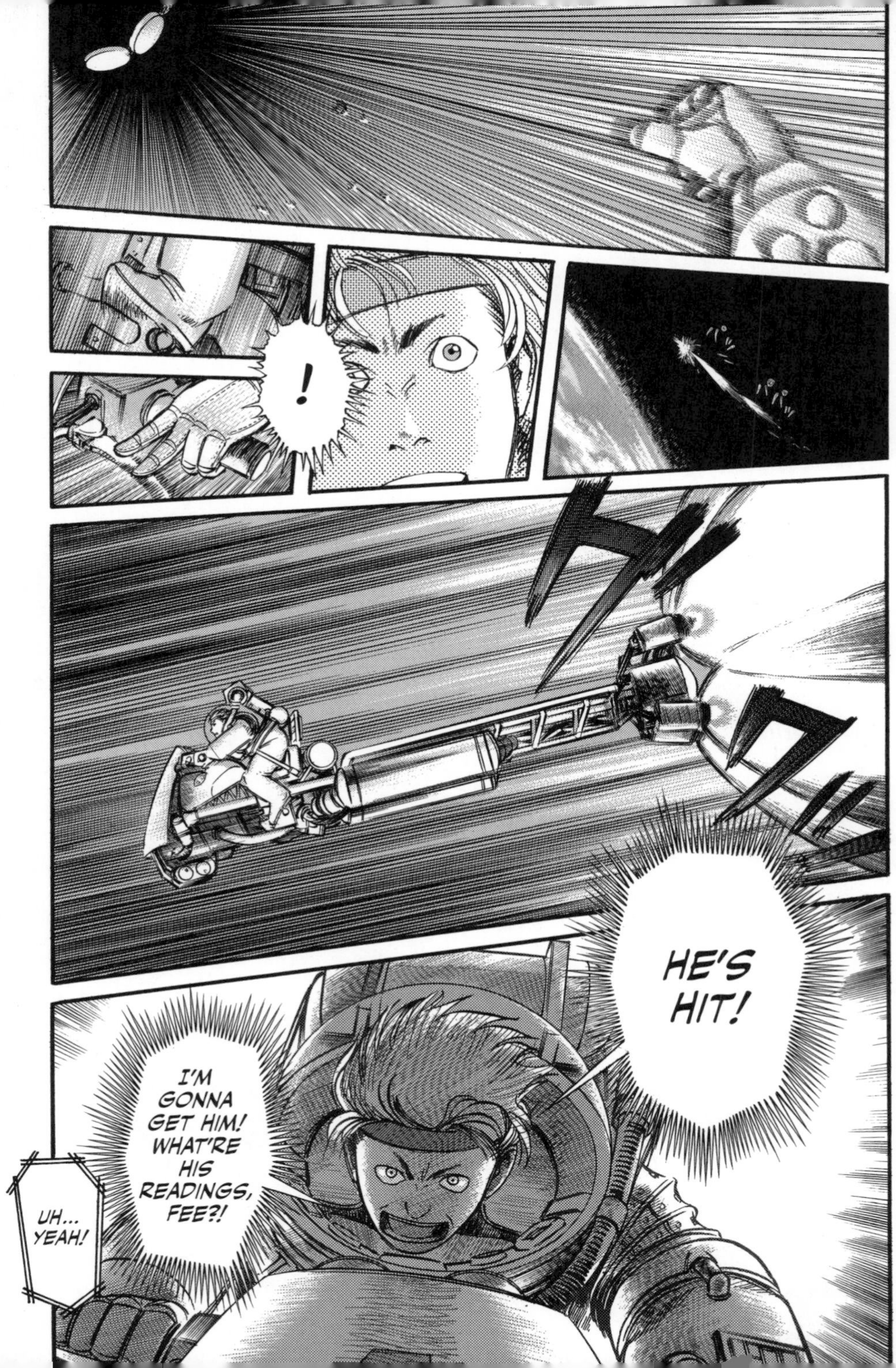
!
HE'S HIT!
I'M GONNA GET HIM! WHAT'RE HIS READINGS, FEE?!
UH... YEAH!

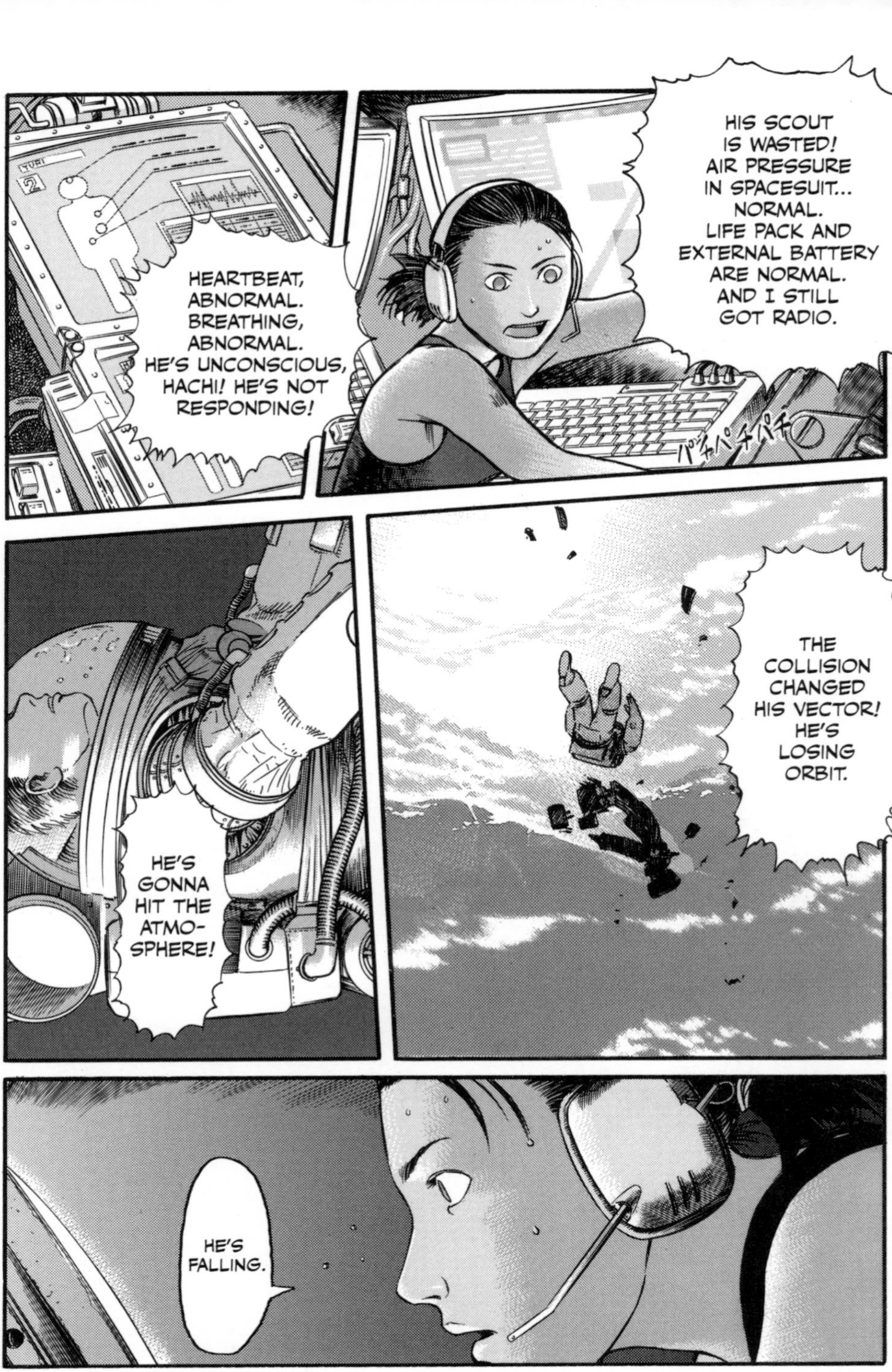
HIS SCOUT IS WASTED! AIR PRESSURE IN SPACESUIT... NORMAL. LIFE PACK AND EXTERNAL BATTERY ARE NORMAL. AND I STILL GOT RADIO.
パチパチパチ
HEARTBEAT, ABNORMAL. BREATHING, ABNORMAL. HE'S UNCONSCIOUS, HACHI! HE'S NOT RESPONDING!
THE COLLISION CHANGED HIS VECTOR! HE'S LOSING ORBIT.
HE'S GONNA HIT THE ATMOSPHERE!
HE'S FALLING.

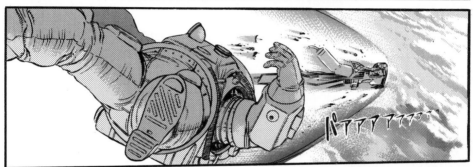

SUIT TEMPERA-TURE RISING FAST!

HURRY UP!

120...

125...

ALTI-TUDE, 130 KM.

WAKE UP, YURI!

YURI!

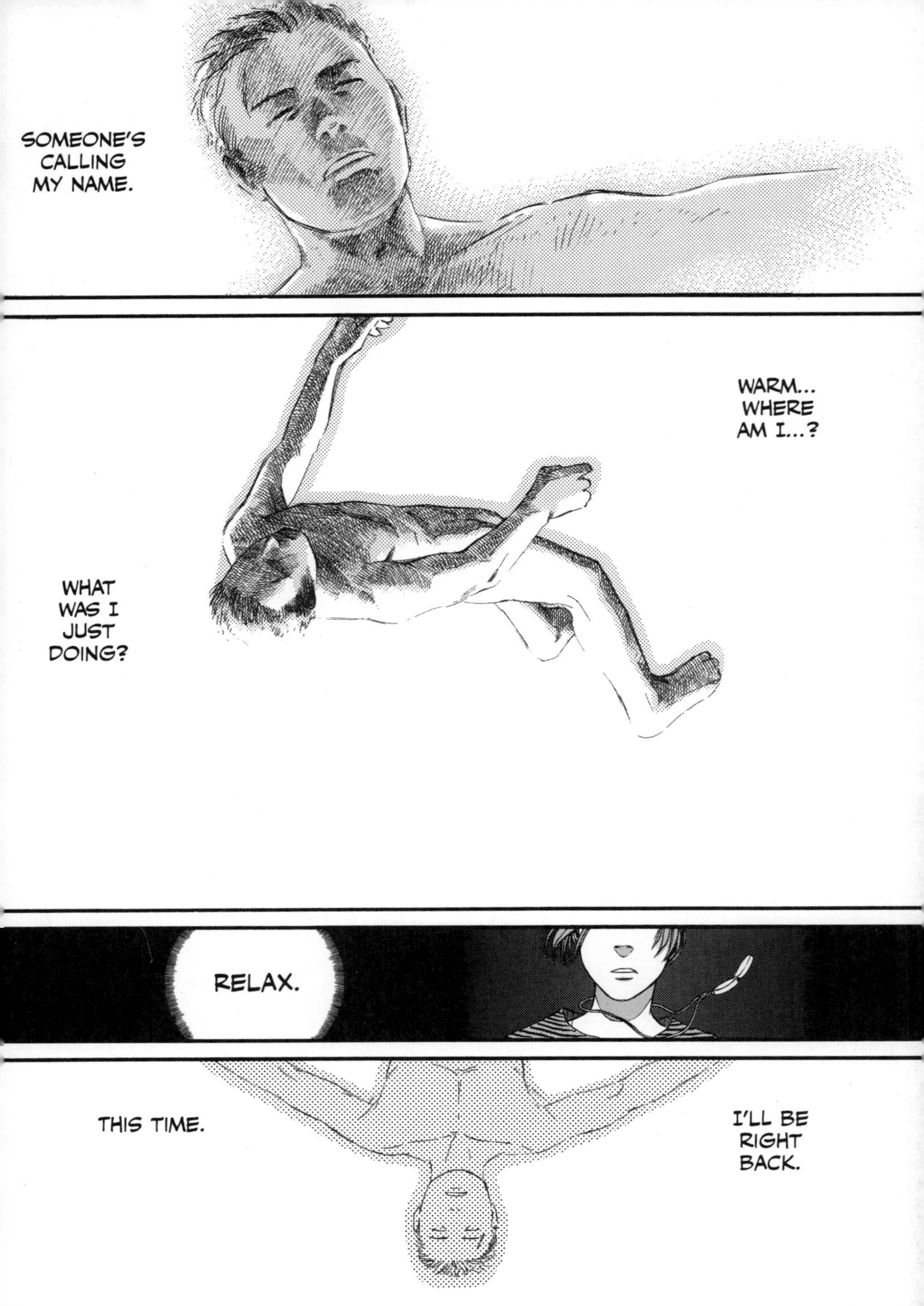
SOMEONE'S CALLING MY NAME.
WARM... WHERE AM I...?
WHAT WAS I JUST DOING?
RELAX.
I'LL BE RIGHT BACK.
THIS TIME.

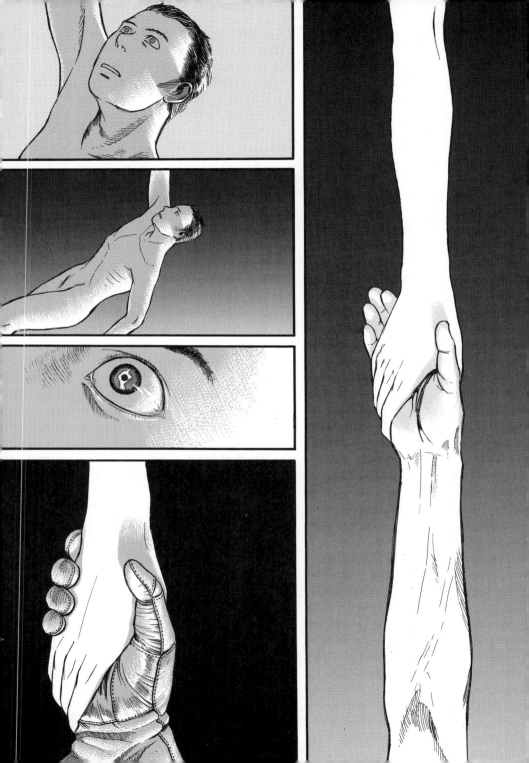

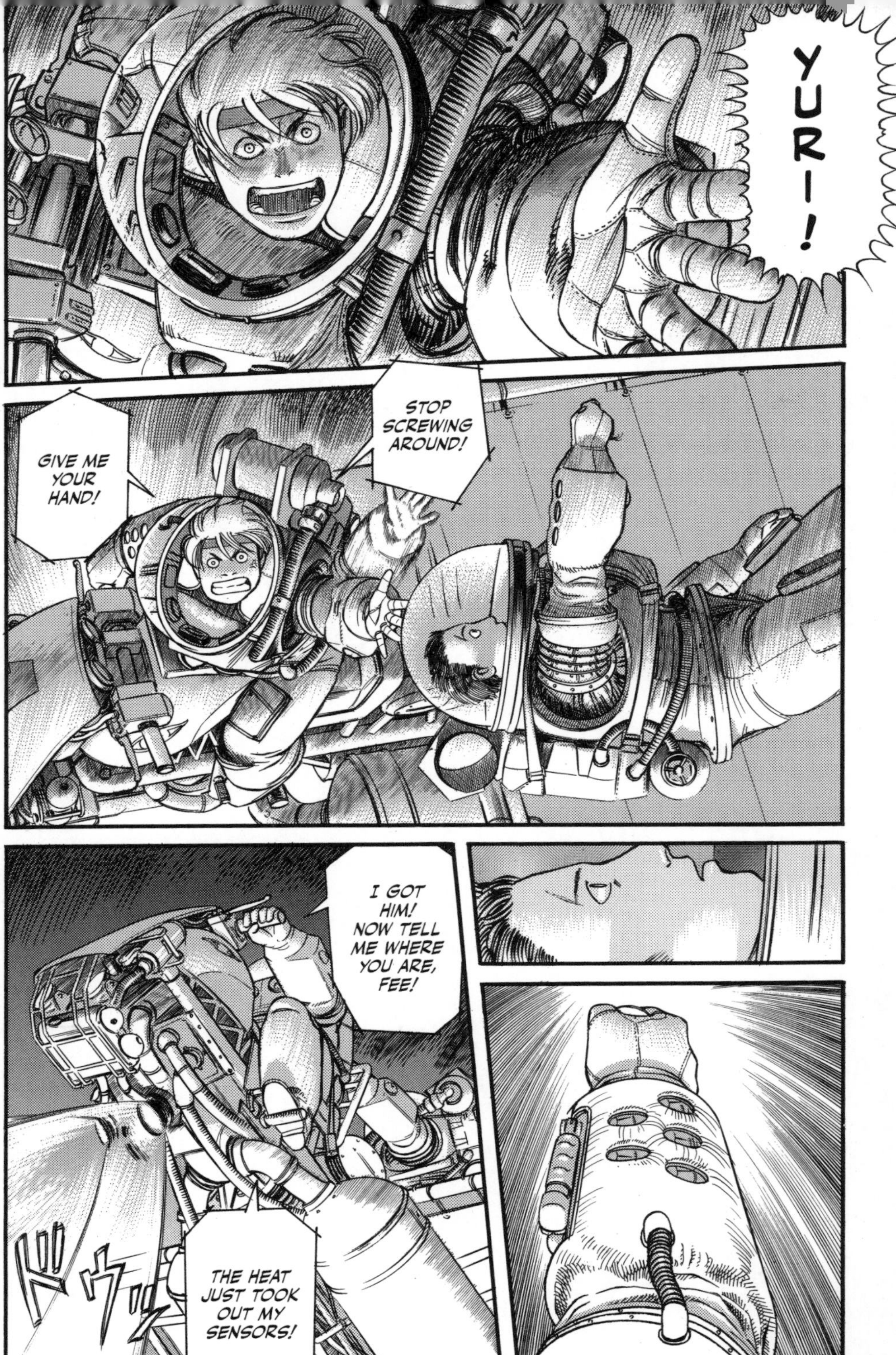
YURI-!
STOP SCREWING AROUND!
GIVE ME YOUR HAND!
I GOT HIM! NOW TELL ME WHERE YOU ARE, FEE!
THE HEAT JUST TOOK OUT MY SENSORS!

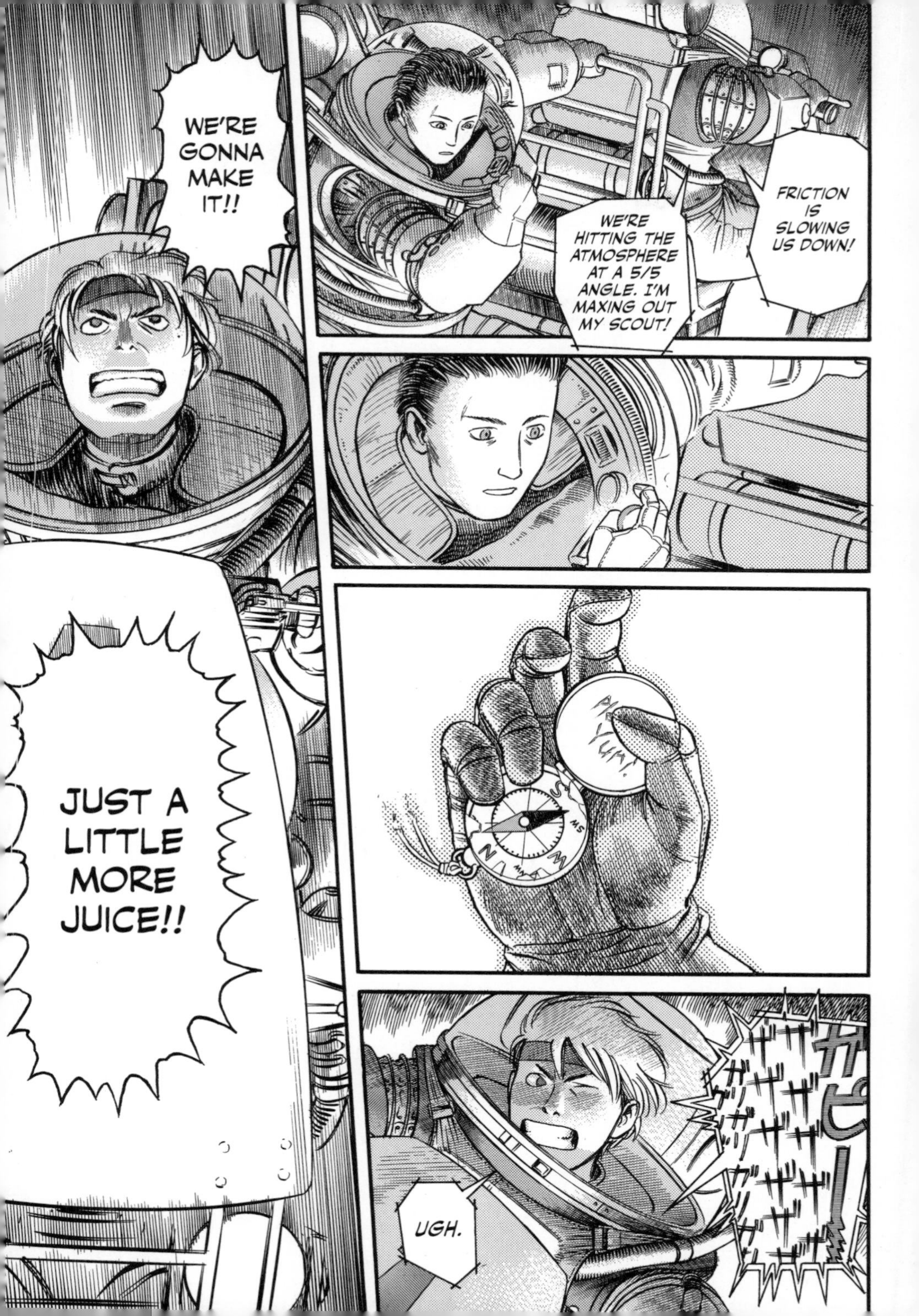
FRICTION IS SLOWING US DOWN!
WE'RE HITTING THE ATMOSPHERE AT A 5/5 ANGLE. I'M MAXING OUT MY SCOUT!
UGH.
WE'RE GONNA MAKE IT!!
JUST A LITTLE MORE JUICE!!

Please save Yuri.

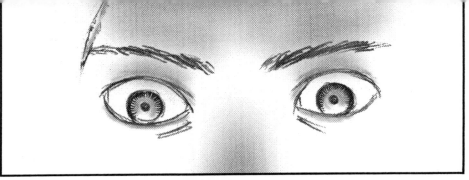

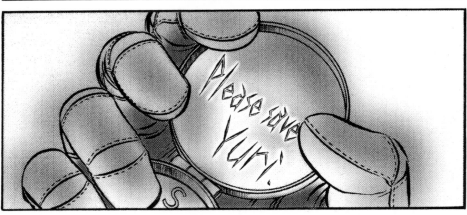

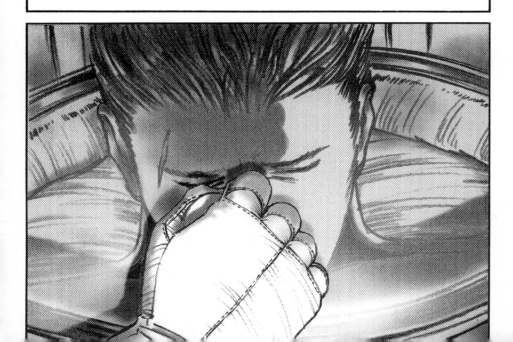

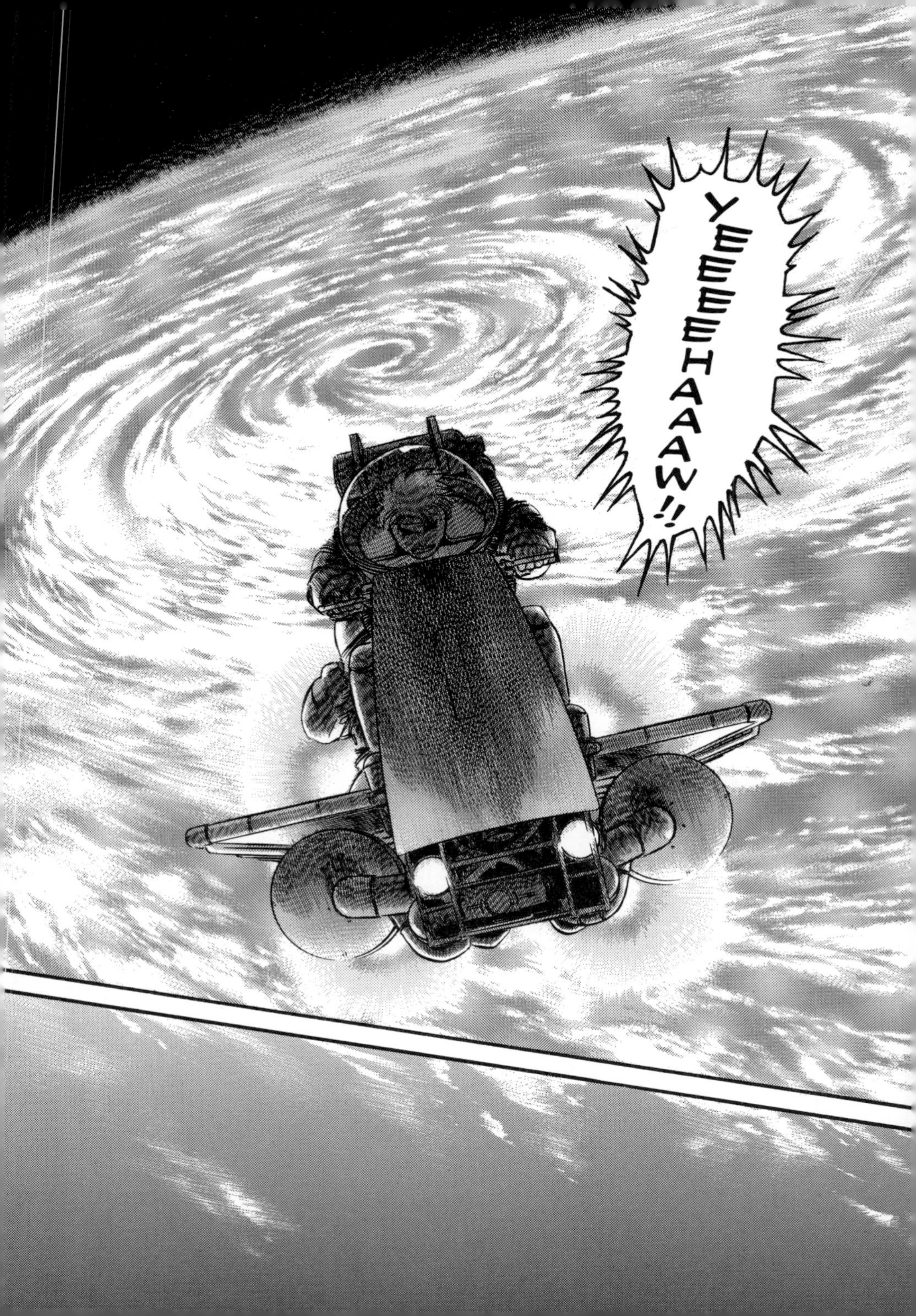
YEEEEHAAAAW!!

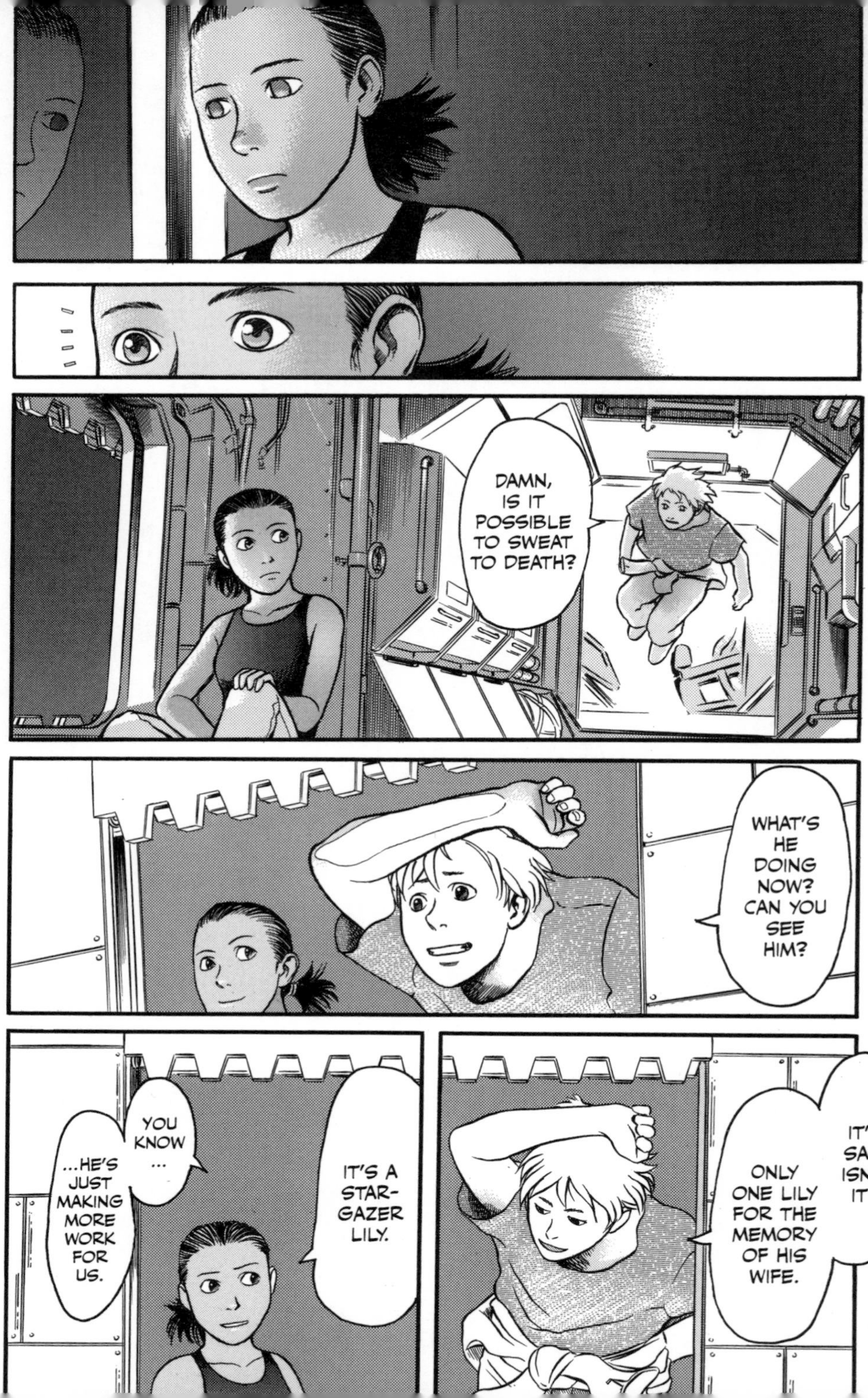
DAMN, IS IT POSSIBLE TO SWEAT TO DEATH?
WHAT'S HE DOING NOW? CAN YOU SEE HIM?
IT'S SAD, ISN'T IT?
ONLY ONE LILY FOR THE MEMORY OF HIS WIFE.
IT'S A STAR-GAZER LILY.
YOU KNOW ...
...HE'S JUST MAKING MORE WORK FOR US.

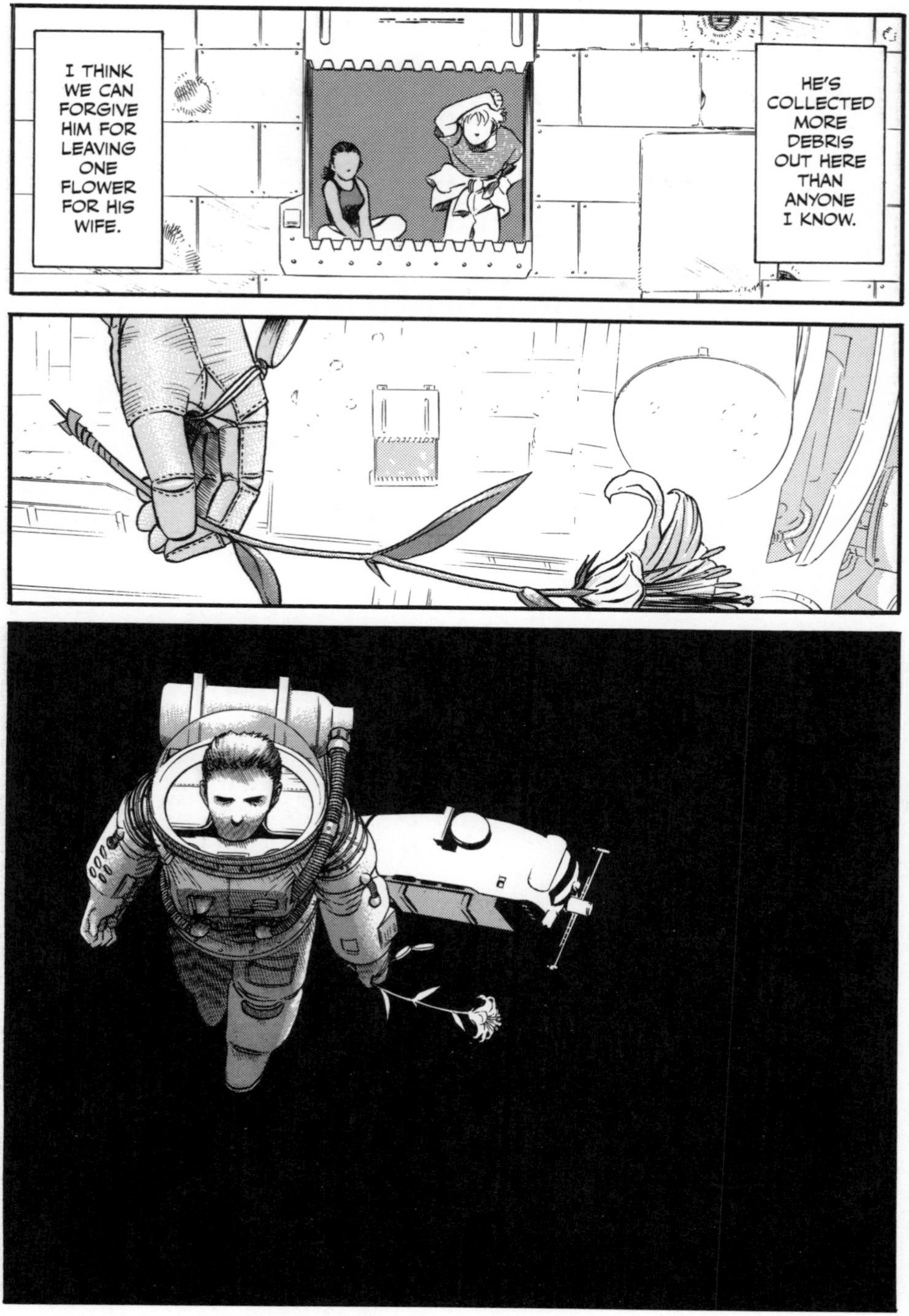
HE'S COLLECTED MORE DEBRIS OUT HERE THAN ANYONE I KNOW.
I THINK WE CAN FORGIVE HIM FOR LEAVING ONE FLOWER FOR HIS WIFE.

シュ
ボッ

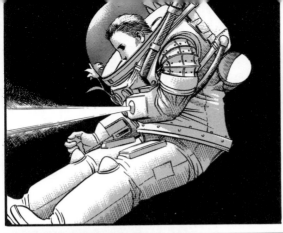

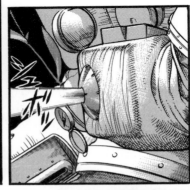

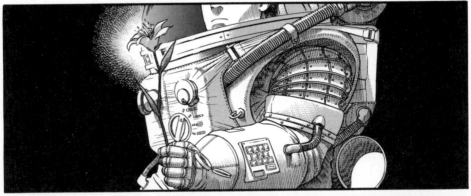

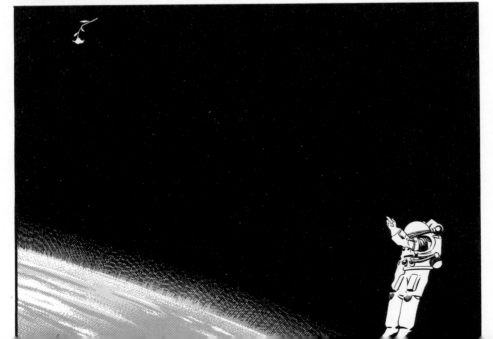

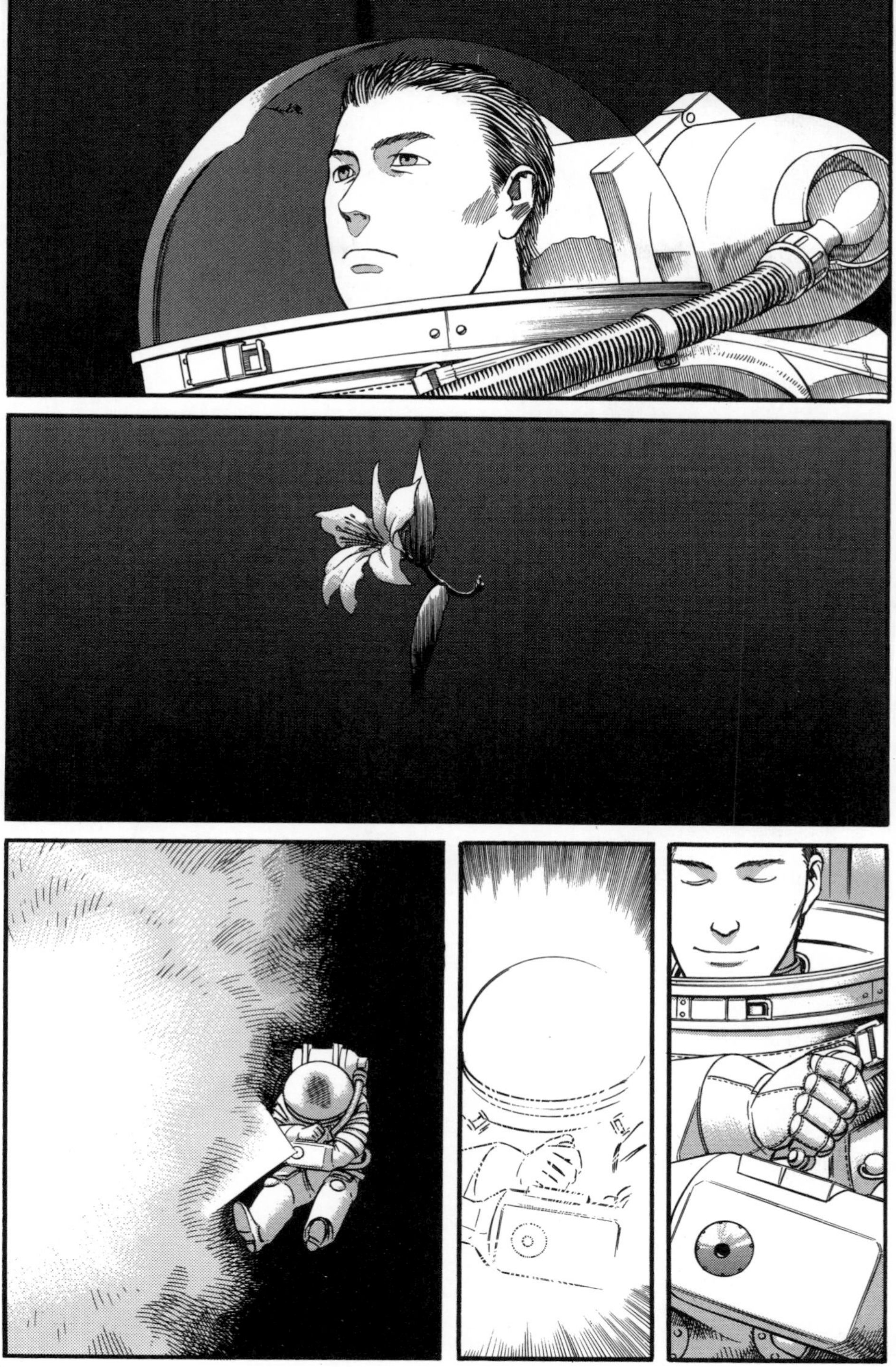

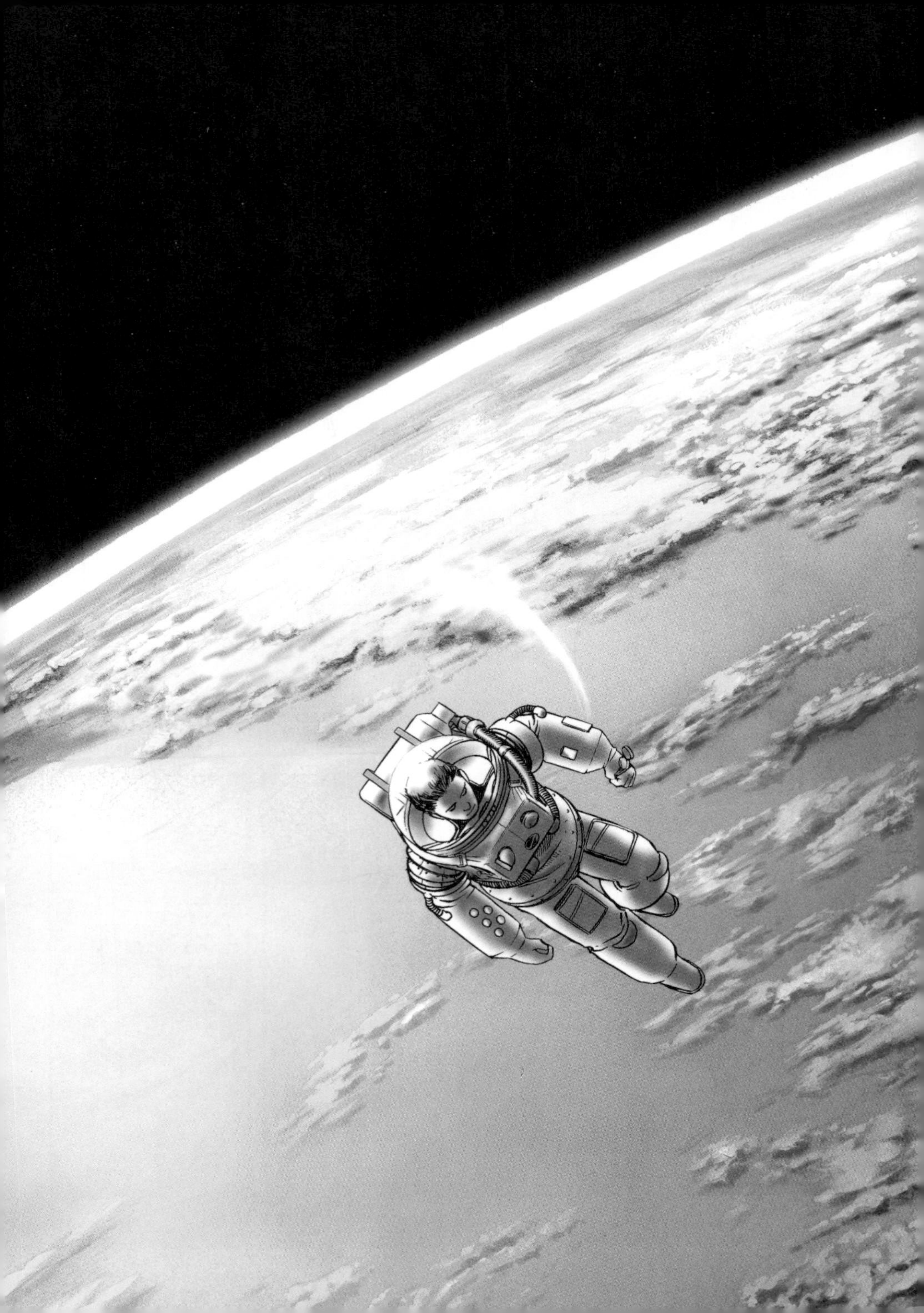

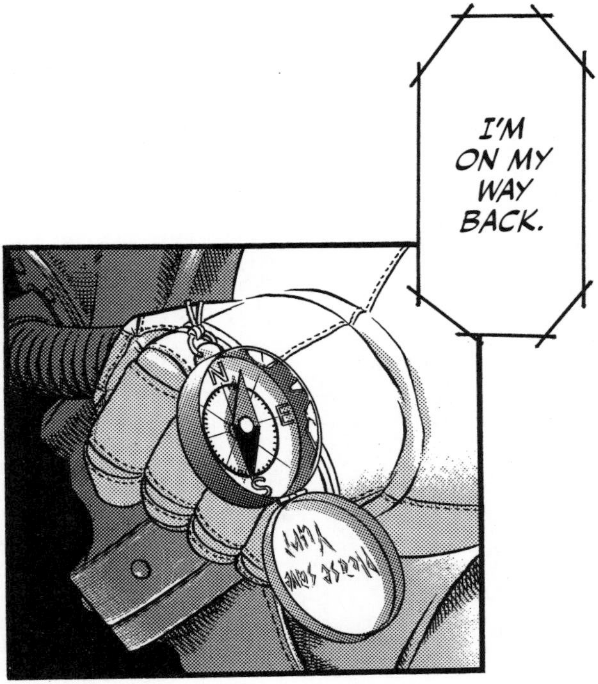
I'M ON MY WAY BACK.

PHASE 1
END

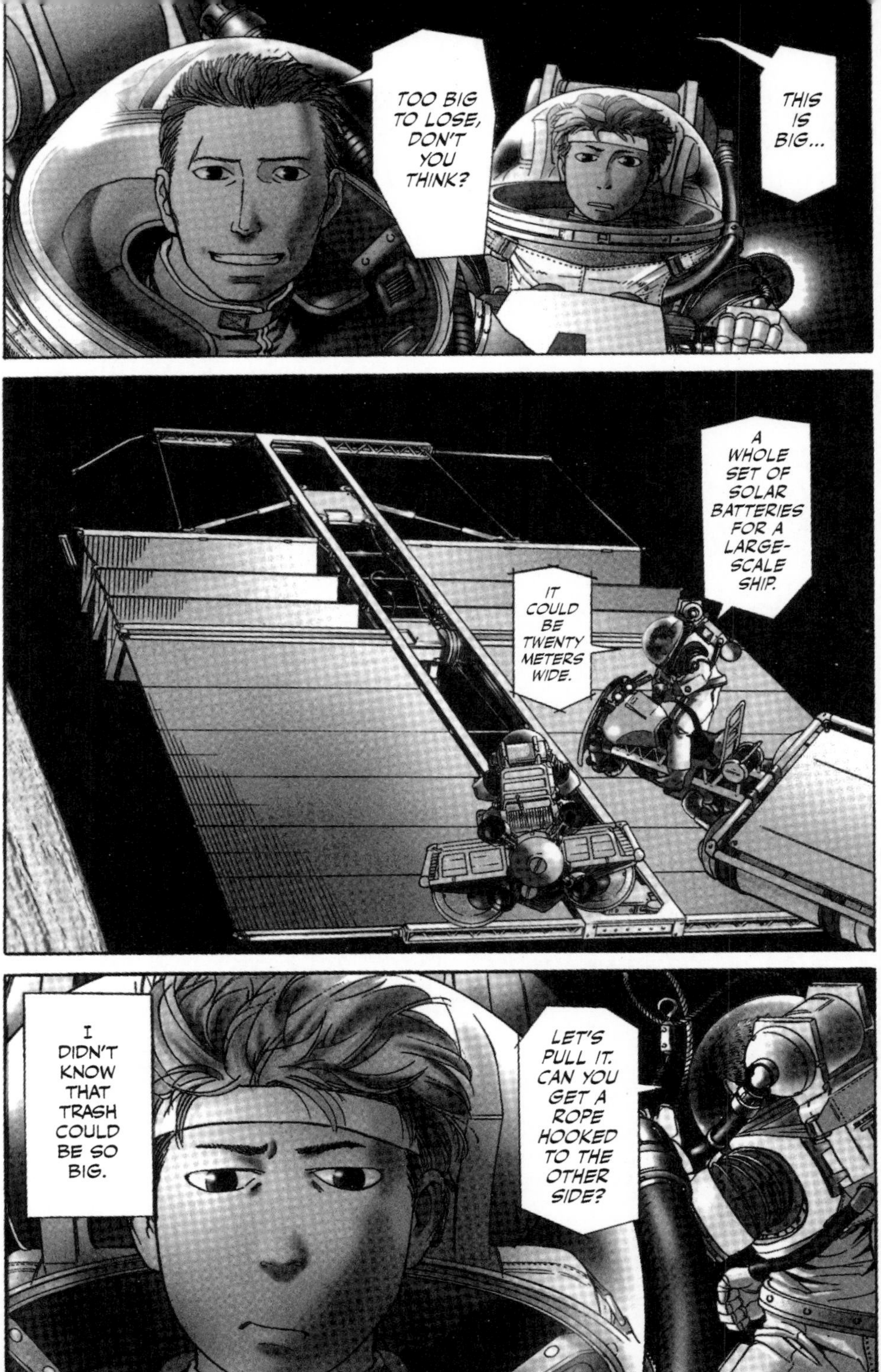
THIS IS BIG...
TOO BIG TO LOSE, DON'T YOU THINK?
A WHOLE SET OF SOLAR BATTERIES FOR A LARGE-SCALE SHIP.
IT COULD BE TWENTY METERS WIDE.
LET'S PULL IT. CAN YOU GET A ROPE HOOKED TO THE OTHER SIDE?
I DIDN'T KNOW THAT TRASH COULD BE SO BIG.

PHASE 2
A GIRL FROM BEYOND THE EARTH

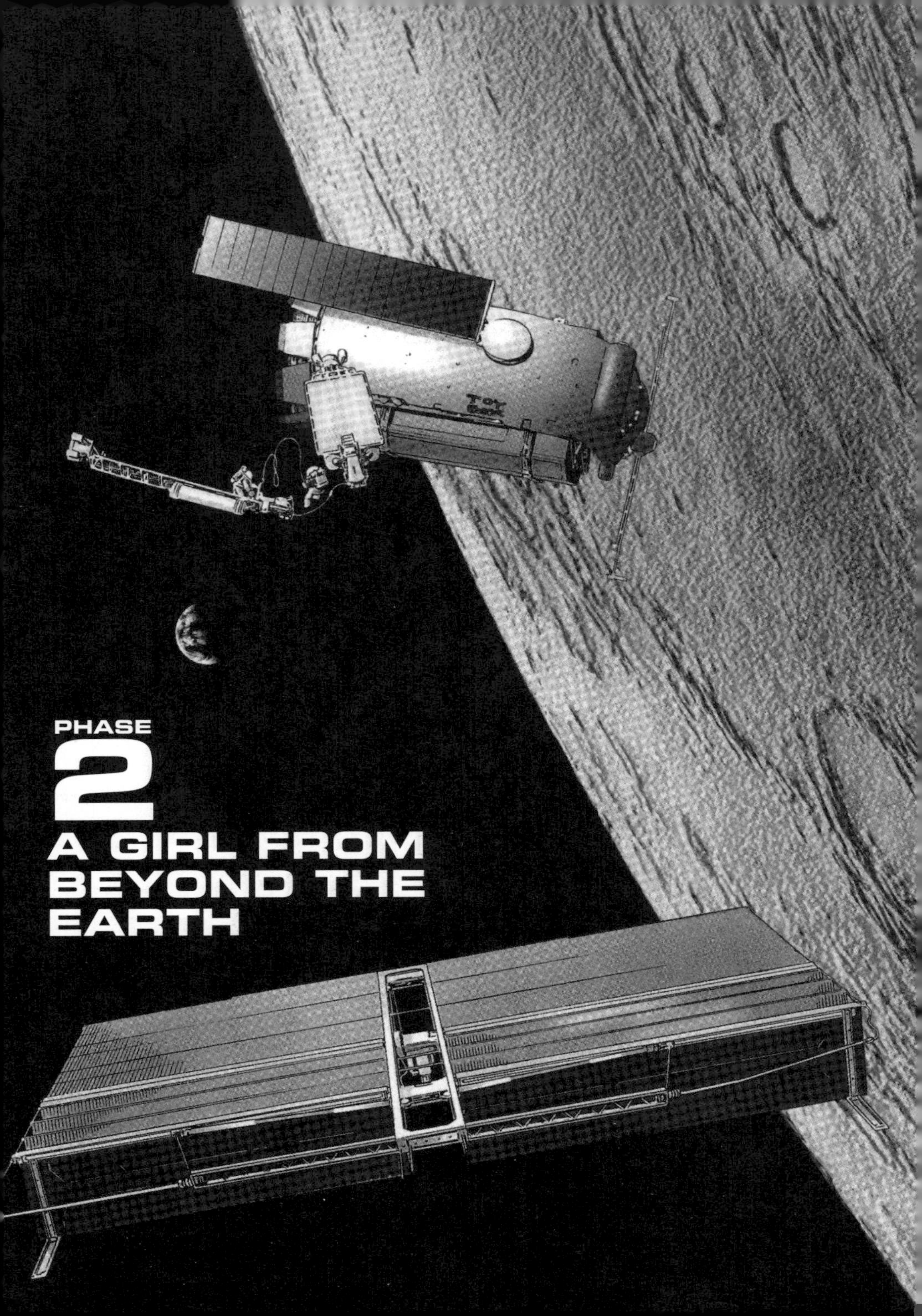

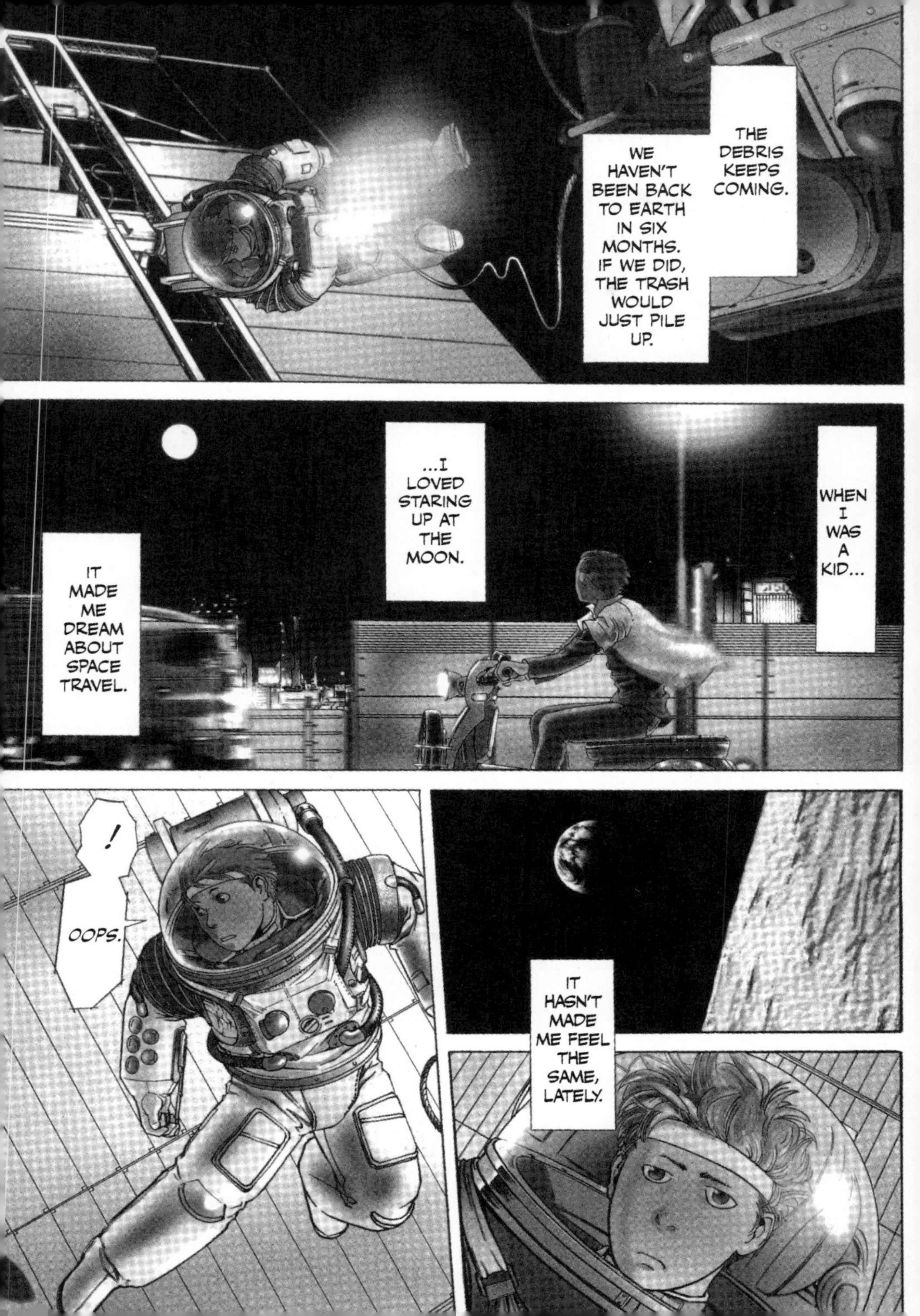
THE DEBRIS KEEPS COMING.
WE HAVEN'T BEEN BACK TO EARTH IN SIX MONTHS. IF WE DID, THE TRASH WOULD JUST PILE UP.
WHEN I WAS A KID...
...I LOVED STARING UP AT THE MOON.
IT MADE ME DREAM ABOUT SPACE TRAVEL.
IT HASN'T MADE ME FEEL THE SAME, LATELY.
!
OOPS.

UGH, IT HURTS!!

THIS IS MOTHER SHIP TO FIRST BORN. HOW YA FEELING, HACHIMAKI?

?

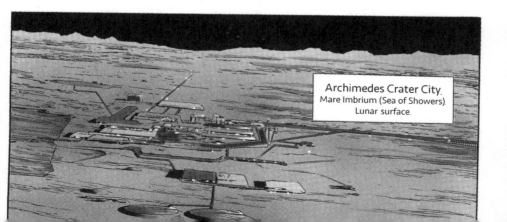

Archimedes Crater City.
Mare Imbrium (Sea of Showers).
Lunar surface.

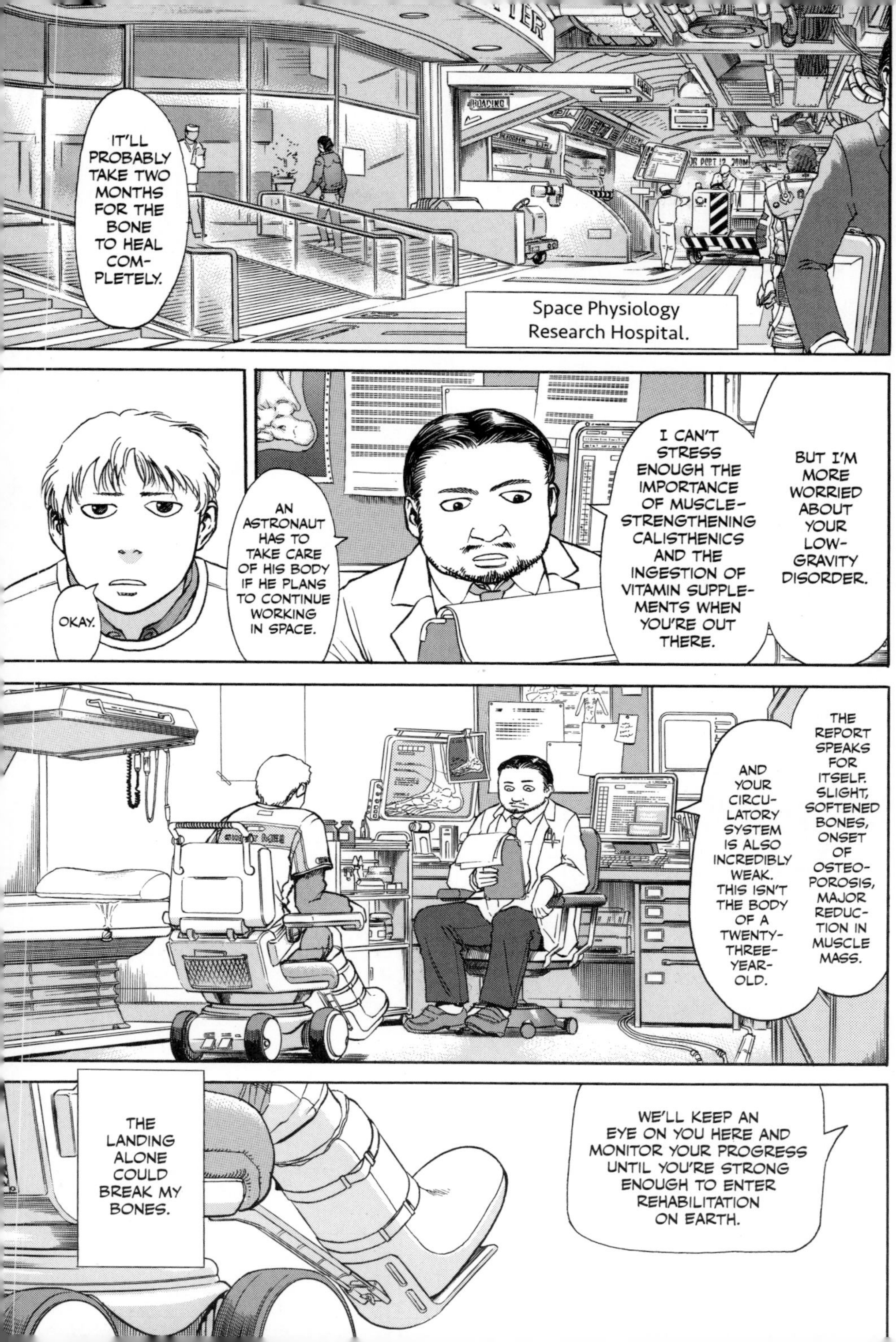
Space Physiology Research Hospital.
IT'LL PROBABLY TAKE TWO MONTHS FOR THE BONE TO HEAL COMPLETELY.
BUT I'M MORE WORRIED ABOUT YOUR LOW-GRAVITY DISORDER.
I CAN'T STRESS ENOUGH THE IMPORTANCE OF MUSCLE-STRENGTHENING CALISTHENICS AND THE INGESTION OF VITAMIN SUPPLEMENTS WHEN YOU'RE OUT THERE.
AN ASTRONAUT HAS TO TAKE CARE OF HIS BODY IF HE PLANS TO CONTINUE WORKING IN SPACE.
OKAY.
THE REPORT SPEAKS FOR ITSELF. SLIGHT, SOFTENED BONES, ONSET OF OSTEOPOROSIS, MAJOR REDUCTION IN MUSCLE MASS.
AND YOUR CIRCULATORY SYSTEM IS ALSO INCREDIBLY WEAK. THIS ISN'T THE BODY OF A TWENTY-THREE-YEAR-OLD.
WE'LL KEEP AN EYE ON YOU HERE AND MONITOR YOUR PROGRESS UNTIL YOU'RE STRONG ENOUGH TO ENTER REHABILITATION ON EARTH.
THE LANDING ALONE COULD BREAK MY BONES.

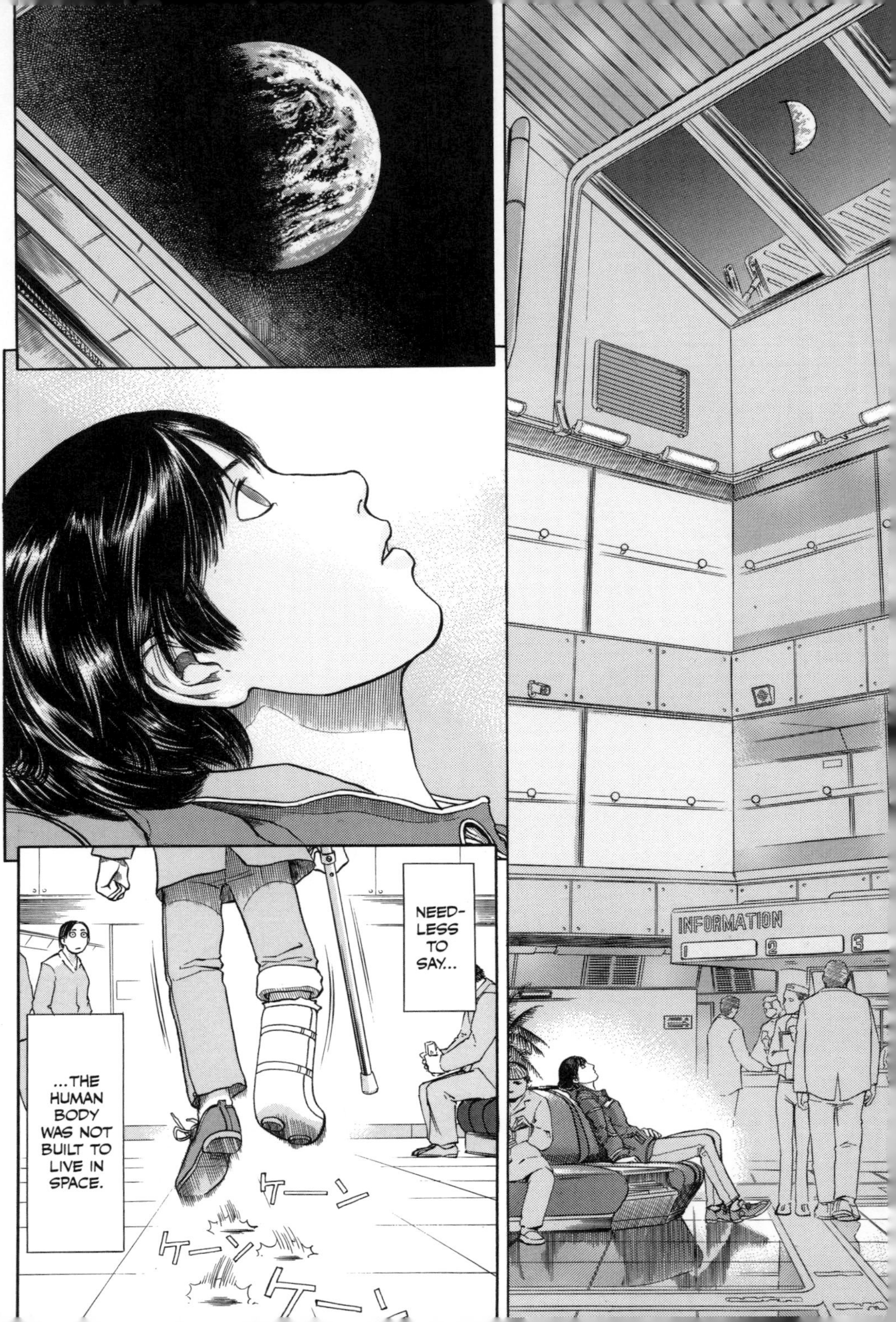

INFORMATION
1
2
3
NEED-LESS TO SAY...
...THE HUMAN BODY WAS NOT BUILT TO LIVE IN SPACE.
ケーン
ケーン
ケーン

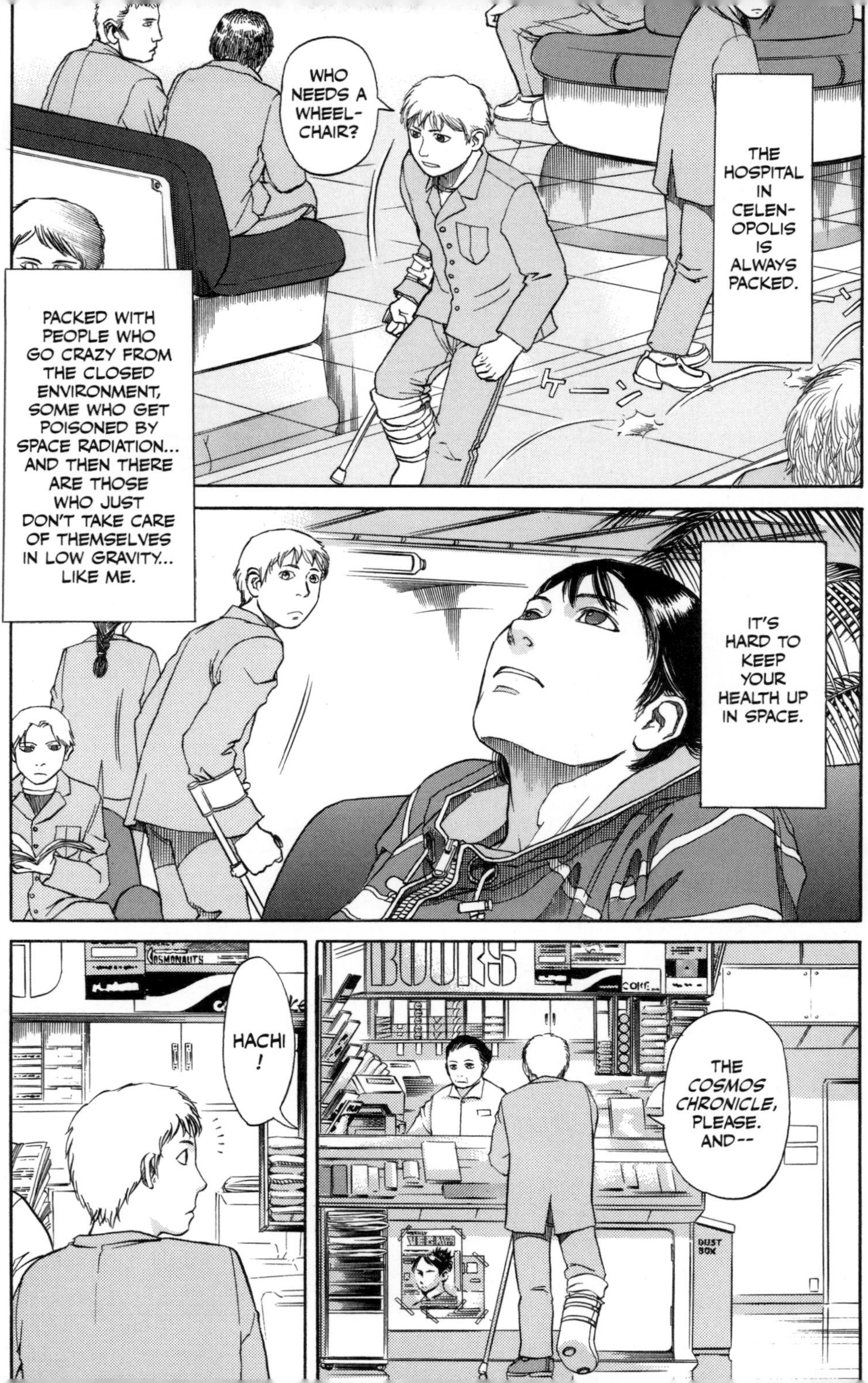
THE HOSPITAL IN CELEN-OPOLIS IS ALWAYS PACKED.
WHO NEEDS A WHEEL-CHAIR?
ケーン
PACKED WITH PEOPLE WHO GO CRAZY FROM THE CLOSED ENVIRONMENT, SOME WHO GET POISONED BY SPACE RADIATION... AND THEN THERE ARE THOSE WHO JUST DON'T TAKE CARE OF THEMSELVES IN LOW GRAVITY... LIKE ME.
IT'S HARD TO KEEP YOUR HEALTH UP IN SPACE.
BOOKS
THE COSMOS CHRONICLE, PLEASE. AND--
DUST BOX
COSMONAUTS
HACHI!

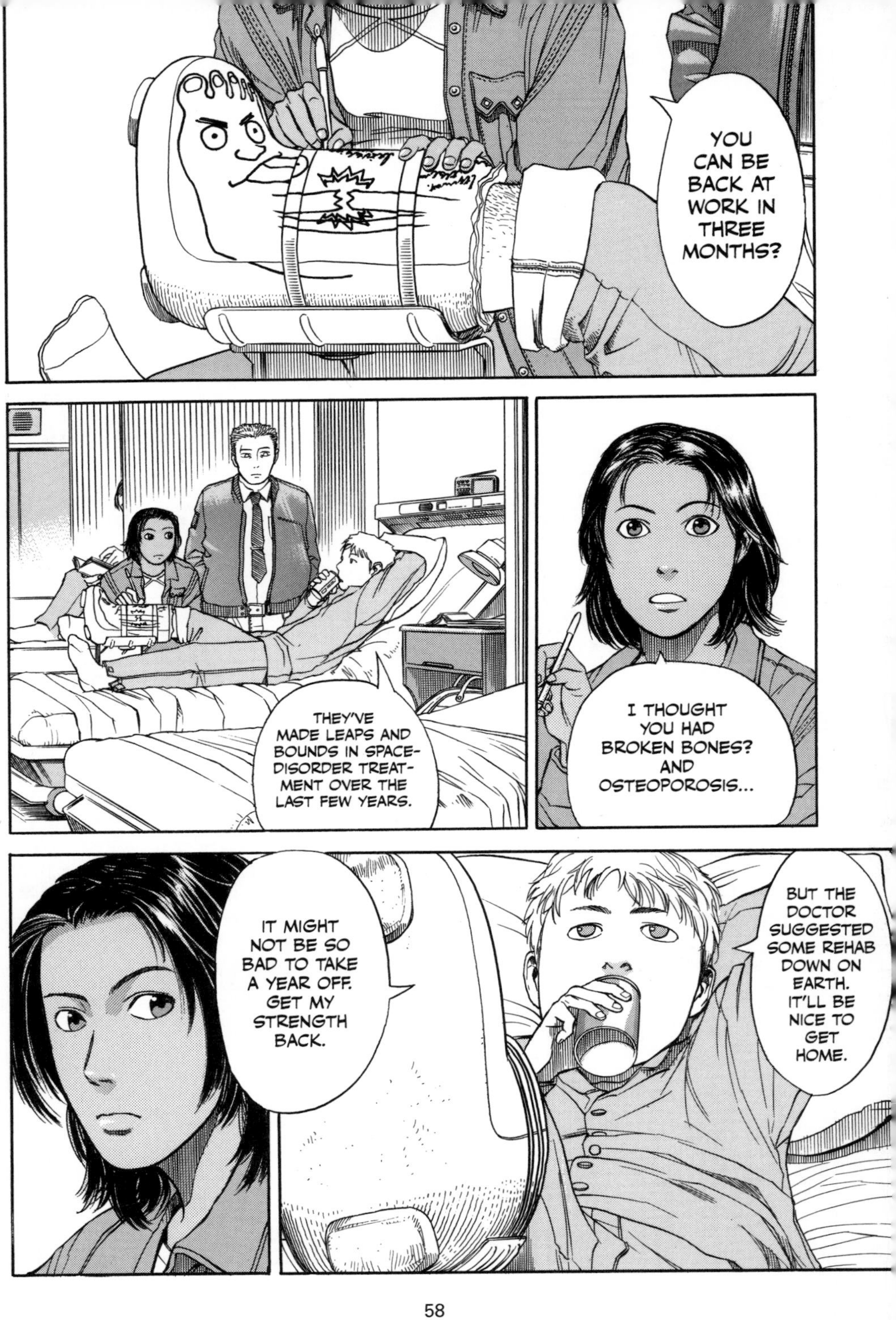
YOU CAN BE BACK AT WORK IN THREE MONTHS?
I THOUGHT YOU HAD BROKEN BONES? AND OSTEOPOROSIS...
THEY'VE MADE LEAPS AND BOUNDS IN SPACE-DISORDER TREATMENT OVER THE LAST FEW YEARS.
BUT THE DOCTOR SUGGESTED SOME REHAB DOWN ON EARTH. IT'LL BE NICE TO GET HOME.
IT MIGHT NOT BE SO BAD TO TAKE A YEAR OFF. GET MY STRENGTH BACK.

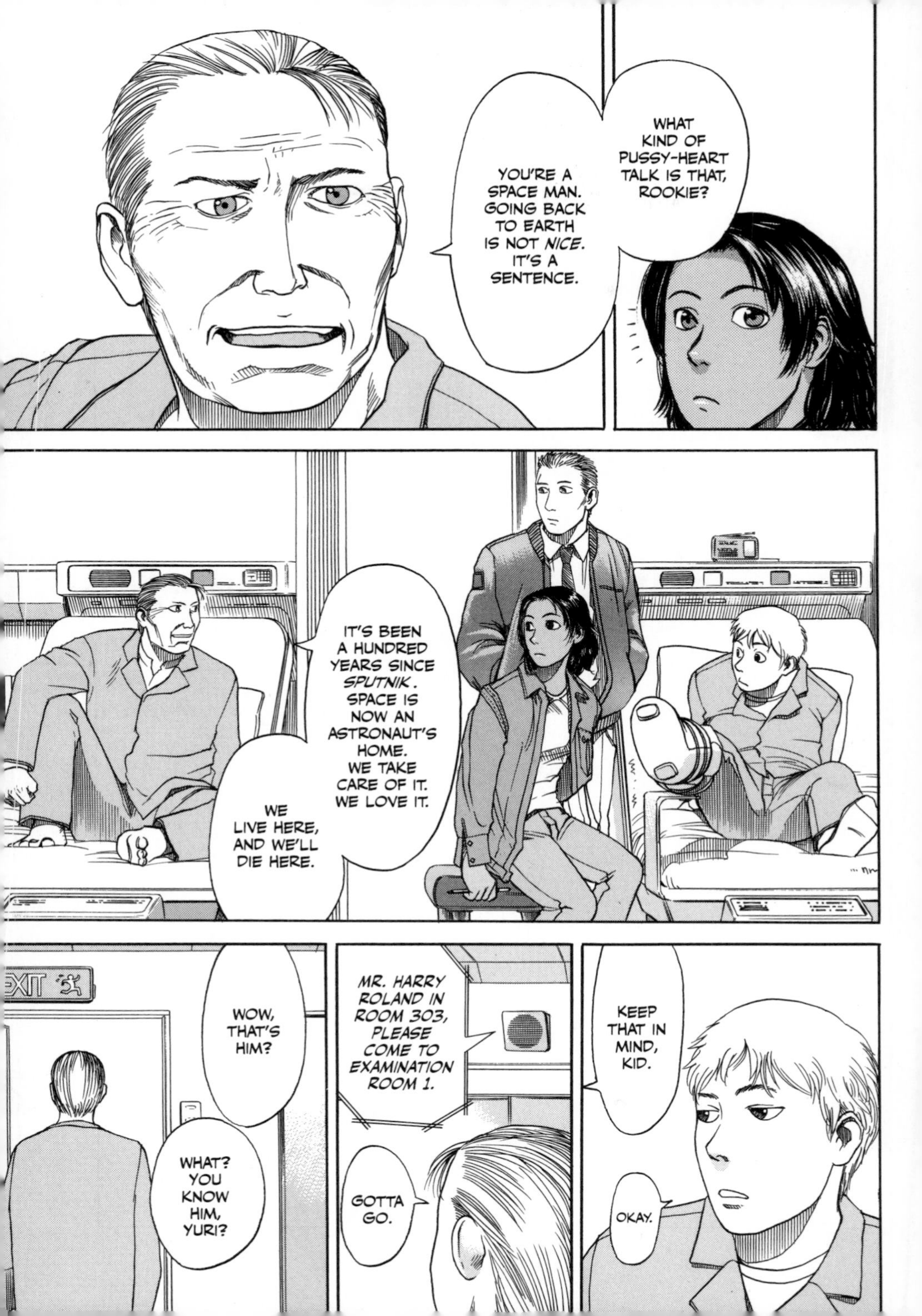
WHAT KIND OF PUSSY-HEART TALK IS THAT, ROOKIE?
YOU'RE A SPACE MAN. GOING BACK TO EARTH IS NOT *NICE*. IT'S A SENTENCE.
IT'S BEEN A HUNDRED YEARS SINCE *SPUTNIK*. SPACE IS NOW AN ASTRONAUT'S HOME. WE TAKE CARE OF IT. WE LOVE IT.
WE LIVE HERE, AND WE'LL DIE HERE.
KEEP THAT IN MIND, KID.
OKAY.
MR. HARRY ROLAND IN ROOM 303, PLEASE COME TO EXAMINATION ROOM 1.
GOTTA GO.
WOW, THAT'S HIM?
EXIT
WHAT? YOU KNOW HIM, YURI?

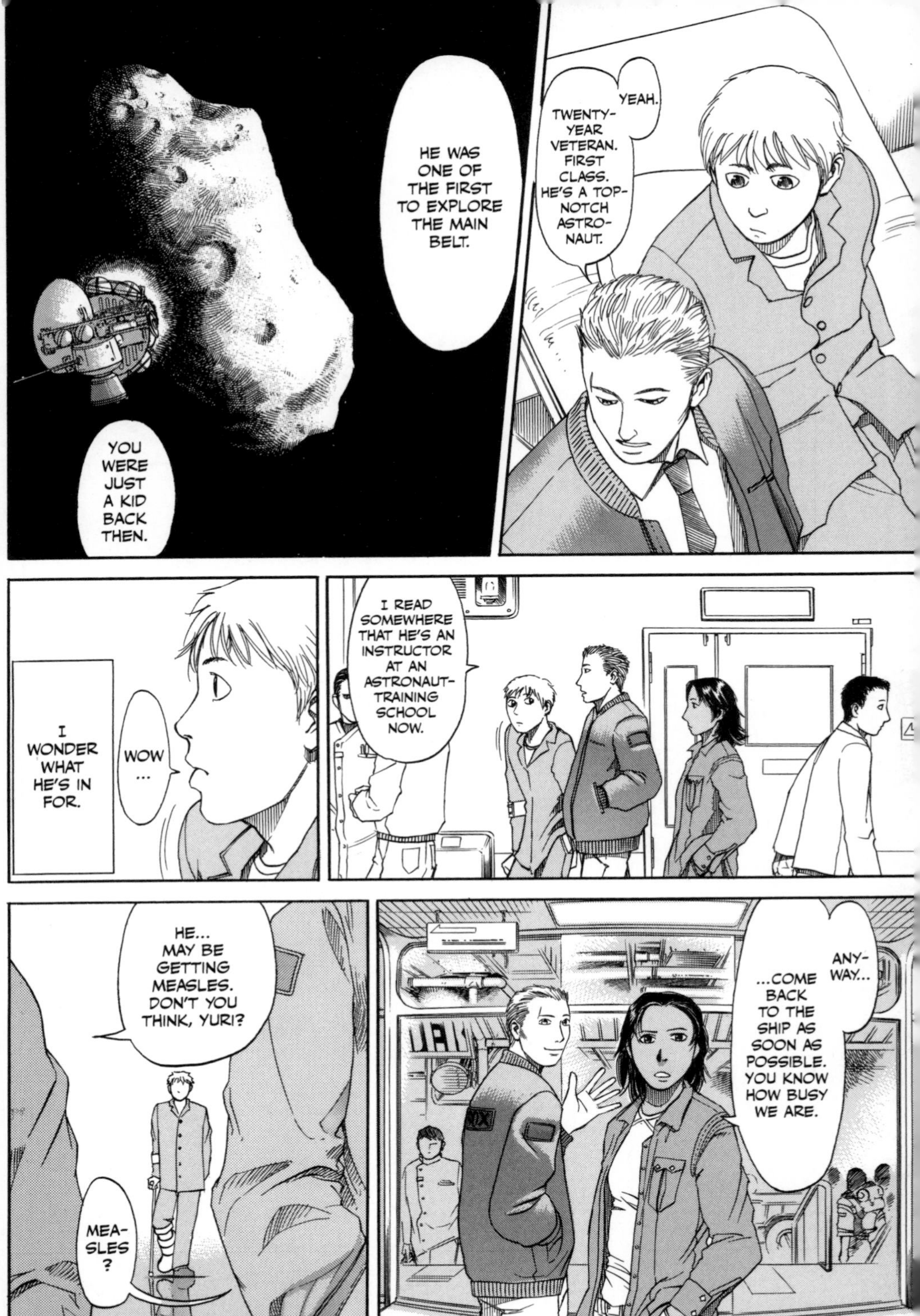
YEAH.
TWENTY-YEAR VETERAN. FIRST CLASS. HE'S A TOP-NOTCH ASTRONAUT.
HE WAS ONE OF THE FIRST TO EXPLORE THE MAIN BELT.
YOU WERE JUST A KID BACK THEN.
I READ SOMEWHERE THAT HE'S AN INSTRUCTOR AT AN ASTRONAUT-TRAINING SCHOOL NOW.
WOW ...
I WONDER WHAT HE'S IN FOR.
ANY-WAY...
...COME BACK TO THE SHIP AS SOON AS POSSIBLE. YOU KNOW HOW BUSY WE ARE.
HE... MAY BE GETTING MEASLES. DON'T YOU THINK, YURI?
MEA-SLES ?

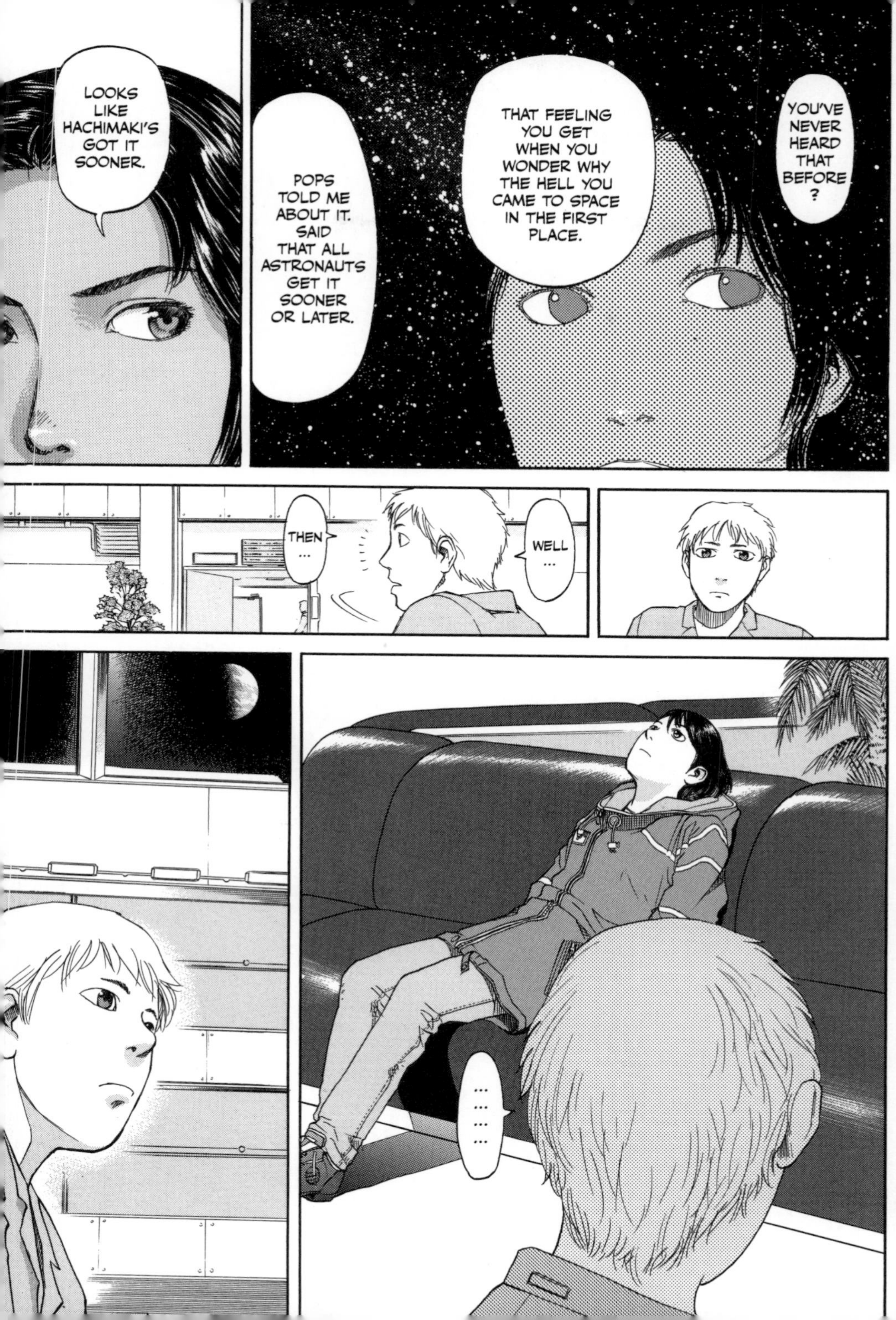
YOU'VE NEVER HEARD THAT BEFORE?
THAT FEELING YOU GET WHEN YOU WONDER WHY THE HELL YOU CAME TO SPACE IN THE FIRST PLACE.
POPS TOLD ME ABOUT IT. SAID THAT ALL ASTRONAUTS GET IT SOONER OR LATER.
LOOKS LIKE HACHIMAKI'S GOT IT SOONER.
WELL ...
THEN ...
... ...

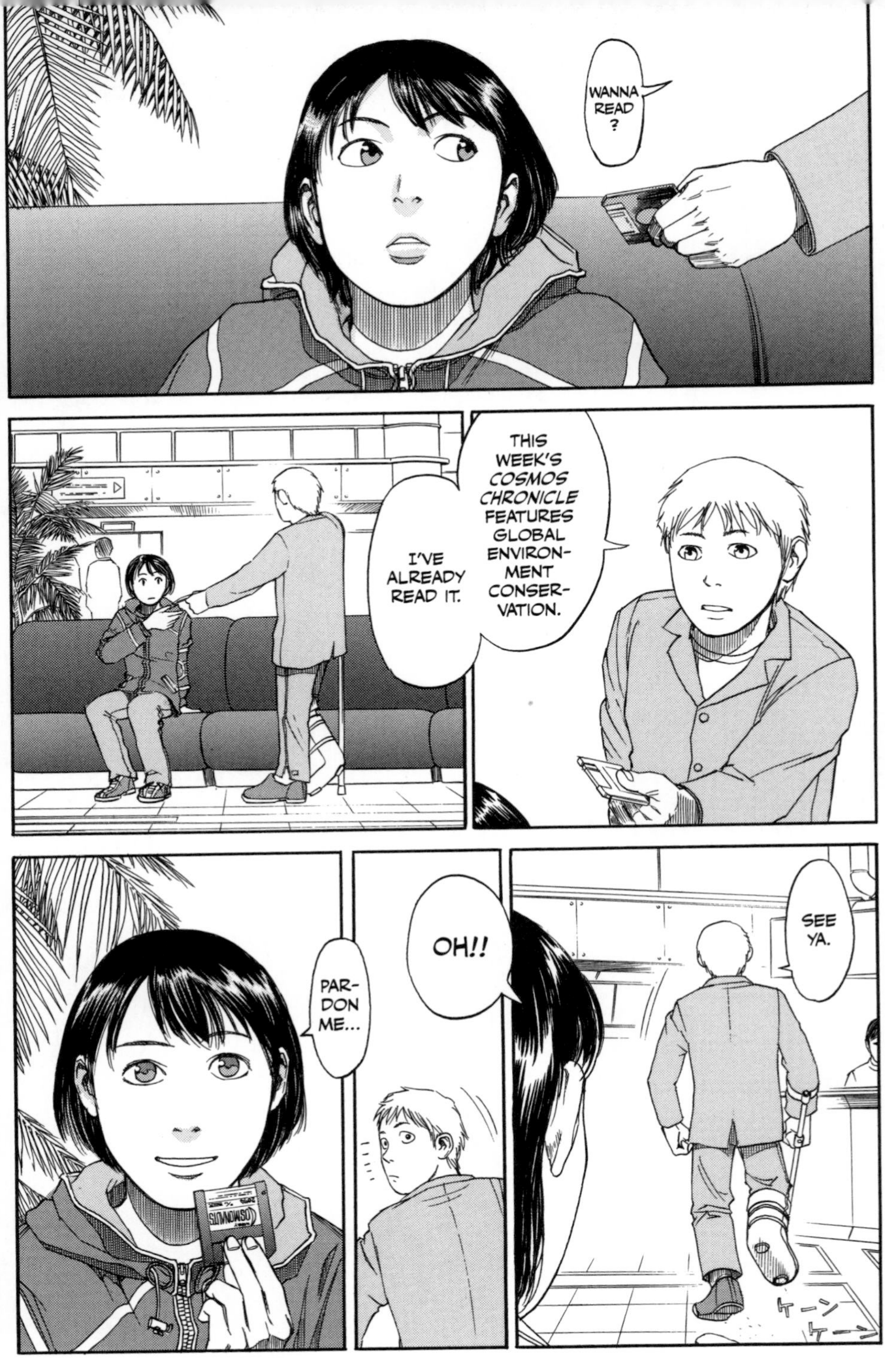
WANNA READ ?
THIS WEEK'S *COSMOS CHRONICLE* FEATURES GLOBAL ENVIRONMENT CONSERVATION.
I'VE ALREADY READ IT.
SEE YA.
ケーン
ケーン
OH!!
PAR-DON ME...

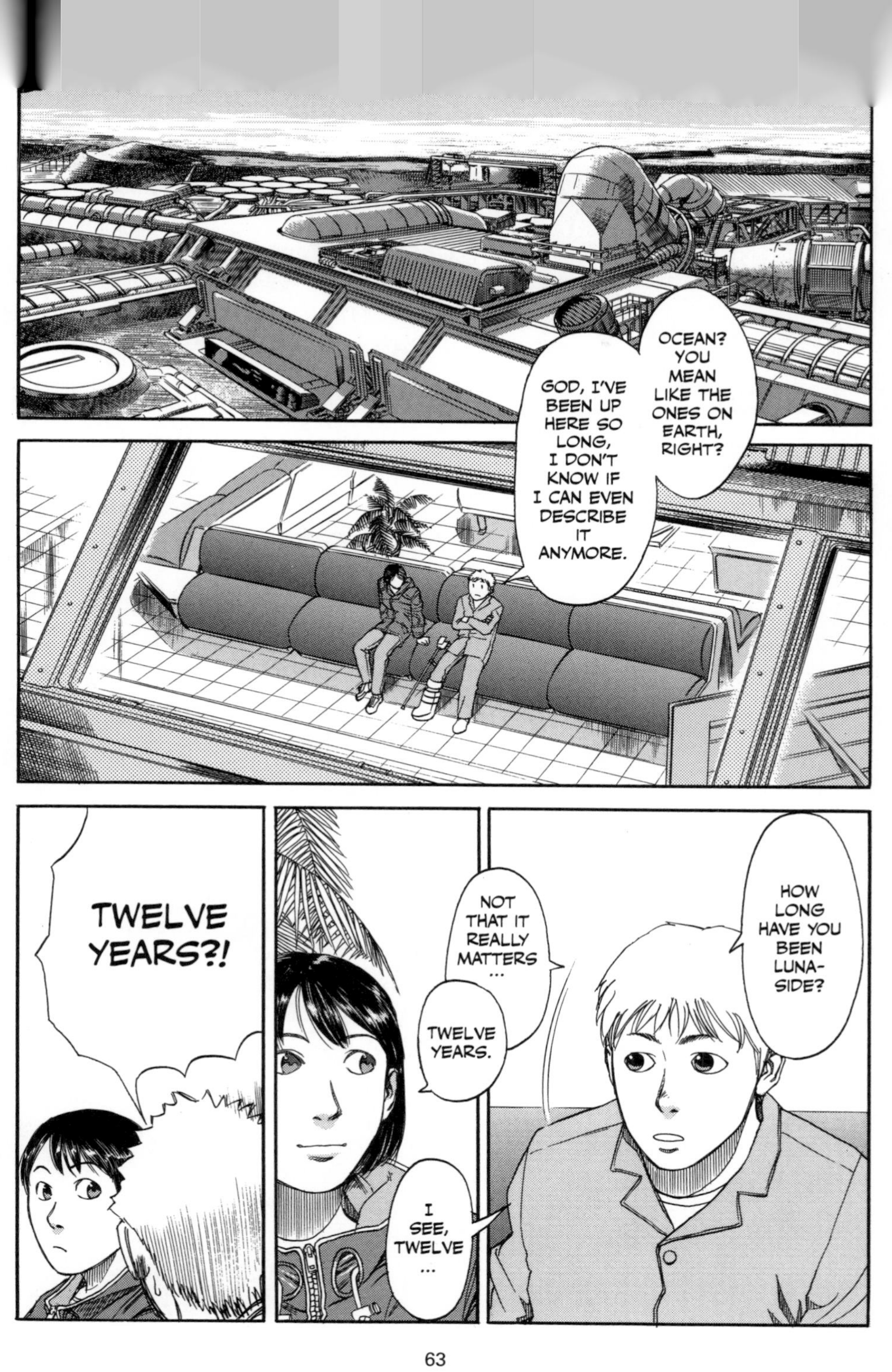
OCEAN? YOU MEAN LIKE THE ONES ON EARTH, RIGHT?
GOD, I'VE BEEN UP HERE SO LONG, I DON'T KNOW IF I CAN EVEN DESCRIBE IT ANYMORE.
HOW LONG HAVE YOU BEEN LUNA-SIDE?
NOT THAT IT REALLY MATTERS...
TWELVE YEARS.
I SEE, TWELVE...
TWELVE YEARS?!

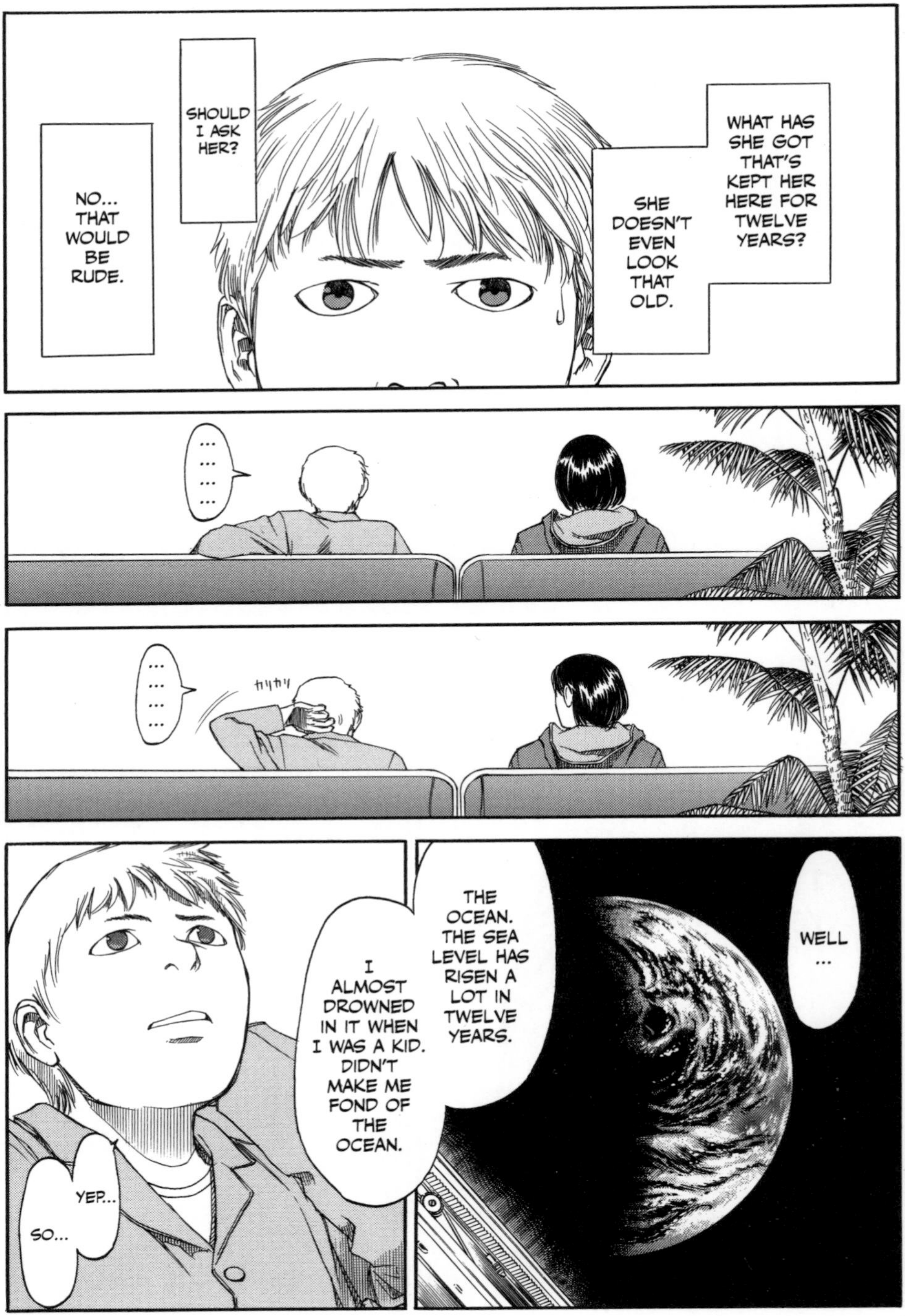
WHAT HAS SHE GOT THAT'S KEPT HER HERE FOR TWELVE YEARS?
SHE DOESN'T EVEN LOOK THAT OLD.
SHOULD I ASK HER?
NO... THAT WOULD BE RUDE.
... ...
カリカリ
... ...
WELL ...
THE OCEAN. THE SEA LEVEL HAS RISEN A LOT IN TWELVE YEARS.
I ALMOST DROWNED IN IT WHEN I WAS A KID. DIDN'T MAKE ME FOND OF THE OCEAN.
YEP... SO...

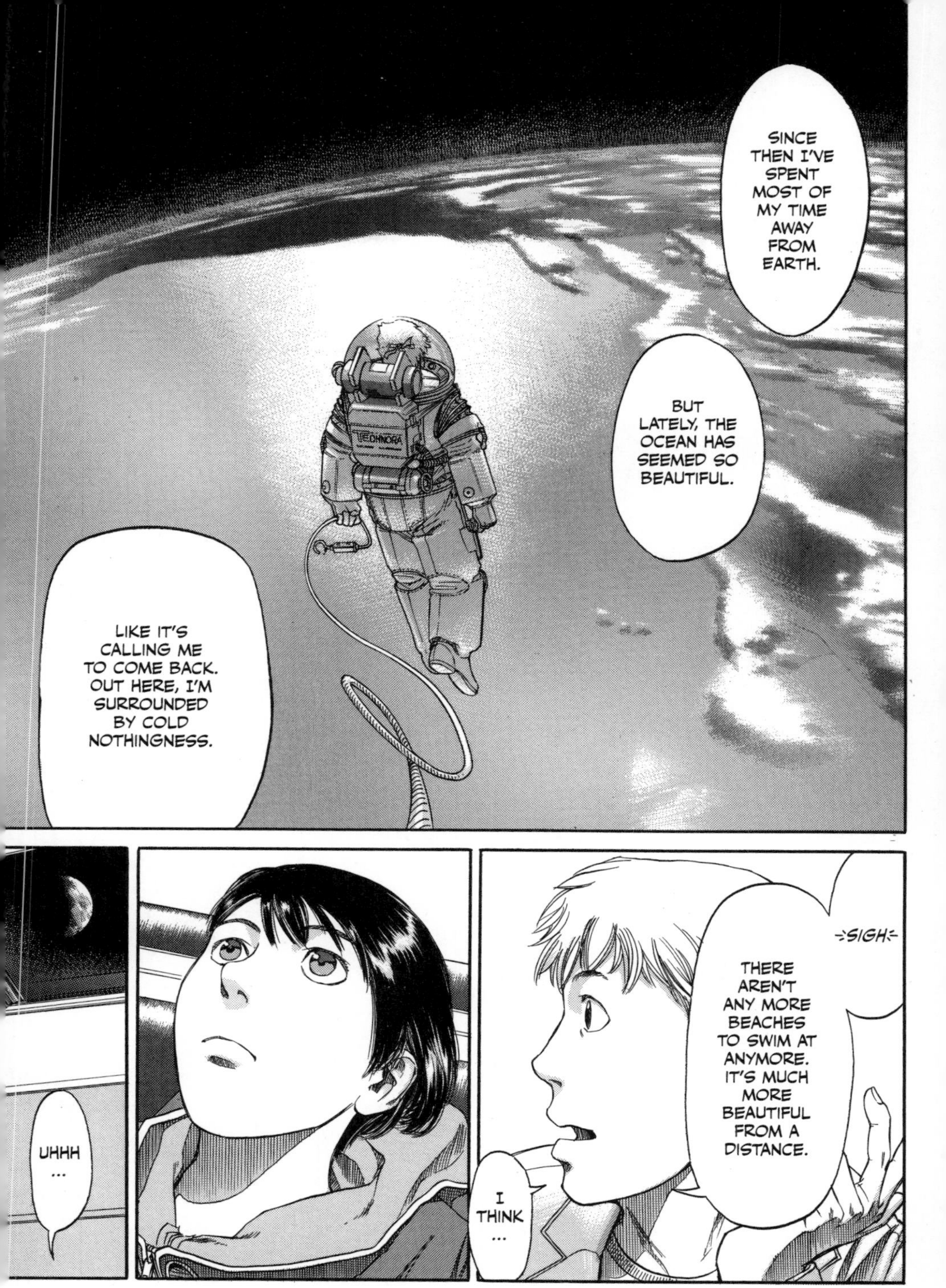
SINCE THEN I'VE SPENT MOST OF MY TIME AWAY FROM EARTH.
BUT LATELY, THE OCEAN HAS SEEMED SO BEAUTIFUL.
LIKE IT'S CALLING ME TO COME BACK. OUT HERE, I'M SURROUNDED BY COLD NOTHINGNESS.
TECHNORA
SIGH
THERE AREN'T ANY MORE BEACHES TO SWIM AT ANYMORE. IT'S MUCH MORE BEAUTIFUL FROM A DISTANCE.
I THINK ...
UHHH ...

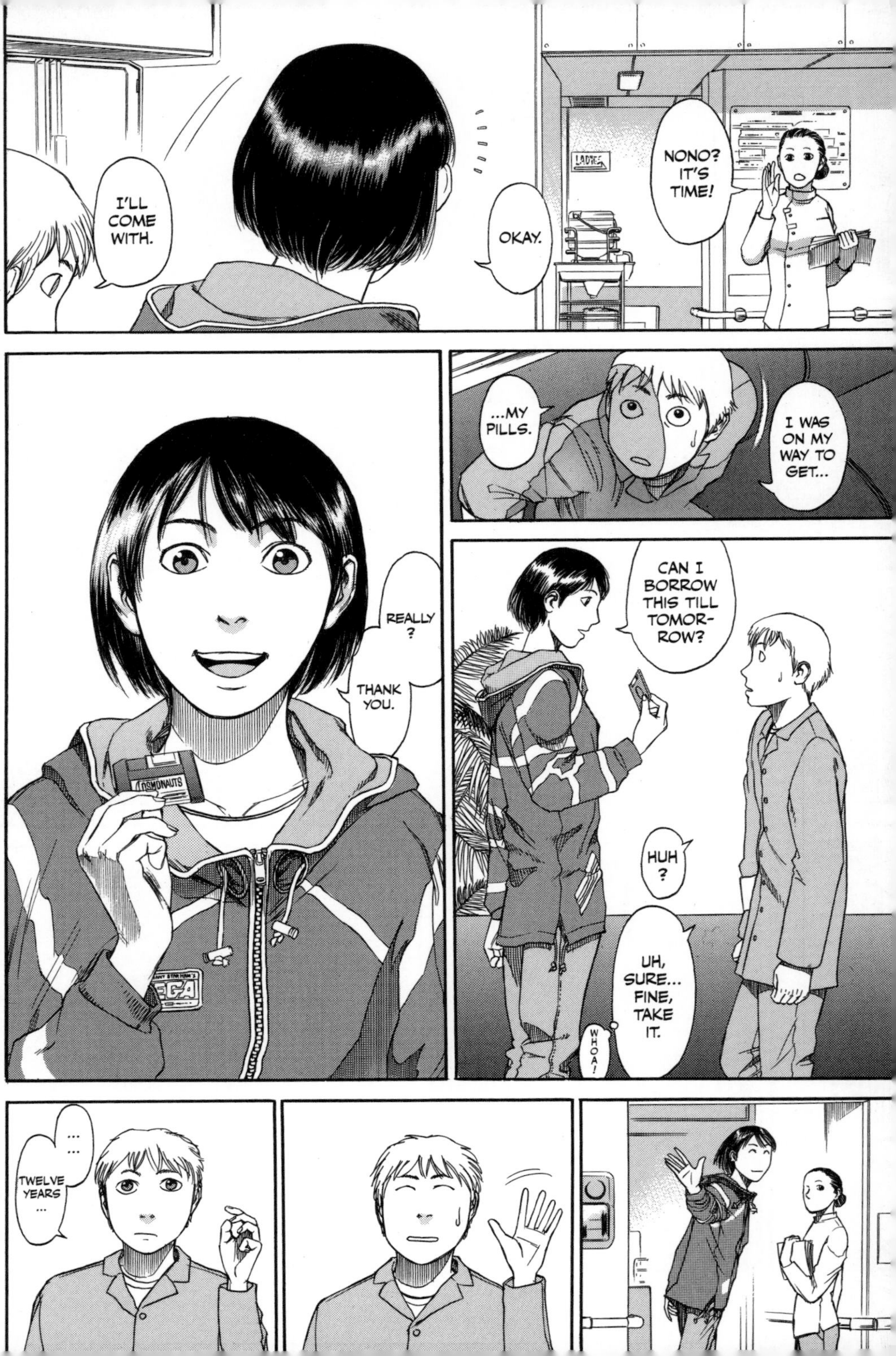
NONO? IT'S TIME!
OKAY.
I'LL COME WITH.
I WAS ON MY WAY TO GET...
...MY PILLS.
CAN I BORROW THIS TILL TOMOR-ROW?
HUH?
UH, SURE... FINE, TAKE IT.
WHOA!
REALLY?
THANK YOU.
...
...
TWELVE YEARS
...

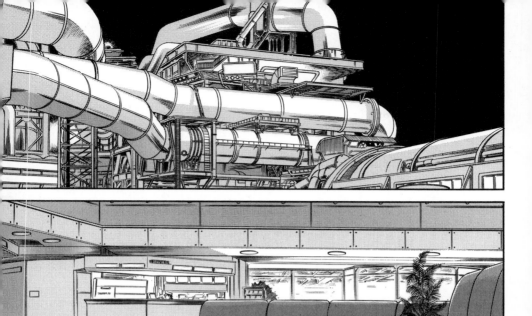

LONG-TERM TREATMENT FOR REAL ILLNESSES IS USUALLY DONE ON EARTH. THE ONLY PEOPLE UP HERE HAVE EITHER GONE WEAK OR CRAZY, AND IF ANYTHING IS THAT SERIOUS, ZIP RIGHT ON BACK TO EARTH.
TWELVE YEARS...
I DON'T THINK I COULD STAND IT.
NO...
BEING A PATIENT FOR THAT LONG...

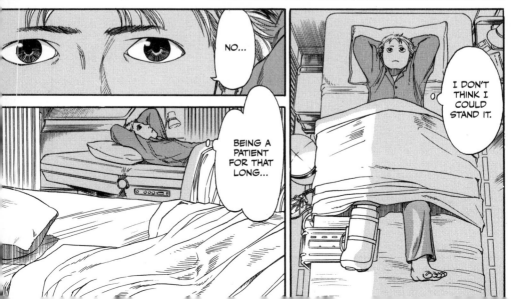

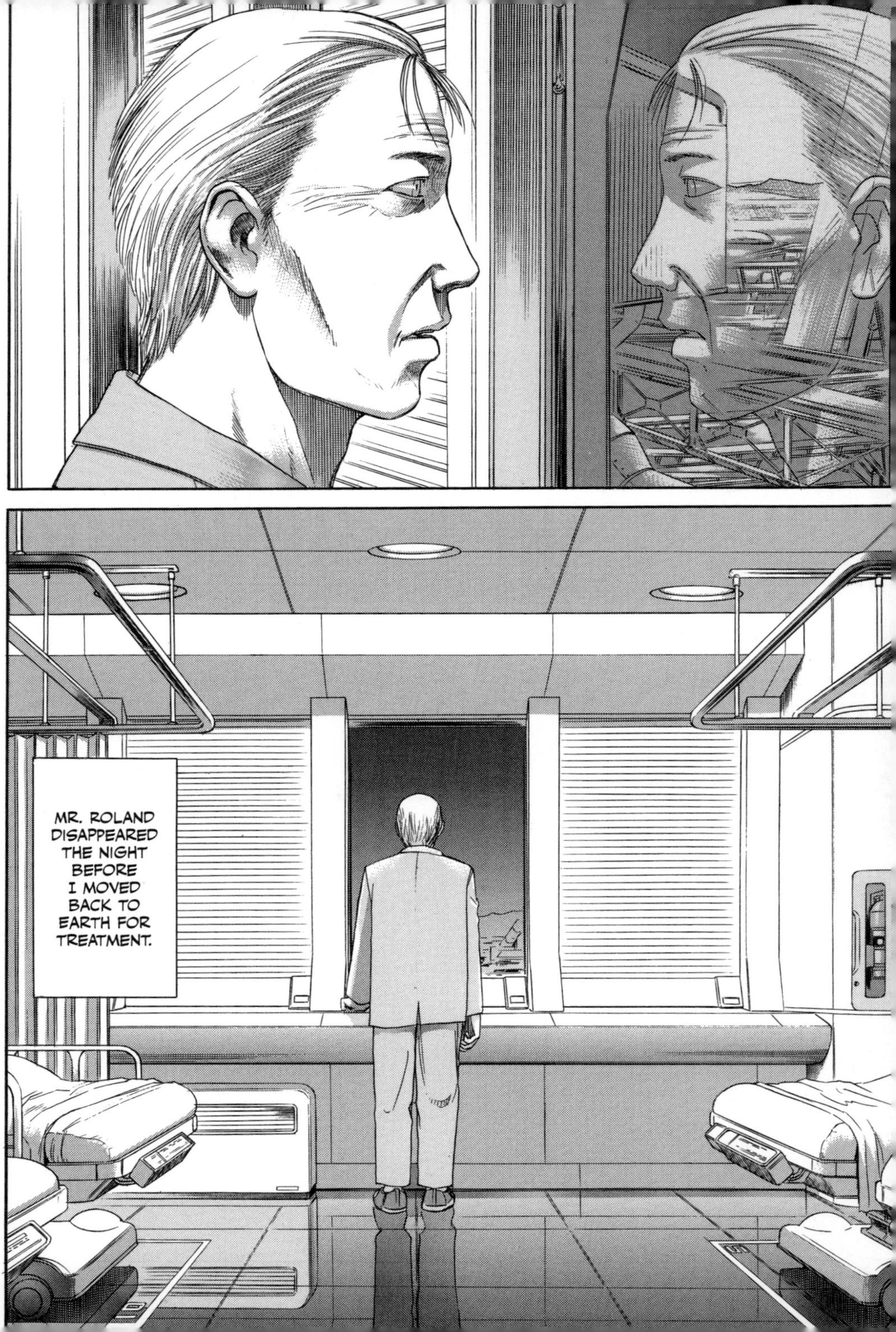
MR. ROLAND DISAPPEARED THE NIGHT BEFORE I MOVED BACK TO EARTH FOR TREATMENT.

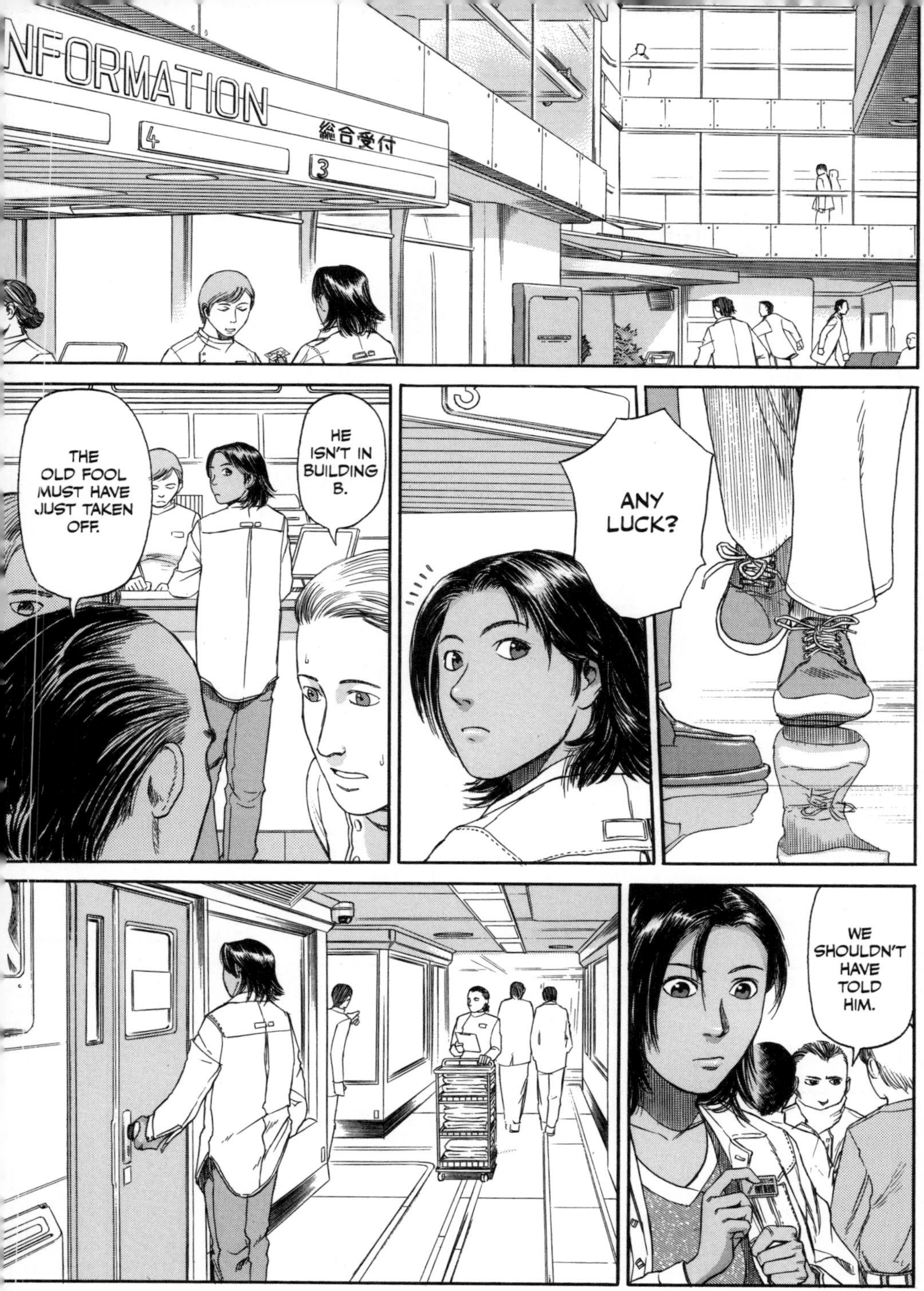
NFORMATION
4
総合受付
3
ANY LUCK?
HE ISN'T IN BUILDING B.
THE OLD FOOL MUST HAVE JUST TAKEN OFF.
WE SHOULDN'T HAVE TOLD HIM.

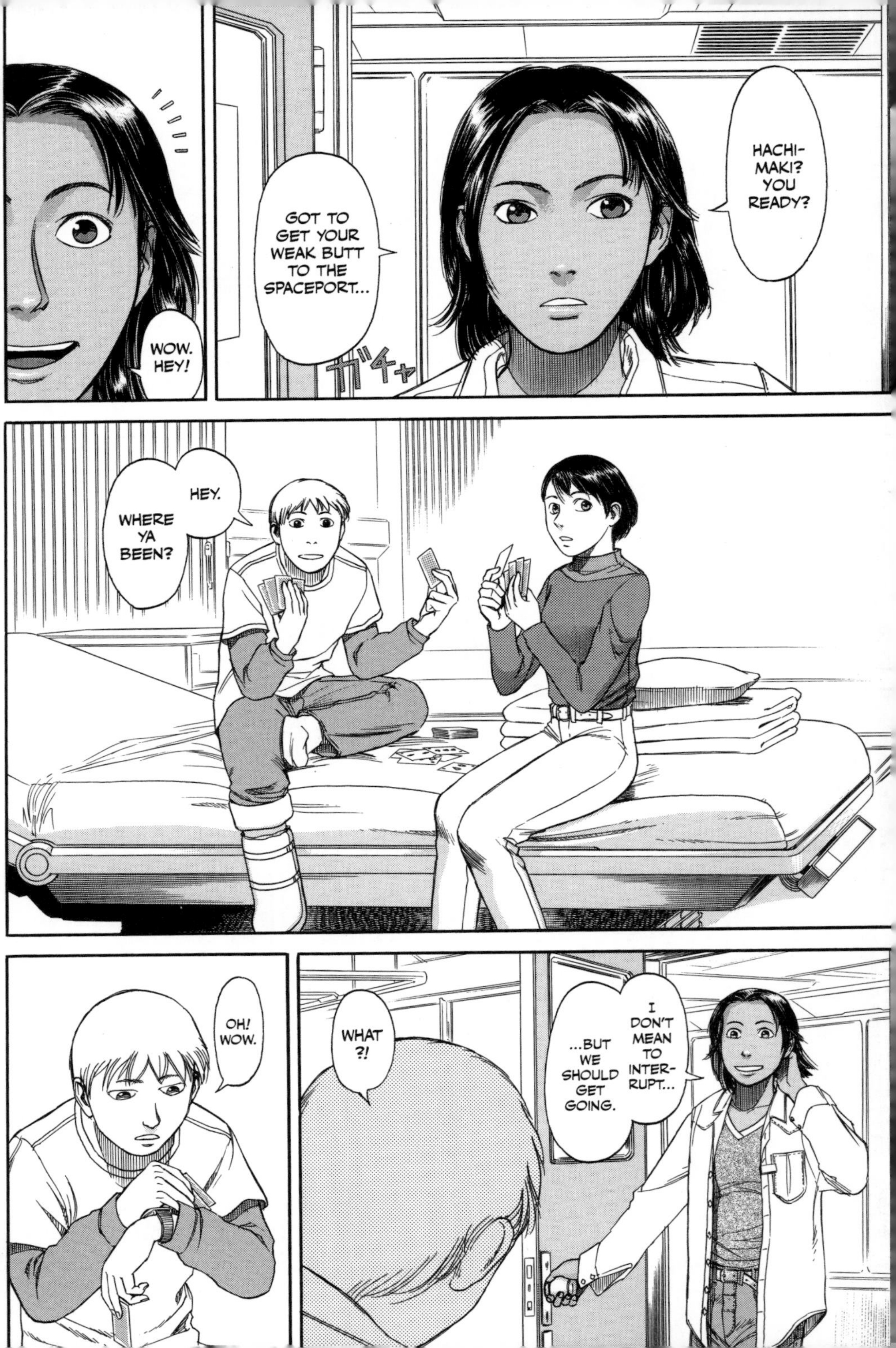
HACHI-MAKI? YOU READY?
GOT TO GET YOUR WEAK BUTT TO THE SPACEPORT...
ガチャ
WOW. HEY!
HEY. WHERE YA BEEN?
I DON'T MEAN TO INTERRUPT...
...BUT WE SHOULD GET GOING.
WHAT?!
OH! WOW.

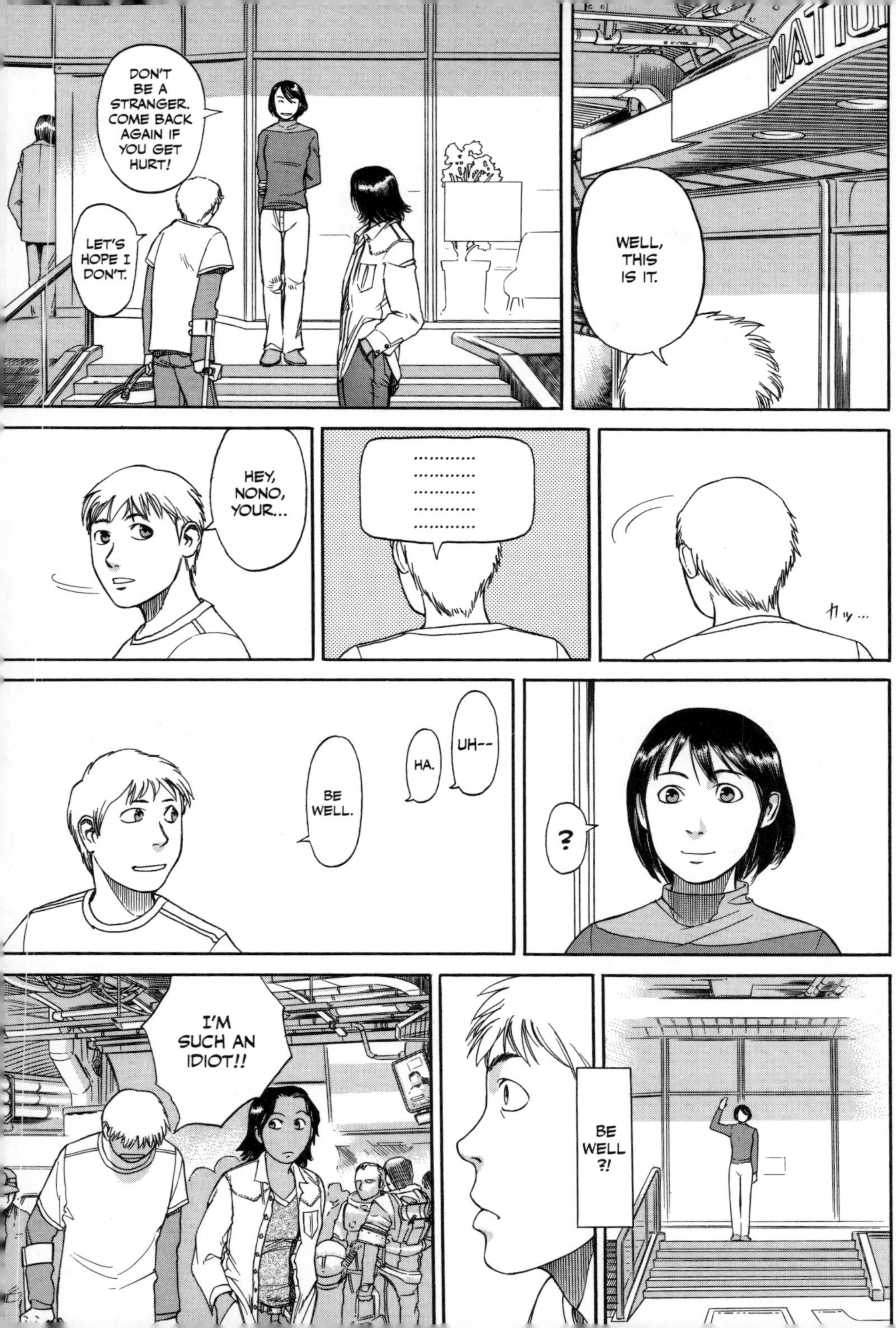
WELL, THIS IS IT.
DON'T BE A STRANGER. COME BACK AGAIN IF YOU GET HURT!
LET'S HOPE I DON'T.
カッ...
....
HEY, NONO, YOUR...
?
UH--
HA.
BE WELL.
BE WELL ?!
I'M SUCH AN IDIOT!!

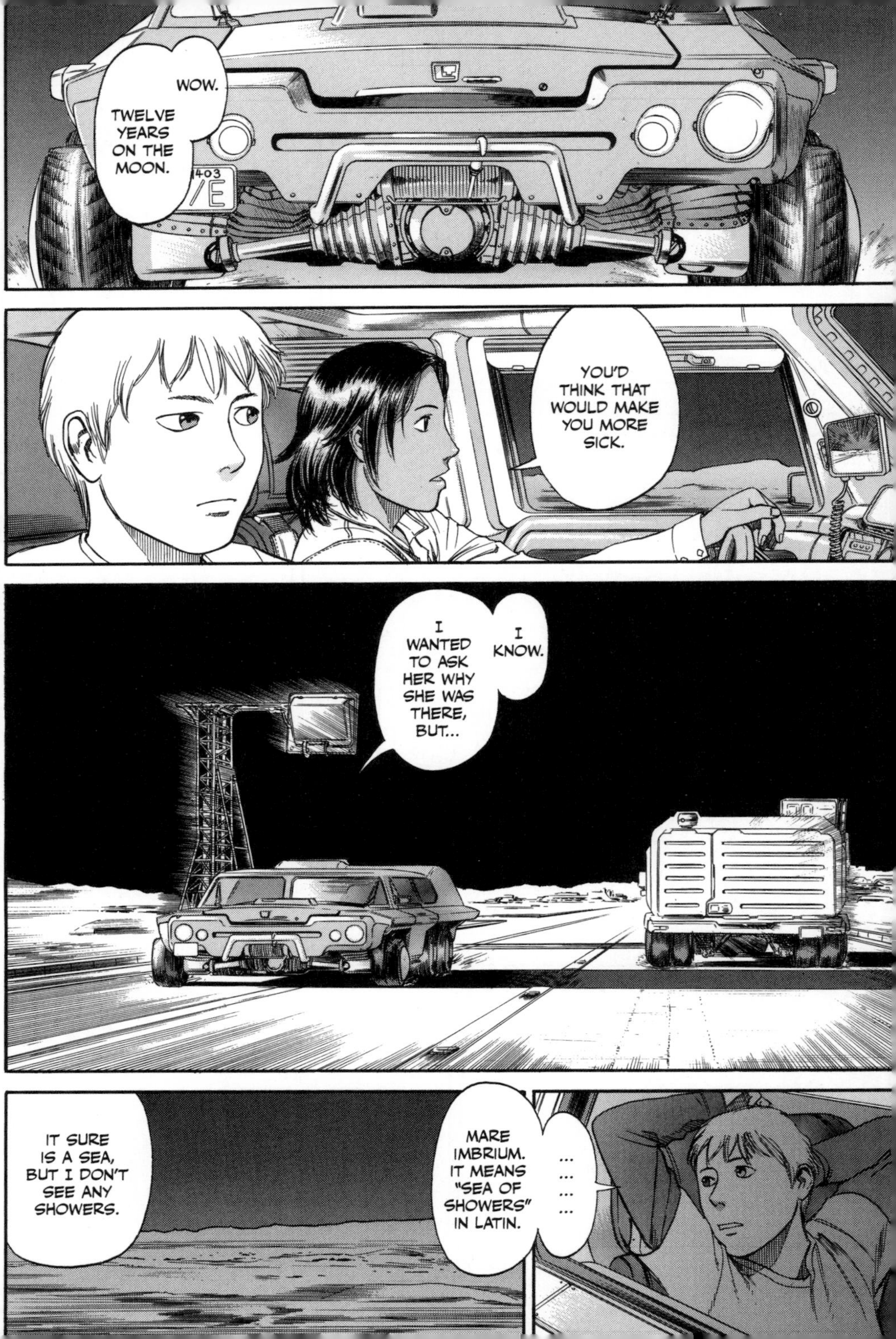
WOW.
TWELVE YEARS ON THE MOON.
YOU'D THINK THAT WOULD MAKE YOU MORE SICK.
I KNOW.
I WANTED TO ASK HER WHY SHE WAS THERE, BUT...
....
MARE IMBRIUM. IT MEANS "SEA OF SHOWERS" IN LATIN.
IT SURE IS A SEA, BUT I DON'T SEE ANY SHOWERS.

...ON EARTH.

I WISH THIS WERE A REAL OCEAN...

ガクッ

OUCH!

!

ピタッ

WHAT?! OWWW!

HACHIMAKI! LOOK, IT'S...

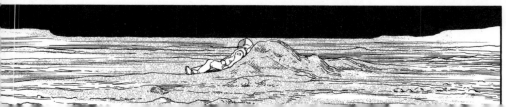

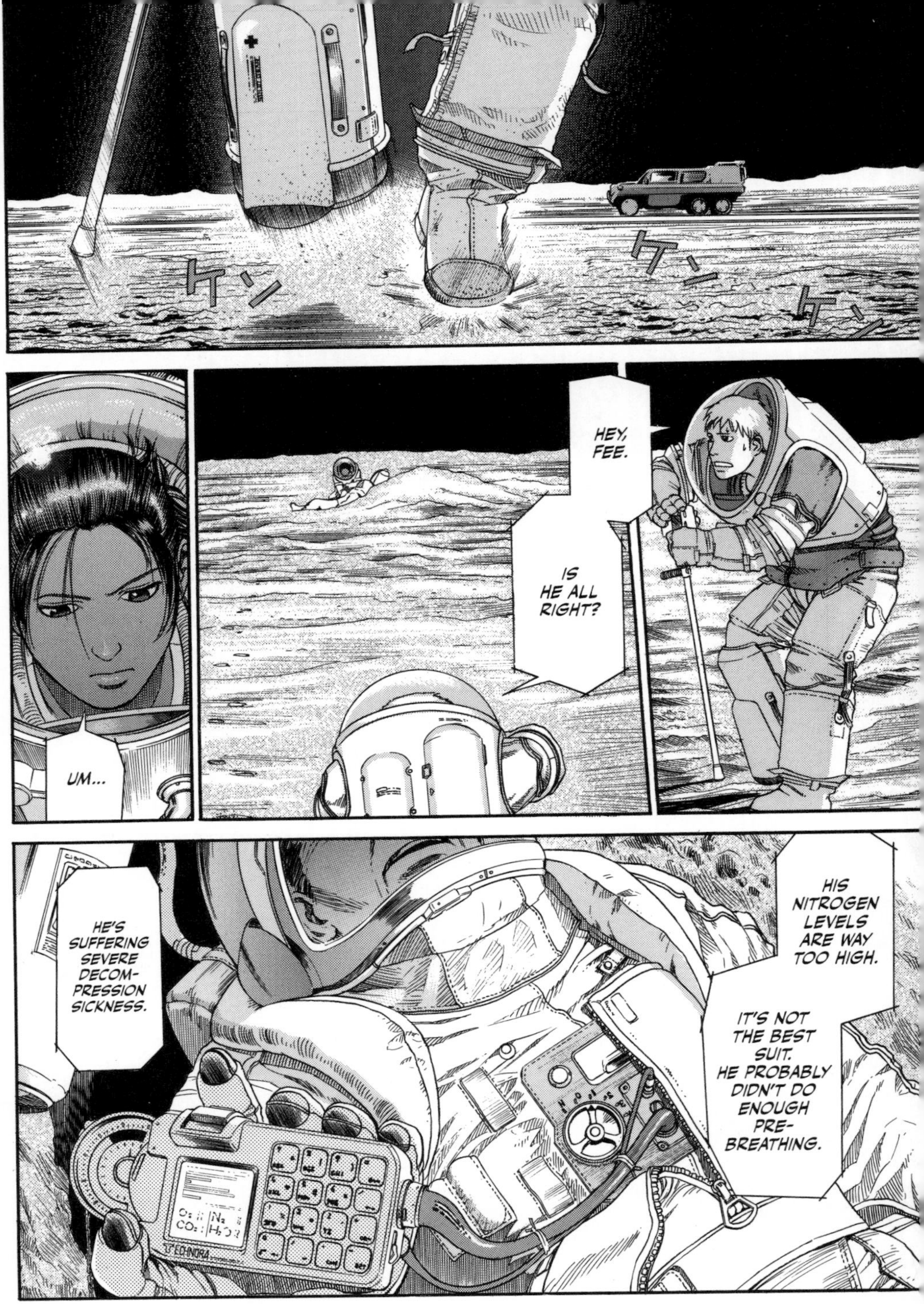
ケン
ケン
ケン
HEY, FEE.
IS HE ALL RIGHT?
UM...
HIS NITROGEN LEVELS ARE WAY TOO HIGH.
IT'S NOT THE BEST SUIT. HE PROBABLY DIDN'T DO ENOUGH PRE-BREATHING.
HE'S SUFFERING SEVERE DECOM-PRESSION SICKNESS.

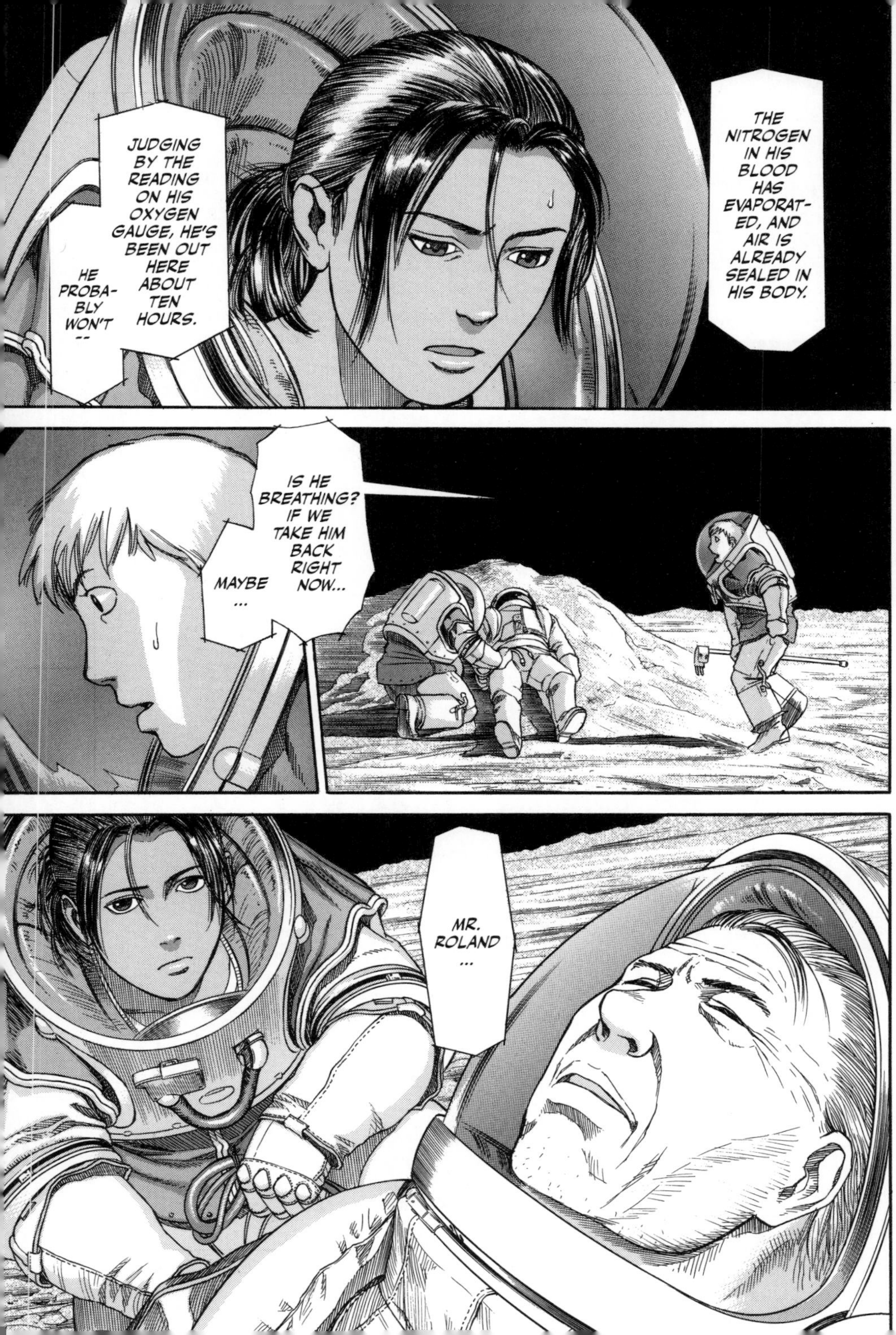
THE NITROGEN IN HIS BLOOD HAS EVAPORATED, AND AIR IS ALREADY SEALED IN HIS BODY.
JUDGING BY THE READING ON HIS OXYGEN GAUGE, HE'S BEEN OUT HERE ABOUT TEN HOURS.
HE PROBABLY WON'T --
IS HE BREATHING? IF WE TAKE HIM BACK RIGHT NOW...
MAYBE ...
MR. ROLAND ...

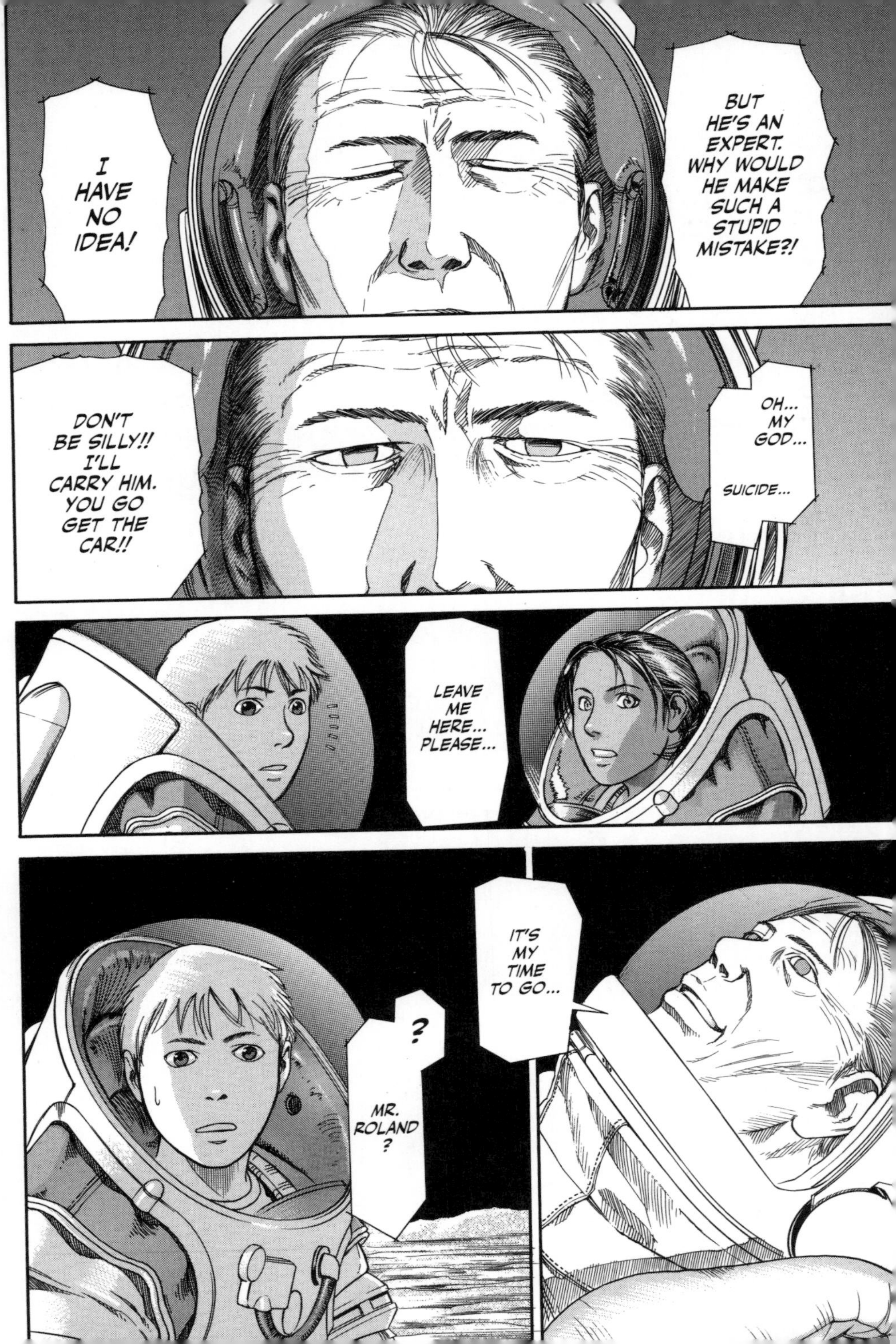
BUT HE'S AN EXPERT. WHY WOULD HE MAKE SUCH A STUPID MISTAKE?!
I HAVE NO IDEA!
OH... MY GOD...
SUICIDE...
DON'T BE SILLY!! I'LL CARRY HIM. YOU GO GET THE CAR!!
LEAVE ME HERE... PLEASE...
IT'S MY TIME TO GO...
?
MR. ROLAND?

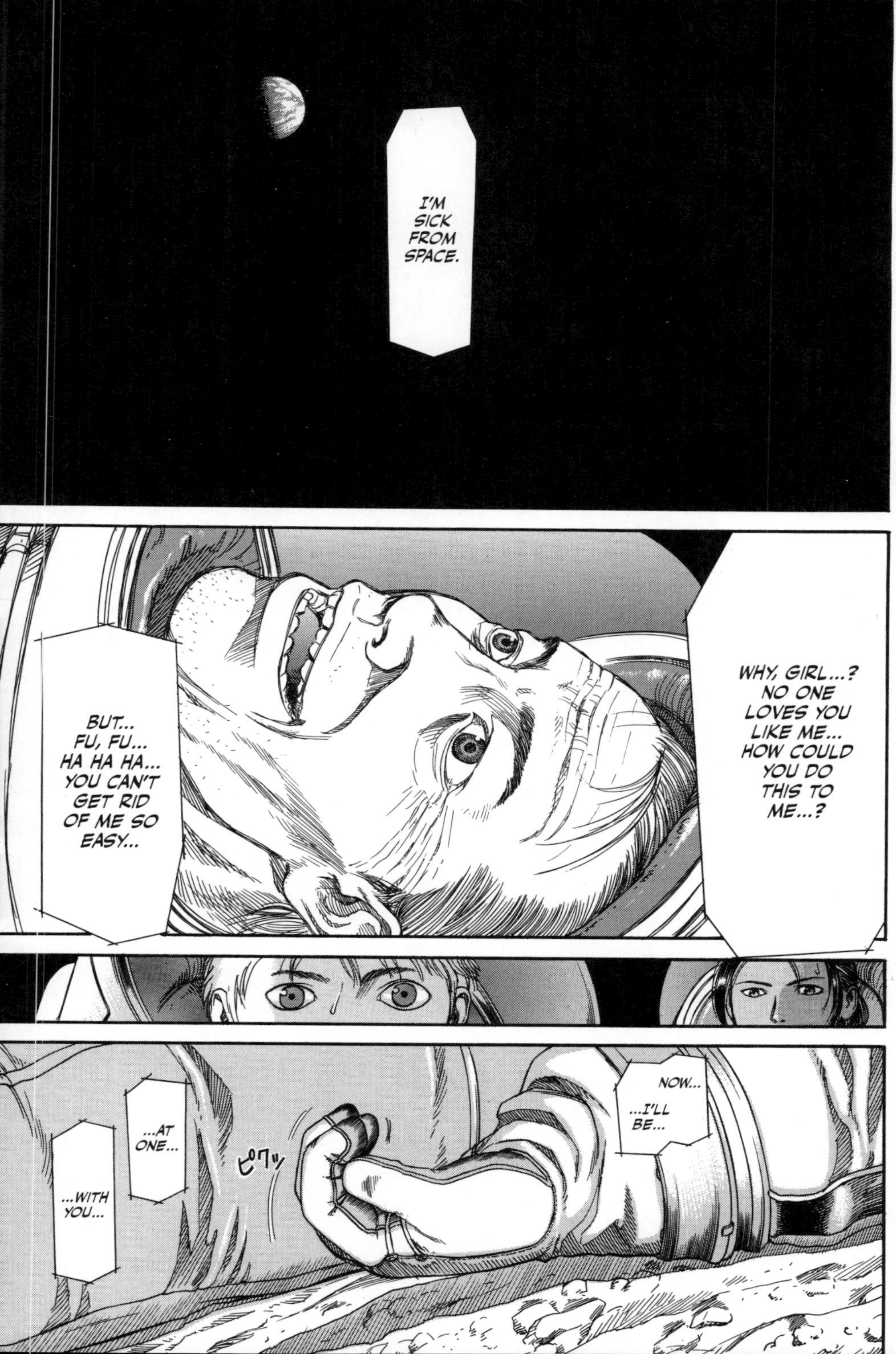
I'M SICK FROM SPACE.
WHY, GIRL...? NO ONE LOVES YOU LIKE ME... HOW COULD YOU DO THIS TO ME...?
BUT... FU, FU... HA HA HA... YOU CAN'T GET RID OF ME SO EASY...
NOW...
...I'LL BE...
...AT ONE...
ピクッ
...WITH YOU...

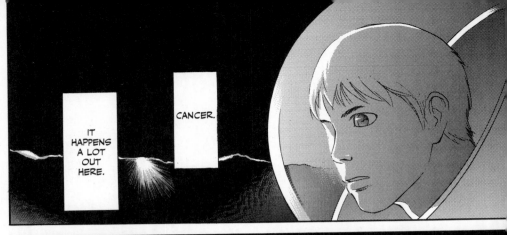

CANCER.
IT HAPPENS A LOT OUT HERE.
SPACE IS FILLED WITH RADIATION. SINCE THERE'S NO ATMOSPHERE, THE MOON IS EXPOSED TO A HUNDRED TIMES MORE RADIATION THAN THE EARTH.
AND RADIA-TION CAUSES CANCER.
THIS PARTI-CULAR CANCER ISN'T FATAL.
BUT IT TRIG-GERS A TYPE OF ANEMIA.
AND WHEN THAT HAPPENS, AN ASTRONAUT HAS TO GIVE UP SPACE.
... ...
HE'S GONE.

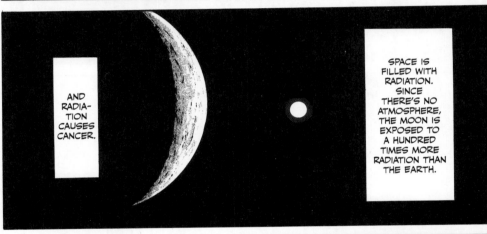

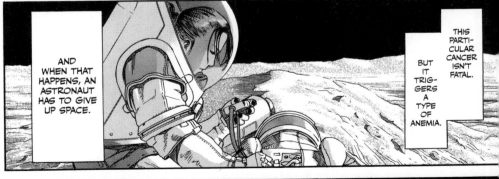

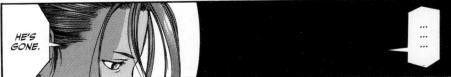

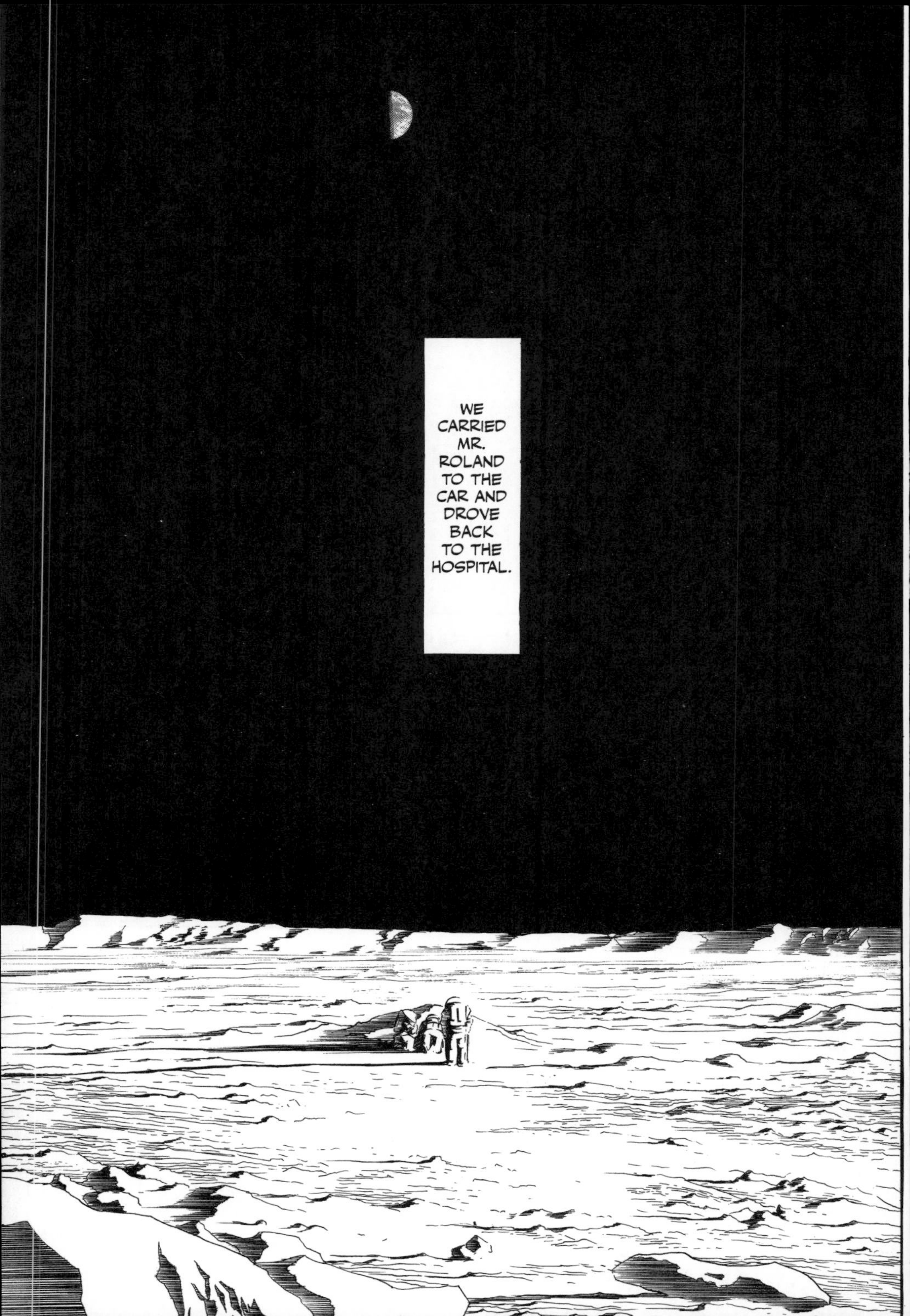
WE CARRIED MR. ROLAND TO THE CAR AND DROVE BACK TO THE HOSPITAL.

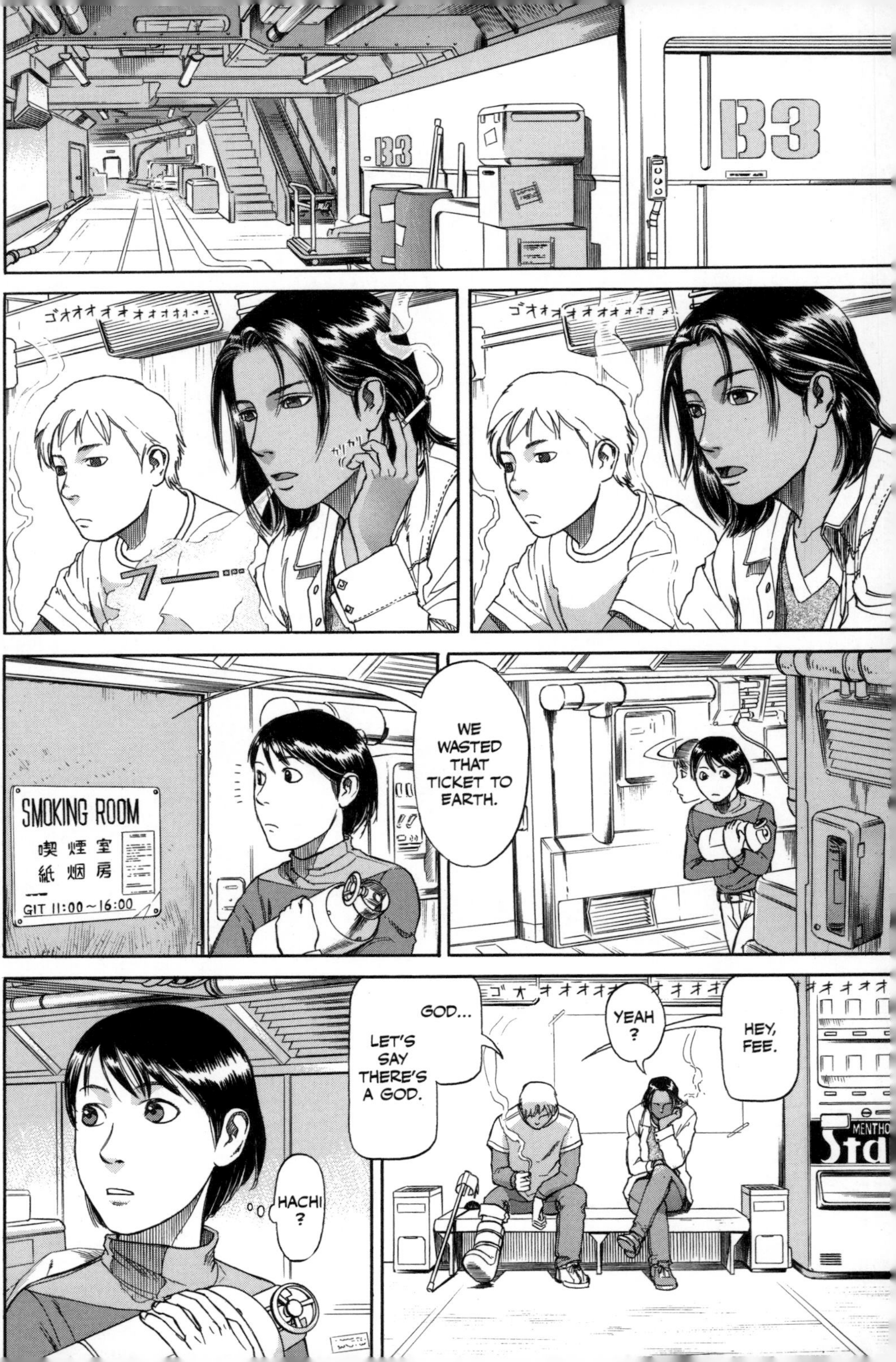
B33
B33
ゴオオオオオオオオオオ
ゴオオオオオオオオオ
ガリガリ
WE WASTED THAT TICKET TO EARTH.
SMOKING ROOM
喫煙室
紙烟房
GIT 11:00～16:00
ゴオオオオオオオオオオオ
HEY, FEE.
YEAH?
GOD...
LET'S SAY THERE'S A GOD.
HACHI?

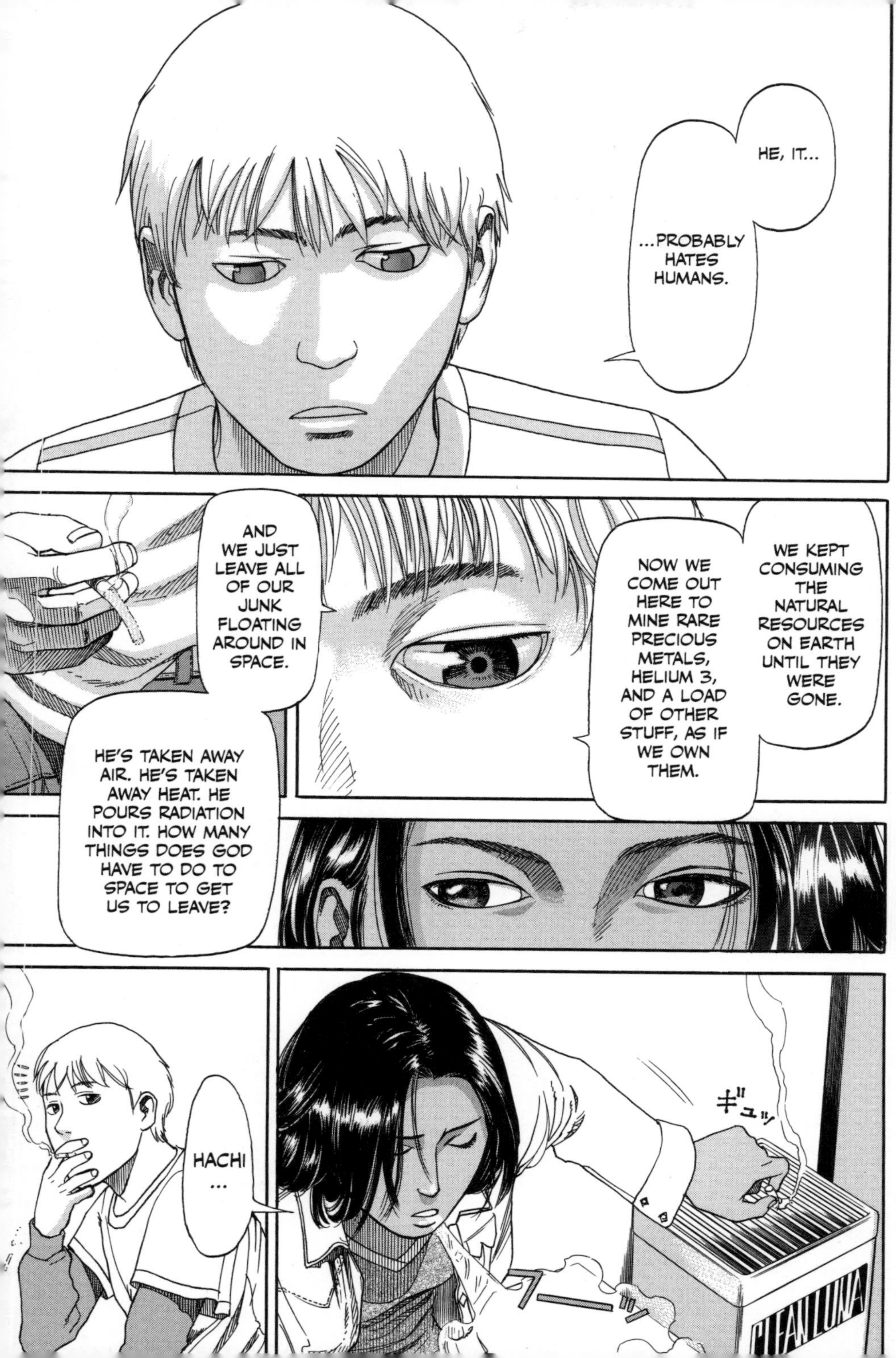
HE, IT...
...PROBABLY HATES HUMANS.
WE KEPT CONSUMING THE NATURAL RESOURCES ON EARTH UNTIL THEY WERE GONE.
NOW WE COME OUT HERE TO MINE RARE PRECIOUS METALS, HELIUM 3, AND A LOAD OF OTHER STUFF, AS IF WE OWN THEM.
AND WE JUST LEAVE ALL OF OUR JUNK FLOATING AROUND IN SPACE.
HE'S TAKEN AWAY AIR. HE'S TAKEN AWAY HEAT. HE POURS RADIATION INTO IT. HOW MANY THINGS DOES GOD HAVE TO DO TO SPACE TO GET US TO LEAVE?
ギュッ
CLEAN LUNA
HACHI ...

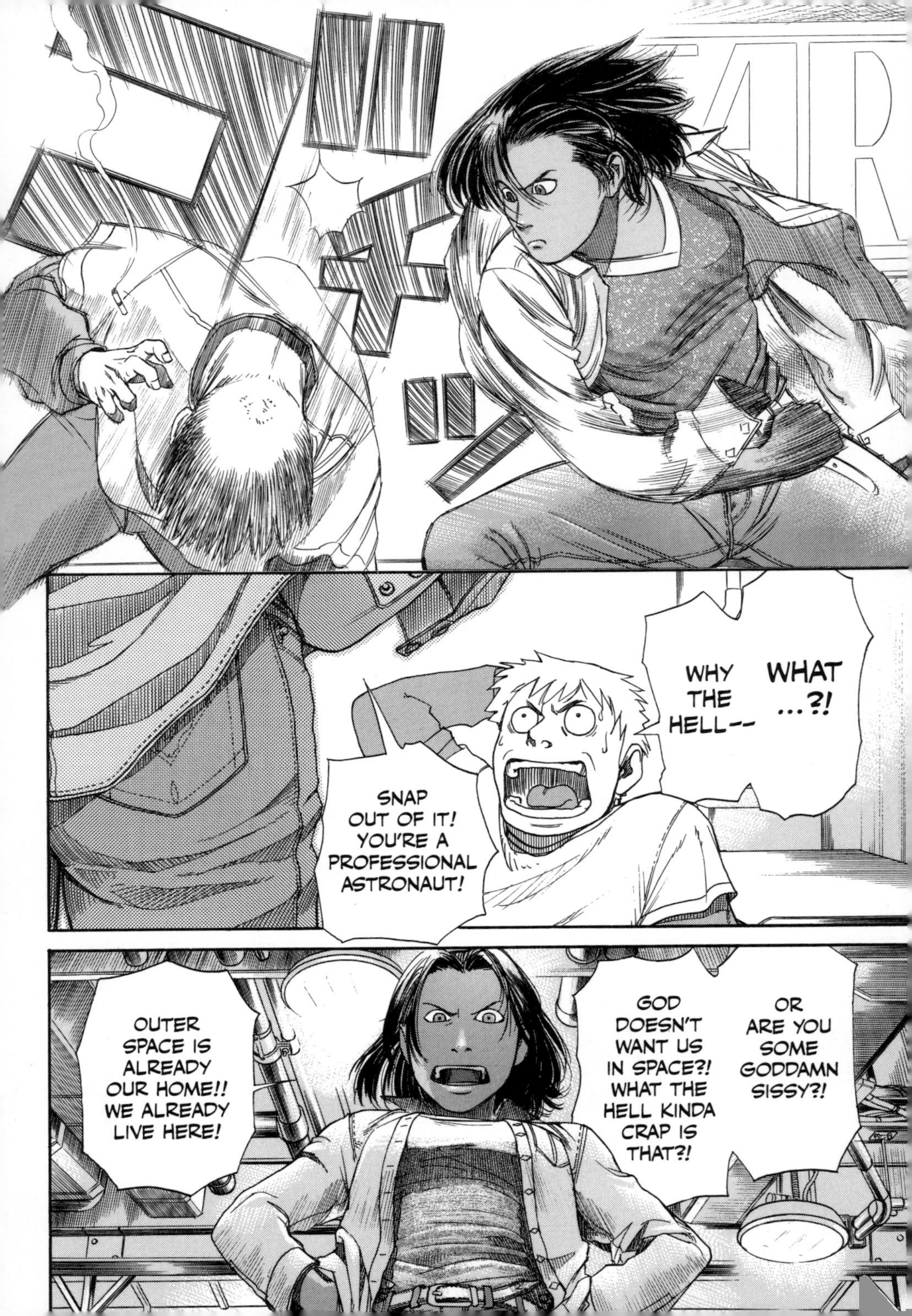
WHAT ...?!
WHY THE HELL--
SNAP OUT OF IT! YOU'RE A PROFESSIONAL ASTRONAUT!
OR ARE YOU SOME GODDAMN SISSY?!
GOD DOESN'T WANT US IN SPACE?! WHAT THE HELL KINDA CRAP IS THAT?!
OUTER SPACE IS ALREADY OUR HOME!! WE ALREADY LIVE HERE!

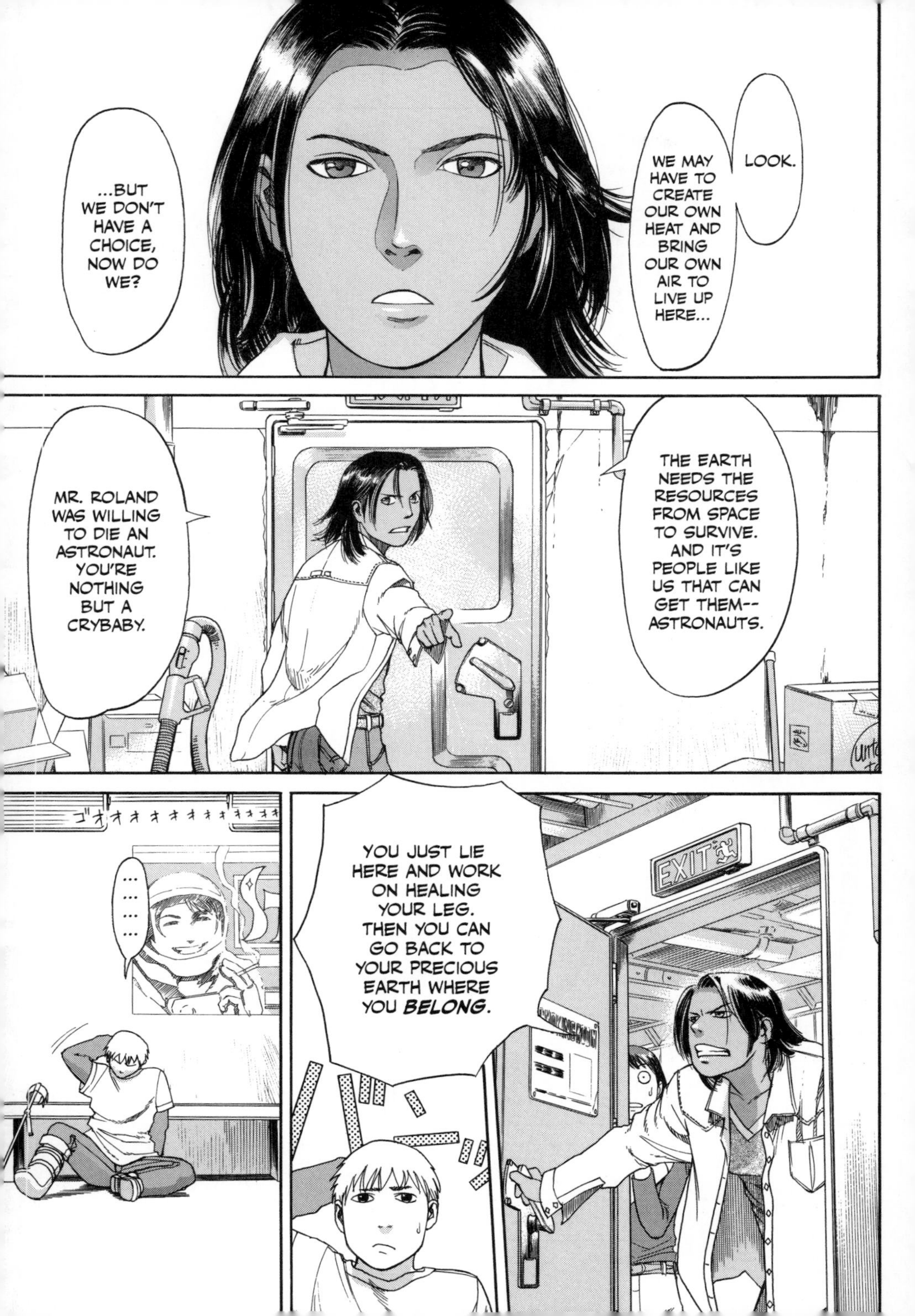

LOOK.
WE MAY HAVE TO CREATE OUR OWN HEAT AND BRING OUR OWN AIR TO LIVE UP HERE...
...BUT WE DON'T HAVE A CHOICE, NOW DO WE?
THE EARTH NEEDS THE RESOURCES FROM SPACE TO SURVIVE. AND IT'S PEOPLE LIKE US THAT CAN GET THEM--ASTRONAUTS.
MR. ROLAND WAS WILLING TO DIE AN ASTRONAUT. YOU'RE NOTHING BUT A CRYBABY.
EXIT
YOU JUST LIE HERE AND WORK ON HEALING YOUR LEG. THEN YOU CAN GO BACK TO YOUR PRECIOUS EARTH WHERE YOU ***BELONG***.
ゴオオオオオオオオオオ
... ...

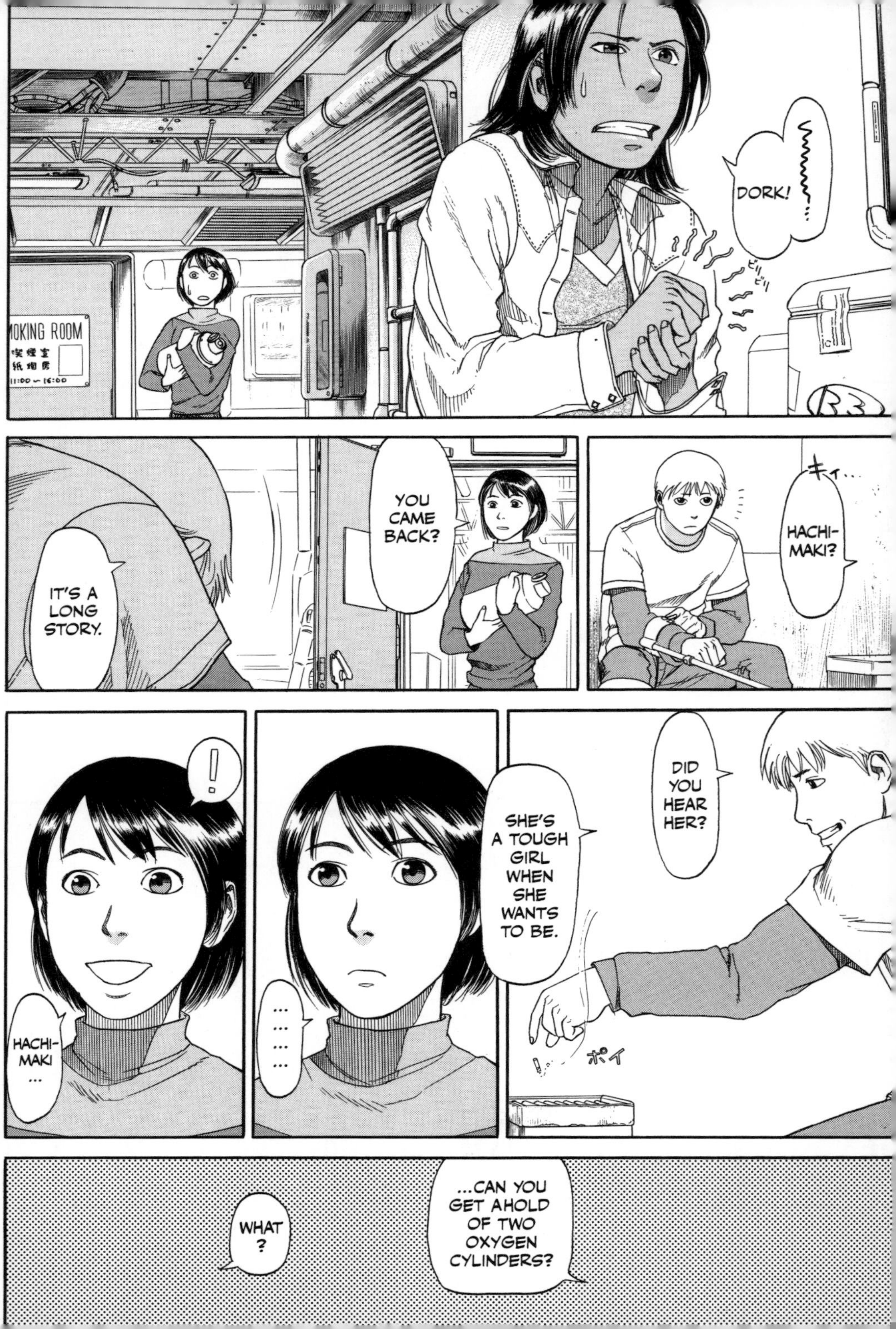

DORK!
ビリビリ
MOKING ROOM
キィ…
HACHI-MAKI?
YOU CAME BACK?
IT'S A LONG STORY.
DID YOU HEAR HER?
SHE'S A TOUGH GIRL WHEN SHE WANTS TO BE.
ポイ
....
!
HACHI-MAKI...
...CAN YOU GET AHOLD OF TWO OXYGEN CYLINDERS?
WHAT?

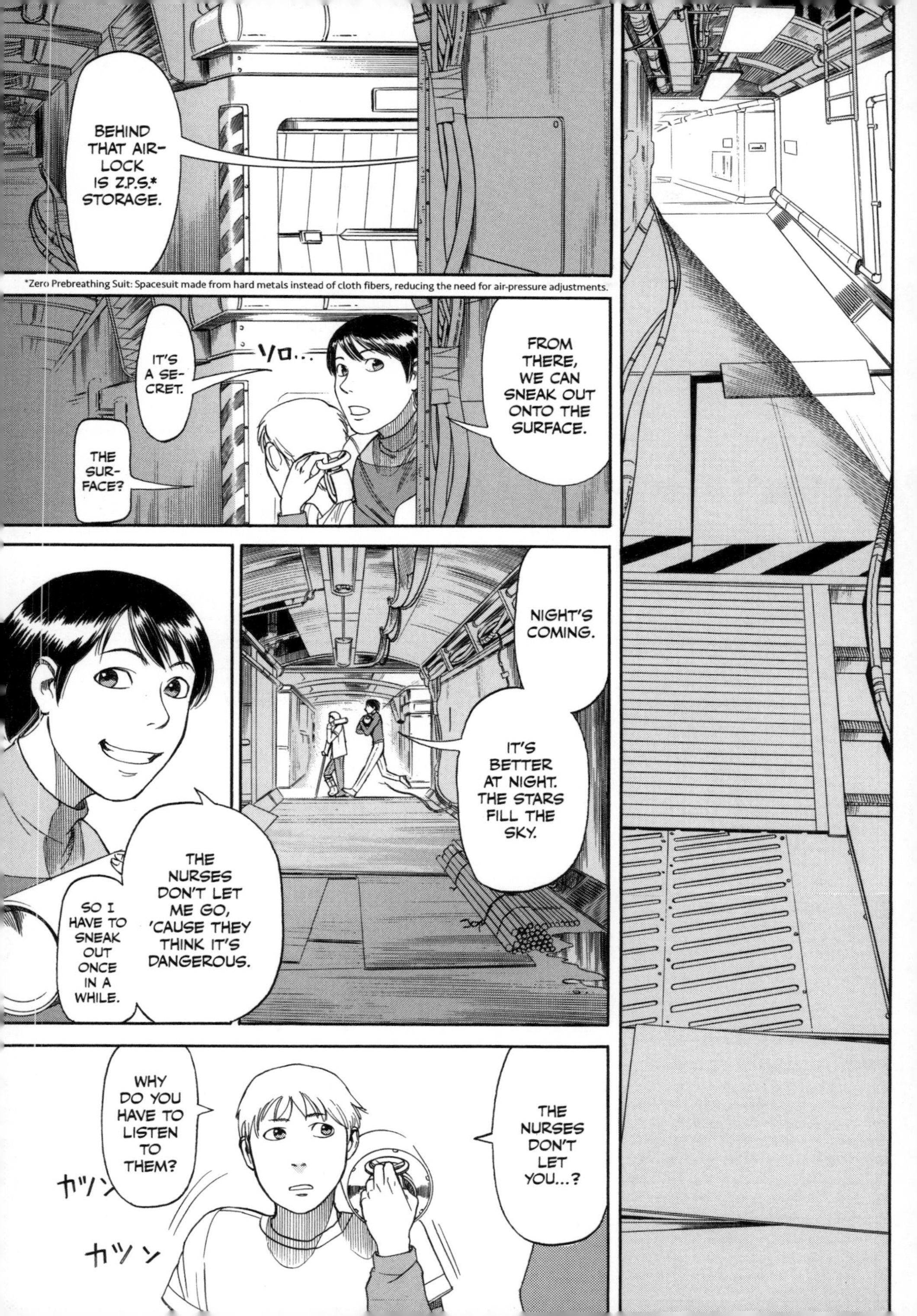
BEHIND THAT AIR-LOCK IS Z.P.S.* STORAGE.
FROM THERE, WE CAN SNEAK OUT ONTO THE SURFACE.
ソロ…
IT'S A SE-CRET.
THE SUR-FACE?
NIGHT'S COMING.
IT'S BETTER AT NIGHT. THE STARS FILL THE SKY.
THE NURSES DON'T LET ME GO, 'CAUSE THEY THINK IT'S DANGEROUS.
SO I HAVE TO SNEAK OUT ONCE IN A WHILE.
THE NURSES DON'T LET YOU...?
WHY DO YOU HAVE TO LISTEN TO THEM?
カツン
カツン

*Zero Prebreathing Suit: Spacesuit made from hard metals instead of cloth fibers, reducing the need for air-pressure adjustments.

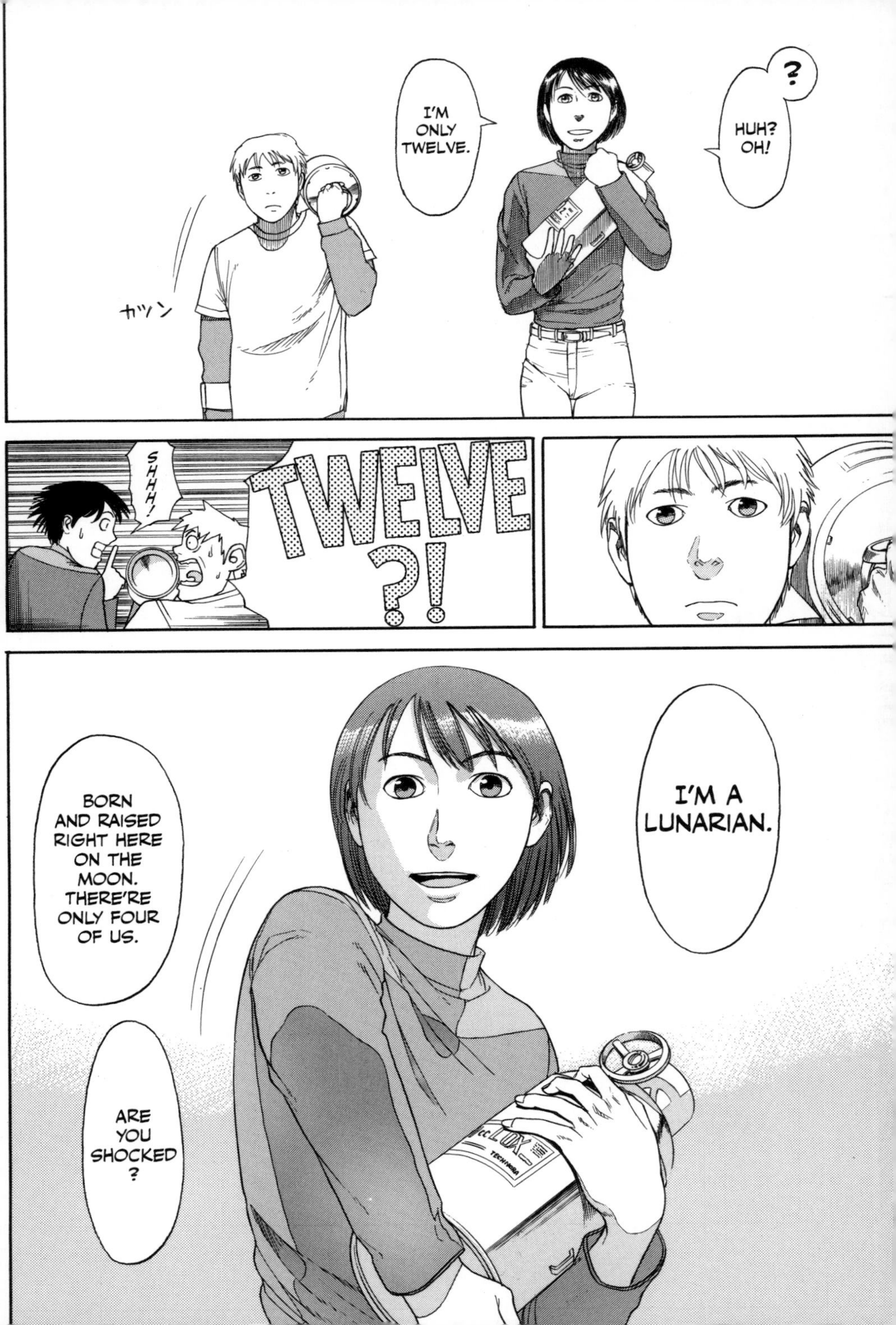
?
HUH? OH!
I'M ONLY TWELVE.
カツン
TWELVE ?!
SHHH!
I'M A LUNARIAN.
BORN AND RAISED RIGHT HERE ON THE MOON. THERE'RE ONLY FOUR OF US.
ARE YOU SHOCKED?

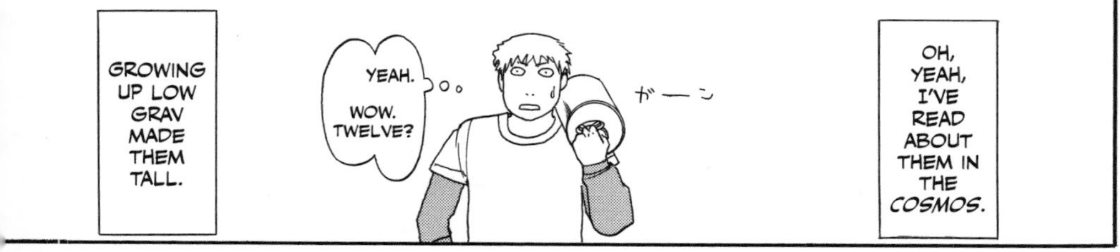
OH, YEAH, I'VE READ ABOUT THEM IN THE *COSMOS.*
ガーン
YEAH.
WOW. TWELVE?
GROWING UP LOW GRAV MADE THEM TALL.

*Ilmenite: Iron titanium oxide. On Earth, it is one of the best ore sources for titanium, a lightweight, noncorrosive metal that has supplanted many other commercial metals. Its discovery on the moon spurred massive mining operations there.

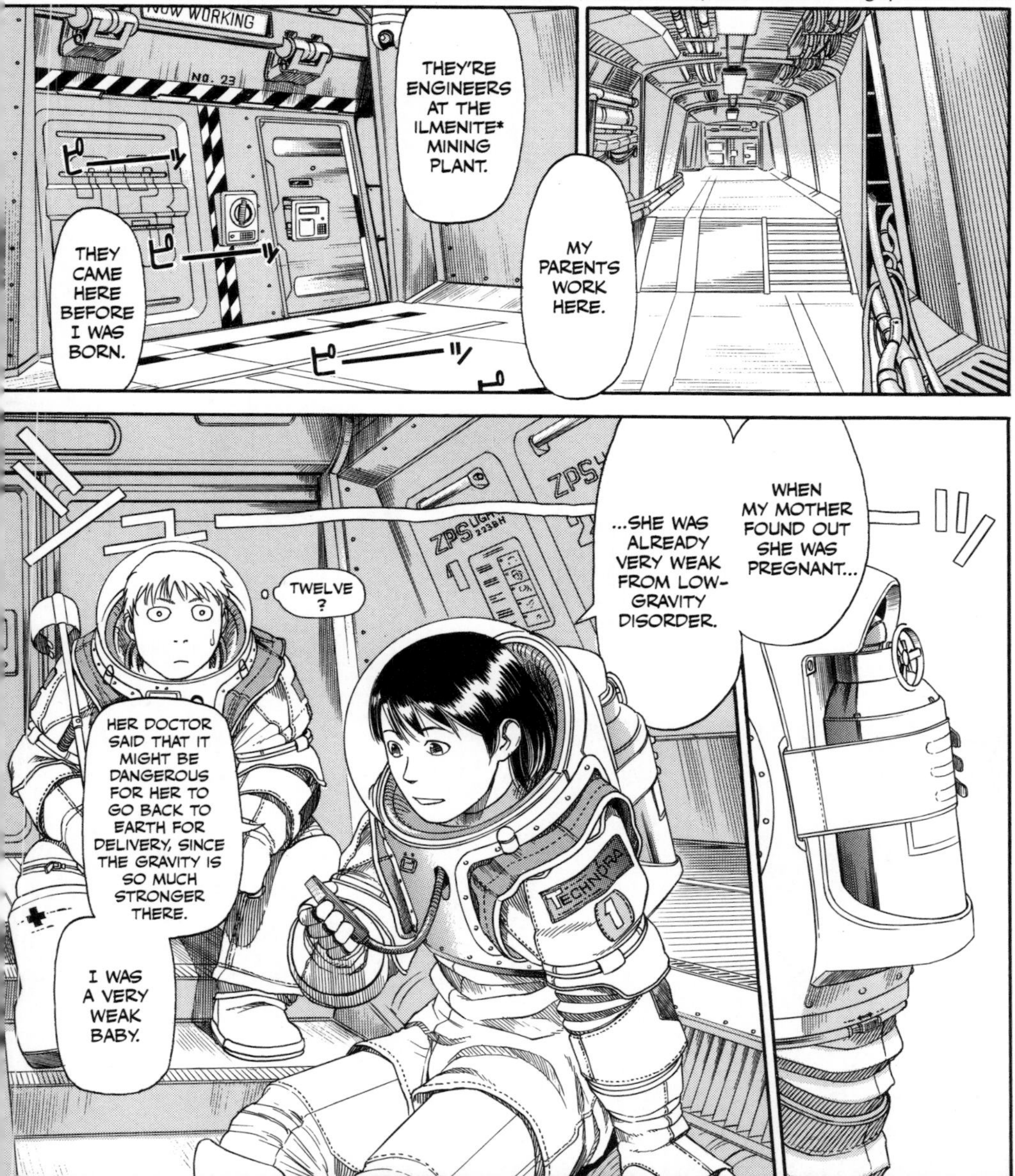
MY PARENTS WORK HERE.
NOW WORKING
NO. 23
THEY'RE ENGINEERS AT THE ILMENITE* MINING PLANT.
ピーーッ
THEY CAME HERE BEFORE I WAS BORN.
WHEN MY MOTHER FOUND OUT SHE WAS PREGNANT...
...SHE WAS ALREADY VERY WEAK FROM LOW-GRAVITY DISORDER.
TWELVE ?
HER DOCTOR SAID THAT IT MIGHT BE DANGEROUS FOR HER TO GO BACK TO EARTH FOR DELIVERY, SINCE THE GRAVITY IS SO MUCH STRONGER THERE.
I WAS A VERY WEAK BABY.
TECHNORA

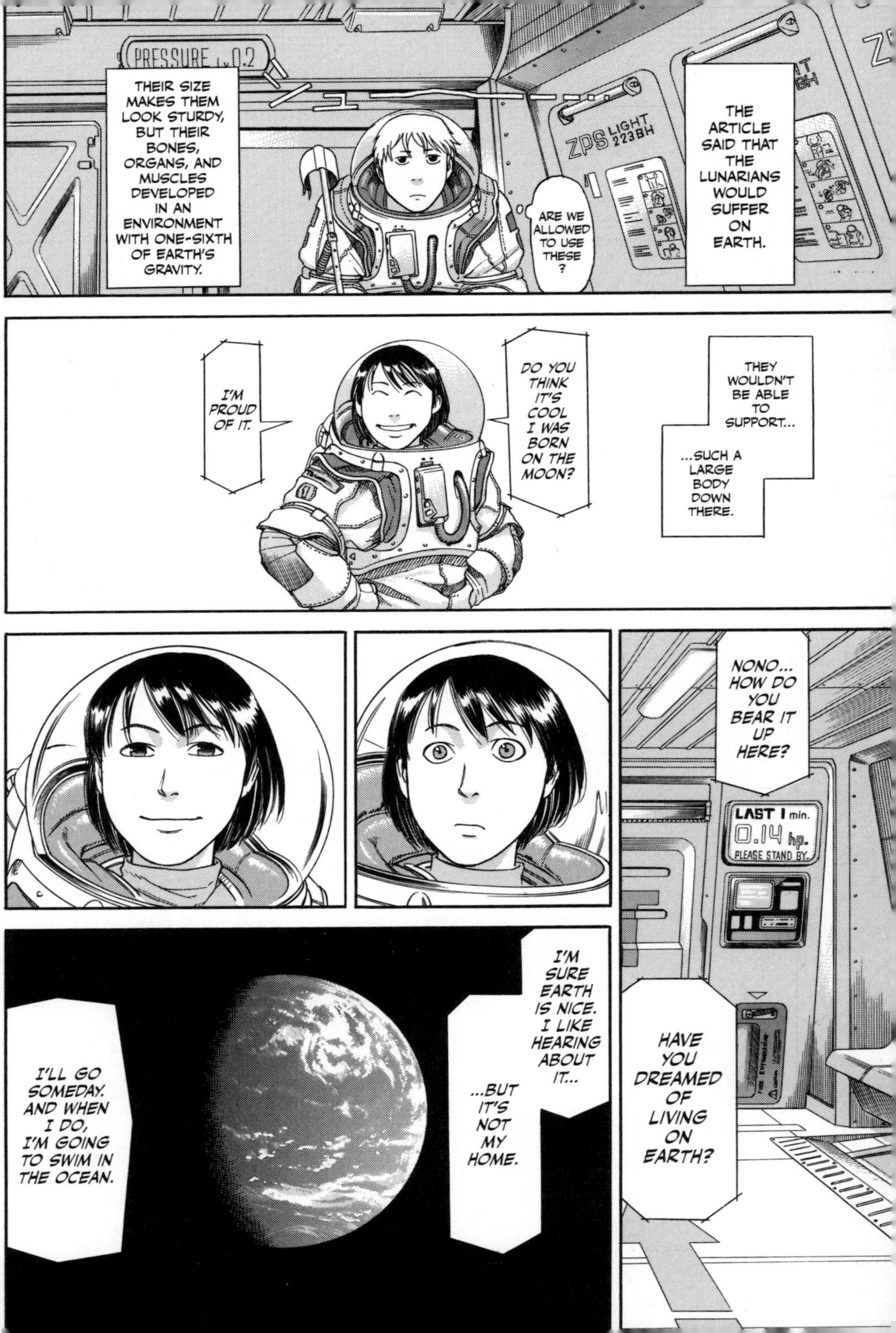
THE ARTICLE SAID THAT THE LUNARIANS WOULD SUFFER ON EARTH.
ZPS LIGHT 223BH
ARE WE ALLOWED TO USE THESE?
THEIR SIZE MAKES THEM LOOK STURDY, BUT THEIR BONES, ORGANS, AND MUSCLES DEVELOPED IN AN ENVIRONMENT WITH ONE-SIXTH OF EARTH'S GRAVITY.
PRESSURE
THEY WOULDN'T BE ABLE TO SUPPORT...
...SUCH A LARGE BODY DOWN THERE.
DO YOU THINK IT'S COOL I WAS BORN ON THE MOON?
I'M PROUD OF IT.
NONO... HOW DO YOU BEAR IT UP HERE?
LAST 1 min.
0.14 hp.
PLEASE STAND BY.
HAVE YOU DREAMED OF LIVING ON EARTH?
I'M SURE EARTH IS NICE. I LIKE HEARING ABOUT IT...
...BUT IT'S NOT MY HOME.
I'LL GO SOMEDAY. AND WHEN I DO, I'M GOING TO SWIM IN THE OCEAN.

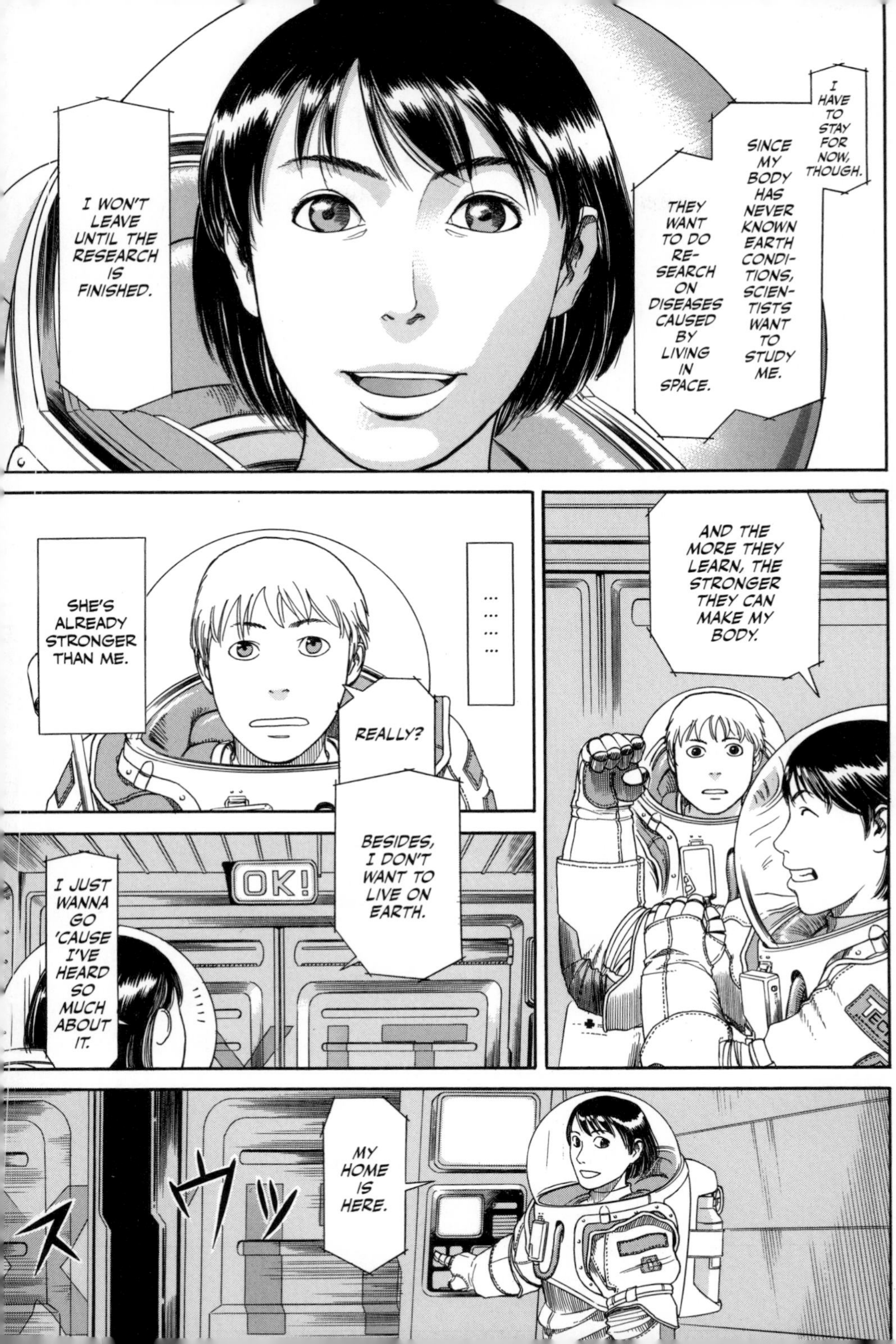
I HAVE TO STAY FOR NOW, THOUGH.
SINCE MY BODY HAS NEVER KNOWN EARTH CONDITIONS, SCIENTISTS WANT TO STUDY ME.
THEY WANT TO DO RE-SEARCH ON DISEASES CAUSED BY LIVING IN SPACE.
I WON'T LEAVE UNTIL THE RESEARCH IS FINISHED.
AND THE MORE THEY LEARN, THE STRONGER THEY CAN MAKE MY BODY.
....
REALLY?
SHE'S ALREADY STRONGER THAN ME.
BESIDES, I DON'T WANT TO LIVE ON EARTH.
OK!
I JUST WANNA GO 'CAUSE I'VE HEARD SO MUCH ABOUT IT.
MY HOME IS HERE.
スウッ

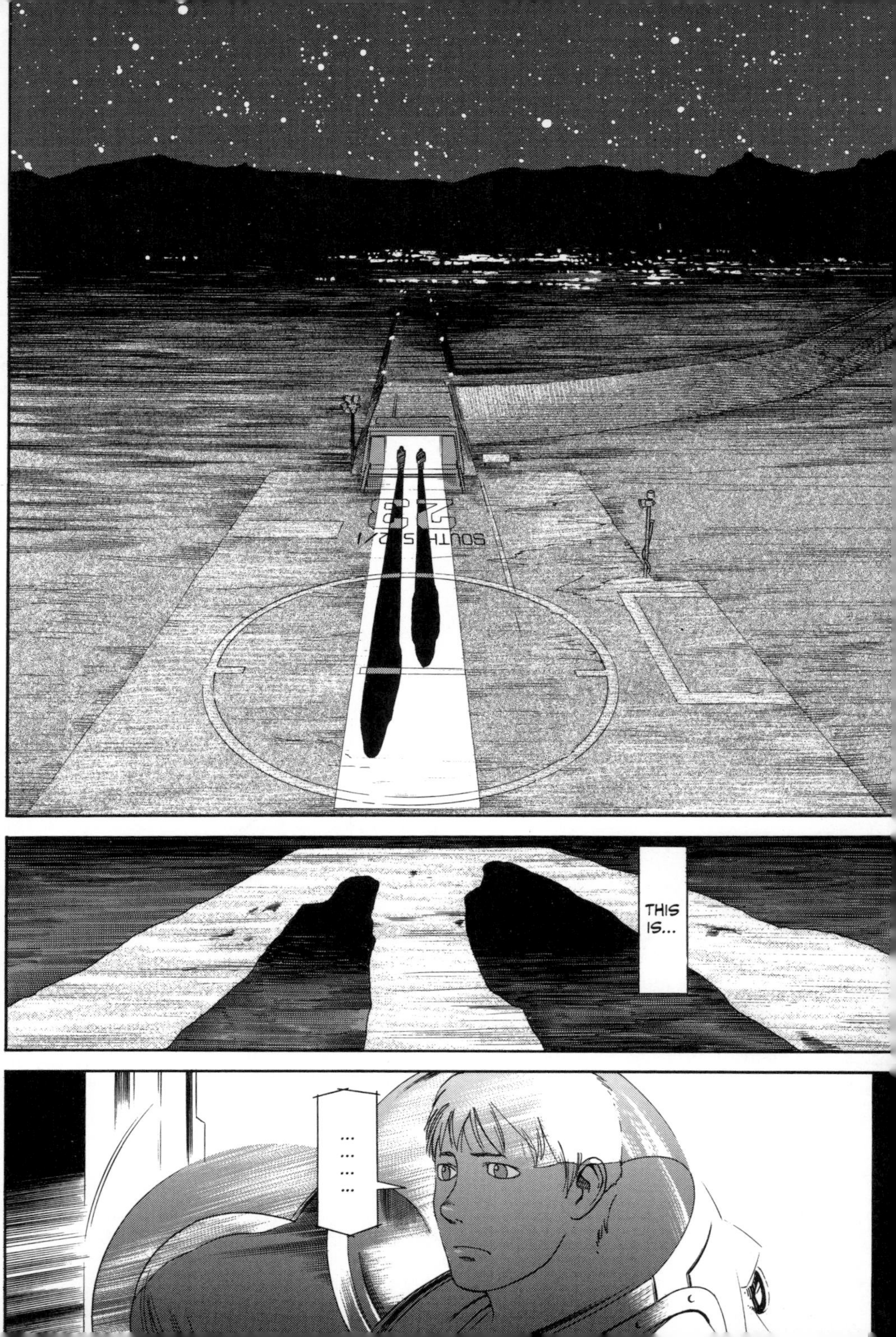
THIS IS...
....

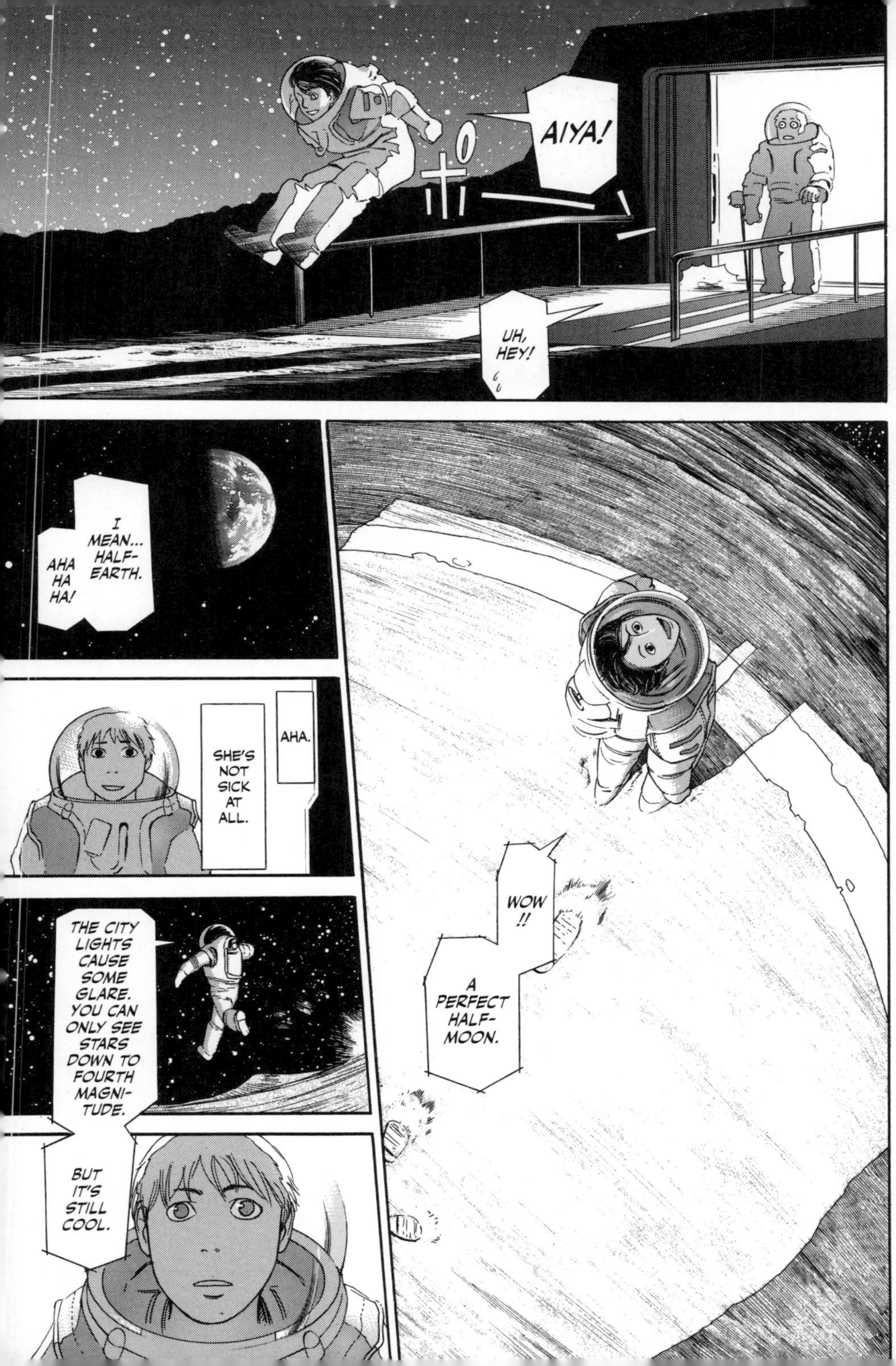
AIYA!
UH, HEY!
WOW!!
A PERFECT HALF-MOON.
I MEAN... HALF-EARTH.
AHA HA HA!
AHA.
SHE'S NOT SICK AT ALL.
THE CITY LIGHTS CAUSE SOME GLARE. YOU CAN ONLY SEE STARS DOWN TO FOURTH MAGNITUDE.
BUT IT'S STILL COOL.

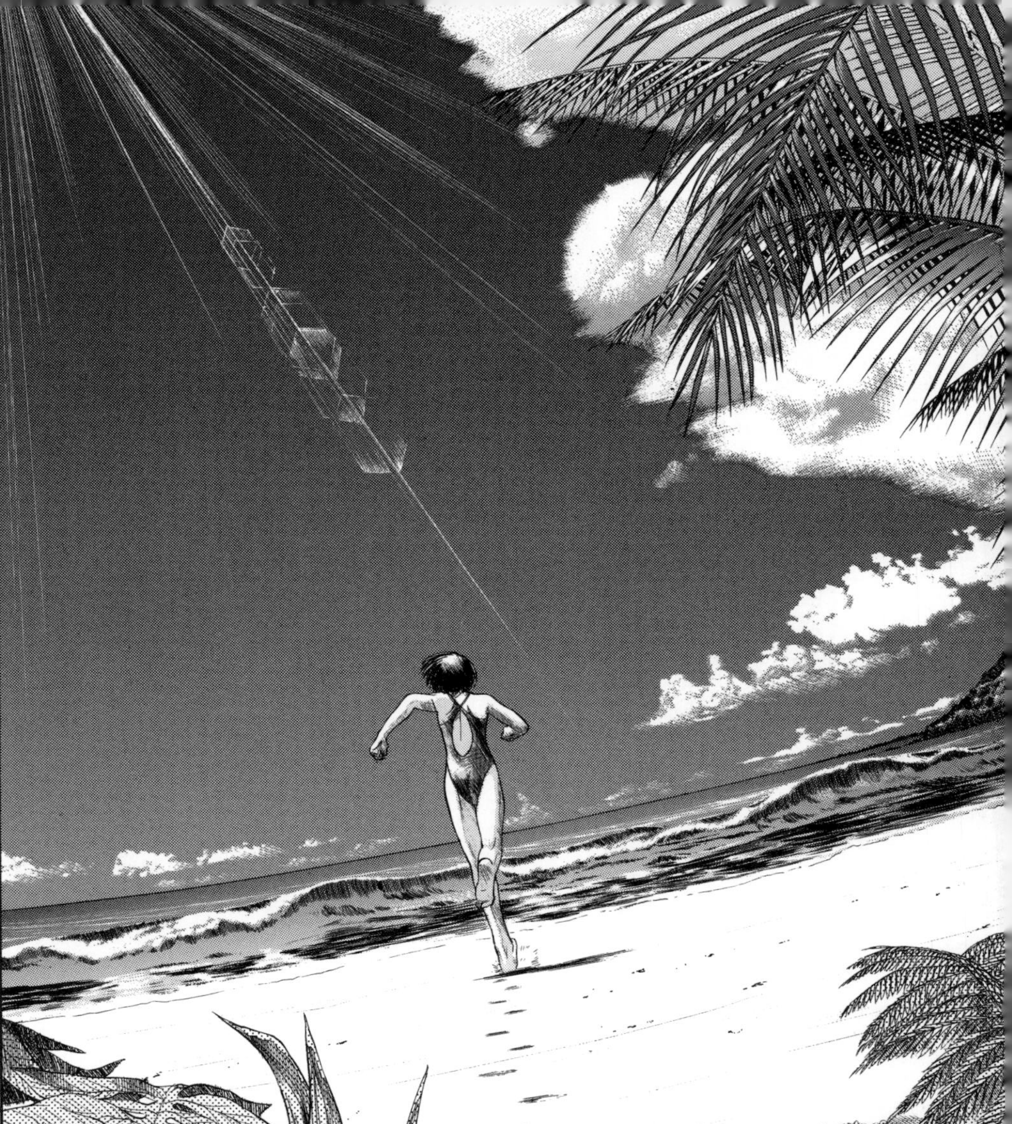

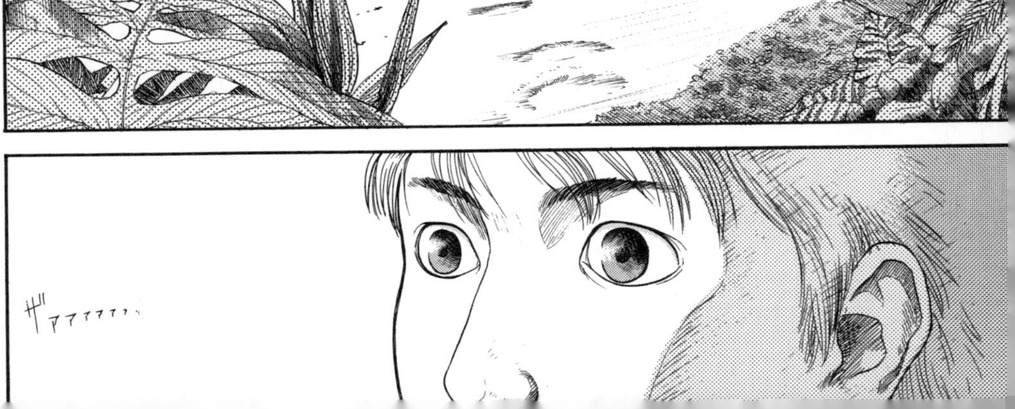
ザァァァァァァ…

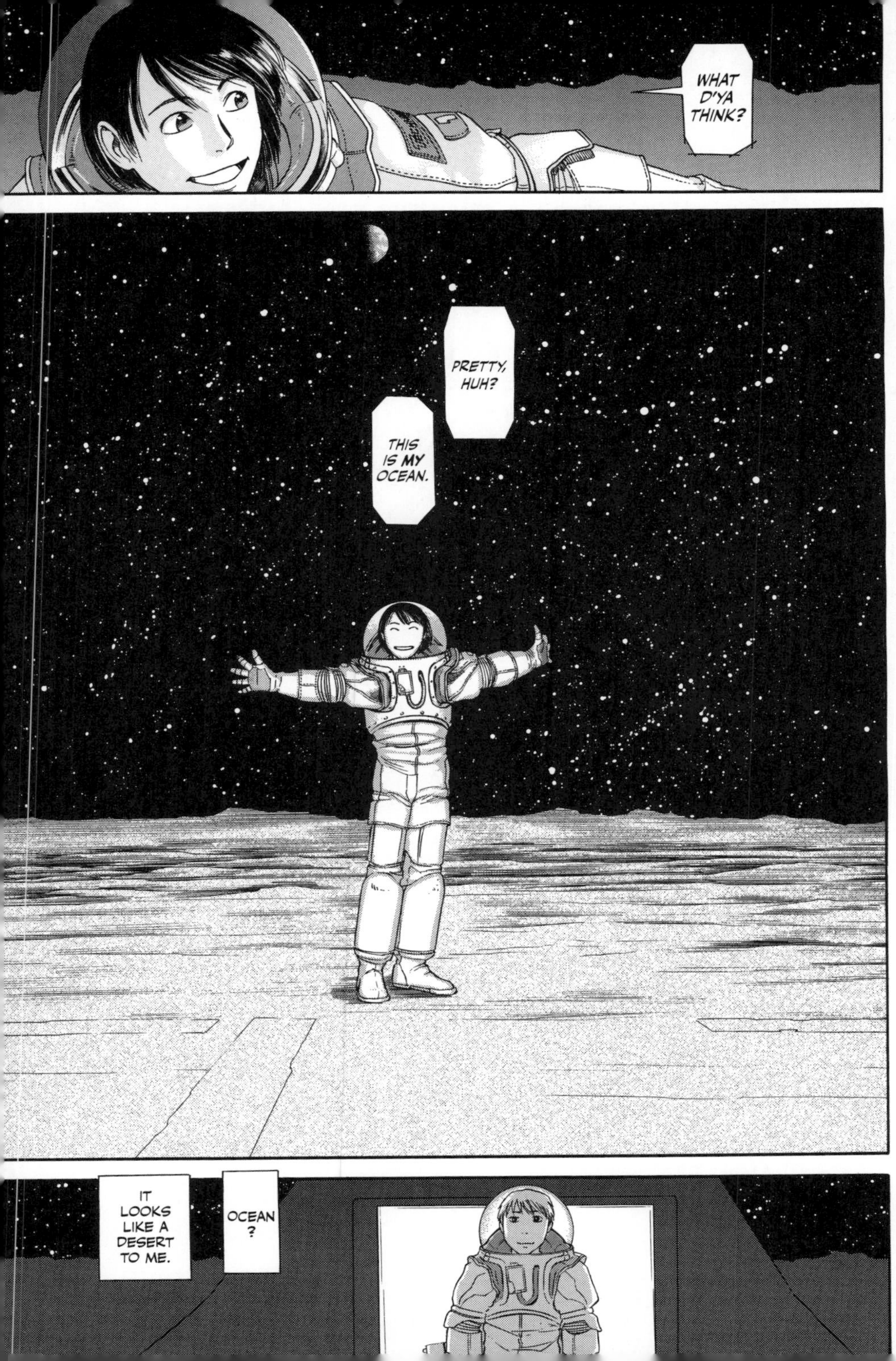
WHAT D'YA THINK?
PRETTY, HUH?
THIS IS MY OCEAN.
OCEAN?
IT LOOKS LIKE A DESERT TO ME.

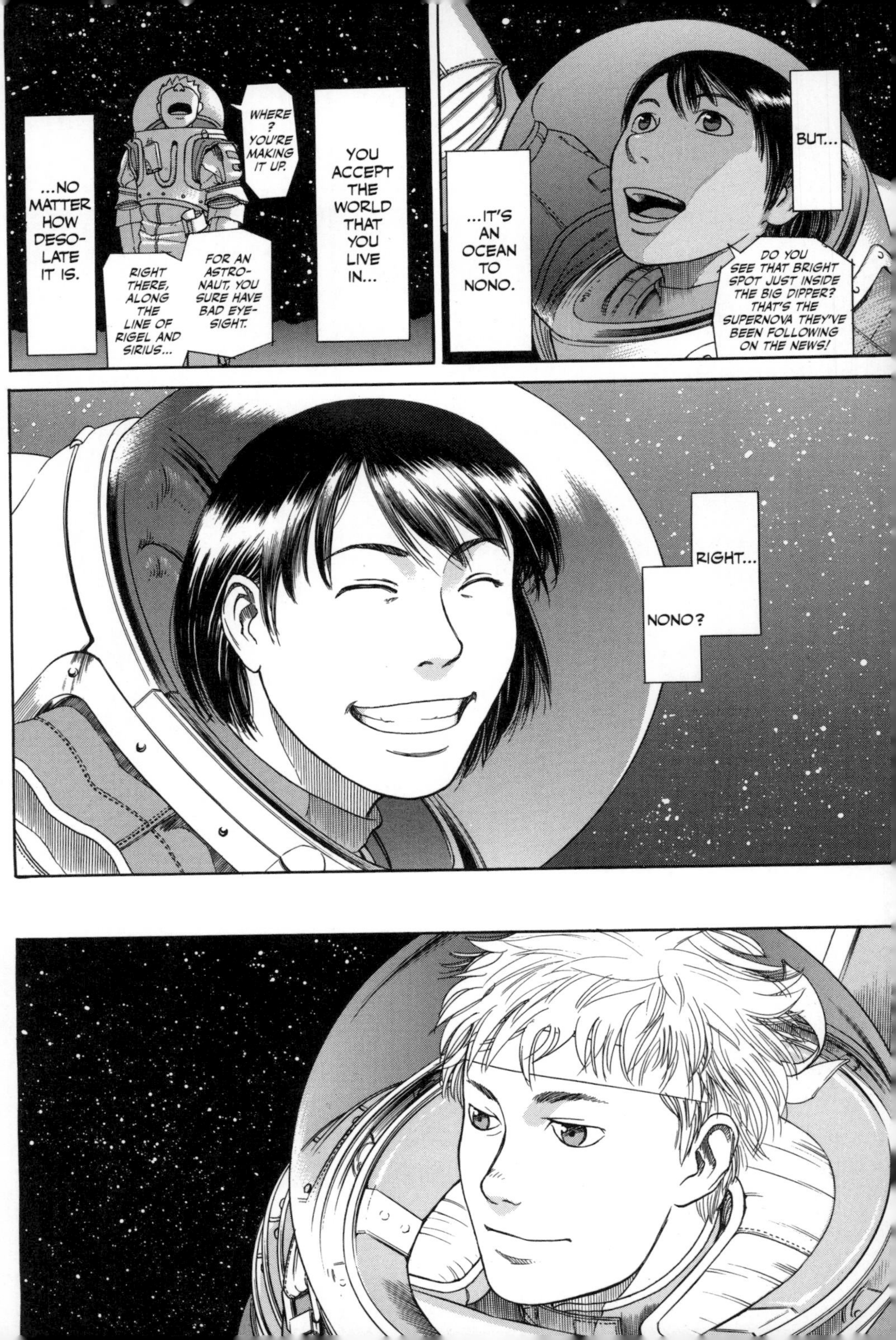
BUT...
...IT'S AN OCEAN TO NONO.
DO YOU SEE THAT BRIGHT SPOT JUST INSIDE THE BIG DIPPER? THAT'S THE SUPERNOVA THEY'VE BEEN FOLLOWING ON THE NEWS!
YOU ACCEPT THE WORLD THAT YOU LIVE IN...
WHERE? YOU'RE MAKING IT UP.
FOR AN ASTRONAUT, YOU SURE HAVE BAD EYESIGHT.
RIGHT THERE, ALONG THE LINE OF RIGEL AND SIRIUS...
...NO MATTER HOW DESOLATE IT IS.
RIGHT...
NONO?

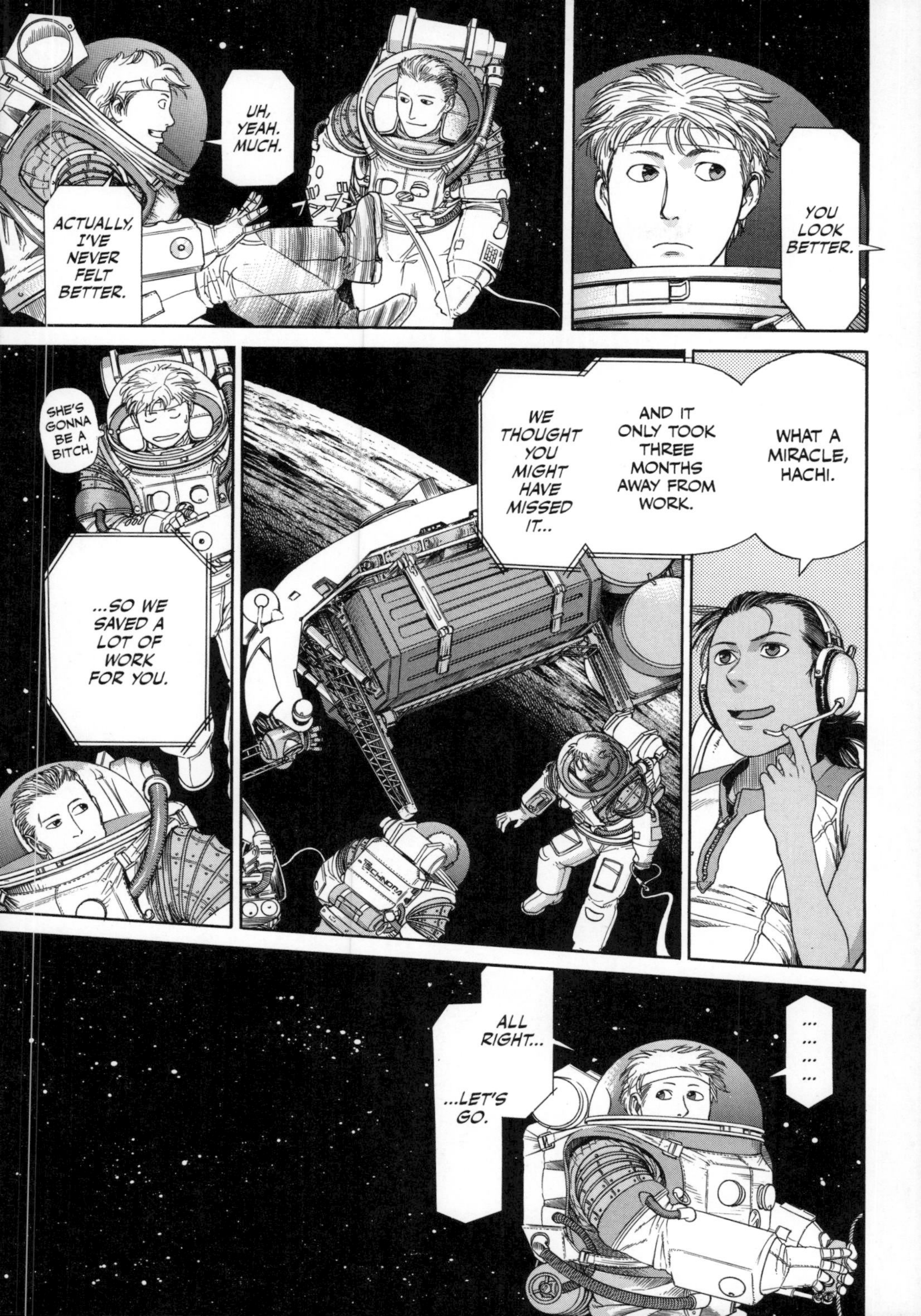
YOU LOOK BETTER.
UH, YEAH. MUCH.
ACTUALLY, I'VE NEVER FELT BETTER.
WHAT A MIRACLE, HACHI.
AND IT ONLY TOOK THREE MONTHS AWAY FROM WORK.
WE THOUGHT YOU MIGHT HAVE MISSED IT...
TECHNORA
SHE'S GONNA BE A BITCH.
...SO WE SAVED A LOT OF WORK FOR YOU.
....
ALL RIGHT...
...LET'S GO.

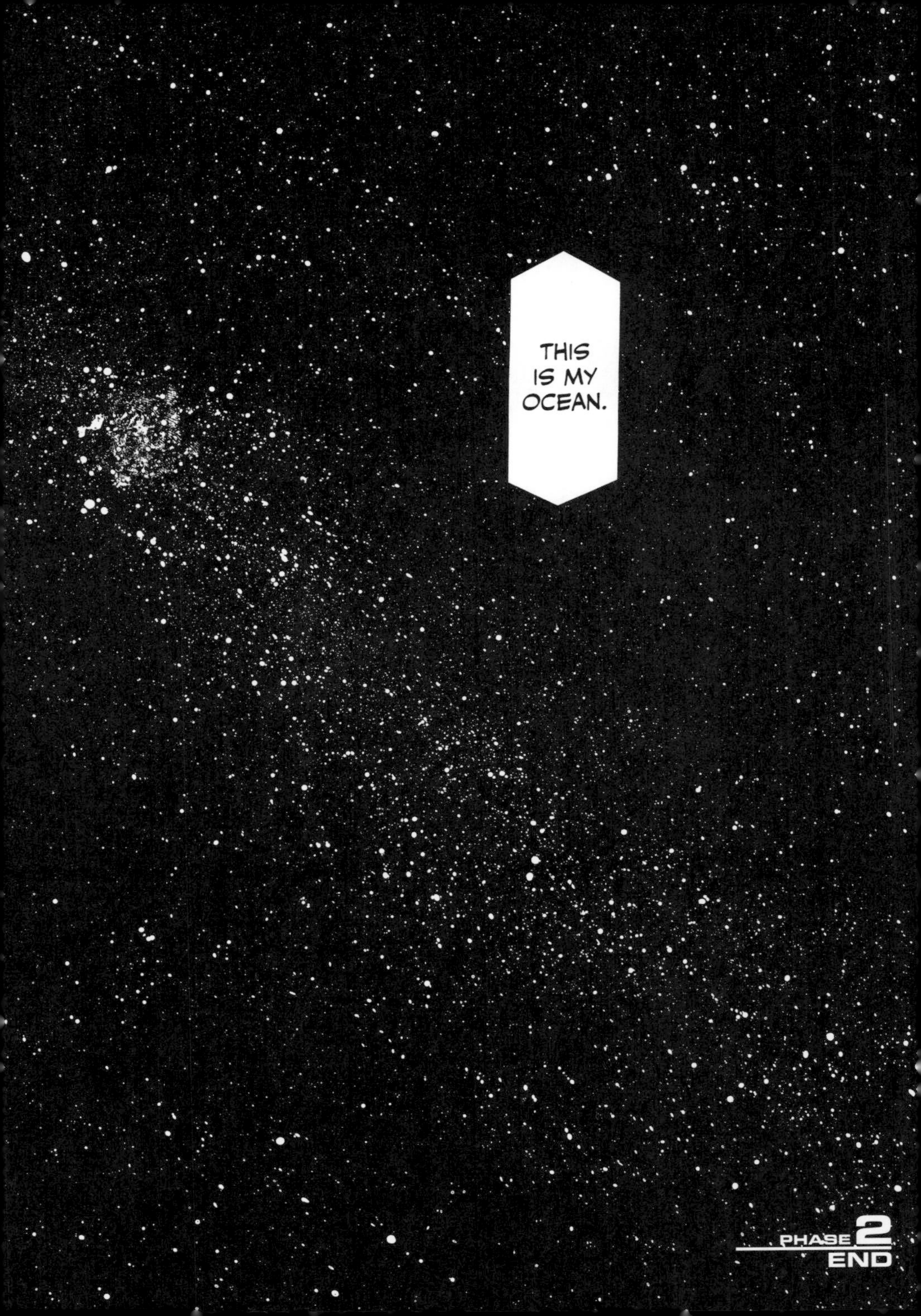
THIS IS MY OCEAN.
PHASE 2 END

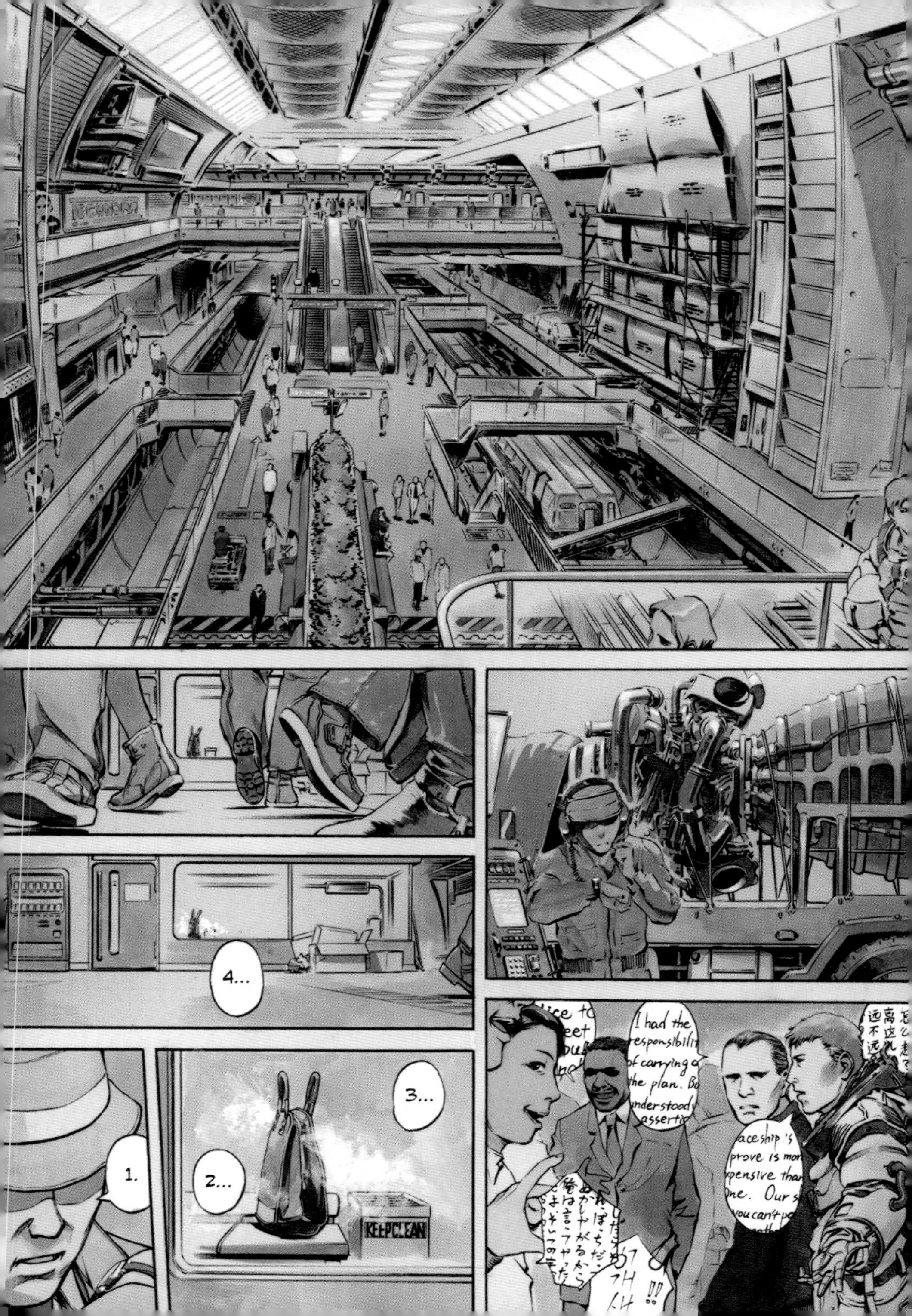
4...
怎么走？
高这儿
远不远
aceship 's
prove is mor
pensive thar
ne. Our s
you can't p
I had the
esponsibilit
f carrying
the plan. B
nderstood
assert
ice to
eet
俺は言ってやったよ
れ、ぼっちだ
おかしやがるから
!!
3...
2...
KEEPCLEAN
1.

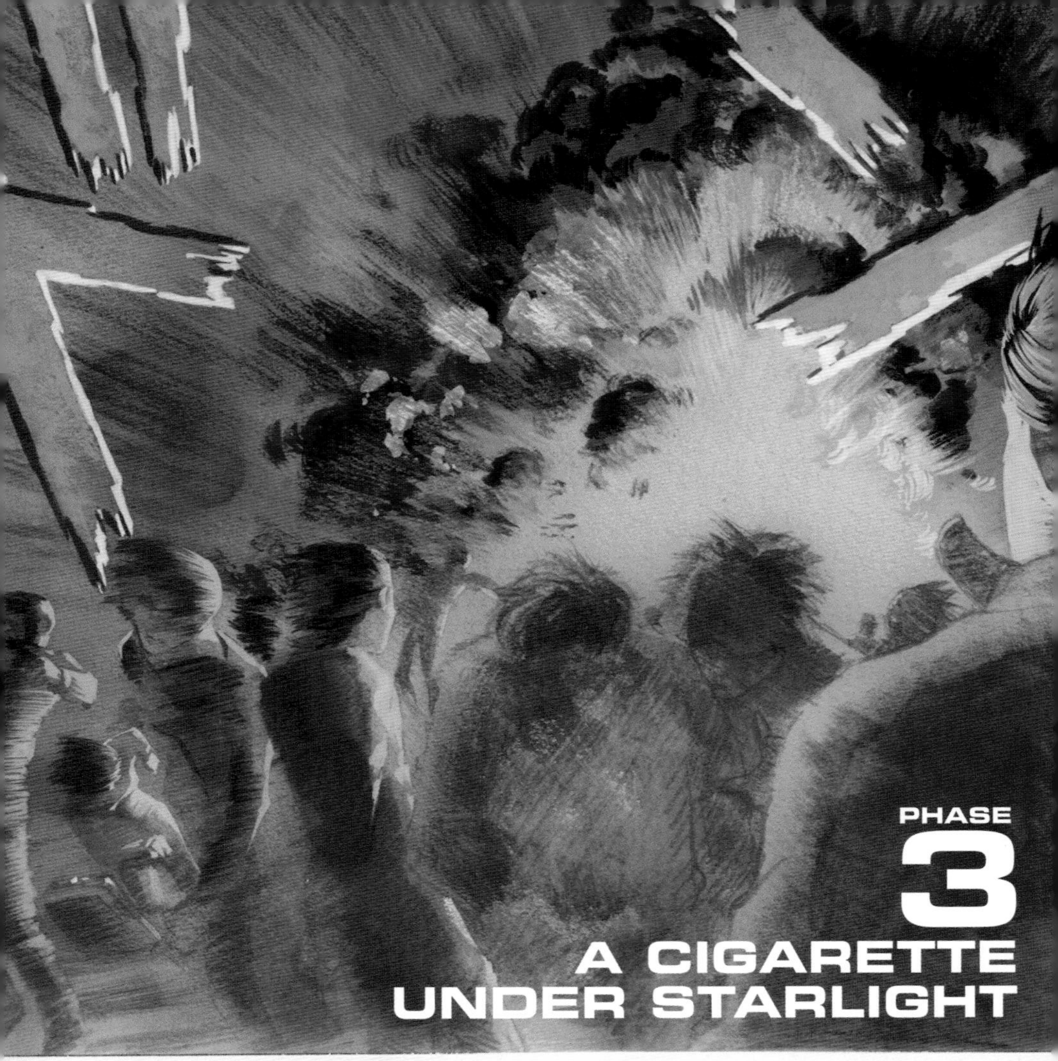
PHASE
3
A CIGARETTE
UNDER STARLIGHT
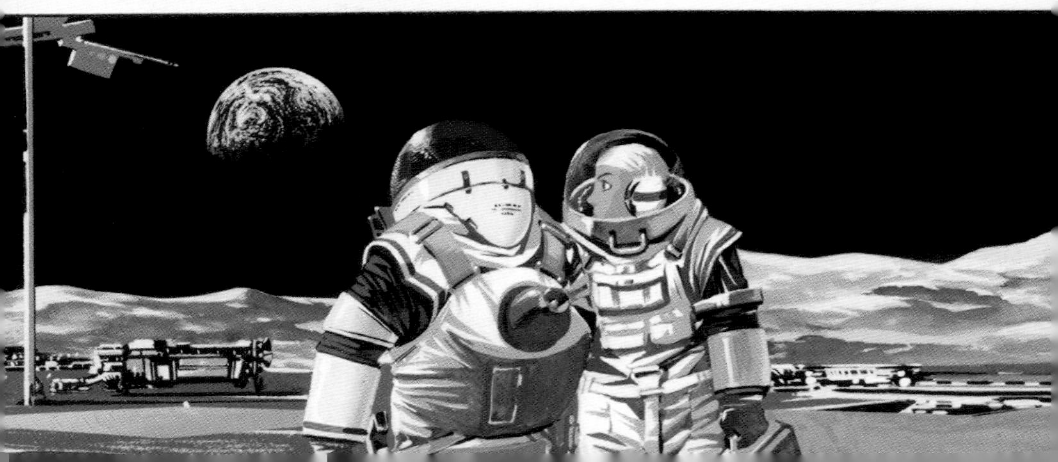

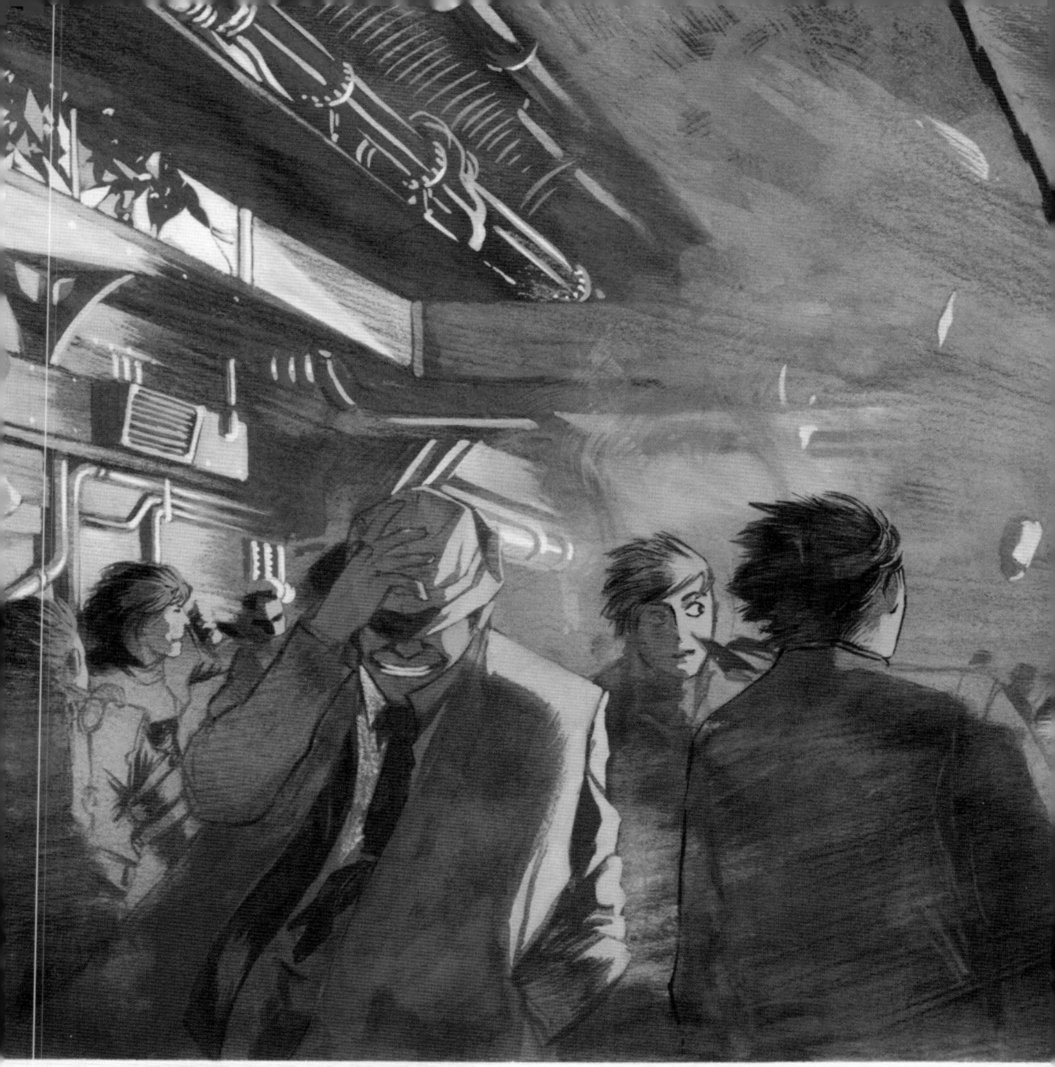

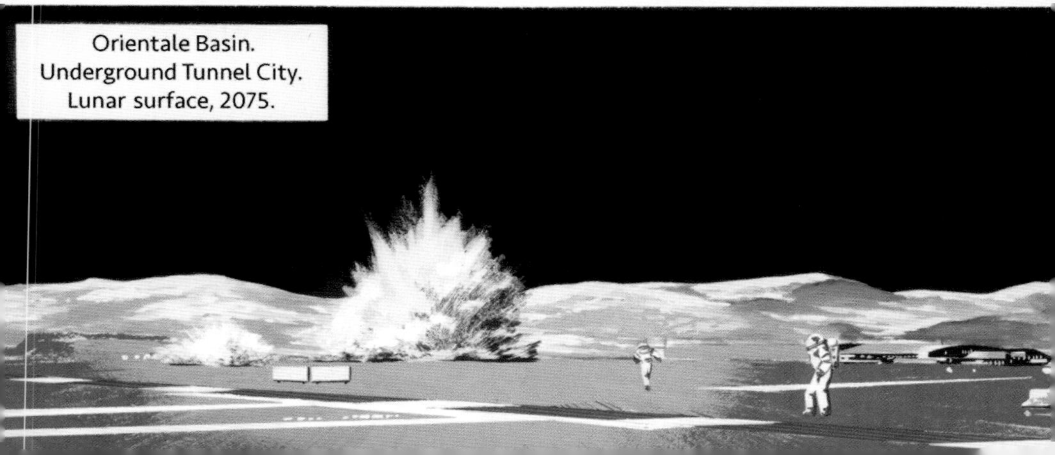
Orientale Basin.
Underground Tunnel City.
Lunar surface, 2075.

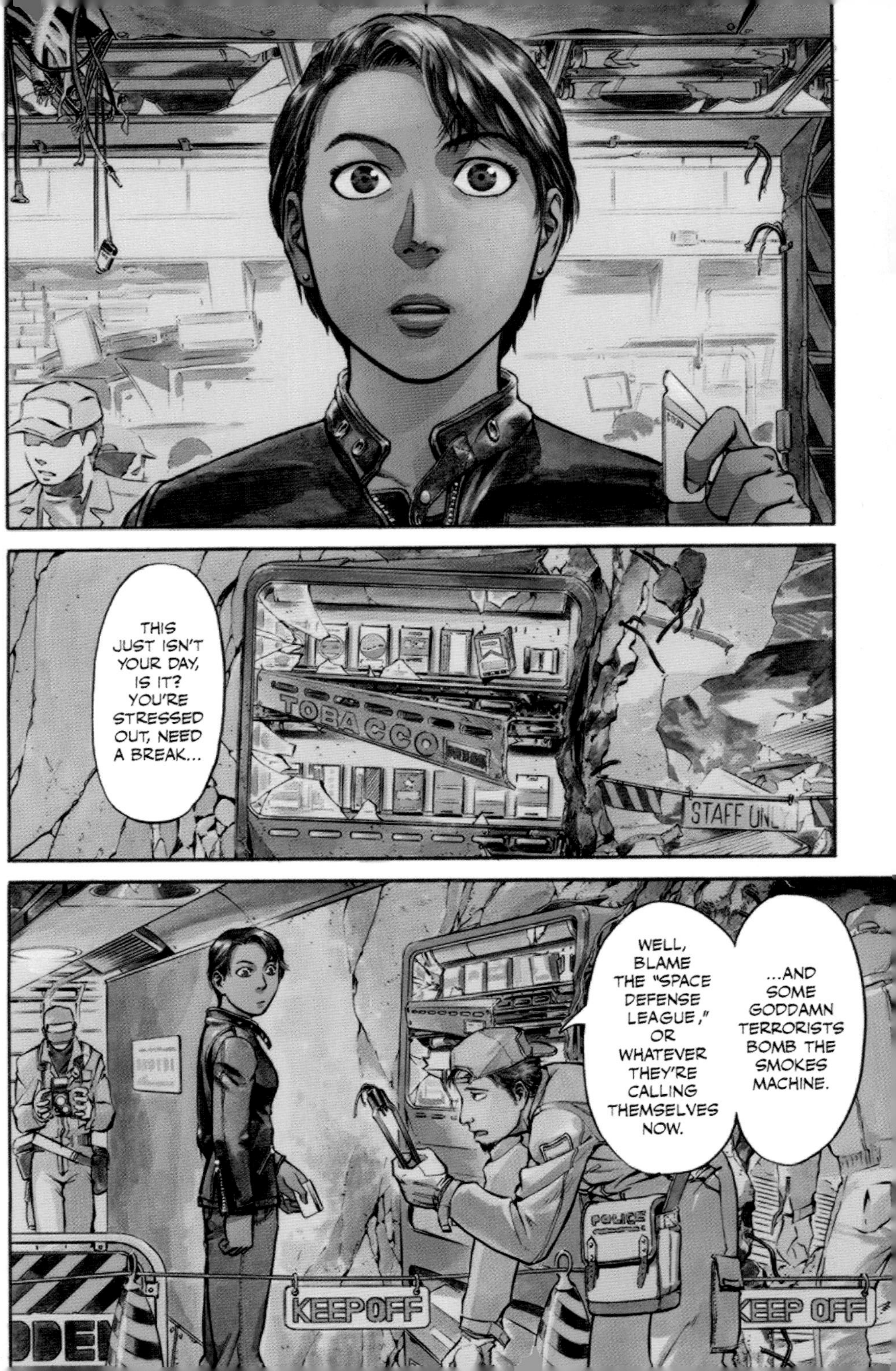
THIS JUST ISN'T YOUR DAY, IS IT? YOU'RE STRESSED OUT, NEED A BREAK...
TOBACCO
...AND SOME GODDAMN TERRORISTS BOMB THE SMOKES MACHINE.
WELL, BLAME THE "SPACE DEFENSE LEAGUE," OR WHATEVER THEY'RE CALLING THEMSELVES NOW.
POLICE
KEEP OFF
KEEPOFF

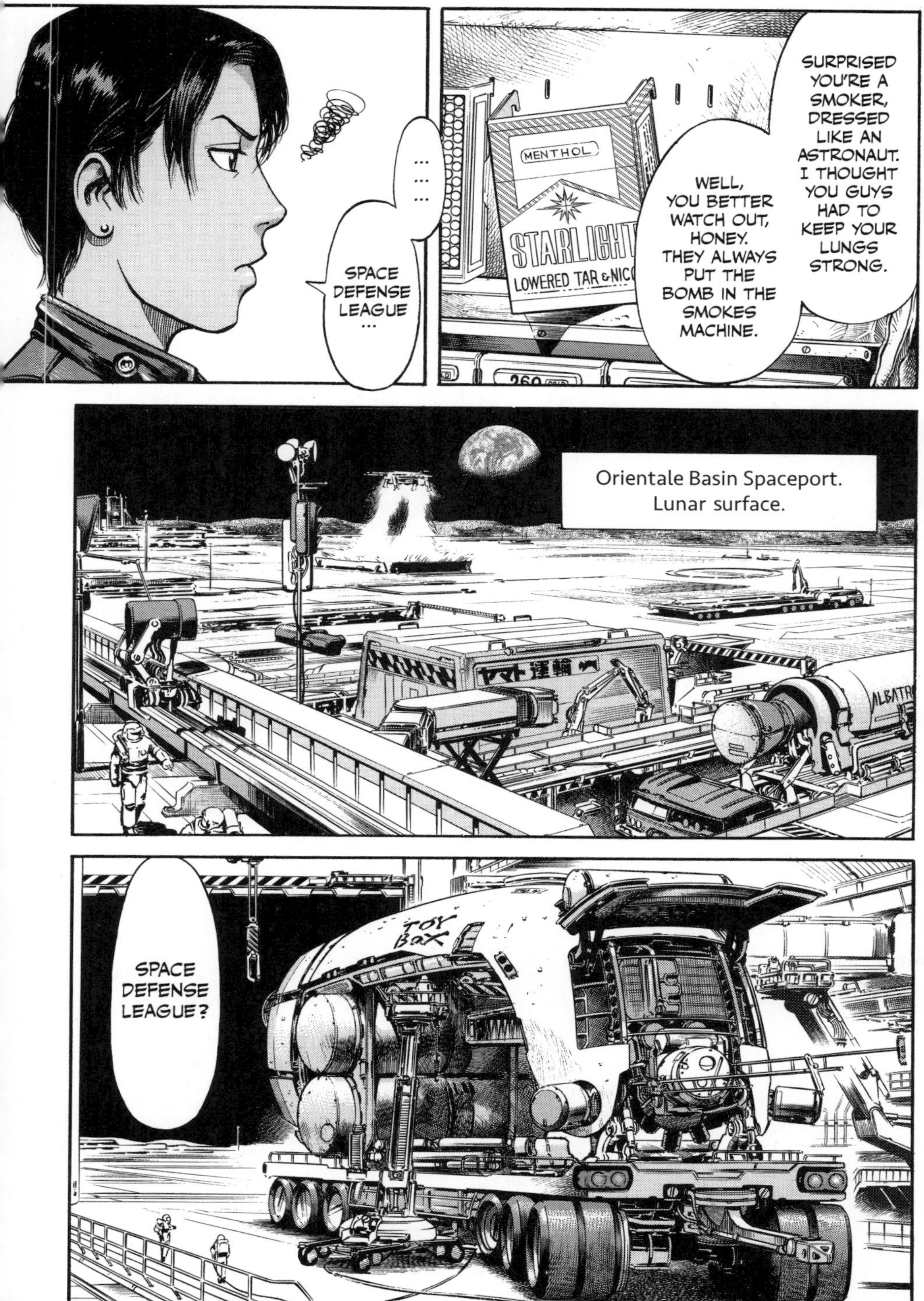
SURPRISED YOU'RE A SMOKER, DRESSED LIKE AN ASTRONAUT. I THOUGHT YOU GUYS HAD TO KEEP YOUR LUNGS STRONG.
WELL, YOU BETTER WATCH OUT, HONEY. THEY ALWAYS PUT THE BOMB IN THE SMOKES MACHINE.
MENTHOL
STARLIGHT
… … …
SPACE DEFENSE LEAGUE …
Orientale Basin Spaceport. Lunar surface.
ヤマト運輸
SPACE DEFENSE LEAGUE?
TOY BOX

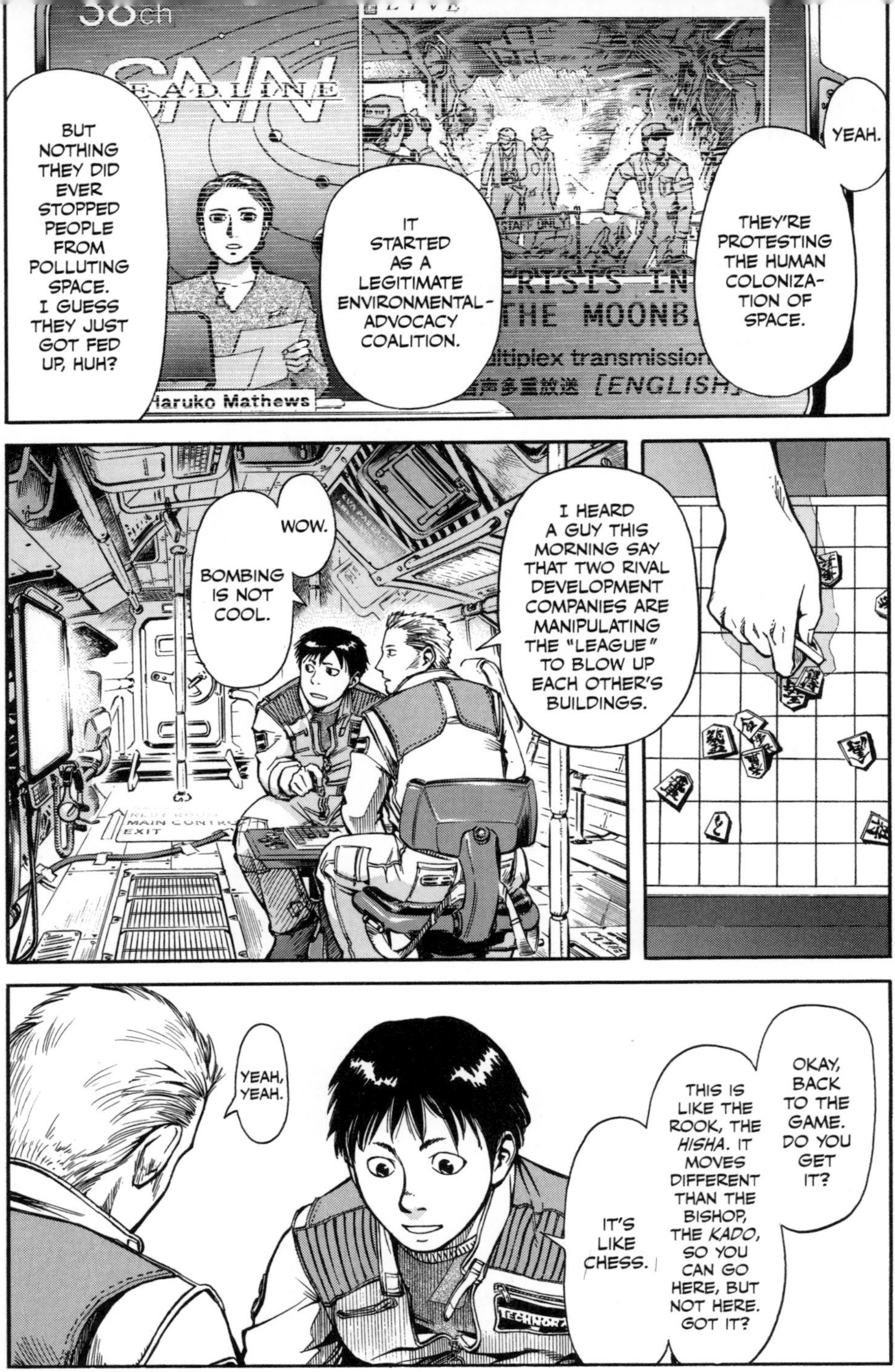
YEAH.
THEY'RE PROTESTING THE HUMAN COLONIZATION OF SPACE.
IT STARTED AS A LEGITIMATE ENVIRONMENTAL-ADVOCACY COALITION.
BUT NOTHING THEY DID EVER STOPPED PEOPLE FROM POLLUTING SPACE. I GUESS THEY JUST GOT FED UP, HUH?
Haruko Mathews
[ENGLISH]
I HEARD A GUY THIS MORNING SAY THAT TWO RIVAL DEVELOPMENT COMPANIES ARE MANIPULATING THE "LEAGUE" TO BLOW UP EACH OTHER'S BUILDINGS.
WOW.
BOMBING IS NOT COOL.
OKAY, BACK TO THE GAME. DO YOU GET IT?
THIS IS LIKE THE ROOK, THE *HISHA*. IT MOVES DIFFERENT THAN THE BISHOP, THE *KADO*, SO YOU CAN GO HERE, BUT NOT HERE. GOT IT?
IT'S LIKE CHESS.
YEAH, YEAH.

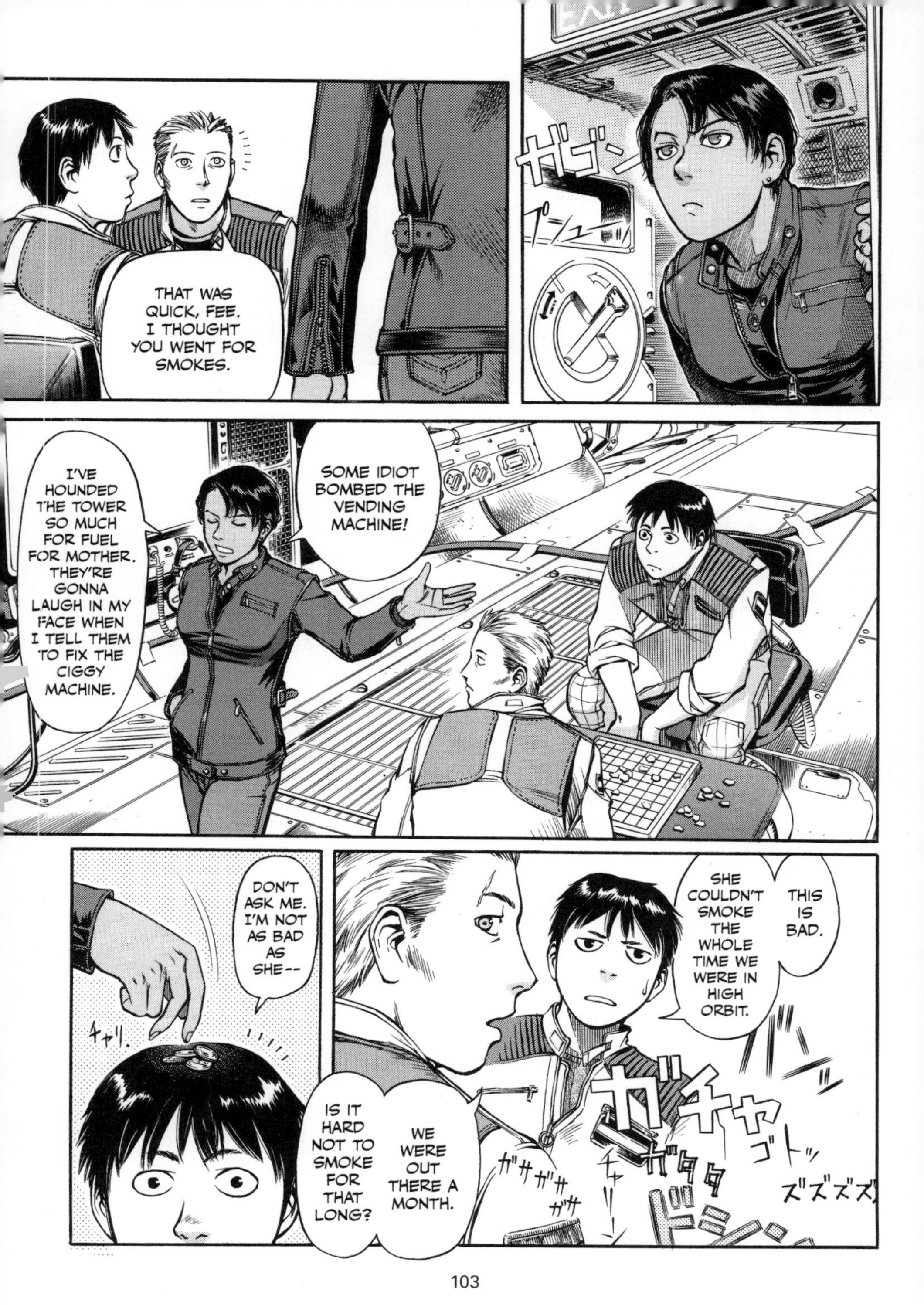
ガゴン
プシューッ
THAT WAS QUICK, FEE. I THOUGHT YOU WENT FOR SMOKES.
SOME IDIOT BOMBED THE VENDING MACHINE!
I'VE HOUNDED THE TOWER SO MUCH FOR FUEL FOR MOTHER. THEY'RE GONNA LAUGH IN MY FACE WHEN I TELL THEM TO FIX THE CIGGY MACHINE.
THIS IS BAD.
SHE COULDN'T SMOKE THE WHOLE TIME WE WERE IN HIGH ORBIT.
ガチャ
ゴトッ
チャリ
DON'T ASK ME. I'M NOT AS BAD AS SHE--
WE WERE OUT THERE A MONTH.
IS IT HARD NOT TO SMOKE FOR THAT LONG?

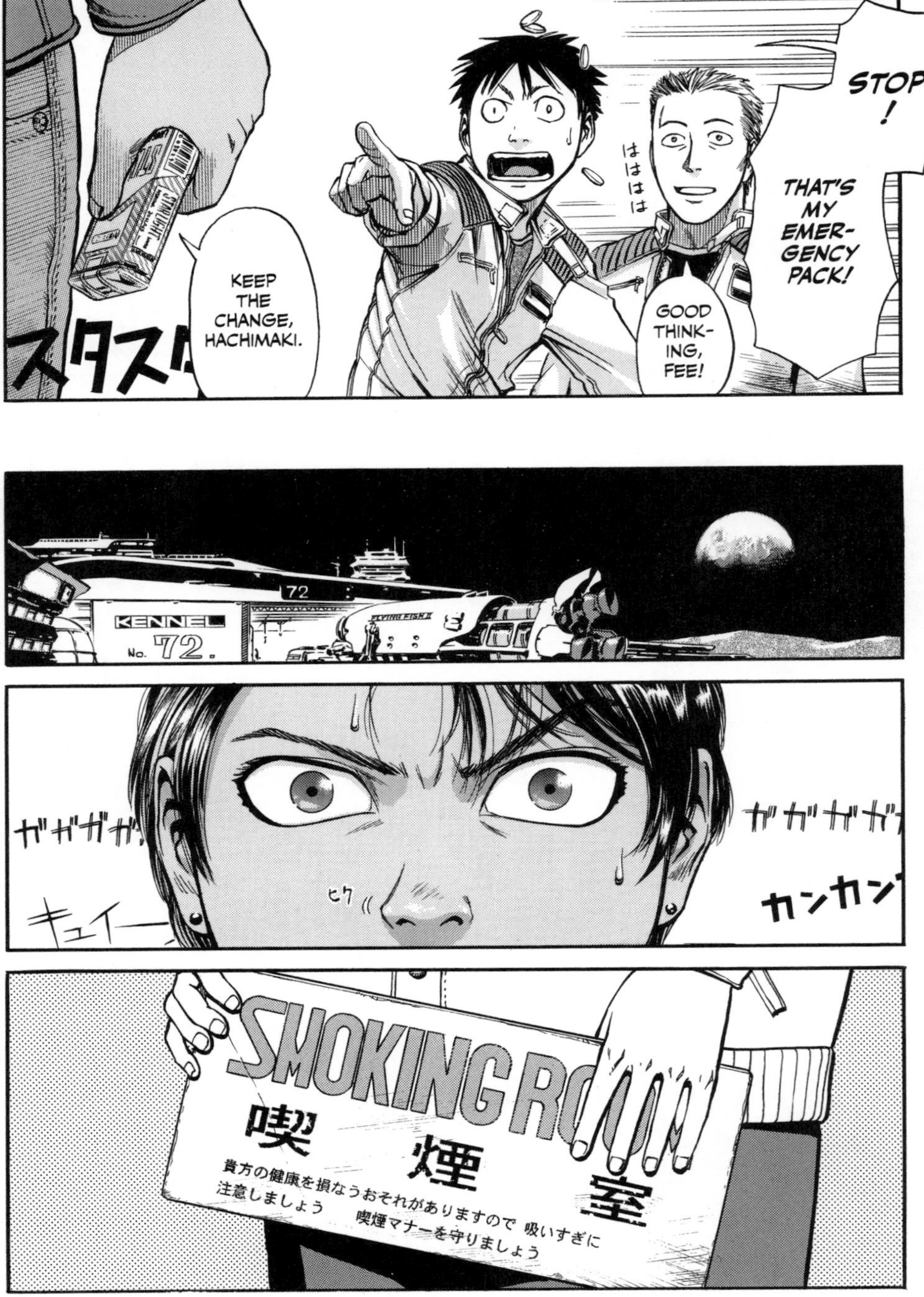
STOP!
THAT'S MY EMERGENCY PACK!
ははは
GOOD THINKING, FEE!
KEEP THE CHANGE, HACHIMAKI.
KENNEL No. 72.
72
FLYING FISH II
ガガガガ
カンカン
ヒク
ガガガガ
キュイー
SMOKING RO
喫煙室
貴方の健康を損なうおそれがありますので 吸いすぎに
注意しましょう 喫煙マナーを守りましょう

THIS IS THE FIFTH ONE THE S.D.L. HAS SET OFF.
AND FOUR OF THOSE TARGETED SMOKING ROOMS.
BUT THOSE LITTLE BASTARDS WON'T GET US AGAIN. WE'RE CLOSING ALL THE SMOKING ROOMS IN THE CITY.
WHAT? YOU CLOSED... ALL?!
I'M THE BASIN CITY EPA.
AND YOU ARE? WHAT? AN ASTRONAUT?
?
HUH ?
DO YOU HAVE ANY IDEA HOW RUDE IT IS TO SMOKE IN SPACE?
CLEAN AIR IS ESSENTIAL FOR HEALTHY LIVING UP HERE, AND YOU SMOKERS SPOIL IT WITH YOUR FOUL ADDICTION.
うっ
DO YOU KNOW HOW MUCH IT COSTS TO CLEAN THE AIR YOU POLLUTE WITH JUST ONE HOUR OF SMOKING?
EVERY-ONE'S A PREACHER.
IT WAS A MISTAKE TO SET UP SMOKING AREAS TO BEGIN WITH. IT NOT ONLY WASTED OUR TAX MONEY TO BUILD THEM INITIALLY, BUT THEY CONTINUE TO DRAIN OUR CITY BUDGET $400 A DAY IN MAINTENANCE FEES. AND NOW, THE S.D.L. ATTACKS ON SMOKING AREAS HAVE COST US EVEN MORE. SMOKERS ONLY REPRESENT A SLIVER OF THE POPULATION, YET THE MAJORITY OF JAPANESE SPACE MEN ARE STILL SMOKERS. AND FOR WHAT? TO LOOK COOL AND FORLORN? I THOUGHT THAT ATTITUDE PASSED WITH THE TWENTIETH CENTURY. WHEN THE SPACE PROGRAM FIRST BEGAN, IT WAS FULL OF HEALTHY, FIT INDIVIDUALS. BUT ONCE IT BECAME COMMERCIAL, IT GOT INVADED WITH HUFFING, PUFFING SLACKERS. DON'T YOU REALIZE THAT YOU ONCE HAD BEAUTIFUL, PINK, FULL LUNGS AND NOW THEY'RE PROBABLY THE SHADE OF CHARCOAL? DID YOU READ THE EXPOSÉ ON SMOKING IN THIS WEEK'S COSMOS? THE VIVISECTION OF A SMOKER'S LUNG WAS QUITE FRIGHTENING AND ENLIGHTENING. LET ME TELL YOU, IT WAS NOT A PRETTY SIGHT...
そそ…
G ROOM

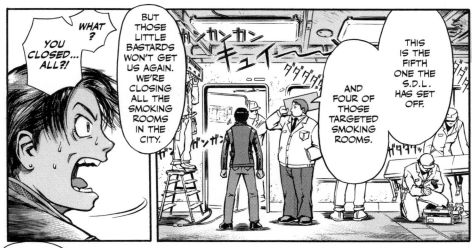

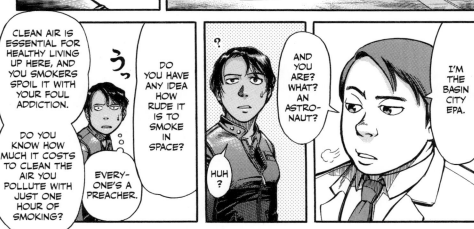

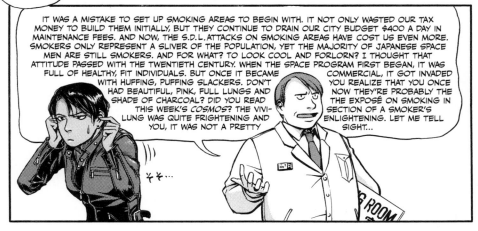

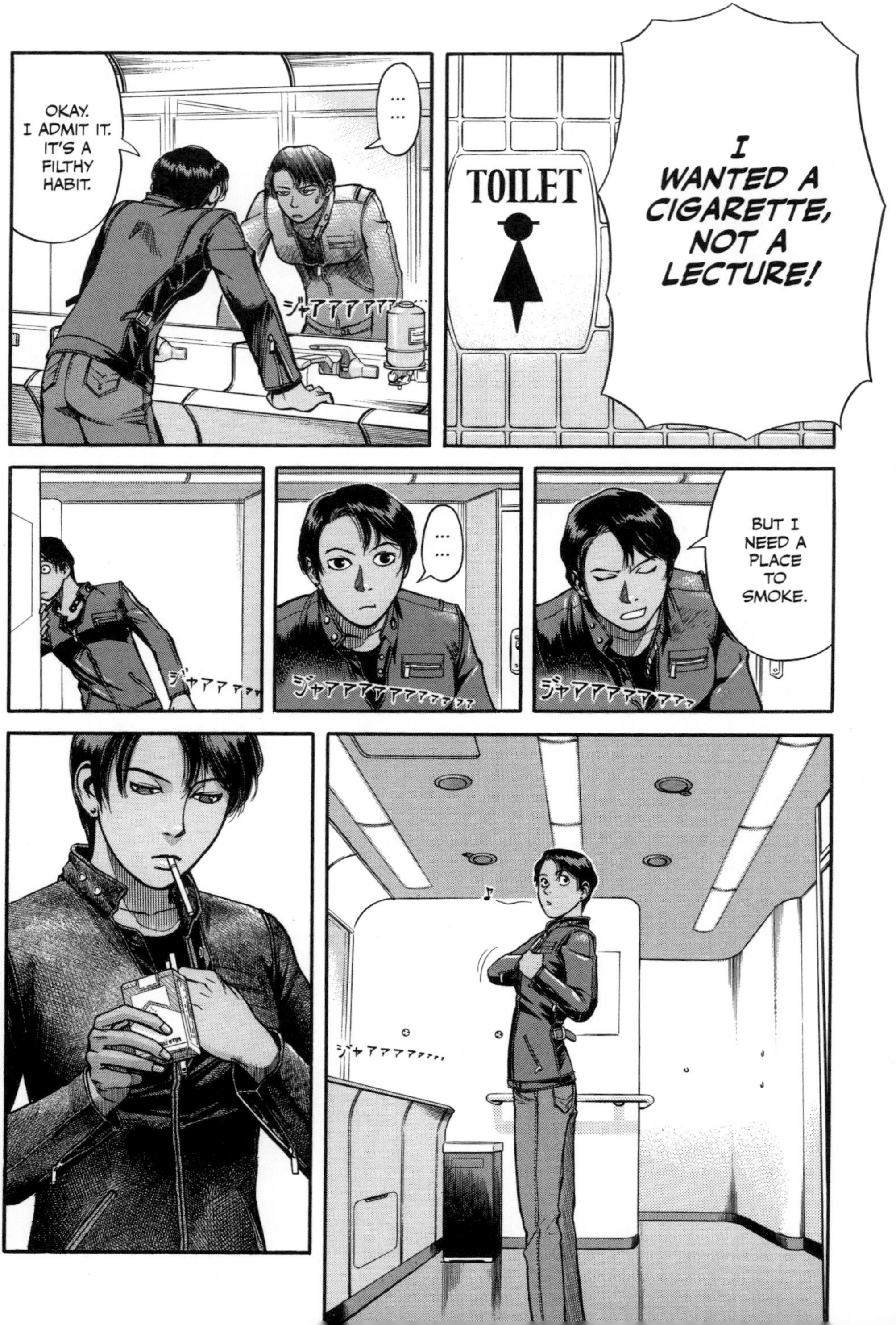
TOILET
I WANTED A CIGARETTE, NOT A LECTURE!
……
OKAY. I ADMIT IT. IT'S A FILTHY HABIT.
ジャアアアアア
BUT I NEED A PLACE TO SMOKE.
ジャアアアアアアァ
……
ジャアアアアアアアァァァ
ジャアアアァァァ
ジャアアアアァァ

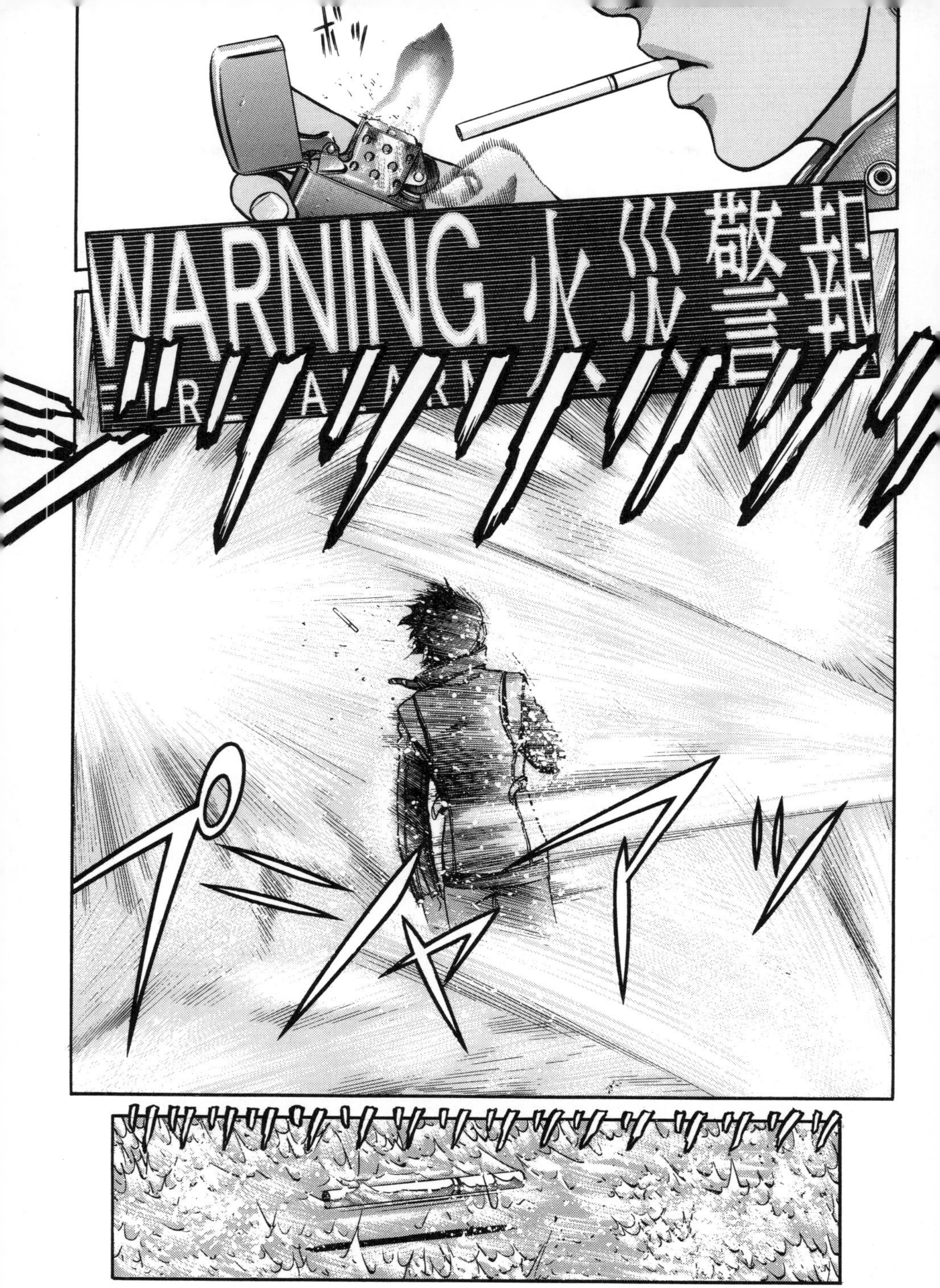
ボッ
WARNING 火災警報

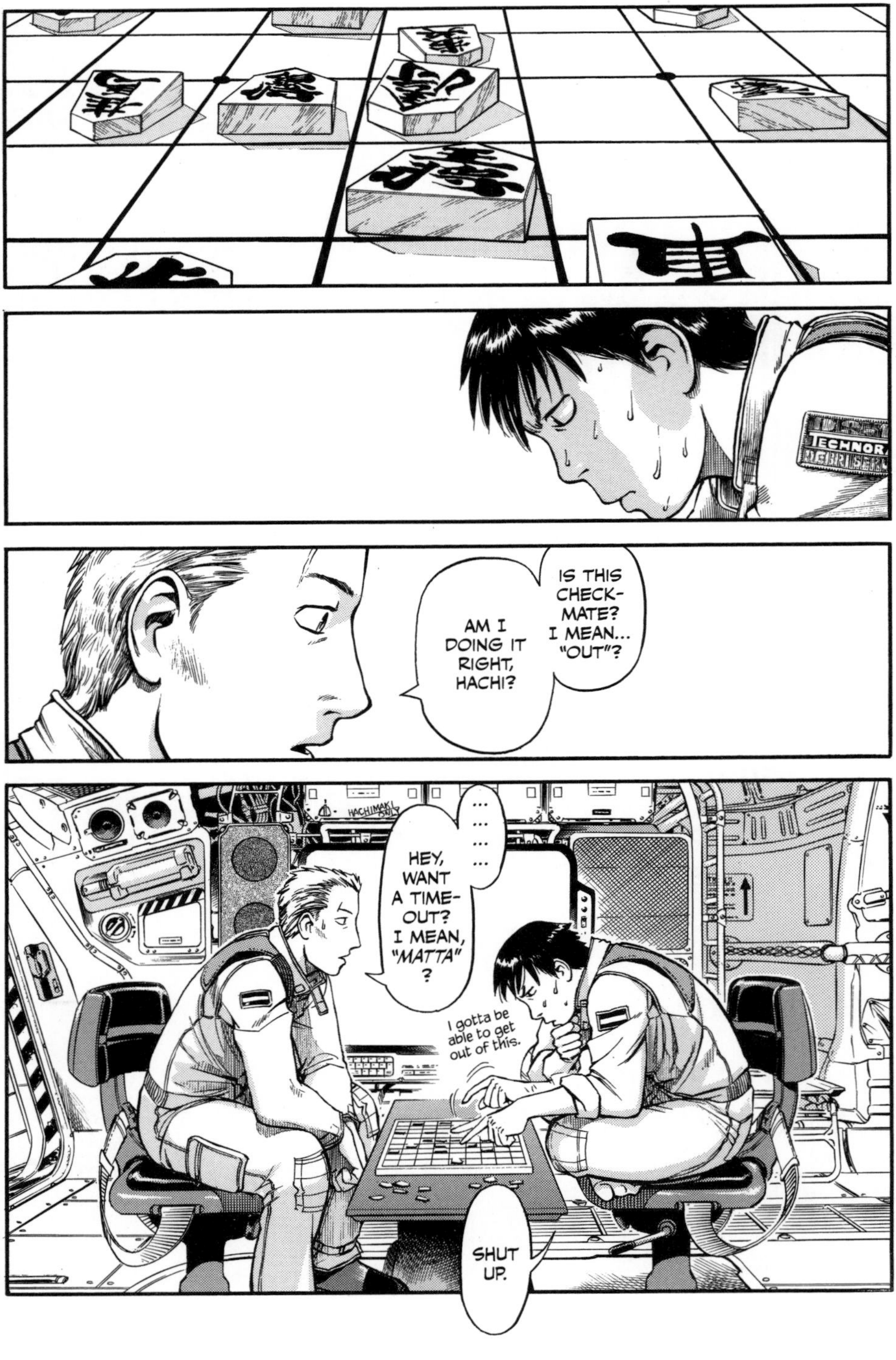
IS THIS CHECK-MATE? I MEAN... "OUT"?
AM I DOING IT RIGHT, HACHI?
....
HEY, WANT A TIME-OUT? I MEAN, "MATTA"?
I gotta be able to get out of this.
SHUT UP.

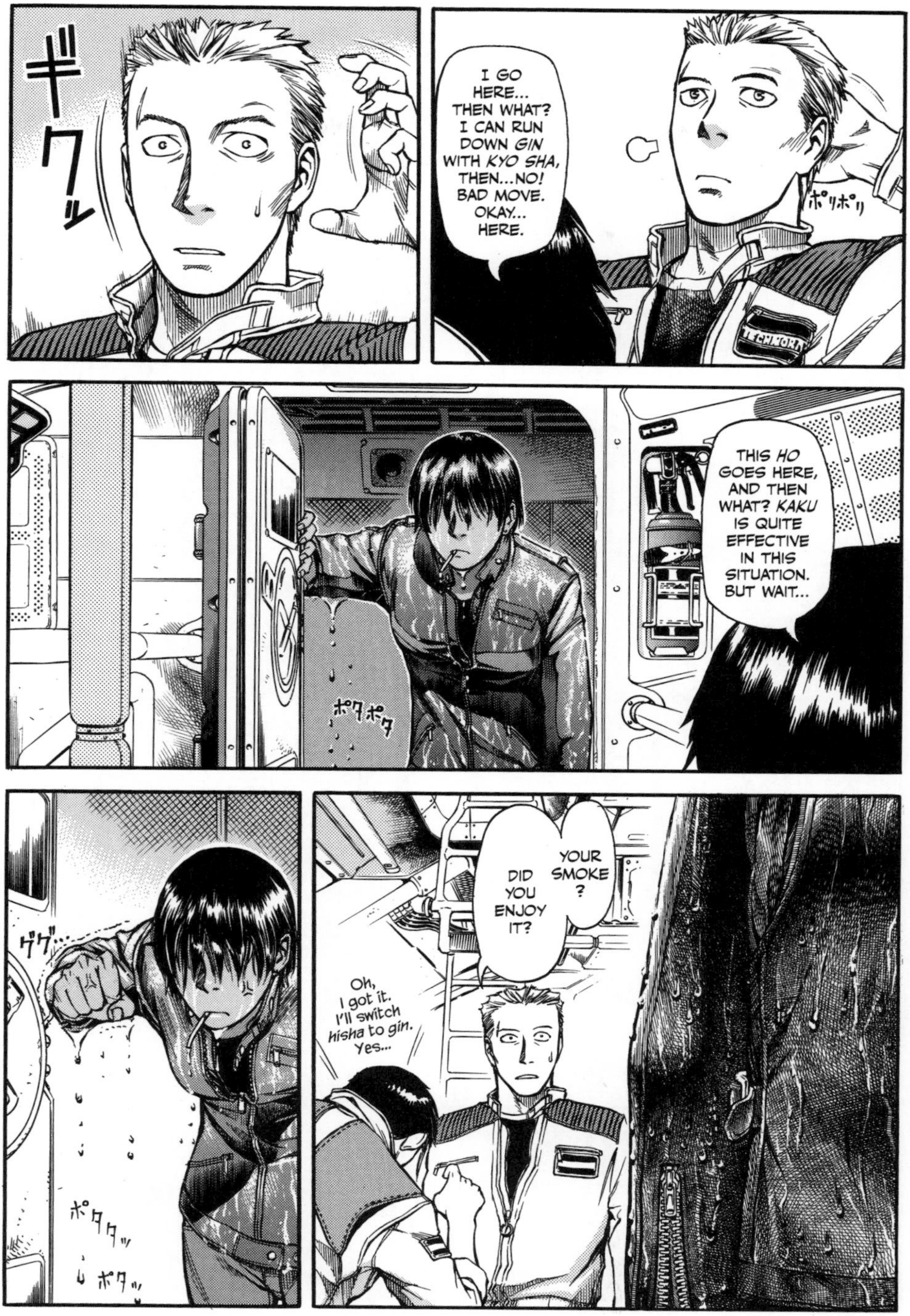
I GO HERE... THEN WHAT? I CAN RUN DOWN *GIN* WITH *KYO SHA*, THEN...NO! BAD MOVE. OKAY... HERE.
ポリポリ
ギクッ
THIS *HO* GOES HERE, AND THEN WHAT? *KAKU* IS QUITE EFFECTIVE IN THIS SITUATION. BUT WAIT...
ポタポタ
YOUR SMOKE?
DID YOU ENJOY IT?
Oh, I got it. I'll switch *hisha* to *gin*. Yes...
ググ…
ポタタッ
ポタッ

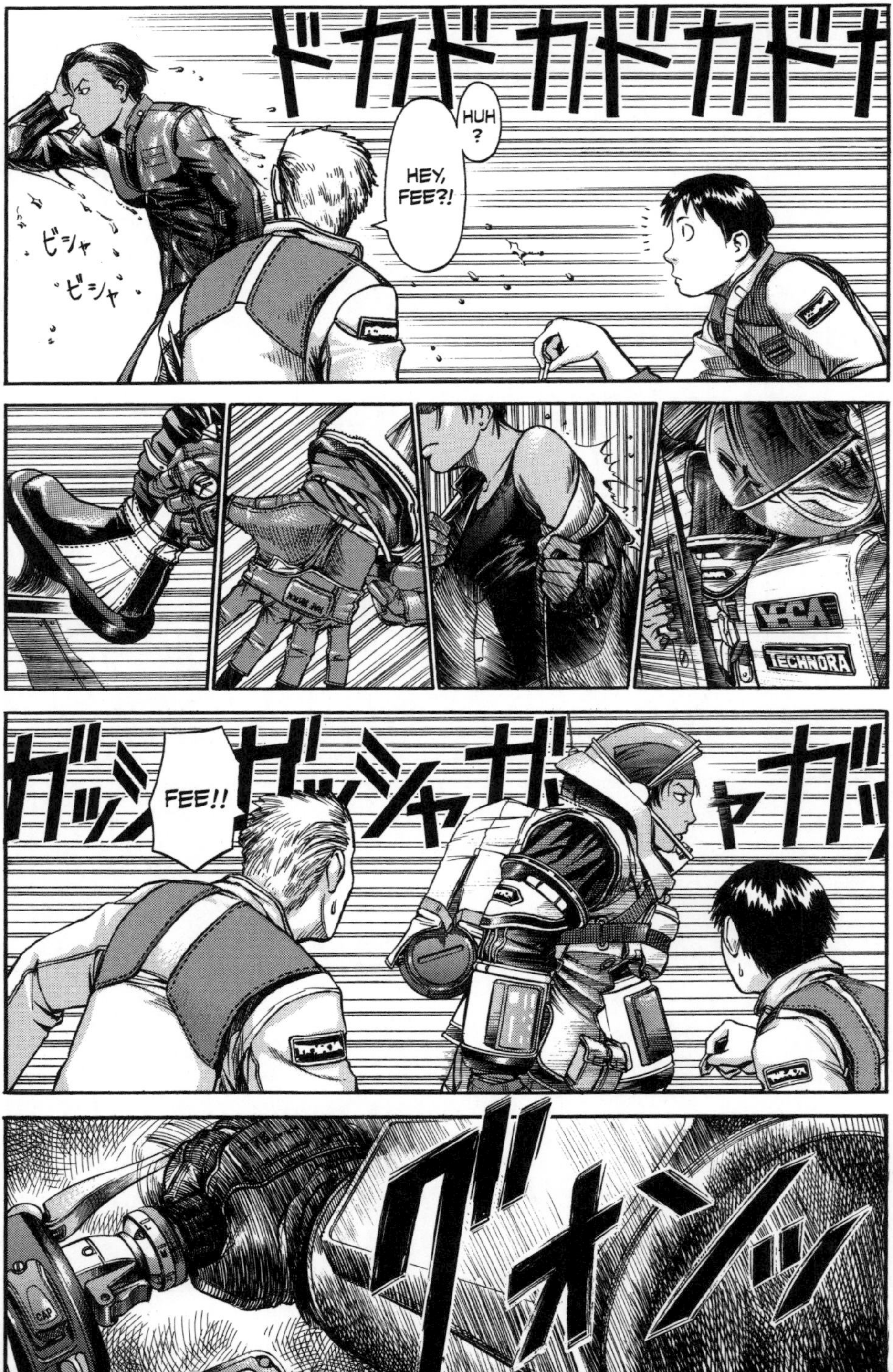
ドカドカドカドカ
HUH ?
HEY, FEE?!
ビシャ
ビシャ
TECHNORA
ガッシャガッシャガッシャガッ
FEE!!
グオンッ

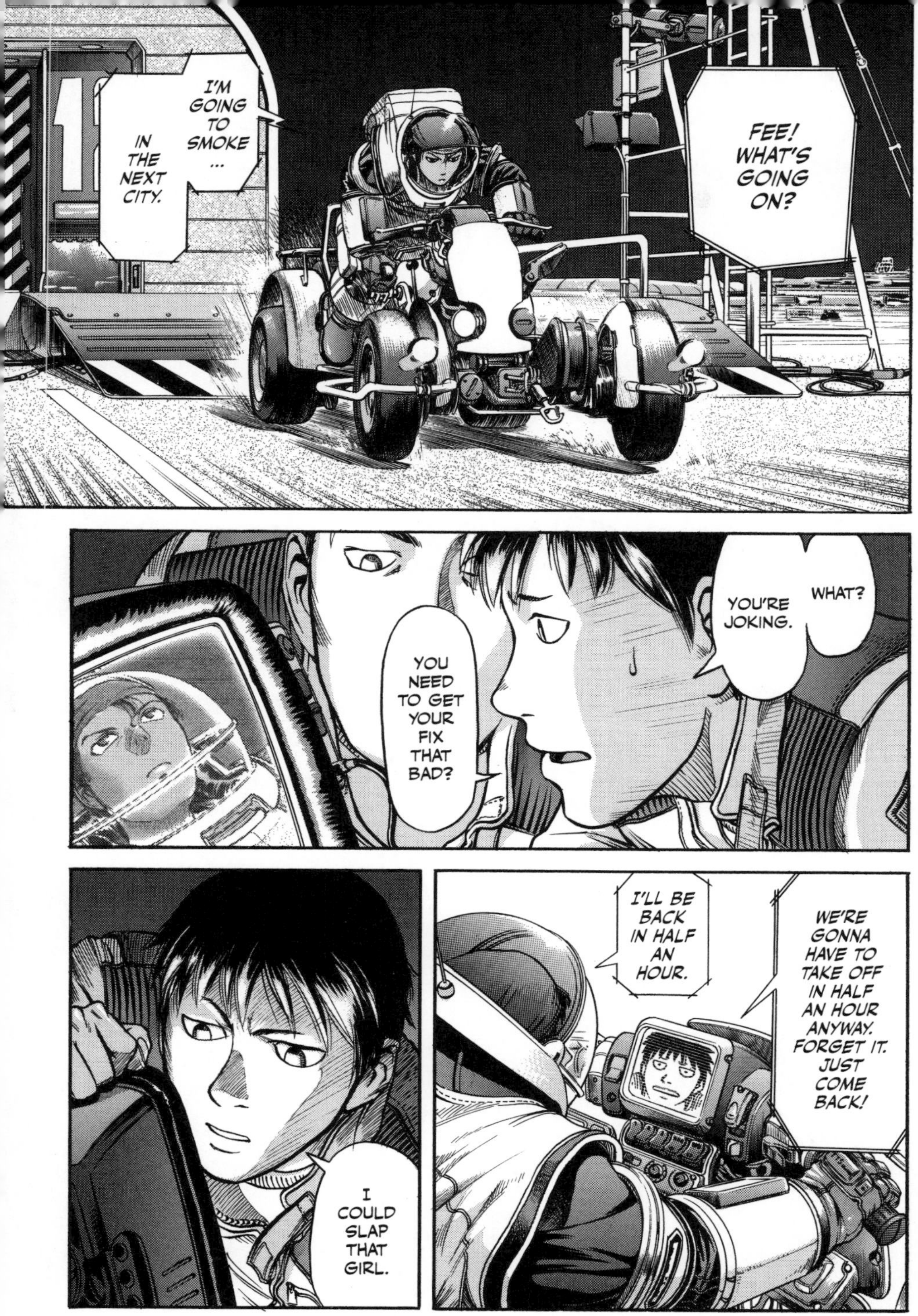
FEE! WHAT'S GOING ON?
I'M GOING TO SMOKE ...
IN THE NEXT CITY.
WHAT?
YOU'RE JOKING.
YOU NEED TO GET YOUR FIX THAT BAD?
WE'RE GONNA HAVE TO TAKE OFF IN HALF AN HOUR ANYWAY. FORGET IT. JUST COME BACK!
I'LL BE BACK IN HALF AN HOUR.
I COULD SLAP THAT GIRL.

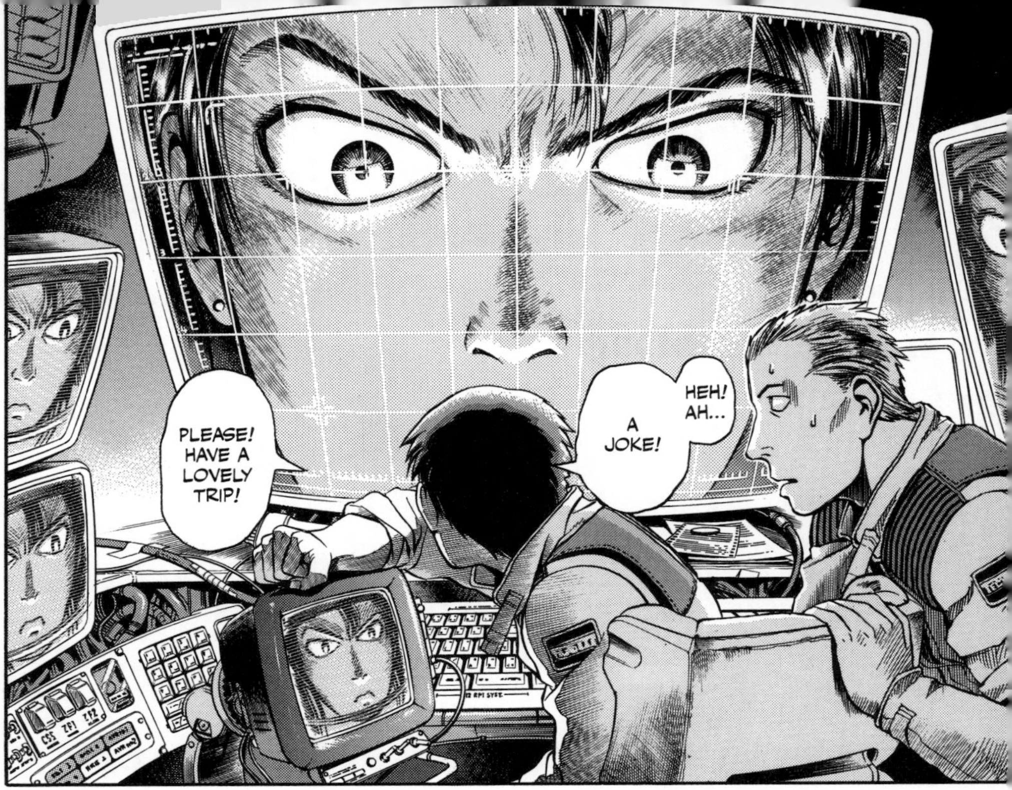
HEH! AH...
A JOKE!
PLEASE! HAVE A LOVELY TRIP!

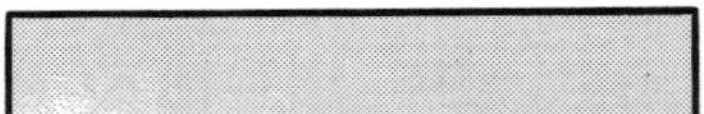

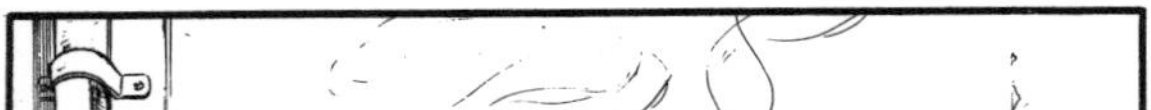

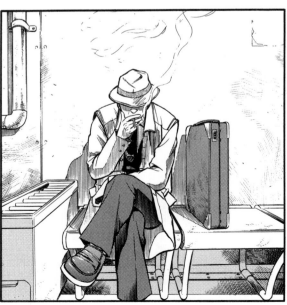

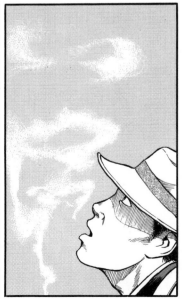

Pi
Pi Pi Pi
Pi Pi!
トッ
スウ…
SMOKING ROOM!
喫煙室
ギッ
WHEW!

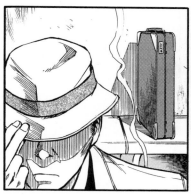

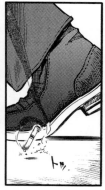

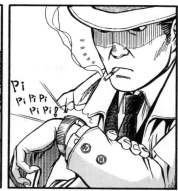

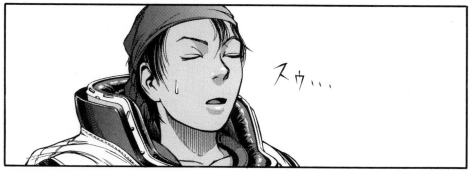

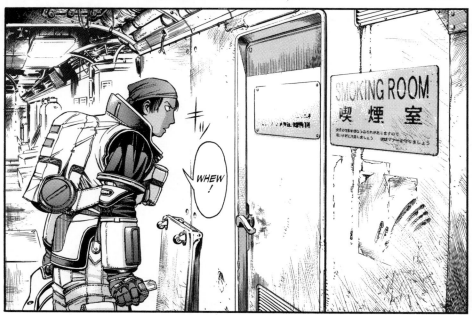

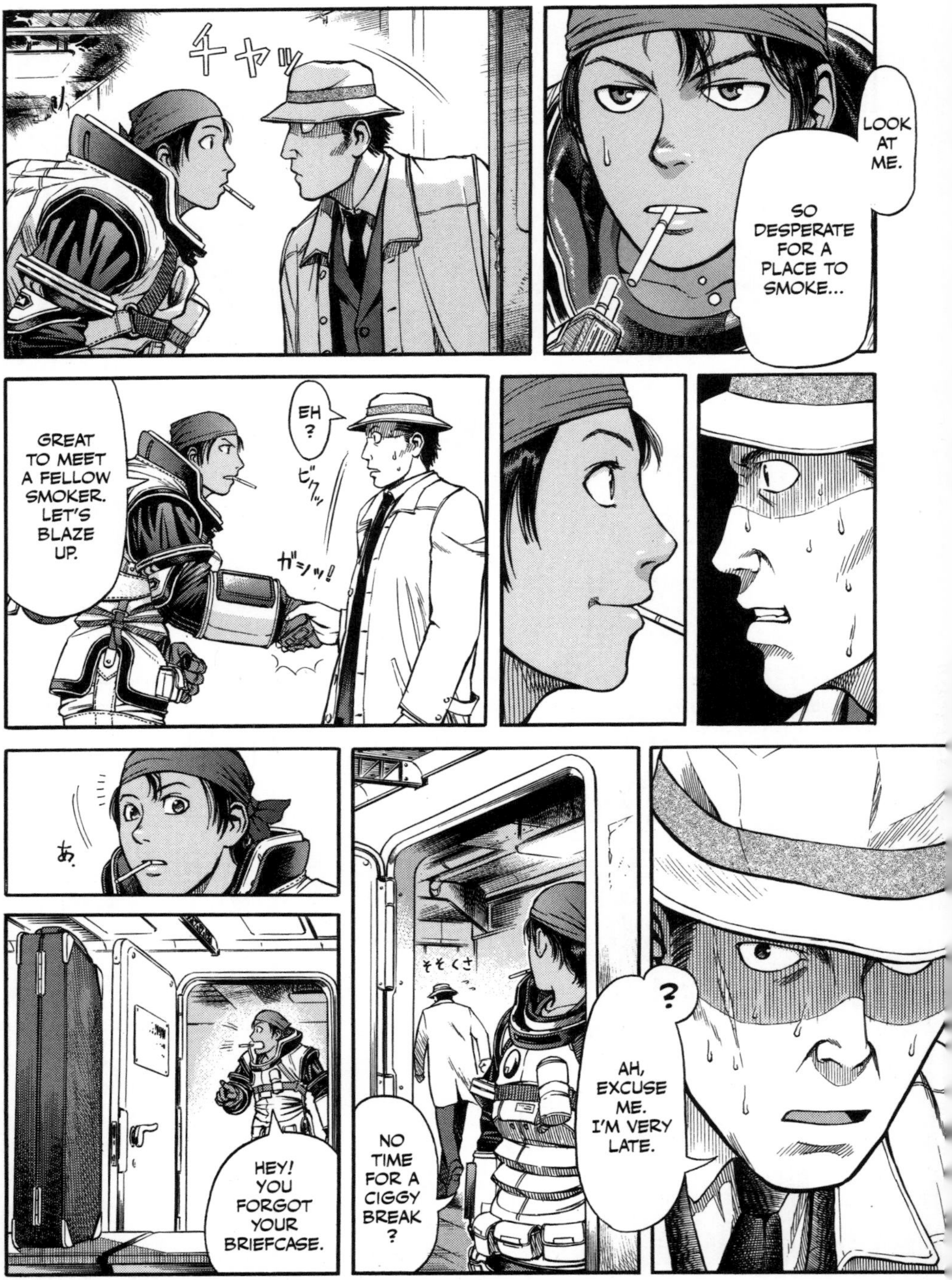

LOOK AT ME.
SO DESPERATE FOR A PLACE TO SMOKE...
チャッ
EH?
ビクッ
GREAT TO MEET A FELLOW SMOKER. LET'S BLAZE UP.
ガシッ!
?
AH, EXCUSE ME. I'M VERY LATE.
そそくさ
NO TIME FOR A CIGGY BREAK?
あ.
HEY! YOU FORGOT YOUR BRIEFCASE.

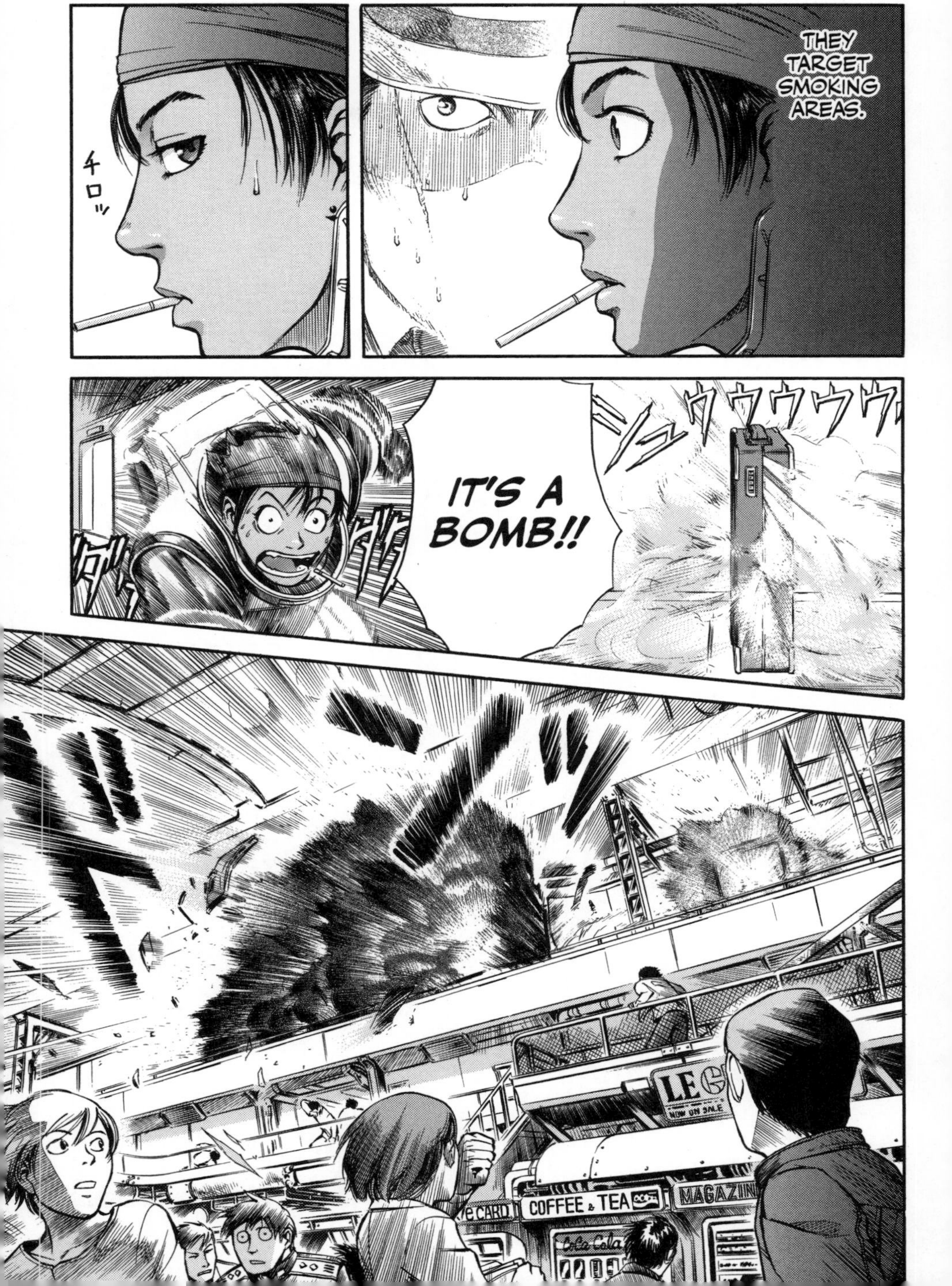
THEY TARGET SMOKING AREAS.
チロッ
シュウウウウウ
IT'S A BOMB!!
COFFEE & TEA
Coca-Cola

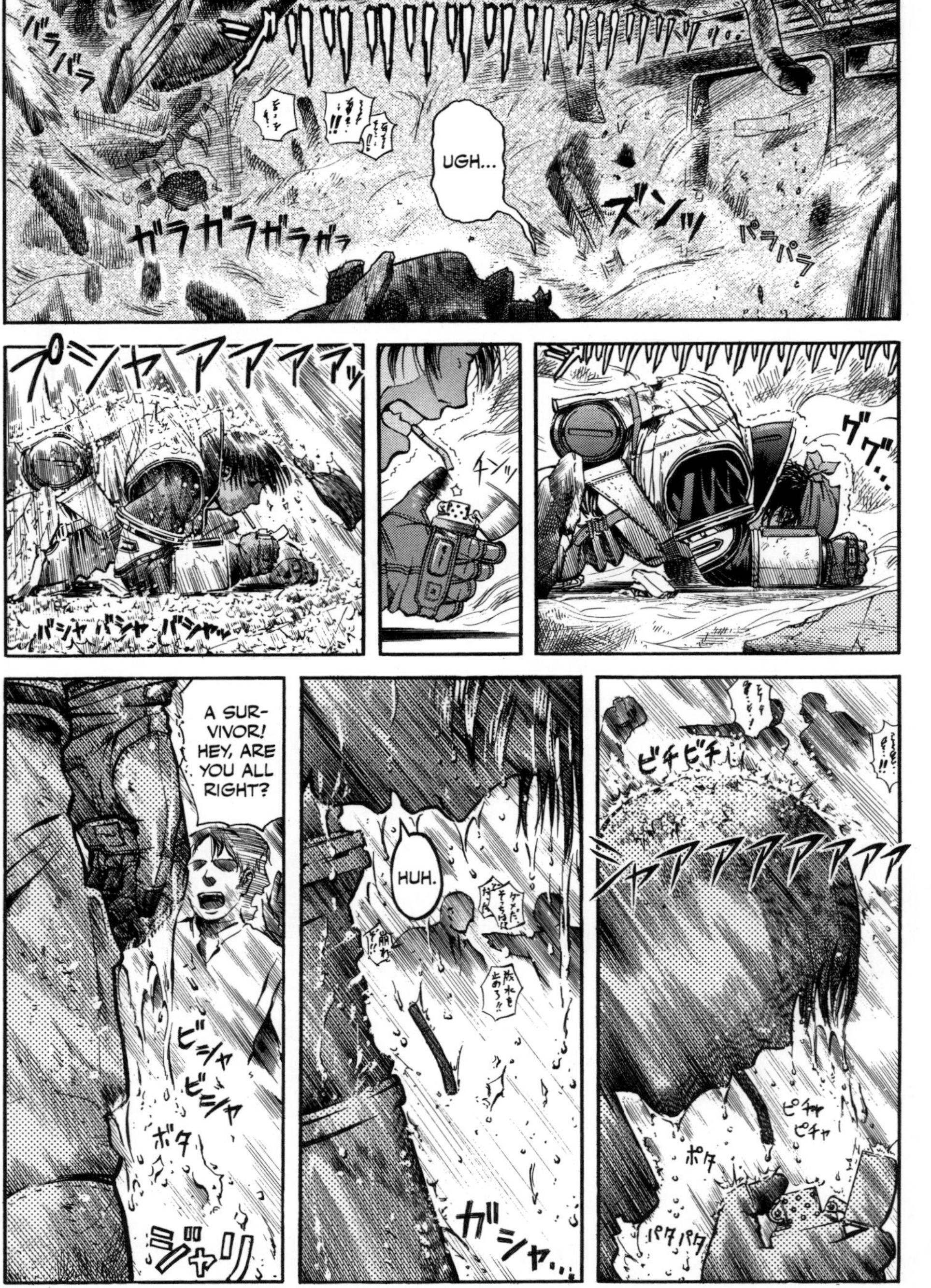
UGH...
バラバラ
ガラガラガラガラ
ズンッ
パラパラ
ググ…
チンッ
プシャアアアアッ
バシャバシャバシャッ
ビチビチ
シャアアアアアア
ピチャピチャ
ポタ
パタパタ
HUH.
ガシャ…
A SUR-VIVOR! HEY, ARE YOU ALL RIGHT?
ビシャビシャ
ボタ
ジャリ

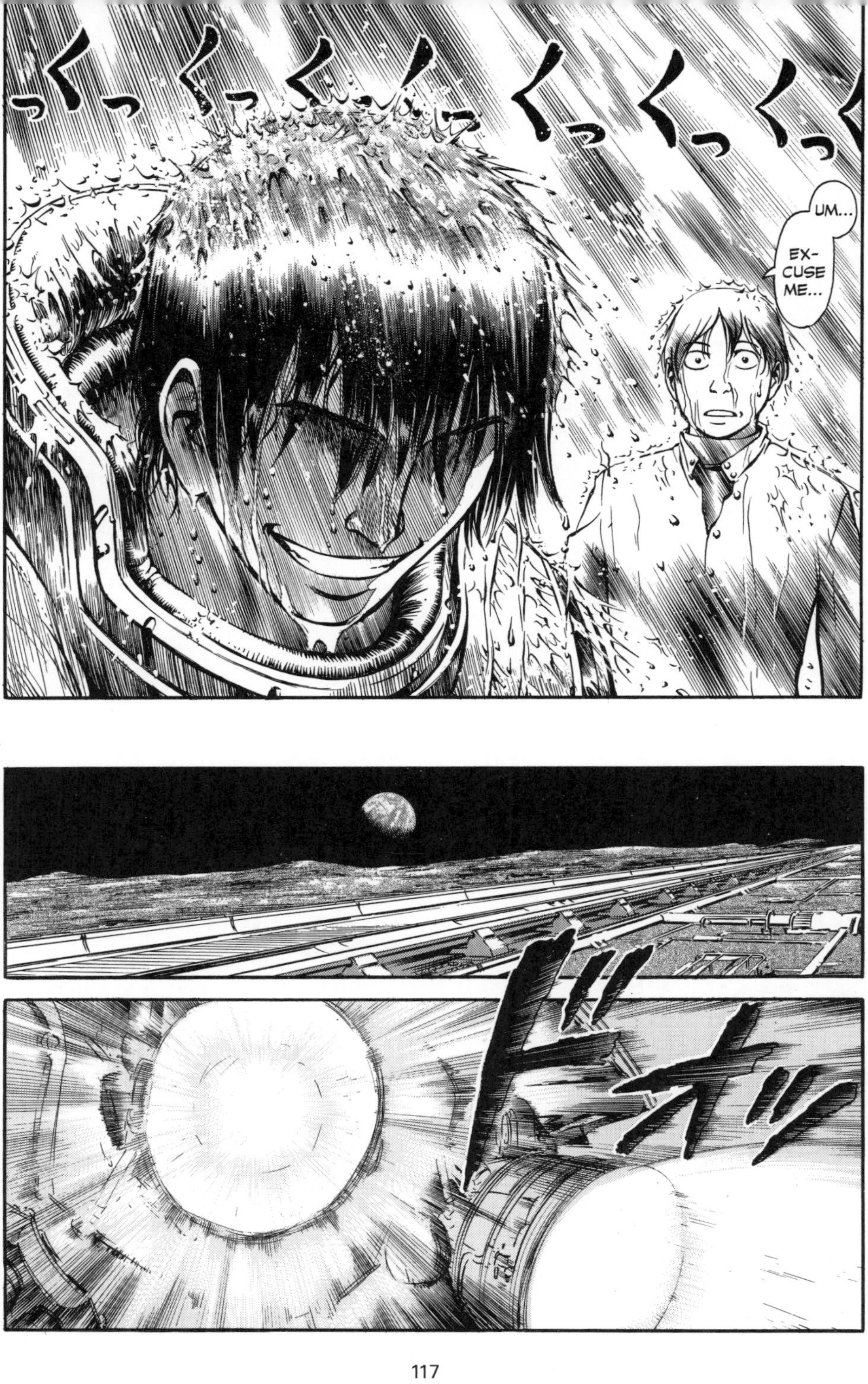
UM...
EX-CUSE ME...

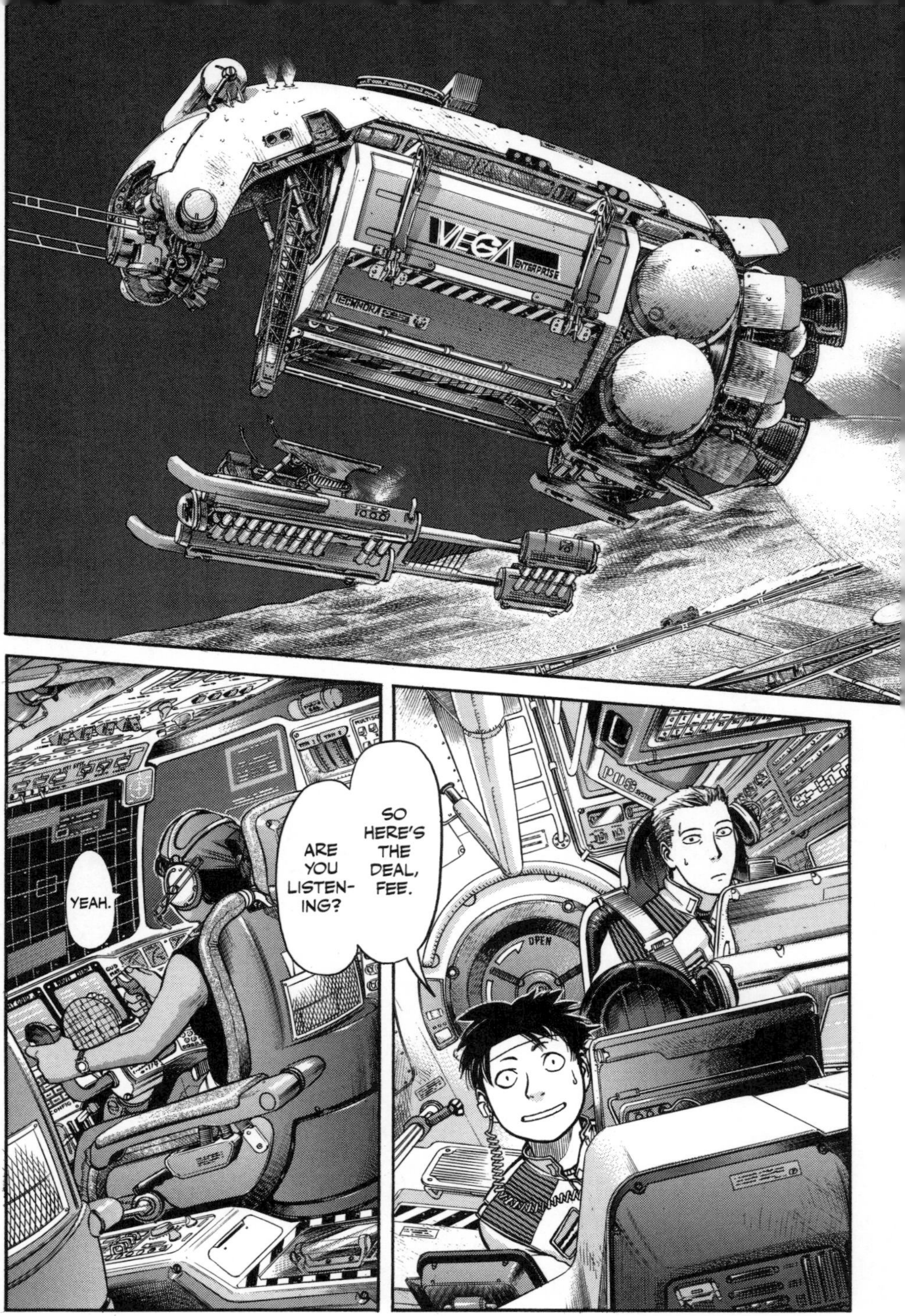
VEGA
ENTERPRISE
SO HERE'S THE DEAL, FEE.
ARE YOU LISTENING?
OPEN
YEAH.

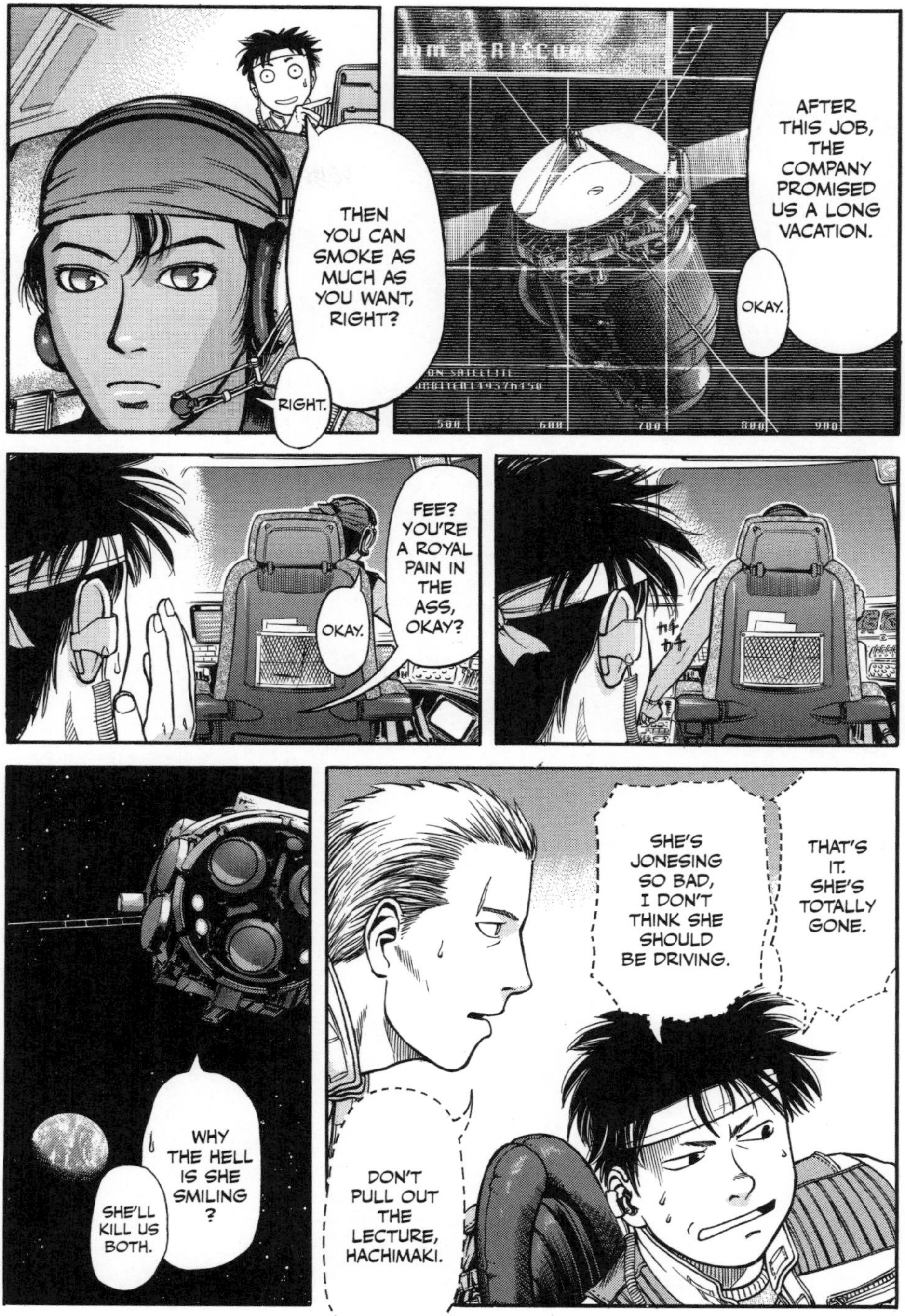
AFTER THIS JOB, THE COMPANY PROMISED US A LONG VACATION.
OKAY.
THEN YOU CAN SMOKE AS MUCH AS YOU WANT, RIGHT?
RIGHT.
カチ カチ
FEE? YOU'RE A ROYAL PAIN IN THE ASS, OKAY?
OKAY.
THAT'S IT. SHE'S TOTALLY GONE.
SHE'S JONESING SO BAD, I DON'T THINK SHE SHOULD BE DRIVING.
DON'T PULL OUT THE LECTURE, HACHIMAKI.
WHY THE HELL IS SHE SMILING?
SHE'LL KILL US BOTH.

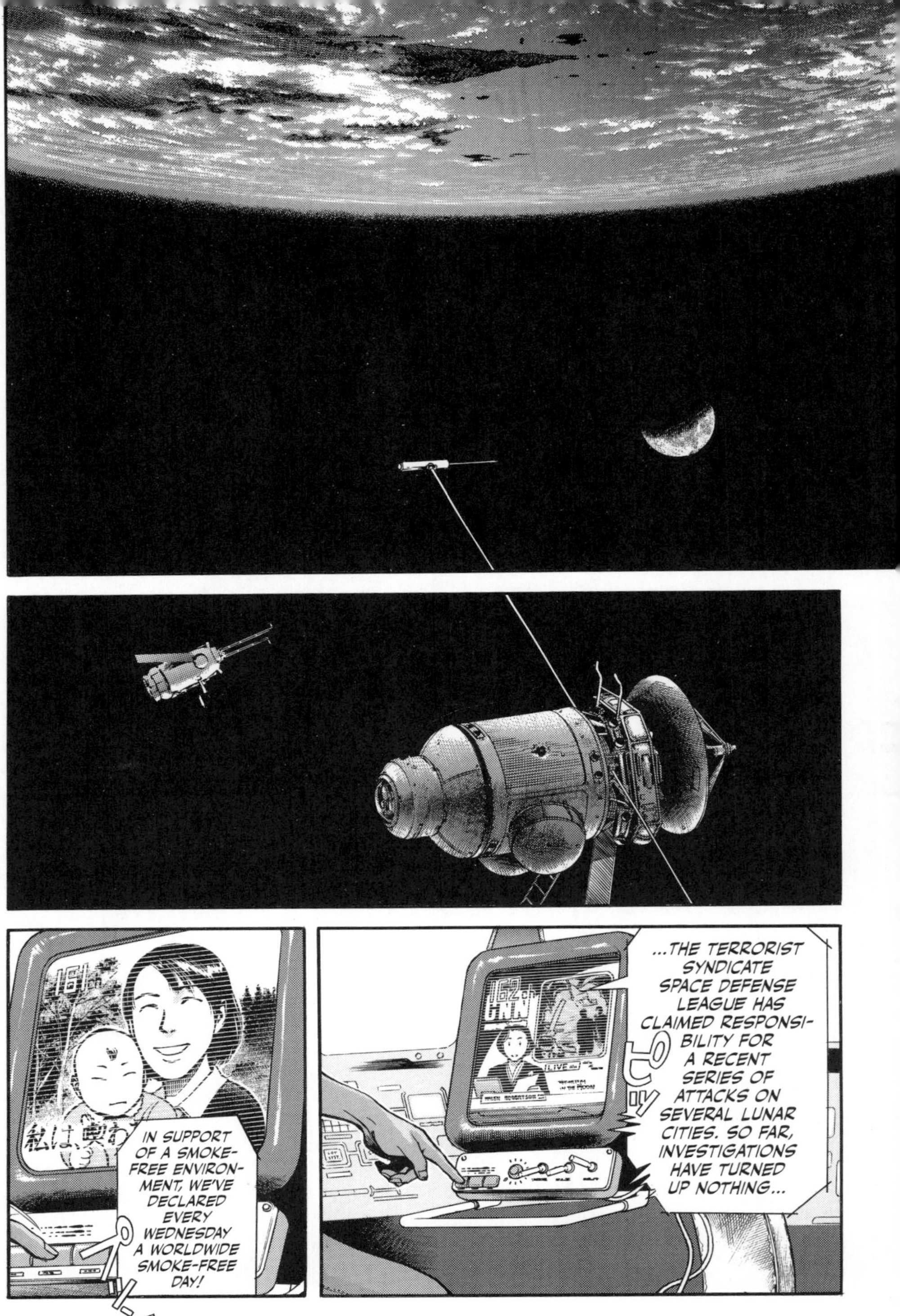
...THE TERRORIST SYNDICATE SPACE DEFENSE LEAGUE HAS CLAIMED RESPONSIBILITY FOR A RECENT SERIES OF ATTACKS ON SEVERAL LUNAR CITIES. SO FAR, INVESTIGATIONS HAVE TURNED UP NOTHING...
IN SUPPORT OF A SMOKE-FREE ENVIRONMENT, WE'VE DECLARED EVERY WEDNESDAY A WORLDWIDE SMOKE-FREE DAY!

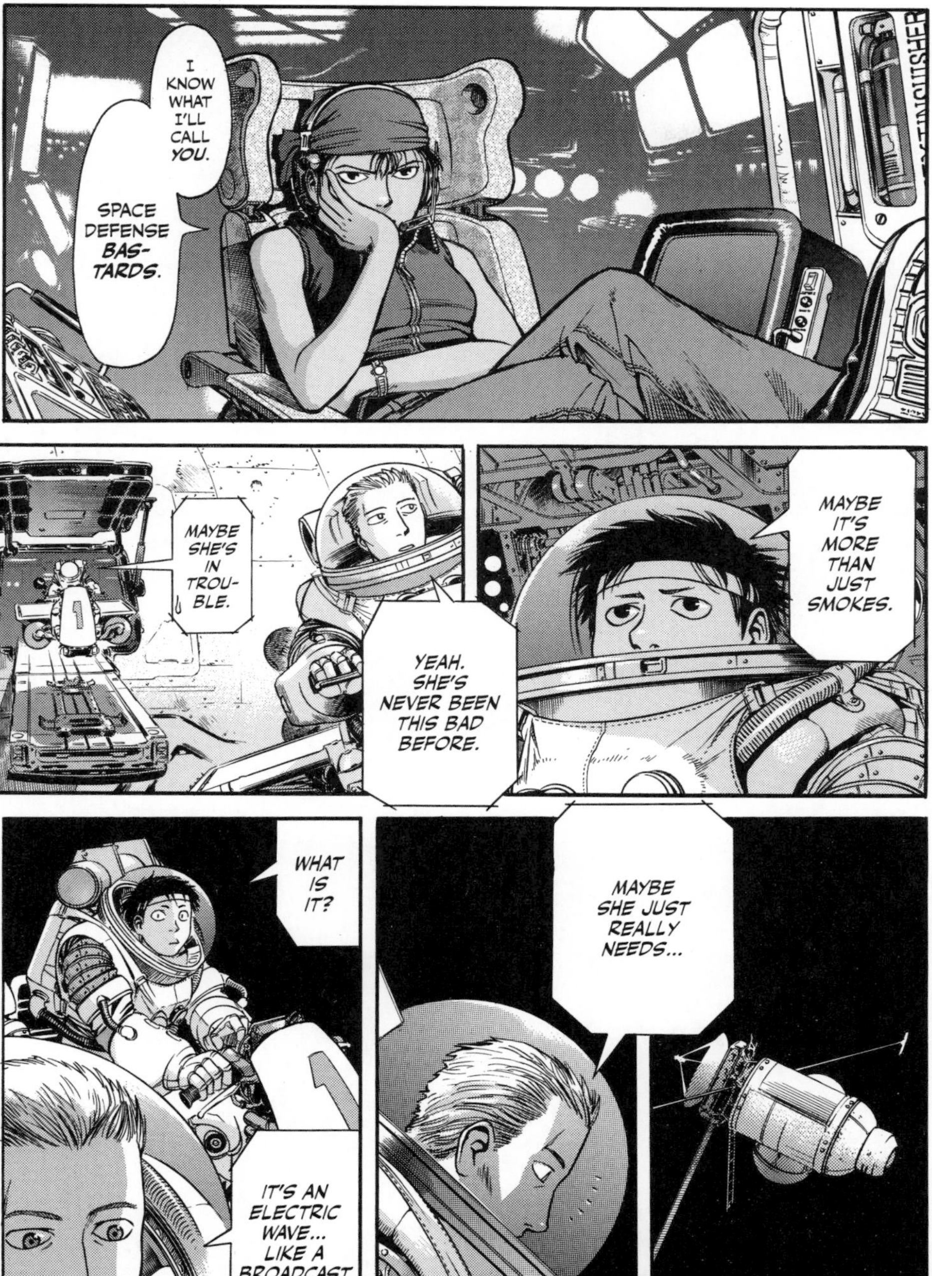
I KNOW WHAT I'LL CALL *YOU*.
SPACE DEFENSE *BASTARDS*.
MAYBE IT'S MORE THAN JUST SMOKES.
YEAH. SHE'S NEVER BEEN THIS BAD BEFORE.
MAYBE SHE'S IN TROUBLE.
MAYBE SHE JUST REALLY NEEDS...
WHAT IS IT?
IT'S AN ELECTRIC WAVE... LIKE A BROADCAST SIGNAL.

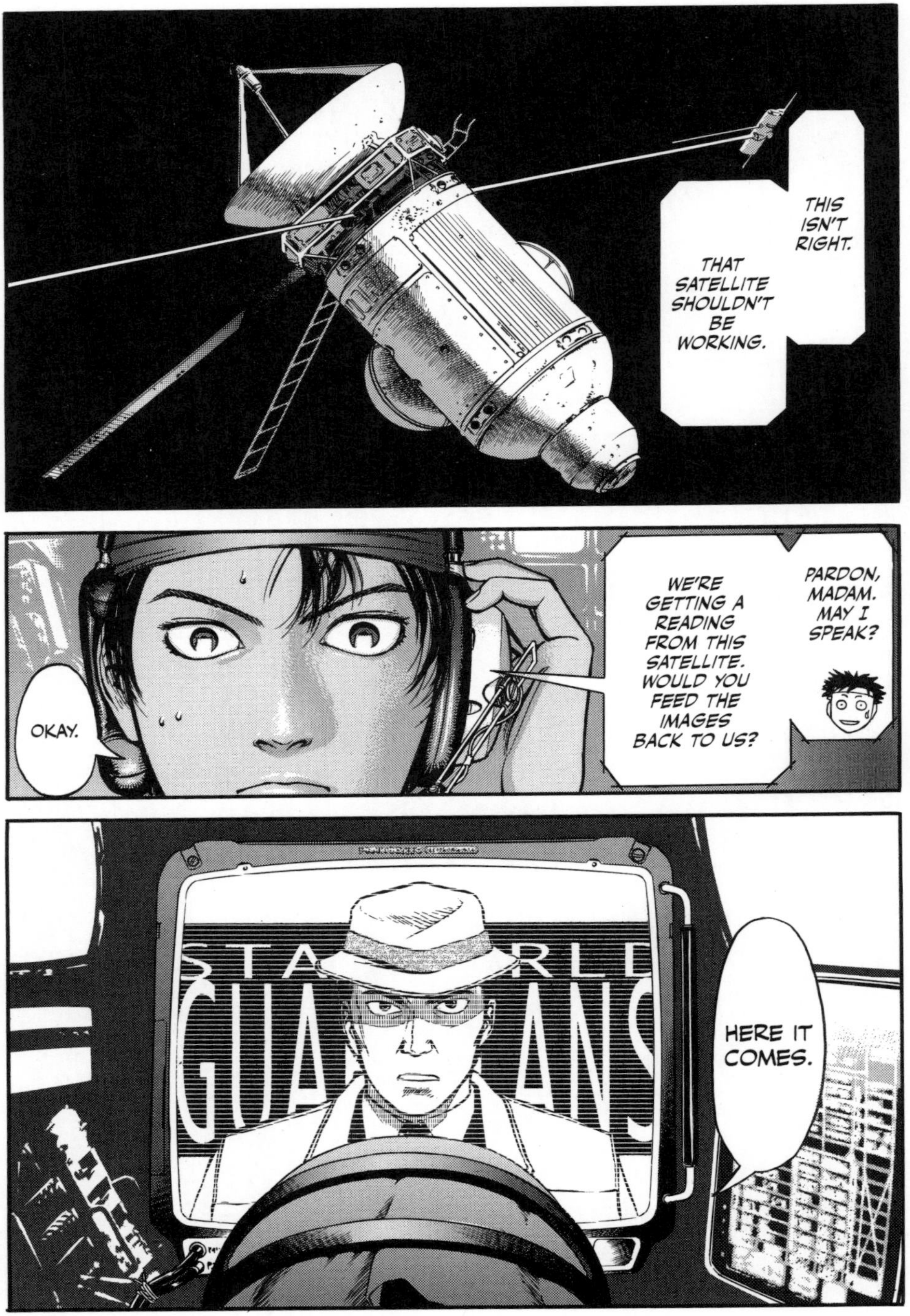
THIS ISN'T RIGHT.
THAT SATELLITE SHOULDN'T BE WORKING.
PARDON, MADAM. MAY I SPEAK?
WE'RE GETTING A READING FROM THIS SATELLITE. WOULD YOU FEED THE IMAGES BACK TO US?
OKAY.
HERE IT COMES.

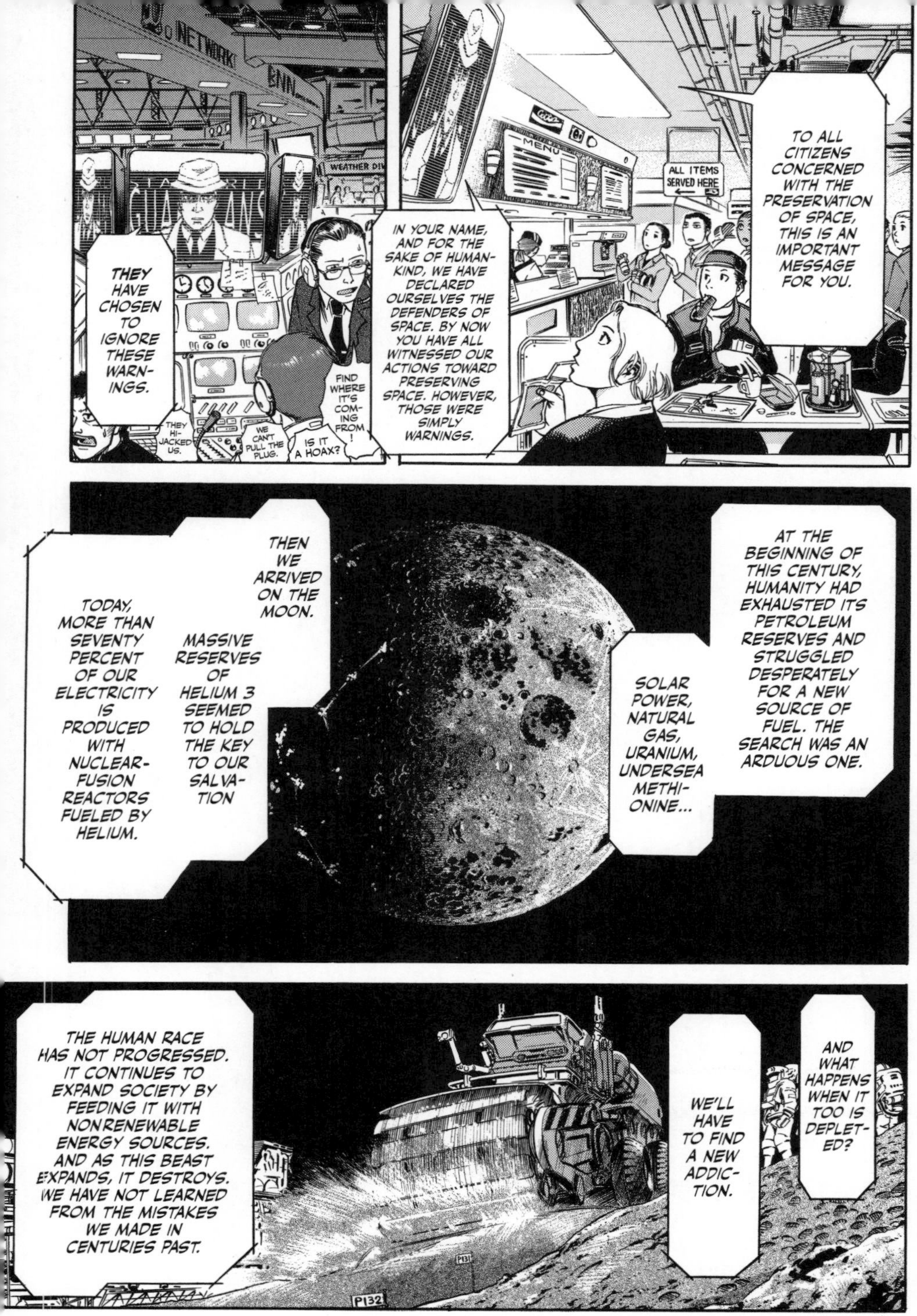
ALL ITEMS SERVED HERE
MENU
TO ALL CITIZENS CONCERNED WITH THE PRESERVATION OF SPACE, THIS IS AN IMPORTANT MESSAGE FOR YOU.
IN YOUR NAME, AND FOR THE SAKE OF HUMAN-KIND, WE HAVE DECLARED OURSELVES THE DEFENDERS OF SPACE. BY NOW YOU HAVE ALL WITNESSED OUR ACTIONS TOWARD PRESERVING SPACE. HOWEVER, THOSE WERE SIMPLY WARNINGS.
FIND WHERE IT'S COMING FROM!
IS IT A HOAX?
WE CAN'T PULL THE PLUG.
THEY HIJACKED US.
THEY HAVE CHOSEN TO IGNORE THESE WARNINGS.
AT THE BEGINNING OF THIS CENTURY, HUMANITY HAD EXHAUSTED ITS PETROLEUM RESERVES AND STRUGGLED DESPERATELY FOR A NEW SOURCE OF FUEL. THE SEARCH WAS AN ARDUOUS ONE.
SOLAR POWER, NATURAL GAS, URANIUM, UNDERSEA METHI-ONINE...
THEN WE ARRIVED ON THE MOON.
MASSIVE RESERVES OF HELIUM 3 SEEMED TO HOLD THE KEY TO OUR SALVA-TION
TODAY, MORE THAN SEVENTY PERCENT OF OUR ELECTRICITY IS PRODUCED WITH NUCLEAR-FUSION REACTORS FUELED BY HELIUM.
AND WHAT HAPPENS WHEN IT TOO IS DEPLET-ED?
WE'LL HAVE TO FIND A NEW ADDIC-TION.
THE HUMAN RACE HAS NOT PROGRESSED. IT CONTINUES TO EXPAND SOCIETY BY FEEDING IT WITH NONRENEWABLE ENERGY SOURCES. AND AS THIS BEAST EXPANDS, IT DESTROYS. WE HAVE NOT LEARNED FROM THE MISTAKES WE MADE IN CENTURIES PAST.

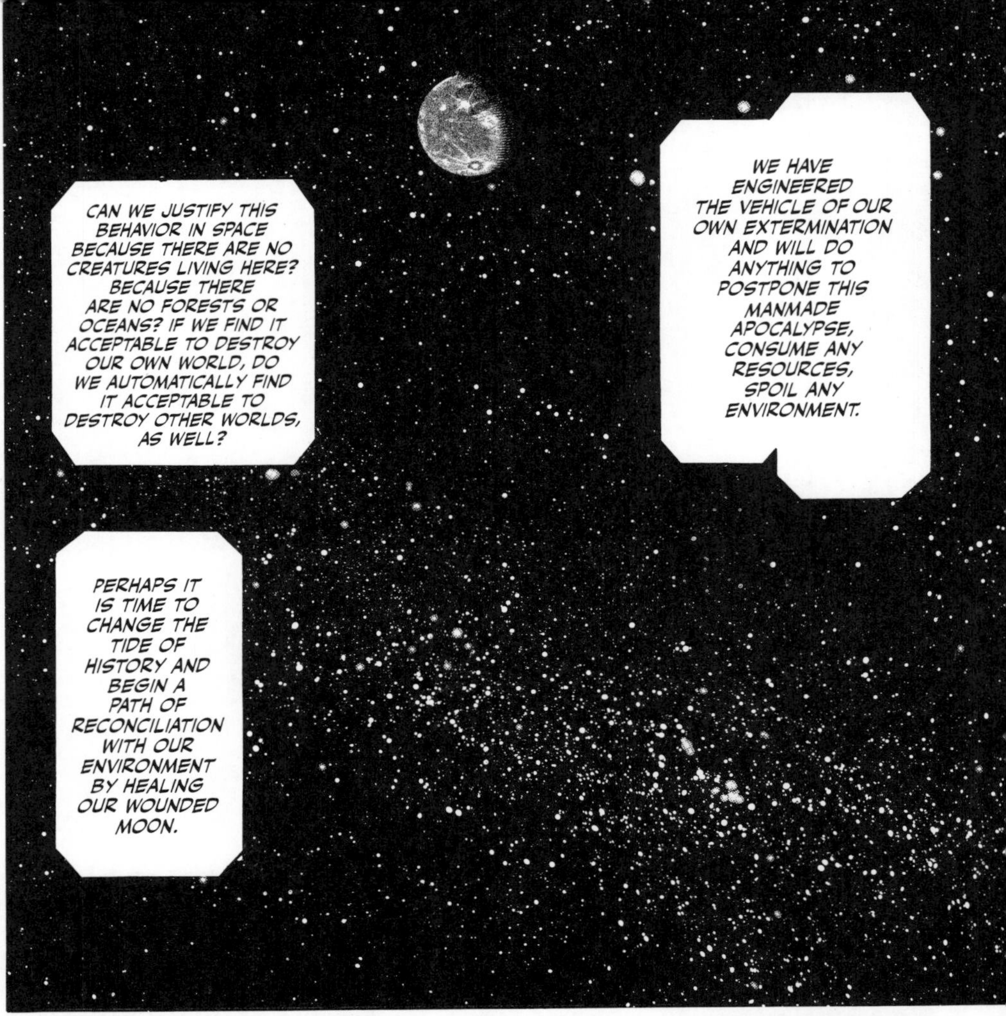
WE HAVE ENGINEERED THE VEHICLE OF OUR OWN EXTERMINATION AND WILL DO ANYTHING TO POSTPONE THIS MANMADE APOCALYPSE, CONSUME ANY RESOURCES, SPOIL ANY ENVIRONMENT.
CAN WE JUSTIFY THIS BEHAVIOR IN SPACE BECAUSE THERE ARE NO CREATURES LIVING HERE? BECAUSE THERE ARE NO FORESTS OR OCEANS? IF WE FIND IT ACCEPTABLE TO DESTROY OUR OWN WORLD, DO WE AUTOMATICALLY FIND IT ACCEPTABLE TO DESTROY OTHER WORLDS, AS WELL?
PERHAPS IT IS TIME TO CHANGE THE TIDE OF HISTORY AND BEGIN A PATH OF RECONCILIATION WITH OUR ENVIRONMENT BY HEALING OUR WOUNDED MOON.
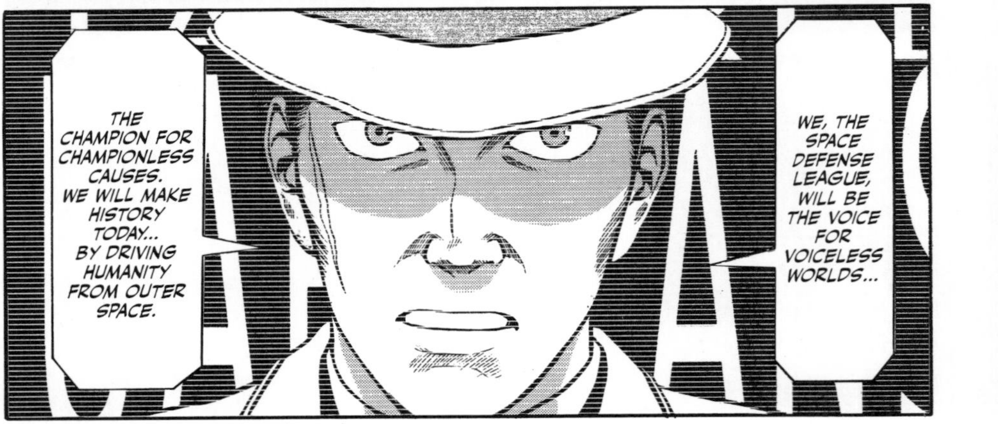
WE, THE SPACE DEFENSE LEAGUE, WILL BE THE VOICE FOR VOICELESS WORLDS...
THE CHAMPION FOR CHAMPIONLESS CAUSES. WE WILL MAKE HISTORY TODAY... BY DRIVING HUMANITY FROM OUTER SPACE.

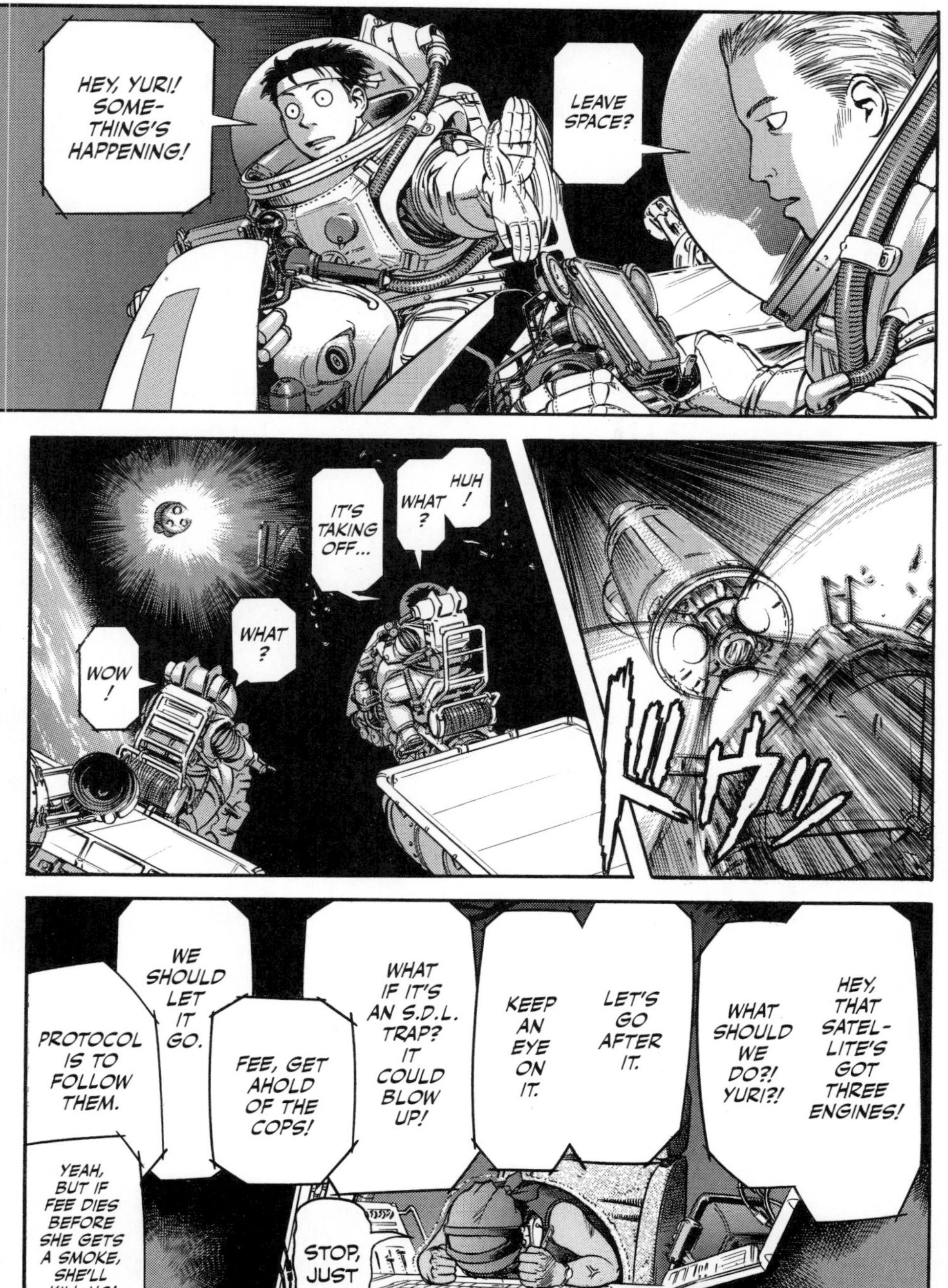
LEAVE SPACE?
HEY, YURI! SOME-THING'S HAPPENING!
HUH!
WHAT?
IT'S TAKING OFF...
WHAT?
WOW!
HEY, THAT SATEL-LITE'S GOT THREE ENGINES!
WHAT SHOULD WE DO?! YURI?!
LET'S GO AFTER IT.
KEEP AN EYE ON IT.
WHAT IF IT'S AN S.D.L. TRAP? IT COULD BLOW UP!
WE SHOULD LET IT GO.
FEE, GET AHOLD OF THE COPS!
PROTOCOL IS TO FOLLOW THEM.
YEAH, BUT IF FEE DIES BEFORE SHE GETS A SMOKE, SHE'LL KILL US!
STOP, JUST STOP!

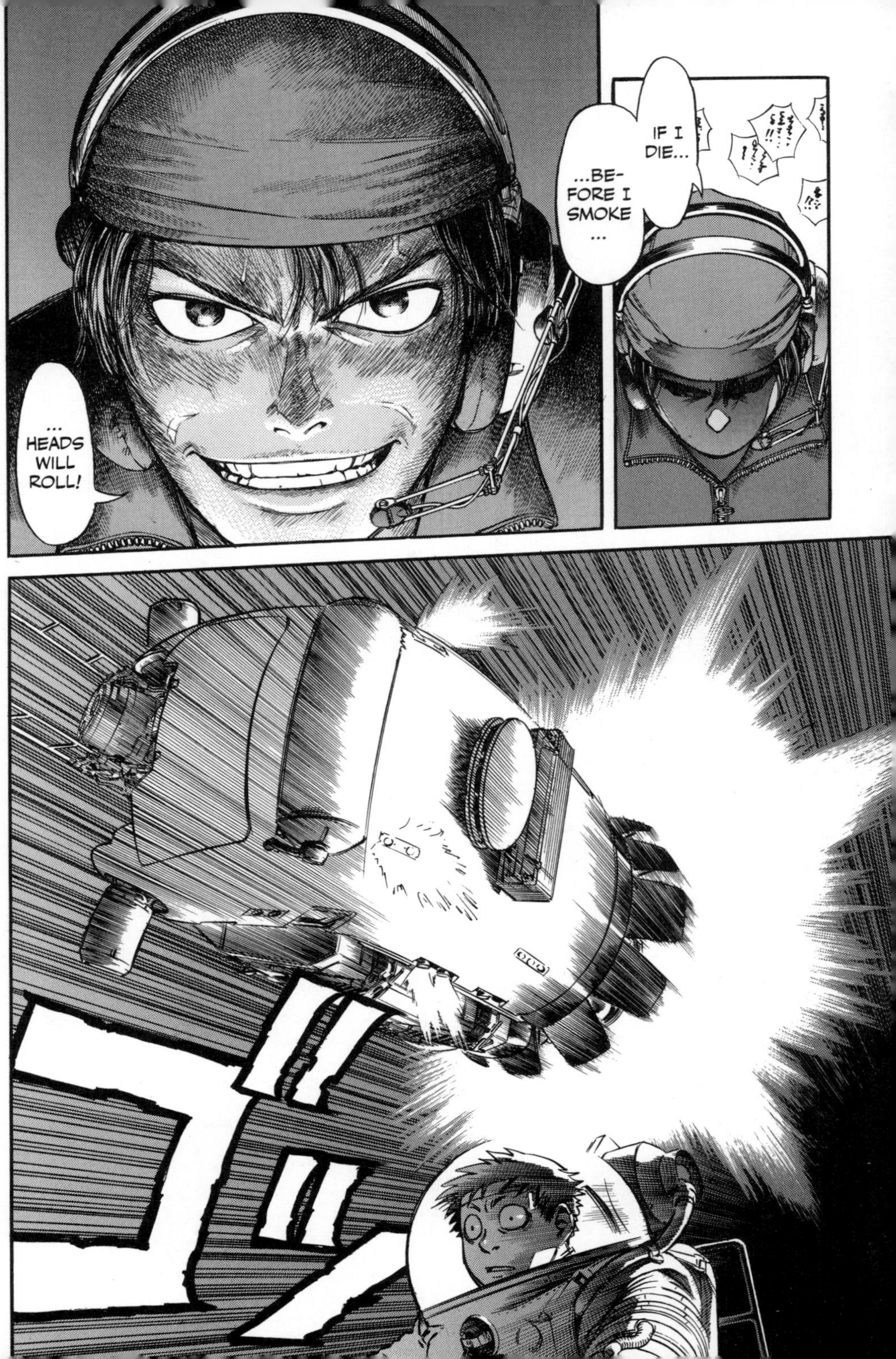
IF I DIE...
...BEFORE I SMOKE...
...HEADS WILL ROLL!

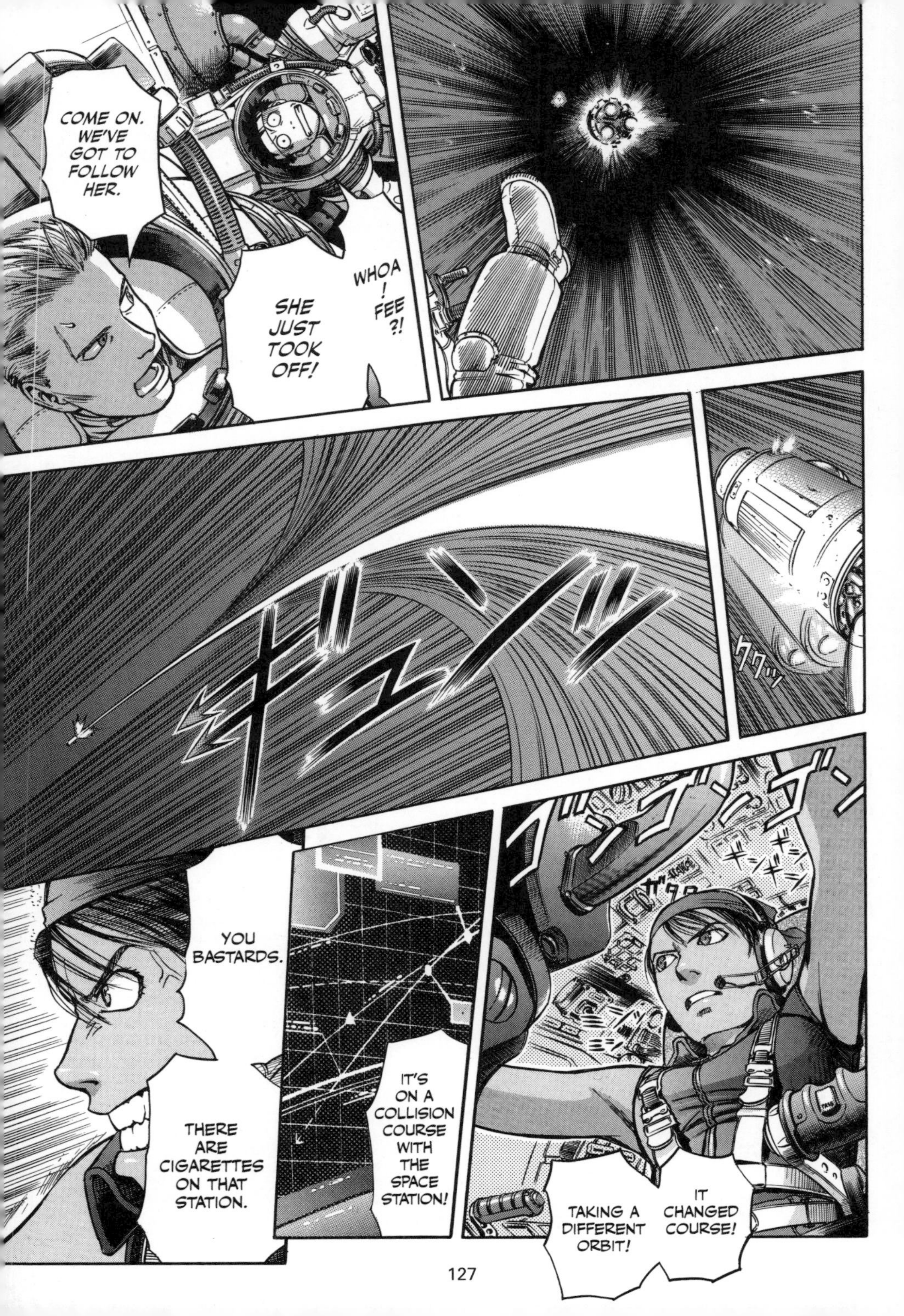
WHOA! FEE?!
SHE JUST TOOK OFF!
COME ON. WE'VE GOT TO FOLLOW HER.
IT CHANGED COURSE!
TAKING A DIFFERENT ORBIT!
IT'S ON A COLLISION COURSE WITH THE SPACE STATION!
YOU BASTARDS.
THERE ARE CIGARETTES ON THAT STATION.

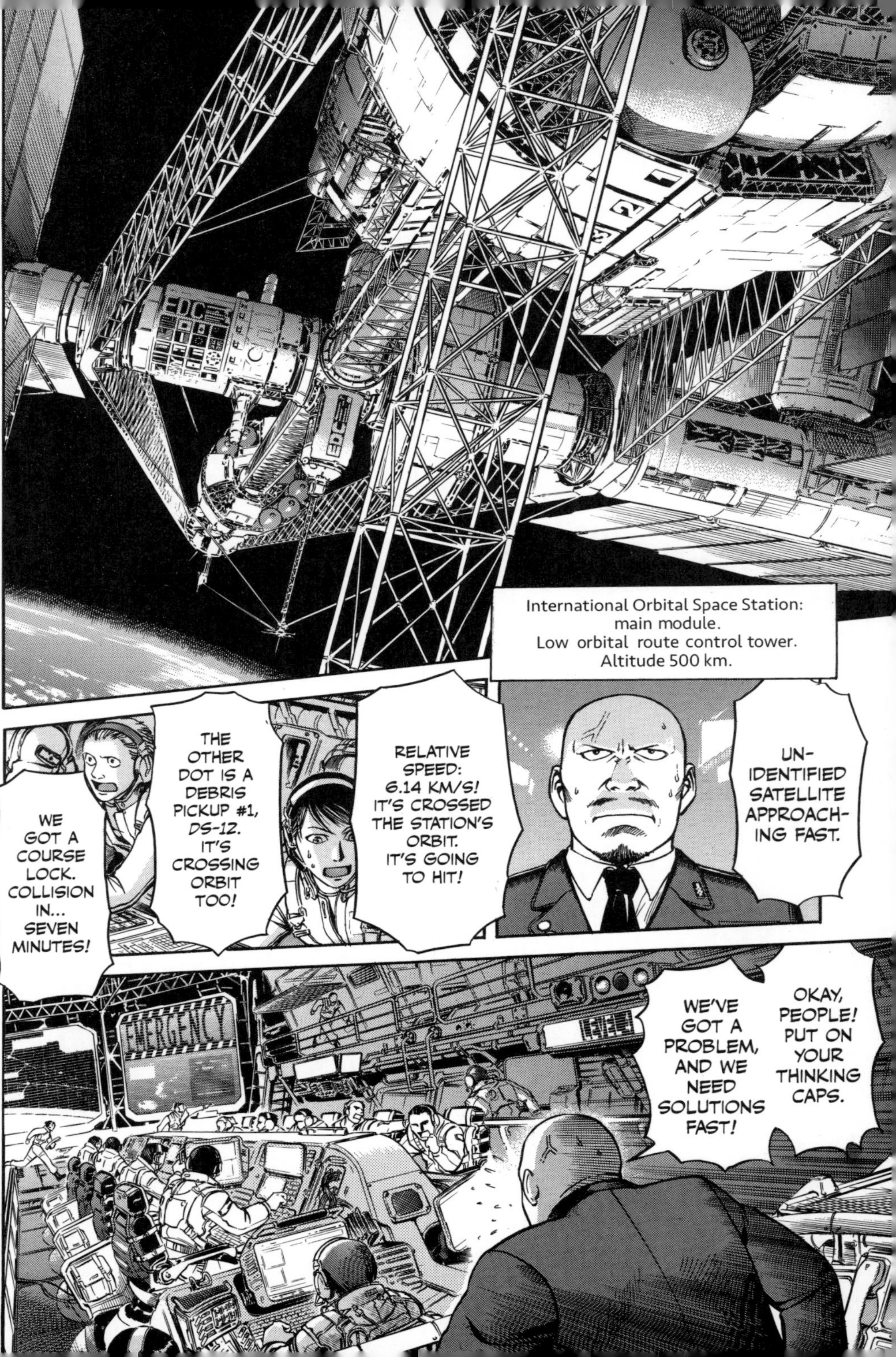
International Orbital Space Station: main module.
Low orbital route control tower.
Altitude 500 km.
UN-IDENTIFIED SATELLITE APPROACHING FAST.
RELATIVE SPEED: 6.14 KM/S! IT'S CROSSED THE STATION'S ORBIT. IT'S GOING TO HIT!
THE OTHER DOT IS A DEBRIS PICKUP #1, DS-12. IT'S CROSSING ORBIT TOO!
WE GOT A COURSE LOCK. COLLISION IN... SEVEN MINUTES!
EMERGENCY
OKAY, PEOPLE! PUT ON YOUR THINKING CAPS.
WE'VE GOT A PROBLEM, AND WE NEED SOLUTIONS FAST!

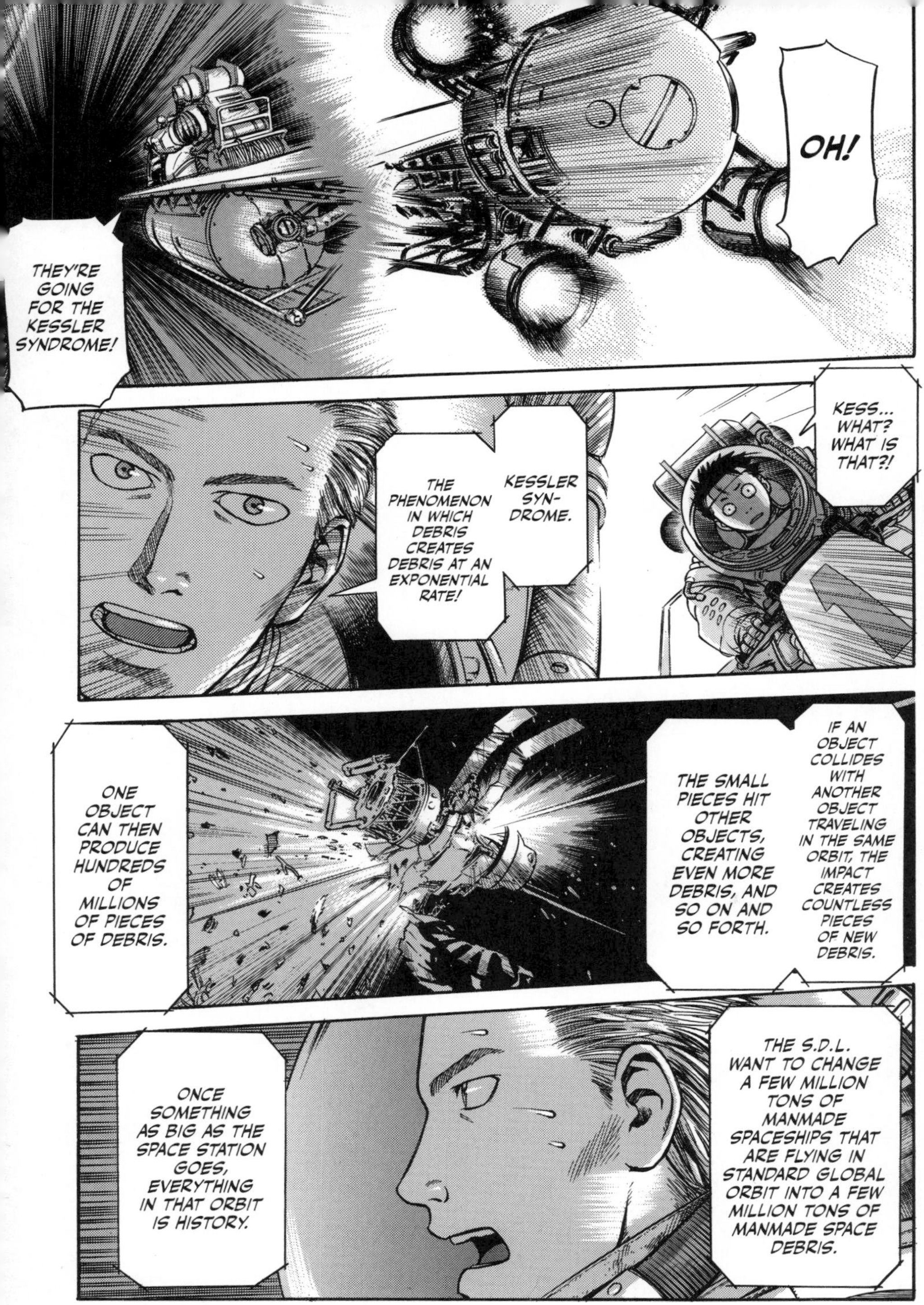
OH!
THEY'RE GOING FOR THE KESSLER SYNDROME!
KESS... WHAT? WHAT IS THAT?!
KESSLER SYNDROME.
THE PHENOMENON IN WHICH DEBRIS CREATES DEBRIS AT AN EXPONENTIAL RATE!
IF AN OBJECT COLLIDES WITH ANOTHER OBJECT TRAVELING IN THE SAME ORBIT, THE IMPACT CREATES COUNTLESS PIECES OF NEW DEBRIS.
THE SMALL PIECES HIT OTHER OBJECTS, CREATING EVEN MORE DEBRIS, AND SO ON AND SO FORTH.
ONE OBJECT CAN THEN PRODUCE HUNDREDS OF MILLIONS OF PIECES OF DEBRIS.
THE S.D.L. WANT TO CHANGE A FEW MILLION TONS OF MANMADE SPACESHIPS THAT ARE FLYING IN STANDARD GLOBAL ORBIT INTO A FEW MILLION TONS OF MANMADE SPACE DEBRIS.
ONCE SOMETHING AS BIG AS THE SPACE STATION GOES, EVERYTHING IN THAT ORBIT IS HISTORY.

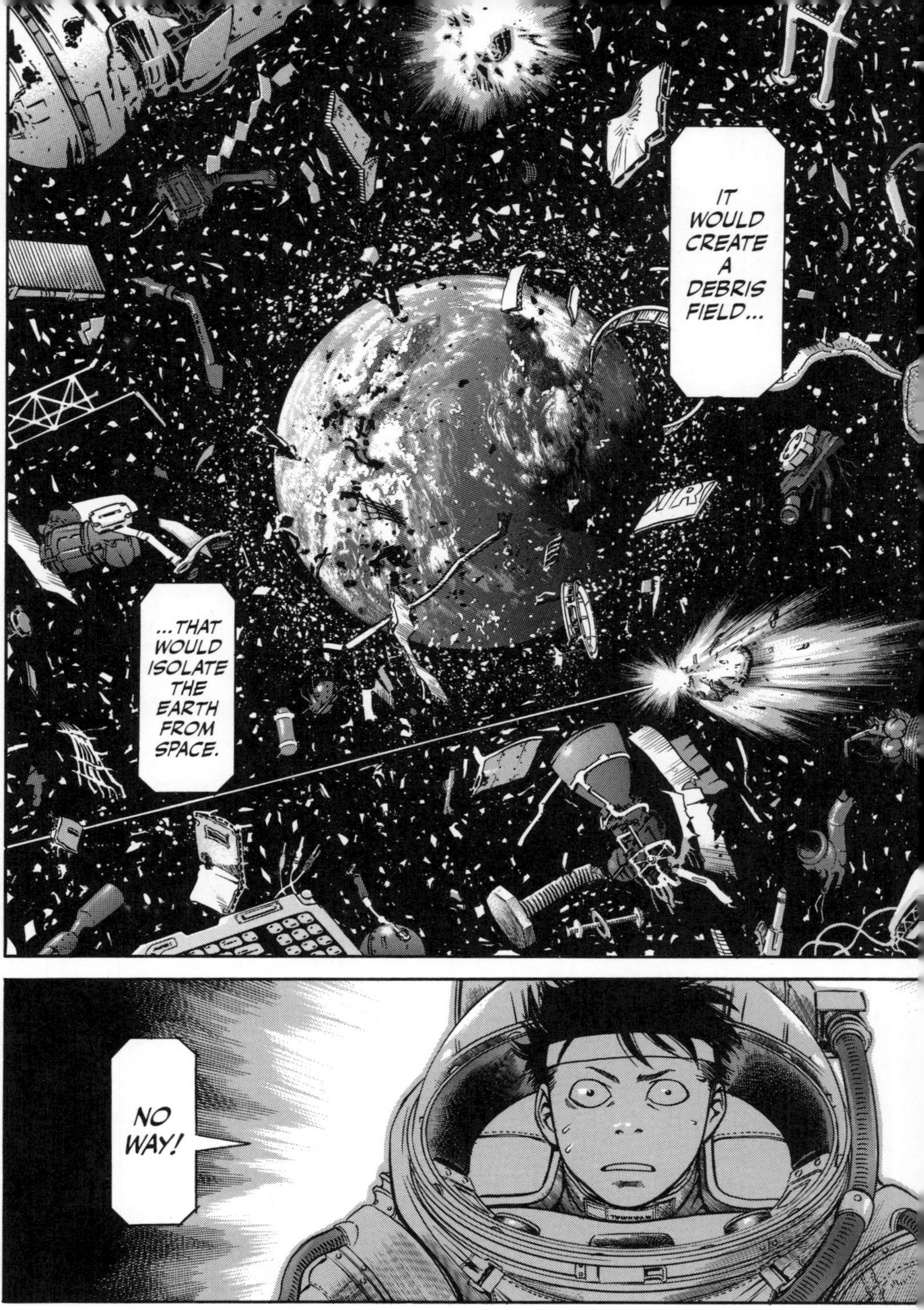
IT WOULD CREATE A DEBRIS FIELD...
...THAT WOULD ISOLATE THE EARTH FROM SPACE.
NO WAY!

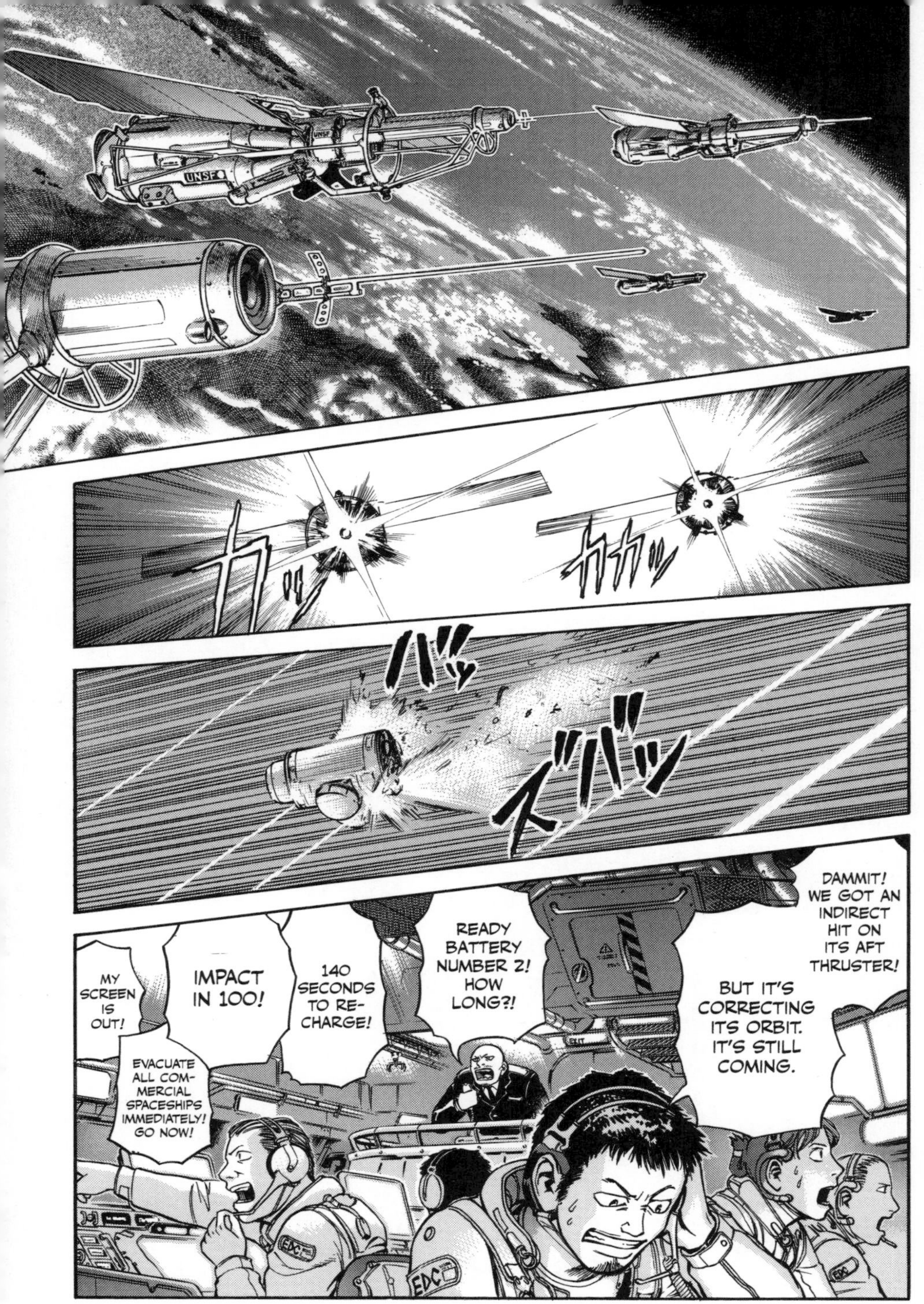
カカッ
カッ
バッ
ズバッ
DAMMIT! WE GOT AN INDIRECT HIT ON ITS AFT THRUSTER!
BUT IT'S CORRECTING ITS ORBIT. IT'S STILL COMING.
READY BATTERY NUMBER 2! HOW LONG?!
140 SECONDS TO RE-CHARGE!
IMPACT IN 100!
MY SCREEN IS OUT!
EVACUATE ALL COM-MERCIAL SPACESHIPS IMMEDIATELY! GO NOW!

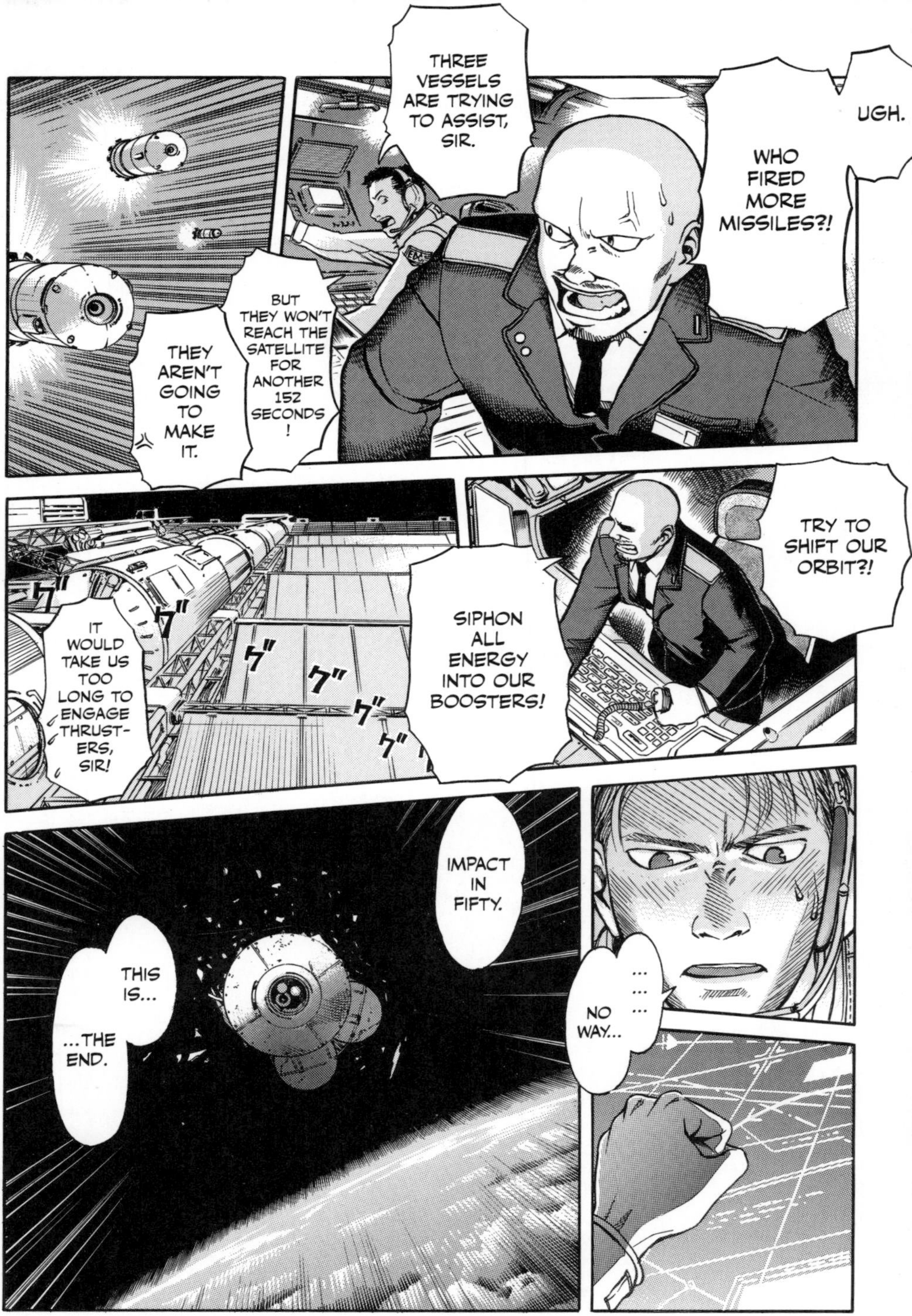
UGH.
WHO FIRED MORE MISSILES?!
THREE VESSELS ARE TRYING TO ASSIST, SIR.
BUT THEY WON'T REACH THE SATELLITE FOR ANOTHER 152 SECONDS!
THEY AREN'T GOING TO MAKE IT.
TRY TO SHIFT OUR ORBIT?!
SIPHON ALL ENERGY INTO OUR BOOSTERS!
IT WOULD TAKE US TOO LONG TO ENGAGE THRUSTERS, SIR!
....
NO WAY...
IMPACT IN FIFTY.
THIS IS...
...THE END.

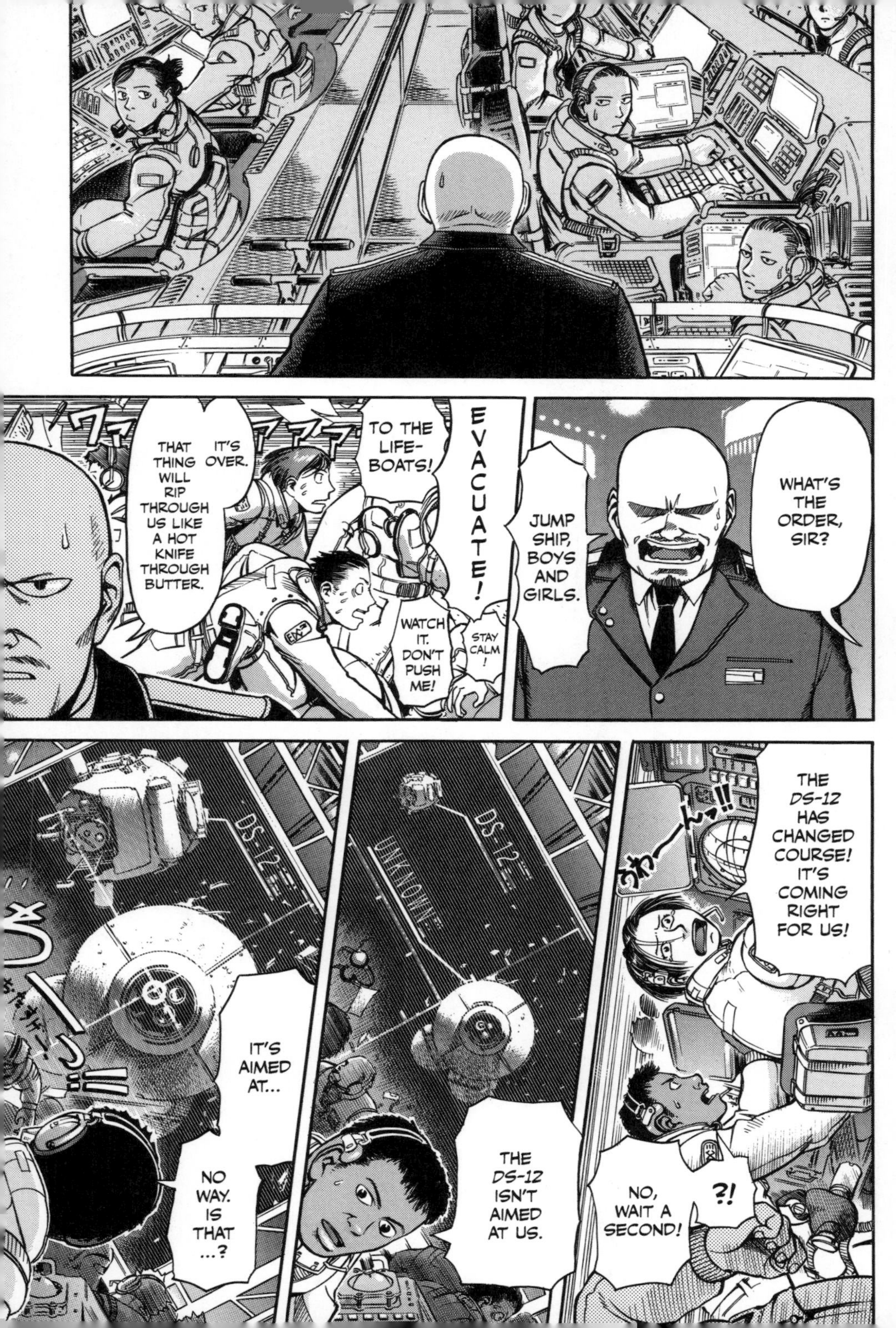
WHAT'S THE ORDER, SIR?
JUMP SHIP, BOYS AND GIRLS.
EVACUATE!
TO THE LIFE-BOATS!
IT'S OVER.
THAT THING WILL RIP THROUGH US LIKE A HOT KNIFE THROUGH BUTTER.
STAY CALM!
WATCH IT. DON'T PUSH ME!
THE *DS-12* HAS CHANGED COURSE! IT'S COMING RIGHT FOR US!
?!
NO, WAIT A SECOND!
DS-12
UNKNOWN
THE *DS-12* ISN'T AIMED AT US.
DS-12
IT'S AIMED AT...
NO WAY. IS THAT ...?

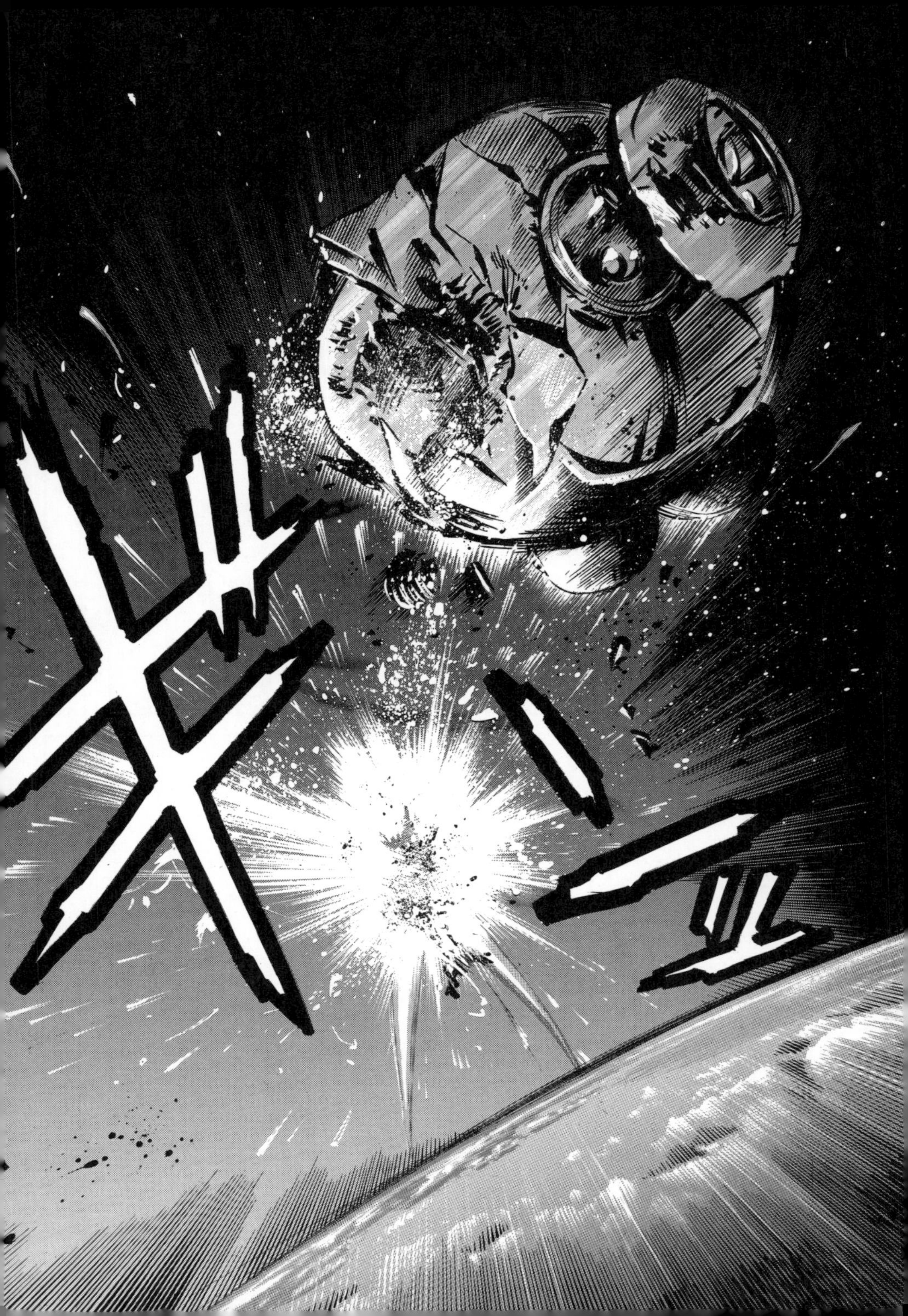

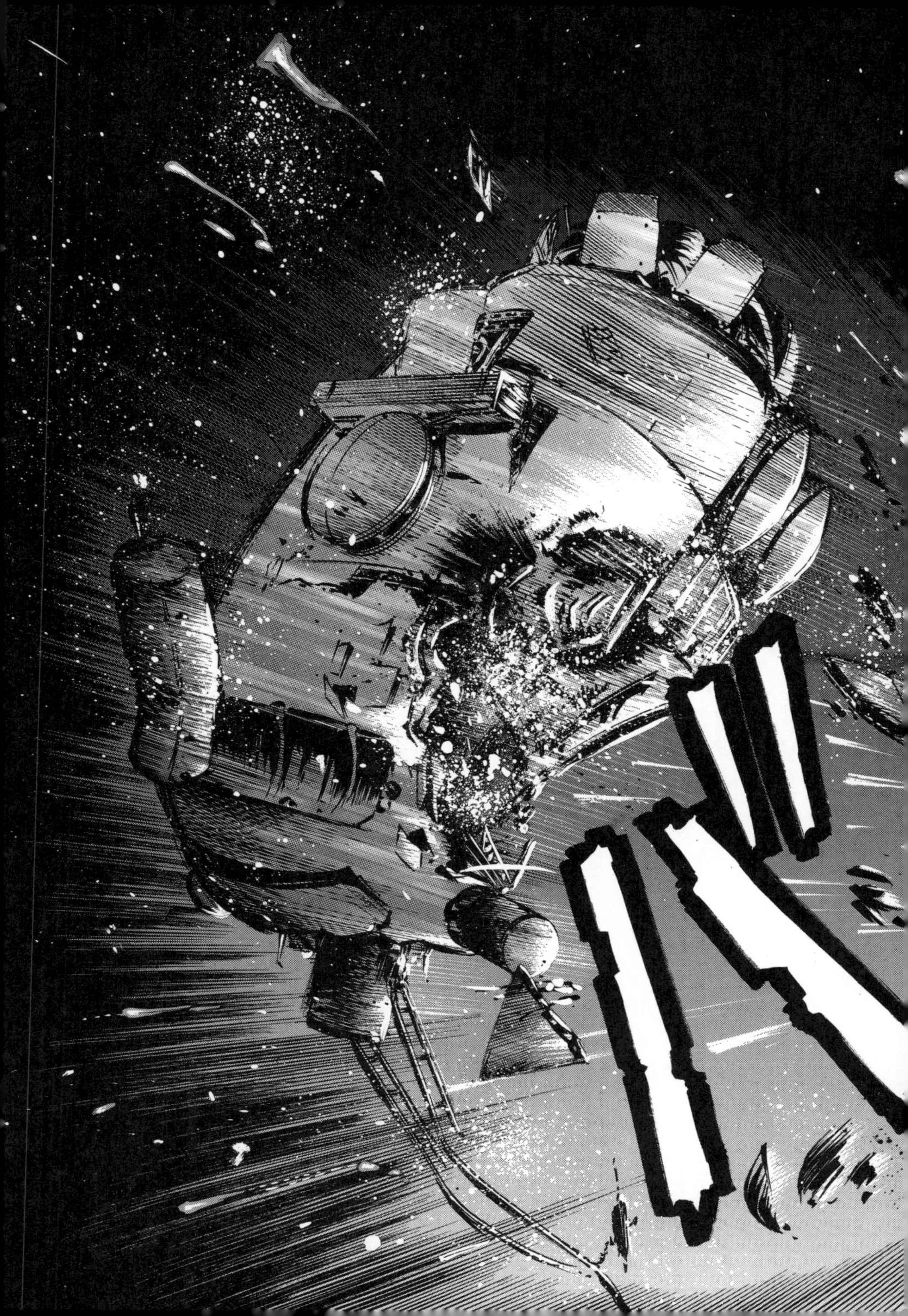

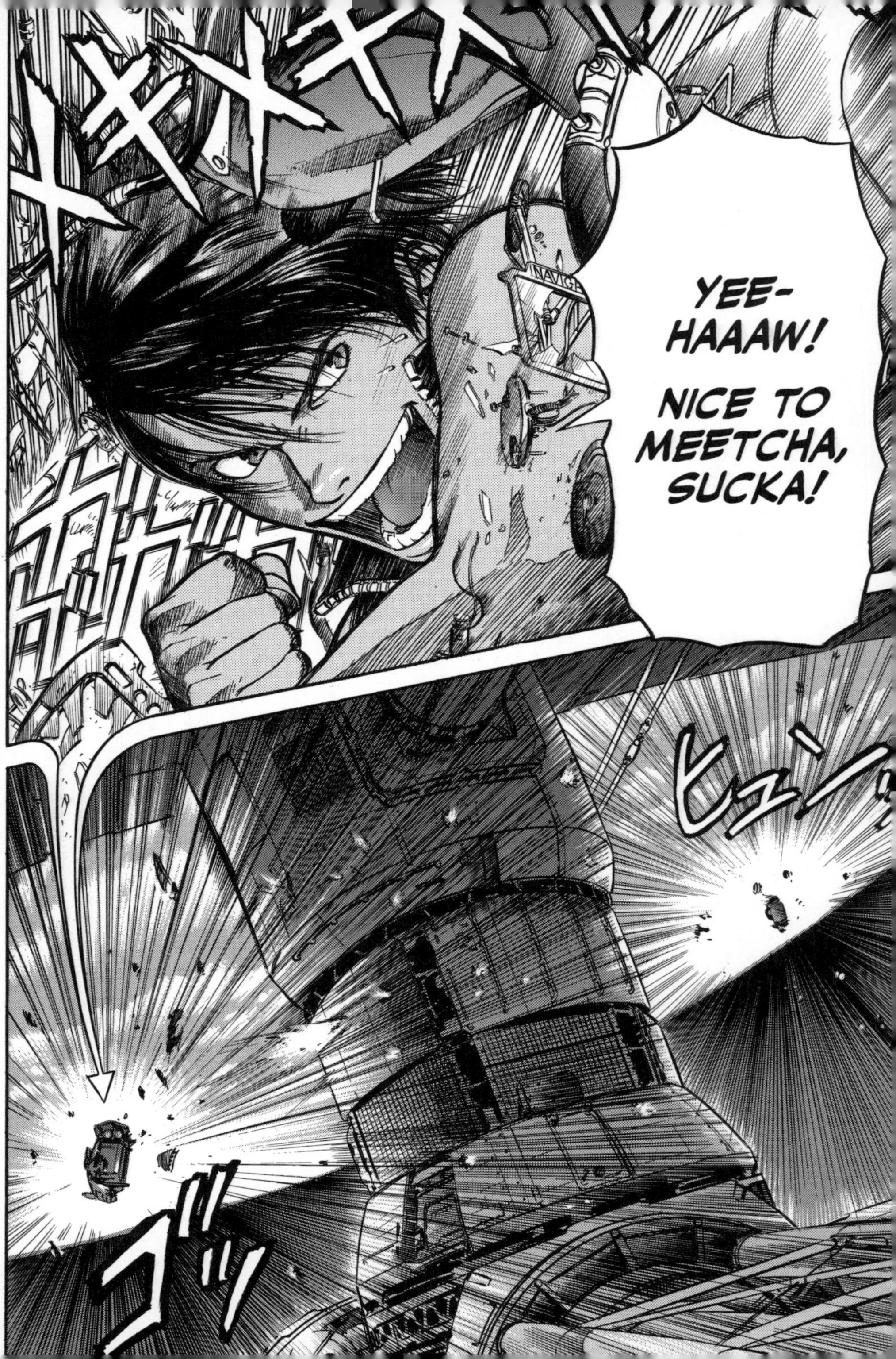
YEE-HAAAW!
NICE TO MEETCHA, SUCKA!

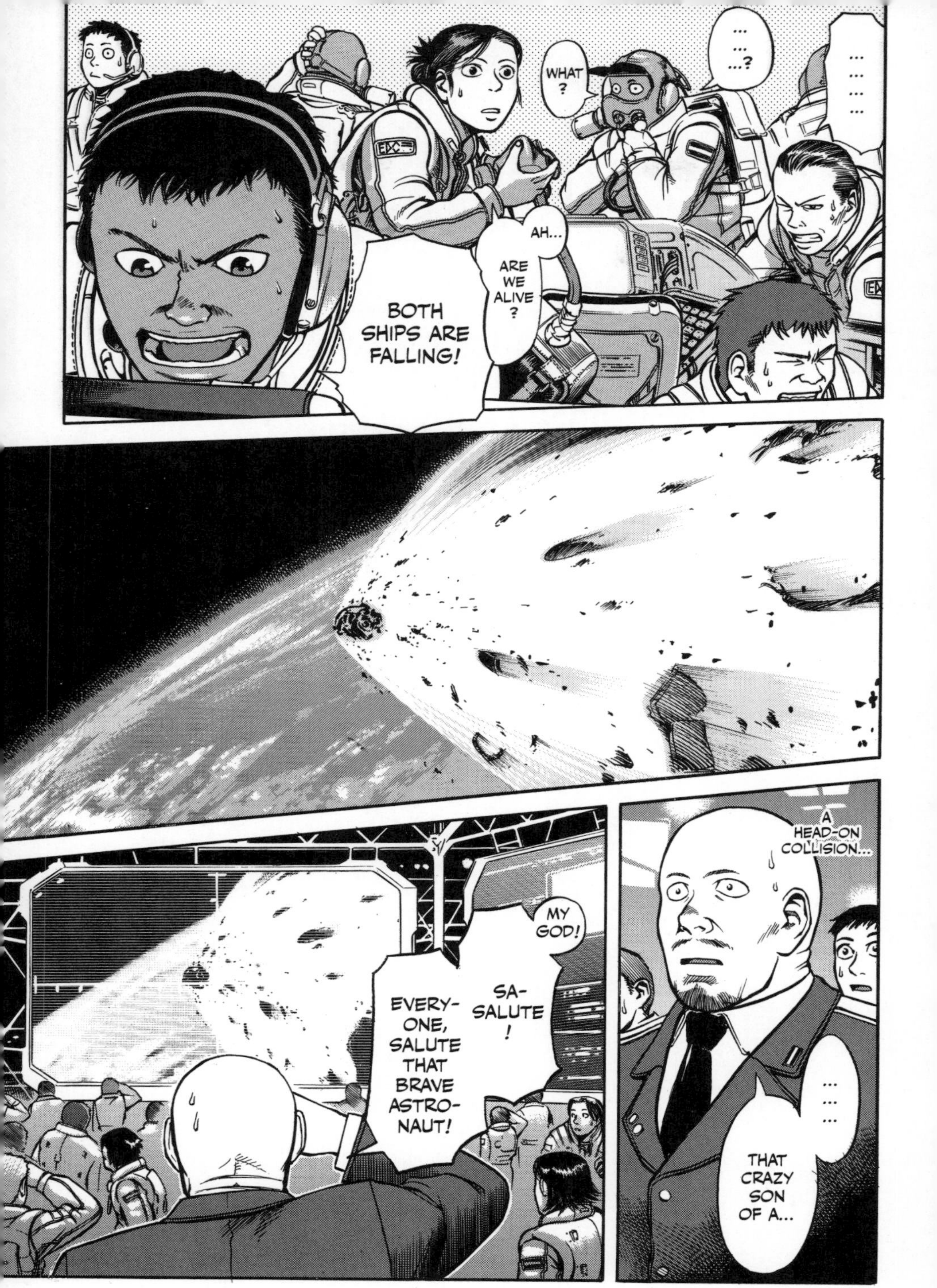
... ...
... ...?
WHAT ?
AH... ARE WE ALIVE ?
BOTH SHIPS ARE FALLING!
A HEAD-ON COLLISION...
... ...
THAT CRAZY SON OF A...
MY GOD!
SA-SALUTE !
EVERY-ONE, SALUTE THAT BRAVE ASTRO-NAUT!

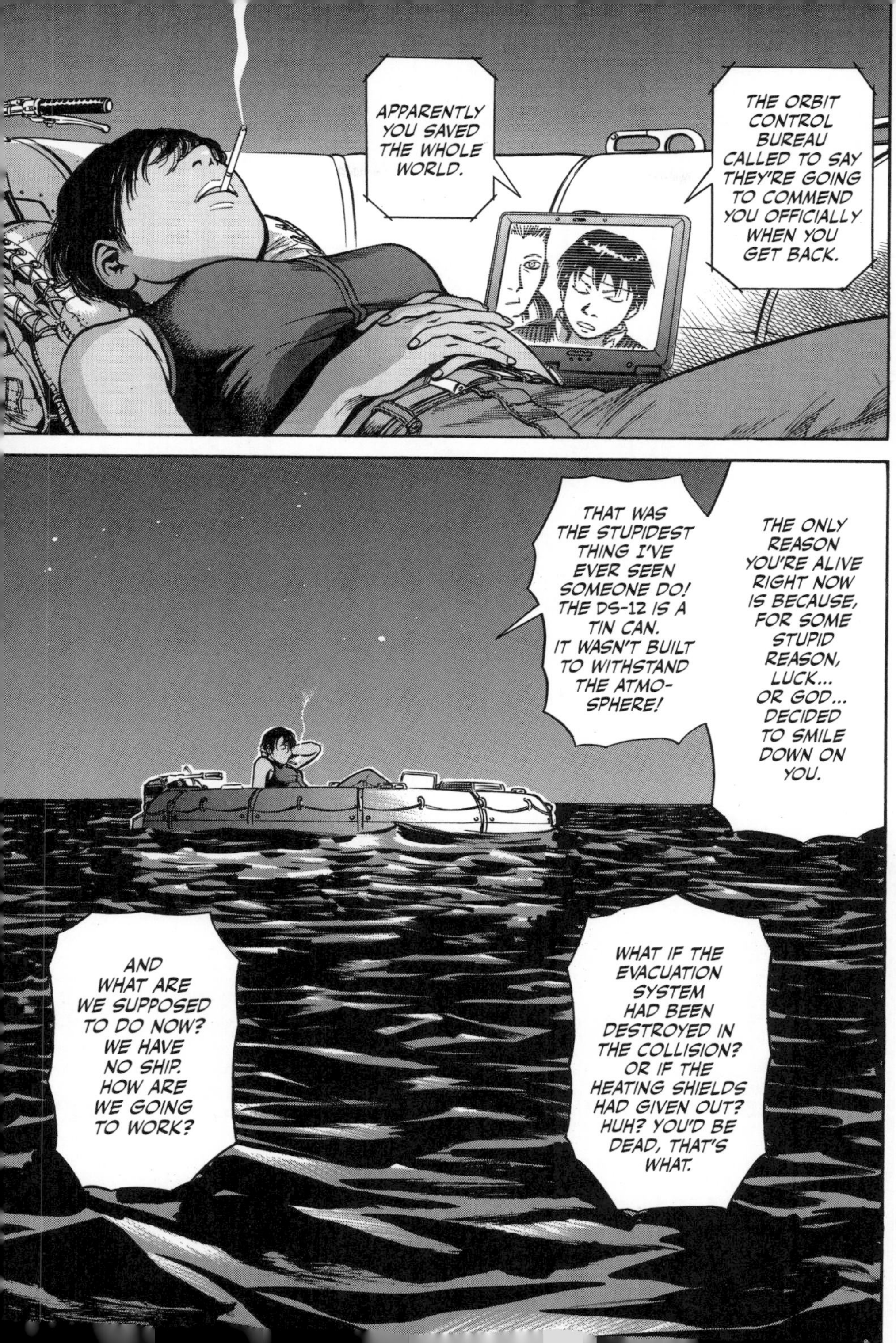
THE ORBIT CONTROL BUREAU CALLED TO SAY THEY'RE GOING TO COMMEND YOU OFFICIALLY WHEN YOU GET BACK.
APPARENTLY YOU SAVED THE WHOLE WORLD.
THAT WAS THE STUPIDEST THING I'VE EVER SEEN SOMEONE DO! THE DS-12 IS A TIN CAN. IT WASN'T BUILT TO WITHSTAND THE ATMO-SPHERE!
THE ONLY REASON YOU'RE ALIVE RIGHT NOW IS BECAUSE, FOR SOME STUPID REASON, LUCK... OR GOD... DECIDED TO SMILE DOWN ON YOU.
WHAT IF THE EVACUATION SYSTEM HAD BEEN DESTROYED IN THE COLLISION? OR IF THE HEATING SHIELDS HAD GIVEN OUT? HUH? YOU'D BE DEAD, THAT'S WHAT.
AND WHAT ARE WE SUPPOSED TO DO NOW? WE HAVE NO SHIP. HOW ARE WE GOING TO WORK?

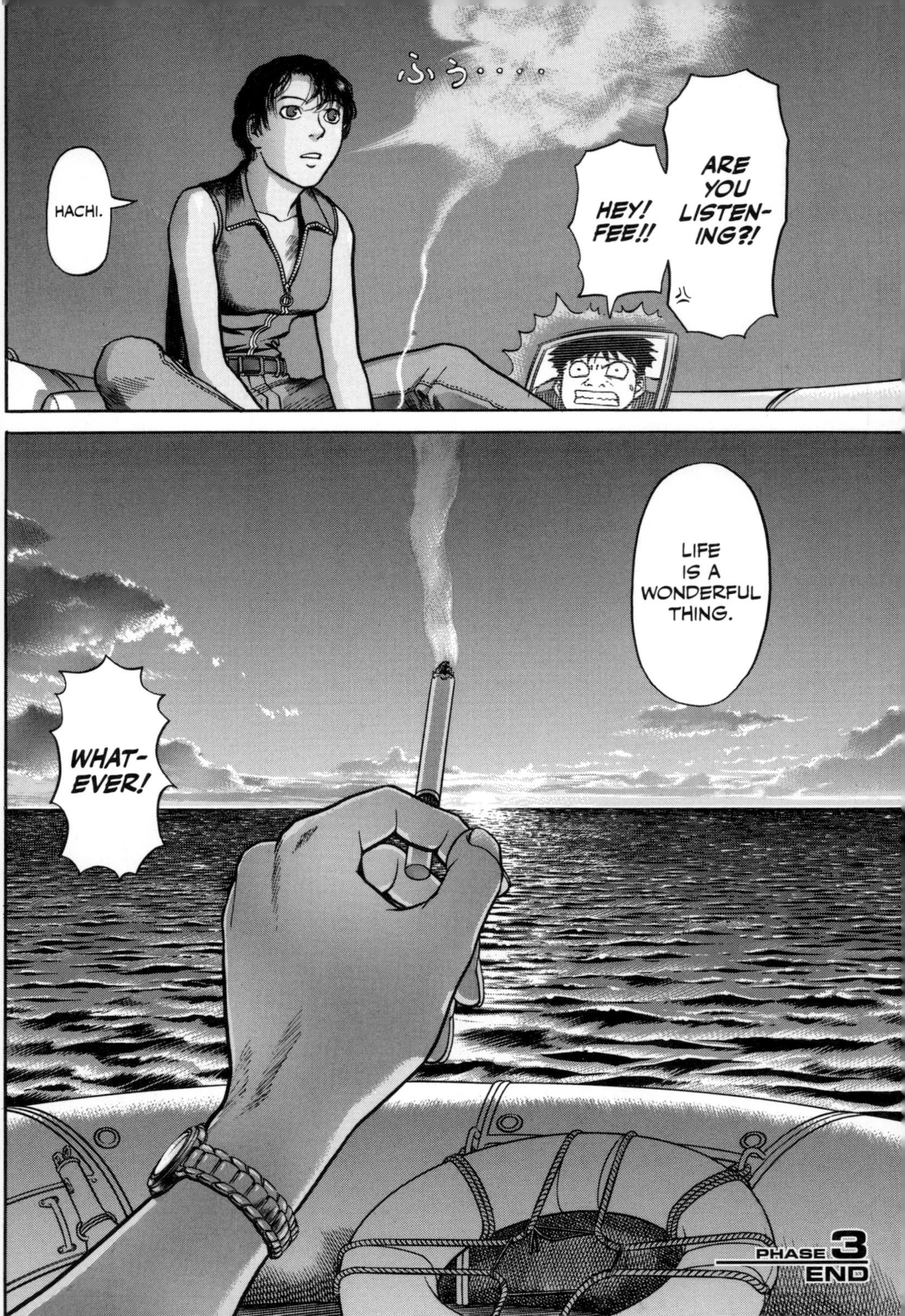
ARE YOU LISTEN-ING?!
HEY! FEE!!
ふう….
HACHI.
LIFE IS A WONDERFUL THING.
WHAT-EVER!
PHASE 3 END

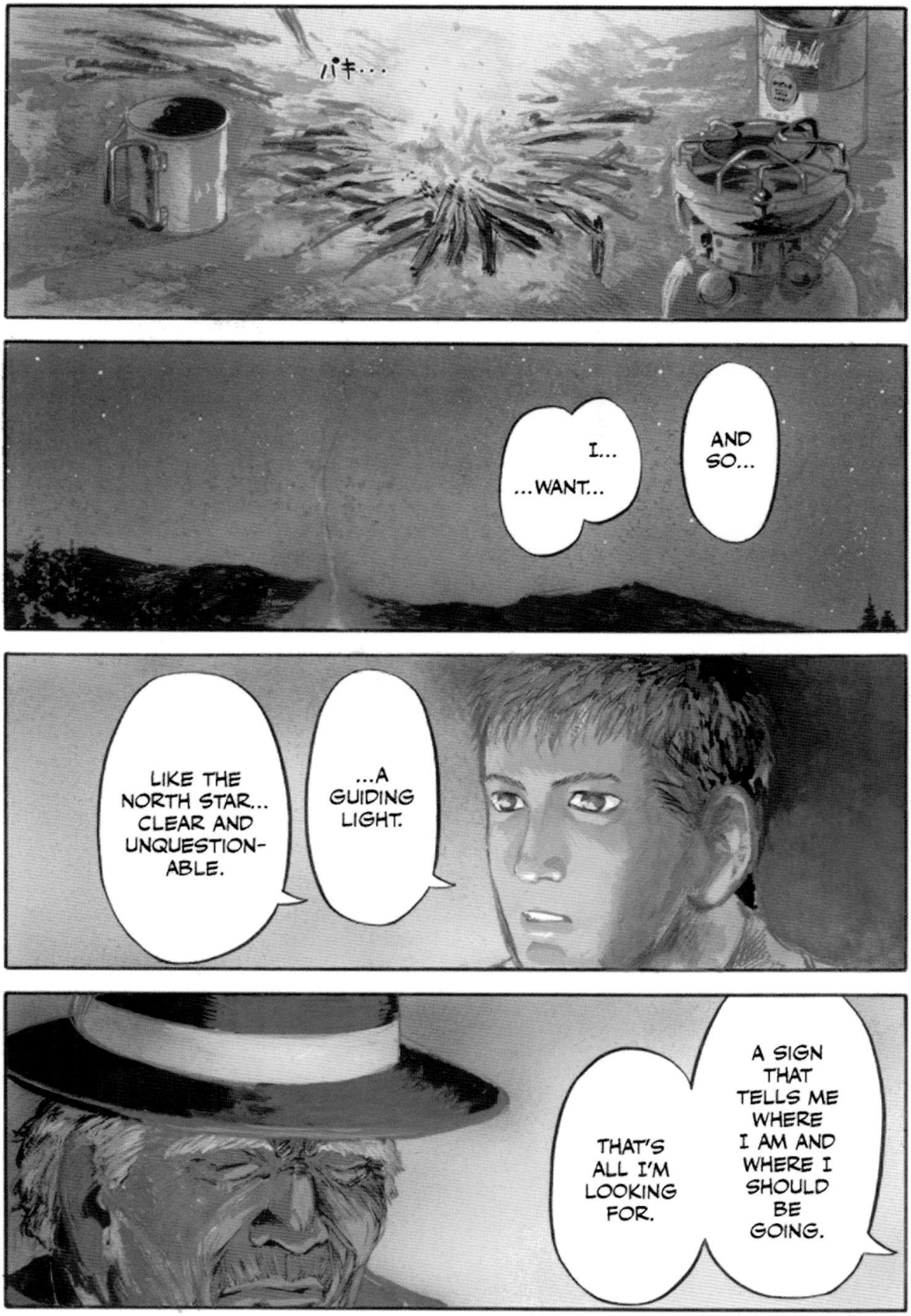
パキ…
AND SO...
I... ...WANT...
...A GUIDING LIGHT.
LIKE THE NORTH STAR... CLEAR AND UNQUESTION-ABLE.
A SIGN THAT TELLS ME WHERE I AM AND WHERE I SHOULD BE GOING.
THAT'S ALL I'M LOOKING FOR.

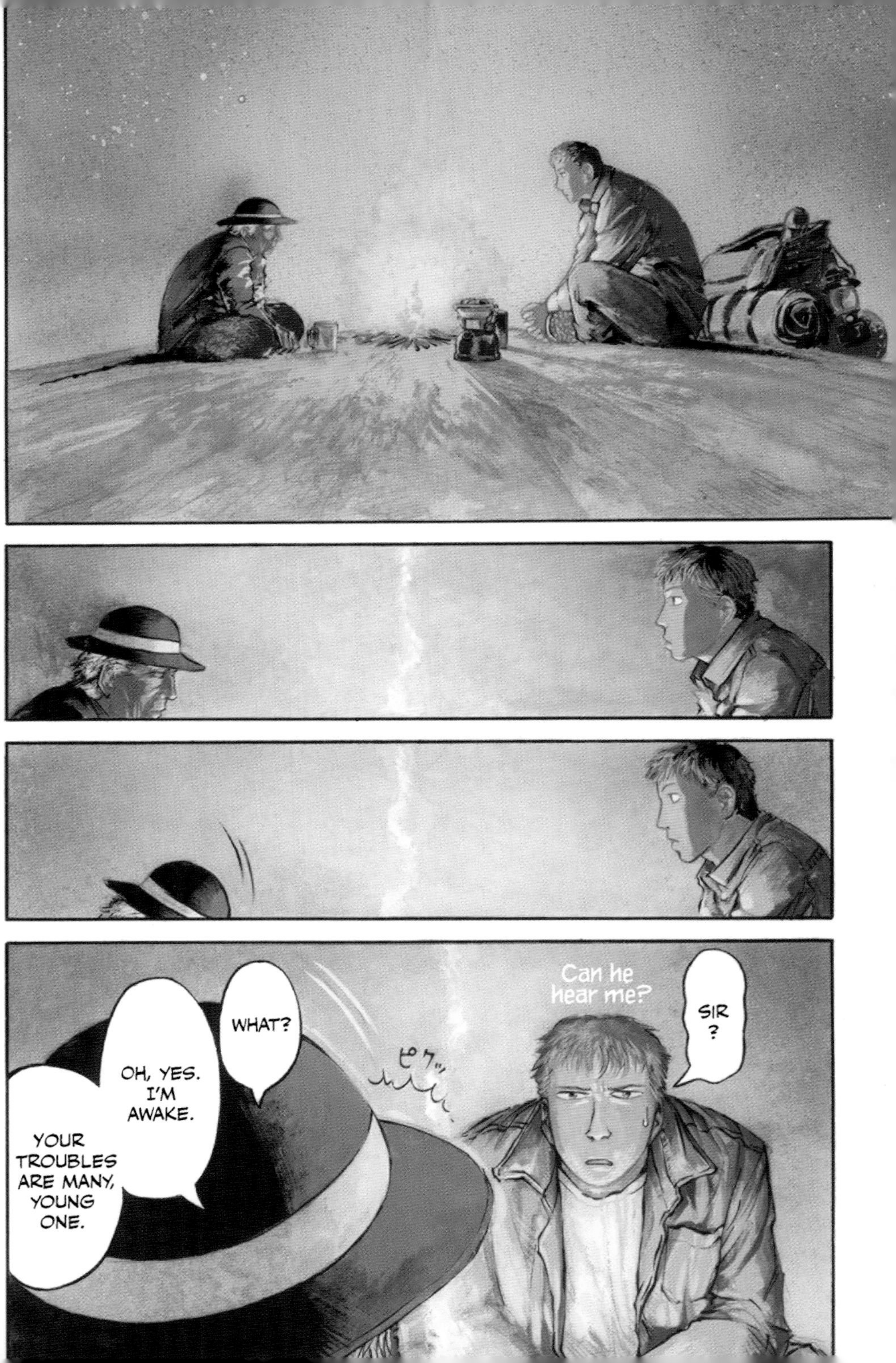
SIR ?
Can he hear me?
WHAT?
ピクッ
OH, YES. I'M AWAKE.
YOUR TROUBLES ARE MANY, YOUNG ONE.

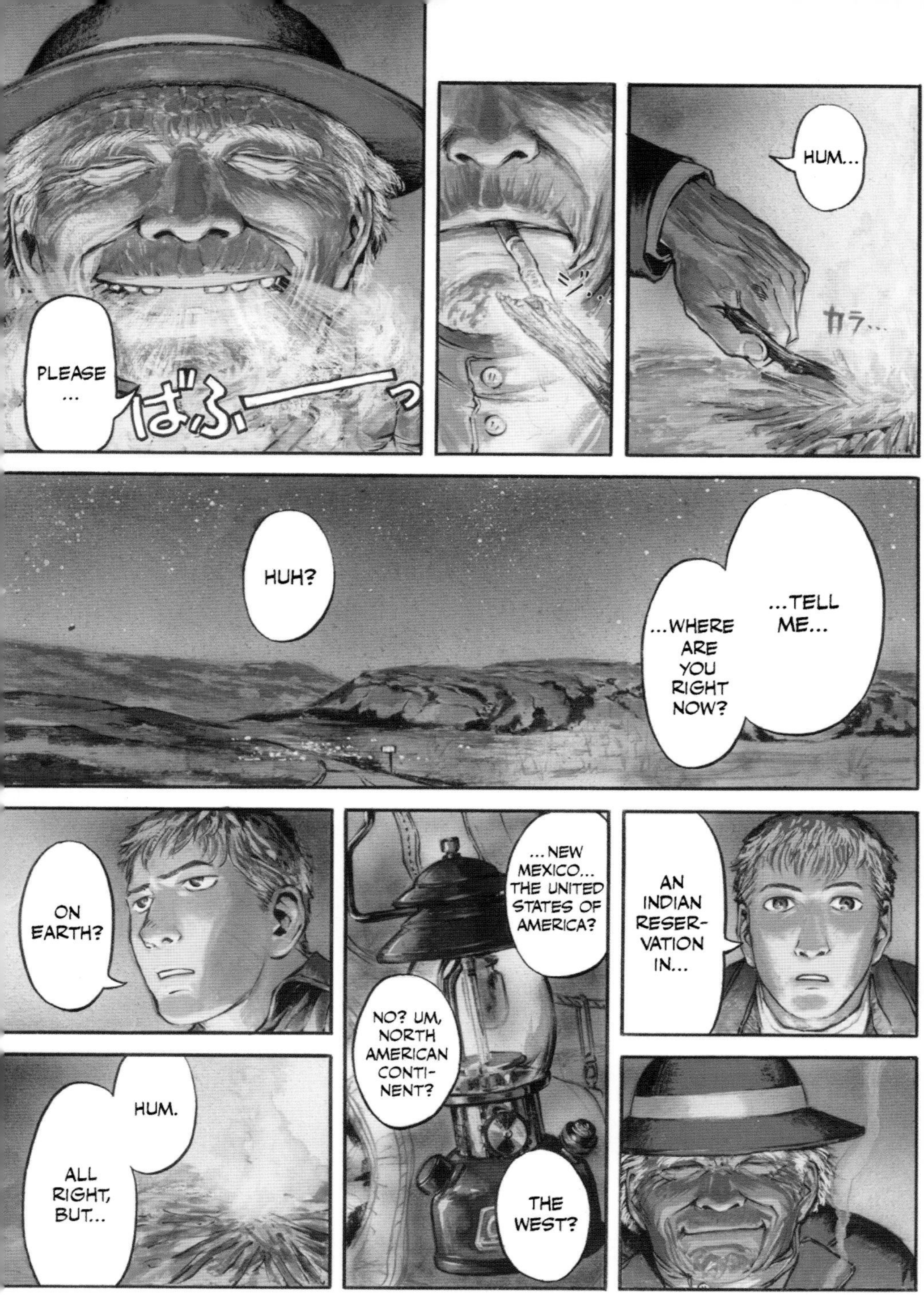
HUM...
カラ...
PLEASE ...
ばふーっ
...TELL ME...
...WHERE ARE YOU RIGHT NOW?
HUH?
AN INDIAN RESERVATION IN...
...NEW MEXICO... THE UNITED STATES OF AMERICA?
NO? UM, NORTH AMERICAN CONTI-NENT?
THE WEST?
ON EARTH?
HUM.
ALL RIGHT, BUT...

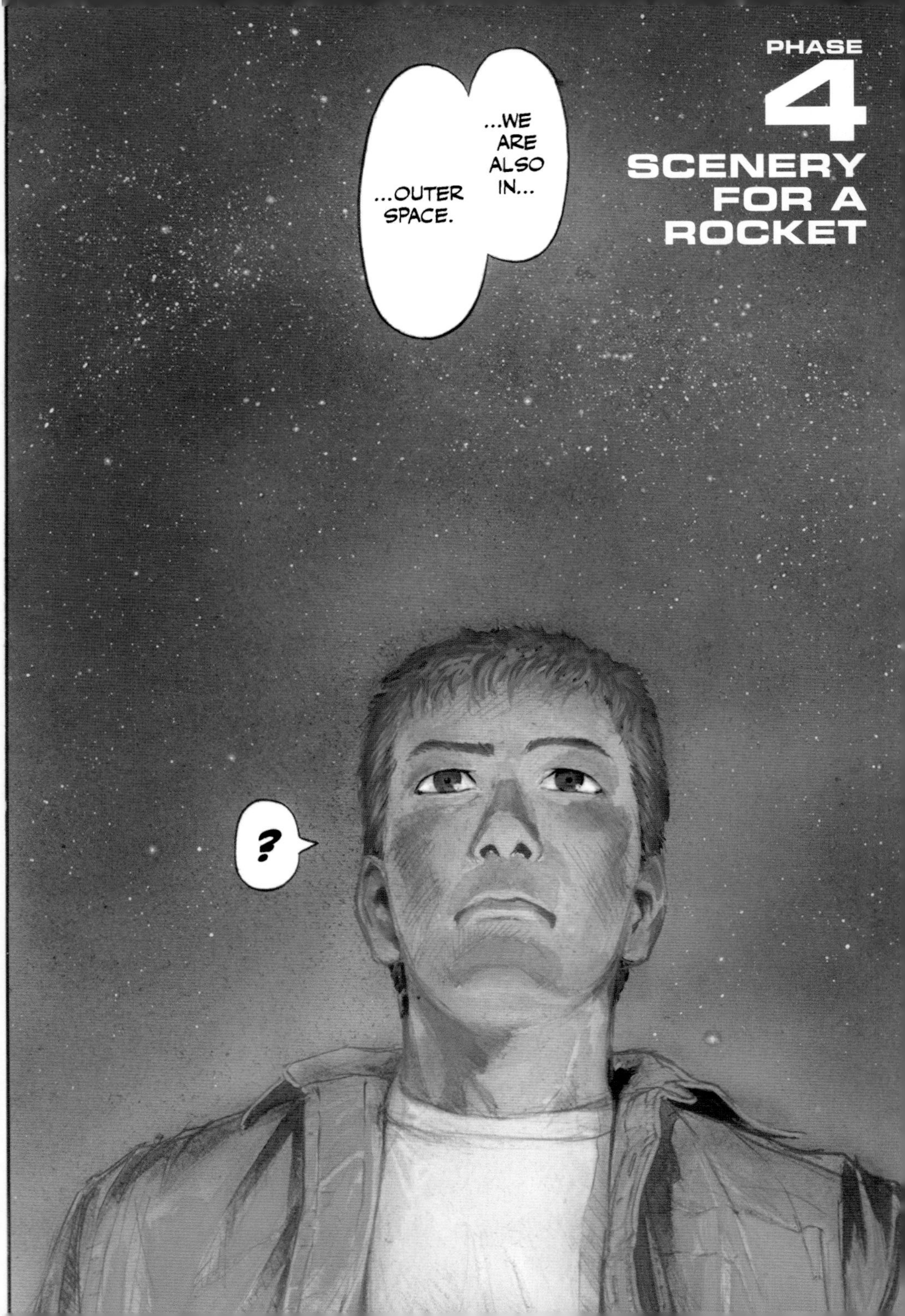
PHASE 4
SCENERY FOR A ROCKET
...WE ARE ALSO IN...
...OUTER SPACE.
?

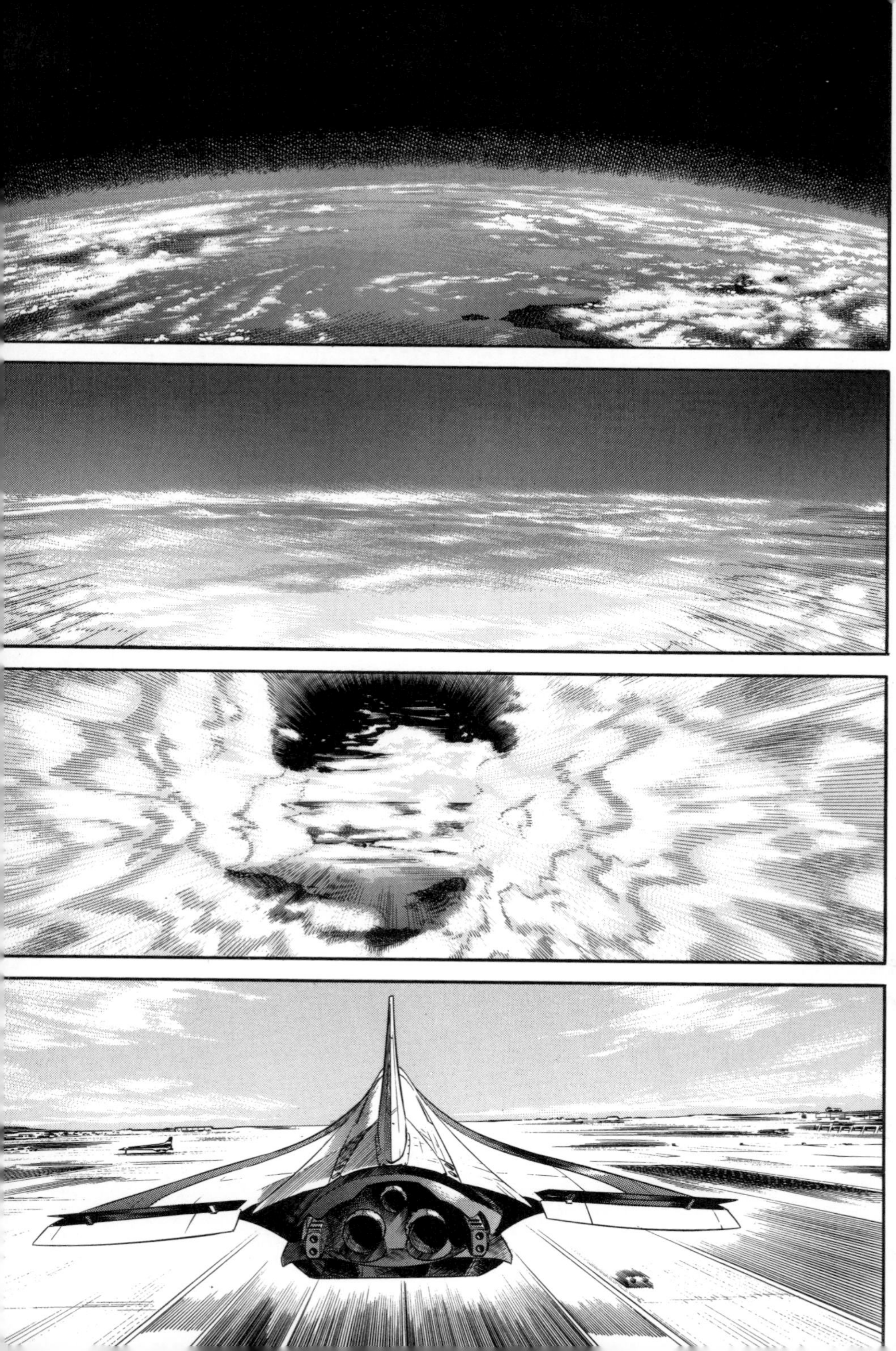

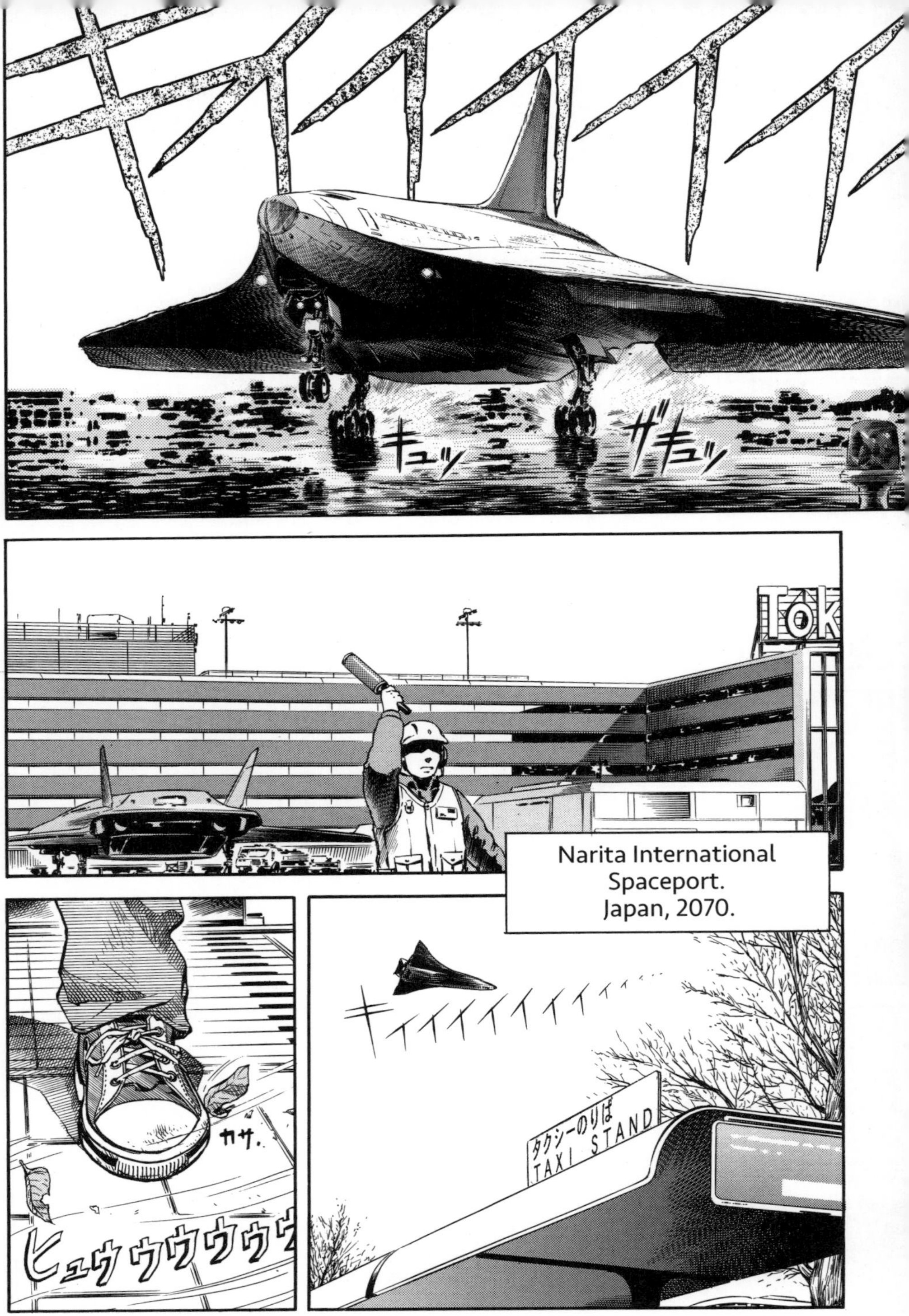
キイイイイイイ
ザギュッ
キュッ
Tok
Narita International
Spaceport.
Japan, 2070.
キイイイイイイイ…
タクシーのりば
TAXI STAND
カサ.
ヒュウウウウウ

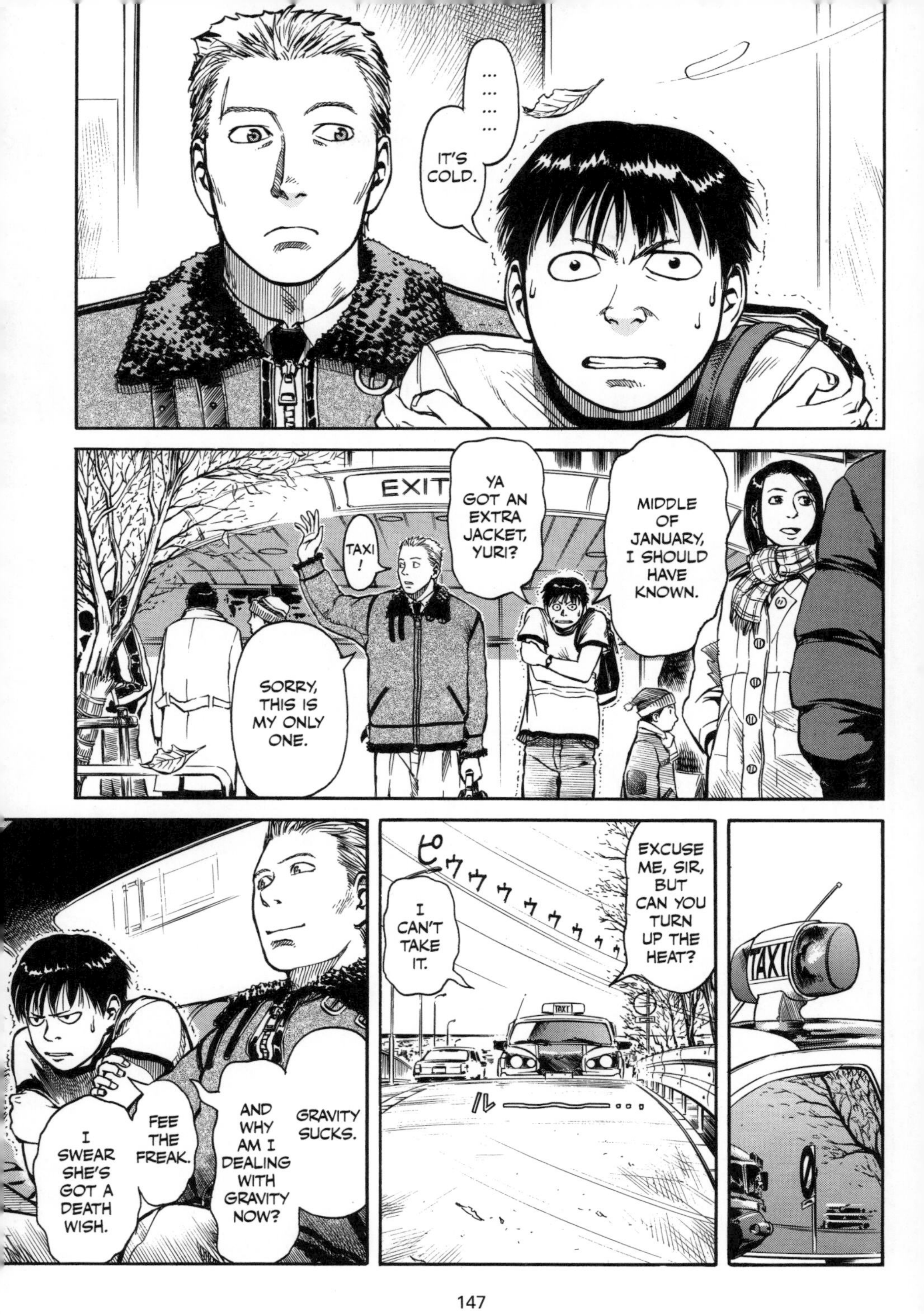
.... IT'S COLD.
MIDDLE OF JANUARY, I SHOULD HAVE KNOWN.
YA GOT AN EXTRA JACKET, YURI?
TAXI!
SORRY, THIS IS MY ONLY ONE.
EXIT
TAXI
EXCUSE ME, SIR, BUT CAN YOU TURN UP THE HEAT?
I CAN'T TAKE IT.
ピウウウウウウウウウ
ル———...
GRAVITY SUCKS.
AND WHY AM I DEALING WITH GRAVITY NOW?
FEE THE FREAK.
I SWEAR SHE'S GOT A DEATH WISH.

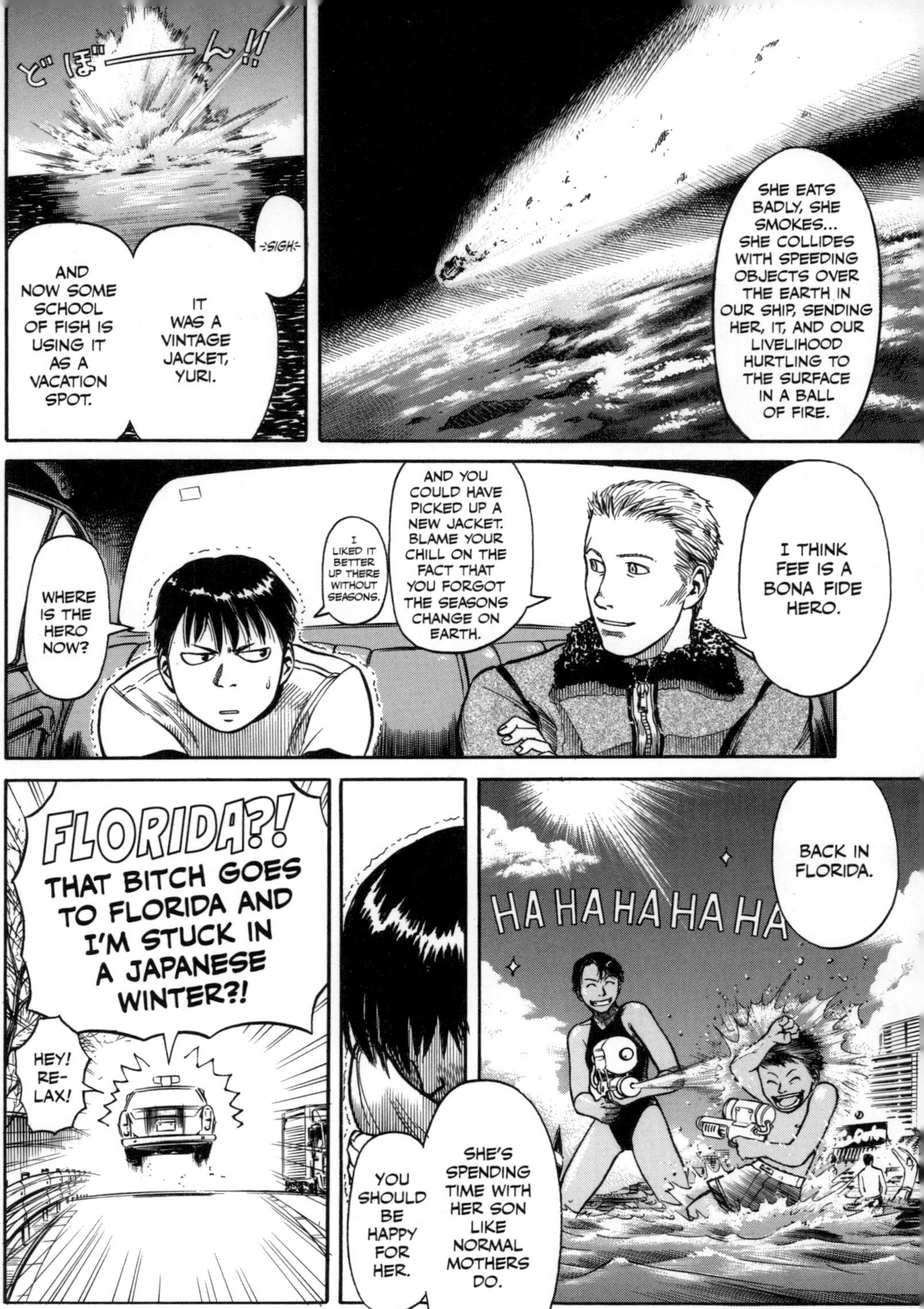
SHE EATS BADLY, SHE SMOKES... SHE COLLIDES WITH SPEEDING OBJECTS OVER THE EARTH IN OUR SHIP, SENDING HER, IT, AND OUR LIVELIHOOD HURTLING TO THE SURFACE IN A BALL OF FIRE.
どぼーーーん!!
SIGH
IT WAS A VINTAGE JACKET, YURI.
AND NOW SOME SCHOOL OF FISH IS USING IT AS A VACATION SPOT.
I THINK FEE IS A BONA FIDE HERO.
AND YOU COULD HAVE PICKED UP A NEW JACKET. BLAME YOUR CHILL ON THE FACT THAT YOU FORGOT THE SEASONS CHANGE ON EARTH.
I LIKED IT BETTER UP THERE WITHOUT SEASONS.
WHERE IS THE HERO NOW?
BACK IN FLORIDA.
HA HA HA HA HA HA
SHE'S SPENDING TIME WITH HER SON LIKE NORMAL MOTHERS DO.
YOU SHOULD BE HAPPY FOR HER.
FLORIDA?!
THAT BITCH GOES TO FLORIDA AND I'M STUCK IN A JAPANESE WINTER?!
HEY! RE-LAX!

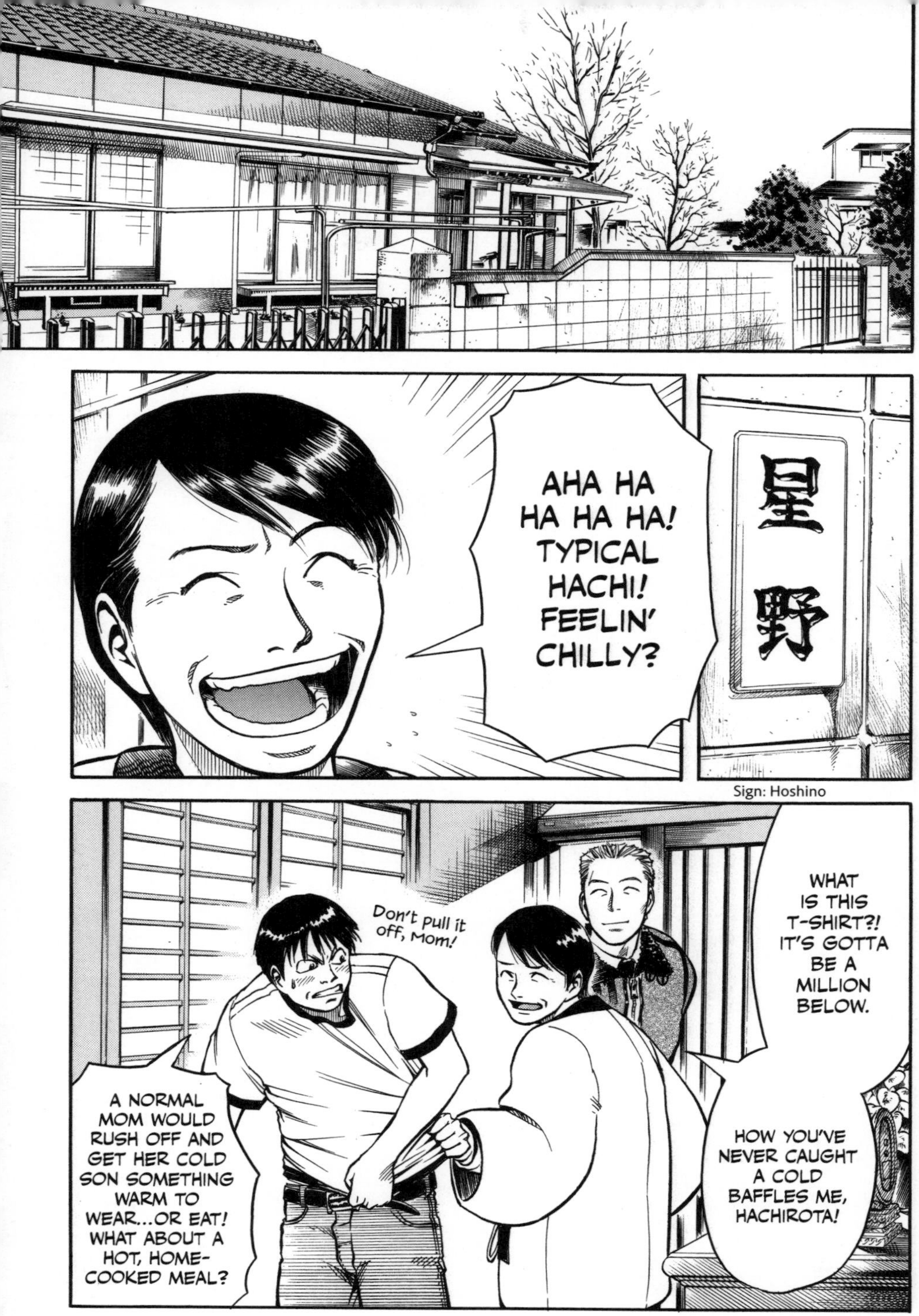
星野
AHA HA HA HA HA! TYPICAL HACHI! FEELIN' CHILLY?
WHAT IS THIS T-SHIRT?! IT'S GOTTA BE A MILLION BELOW.
Don't pull it off, Mom!
HOW YOU'VE NEVER CAUGHT A COLD BAFFLES ME, HACHIROTA!
A NORMAL MOM WOULD RUSH OFF AND GET HER COLD SON SOMETHING WARM TO WEAR...OR EAT! WHAT ABOUT A HOT, HOME-COOKED MEAL?
Sign: Hoshino

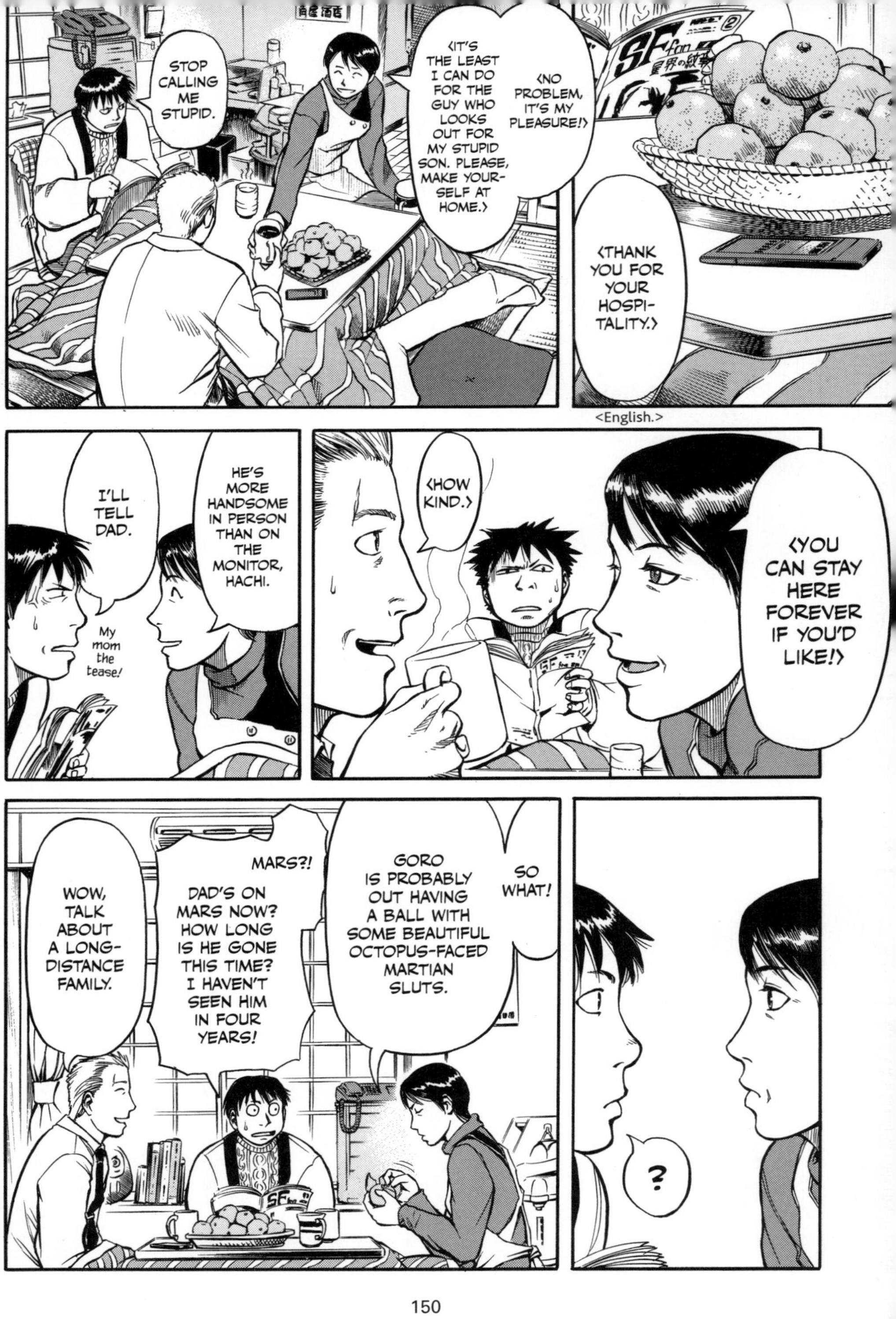
‹THANK YOU FOR YOUR HOSPITALITY.›
<English.>
‹NO PROBLEM, IT'S MY PLEASURE!›
‹IT'S THE LEAST I CAN DO FOR THE GUY WHO LOOKS OUT FOR MY STUPID SON. PLEASE, MAKE YOURSELF AT HOME.›
STOP CALLING ME STUPID.
‹YOU CAN STAY HERE FOREVER IF YOU'D LIKE!›
‹HOW KIND.›
HE'S MORE HANDSOME IN PERSON THAN ON THE MONITOR, HACHI.
I'LL TELL DAD.
My mom the tease!
?
SO WHAT!
GORO IS PROBABLY OUT HAVING A BALL WITH SOME BEAUTIFUL OCTOPUS-FACED MARTIAN SLUTS.
MARS?!
DAD'S ON MARS NOW? HOW LONG IS HE GONE THIS TIME? I HAVEN'T SEEN HIM IN FOUR YEARS!
WOW, TALK ABOUT A LONG-DISTANCE FAMILY.

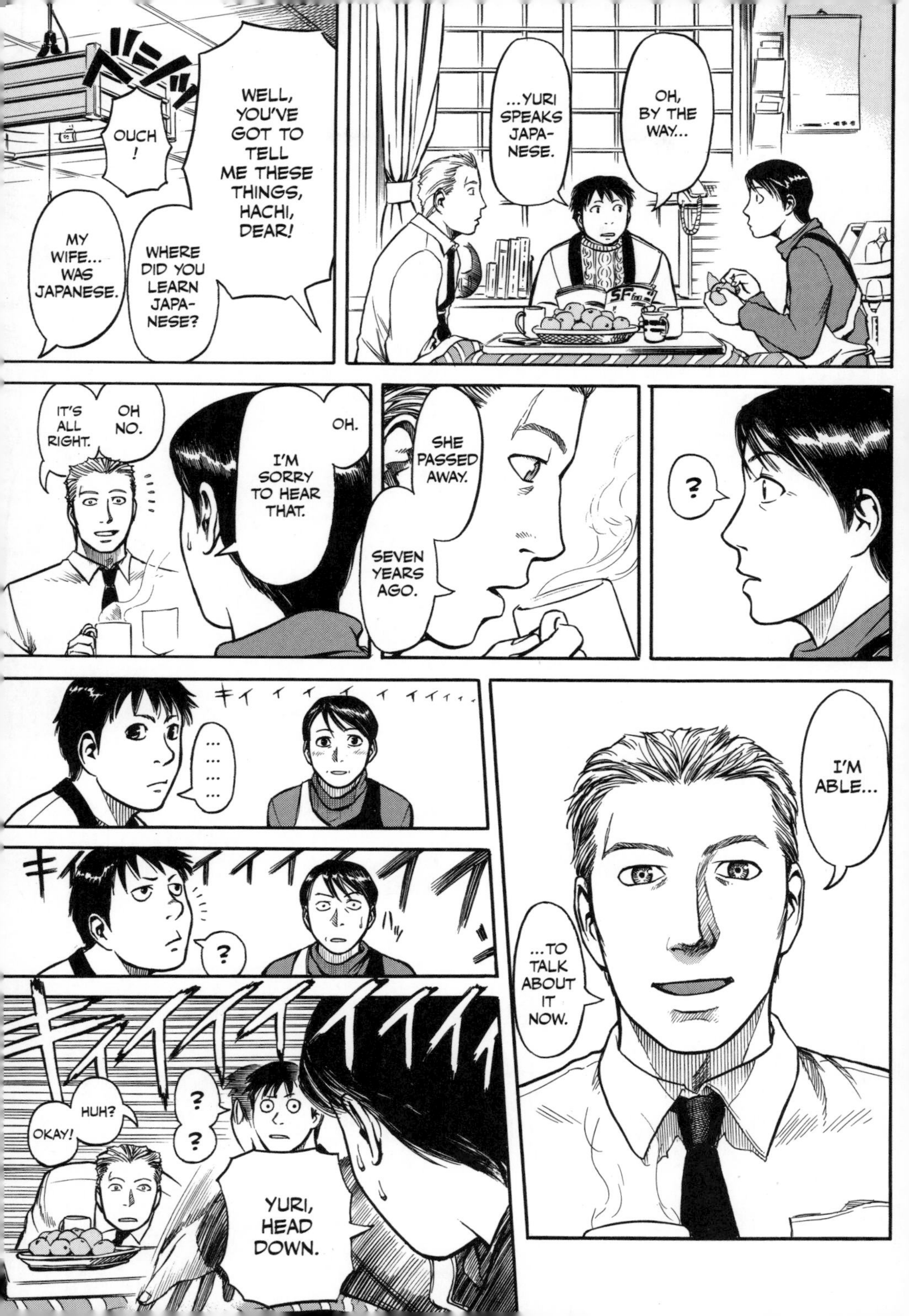
OH, BY THE WAY...
...YURI SPEAKS JAPANESE.
WELL, YOU'VE GOT TO TELL ME THESE THINGS, HACHI, DEAR!
OUCH!
WHERE DID YOU LEARN JAPANESE?
MY WIFE... WAS JAPANESE.
?
SHE PASSED AWAY.
SEVEN YEARS AGO.
OH.
I'M SORRY TO HEAR THAT.
OH NO.
IT'S ALL RIGHT.
I'M ABLE...
...TO TALK ABOUT IT NOW.
キィィィィィィィィ
....
キィィィィィィ
?
キィィィィィィィ
HUH?
OKAY!
?
?
YURI, HEAD DOWN.

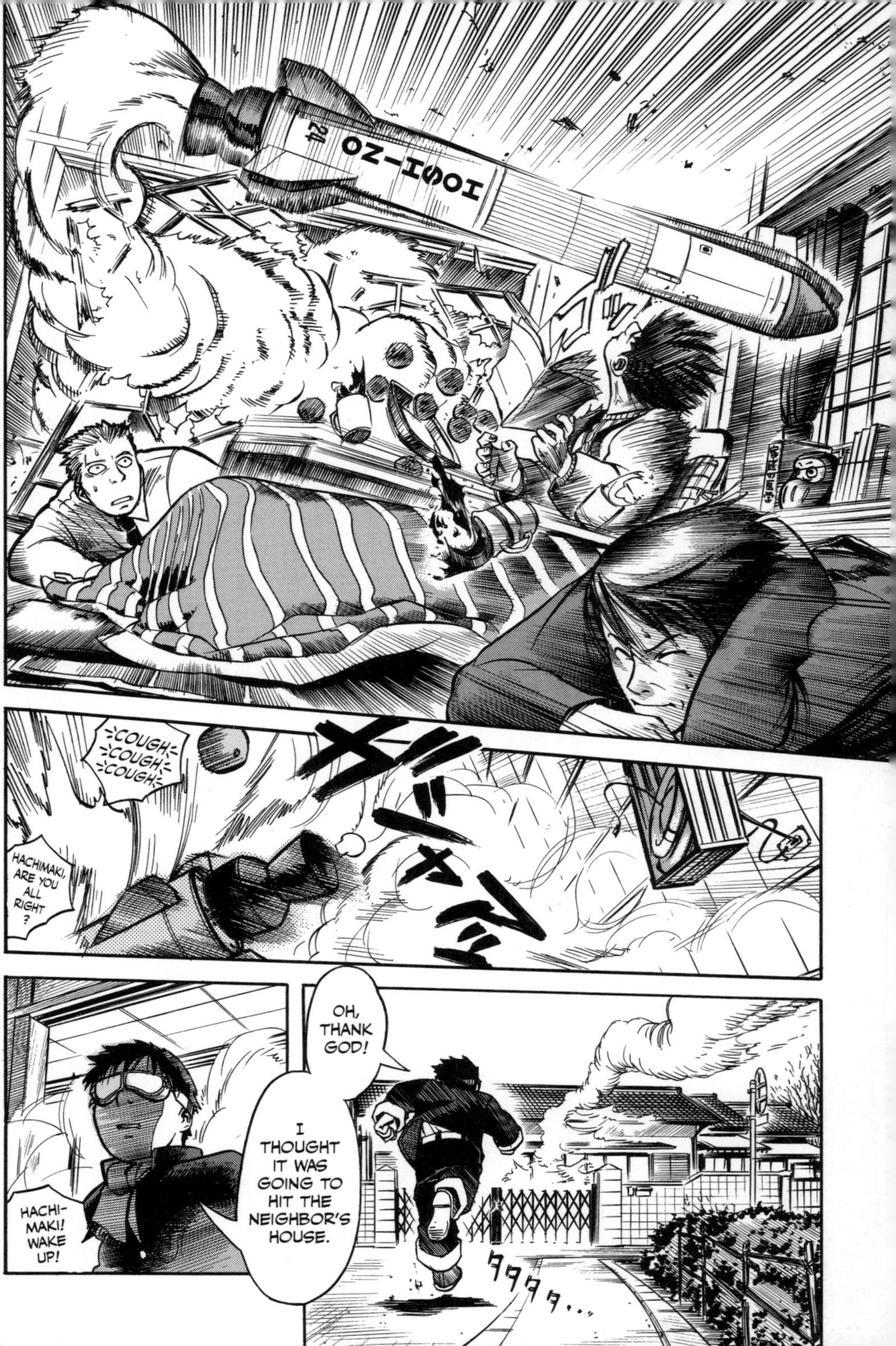
COUGH COUGH COUGH
HACHIMAKI, ARE YOU ALL RIGHT?
OH, THANK GOD!
I THOUGHT IT WAS GOING TO HIT THE NEIGHBOR'S HOUSE.
タタタタ...
HACHI-MAKI! WAKE UP!

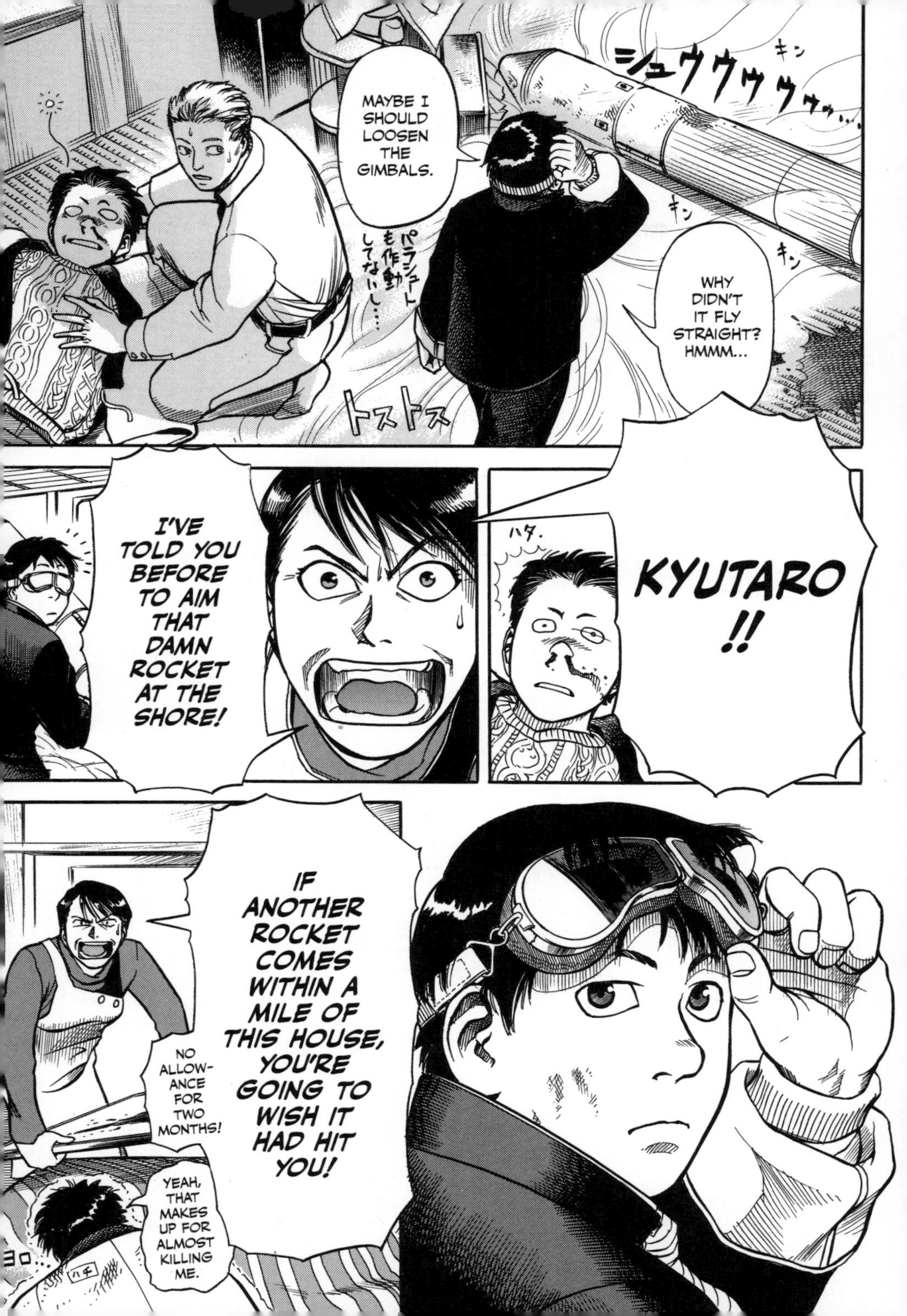
シュウウウウゥ…
キン
キン
キン
WHY DIDN'T IT FLY STRAIGHT? HMMM...
MAYBE I SHOULD LOOSEN THE GIMBALS.
パラシュートも作動してないし…
トストス
KYUTARO!!
ハタ.
I'VE TOLD YOU BEFORE TO AIM THAT DAMN ROCKET AT THE SHORE!
IF ANOTHER ROCKET COMES WITHIN A MILE OF THIS HOUSE, YOU'RE GOING TO WISH IT HAD HIT YOU!
NO ALLOW-ANCE FOR TWO MONTHS!
YEAH, THAT MAKES UP FOR ALMOST KILLING ME.
ヨロ…

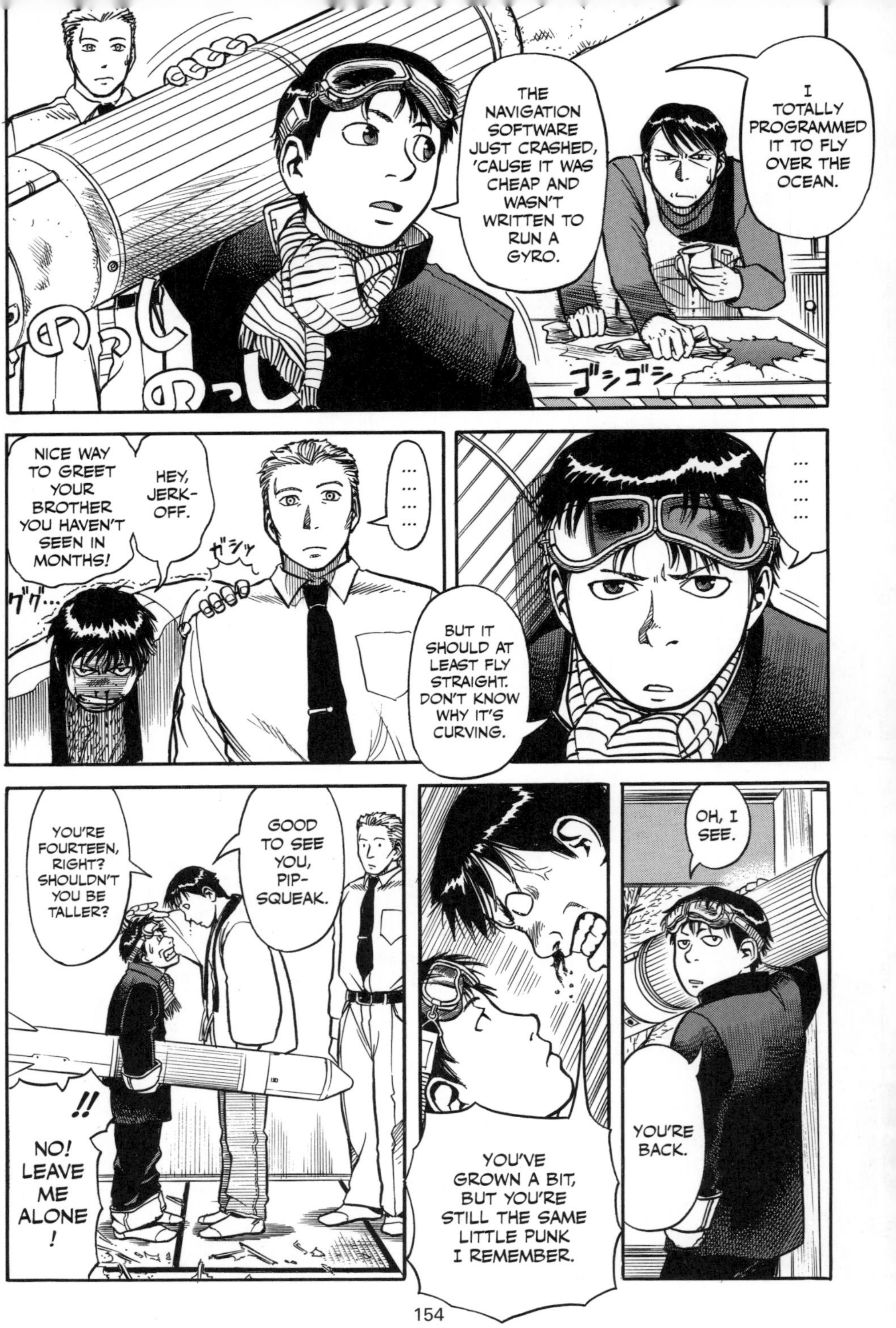
I TOTALLY PROGRAMMED IT TO FLY OVER THE OCEAN.
THE NAVIGATION SOFTWARE JUST CRASHED, 'CAUSE IT WAS CHEAP AND WASN'T WRITTEN TO RUN A GYRO.
ゴシゴシ
のっし のっし
......
BUT IT SHOULD AT LEAST FLY STRAIGHT. DON'T KNOW WHY IT'S CURVING.
......
HEY, JERK-OFF.
NICE WAY TO GREET YOUR BROTHER YOU HAVEN'T SEEN IN MONTHS!
ガシッ
ググ...
OH, I SEE.
YOU'RE BACK.
YOU'VE GROWN A BIT, BUT YOU'RE STILL THE SAME LITTLE PUNK I REMEMBER.
GOOD TO SEE YOU, PIP-SQUEAK.
YOU'RE FOURTEEN, RIGHT? SHOULDN'T YOU BE TALLER?
!!
NO! LEAVE ME ALONE!

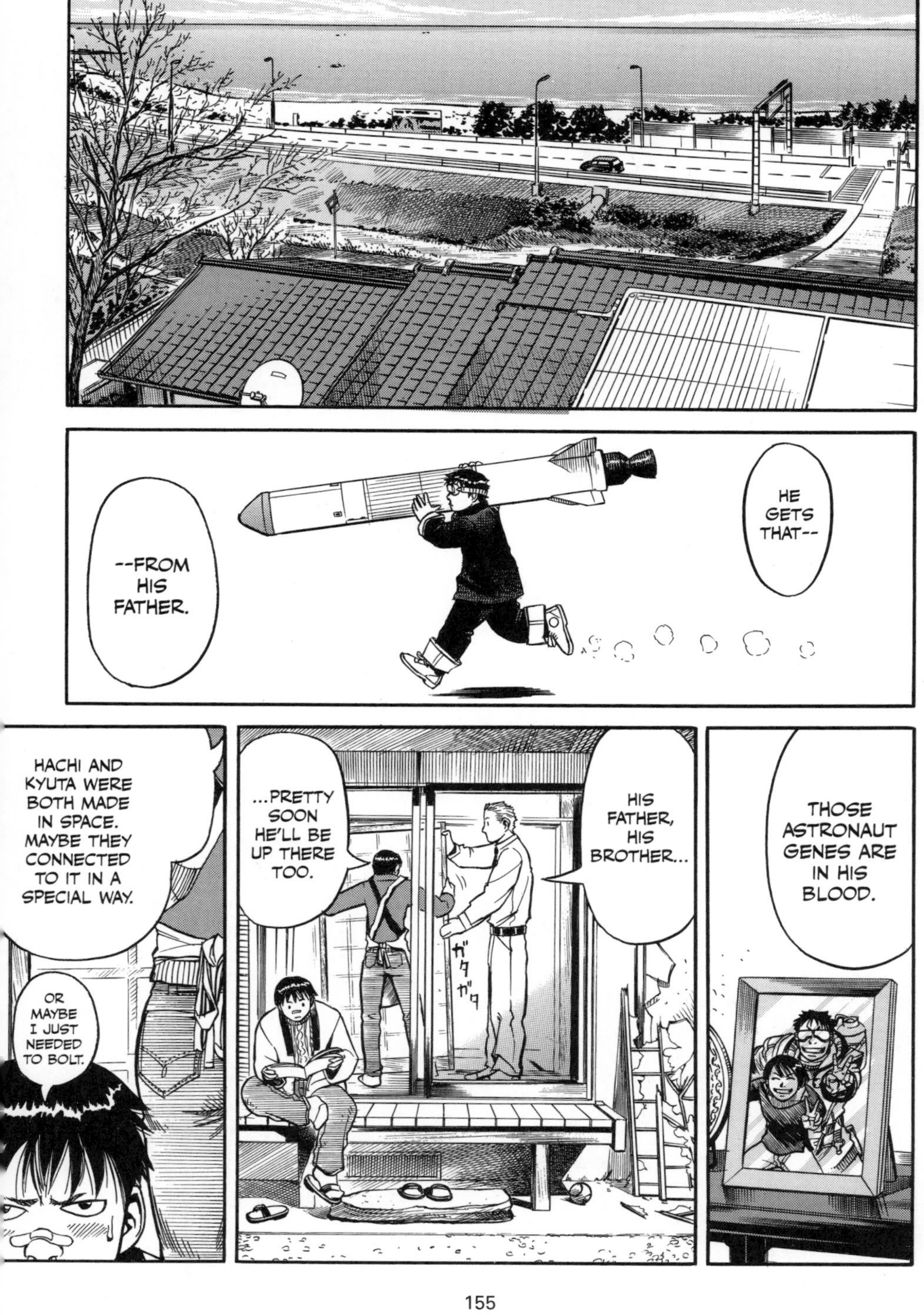
HE GETS THAT--
--FROM HIS FATHER.
THOSE ASTRONAUT GENES ARE IN HIS BLOOD.
HIS FATHER, HIS BROTHER...
...PRETTY SOON HE'LL BE UP THERE TOO.
ガタガタ
HACHI AND KYUTA WERE BOTH MADE IN SPACE. MAYBE THEY CONNECTED TO IT IN A SPECIAL WAY.
OR MAYBE I JUST NEEDED TO BOLT.

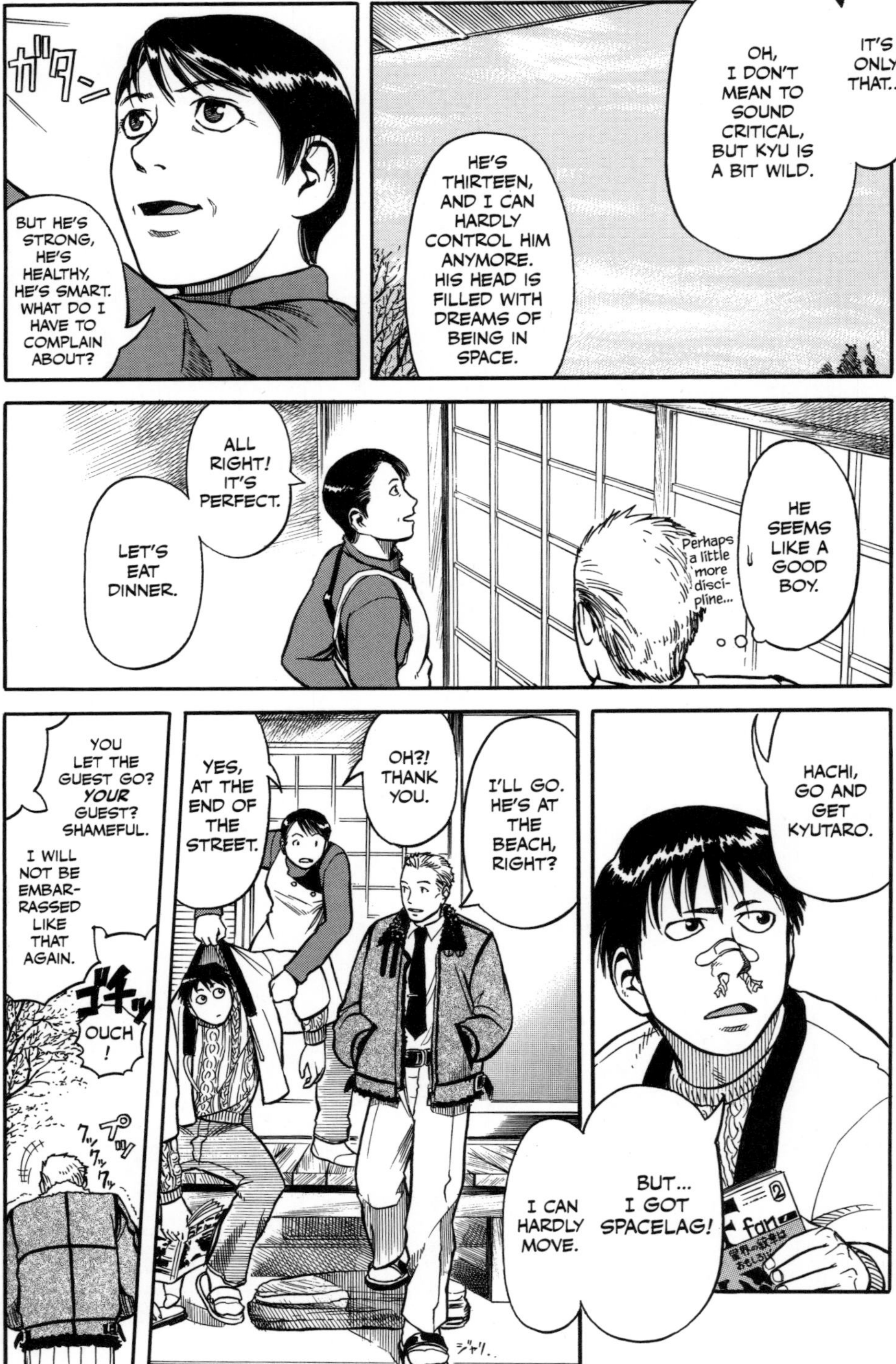
IT'S ONLY THAT...
OH, I DON'T MEAN TO SOUND CRITICAL, BUT KYU IS A BIT WILD.
HE'S THIRTEEN, AND I CAN HARDLY CONTROL HIM ANYMORE. HIS HEAD IS FILLED WITH DREAMS OF BEING IN SPACE.
ガタン
BUT HE'S STRONG, HE'S HEALTHY, HE'S SMART. WHAT DO I HAVE TO COMPLAIN ABOUT?
HE SEEMS LIKE A GOOD BOY.
Perhaps a little more disci-pline...
ALL RIGHT! IT'S PERFECT.
LET'S EAT DINNER.
HACHI, GO AND GET KYUTARO.
BUT... I GOT SPACELAG!
I CAN HARDLY MOVE.
I'LL GO. HE'S AT THE BEACH, RIGHT?
OH?! THANK YOU.
YES, AT THE END OF THE STREET.
ジャリ
YOU LET THE GUEST GO? *YOUR* GUEST? SHAMEFUL.
I WILL NOT BE EMBAR-RASSED LIKE THAT AGAIN.
ゴチッ
OUCH!

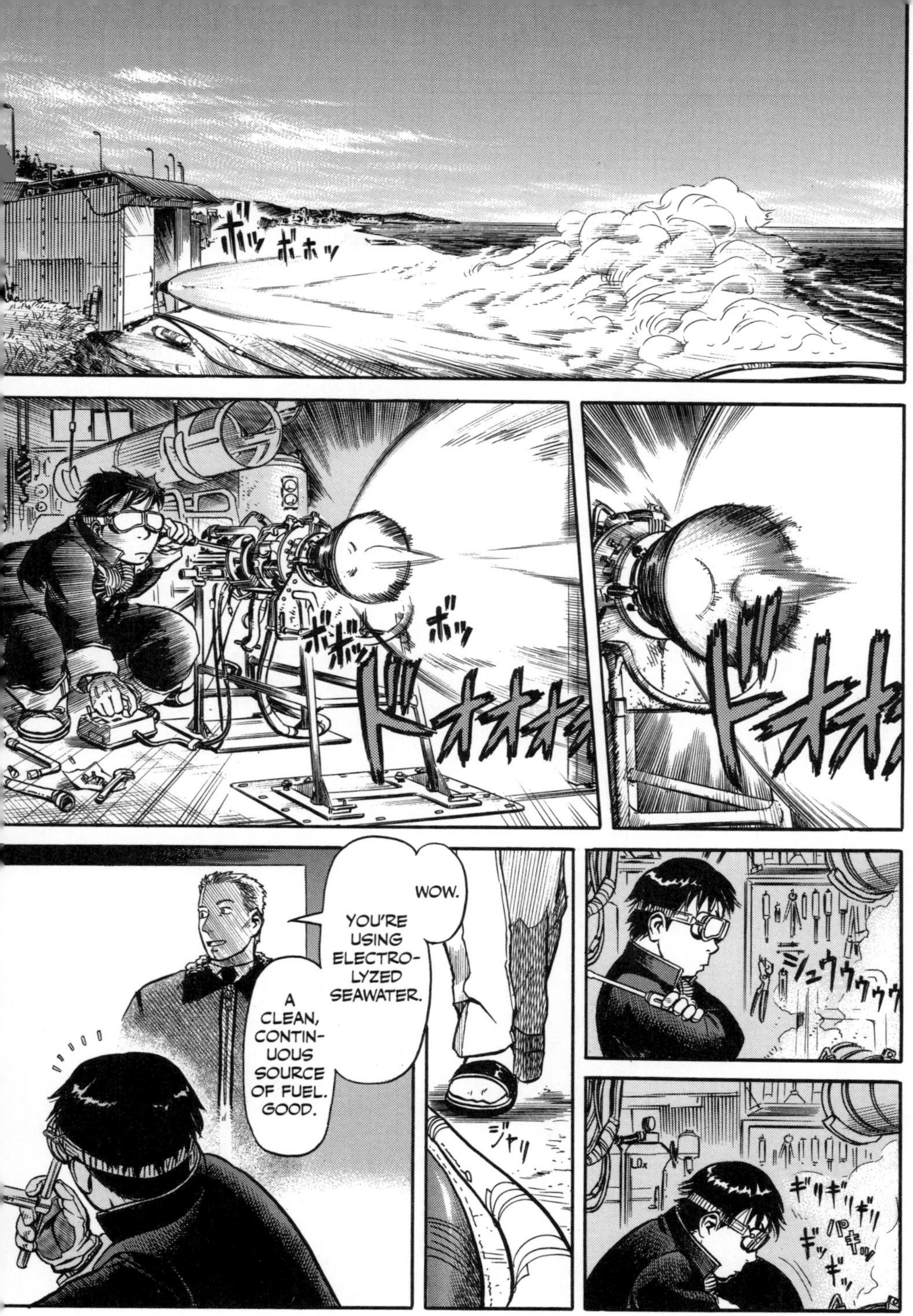
ボッ ボホッ
ドオオッ
ボボッ ボッ
ドオオオッ
シュウウウウウ
ギリギリギリ パキッ ギッギッ
WOW. YOU'RE USING ELECTROLYZED SEAWATER. A CLEAN, CONTINUOUS SOURCE OF FUEL. GOOD.
ジャリ

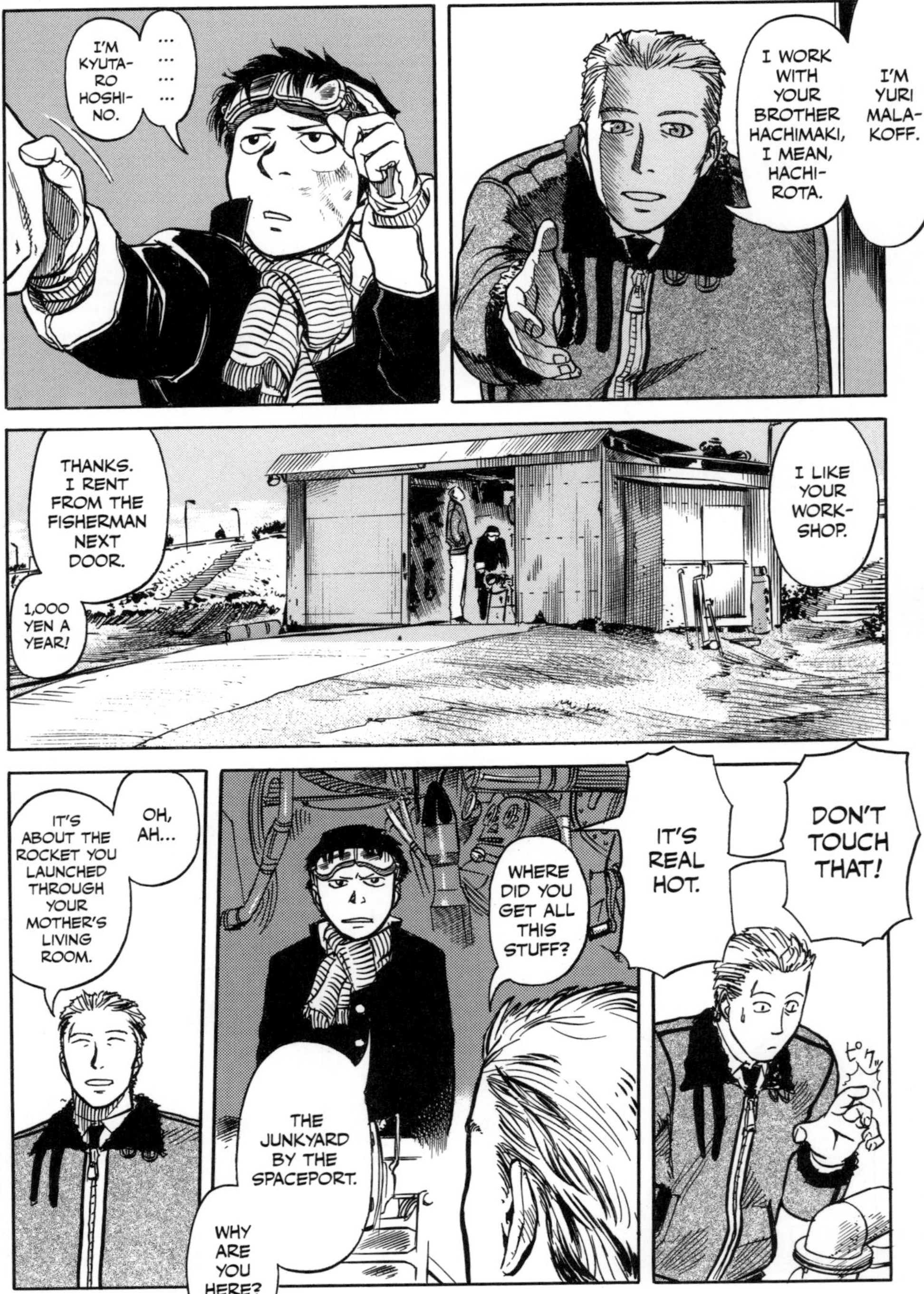
I'M YURI MALAKOFF.
I WORK WITH YOUR BROTHER HACHIMAKI, I MEAN, HACHIROTA.
....
I'M KYUTARO HOSHINO.
I LIKE YOUR WORKSHOP.
THANKS. I RENT FROM THE FISHERMAN NEXT DOOR.
1,000 YEN A YEAR!
DON'T TOUCH THAT!
IT'S REAL HOT.
WHERE DID YOU GET ALL THIS STUFF?
THE JUNKYARD BY THE SPACEPORT.
WHY ARE YOU HERE?
OH, AH...
IT'S ABOUT THE ROCKET YOU LAUNCHED THROUGH YOUR MOTHER'S LIVING ROOM.

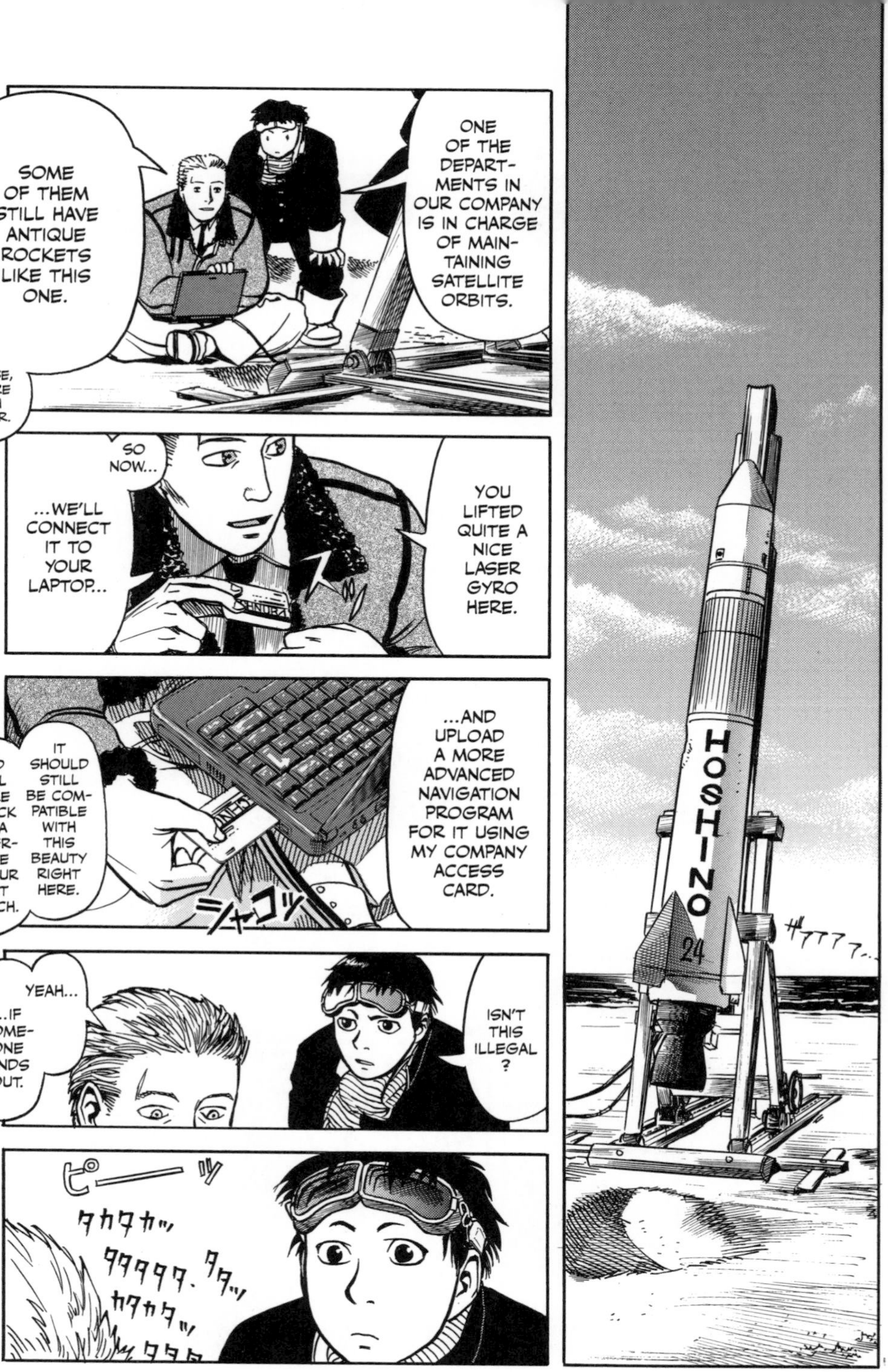
HOSHINO
24
ザァァァァ…
ONE OF THE DEPART-MENTS IN OUR COMPANY IS IN CHARGE OF MAIN-TAINING SATELLITE ORBITS.
SOME OF THEM STILL HAVE ANTIQUE ROCKETS LIKE THIS ONE.
OF COURSE, THEY'RE MUCH BIGGER.
YOU LIFTED QUITE A NICE LASER GYRO HERE.
SO NOW...
...WE'LL CONNECT IT TO YOUR LAPTOP...
...AND UPLOAD A MORE ADVANCED NAVIGATION PROGRAM FOR IT USING MY COMPANY ACCESS CARD.
IT SHOULD STILL BE COM-PATIBLE WITH THIS BEAUTY RIGHT HERE.
AND IT'LL MAKE A HECK OF A DIFFER-ENCE IN YOUR NEXT LAUNCH.
シャコッ
ISN'T THIS ILLEGAL?
YEAH...
...IF SOME-ONE FINDS OUT.
ピーーッ
タカタカッ
タタタタタ. タタッ
カタカタッ
タタタ

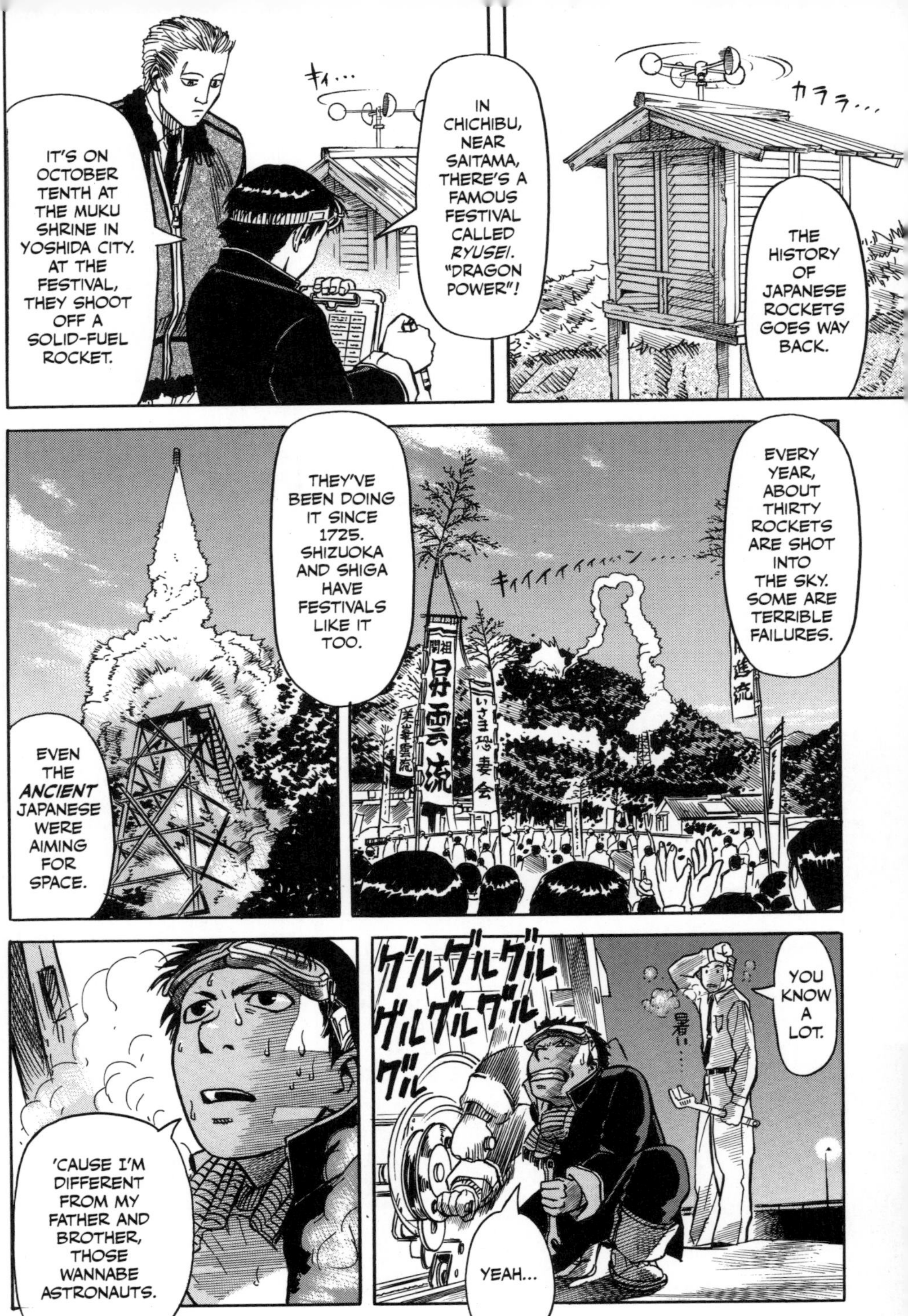

カララ・・・
THE HISTORY OF JAPANESE ROCKETS GOES WAY BACK.
キィ・・・
IN CHICHIBU, NEAR SAITAMA, THERE'S A FAMOUS FESTIVAL CALLED *RYUSEI*. "DRAGON POWER"!
IT'S ON OCTOBER TENTH AT THE MUKU SHRINE IN YOSHIDA CITY. AT THE FESTIVAL, THEY SHOOT OFF A SOLID-FUEL ROCKET.
EVERY YEAR, ABOUT THIRTY ROCKETS ARE SHOT INTO THE SKY. SOME ARE TERRIBLE FAILURES.
キィイイイイィィン・・・
THEY'VE BEEN DOING IT SINCE 1725. SHIZUOKA AND SHIGA HAVE FESTIVALS LIKE IT TOO.
EVEN THE ***ANCIENT*** JAPANESE WERE AIMING FOR SPACE.
YOU KNOW A LOT.
暑い・・・
グルグルグル
グルグルグル
グル
YEAH...
'CAUSE I'M DIFFERENT FROM MY FATHER AND BROTHER, THOSE WANNABE ASTRONAUTS.

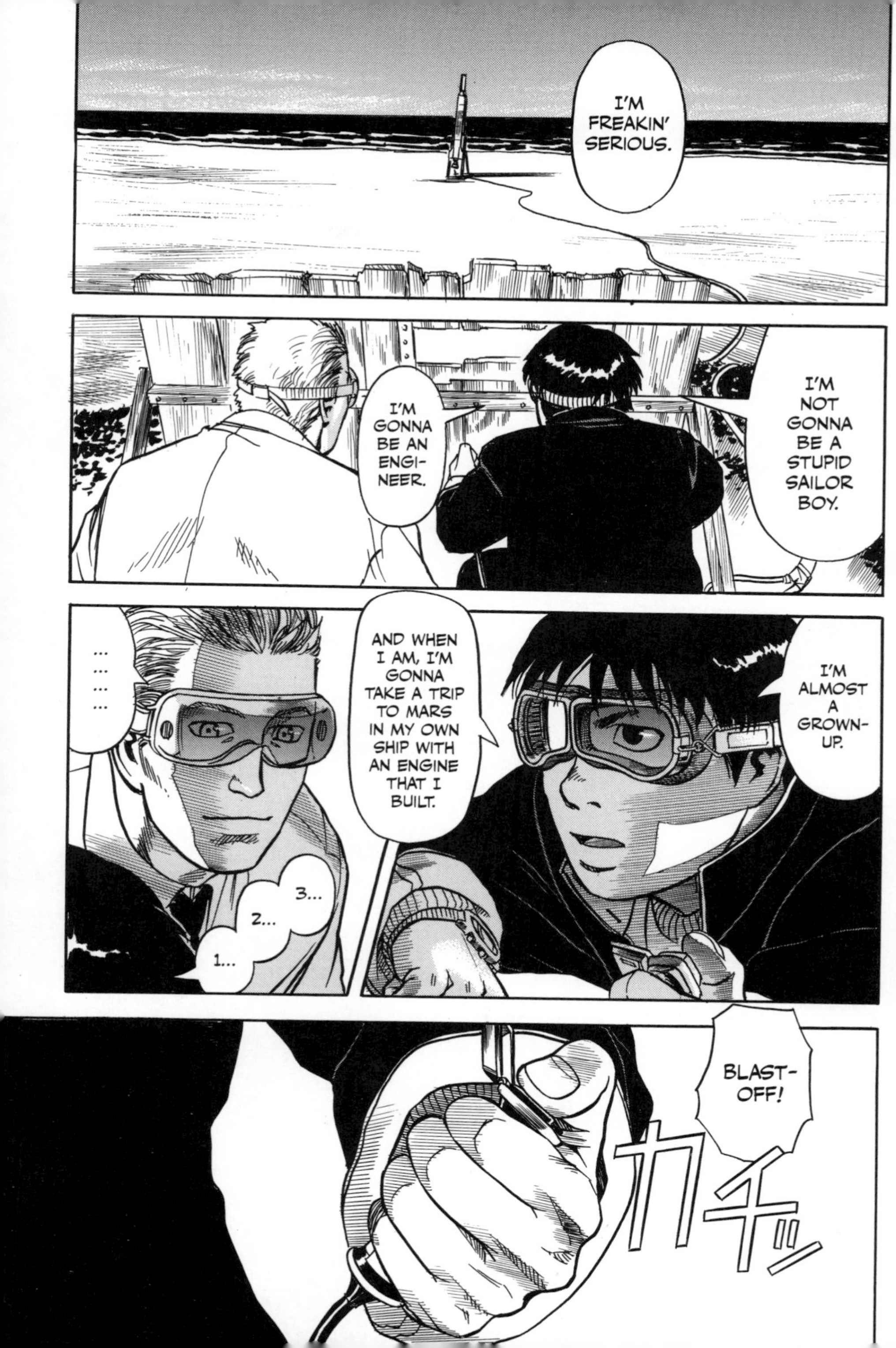
I'M FREAKIN' SERIOUS.
I'M NOT GONNA BE A STUPID SAILOR BOY.
I'M GONNA BE AN ENGI-NEER.
I'M ALMOST A GROWN-UP.
AND WHEN I AM, I'M GONNA TAKE A TRIP TO MARS IN MY OWN SHIP WITH AN ENGINE THAT I BUILT.
... ...
3... 2... 1...
BLAST-OFF!
カチッ

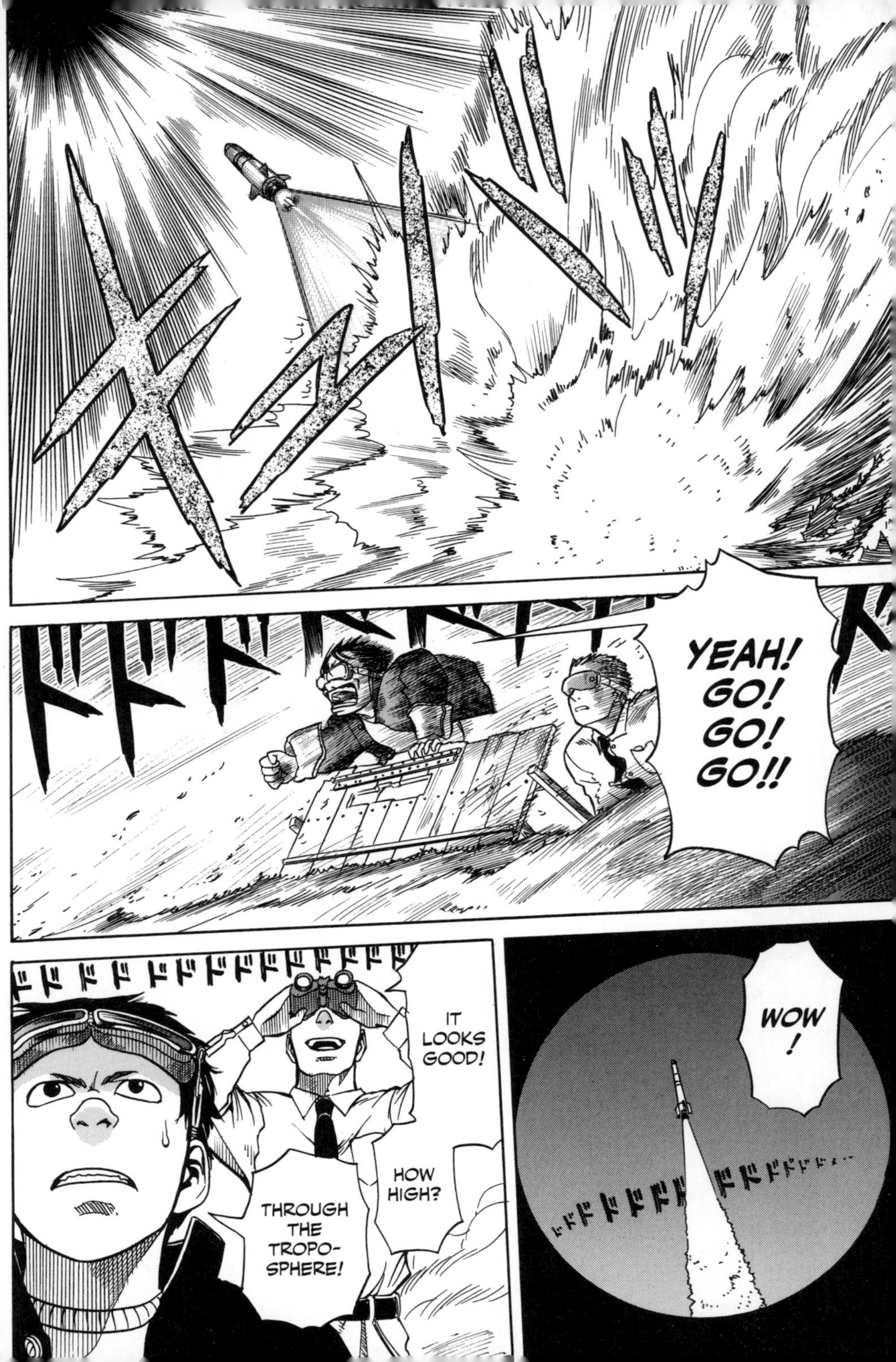
YEAH! GO! GO! GO!!
WOW!
IT LOOKS GOOD!
HOW HIGH?
THROUGH THE TROPOSPHERE!

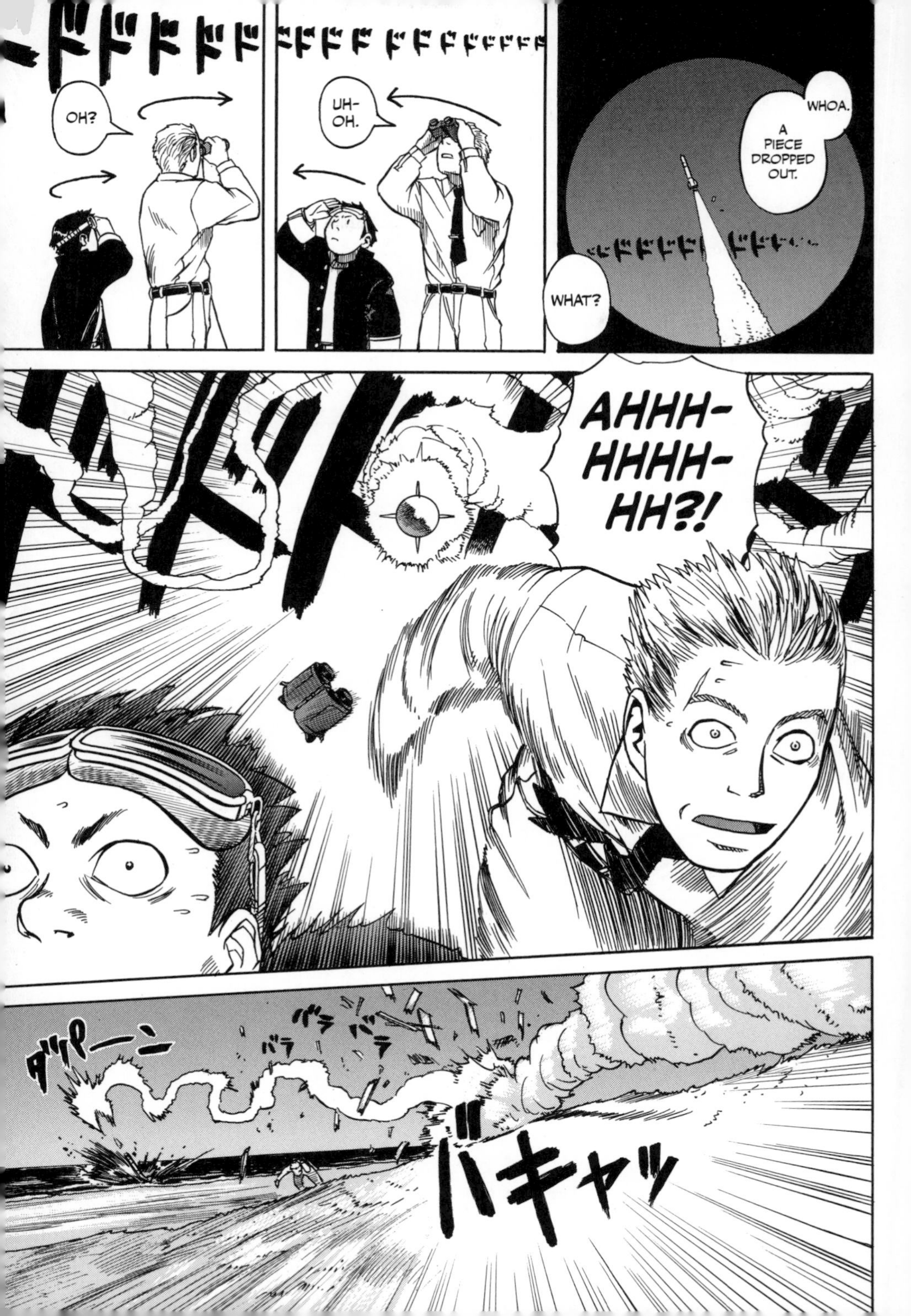
WHOA.
A PIECE DROPPED OUT.
WHAT?
UH-OH.
OH?
AHHH-HHHH-HH?!
バラ
バラ
バキャッ

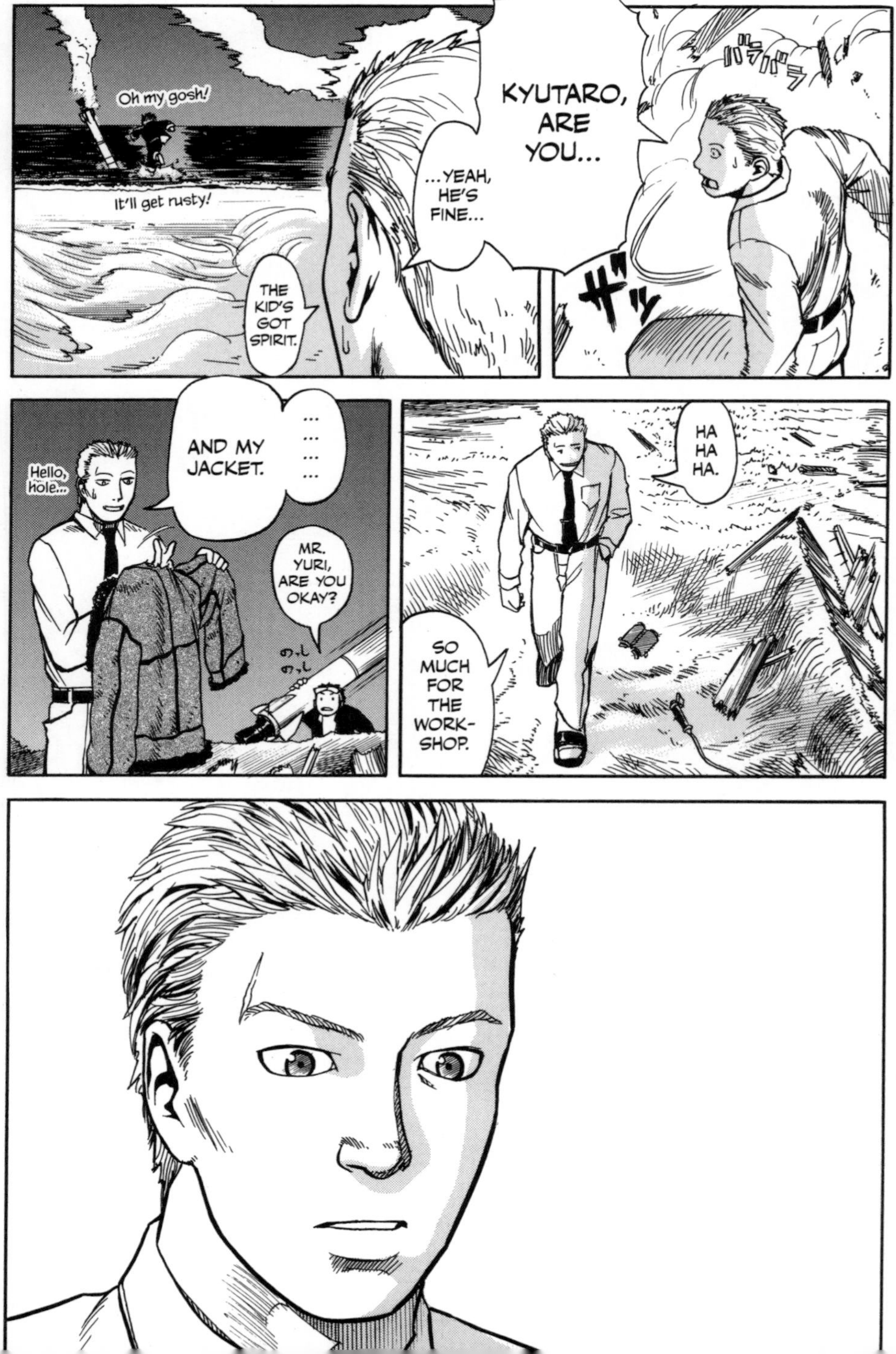
KYUTARO, ARE YOU...
バラバラ
ザッ
...YEAH, HE'S FINE...
THE KID'S GOT SPIRIT.
Oh my gosh!
It'll get rusty!
HA HA HA.
SO MUCH FOR THE WORK-SHOP.
... ...
AND MY JACKET.
Hello, hole...
MR. YURI, ARE YOU OKAY?
のし のし

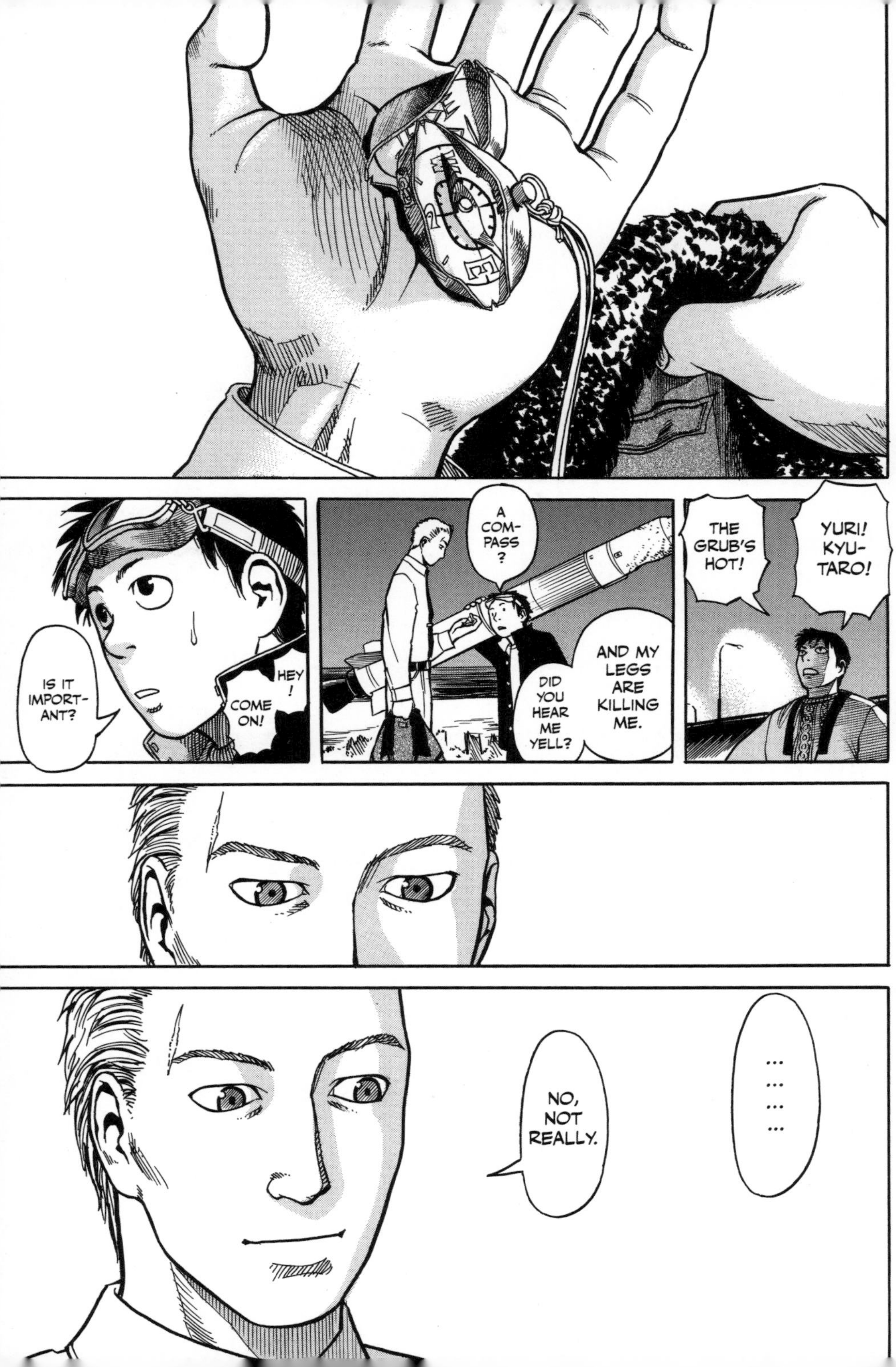
YURI! KYU-TARO!
THE GRUB'S HOT!
A COM-PASS?
AND MY LEGS ARE KILLING ME.
DID YOU HEAR ME YELL?
HEY!
COME ON!
IS IT IMPORT-ANT?
... ...
NO, NOT REALLY.

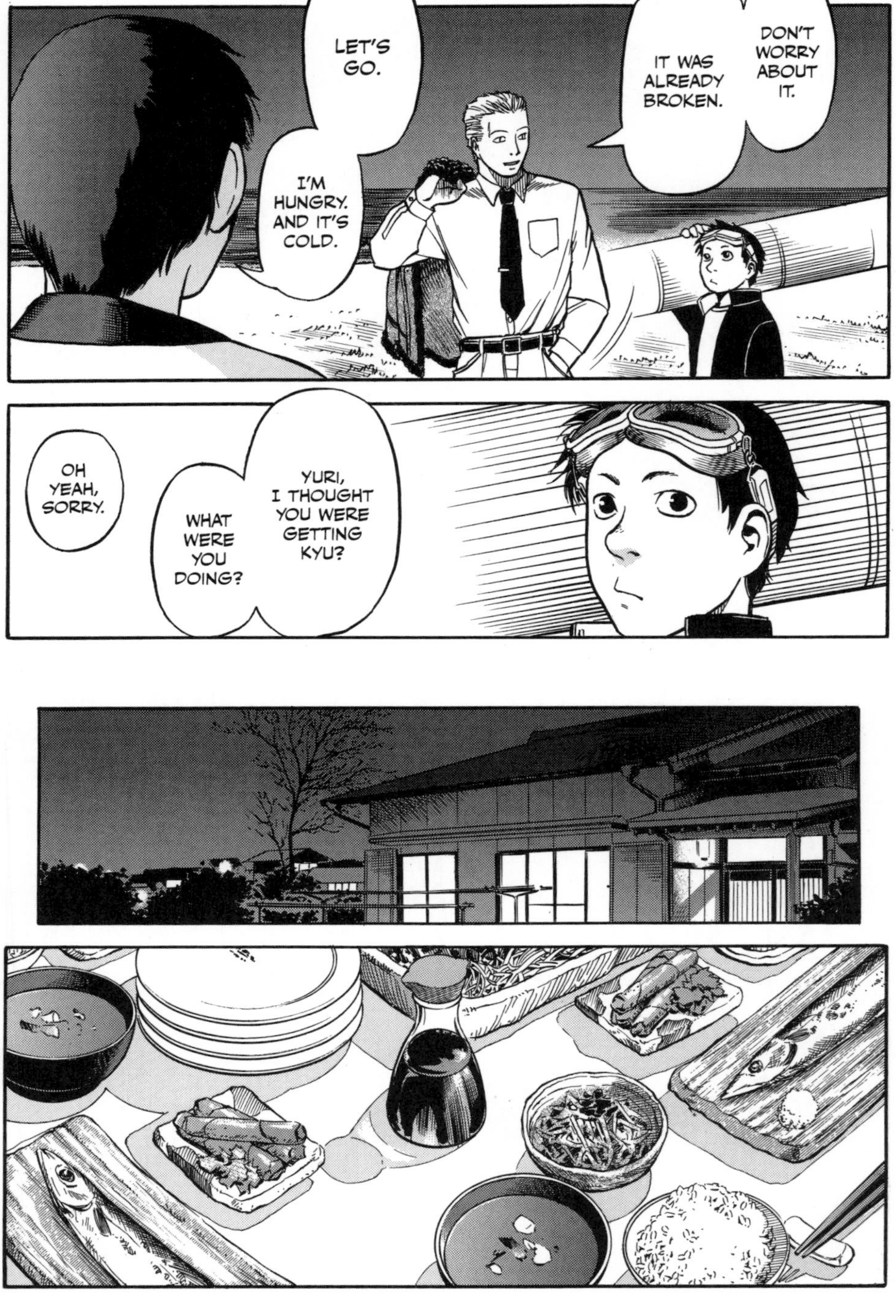
DON'T WORRY ABOUT IT.
IT WAS ALREADY BROKEN.
LET'S GO.
I'M HUNGRY. AND IT'S COLD.
YURI, I THOUGHT YOU WERE GETTING KYU?
WHAT WERE YOU DOING?
OH YEAH, SORRY.

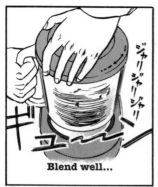

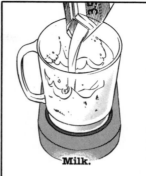

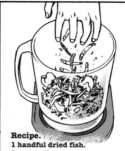

Recipe.
1 handful dried fish.
2 egg shells.
100g. dried baby sardines.
Anything else that suits your fancy.
Milk.
ジャリジャリジャリ
ギュ〜〜
Blend well...
ジャリジャリジャリ
ギュ〜〜〜ン
...and chug!
タンッ

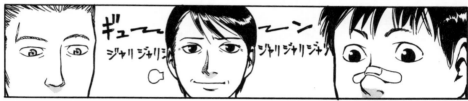

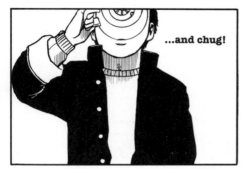

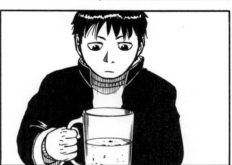

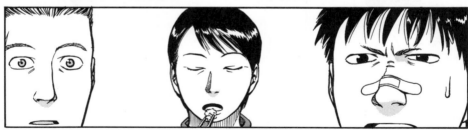

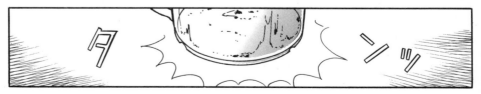

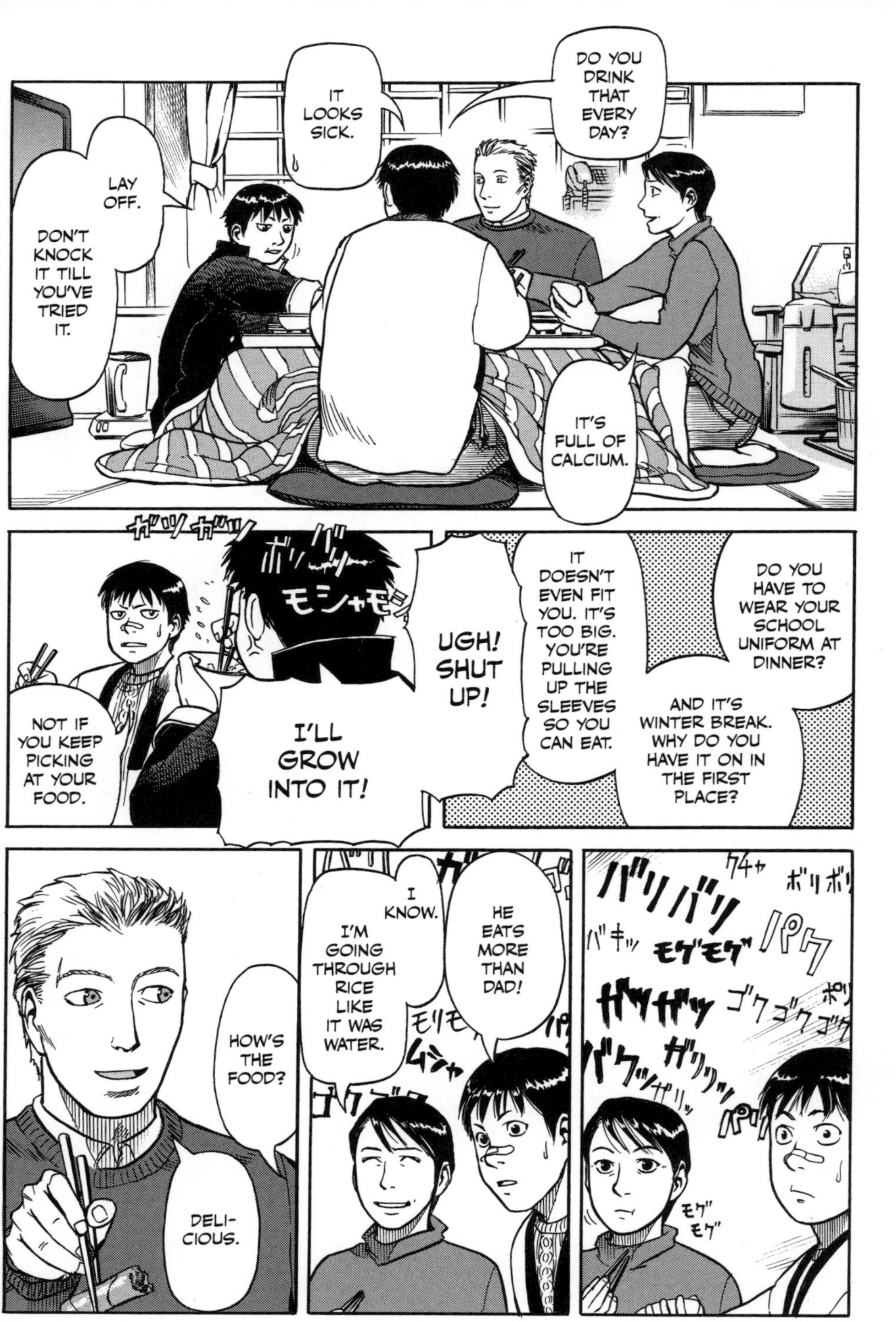
DO YOU DRINK THAT EVERY DAY?
IT LOOKS SICK.
LAY OFF.
DON'T KNOCK IT TILL YOU'VE TRIED IT.
IT'S FULL OF CALCIUM.
DO YOU HAVE TO WEAR YOUR SCHOOL UNIFORM AT DINNER?
AND IT'S WINTER BREAK. WHY DO YOU HAVE IT ON IN THE FIRST PLACE?
IT DOESN'T EVEN FIT YOU. IT'S TOO BIG. YOU'RE PULLING UP THE SLEEVES SO YOU CAN EAT.
UGH! SHUT UP!
I'LL GROW INTO IT!
NOT IF YOU KEEP PICKING AT YOUR FOOD.
クチャ
ボリボリ
バリバリ
パク
バキッ
モグモグ
ガツガツ
ゴクゴク
HE EATS MORE THAN DAD!
I KNOW.
I'M GOING THROUGH RICE LIKE IT WAS WATER.
HOW'S THE FOOD?
DELICIOUS.

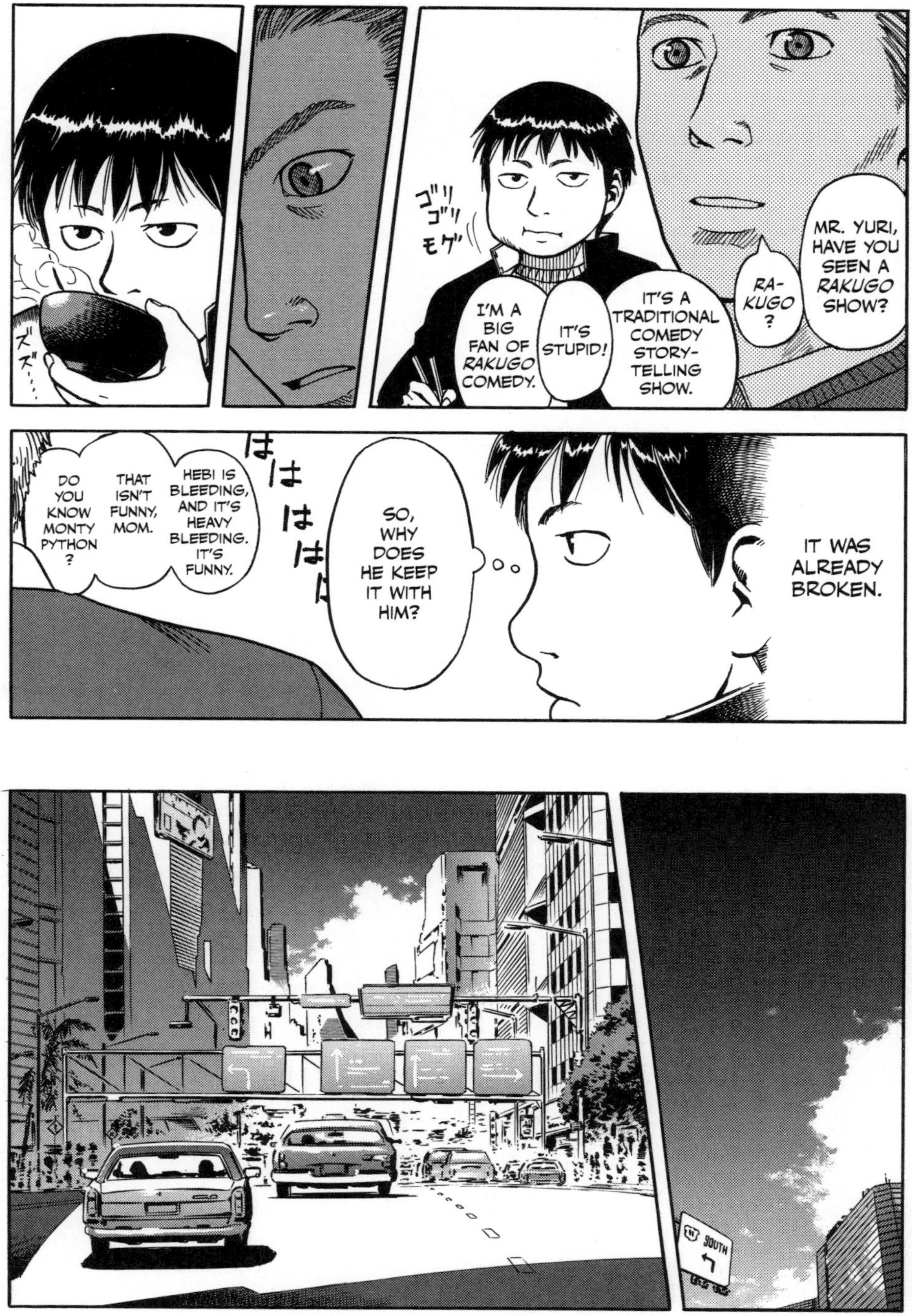
MR. YURI, HAVE YOU SEEN A RAKUGO SHOW?
RAKUGO?
IT'S A TRADITIONAL COMEDY STORY-TELLING SHOW.
IT'S STUPID!
I'M A BIG FAN OF RAKUGO COMEDY.
ゴリゴリモグ
ズズ…
IT WAS ALREADY BROKEN.
SO, WHY DOES HE KEEP IT WITH HIM?
ははは
HEBI IS BLEEDING, AND IT'S HEAVY BLEEDING. IT'S FUNNY.
THAT ISN'T FUNNY, MOM.
DO YOU KNOW MONTY PYTHON?
SOUTH

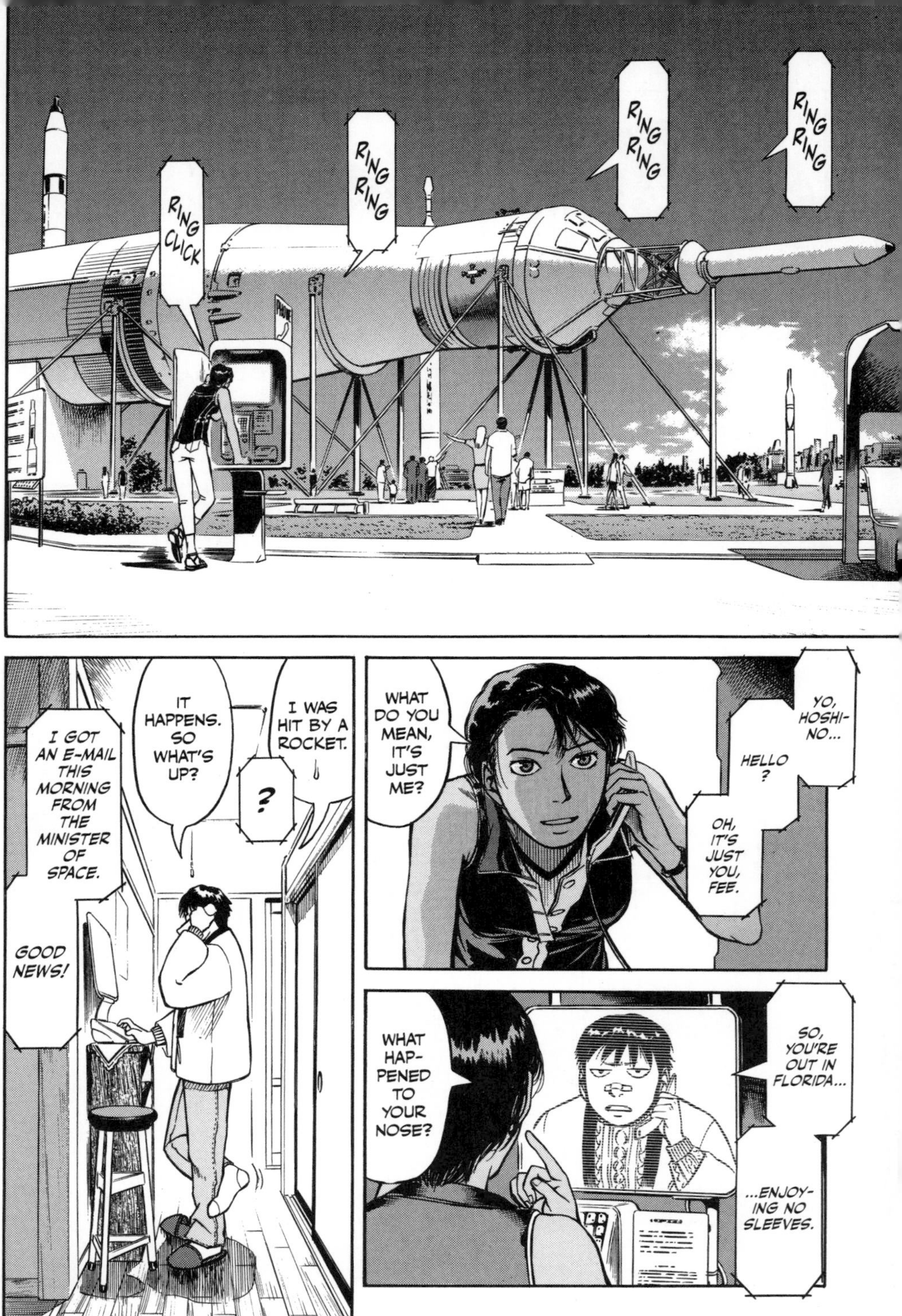
RING RING
RING RING
RING RING
RING CLICK
YO, HOSHINO...
HELLO ?
OH, IT'S JUST YOU, FEE.
WHAT DO YOU MEAN, IT'S JUST ME?
SO, YOU'RE OUT IN FLORIDA...
...ENJOYING NO SLEEVES.
WHAT HAPPENED TO YOUR NOSE?
I WAS HIT BY A ROCKET.
?
IT HAPPENS. SO WHAT'S UP?
I GOT AN E-MAIL THIS MORNING FROM THE MINISTER OF SPACE.
GOOD NEWS!

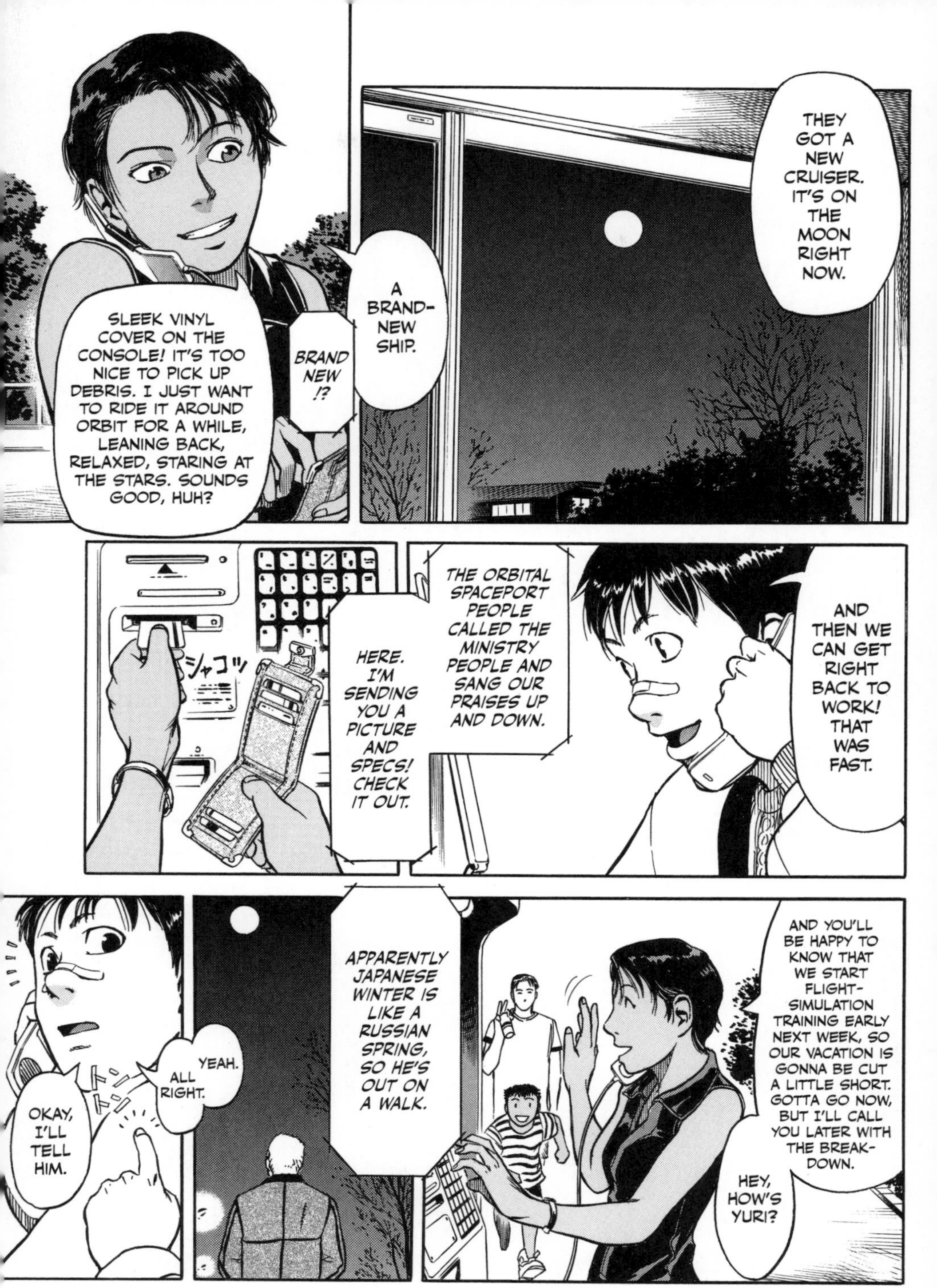
THEY GOT A NEW CRUISER. IT'S ON THE MOON RIGHT NOW.
A BRAND-NEW SHIP.
BRAND NEW !?
SLEEK VINYL COVER ON THE CONSOLE! IT'S TOO NICE TO PICK UP DEBRIS. I JUST WANT TO RIDE IT AROUND ORBIT FOR A WHILE, LEANING BACK, RELAXED, STARING AT THE STARS. SOUNDS GOOD, HUH?
AND THEN WE CAN GET RIGHT BACK TO WORK! THAT WAS FAST.
THE ORBITAL SPACEPORT PEOPLE CALLED THE MINISTRY PEOPLE AND SANG OUR PRAISES UP AND DOWN.
HERE. I'M SENDING YOU A PICTURE AND SPECS! CHECK IT OUT.
シャコッ
AND YOU'LL BE HAPPY TO KNOW THAT WE START FLIGHT-SIMULATION TRAINING EARLY NEXT WEEK, SO OUR VACATION IS GONNA BE CUT A LITTLE SHORT. GOTTA GO NOW, BUT I'LL CALL YOU LATER WITH THE BREAK-DOWN.
HEY, HOW'S YURI?
APPARENTLY JAPANESE WINTER IS LIKE A RUSSIAN SPRING, SO HE'S OUT ON A WALK.
YEAH.
ALL RIGHT.
トントン
OKAY, I'LL TELL HIM.

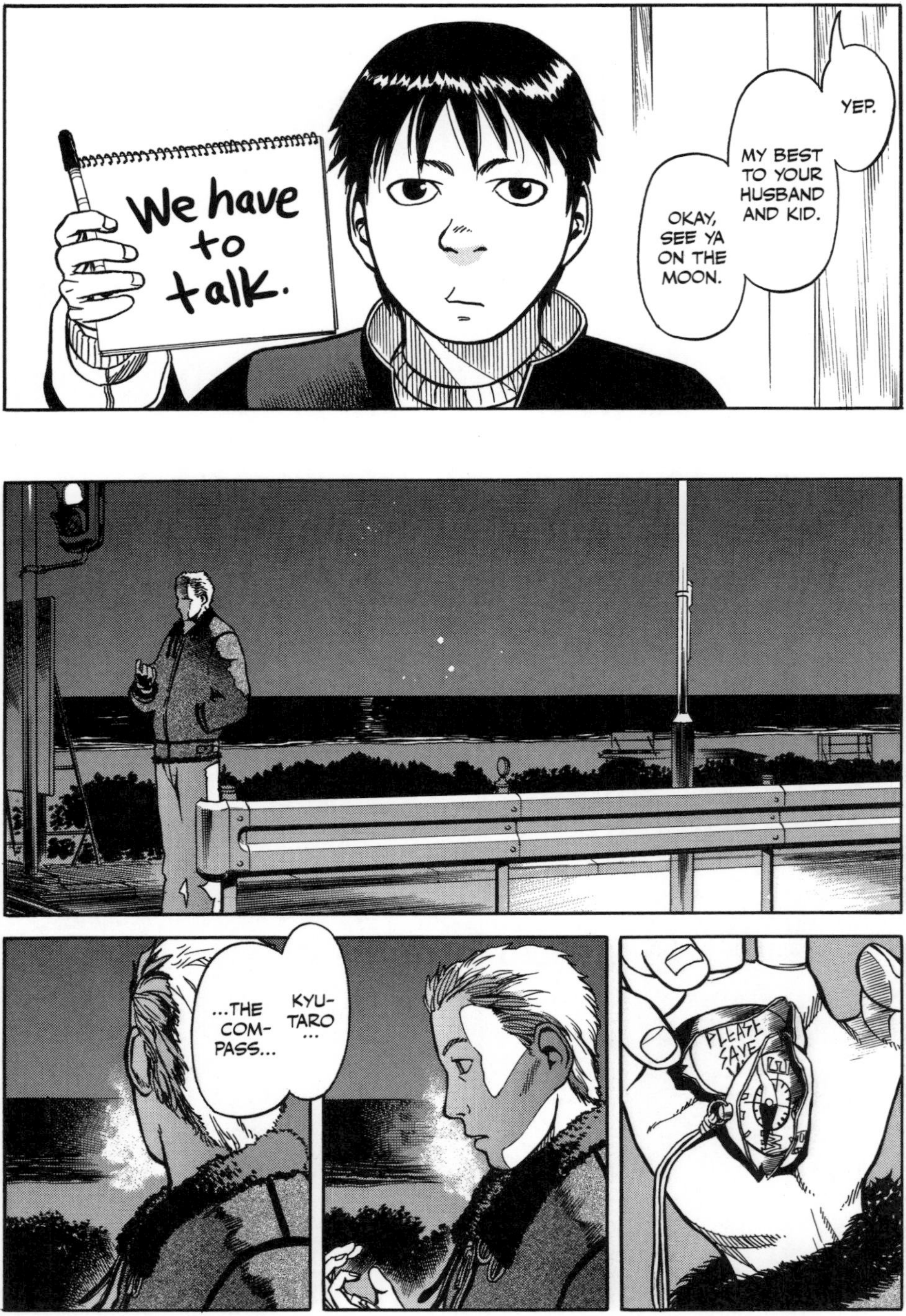
YEP.
MY BEST TO YOUR HUSBAND AND KID.
OKAY, SEE YA ON THE MOON.
We have to talk.
PLEASE SAVE
KYU-TARO ...
...THE COM-PASS...

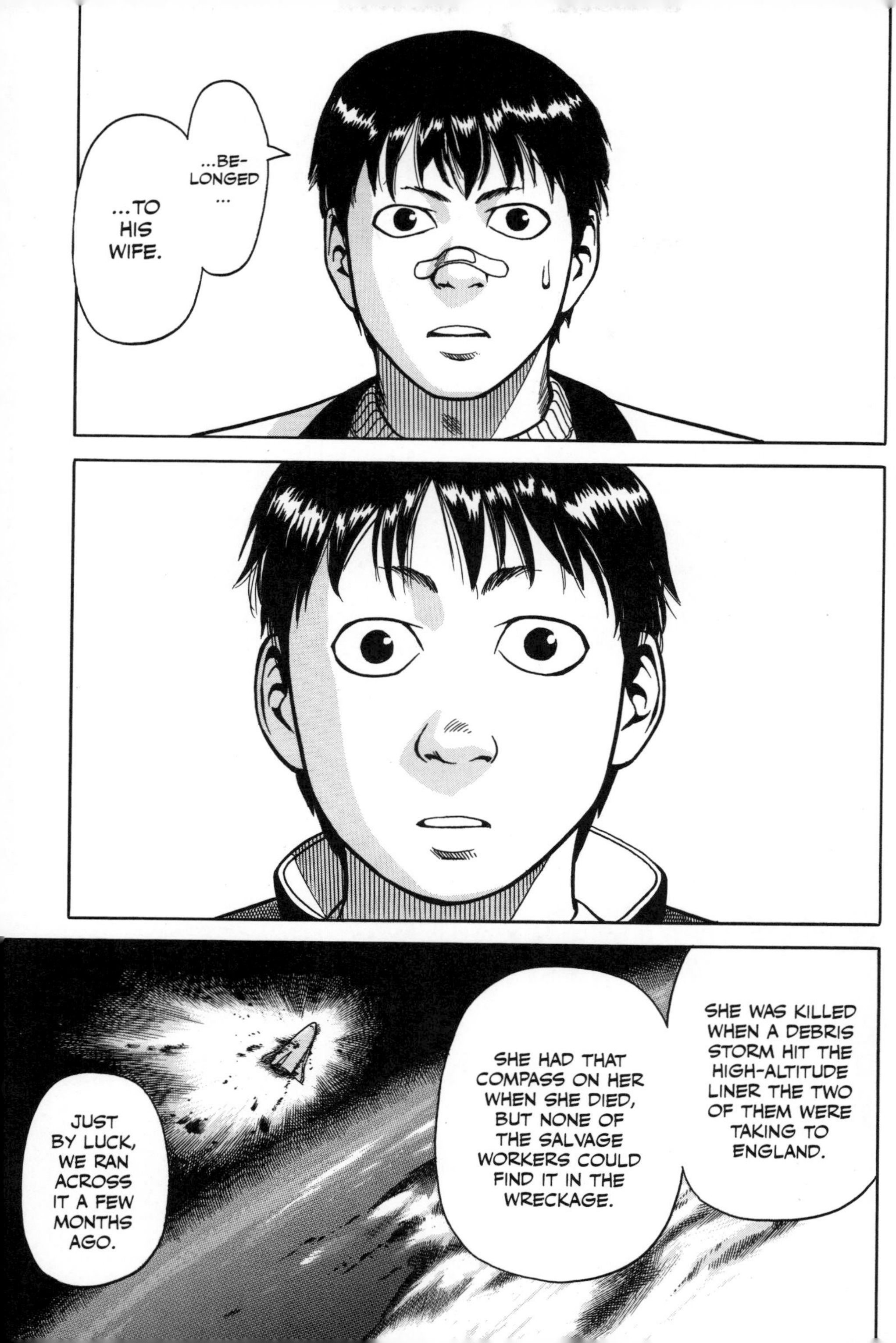
...BE-
LONGED
...
...TO
HIS
WIFE.
SHE WAS KILLED WHEN A DEBRIS STORM HIT THE HIGH-ALTITUDE LINER THE TWO OF THEM WERE TAKING TO ENGLAND.
SHE HAD THAT COMPASS ON HER WHEN SHE DIED, BUT NONE OF THE SALVAGE WORKERS COULD FIND IT IN THE WRECKAGE.
JUST BY LUCK, WE RAN ACROSS IT A FEW MONTHS AGO.

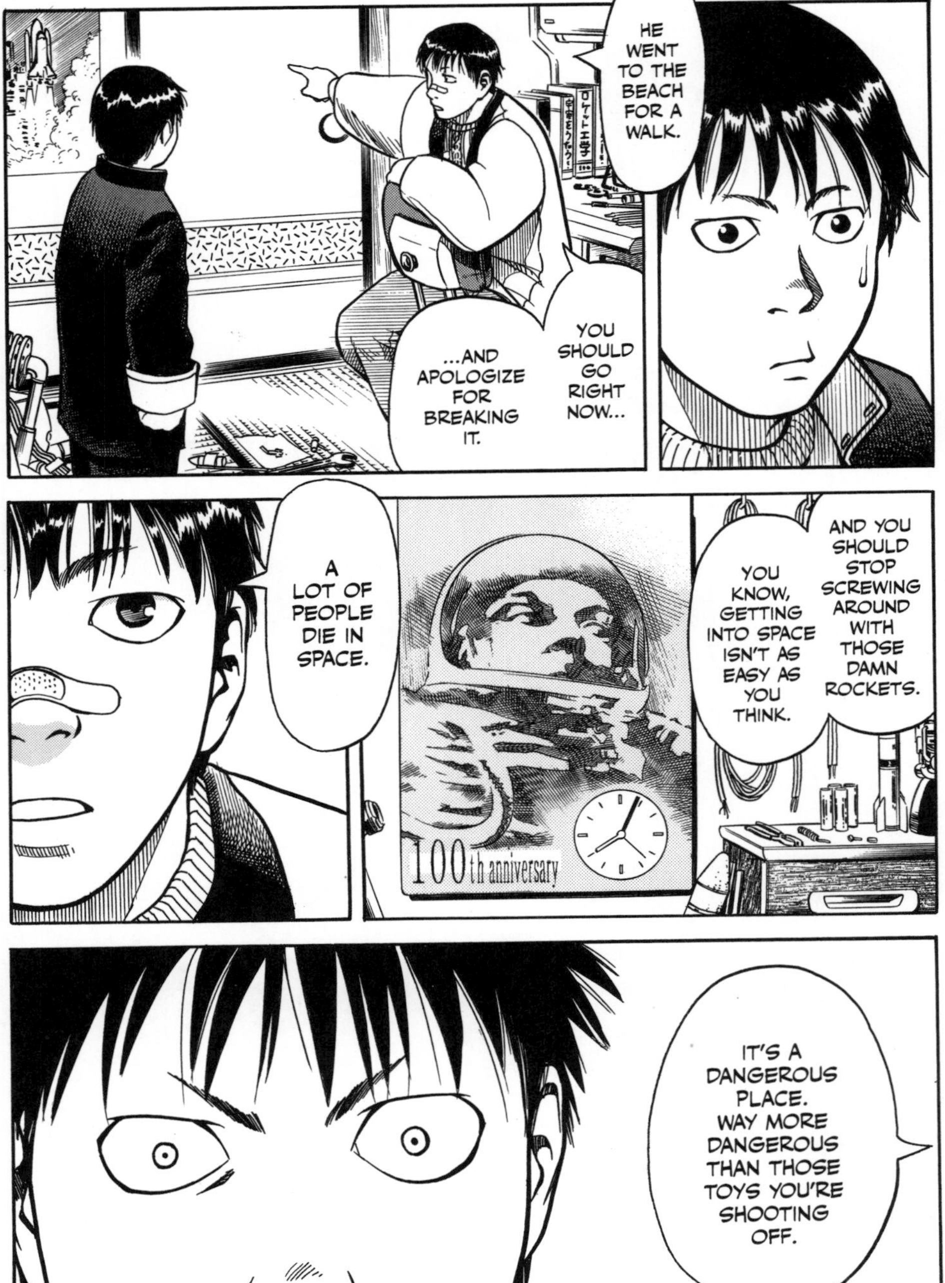
HE WENT TO THE BEACH FOR A WALK.
YOU SHOULD GO RIGHT NOW...
...AND APOLOGIZE FOR BREAKING IT.
AND YOU SHOULD STOP SCREWING AROUND WITH THOSE DAMN ROCKETS.
YOU KNOW, GETTING INTO SPACE ISN'T AS EASY AS YOU THINK.
100th anniversary
A LOT OF PEOPLE DIE IN SPACE.
IT'S A DANGEROUS PLACE. WAY MORE DANGEROUS THAN THOSE TOYS YOU'RE SHOOTING OFF.

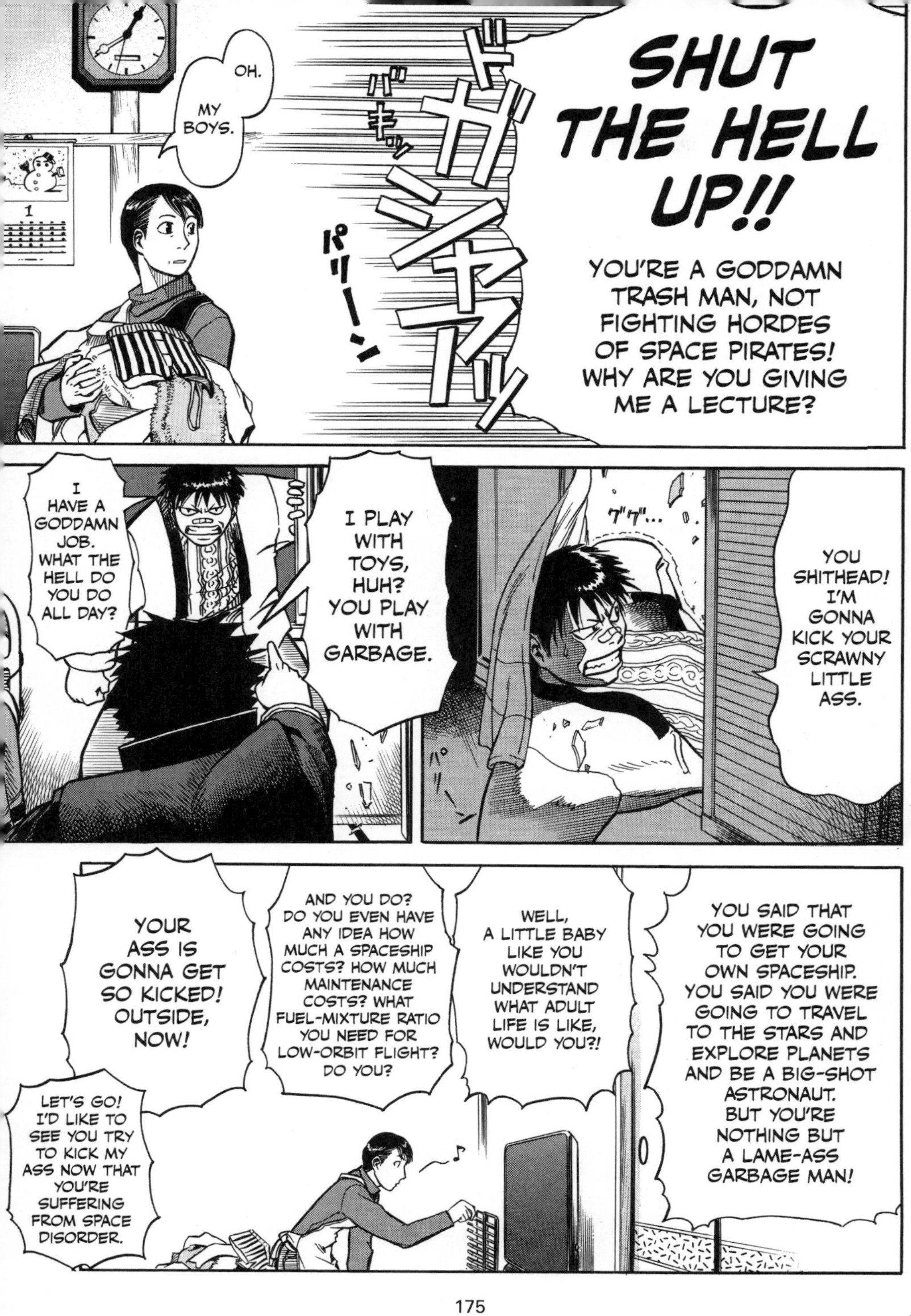
SHUT THE HELL UP!!
YOU'RE A GODDAMN TRASH MAN, NOT FIGHTING HORDES OF SPACE PIRATES! WHY ARE YOU GIVING ME A LECTURE?
ドガシャアッ
バキッ
パリーン
OH.
MY BOYS.
YOU SHITHEAD! I'M GONNA KICK YOUR SCRAWNY LITTLE ASS.
I PLAY WITH TOYS, HUH? YOU PLAY WITH GARBAGE.
I HAVE A GODDAMN JOB. WHAT THE HELL DO YOU DO ALL DAY?
YOU SAID THAT YOU WERE GOING TO GET YOUR OWN SPACESHIP. YOU SAID YOU WERE GOING TO TRAVEL TO THE STARS AND EXPLORE PLANETS AND BE A BIG-SHOT ASTRONAUT. BUT YOU'RE NOTHING BUT A LAME-ASS GARBAGE MAN!
WELL, A LITTLE BABY LIKE YOU WOULDN'T UNDERSTAND WHAT ADULT LIFE IS LIKE, WOULD YOU?!
AND YOU DO? DO YOU EVEN HAVE ANY IDEA HOW MUCH A SPACESHIP COSTS? HOW MUCH MAINTENANCE COSTS? WHAT FUEL-MIXTURE RATIO YOU NEED FOR LOW-ORBIT FLIGHT? DO YOU?
YOUR ASS IS GONNA GET SO KICKED! OUTSIDE, NOW!
LET'S GO! I'D LIKE TO SEE YOU TRY TO KICK MY ASS NOW THAT YOU'RE SUFFERING FROM SPACE DISORDER.

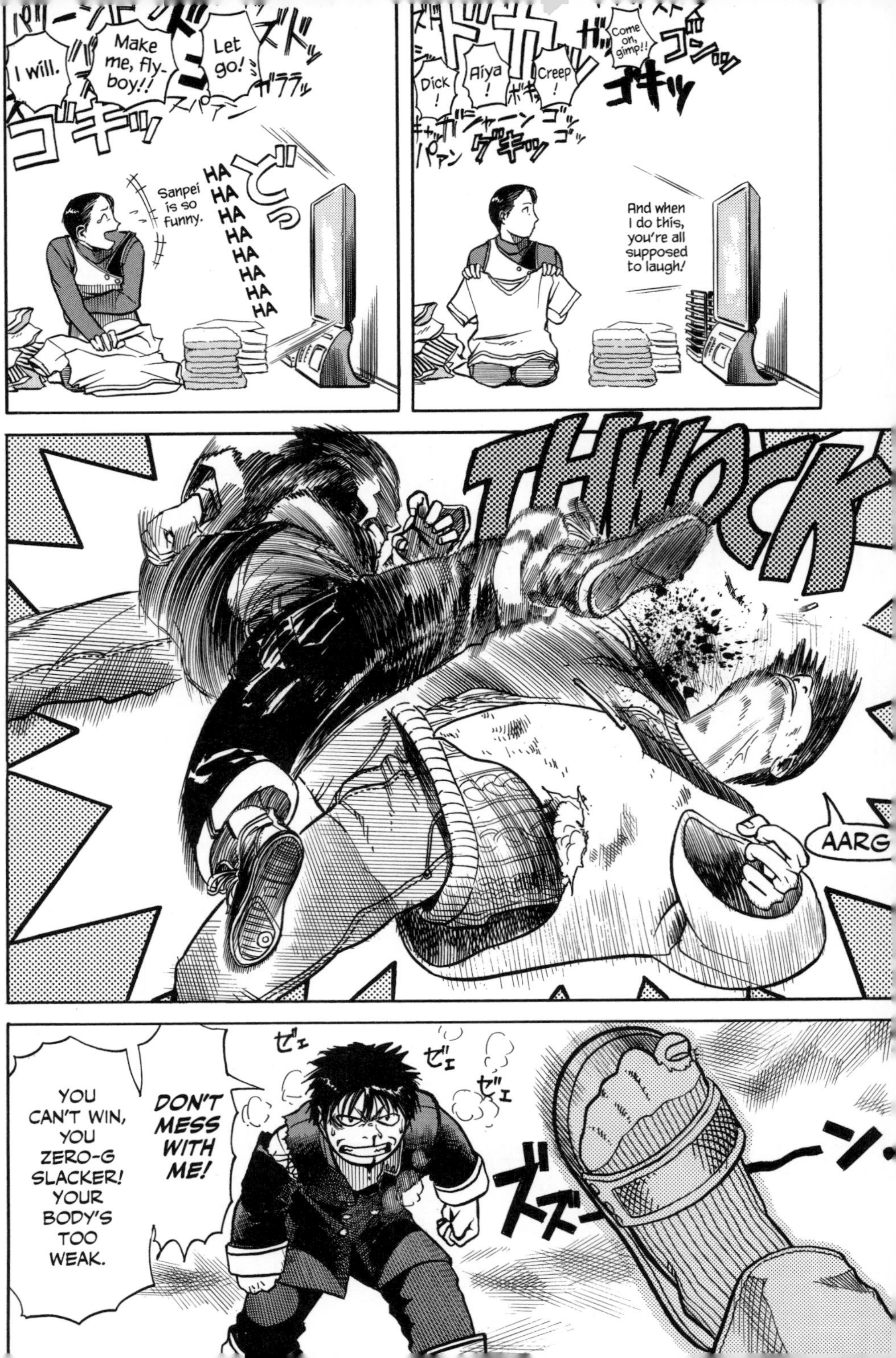
Come on, gimp!!
Creep!
Aiya!
Dick!
And when I do this, you're all supposed to laugh!
Let go!
Make me, fly-boy!!
I will.
HA HA HA HA HA HA HA HA
Sanpei is so funny.
THWOCK
AARG
DON'T MESS WITH ME!
YOU CAN'T WIN, YOU ZERO-G SLACKER! YOUR BODY'S TOO WEAK.

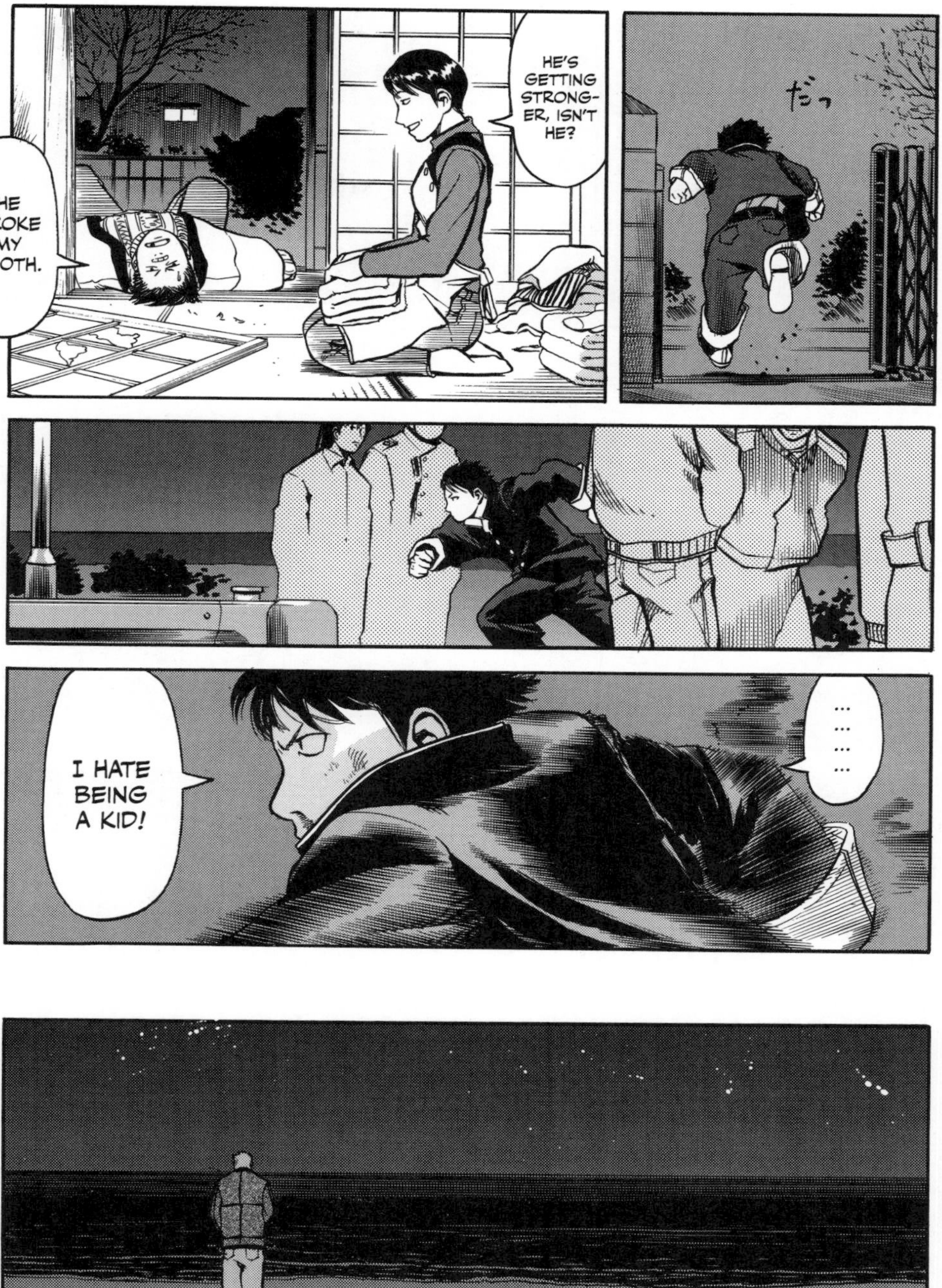
だっ
HE'S GETTING STRONGER, ISN'T HE?
HE BROKE MY TOOTH.
....
I HATE BEING A KID!

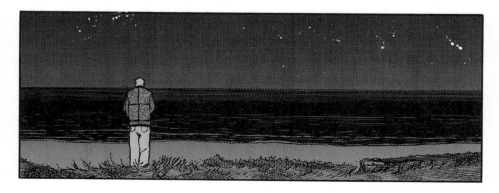

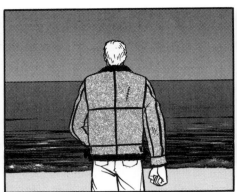

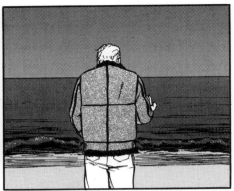

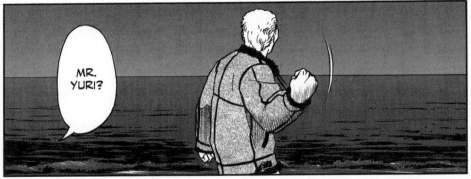

MR. YURI?
HEY, KYU. WHAT'RE YOU DOIN' UP?
EVENING LAUNCH?
ジャリ.
... ...
UM, THAT COMPASS ...

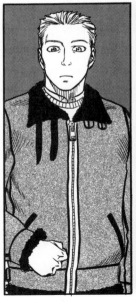

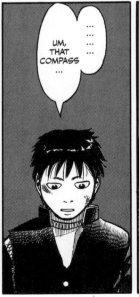

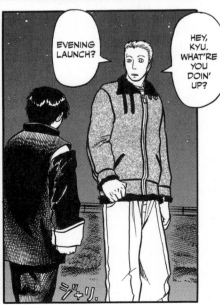

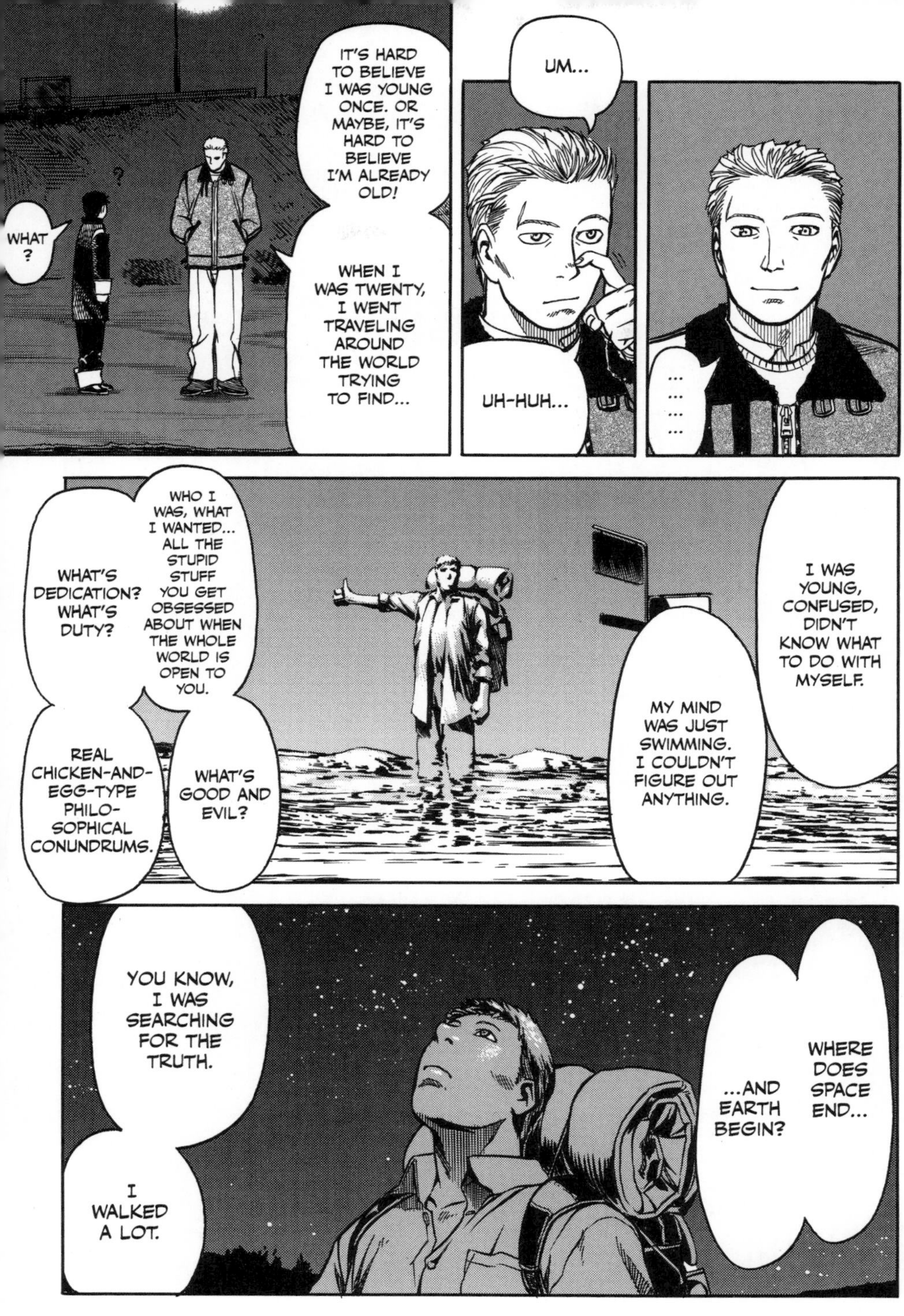
... ...
UM...
UH-HUH...
IT'S HARD TO BELIEVE I WAS YOUNG ONCE. OR MAYBE, IT'S HARD TO BELIEVE I'M ALREADY OLD!
WHEN I WAS TWENTY, I WENT TRAVELING AROUND THE WORLD TRYING TO FIND...
WHAT?
I WAS YOUNG, CONFUSED, DIDN'T KNOW WHAT TO DO WITH MYSELF.
MY MIND WAS JUST SWIMMING. I COULDN'T FIGURE OUT ANYTHING.
WHO I WAS, WHAT I WANTED... ALL THE STUPID STUFF YOU GET OBSESSED ABOUT WHEN THE WHOLE WORLD IS OPEN TO YOU.
WHAT'S DEDICATION? WHAT'S DUTY?
WHAT'S GOOD AND EVIL?
REAL CHICKEN-AND-EGG-TYPE PHILOSOPHICAL CONUNDRUMS.
WHERE DOES SPACE END...
...AND EARTH BEGIN?
YOU KNOW, I WAS SEARCHING FOR THE TRUTH.
I WALKED A LOT.

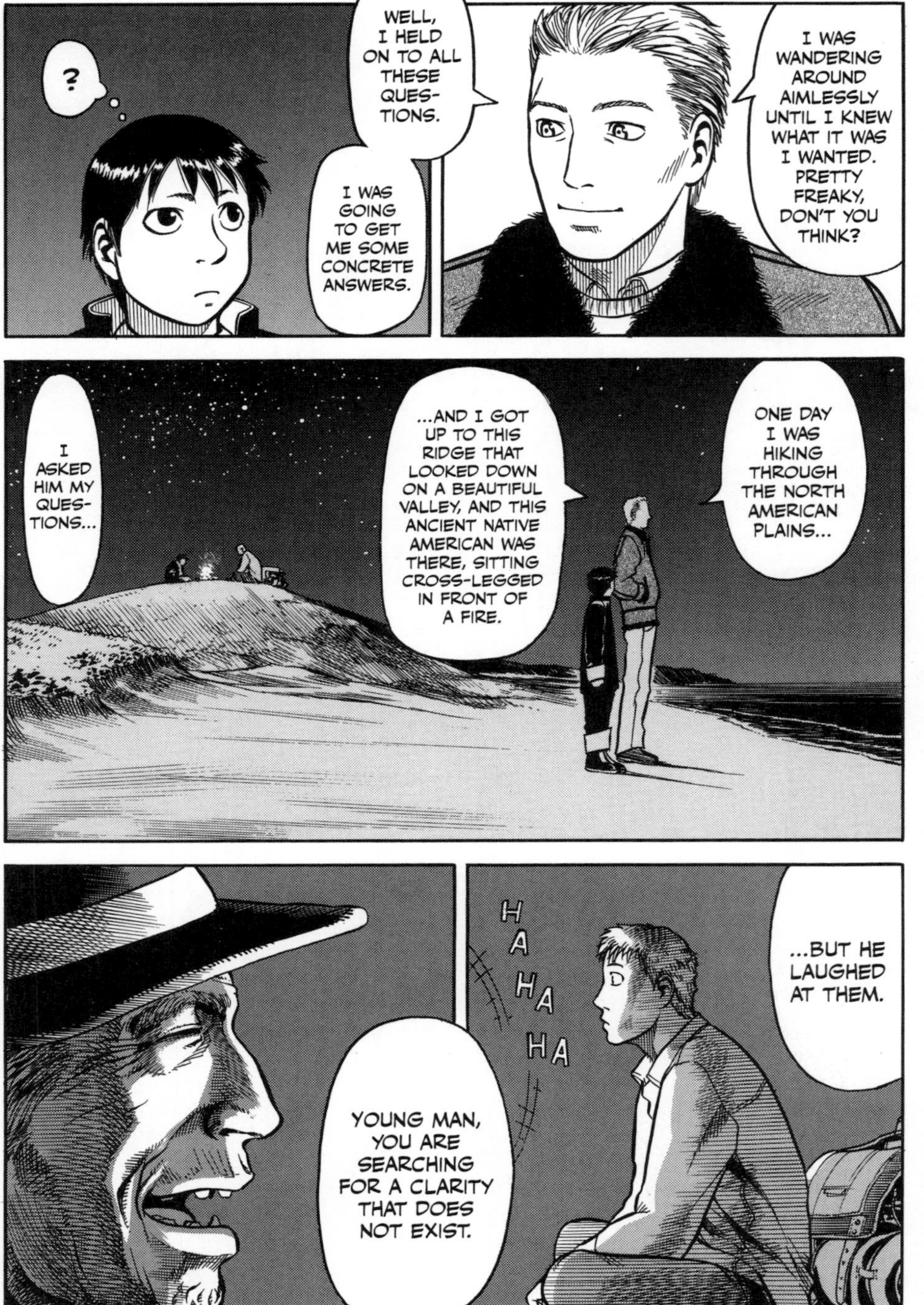
I WAS WANDERING AROUND AIMLESSLY UNTIL I KNEW WHAT IT WAS I WANTED. PRETTY FREAKY, DON'T YOU THINK?
WELL, I HELD ON TO ALL THESE QUES-TIONS.
I WAS GOING TO GET ME SOME CONCRETE ANSWERS.
?
ONE DAY I WAS HIKING THROUGH THE NORTH AMERICAN PLAINS...
...AND I GOT UP TO THIS RIDGE THAT LOOKED DOWN ON A BEAUTIFUL VALLEY, AND THIS ANCIENT NATIVE AMERICAN WAS THERE, SITTING CROSS-LEGGED IN FRONT OF A FIRE.
I ASKED HIM MY QUES-TIONS...
...BUT HE LAUGHED AT THEM.
HA HA HA HA
YOUNG MAN, YOU ARE SEARCHING FOR A CLARITY THAT DOES NOT EXIST.

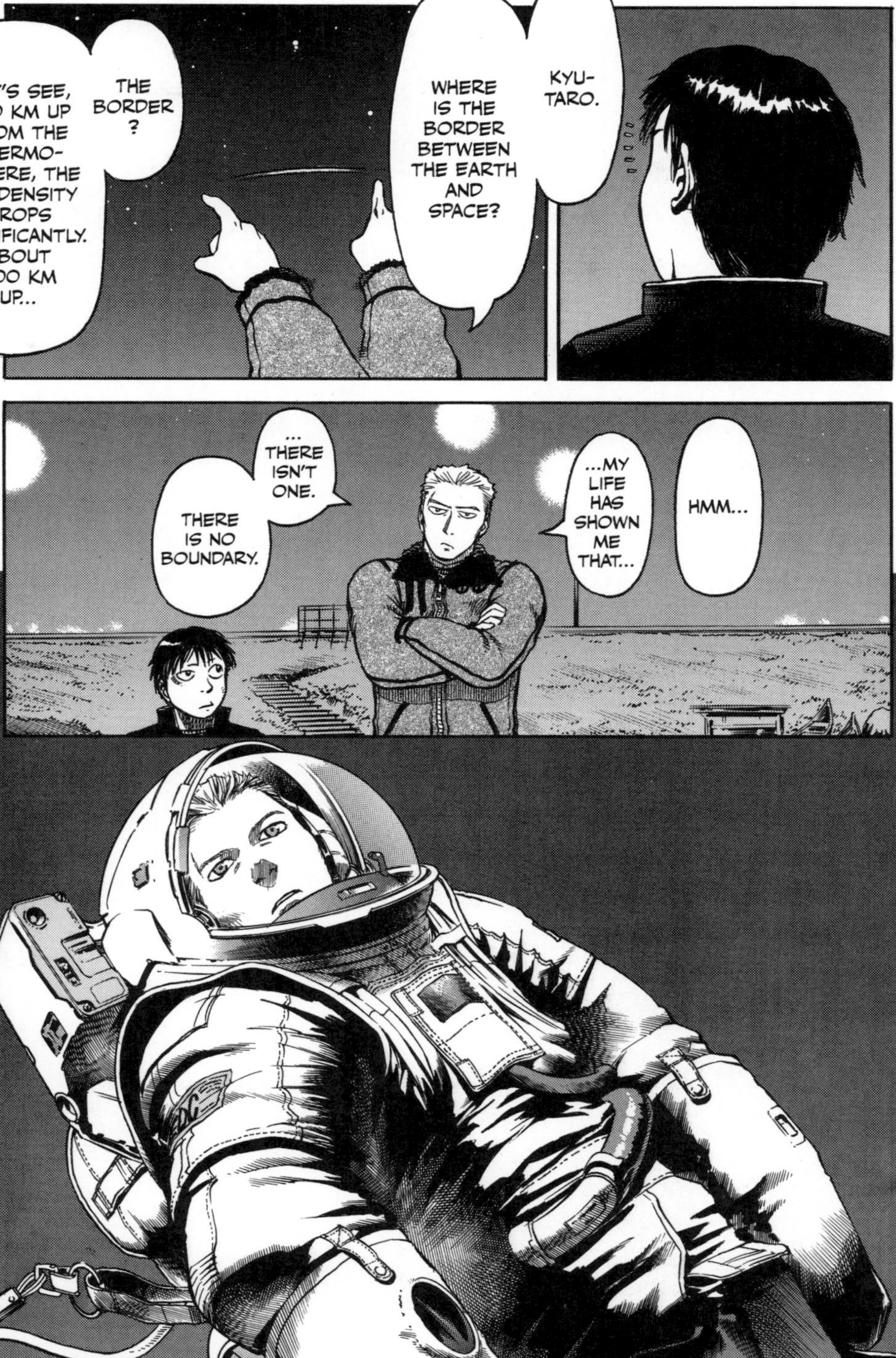
KYU-TARO.
WHERE IS THE BORDER BETWEEN THE EARTH AND SPACE?
THE BORDER?
LET'S SEE, 100 KM UP FROM THE THERMO-SPHERE, THE AIR DENSITY DROPS SIGNIFICANTLY. ABOUT 200 KM UP...
HMM...
...MY LIFE HAS SHOWN ME THAT...
... THERE ISN'T ONE.
THERE IS NO BOUNDARY.

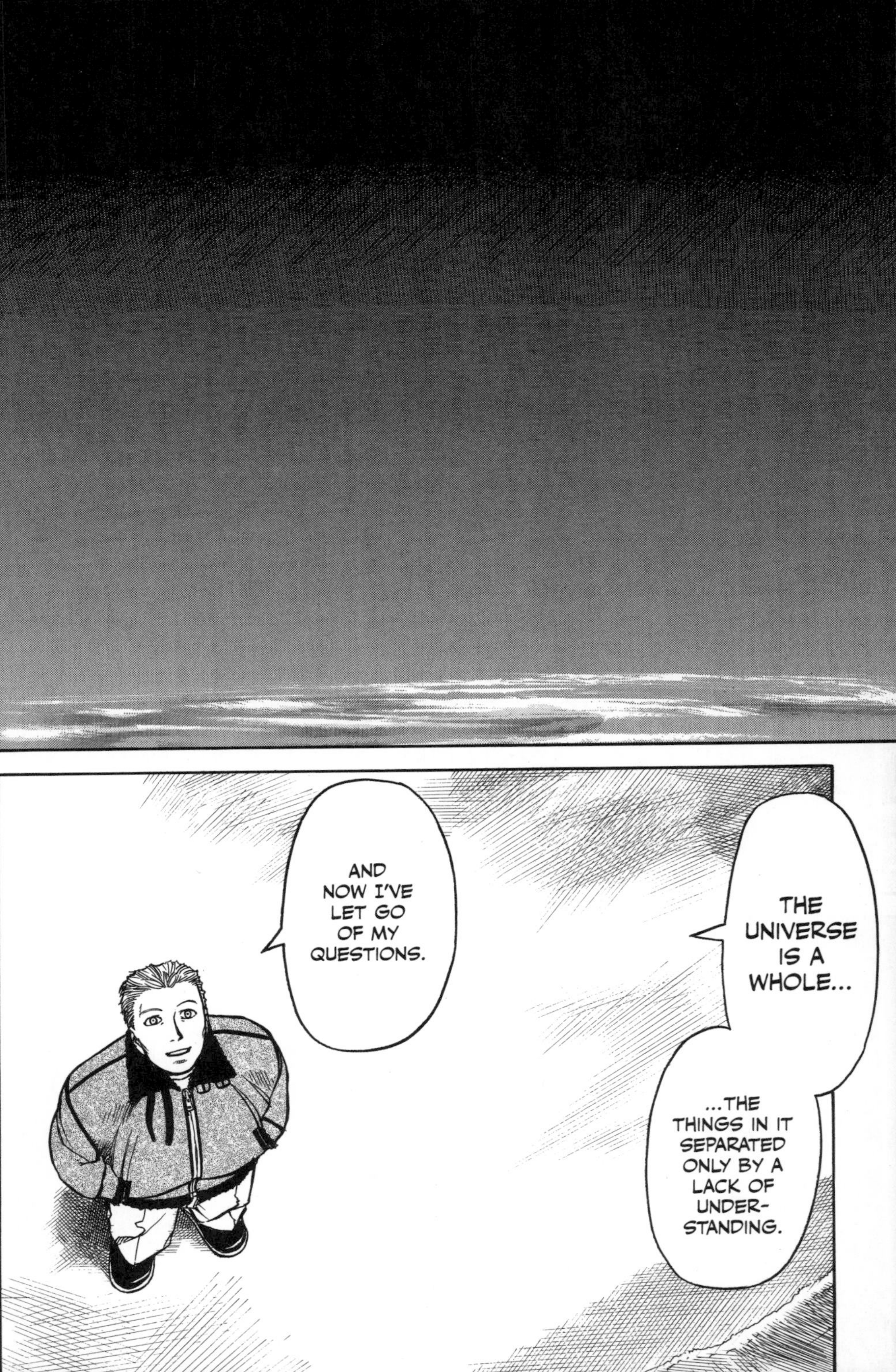
THE UNIVERSE IS A WHOLE...
...THE THINGS IN IT SEPARATED ONLY BY A LACK OF UNDER-STANDING.
AND NOW I'VE LET GO OF MY QUESTIONS.

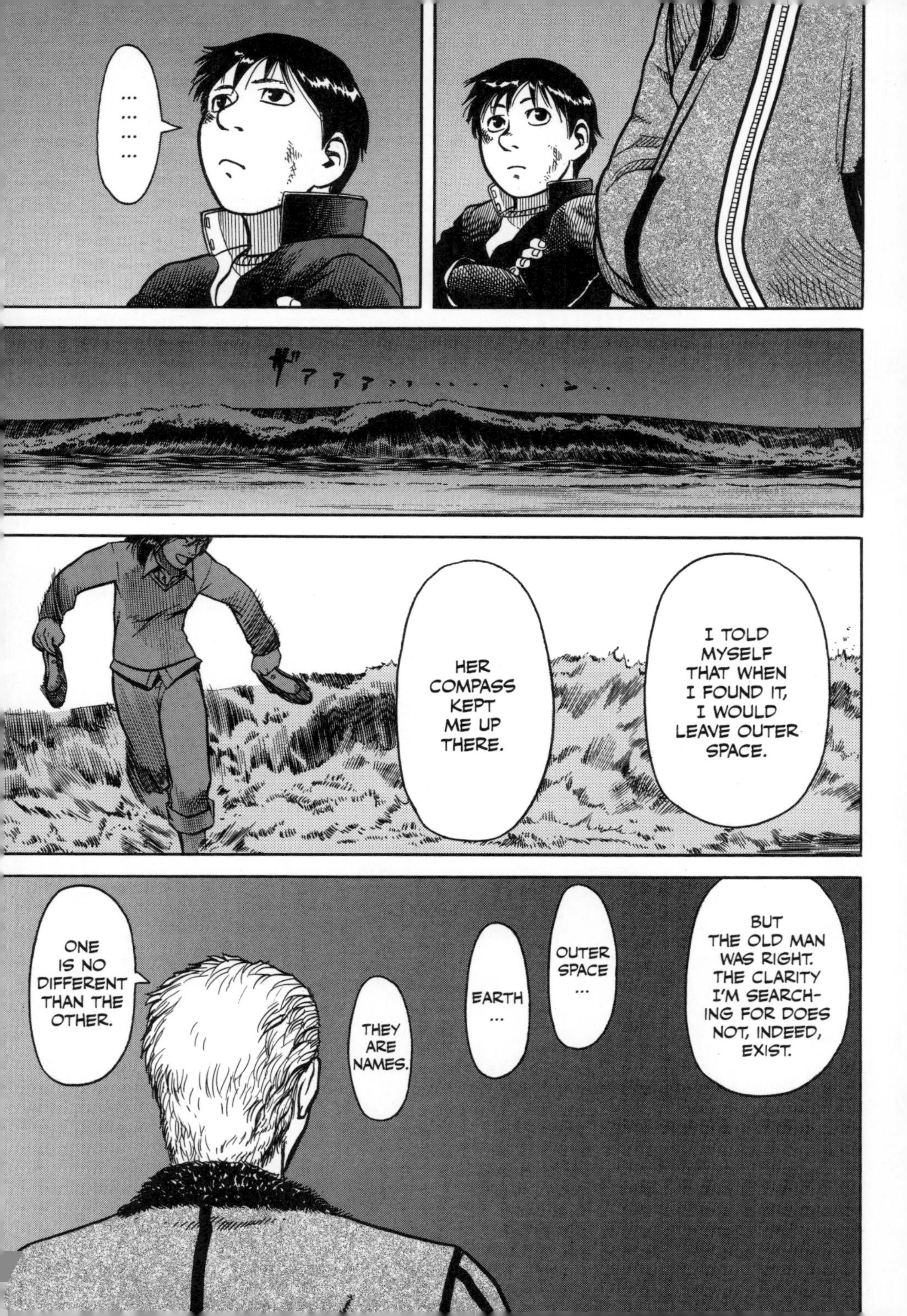
......
I TOLD MYSELF THAT WHEN I FOUND IT, I WOULD LEAVE OUTER SPACE.
HER COMPASS KEPT ME UP THERE.
BUT THE OLD MAN WAS RIGHT. THE CLARITY I'M SEARCHING FOR DOES NOT, INDEED, EXIST.
OUTER SPACE ...
EARTH ...
THEY ARE NAMES.
ONE IS NO DIFFERENT THAN THE OTHER.

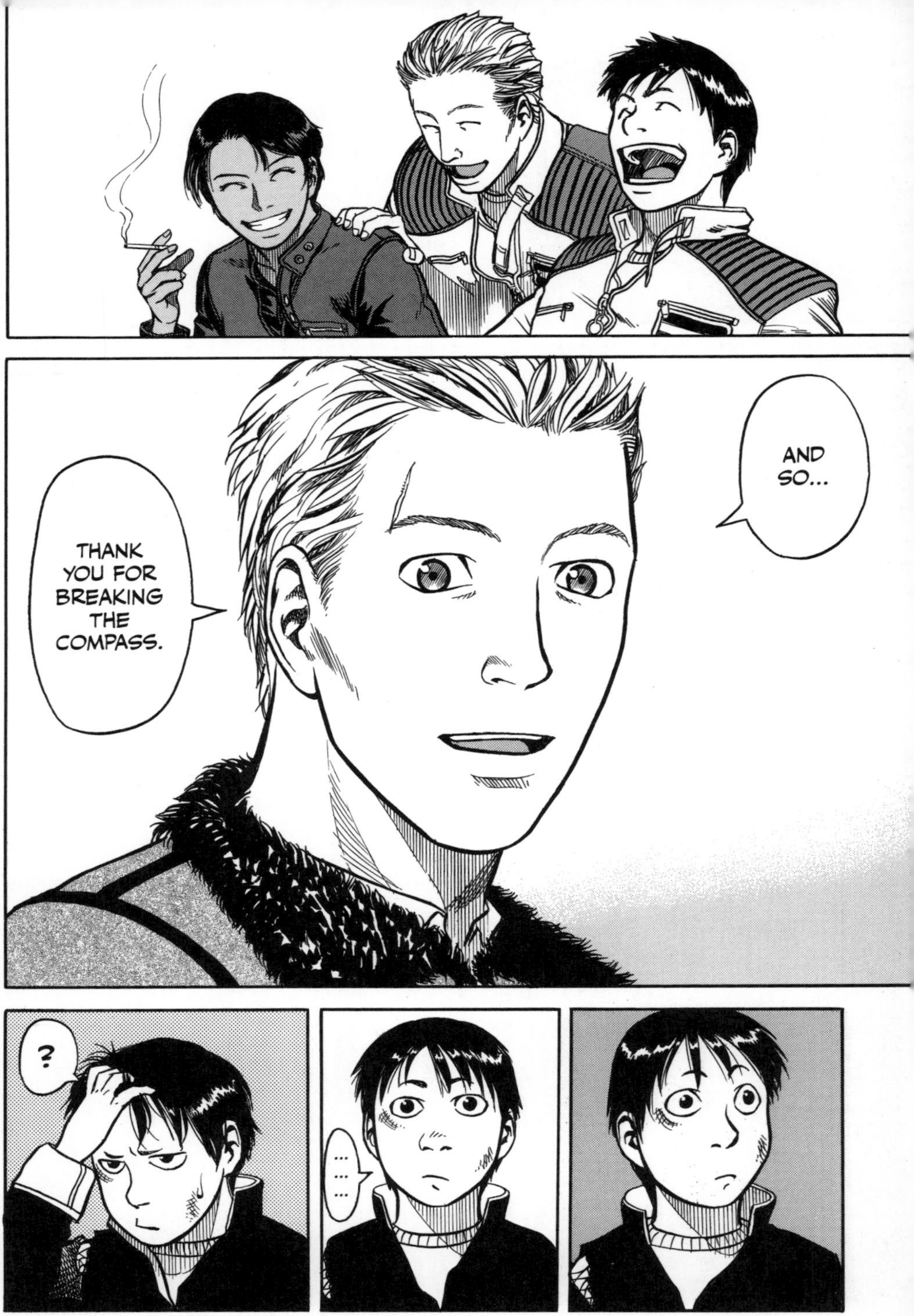
AND SO...
THANK YOU FOR BREAKING THE COMPASS.
....
?

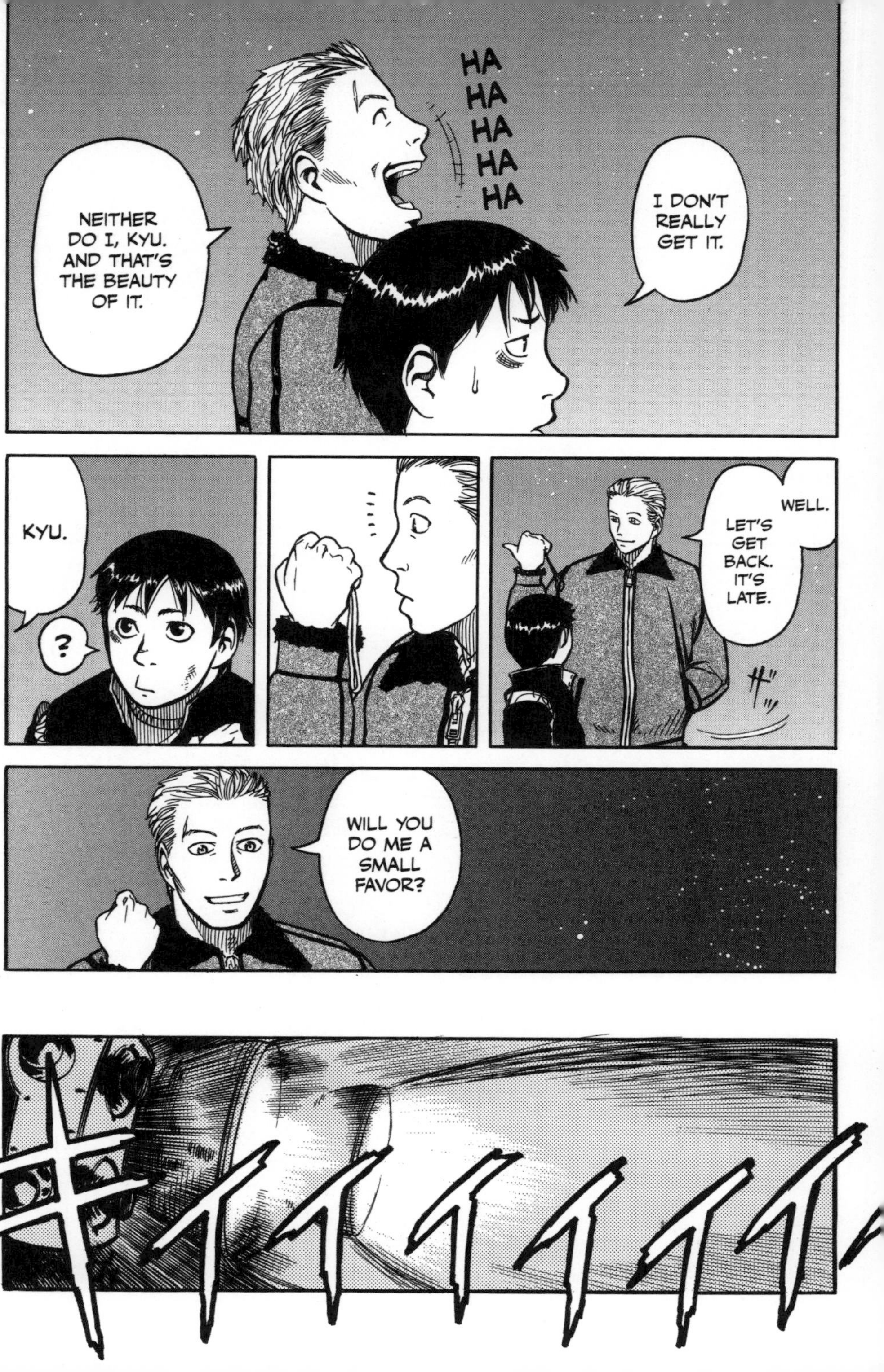
I DON'T REALLY GET IT.
HA HA HA HA HA
NEITHER DO I, KYU. AND THAT'S THE BEAUTY OF IT.
WELL.
LET'S GET BACK. IT'S LATE.
ザッ
KYU.
?
WILL YOU DO ME A SMALL FAVOR?
キイイイイイイ

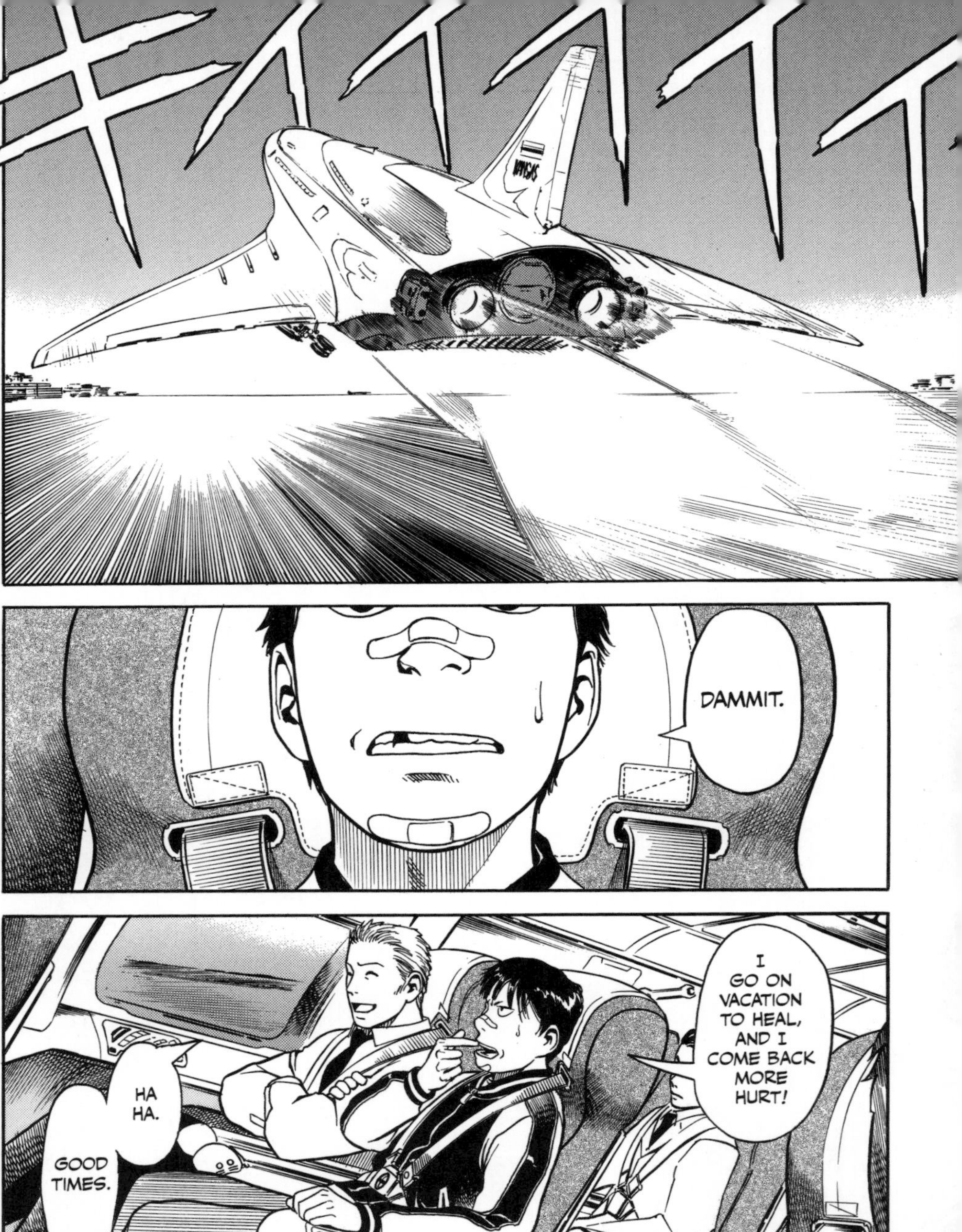
キイイイイ
DAMMIT.
I GO ON VACATION TO HEAL, AND I COME BACK MORE HURT!
HA HA. GOOD TIMES.

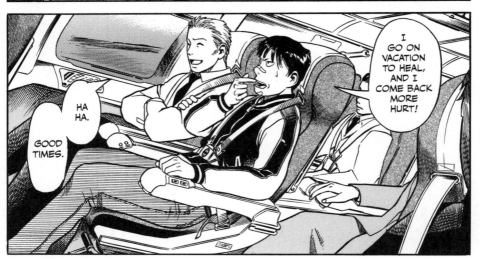

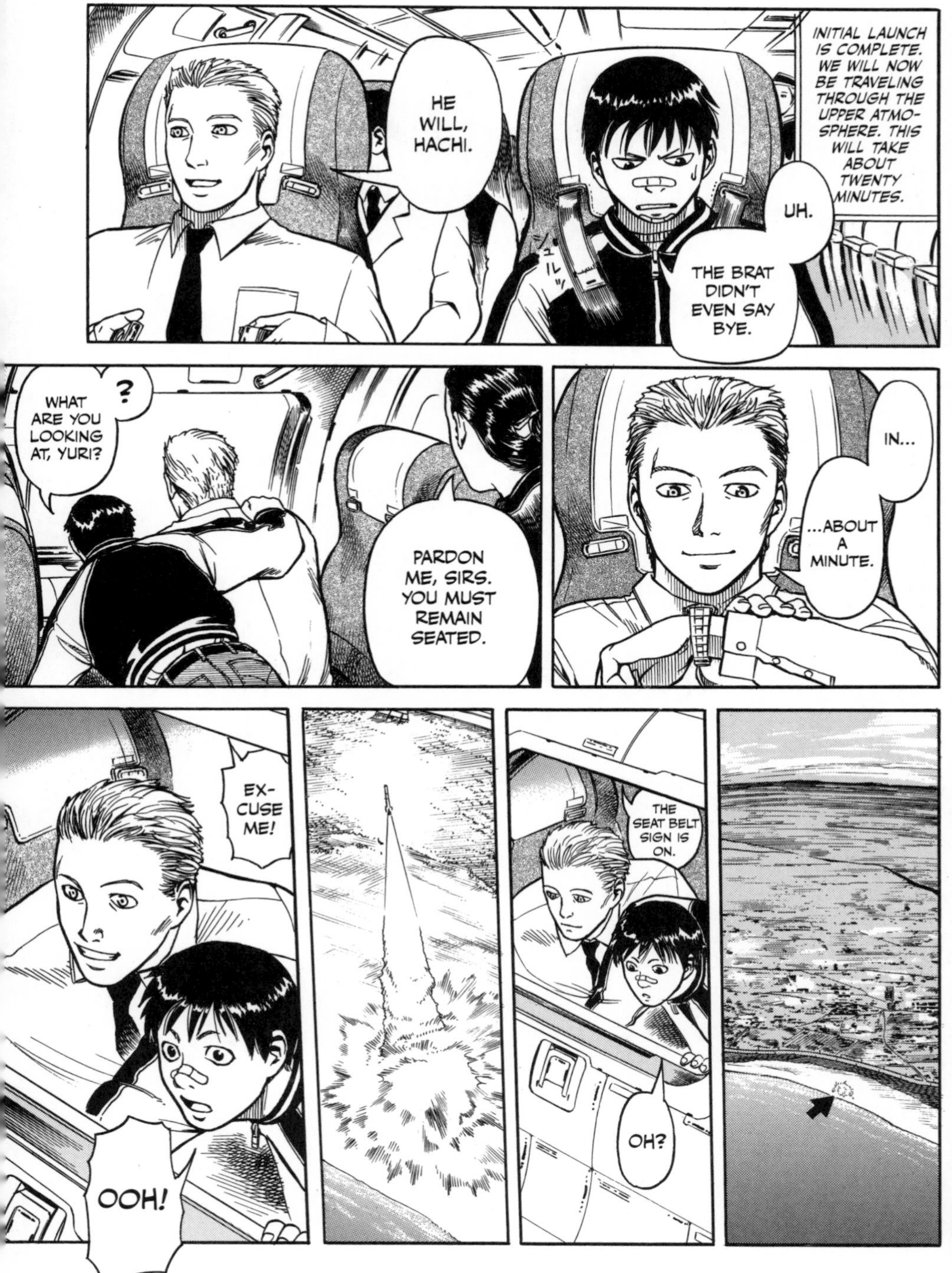
INITIAL LAUNCH IS COMPLETE. WE WILL NOW BE TRAVELING THROUGH THE UPPER ATMOSPHERE. THIS WILL TAKE ABOUT TWENTY MINUTES.
UH.
THE BRAT DIDN'T EVEN SAY BYE.
シュルッ
HE WILL, HACHI.
IN...
...ABOUT A MINUTE.
?
WHAT ARE YOU LOOKING AT, YURI?
PARDON ME, SIRS. YOU MUST REMAIN SEATED.
THE SEAT BELT SIGN IS ON.
OH?
EX-CUSE ME!
OOH!

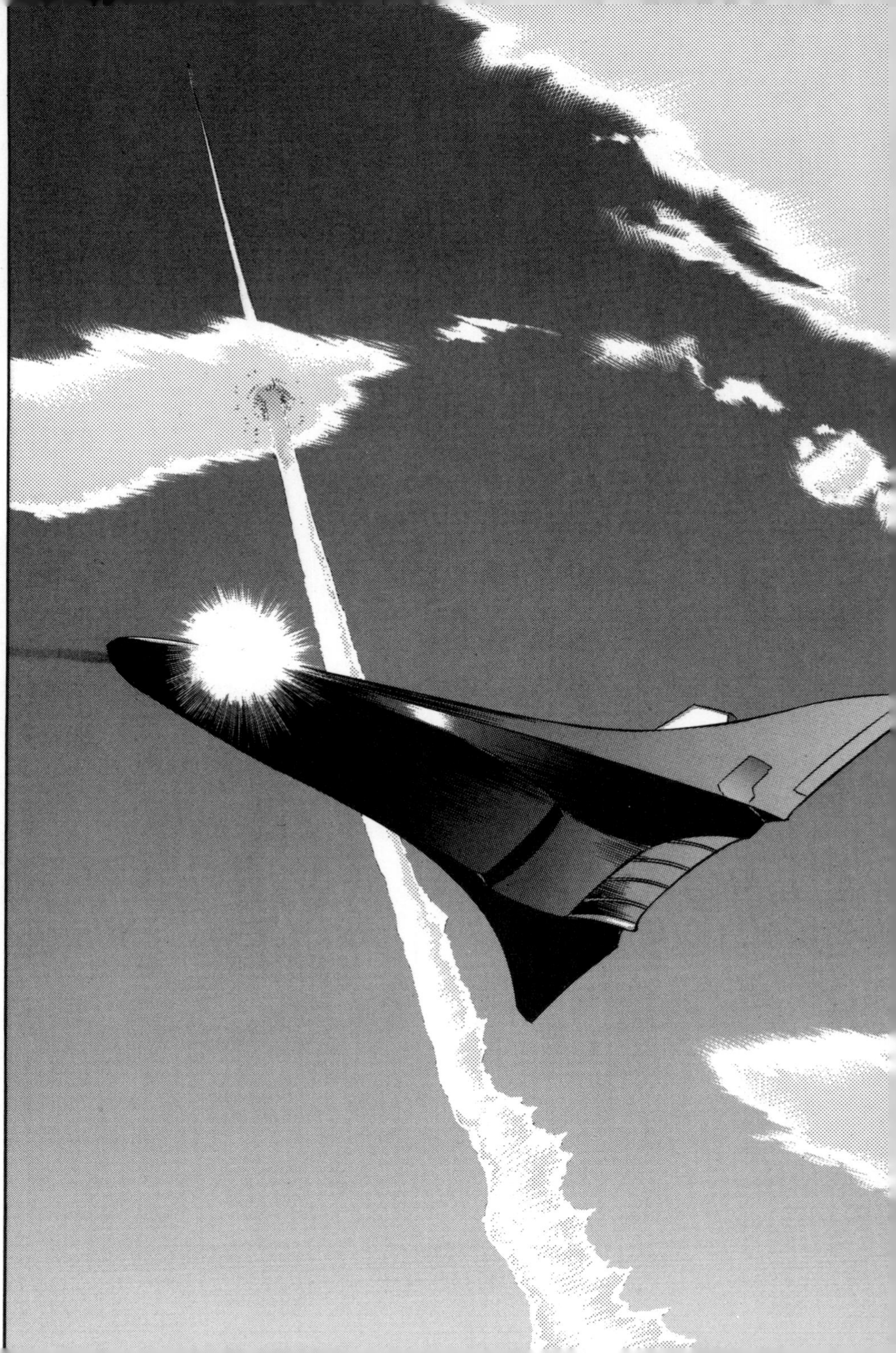

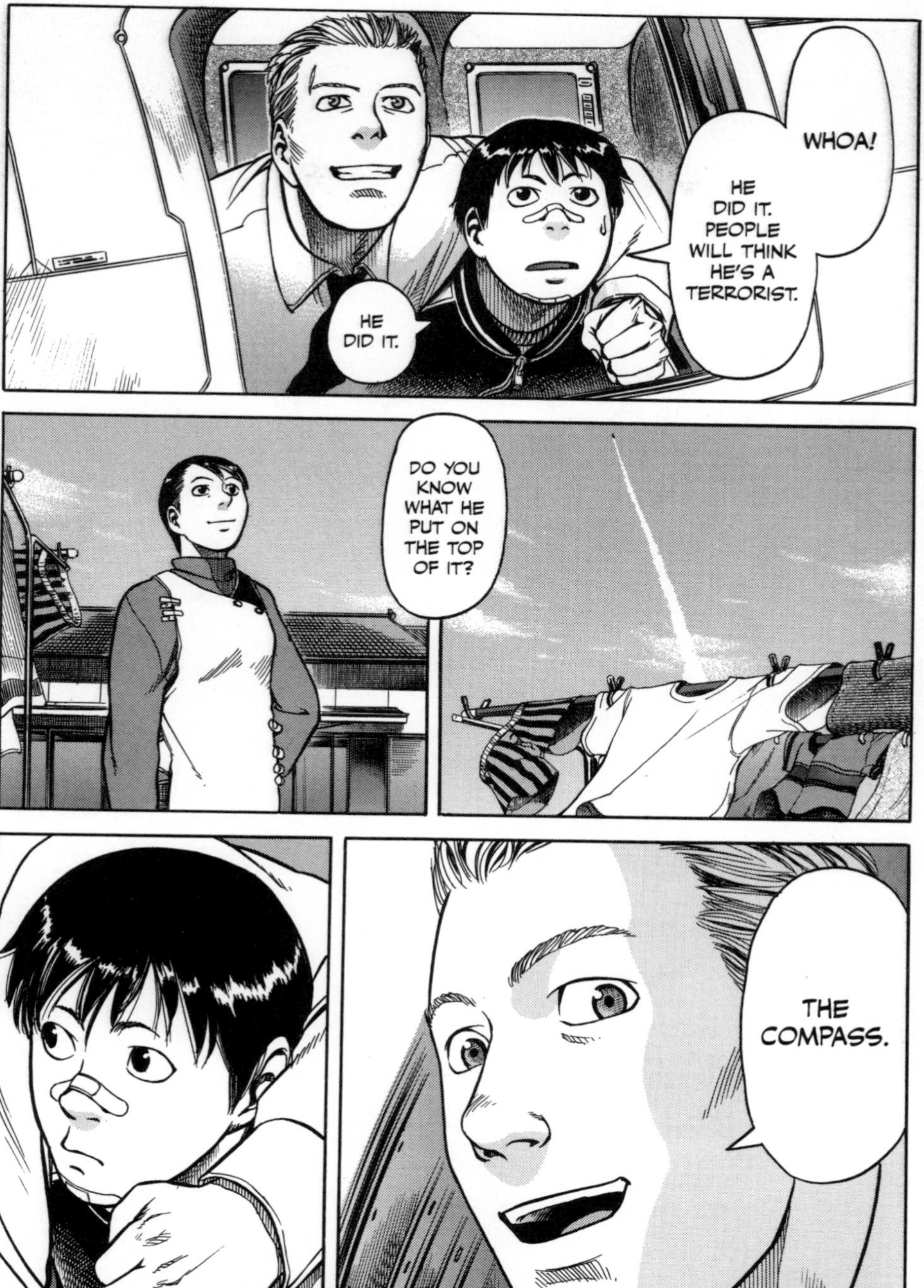
WHOA!
HE DID IT. PEOPLE WILL THINK HE'S A TERRORIST.
HE DID IT.
DO YOU KNOW WHAT HE PUT ON THE TOP OF IT?
THE COMPASS.

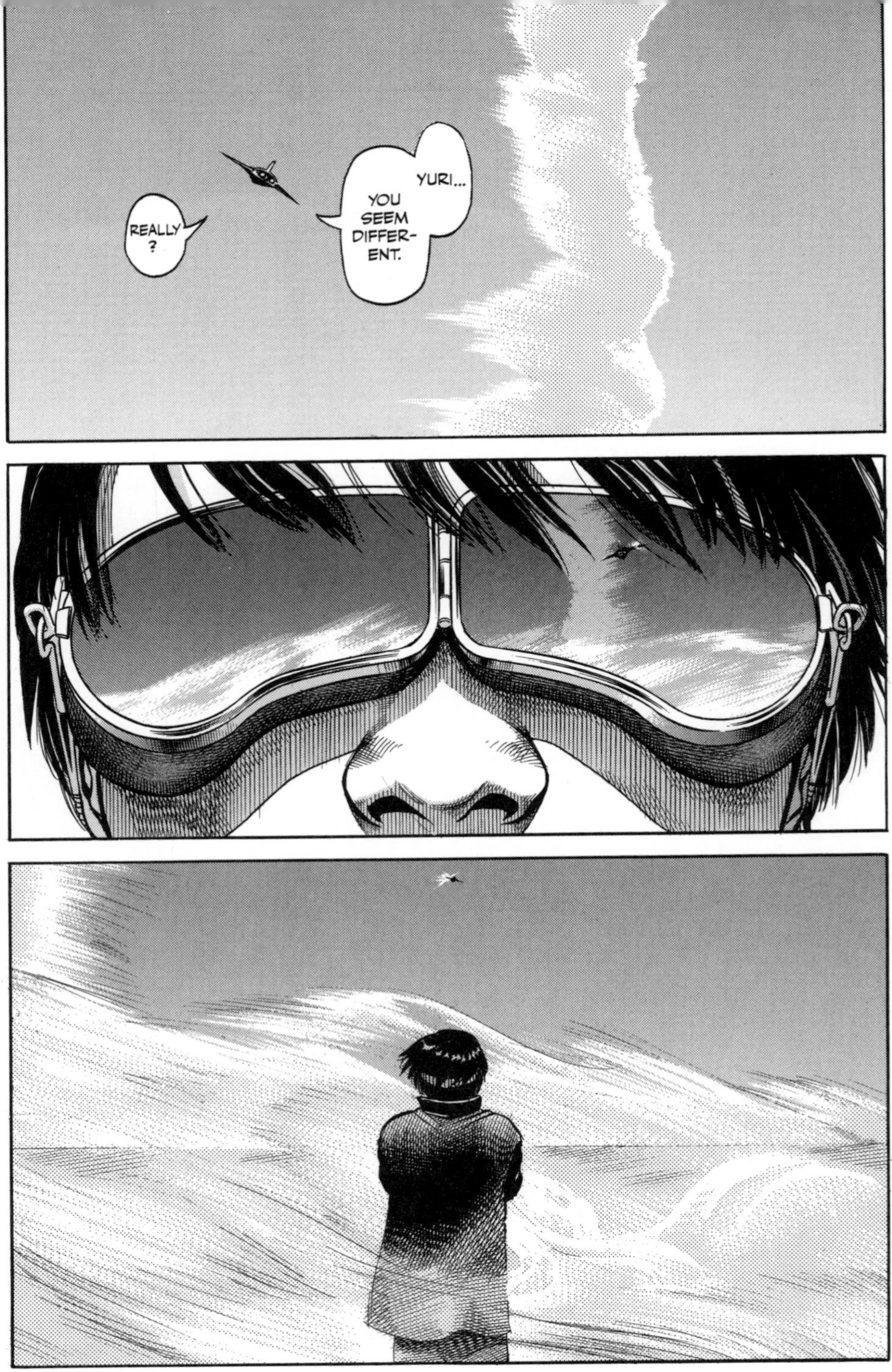
YURI... YOU SEEM DIFFERENT.
REALLY?

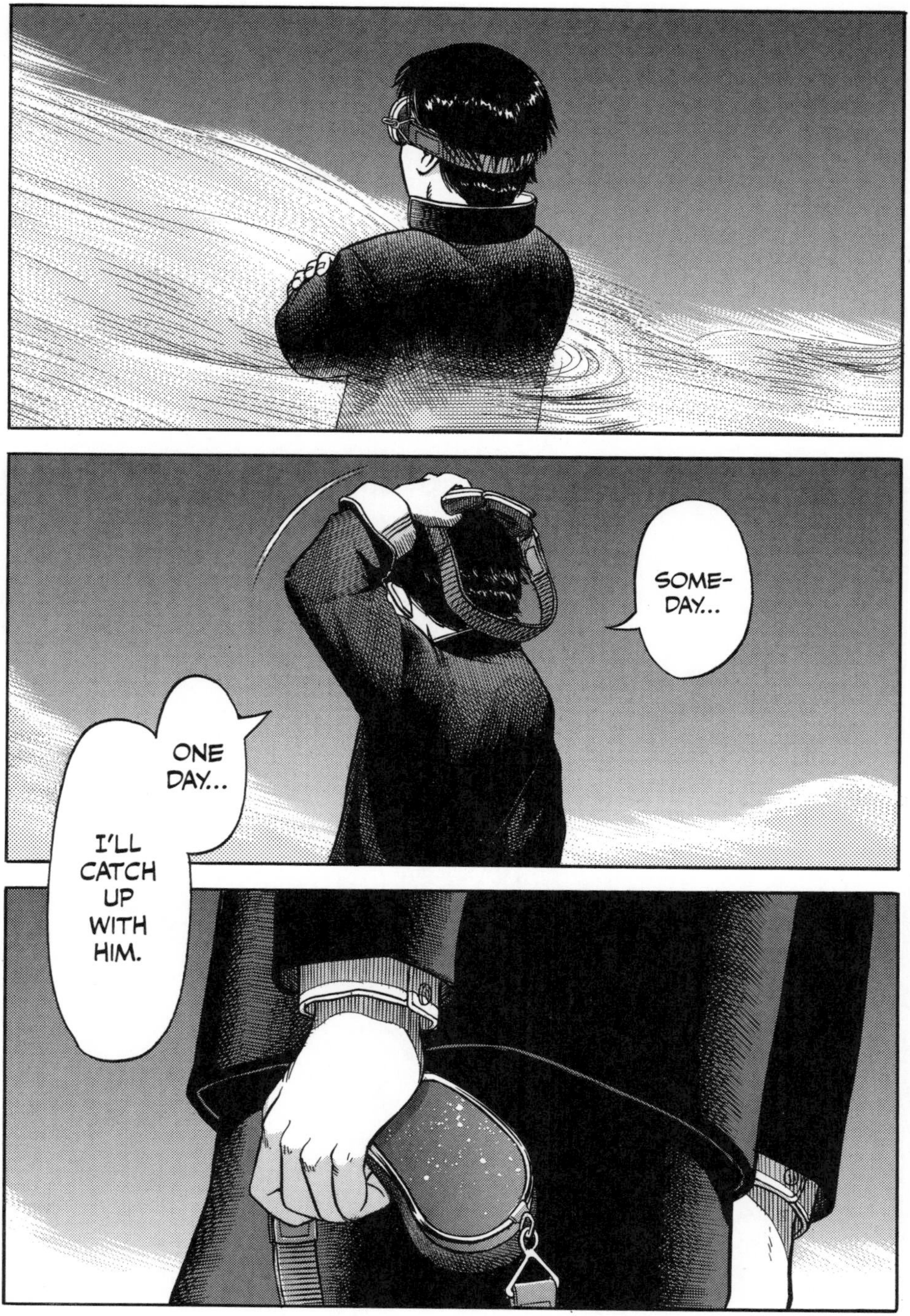
SOME-DAY...
ONE DAY... I'LL CATCH UP WITH HIM.

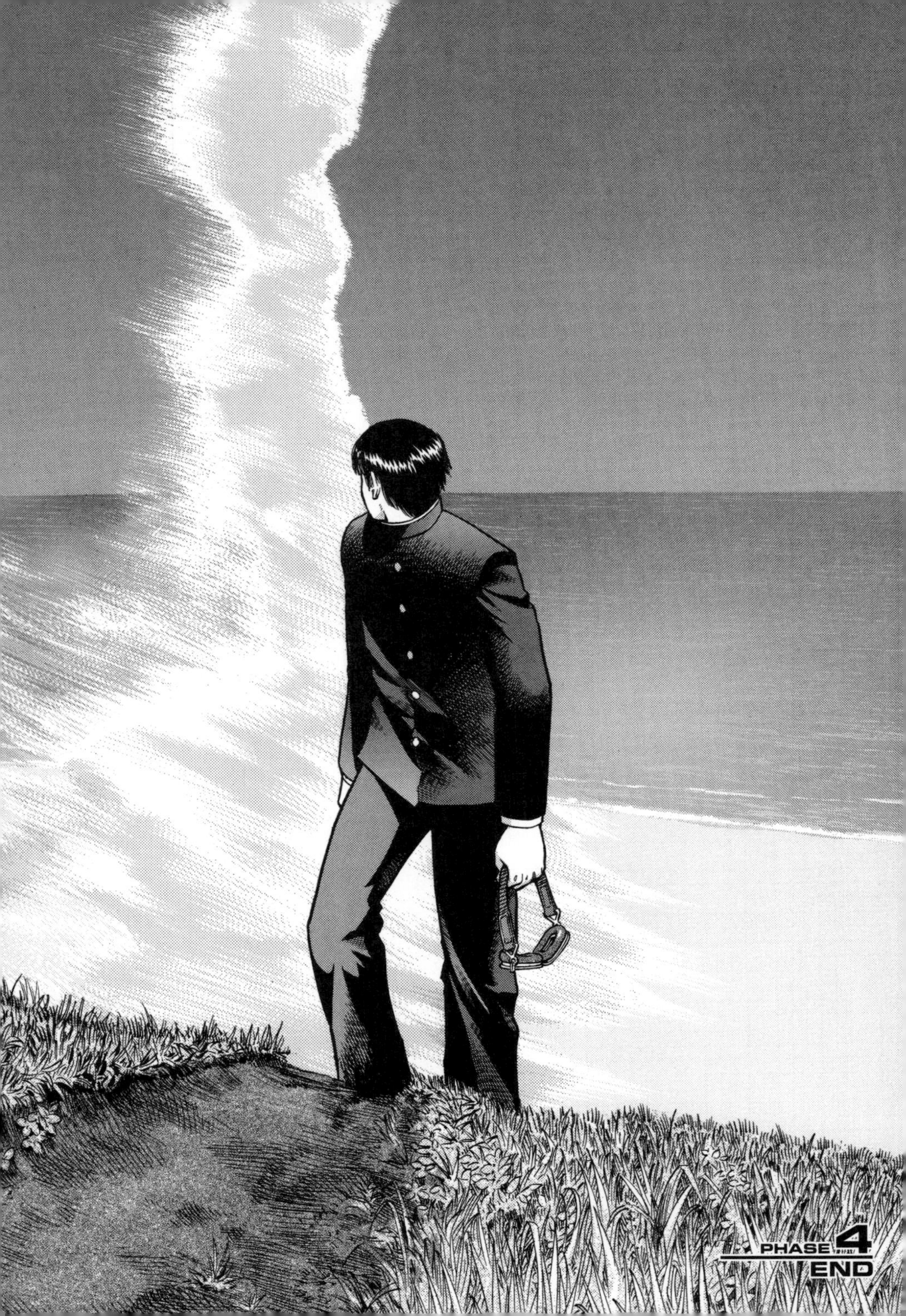
PHASE 4
END

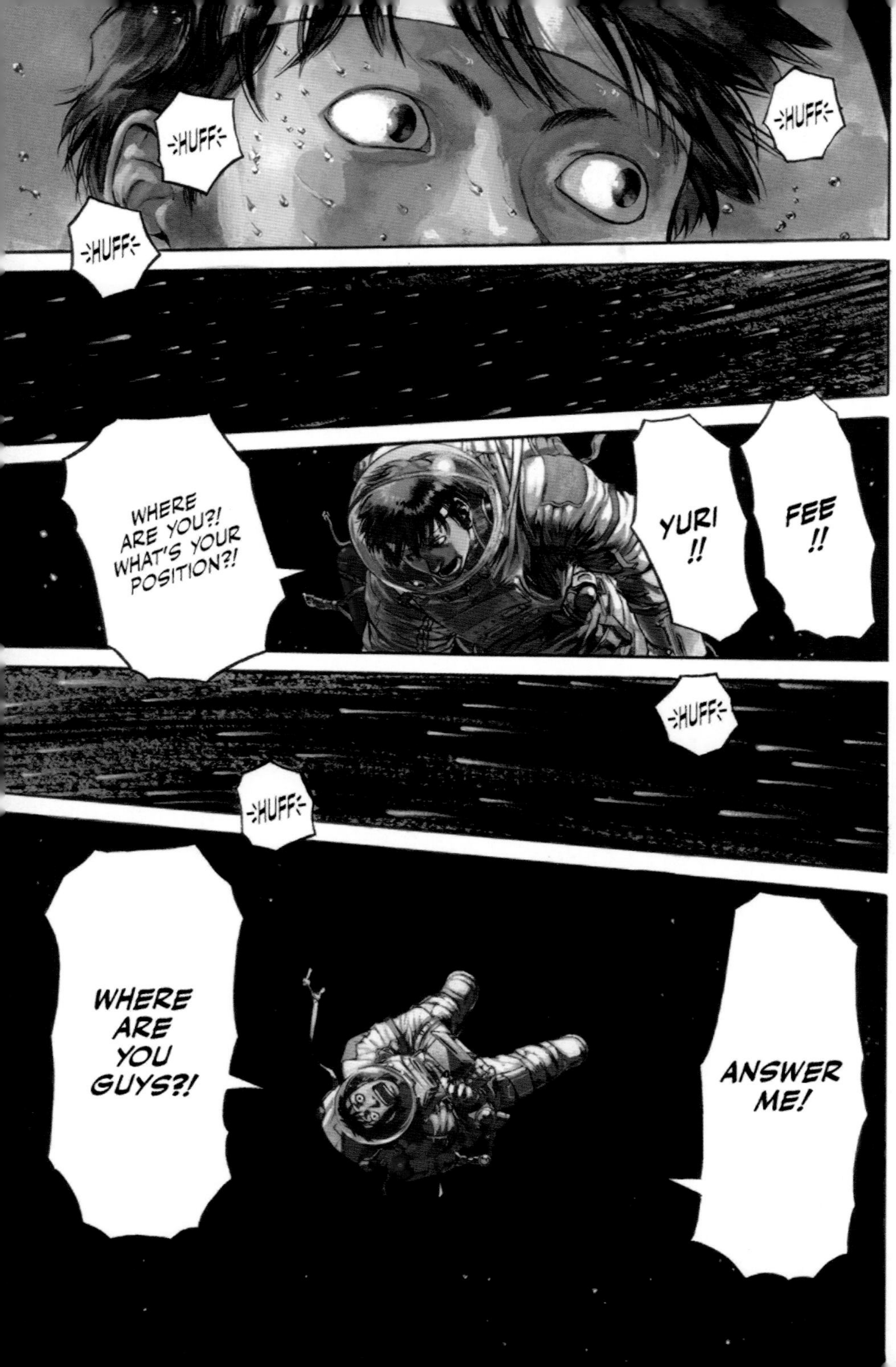

HUFF
HUFF
HUFF
FEE !!
YURI !!
WHERE ARE YOU?! WHAT'S YOUR POSITION?!
HUFF
HUFF
ANSWER ME!
WHERE ARE YOU GUYS?!

PHASE
5
IGNITION

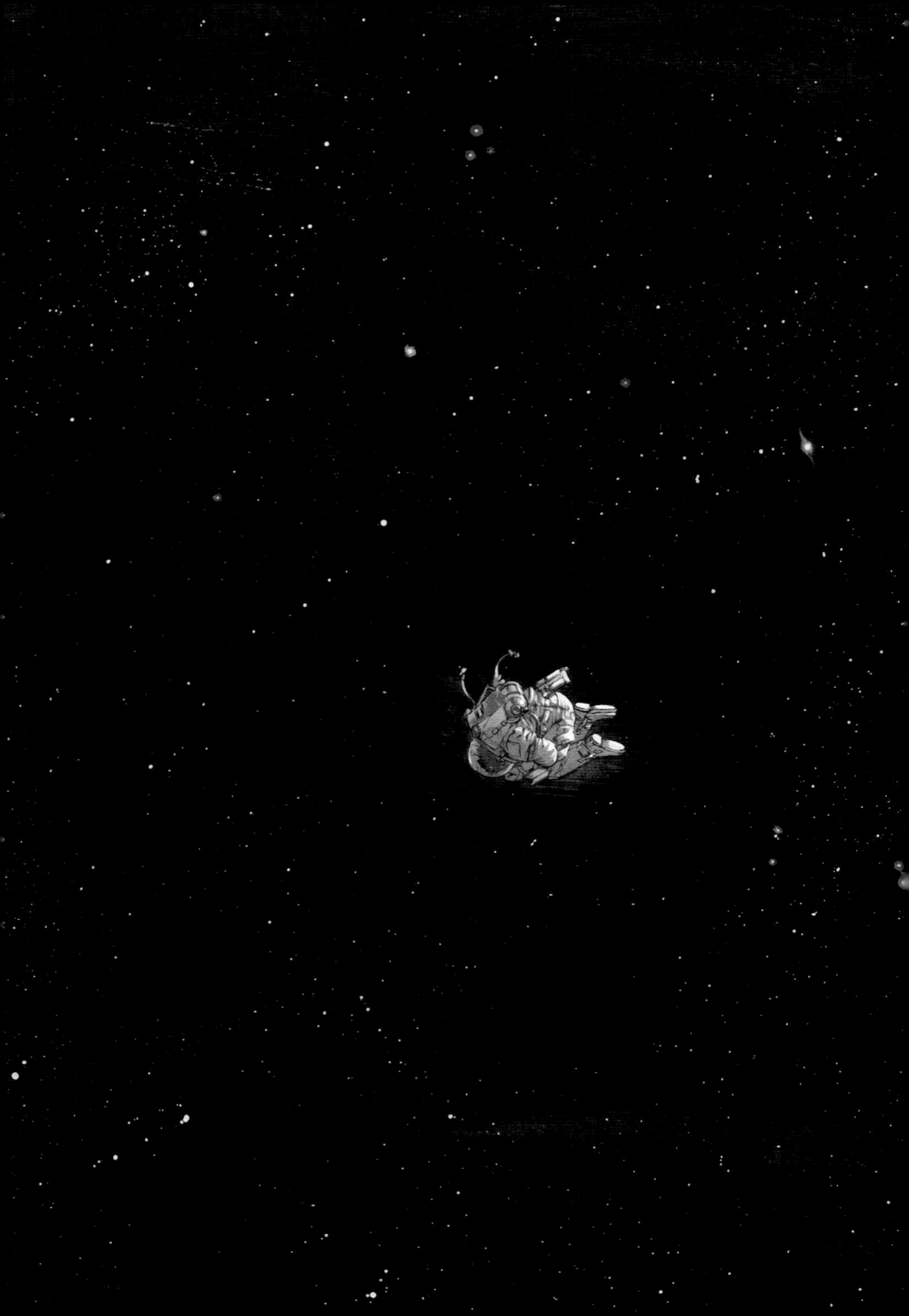

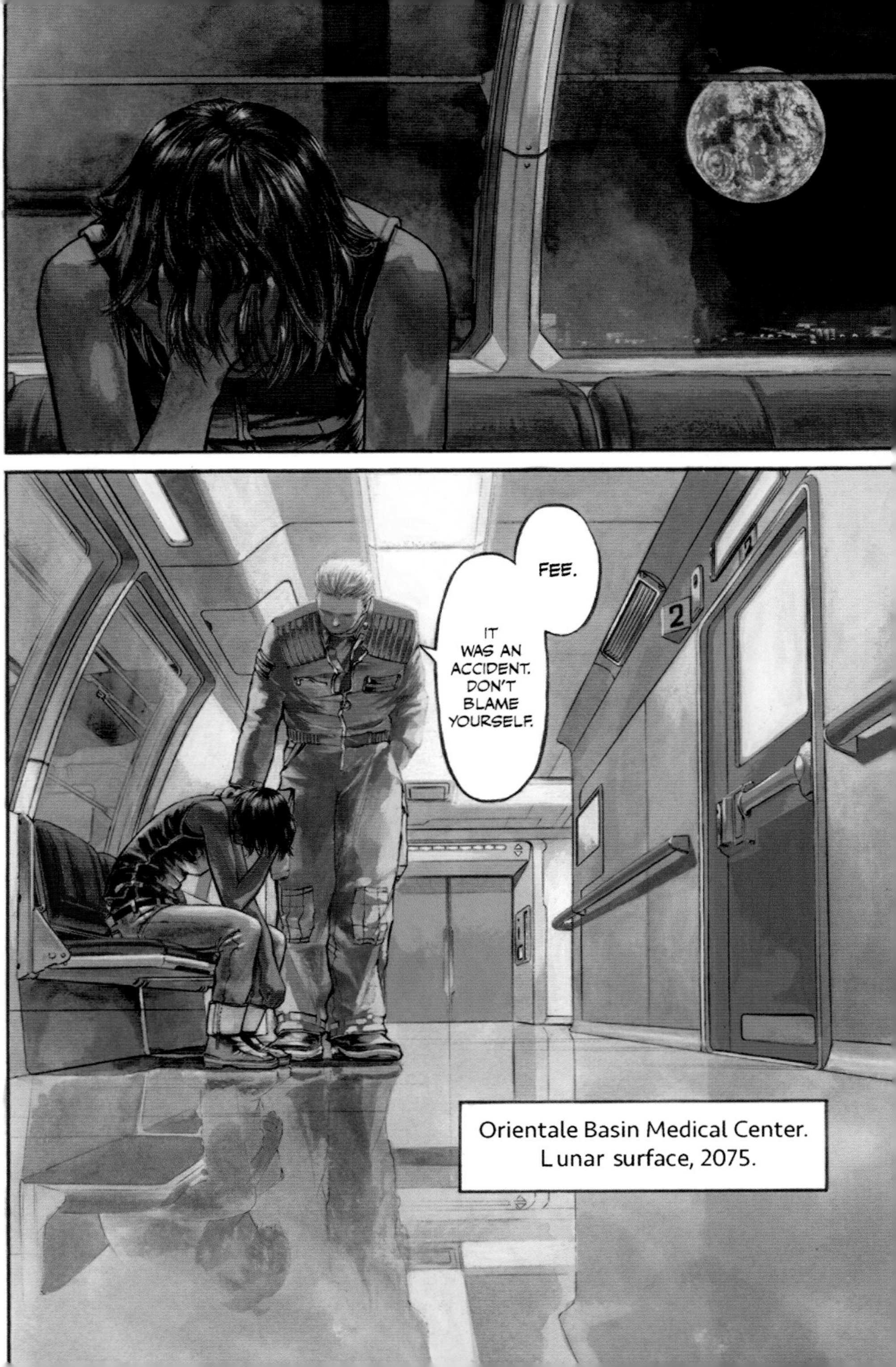
FEE.
IT WAS AN ACCIDENT. DON'T BLAME YOURSELF.
Orientale Basin Medical Center. Lunar surface, 2075.

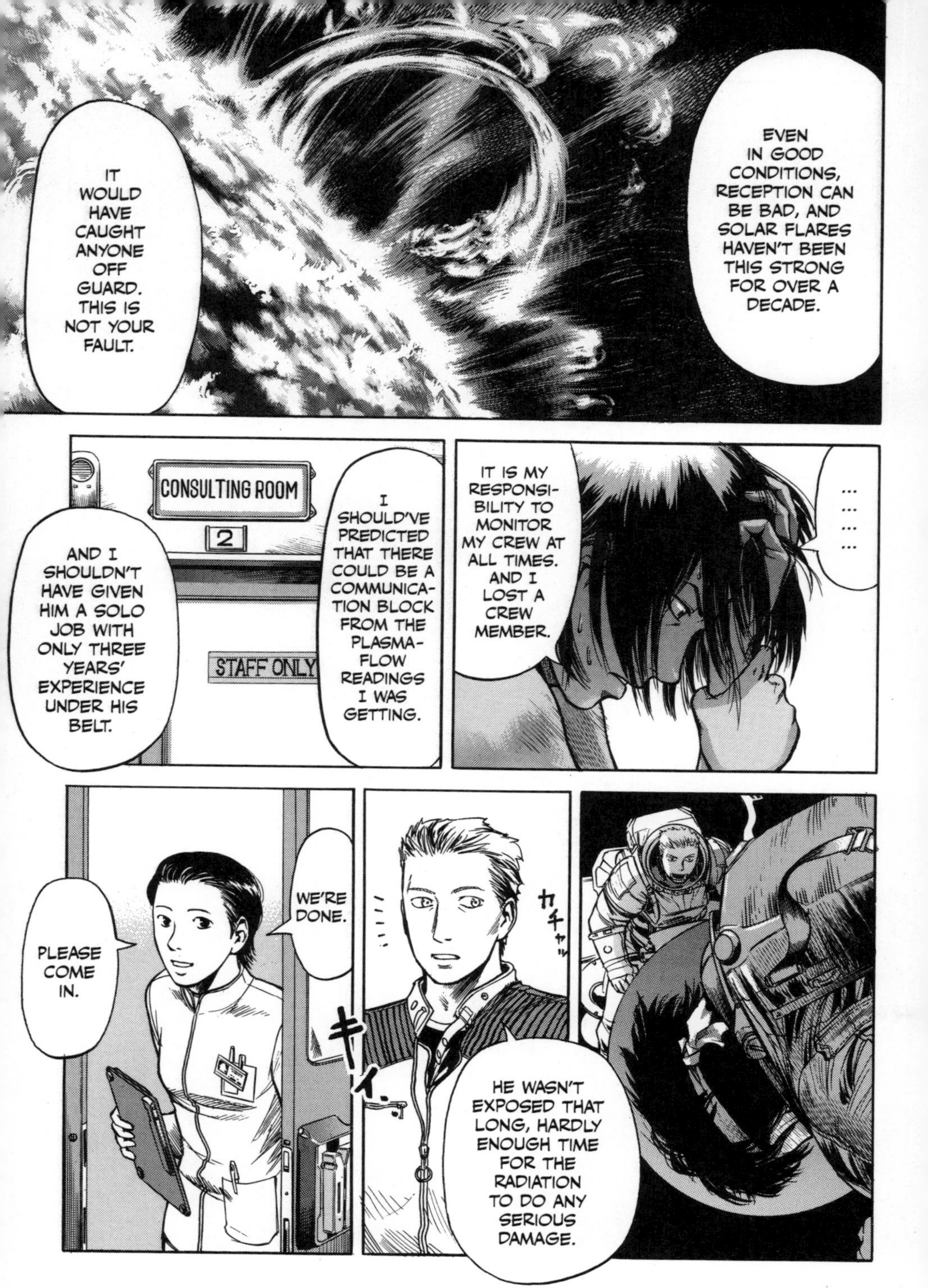
EVEN IN GOOD CONDITIONS, RECEPTION CAN BE BAD, AND SOLAR FLARES HAVEN'T BEEN THIS STRONG FOR OVER A DECADE.
IT WOULD HAVE CAUGHT ANYONE OFF GUARD. THIS IS NOT YOUR FAULT.
... ...
IT IS MY RESPONSIBILITY TO MONITOR MY CREW AT ALL TIMES. AND I LOST A CREW MEMBER.
CONSULTING ROOM
2
STAFF ONLY
I SHOULD'VE PREDICTED THAT THERE COULD BE A COMMUNICATION BLOCK FROM THE PLASMA-FLOW READINGS I WAS GETTING.
AND I SHOULDN'T HAVE GIVEN HIM A SOLO JOB WITH ONLY THREE YEARS' EXPERIENCE UNDER HIS BELT.
HE WASN'T EXPOSED THAT LONG, HARDLY ENOUGH TIME FOR THE RADIATION TO DO ANY SERIOUS DAMAGE.
カチャッ
キィ
WE'RE DONE.
PLEASE COME IN.

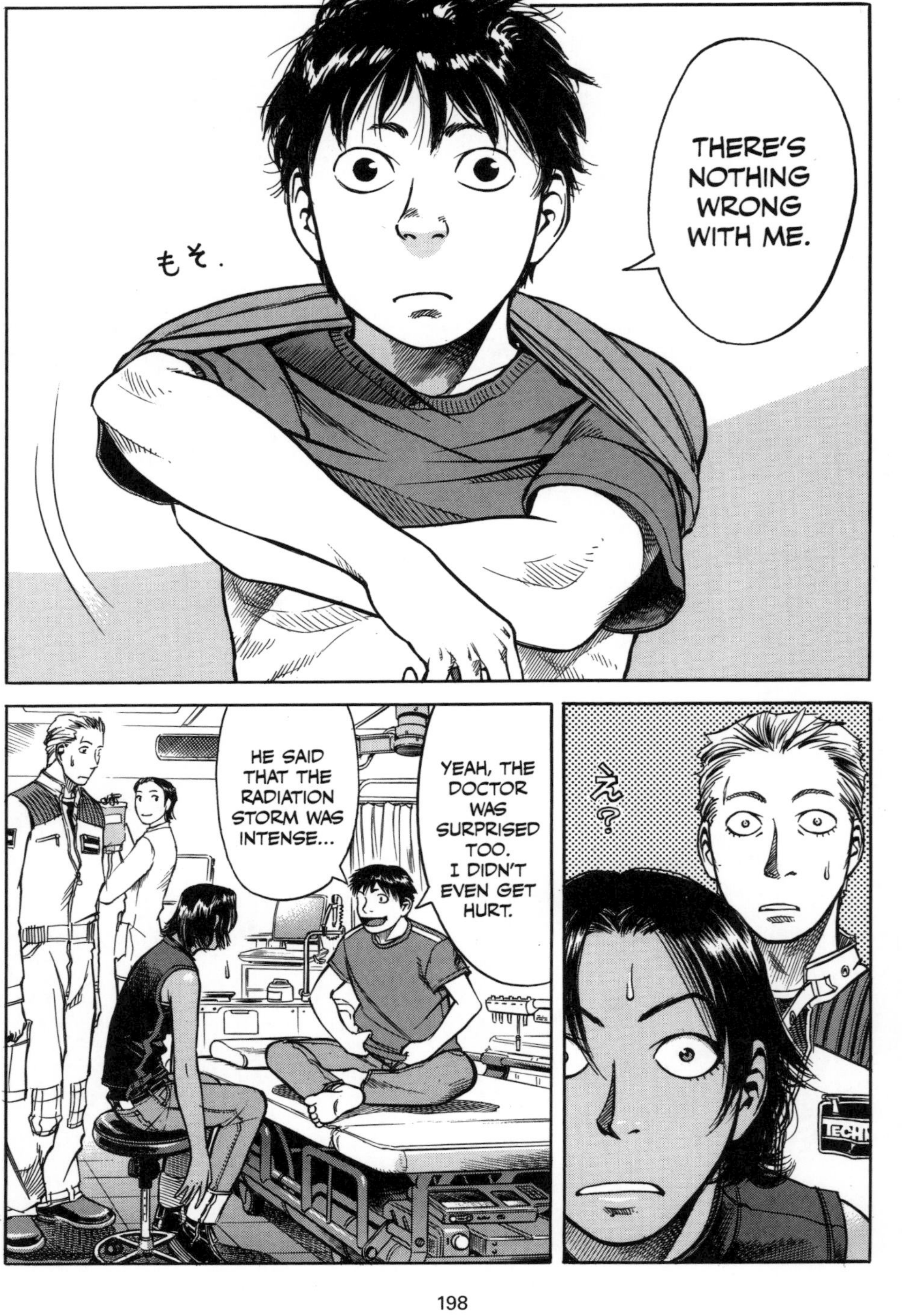
THERE'S NOTHING WRONG WITH ME.
もそ.
え？
YEAH, THE DOCTOR WAS SURPRISED TOO. I DIDN'T EVEN GET HURT.
HE SAID THAT THE RADIATION STORM WAS INTENSE...

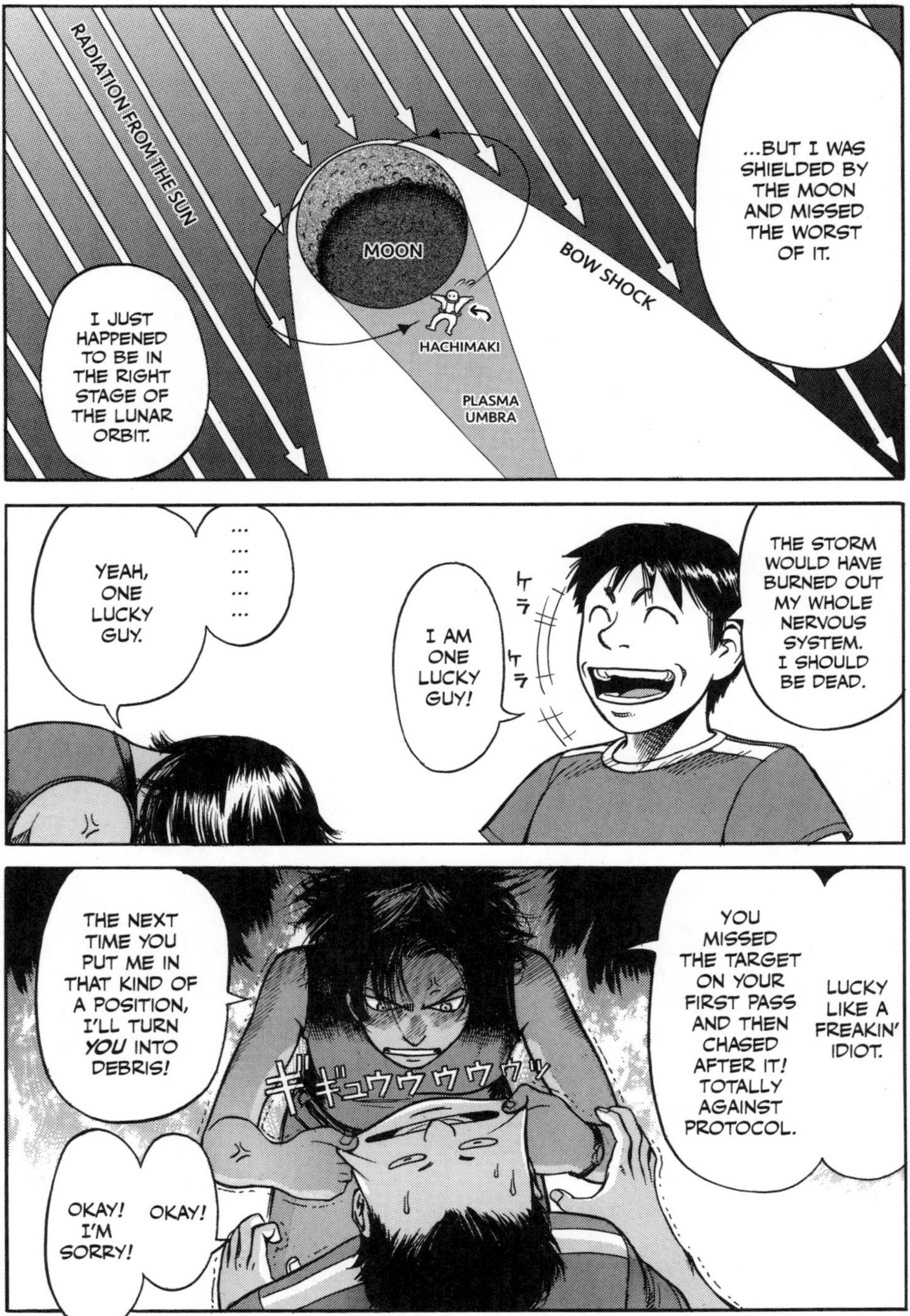

...BUT I WAS SHIELDED BY THE MOON AND MISSED THE WORST OF IT.
RADIATION FROM THE SUN
BOW SHOCK
MOON
HACHIMAKI
PLASMA UMBRA
I JUST HAPPENED TO BE IN THE RIGHT STAGE OF THE LUNAR ORBIT.
THE STORM WOULD HAVE BURNED OUT MY WHOLE NERVOUS SYSTEM. I SHOULD BE DEAD.
ケラ
ケラ
I AM ONE LUCKY GUY!
...
....
.....
......
YEAH, ONE LUCKY GUY.
YOU MISSED THE TARGET ON YOUR FIRST PASS AND THEN CHASED AFTER IT! TOTALLY AGAINST PROTOCOL.
LUCKY LIKE A FREAKIN' IDIOT.
THE NEXT TIME YOU PUT ME IN THAT KIND OF A POSITION, I'LL TURN *YOU* INTO DEBRIS!
ギギュウウウウウッ
OKAY!
OKAY! I'M SORRY!

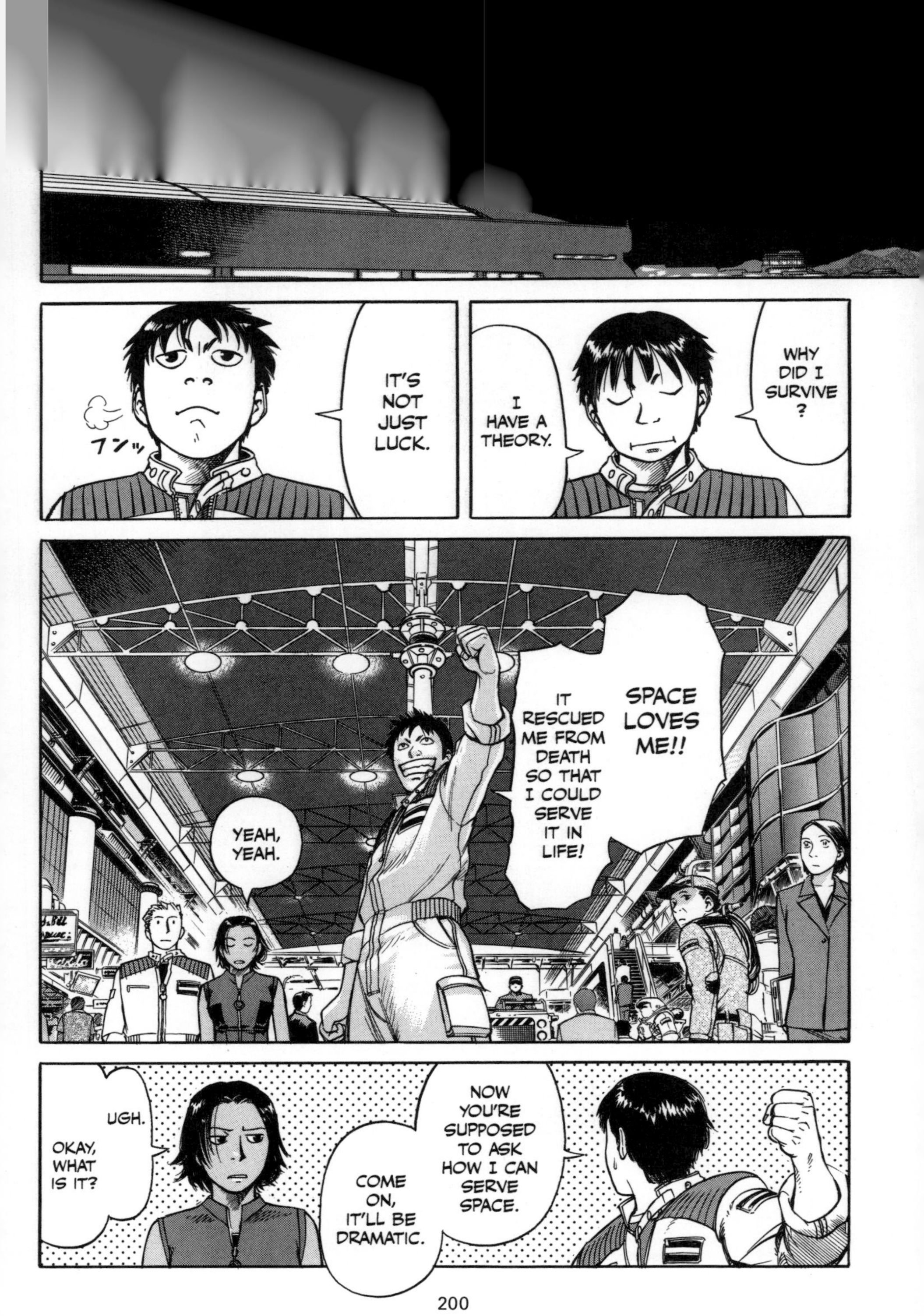
WHY DID I SURVIVE ?
I HAVE A THEORY.
IT'S NOT JUST LUCK.
フンッ
SPACE LOVES ME!!
IT RESCUED ME FROM DEATH SO THAT I COULD SERVE IT IN LIFE!
YEAH, YEAH.
NOW YOU'RE SUPPOSED TO ASK HOW I CAN SERVE SPACE.
COME ON, IT'LL BE DRAMATIC.
UGH.
OKAY, WHAT IS IT?

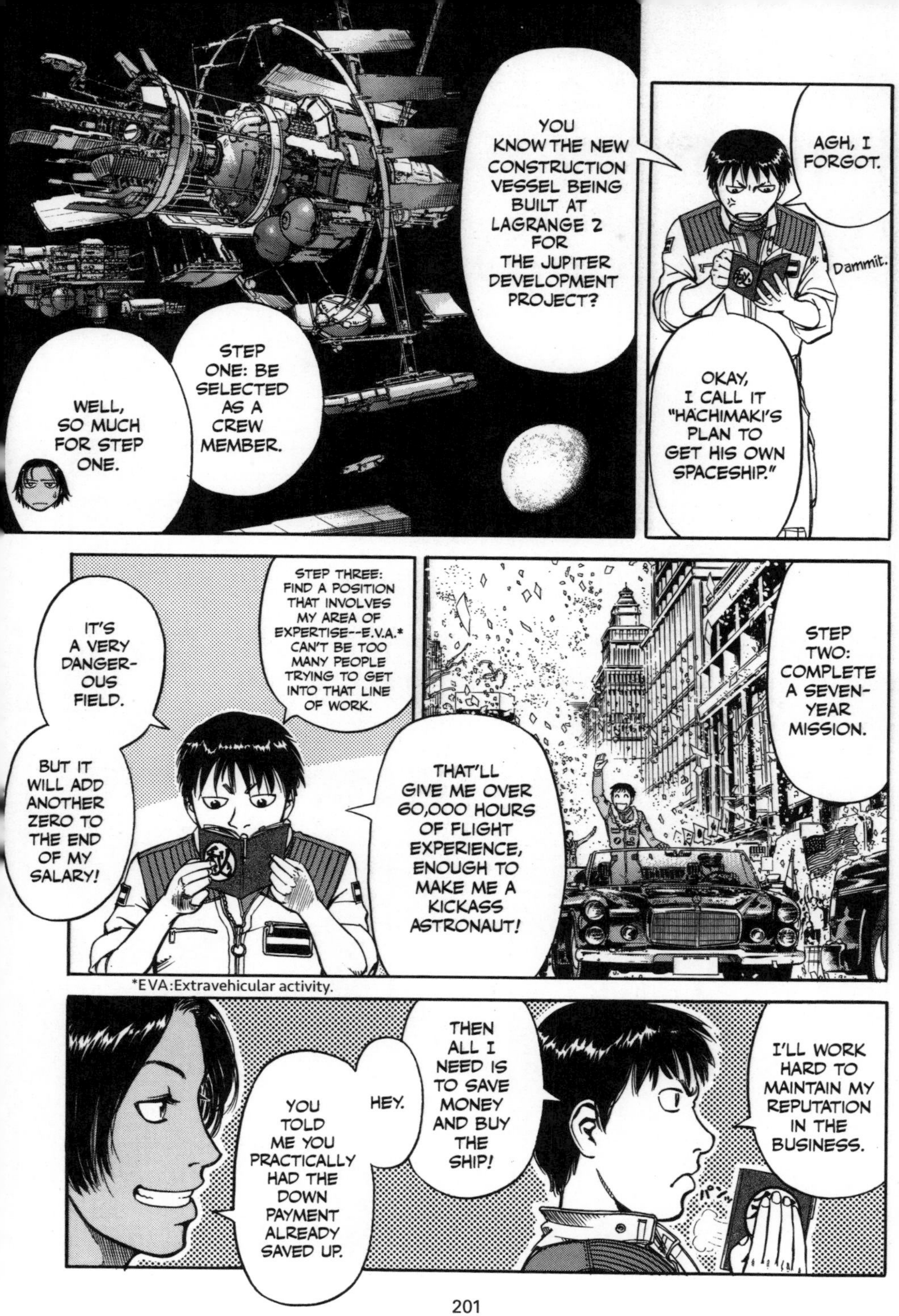
AGH, I FORGOT.
Dammit.
OKAY, I CALL IT "HACHIMAKI'S PLAN TO GET HIS OWN SPACESHIP."
YOU KNOW THE NEW CONSTRUCTION VESSEL BEING BUILT AT LAGRANGE 2 FOR THE JUPITER DEVELOPMENT PROJECT?
STEP ONE: BE SELECTED AS A CREW MEMBER.
WELL, SO MUCH FOR STEP ONE.
STEP TWO: COMPLETE A SEVEN-YEAR MISSION.
THAT'LL GIVE ME OVER 60,000 HOURS OF FLIGHT EXPERIENCE, ENOUGH TO MAKE ME A KICKASS ASTRONAUT!
STEP THREE: FIND A POSITION THAT INVOLVES MY AREA OF EXPERTISE--E.V.A.* CAN'T BE TOO MANY PEOPLE TRYING TO GET INTO THAT LINE OF WORK.
IT'S A VERY DANGER-OUS FIELD.
BUT IT WILL ADD ANOTHER ZERO TO THE END OF MY SALARY!
I'LL WORK HARD TO MAINTAIN MY REPUTATION IN THE BUSINESS.
THEN ALL I NEED IS TO SAVE MONEY AND BUY THE SHIP!
HEY.
YOU TOLD ME YOU PRACTICALLY HAD THE DOWN PAYMENT ALREADY SAVED UP.

*EVA:Extravehicular activity.

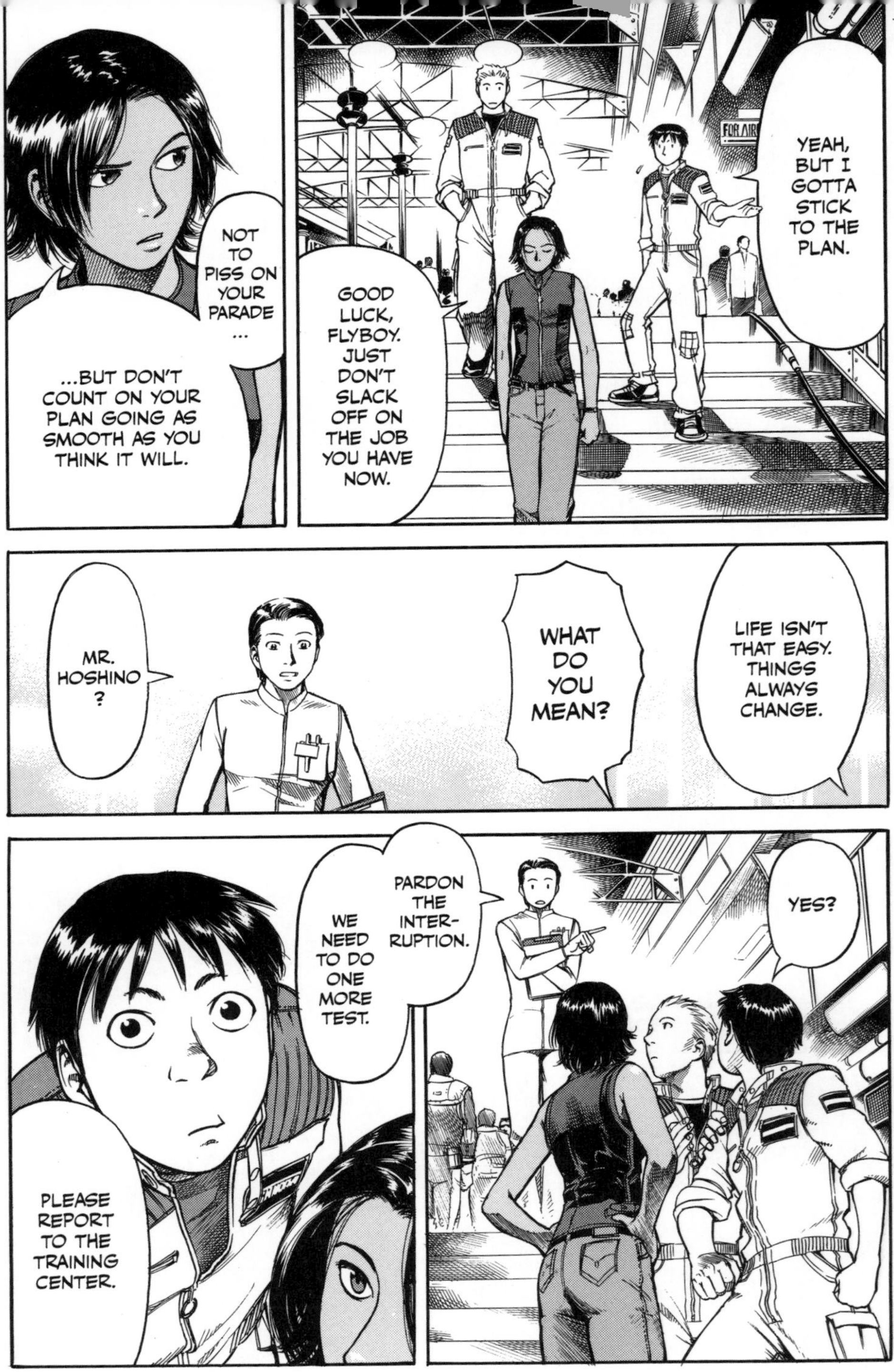
YEAH, BUT I GOTTA STICK TO THE PLAN.
GOOD LUCK, FLYBOY. JUST DON'T SLACK OFF ON THE JOB YOU HAVE NOW.
NOT TO PISS ON YOUR PARADE ...
...BUT DON'T COUNT ON YOUR PLAN GOING AS SMOOTH AS YOU THINK IT WILL.
LIFE ISN'T THAT EASY. THINGS ALWAYS CHANGE.
WHAT DO YOU MEAN?
MR. HOSHINO?
YES?
PARDON THE INTER-RUPTION.
WE NEED TO DO ONE MORE TEST.
PLEASE REPORT TO THE TRAINING CENTER.

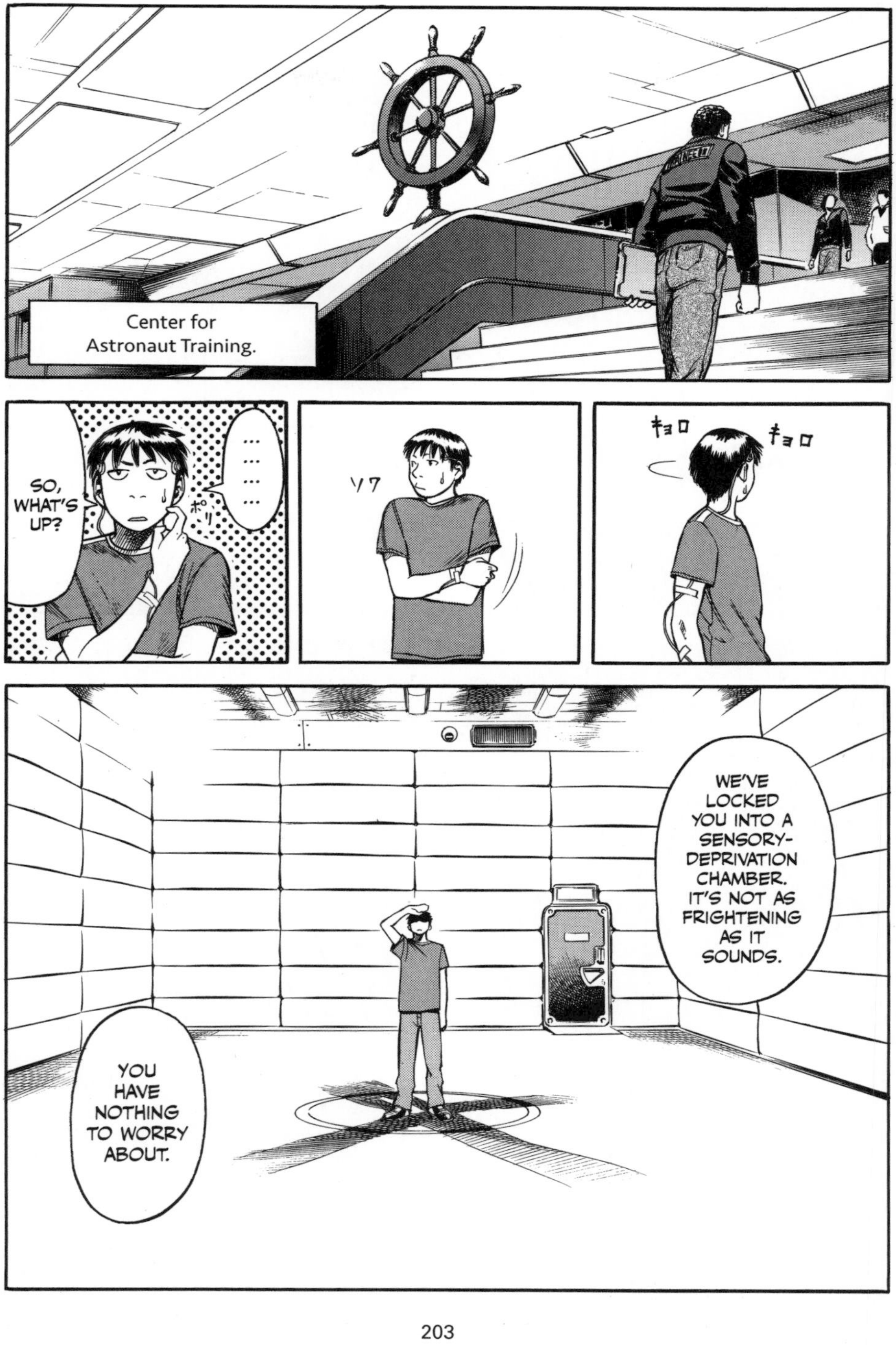
Center for Astronaut Training.
キョロ
キョロ
ソワ
…… …… …… ……
ポリ
SO, WHAT'S UP?
WE'VE LOCKED YOU INTO A SENSORY-DEPRIVATION CHAMBER. IT'S NOT AS FRIGHTENING AS IT SOUNDS.
YOU HAVE NOTHING TO WORRY ABOUT.

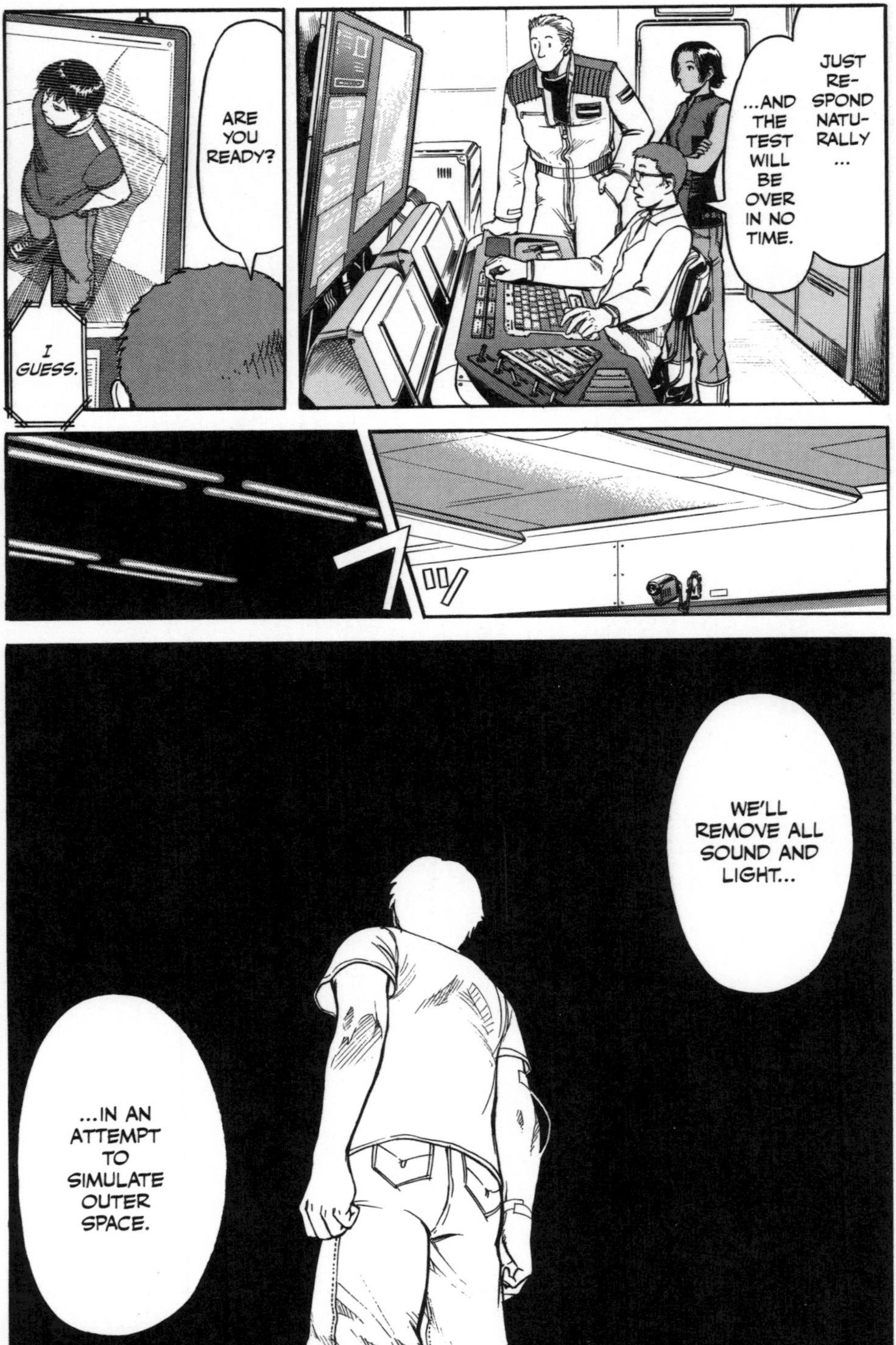
JUST RE-SPOND NATU-RALLY ...
...AND THE TEST WILL BE OVER IN NO TIME.
ARE YOU READY?
I GUESS.
WE'LL REMOVE ALL SOUND AND LIGHT...
...IN AN ATTEMPT TO SIMULATE OUTER SPACE.

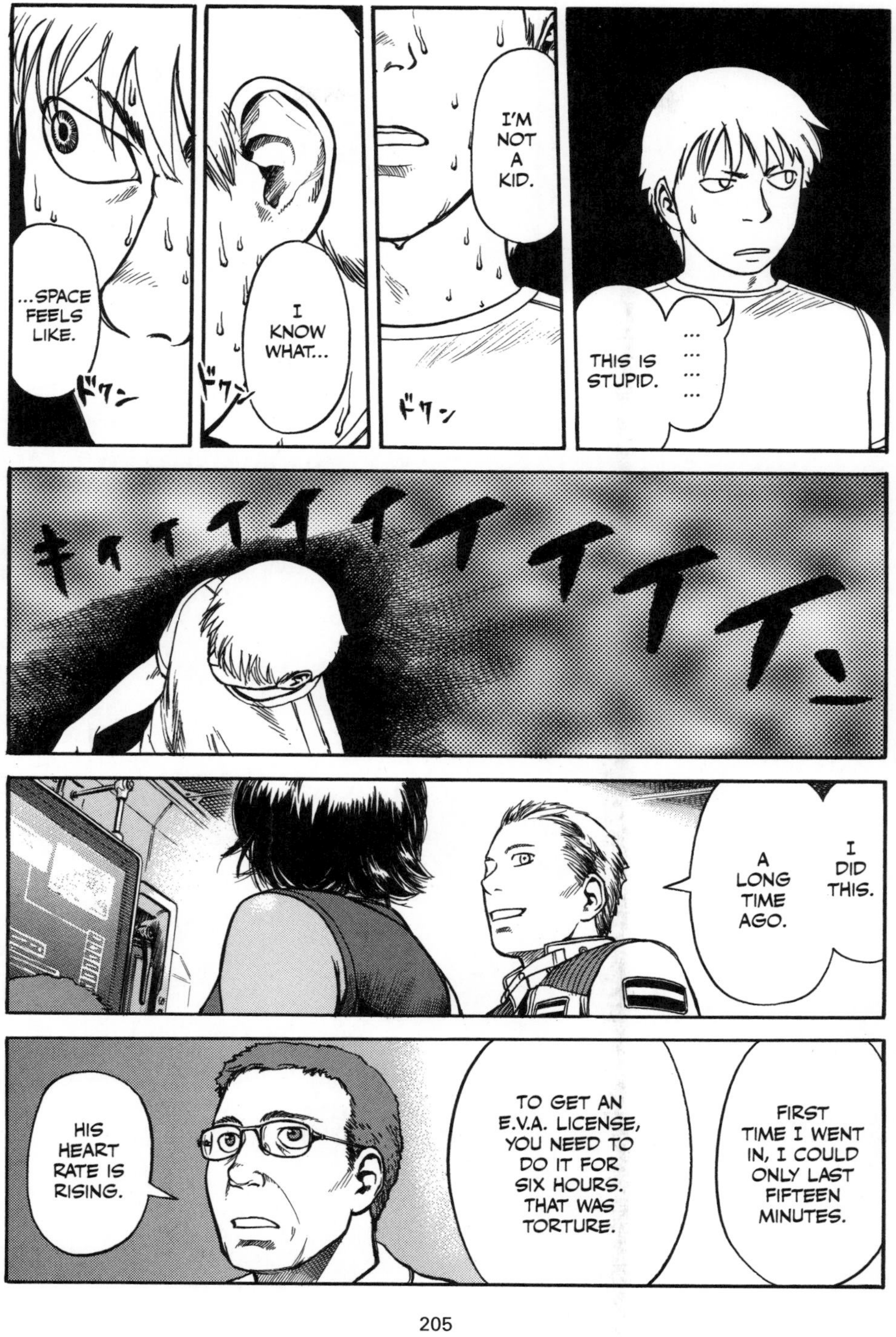

......
THIS IS STUPID.
I'M NOT A KID.
ドクン
I KNOW WHAT...
ドクン
...SPACE FEELS LIKE.
ドクン
キィイイイイイイイン
I DID THIS.
A LONG TIME AGO.
FIRST TIME I WENT IN, I COULD ONLY LAST FIFTEEN MINUTES.
TO GET AN E.V.A. LICENSE, YOU NEED TO DO IT FOR SIX HOURS. THAT WAS TORTURE.
HIS HEART RATE IS RISING.

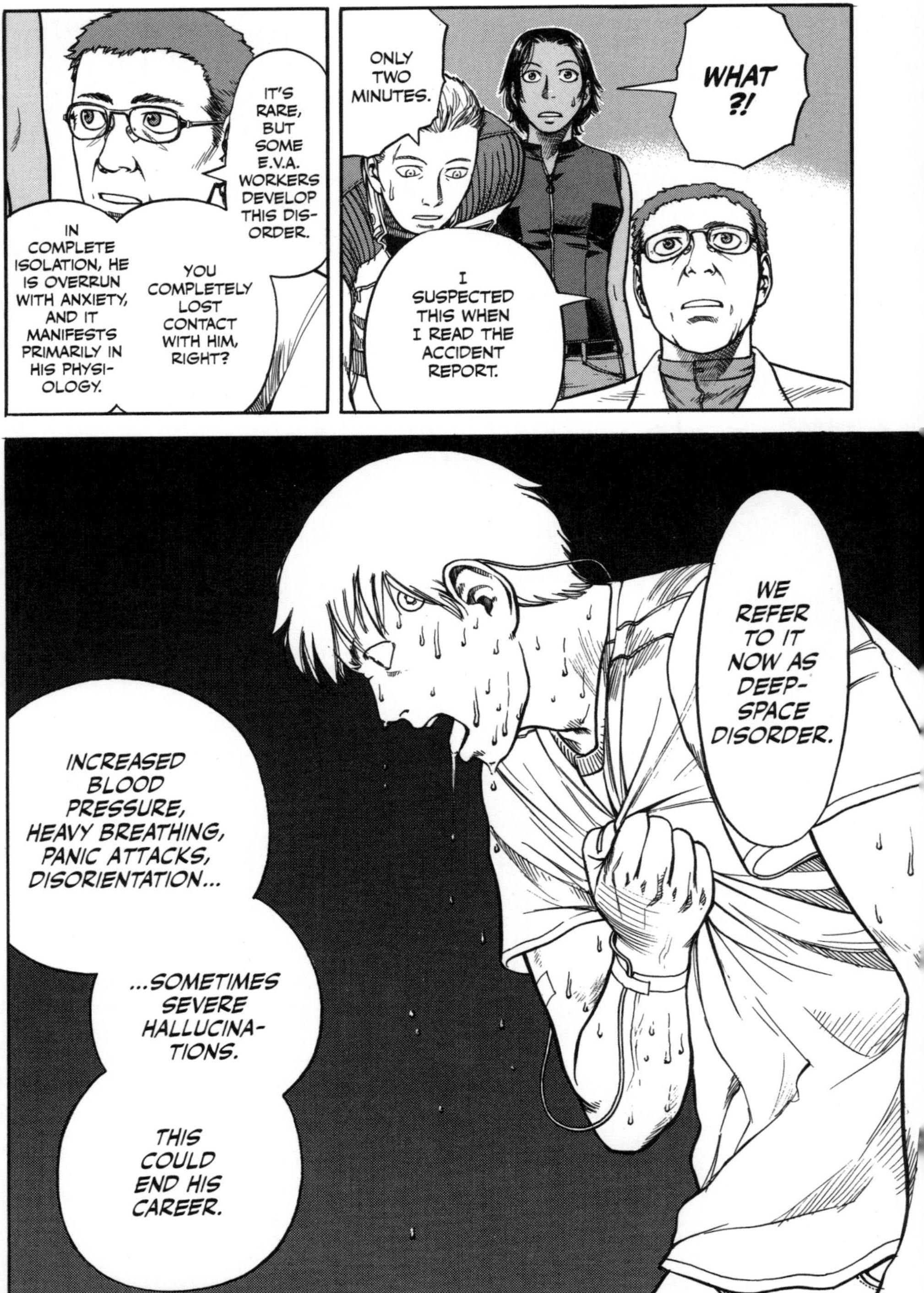
IT'S RARE, BUT SOME E.V.A. WORKERS DEVELOP THIS DISORDER.
IN COMPLETE ISOLATION, HE IS OVERRUN WITH ANXIETY, AND IT MANIFESTS PRIMARILY IN HIS PHYSIOLOGY.
YOU COMPLETELY LOST CONTACT WITH HIM, RIGHT?
ONLY TWO MINUTES.
WHAT ?!
I SUSPECTED THIS WHEN I READ THE ACCIDENT REPORT.
WE REFER TO IT NOW AS DEEP-SPACE DISORDER.
INCREASED BLOOD PRESSURE, HEAVY BREATHING, PANIC ATTACKS, DISORIENTATION...
...SOMETIMES SEVERE HALLUCINATIONS.
THIS COULD END HIS CAREER.

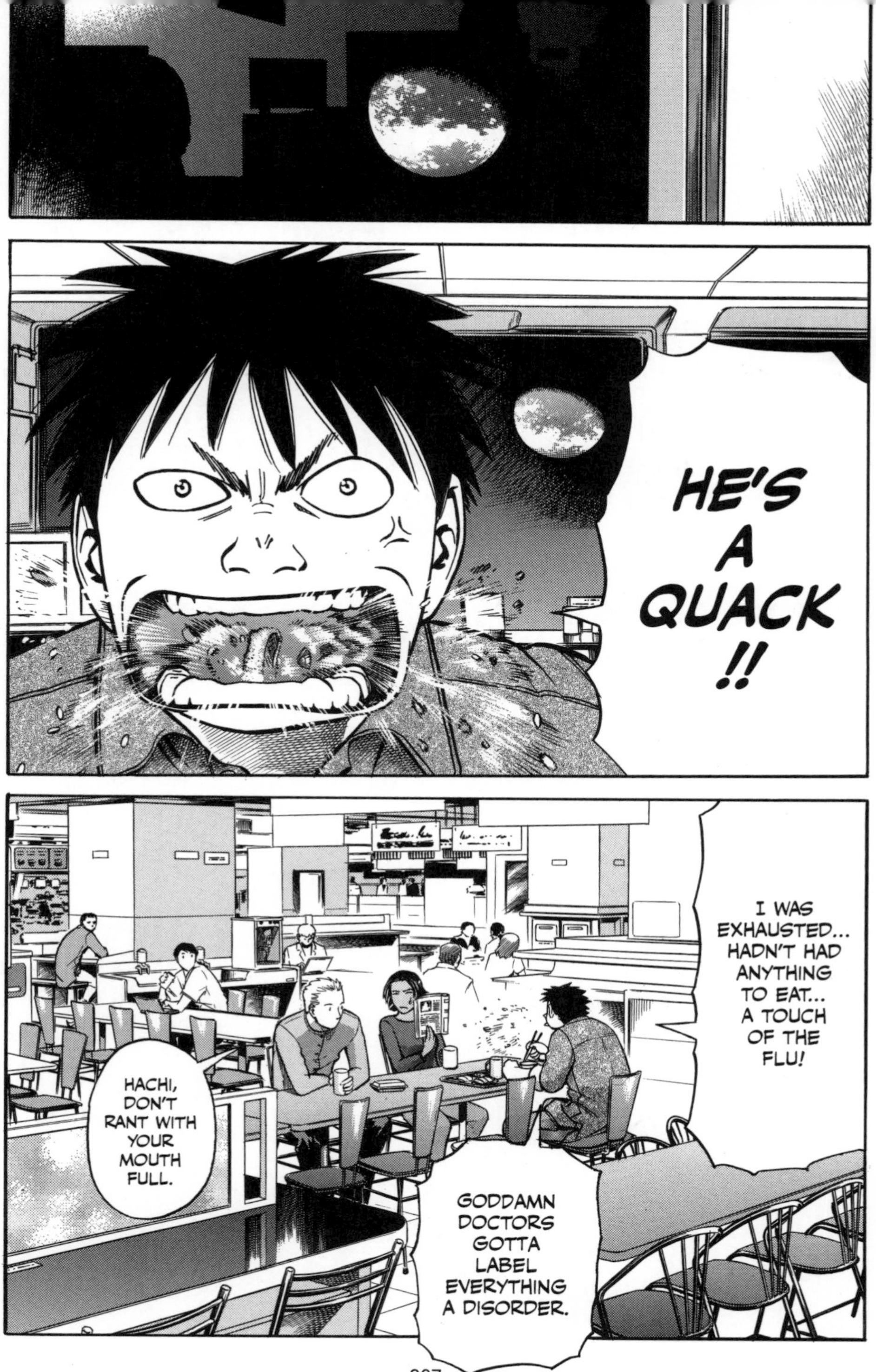
HE'S A QUACK!!
I WAS EXHAUSTED... HADN'T HAD ANYTHING TO EAT... A TOUCH OF THE FLU!
GODDAMN DOCTORS GOTTA LABEL EVERYTHING A DISORDER.
HACHI, DON'T RANT WITH YOUR MOUTH FULL.

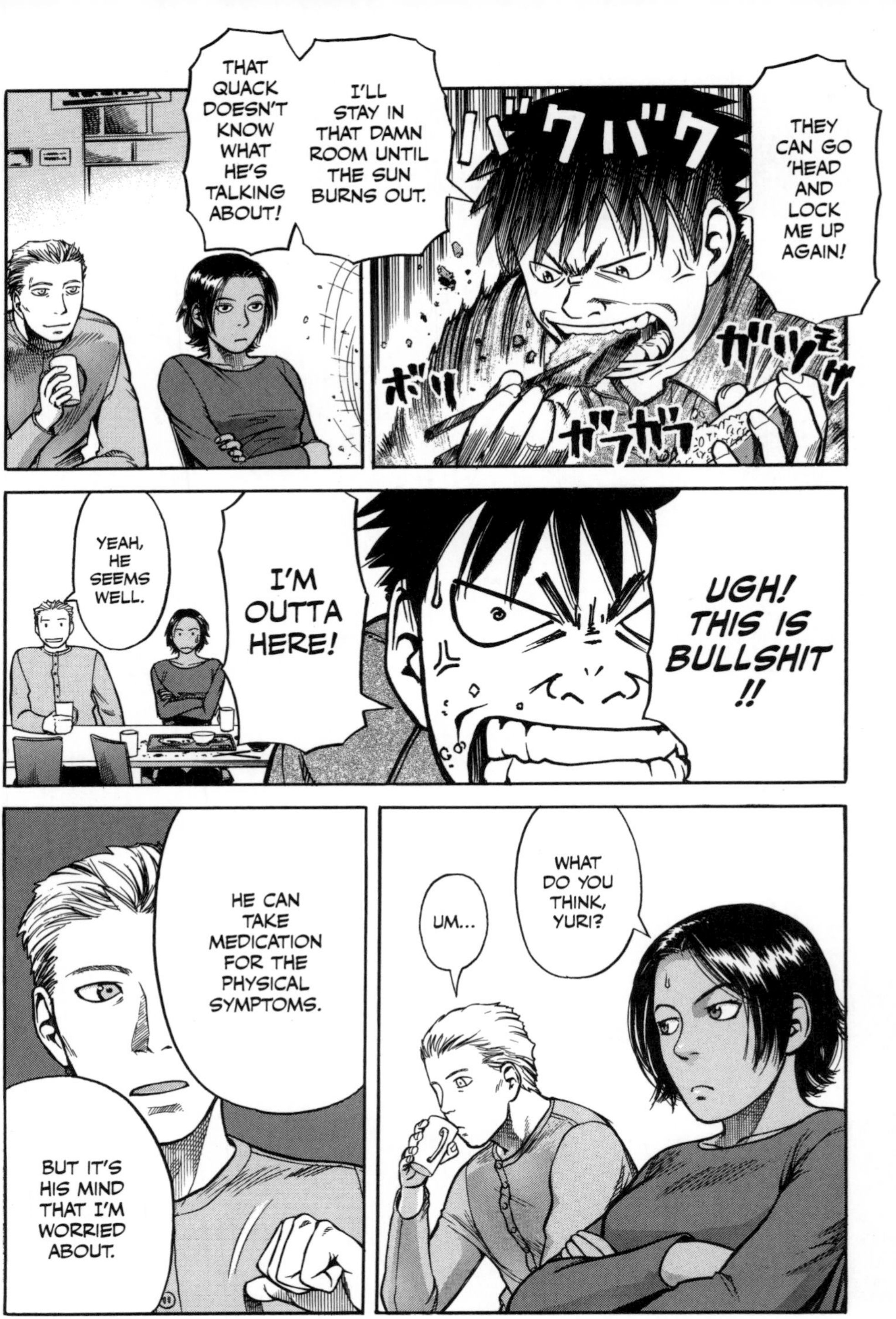
THEY CAN GO 'HEAD AND LOCK ME UP AGAIN!
バクバク
ボリ
I'LL STAY IN THAT DAMN ROOM UNTIL THE SUN BURNS OUT.
THAT QUACK DOESN'T KNOW WHAT HE'S TALKING ABOUT!
UGH! THIS IS BULLSHIT!!
I'M OUTTA HERE!
YEAH, HE SEEMS WELL.
WHAT DO YOU THINK, YURI?
UM...
HE CAN TAKE MEDICATION FOR THE PHYSICAL SYMPTOMS.
BUT IT'S HIS MIND THAT I'M WORRIED ABOUT.

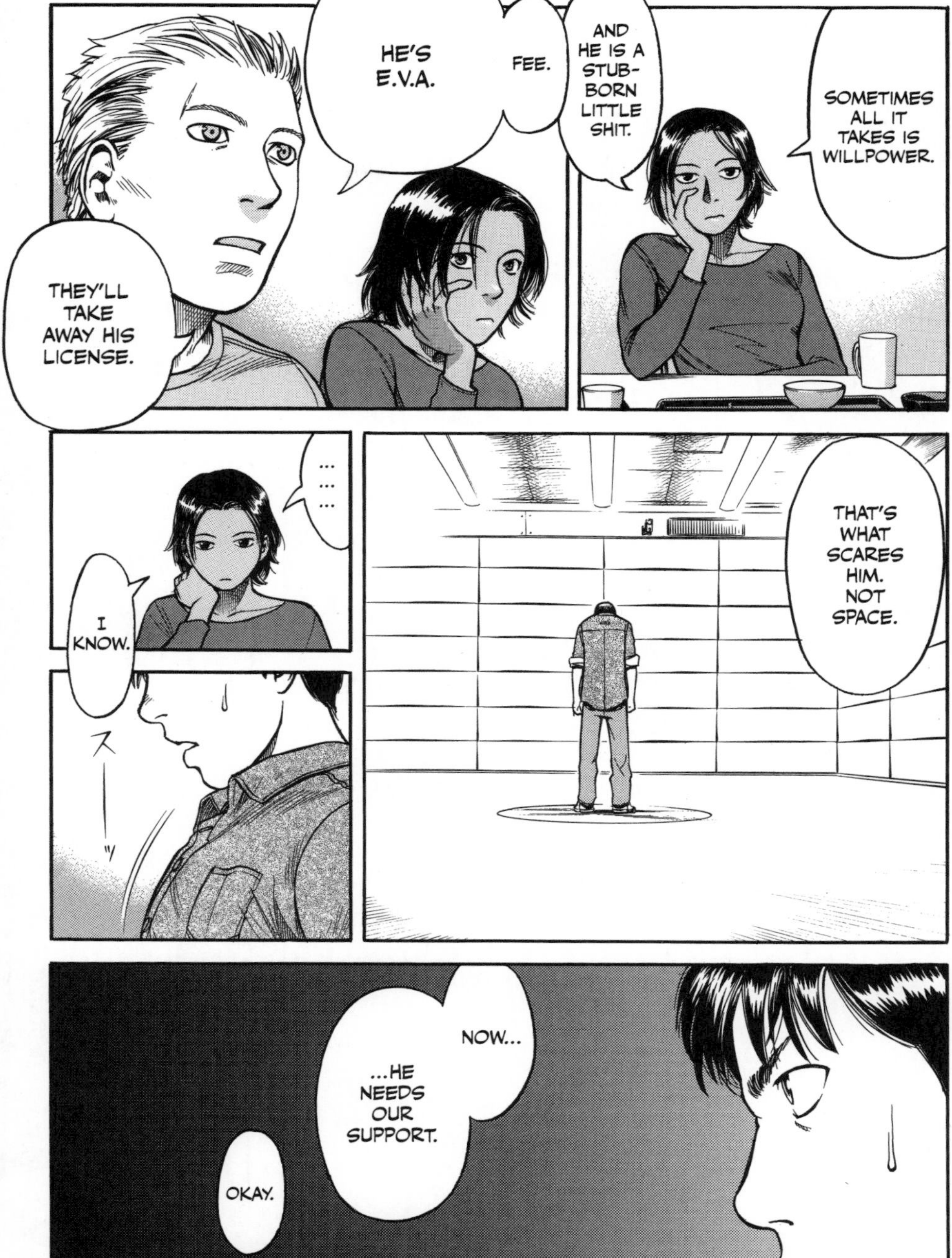
SOMETIMES ALL IT TAKES IS WILLPOWER.
AND HE IS A STUB-BORN LITTLE SHIT.
HE'S E.V.A.
FEE.
THEY'LL TAKE AWAY HIS LICENSE.
THAT'S WHAT SCARES HIM. NOT SPACE.
... ...
I KNOW.
スーッ
NOW...
...HE NEEDS OUR SUPPORT.
OKAY.

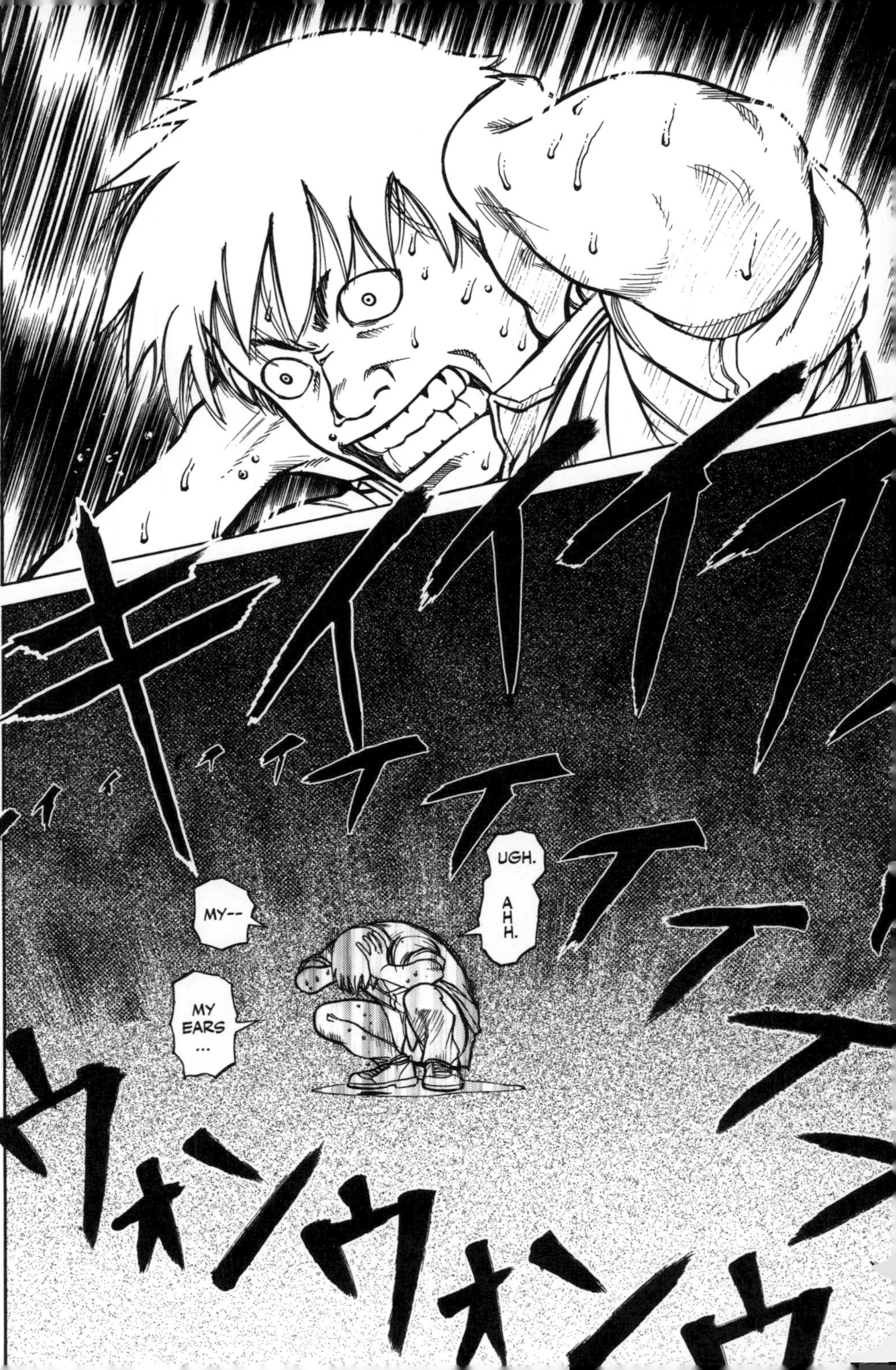
UGH.
AHH.
MY--
MY EARS ...

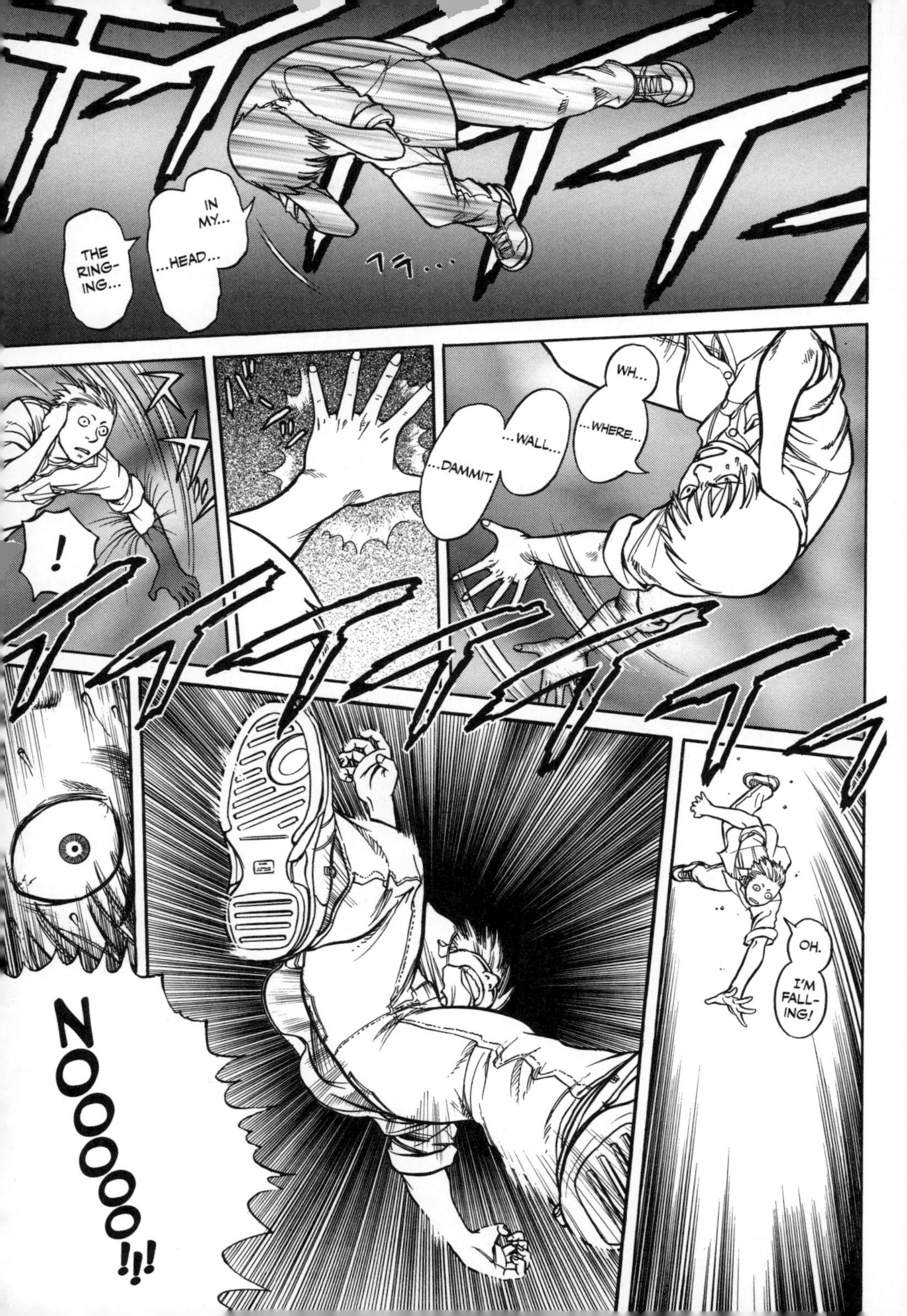
IN MY... ...HEAD...
THE RING-ING...
WH...
...WHERE...
...WALL...
...DAMMIT.
!
OH.
I'M FALL-ING!
NOOOOOO!!!

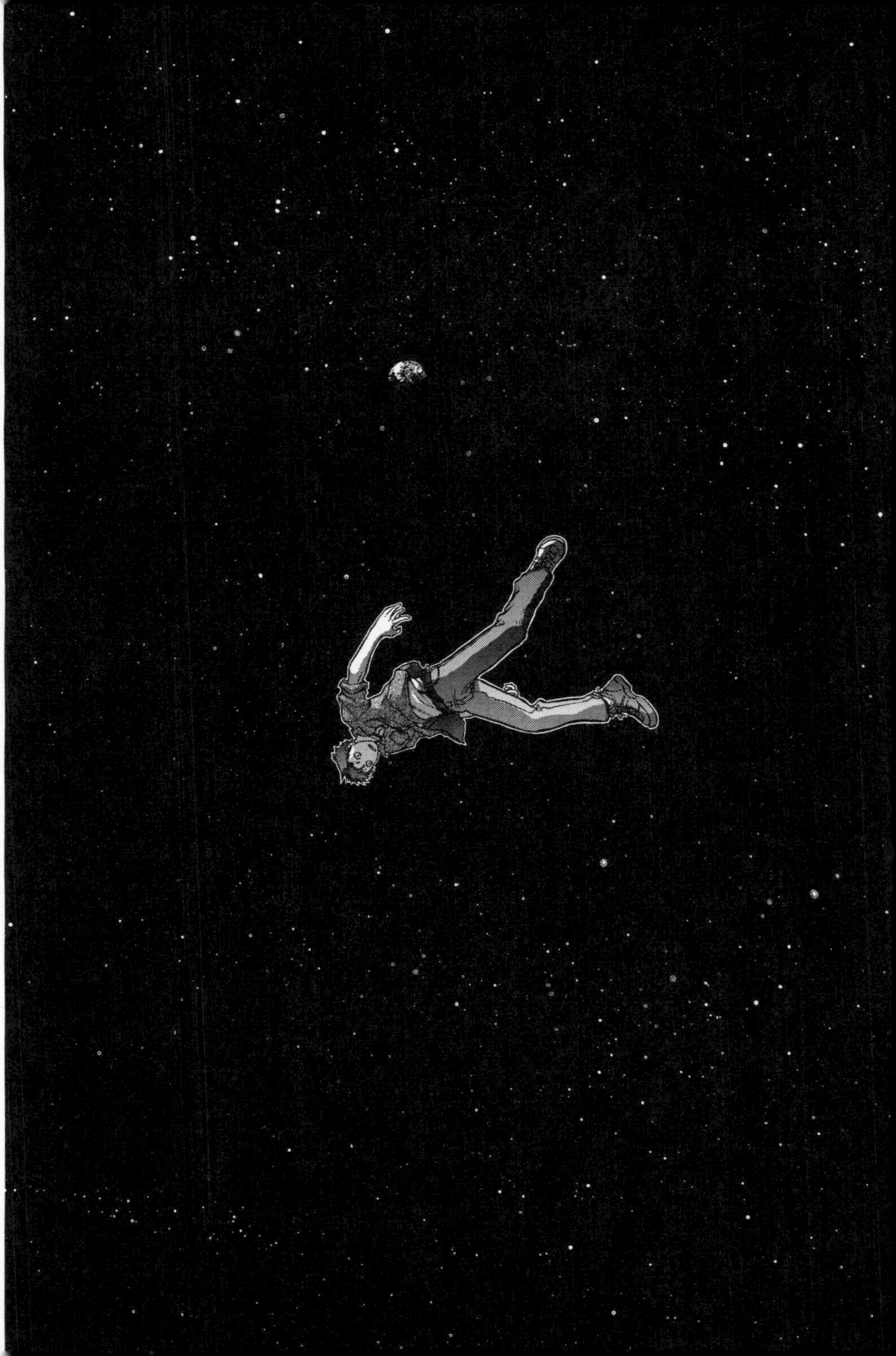

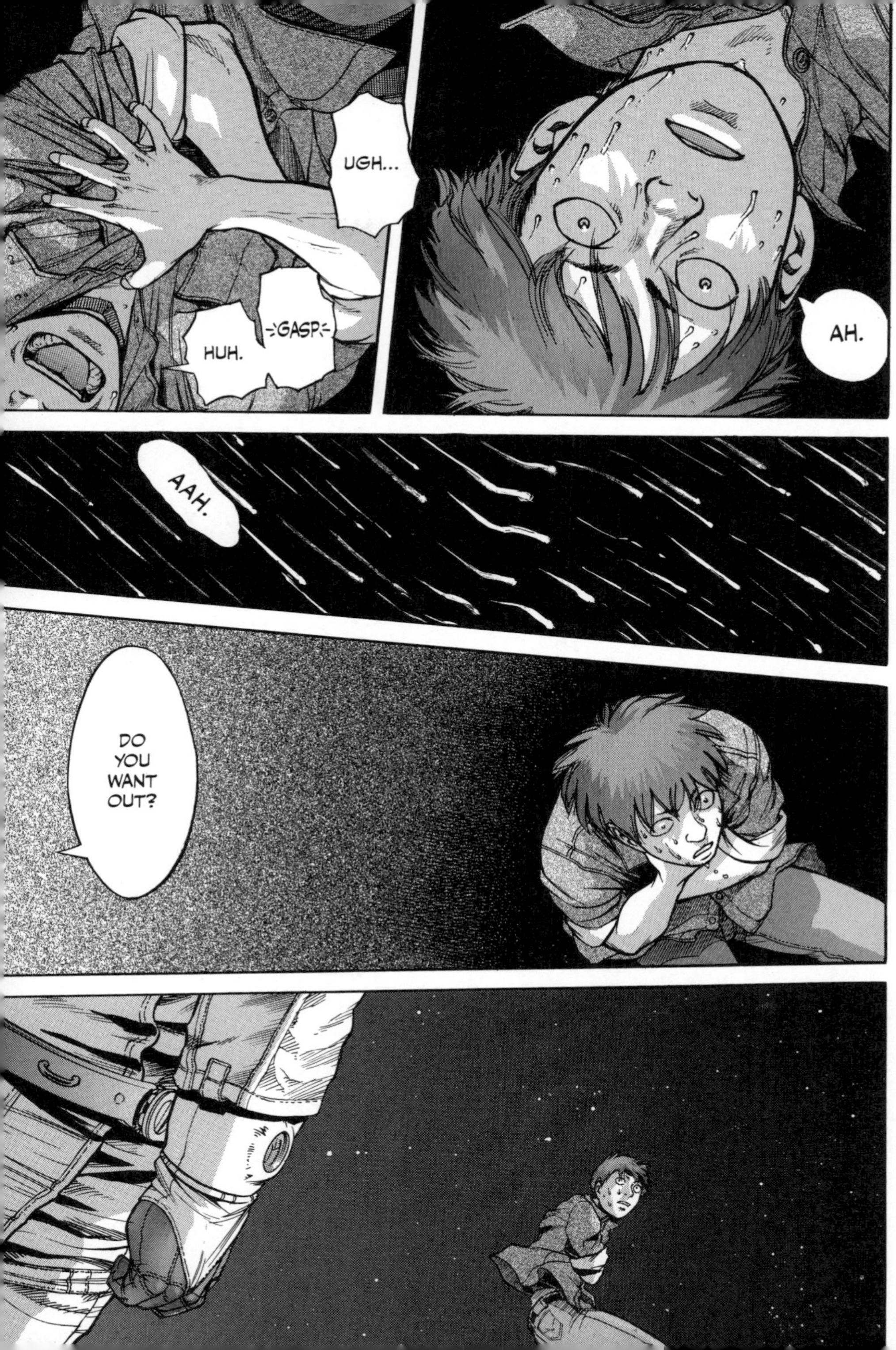
AH.
UGH...
-GASP-
HUH.
AAH.
DO YOU WANT OUT?

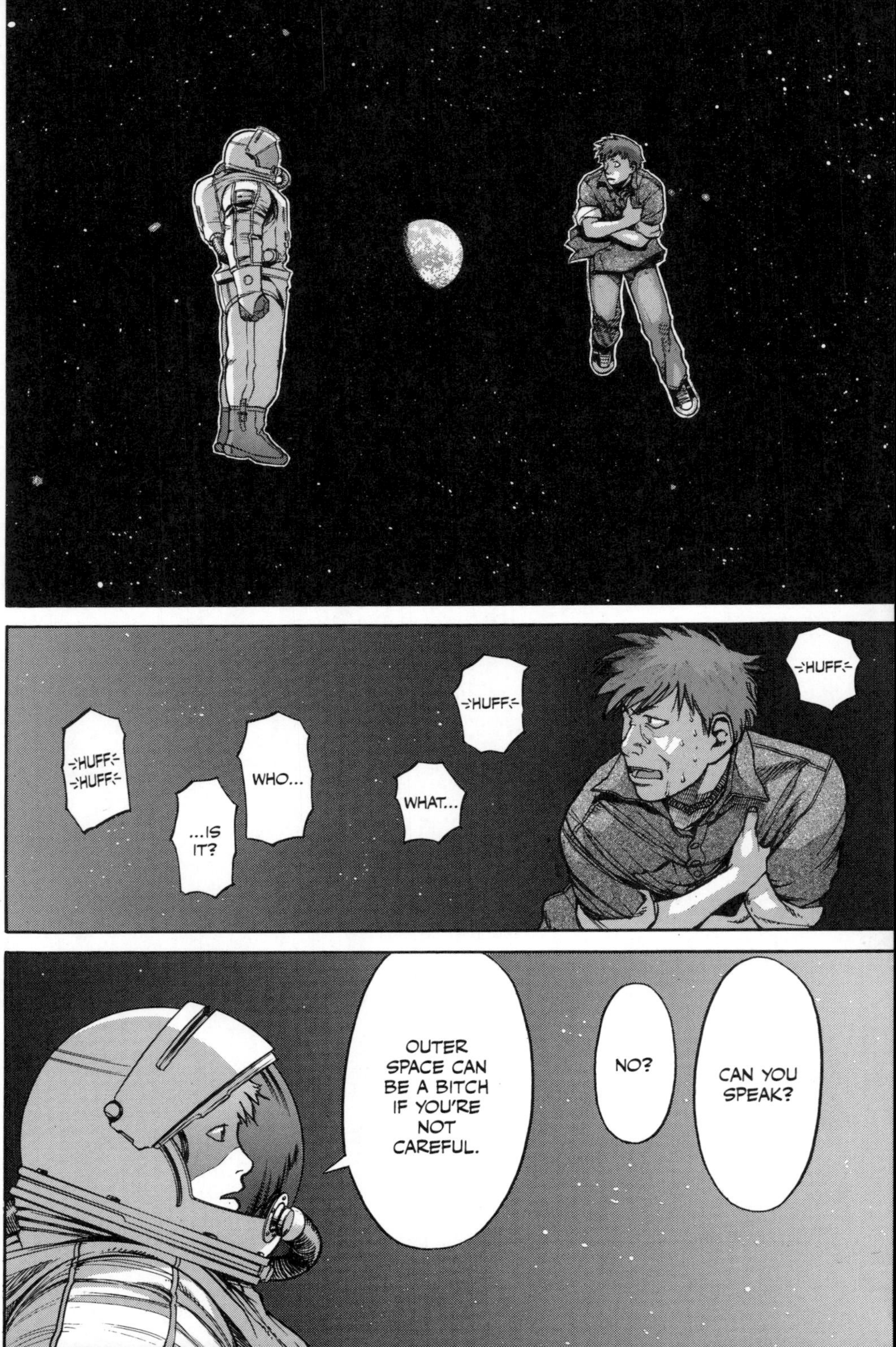
HUFF
HUFF
WHAT...
WHO...
...IS IT?
HUFF HUFF
CAN YOU SPEAK?
NO?
OUTER SPACE CAN BE A BITCH IF YOU'RE NOT CAREFUL.

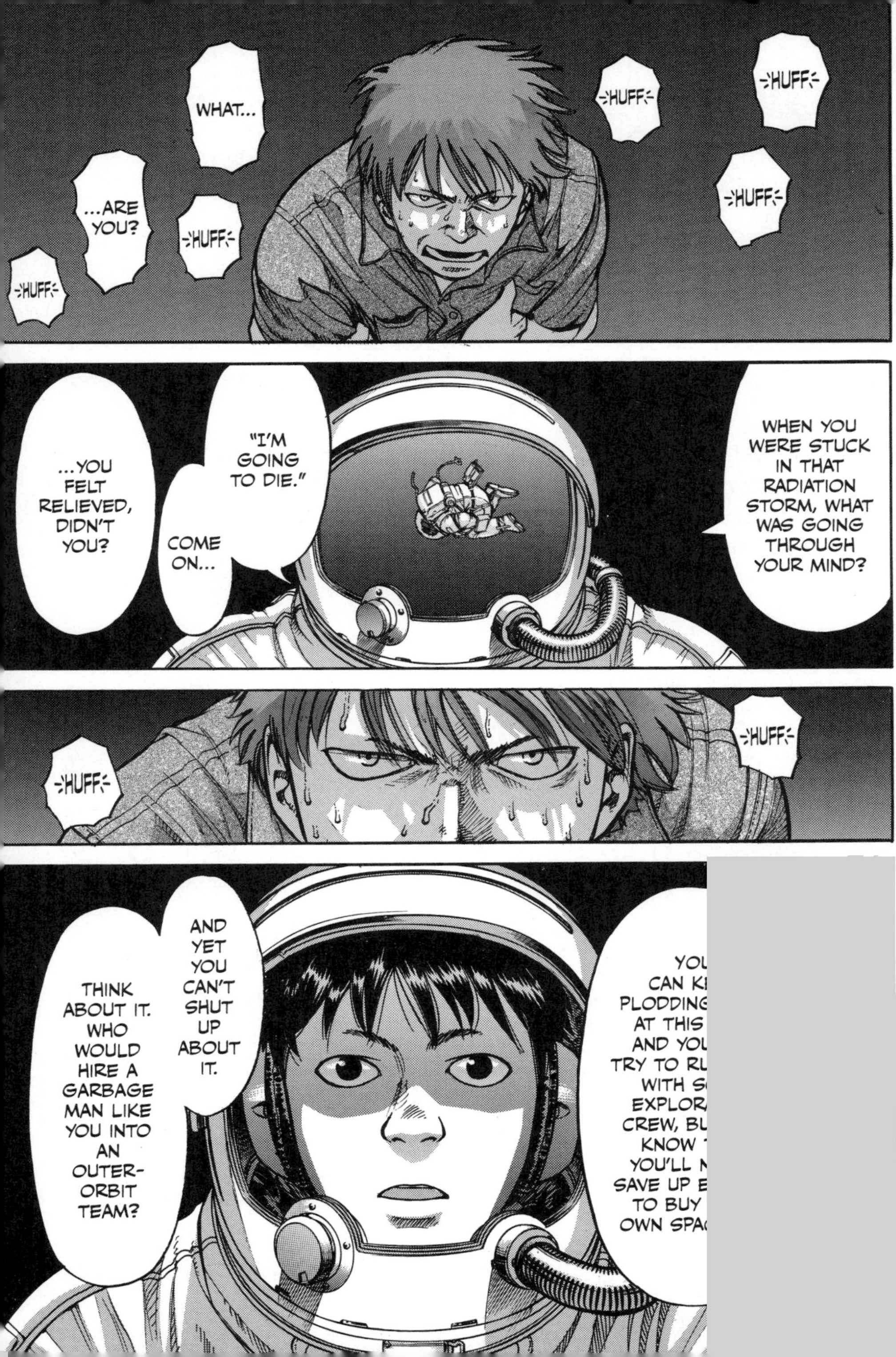
HUFF
HUFF
WHAT...
HUFF
...ARE YOU?
HUFF
HUFF
WHEN YOU WERE STUCK IN THAT RADIATION STORM, WHAT WAS GOING THROUGH YOUR MIND?
"I'M GOING TO DIE."
COME ON...
...YOU FELT RELIEVED, DIDN'T YOU?
HUFF
HUFF
AND YET YOU CAN'T SHUT UP ABOUT IT.
THINK ABOUT IT. WHO WOULD HIRE A GARBAGE MAN LIKE YOU INTO AN OUTER-ORBIT TEAM?

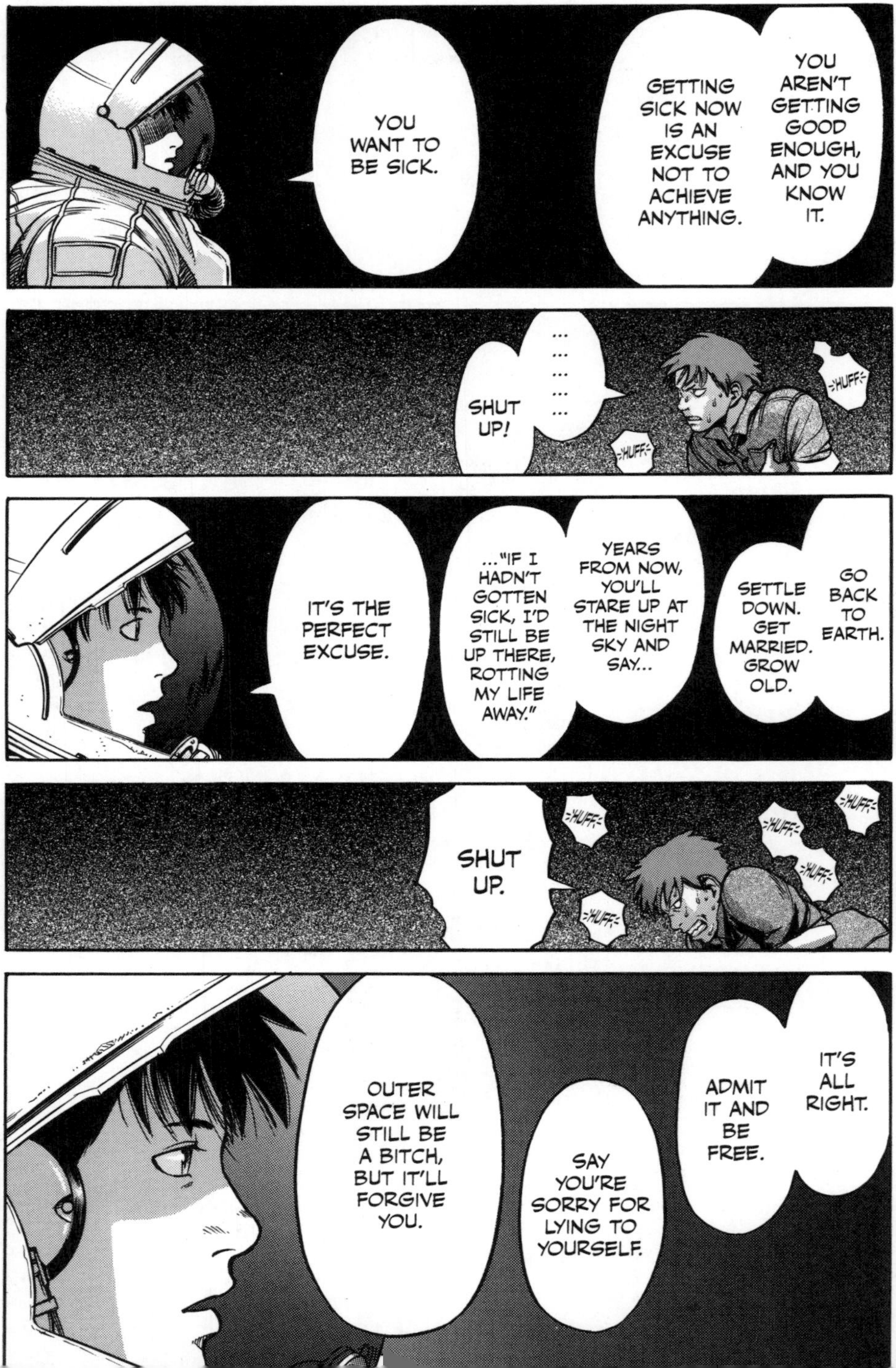
YOU AREN'T GETTING GOOD ENOUGH, AND YOU KNOW IT.
GETTING SICK NOW IS AN EXCUSE NOT TO ACHIEVE ANYTHING.
YOU WANT TO BE SICK.
HUFF
....
SHUT UP!
HUFF
GO BACK TO EARTH.
SETTLE DOWN. GET MARRIED. GROW OLD.
YEARS FROM NOW, YOU'LL STARE UP AT THE NIGHT SKY AND SAY...
..."IF I HADN'T GOTTEN SICK, I'D STILL BE UP THERE, ROTTING MY LIFE AWAY."
IT'S THE PERFECT EXCUSE.
HUFF
HUFF
HUFF
HUFF
SHUT UP.
HUFF
IT'S ALL RIGHT.
ADMIT IT AND BE FREE.
SAY YOU'RE SORRY FOR LYING TO YOURSELF.
OUTER SPACE WILL STILL BE A BITCH, BUT IT'LL FORGIVE YOU.

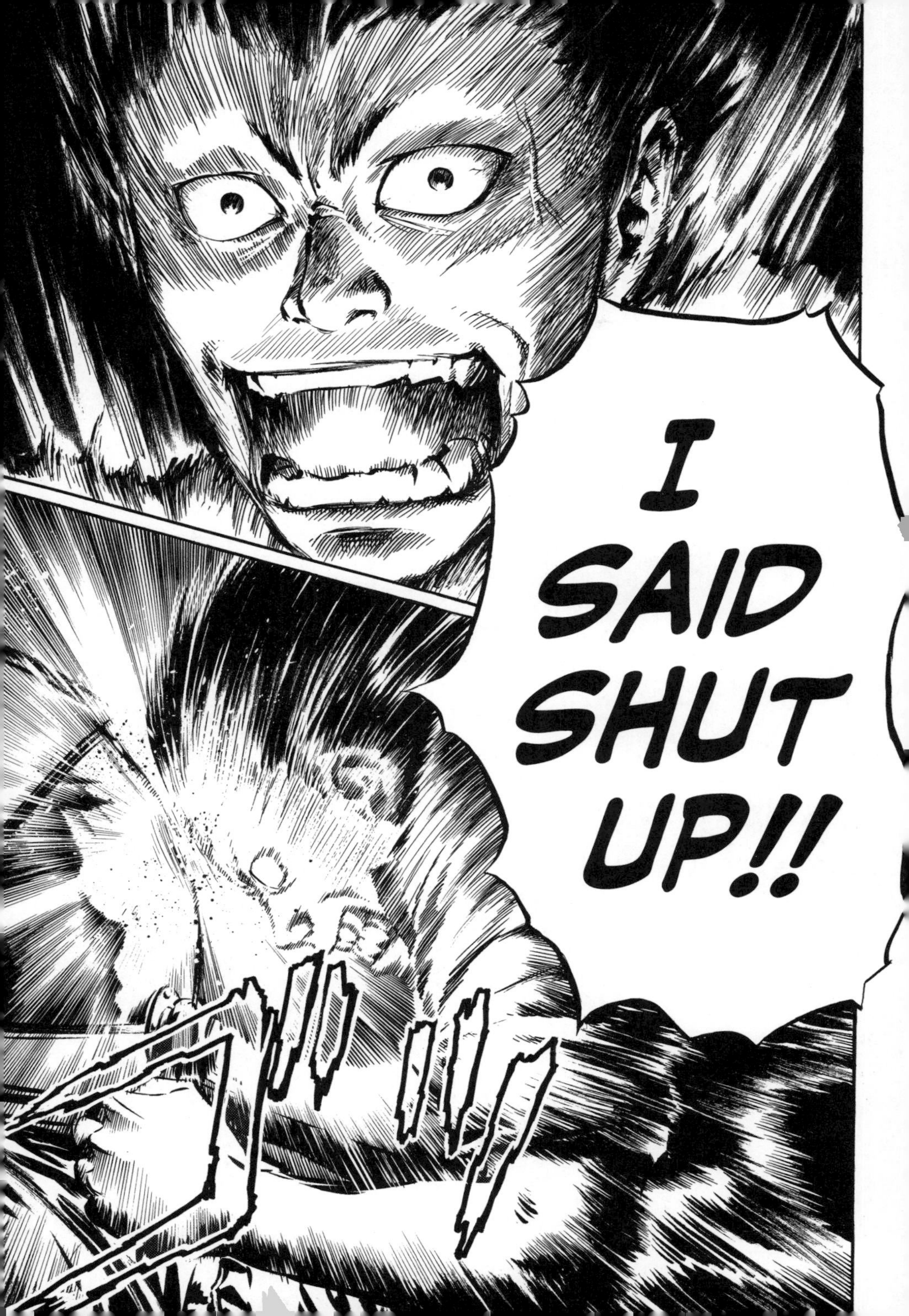
I SAID SHUT UP!!

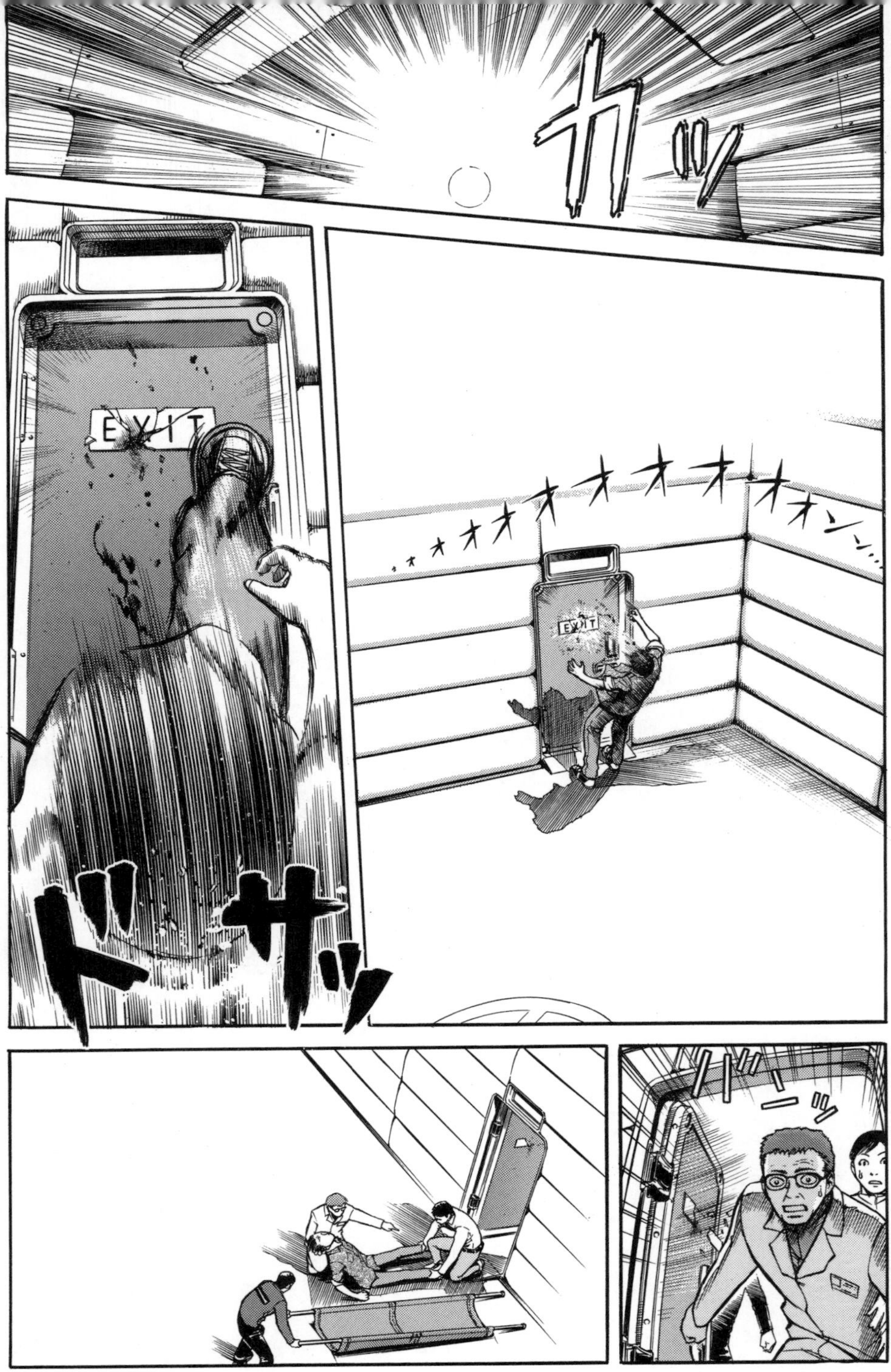
カッ
ォォォオオオオオオオオン…
EXIT
ドサッ
バーッ

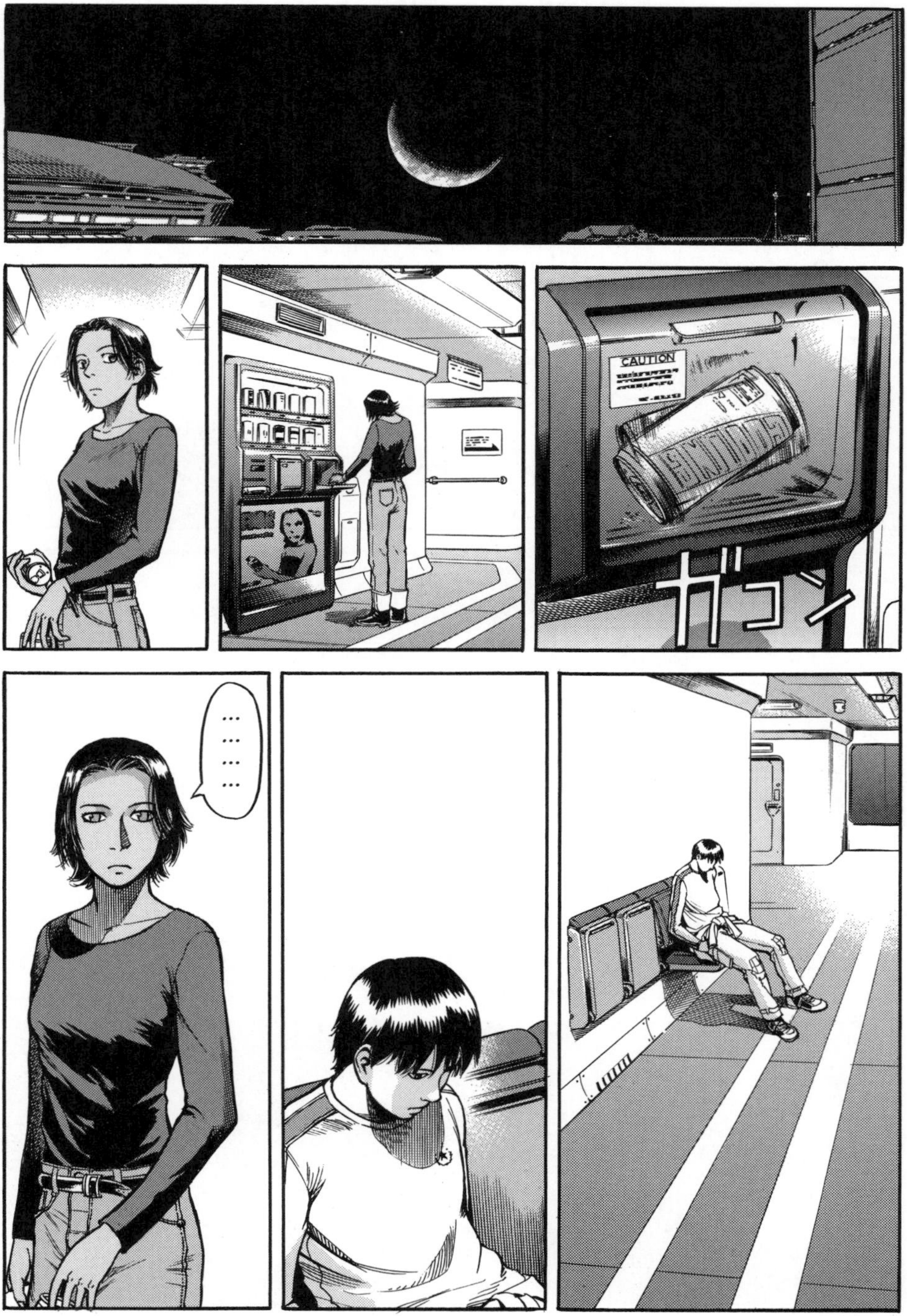
CAUTION
ガコン
…………

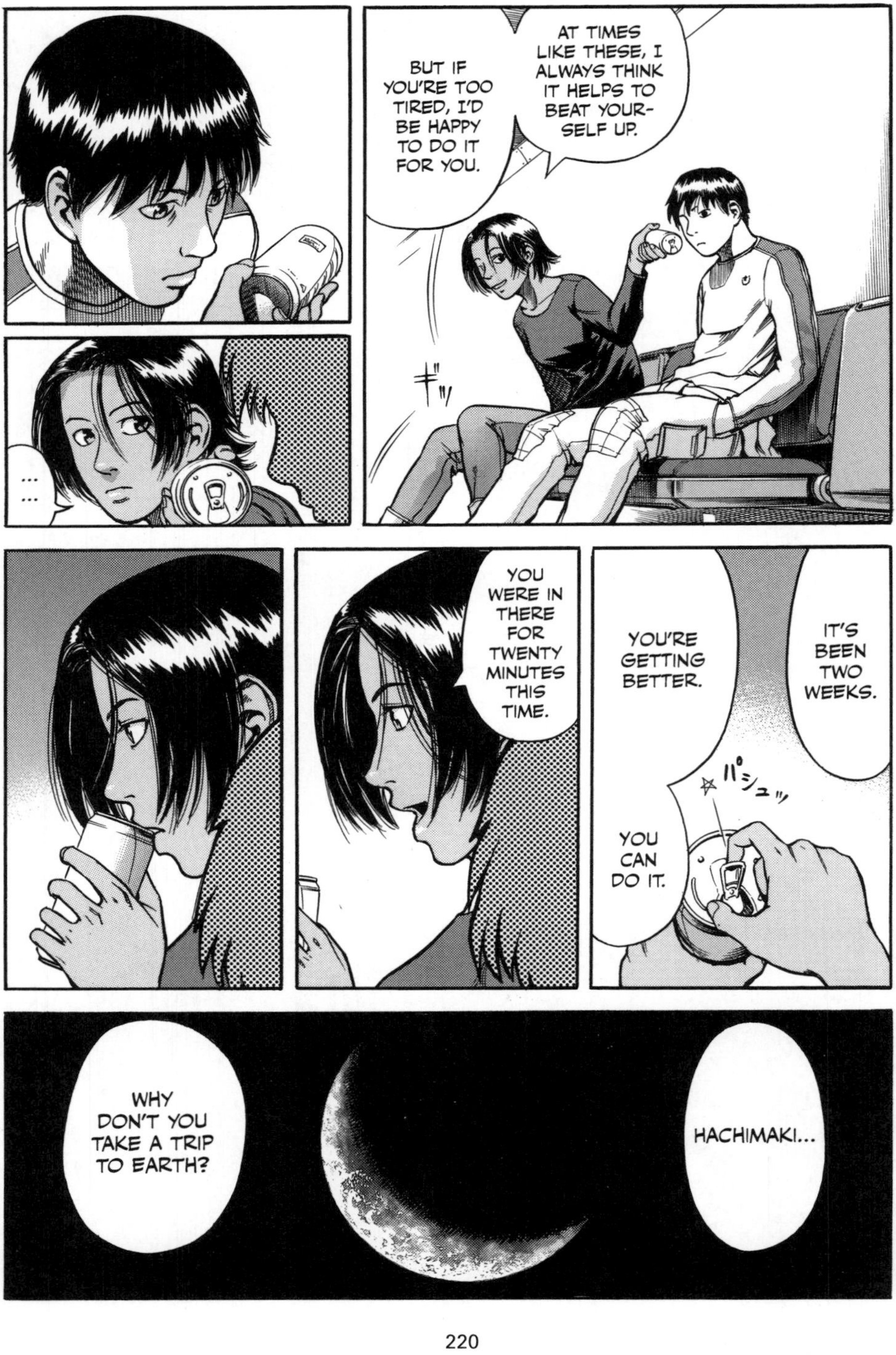
AT TIMES LIKE THESE, I ALWAYS THINK IT HELPS TO BEAT YOUR-SELF UP.
BUT IF YOU'RE TOO TIRED, I'D BE HAPPY TO DO IT FOR YOU.
ギッ
…… ……
IT'S BEEN TWO WEEKS.
YOU'RE GETTING BETTER.
パシュッ
YOU CAN DO IT.
YOU WERE IN THERE FOR TWENTY MINUTES THIS TIME.
HACHIMAKI...
WHY DON'T YOU TAKE A TRIP TO EARTH?

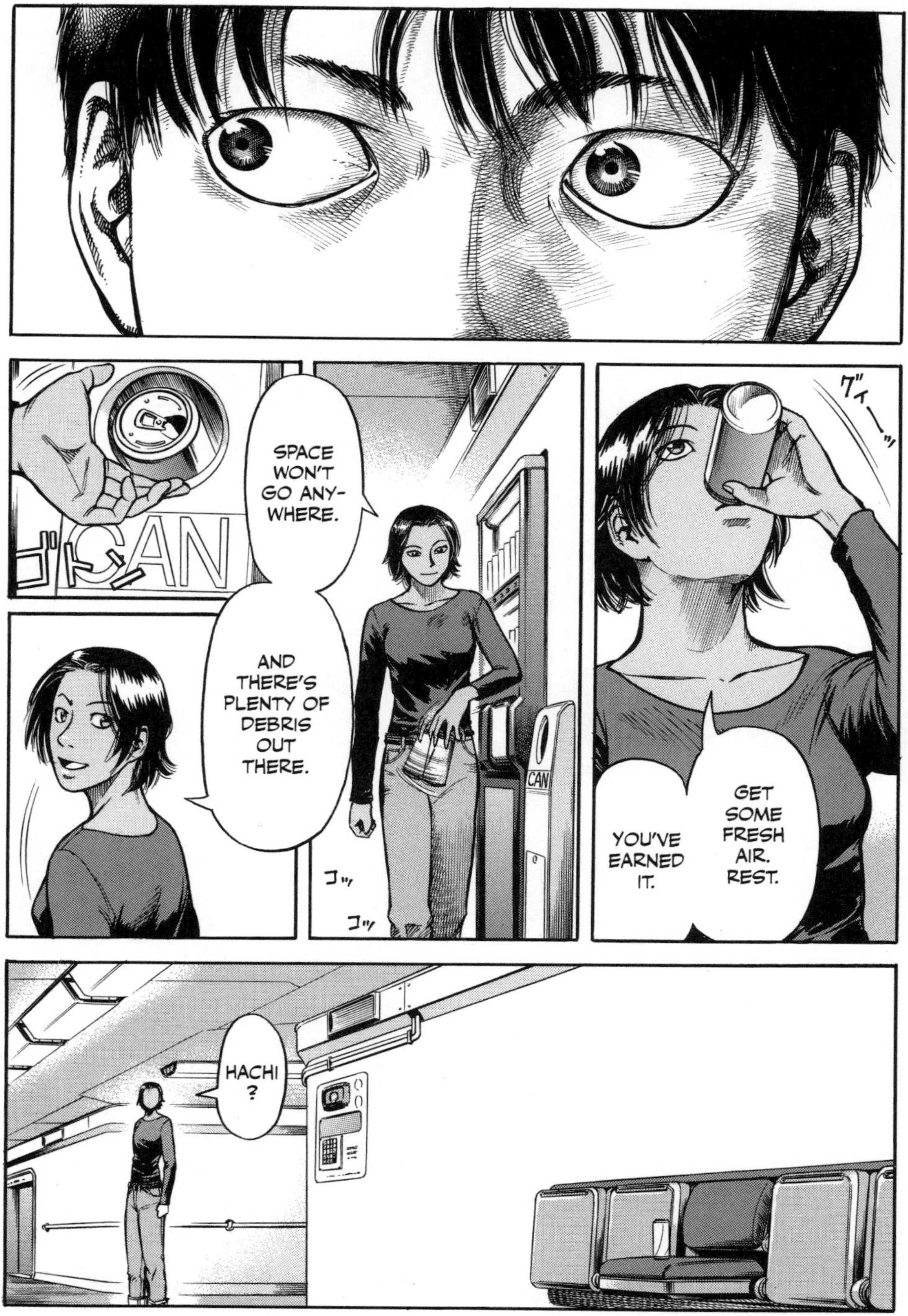
グィーッ
GET SOME FRESH AIR. REST.
YOU'VE EARNED IT.
SPACE WON'T GO ANY-WHERE.
AND THERE'S PLENTY OF DEBRIS OUT THERE.
CAN
ゴッ
ゴッ
CAN
HACHI ?

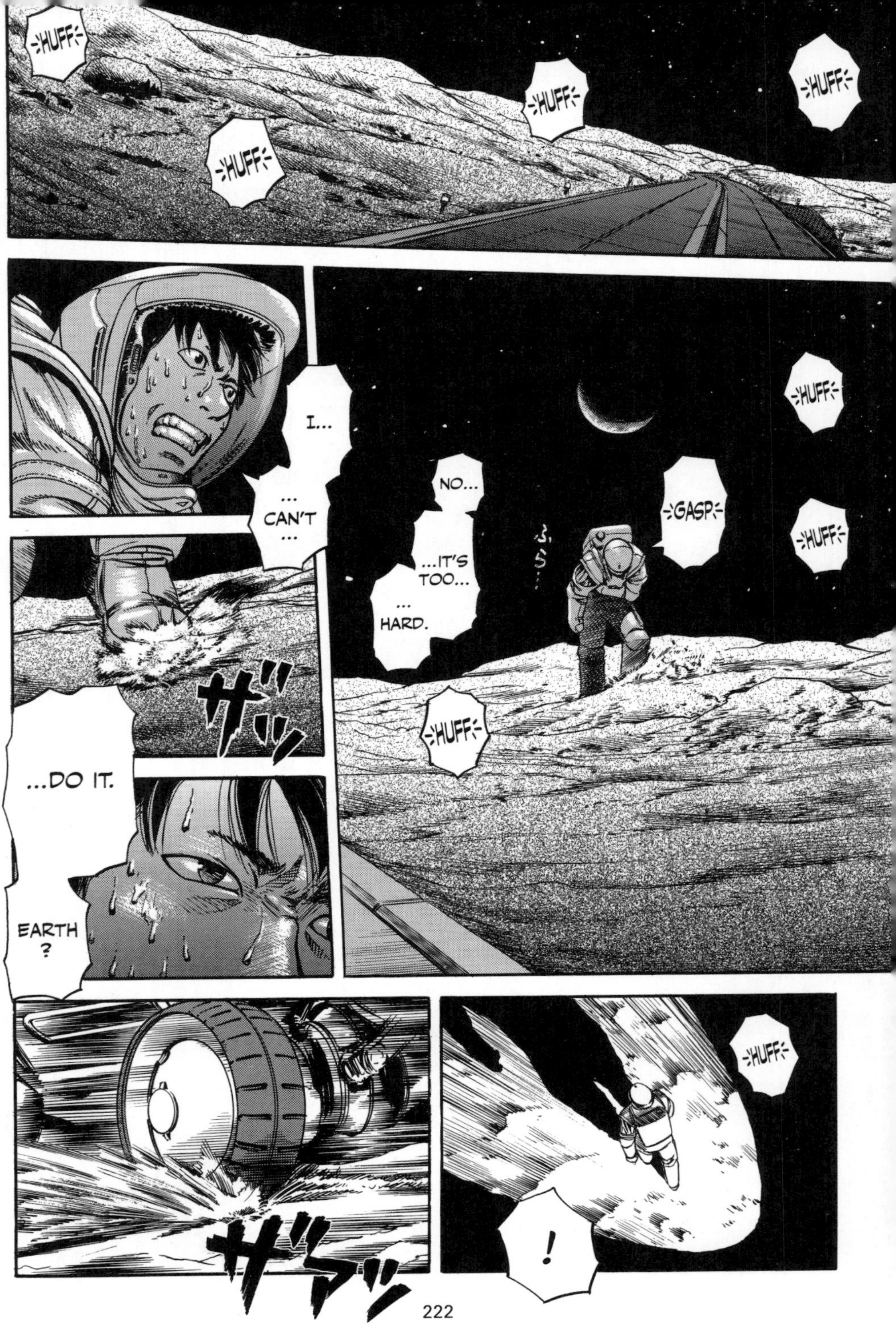
HUFF
HUFF
HUFF
HUFF
HUFF
GASP
HUFF
NO...
...IT'S TOO...
...HARD.
ふら…
HUFF
I...
...CAN'T...
ザッ
...DO IT.
EARTH?
HUFF
!
ザザァッ

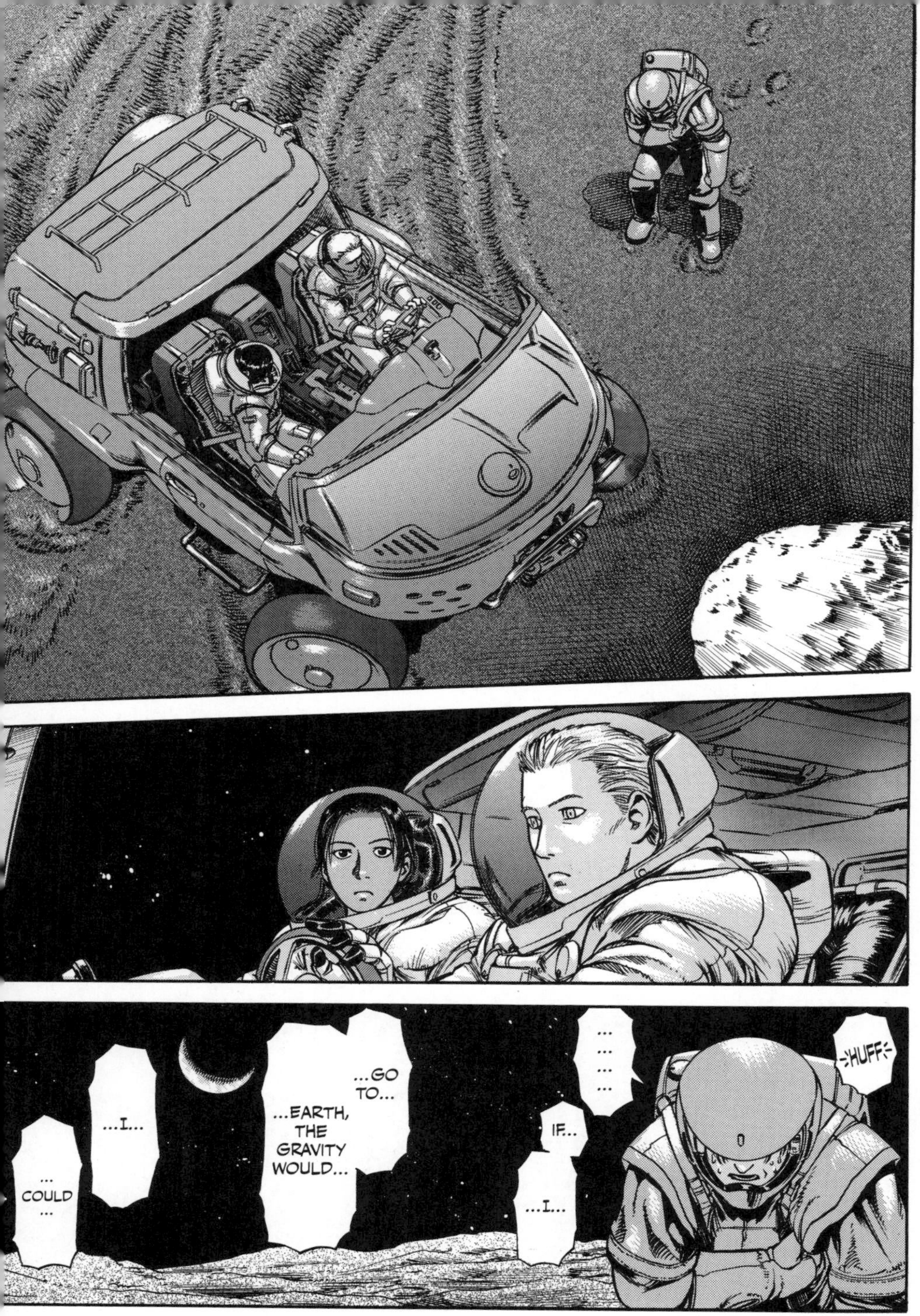
HUFF
... ...
IF...
...I...
...GO TO...
...EARTH, THE GRAVITY WOULD...
...I...
... COULD ...

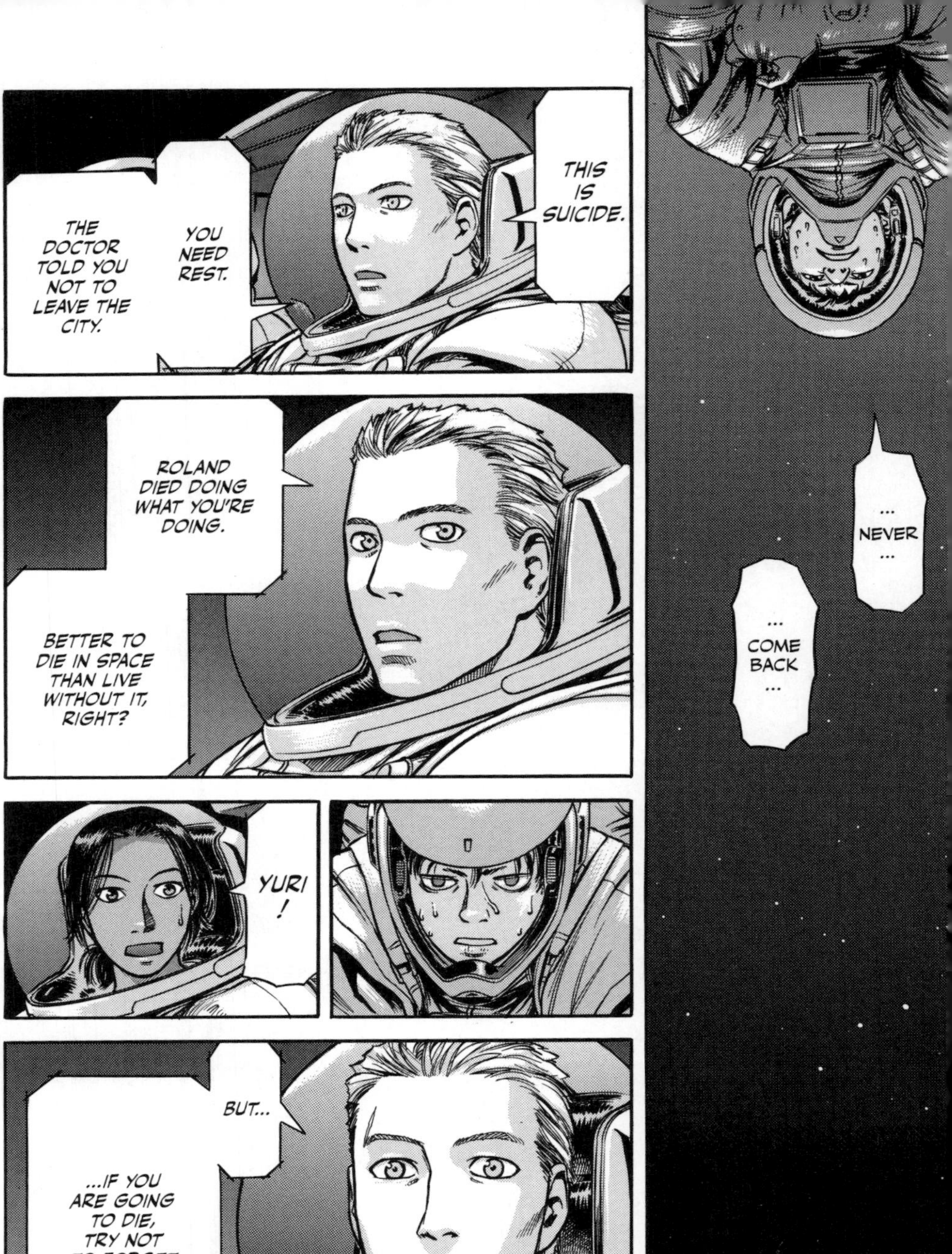
... NEVER ...
... COME BACK ...
THIS IS SUICIDE.
YOU NEED REST.
THE DOCTOR TOLD YOU NOT TO LEAVE THE CITY.
ROLAND DIED DOING WHAT YOU'RE DOING.
BETTER TO DIE IN SPACE THAN LIVE WITHOUT IT, RIGHT?
YURI!
BUT...
...IF YOU ARE GOING TO DIE, TRY NOT TO FORGET ABOUT US. OKAY?

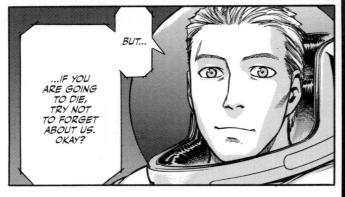

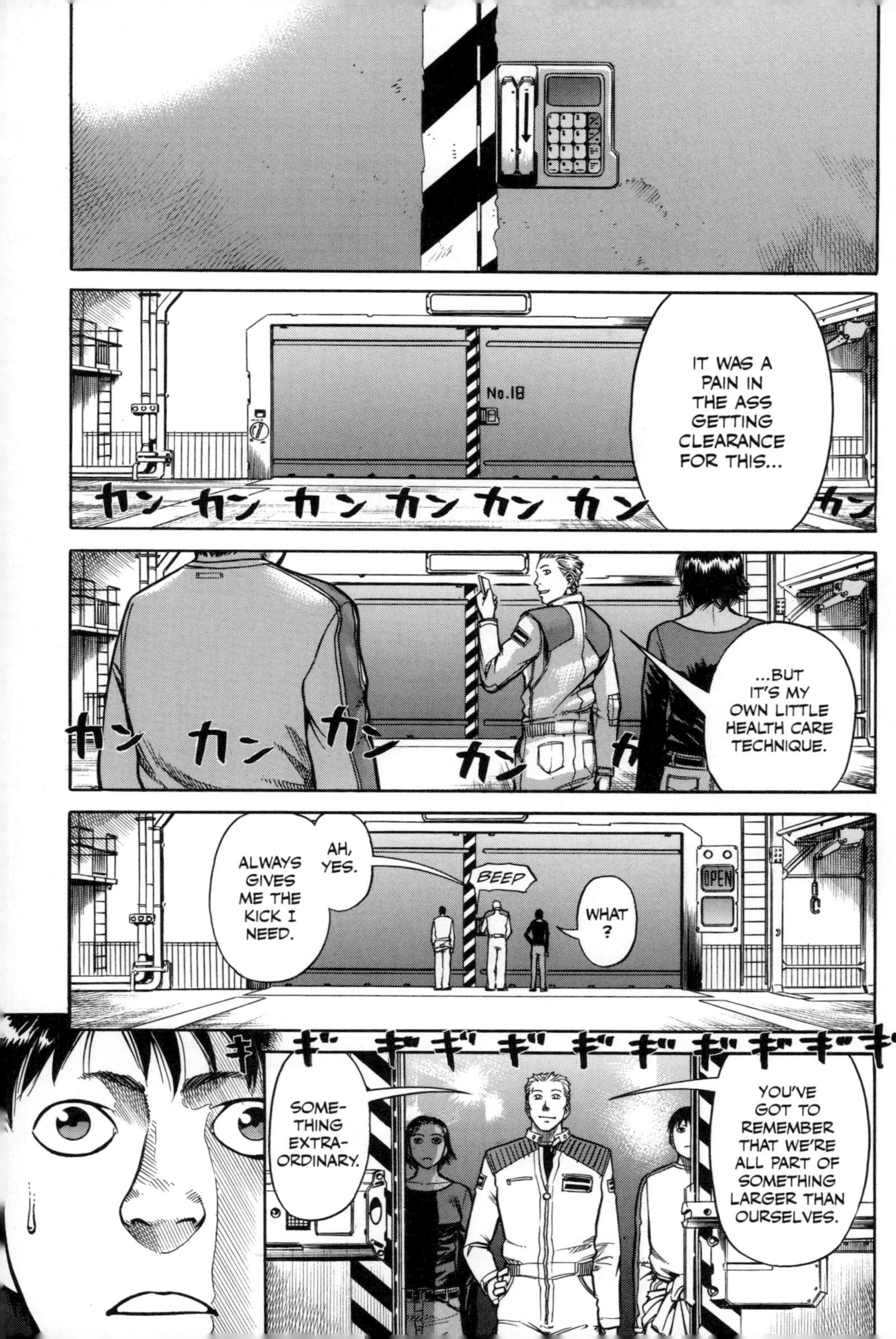

IT WAS A PAIN IN THE ASS GETTING CLEARANCE FOR THIS...
カン カン カン カン カン カン カン
...BUT IT'S MY OWN LITTLE HEALTH CARE TECHNIQUE.
カン カン カン カン カン
No.18
OPEN
WHAT ?
BEEP
AH, YES.
ALWAYS GIVES ME THE KICK I NEED.
ギ ギ ギ ギ ギ ギ ギ ギ ギ ギ ギ ギ
YOU'VE GOT TO REMEMBER THAT WE'RE ALL PART OF SOMETHING LARGER THAN OURSELVES.
SOME-THING EXTRA-ORDINARY.

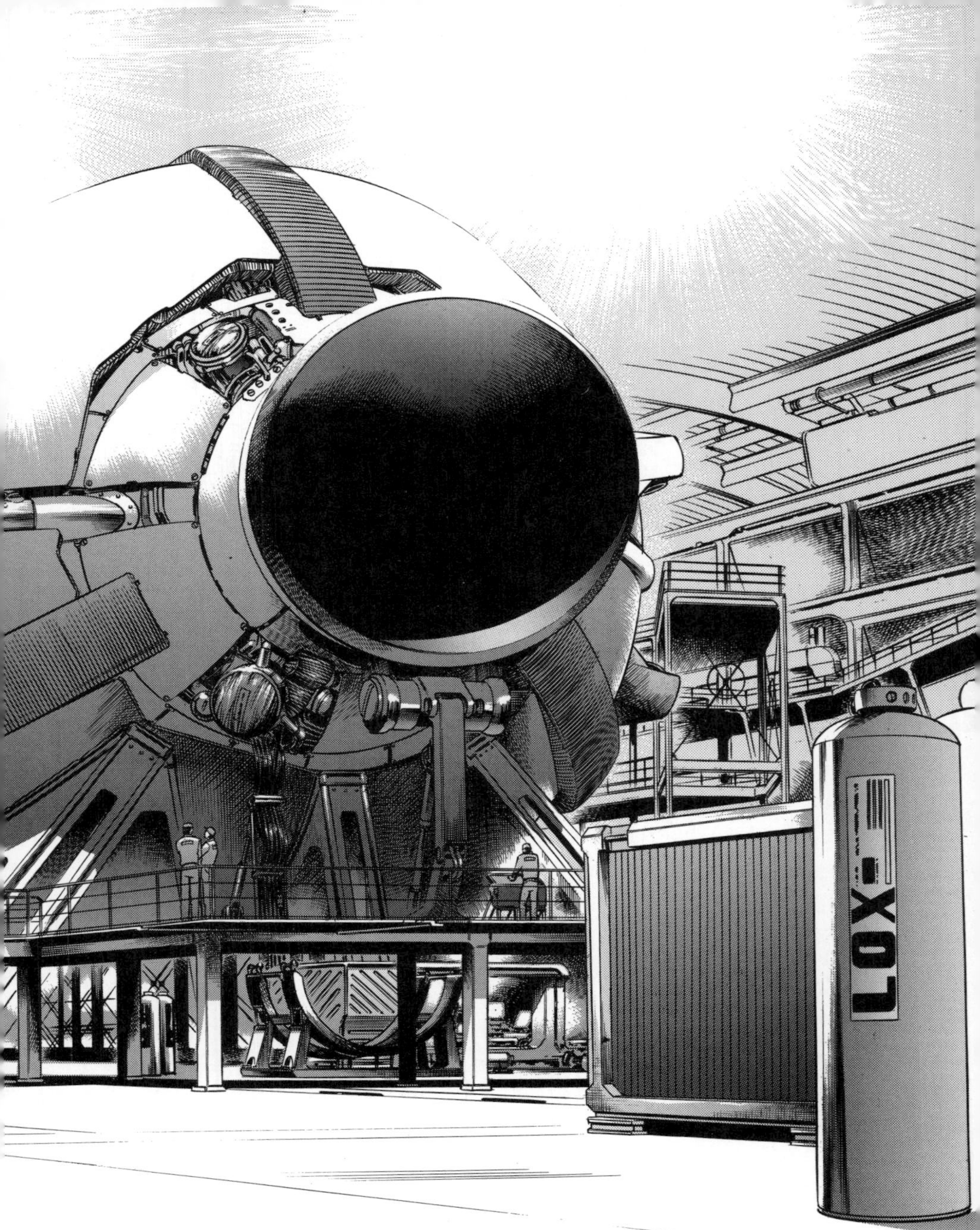
LOX

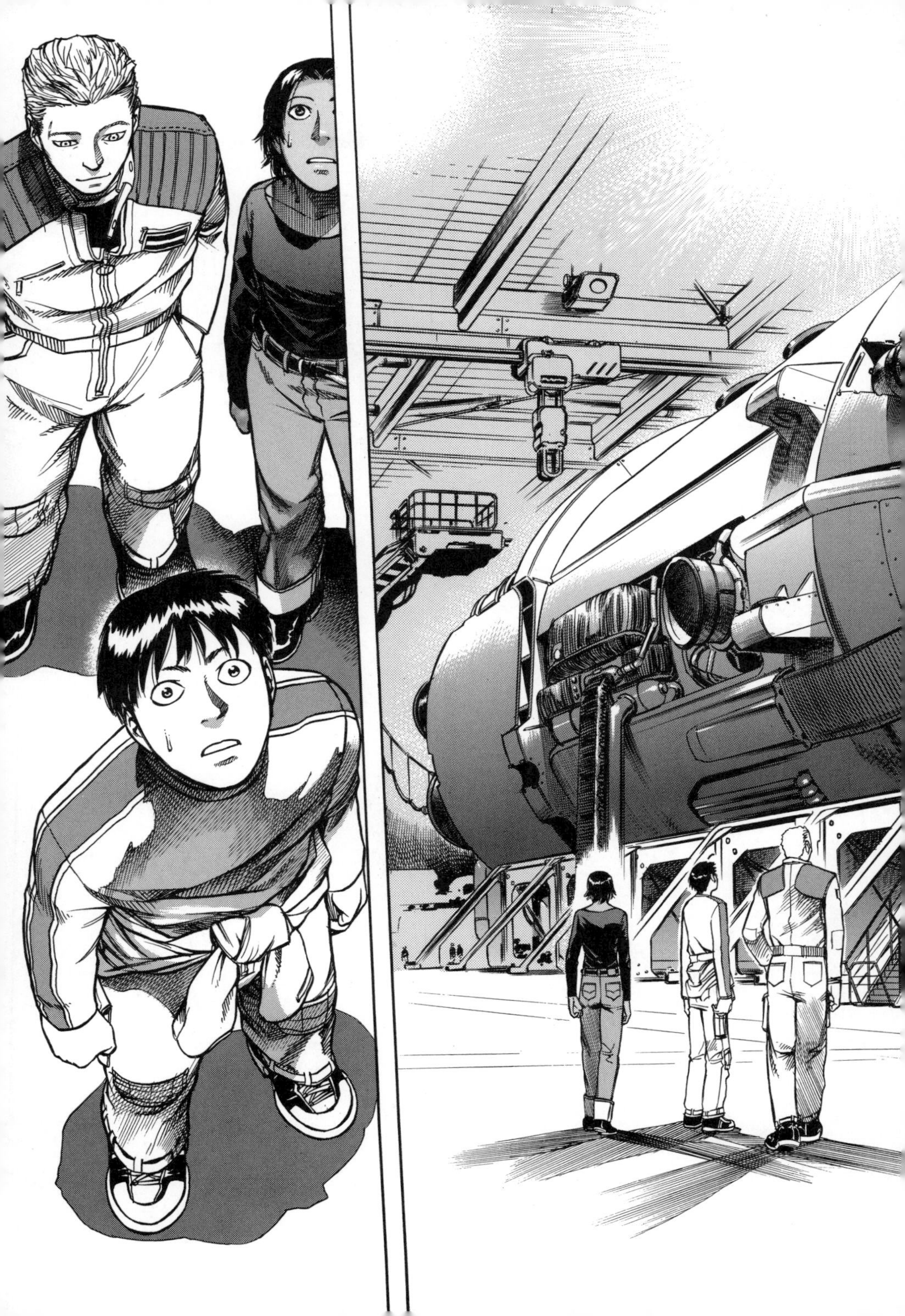

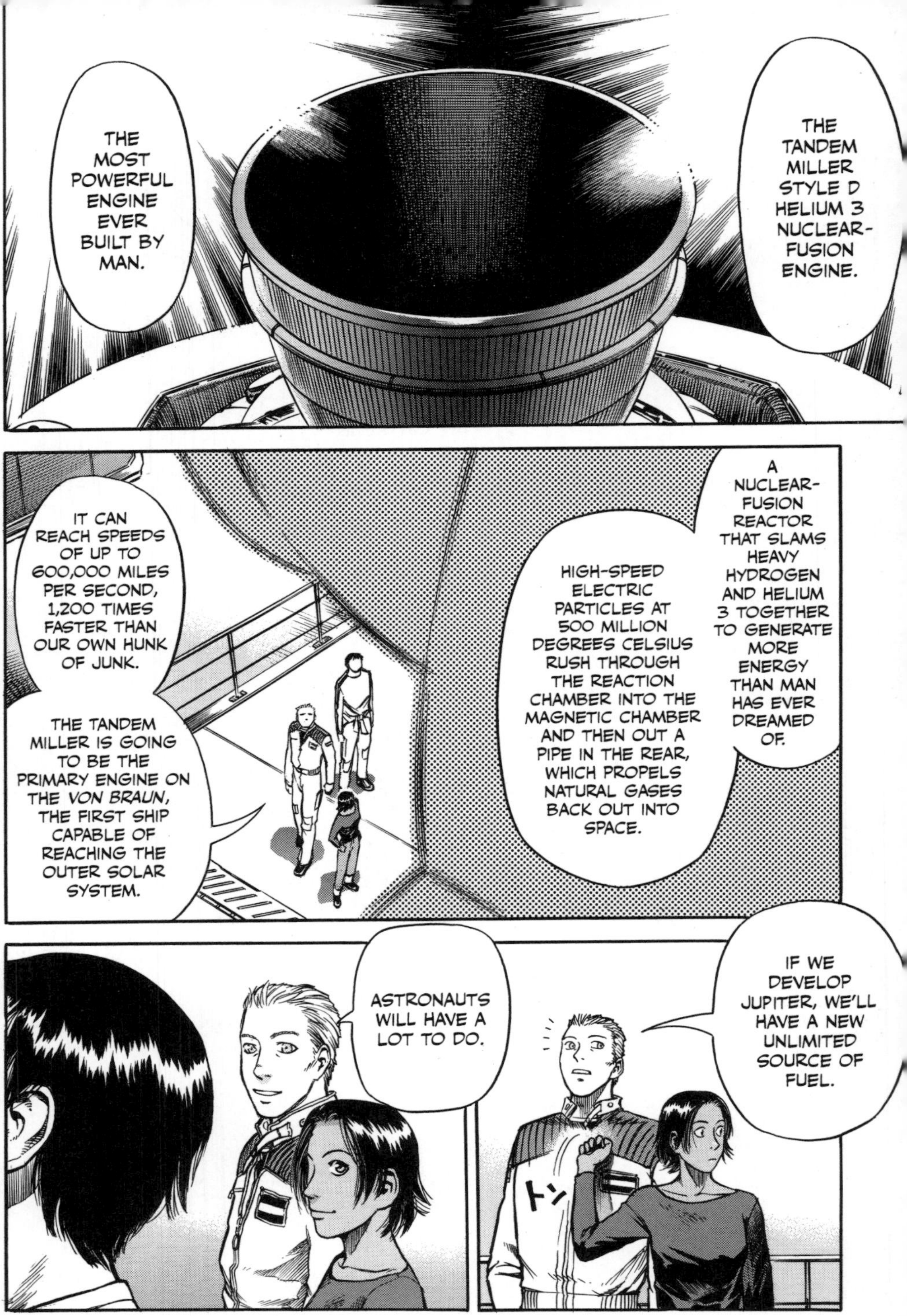
THE TANDEM MILLER STYLE D HELIUM 3 NUCLEAR-FUSION ENGINE.
THE MOST POWERFUL ENGINE EVER BUILT BY MAN.
A NUCLEAR-FUSION REACTOR THAT SLAMS HEAVY HYDROGEN AND HELIUM 3 TOGETHER TO GENERATE MORE ENERGY THAN MAN HAS EVER DREAMED OF.
HIGH-SPEED ELECTRIC PARTICLES AT 500 MILLION DEGREES CELSIUS RUSH THROUGH THE REACTION CHAMBER INTO THE MAGNETIC CHAMBER AND THEN OUT A PIPE IN THE REAR, WHICH PROPELS NATURAL GASES BACK OUT INTO SPACE.
IT CAN REACH SPEEDS OF UP TO 600,000 MILES PER SECOND, 1,200 TIMES FASTER THAN OUR OWN HUNK OF JUNK.
THE TANDEM MILLER IS GOING TO BE THE PRIMARY ENGINE ON THE *VON BRAUN*, THE FIRST SHIP CAPABLE OF REACHING THE OUTER SOLAR SYSTEM.
IF WE DEVELOP JUPITER, WE'LL HAVE A NEW UNLIMITED SOURCE OF FUEL.
トン
ASTRONAUTS WILL HAVE A LOT TO DO.

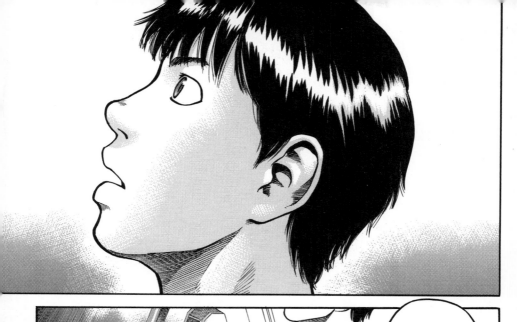

OUR CONCEPT OF THE SOLAR SYSTEM WILL CHANGE RADICALLY.

WE'LL NEED AMBITIOUS AND ENERGETIC ASTRONAUTS TO HELP USHER IN THIS FUTURE, HACHI.

GUYS LIKE YOU.

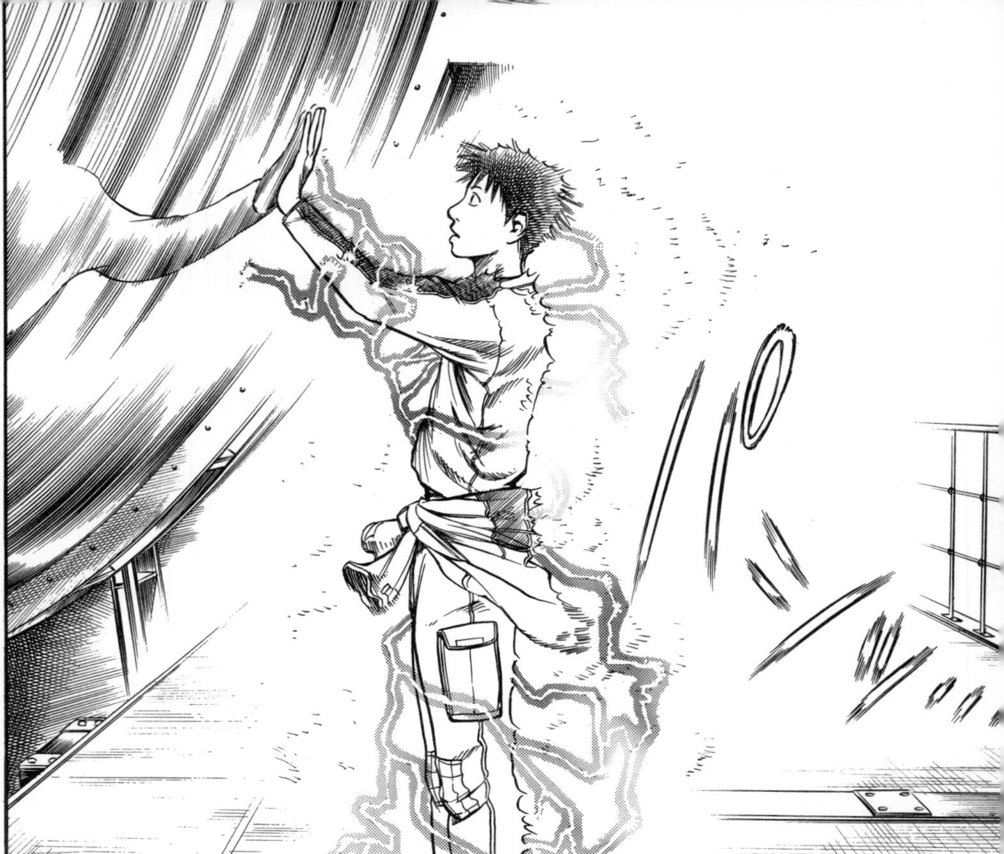

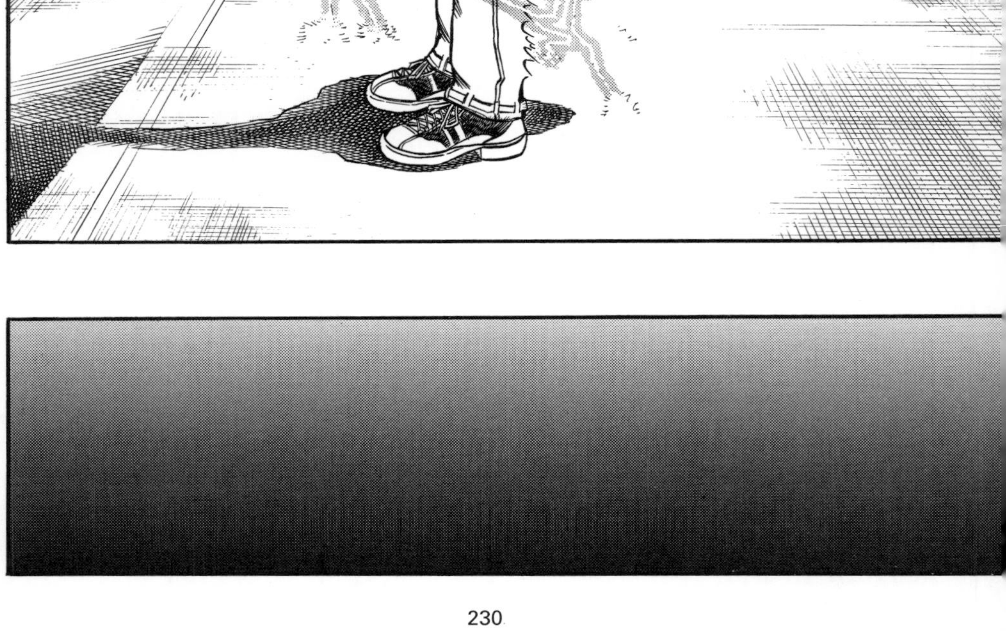

YOU SEEM RELAXED.
TELL ME.
WHAT'S ON YOUR MIND?

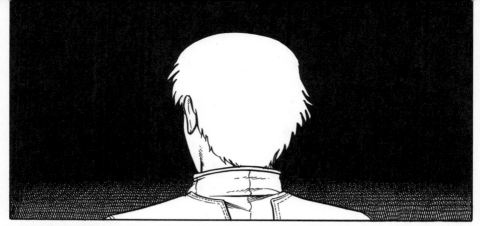

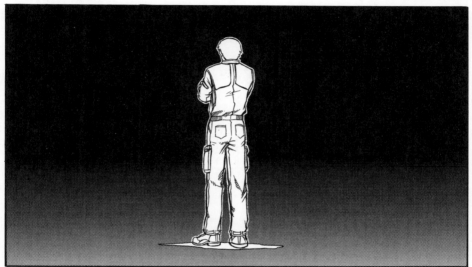

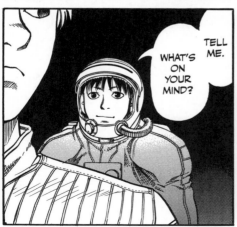

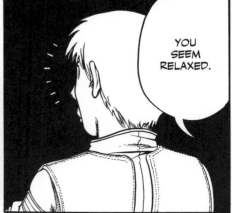

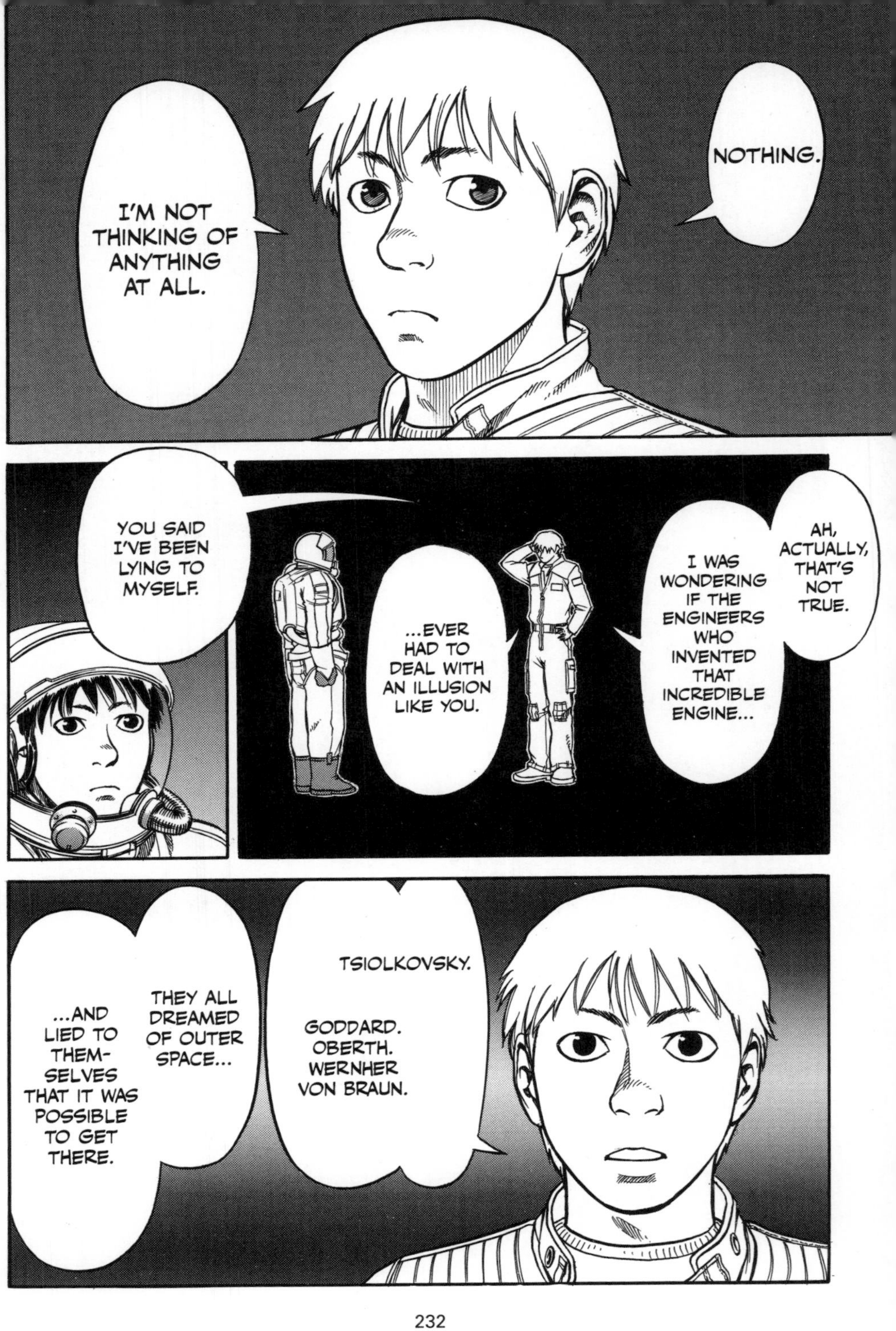
NOTHING.
I'M NOT THINKING OF ANYTHING AT ALL.
AH, ACTUALLY, THAT'S NOT TRUE.
I WAS WONDERING IF THE ENGINEERS WHO INVENTED THAT INCREDIBLE ENGINE...
...EVER HAD TO DEAL WITH AN ILLUSION LIKE YOU.
YOU SAID I'VE BEEN LYING TO MYSELF.
TSIOLKOVSKY.
GODDARD. OBERTH. WERNHER VON BRAUN.
THEY ALL DREAMED OF OUTER SPACE...
...AND LIED TO THEM-SELVES THAT IT WAS POSSIBLE TO GET THERE.

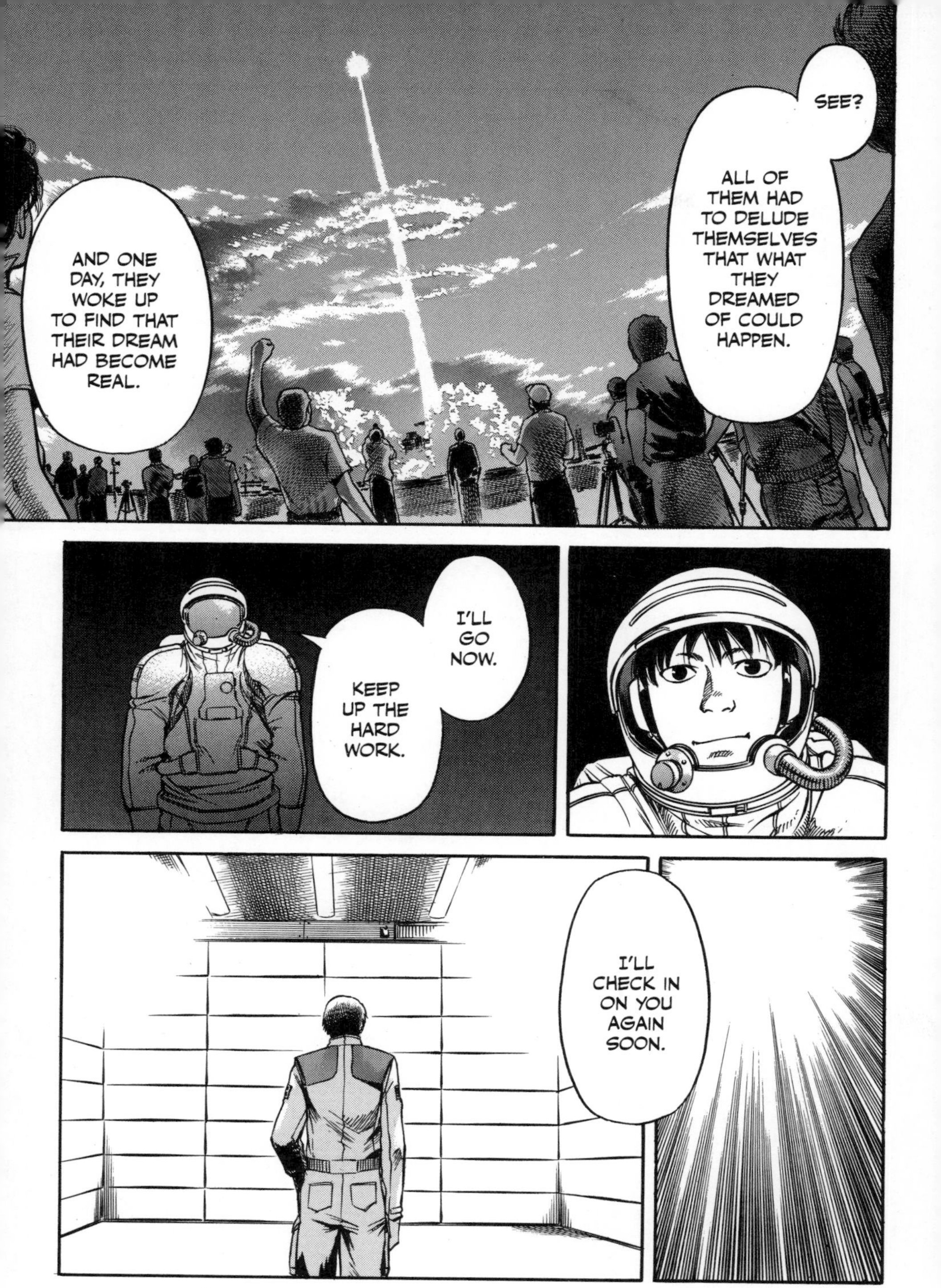
SEE?
ALL OF THEM HAD TO DELUDE THEMSELVES THAT WHAT THEY DREAMED OF COULD HAPPEN.
AND ONE DAY, THEY WOKE UP TO FIND THAT THEIR DREAM HAD BECOME REAL.
I'LL GO NOW.
KEEP UP THE HARD WORK.
I'LL CHECK IN ON YOU AGAIN SOON.

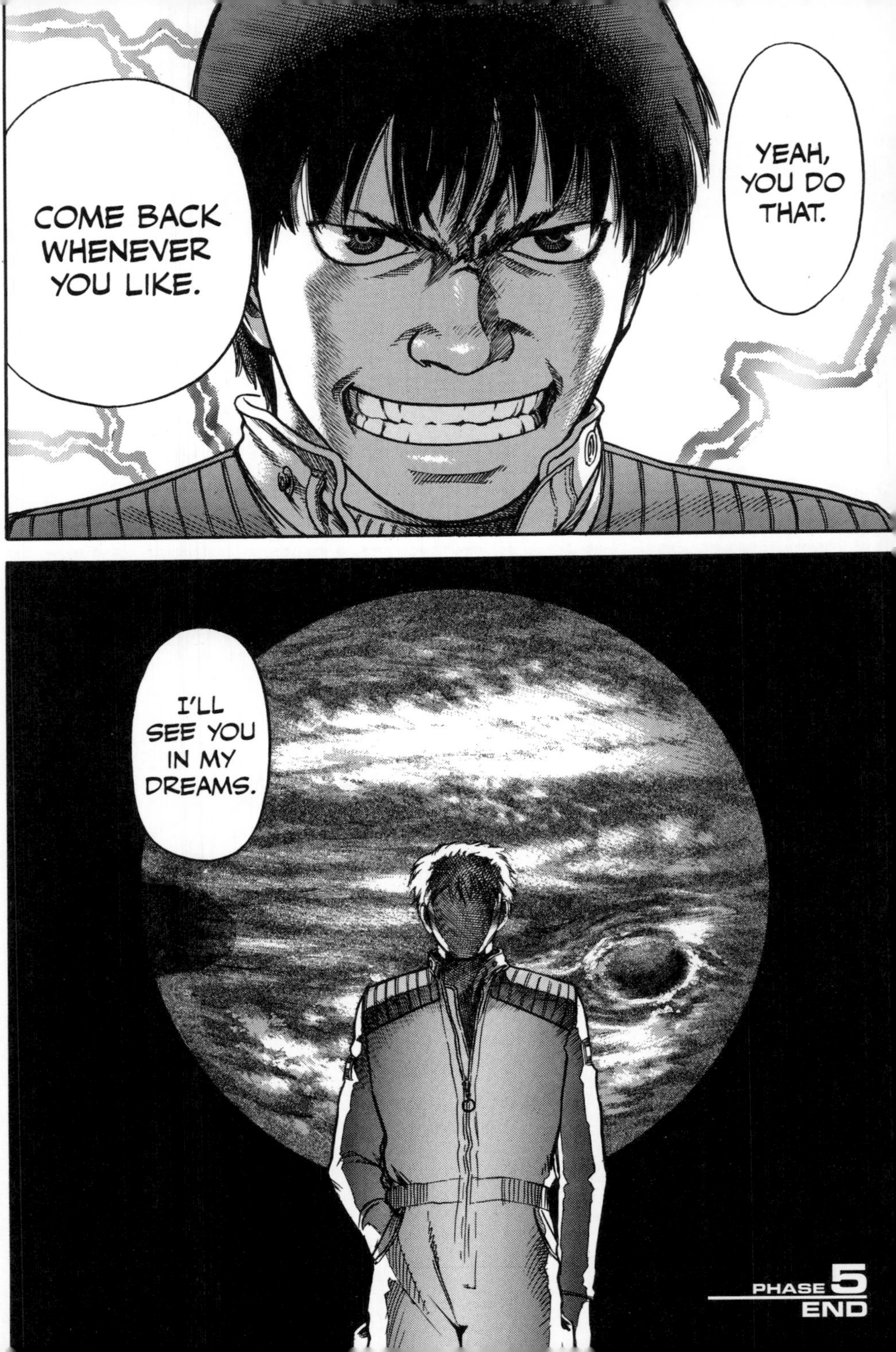
YEAH, YOU DO THAT.
COME BACK WHENEVER YOU LIKE.
I'LL SEE YOU IN MY DREAMS.
PHASE 5 END

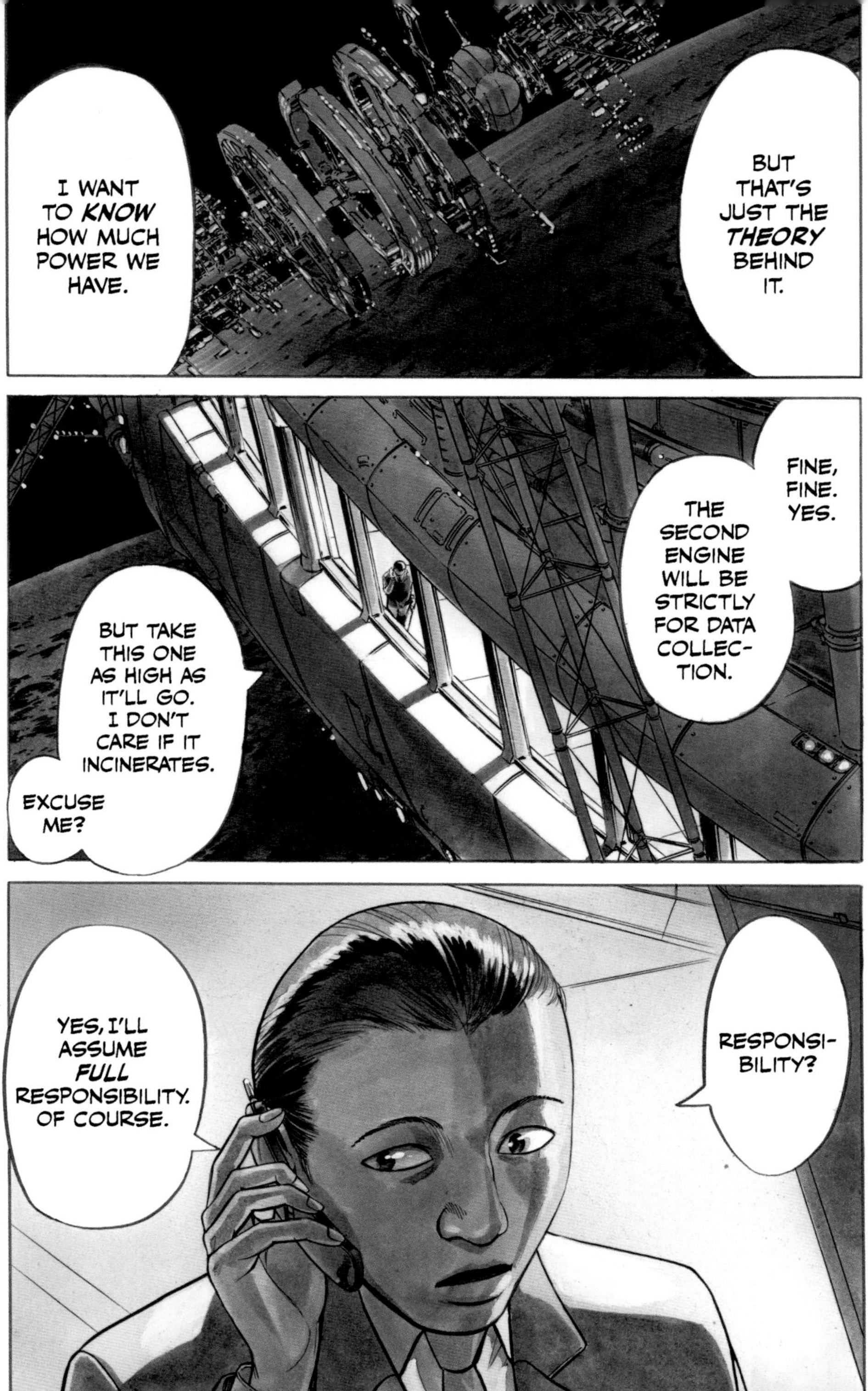
BUT THAT'S JUST THE *THEORY* BEHIND IT.
I WANT TO *KNOW* HOW MUCH POWER WE HAVE.
FINE, FINE. YES.
THE SECOND ENGINE WILL BE STRICTLY FOR DATA COLLEC-TION.
BUT TAKE THIS ONE AS HIGH AS IT'LL GO. I DON'T CARE IF IT INCINERATES.
EXCUSE ME?
RESPONSI-BILITY?
YES, I'LL ASSUME *FULL* RESPONSIBILITY. OF COURSE.

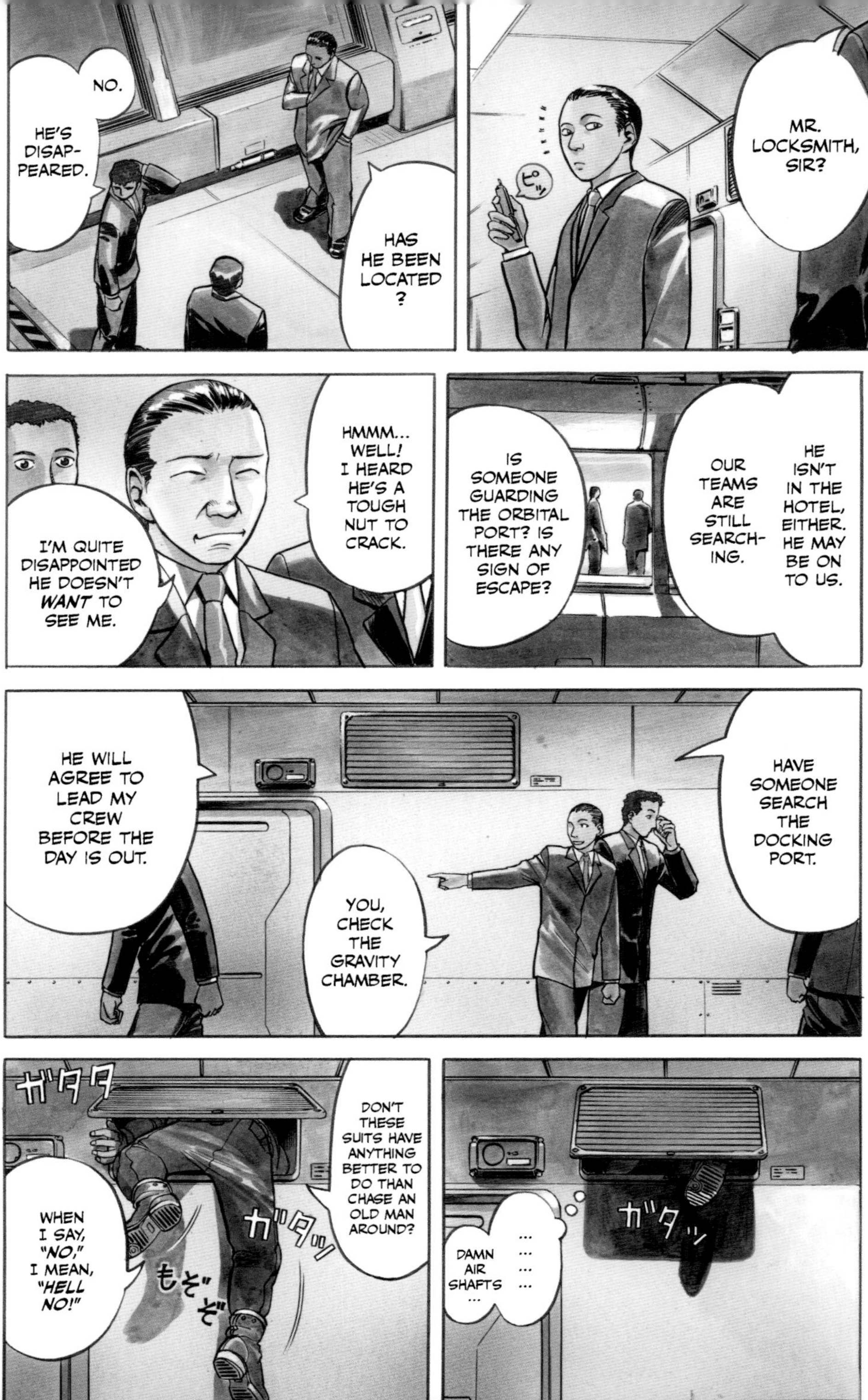
MR. LOCKSMITH, SIR?
ピッ
HAS HE BEEN LOCATED?
NO.
HE'S DISAP-PEARED.
HE ISN'T IN THE HOTEL, EITHER. HE MAY BE ON TO US.
OUR TEAMS ARE STILL SEARCH-ING.
IS SOMEONE GUARDING THE ORBITAL PORT? IS THERE ANY SIGN OF ESCAPE?
HMMM... WELL! I HEARD HE'S A TOUGH NUT TO CRACK.
I'M QUITE DISAPPOINTED HE DOESN'T *WANT* TO SEE ME.
HAVE SOMEONE SEARCH THE DOCKING PORT.
YOU, CHECK THE GRAVITY CHAMBER.
HE WILL AGREE TO LEAD MY CREW BEFORE THE DAY IS OUT.
ガタッ
... ...
DAMN AIR SHAFTS ...
ガタタ
DON'T THESE SUITS HAVE ANYTHING BETTER TO DO THAN CHASE AN OLD MAN AROUND?
ガタッ
もぞぞ
WHEN I SAY, "*NO*," I MEAN, "*HELL NO!*"

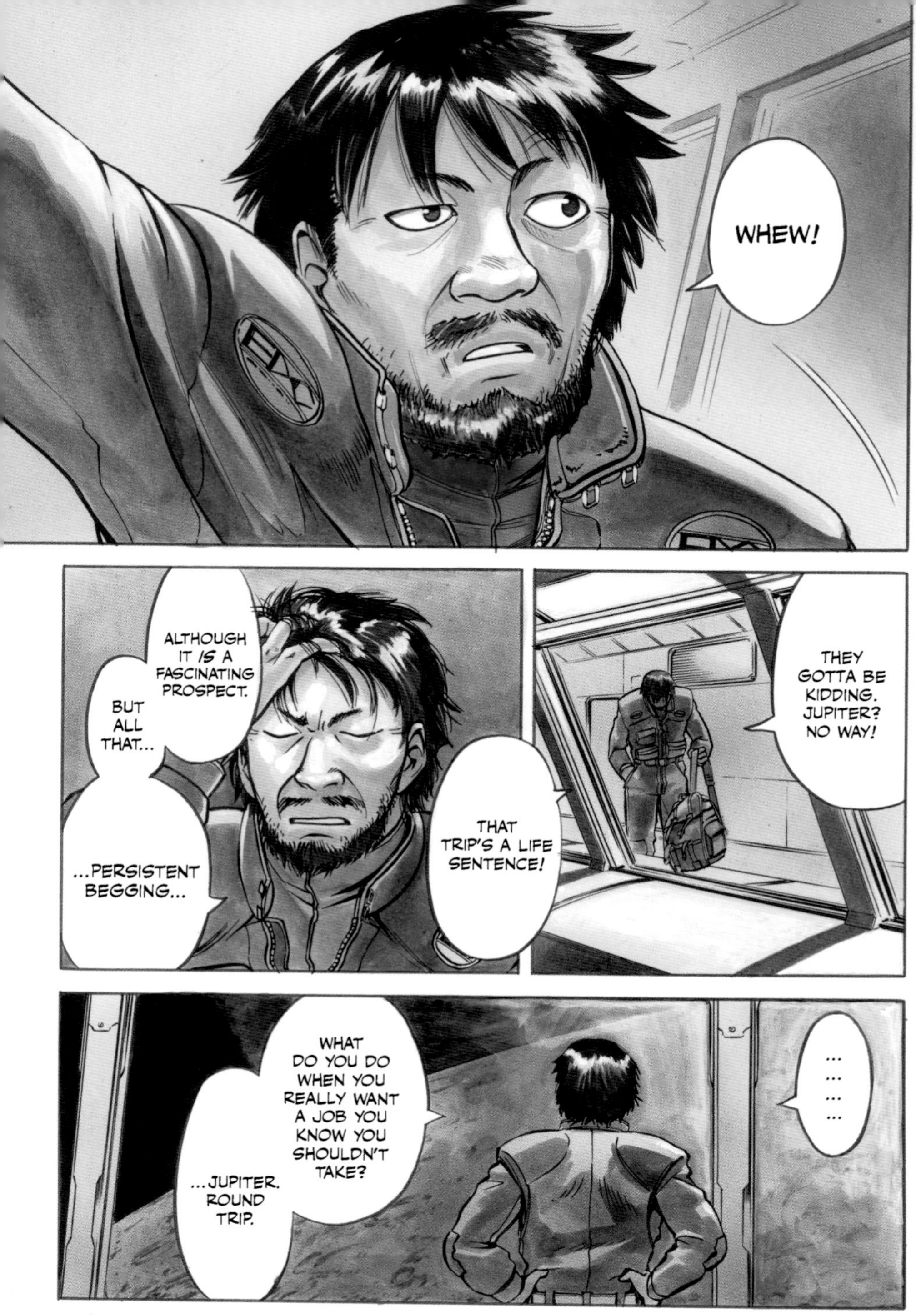
WHEW!
THEY GOTTA BE KIDDING. JUPITER? NO WAY!
THAT TRIP'S A LIFE SENTENCE!
ALTHOUGH IT *IS* A FASCINATING PROSPECT.
BUT ALL THAT...
...PERSISTENT BEGGING...
...
...
...
...
WHAT DO YOU DO WHEN YOU REALLY WANT A JOB YOU KNOW YOU SHOULDN'T TAKE?
...JUPITER. ROUND TRIP.

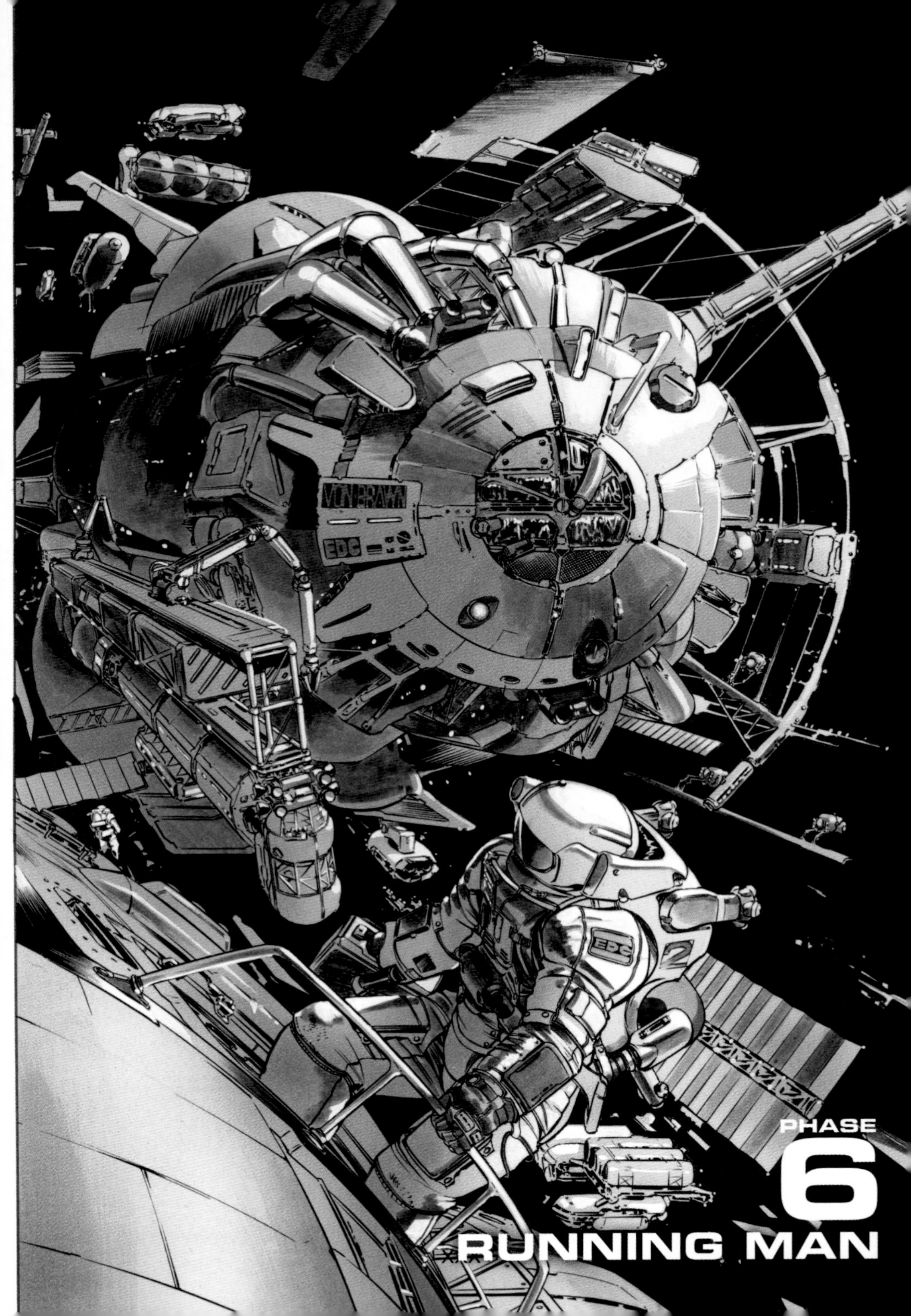
VON BRAUN
EDC
EDC
2
PHASE
6
RUNNING MAN

November 2075.

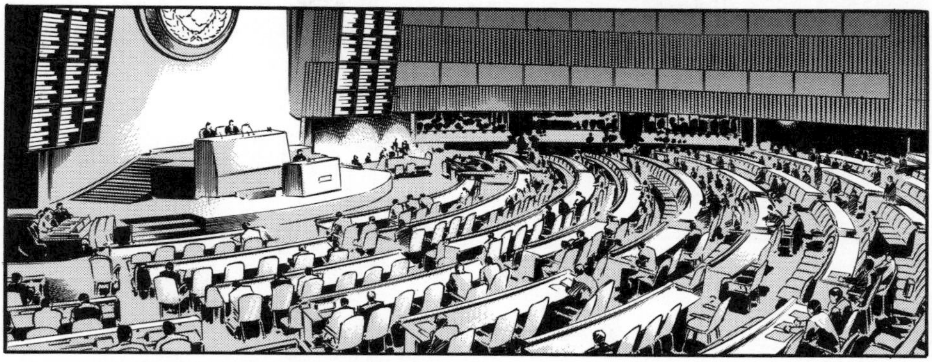

The EDC (Earth Development Community) has declared it will begin construction on a permanent resource base--a mine--on Jupiter before the end of the century.

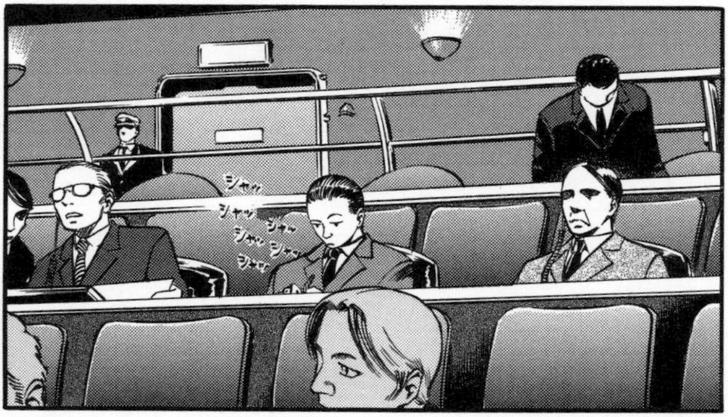
シャッ
シャッ
シャッ
シャッ
シャッ
シャッ

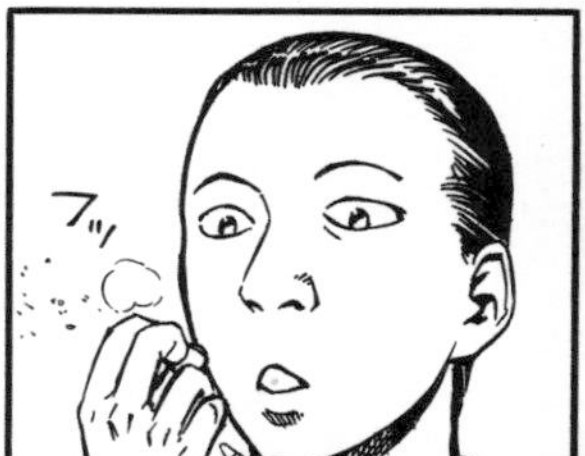
フッ

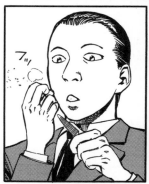

The first-ever manned mission to Jupiter will take place on the spaceship *Von Braun*.
Scheduled completion of the *Von Braun*: 2078.

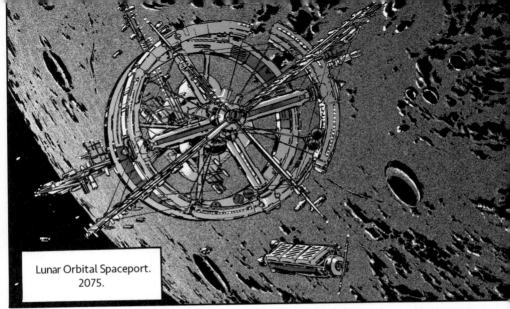

Lunar Orbital Spaceport.
2075.

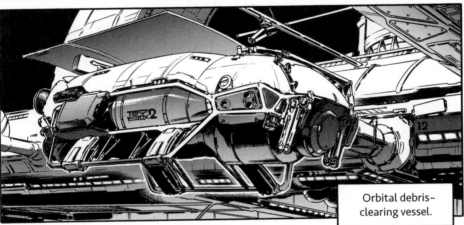

Orbital debris–
clearing vessel.

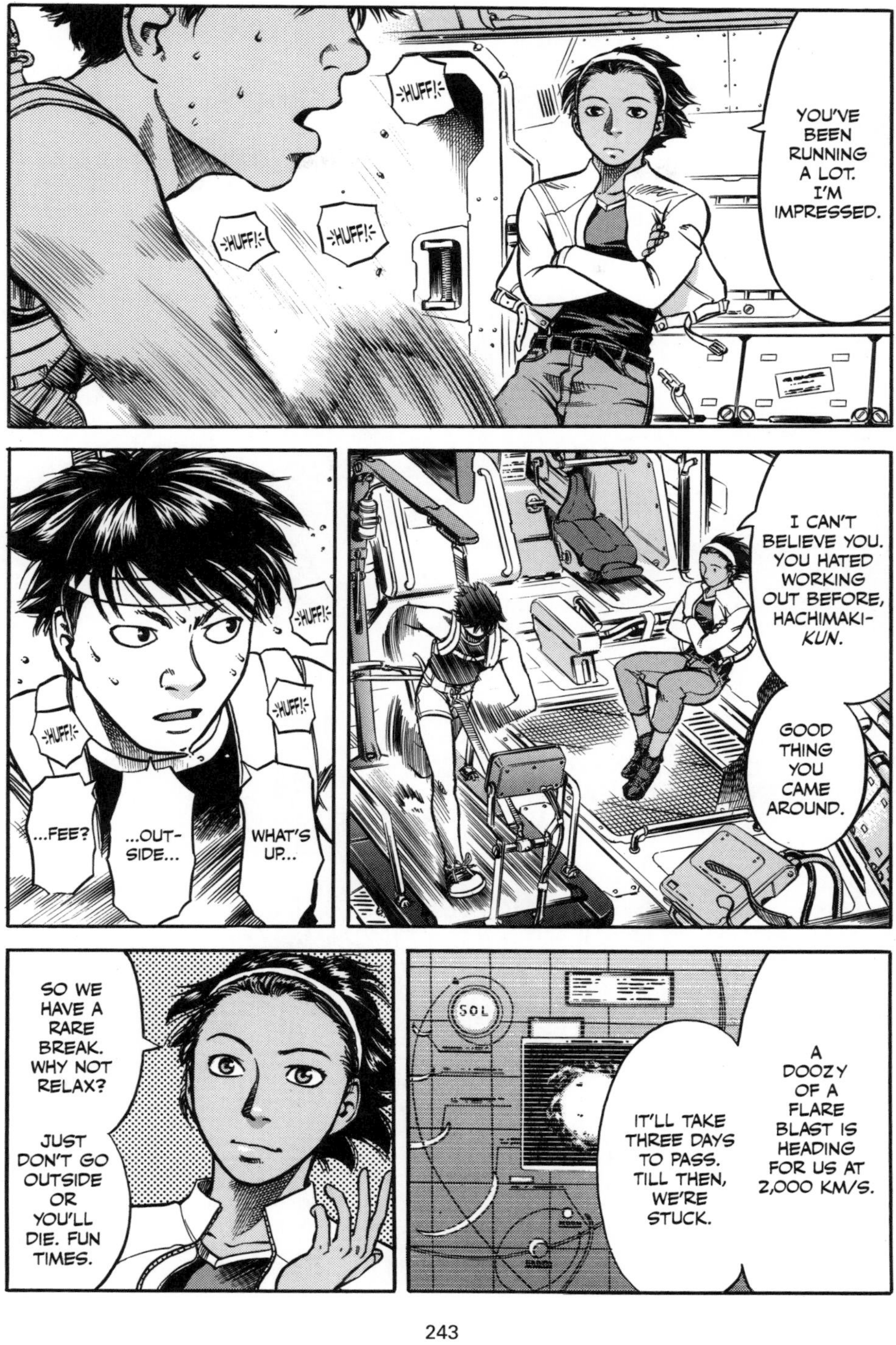
YOU'VE BEEN RUNNING A LOT. I'M IMPRESSED.
-HUFF!-
-HUFF!-
-HUFF!-
I CAN'T BELIEVE YOU. YOU HATED WORKING OUT BEFORE, HACHIMAKI-*KUN*.
GOOD THING YOU CAME AROUND.
-HUFF!-
-HUFF!-
-HUFF!-
WHAT'S UP...
...OUT-SIDE...
...FEE?
A DOOZY OF A FLARE BLAST IS HEADING FOR US AT 2,000 KM/S.
SOL
IT'LL TAKE THREE DAYS TO PASS. TILL THEN, WE'RE STUCK.
SO WE HAVE A RARE BREAK. WHY NOT RELAX?
JUST DON'T GO OUTSIDE OR YOU'LL DIE. FUN TIMES.

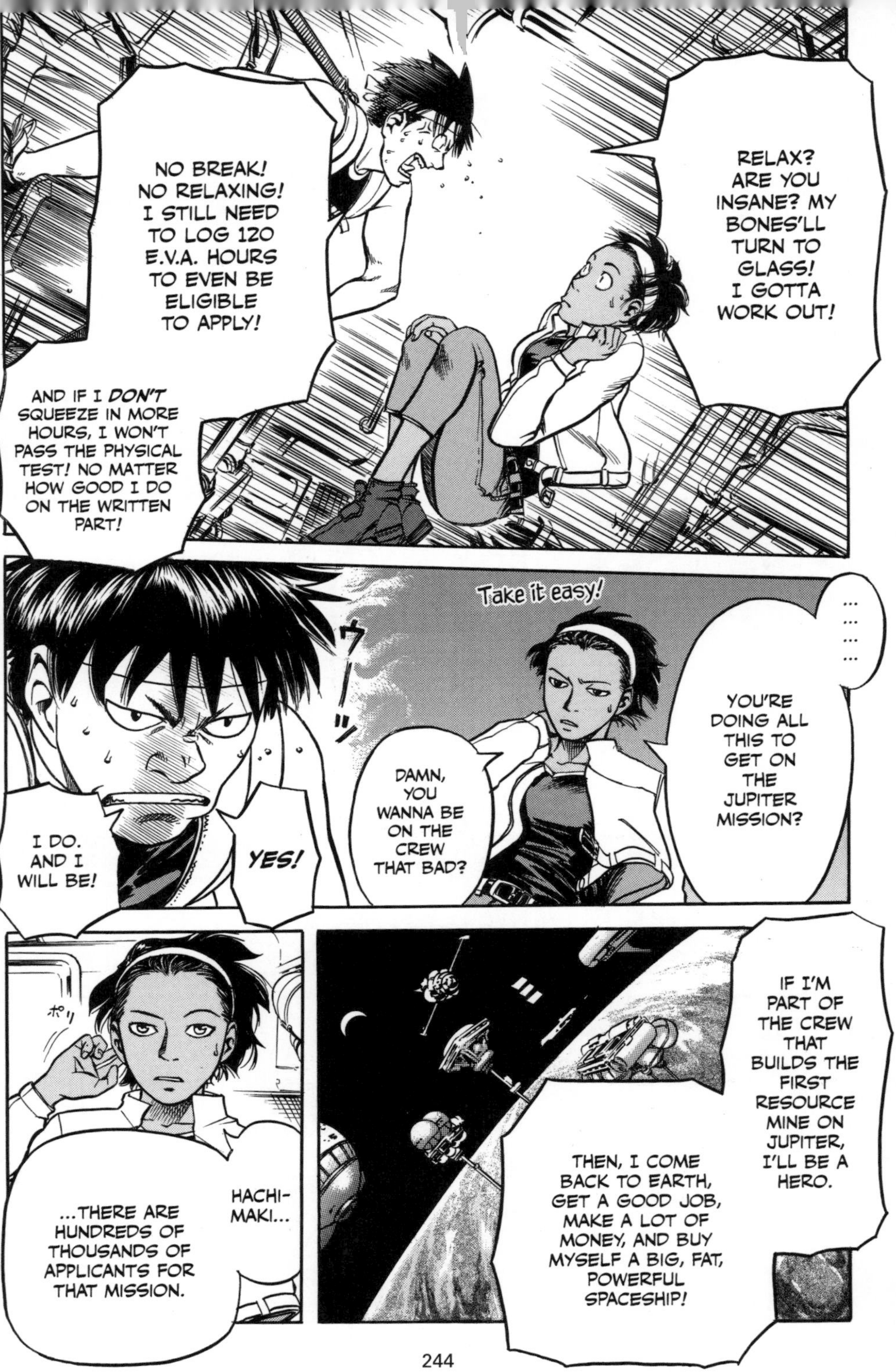
RELAX? ARE YOU INSANE? MY BONES'LL TURN TO GLASS! I GOTTA WORK OUT!
NO BREAK! NO RELAXING! I STILL NEED TO LOG 120 E.V.A. HOURS TO EVEN BE ELIGIBLE TO APPLY!
AND IF I *DON'T* SQUEEZE IN MORE HOURS, I WON'T PASS THE PHYSICAL TEST! NO MATTER HOW GOOD I DO ON THE WRITTEN PART!
...
...
...
...
Take it easy!
YOU'RE DOING ALL THIS TO GET ON THE JUPITER MISSION?
DAMN, YOU WANNA BE ON THE CREW THAT BAD?
YES!
I DO. AND I WILL BE!
IF I'M PART OF THE CREW THAT BUILDS THE FIRST RESOURCE MINE ON JUPITER, I'LL BE A HERO.
THEN, I COME BACK TO EARTH, GET A GOOD JOB, MAKE A LOT OF MONEY, AND BUY MYSELF A BIG, FAT, POWERFUL SPACESHIP!
HACHI-MAKI...
ポリ
...THERE ARE HUNDREDS OF THOUSANDS OF APPLICANTS FOR THAT MISSION.

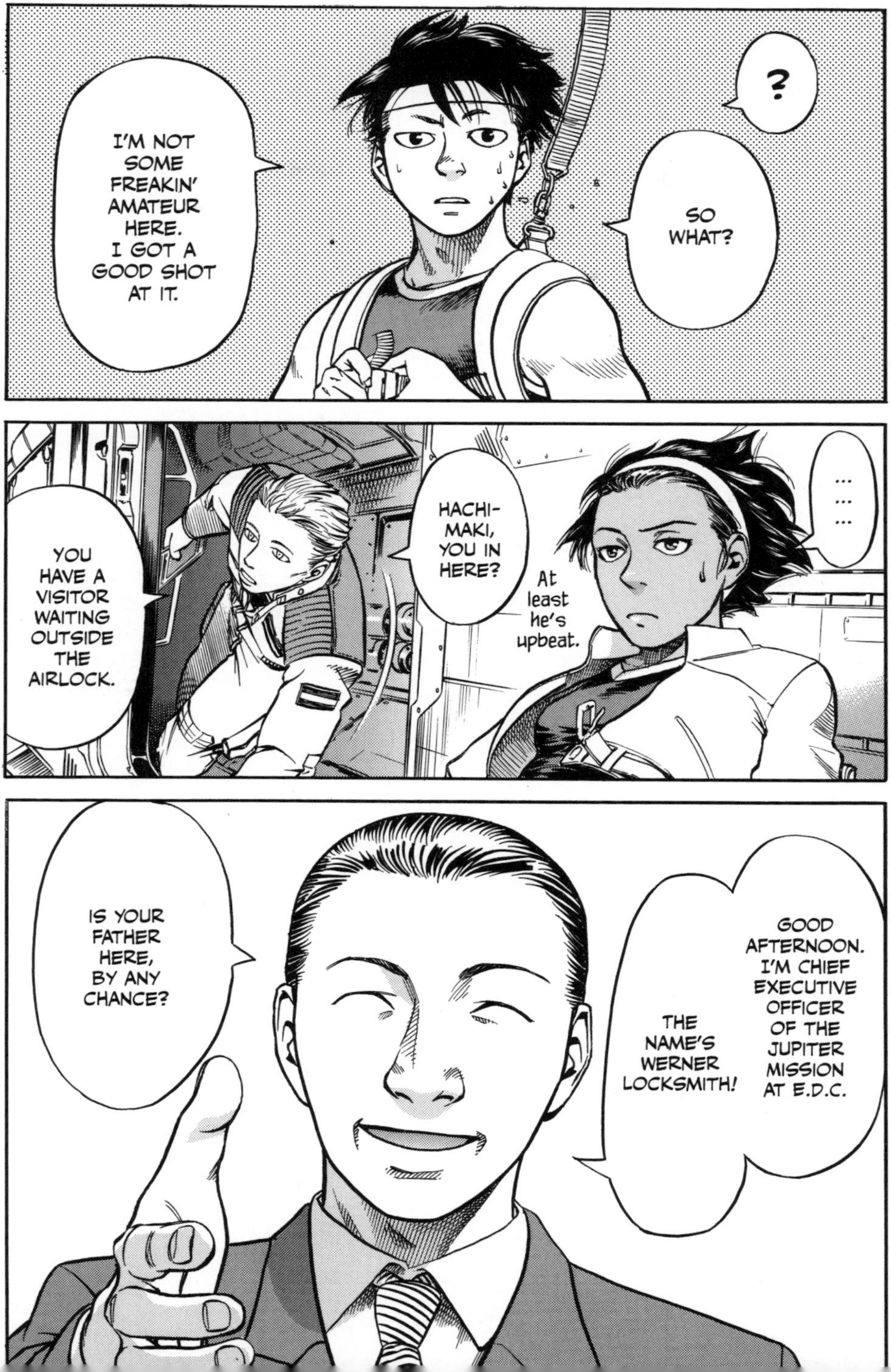
?
SO WHAT?
I'M NOT SOME FREAKIN' AMATEUR HERE. I GOT A GOOD SHOT AT IT.
....
At least he's upbeat.
HACHI-MAKI, YOU IN HERE?
YOU HAVE A VISITOR WAITING OUTSIDE THE AIRLOCK.
GOOD AFTERNOON. I'M CHIEF EXECUTIVE OFFICER OF THE JUPITER MISSION AT E.D.C.
THE NAME'S WERNER LOCKSMITH!
IS YOUR FATHER HERE, BY ANY CHANCE?

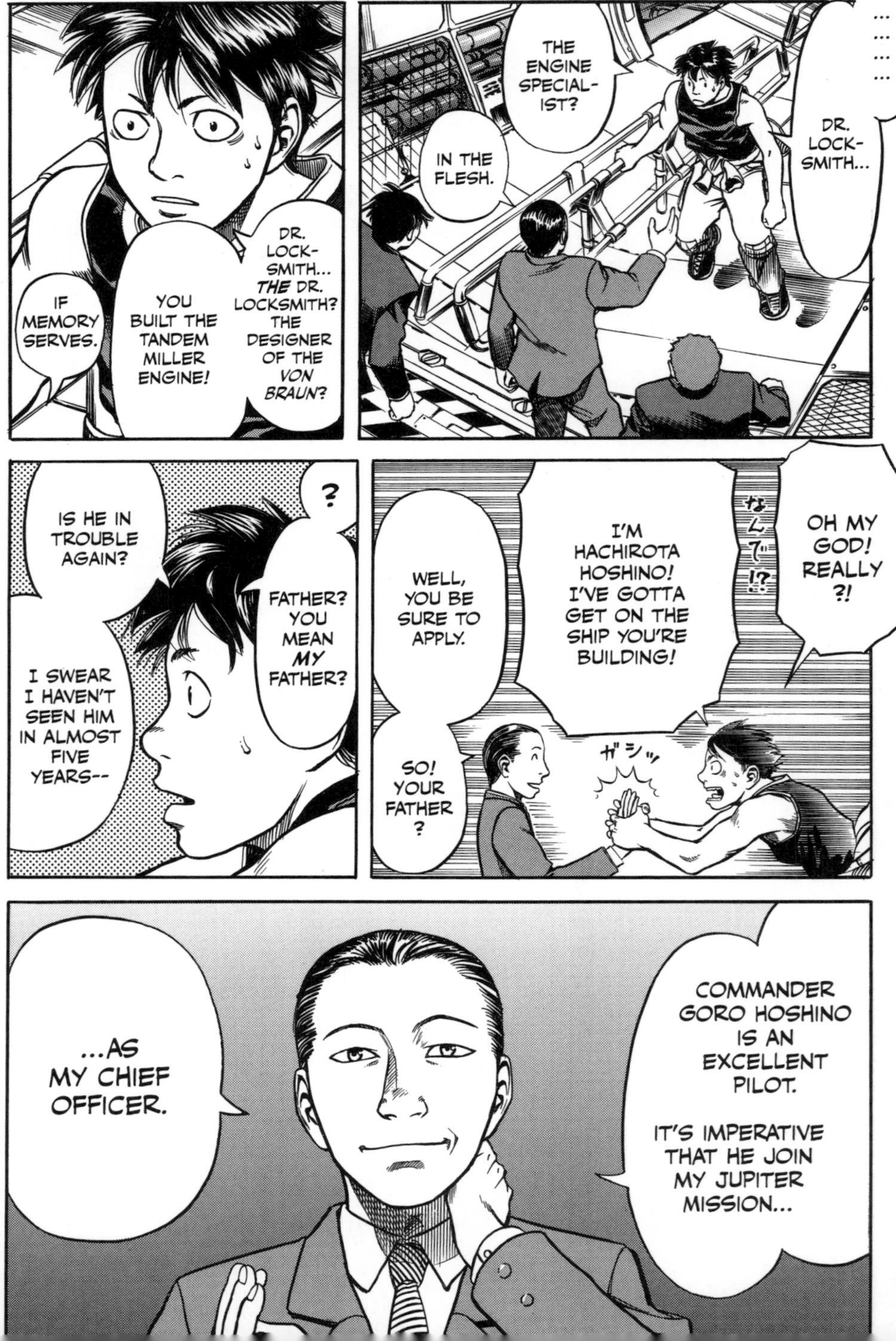
....
DR. LOCKSMITH...
THE ENGINE SPECIALIST?
IN THE FLESH.
DR. LOCKSMITH... *THE* DR. LOCKSMITH? THE DESIGNER OF THE *VON BRAUN*?
YOU BUILT THE TANDEM MILLER ENGINE!
IF MEMORY SERVES.
OH MY GOD! REALLY?!
なんで!?
I'M HACHIROTA HOSHINO! I'VE GOTTA GET ON THE SHIP YOU'RE BUILDING!
WELL, YOU BE SURE TO APPLY.
ガシッ
SO! YOUR FATHER?
?
FATHER? YOU MEAN *MY* FATHER?
IS HE IN TROUBLE AGAIN?
I SWEAR I HAVEN'T SEEN HIM IN ALMOST FIVE YEARS--
COMMANDER GORO HOSHINO IS AN EXCELLENT PILOT.
IT'S IMPERATIVE THAT HE JOIN MY JUPITER MISSION...
...AS MY CHIEF OFFICER.

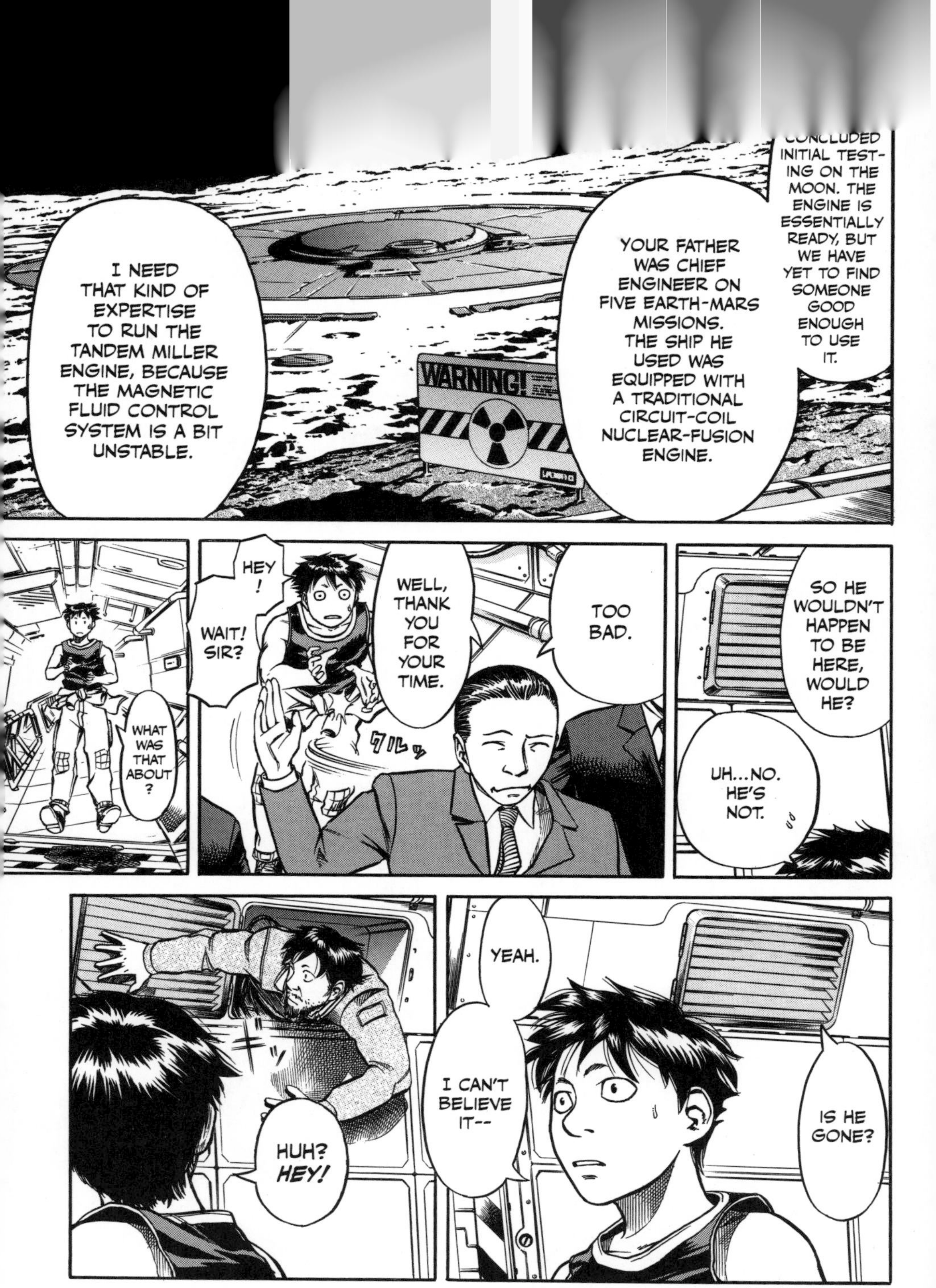
CONCLUDED INITIAL TESTING ON THE MOON. THE ENGINE IS ESSENTIALLY READY, BUT WE HAVE YET TO FIND SOMEONE GOOD ENOUGH TO USE IT.
YOUR FATHER WAS CHIEF ENGINEER ON FIVE EARTH-MARS MISSIONS. THE SHIP HE USED WAS EQUIPPED WITH A TRADITIONAL CIRCUIT-COIL NUCLEAR-FUSION ENGINE.
WARNING!
I NEED THAT KIND OF EXPERTISE TO RUN THE TANDEM MILLER ENGINE, BECAUSE THE MAGNETIC FLUID CONTROL SYSTEM IS A BIT UNSTABLE.
SO HE WOULDN'T HAPPEN TO BE HERE, WOULD HE?
UH...NO. HE'S NOT.
TOO BAD.
WELL, THANK YOU FOR YOUR TIME.
HEY!
WAIT! SIR?
クルッ
WHAT WAS THAT ABOUT?
IS HE GONE?
YEAH.
I CAN'T BELIEVE IT--
HUH? *HEY!*

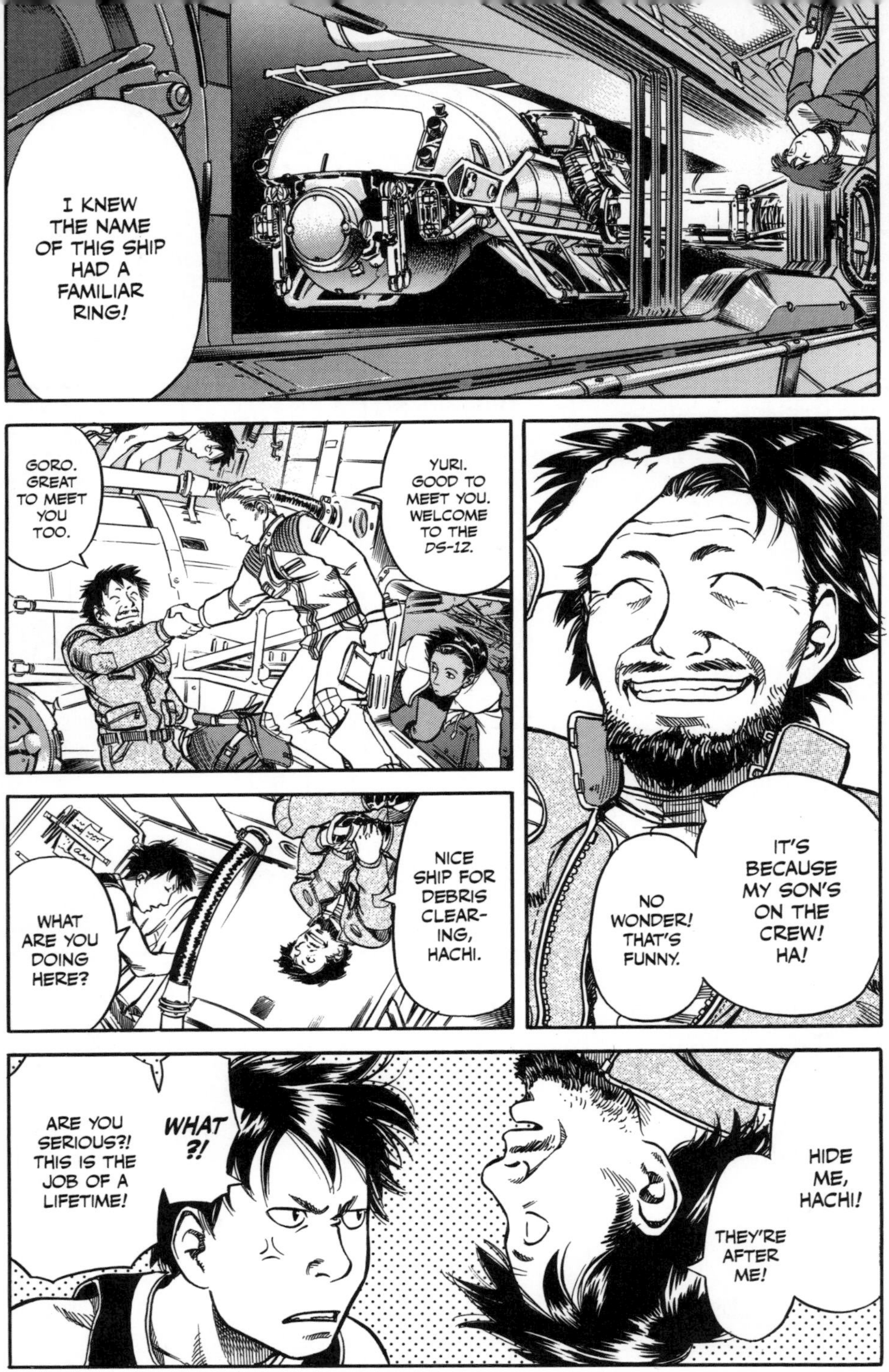
I KNEW THE NAME OF THIS SHIP HAD A FAMILIAR RING!
IT'S BECAUSE MY SON'S ON THE CREW! HA!
NO WONDER! THAT'S FUNNY.
YURI. GOOD TO MEET YOU. WELCOME TO THE *DS-12.*
GORO. GREAT TO MEET YOU TOO.
NICE SHIP FOR DEBRIS CLEAR-ING, HACHI.
WHAT ARE YOU DOING HERE?
HIDE ME, HACHI!
THEY'RE AFTER ME!
WHAT ?!
ARE YOU SERIOUS?! THIS IS THE JOB OF A LIFETIME!

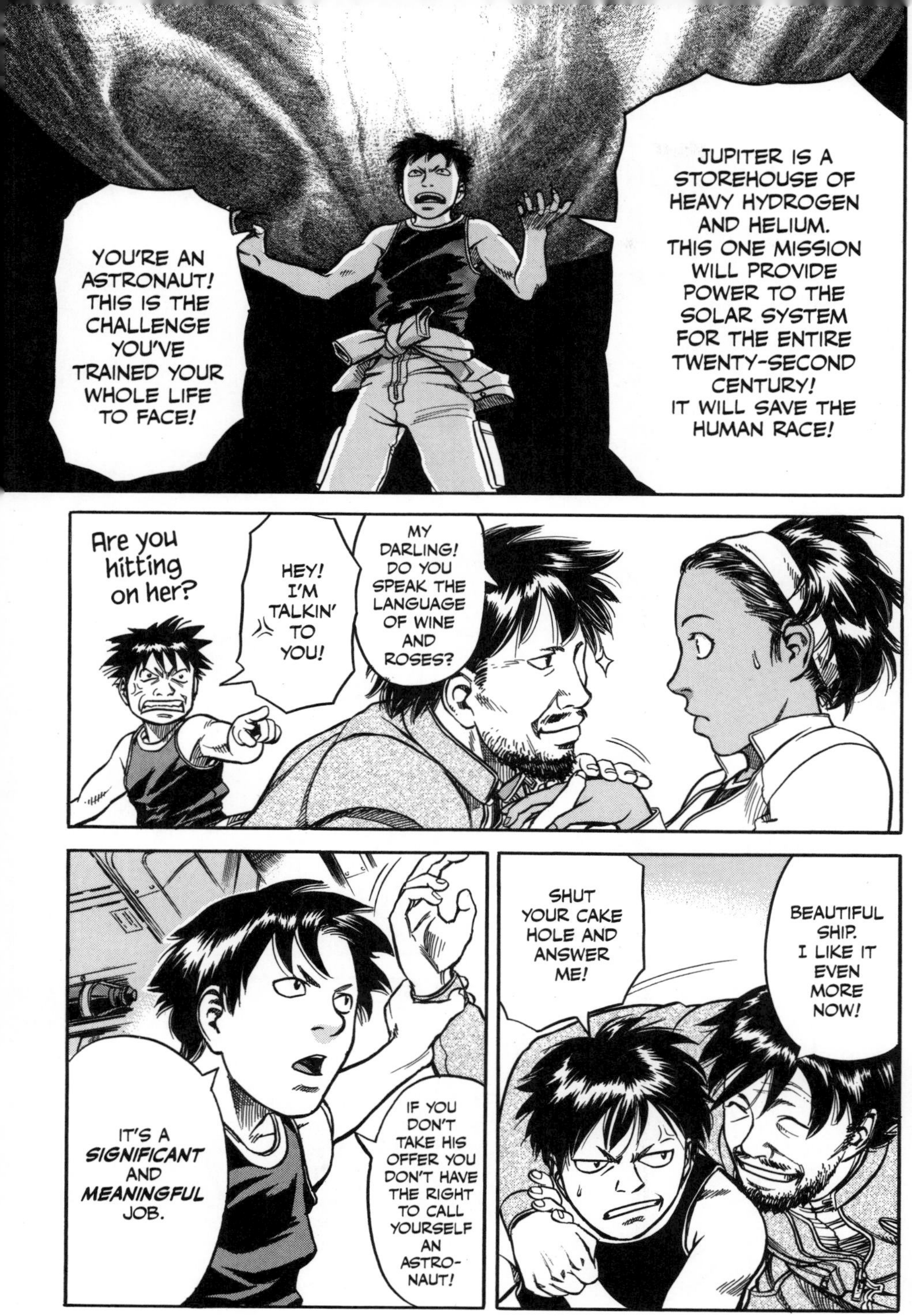
JUPITER IS A STOREHOUSE OF HEAVY HYDROGEN AND HELIUM. THIS ONE MISSION WILL PROVIDE POWER TO THE SOLAR SYSTEM FOR THE ENTIRE TWENTY-SECOND CENTURY! IT WILL SAVE THE HUMAN RACE!
YOU'RE AN ASTRONAUT! THIS IS THE CHALLENGE YOU'VE TRAINED YOUR WHOLE LIFE TO FACE!
MY DARLING! DO YOU SPEAK THE LANGUAGE OF WINE AND ROSES?
HEY! I'M TALKIN' TO YOU!
Are you hitting on her?
BEAUTIFUL SHIP. I LIKE IT EVEN MORE NOW!
SHUT YOUR CAKE HOLE AND ANSWER ME!
IF YOU DON'T TAKE HIS OFFER YOU DON'T HAVE THE RIGHT TO CALL YOURSELF AN ASTRONAUT!
IT'S A *SIGNIFICANT* AND *MEANINGFUL* JOB.

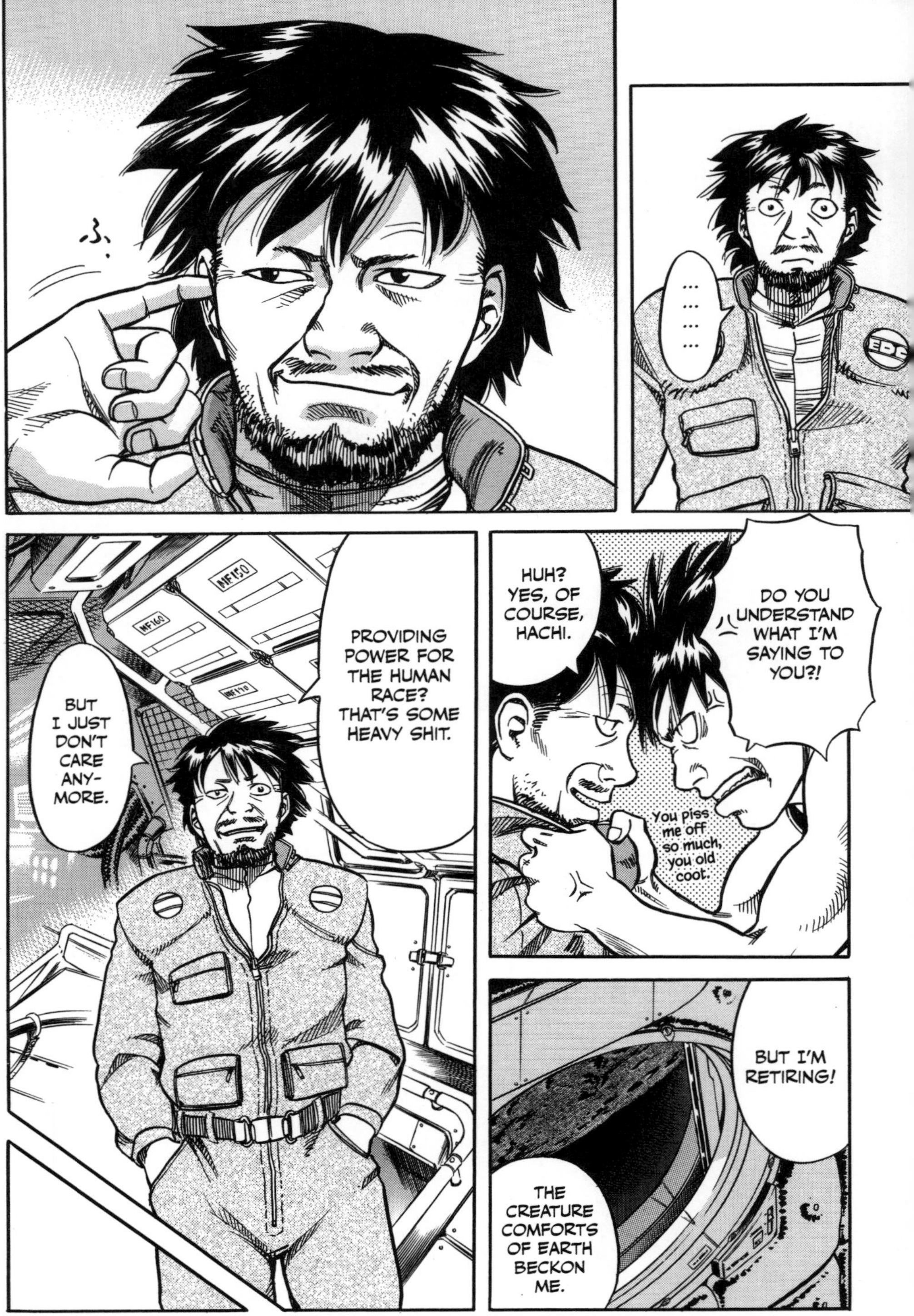

... ...
ふ
DO YOU UNDERSTAND WHAT I'M SAYING TO YOU?!
HUH? YES, OF COURSE, HACHI.
You piss me off so much, you old coot.
BUT I'M RETIRING!
THE CREATURE COMFORTS OF EARTH BECKON ME.
PROVIDING POWER FOR THE HUMAN RACE? THAT'S SOME HEAVY SHIT.
BUT I JUST DON'T CARE ANY-MORE.

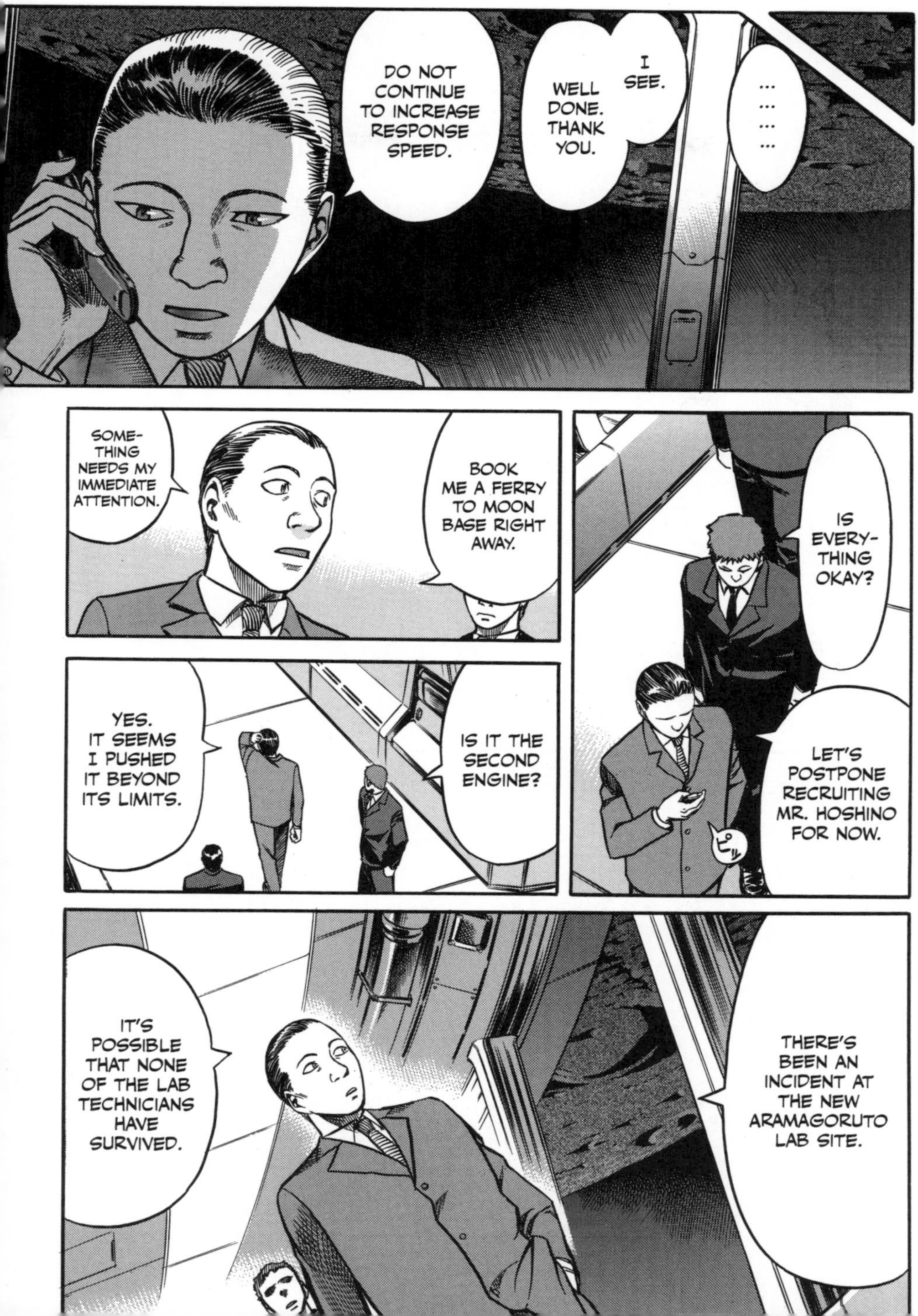
......
I SEE.
WELL DONE. THANK YOU.
DO NOT CONTINUE TO INCREASE RESPONSE SPEED.
IS EVERYTHING OKAY?
LET'S POSTPONE RECRUITING MR. HOSHINO FOR NOW.
ピッ
BOOK ME A FERRY TO MOON BASE RIGHT AWAY.
SOMETHING NEEDS MY IMMEDIATE ATTENTION.
IS IT THE SECOND ENGINE?
YES. IT SEEMS I PUSHED IT BEYOND ITS LIMITS.
THERE'S BEEN AN INCIDENT AT THE NEW ARAMAGORUTO LAB SITE.
IT'S POSSIBLE THAT NONE OF THE LAB TECHNICIANS HAVE SURVIVED.

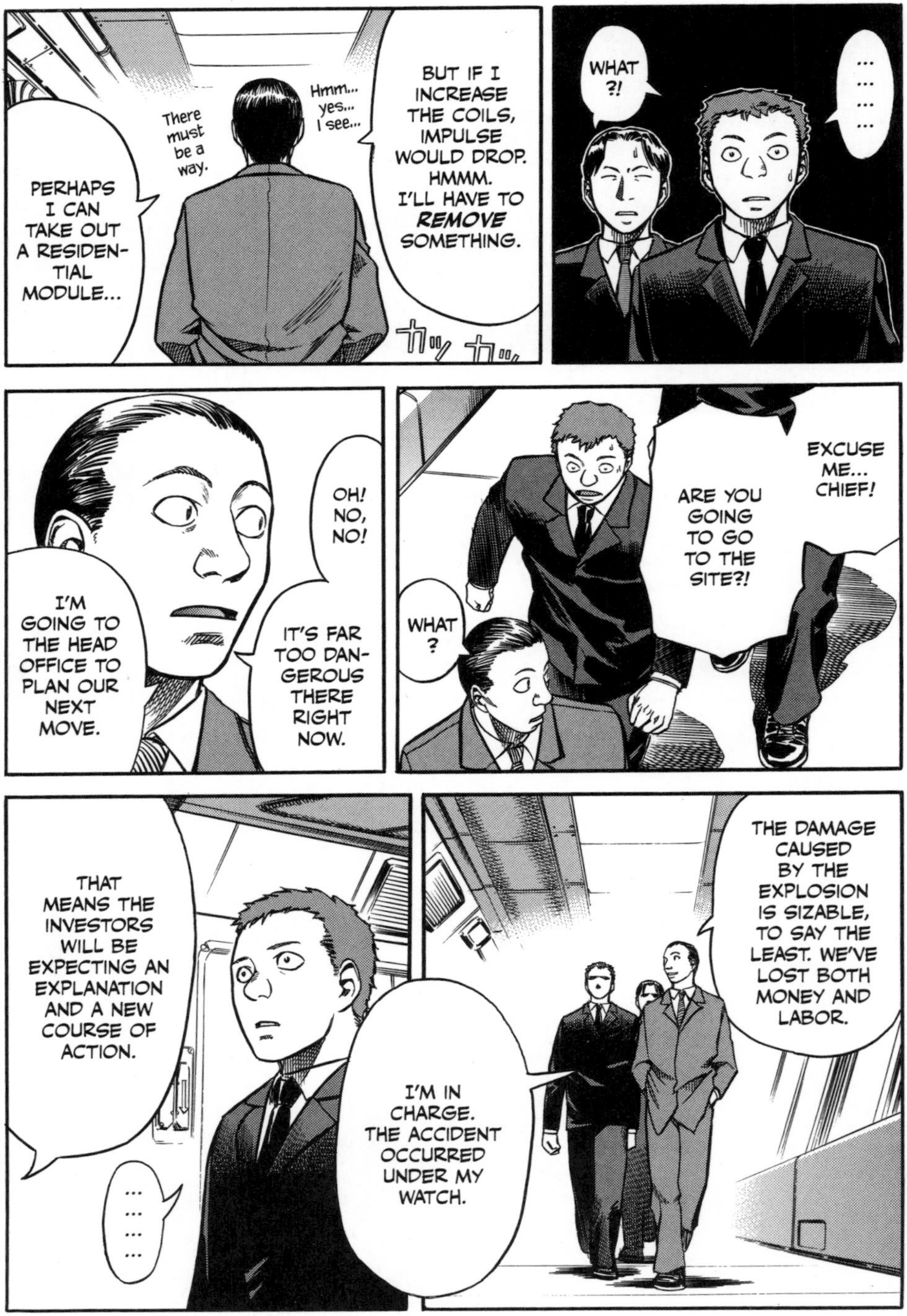
... ...
WHAT ?!
BUT IF I INCREASE THE COILS, IMPULSE WOULD DROP. HMMM. I'LL HAVE TO ***REMOVE*** SOMETHING.
Hmm... yes... I see...
There must be a way.
PERHAPS I CAN TAKE OUT A RESIDEN-TIAL MODULE...
カッ カッ
EXCUSE ME... CHIEF!
ARE YOU GOING TO GO TO THE SITE?!
WHAT ?
OH! NO, NO!
IT'S FAR TOO DAN-GEROUS THERE RIGHT NOW.
I'M GOING TO THE HEAD OFFICE TO PLAN OUR NEXT MOVE.
THE DAMAGE CAUSED BY THE EXPLOSION IS SIZABLE, TO SAY THE LEAST. WE'VE LOST BOTH MONEY AND LABOR.
I'M IN CHARGE. THE ACCIDENT OCCURRED UNDER MY WATCH.
THAT MEANS THE INVESTORS WILL BE EXPECTING AN EXPLANATION AND A NEW COURSE OF ACTION.
... ...

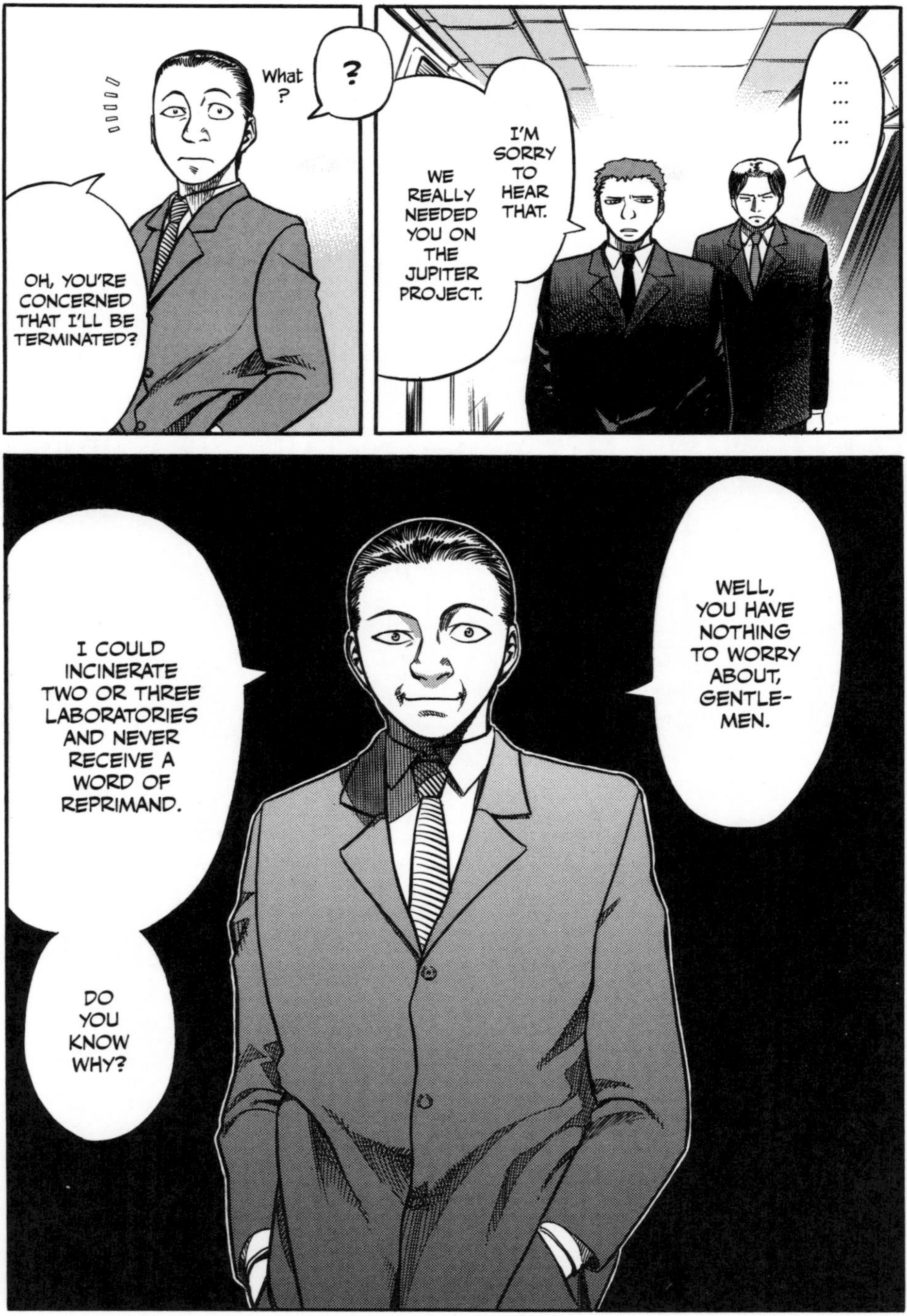
......
I'M SORRY TO HEAR THAT.
WE REALLY NEEDED YOU ON THE JUPITER PROJECT.
?
What?
OH, YOU'RE CONCERNED THAT I'LL BE TERMINATED?
WELL, YOU HAVE NOTHING TO WORRY ABOUT, GENTLE-MEN.
I COULD INCINERATE TWO OR THREE LABORATORIES AND NEVER RECEIVE A WORD OF REPRIMAND.
DO YOU KNOW WHY?

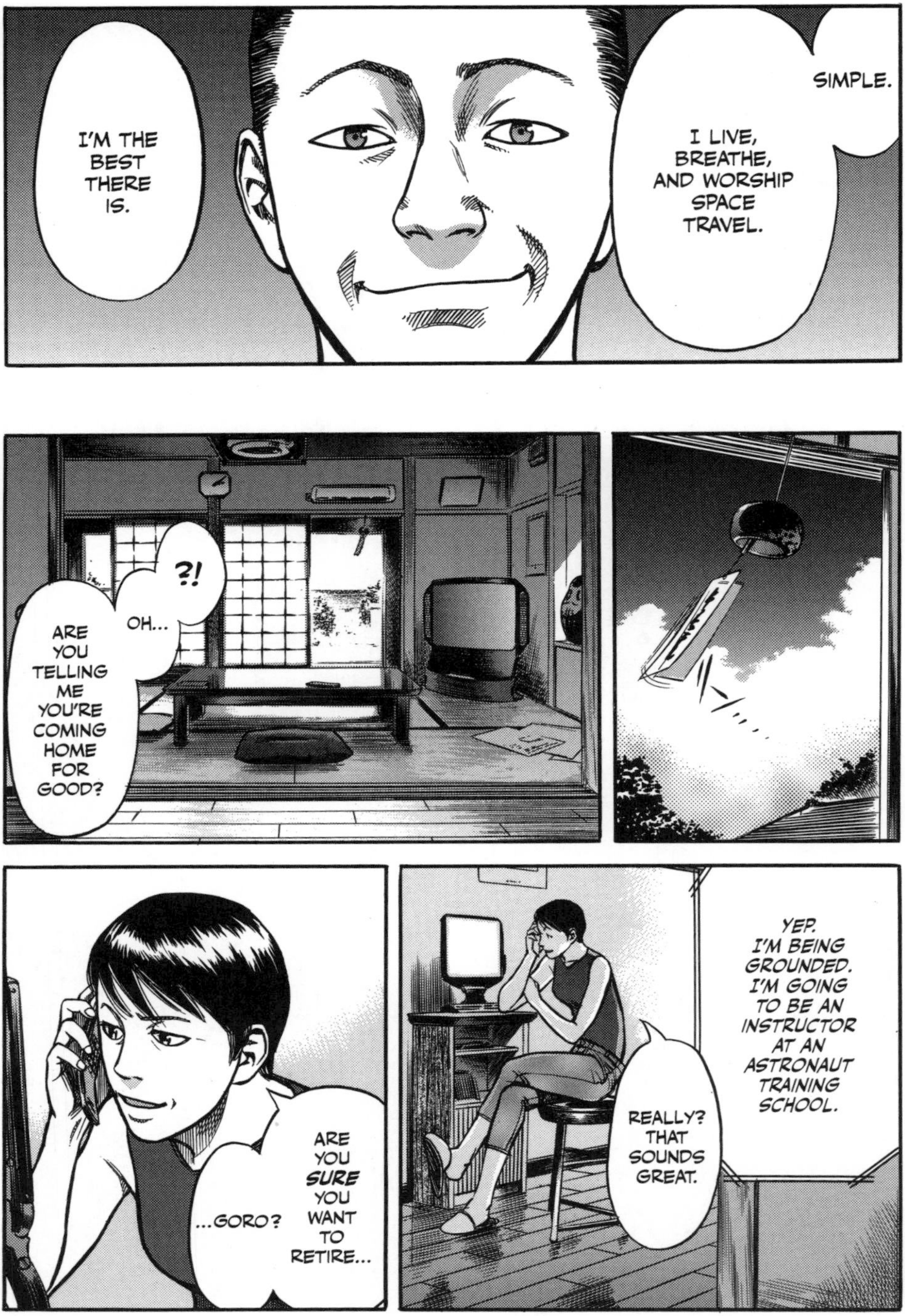
SIMPLE.
I LIVE, BREATHE, AND WORSHIP SPACE TRAVEL.
I'M THE BEST THERE IS.
?!
OH...
ARE YOU TELLING ME YOU'RE COMING HOME FOR GOOD?
YEP. I'M BEING GROUNDED. I'M GOING TO BE AN INSTRUCTOR AT AN ASTRONAUT TRAINING SCHOOL.
REALLY? THAT SOUNDS GREAT.
ARE YOU SURE YOU WANT TO RETIRE...
...GORO?

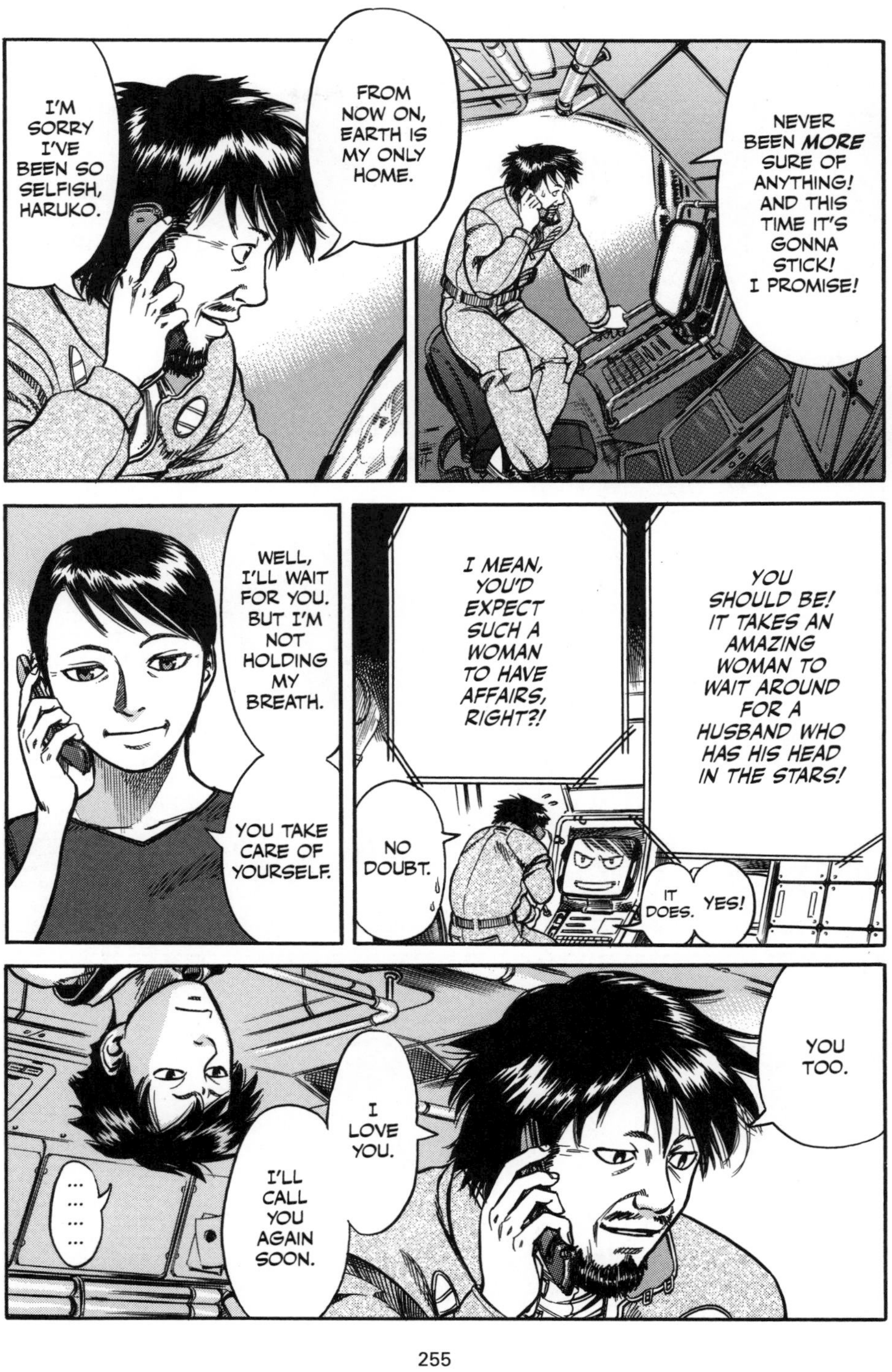
I'M SORRY I'VE BEEN SO SELFISH, HARUKO.
FROM NOW ON, EARTH IS MY ONLY HOME.
NEVER BEEN MORE SURE OF ANYTHING! AND THIS TIME IT'S GONNA STICK! I PROMISE!
WELL, I'LL WAIT FOR YOU. BUT I'M NOT HOLDING MY BREATH.
YOU TAKE CARE OF YOURSELF.
YOU SHOULD BE! IT TAKES AN AMAZING WOMAN TO WAIT AROUND FOR A HUSBAND WHO HAS HIS HEAD IN THE STARS!
I MEAN, YOU'D EXPECT SUCH A WOMAN TO HAVE AFFAIRS, RIGHT?!
YES!
IT DOES.
NO DOUBT.
I LOVE YOU.
I'LL CALL YOU AGAIN SOON.
....
YOU TOO.

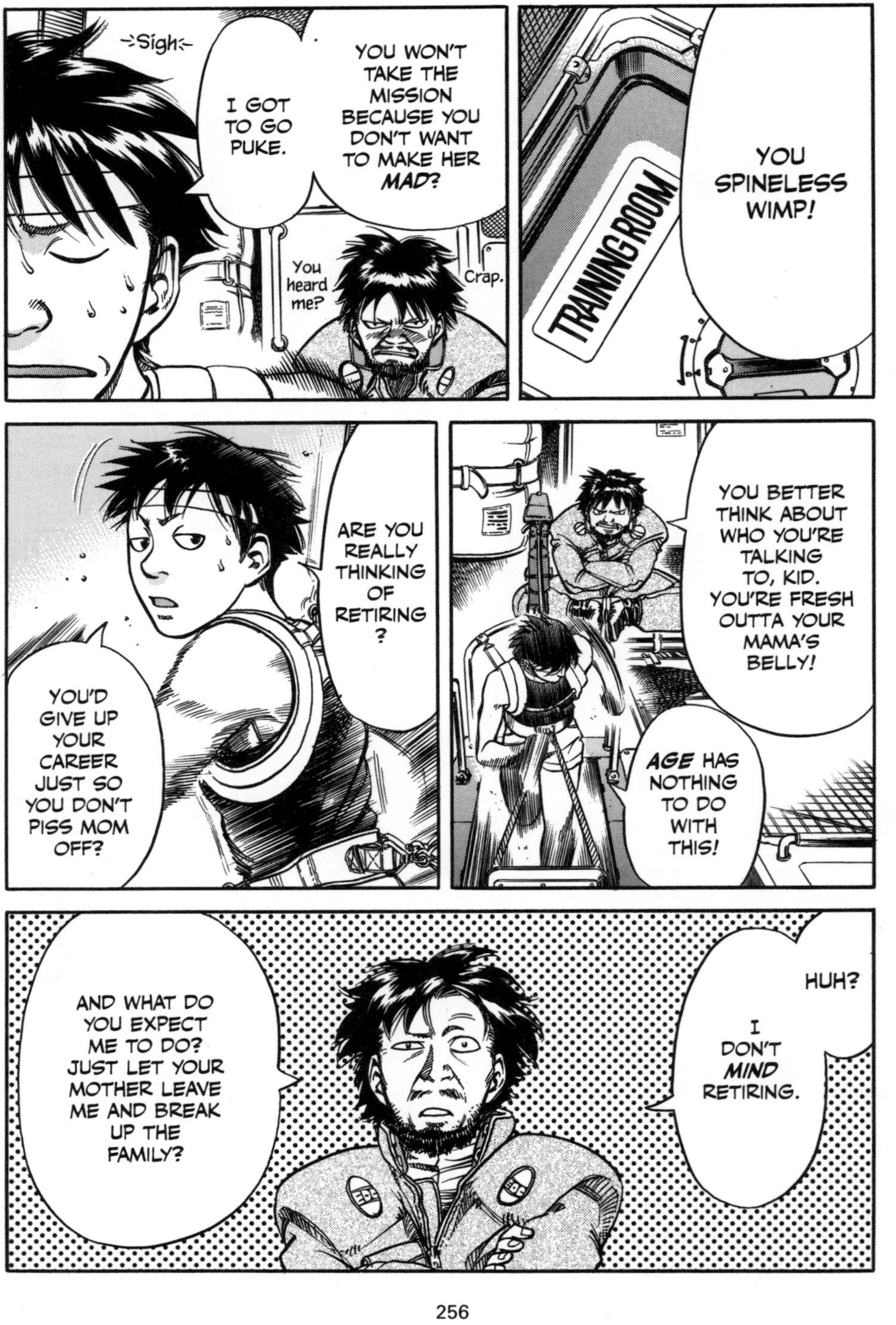
YOU SPINELESS WIMP!
TRAINING ROOM
YOU WON'T TAKE THE MISSION BECAUSE YOU DON'T WANT TO MAKE HER *MAD*?
I GOT TO GO PUKE.
Sigh
Crap.
You heard me?
YOU BETTER THINK ABOUT WHO YOU'RE TALKING TO, KID. YOU'RE FRESH OUTTA YOUR MAMA'S BELLY!
AGE HAS NOTHING TO DO WITH THIS!
ARE YOU REALLY THINKING OF RETIRING?
YOU'D GIVE UP YOUR CAREER JUST SO YOU DON'T PISS MOM OFF?
HUH?
I DON'T *MIND* RETIRING.
AND WHAT DO YOU EXPECT ME TO DO? JUST LET YOUR MOTHER LEAVE ME AND BREAK UP THE FAMILY?

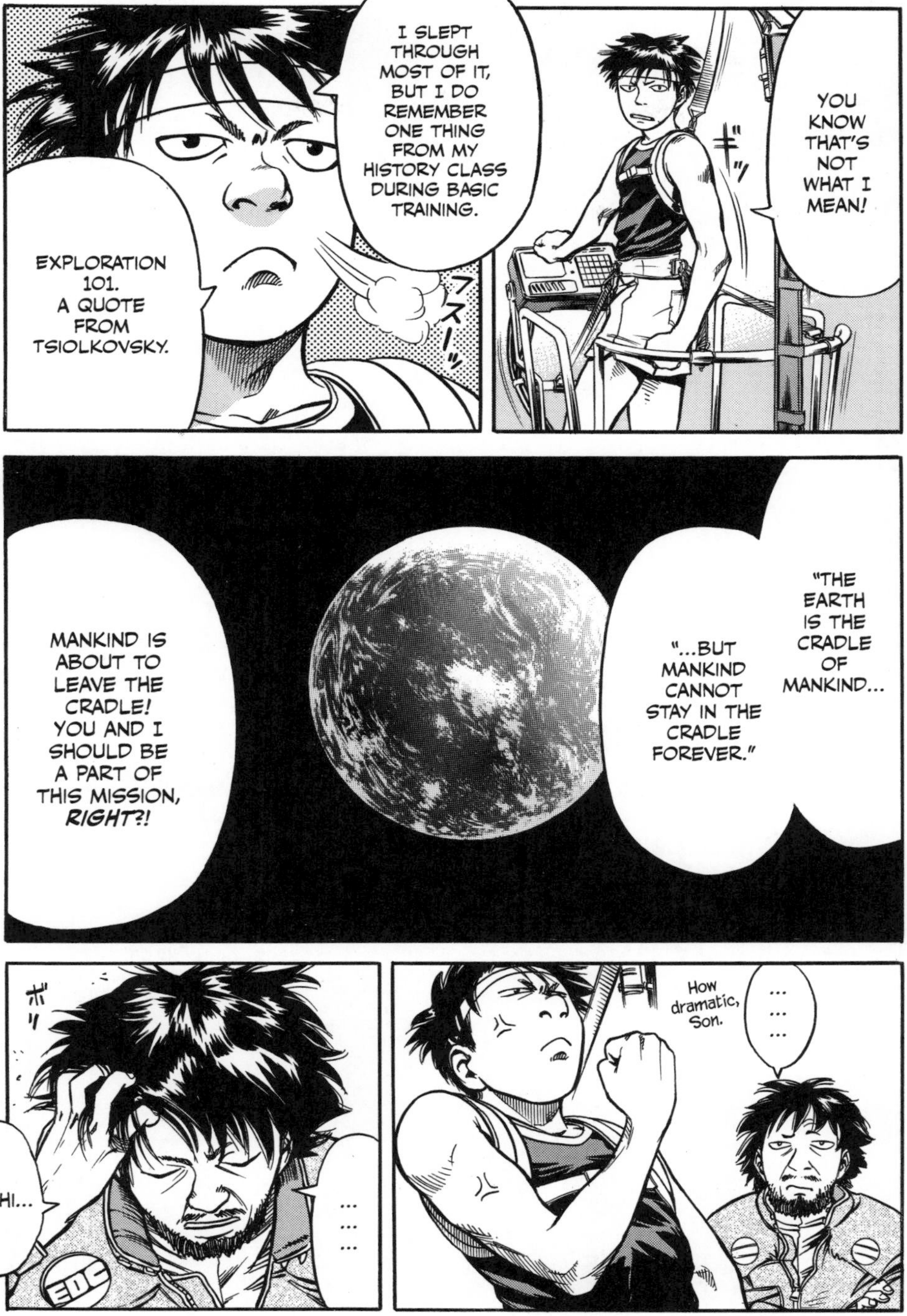
YOU KNOW THAT'S NOT WHAT I MEAN!
ギッ
I SLEPT THROUGH MOST OF IT, BUT I DO REMEMBER ONE THING FROM MY HISTORY CLASS DURING BASIC TRAINING.
EXPLORATION 101. A QUOTE FROM TSIOLKOVSKY.
フスーッ
"THE EARTH IS THE CRADLE OF MANKIND...
"...BUT MANKIND CANNOT STAY IN THE CRADLE FOREVER."
MANKIND IS ABOUT TO LEAVE THE CRADLE! YOU AND I SHOULD BE A PART OF THIS MISSION, *RIGHT*?!
... ...
How dramatic, Son.
ボリ
... ...
HACHI...

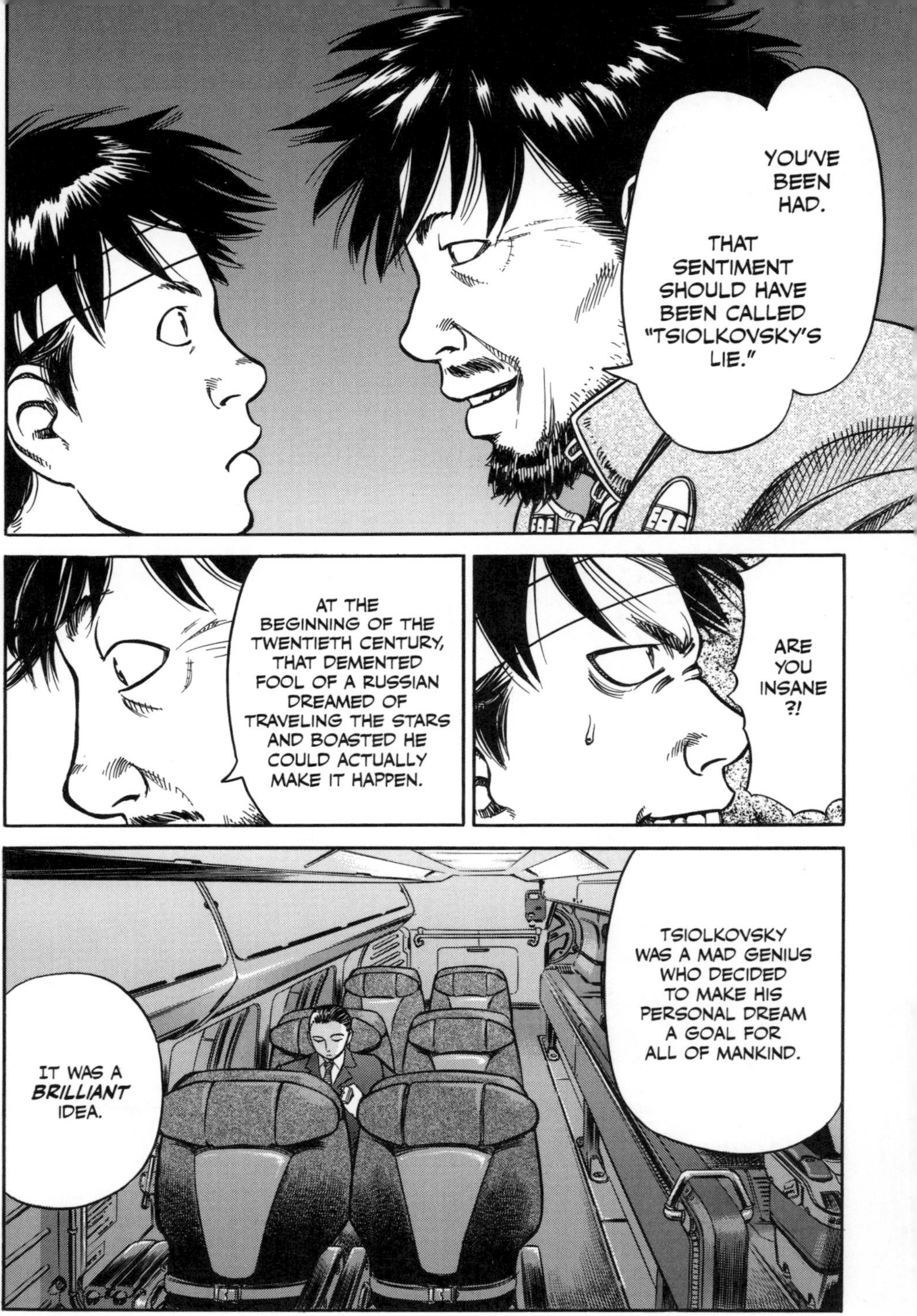
YOU'VE BEEN HAD.
THAT SENTIMENT SHOULD HAVE BEEN CALLED "TSIOLKOVSKY'S LIE."
ARE YOU INSANE ?!
AT THE BEGINNING OF THE TWENTIETH CENTURY, THAT DEMENTED FOOL OF A RUSSIAN DREAMED OF TRAVELING THE STARS AND BOASTED HE COULD ACTUALLY MAKE IT HAPPEN.
TSIOLKOVSKY WAS A MAD GENIUS WHO DECIDED TO MAKE HIS PERSONAL DREAM A GOAL FOR ALL OF MANKIND.
IT WAS A *BRILLIANT* IDEA.

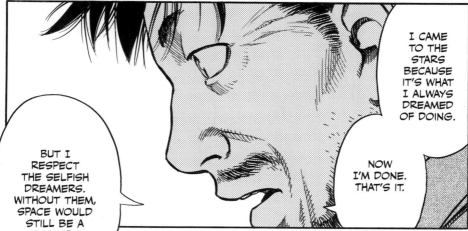

I CAME TO THE STARS BECAUSE IT'S WHAT I ALWAYS DREAMED OF DOING.

NOW I'M DONE. THAT'S IT.

BUT I RESPECT THE SELFISH DREAMERS. WITHOUT THEM, SPACE WOULD STILL BE A MYSTERY.

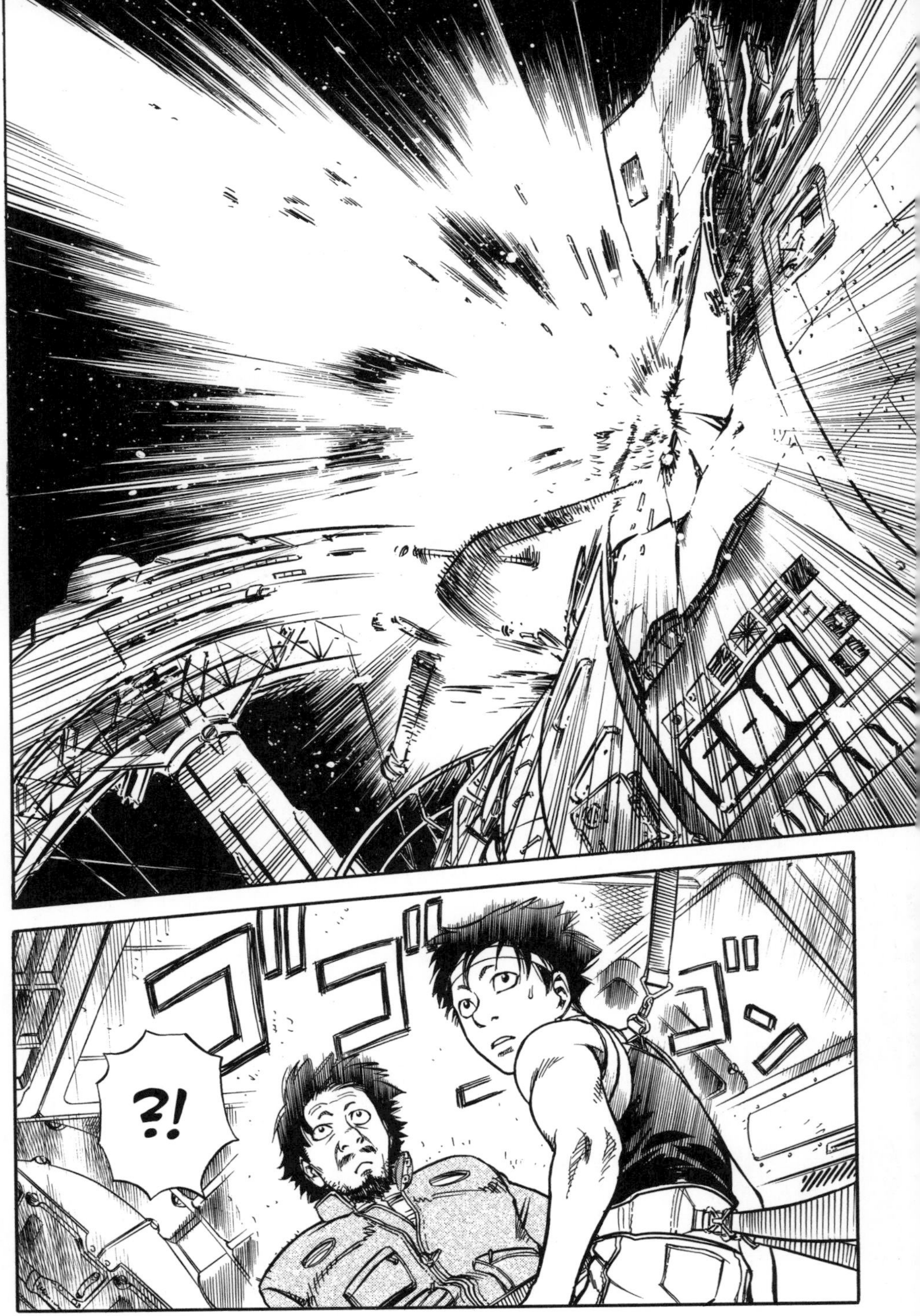
ゴン
ゴゴ
?!

SOMETHING'S HIT A SHAFT IN THE ORBITAL PORT.

THE CONTROL CENTER IS ORDERING US TO EVACUATE.

YURI-- STATUS!

I DON'T KNOW, BUT IF WE DON'T LEAVE NOW *WE'LL* BE DEBRIS. STRAP YOURSELF IN.

DEBRIS?

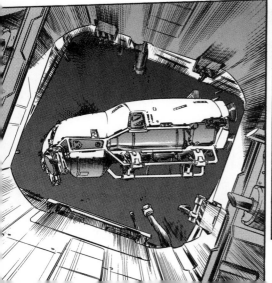

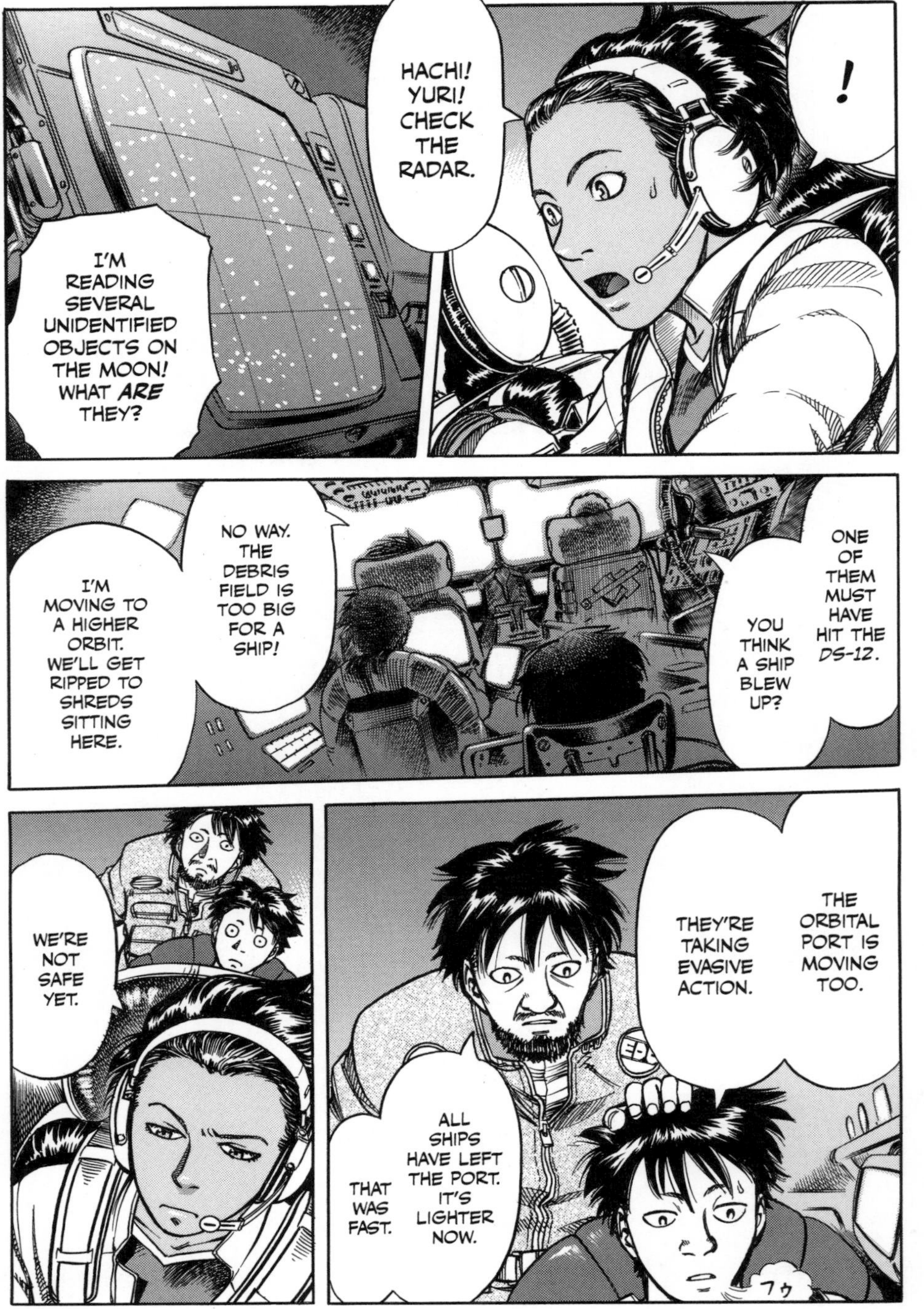
HACHI! YURI! CHECK THE RADAR.
!
I'M READING SEVERAL UNIDENTIFIED OBJECTS ON THE MOON! WHAT *ARE* THEY?
ONE OF THEM MUST HAVE HIT THE *DS-12*.
YOU THINK A SHIP BLEW UP?
NO WAY. THE DEBRIS FIELD IS TOO BIG FOR A SHIP!
I'M MOVING TO A HIGHER ORBIT. WE'LL GET RIPPED TO SHREDS SITTING HERE.
THE ORBITAL PORT IS MOVING TOO.
THEY'RE TAKING EVASIVE ACTION.
ALL SHIPS HAVE LEFT THE PORT. IT'S LIGHTER NOW.
THAT WAS FAST.
フゥ
WE'RE NOT SAFE YET.

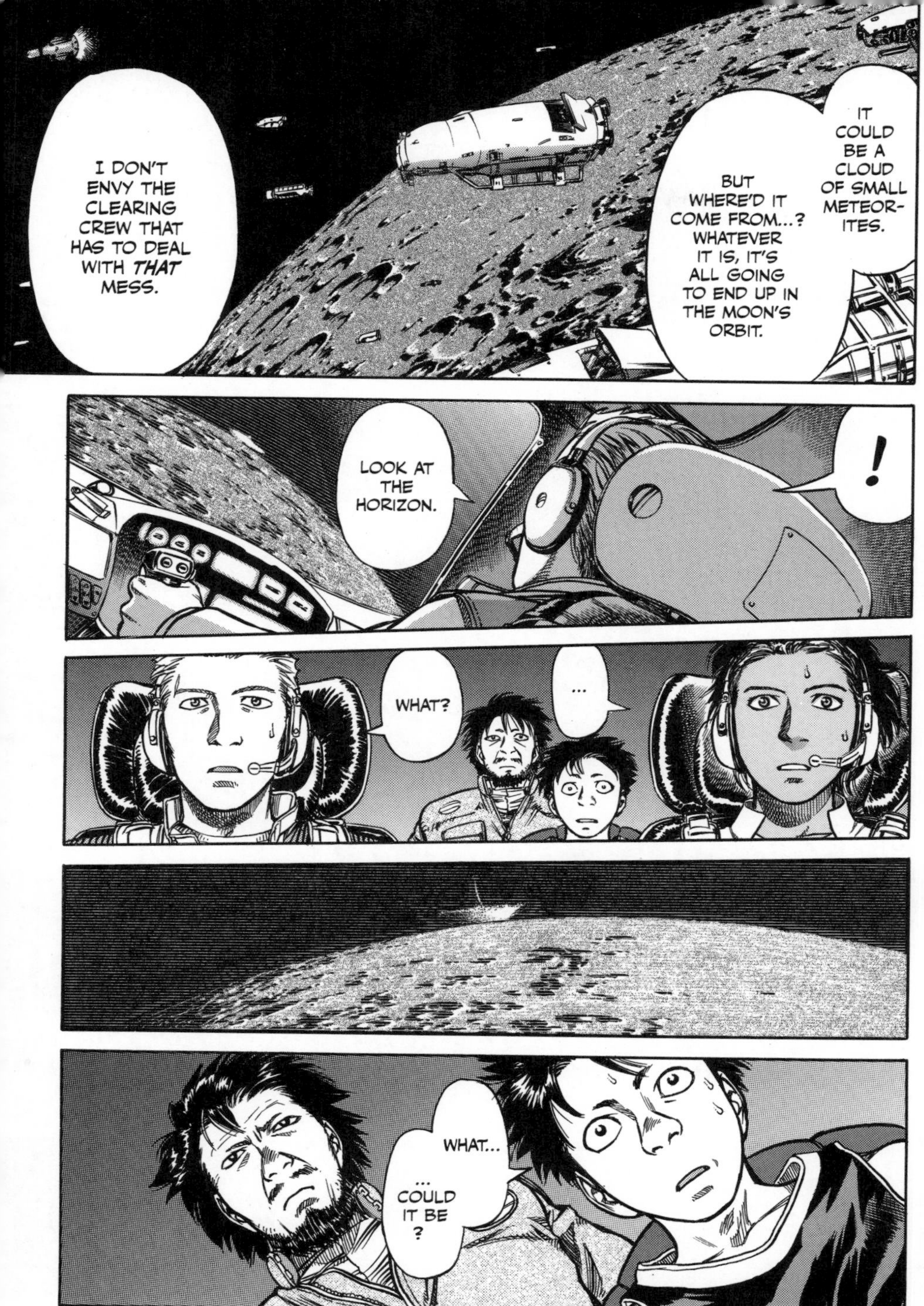
IT COULD BE A CLOUD OF SMALL METEOR-ITES.
BUT WHERE'D IT COME FROM...? WHATEVER IT IS, IT'S ALL GOING TO END UP IN THE MOON'S ORBIT.
I DON'T ENVY THE CLEARING CREW THAT HAS TO DEAL WITH *THAT* MESS.
!
LOOK AT THE HORIZON.
...
WHAT?
WHAT...
...COULD IT BE?

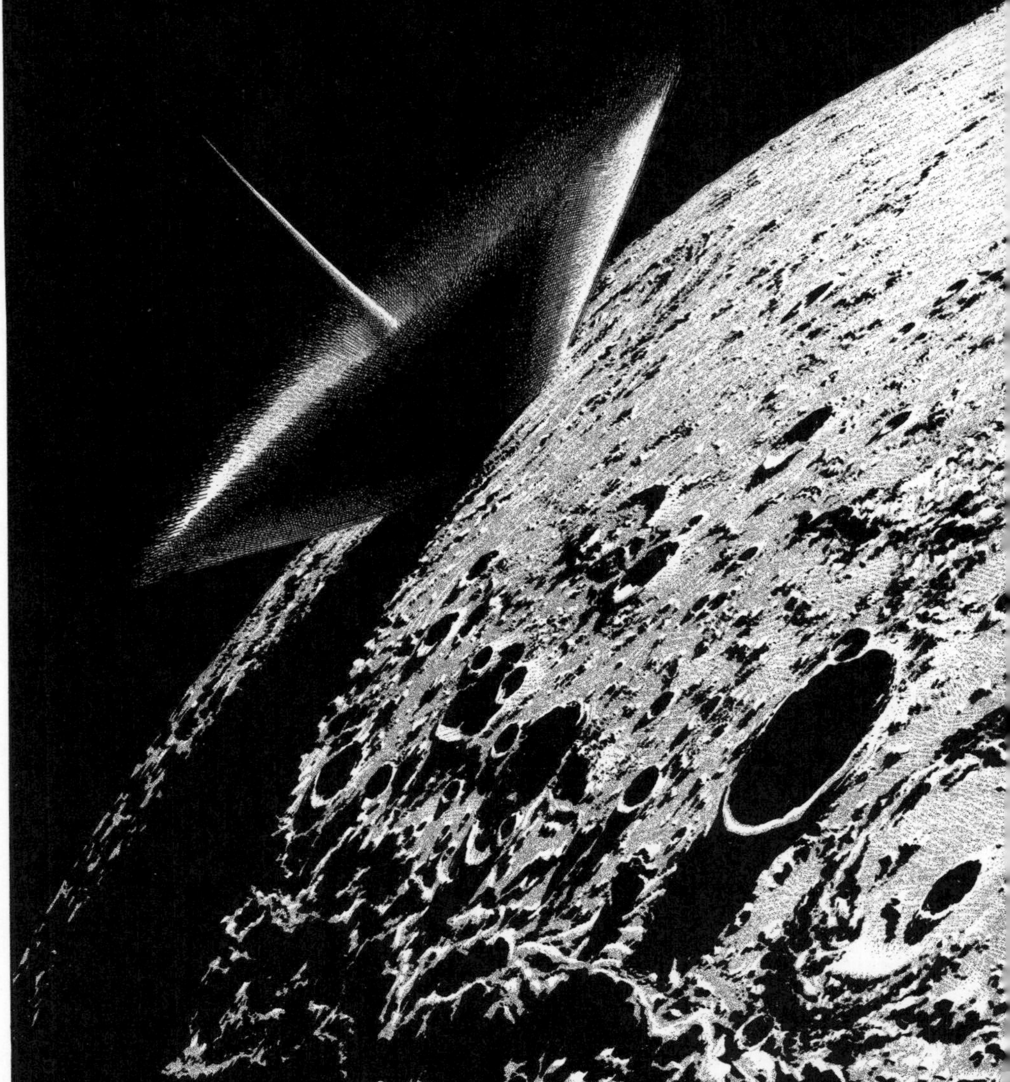

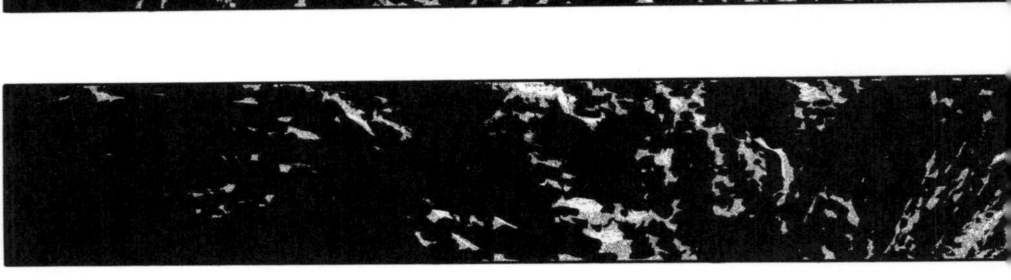

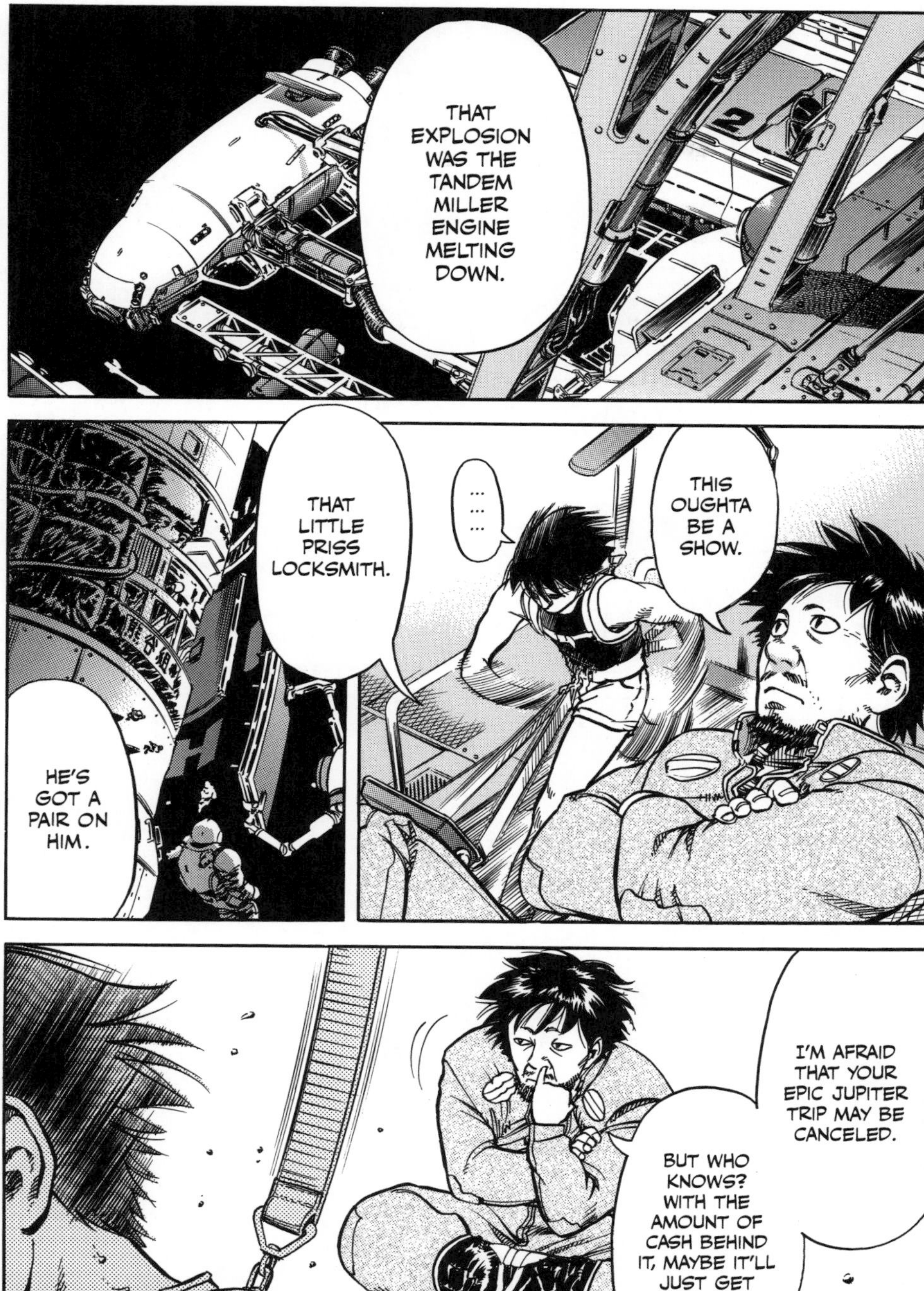
THAT EXPLOSION WAS THE TANDEM MILLER ENGINE MELTING DOWN.
THIS OUGHTA BE A SHOW.
... ...
THAT LITTLE PRISS LOCKSMITH.
HE'S GOT A PAIR ON HIM.
I'M AFRAID THAT YOUR EPIC JUPITER TRIP MAY BE CANCELED.
BUT WHO KNOWS? WITH THE AMOUNT OF CASH BEHIND IT, MAYBE IT'LL JUST GET DELAYED.

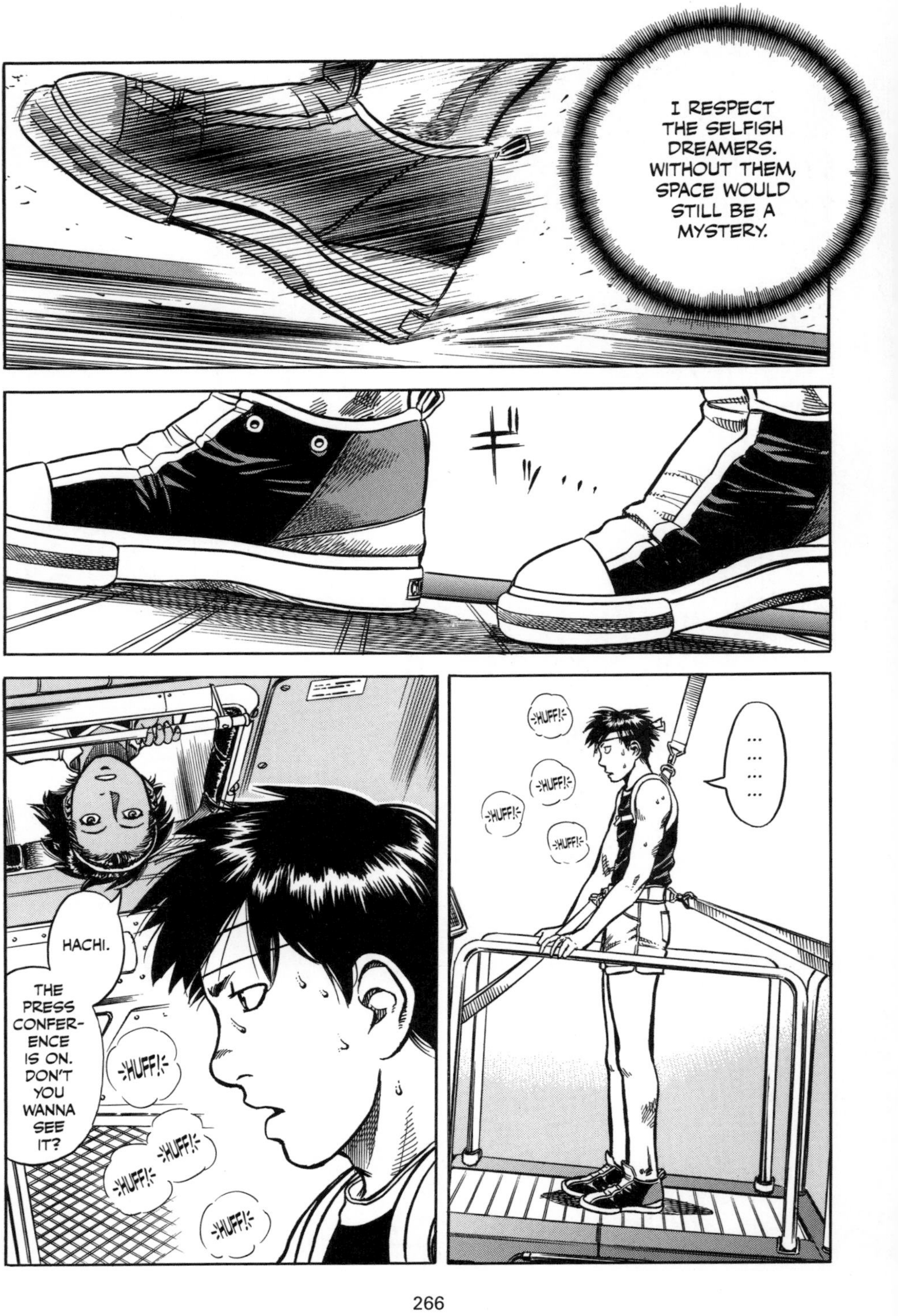
I RESPECT THE SELFISH DREAMERS. WITHOUT THEM, SPACE WOULD STILL BE A MYSTERY.
ザッ...
HUFF!
HUFF!
HUFF!
HUFF!
... ...
HACHI.
THE PRESS CONFERENCE IS ON. DON'T YOU WANNA SEE IT?
HUFF!
HUFF!
HUFF!
HUFF!

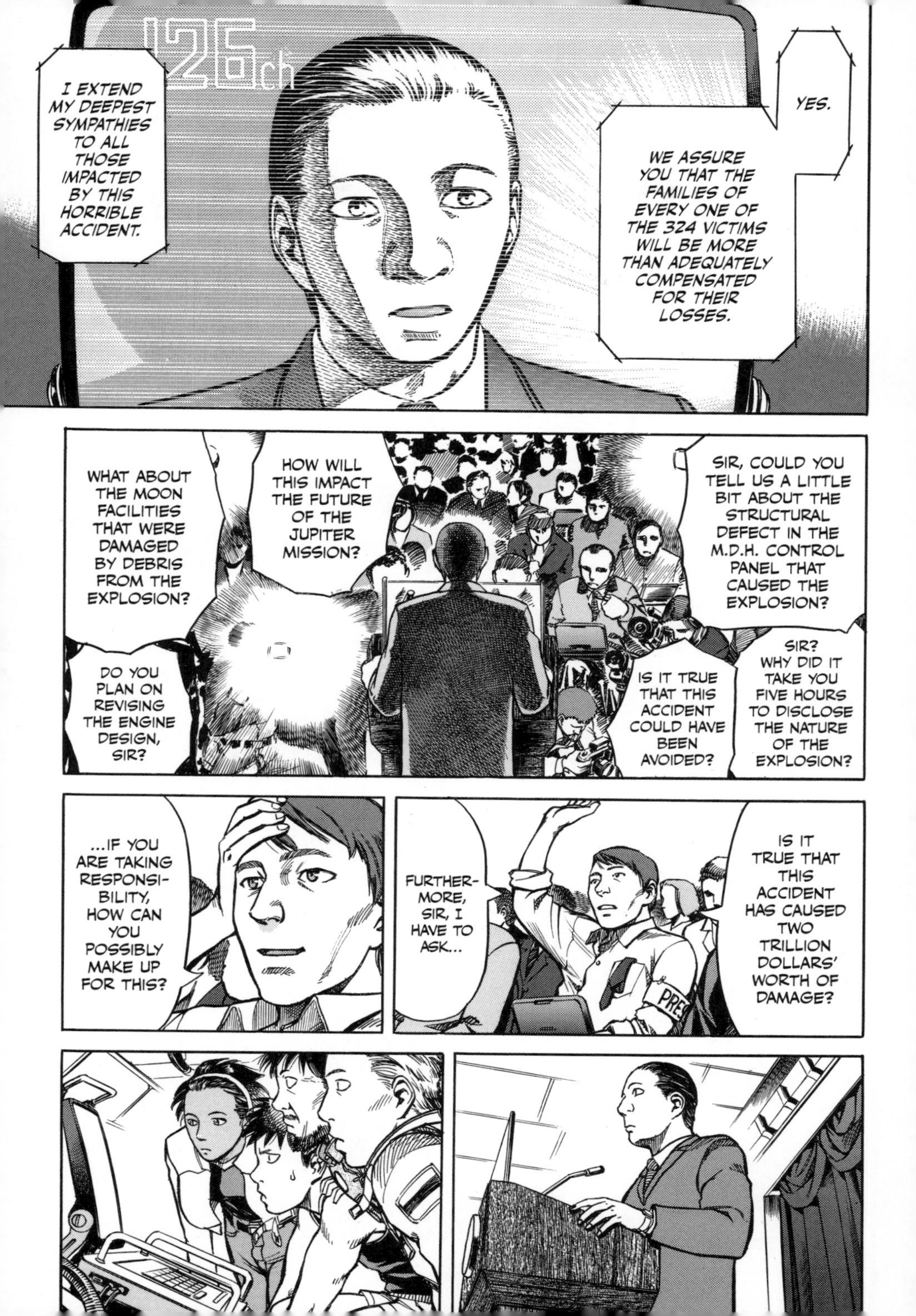
126ch
YES.
WE ASSURE YOU THAT THE FAMILIES OF EVERY ONE OF THE 324 VICTIMS WILL BE MORE THAN ADEQUATELY COMPENSATED FOR THEIR LOSSES.
I EXTEND MY DEEPEST SYMPATHIES TO ALL THOSE IMPACTED BY THIS HORRIBLE ACCIDENT.
SIR, COULD YOU TELL US A LITTLE BIT ABOUT THE STRUCTURAL DEFECT IN THE M.D.H. CONTROL PANEL THAT CAUSED THE EXPLOSION?
SIR? WHY DID IT TAKE YOU FIVE HOURS TO DISCLOSE THE NATURE OF THE EXPLOSION?
IS IT TRUE THAT THIS ACCIDENT COULD HAVE BEEN AVOIDED?
HOW WILL THIS IMPACT THE FUTURE OF THE JUPITER MISSION?
WHAT ABOUT THE MOON FACILITIES THAT WERE DAMAGED BY DEBRIS FROM THE EXPLOSION?
DO YOU PLAN ON REVISING THE ENGINE DESIGN, SIR?
IS IT TRUE THAT THIS ACCIDENT HAS CAUSED TWO TRILLION DOLLARS' WORTH OF DAMAGE?
FURTHER-MORE, SIR, I HAVE TO ASK...
...IF YOU ARE TAKING RESPONSI-BILITY, HOW CAN YOU POSSIBLY MAKE UP FOR THIS?

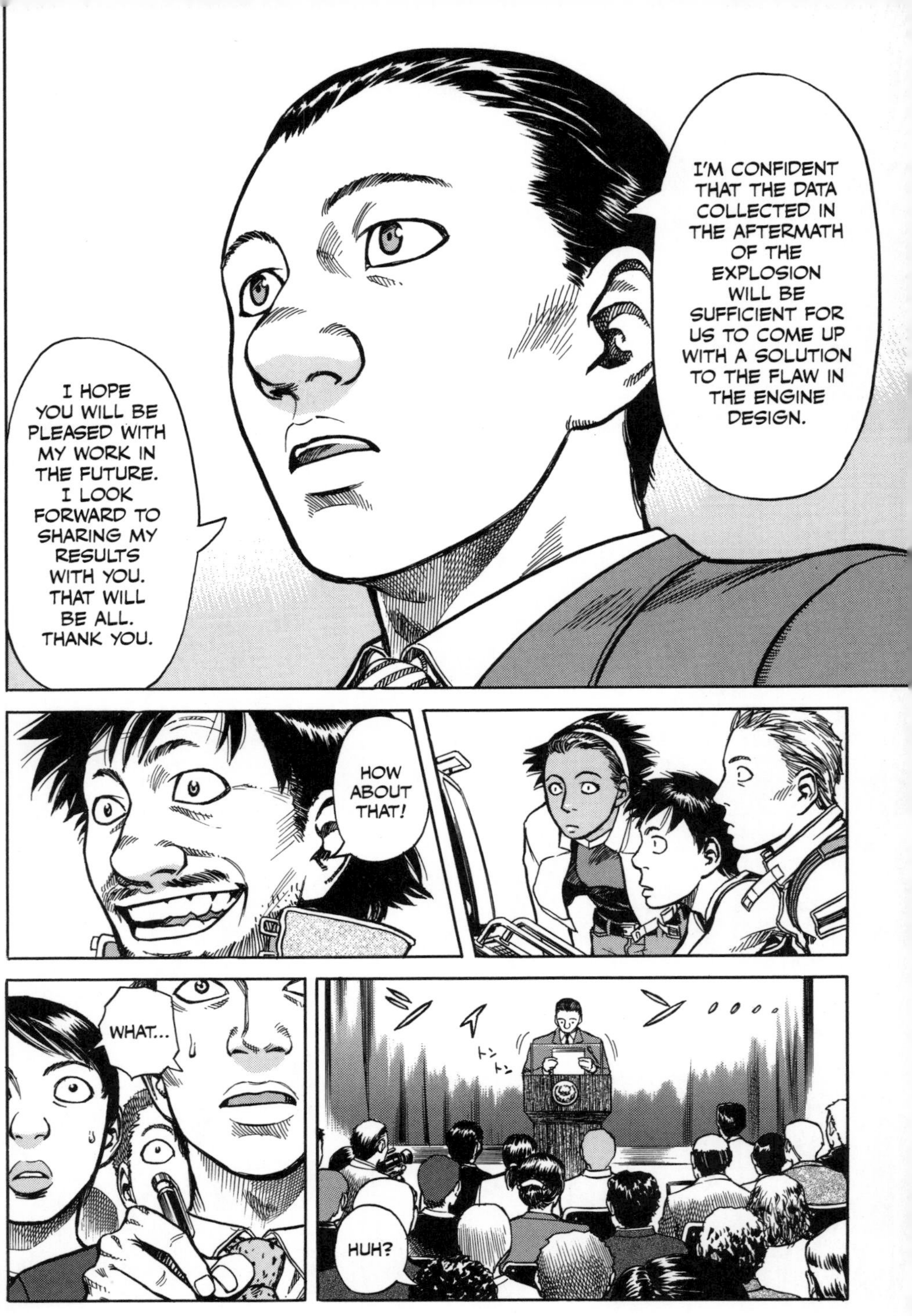
I'M CONFIDENT THAT THE DATA COLLECTED IN THE AFTERMATH OF THE EXPLOSION WILL BE SUFFICIENT FOR US TO COME UP WITH A SOLUTION TO THE FLAW IN THE ENGINE DESIGN.
I HOPE YOU WILL BE PLEASED WITH MY WORK IN THE FUTURE. I LOOK FORWARD TO SHARING MY RESULTS WITH YOU. THAT WILL BE ALL. THANK YOU.
HOW ABOUT THAT!
トン トン
HUH?
WHAT...

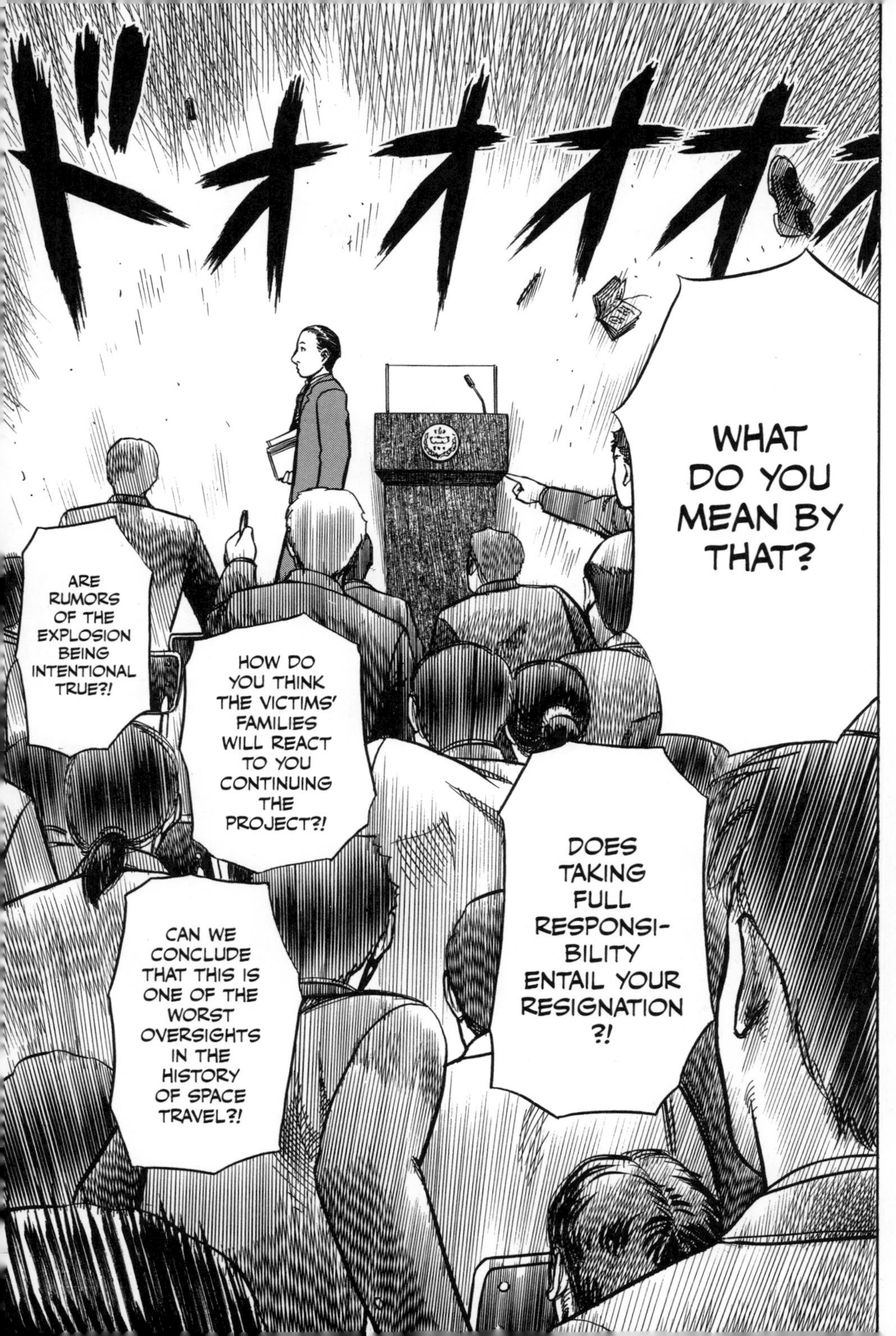
ドオオオオ
WHAT DO YOU MEAN BY THAT?
HOW DO YOU THINK THE VICTIMS' FAMILIES WILL REACT TO YOU CONTINUING THE PROJECT?!
ARE RUMORS OF THE EXPLOSION BEING INTENTIONAL TRUE?!
DOES TAKING FULL RESPONSI-BILITY ENTAIL YOUR RESIGNATION ?!
CAN WE CONCLUDE THAT THIS IS ONE OF THE WORST OVERSIGHTS IN THE HISTORY OF SPACE TRAVEL?!

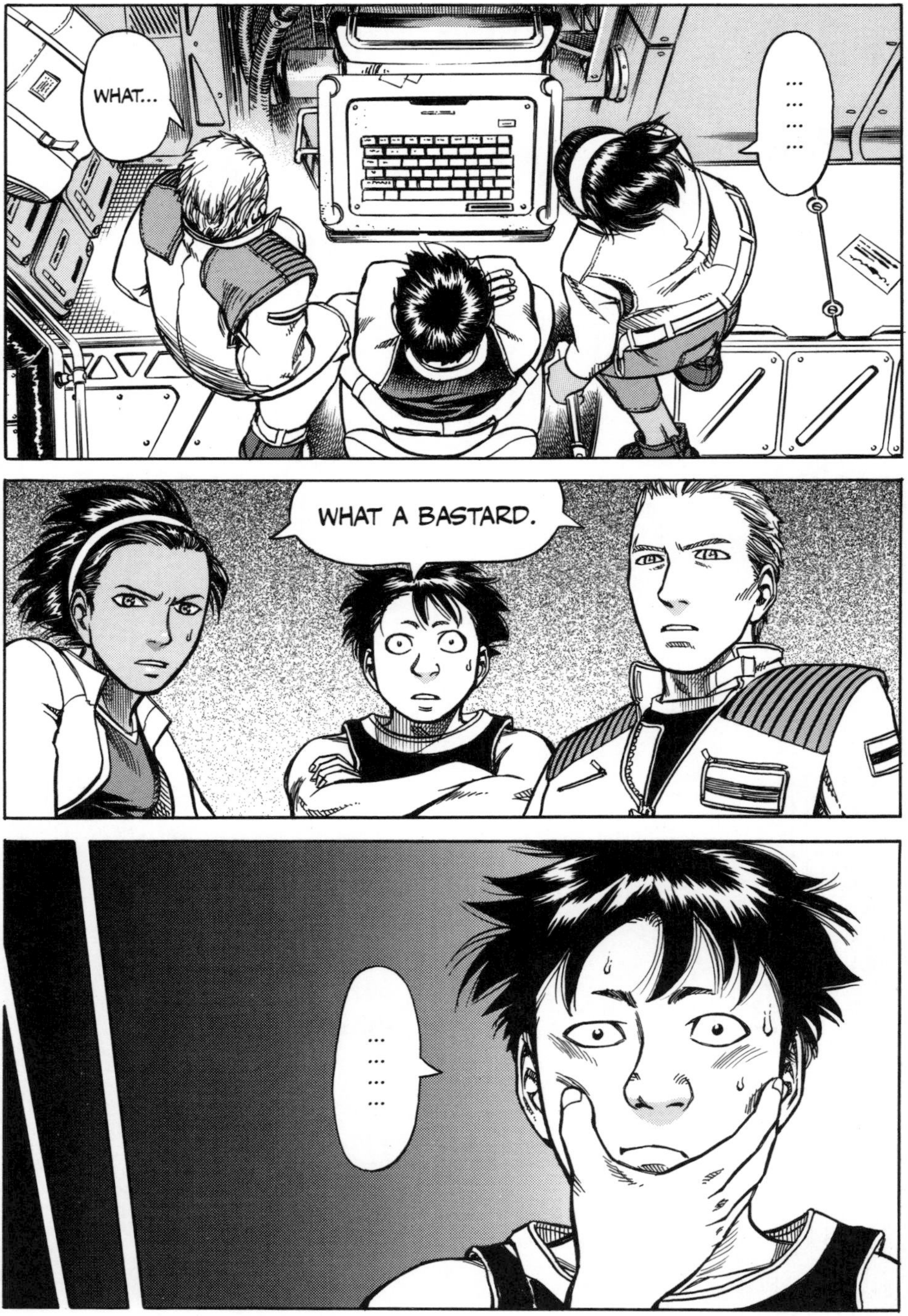
....
WHAT...
WHAT A BASTARD.
....

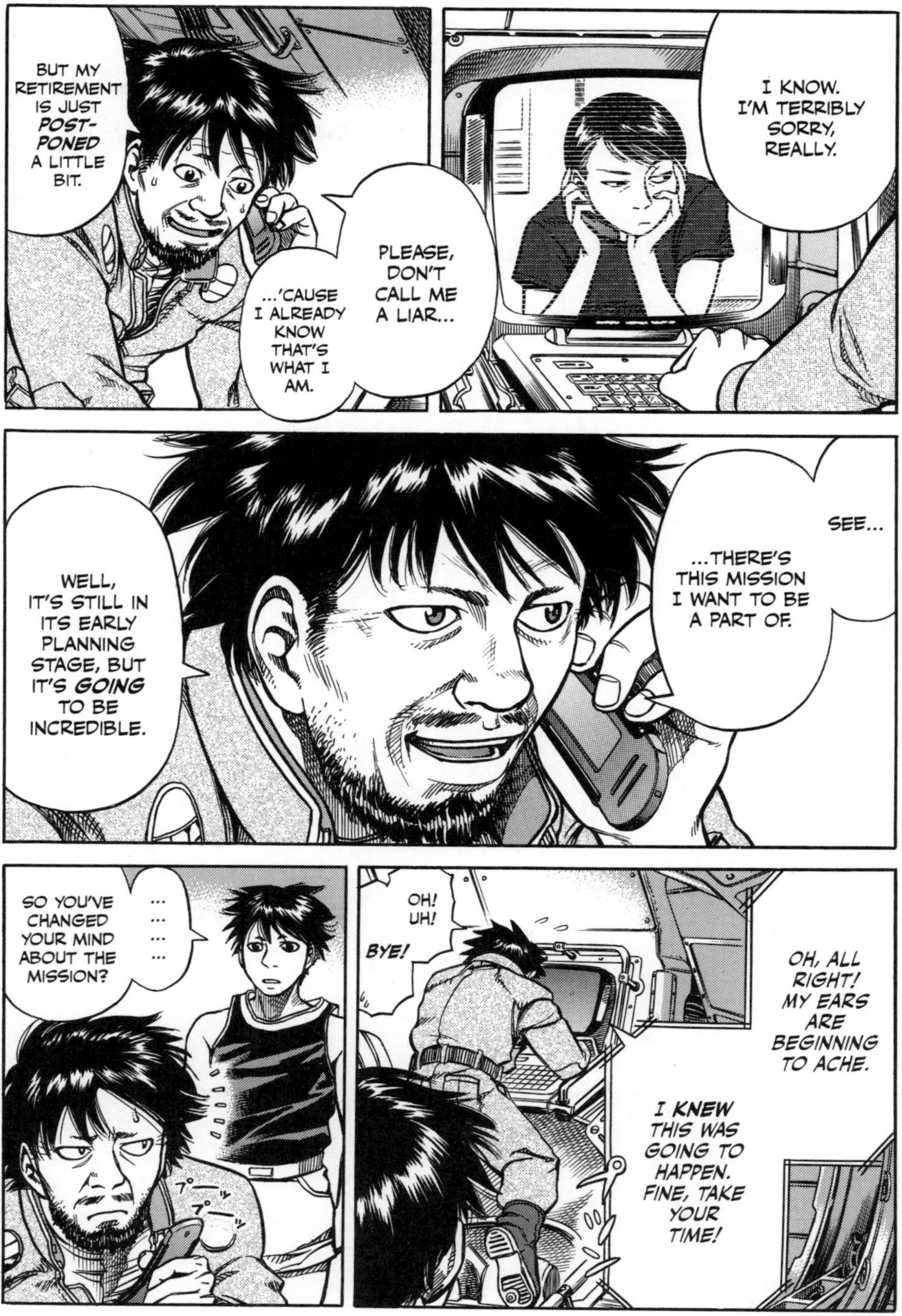
I KNOW. I'M TERRIBLY SORRY, REALLY.
BUT MY RETIREMENT IS JUST ***POST-PONED*** A LITTLE BIT.
PLEASE, DON'T CALL ME A LIAR...
...'CAUSE I ALREADY KNOW THAT'S WHAT I AM.
SEE...
...THERE'S THIS MISSION I WANT TO BE A PART OF.
WELL, IT'S STILL IN ITS EARLY PLANNING STAGE, BUT IT'S ***GOING*** TO BE INCREDIBLE.
OH, ALL RIGHT! MY EARS ARE BEGINNING TO ACHE.
*I **KNEW** THIS WAS GOING TO HAPPEN. FINE, TAKE YOUR TIME!*
OH! UH!
BYE!
SO YOU'VE CHANGED YOUR MIND ABOUT THE MISSION?
....
プーッ
プーッ

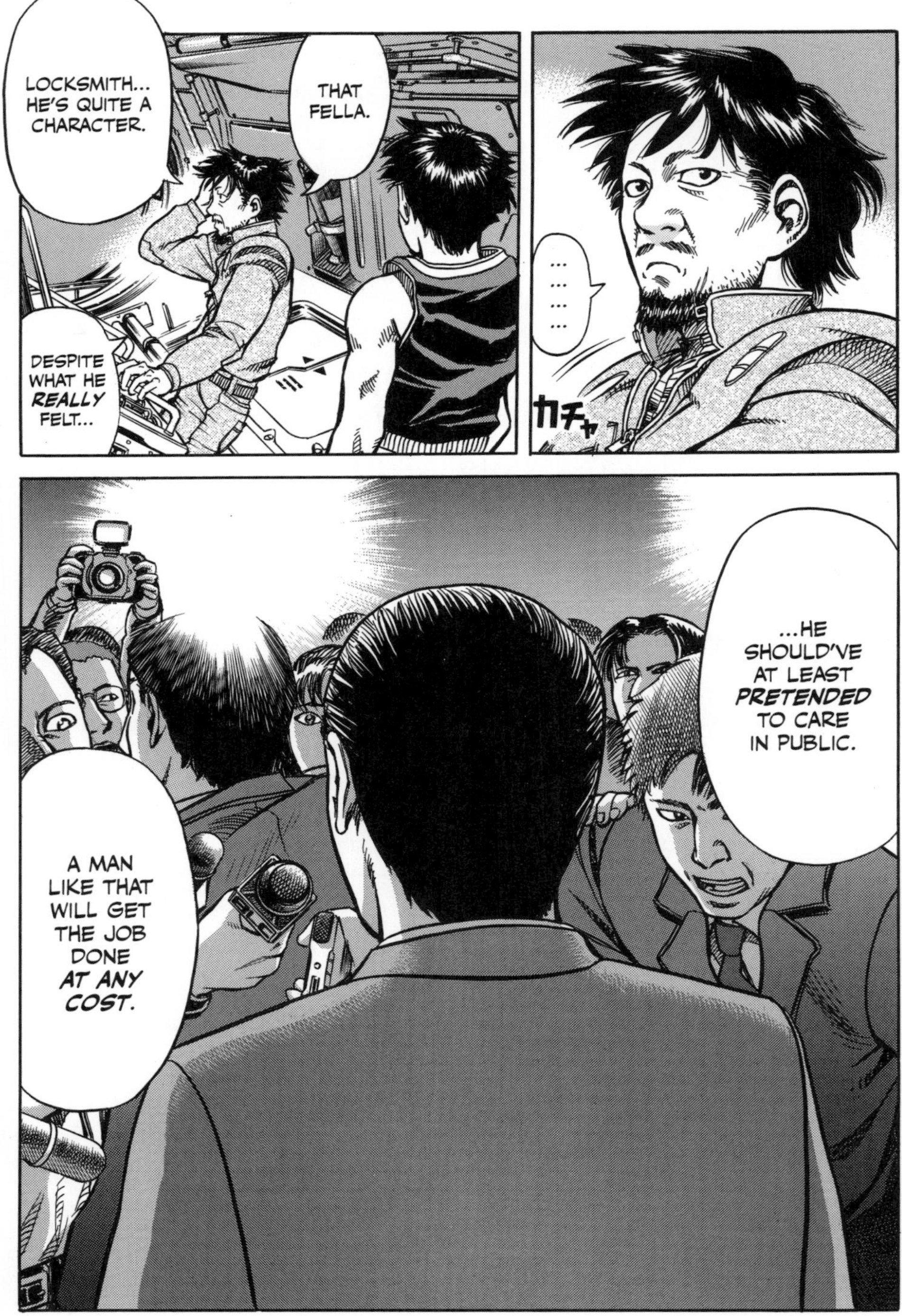
....
....
....
....
カチャ
LOCKSMITH... HE'S QUITE A CHARACTER.
THAT FELLA.
DESPITE WHAT HE *REALLY* FELT...
...HE SHOULD'VE AT LEAST *PRETENDED* TO CARE IN PUBLIC.
A MAN LIKE THAT WILL GET THE JOB DONE *AT ANY COST*.

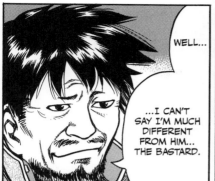

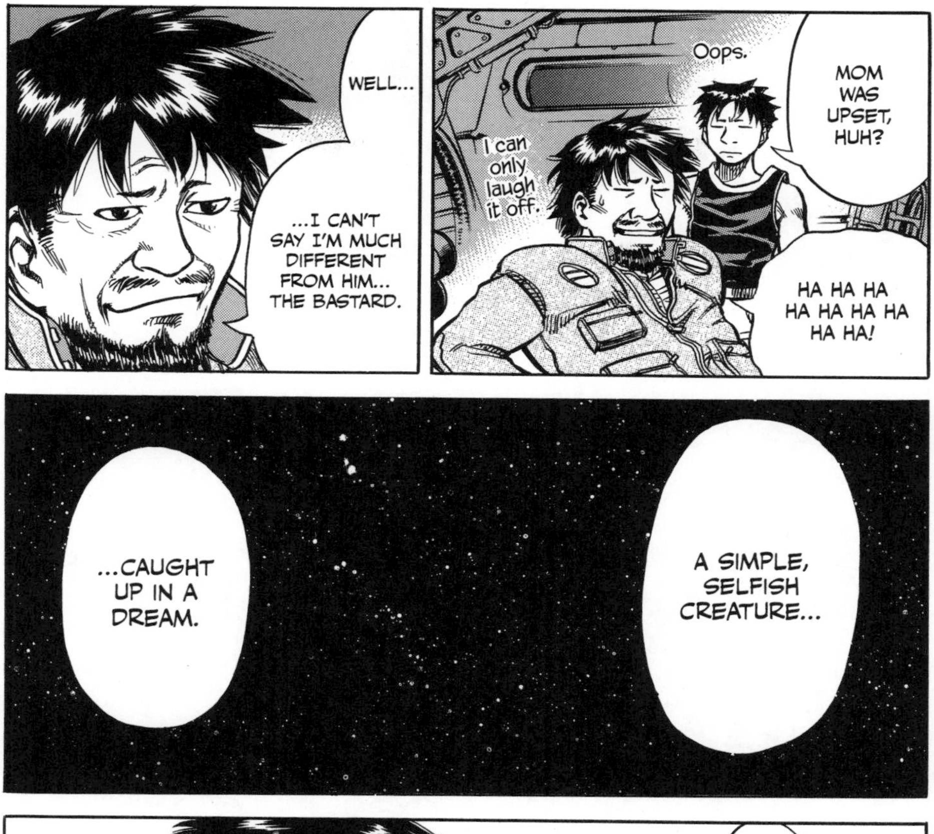

MOM WAS UPSET, HUH?
Oops.
I can only laugh it off.
HA HA HA HA HA HA HA HA HA!
WELL...
...I CAN'T SAY I'M MUCH DIFFERENT FROM HIM... THE BASTARD.
A SIMPLE, SELFISH CREATURE...
...CAUGHT UP IN A DREAM.
AND YOU...
...YOU'RE JUST LIKE THE BOTH OF US, AREN'T YOU?
....

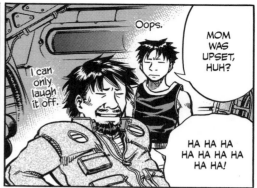

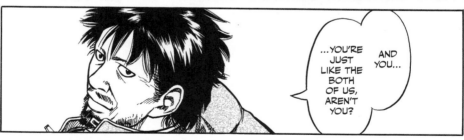

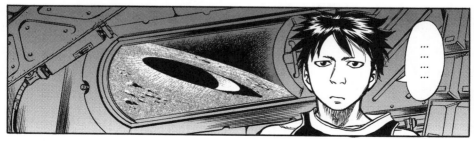

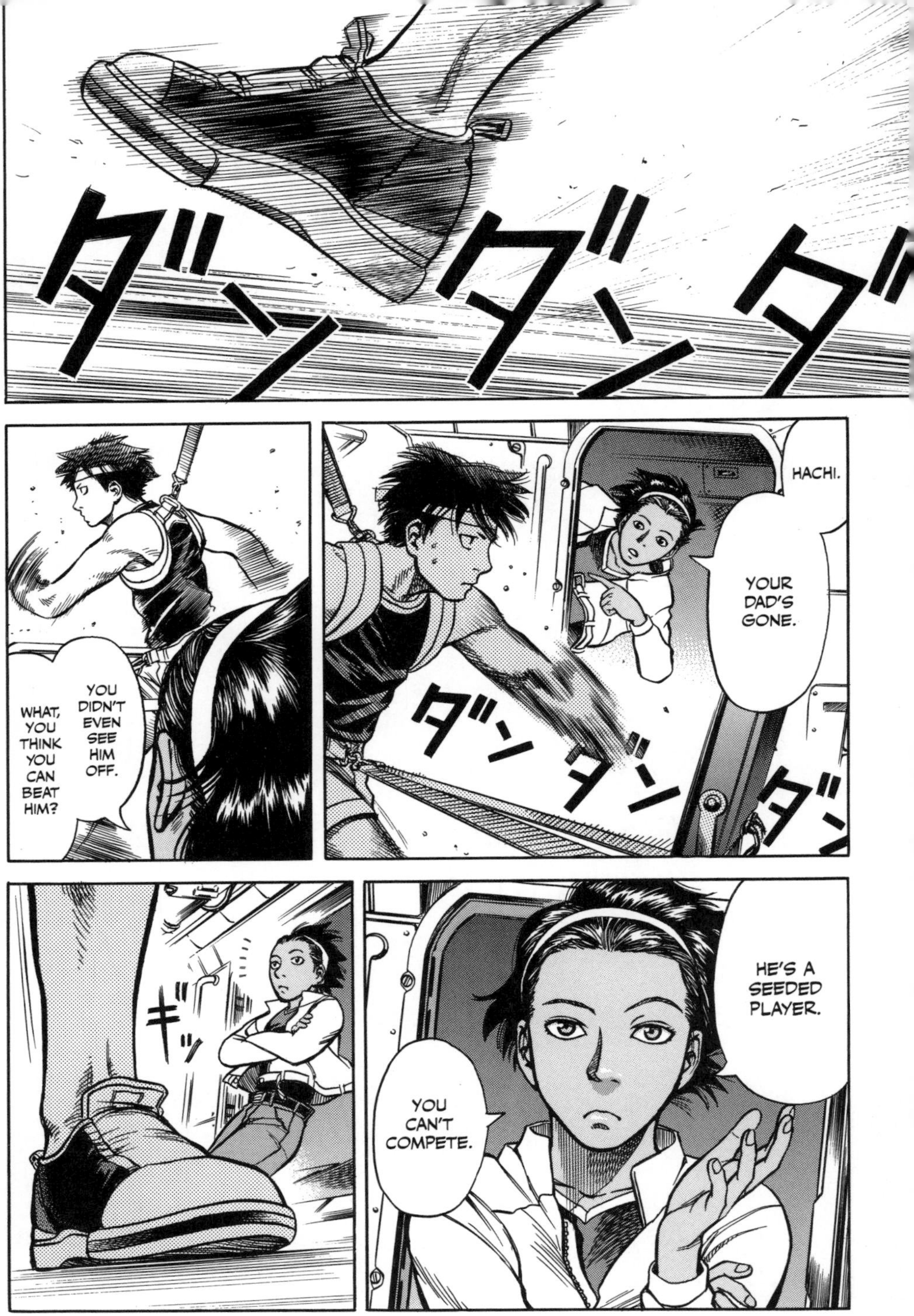
ダ
ダン
ダン
HACHI.
YOUR DAD'S GONE.
ダン
ダン
ダン
YOU DIDN'T EVEN SEE HIM OFF.
WHAT, YOU THINK YOU CAN BEAT HIM?
HE'S A SEEDED PLAYER.
YOU CAN'T COMPETE.
ギッ

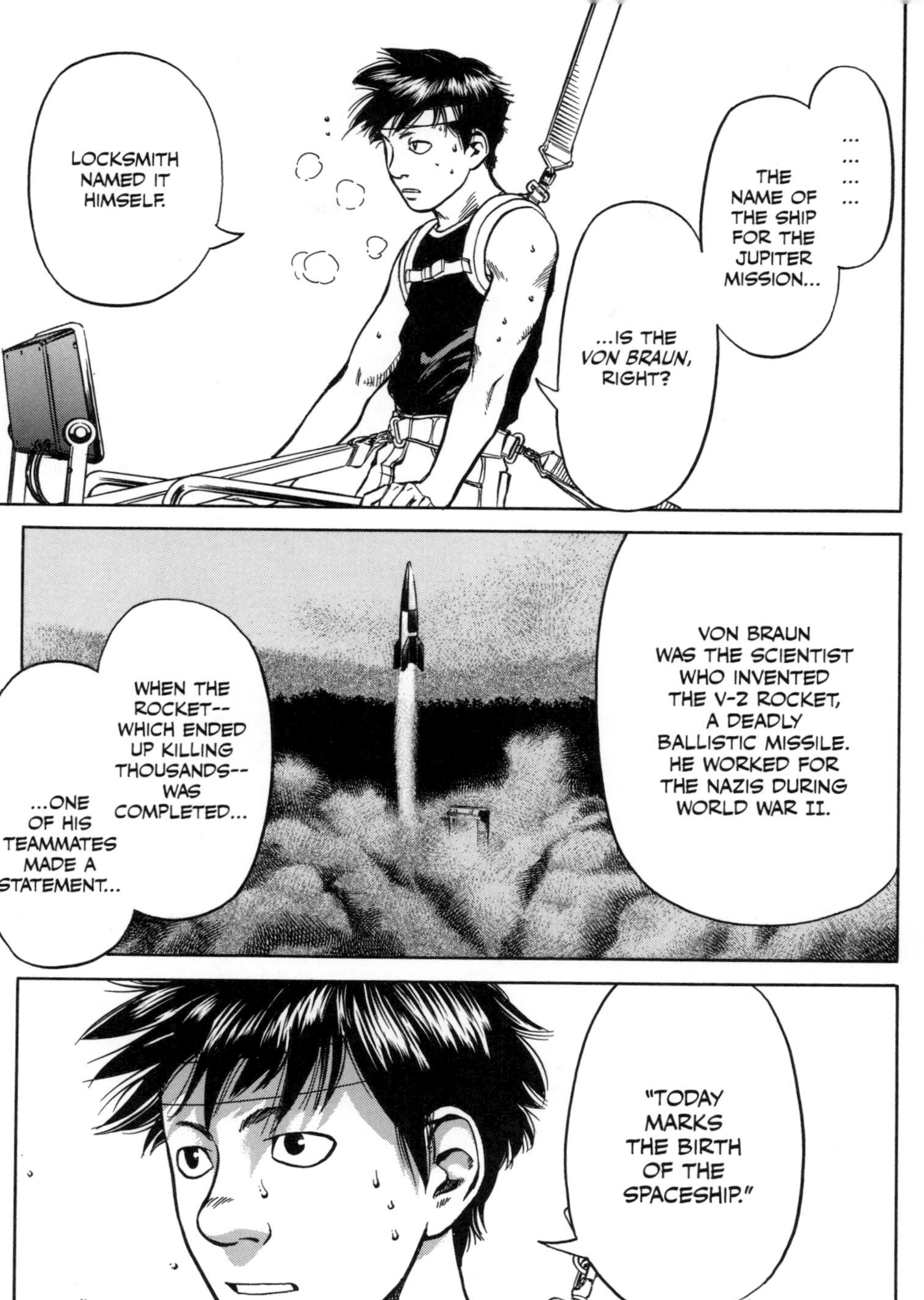
... ...
THE NAME OF THE SHIP FOR THE JUPITER MISSION...
...IS THE *VON BRAUN*, RIGHT?
LOCKSMITH NAMED IT HIMSELF.
VON BRAUN WAS THE SCIENTIST WHO INVENTED THE V-2 ROCKET, A DEADLY BALLISTIC MISSILE. HE WORKED FOR THE NAZIS DURING WORLD WAR II.
WHEN THE ROCKET--WHICH ENDED UP KILLING THOUSANDS--WAS COMPLETED...
...ONE OF HIS TEAMMATES MADE A STATEMENT...
"TODAY MARKS THE BIRTH OF THE SPACESHIP."

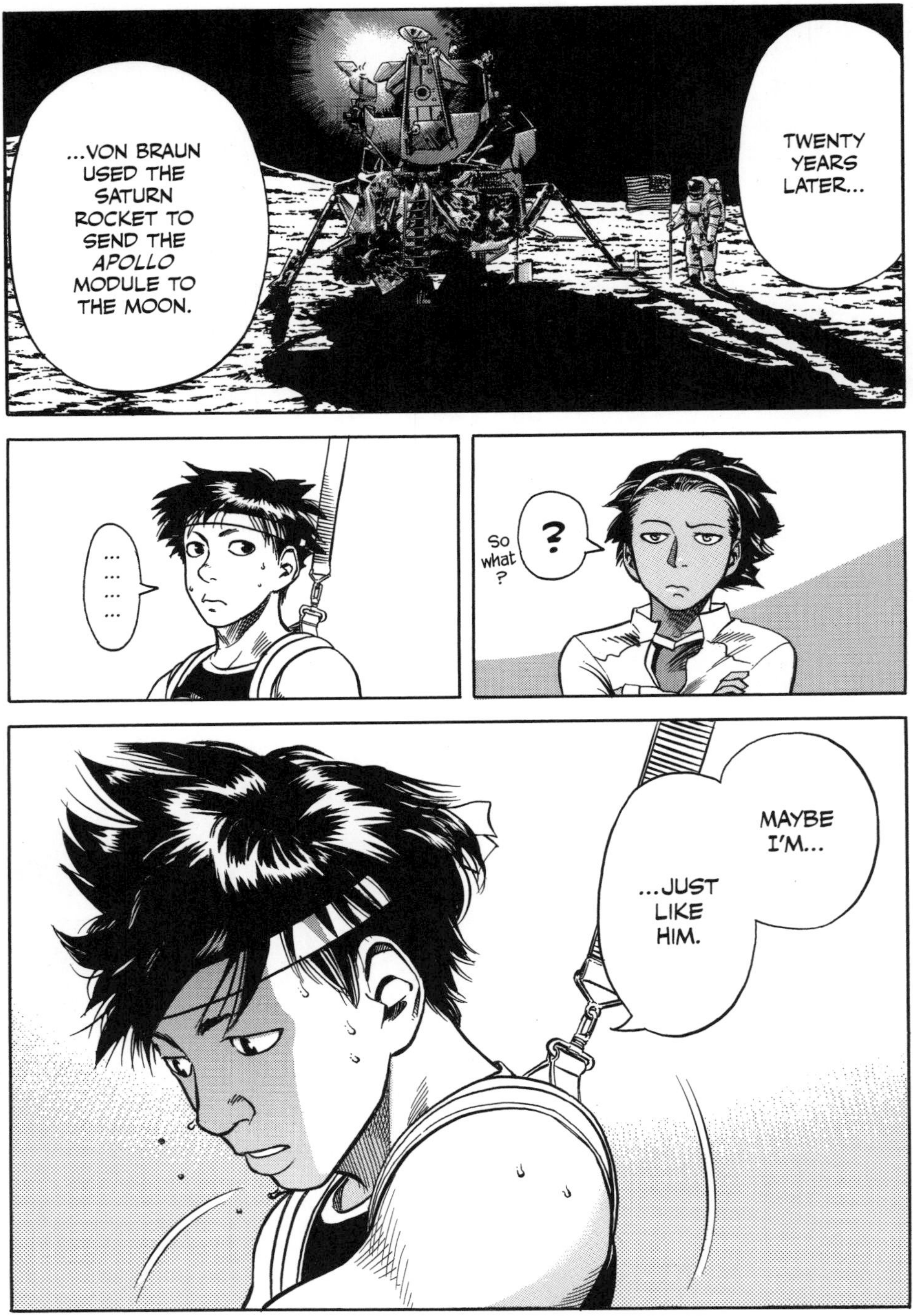
TWENTY YEARS LATER...
...VON BRAUN USED THE SATURN ROCKET TO SEND THE *APOLLO* MODULE TO THE MOON.
?
So what?
... ...
MAYBE I'M...
...JUST LIKE HIM.

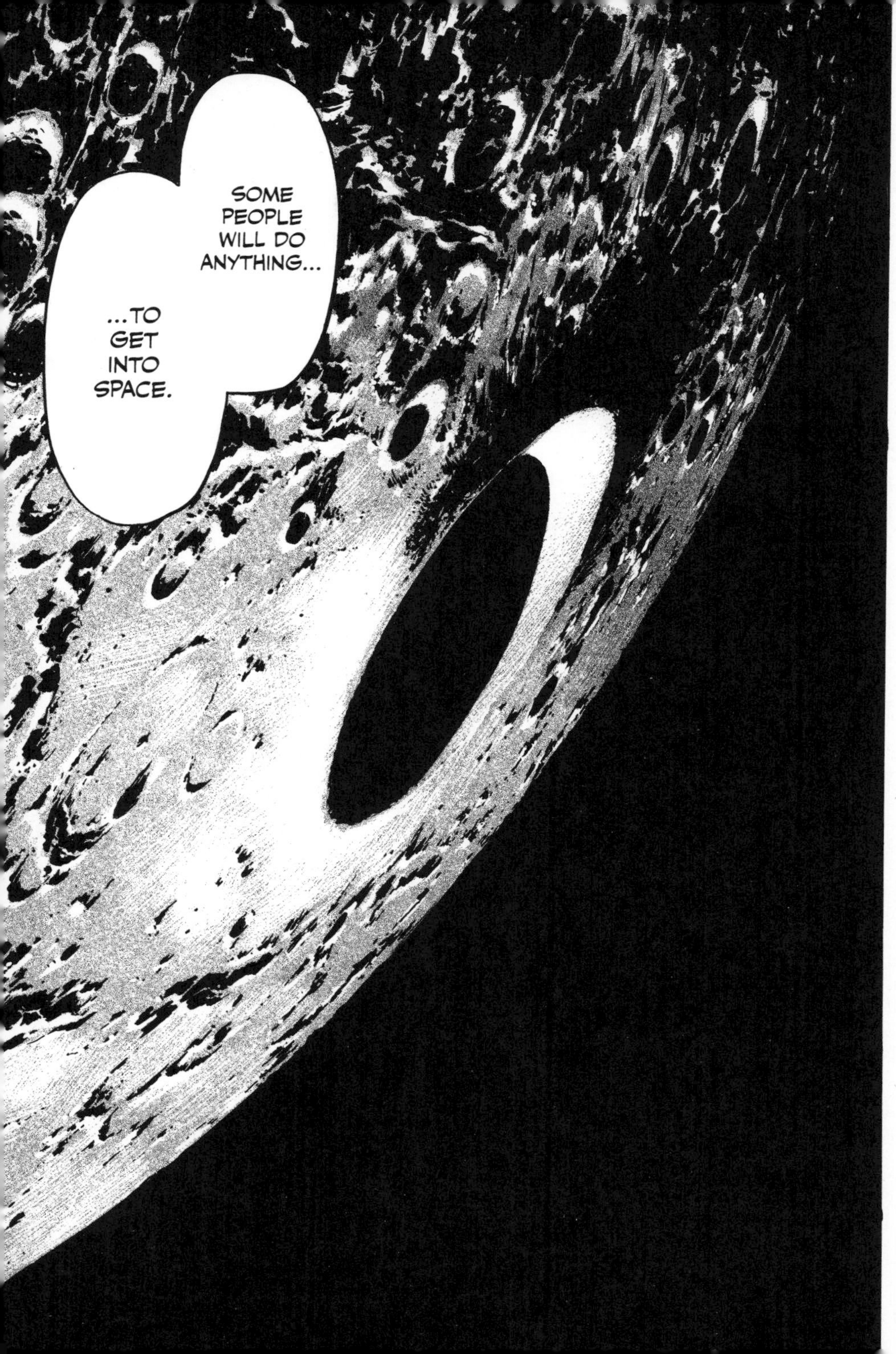
SOME PEOPLE WILL DO ANYTHING...
...TO GET INTO SPACE.

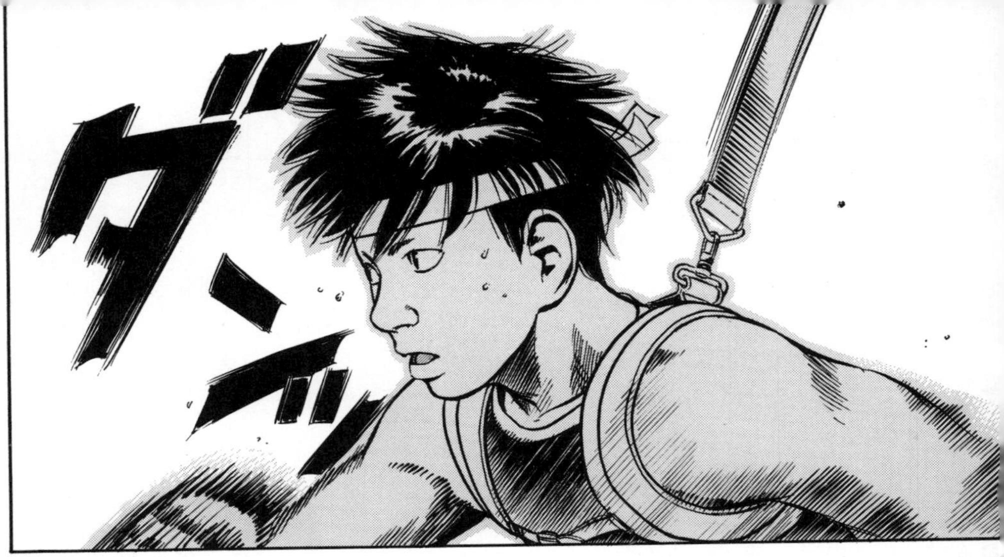
ダン
ダッ

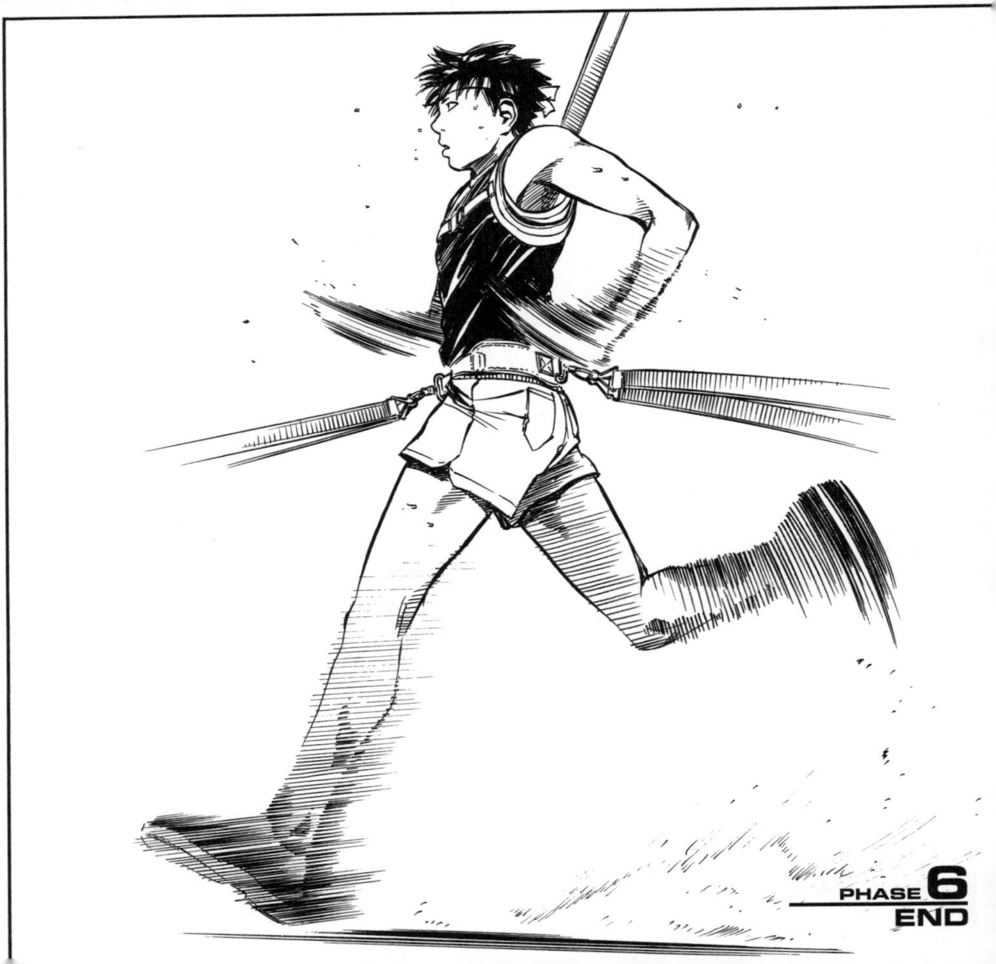

PHASE 6 END

Helmet latches separately
Life Pack SE 73
Pressure tank on his back
Suit opens from back
Guard
Arm bolt
Guard
Wrist bolt
Buttocks 73
SE 73
SE 73
Kiji-type ring
Ankle bolt
TECHNORA

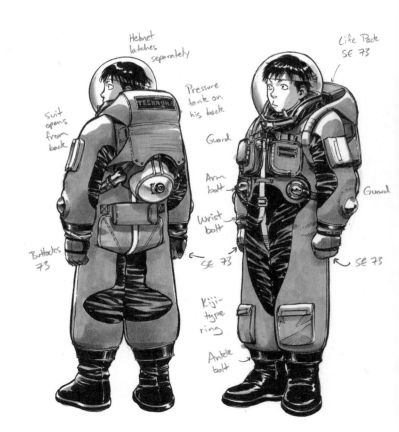

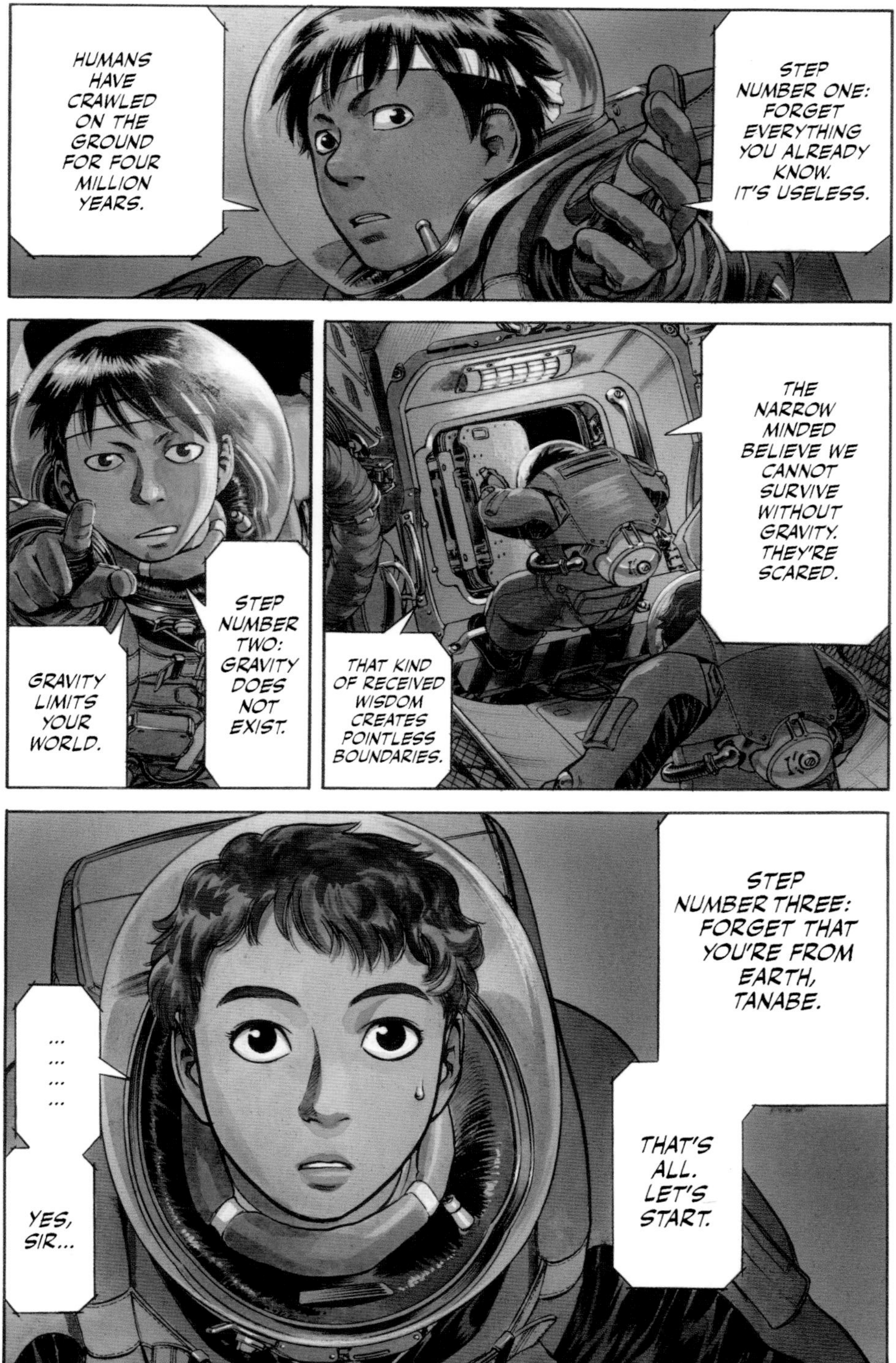
STEP NUMBER ONE: FORGET EVERYTHING YOU ALREADY KNOW. IT'S USELESS.
HUMANS HAVE CRAWLED ON THE GROUND FOR FOUR MILLION YEARS.
THE NARROW MINDED BELIEVE WE CANNOT SURVIVE WITHOUT GRAVITY. THEY'RE SCARED.
THAT KIND OF RECEIVED WISDOM CREATES POINTLESS BOUNDARIES.
STEP NUMBER TWO: GRAVITY DOES NOT EXIST.
GRAVITY LIMITS YOUR WORLD.
STEP NUMBER THREE: FORGET THAT YOU'RE FROM EARTH, TANABE.
... ...
THAT'S ALL. LET'S START.
YES, SIR...

PHASE 7
TANABE

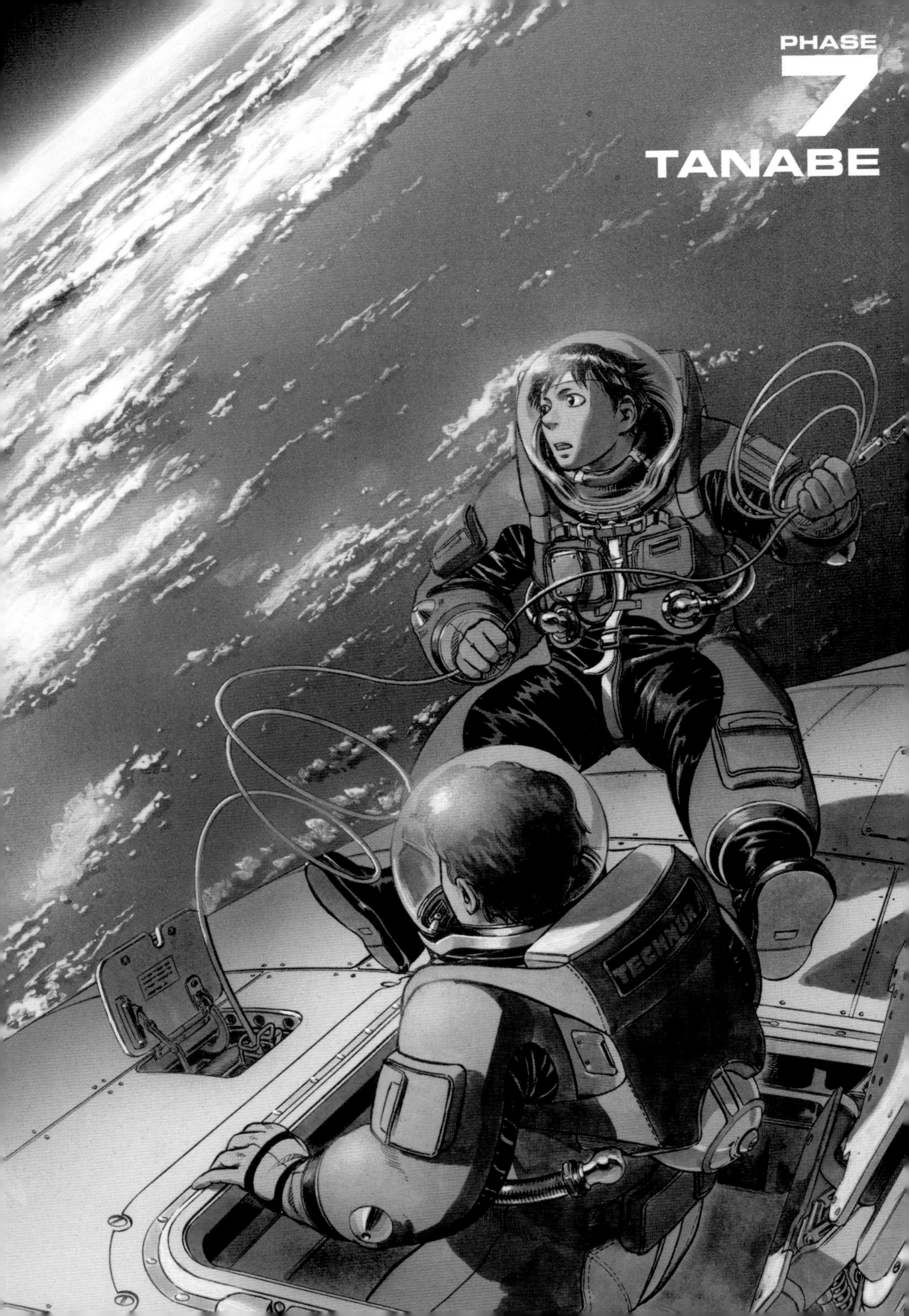

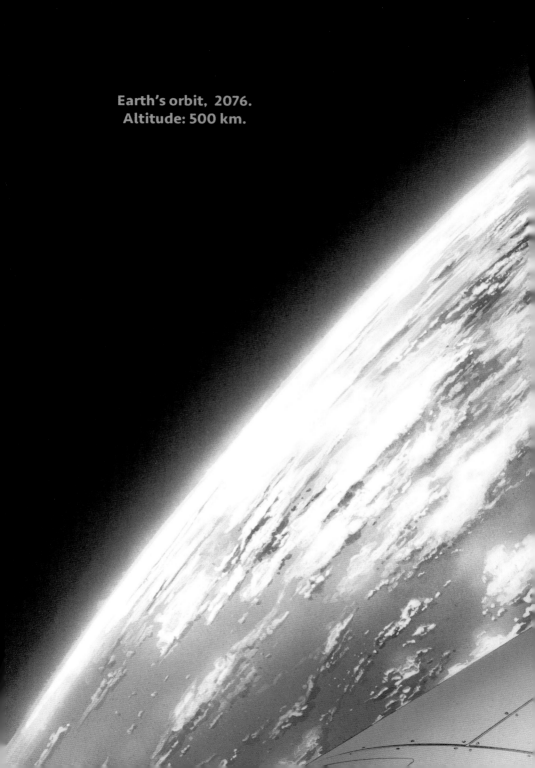

Earth's orbit, 2076.
Altitude: 500 km.

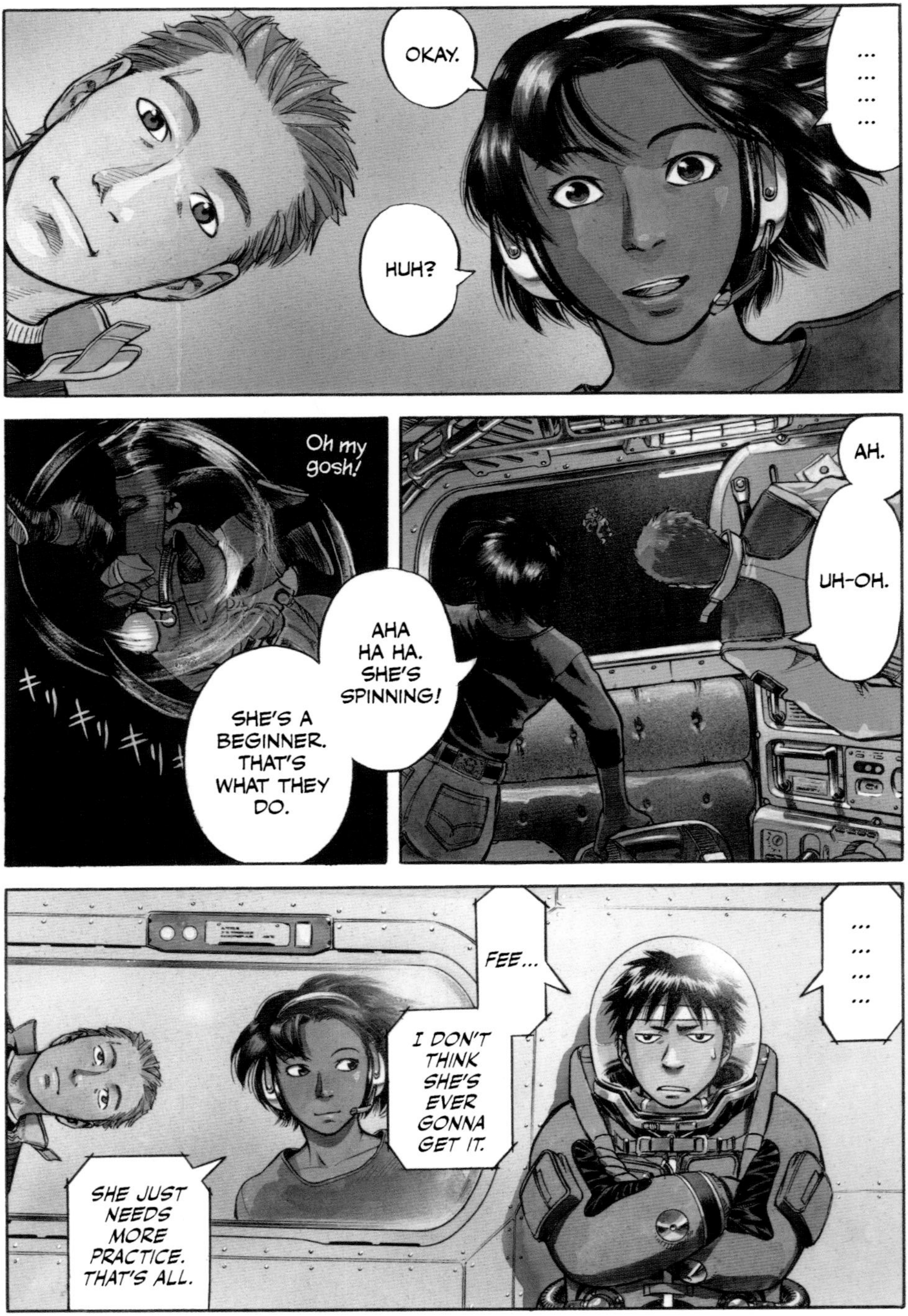
....
OKAY.
HUH?
AH.
UH-OH.
AHA HA HA. SHE'S SPINNING!
Oh my gosh!
SHE'S A BEGINNER. THAT'S WHAT THEY DO.
キリキリキリ
....
FEE...
I DON'T THINK SHE'S EVER GONNA GET IT.
SHE JUST NEEDS MORE PRACTICE. THAT'S ALL.

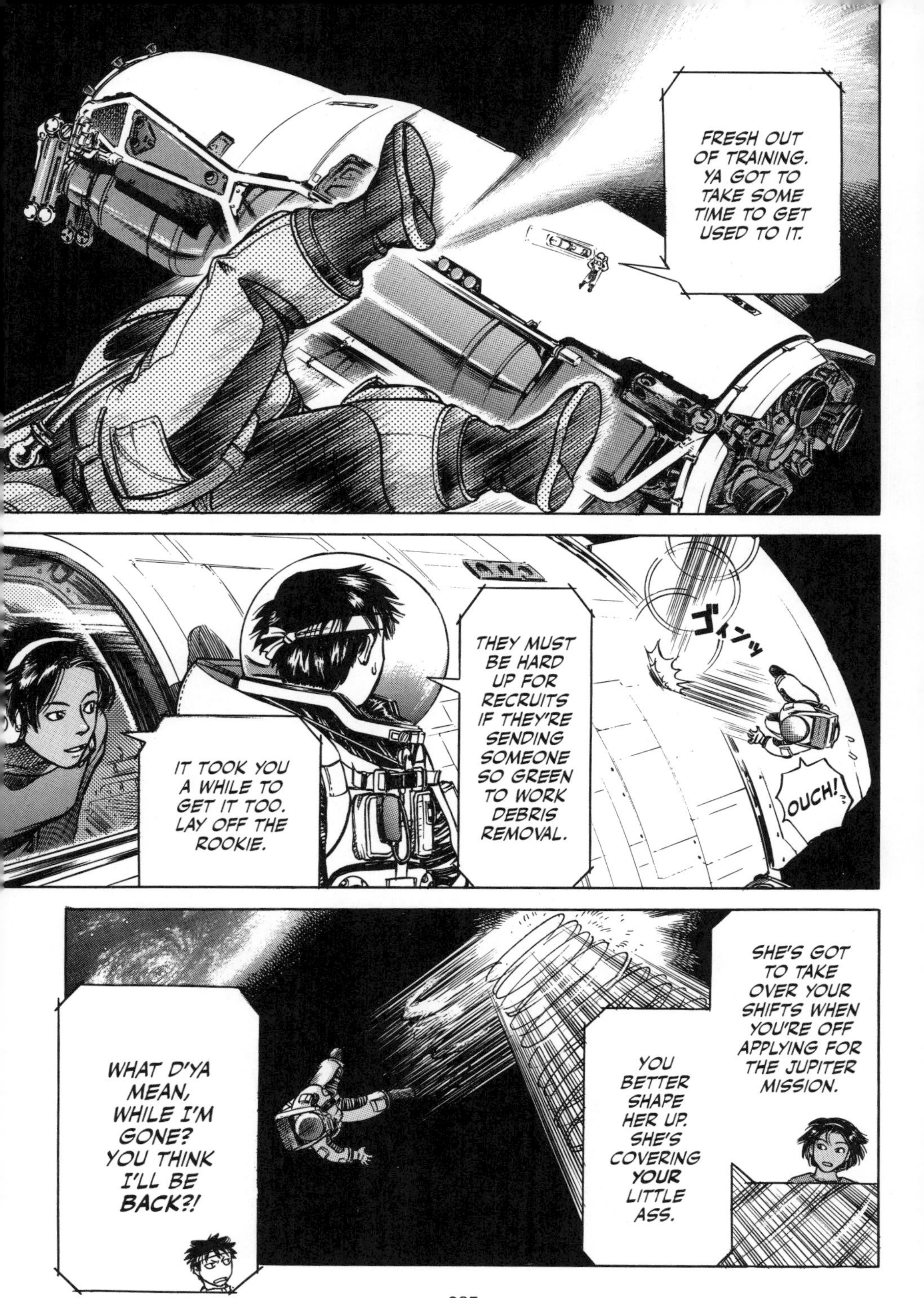
FRESH OUT OF TRAINING. YA GOT TO TAKE SOME TIME TO GET USED TO IT.
ゴィンッ
OUCH!?
THEY MUST BE HARD UP FOR RECRUITS IF THEY'RE SENDING SOMEONE SO GREEN TO WORK DEBRIS REMOVAL.
IT TOOK YOU A WHILE TO GET IT TOO. LAY OFF THE ROOKIE.
SHE'S GOT TO TAKE OVER YOUR SHIFTS WHEN YOU'RE OFF APPLYING FOR THE JUPITER MISSION.
YOU BETTER SHAPE HER UP. SHE'S COVERING YOUR LITTLE ASS.
WHAT D'YA MEAN, WHILE I'M GONE? YOU THINK I'LL BE BACK?!

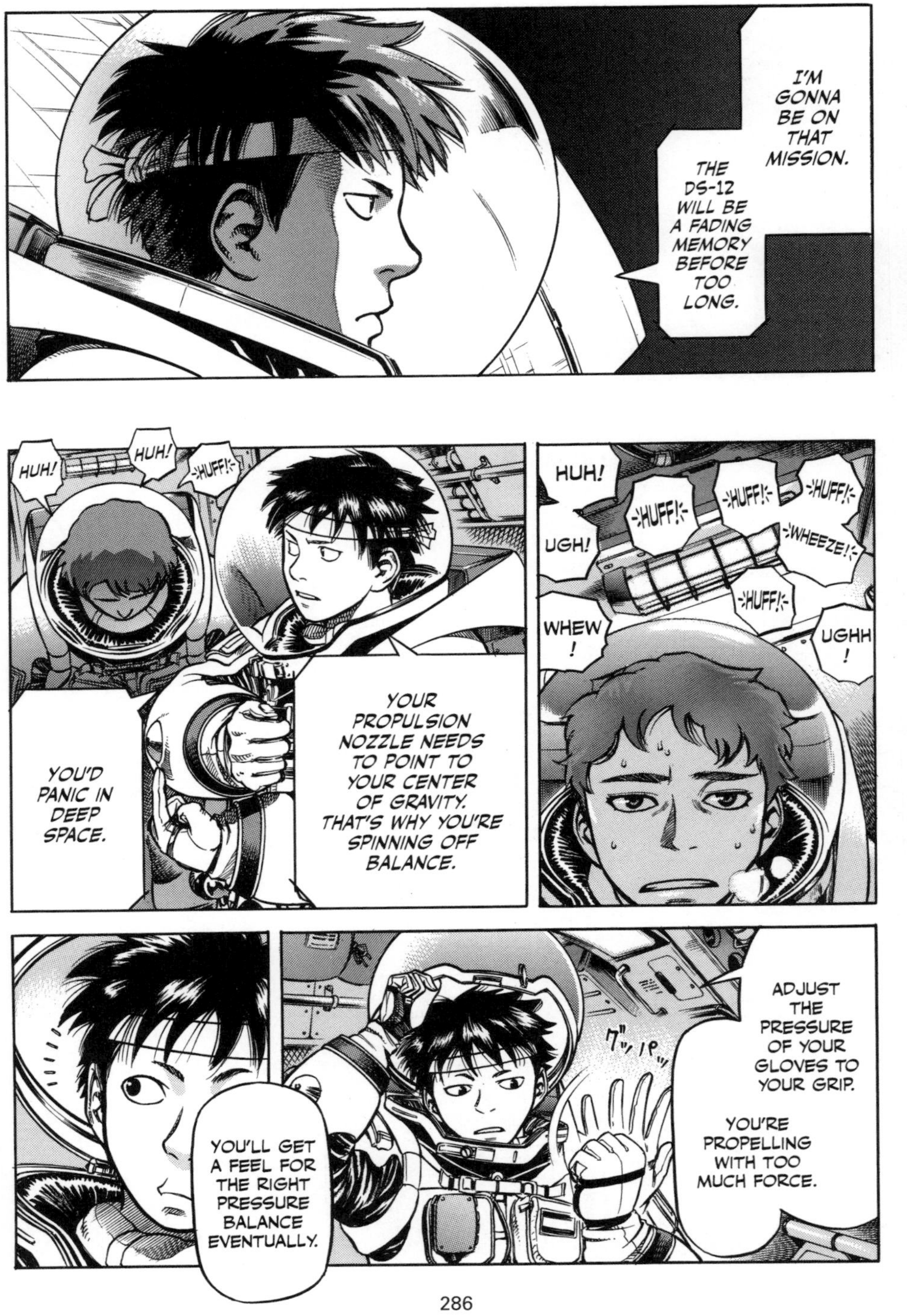
I'M GONNA BE ON THAT MISSION.
THE DS-12 WILL BE A FADING MEMORY BEFORE TOO LONG.
-HUFF!-
-HUFF!-
HUH!
-HUFF!-
-WHEEZE!-
UGH!
-HUFF!-
UGHH!
WHEW!
-HUFF!-
HUH!
HUH!
YOUR PROPULSION NOZZLE NEEDS TO POINT TO YOUR CENTER OF GRAVITY. THAT'S WHY YOU'RE SPINNING OFF BALANCE.
YOU'D PANIC IN DEEP SPACE.
ADJUST THE PRESSURE OF YOUR GLOVES TO YOUR GRIP.
YOU'RE PROPELLING WITH TOO MUCH FORCE.
グッ パッ
YOU'LL GET A FEEL FOR THE RIGHT PRESSURE BALANCE EVENTUALLY.

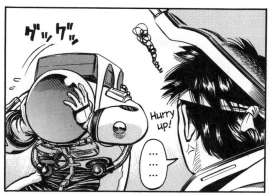

モタ.
ヨロ
グッグッ
Hurry up!
...
...
...
TAKE OFF YOUR GLOVES FIRST... HERE! *I'LL* DO IT!
SAY, HOW DOES A TURTLE MANAGE TO GET AN ASTRONAUT'S LICENSE?
YA GOT TO LEARN FASTER, TANABE.
I'M NOT GONNA BE ABLE TO LEAVE IF YOU'RE NOT GOOD ENOUGH TO DO MY JOB.
YOU KNOW THE JAPANESE SAYING, "BIRDS LEAVE THE WATER UNDIS-TURBED"?
...TANABE
...?

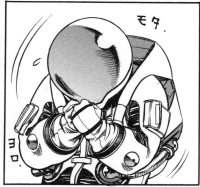

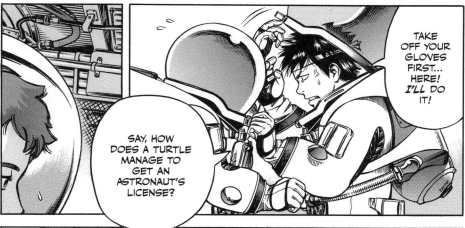

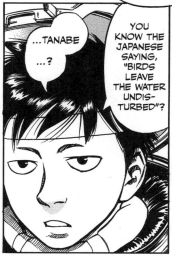

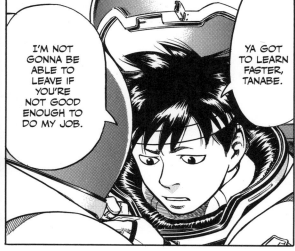

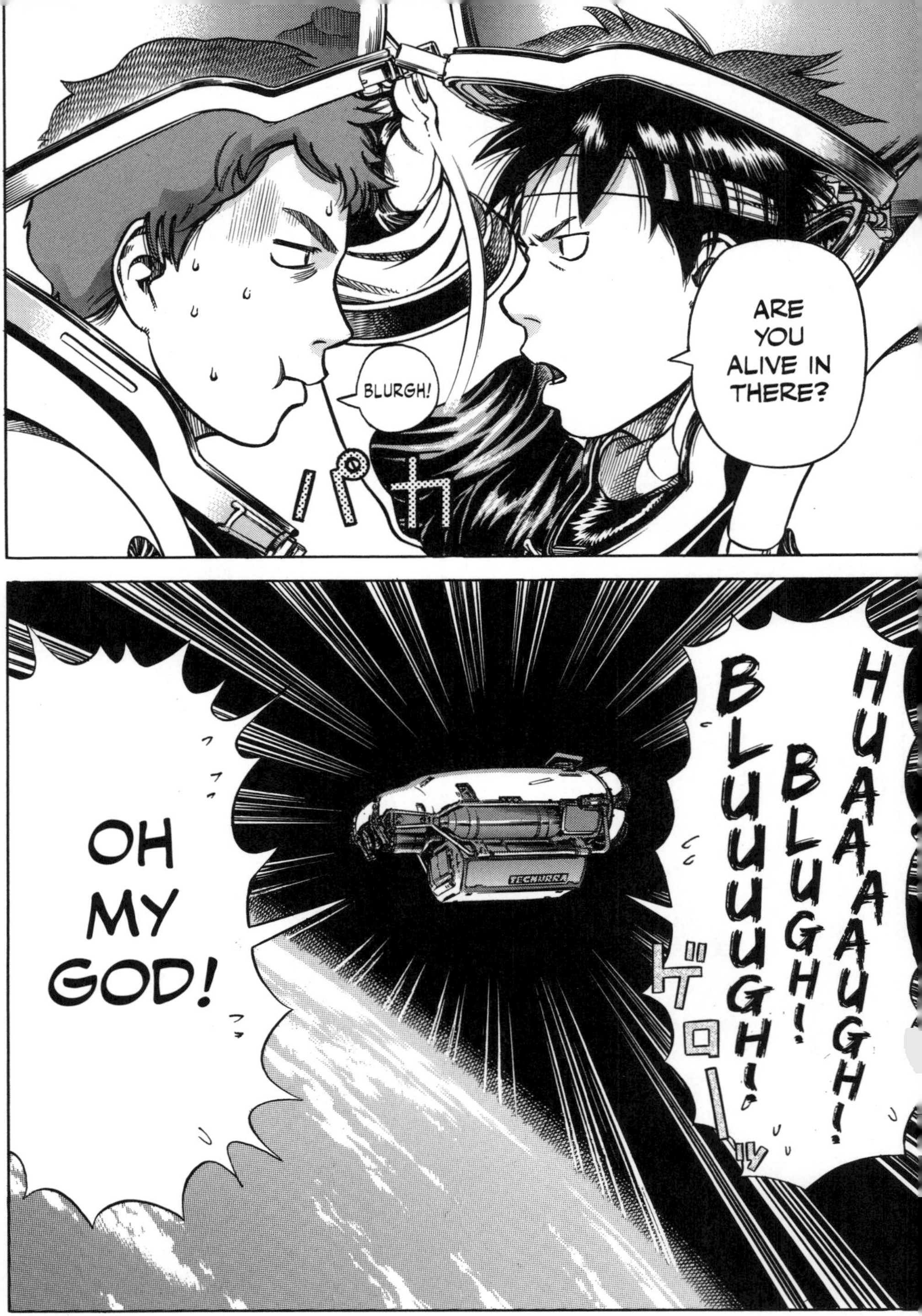
ARE YOU ALIVE IN THERE?
BLURGH!
パカ
HUAAAAAUGH!
BLUGH!
BLUUUUGH!
ゲロ〜ッ
OH MY GOD!

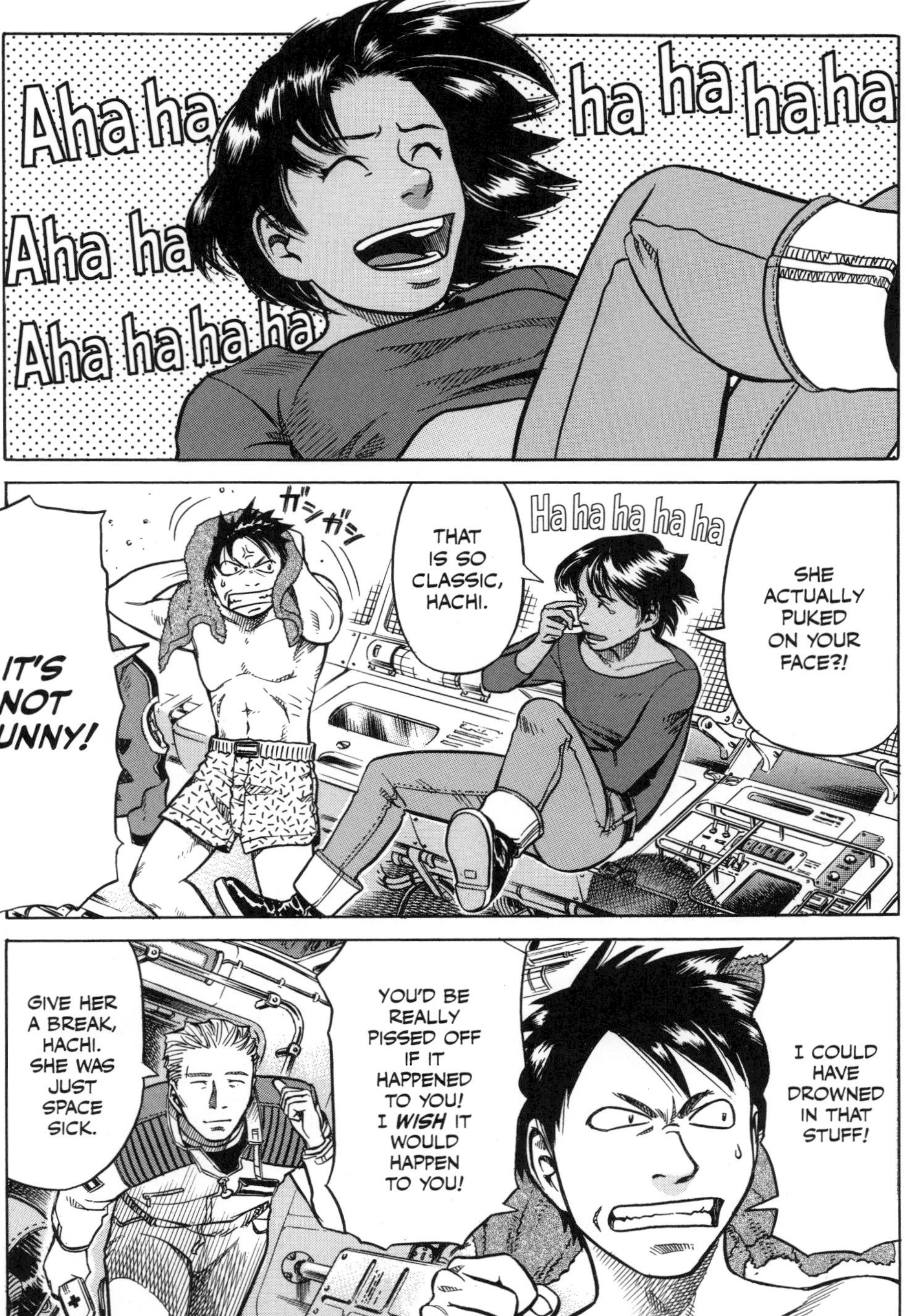
ha ha ha ha
Aha ha
Aha ha
Aha ha ha ha
SHE ACTUALLY PUKED ON YOUR FACE?!
Ha ha ha ha ha
THAT IS SO CLASSIC, HACHI.
ガシガシ
IT'S NOT FUNNY!
I COULD HAVE DROWNED IN THAT STUFF!
YOU'D BE REALLY PISSED OFF IF IT HAPPENED TO YOU! I WISH IT WOULD HAPPEN TO YOU!
GIVE HER A BREAK, HACHI. SHE WAS JUST SPACE SICK.

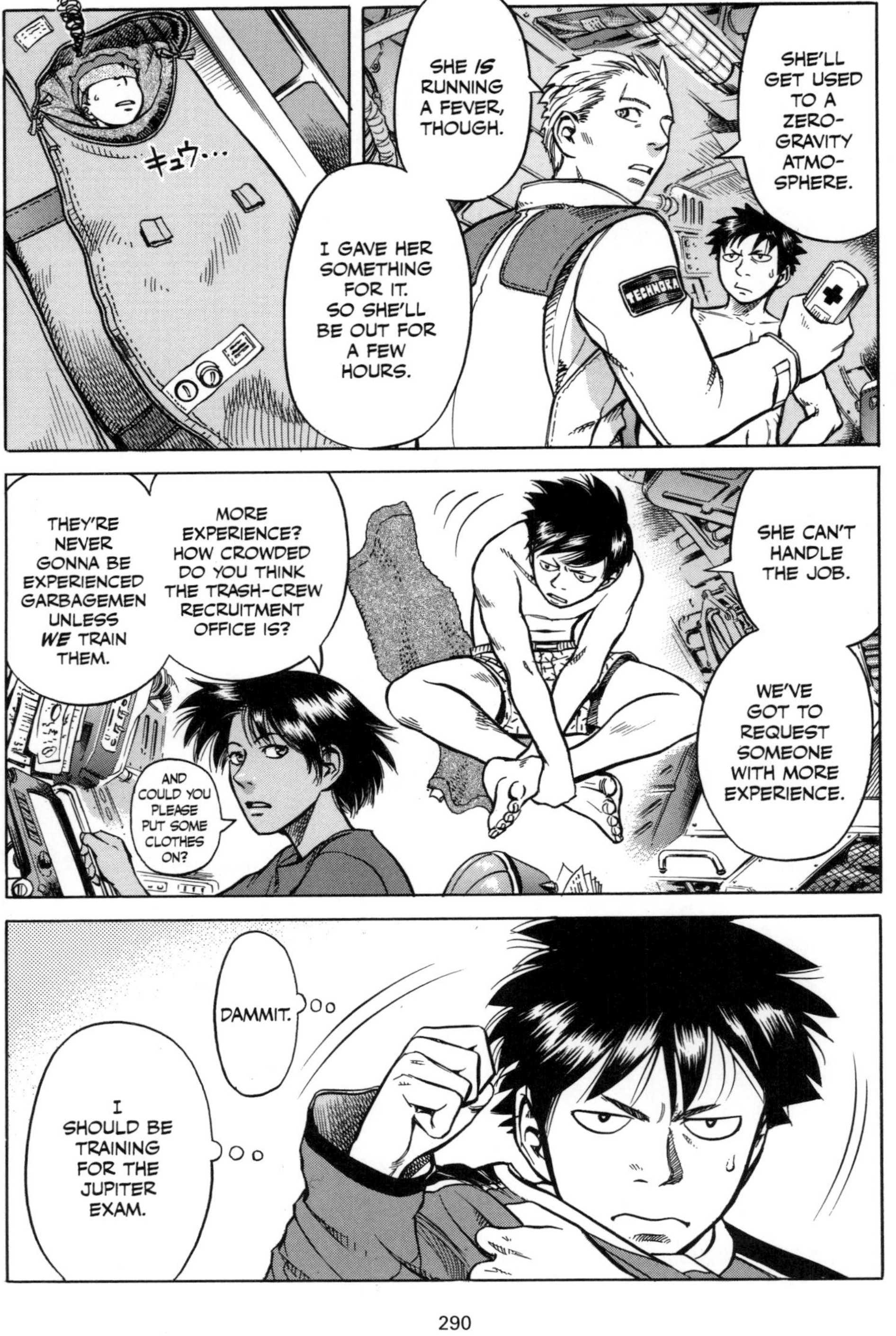
SHE'LL GET USED TO A ZERO-GRAVITY ATMOSPHERE.
SHE *IS* RUNNING A FEVER, THOUGH.
TECHNORA
I GAVE HER SOMETHING FOR IT. SO SHE'LL BE OUT FOR A FEW HOURS.
キュウ…
SHE CAN'T HANDLE THE JOB.
WE'VE GOT TO REQUEST SOMEONE WITH MORE EXPERIENCE.
MORE EXPERIENCE? HOW CROWDED DO YOU THINK THE TRASH-CREW RECRUITMENT OFFICE IS?
THEY'RE NEVER GONNA BE EXPERIENCED GARBAGEMEN UNLESS ***WE*** TRAIN THEM.
AND COULD YOU PLEASE PUT SOME CLOTHES ON?
DAMMIT.
I SHOULD BE TRAINING FOR THE JUPITER EXAM.

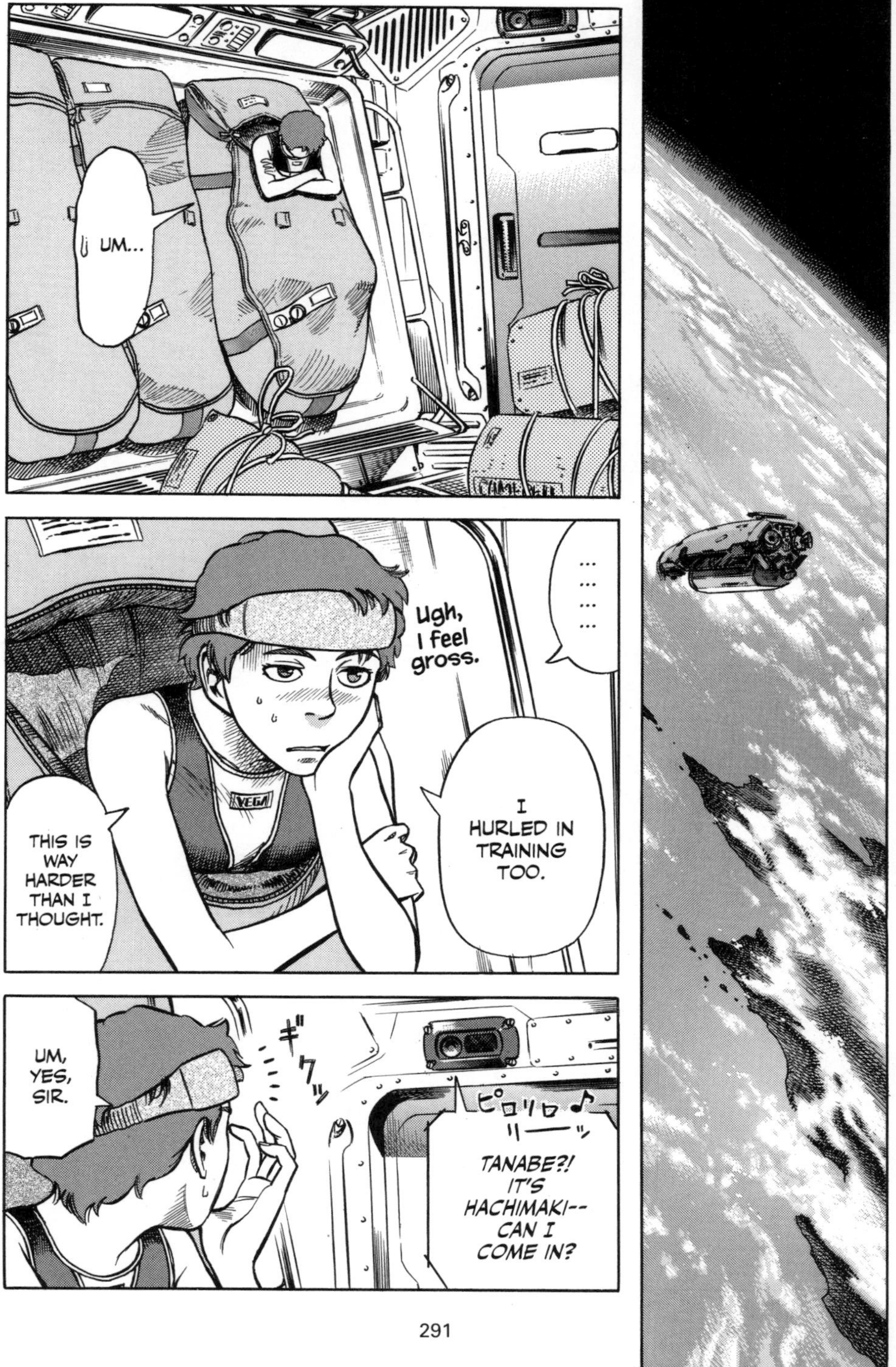
UM...
....
Ugh, I feel gross.
I HURLED IN TRAINING TOO.
THIS IS WAY HARDER THAN I THOUGHT.
ピロリロ♪
リーッ
TANABE?! IT'S HACHIMAKI-- CAN I COME IN?
ギクッ
UM, YES, SIR.

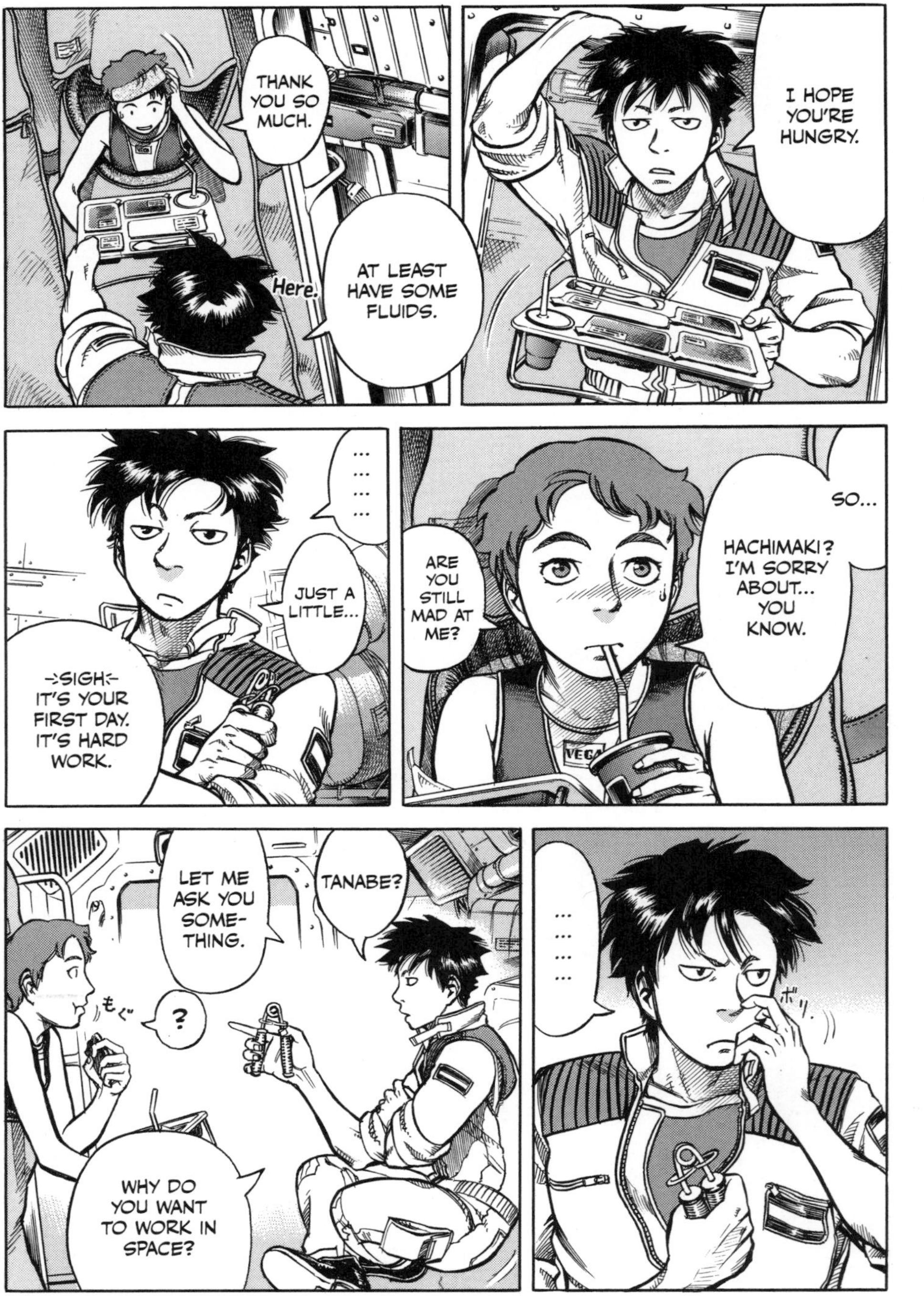
I HOPE YOU'RE HUNGRY.
Here.
AT LEAST HAVE SOME FLUIDS.
THANK YOU SO MUCH.
SO...
HACHIMAKI? I'M SORRY ABOUT... YOU KNOW.
ARE YOU STILL MAD AT ME?
...
...
...
...
JUST A LITTLE...
SIGH IT'S YOUR FIRST DAY. IT'S HARD WORK.
...
...
...
...
ポリ
TANABE?
LET ME ASK YOU SOME-THING.
もぐ
?
WHY DO YOU WANT TO WORK IN SPACE?

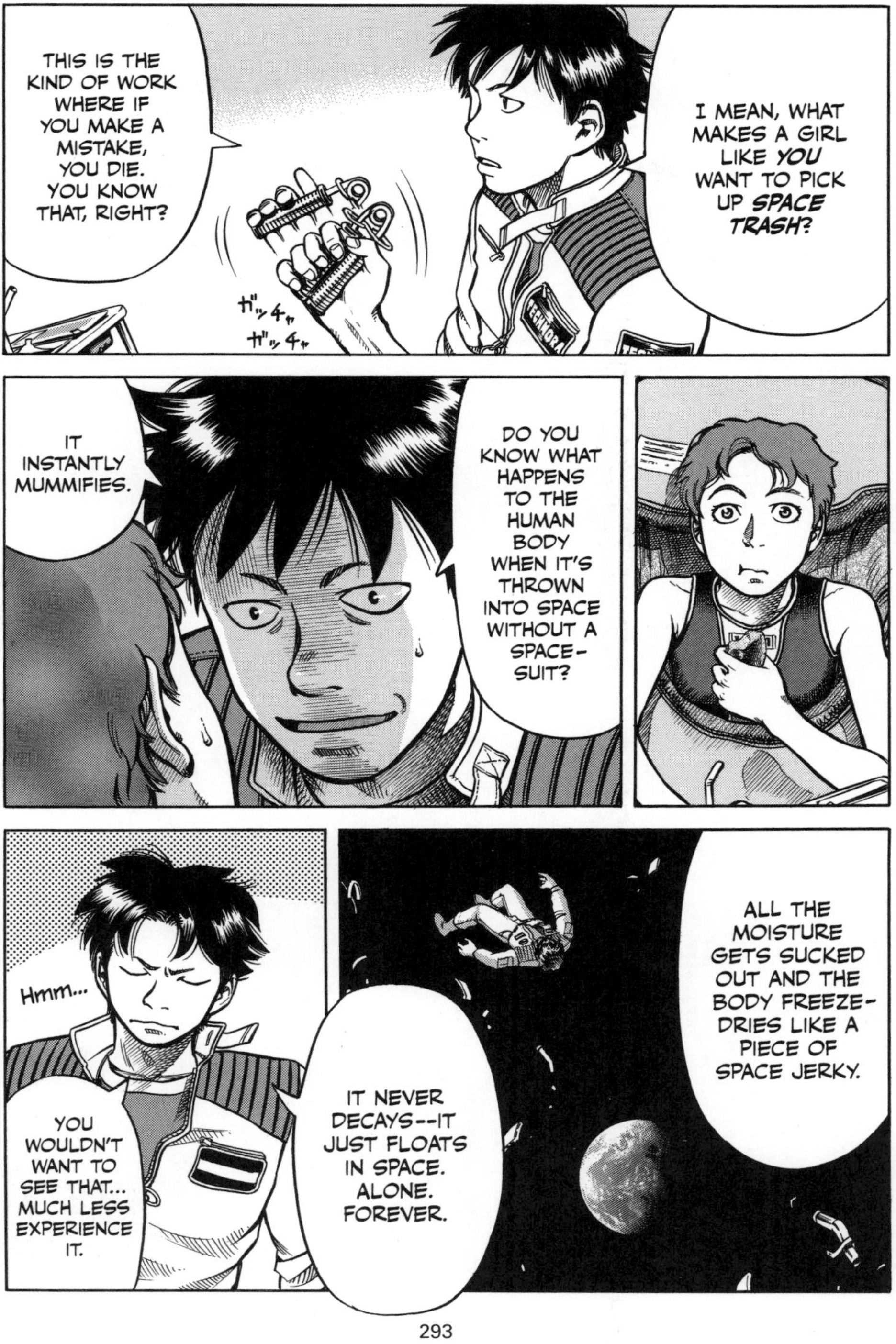
I MEAN, WHAT MAKES A GIRL LIKE ***YOU*** WANT TO PICK UP ***SPACE TRASH***?
THIS IS THE KIND OF WORK WHERE IF YOU MAKE A MISTAKE, YOU DIE. YOU KNOW THAT, RIGHT?
ガッチャ
ガッチャ
DO YOU KNOW WHAT HAPPENS TO THE HUMAN BODY WHEN IT'S THROWN INTO SPACE WITHOUT A SPACE-SUIT?
IT INSTANTLY MUMMIFIES.
ALL THE MOISTURE GETS SUCKED OUT AND THE BODY FREEZE-DRIES LIKE A PIECE OF SPACE JERKY.
IT NEVER DECAYS--IT JUST FLOATS IN SPACE. ALONE. FOREVER.
Hmm...
YOU WOULDN'T WANT TO SEE THAT... MUCH LESS EXPERIENCE IT.

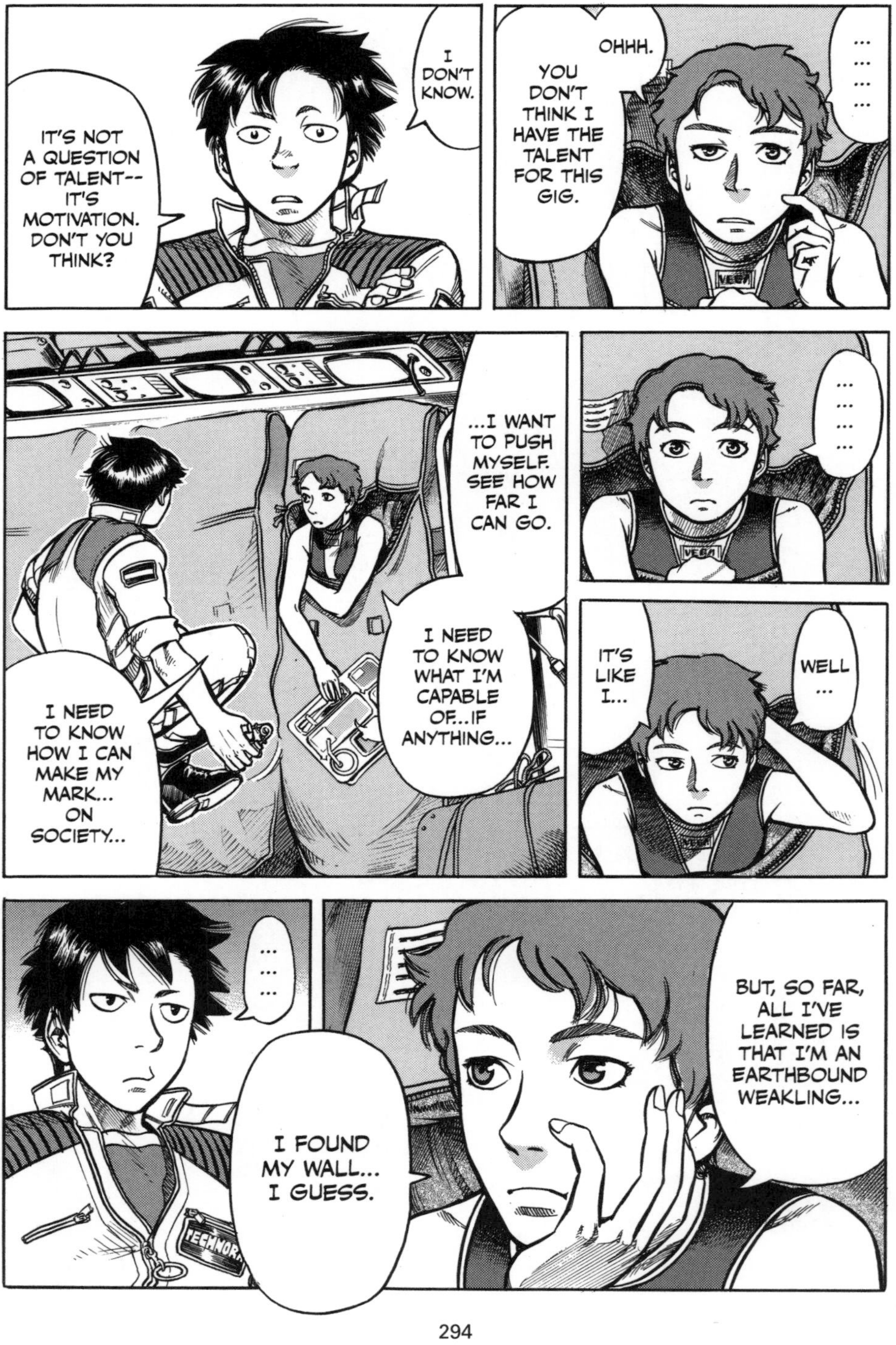
....
OHHH.
YOU DON'T THINK I HAVE THE TALENT FOR THIS GIG.
I DON'T KNOW.
IT'S NOT A QUESTION OF TALENT-- IT'S MOTIVATION. DON'T YOU THINK?
....
WELL ...
IT'S LIKE I...
...I WANT TO PUSH MYSELF. SEE HOW FAR I CAN GO.
I NEED TO KNOW WHAT I'M CAPABLE OF...IF ANYTHING...
I NEED TO KNOW HOW I CAN MAKE MY MARK... ON SOCIETY...
BUT, SO FAR, ALL I'VE LEARNED IS THAT I'M AN EARTHBOUND WEAKLING...
I FOUND MY WALL... I GUESS.
....

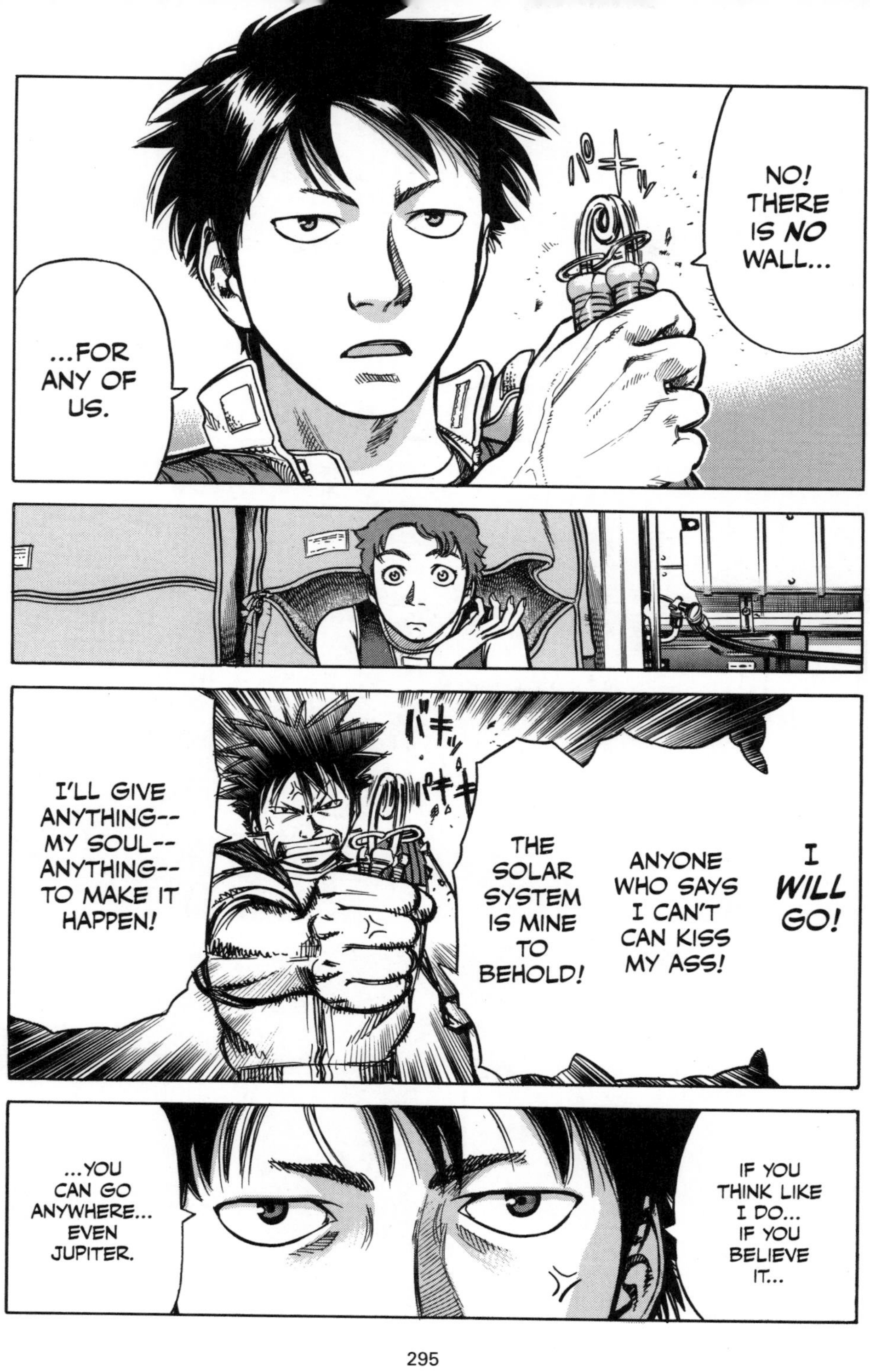
NO! THERE IS **NO** WALL...
...FOR ANY OF US.
I ***WILL*** GO!
ANYONE WHO SAYS I CAN'T CAN KISS MY ASS!
THE SOLAR SYSTEM IS MINE TO BEHOLD!
I'LL GIVE ANYTHING-- MY SOUL-- ANYTHING-- TO MAKE IT HAPPEN!
IF YOU THINK LIKE I DO... IF YOU BELIEVE IT...
...YOU CAN GO ANYWHERE... EVEN JUPITER.

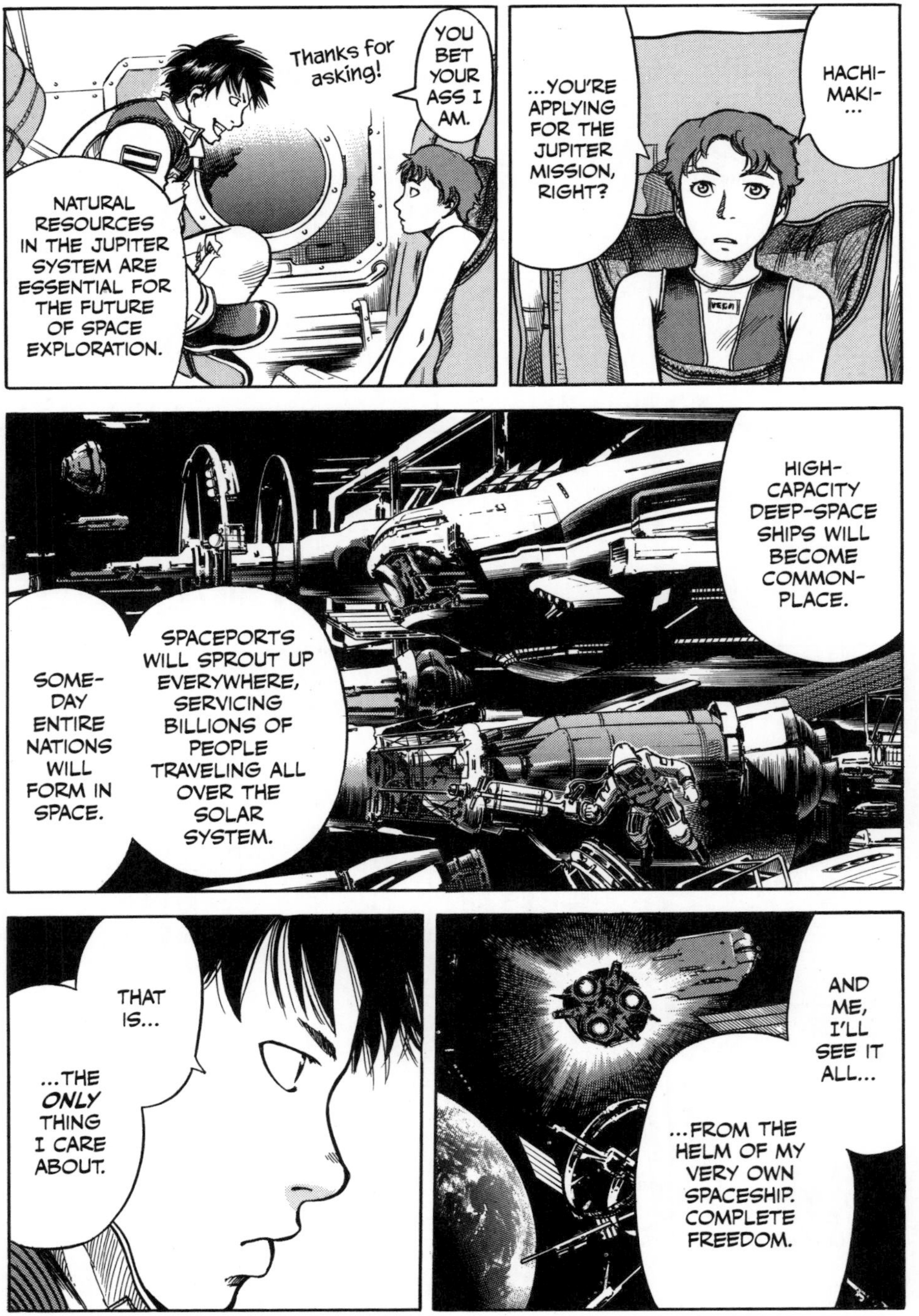
HACHI-MAKI-...
...YOU'RE APPLYING FOR THE JUPITER MISSION, RIGHT?
YOU BET YOUR ASS I AM.
Thanks for asking!
NATURAL RESOURCES IN THE JUPITER SYSTEM ARE ESSENTIAL FOR THE FUTURE OF SPACE EXPLORATION.
HIGH-CAPACITY DEEP-SPACE SHIPS WILL BECOME COMMON-PLACE.
SPACEPORTS WILL SPROUT UP EVERYWHERE, SERVICING BILLIONS OF PEOPLE TRAVELING ALL OVER THE SOLAR SYSTEM.
SOME-DAY ENTIRE NATIONS WILL FORM IN SPACE.
AND ME, I'LL SEE IT ALL...
...FROM THE HELM OF MY VERY OWN SPACESHIP. COMPLETE FREEDOM.
THAT IS...
...THE *ONLY* THING I CARE ABOUT.

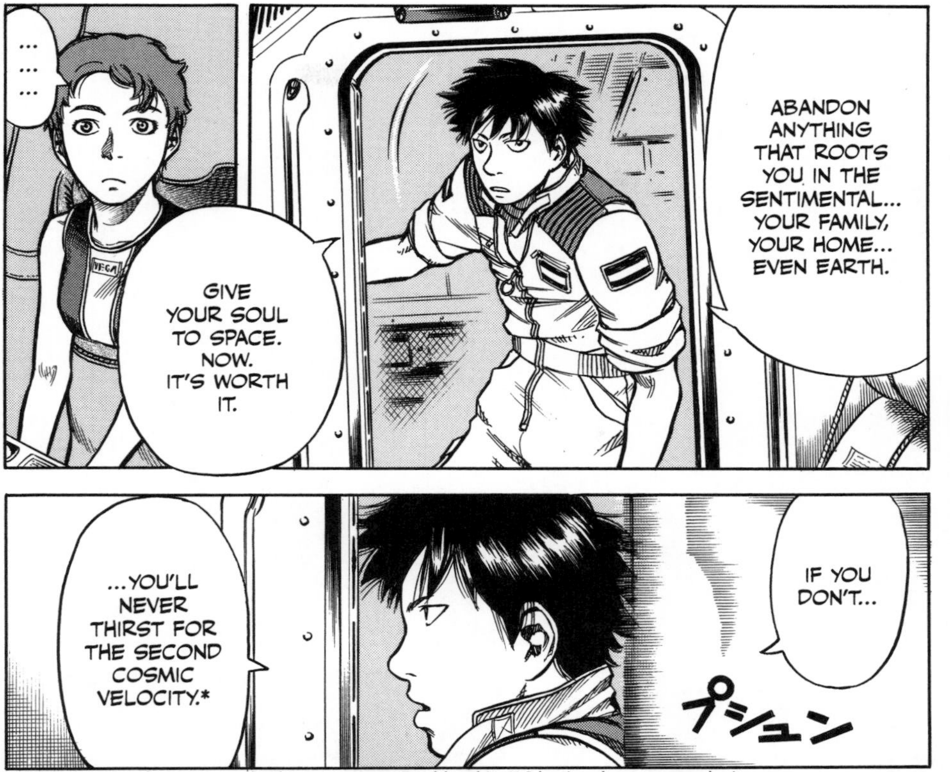
ABANDON ANYTHING THAT ROOTS YOU IN THE SENTIMENTAL... YOUR FAMILY, YOUR HOME... EVEN EARTH.
GIVE YOUR SOUL TO SPACE. NOW. IT'S WORTH IT.
....
IF YOU DON'T...
プシュン
...YOU'LL NEVER THIRST FOR THE SECOND COSMIC VELOCITY.*

*Speed necessary for a manmade object to escape Earth's orbit. 11.2 km/s, a.k.a. escape velocity.

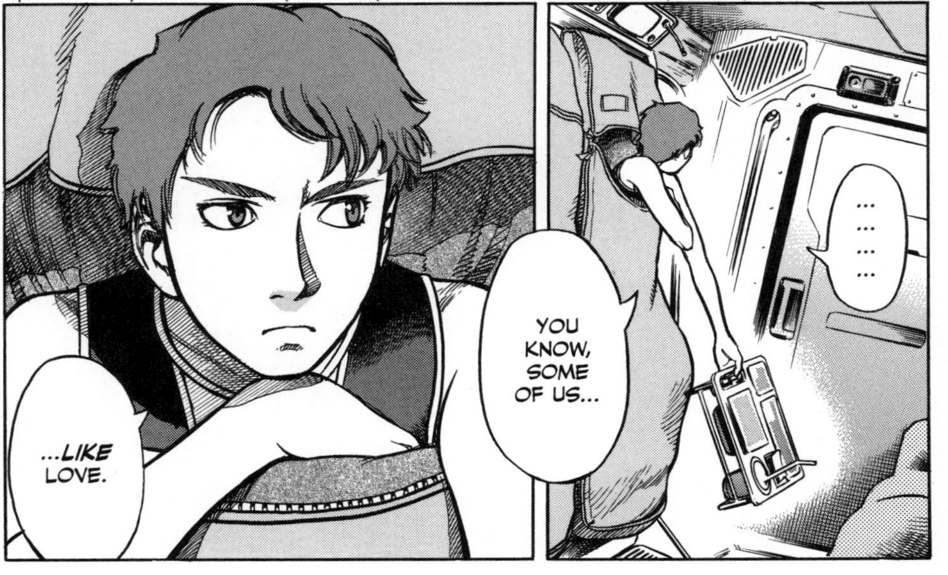
....
YOU KNOW, SOME OF US...
...LIKE LOVE.

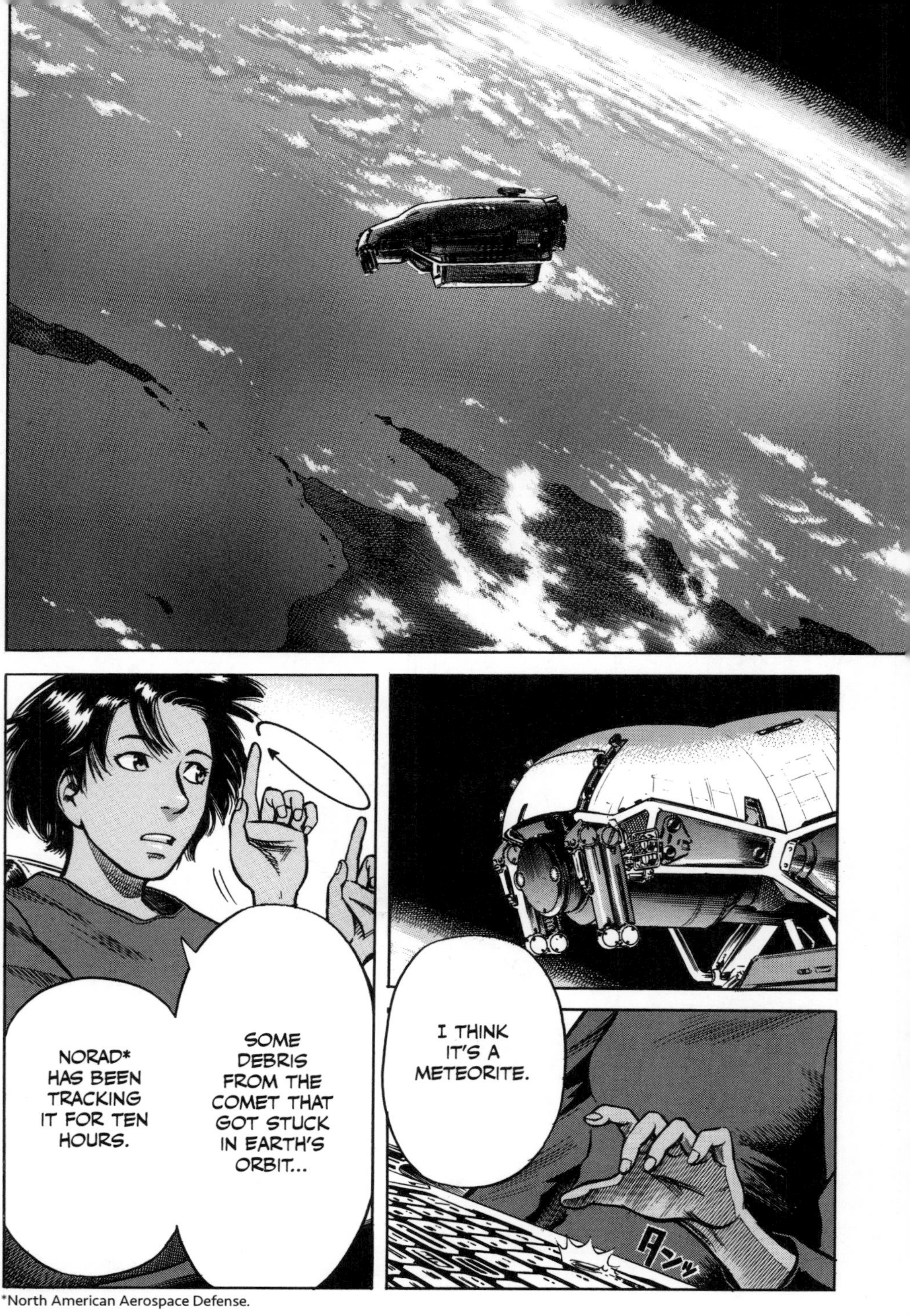
I THINK IT'S A METEORITE.
タンッ
SOME DEBRIS FROM THE COMET THAT GOT STUCK IN EARTH'S ORBIT...
NORAD* HAS BEEN TRACKING IT FOR TEN HOURS.

*North American Aerospace Defense.

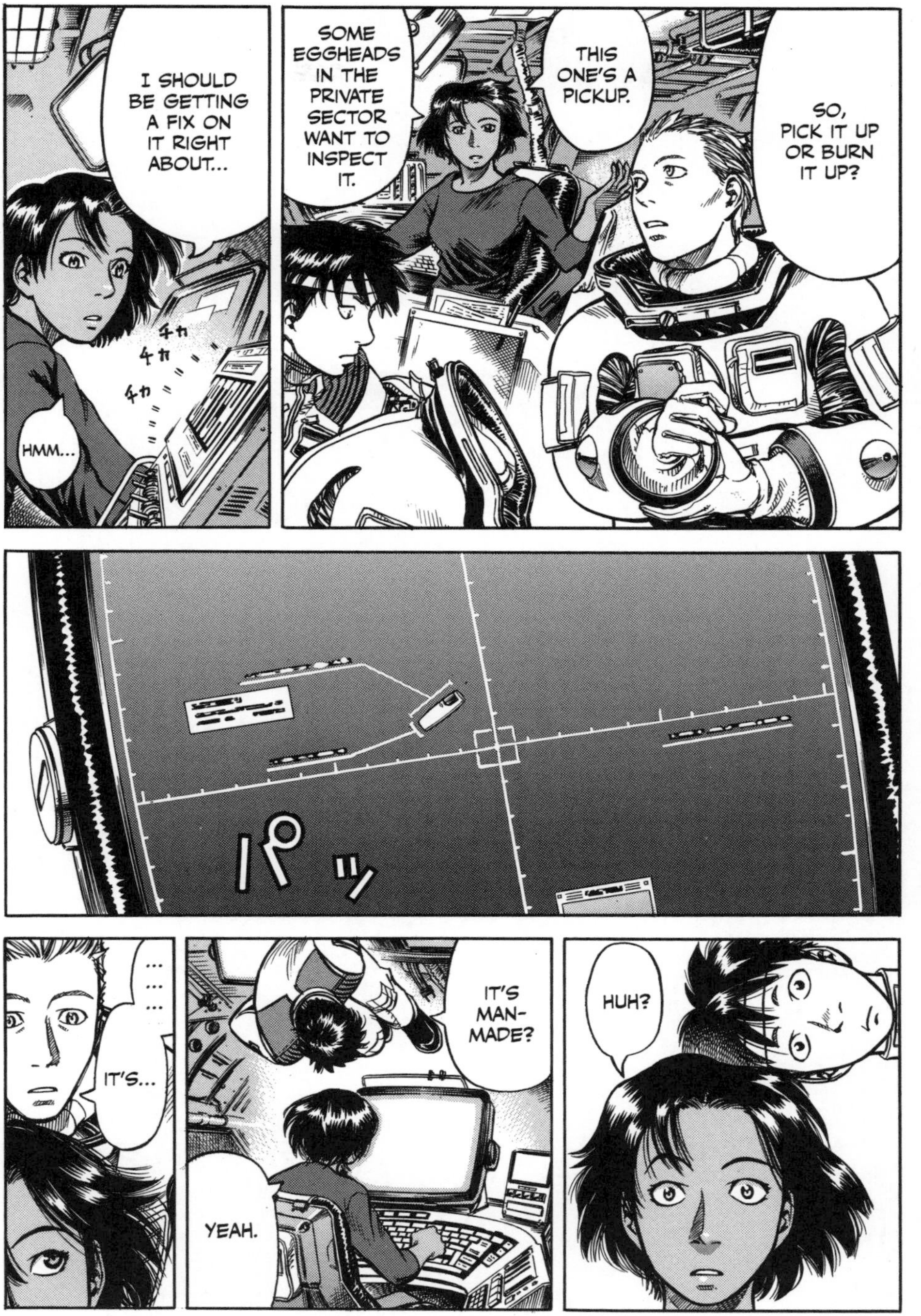
SO, PICK IT UP OR BURN IT UP?
THIS ONE'S A PICKUP.
SOME EGGHEADS IN THE PRIVATE SECTOR WANT TO INSPECT IT.
I SHOULD BE GETTING A FIX ON IT RIGHT ABOUT...
HMM...
パッ
HUH?
IT'S MAN-MADE?
YEAH.
... ...
IT'S...

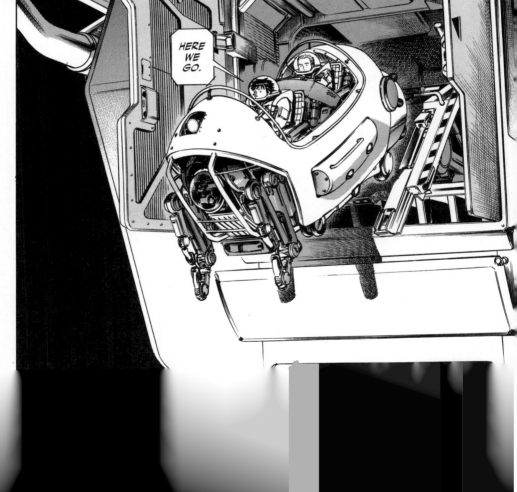

HERE
WE
GO.

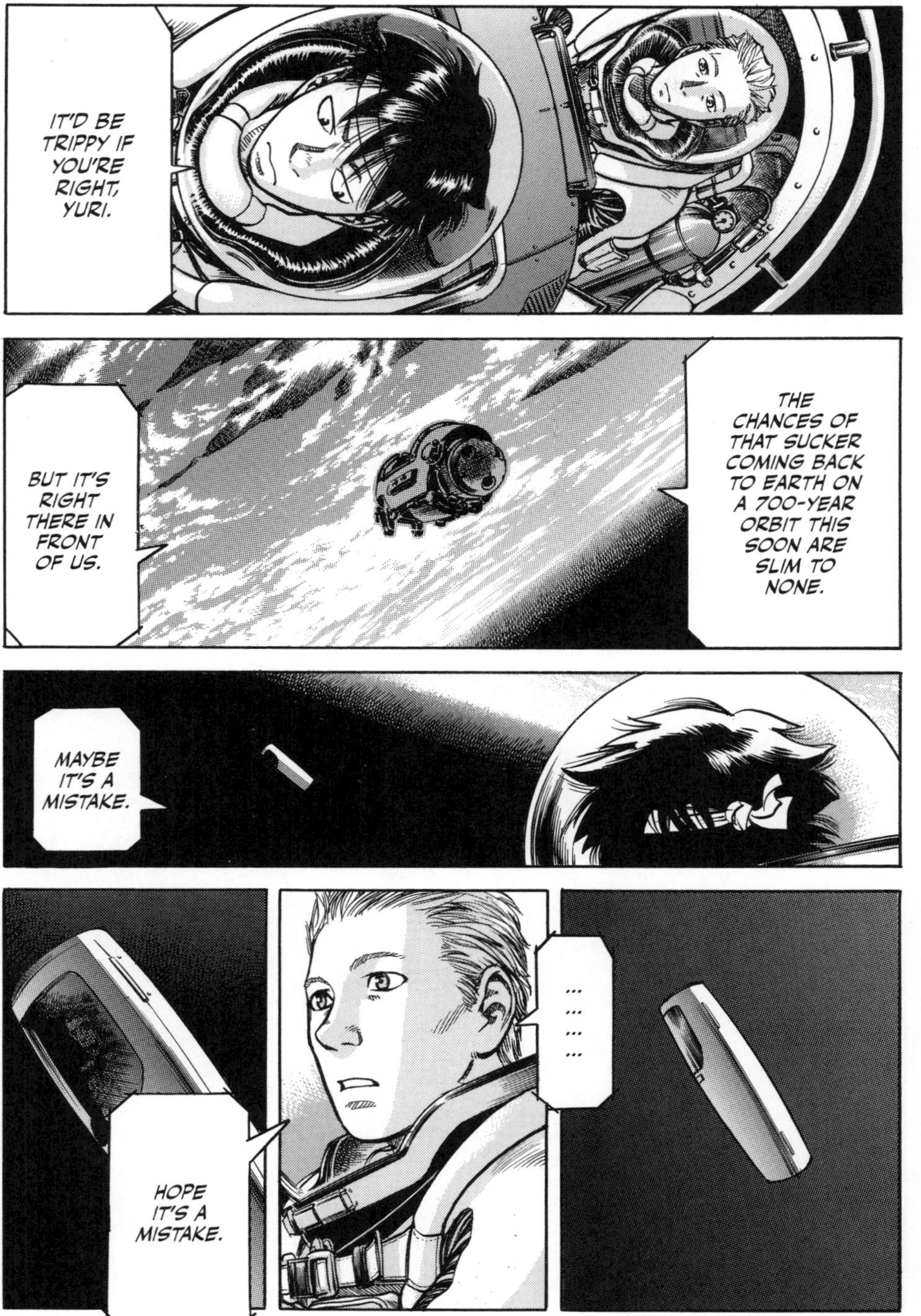
IT'D BE TRIPPY IF YOU'RE RIGHT, YURI.
THE CHANCES OF THAT SUCKER COMING BACK TO EARTH ON A 700-YEAR ORBIT THIS SOON ARE SLIM TO NONE.
BUT IT'S RIGHT THERE IN FRONT OF US.
MAYBE IT'S A MISTAKE.
... ...
HOPE IT'S A MISTAKE.

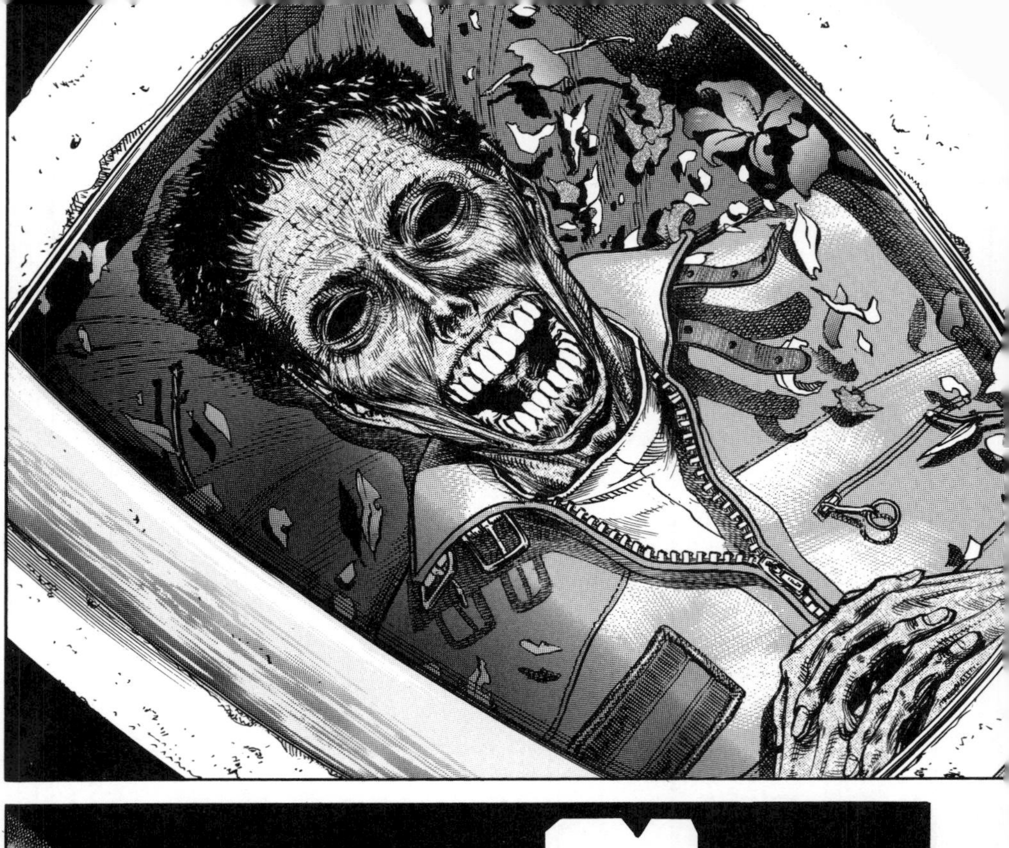

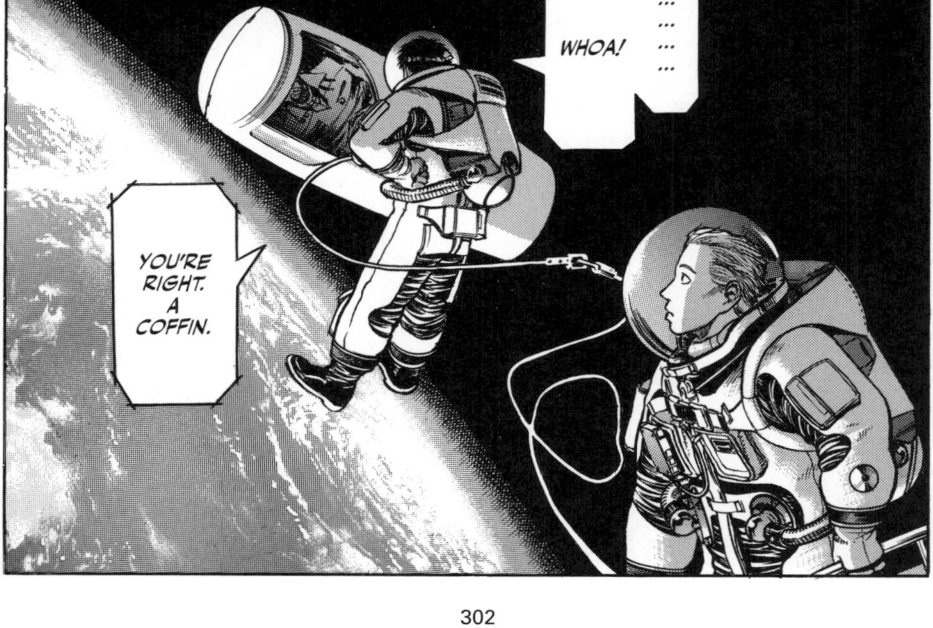
...
...
...
...
WHOA!
YOU'RE RIGHT. A COFFIN.

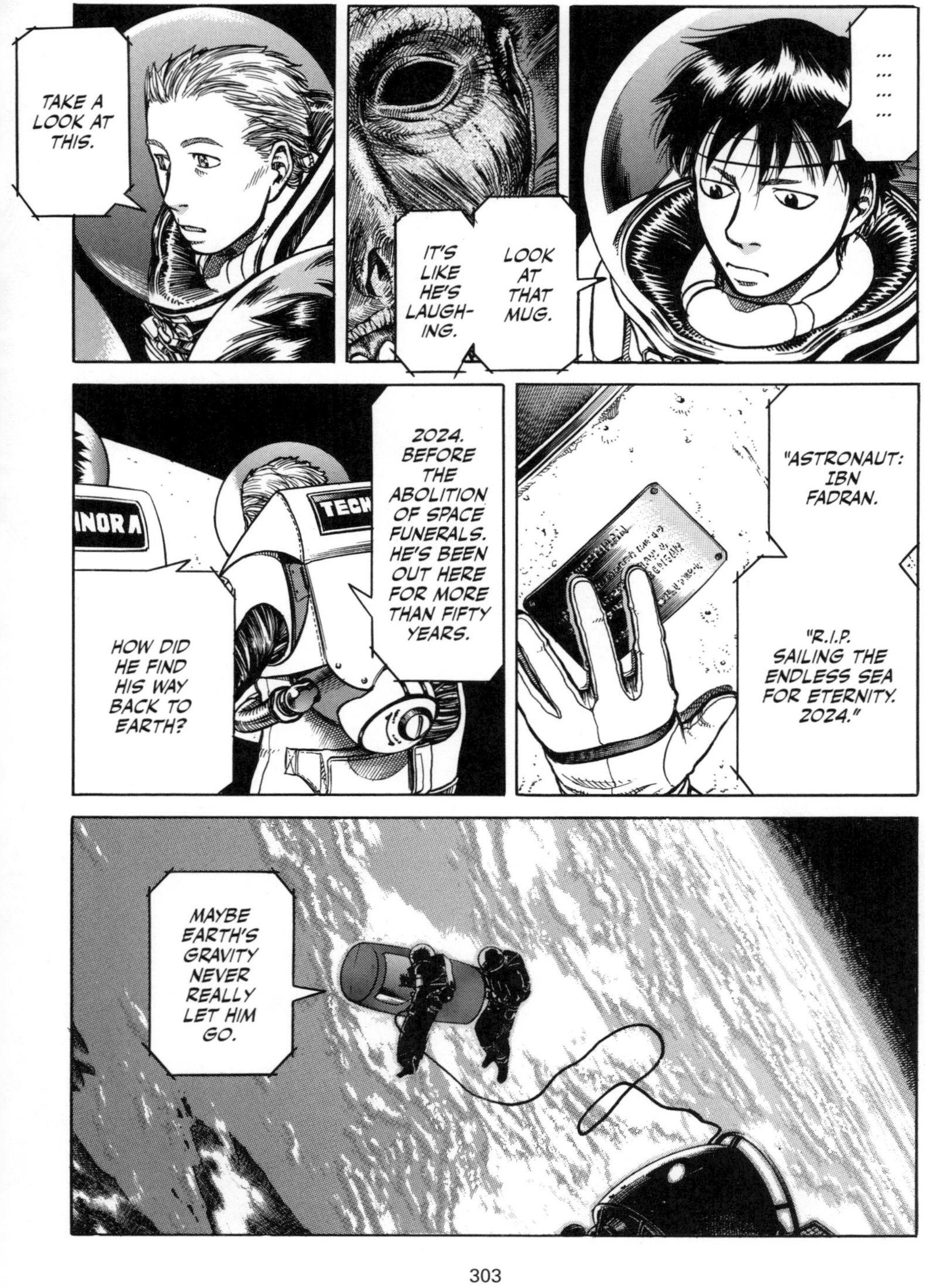
...
...
...
...
LOOK AT THAT MUG.
IT'S LIKE HE'S LAUGHING.
TAKE A LOOK AT THIS.
"ASTRONAUT: IBN FADRAN.
"R.I.P. SAILING THE ENDLESS SEA FOR ETERNITY. 2024."
2024. BEFORE THE ABOLITION OF SPACE FUNERALS. HE'S BEEN OUT HERE FOR MORE THAN FIFTY YEARS.
TECH
INORA
HOW DID HE FIND HIS WAY BACK TO EARTH?
MAYBE EARTH'S GRAVITY NEVER REALLY LET HIM GO.

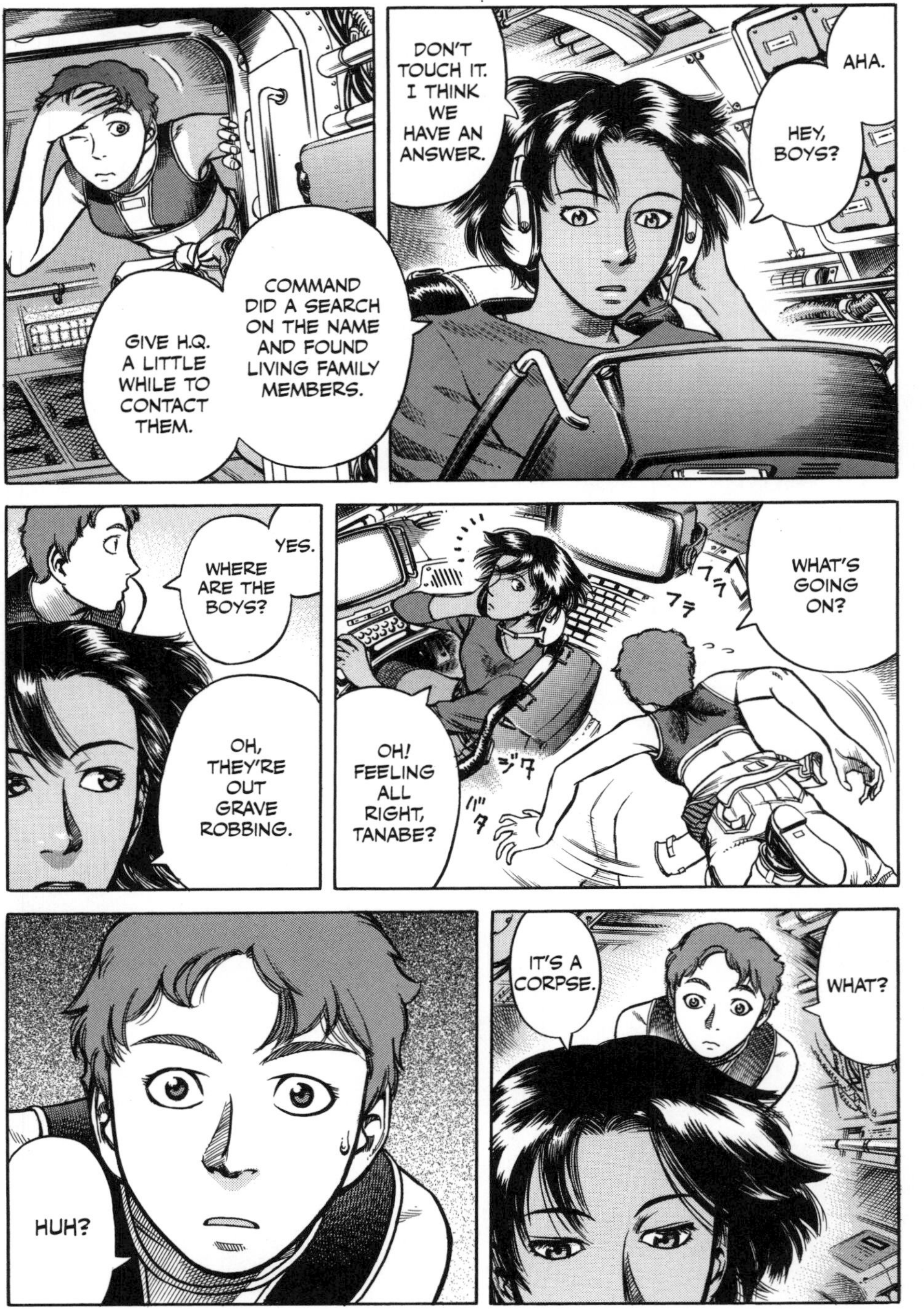
AHA.
HEY, BOYS?
DON'T TOUCH IT. I THINK WE HAVE AN ANSWER.
COMMAND DID A SEARCH ON THE NAME AND FOUND LIVING FAMILY MEMBERS.
GIVE H.Q. A LITTLE WHILE TO CONTACT THEM.
WHAT'S GOING ON?
フラ
フラ
OH! FEELING ALL RIGHT, TANABE?
ジタ
バタ
YES.
WHERE ARE THE BOYS?
OH, THEY'RE OUT GRAVE ROBBING.
WHAT?
IT'S A CORPSE.
HUH?

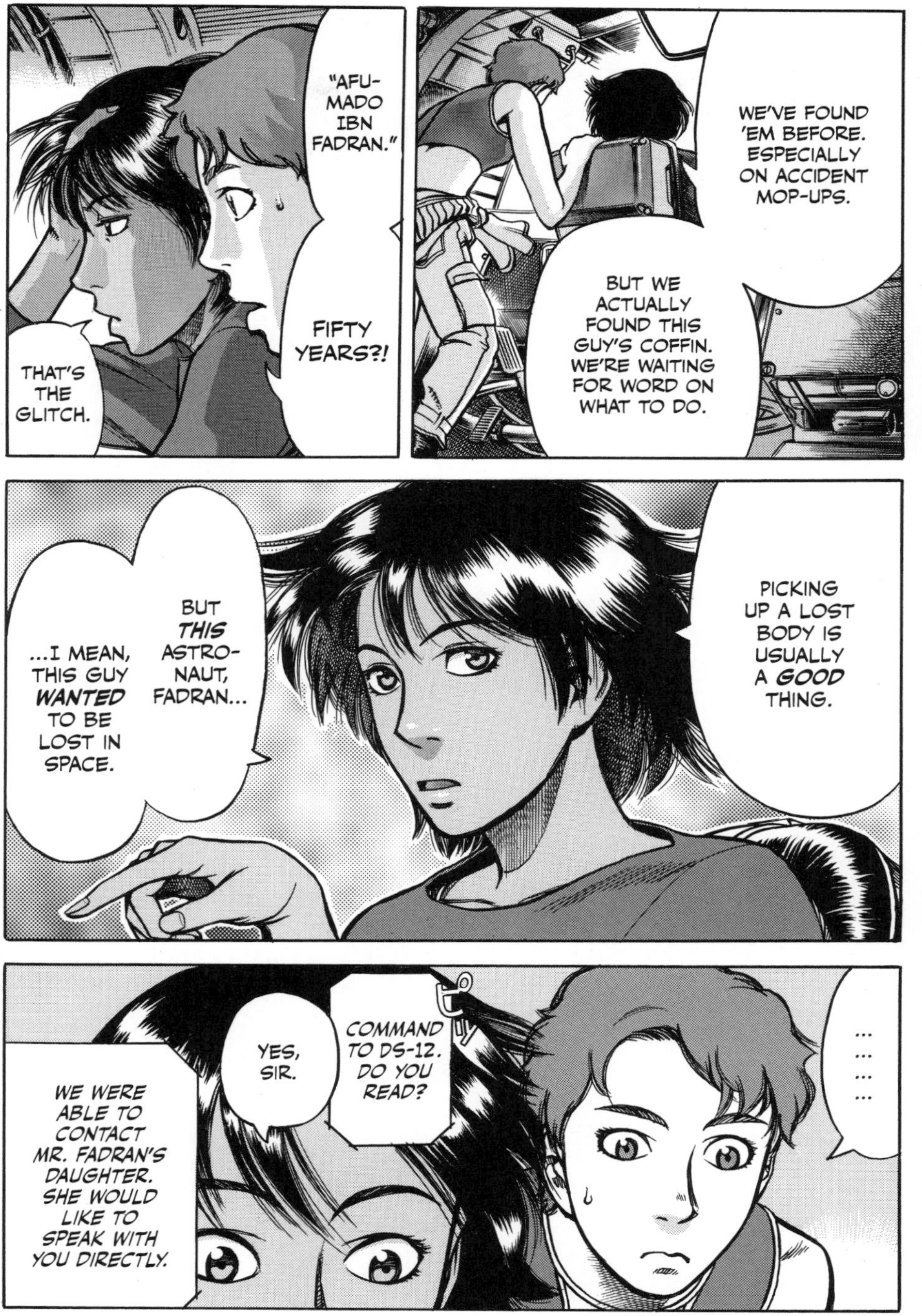
WE'VE FOUND 'EM BEFORE. ESPECIALLY ON ACCIDENT MOP-UPS.
BUT WE ACTUALLY FOUND THIS GUY'S COFFIN. WE'RE WAITING FOR WORD ON WHAT TO DO.
"AFU-MADO IBN FADRAN."
FIFTY YEARS?!
THAT'S THE GLITCH.
PICKING UP A LOST BODY IS USUALLY A GOOD THING.
BUT THIS ASTRONAUT, FADRAN...
...I MEAN, THIS GUY WANTED TO BE LOST IN SPACE.
....
COMMAND TO DS-12. DO YOU READ?
YES, SIR.
WE WERE ABLE TO CONTACT MR. FADRAN'S DAUGHTER. SHE WOULD LIKE TO SPEAK WITH YOU DIRECTLY.

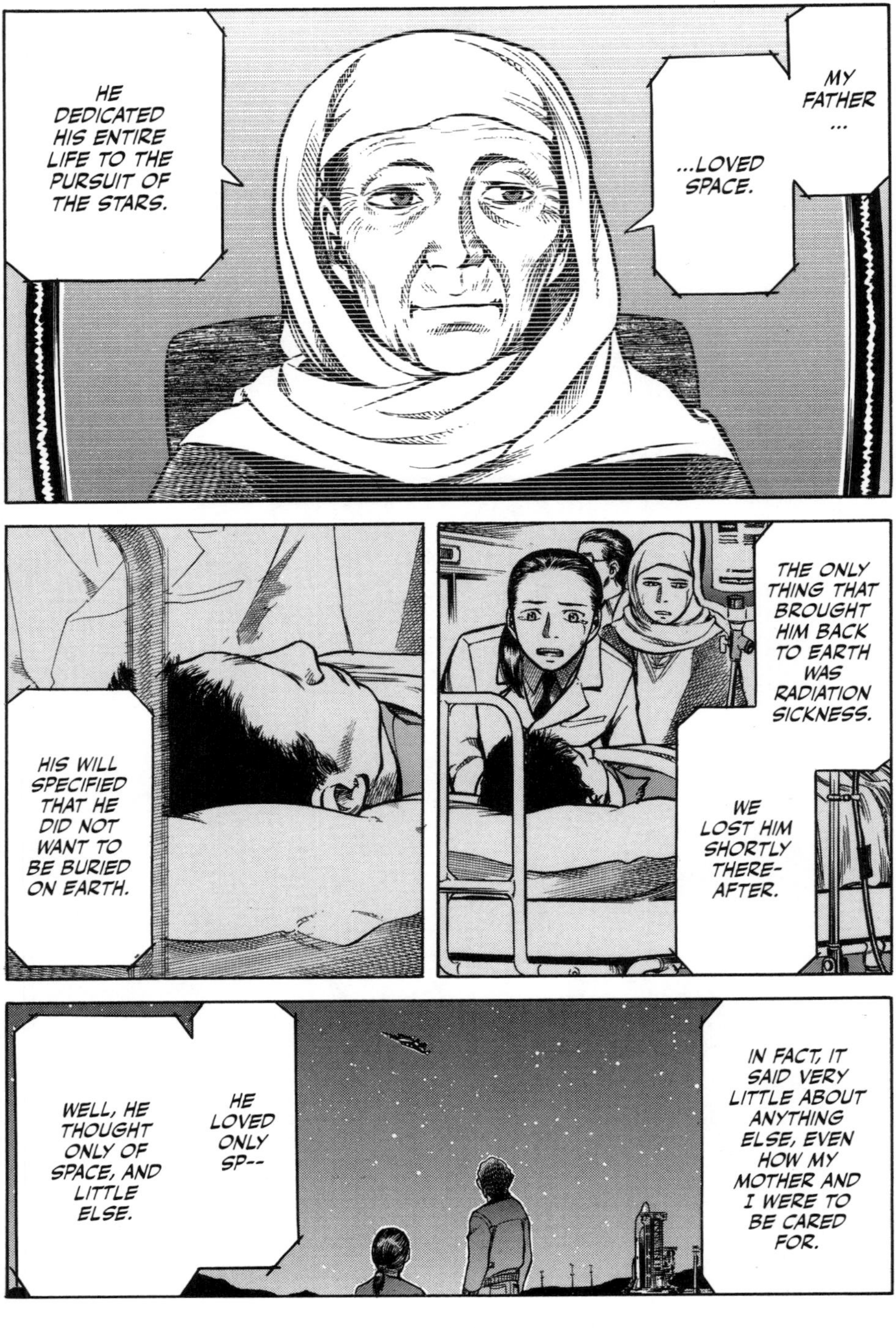
MY FATHER ...
...LOVED SPACE.
HE DEDICATED HIS ENTIRE LIFE TO THE PURSUIT OF THE STARS.
THE ONLY THING THAT BROUGHT HIM BACK TO EARTH WAS RADIATION SICKNESS.
WE LOST HIM SHORTLY THERE-AFTER.
HIS WILL SPECIFIED THAT HE DID NOT WANT TO BE BURIED ON EARTH.
IN FACT, IT SAID VERY LITTLE ABOUT ANYTHING ELSE, EVEN HOW MY MOTHER AND I WERE TO BE CARED FOR.
HE LOVED ONLY SP--
WELL, HE THOUGHT ONLY OF SPACE, AND LITTLE ELSE.

HE ALWAYS LONGED...

...TO BECOME ONE WITH THE IMMORTAL DEEP.

SO SHOULD WE...

WE CAN HAUL HIM TO THE MOON ORBIT PORT AND SHOOT HIM BACK FROM THERE?

...

VEGA

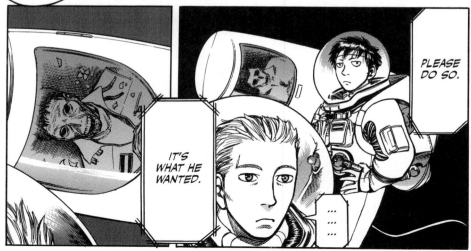

PLEASE DO SO.

IT'S WHAT HE WANTED.

...

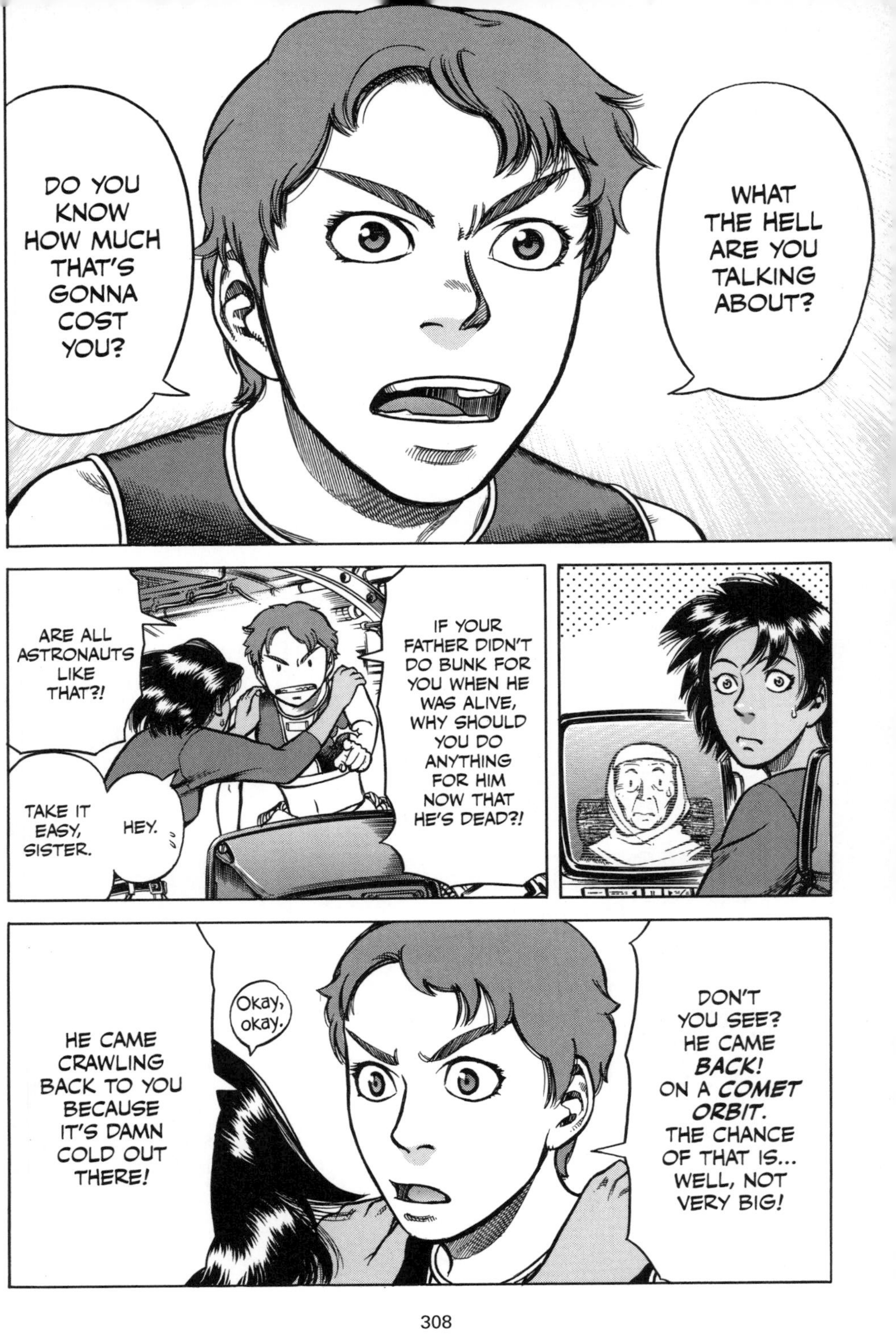
WHAT THE HELL ARE YOU TALKING ABOUT?
DO YOU KNOW HOW MUCH THAT'S GONNA COST YOU?
IF YOUR FATHER DIDN'T DO BUNK FOR YOU WHEN HE WAS ALIVE, WHY SHOULD YOU DO ANYTHING FOR HIM NOW THAT HE'S DEAD?!
ARE ALL ASTRONAUTS LIKE THAT?!
HEY.
TAKE IT EASY, SISTER.
DON'T YOU SEE? HE CAME ***BACK!*** ON A ***COMET ORBIT***. THE CHANCE OF THAT IS... WELL, NOT VERY BIG!
Okay, okay.
HE CAME CRAWLING BACK TO YOU BECAUSE IT'S DAMN COLD OUT THERE!

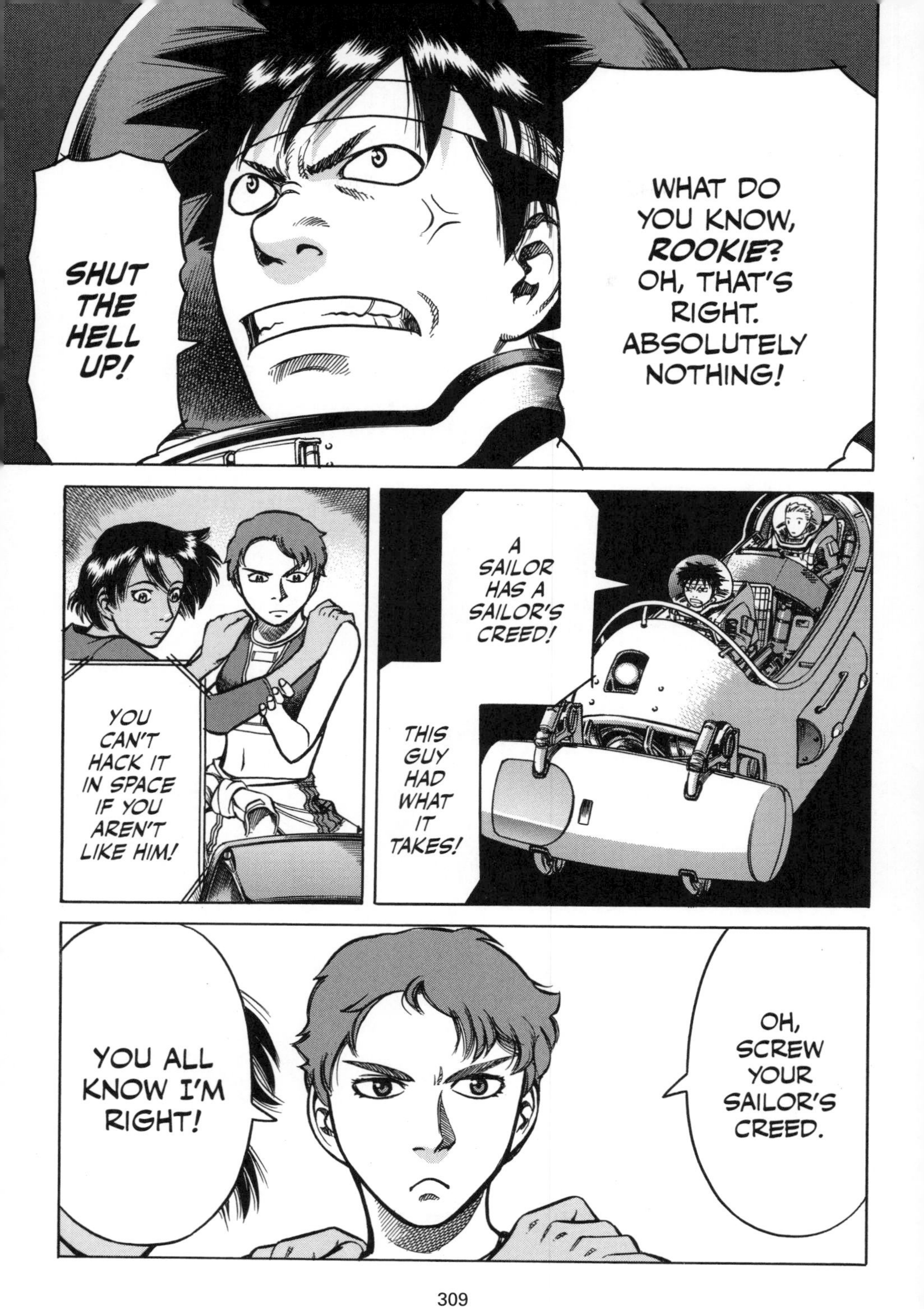
WHAT DO YOU KNOW, ***ROOKIE?*** OH, THAT'S RIGHT. ABSOLUTELY NOTHING!
SHUT THE HELL UP!
A SAILOR HAS A SAILOR'S CREED!
THIS GUY HAD WHAT IT TAKES!
YOU CAN'T HACK IT IN SPACE IF YOU AREN'T LIKE HIM!
OH, SCREW YOUR SAILOR'S CREED.
YOU ALL KNOW I'M RIGHT!

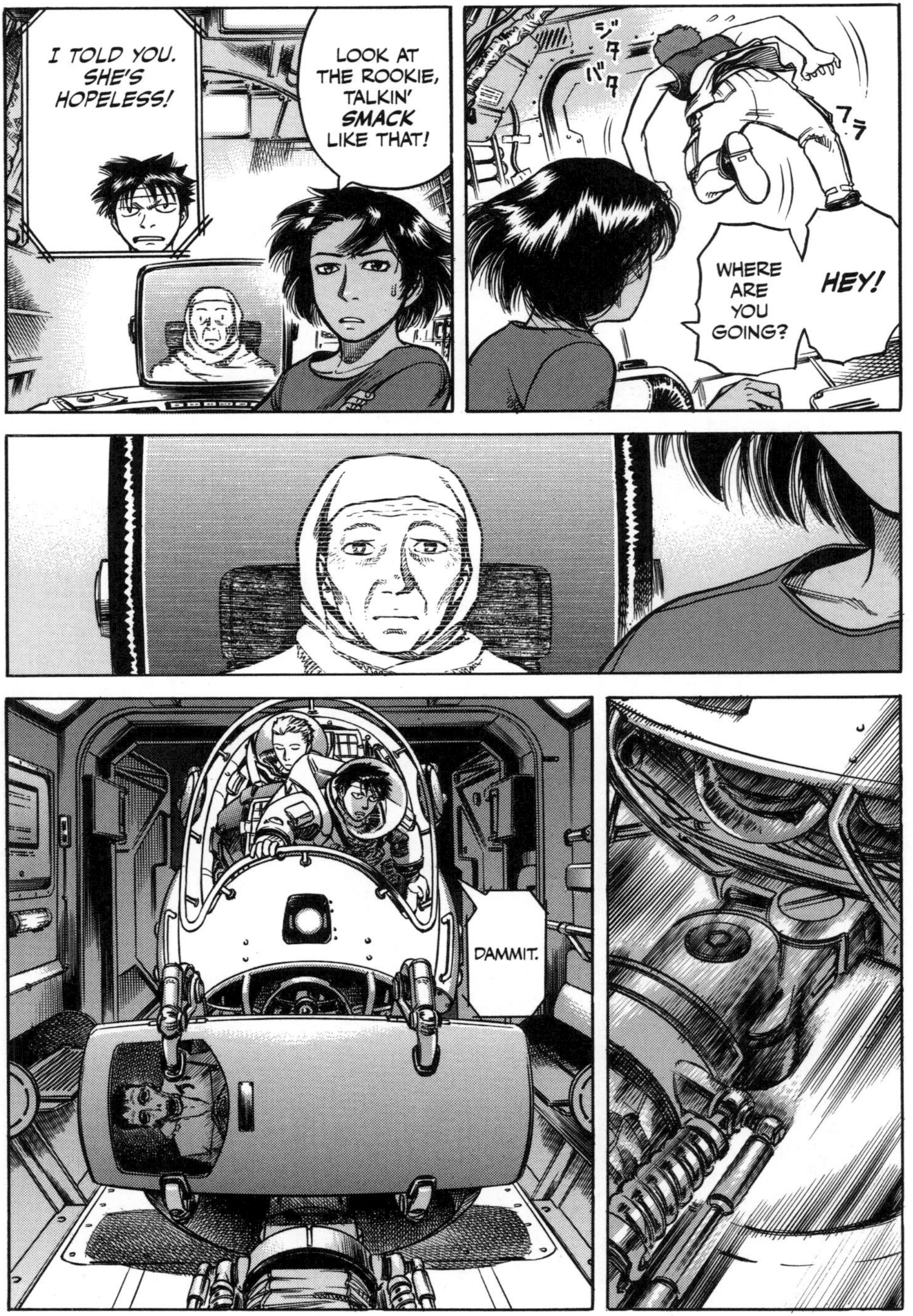

フワ
ジタバタ
HEY!
WHERE ARE YOU GOING?
LOOK AT THE ROOKIE, TALKIN' SMACK LIKE THAT!
I TOLD YOU. SHE'S HOPELESS!
DAMMIT.

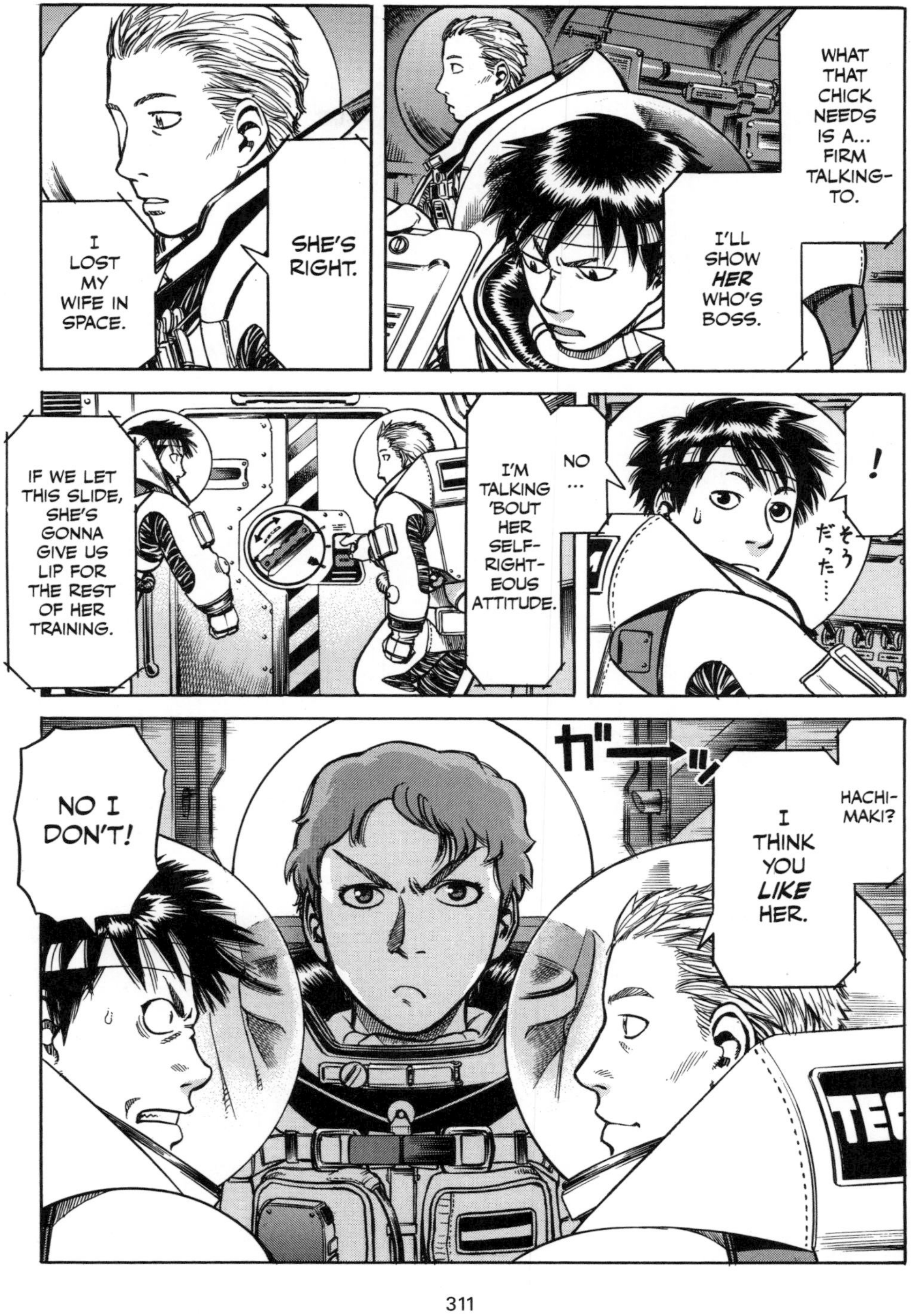
WHAT THAT CHICK NEEDS IS A... FIRM TALKING-TO.
I'LL SHOW HER WHO'S BOSS.
SHE'S RIGHT.
I LOST MY WIFE IN SPACE.
!
そうだった…
NO ...
I'M TALKING 'BOUT HER SELF-RIGHTEOUS ATTITUDE.
IF WE LET THIS SLIDE, SHE'S GONNA GIVE US LIP FOR THE REST OF HER TRAINING.
ガー
HACHI-MAKI?
I THINK YOU LIKE HER.
NO I DON'T!

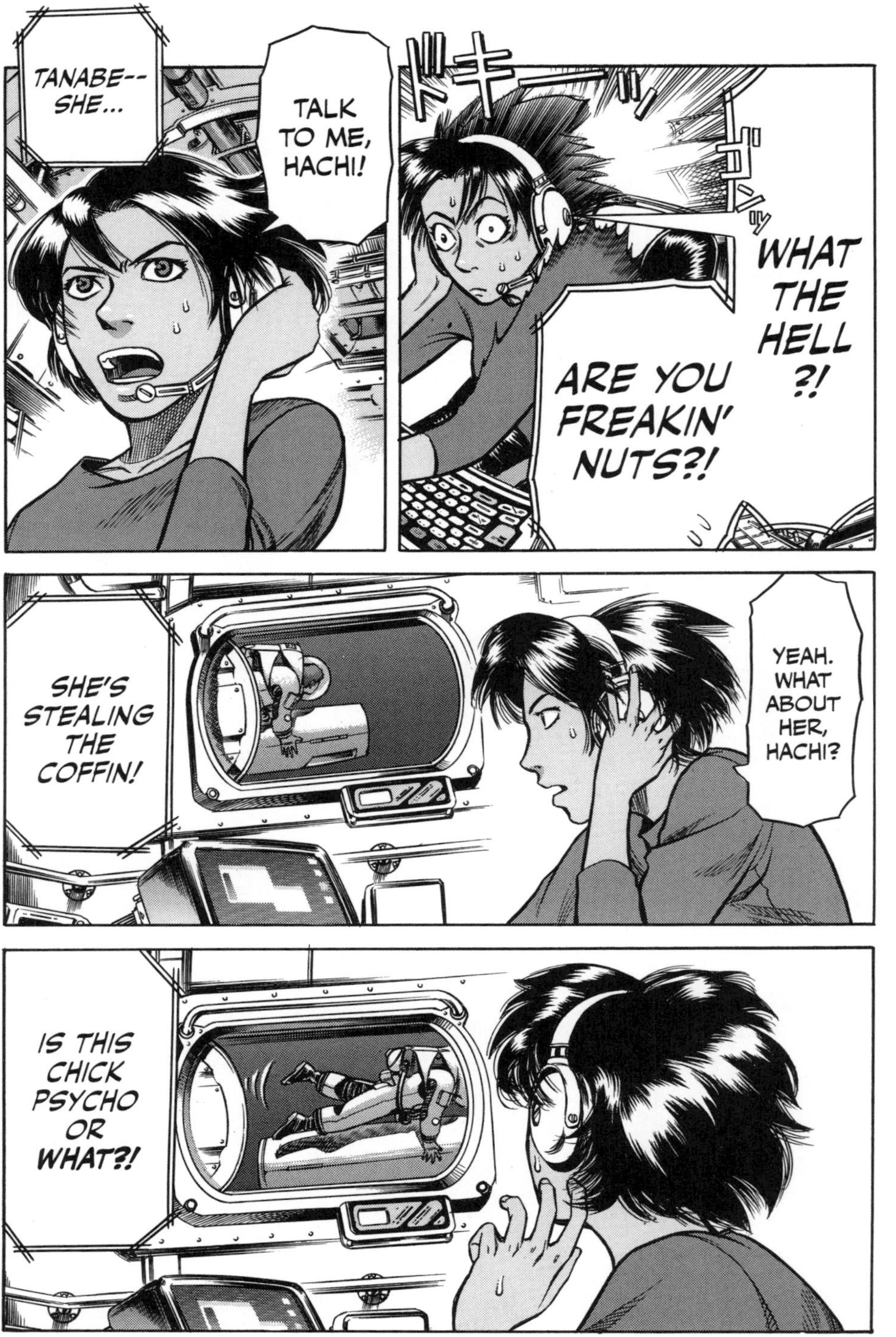
WHAT THE HELL ?!
ARE YOU FREAKIN' NUTS?!
TALK TO ME, HACHI!
TANABE-- SHE...
YEAH. WHAT ABOUT HER, HACHI?
SHE'S STEALING THE COFFIN!
IS THIS CHICK PSYCHO OR WHAT?!

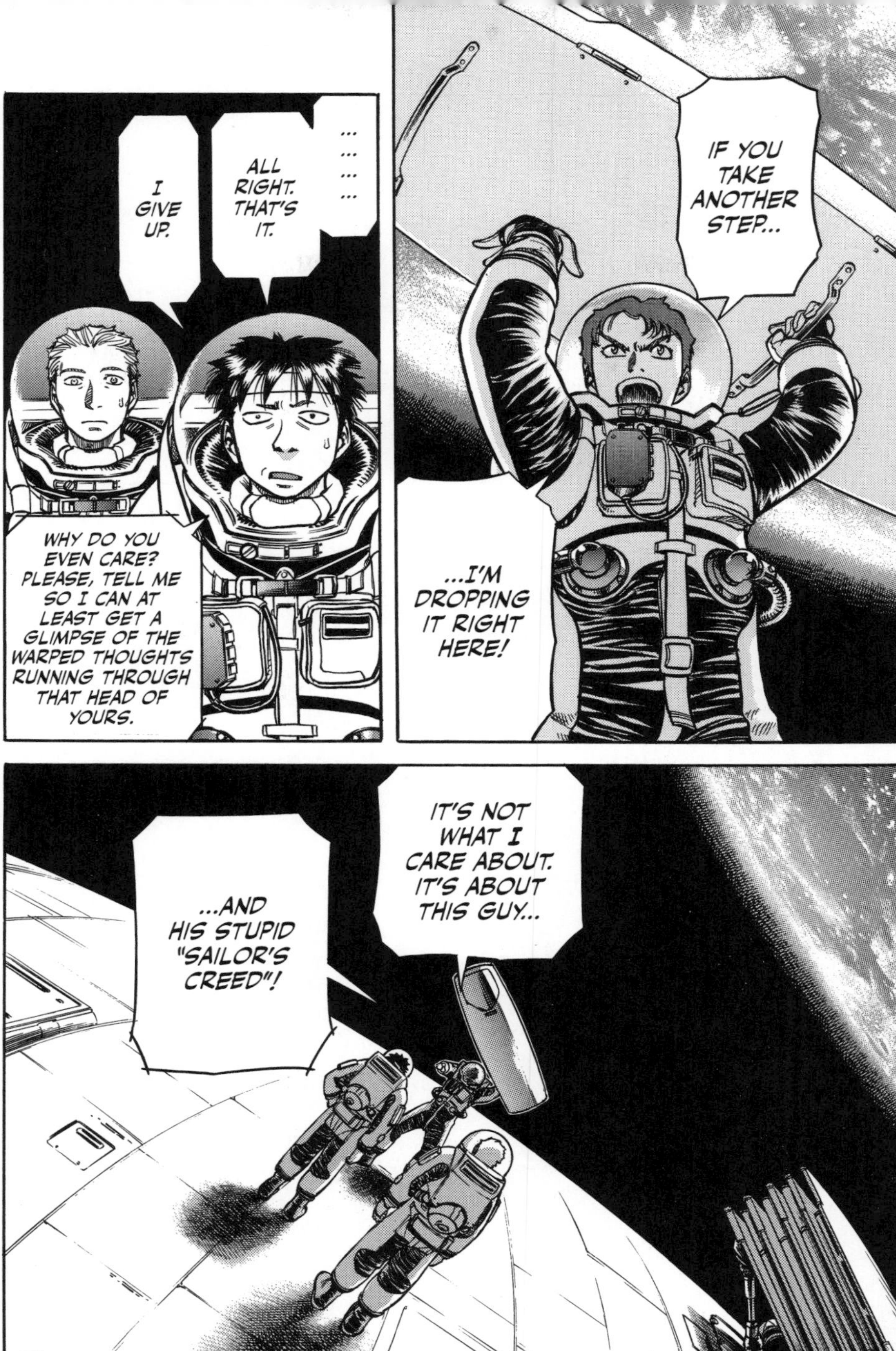
IF YOU TAKE ANOTHER STEP...
...I'M DROPPING IT RIGHT HERE!
... ...
ALL RIGHT. THAT'S IT.
I GIVE UP.
WHY DO YOU EVEN CARE? PLEASE, TELL ME SO I CAN AT LEAST GET A GLIMPSE OF THE WARPED THOUGHTS RUNNING THROUGH THAT HEAD OF YOURS.
IT'S NOT WHAT I CARE ABOUT. IT'S ABOUT THIS GUY...
...AND HIS STUPID "SAILOR'S CREED"!

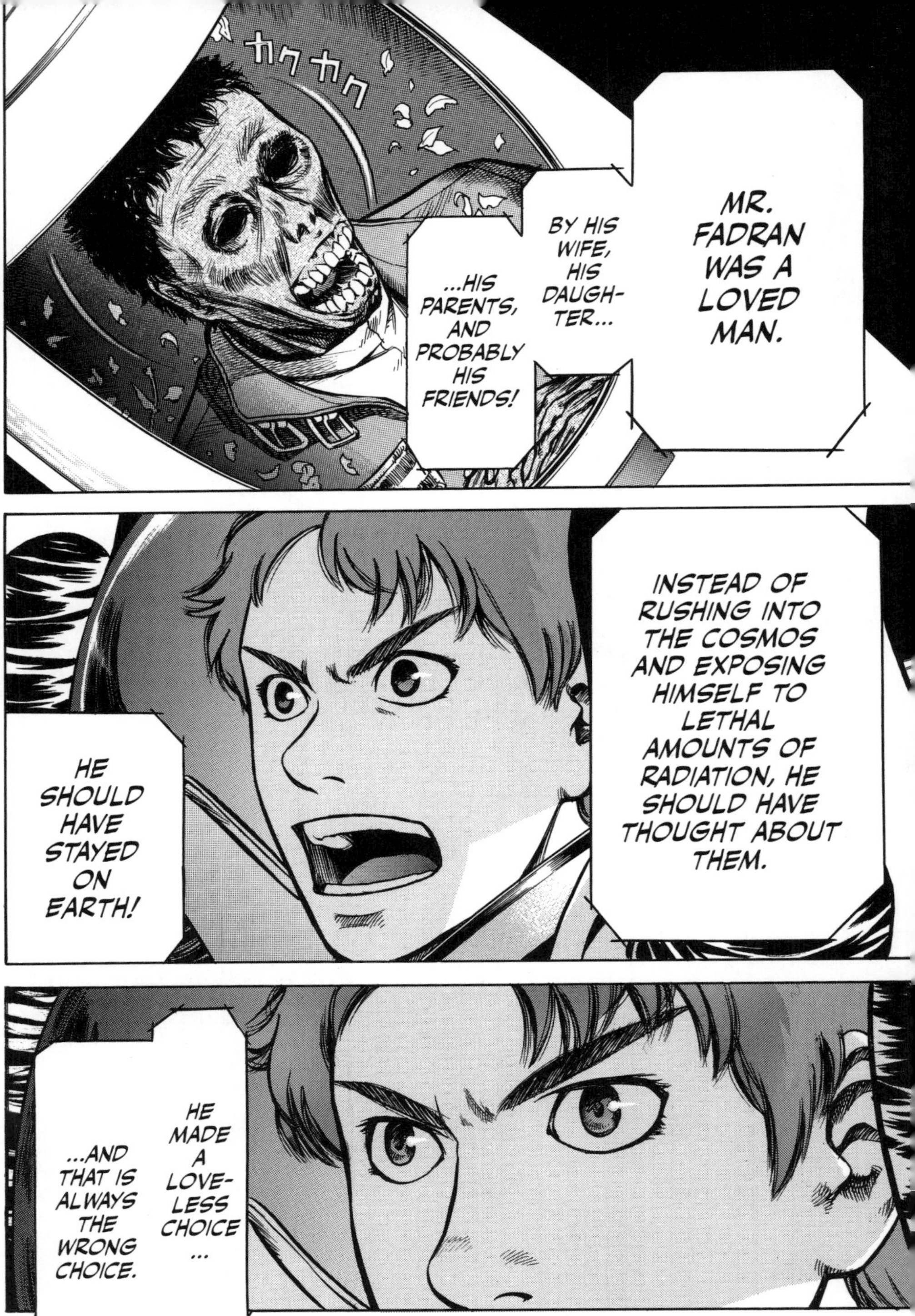
カクカク
MR. FADRAN WAS A LOVED MAN.
BY HIS WIFE, HIS DAUGH-TER...
...HIS PARENTS, AND PROBABLY HIS FRIENDS!
INSTEAD OF RUSHING INTO THE COSMOS AND EXPOSING HIMSELF TO LETHAL AMOUNTS OF RADIATION, HE SHOULD HAVE THOUGHT ABOUT THEM.
HE SHOULD HAVE STAYED ON EARTH!
HE MADE A LOVE-LESS CHOICE ...
...AND THAT IS ALWAYS THE WRONG CHOICE.

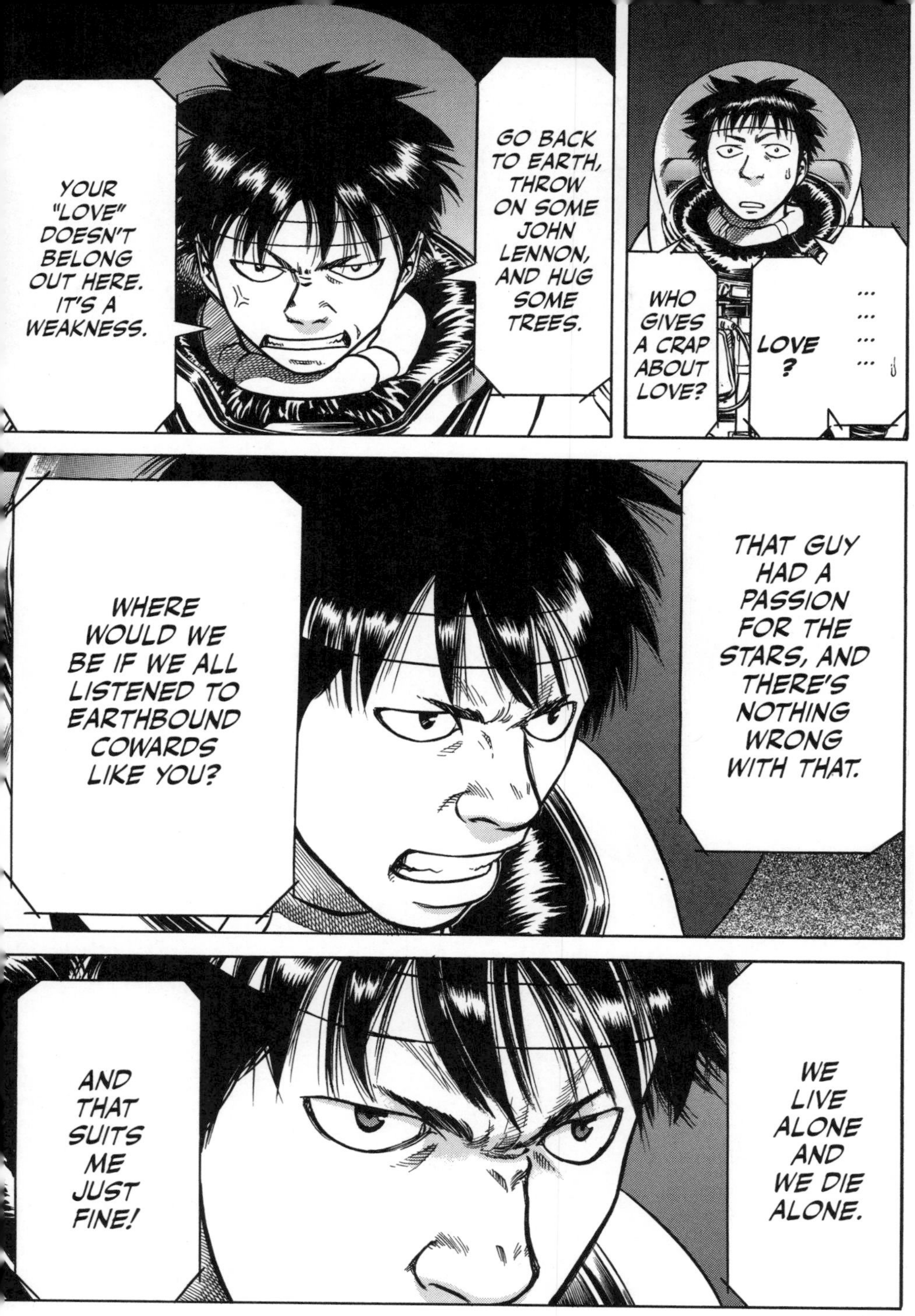

... ...
LOVE?
WHO GIVES A CRAP ABOUT LOVE?
GO BACK TO EARTH, THROW ON SOME JOHN LENNON, AND HUG SOME TREES.
YOUR "LOVE" DOESN'T BELONG OUT HERE. IT'S A WEAKNESS.
THAT GUY HAD A PASSION FOR THE STARS, AND THERE'S NOTHING WRONG WITH THAT.
WHERE WOULD WE BE IF WE ALL LISTENED TO EARTHBOUND COWARDS LIKE YOU?
WE LIVE ALONE AND WE DIE ALONE.
AND THAT SUITS ME JUST FINE!

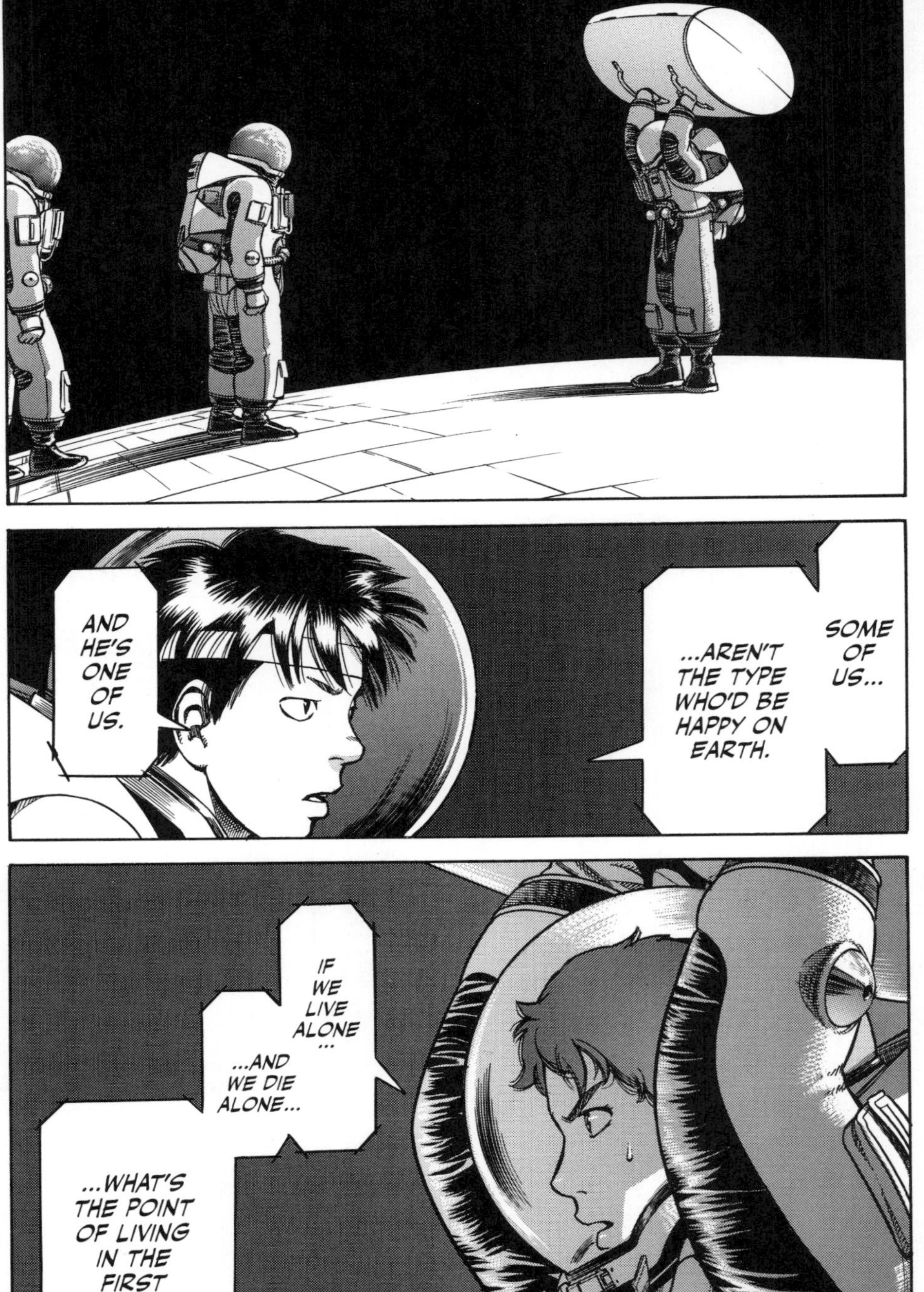
SOME OF US...
...AREN'T THE TYPE WHO'D BE HAPPY ON EARTH.
AND HE'S ONE OF US.
IF WE LIVE ALONE...
...AND WE DIE ALONE...
...WHAT'S THE POINT OF LIVING IN THE FIRST PLACE?

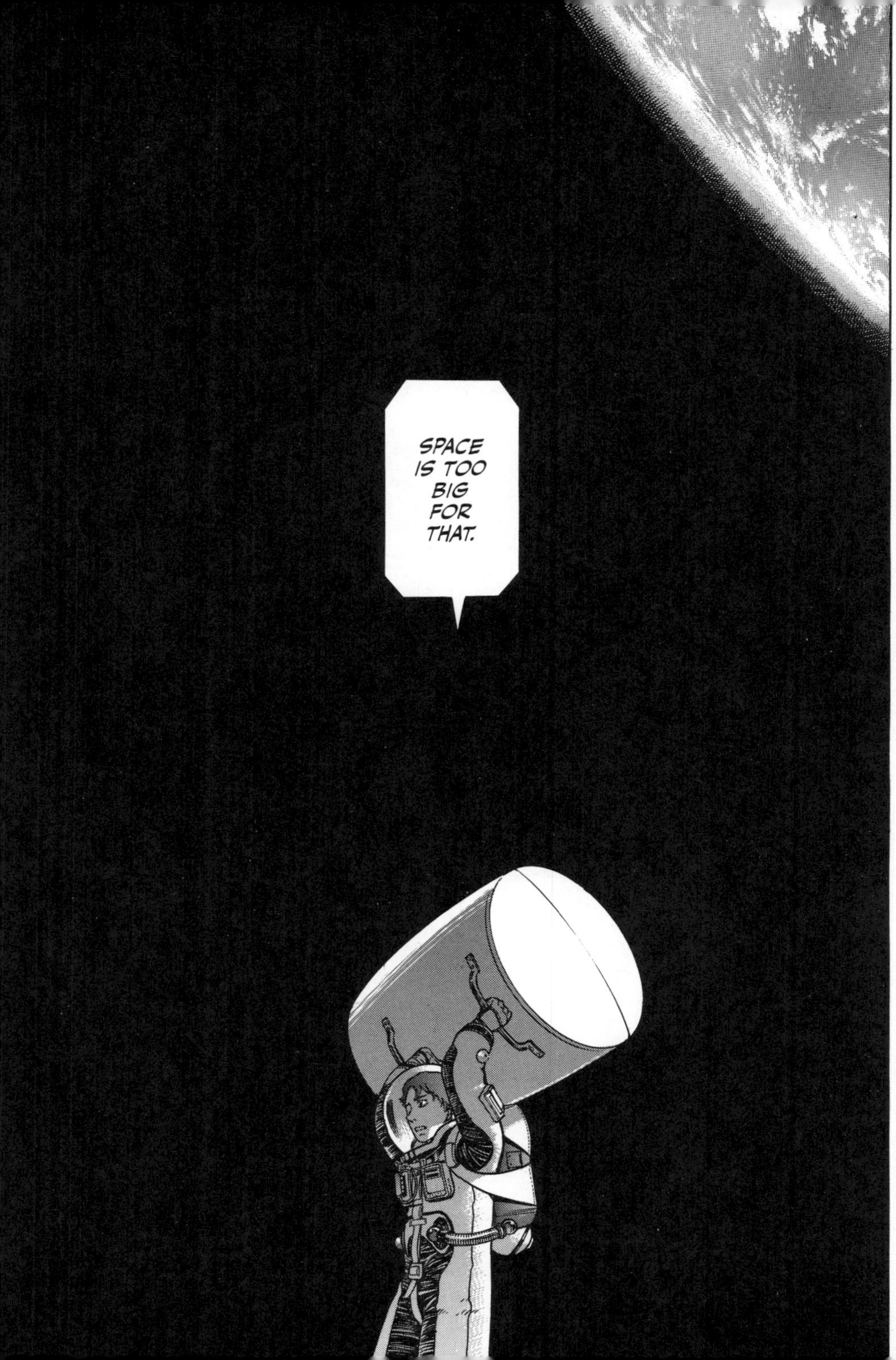
SPACE IS TOO BIG FOR THAT.

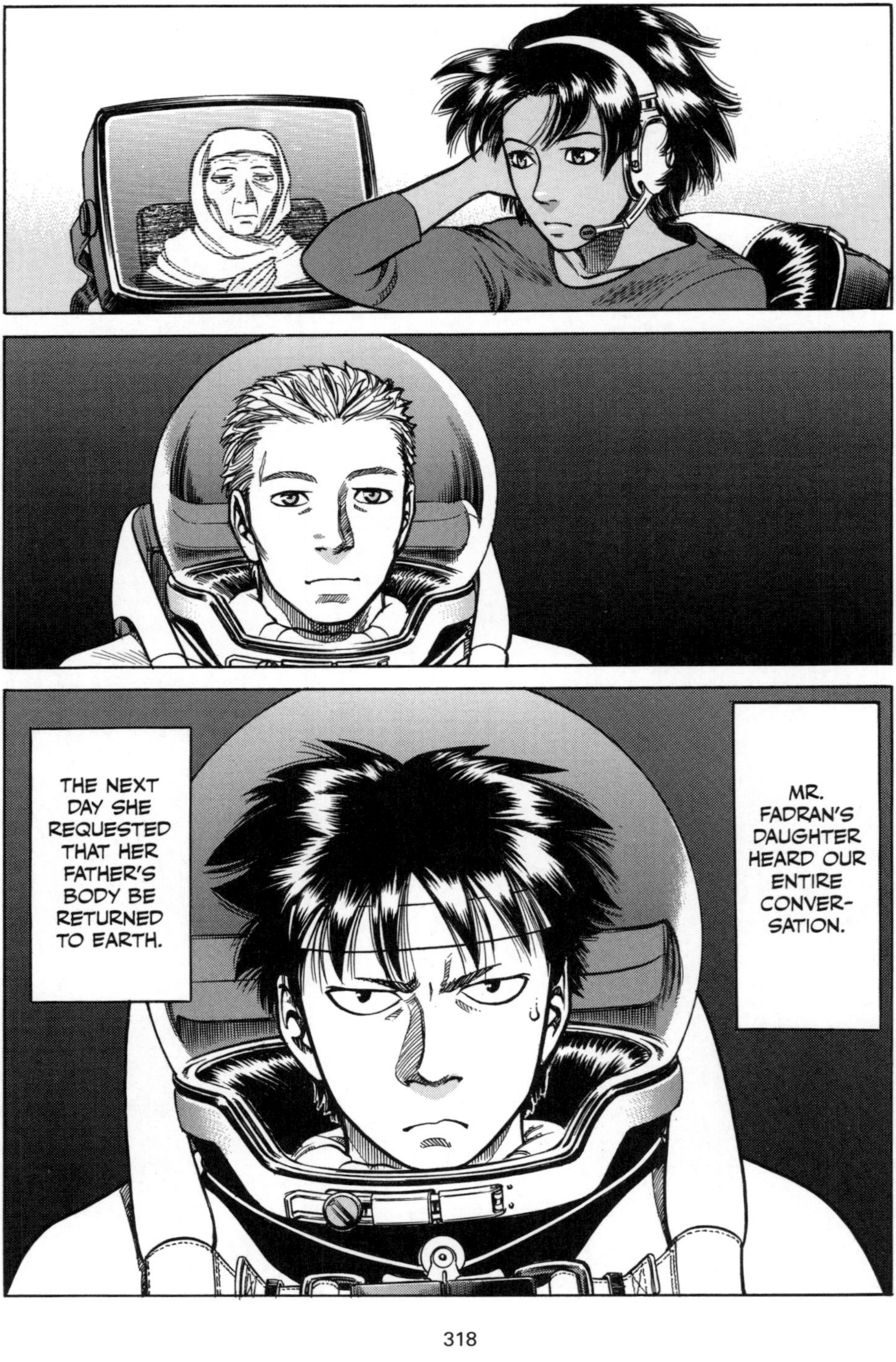
MR. FADRAN'S DAUGHTER HEARD OUR ENTIRE CONVER-SATION.
THE NEXT DAY SHE REQUESTED THAT HER FATHER'S BODY BE RETURNED TO EARTH.

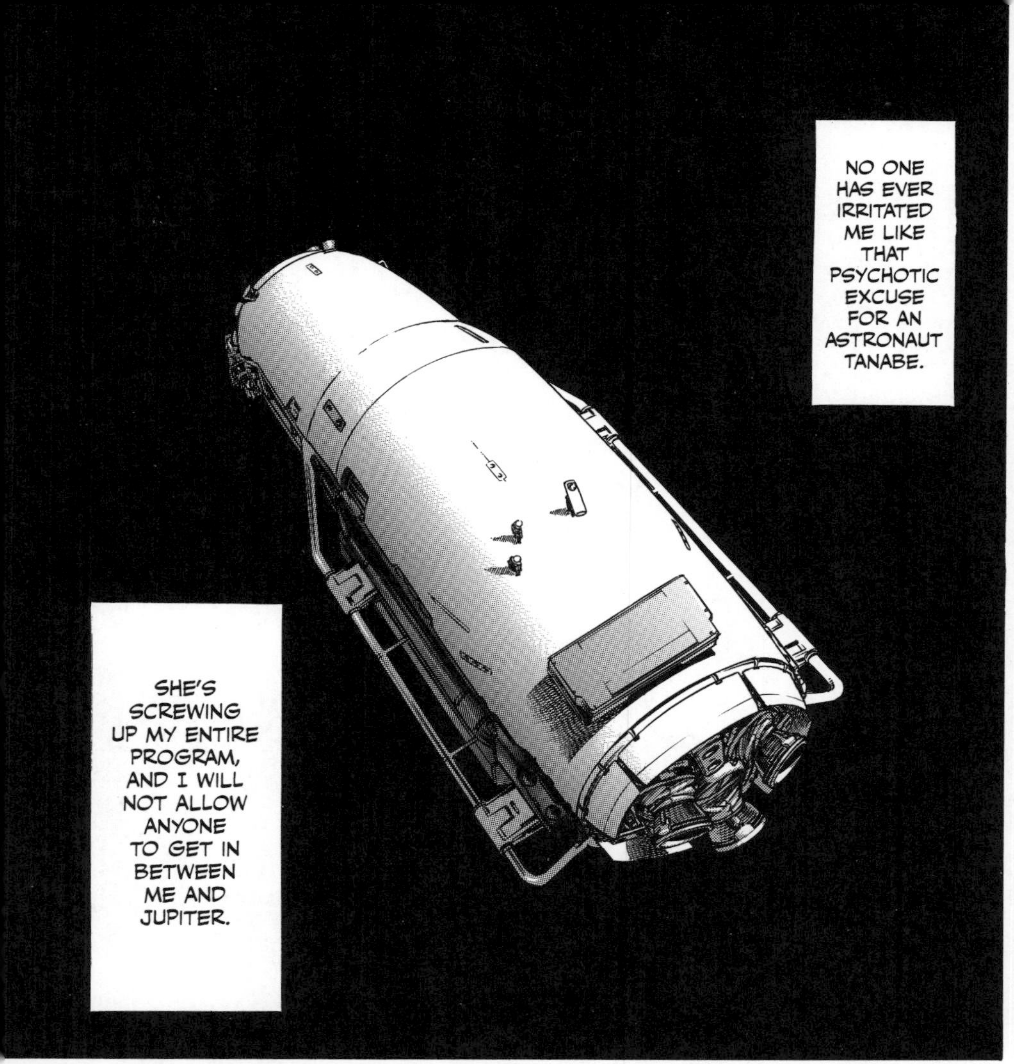
NO ONE HAS EVER IRRITATED ME LIKE THAT PSYCHOTIC EXCUSE FOR AN ASTRONAUT TANABE.
SHE'S SCREWING UP MY ENTIRE PROGRAM, AND I WILL NOT ALLOW ANYONE TO GET IN BETWEEN ME AND JUPITER.
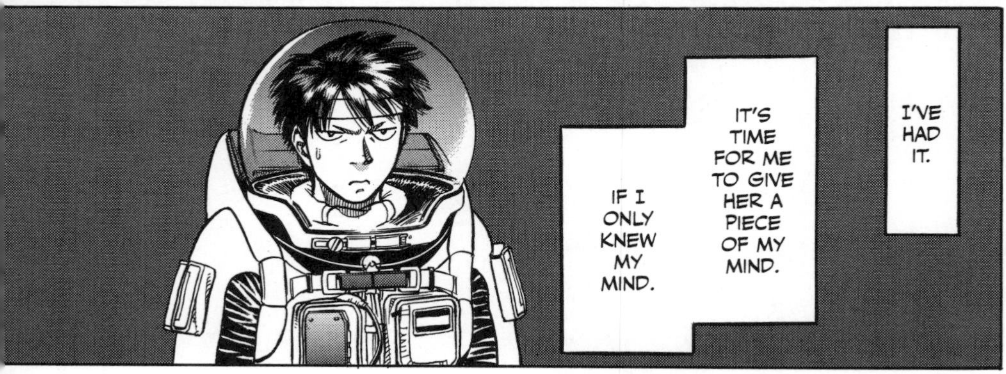
I'VE HAD IT.
IT'S TIME FOR ME TO GIVE HER A PIECE OF MY MIND.
IF I ONLY KNEW MY MIND.

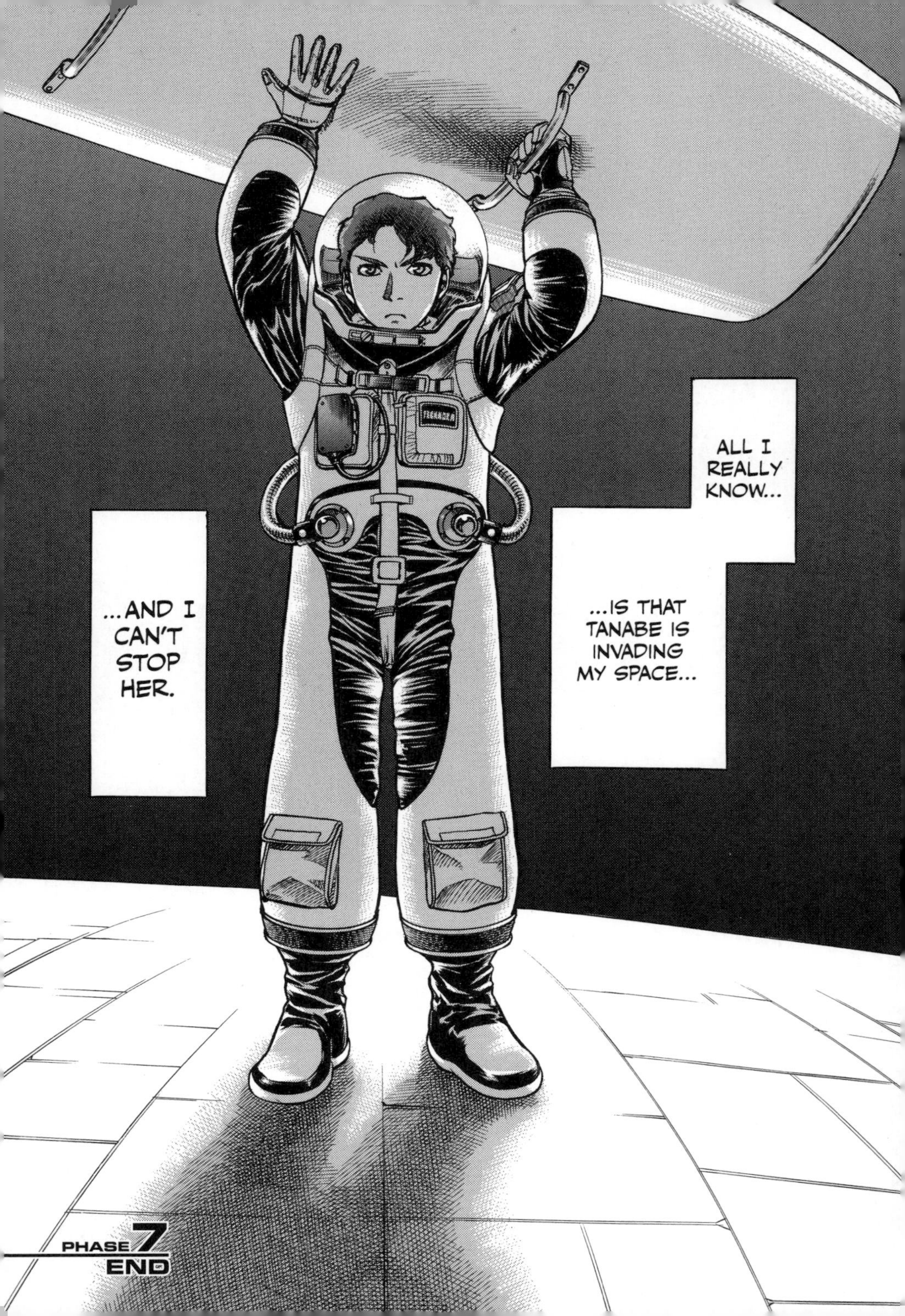
ALL I REALLY KNOW...
...IS THAT TANABE IS INVADING MY SPACE...
...AND I CAN'T STOP HER.
PHASE 7 END

THIS IS
A HAPPY
LIFE, FROM
A CERTAIN
POINT OF *PLANETES*
VIEW. SUPPLEMENT

BY MAKOTO
YUKIMURA

A FOUR-PANEL COMIC

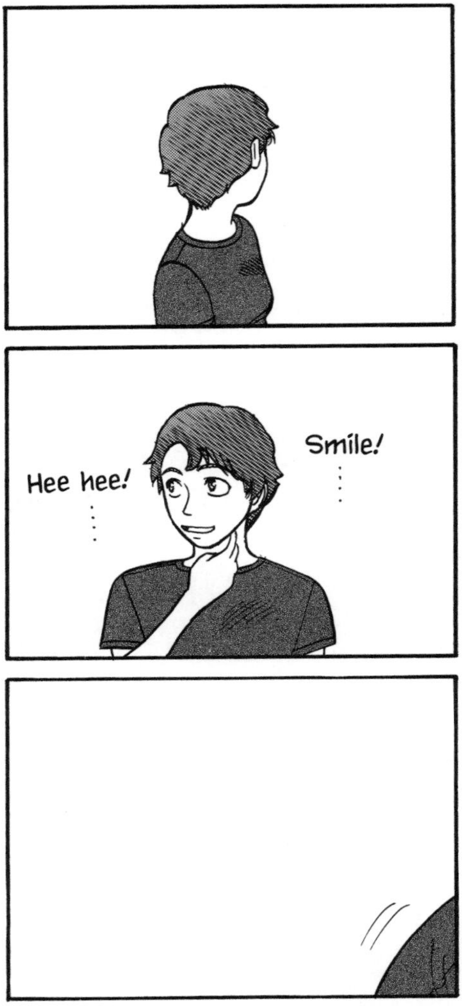
Smile!
Hee hee!
LET ME INTRODUCE MY PET... OH!! WE'RE ON THE FOURTH PANEL ALREADY?!
PICK UP THE PACE.
But I haven't finished!

NAMAO (PRESUMABLY MALE)

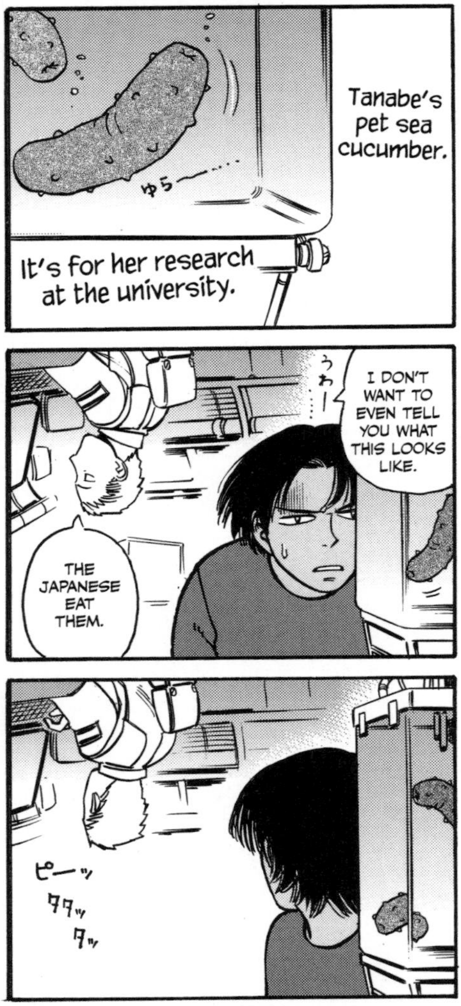
Tanabe's pet sea cucumber.
ゆら～…
It's for her research at the university.
うわ…
I DON'T WANT TO EVEN TELL YOU WHAT THIS LOOKS LIKE.
THE JAPANESE EAT THEM.
ピーッ
タタッ
タッ
AS A PUNISHMENT?
NO, AS AN APPETIZER.
With ponzu sauce. Delicious.

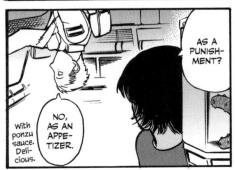

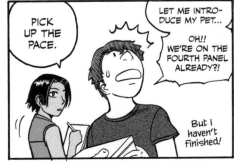

EAT? THAT THING?!

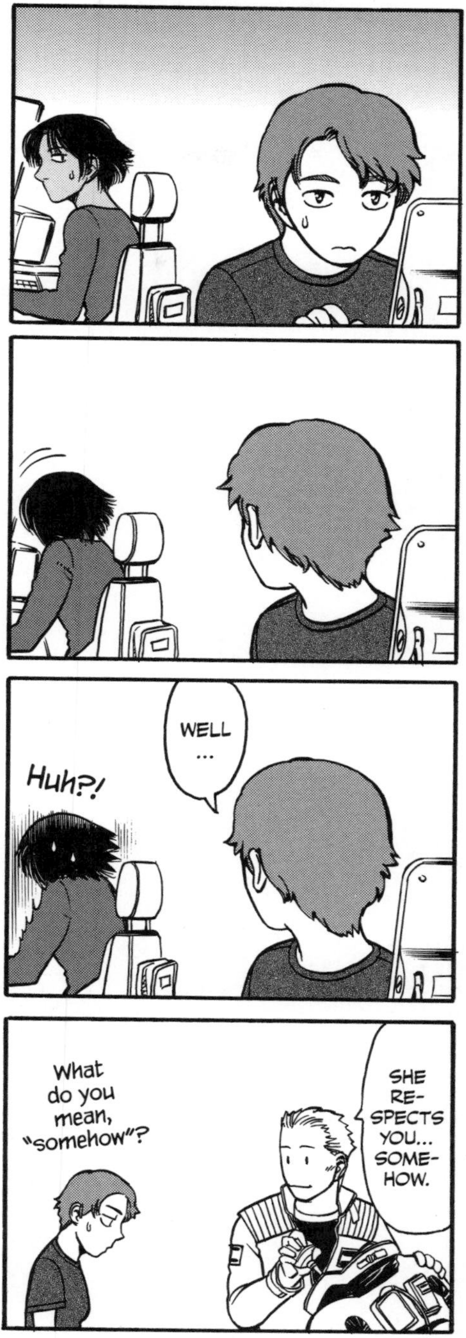
WELL ...
Huh?!
SHE RE-SPECTS YOU... SOME-HOW.
What do you mean, "somehow"?

DRINKING HOT COFFEE THROUGH A STRAW

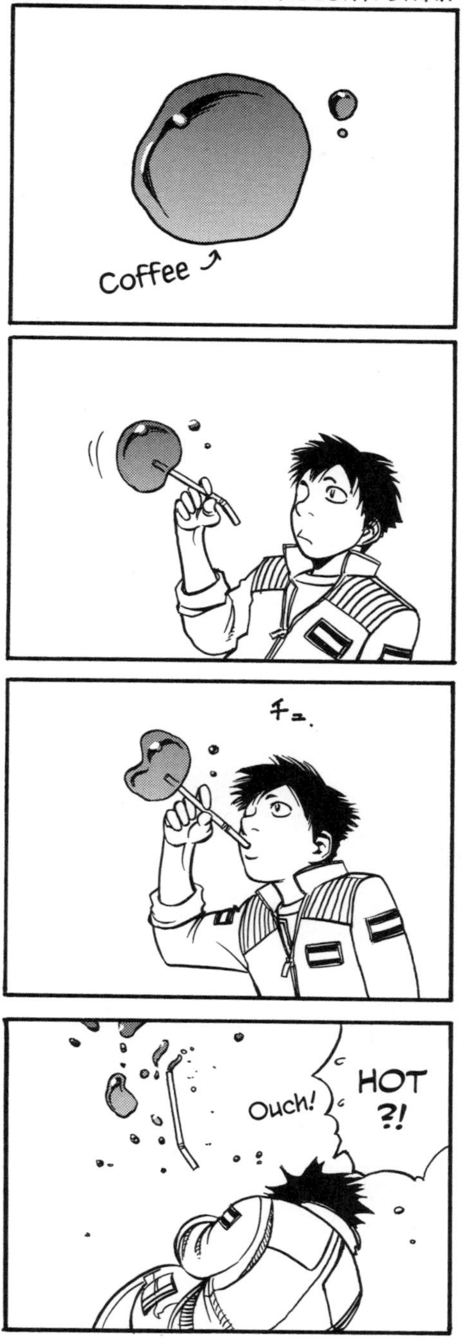
Coffee
チュ
HOT ?!
Ouch!

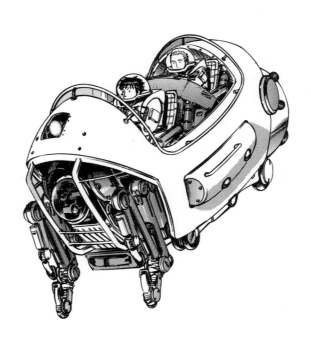

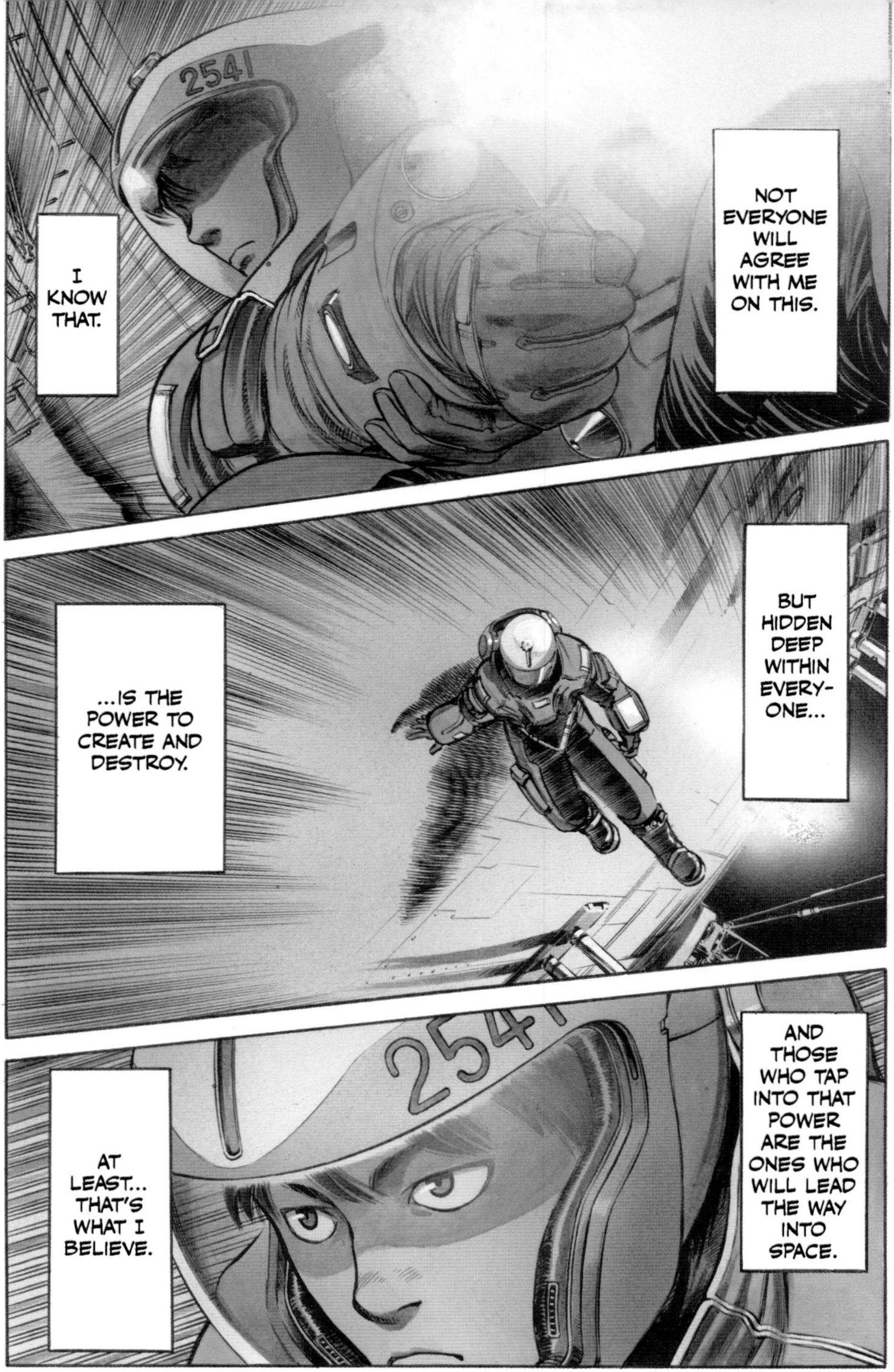
NOT EVERYONE WILL AGREE WITH ME ON THIS.
I KNOW THAT.
BUT HIDDEN DEEP WITHIN EVERY-ONE...
...IS THE POWER TO CREATE AND DESTROY.
AND THOSE WHO TAP INTO THAT POWER ARE THE ONES WHO WILL LEAD THE WAY INTO SPACE.
AT LEAST... THAT'S WHAT I BELIEVE.

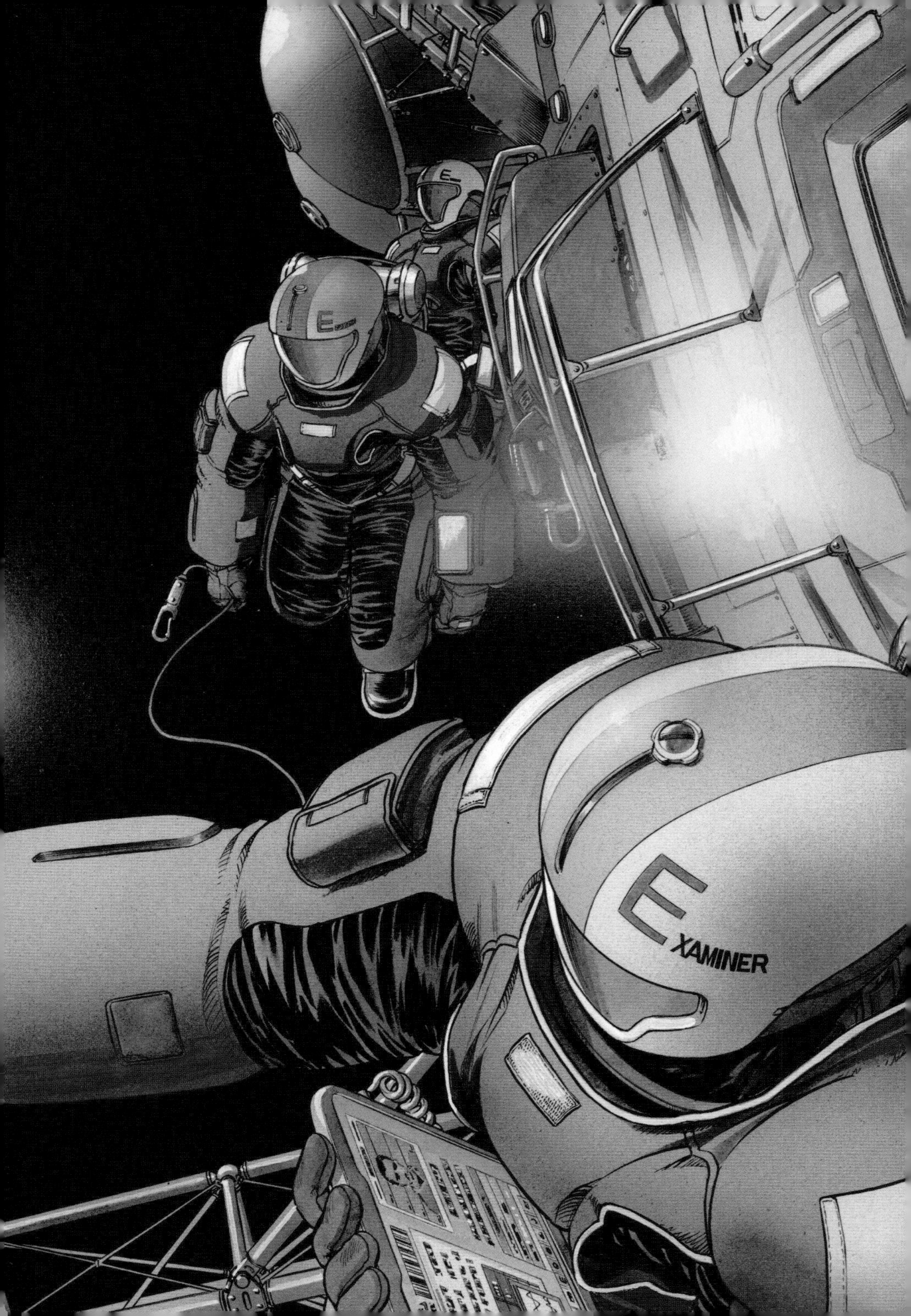
EXAMINER

8

A BLACK FLOWER NAMED
SAKINOHAKA (PART 1)

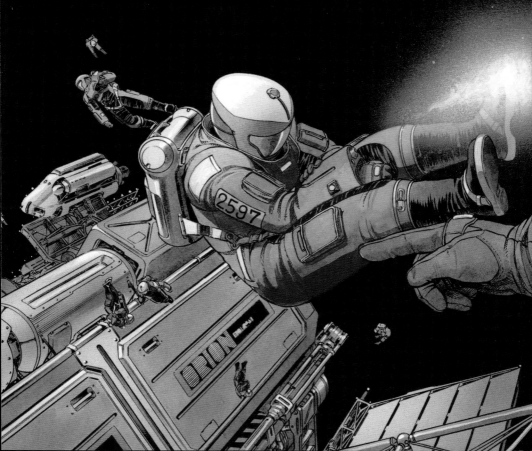

Jupiter mission EVA
crew evaluation site 2.
Lagrange 1, 2076.

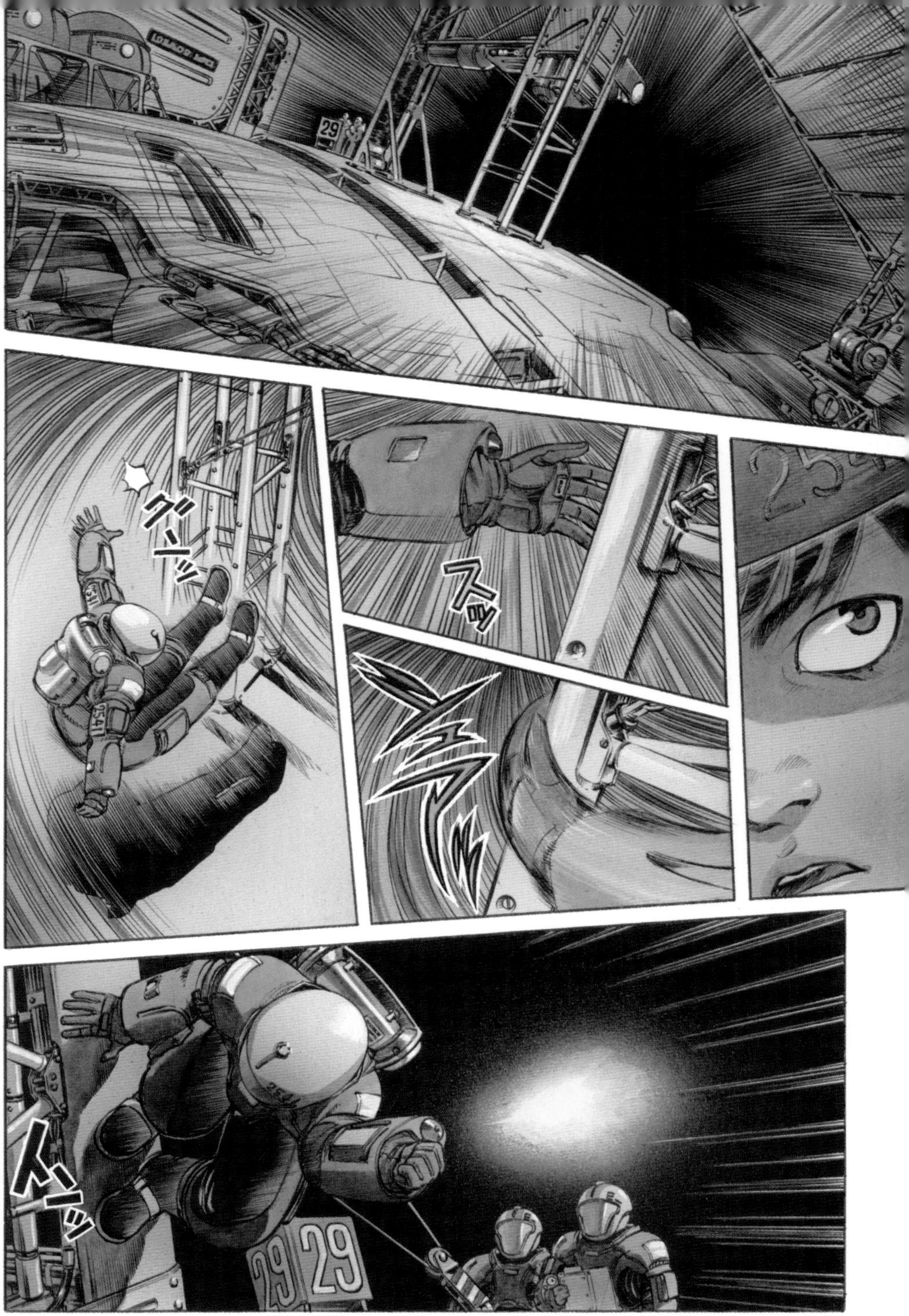
スッ

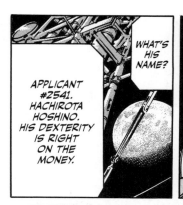

IMPRESSIVE.
DID YOU SEE THAT KID MOVE?
YEAH. ALL MOMENTUM, NO JETS.
WHAT'S HIS NAME?
APPLICANT #2541. HACHIROTA HOSHINO. HIS DEXTERITY IS RIGHT ON THE MONEY.
HE WORKED E.V.A. CREW FOR A COMMERCIAL DEBRIS-PICKUP SERVICE FOR THREE AND A HALF YEARS. JUST LEFT IT LAST MONTH.
HE'S GOOD.
HE'S STILL FULL ON FUEL... STILL HAS PLENTY OF OXYGEN... PERFECT TIMING. EVERYTHING'S PRETTY TIGHT.
E.V.A., HUH? THAT'S A TOUGH WAY TO CUT YOUR TEETH.
HIS WRITTEN SCORES AREN'T SO GOOD, BUT WITH THAT RAW TALENT...
I SAY WE ADVANCE HIM TO THE NEXT ROUND.
RIGHT ON.

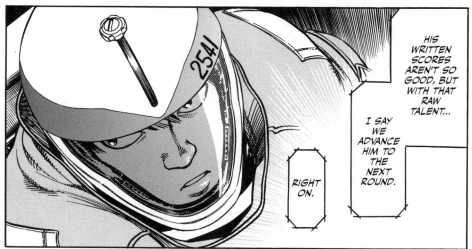

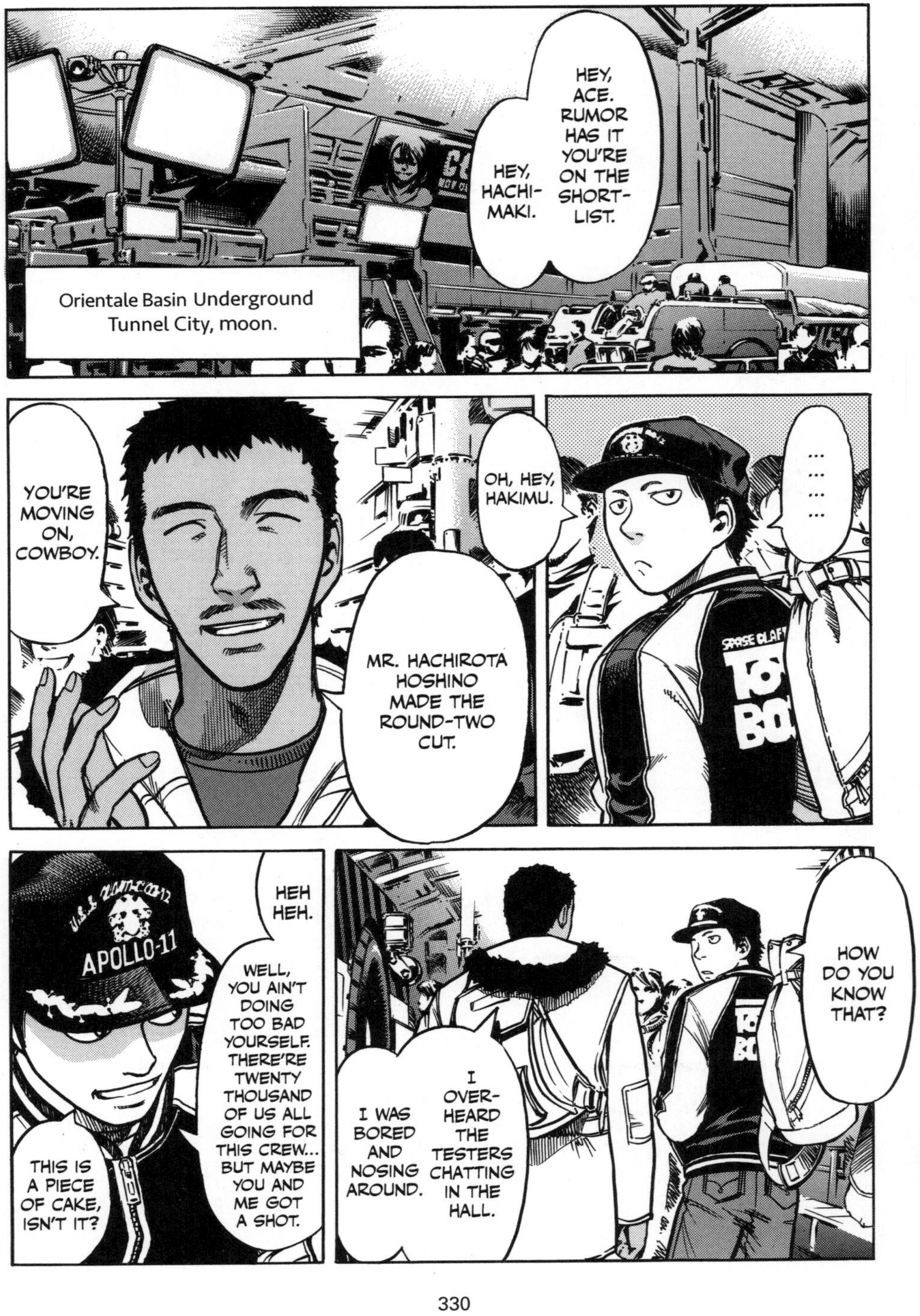
HEY, ACE. RUMOR HAS IT YOU'RE ON THE SHORT-LIST.
HEY, HACHI-MAKI.
Orientale Basin Underground Tunnel City, moon.
...
...
...
...
OH, HEY, HAKIMU.
MR. HACHIROTA HOSHINO MADE THE ROUND-TWO CUT.
YOU'RE MOVING ON, COWBOY.
HOW DO YOU KNOW THAT?
I OVERHEARD THE TESTERS CHATTING IN THE HALL.
I WAS BORED AND NOSING AROUND.
HEH HEH.
APOLLO-11
WELL, YOU AIN'T DOING TOO BAD YOURSELF. THERE'RE TWENTY THOUSAND OF US ALL GOING FOR THIS CREW... BUT MAYBE YOU AND ME GOT A SHOT.
THIS IS A PIECE OF CAKE, ISN'T IT?

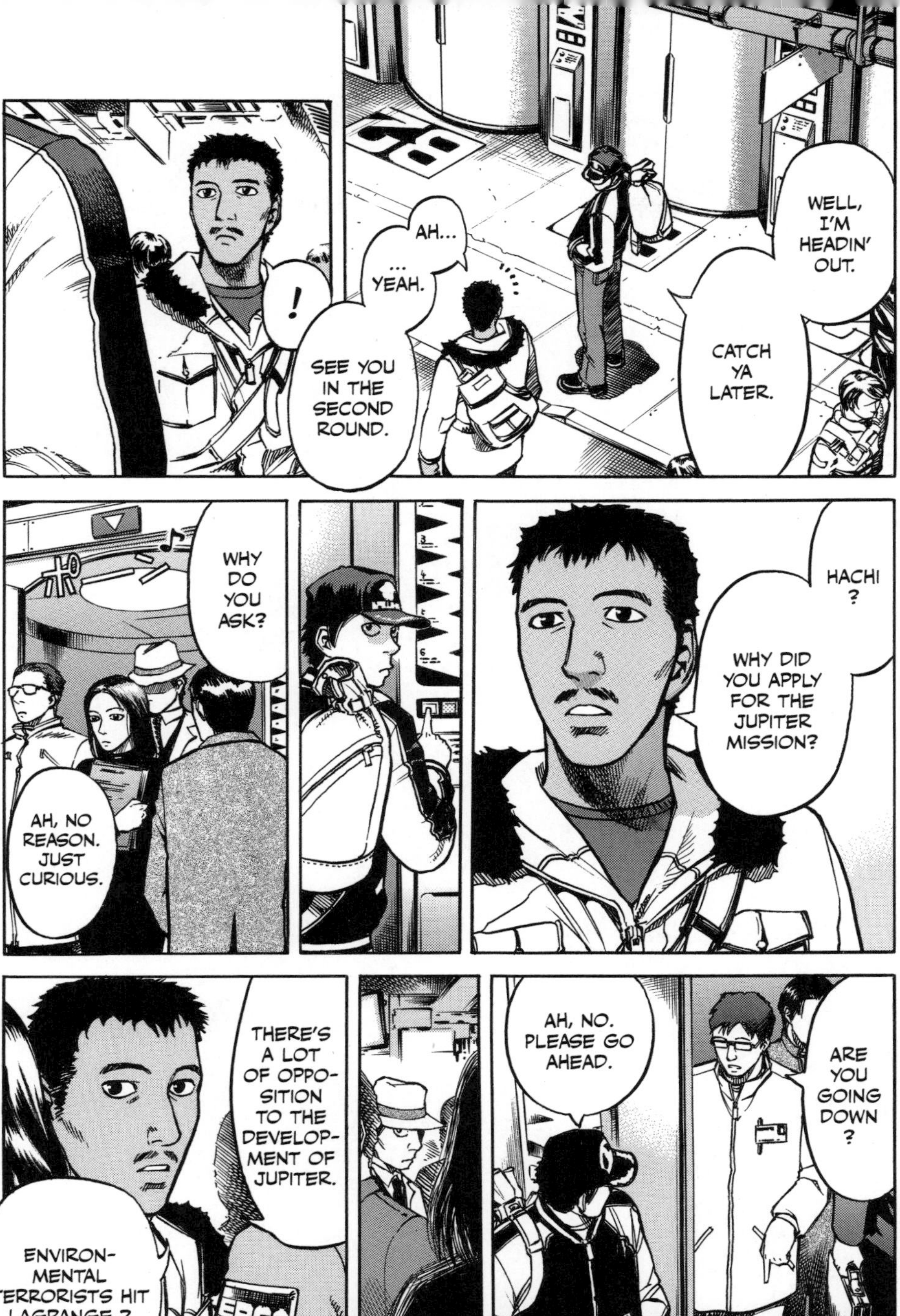
WELL, I'M HEADIN' OUT.
CATCH YA LATER.
AH...
... YEAH.
SEE YOU IN THE SECOND ROUND.
!
HACHI?
WHY DID YOU APPLY FOR THE JUPITER MISSION?
WHY DO YOU ASK?
AH, NO REASON. JUST CURIOUS.
ARE YOU GOING DOWN?
AH, NO. PLEASE GO AHEAD.
THERE'S A LOT OF OPPO-SITION TO THE DEVELOP-MENT OF JUPITER.
ENVIRON-MENTAL TERRORISTS HIT LAGRANGE 2 LAST WEEK.

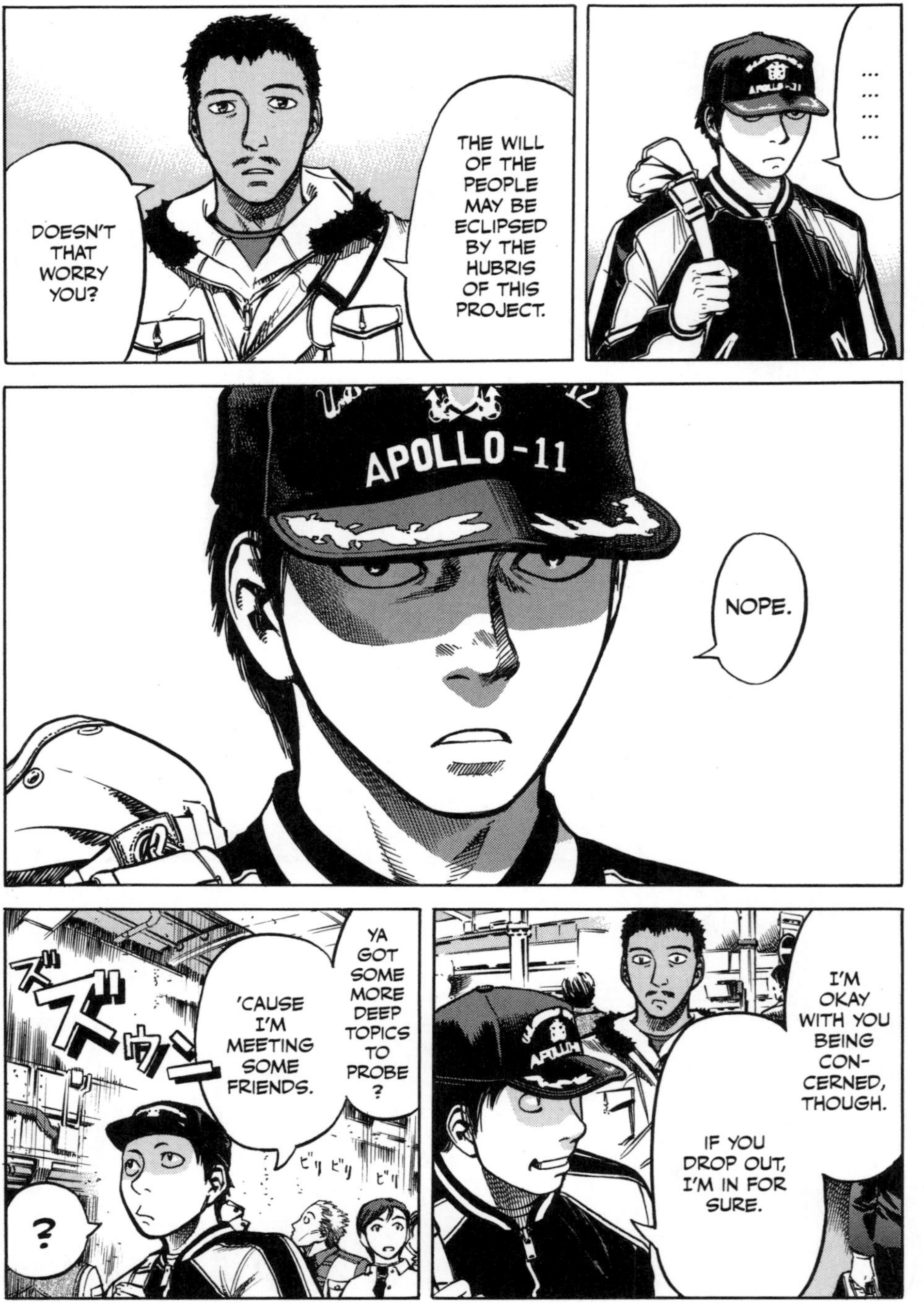
…
…
…
…
APOLLO-11
THE WILL OF THE PEOPLE MAY BE ECLIPSED BY THE HUBRIS OF THIS PROJECT.
DOESN'T THAT WORRY YOU?
APOLLO-11
NOPE.
I'M OKAY WITH YOU BEING CON-CERNED, THOUGH.
IF YOU DROP OUT, I'M IN FOR SURE.
YA GOT SOME MORE DEEP TOPICS TO PROBE?
'CAUSE I'M MEETING SOME FRIENDS.
ビリ ビリ ビリ
?

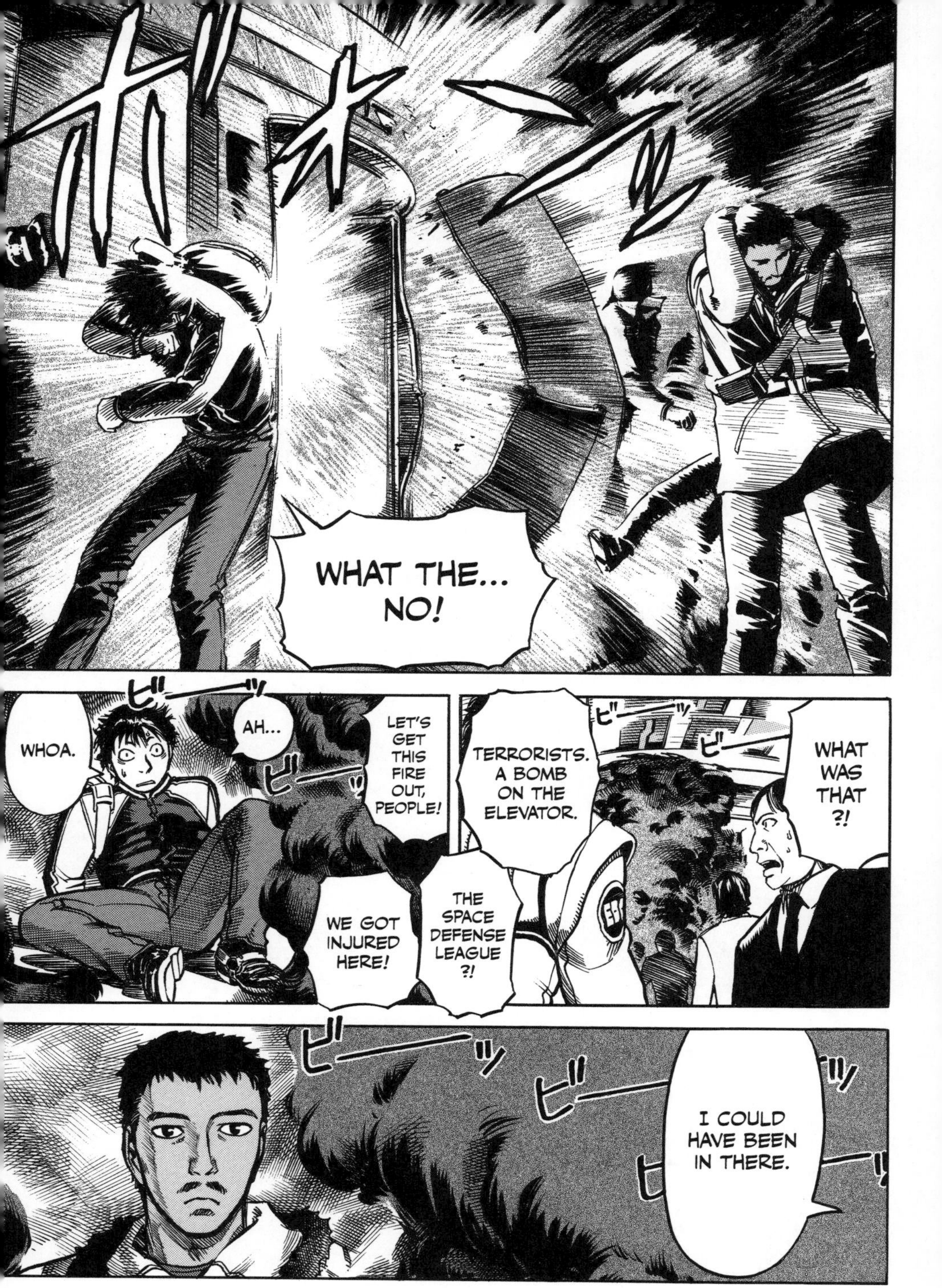
WHAT THE... NO!
WHAT WAS THAT ?!
TERRORISTS. A BOMB ON THE ELEVATOR.
THE SPACE DEFENSE LEAGUE ?!
LET'S GET THIS FIRE OUT, PEOPLE!
AH...
WHOA.
WE GOT INJURED HERE!
I COULD HAVE BEEN IN THERE.

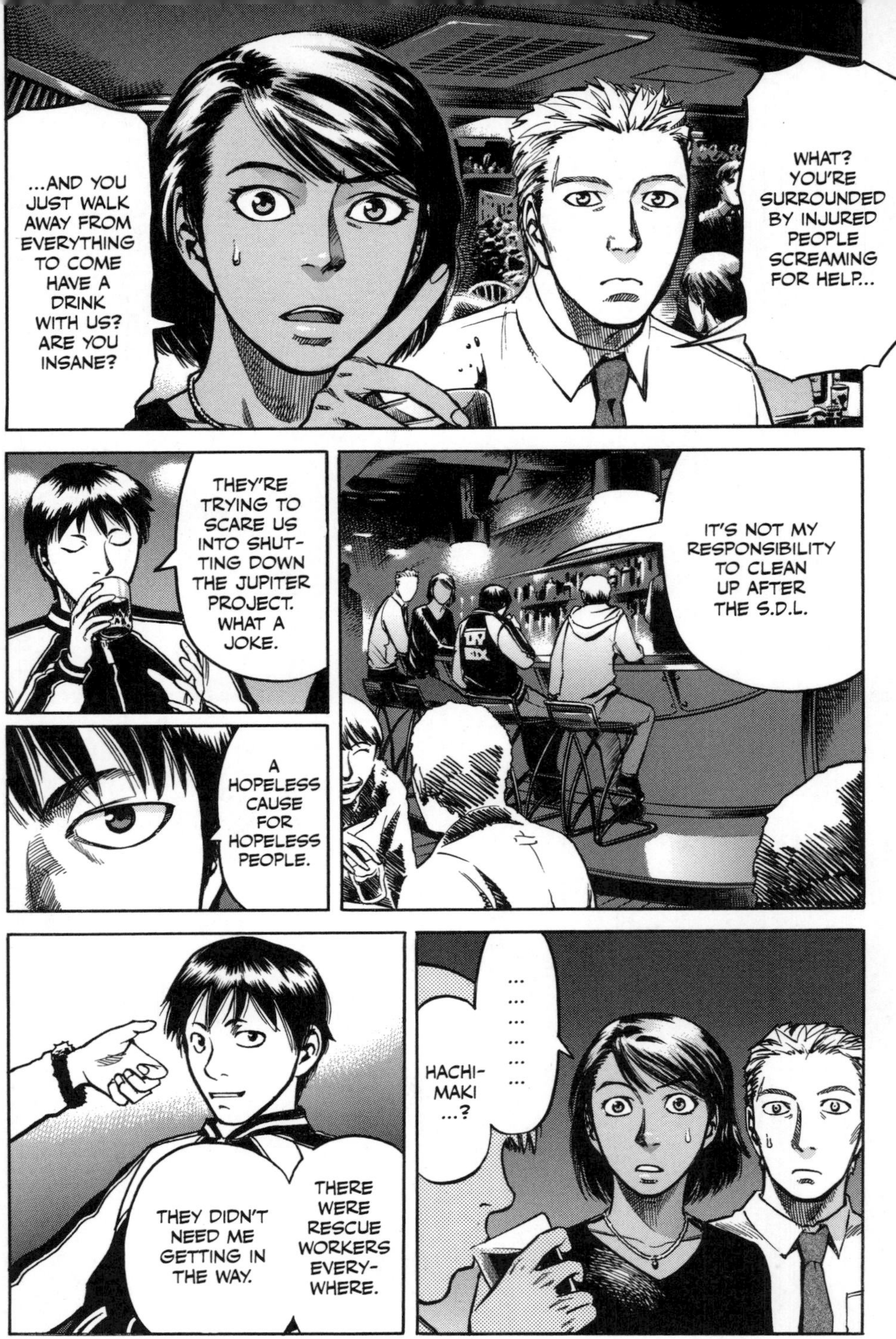
WHAT? YOU'RE SURROUNDED BY INJURED PEOPLE SCREAMING FOR HELP...
...AND YOU JUST WALK AWAY FROM EVERYTHING TO COME HAVE A DRINK WITH US? ARE YOU INSANE?
IT'S NOT MY RESPONSIBILITY TO CLEAN UP AFTER THE S.D.L.
THEY'RE TRYING TO SCARE US INTO SHUTTING DOWN THE JUPITER PROJECT. WHAT A JOKE.
A HOPELESS CAUSE FOR HOPELESS PEOPLE.
... ...
HACHI-MAKI ...?
THERE WERE RESCUE WORKERS EVERYWHERE.
THEY DIDN'T NEED ME GETTING IN THE WAY.

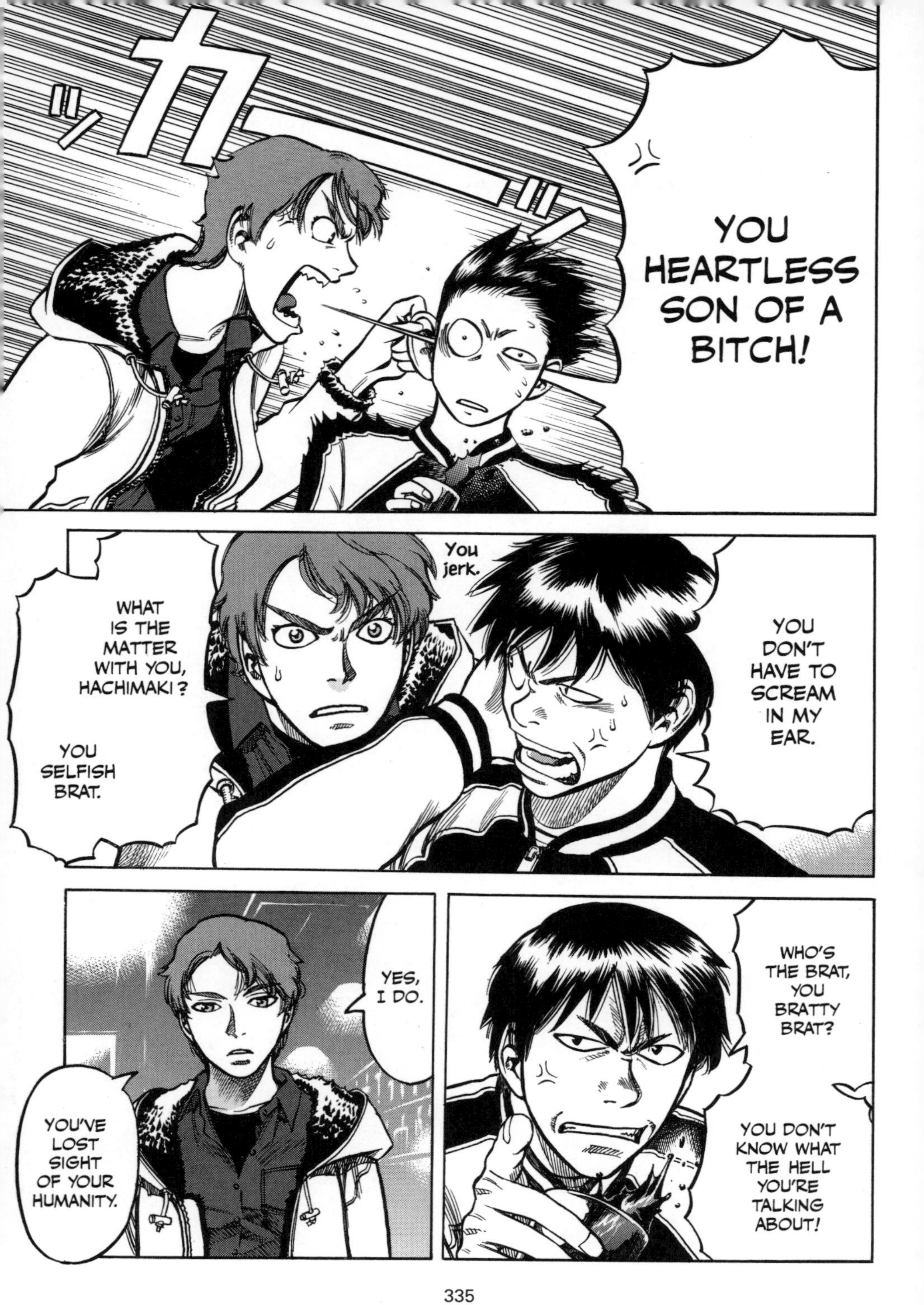
YOU HEARTLESS SON OF A BITCH!
YOU DON'T HAVE TO SCREAM IN MY EAR.
You jerk.
WHAT IS THE MATTER WITH YOU, HACHIMAKI?
YOU SELFISH BRAT.
WHO'S THE BRAT, YOU BRATTY BRAT?
YOU DON'T KNOW WHAT THE HELL YOU'RE TALKING ABOUT!
YES, I DO.
YOU'VE LOST SIGHT OF YOUR HUMANITY.

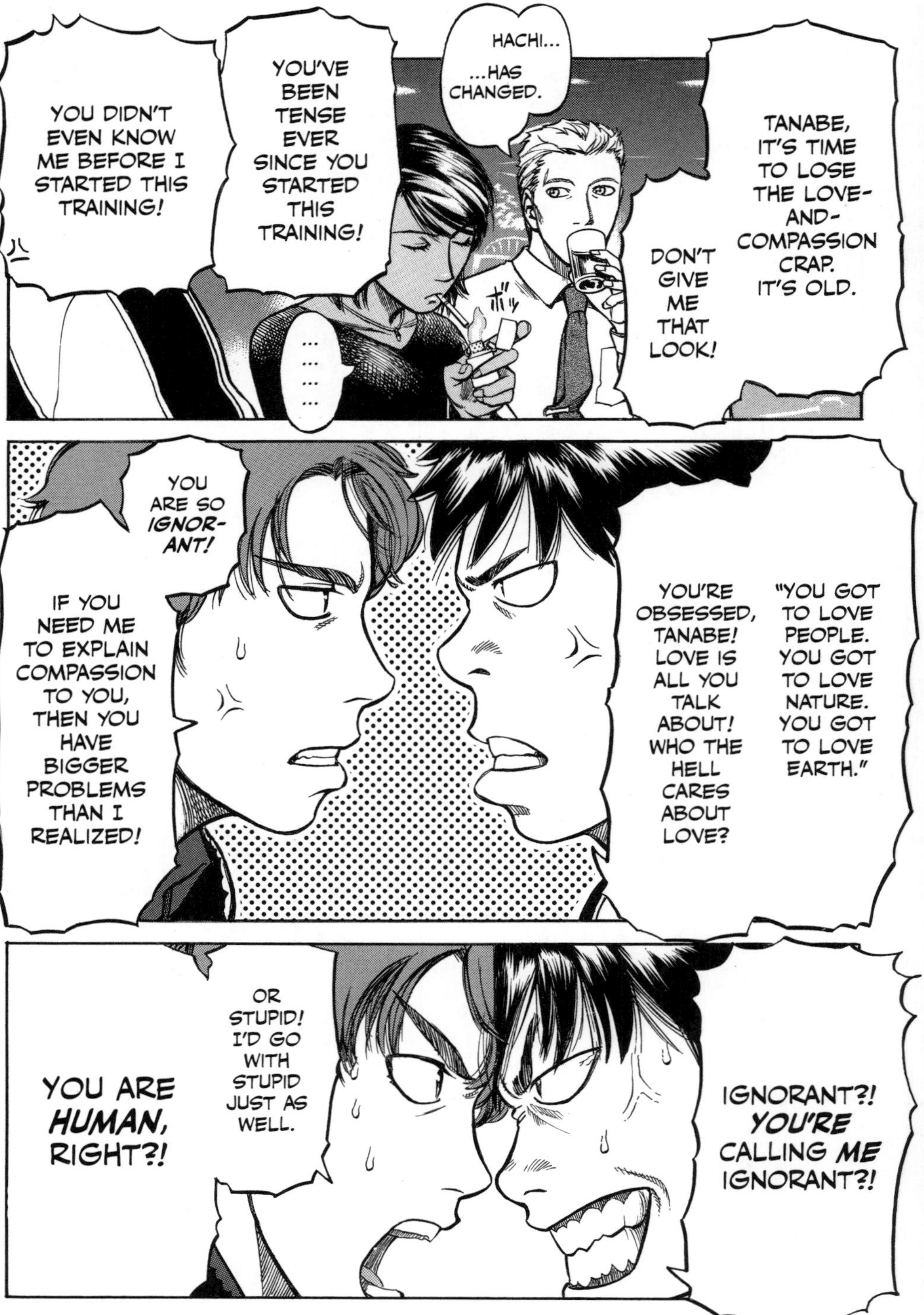
TANABE, IT'S TIME TO LOSE THE LOVE-AND-COMPASSION CRAP. IT'S OLD.
HACHI... ...HAS CHANGED.
DON'T GIVE ME THAT LOOK!
ボッ
YOU'VE BEEN TENSE EVER SINCE YOU STARTED THIS TRAINING!
YOU DIDN'T EVEN KNOW ME BEFORE I STARTED THIS TRAINING!
... ...
"YOU GOT TO LOVE PEOPLE. YOU GOT TO LOVE NATURE. YOU GOT TO LOVE EARTH."
YOU'RE OBSESSED, TANABE! LOVE IS ALL YOU TALK ABOUT! WHO THE HELL CARES ABOUT LOVE?
YOU ARE SO *IGNORANT!*
IF YOU NEED ME TO EXPLAIN COMPASSION TO YOU, THEN YOU HAVE BIGGER PROBLEMS THAN I REALIZED!
IGNORANT?! *YOU'RE* CALLING *ME* IGNORANT?!
OR STUPID! I'D GO WITH STUPID JUST AS WELL.
YOU ARE *HUMAN,* RIGHT?!

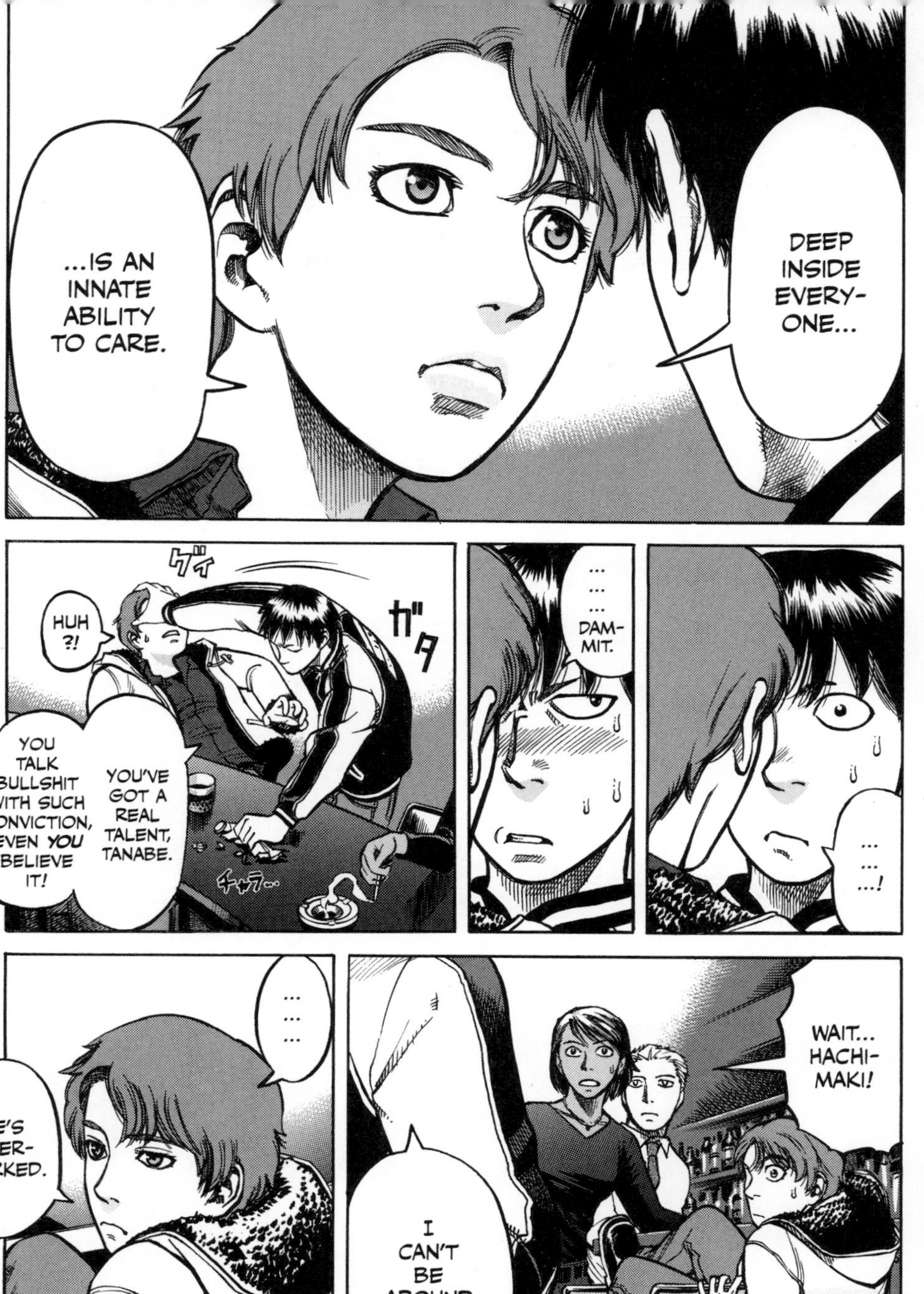
DEEP INSIDE EVERY-ONE...
...IS AN INNATE ABILITY TO CARE.
...
...
...!
...
...
...
DAM-MIT.
ガタ
グィ
HUH?!
YOU'VE GOT A REAL TALENT, TANABE.
YOU TALK BULLSHIT WITH SUCH CONVICTION, EVEN *YOU* BELIEVE IT!
チャラ…
WAIT... HACHI-MAKI!
I CAN'T BE AROUND HER.
...
...
...
HE'S OVER-WORKED.

グギギギギギ
ギギ
EIYA!
ガシャ…
ギギギギ

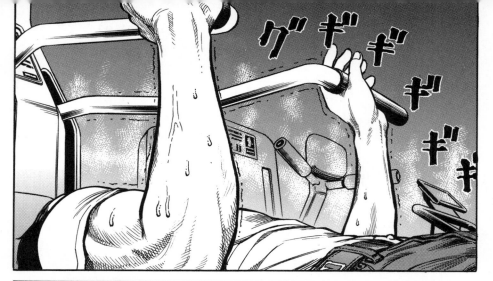

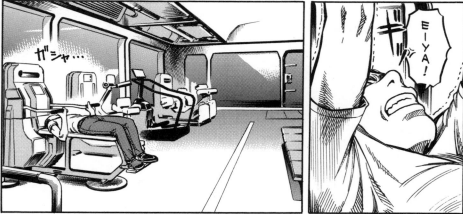

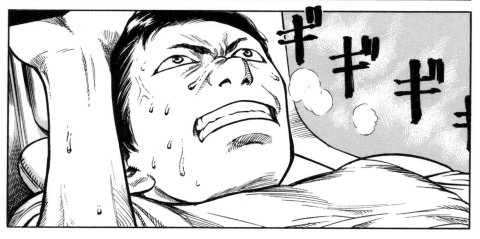

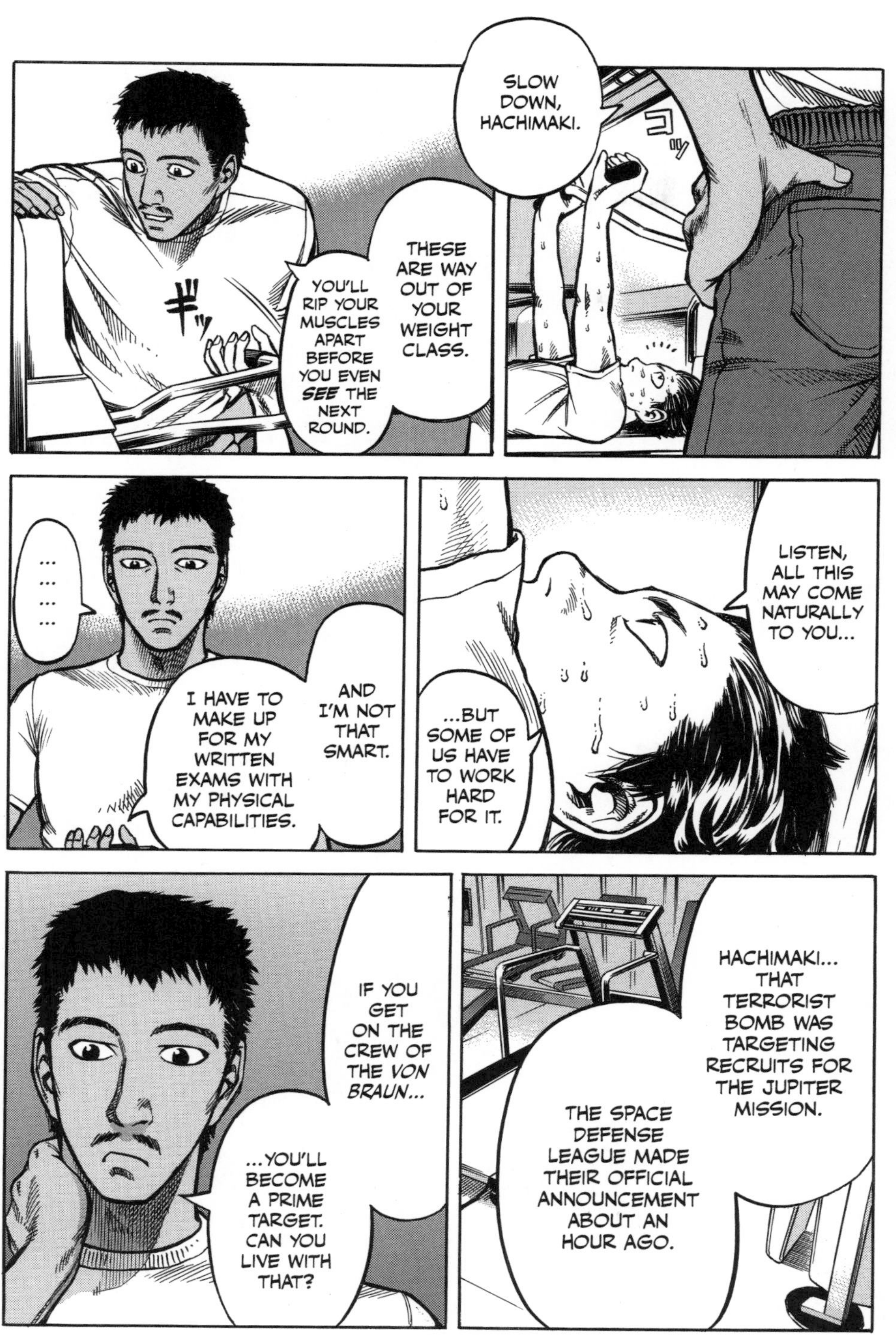
SLOW DOWN, HACHIMAKI.
コッ
THESE ARE WAY OUT OF YOUR WEIGHT CLASS.
YOU'LL RIP YOUR MUSCLES APART BEFORE YOU EVEN *SEE* THE NEXT ROUND.
ギッ
LISTEN, ALL THIS MAY COME NATURALLY TO YOU...
...BUT SOME OF US HAVE TO WORK HARD FOR IT.
AND I'M NOT THAT SMART.
I HAVE TO MAKE UP FOR MY WRITTEN EXAMS WITH MY PHYSICAL CAPABILITIES.
....
HACHIMAKI... THAT TERRORIST BOMB WAS TARGETING RECRUITS FOR THE JUPITER MISSION.
THE SPACE DEFENSE LEAGUE MADE THEIR OFFICIAL ANNOUNCEMENT ABOUT AN HOUR AGO.
IF YOU GET ON THE CREW OF THE *VON BRAUN*...
...YOU'LL BECOME A PRIME TARGET. CAN YOU LIVE WITH THAT?

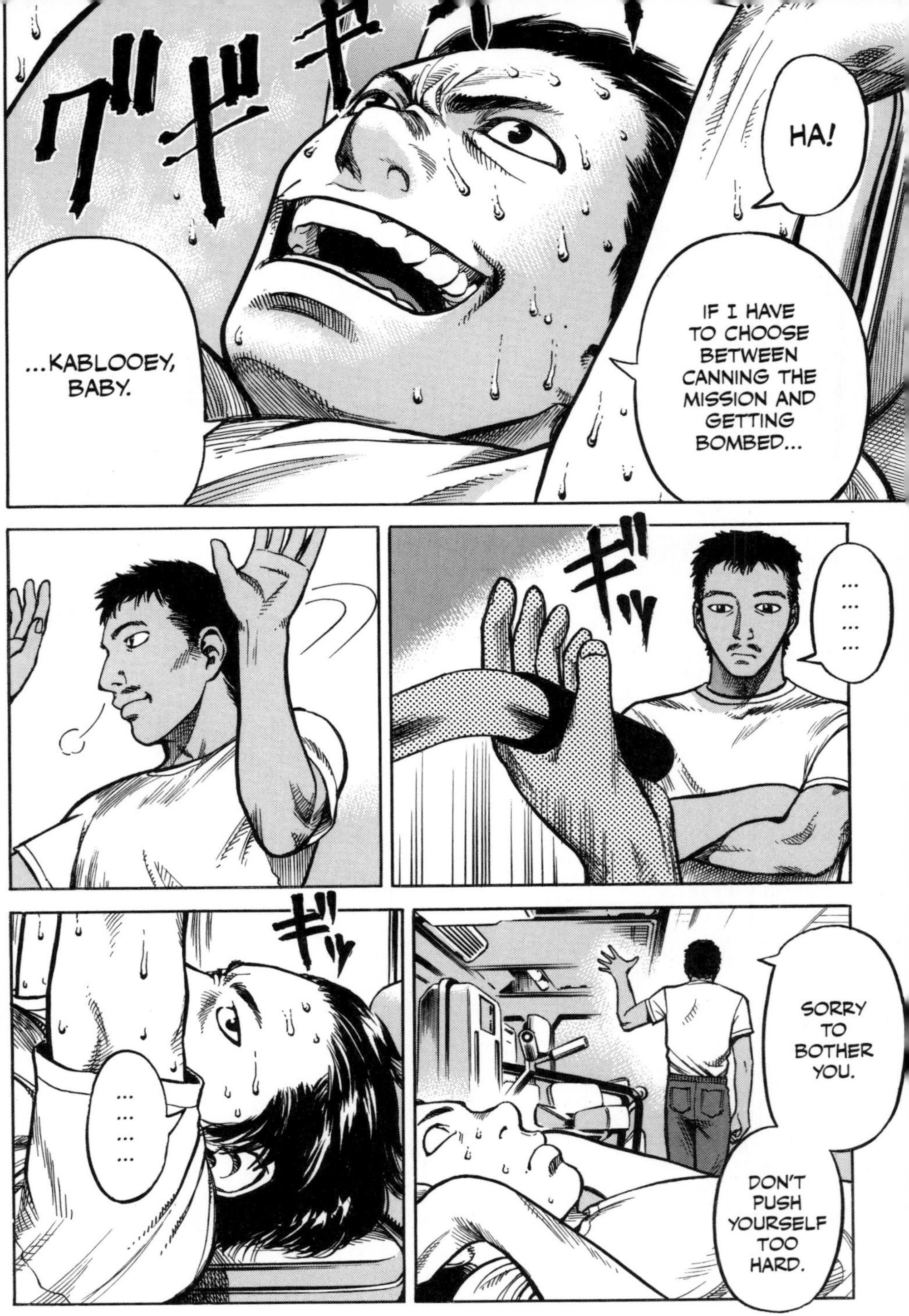
HA!
IF I HAVE TO CHOOSE BETWEEN CANNING THE MISSION AND GETTING BOMBED...
...KABLOOEY, BABY.
ギッ
...
...
...
...
...
SORRY TO BOTHER YOU.
DON'T PUSH YOURSELF TOO HARD.
ギッ
...
...
...
...

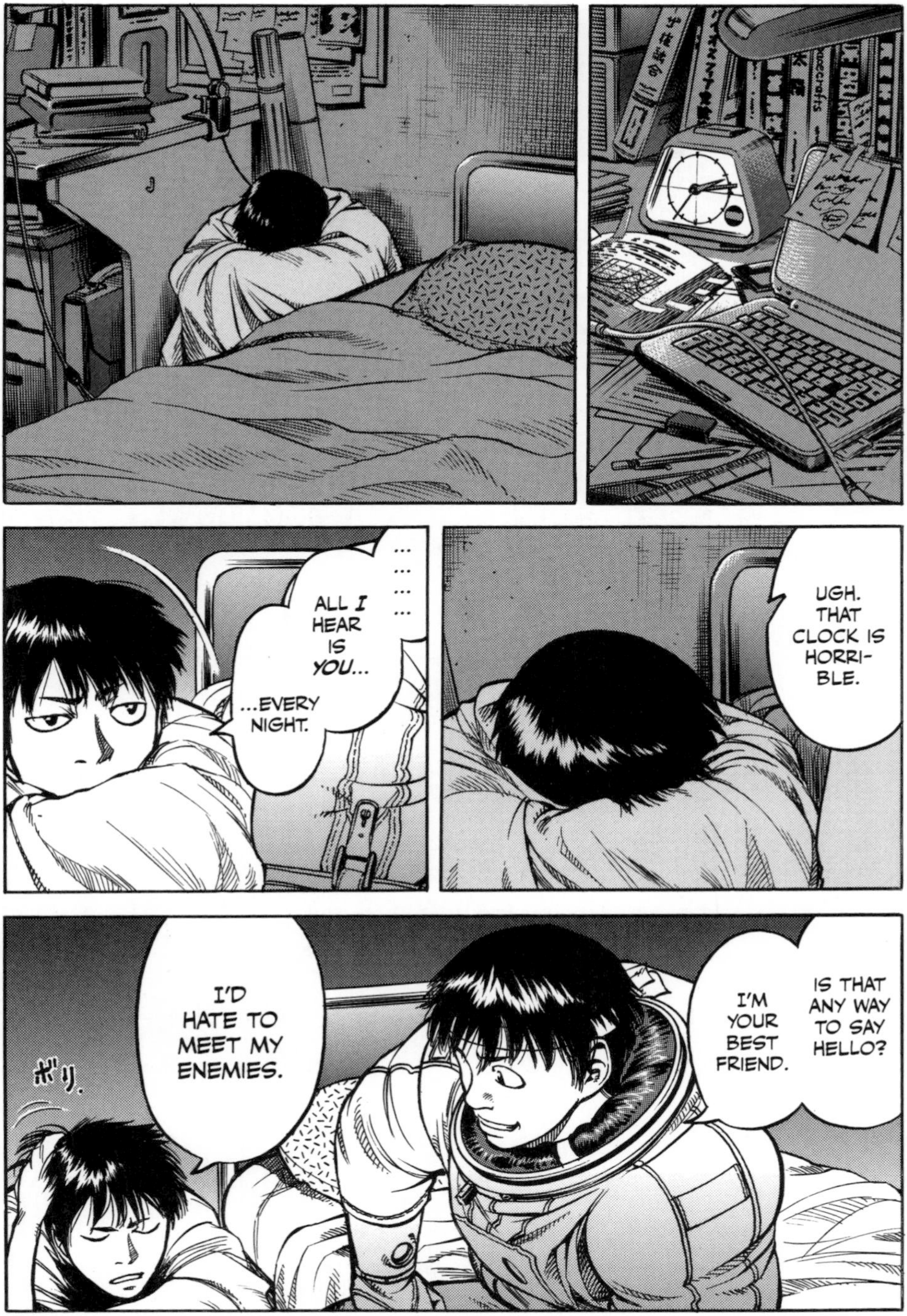
UGH. THAT CLOCK IS HORRIBLE.
... ...
ALL *I* HEAR IS *YOU*...
...EVERY NIGHT.
IS THAT ANY WAY TO SAY HELLO?
I'M YOUR BEST FRIEND.
I'D HATE TO MEET MY ENEMIES.
ボリ.

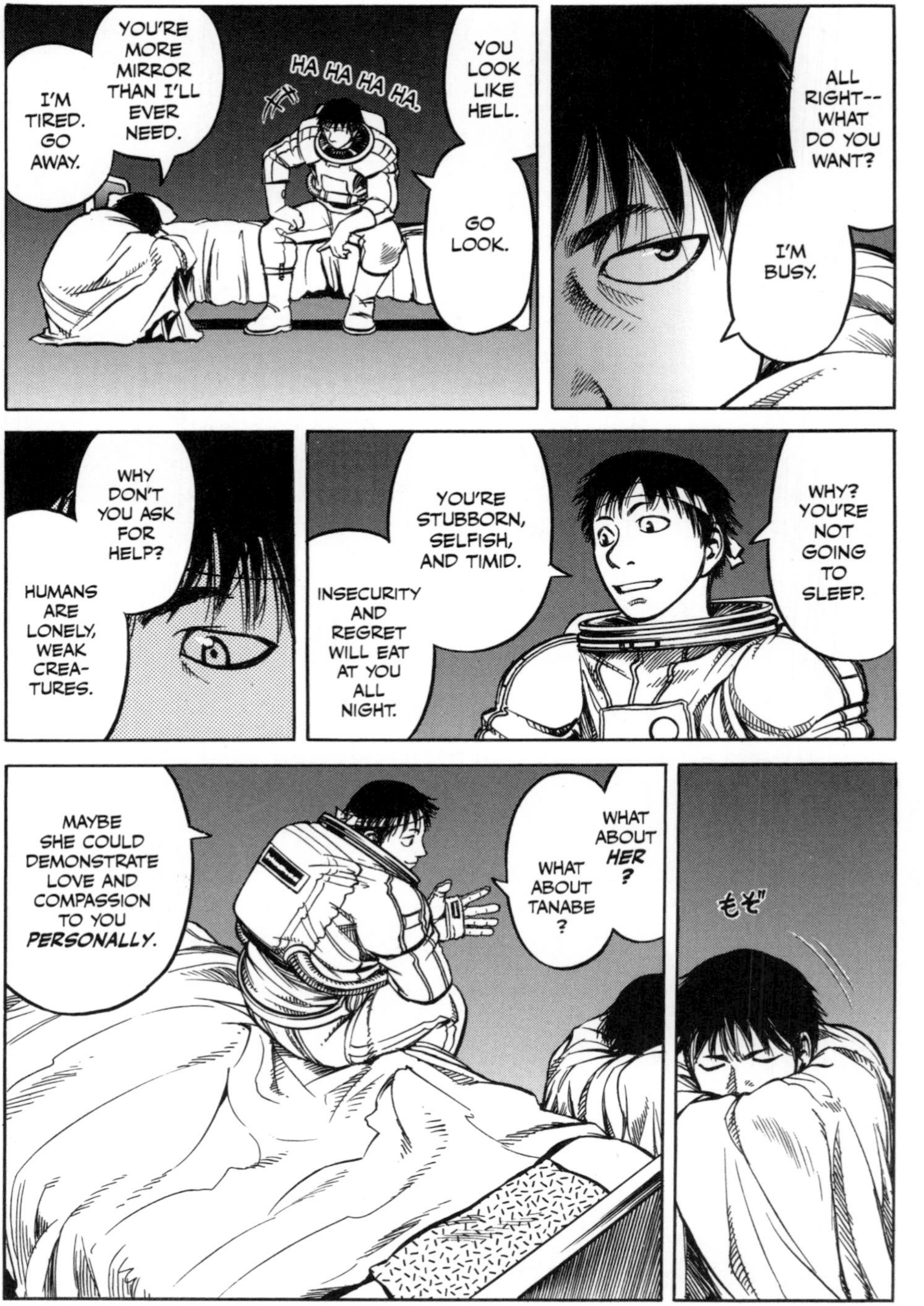
ALL RIGHT-- WHAT DO YOU WANT?
I'M BUSY.
YOU LOOK LIKE HELL.
GO LOOK.
HA HA HA HA.
YOU'RE MORE MIRROR THAN I'LL EVER NEED.
I'M TIRED. GO AWAY.
WHY? YOU'RE NOT GOING TO SLEEP.
YOU'RE STUBBORN, SELFISH, AND TIMID.
INSECURITY AND REGRET WILL EAT AT YOU ALL NIGHT.
WHY DON'T YOU ASK FOR HELP?
HUMANS ARE LONELY, WEAK CREA-TURES.
もぞ
WHAT ABOUT *HER*?
WHAT ABOUT TANABE?
MAYBE SHE COULD DEMONSTRATE LOVE AND COMPASSION TO YOU *PERSONALLY*.

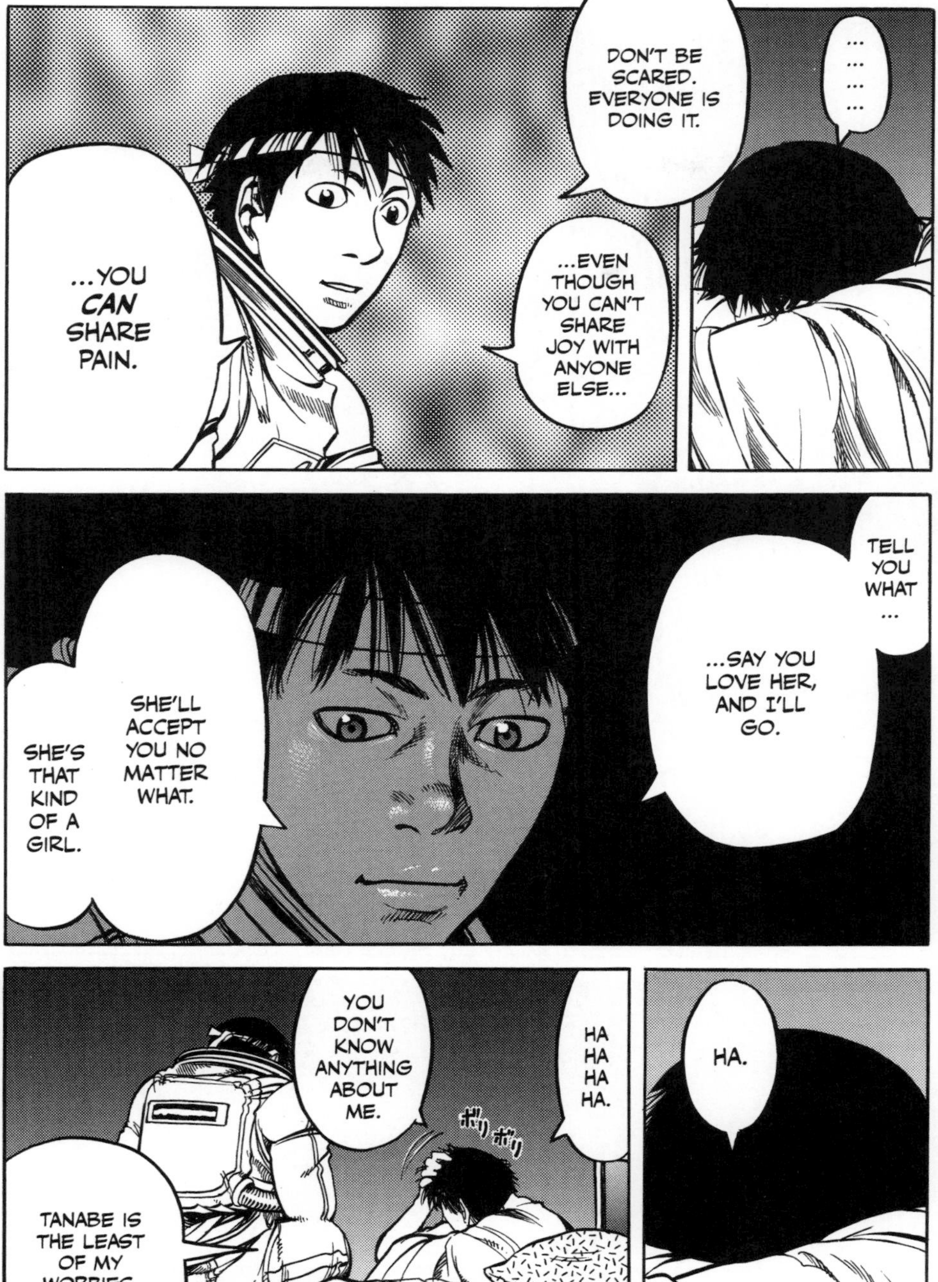
... ...
DON'T BE SCARED. EVERYONE IS DOING IT.
...EVEN THOUGH YOU CAN'T SHARE JOY WITH ANYONE ELSE...
...YOU *CAN* SHARE PAIN.
TELL YOU WHAT ...
...SAY YOU LOVE HER, AND I'LL GO.
SHE'LL ACCEPT YOU NO MATTER WHAT.
SHE'S THAT KIND OF A GIRL.
HA.
HA HA HA HA.
YOU DON'T KNOW ANYTHING ABOUT ME.
ボリ ボリ
TANABE IS THE LEAST OF MY WORRIES.

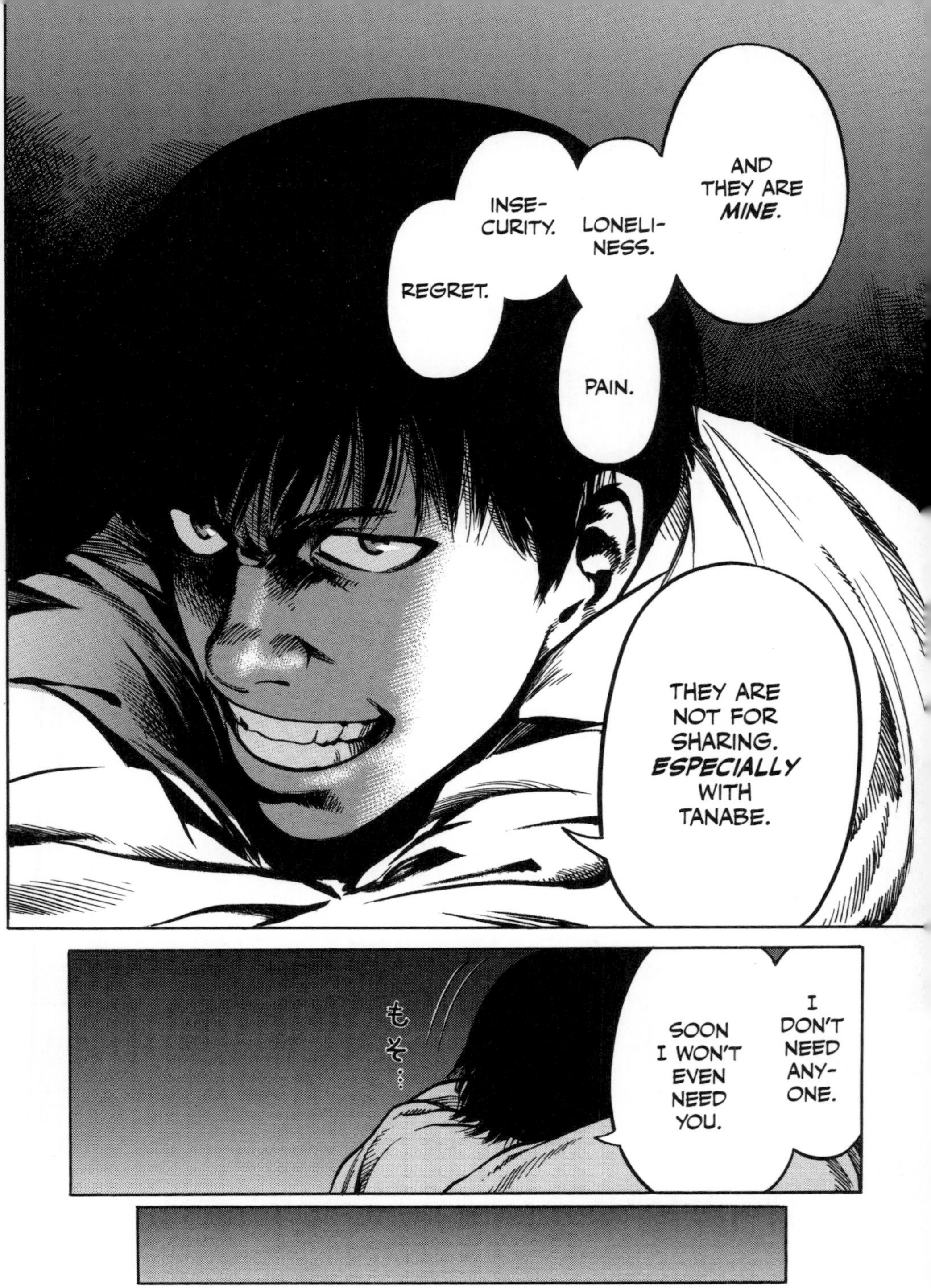
AND THEY ARE *MINE.*
LONELI-NESS.
INSE-CURITY.
REGRET.
PAIN.
THEY ARE NOT FOR SHARING. ***ESPECIALLY*** WITH TANABE.
I DON'T NEED ANY-ONE.
SOON I WON'T EVEN NEED YOU.
もぞ…

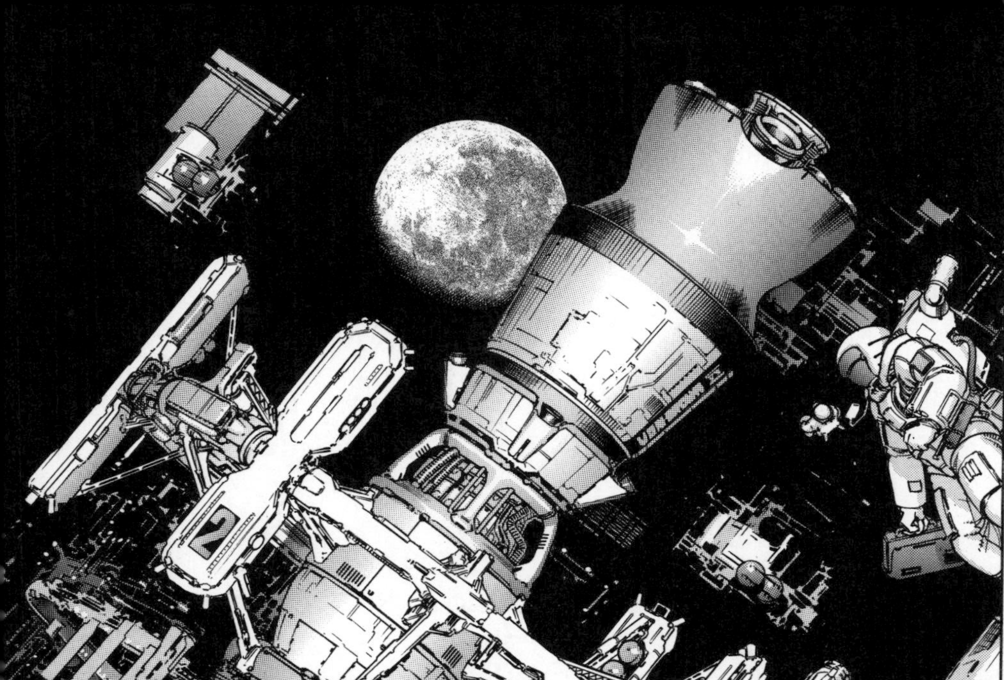
Manned Jupiter mission vessel *Von Braun*. Lagrange 2.

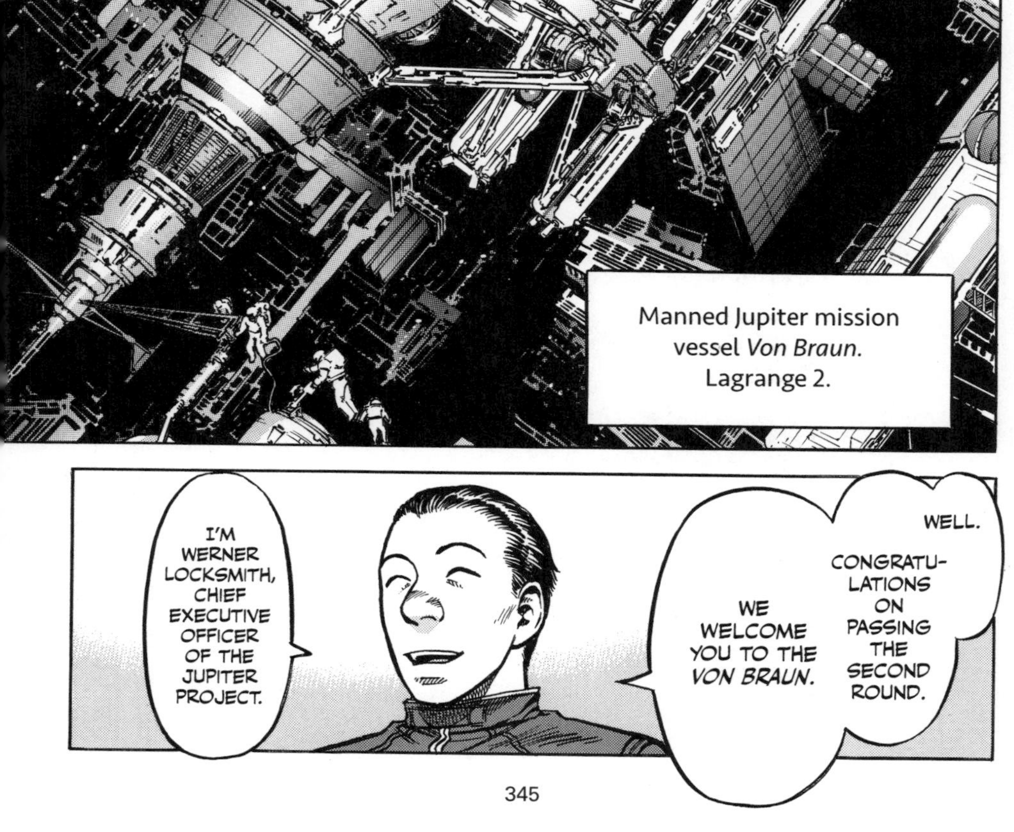
WELL.
CONGRATU-LATIONS ON PASSING THE SECOND ROUND.
WE WELCOME YOU TO THE *VON BRAUN*.
I'M WERNER LOCKSMITH, CHIEF EXECUTIVE OFFICER OF THE JUPITER PROJECT.

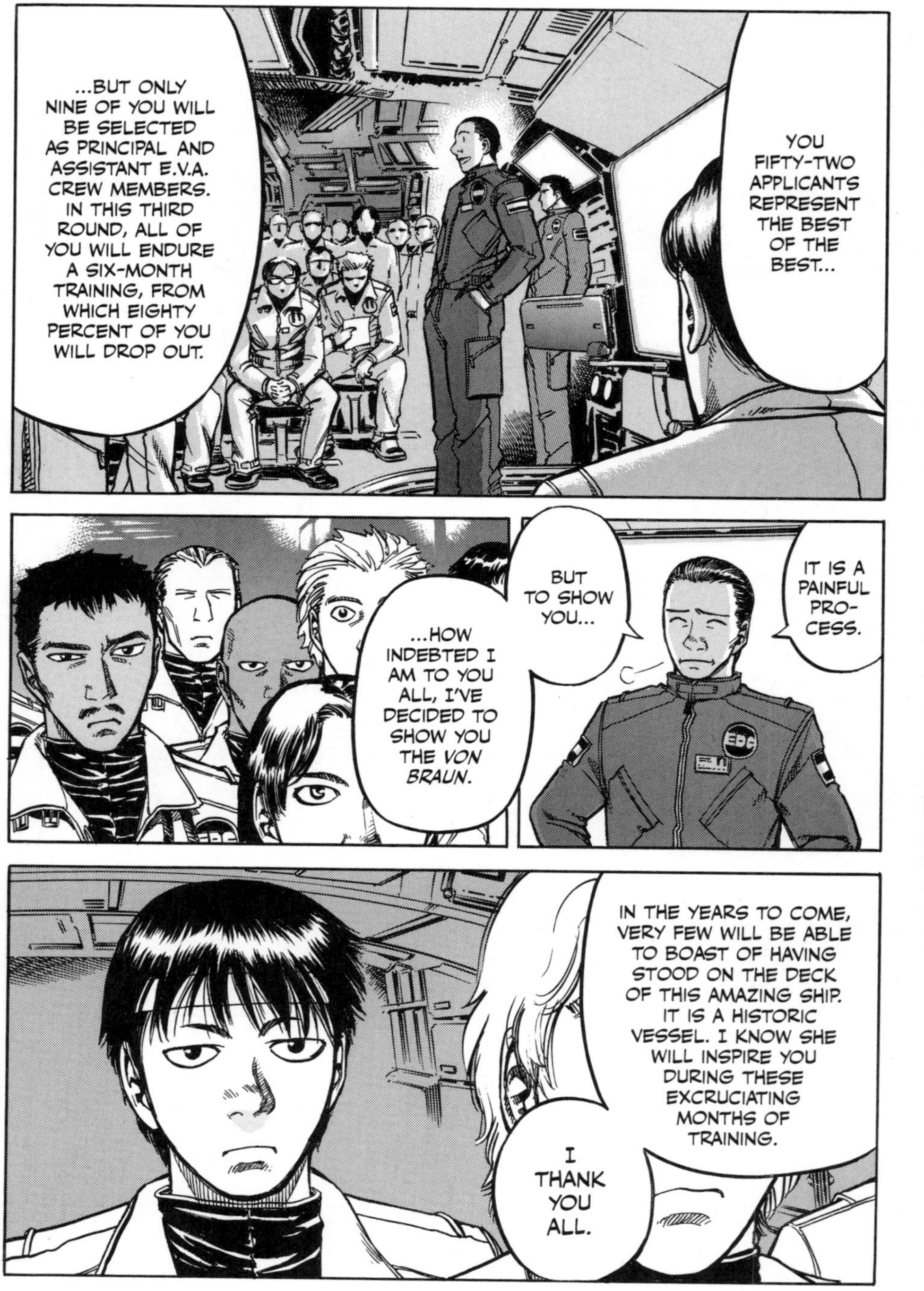
YOU FIFTY-TWO APPLICANTS REPRESENT THE BEST OF THE BEST...
...BUT ONLY NINE OF YOU WILL BE SELECTED AS PRINCIPAL AND ASSISTANT E.V.A. CREW MEMBERS. IN THIS THIRD ROUND, ALL OF YOU WILL ENDURE A SIX-MONTH TRAINING, FROM WHICH EIGHTY PERCENT OF YOU WILL DROP OUT.
IT IS A PAINFUL PRO-CESS.
BUT TO SHOW YOU...
...HOW INDEBTED I AM TO YOU ALL, I'VE DECIDED TO SHOW YOU THE *VON BRAUN*.
IN THE YEARS TO COME, VERY FEW WILL BE ABLE TO BOAST OF HAVING STOOD ON THE DECK OF THIS AMAZING SHIP. IT IS A HISTORIC VESSEL. I KNOW SHE WILL INSPIRE YOU DURING THESE EXCRUCIATING MONTHS OF TRAINING.
I THANK YOU ALL.

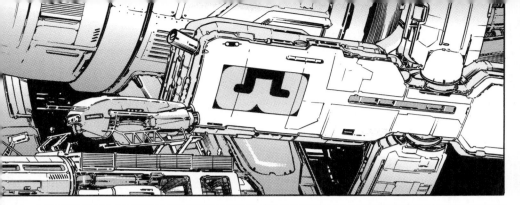

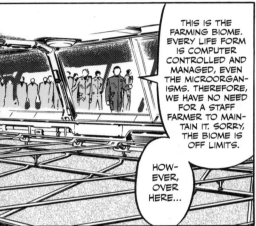

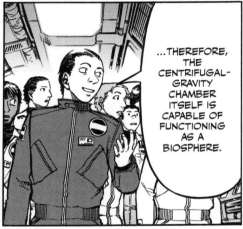

...THEREFORE, THE CENTRIFUGAL-GRAVITY CHAMBER ITSELF IS CAPABLE OF FUNCTIONING AS A BIOSPHERE.
THIS IS THE FARMING BIOME. EVERY LIFE FORM IS COMPUTER CONTROLLED AND MANAGED, EVEN THE MICROORGANISMS. THEREFORE, WE HAVE NO NEED FOR A STAFF FARMER TO MAINTAIN IT. SORRY, THE BIOME IS OFF LIMITS.
HOWEVER, OVER HERE...
ス....
HEY!
YOU LOST?

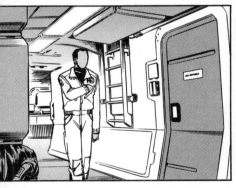

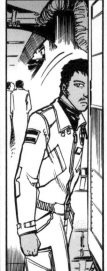

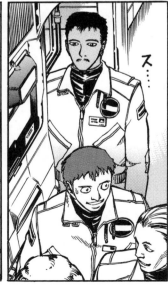

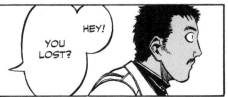

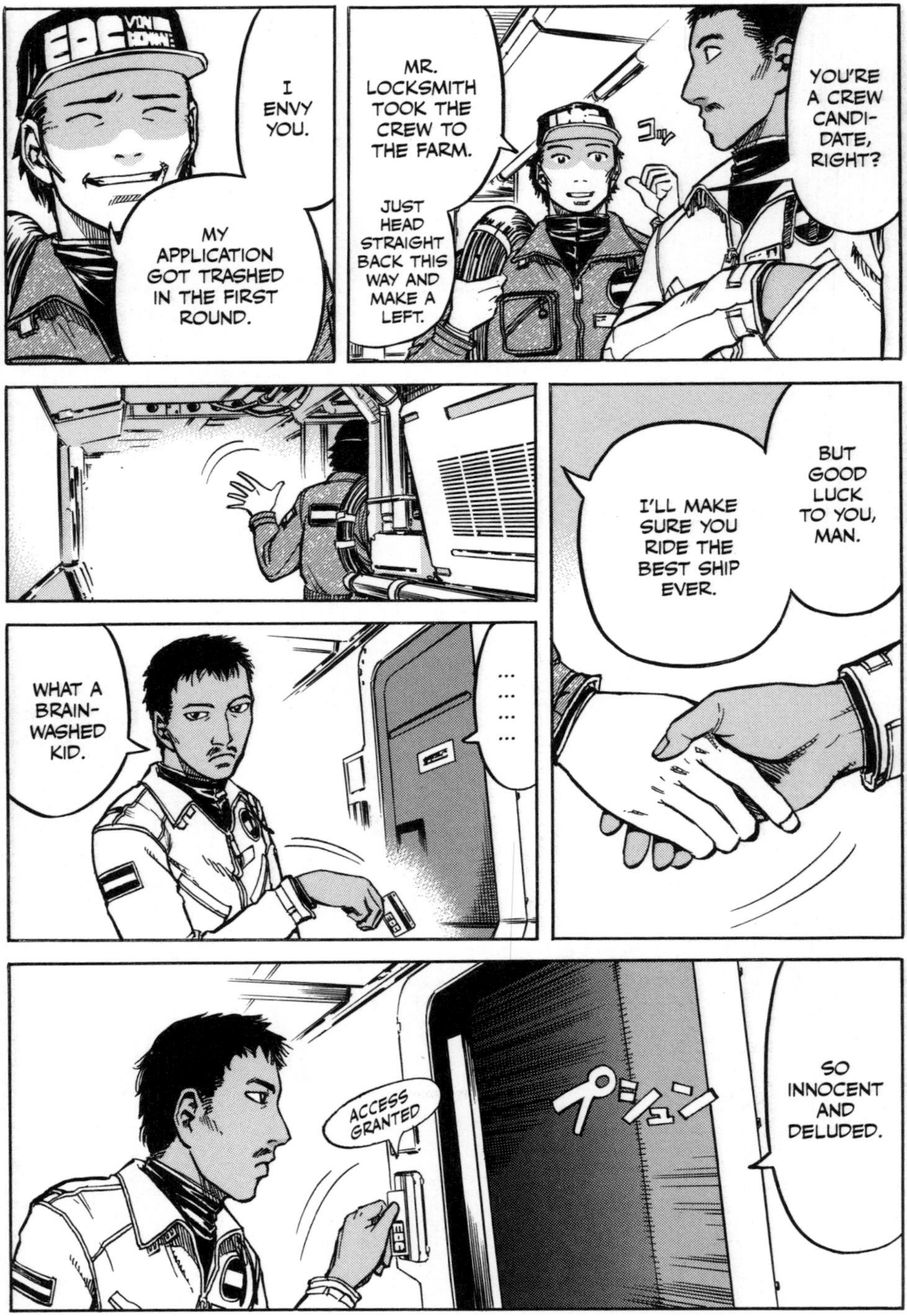
YOU'RE A CREW CANDI- DATE, RIGHT?
コッ
MR. LOCKSMITH TOOK THE CREW TO THE FARM.
JUST HEAD STRAIGHT BACK THIS WAY AND MAKE A LEFT.
I ENVY YOU.
MY APPLICATION GOT TRASHED IN THE FIRST ROUND.
BUT GOOD LUCK TO YOU, MAN.
I'LL MAKE SURE YOU RIDE THE BEST SHIP EVER.
... ...
WHAT A BRAIN- WASHED KID.
SO INNOCENT AND DELUDED.
プシュー
ACCESS GRANTED

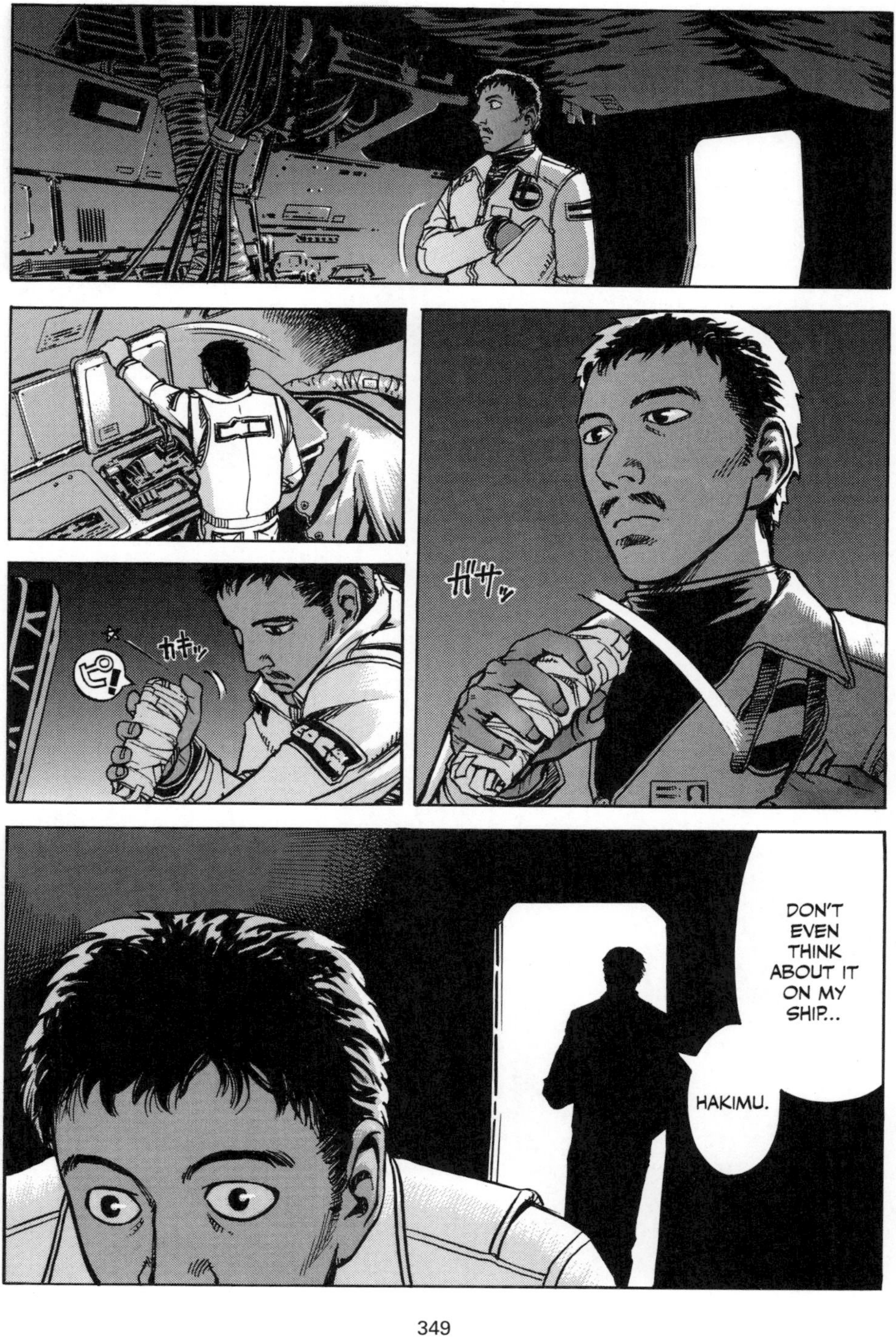
ガサッ
カキッ
ピ!
DON'T EVEN THINK ABOUT IT ON MY SHIP...
HAKIMU.

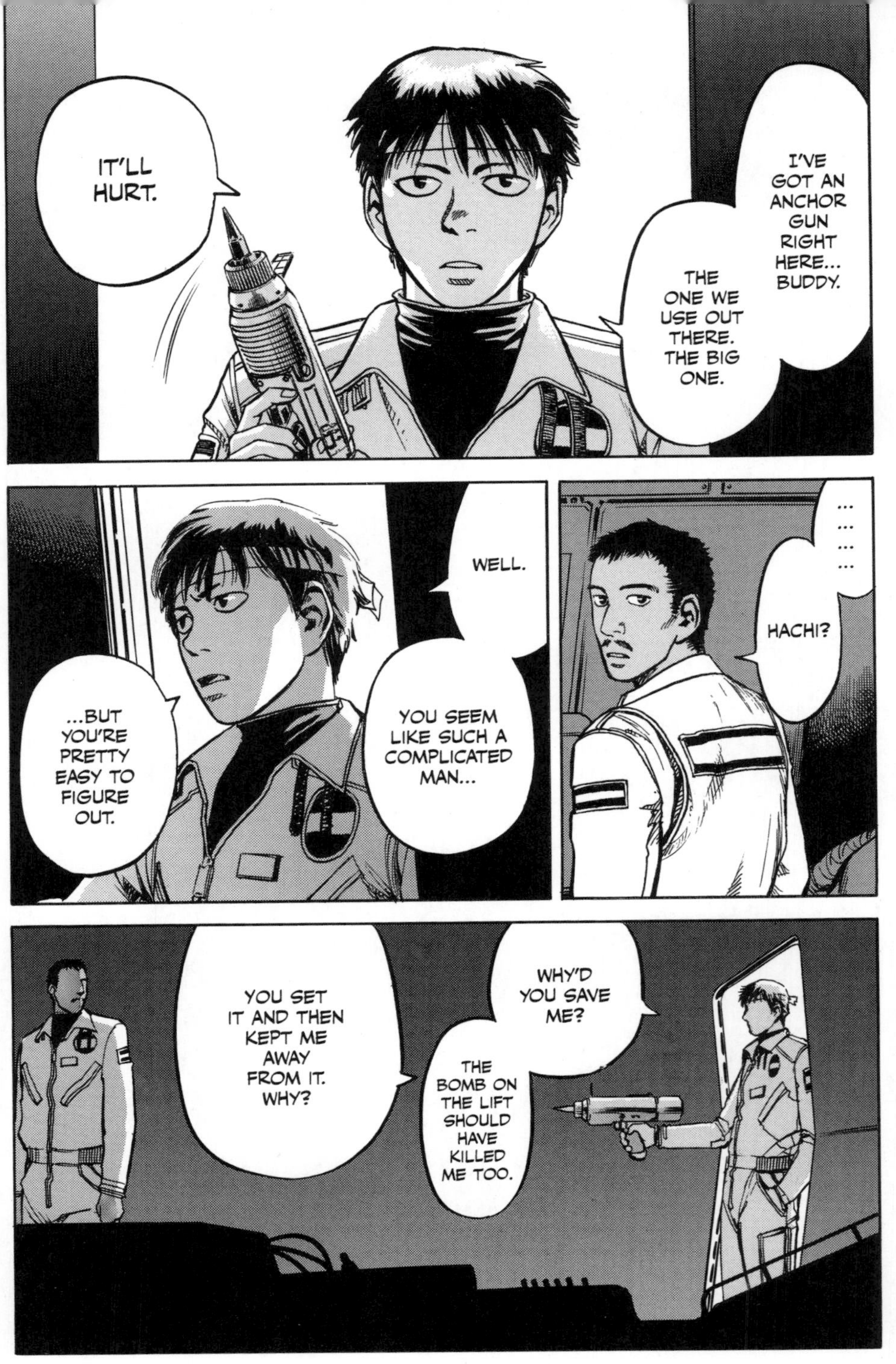

I'VE GOT AN ANCHOR GUN RIGHT HERE... BUDDY.
THE ONE WE USE OUT THERE. THE BIG ONE.
IT'LL HURT.
....
HACHI?
WELL.
YOU SEEM LIKE SUCH A COMPLICATED MAN...
...BUT YOU'RE PRETTY EASY TO FIGURE OUT.
WHY'D YOU SAVE ME?
THE BOMB ON THE LIFT SHOULD HAVE KILLED ME TOO.
YOU SET IT AND THEN KEPT ME AWAY FROM IT. WHY?

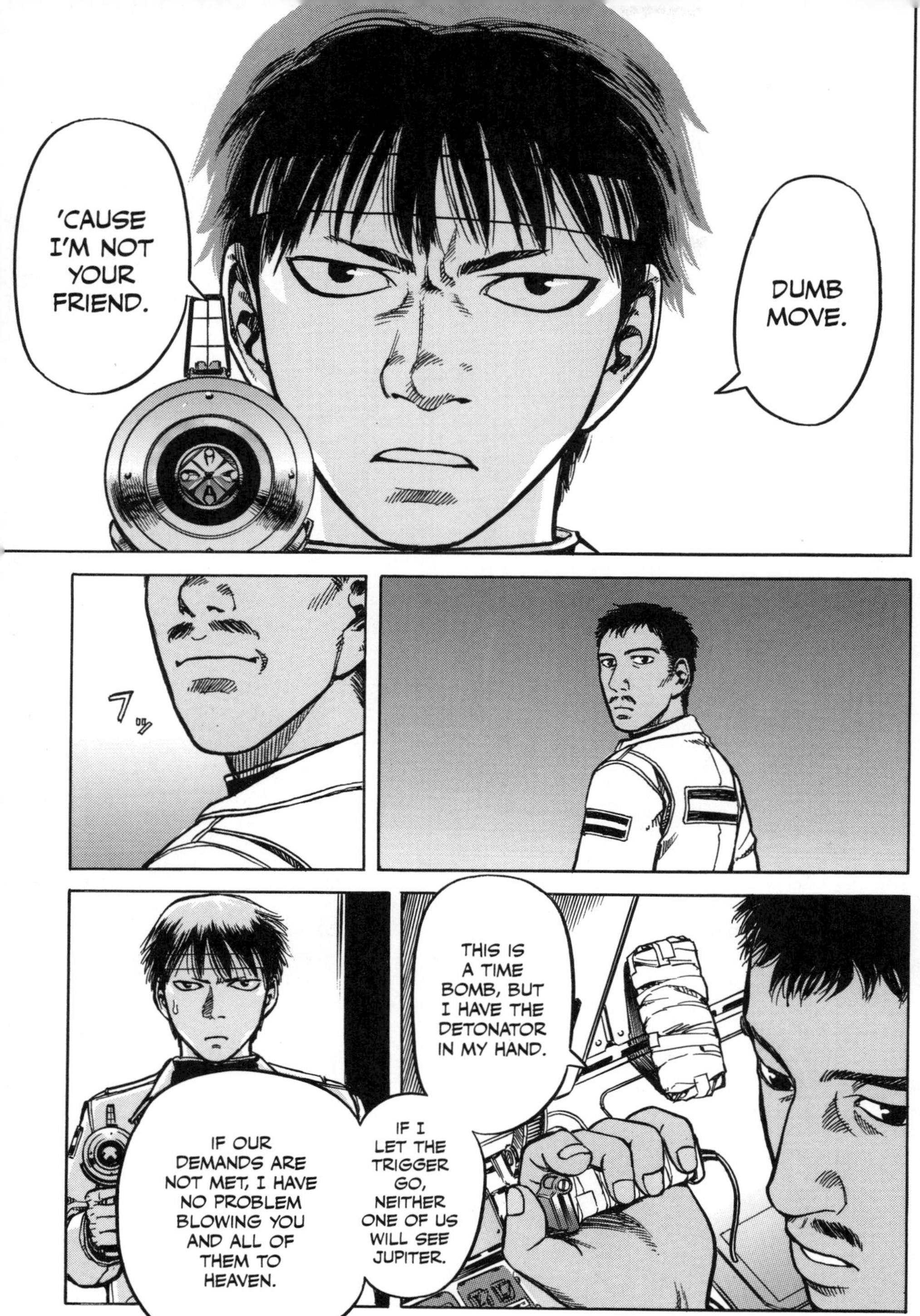
DUMB MOVE.
'CAUSE I'M NOT YOUR FRIEND.
フッ
THIS IS A TIME BOMB, BUT I HAVE THE DETONATOR IN MY HAND.
IF I LET THE TRIGGER GO, NEITHER ONE OF US WILL SEE JUPITER.
IF OUR DEMANDS ARE NOT MET, I HAVE NO PROBLEM BLOWING YOU AND ALL OF THEM TO HEAVEN.

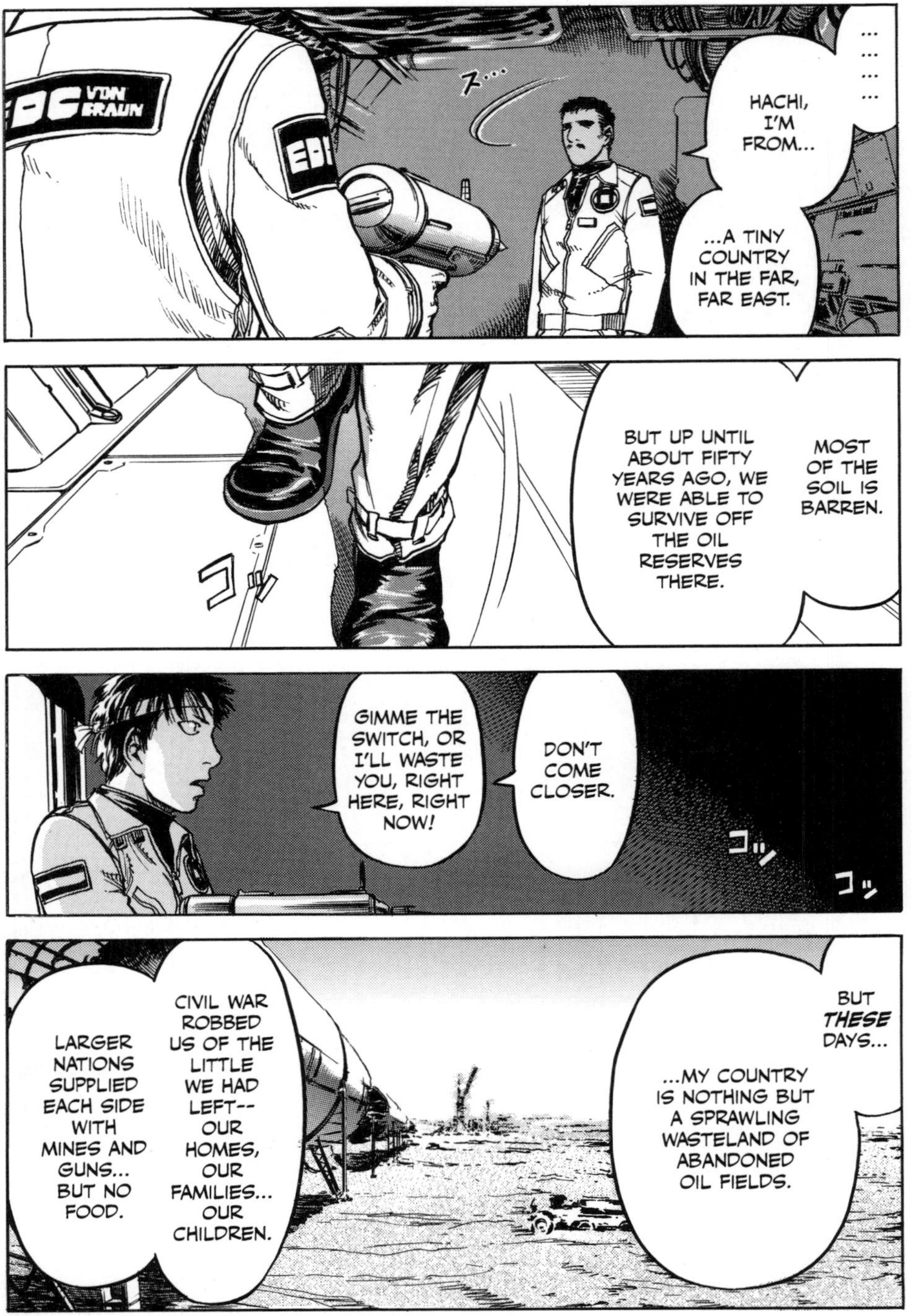
....
ス...
HACHI, I'M FROM...
...A TINY COUNTRY IN THE FAR, FAR EAST.
MOST OF THE SOIL IS BARREN.
BUT UP UNTIL ABOUT FIFTY YEARS AGO, WE WERE ABLE TO SURVIVE OFF THE OIL RESERVES THERE.
コッ
コッ
コッ
DON'T COME CLOSER.
GIMME THE SWITCH, OR I'LL WASTE YOU, RIGHT HERE, RIGHT NOW!
BUT ***THESE*** DAYS...
...MY COUNTRY IS NOTHING BUT A SPRAWLING WASTELAND OF ABANDONED OIL FIELDS.
CIVIL WAR ROBBED US OF THE LITTLE WE HAD LEFT-- OUR HOMES, OUR FAMILIES... OUR CHILDREN.
LARGER NATIONS SUPPLIED EACH SIDE WITH MINES AND GUNS... BUT NO FOOD.

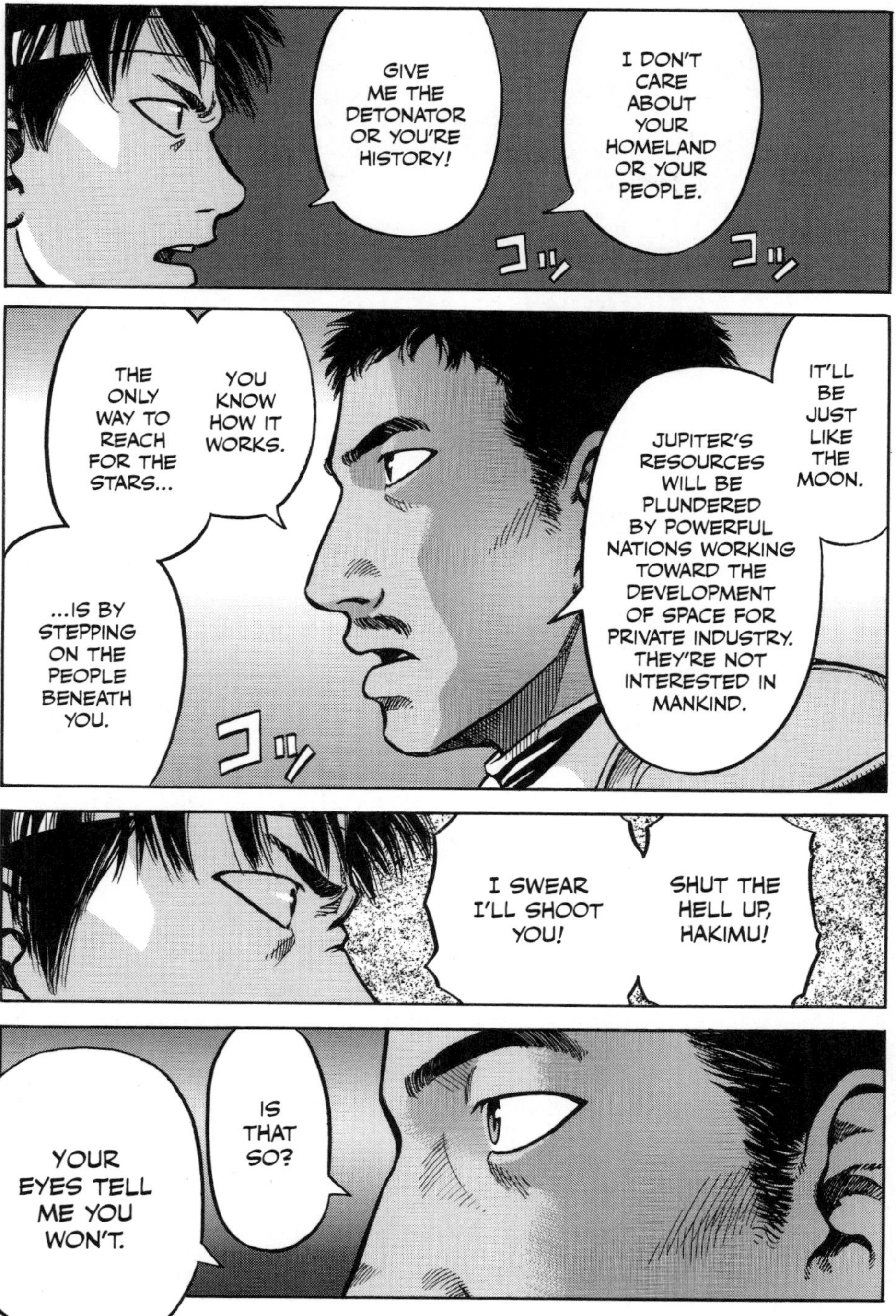
I DON'T CARE ABOUT YOUR HOMELAND OR YOUR PEOPLE.
GIVE ME THE DETONATOR OR YOU'RE HISTORY!
コッ
コッ
IT'LL BE JUST LIKE THE MOON.
JUPITER'S RESOURCES WILL BE PLUNDERED BY POWERFUL NATIONS WORKING TOWARD THE DEVELOPMENT OF SPACE FOR PRIVATE INDUSTRY. THEY'RE NOT INTERESTED IN MANKIND.
YOU KNOW HOW IT WORKS.
THE ONLY WAY TO REACH FOR THE STARS...
...IS BY STEPPING ON THE PEOPLE BENEATH YOU.
コッ
SHUT THE HELL UP, HAKIMU!
I SWEAR I'LL SHOOT YOU!
IS THAT SO?
YOUR EYES TELL ME YOU WON'T.

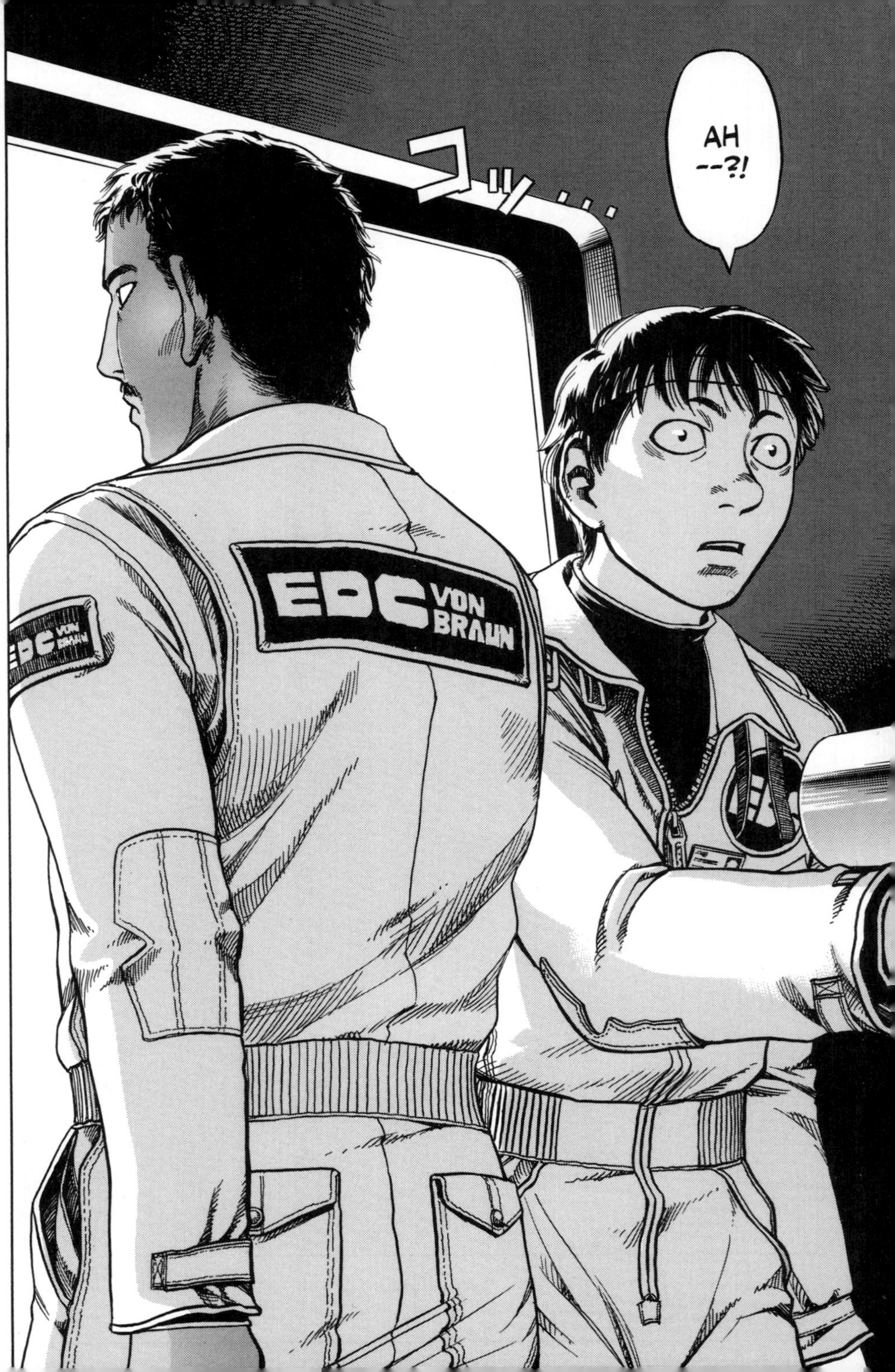
AH --?!
コッ・・・
EDC VON BRAUN
EDC VON BRAUN

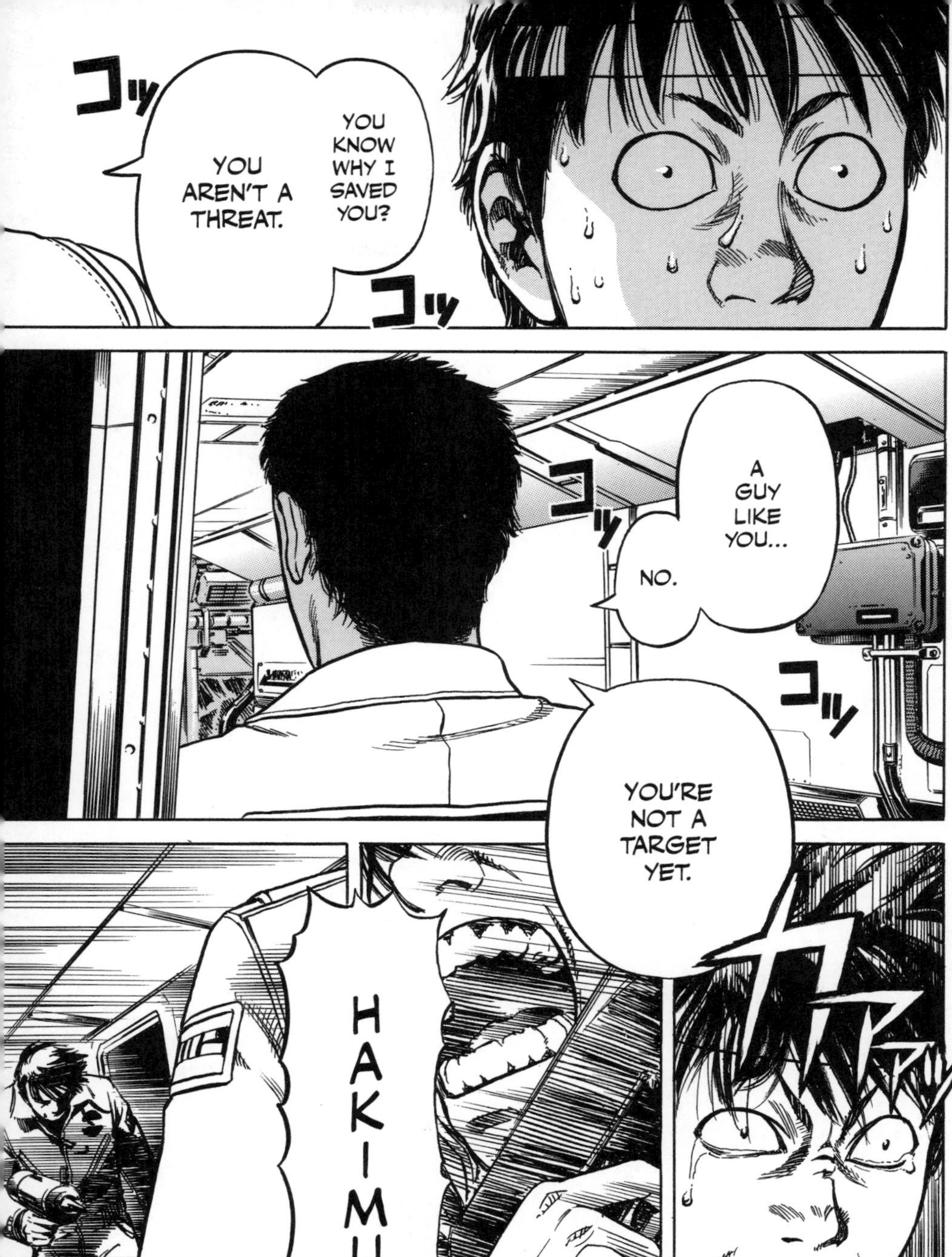
コッ
YOU KNOW WHY I SAVED YOU?
YOU AREN'T A THREAT.
コッ
A GUY LIKE YOU...
NO.
コッ
コッ
YOU'RE NOT A TARGET YET.
HAKIMU!

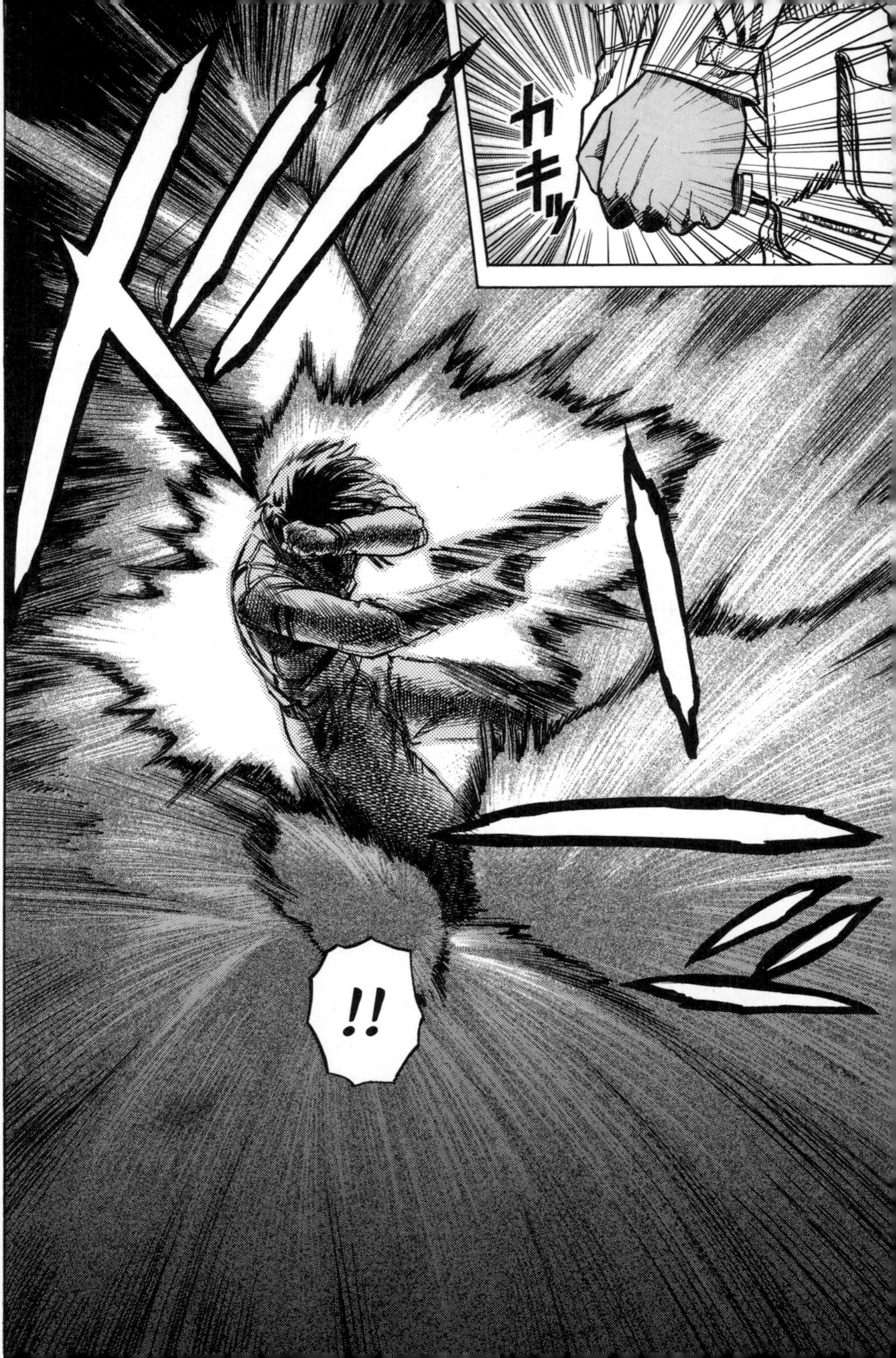
カキッ
!!

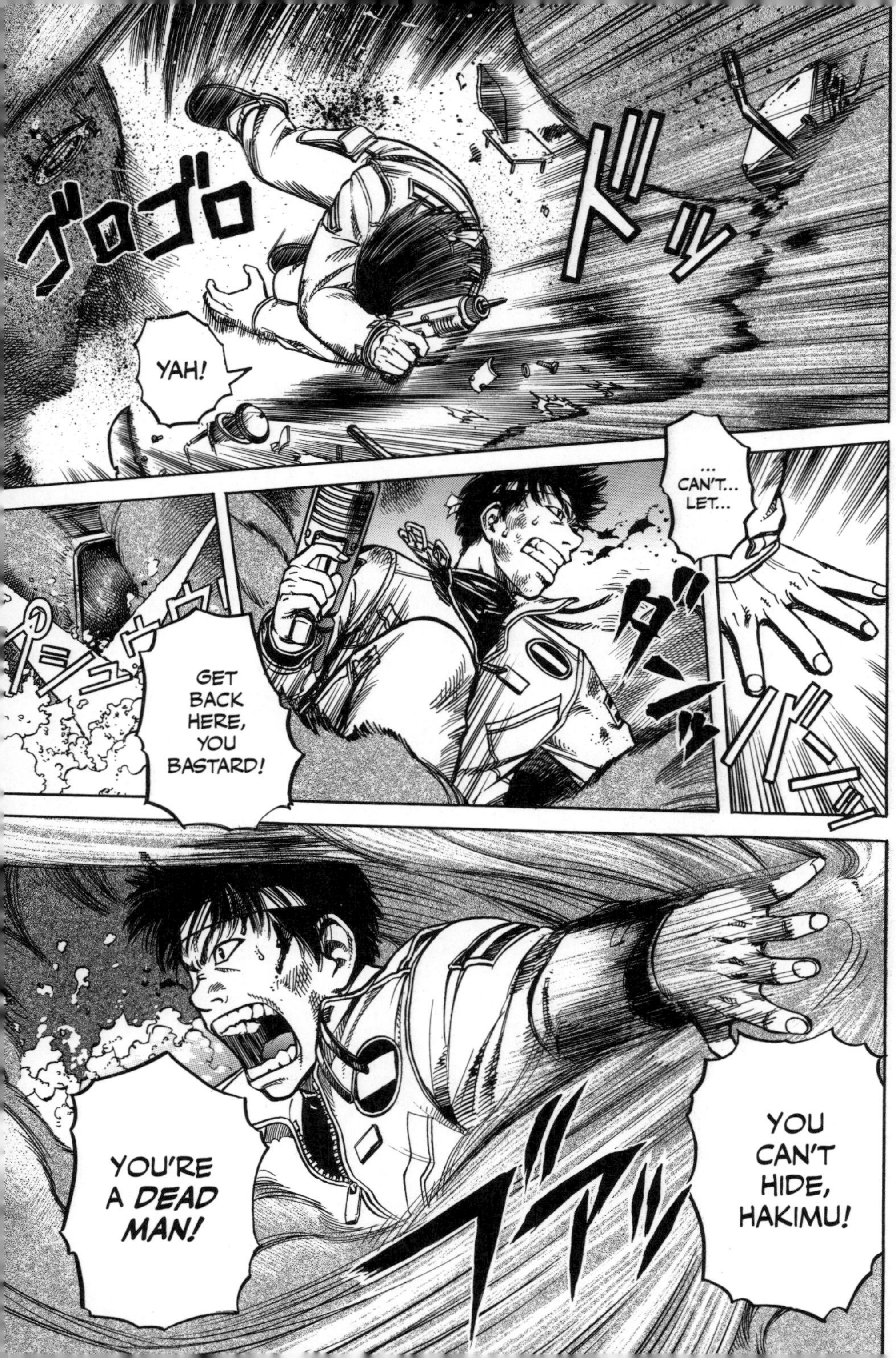
ゴロゴロ
YAH!
...CAN'T... LET...
GET BACK HERE, YOU BASTARD!
YOU CAN'T HIDE, HAKIMU!
YOU'RE A DEAD MAN!

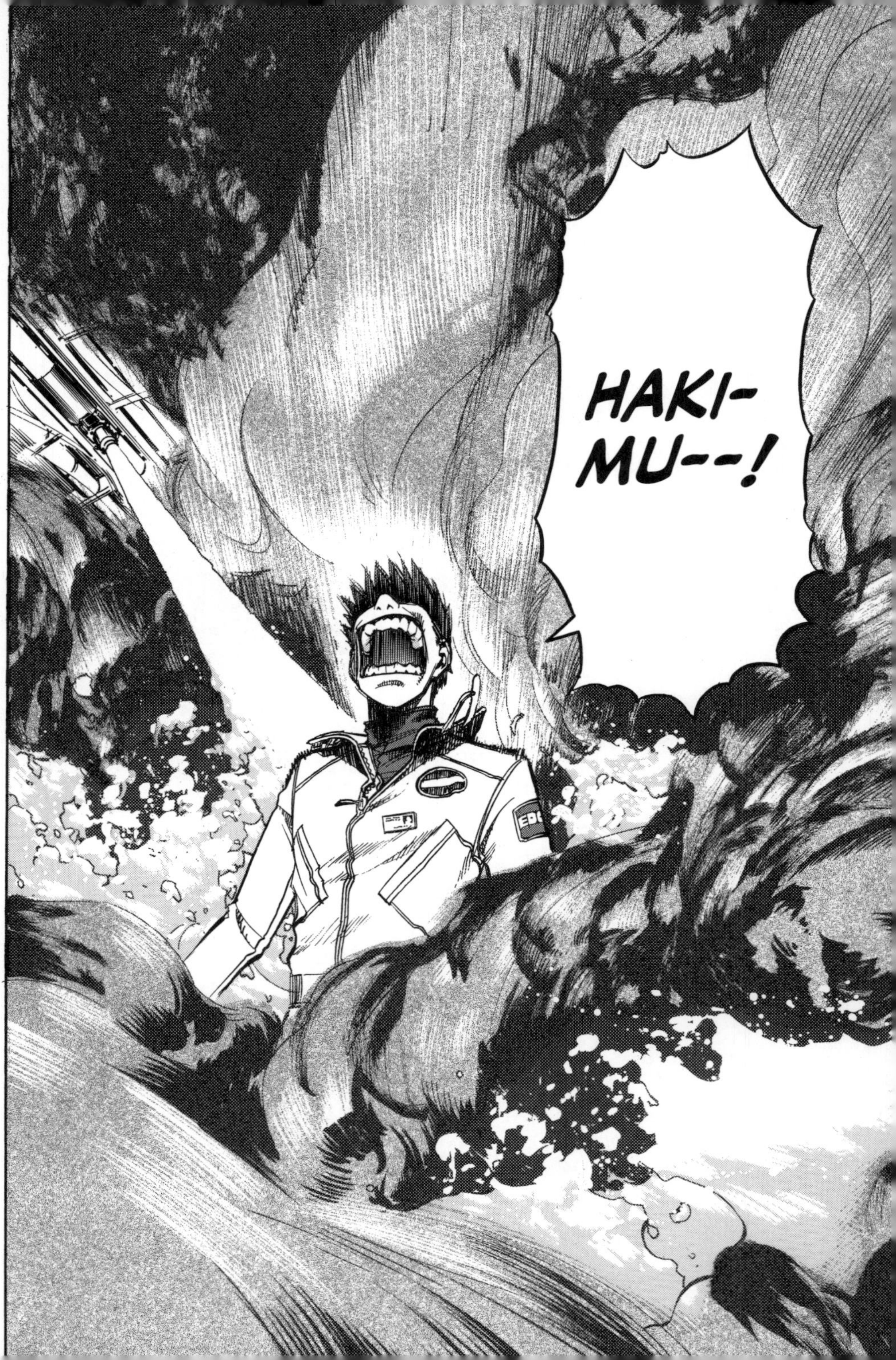
HAKI-MU--!

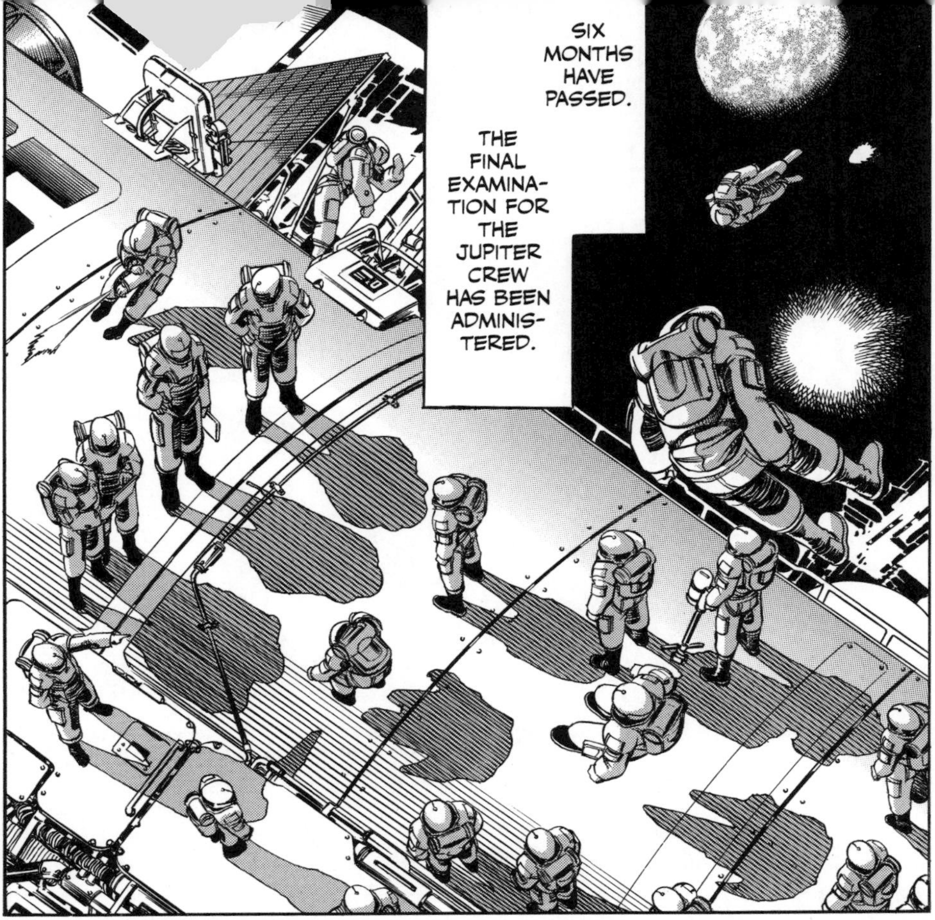
SIX MONTHS HAVE PASSED.
THE FINAL EXAMINATION FOR THE JUPITER CREW HAS BEEN ADMINISTERED.

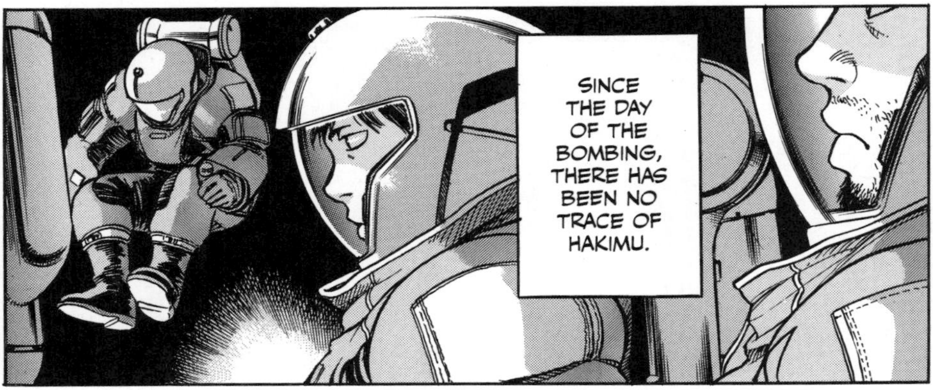
SINCE THE DAY OF THE BOMBING, THERE HAS BEEN NO TRACE OF HAKIMU.

ALL RIGHT, EVERYONE, THE EXAM RESULTS ARE IN.

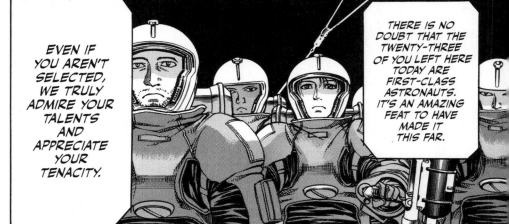

THERE IS NO DOUBT THAT THE TWENTY-THREE OF YOU LEFT HERE TODAY ARE FIRST-CLASS ASTRONAUTS. IT'S AN AMAZING FEAT TO HAVE MADE IT THIS FAR.

EVEN IF YOU AREN'T SELECTED, WE TRULY ADMIRE YOUR TALENTS AND APPRECIATE YOUR TENACITY.

I'M SURE ALL OF YOU WILL PLAY A CRUCIAL ROLE IN THE FUTURE OF THE SOLAR SYSTEM.

YOU SHOULD BE VERY PROUD OF YOUR-SELVES.

NONE OF THE EXAMINERS HAVE SAID A WORD ABOUT HIM.

"YOU'RE NOT OUR TARGET YET."   "NO.   "A GUY LIKE YOU...

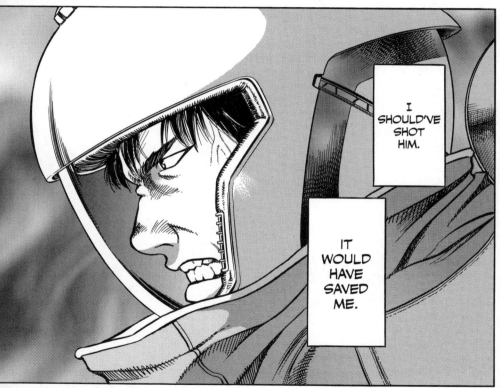

I SHOULD'VE SHOT HIM.

IT WOULD HAVE SAVED ME.

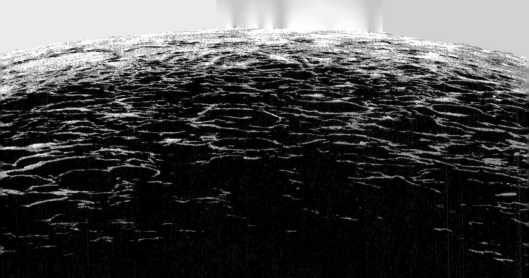

Beat them down! Beat them down!
Those who have worked hard only to waste away
 drinking . . .
Those who have sought to learn about the world
 only to conclude that it is a barren wasteland . . .
Those who have excelled in life only to lord over
 their fellow man . . .
Tear them all down!
Get those devils out!
Make them work under the fish and pigs!
We must temper the steel of the new generation . . .
We must surmount the blue majesty of the
 mountains . . .
We must look to the galaxy for our power . . .

—Excerpt from *Black Flowers Called Sakinohaka,*
 by Kenji Miyazawa

PHASE

9
A BLACK FLOWER NAMED
SAKINOHAKA [PART 2]

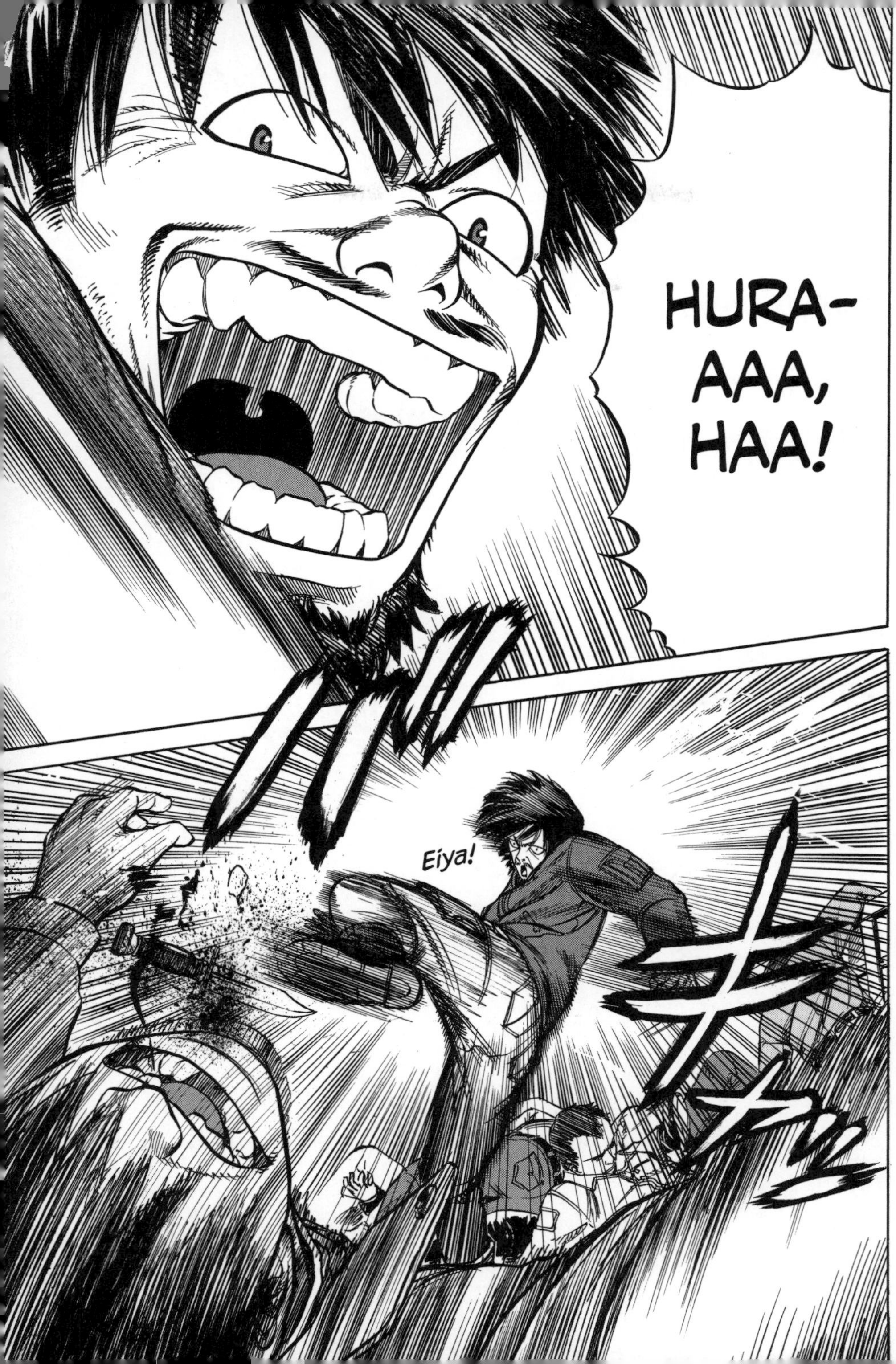
HURA-
AAA,
HAA!
Eiya!

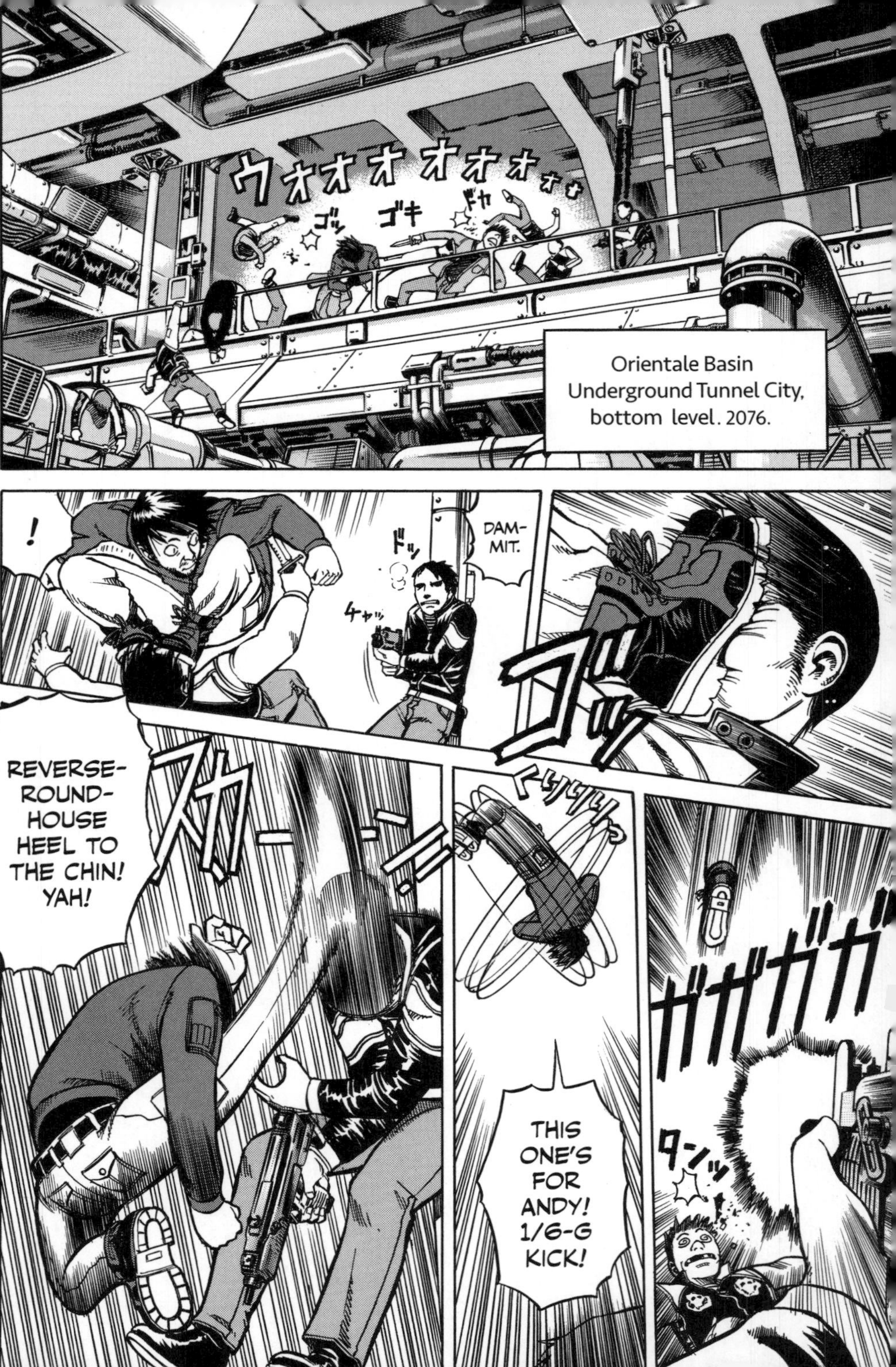
ウォオオオオオォォォ
ドカ
ゴキ
ゴッ
Orientale Basin
Underground Tunnel City,
bottom level. 2076.
ゴッ
DAM-MIT.
ドッ
!
ガガガガ
ターンッ
THIS ONE'S FOR ANDY! 1/6-G KICK!
スカーーー!
REVERSE-ROUNDHOUSE HEEL TO THE CHIN! YAH!

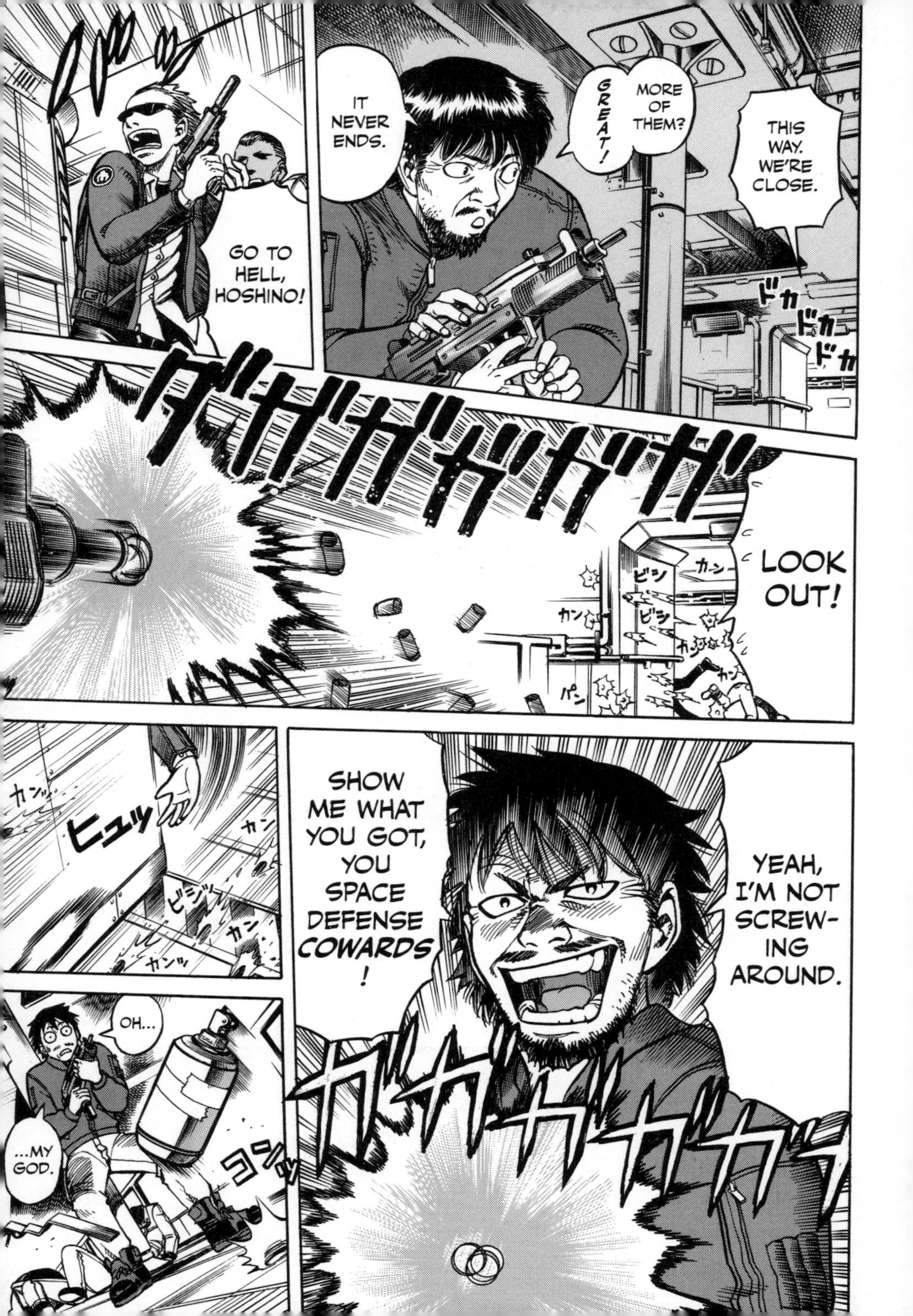
THIS WAY. WE'RE CLOSE.
MORE OF THEM?
GREAT!
IT NEVER ENDS.
ドカ ドカ ドカ
GO TO HELL, HOSHINO!
LOOK OUT!
YEAH, I'M NOT SCREWING AROUND.
SHOW ME WHAT YOU GOT, YOU SPACE DEFENSE COWARDS!
ヒュッ
OH...
...MY GOD.

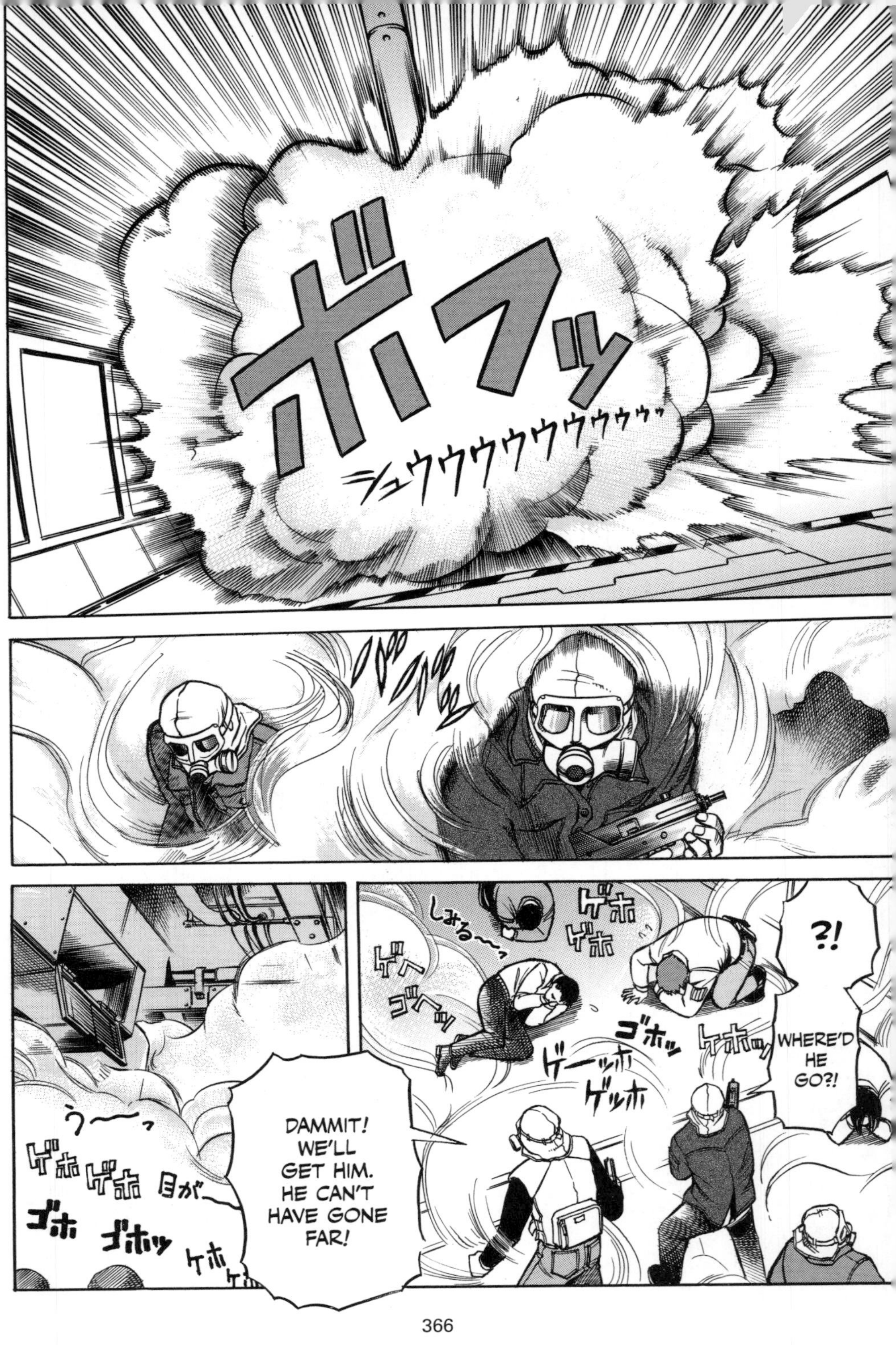
ボフッ
シュウウウウウウウゥ
?!
WHERE'D HE GO?!
しみる〜っ
ゲホ ゲホ
ゲヘ ゴヘッ
ゴホッ
ケホッ
ゲーッホ ゲッホ
DAMMIT! WE'LL GET HIM. HE CAN'T HAVE GONE FAR!
う〜っ
ゲホ ゲホ 目が
ゴホ ゴホッ ケホ

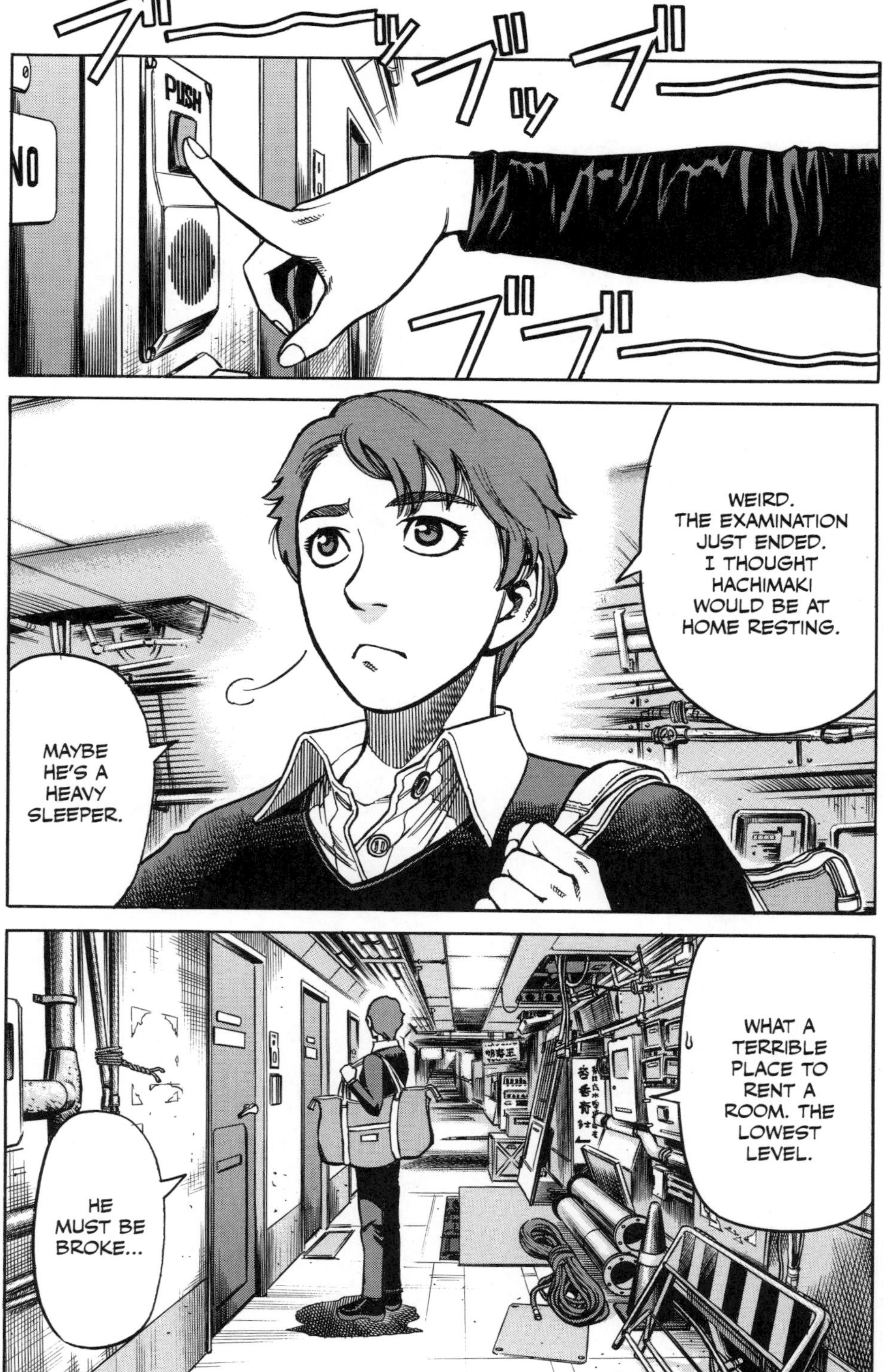
ブーーーッ
ブッ
ブーー
PUSH
NO
ブブー
WEIRD. THE EXAMINATION JUST ENDED. I THOUGHT HACHIMAKI WOULD BE AT HOME RESTING.
MAYBE HE'S A HEAVY SLEEPER.
WHAT A TERRIBLE PLACE TO RENT A ROOM. THE LOWEST LEVEL.
HE MUST BE BROKE...

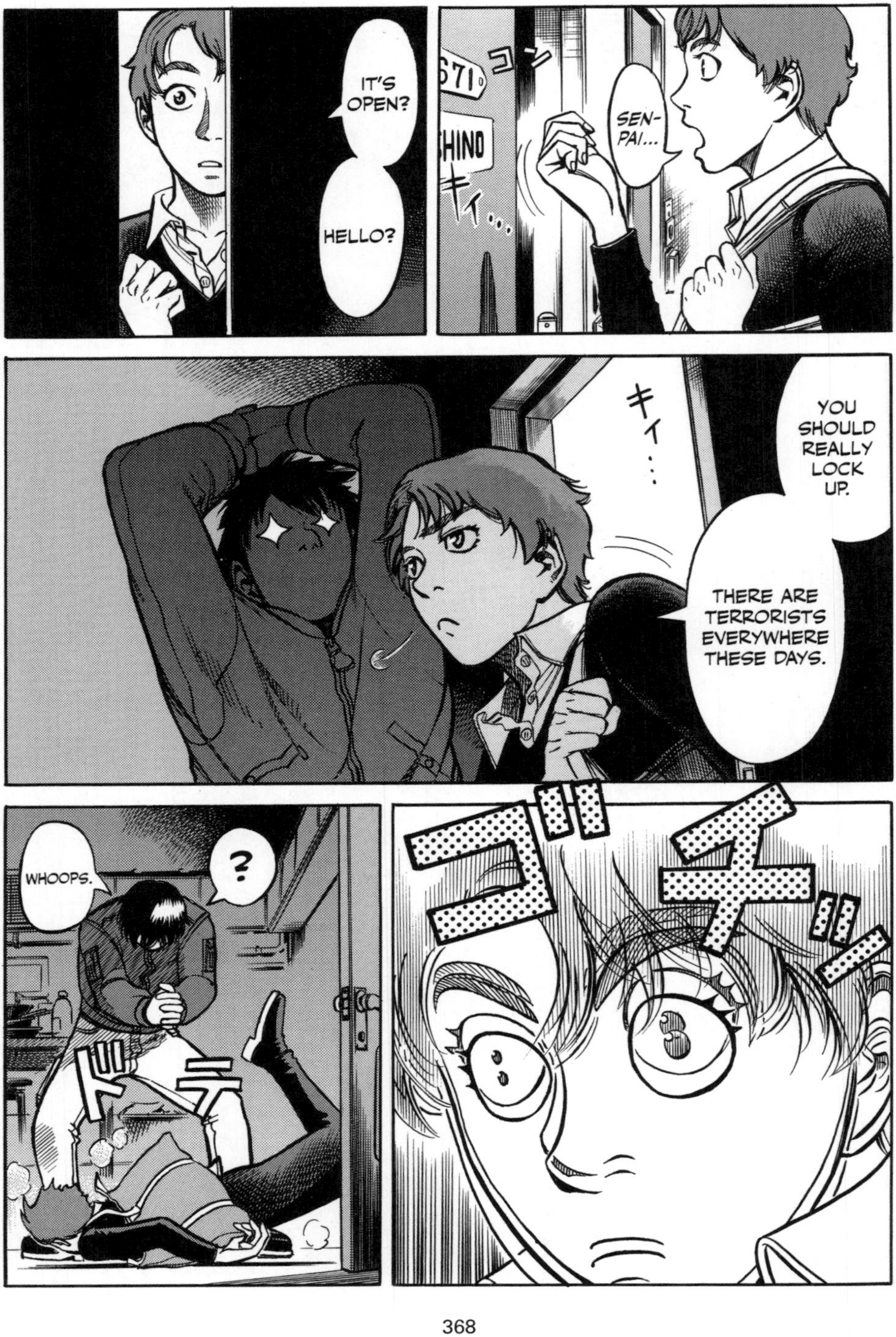
671
コン
SHINO
キィ…
SEN-PAI…
IT'S OPEN?
HELLO?
キィ…
YOU SHOULD REALLY LOCK UP.
THERE ARE TERRORISTS EVERYWHERE THESE DAYS.
?
WHOOPS.
ドテ

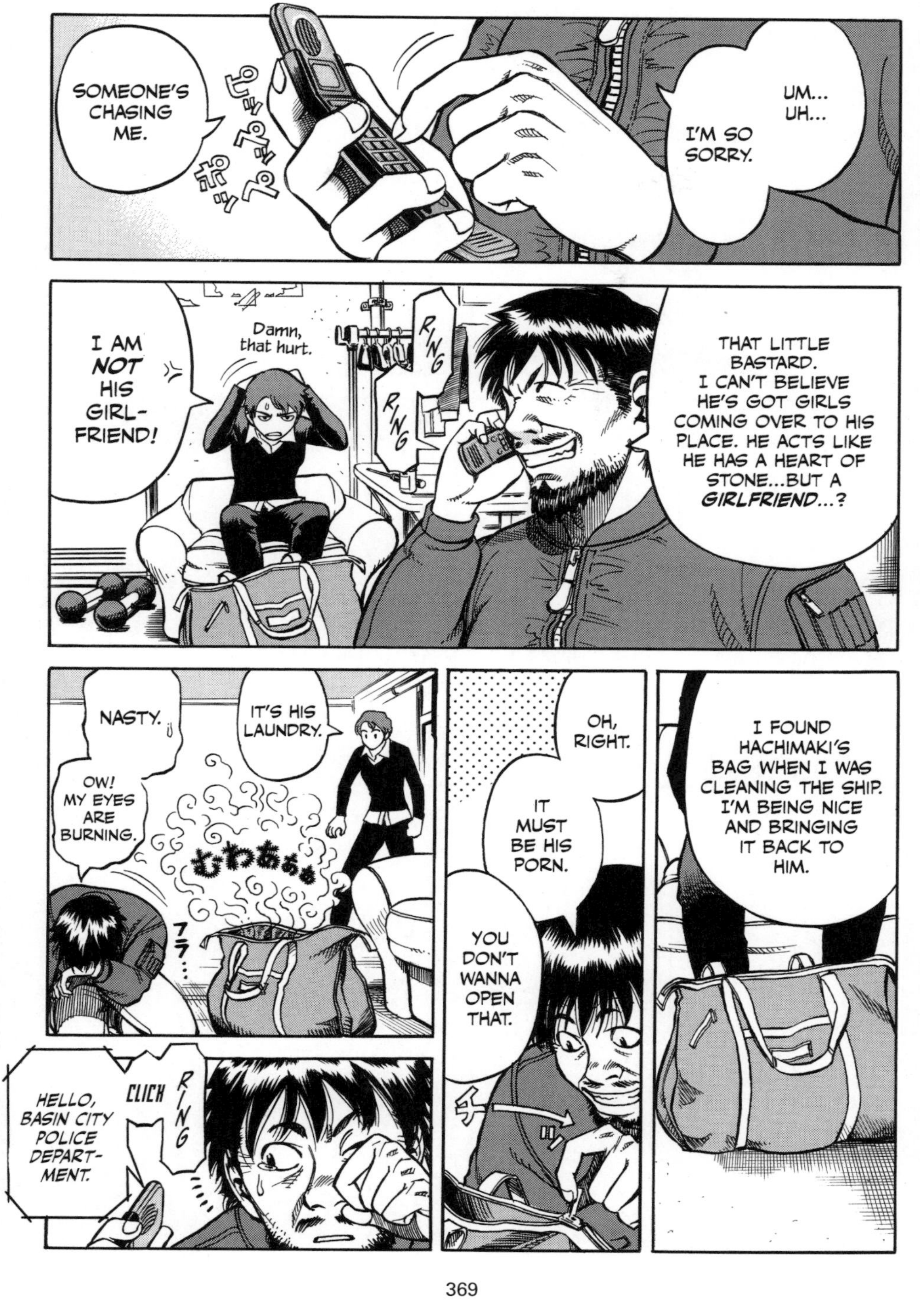
UM... UH...
I'M SO SORRY.
SOMEONE'S CHASING ME.
THAT LITTLE BASTARD. I CAN'T BELIEVE HE'S GOT GIRLS COMING OVER TO HIS PLACE. HE ACTS LIKE HE HAS A HEART OF STONE...BUT A GIRLFRIEND...?
RING RING
Damn, that hurt.
I AM NOT HIS GIRL-FRIEND!
I FOUND HACHIMAKI'S BAG WHEN I WAS CLEANING THE SHIP. I'M BEING NICE AND BRINGING IT BACK TO HIM.
OH, RIGHT.
IT MUST BE HIS PORN.
YOU DON'T WANNA OPEN THAT.
IT'S HIS LAUNDRY.
NASTY.
OW! MY EYES ARE BURNING.
むわぁぁぁ
RING
CLICK
HELLO, BASIN CITY POLICE DEPART-MENT.

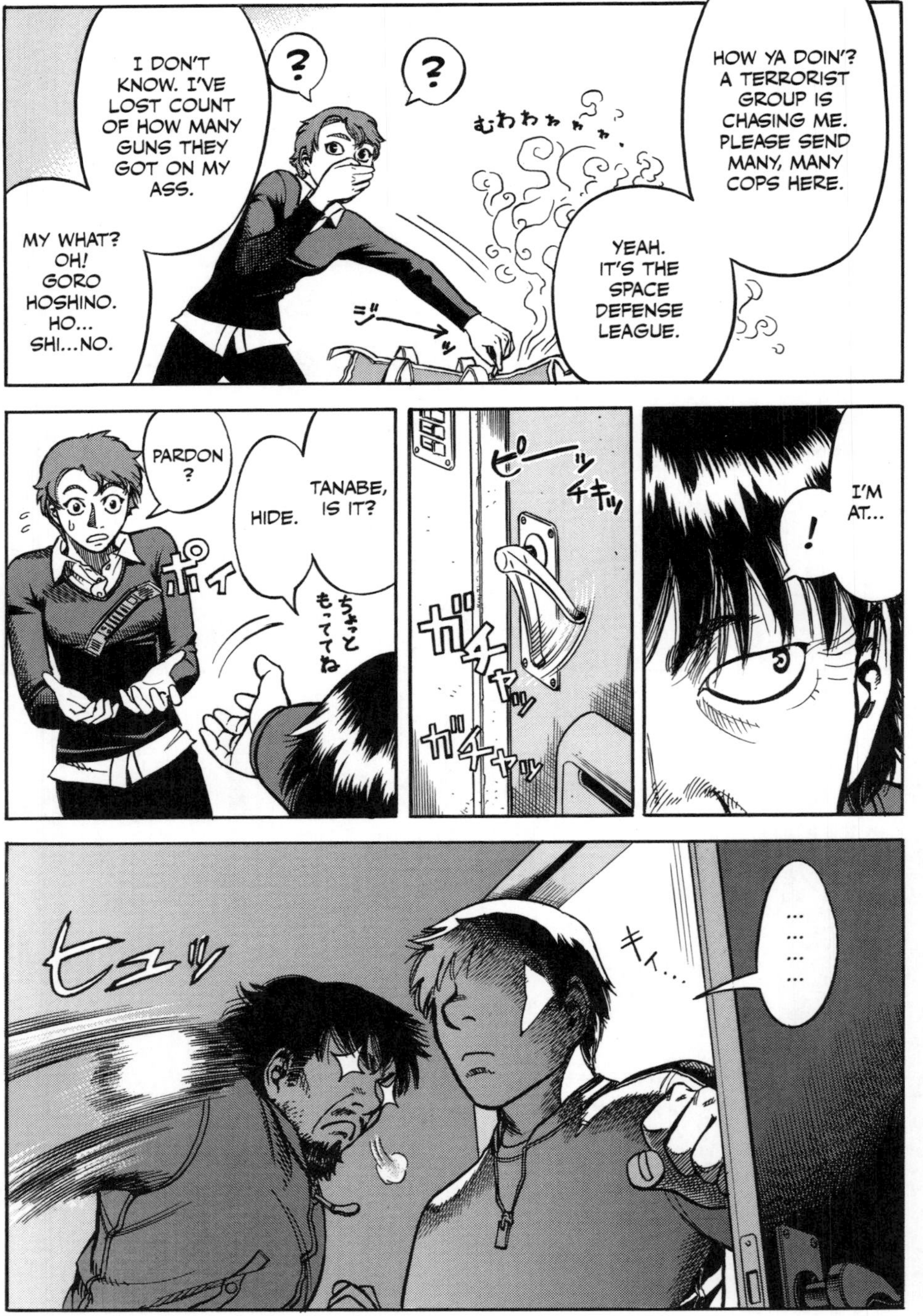
HOW YA DOIN'? A TERRORIST GROUP IS CHASING ME. PLEASE SEND MANY, MANY COPS HERE.
YEAH. IT'S THE SPACE DEFENSE LEAGUE.
むわわぁぁぁ
?
?
I DON'T KNOW. I'VE LOST COUNT OF HOW MANY GUNS THEY GOT ON MY ASS.
MY WHAT? OH! GORO HOSHINO. HO... SHI...NO.
ジ
ッ
I'M AT...
!
ピーッ
チキッ
ガチャッ
ガチャッ
TANABE, IS IT?
PARDON?
HIDE.
ポイ
ちょっともっててね
...
...
...
...
キィ...
ヒュッ

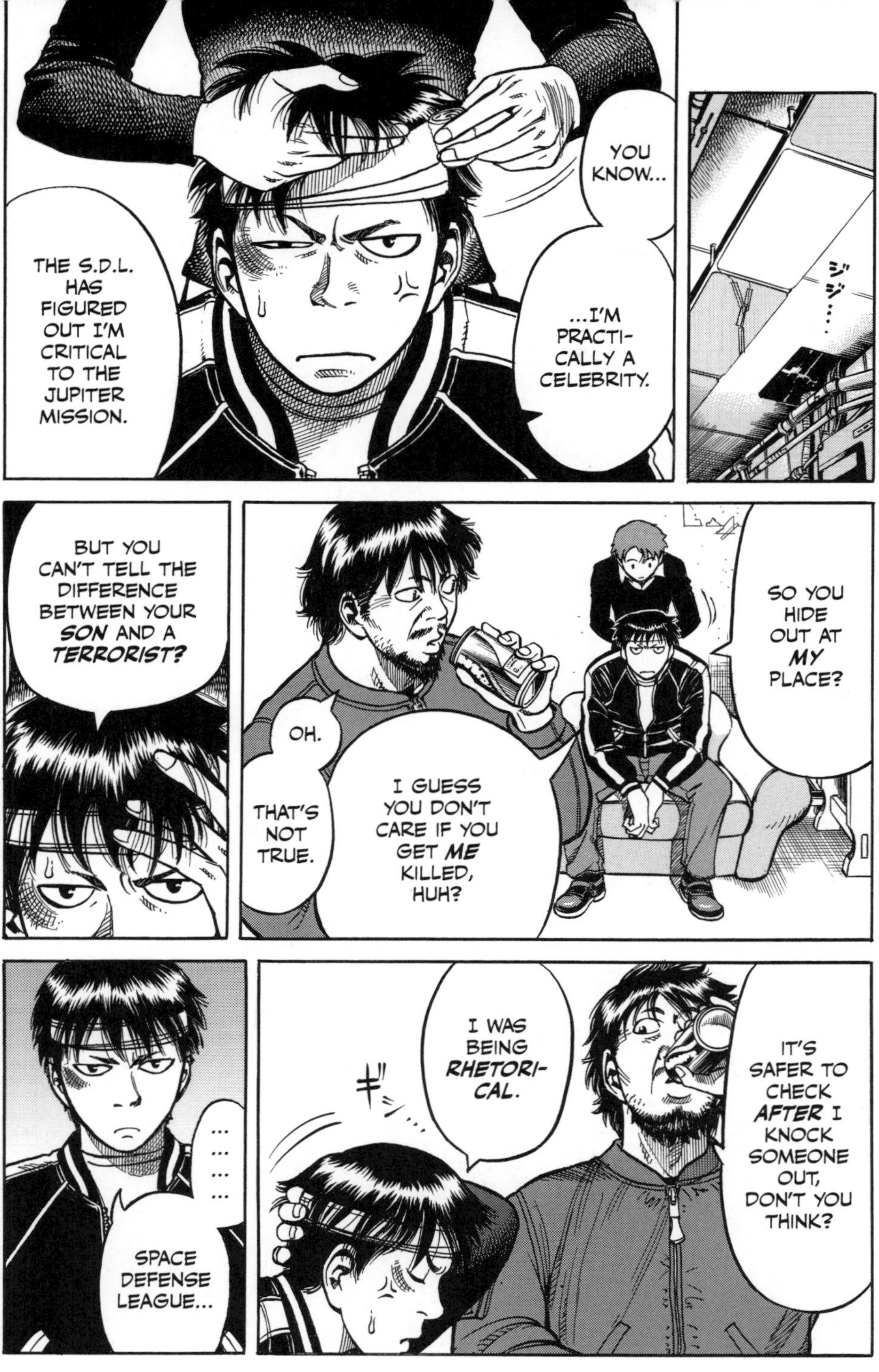
ジジ…
YOU KNOW...
...I'M PRACTI-CALLY A CELEBRITY.
THE S.D.L. HAS FIGURED OUT I'M CRITICAL TO THE JUPITER MISSION.
SO YOU HIDE OUT AT *MY* PLACE?
I GUESS YOU DON'T CARE IF YOU GET *ME* KILLED, HUH?
OH.
THAT'S NOT TRUE.
BUT YOU CAN'T TELL THE DIFFERENCE BETWEEN YOUR *SON* AND A *TERRORIST?*
IT'S SAFER TO CHECK *AFTER* I KNOCK SOMEONE OUT, DON'T YOU THINK?
I WAS BEING *RHETORI-CAL*.
ギシ…
....
SPACE DEFENSE LEAGUE...

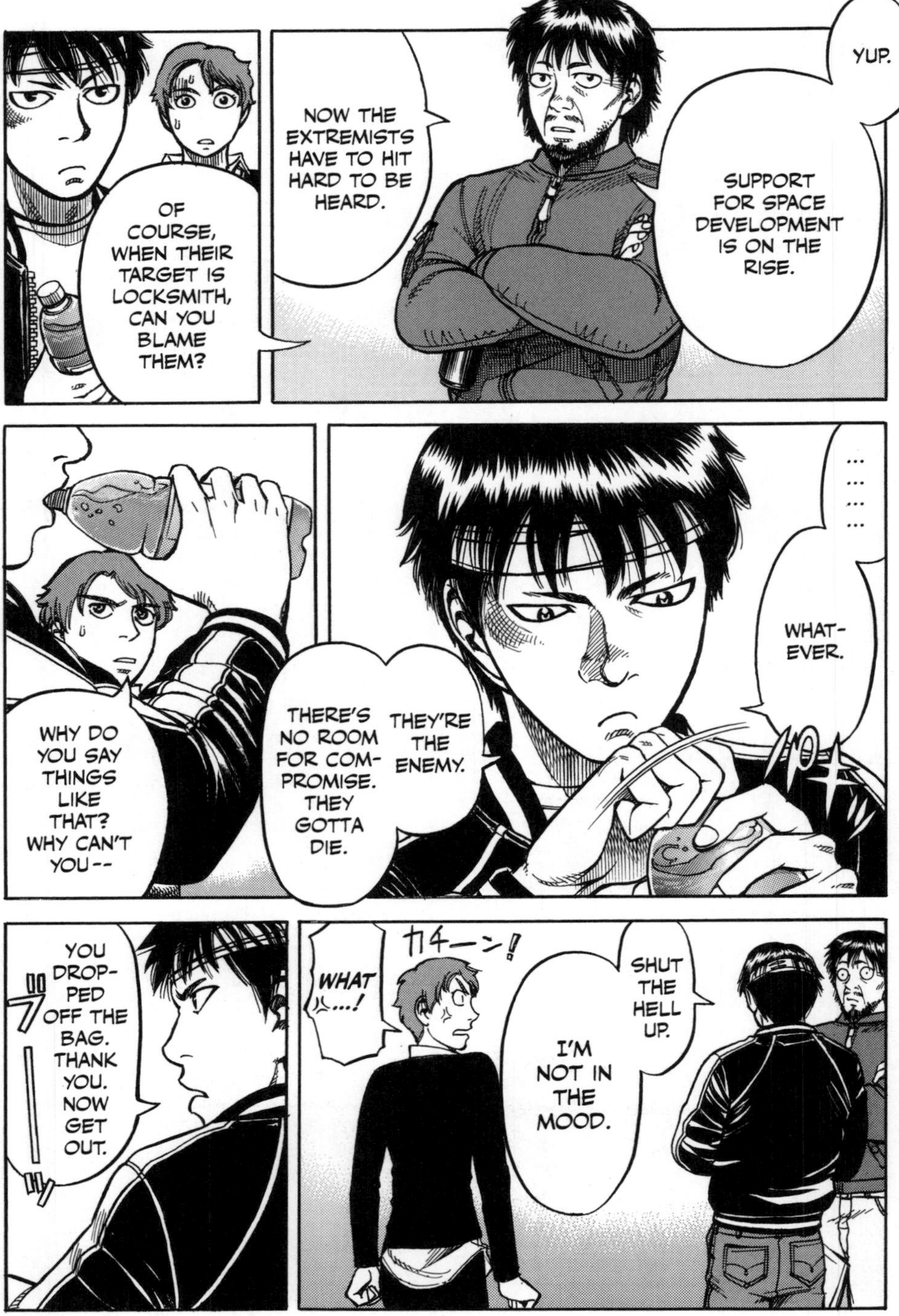
YUP.
SUPPORT FOR SPACE DEVELOPMENT IS ON THE RISE.
NOW THE EXTREMISTS HAVE TO HIT HARD TO BE HEARD.
OF COURSE, WHEN THEIR TARGET IS LOCKSMITH, CAN YOU BLAME THEM?
....
WHAT-EVER.
THEY'RE THE ENEMY.
THERE'S NO ROOM FOR COM-PROMISE. THEY GOTTA DIE.
WHY DO YOU SAY THINGS LIKE THAT? WHY CAN'T YOU--
SHUT THE HELL UP.
I'M NOT IN THE MOOD.
カチーン!
WHAT...!
YOU DROP-PED OFF THE BAG. THANK YOU. NOW GET OUT.

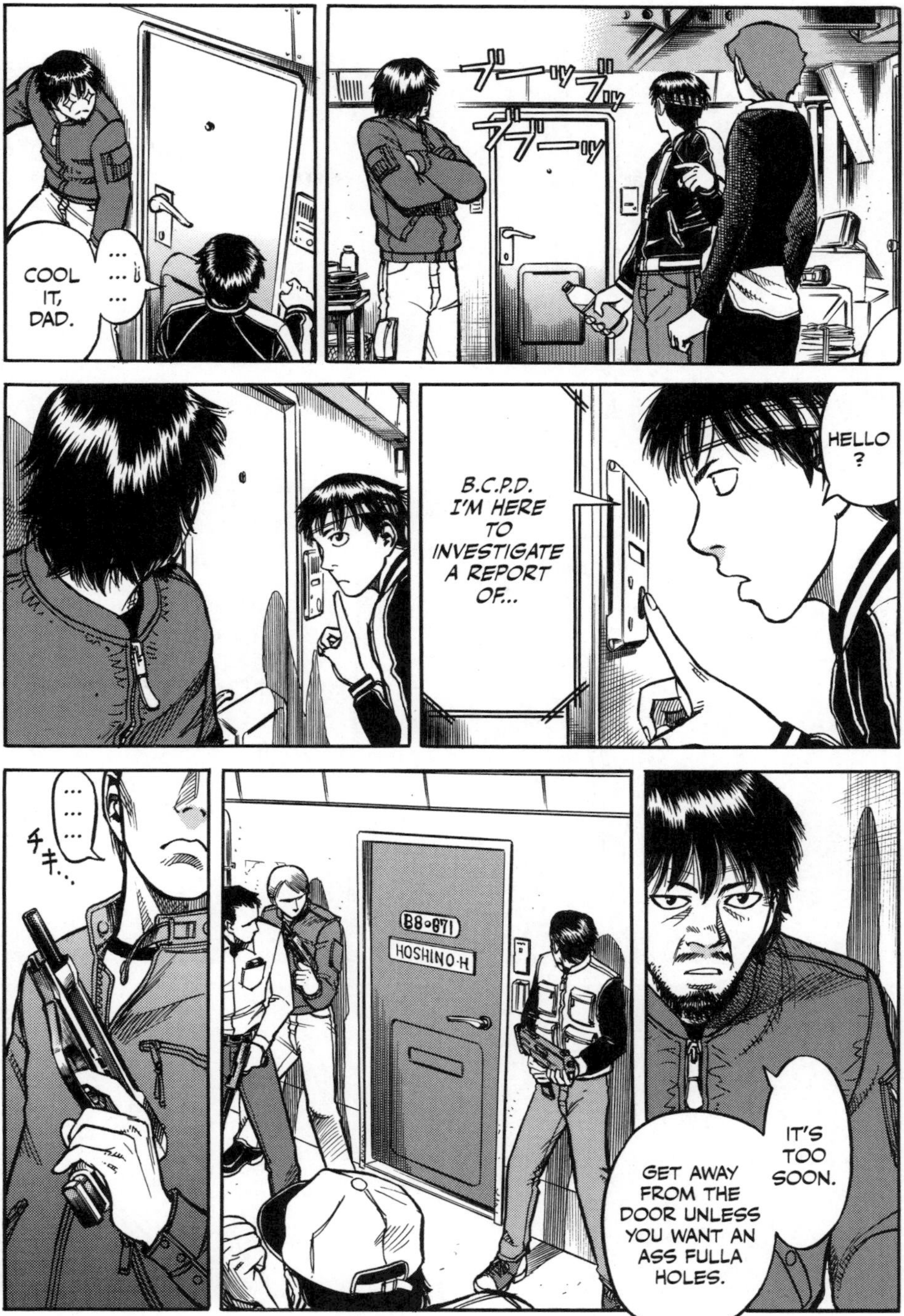
ブーッブッ
ブブーッ
...
...
...
COOL IT, DAD.
HELLO?
B.C.P.D. I'M HERE TO INVESTIGATE A REPORT OF...
IT'S TOO SOON.
GET AWAY FROM THE DOOR UNLESS YOU WANT AN ASS FULLA HOLES.
B8-671
HOSHINO-H
...
...
...
チキ...

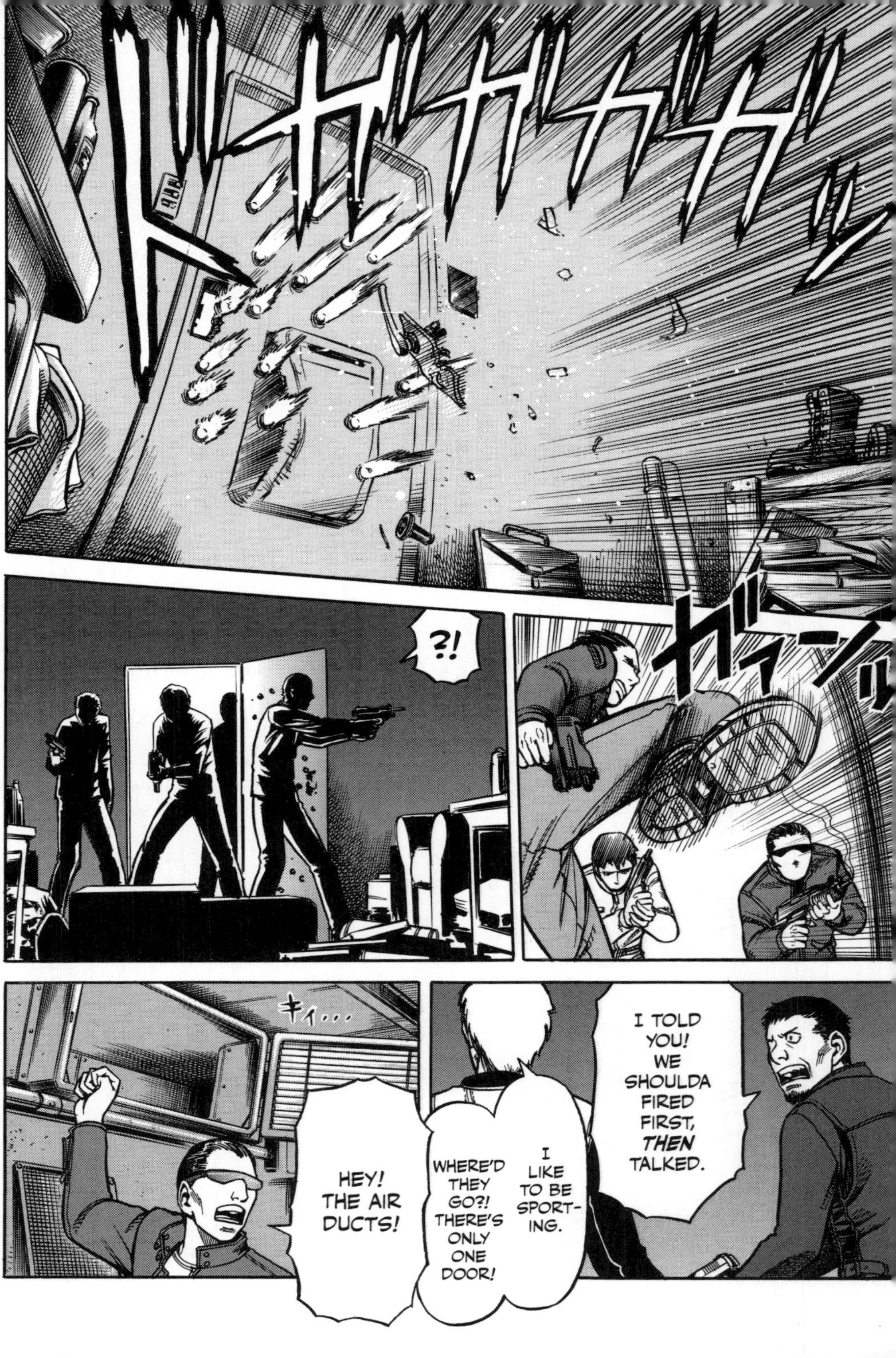

?!
I TOLD YOU! WE SHOULDA FIRED FIRST, *THEN* TALKED.
I LIKE TO BE SPORTING.
WHERE'D THEY GO?! THERE'S ONLY ONE DOOR!
キィ...
HEY! THE AIR DUCTS!

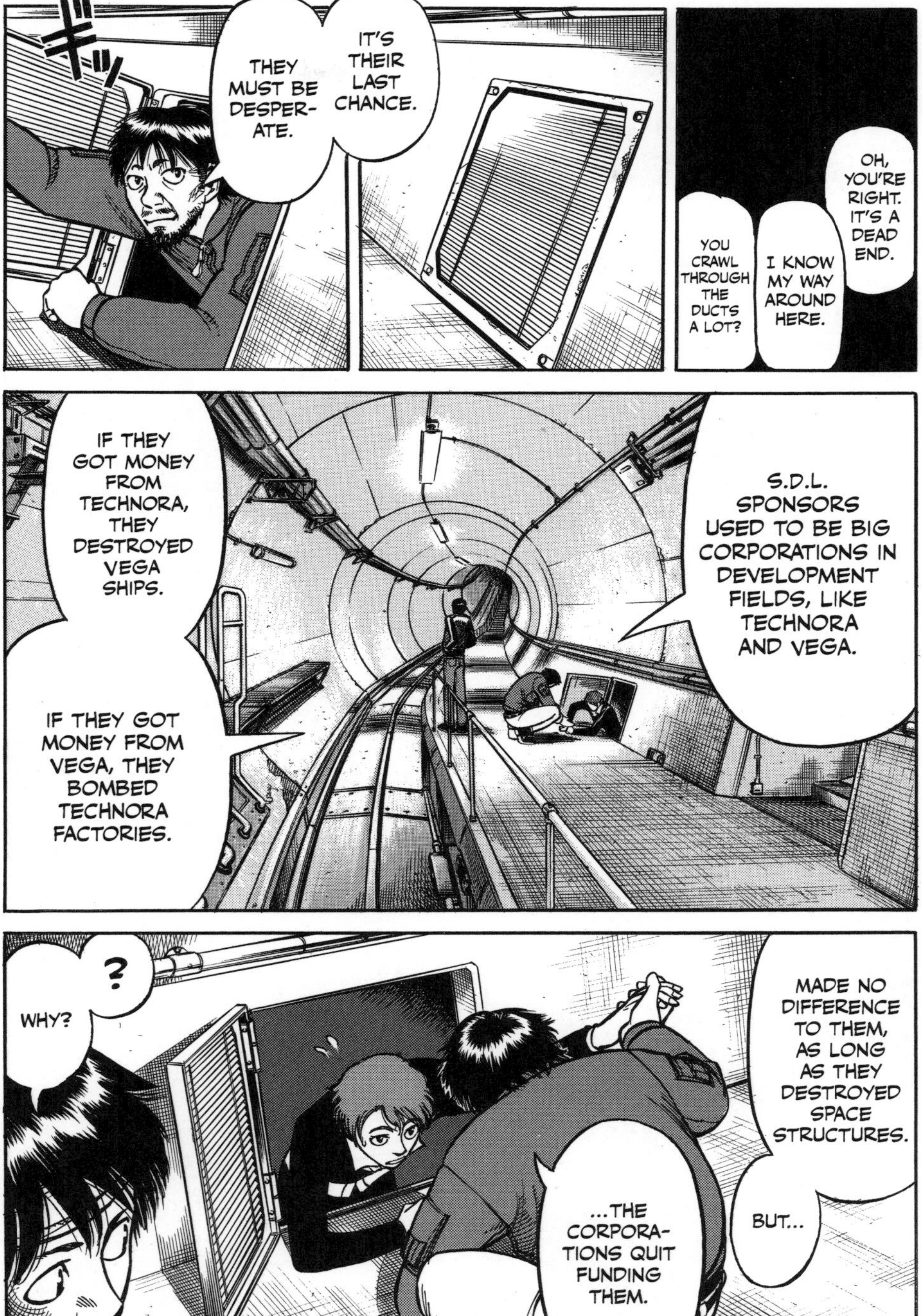
OH, YOU'RE RIGHT. IT'S A DEAD END.
I KNOW MY WAY AROUND HERE.
YOU CRAWL THROUGH THE DUCTS A LOT?
ギッ
IT'S THEIR LAST CHANCE.
THEY MUST BE DESPER-ATE.
S.D.L. SPONSORS USED TO BE BIG CORPORATIONS IN DEVELOPMENT FIELDS, LIKE TECHNORA AND VEGA.
IF THEY GOT MONEY FROM TECHNORA, THEY DESTROYED VEGA SHIPS.
IF THEY GOT MONEY FROM VEGA, THEY BOMBED TECHNORA FACTORIES.
MADE NO DIFFERENCE TO THEM, AS LONG AS THEY DESTROYED SPACE STRUCTURES.
BUT...
...THE CORPORA-TIONS QUIT FUNDING THEM.
?
WHY?

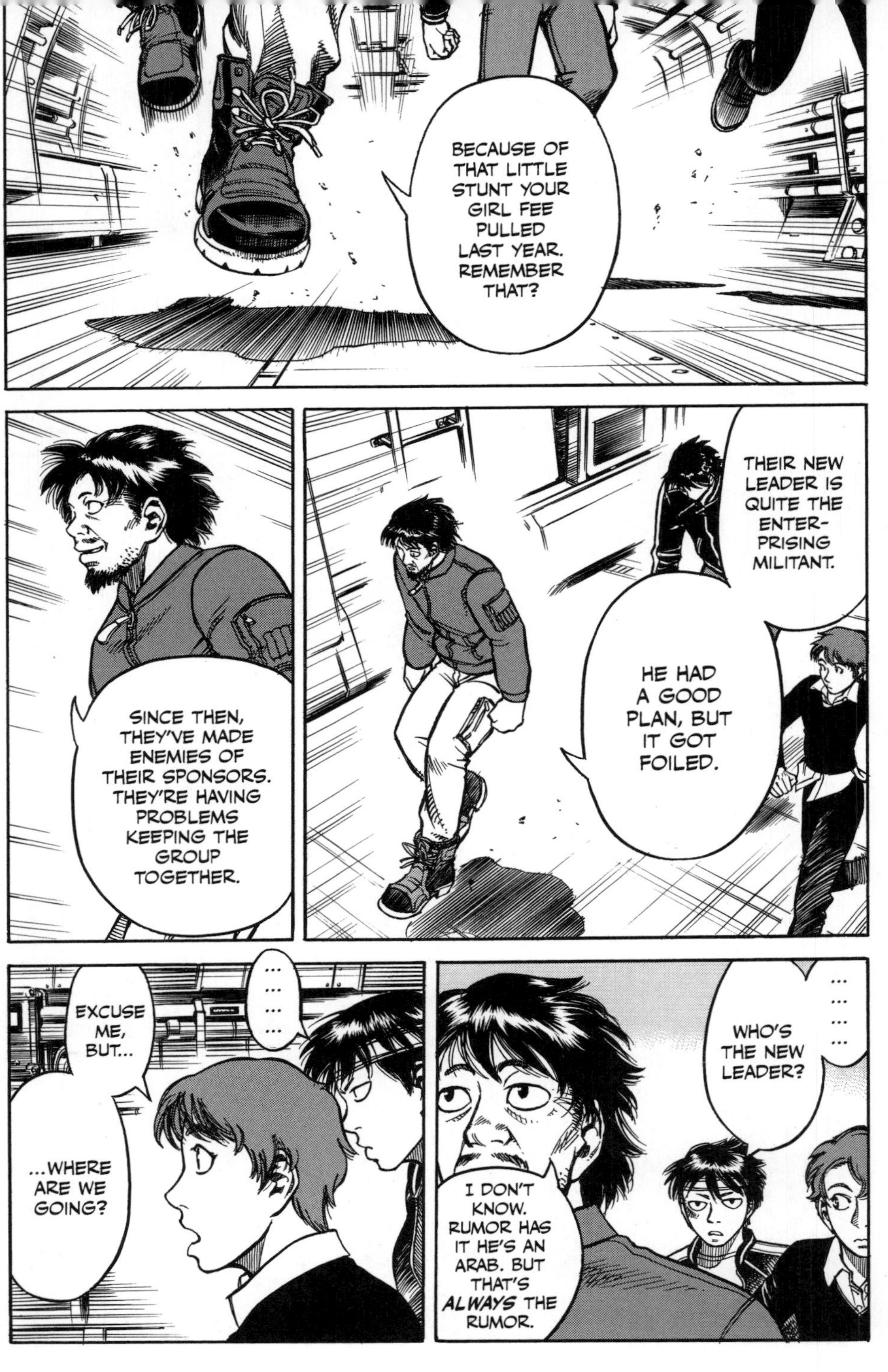
BECAUSE OF THAT LITTLE STUNT YOUR GIRL FEE PULLED LAST YEAR. REMEMBER THAT?
THEIR NEW LEADER IS QUITE THE ENTER-PRISING MILITANT.
HE HAD A GOOD PLAN, BUT IT GOT FOILED.
SINCE THEN, THEY'VE MADE ENEMIES OF THEIR SPONSORS. THEY'RE HAVING PROBLEMS KEEPING THE GROUP TOGETHER.
....
WHO'S THE NEW LEADER?
I DON'T KNOW. RUMOR HAS IT HE'S AN ARAB. BUT THAT'S *ALWAYS* THE RUMOR.
....
EXCUSE ME, BUT...
...WHERE ARE WE GOING?

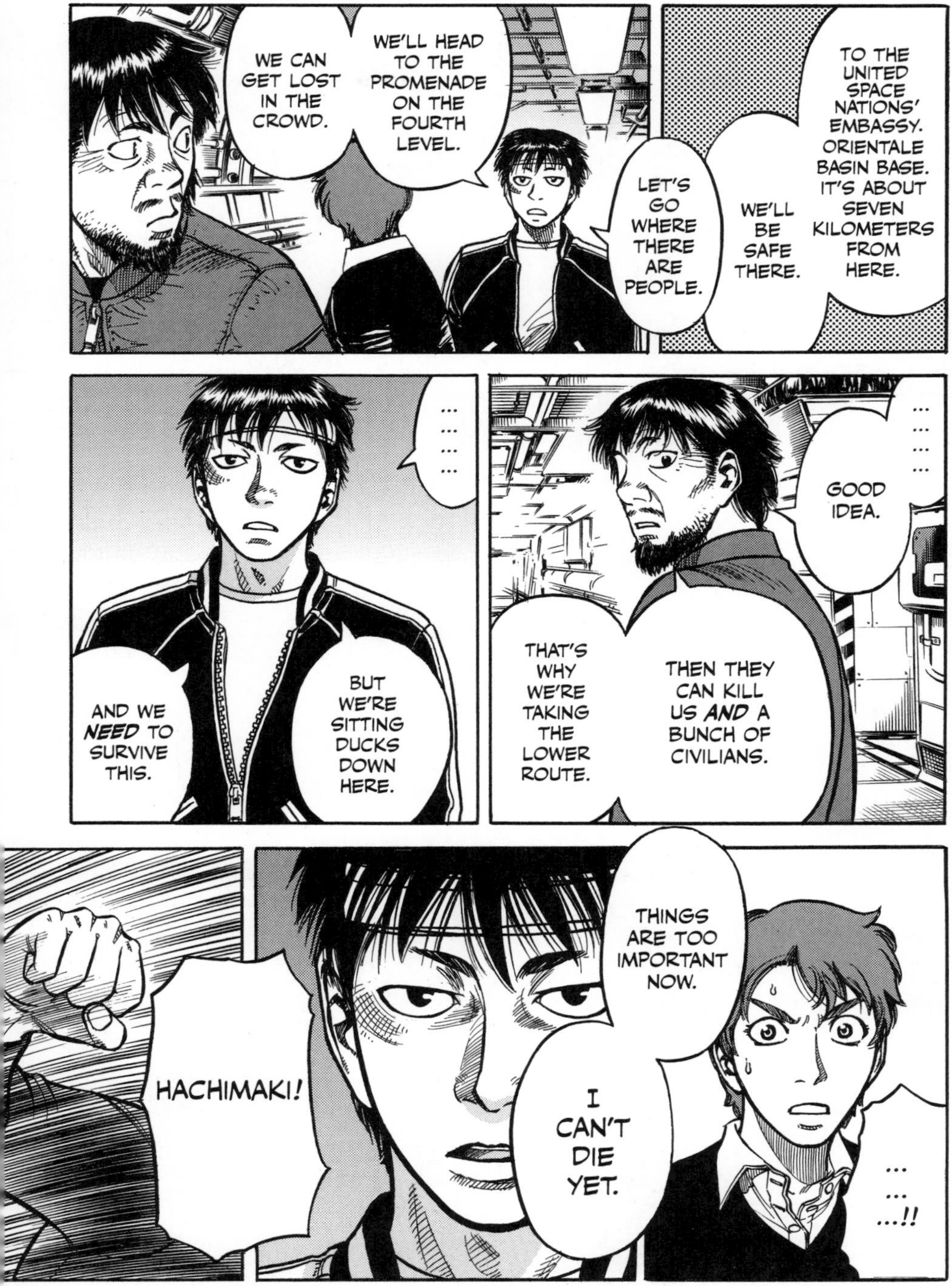
TO THE UNITED SPACE NATIONS' EMBASSY. ORIENTALE BASIN BASE. IT'S ABOUT SEVEN KILOMETERS FROM HERE.
WE'LL BE SAFE THERE.
LET'S GO WHERE THERE ARE PEOPLE.
WE'LL HEAD TO THE PROMENADE ON THE FOURTH LEVEL.
WE CAN GET LOST IN THE CROWD.
... ...
GOOD IDEA.
THEN THEY CAN KILL US *AND* A BUNCH OF CIVILIANS.
THAT'S WHY WE'RE TAKING THE LOWER ROUTE.
... ...
BUT WE'RE SITTING DUCKS DOWN HERE.
AND WE *NEED* TO SURVIVE THIS.
THINGS ARE TOO IMPORTANT NOW.
I CAN'T DIE YET.
... ...!!
HACHIMAKI!

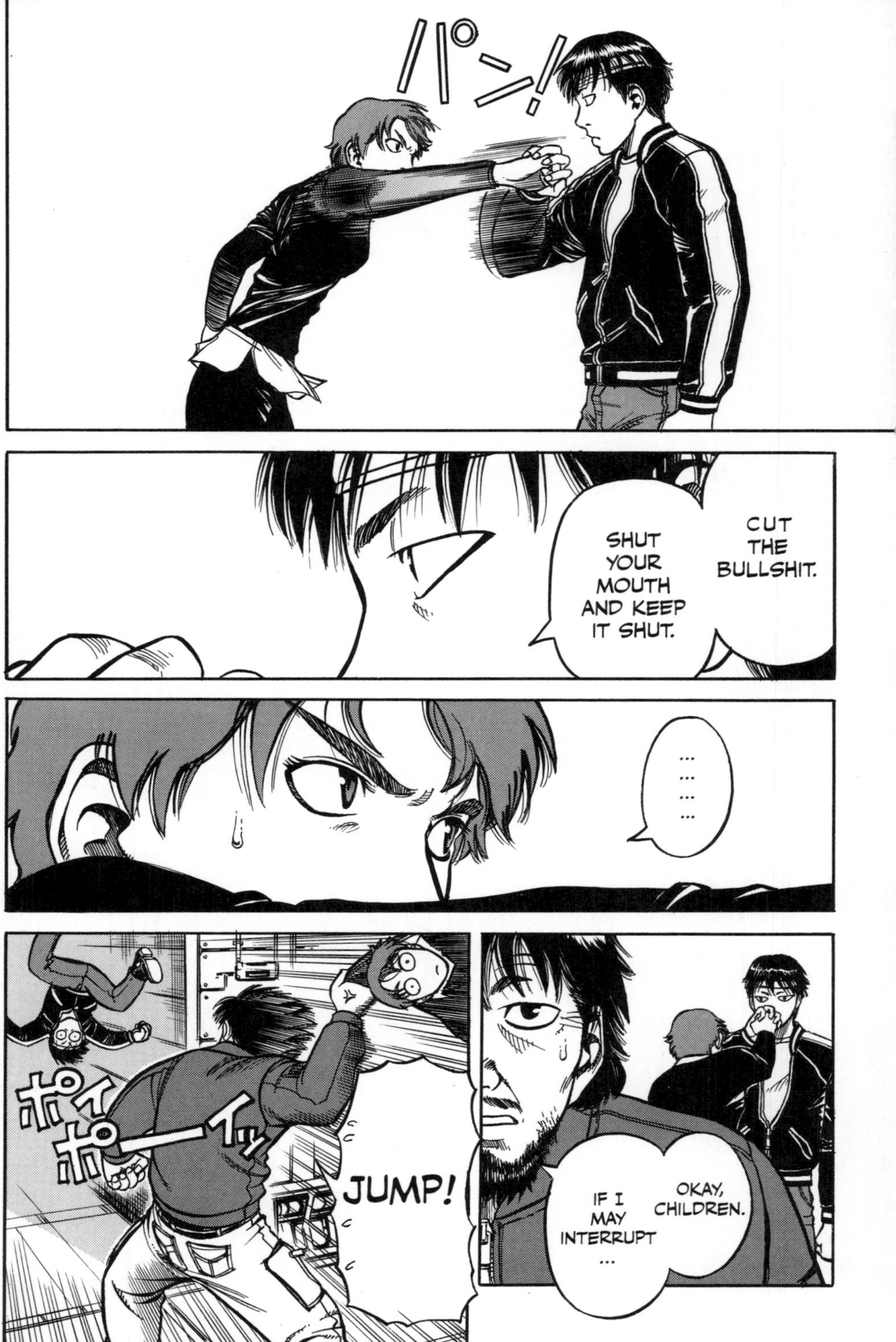
パン!
CUT THE BULLSHIT.
SHUT YOUR MOUTH AND KEEP IT SHUT.
……
OKAY, CHILDREN.
IF I MAY INTERRUPT …
ポイ
ポーイッ
JUMP!

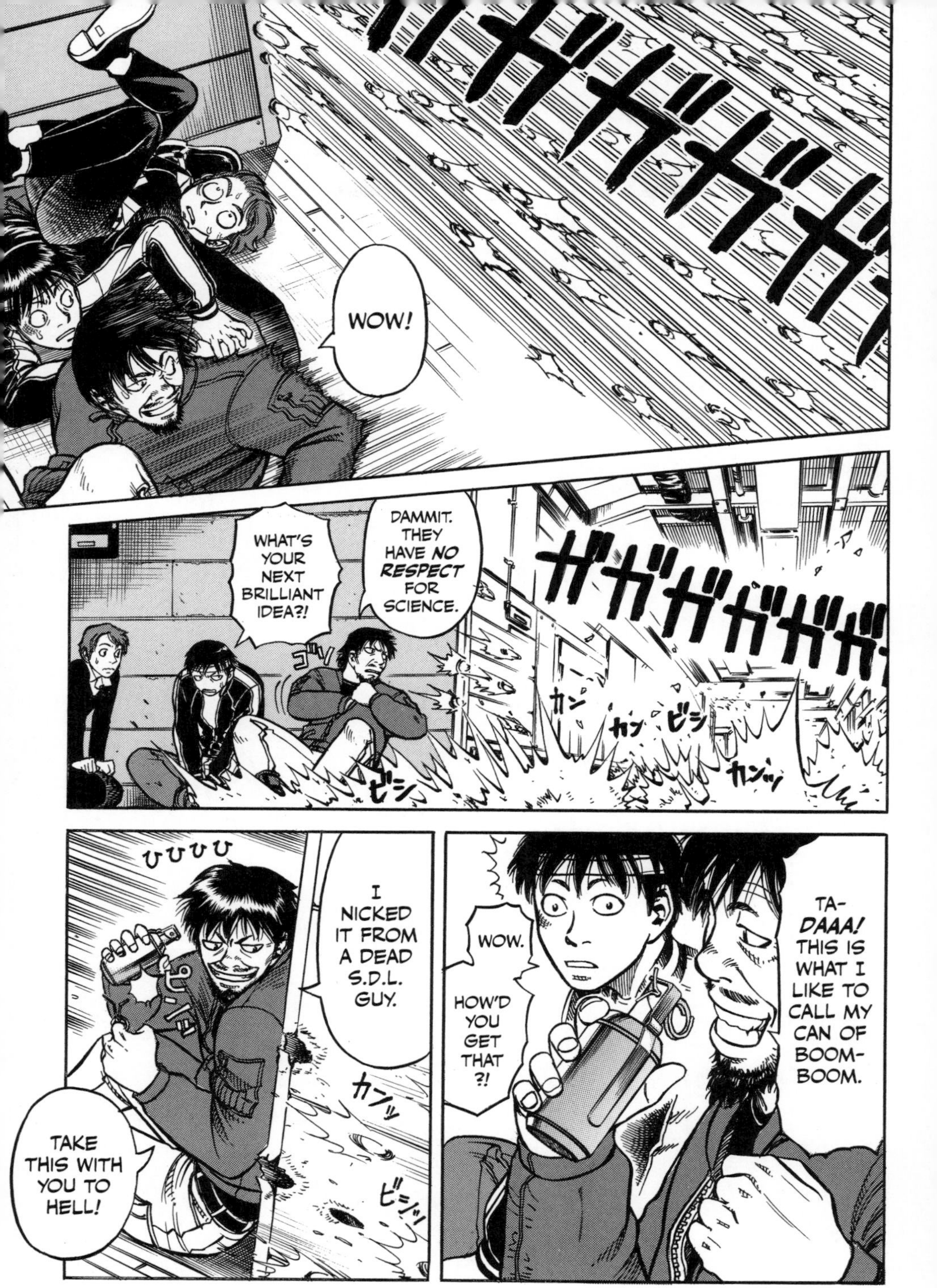
WOW!
DAMMIT. THEY HAVE *NO RESPECT* FOR SCIENCE.
WHAT'S YOUR NEXT BRILLIANT IDEA?!
TA-*DAAA!* THIS IS WHAT I LIKE TO CALL MY CAN OF BOOM-BOOM.
WOW.
HOW'D YOU GET THAT?!
I NICKED IT FROM A DEAD S.D.L. GUY.
TAKE THIS WITH YOU TO HELL!

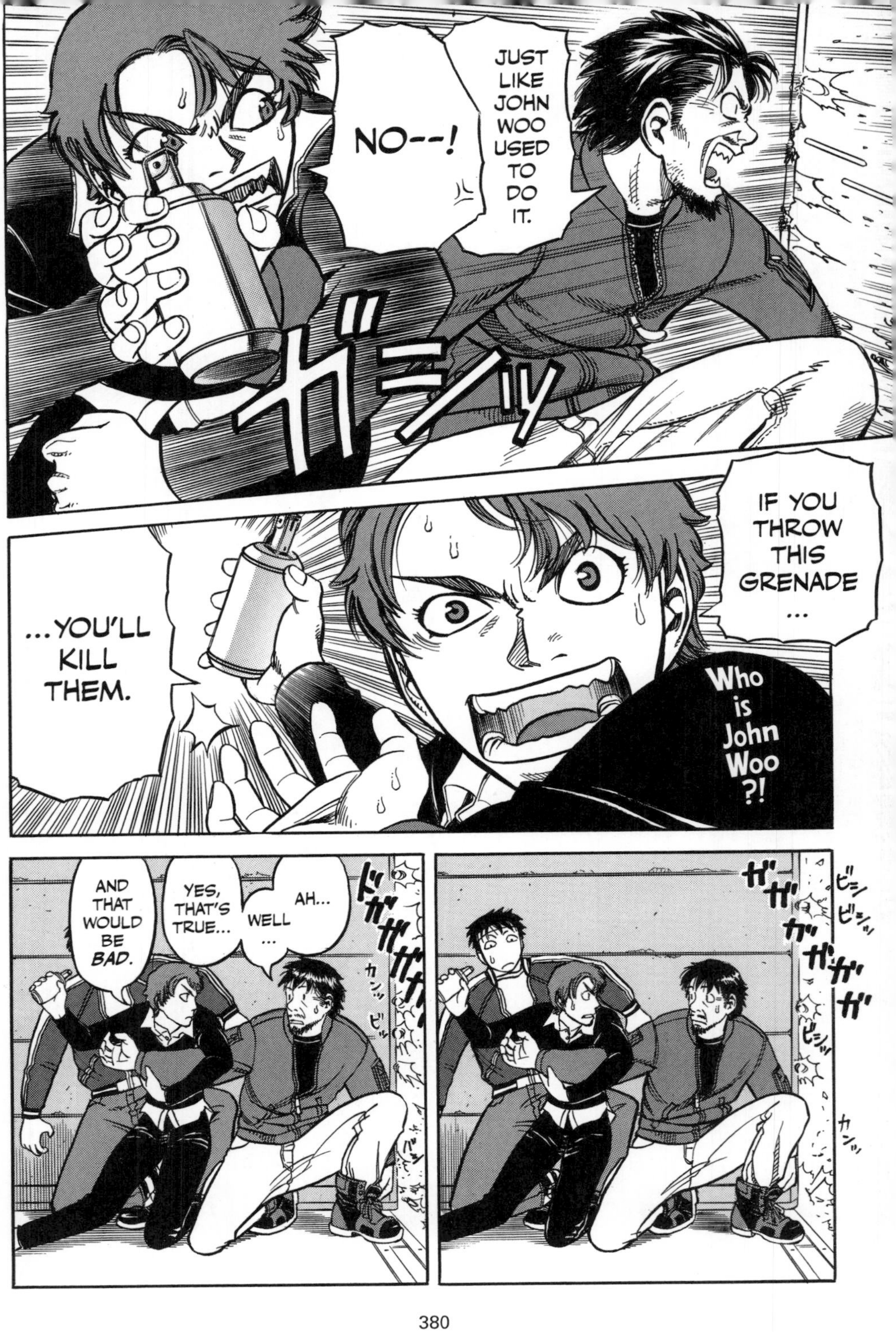
JUST LIKE JOHN WOO USED TO DO IT.
NO--!
ガシッ
IF YOU THROW THIS GRENADE ...
...YOU'LL KILL THEM.
Who is John Woo ?!
AH... WELL ...
YES, THAT'S TRUE...
AND THAT WOULD BE *BAD*.

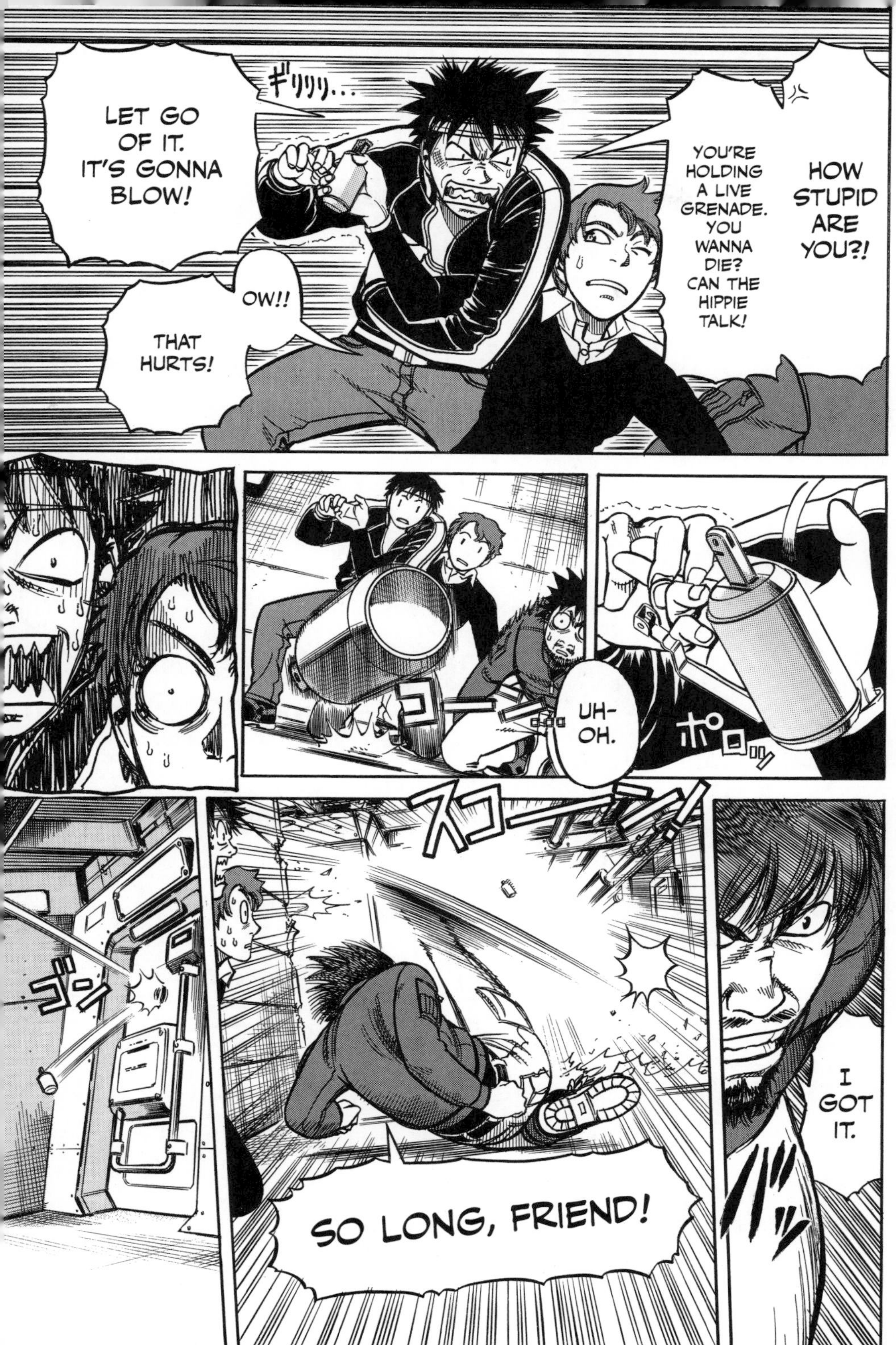
HOW STUPID ARE YOU?!
YOU'RE HOLDING A LIVE GRENADE. YOU WANNA DIE? CAN THE HIPPIE TALK!
ギリリリ…
LET GO OF IT. IT'S GONNA BLOW!
OW!! THAT HURTS!
ポロッ
UH-OH.
コーン
I GOT IT.
スコーン!
SO LONG, FRIEND!
ゴン

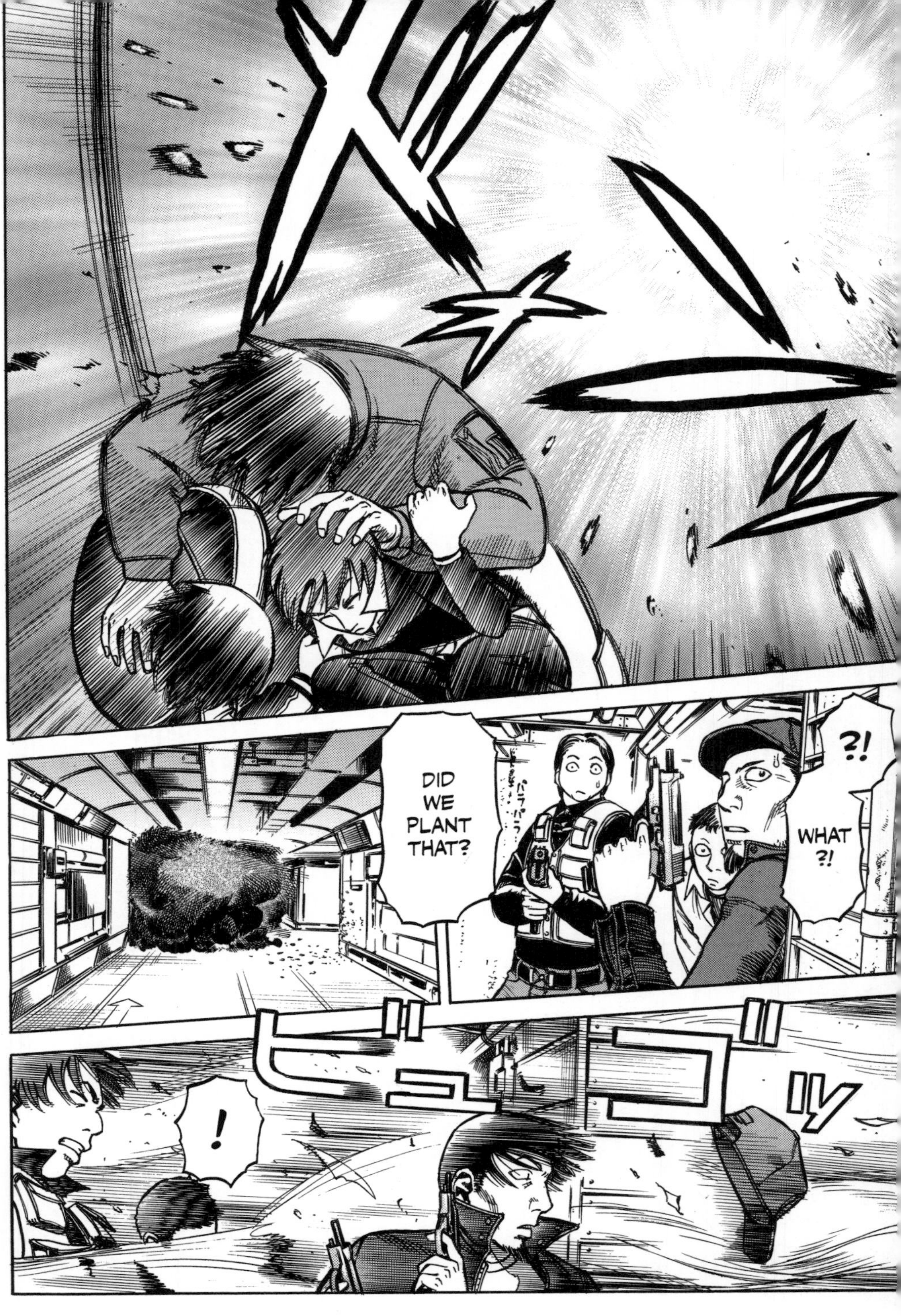
?!
WHAT ?!
DID WE PLANT THAT?
!

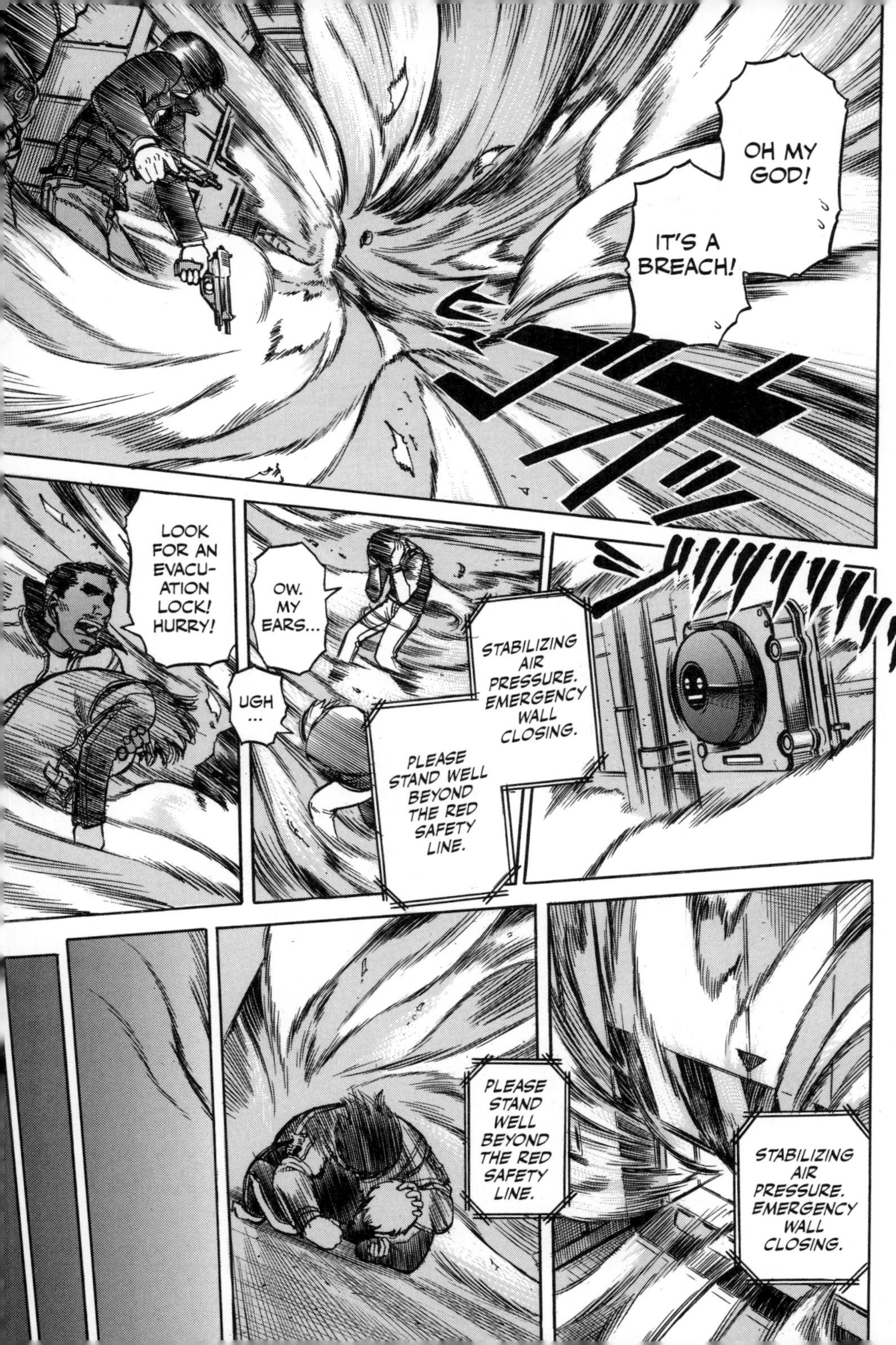
OH MY GOD!
IT'S A BREACH!
STABILIZING AIR PRESSURE. EMERGENCY WALL CLOSING.
PLEASE STAND WELL BEYOND THE RED SAFETY LINE.
OW. MY EARS...
UGH ...
LOOK FOR AN EVACUATION LOCK! HURRY!
STABILIZING AIR PRESSURE. EMERGENCY WALL CLOSING.
PLEASE STAND WELL BEYOND THE RED SAFETY LINE.

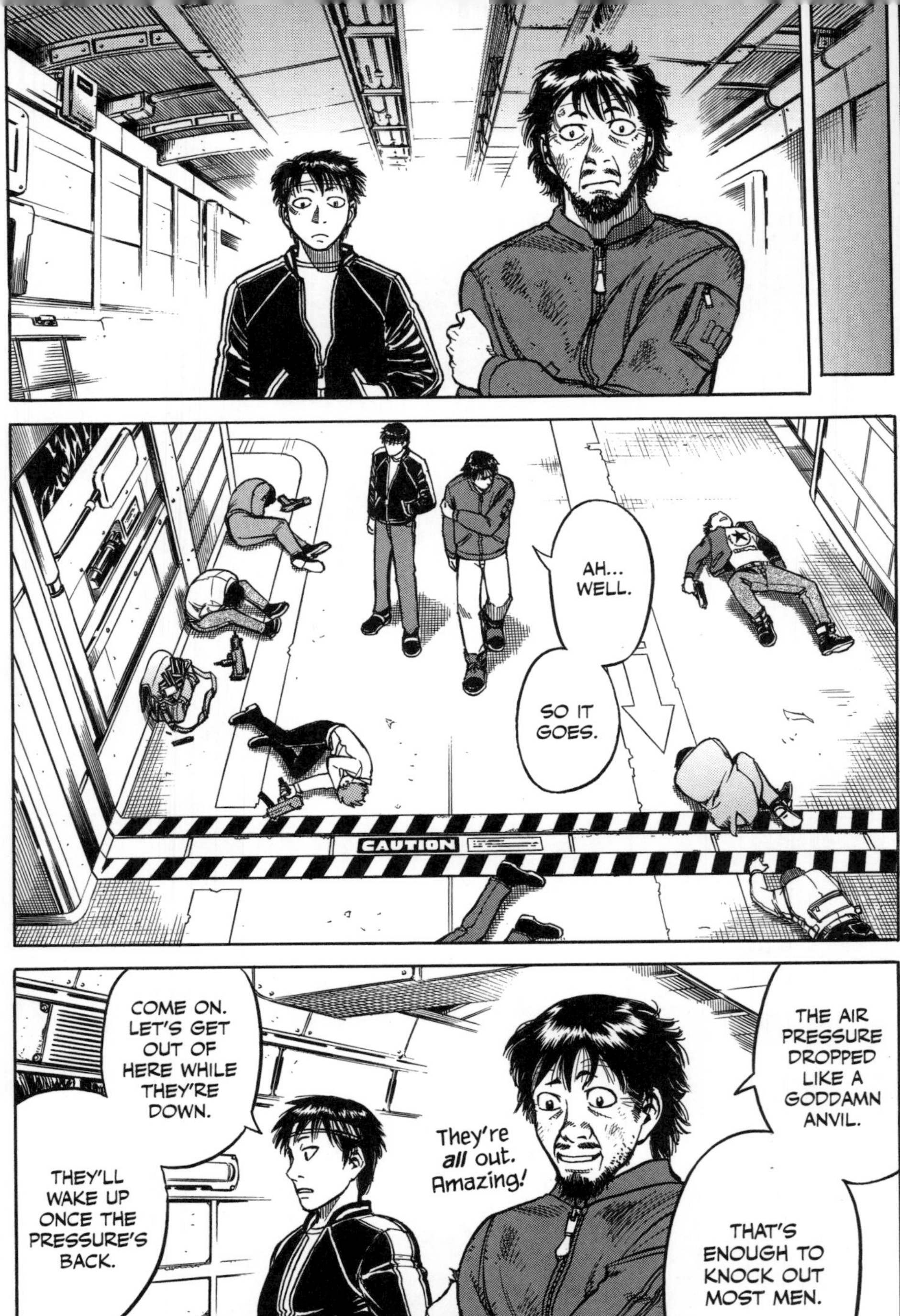
AH... WELL.
SO IT GOES.
CAUTION
THE AIR PRESSURE DROPPED LIKE A GODDAMN ANVIL.
THAT'S ENOUGH TO KNOCK OUT MOST MEN.
They're *all* out. Amazing!
COME ON. LET'S GET OUT OF HERE WHILE THEY'RE DOWN.
THEY'LL WAKE UP ONCE THE PRESSURE'S BACK.

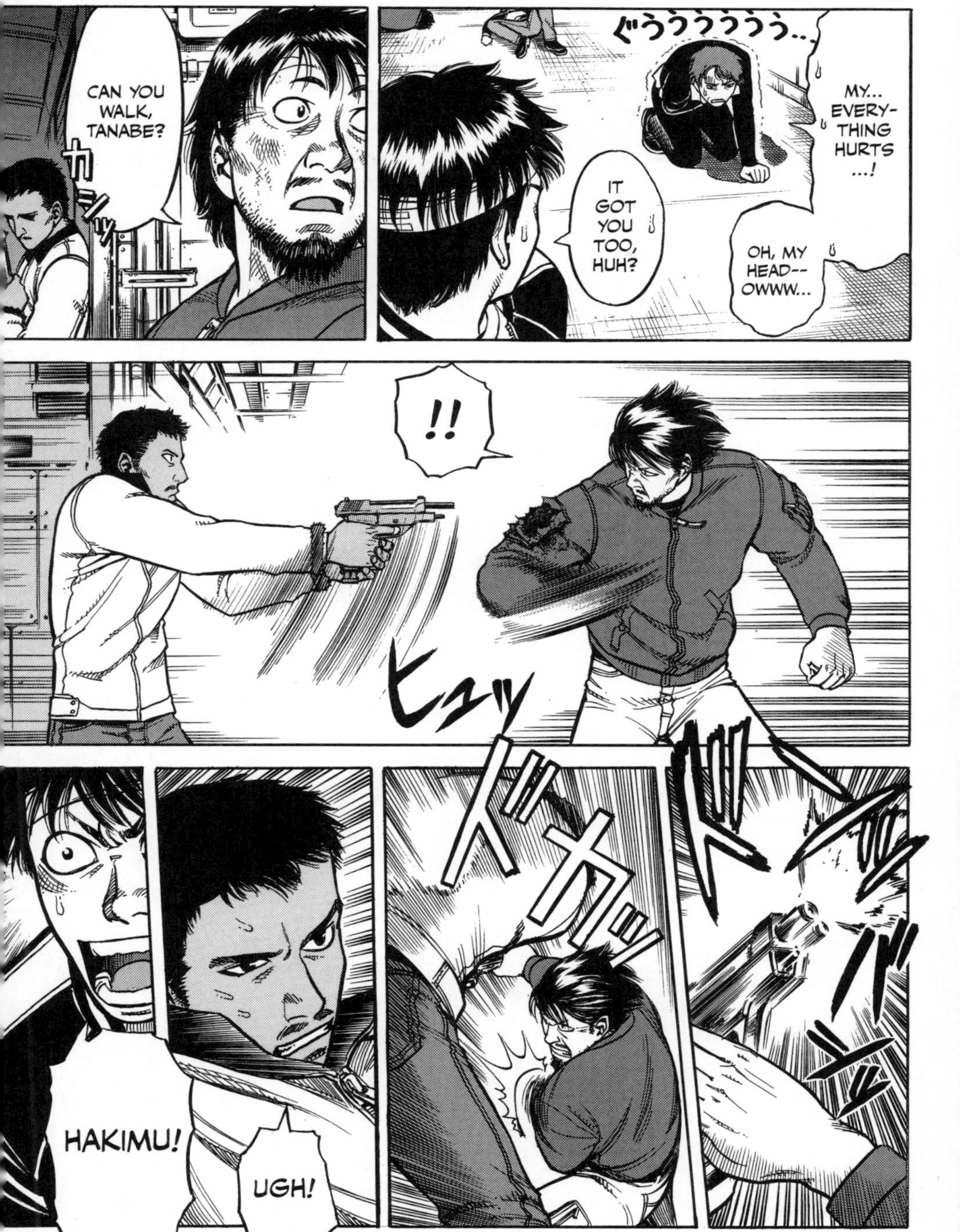
ぐううううううう…
MY... EVERY-THING HURTS ...!
IT GOT YOU TOO, HUH?
OH, MY HEAD-- OWWW...
CAN YOU WALK, TANABE?
!!
ヒュッ
HAKIMU!
UGH!

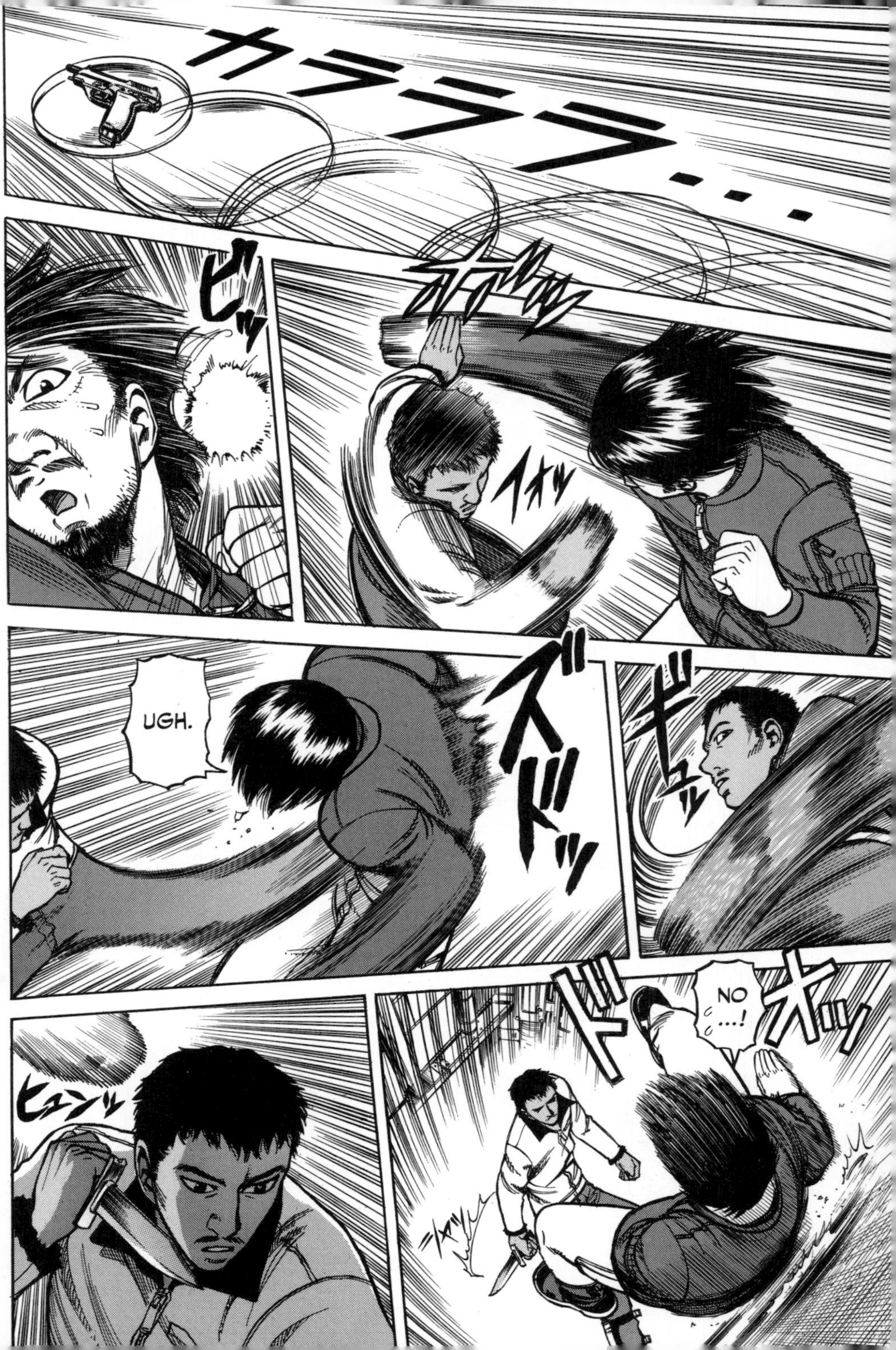
カラララ...
ビッ
ズドッ
UGH.
NO ...!
ヒュンッ

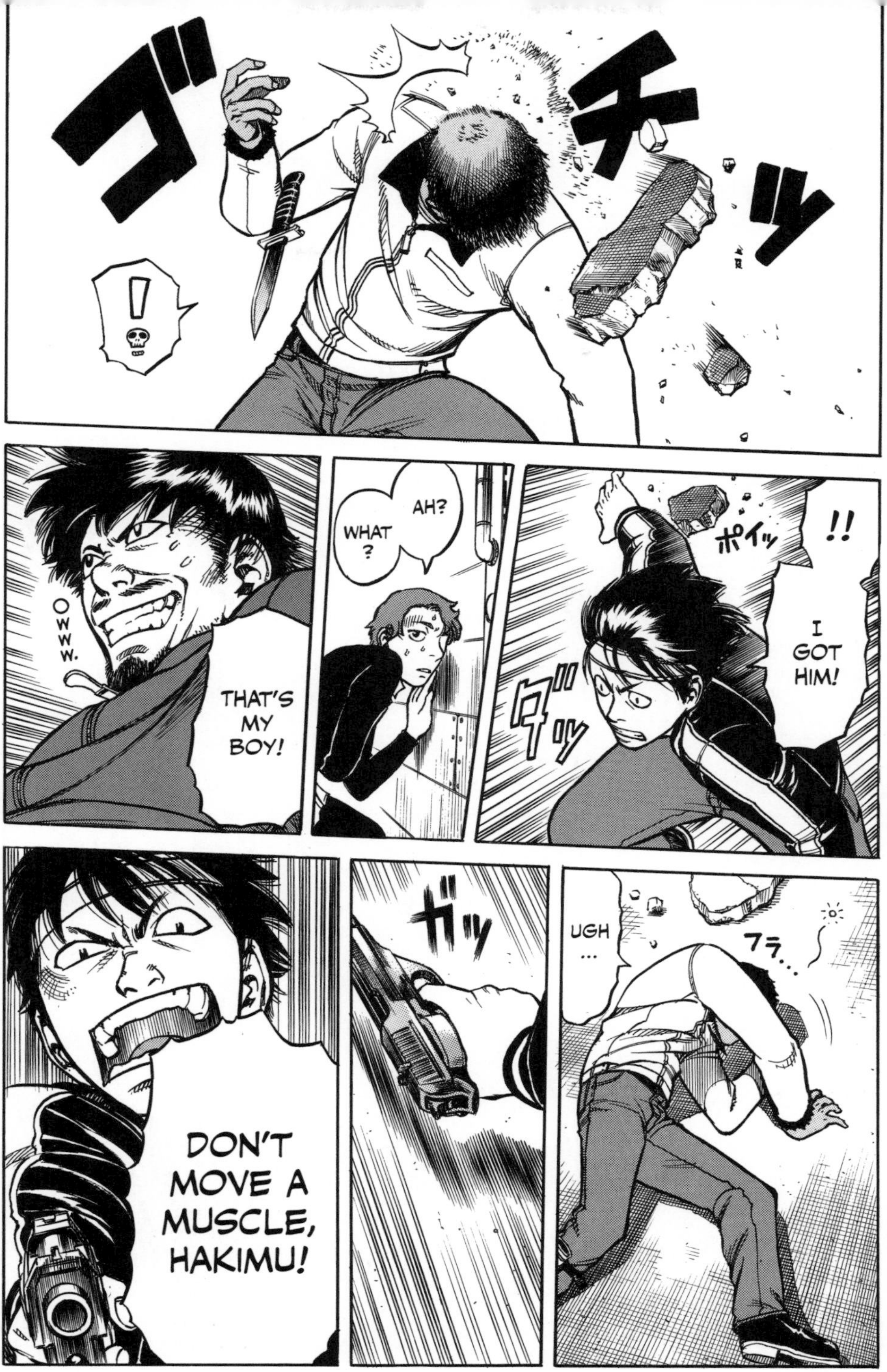
ゴチッ
!
ポイッ
!!
I GOT HIM!
ダッ
AH?
WHAT?
OWWW.
THAT'S MY BOY!
フラ…
UGH…
ガッ
DON'T MOVE A MUSCLE, HAKIMU!

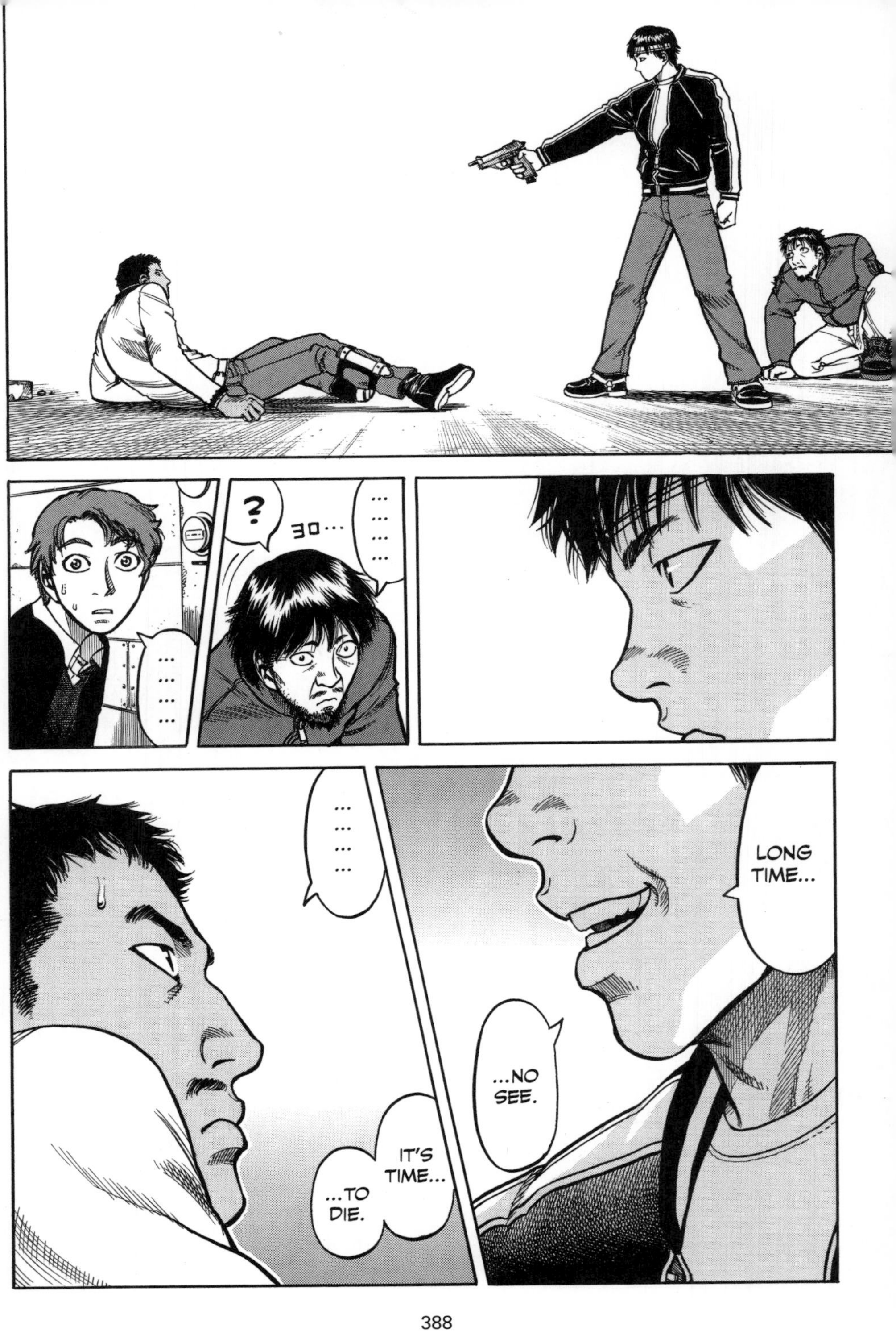

....
?
ЭO...
....
LONG TIME...
...NO SEE.
....
IT'S TIME...
...TO DIE.

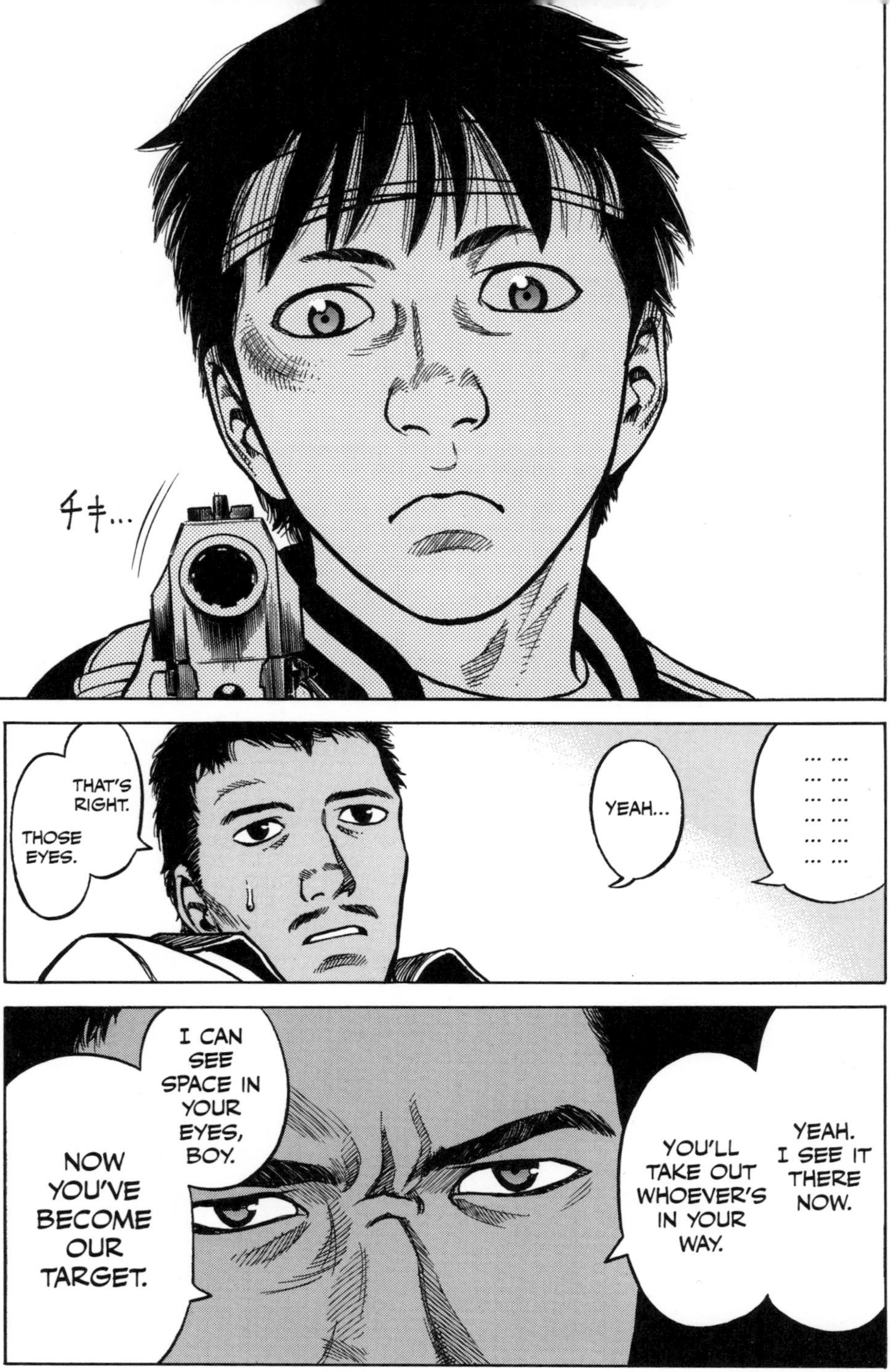

チキ...
... ...
YEAH...
THAT'S RIGHT. THOSE EYES.
YEAH. I SEE IT THERE NOW.
YOU'LL TAKE OUT WHOEVER'S IN YOUR WAY.
I CAN SEE SPACE IN YOUR EYES, BOY.
NOW YOU'VE BECOME OUR TARGET.

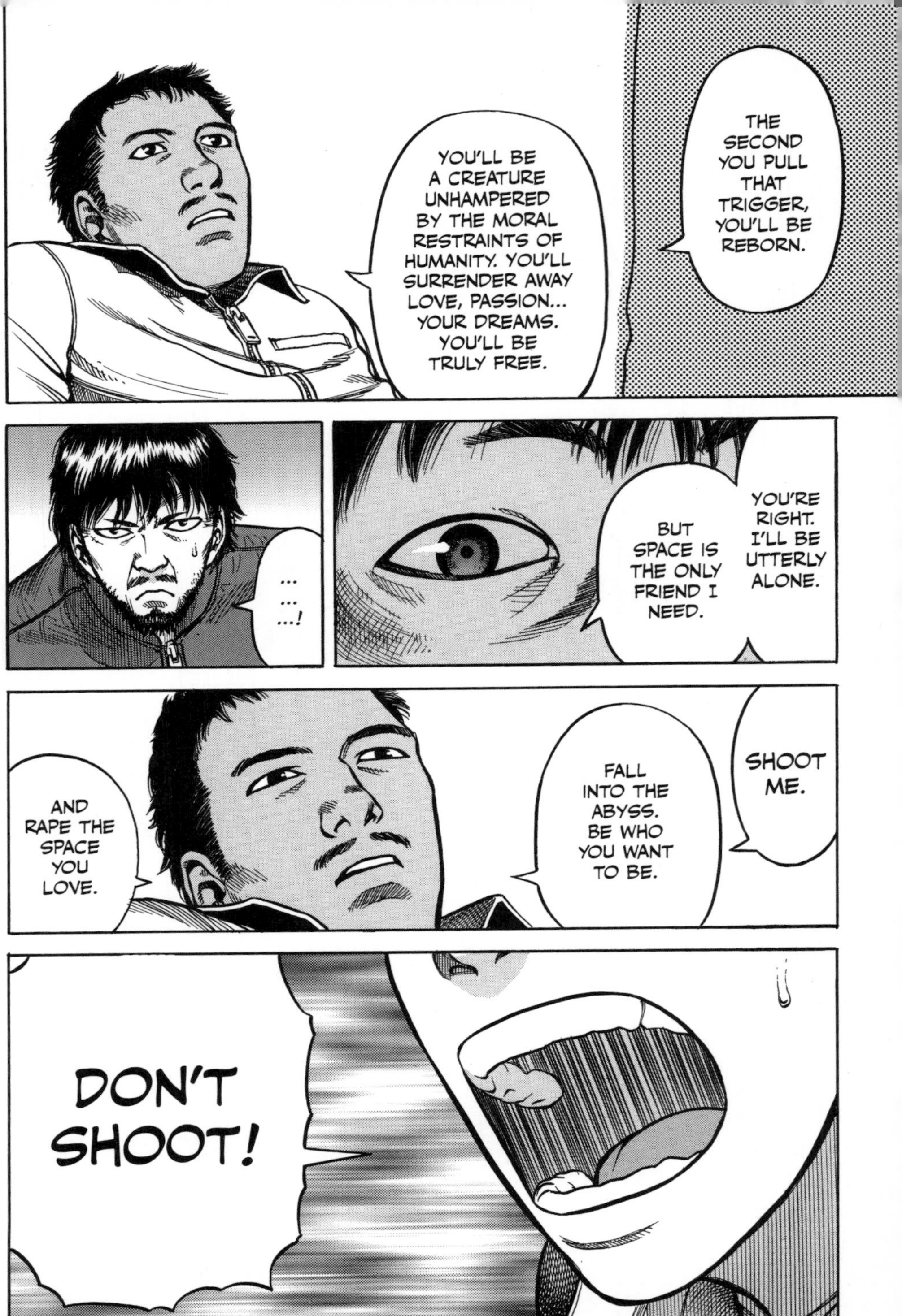
THE SECOND YOU PULL THAT TRIGGER, YOU'LL BE REBORN.
YOU'LL BE A CREATURE UNHAMPERED BY THE MORAL RESTRAINTS OF HUMANITY. YOU'LL SURRENDER AWAY LOVE, PASSION... YOUR DREAMS. YOU'LL BE TRULY FREE.
YOU'RE RIGHT. I'LL BE UTTERLY ALONE.
BUT SPACE IS THE ONLY FRIEND I NEED.
... ...!
SHOOT ME.
FALL INTO THE ABYSS. BE WHO YOU WANT TO BE.
AND RAPE THE SPACE YOU LOVE.
DON'T SHOOT!

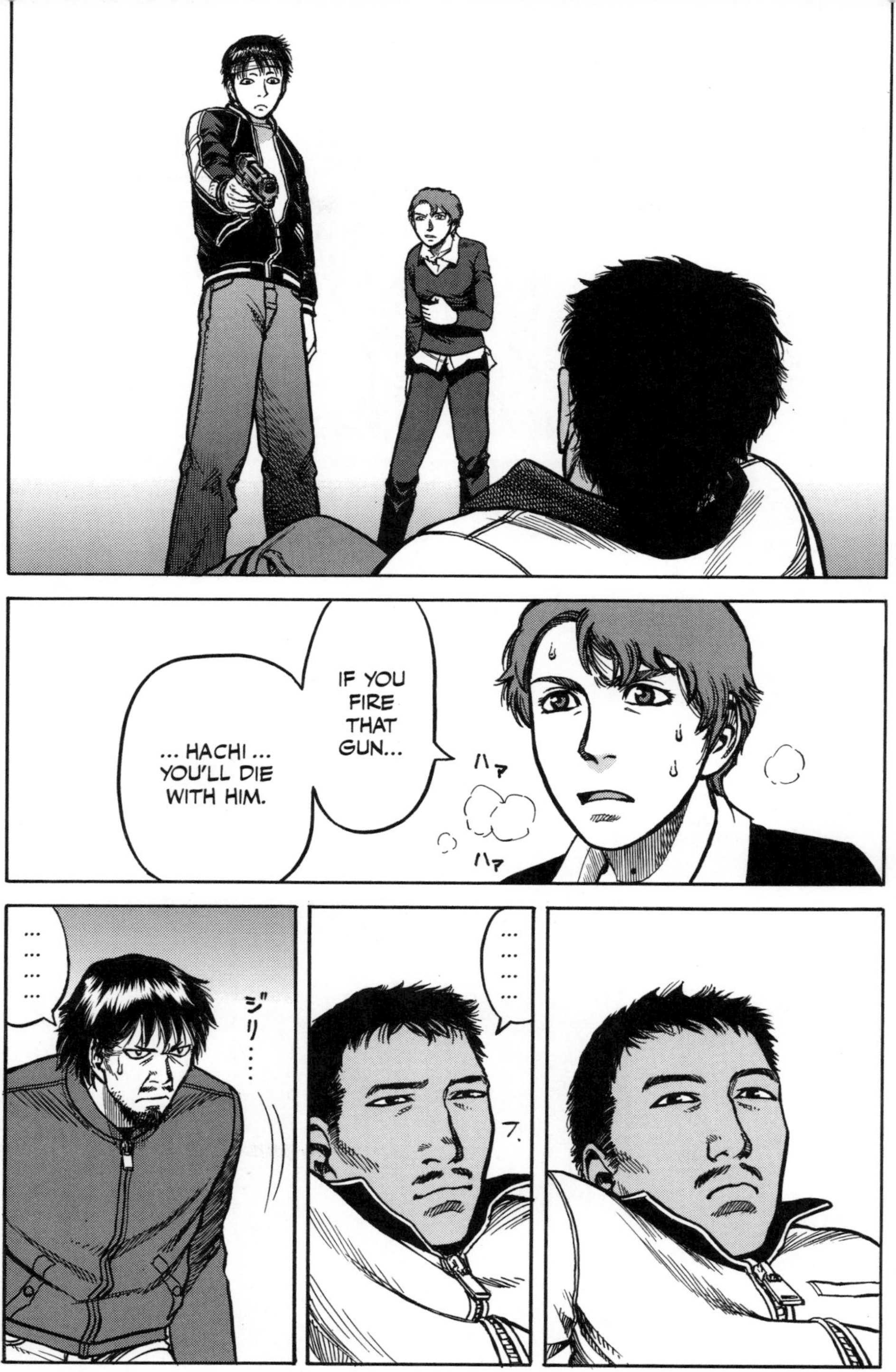
IF YOU FIRE THAT GUN...
... HACHI ... YOU'LL DIE WITH HIM.
ハァ
ハァ
....
....
ジリ....

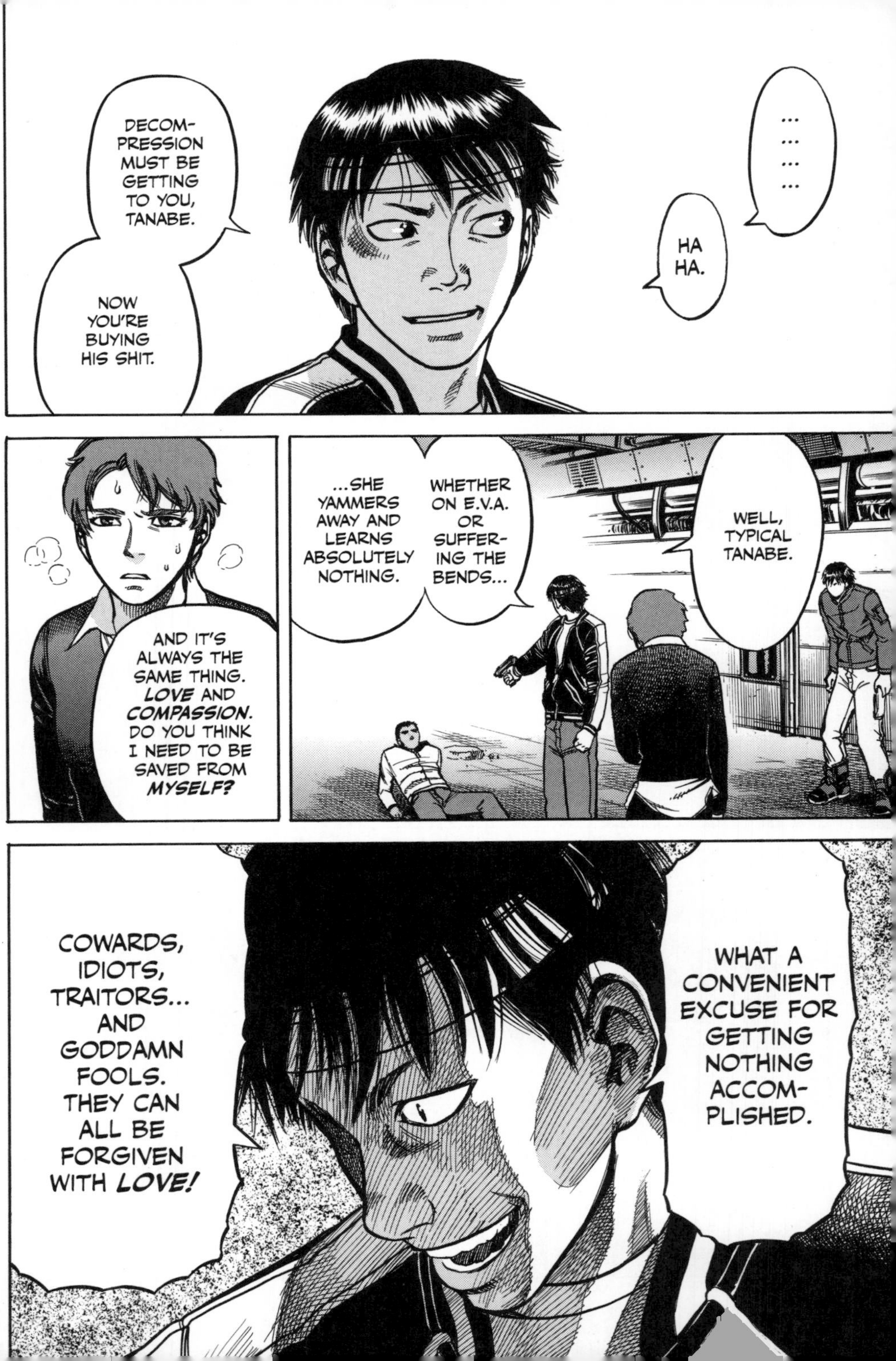
... ...
HA HA.
DECOMPRESSION MUST BE GETTING TO YOU, TANABE.
NOW YOU'RE BUYING HIS SHIT.
WELL, TYPICAL TANABE.
WHETHER ON E.V.A. OR SUFFERING THE BENDS...
...SHE YAMMERS AWAY AND LEARNS ABSOLUTELY NOTHING.
AND IT'S ALWAYS THE SAME THING. LOVE AND COMPASSION. DO YOU THINK I NEED TO BE SAVED FROM MYSELF?
WHAT A CONVENIENT EXCUSE FOR GETTING NOTHING ACCOMPLISHED.
COWARDS, IDIOTS, TRAITORS... AND GODDAMN FOOLS. THEY CAN ALL BE FORGIVEN WITH LOVE!

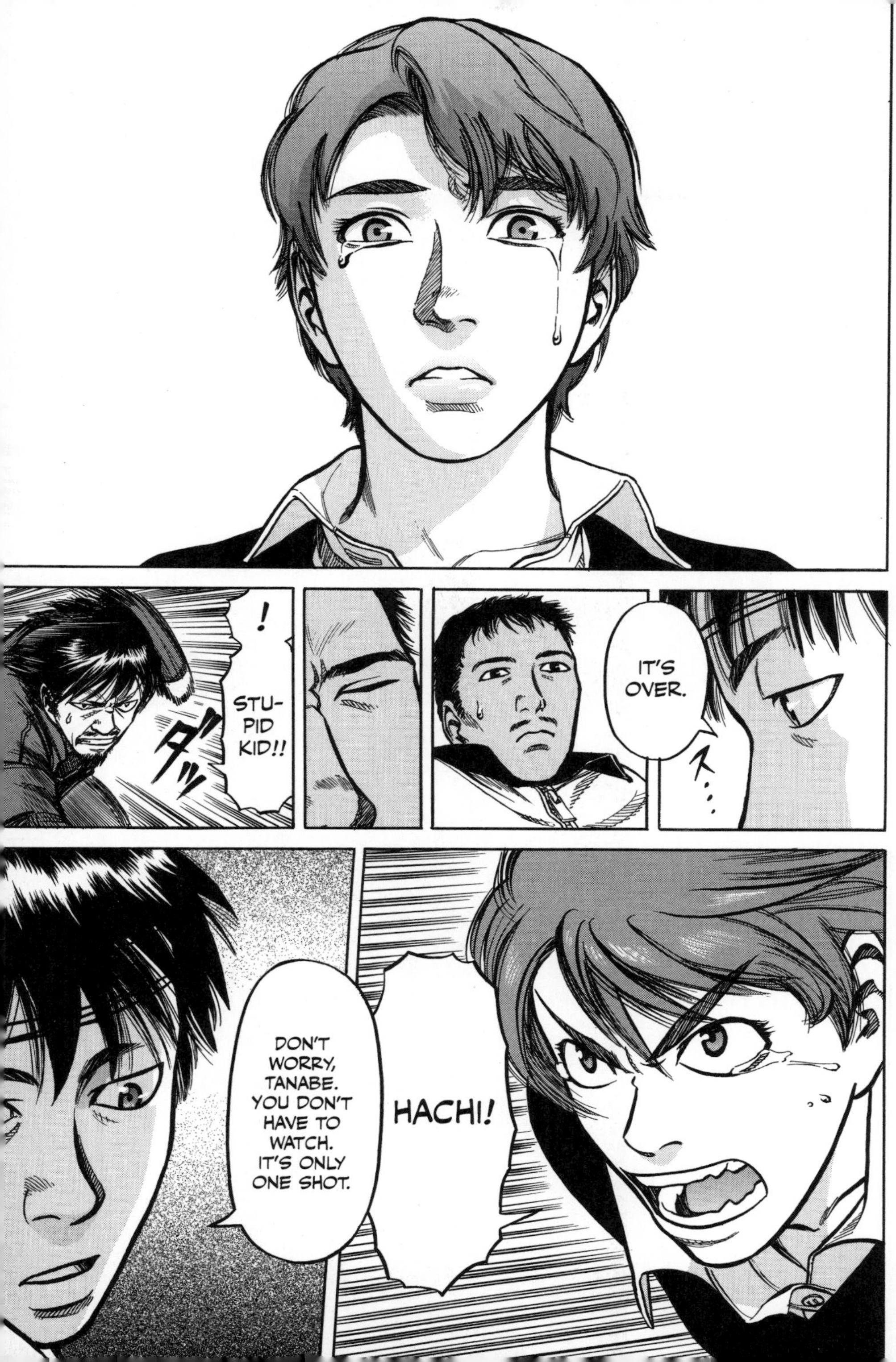
IT'S OVER.
!
STU-PID KID!!
ダッ
HACHI!
DON'T WORRY, TANABE. YOU DON'T HAVE TO WATCH. IT'S ONLY ONE SHOT.

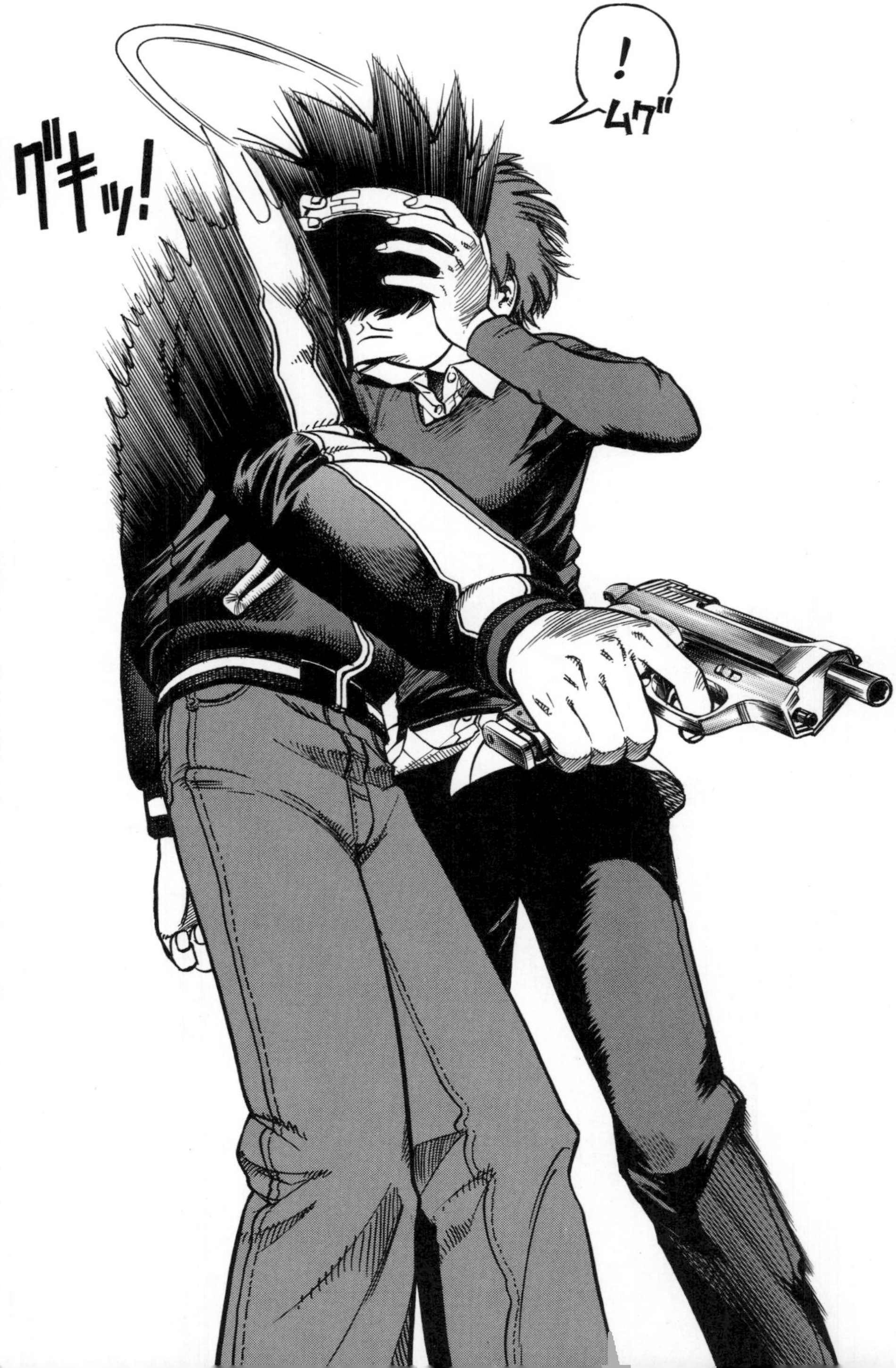
!
ムグ
グキッ!

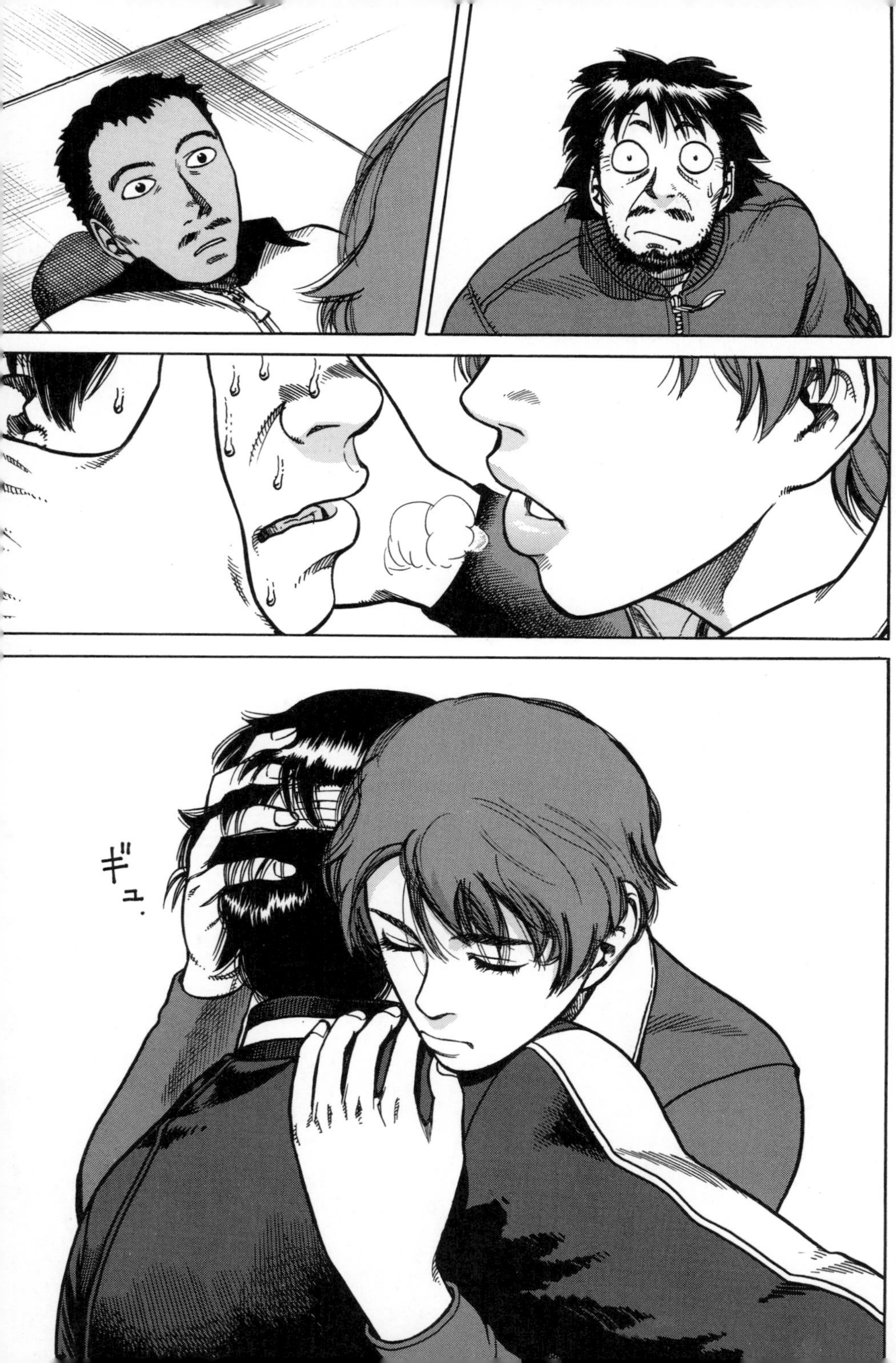
ギュ.

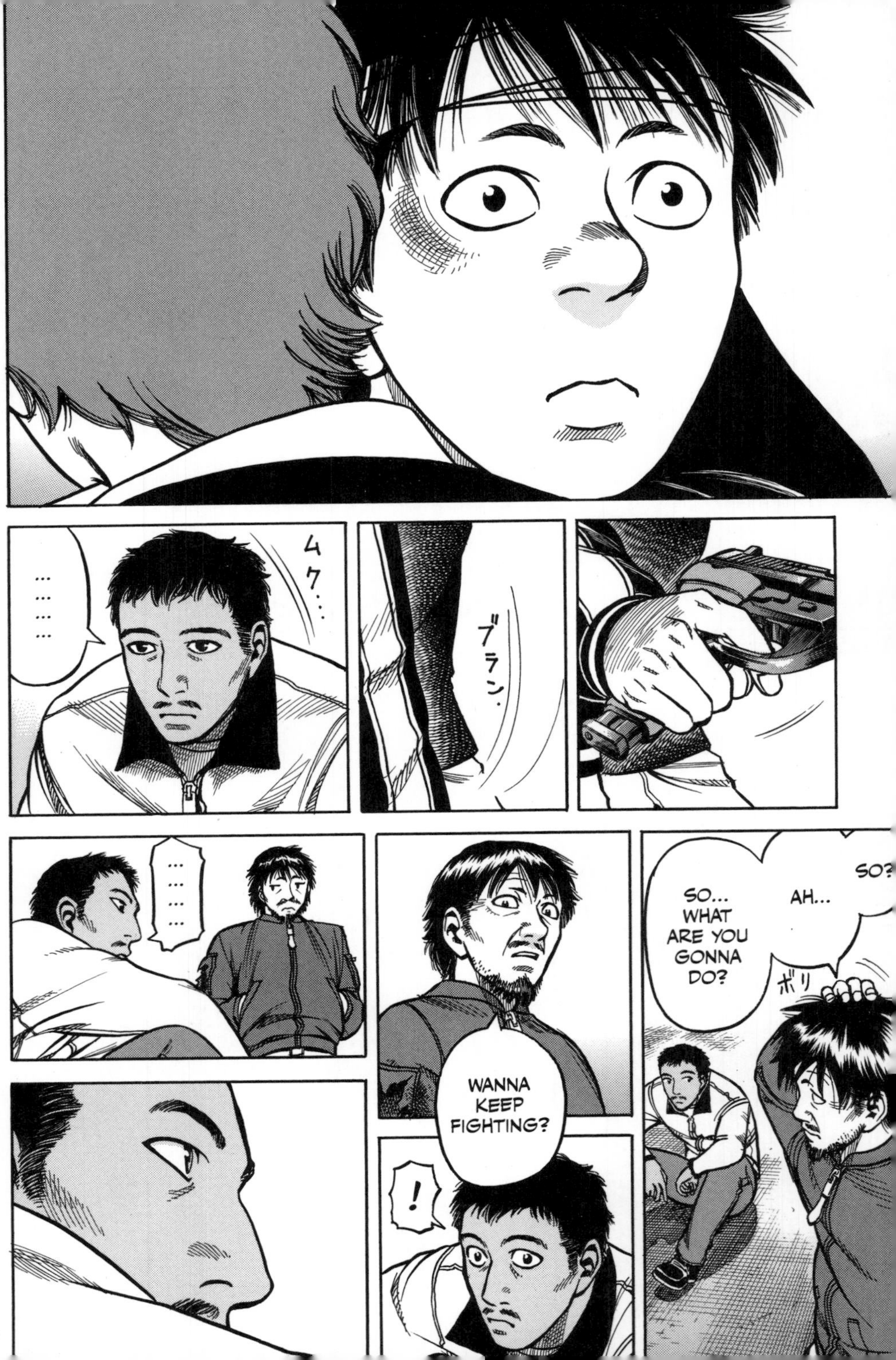
ブラン・
ムク…
……
SO?
AH...
SO... WHAT ARE YOU GONNA DO?
ボリ
……
WANNA KEEP FIGHTING?
!

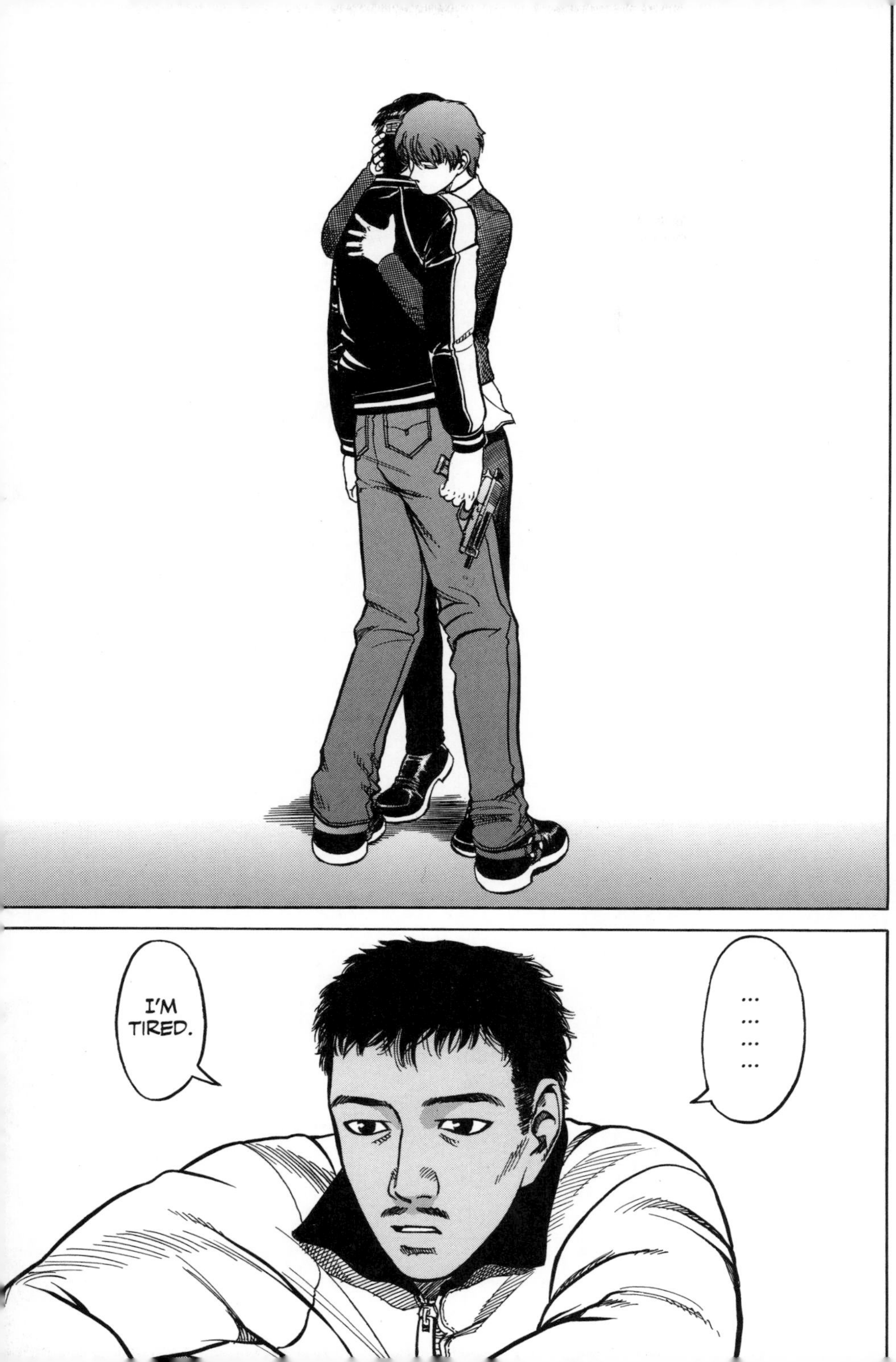

....
I'M TIRED.

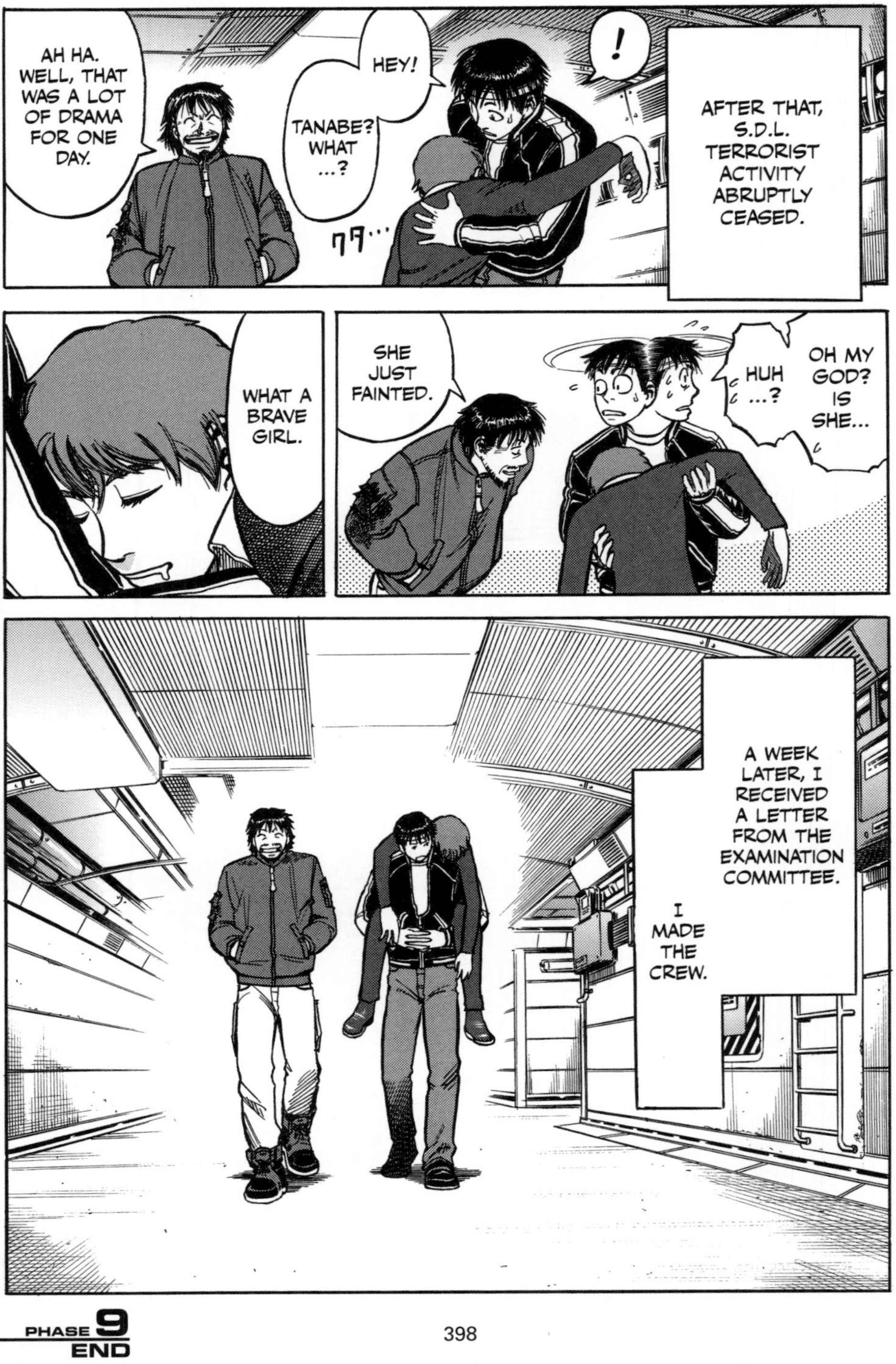
AFTER THAT, S.D.L. TERRORIST ACTIVITY ABRUPTLY CEASED.
!
HEY!
TANABE? WHAT ...?
AH HA. WELL, THAT WAS A LOT OF DRAMA FOR ONE DAY.
OH MY GOD? IS SHE...
HUH ...?
SHE JUST FAINTED.
WHAT A BRAVE GIRL.
A WEEK LATER, I RECEIVED A LETTER FROM THE EXAMINATION COMMITTEE.
I MADE THE CREW.

PHASE 9 END

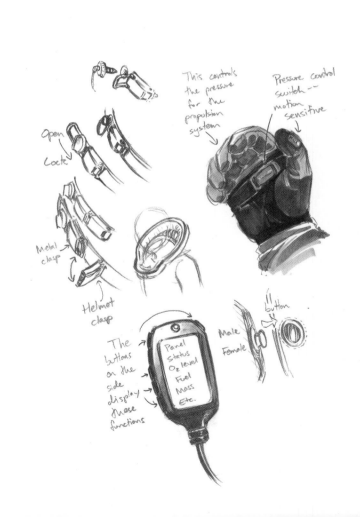

This controls the pressure for the propulsion system

Pressure control switch -- motion sensitive

Open
Close

Metal clasp

Helmet clasp

The buttons on the side display these functions

Panel
Status
O₂ level
Fuel
Mass
Etc.

Male
Female

button

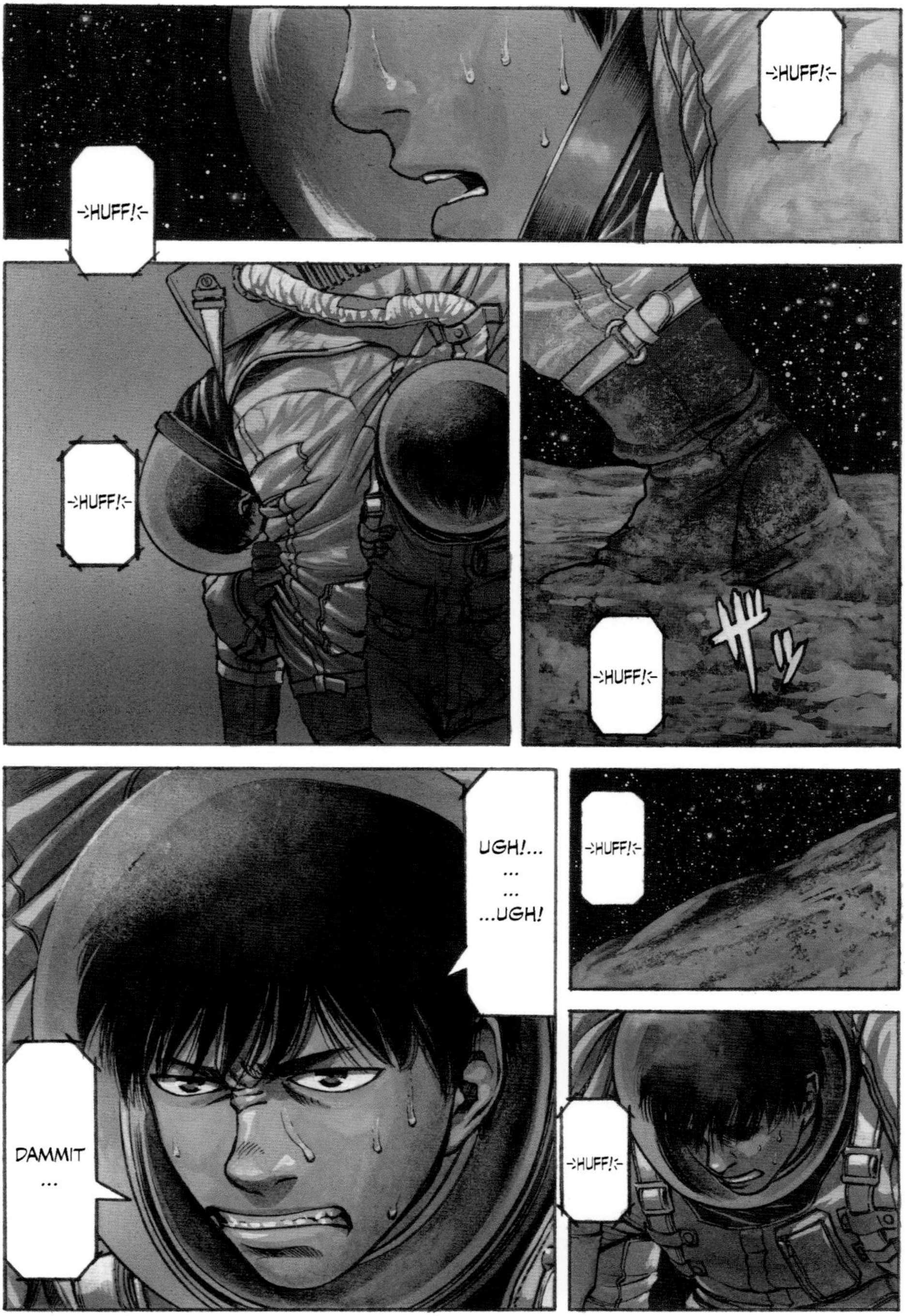
HUFF!
HUFF!
HUFF!
HUFF!
HUFF!
HUFF!
UGH!... ... ...UGH!
DAMMIT ...

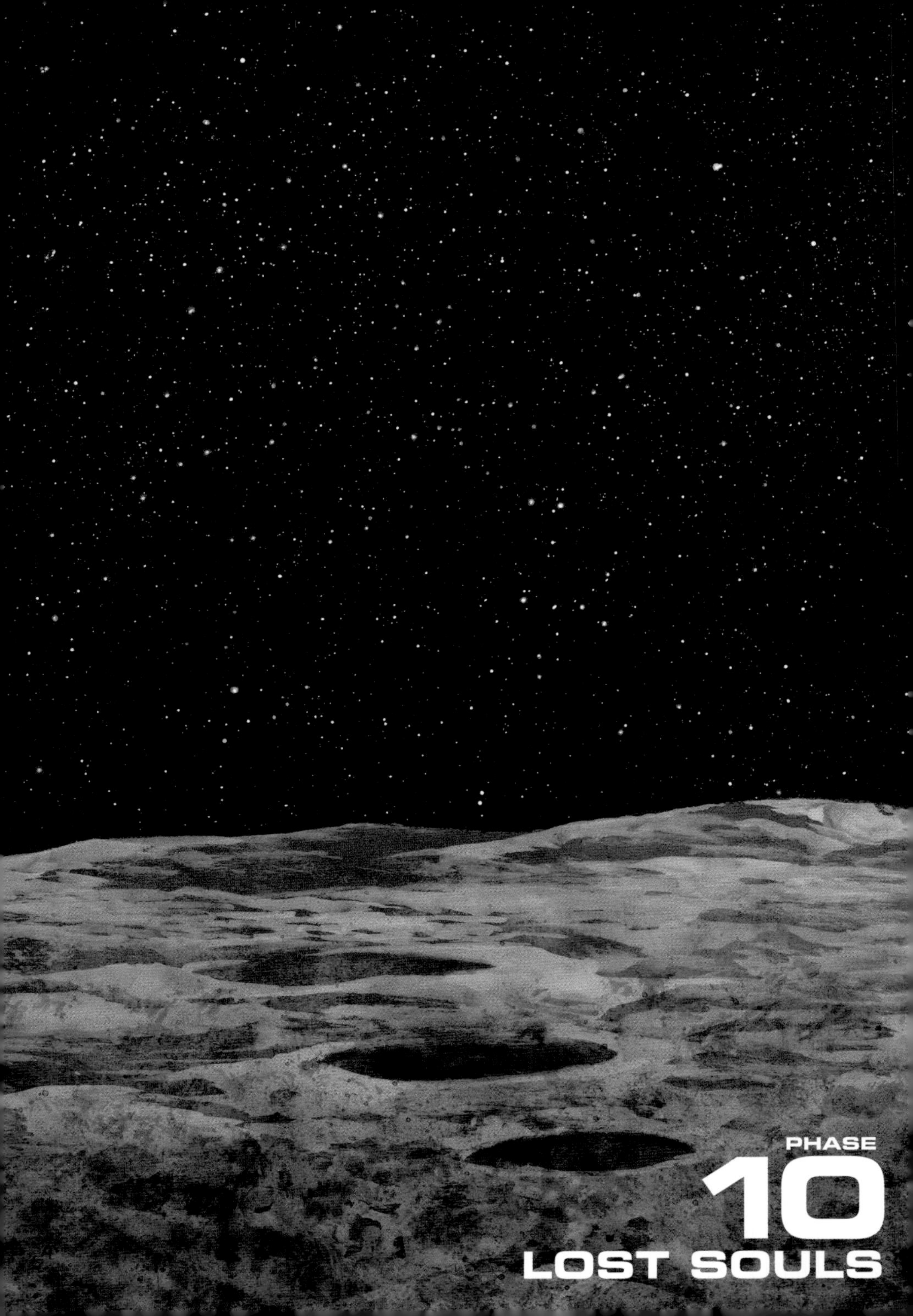
PHASE
10
LOST SOULS

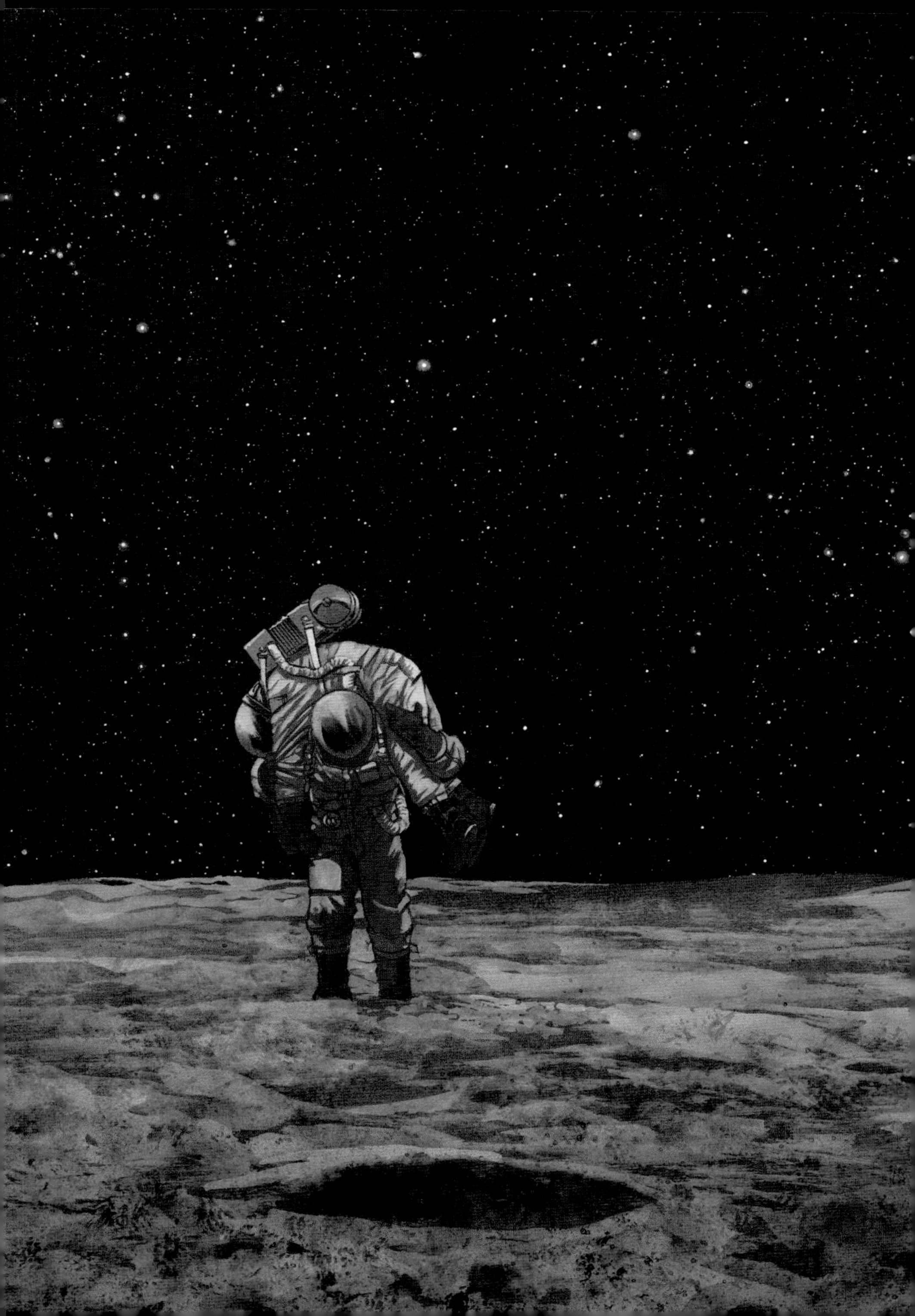

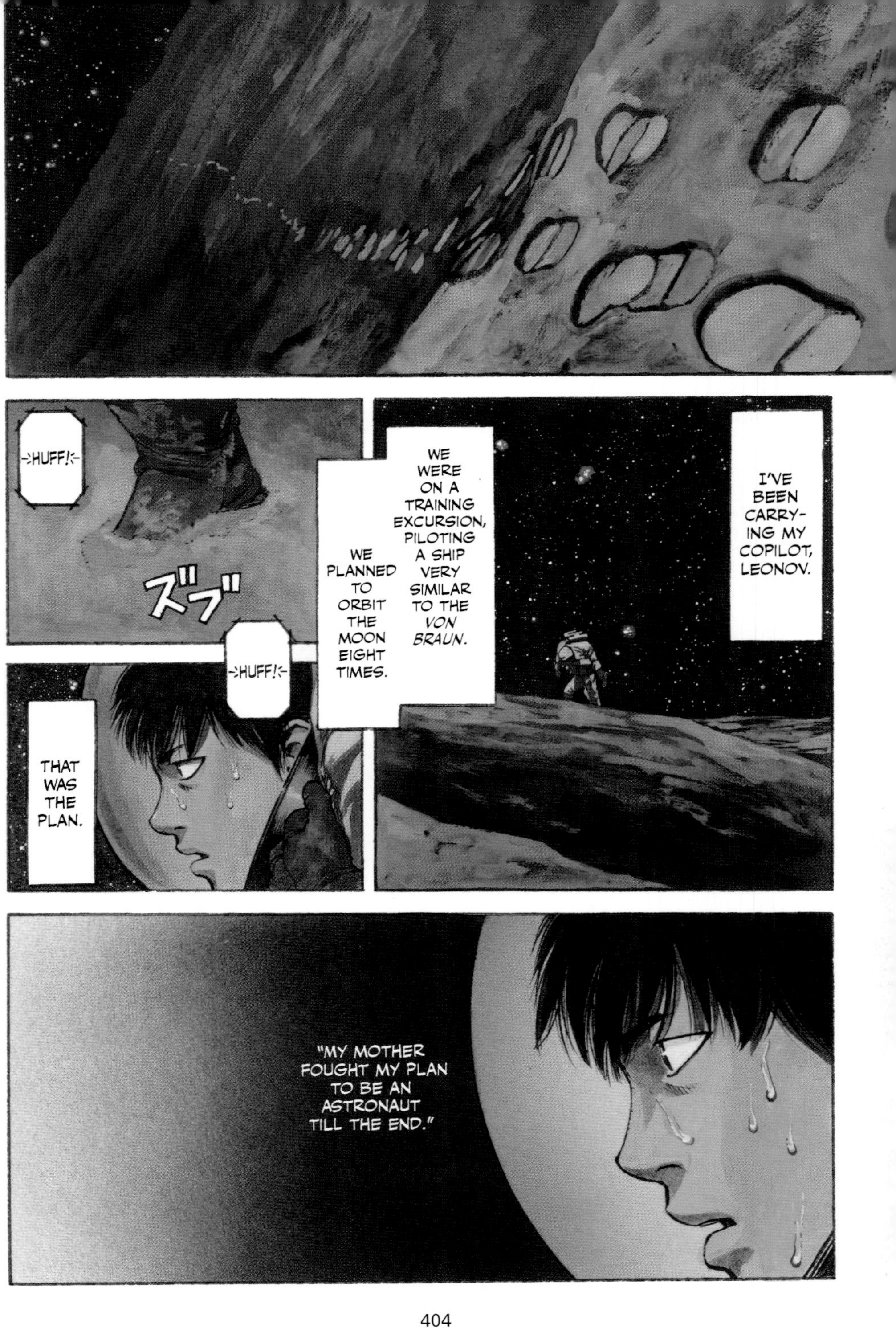
I'VE BEEN CARRYING MY COPILOT, LEONOV.
WE WERE ON A TRAINING EXCURSION, PILOTING A SHIP VERY SIMILAR TO THE *VON BRAUN*.
WE PLANNED TO ORBIT THE MOON EIGHT TIMES.
HUFF!
ズブ
HUFF!
THAT WAS THE PLAN.
"MY MOTHER FOUGHT MY PLAN TO BE AN ASTRONAUT TILL THE END."

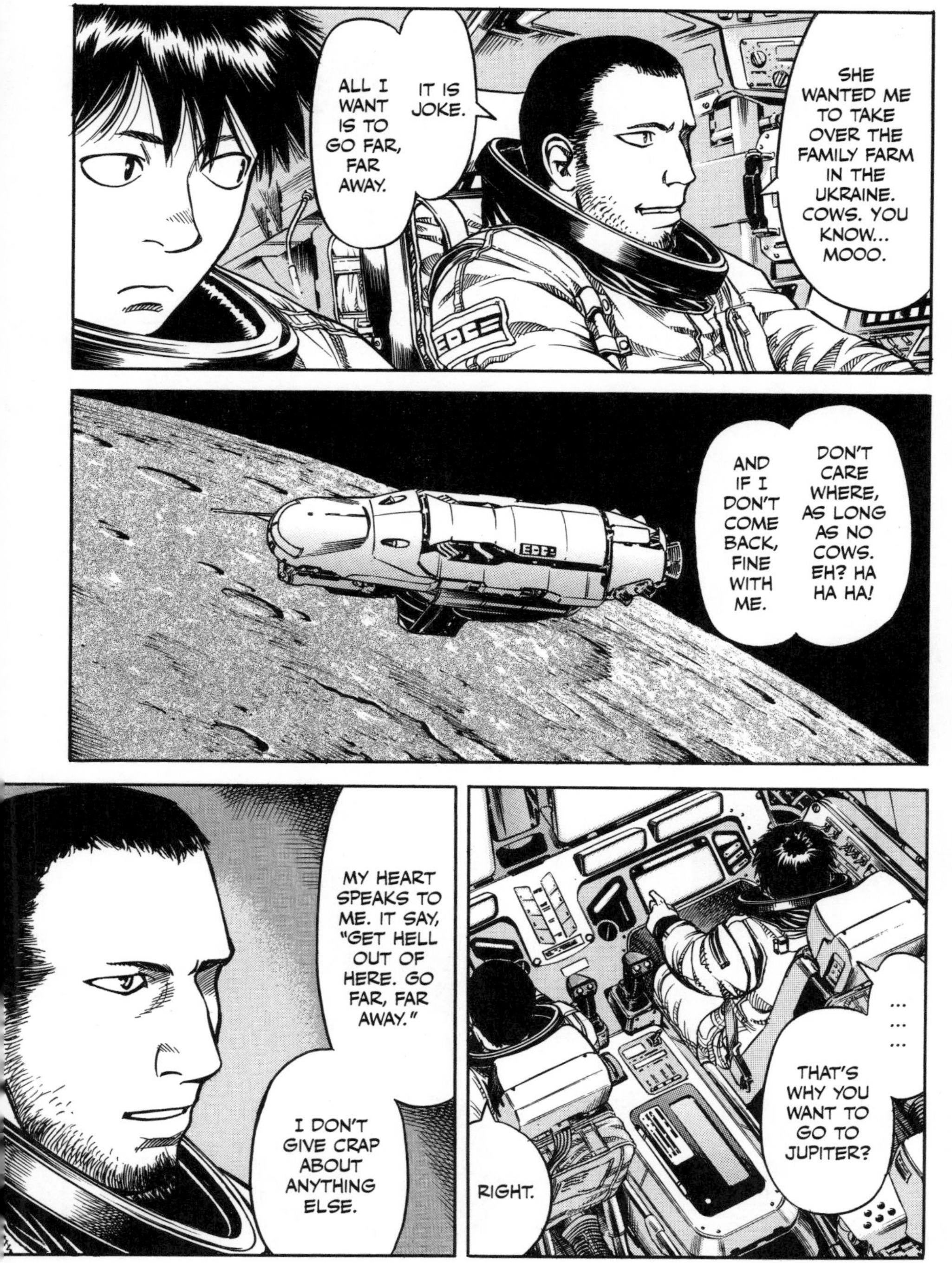
SHE WANTED ME TO TAKE OVER THE FAMILY FARM IN THE UKRAINE. COWS. YOU KNOW... MOOO.
IT IS JOKE.
ALL I WANT IS TO GO FAR, FAR AWAY.
DON'T CARE WHERE, AS LONG AS NO COWS. EH? HA HA HA!
AND IF I DON'T COME BACK, FINE WITH ME.
... ...
THAT'S WHY YOU WANT TO GO TO JUPITER?
RIGHT.
MY HEART SPEAKS TO ME. IT SAY, "GET HELL OUT OF HERE. GO FAR, FAR AWAY."
I DON'T GIVE CRAP ABOUT ANYTHING ELSE.

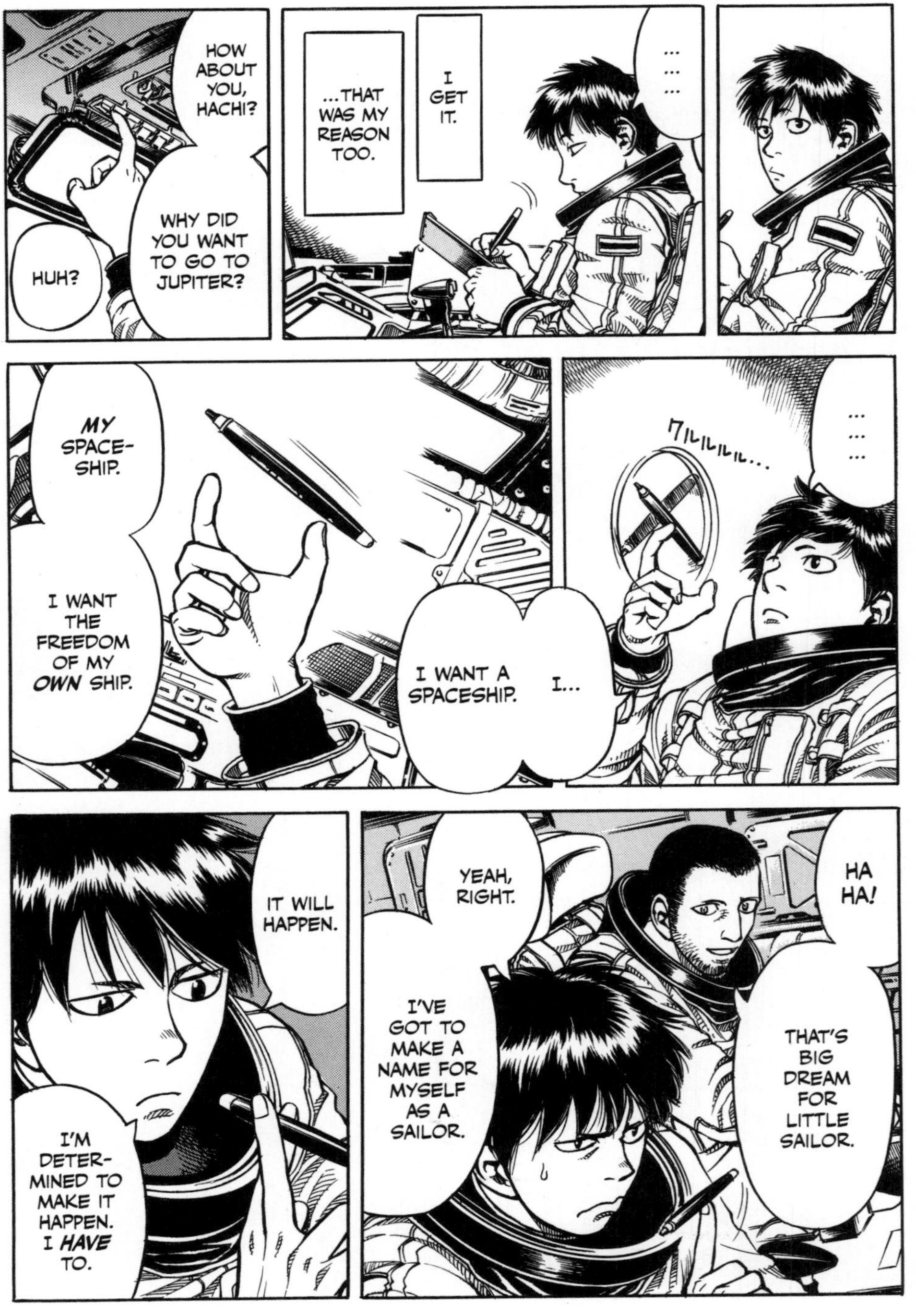
... ...
I GET IT.
...THAT WAS MY REASON TOO.
HOW ABOUT YOU, HACHI?
WHY DID YOU WANT TO GO TO JUPITER?
HUH?
ワルルルル...
... ...
I...
I WANT A SPACESHIP.
MY SPACESHIP.
I WANT THE FREEDOM OF MY *OWN* SHIP.
HA HA!
YEAH, RIGHT.
THAT'S BIG DREAM FOR LITTLE SAILOR.
I'VE GOT TO MAKE A NAME FOR MYSELF AS A SAILOR.
IT WILL HAPPEN.
I'M DETERMINED TO MAKE IT HAPPEN. I *HAVE* TO.

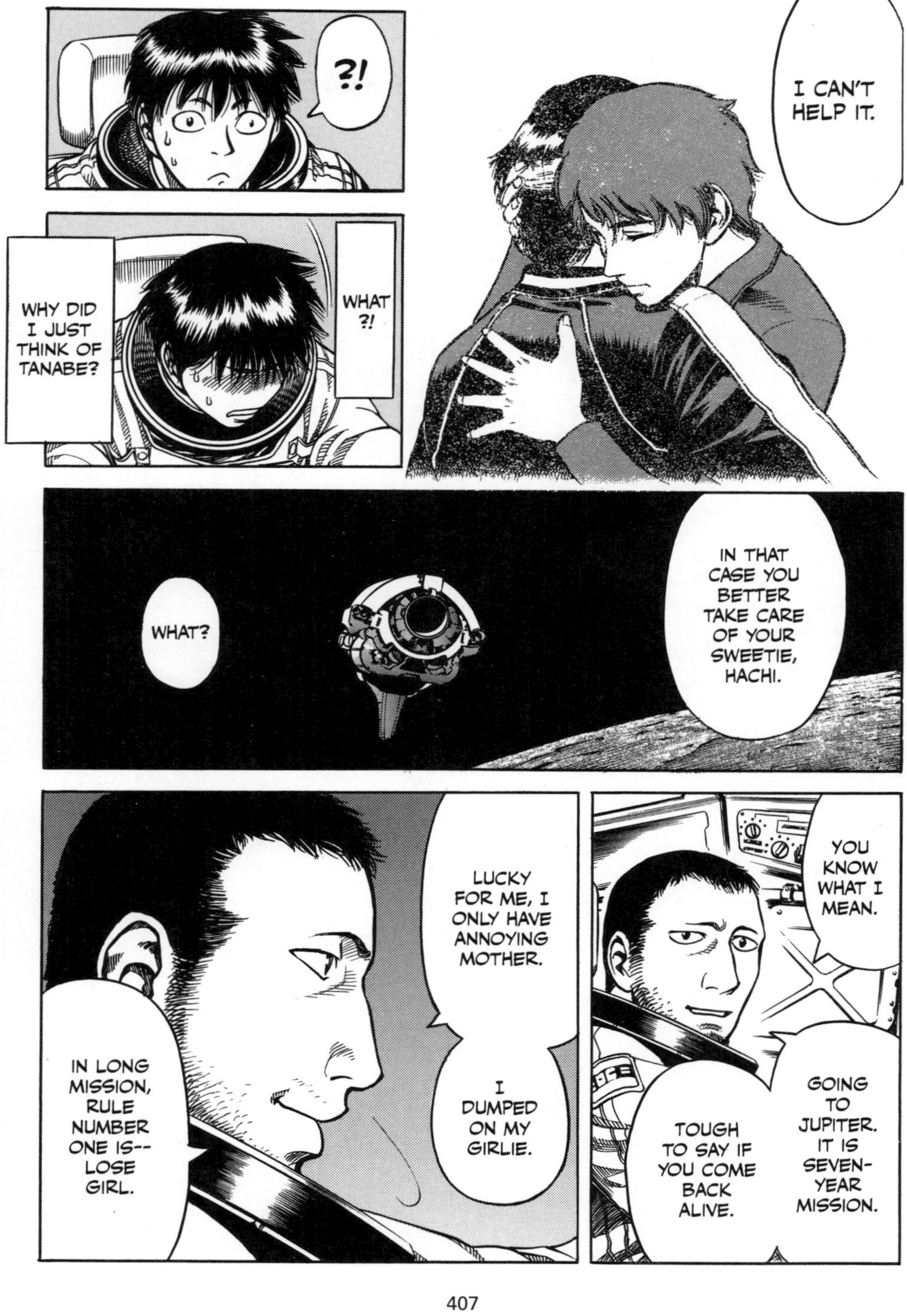
I CAN'T HELP IT.
?!
WHAT ?!
WHY DID I JUST THINK OF TANABE?
IN THAT CASE YOU BETTER TAKE CARE OF YOUR SWEETIE, HACHI.
WHAT?
YOU KNOW WHAT I MEAN.
GOING TO JUPITER. IT IS SEVEN-YEAR MISSION.
TOUGH TO SAY IF YOU COME BACK ALIVE.
LUCKY FOR ME, I ONLY HAVE ANNOYING MOTHER.
I DUMPED ON MY GIRLIE.
IN LONG MISSION, RULE NUMBER ONE IS-- LOSE GIRL.

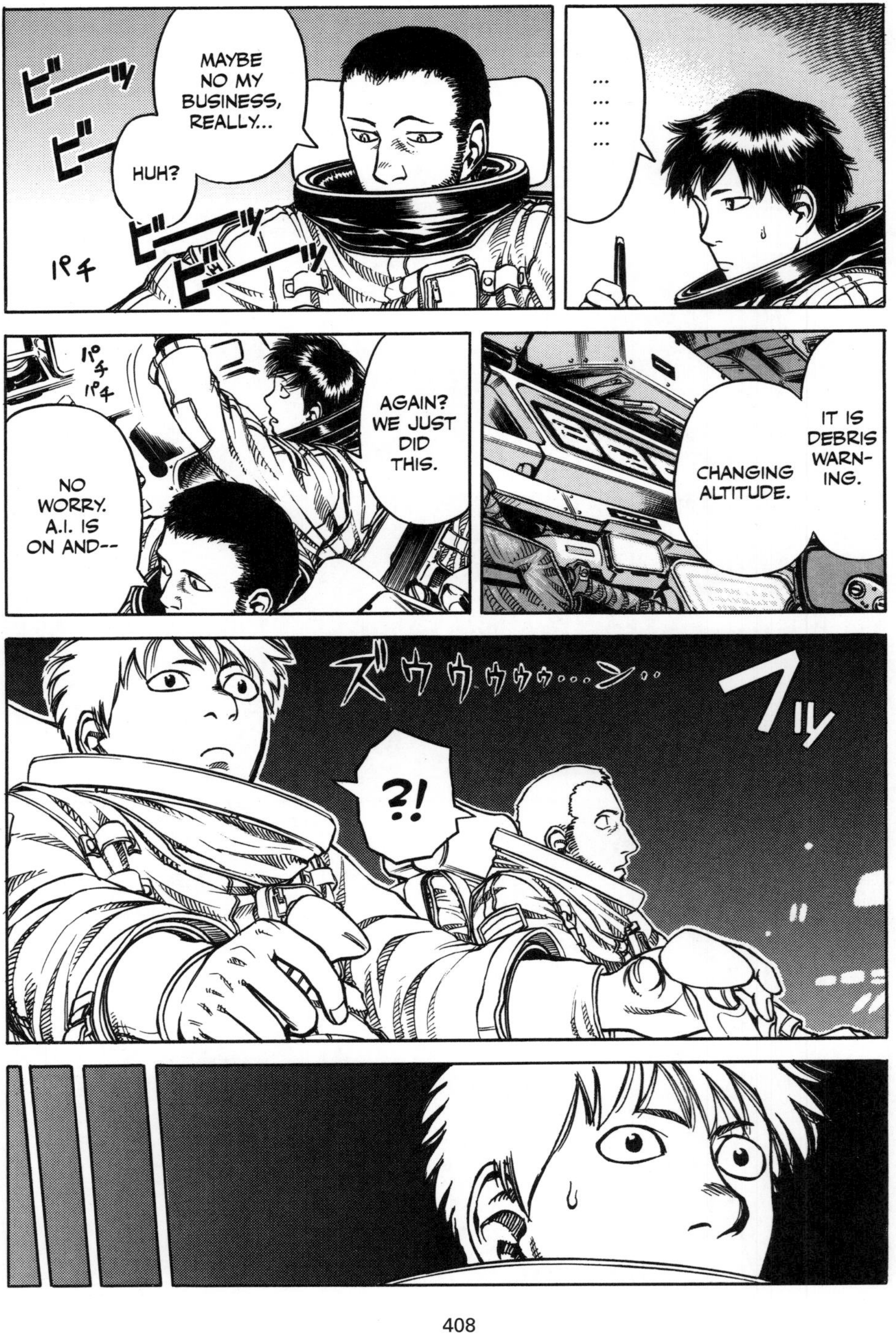
....
....
....
....
MAYBE NO MY BUSINESS, REALLY...
HUH?
ビーーッ
ビー
ビーーッ
ビーーッ
パチ
IT IS DEBRIS WARNING.
CHANGING ALTITUDE.
AGAIN? WE JUST DID THIS.
パチ
パチ
NO WORRY. A.I. IS ON AND--
フッ
ズウウウウウ...ン..
?!

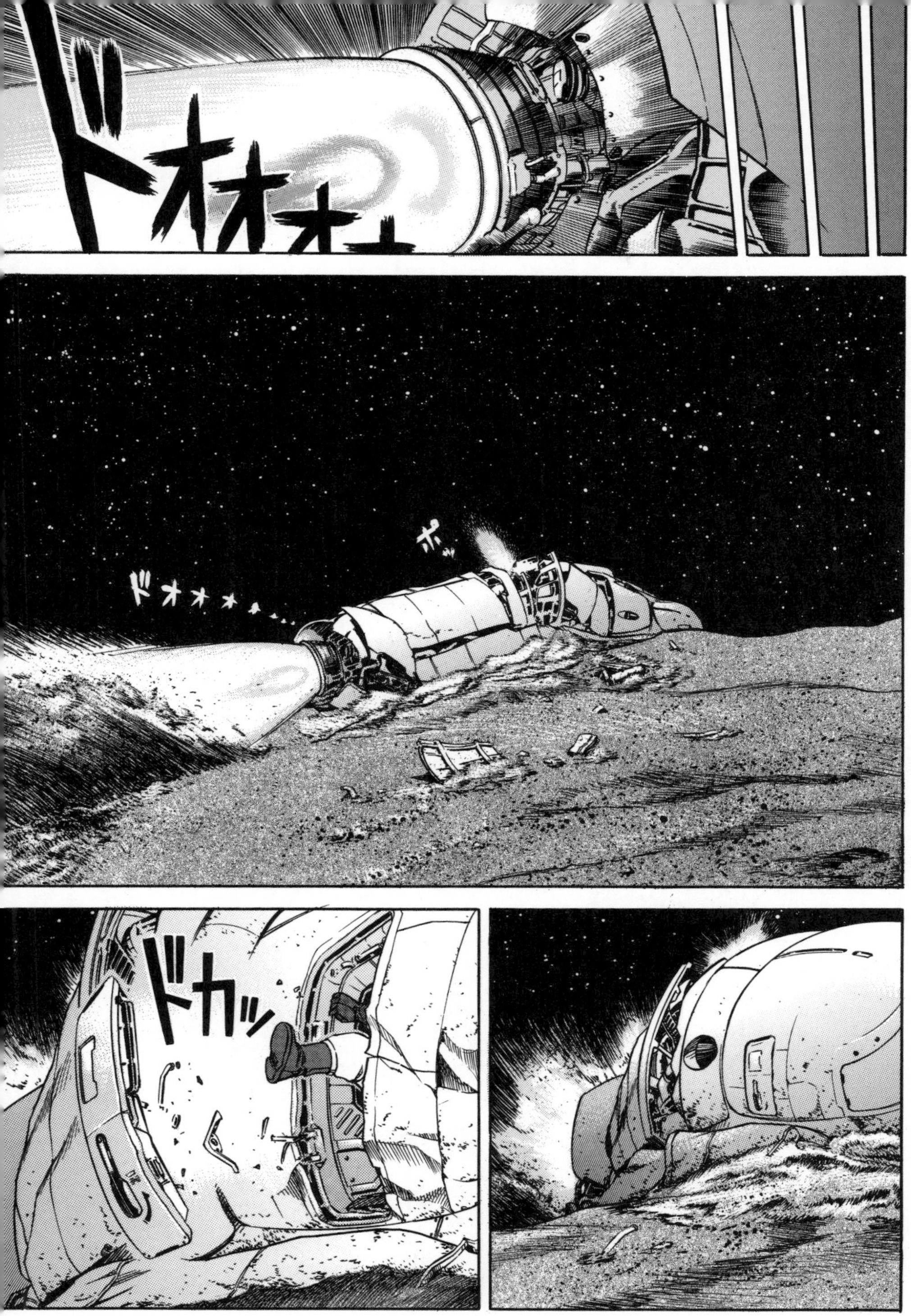
ドオオオ
ポッ
ドオオオォ…
ドカッ

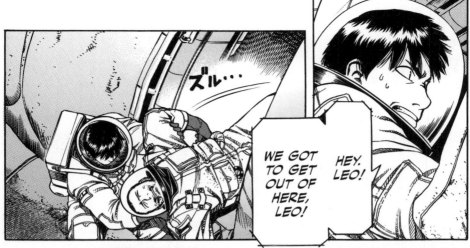

HEY. LEO!
WE GOT TO GET OUT OF HERE, LEO!
ズル…
HEH, HEH...
OH MAN...
THE COOLER PUMP IS DOWN AND THE ENGINE'S STILL GOING!
ポイッ
HACHIMAKI, YOU... VERY ROUGH.
IF YOU'RE STILL ABLE TO BE A SMART ASS YOU SHOULD BE ABLE TO WALK.
THAT'S WHY YOU HAVE NO GIRL TO DUMP.
PRESSURE PUMP'S REDLINING.
EVERY-THING'S GONNA BLOW. INCLUDING THE PROPELLANT TANK!

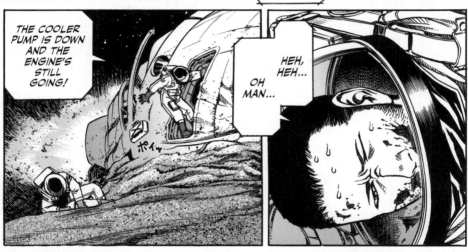

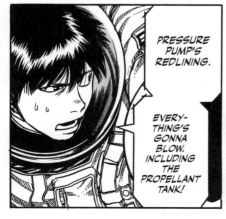

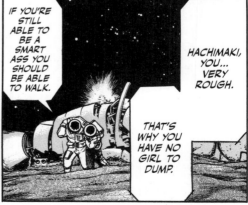

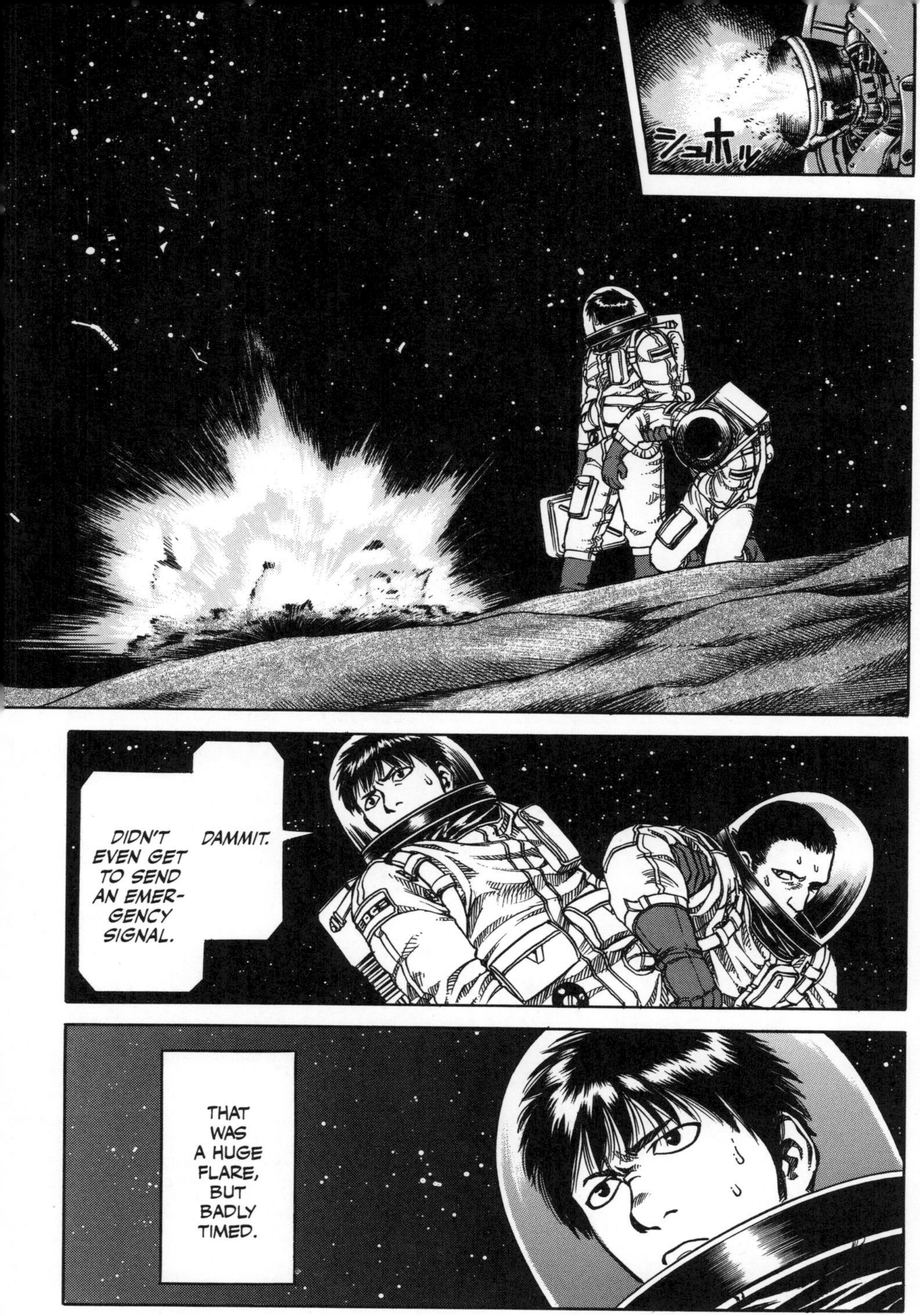
シュボッ
DAMMIT.
DIDN'T EVEN GET TO SEND AN EMERGENCY SIGNAL.
THAT WAS A HUGE FLARE, BUT BADLY TIMED.

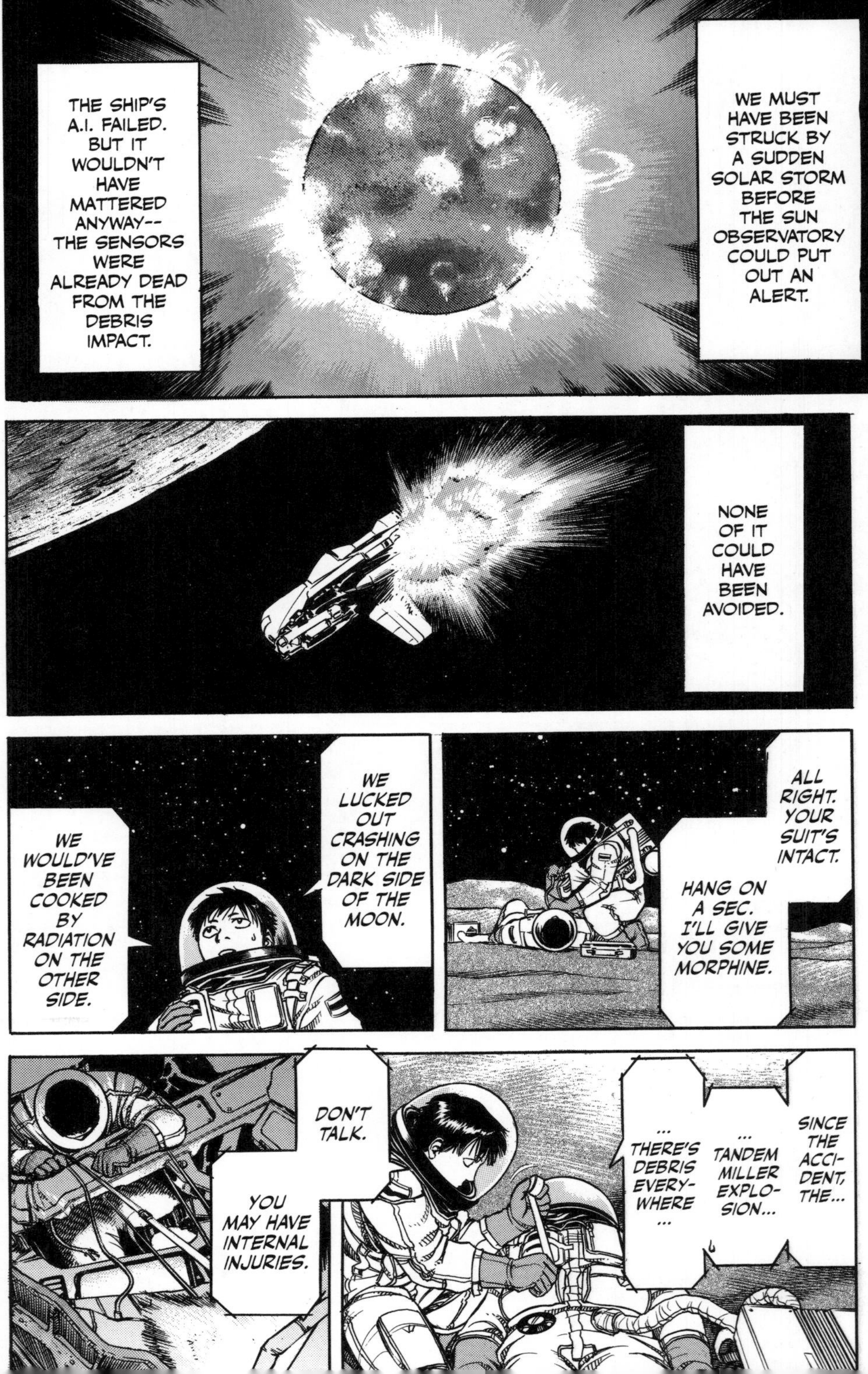
WE MUST HAVE BEEN STRUCK BY A SUDDEN SOLAR STORM BEFORE THE SUN OBSERVATORY COULD PUT OUT AN ALERT.
THE SHIP'S A.I. FAILED. BUT IT WOULDN'T HAVE MATTERED ANYWAY-- THE SENSORS WERE ALREADY DEAD FROM THE DEBRIS IMPACT.
NONE OF IT COULD HAVE BEEN AVOIDED.
ALL RIGHT. YOUR SUIT'S INTACT.
HANG ON A SEC. I'LL GIVE YOU SOME MORPHINE.
WE LUCKED OUT CRASHING ON THE DARK SIDE OF THE MOON.
WE WOULD'VE BEEN COOKED BY RADIATION ON THE OTHER SIDE.
SINCE THE ACCI-DENT, THE...
... TANDEM MILLER EXPLO-SION...
... THERE'S DEBRIS EVERY-WHERE ...
DON'T TALK.
YOU MAY HAVE INTERNAL INJURIES.

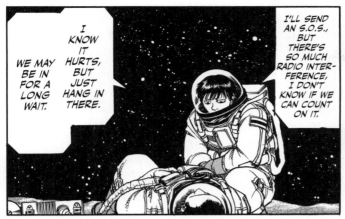

OKAY...
I'LL SEND AN S.O.S., BUT THERE'S SO MUCH RADIO INTERFERENCE, I DON'T KNOW IF WE CAN COUNT ON IT.
I KNOW IT HURTS, BUT JUST HANG IN THERE.
WE MAY BE IN FOR A LONG WAIT.
HUFF!
... ...
ALL RIGHT. JUST IN CASE... I HAVE TO ASK YOU... DO YOU HAVE A ...WILL, OR SOMETHING YOU WANT ME TO DO IF...?
YOU'RE BLEEDING. IT'S JUST A PRECAUTION.
... ...
HUFF!
MY WILL?
THIS JOKE NOT FUNNY ANYMORE.

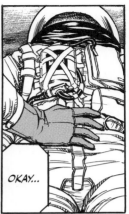

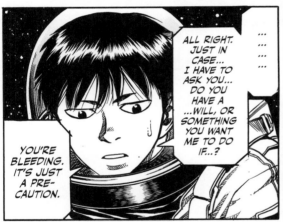

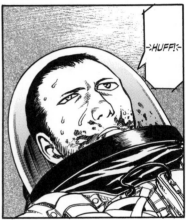

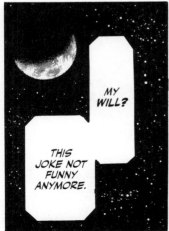

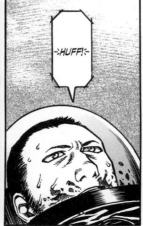

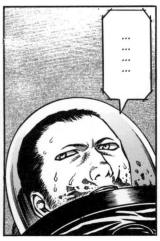

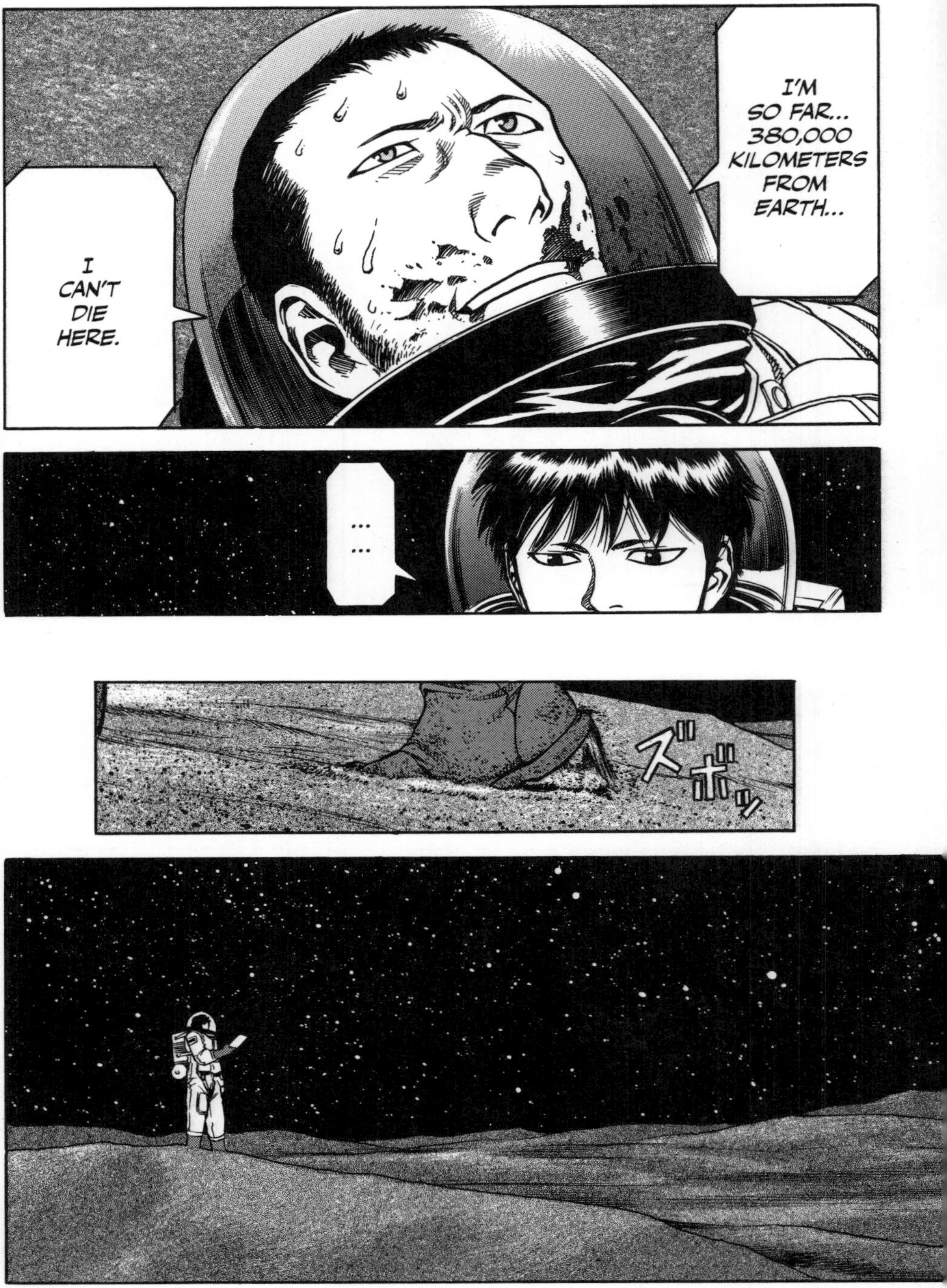
I'M SO FAR... 380,000 KILOMETERS FROM EARTH...
I CAN'T DIE HERE.
... ...
ズボッ

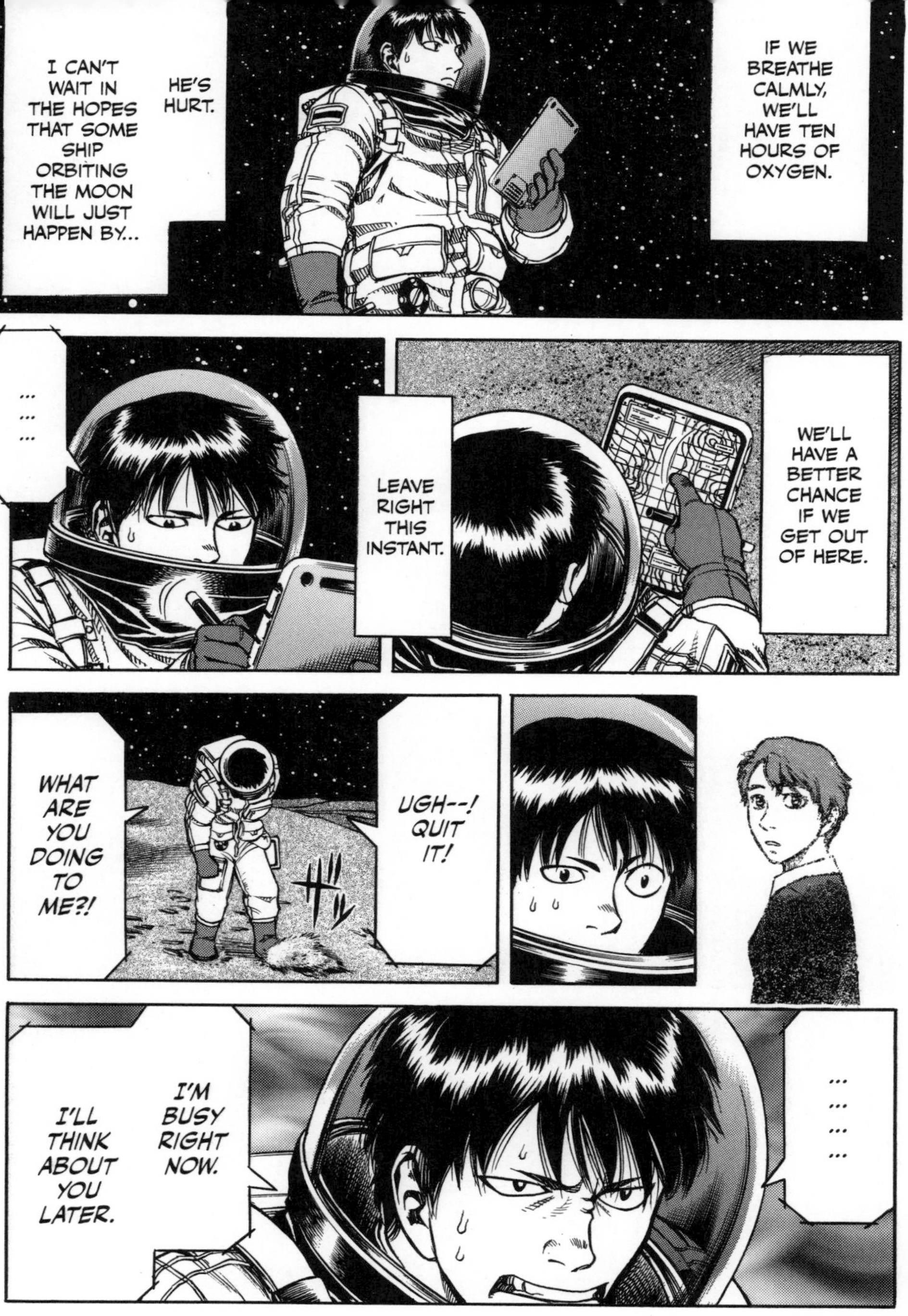
IF WE BREATHE CALMLY, WE'LL HAVE TEN HOURS OF OXYGEN.
HE'S HURT.
I CAN'T WAIT IN THE HOPES THAT SOME SHIP ORBITING THE MOON WILL JUST HAPPEN BY...
WE'LL HAVE A BETTER CHANCE IF WE GET OUT OF HERE.
LEAVE RIGHT THIS INSTANT.
... ...
UGH--! QUIT IT!
WHAT ARE YOU DOING TO ME?!
... ...
I'M BUSY RIGHT NOW.
I'LL THINK ABOUT YOU LATER.

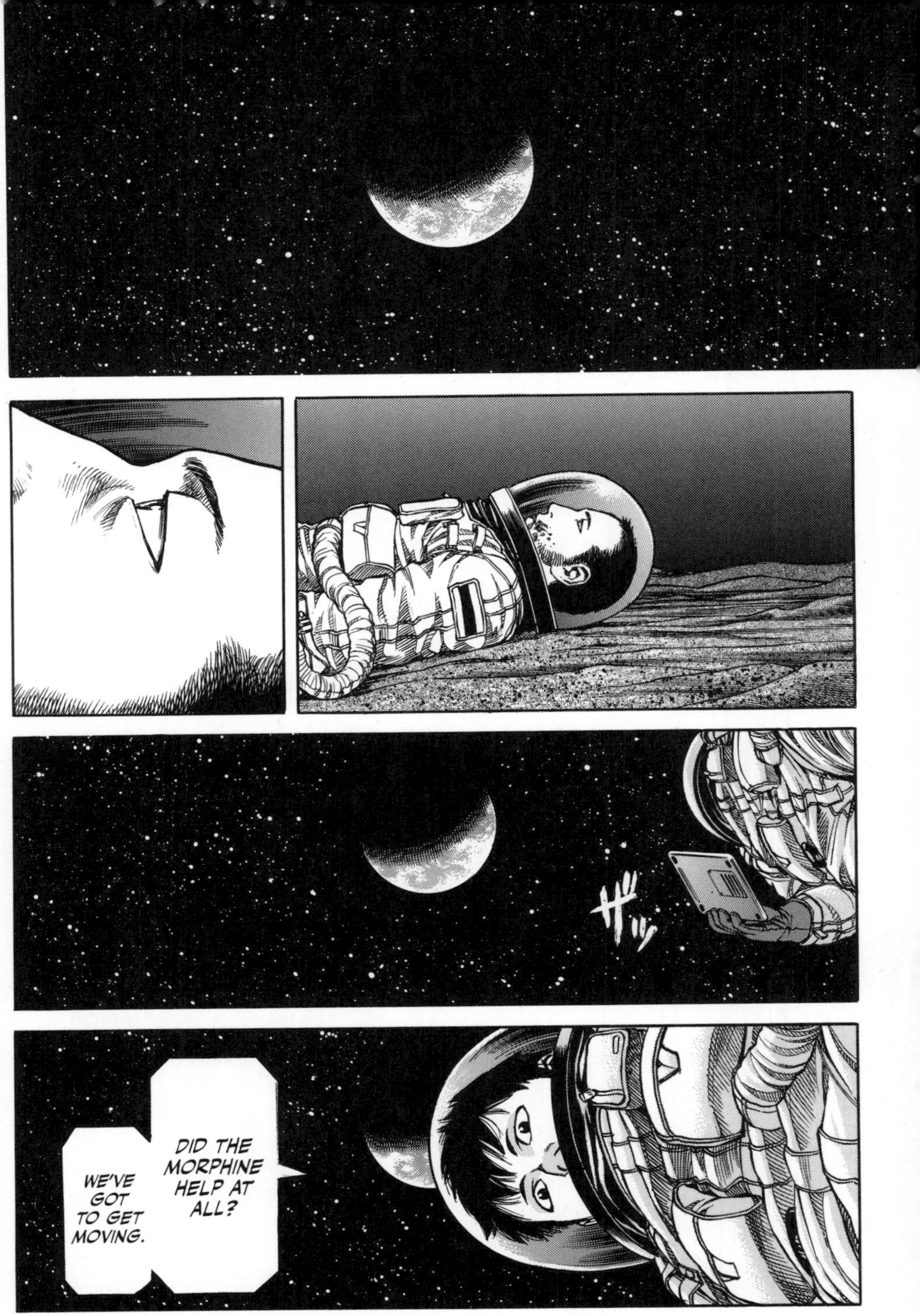
ザッ
DID THE MORPHINE HELP AT ALL?
WE'VE GOT TO GET MOVING.

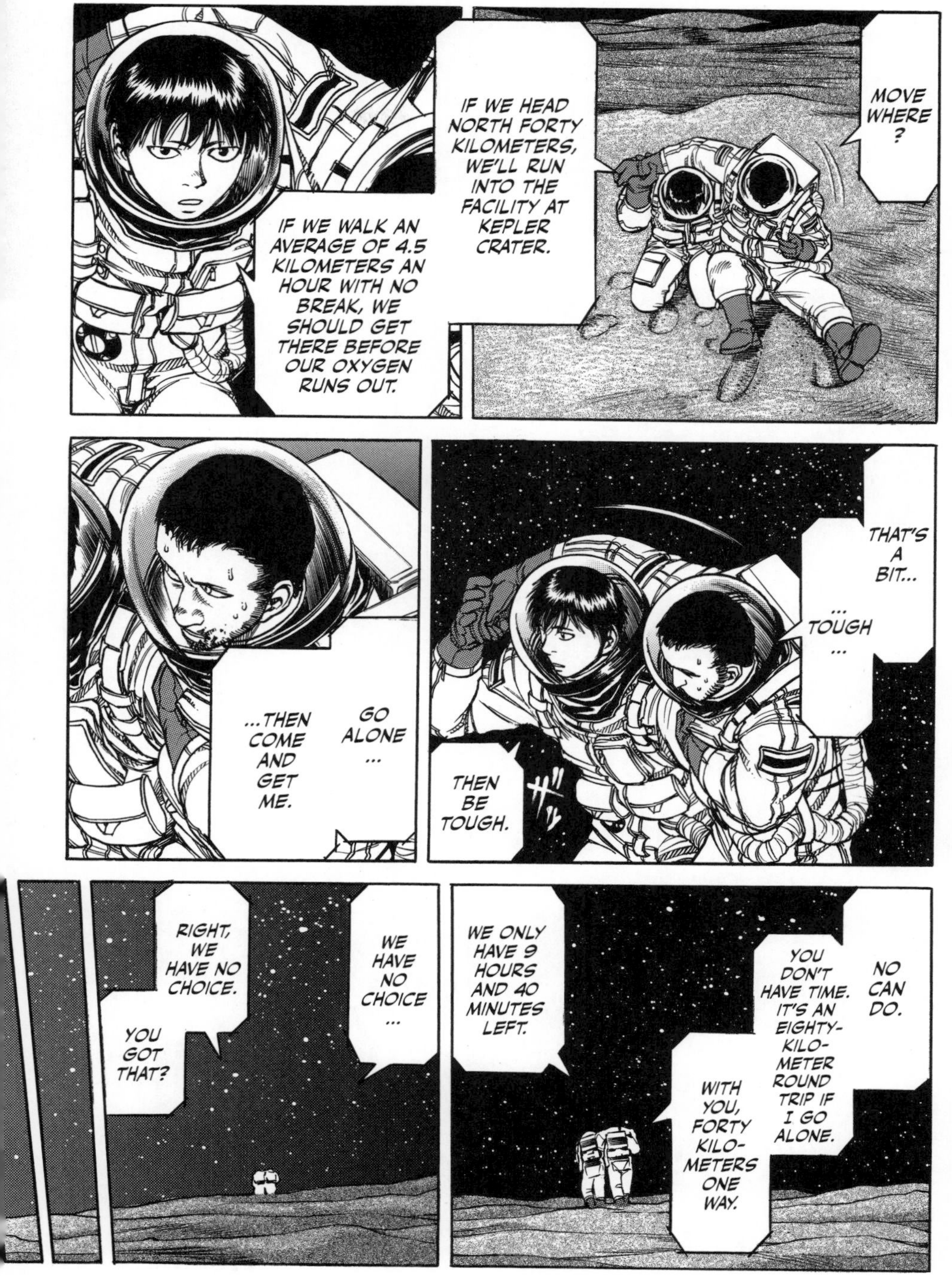
MOVE WHERE ?
IF WE HEAD NORTH FORTY KILOMETERS, WE'LL RUN INTO THE FACILITY AT KEPLER CRATER.
IF WE WALK AN AVERAGE OF 4.5 KILOMETERS AN HOUR WITH NO BREAK, WE SHOULD GET THERE BEFORE OUR OXYGEN RUNS OUT.
THAT'S A BIT...
...TOUGH...
THEN BE TOUGH.
GO ALONE...
...THEN COME AND GET ME.
NO CAN DO.
YOU DON'T HAVE TIME. IT'S AN EIGHTY-KILOMETER ROUND TRIP IF I GO ALONE.
WITH YOU, FORTY KILOMETERS ONE WAY.
WE ONLY HAVE 9 HOURS AND 40 MINUTES LEFT.
WE HAVE NO CHOICE...
RIGHT, WE HAVE NO CHOICE.
YOU GOT THAT?

HUFF!
HUFF!
CLEAR YOUR MIND.

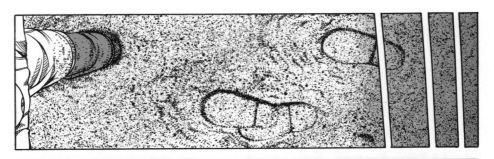

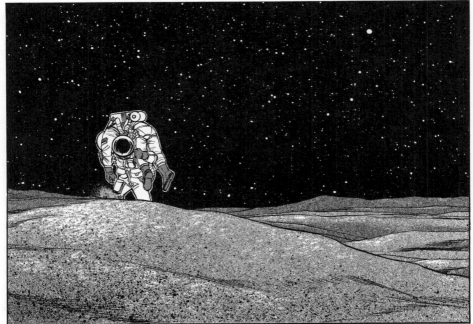

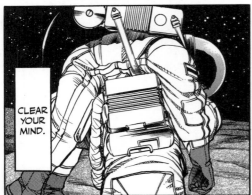

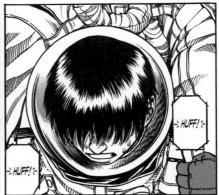

THINK ABOUT NOTH- ING.

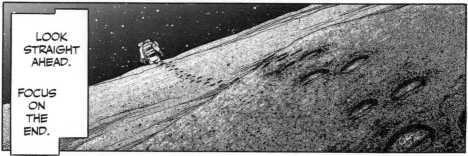

LOOK STRAIGHT AHEAD.

FOCUS ON THE END.

ONE FOOT IN FRONT OF THE OTHER.

FOCUS. EASY. PERFECT.

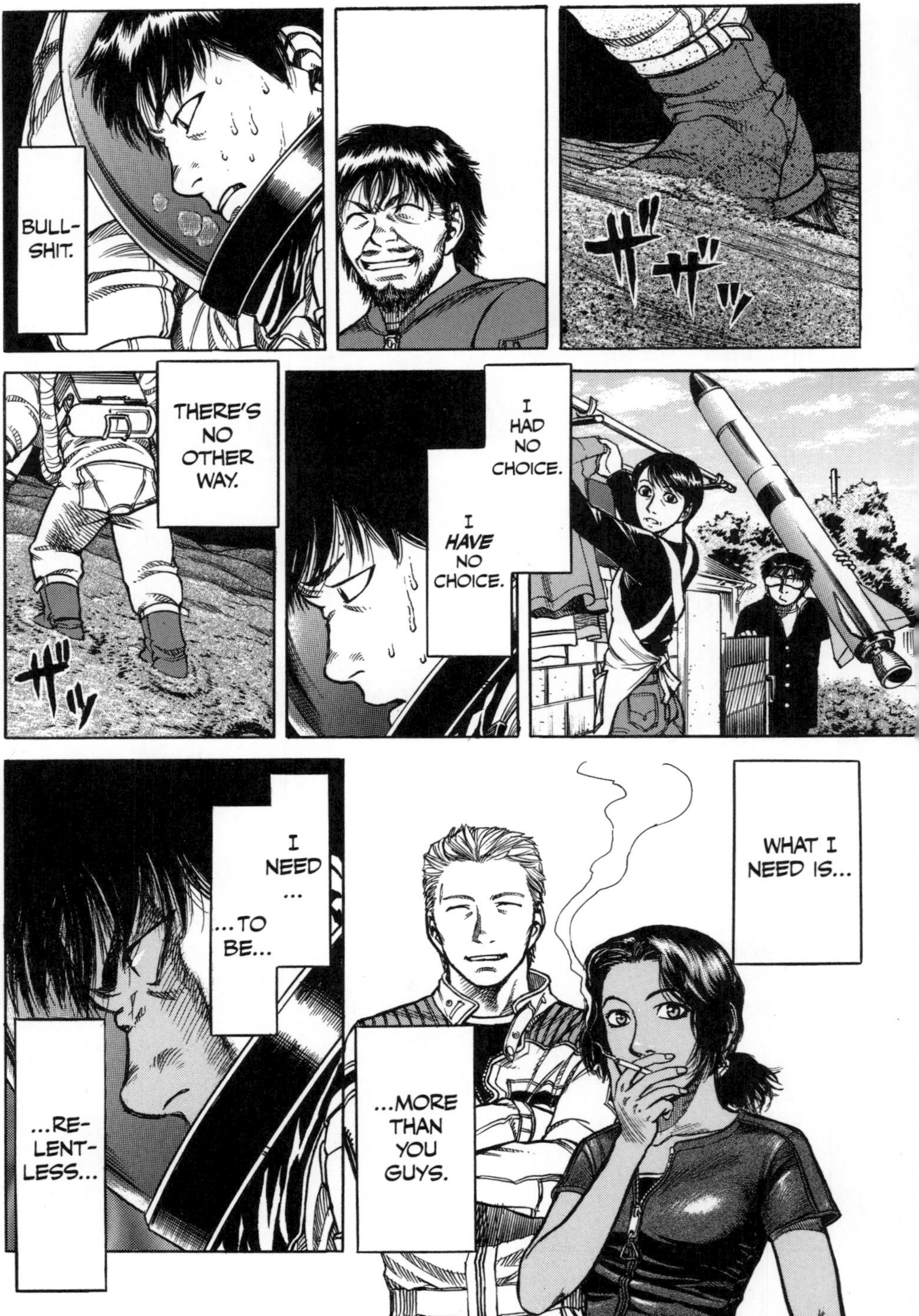

ザザッ
BULL-SHIT.
I HAD NO CHOICE.
I *HAVE* NO CHOICE.
THERE'S NO OTHER WAY.
ザッ
WHAT I NEED IS...
...MORE THAN YOU GUYS.
I NEED ...
...TO BE...
...RE-LENT-LESS...

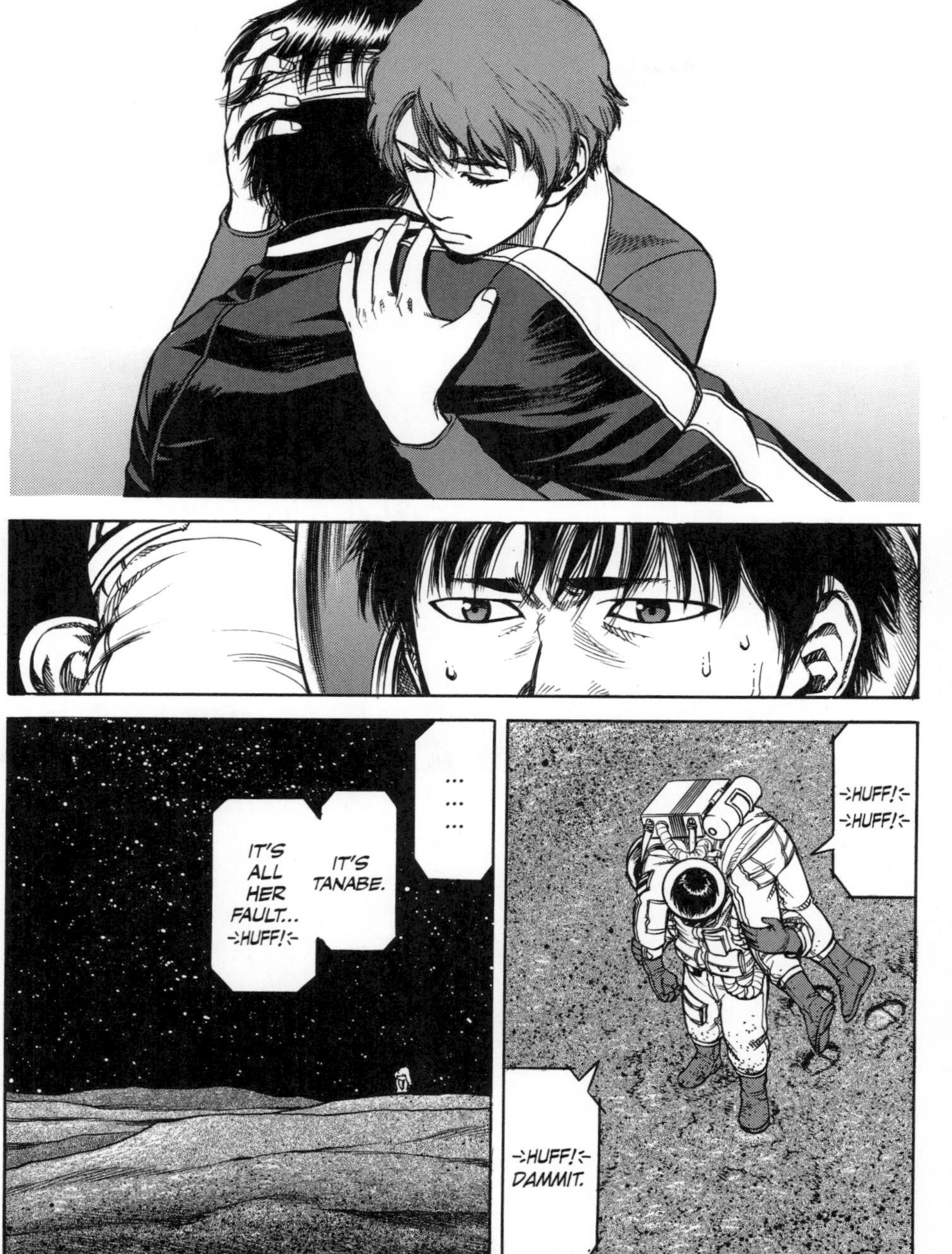

-HUFF!-
-HUFF!-
-HUFF!- DAMMIT.
......
IT'S TANABE.
IT'S ALL HER FAULT... -HUFF!-

HEY! LEO?

≈GASP≈
≈GASP≈

THREE MORE HOURS OR SO.

DO YOU FEEL WORSE?

HACHI...

HOW LONG... NOW...

...
....
.....

LEONOV?

I'M GOING TO...

...PASS OUT...

...THREE MORE HOURS...

...I'LL MAKE IT...

I'M SORRY...

I DON'T THINK...

422

...MOTHER...

I'M SORRY...

...
...
...
...
...
...

WHAT?

WHY NOW?

IT TAKES --

...DID YOU APOLOGIZE TO HER...?

WHY...

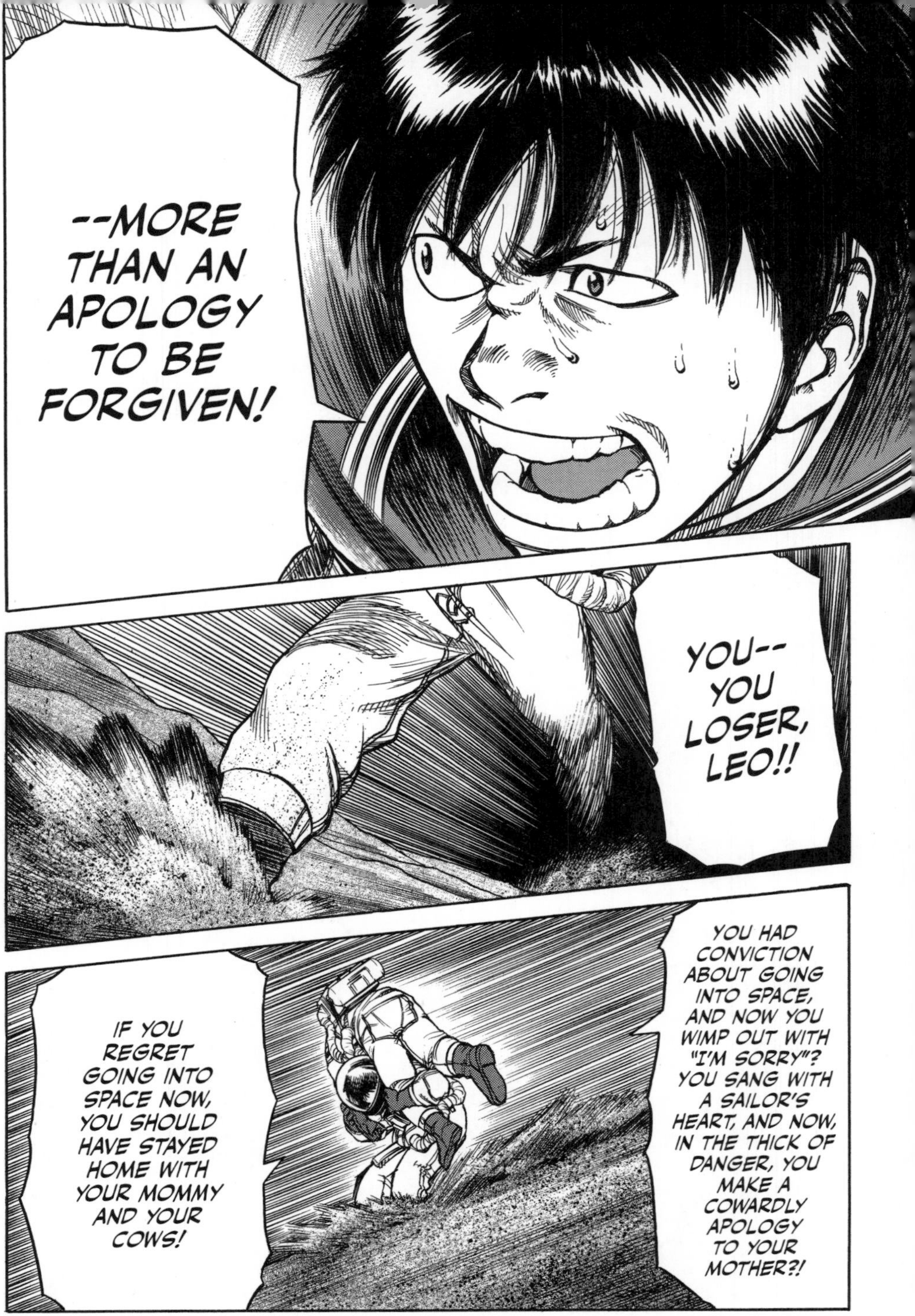
--MORE THAN AN APOLOGY TO BE FORGIVEN!
YOU--
YOU LOSER, LEO!!
YOU HAD CONVICTION ABOUT GOING INTO SPACE, AND NOW YOU WIMP OUT WITH "I'M SORRY"? YOU SANG WITH A SAILOR'S HEART, AND NOW, IN THE THICK OF DANGER, YOU MAKE A COWARDLY APOLOGY TO YOUR MOTHER?!
IF YOU REGRET GOING INTO SPACE NOW, YOU SHOULD HAVE STAYED HOME WITH YOUR MOMMY AND YOUR COWS!

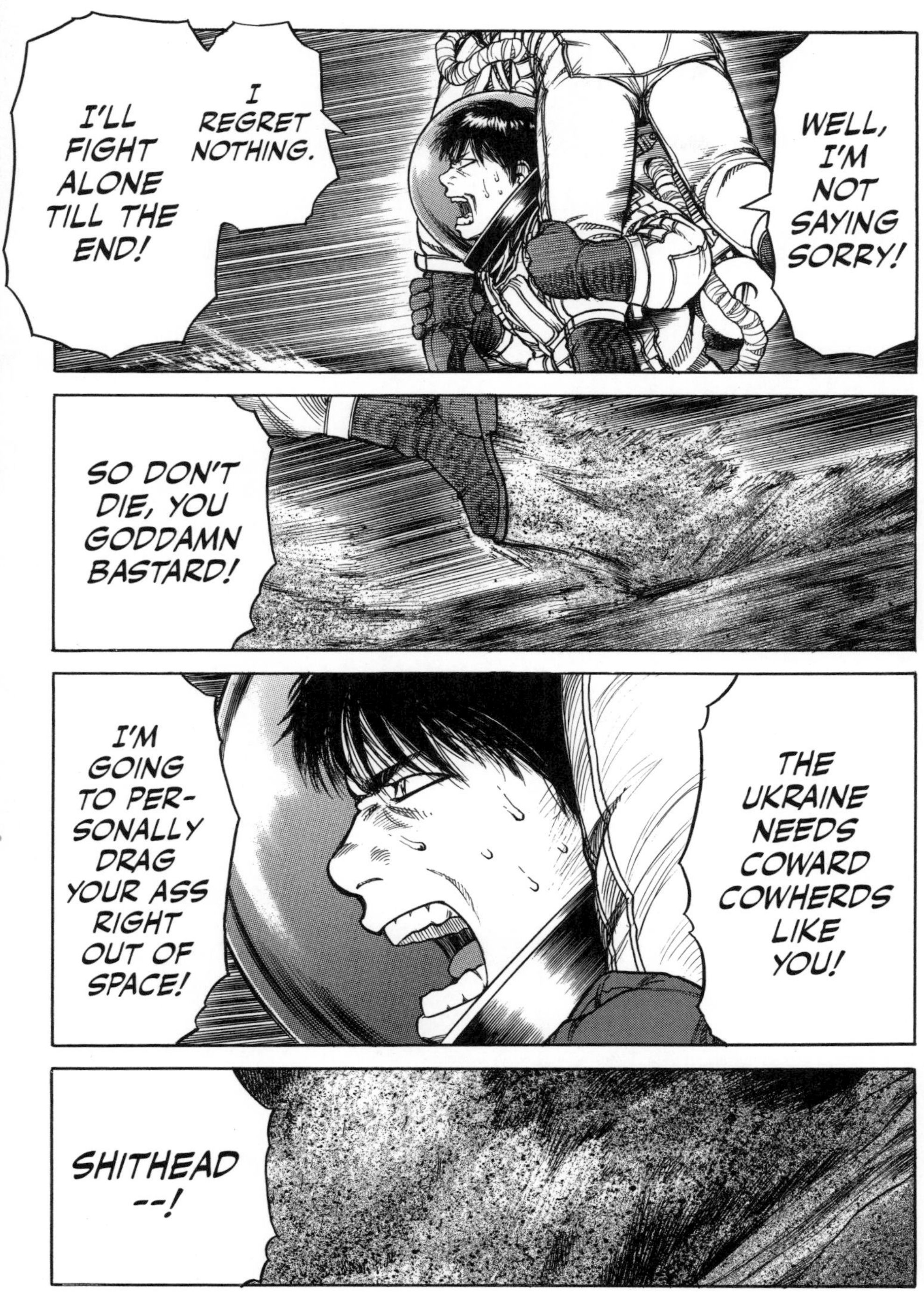
WELL, I'M NOT SAYING SORRY!
I REGRET NOTHING.
I'LL FIGHT ALONE TILL THE END!
SO DON'T DIE, YOU GODDAMN BASTARD!
THE UKRAINE NEEDS COWARD COWHERDS LIKE YOU!
I'M GOING TO PER-SONALLY DRAG YOUR ASS RIGHT OUT OF SPACE!
SHITHEAD --!

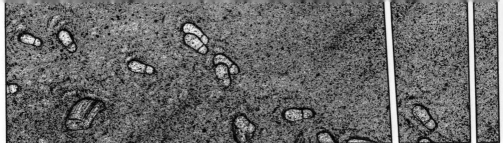

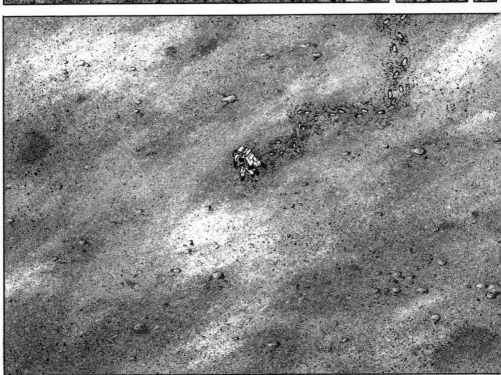

SHIT-
HEAD
...

I
WON'T
FOR-
GIVE
YOU
...

BAS-
TARD
...

ズ
ズ...

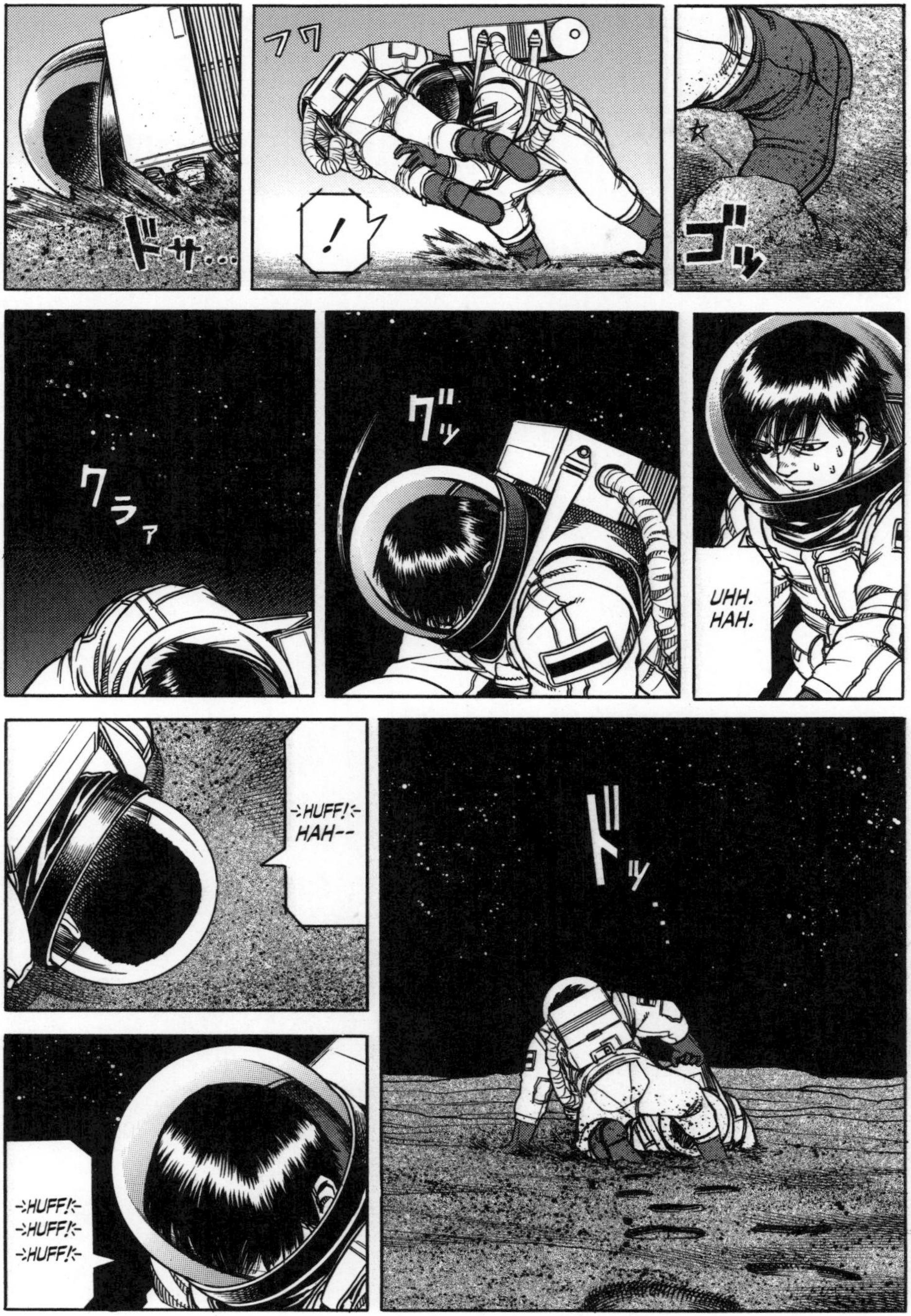
ゴッ
フワ
!
ドサ…
UHH. HAH.
グッ
クラァ
ドッ
HUFF! HAH--
HUFF! HUFF! HUFF!

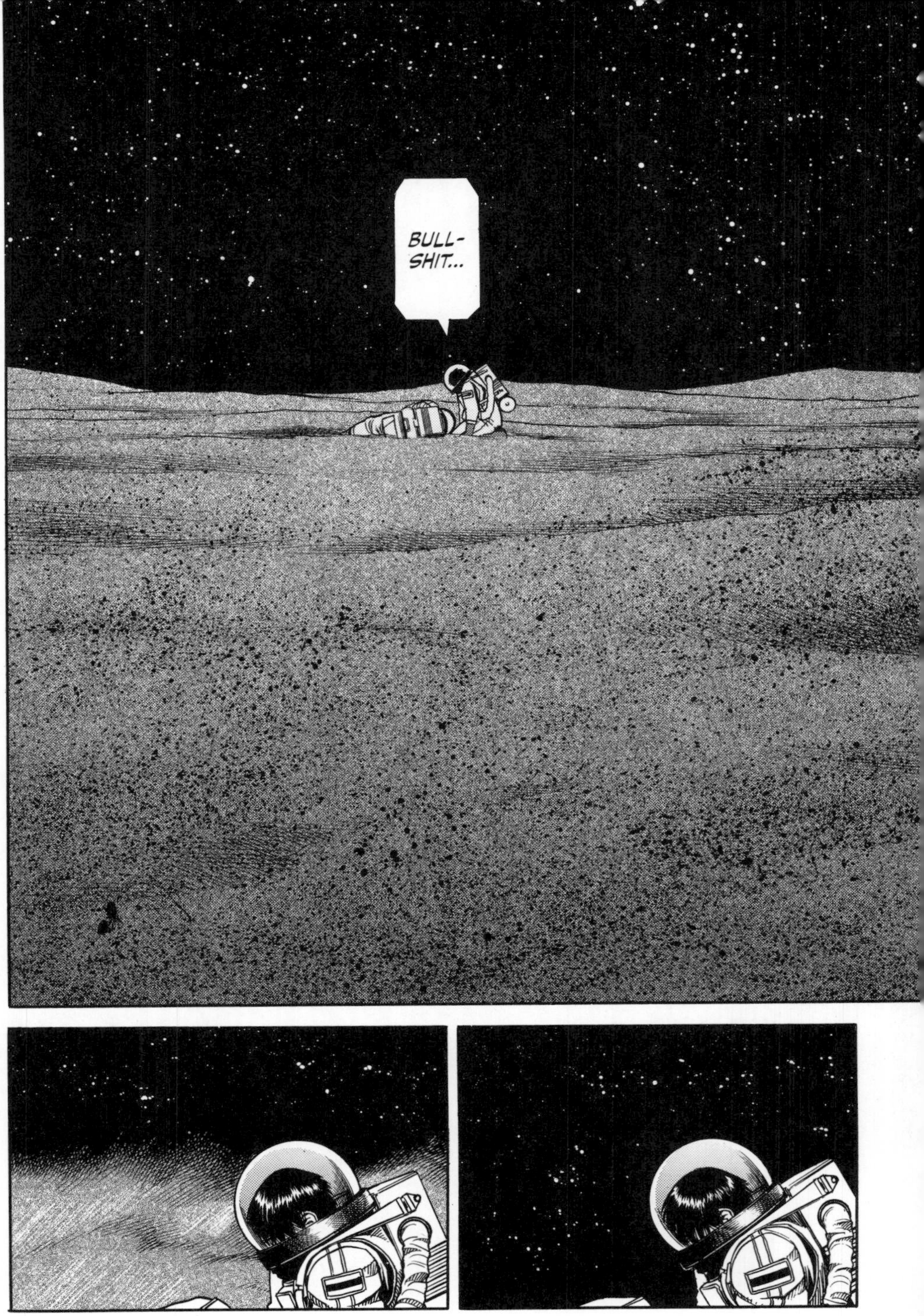
BULL-
SHIT...

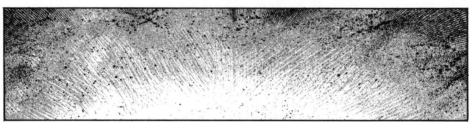
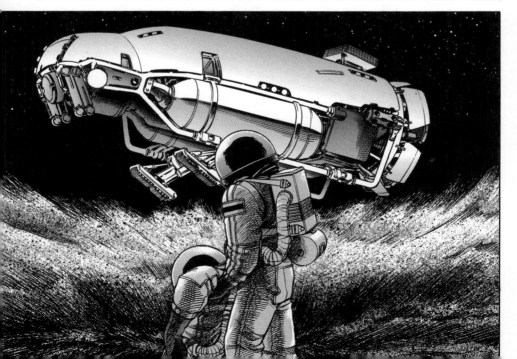

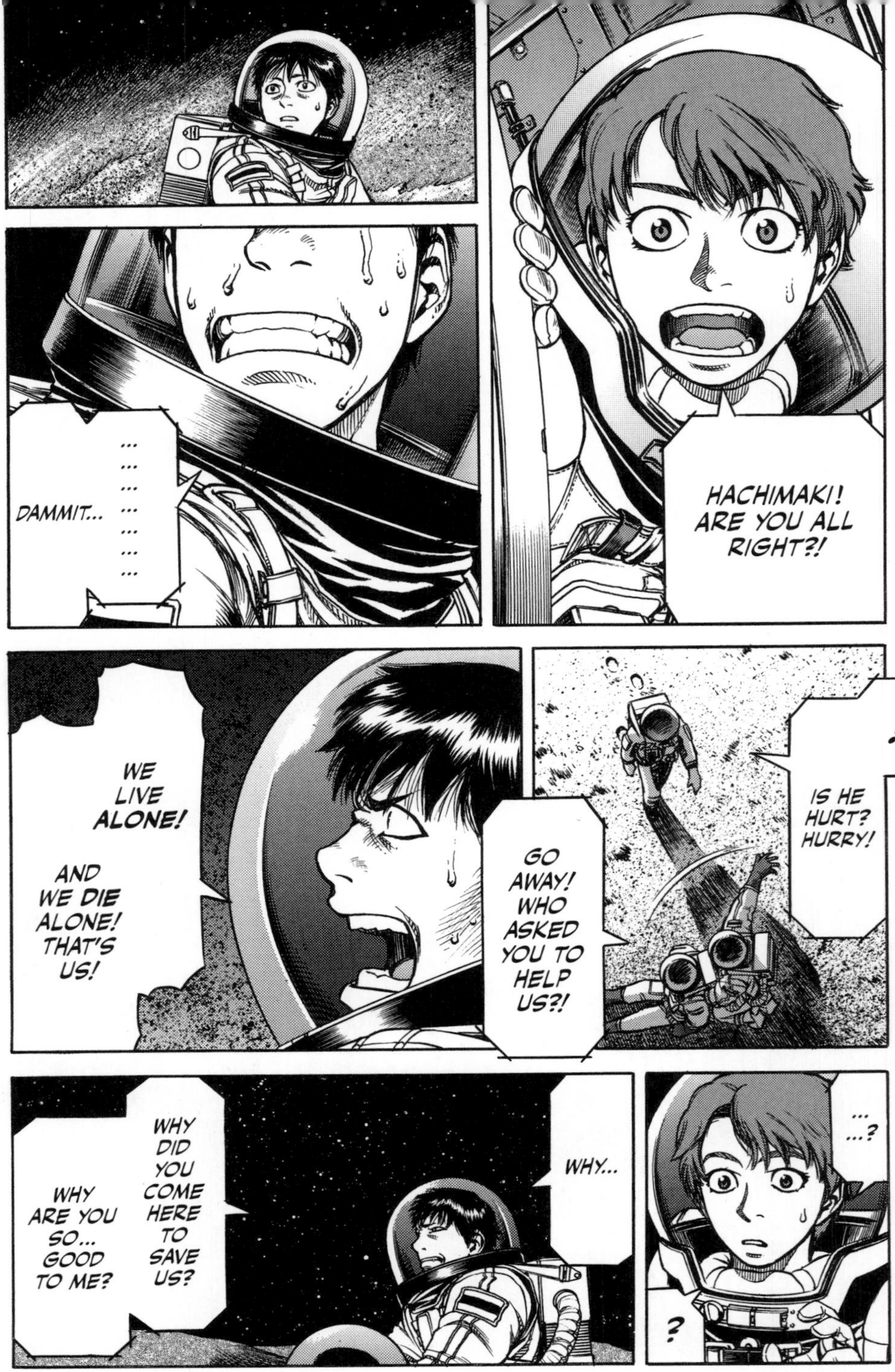
HACHIMAKI! ARE YOU ALL RIGHT?!
DAMMIT...
... ...
!
IS HE HURT? HURRY!
GO AWAY! WHO ASKED YOU TO HELP US?!
WE LIVE ALONE!
AND WE DIE ALONE! THAT'S US!
... ...?
?
WHY...
WHY DID YOU COME HERE TO SAVE US?
WHY ARE YOU SO... GOOD TO ME?

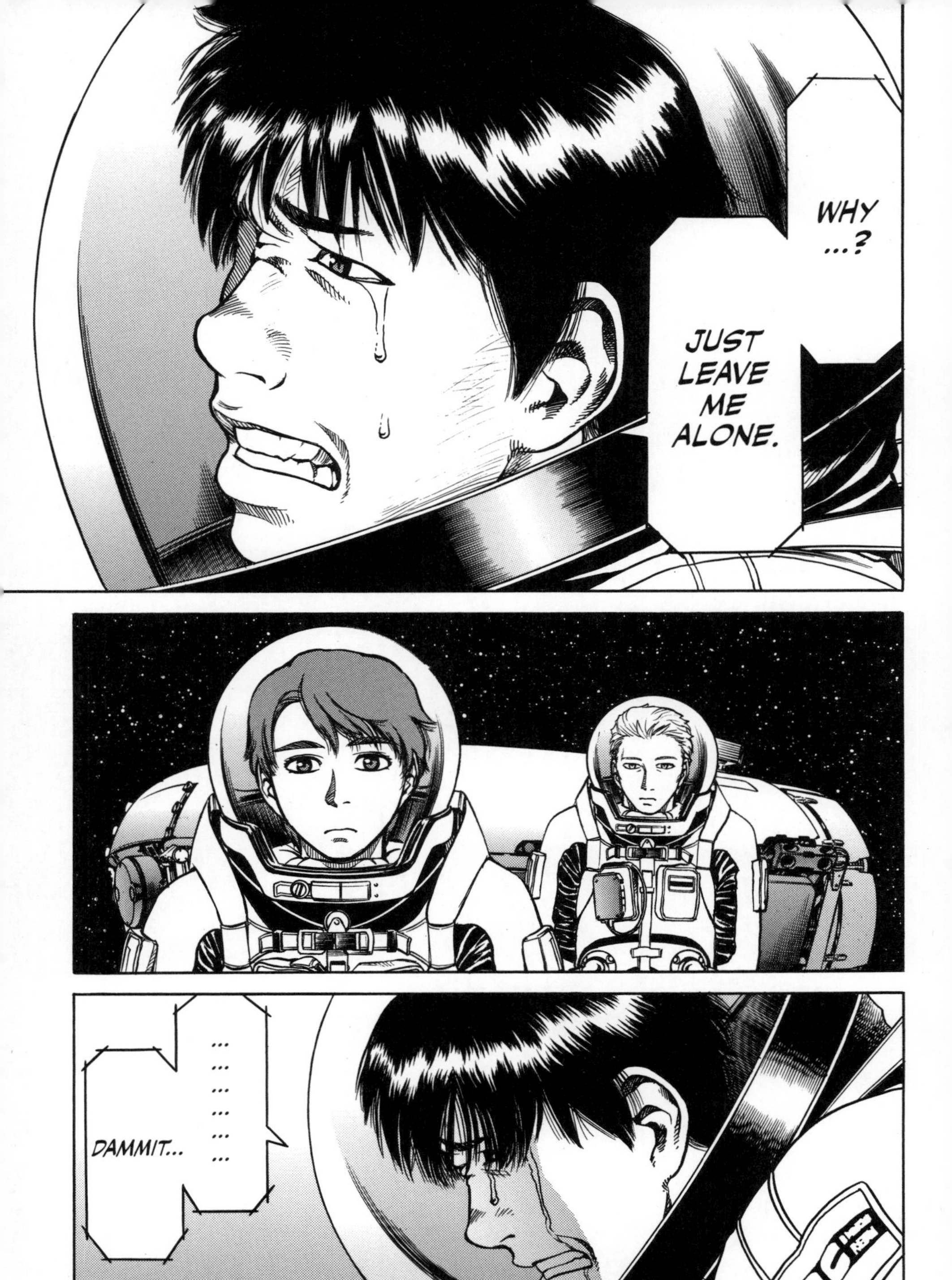
WHY ...?
JUST LEAVE ME ALONE.
... ...
DAMMIT...

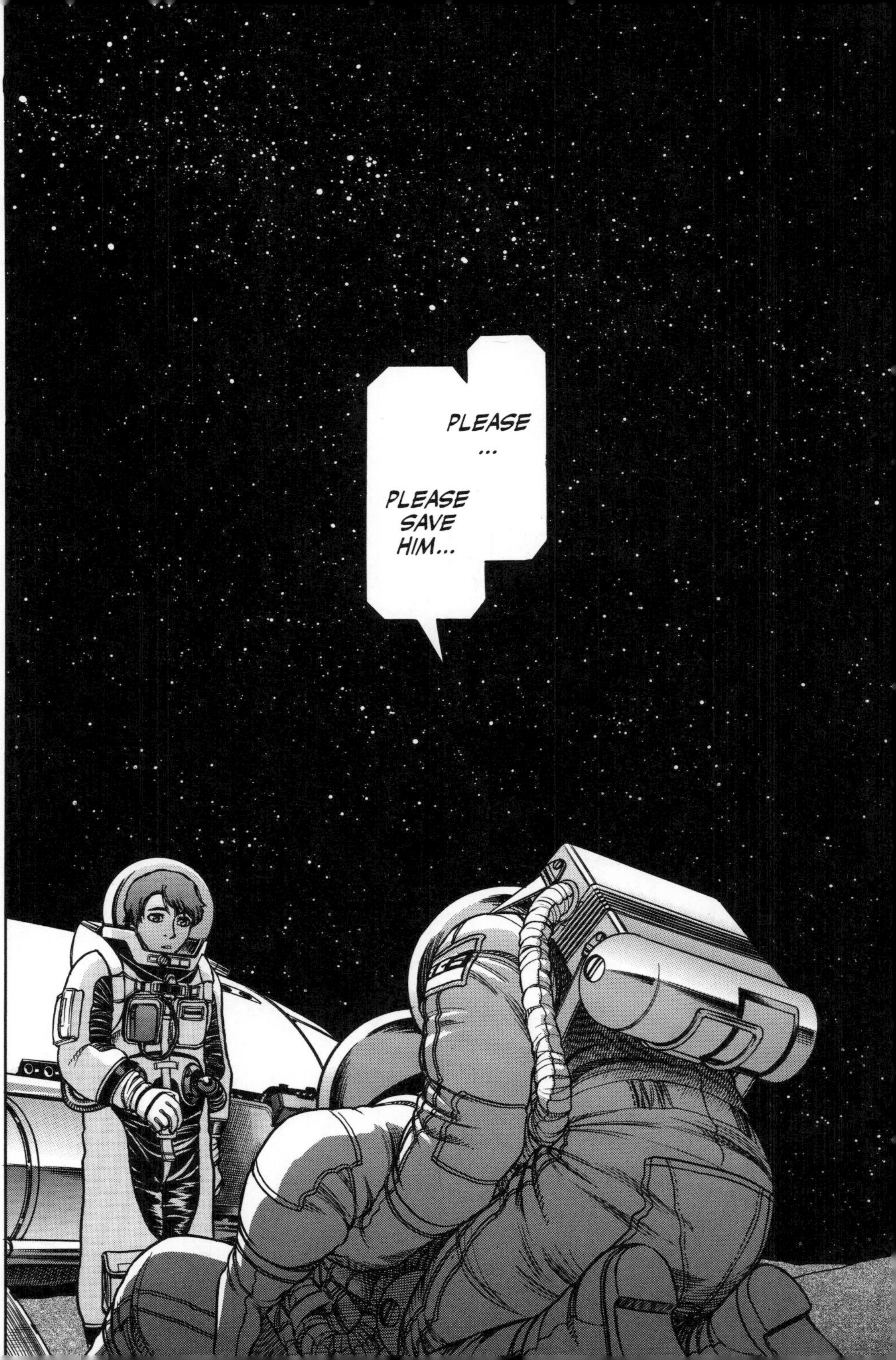
PLEASE
...
PLEASE SAVE HIM...

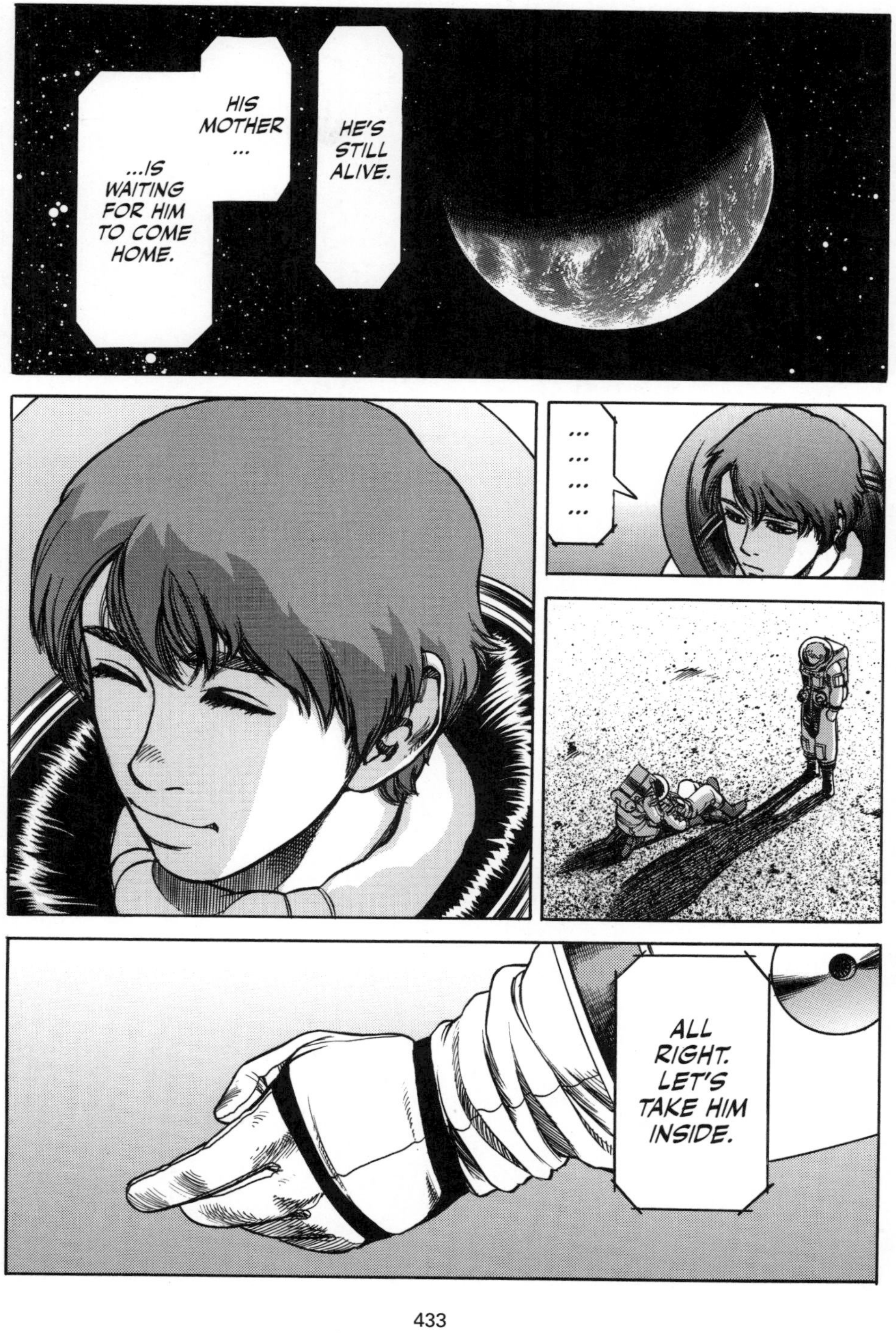
HE'S STILL ALIVE.
HIS MOTHER ...
...IS WAITING FOR HIM TO COME HOME.
... ...
ALL RIGHT. LET'S TAKE HIM INSIDE.

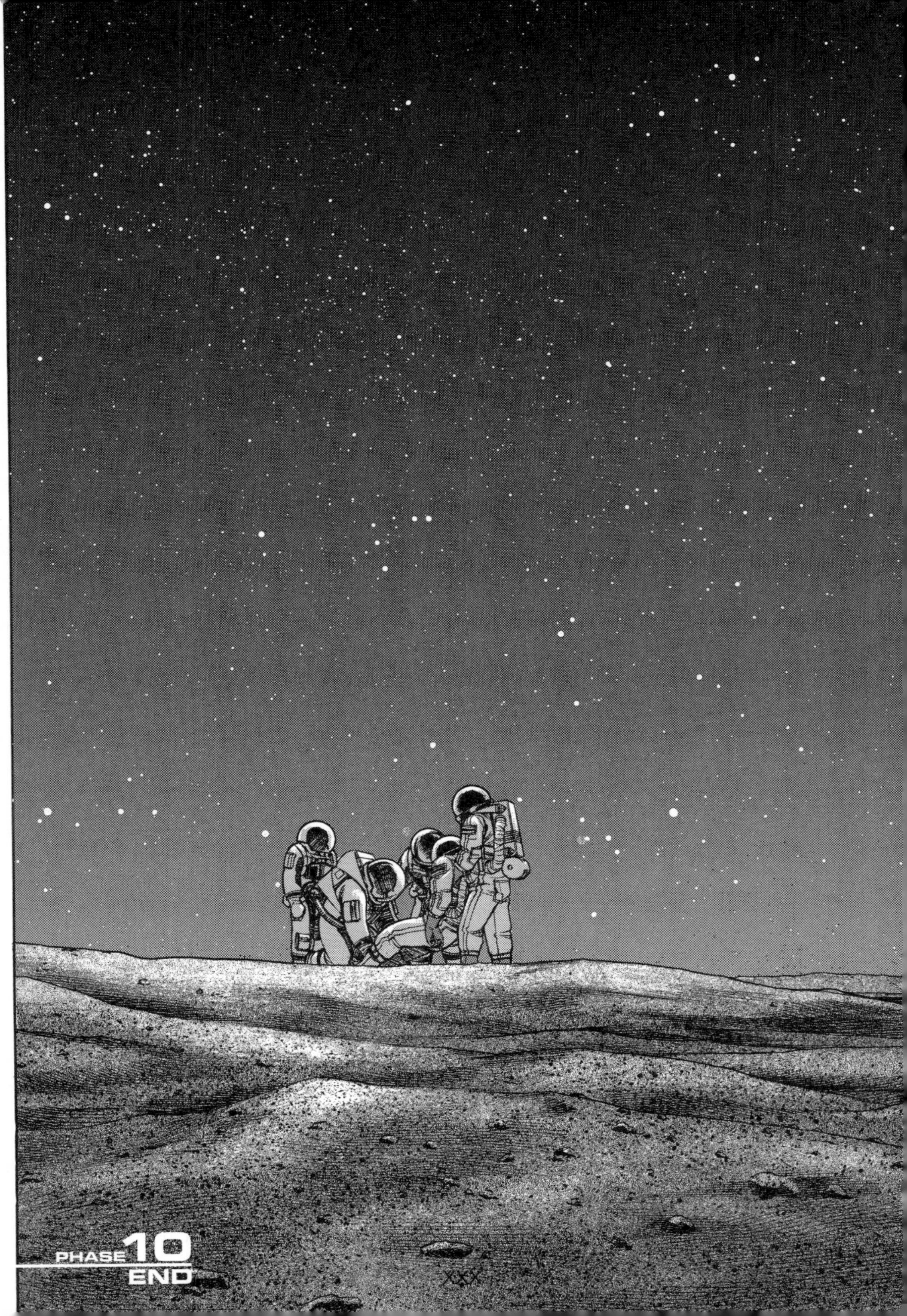
PHASE 10
END

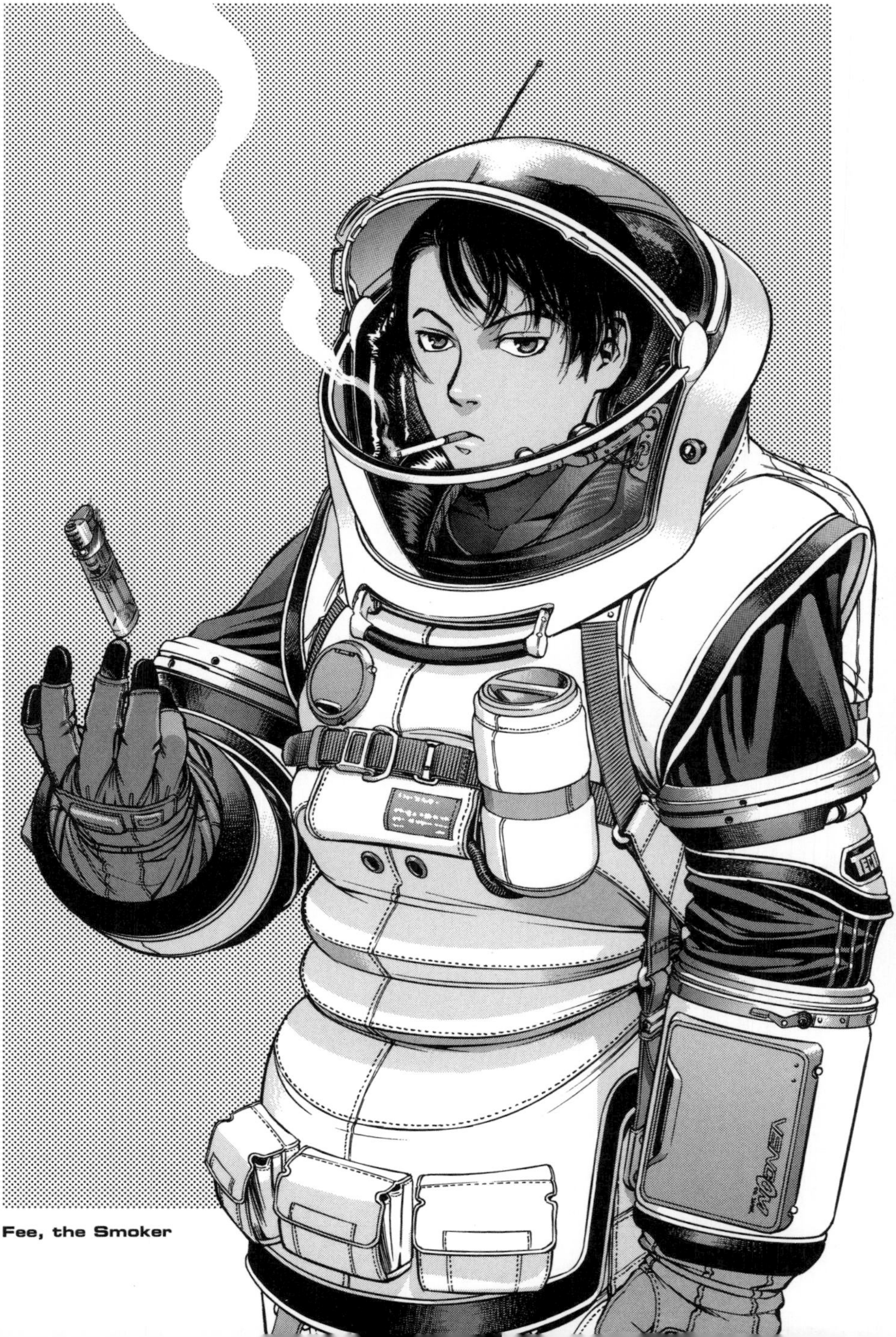

Fee, the Smoker

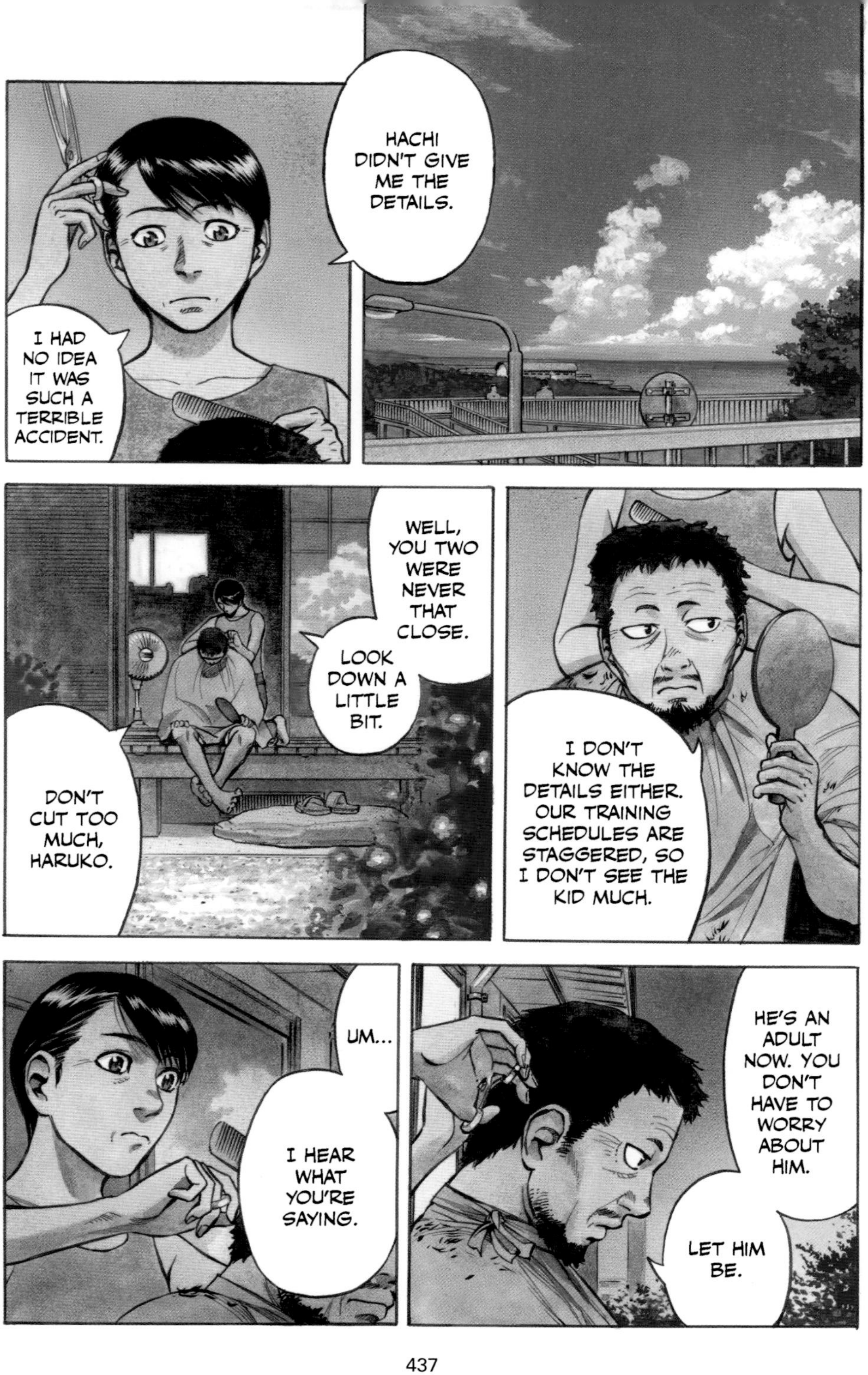
HACHI DIDN'T GIVE ME THE DETAILS.
I HAD NO IDEA IT WAS SUCH A TERRIBLE ACCIDENT.
I DON'T KNOW THE DETAILS EITHER. OUR TRAINING SCHEDULES ARE STAGGERED, SO I DON'T SEE THE KID MUCH.
WELL, YOU TWO WERE NEVER THAT CLOSE.
LOOK DOWN A LITTLE BIT.
DON'T CUT TOO MUCH, HARUKO.
HE'S AN ADULT NOW. YOU DON'T HAVE TO WORRY ABOUT HIM.
LET HIM BE.
UM...
I HEAR WHAT YOU'RE SAYING.

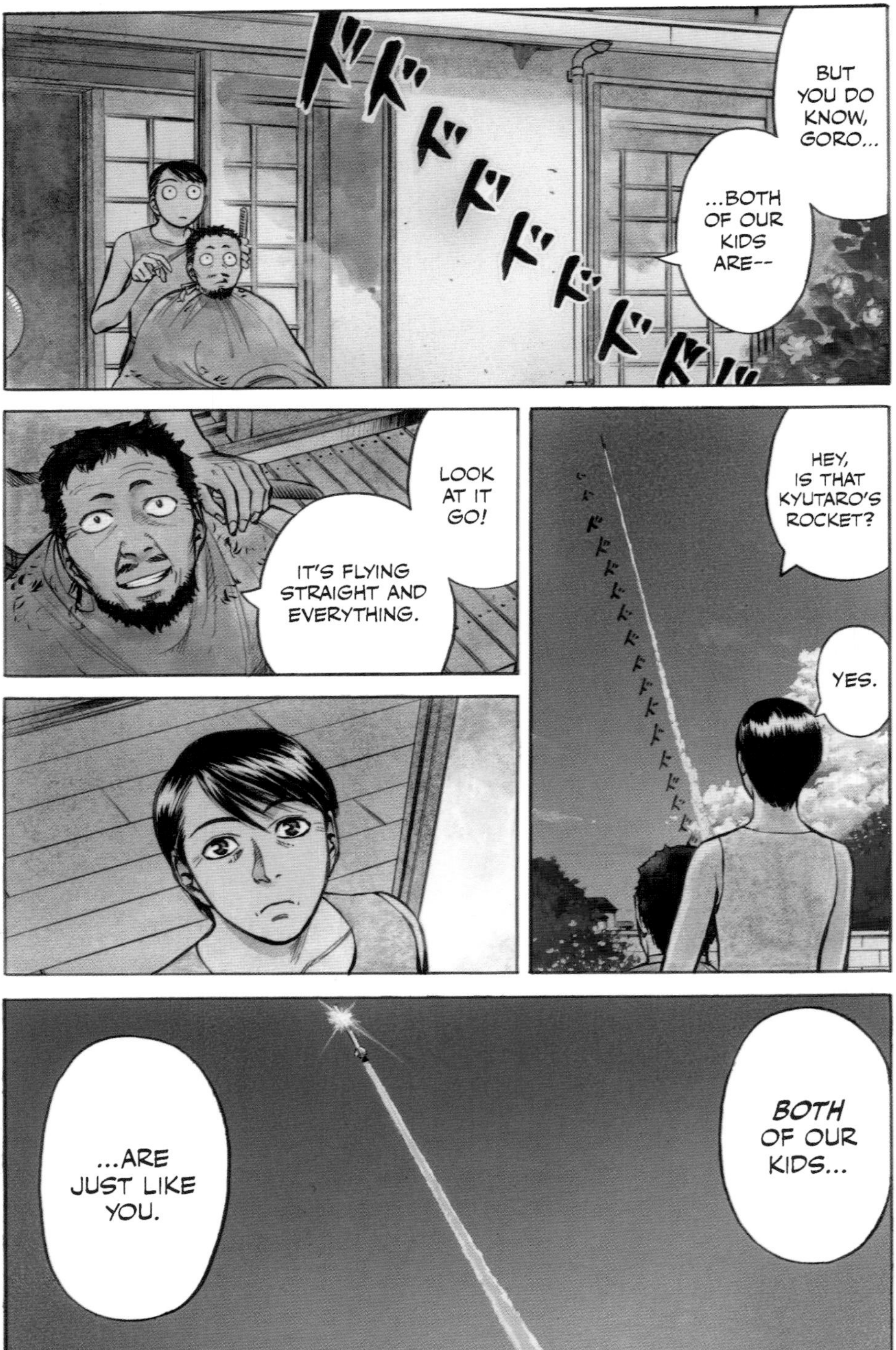
BUT YOU DO KNOW, GORO...
...BOTH OF OUR KIDS ARE--
HEY, IS THAT KYUTARO'S ROCKET?
YES.
LOOK AT IT GO!
IT'S FLYING STRAIGHT AND EVERYTHING.
BOTH OF OUR KIDS...
...ARE JUST LIKE YOU.

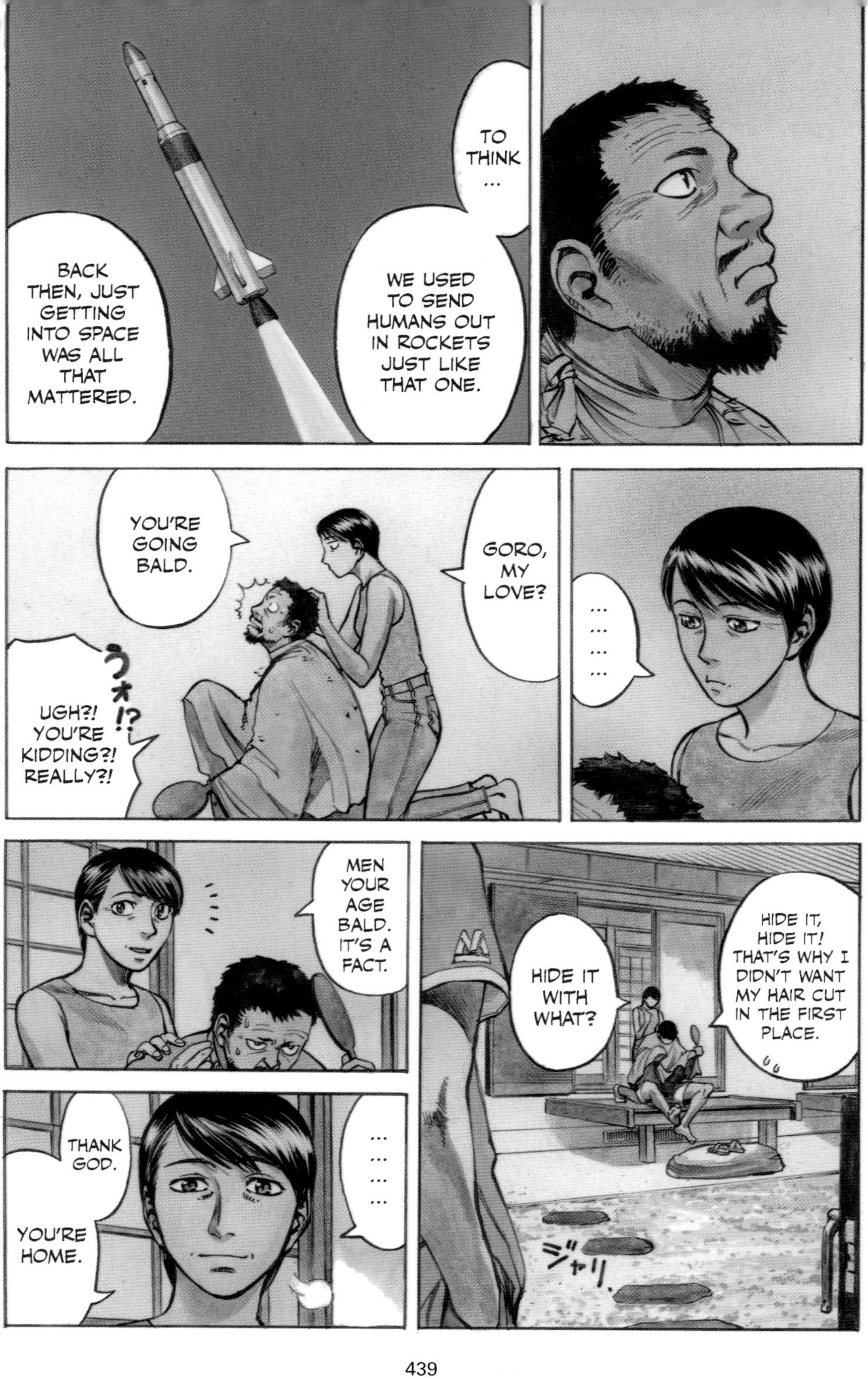
TO THINK ...
WE USED TO SEND HUMANS OUT IN ROCKETS JUST LIKE THAT ONE.
BACK THEN, JUST GETTING INTO SPACE WAS ALL THAT MATTERED.
... ...
GORO, MY LOVE?
YOU'RE GOING BALD.
ウォ!?
UGH?! YOU'RE KIDDING?! REALLY?!
HIDE IT, HIDE IT! THAT'S WHY I DIDN'T WANT MY HAIR CUT IN THE FIRST PLACE.
HIDE IT WITH WHAT?
ジャリ
MEN YOUR AGE BALD. IT'S A FACT.
... ...
THANK GOD.
YOU'RE HOME.

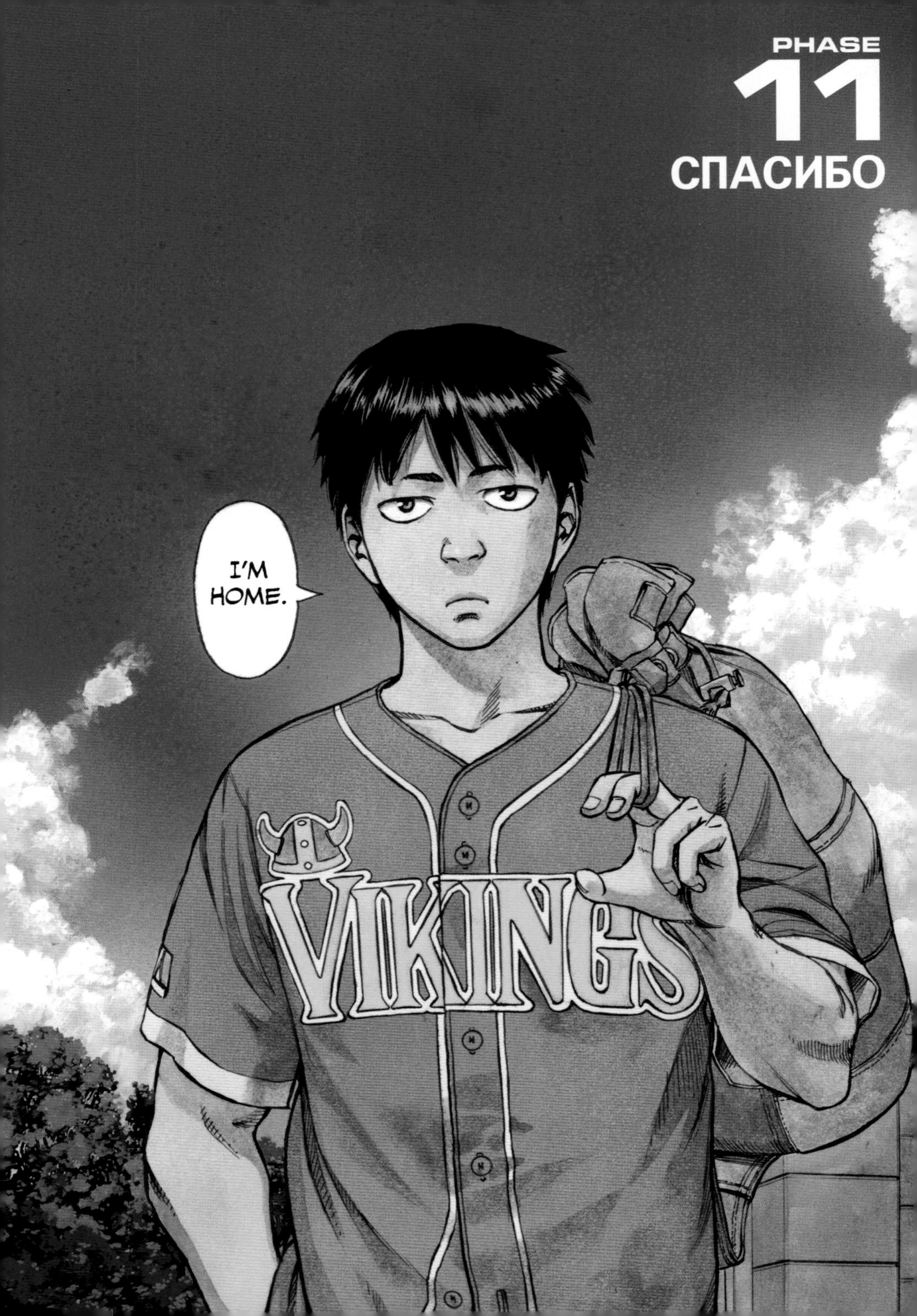
PHASE
11
СПАСИБО
I'M HOME.
VIKINGS

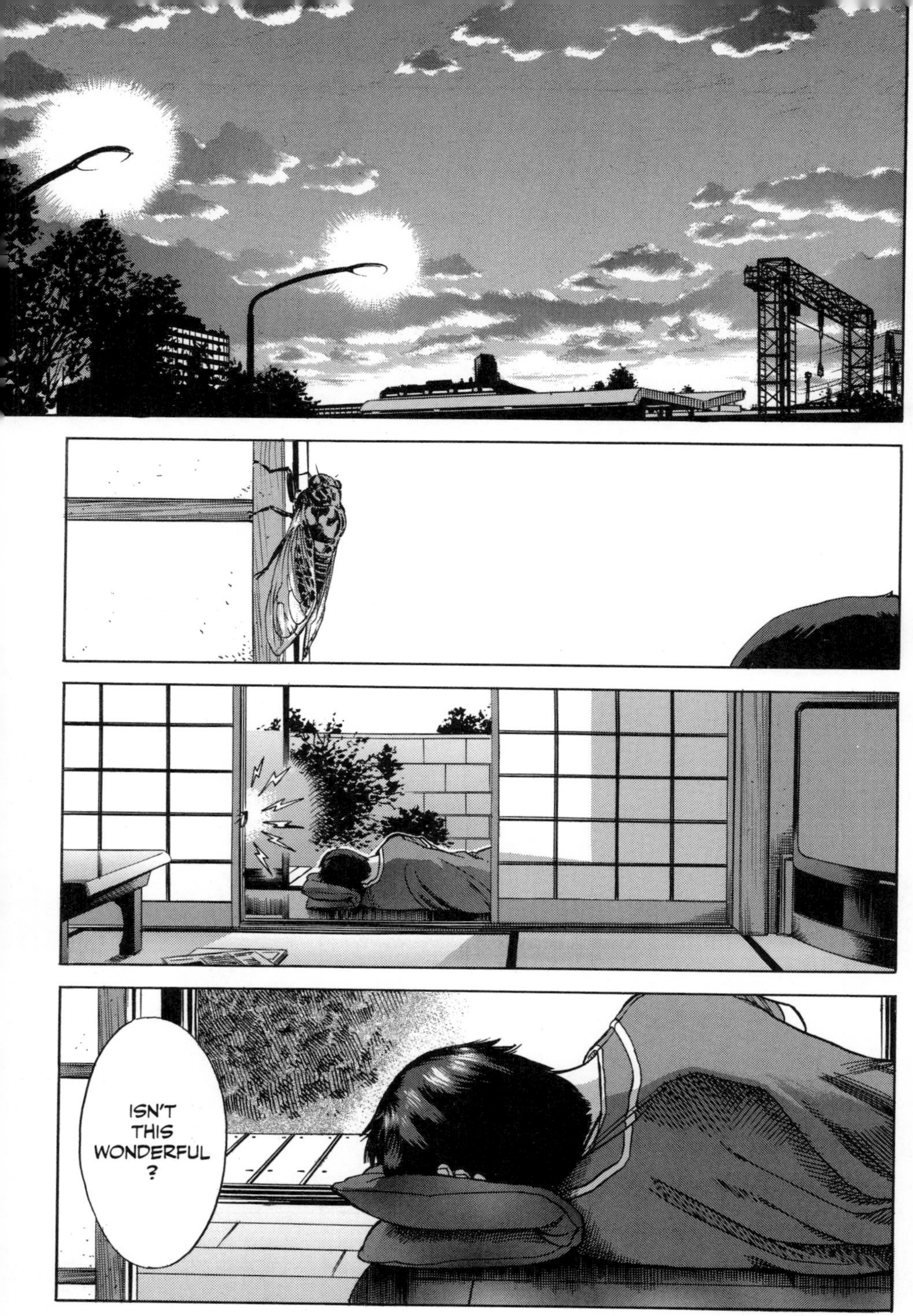
ISN'T THIS WONDERFUL?

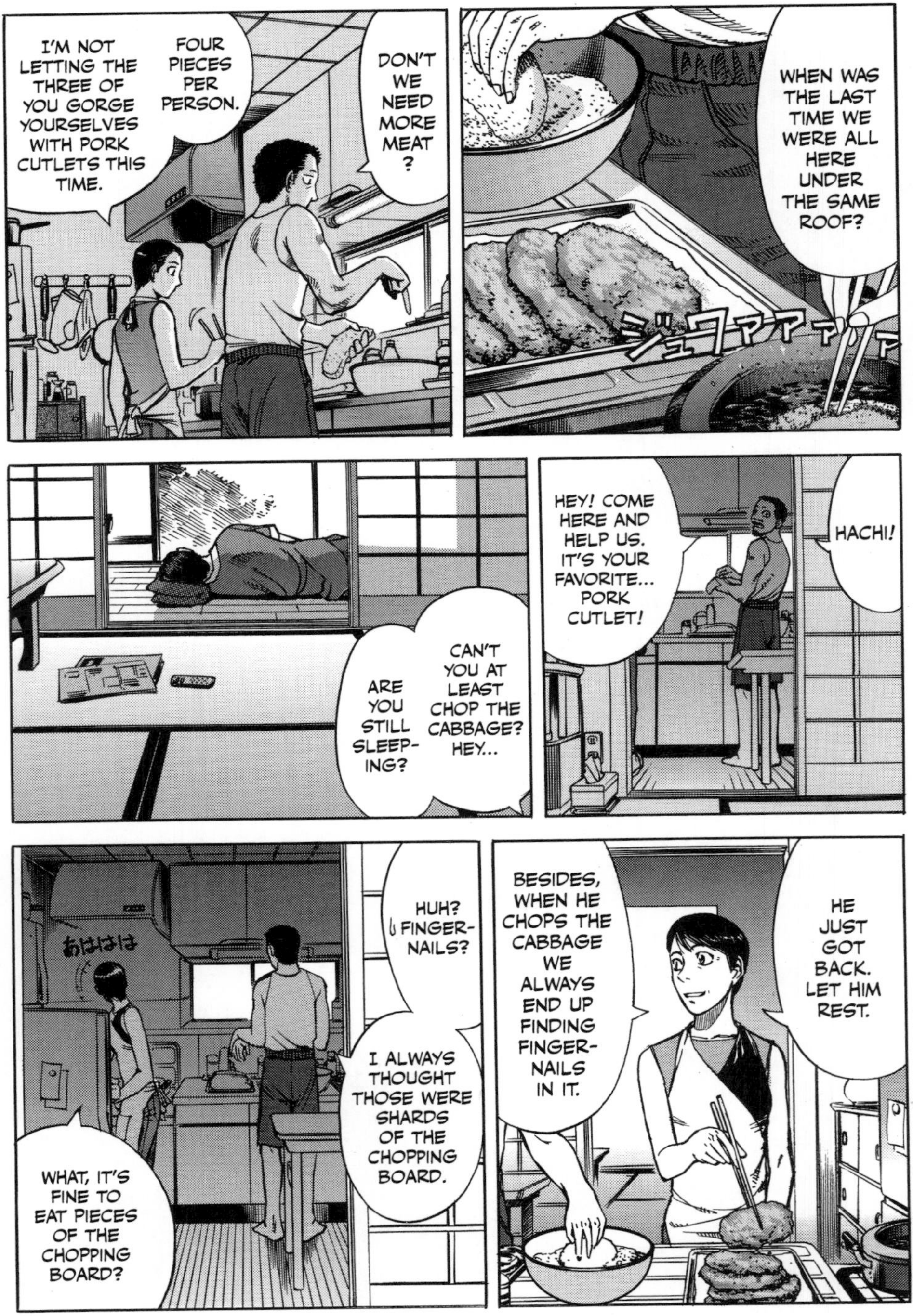
WHEN WAS THE LAST TIME WE WERE ALL HERE UNDER THE SAME ROOF?
ジュワアァァァ
DON'T WE NEED MORE MEAT?
FOUR PIECES PER PERSON.
I'M NOT LETTING THE THREE OF YOU GORGE YOURSELVES WITH PORK CUTLETS THIS TIME.
HACHI!
HEY! COME HERE AND HELP US. IT'S YOUR FAVORITE... PORK CUTLET!
CAN'T YOU AT LEAST CHOP THE CABBAGE? HEY...
ARE YOU STILL SLEEPING?
HE JUST GOT BACK. LET HIM REST.
BESIDES, WHEN HE CHOPS THE CABBAGE WE ALWAYS END UP FINDING FINGERNAILS IN IT.
HUH? FINGERNAILS?
I ALWAYS THOUGHT THOSE WERE SHARDS OF THE CHOPPING BOARD.
あははは
WHAT, IT'S FINE TO EAT PIECES OF THE CHOPPING BOARD?

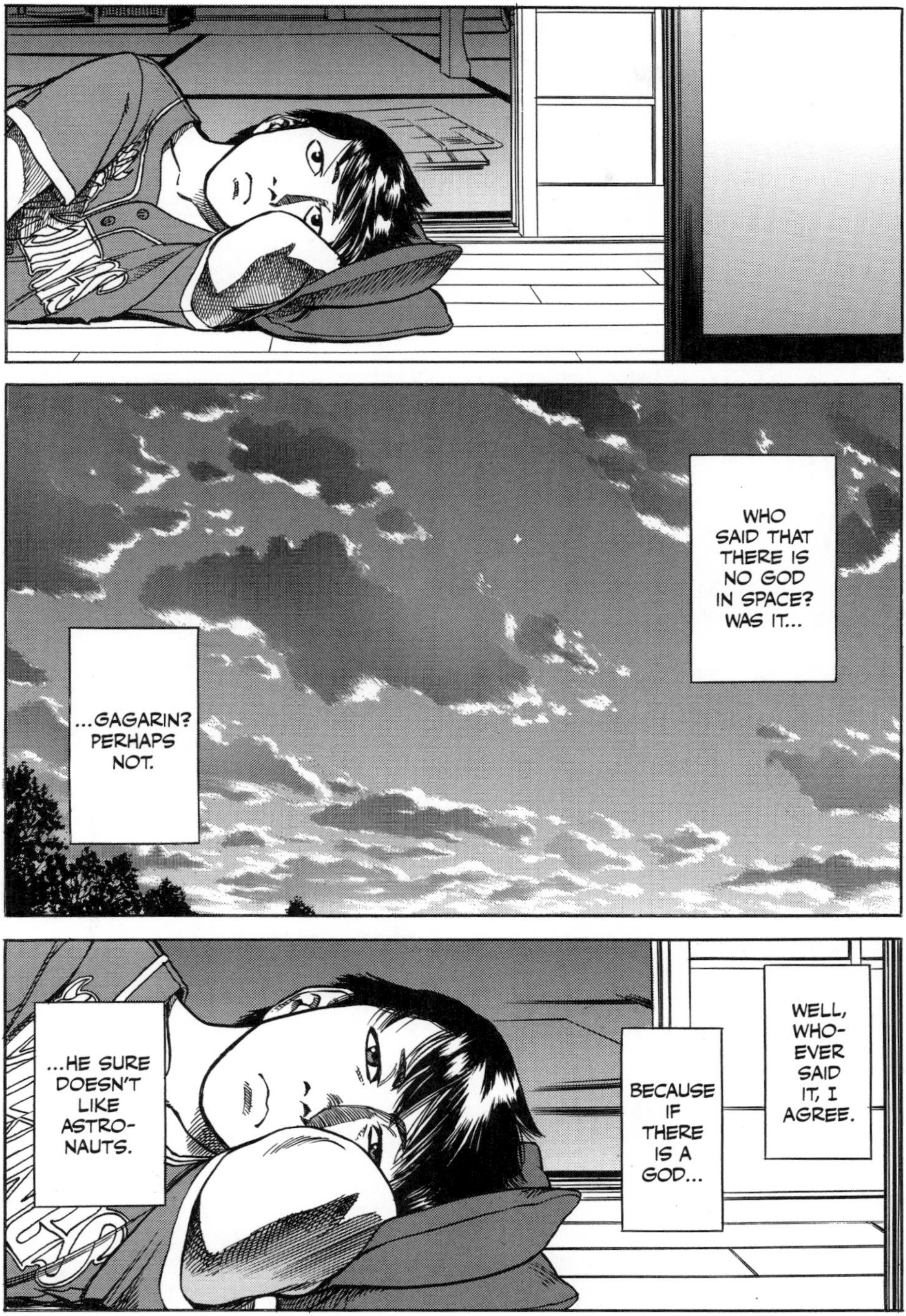
WHO SAID THAT THERE IS NO GOD IN SPACE? WAS IT...
...GAGARIN? PERHAPS NOT.
WELL, WHO-EVER SAID IT, I AGREE.
BECAUSE IF THERE IS A GOD...
...HE SURE DOESN'T LIKE ASTRO-NAUTS.

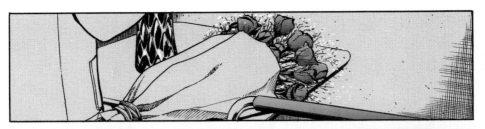

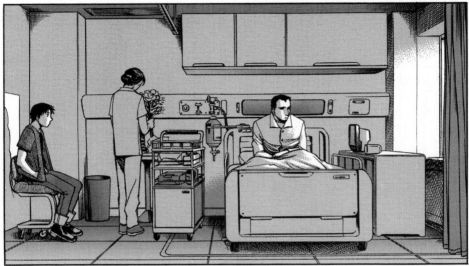

HE'D BE IN FOR SIX MONTHS.

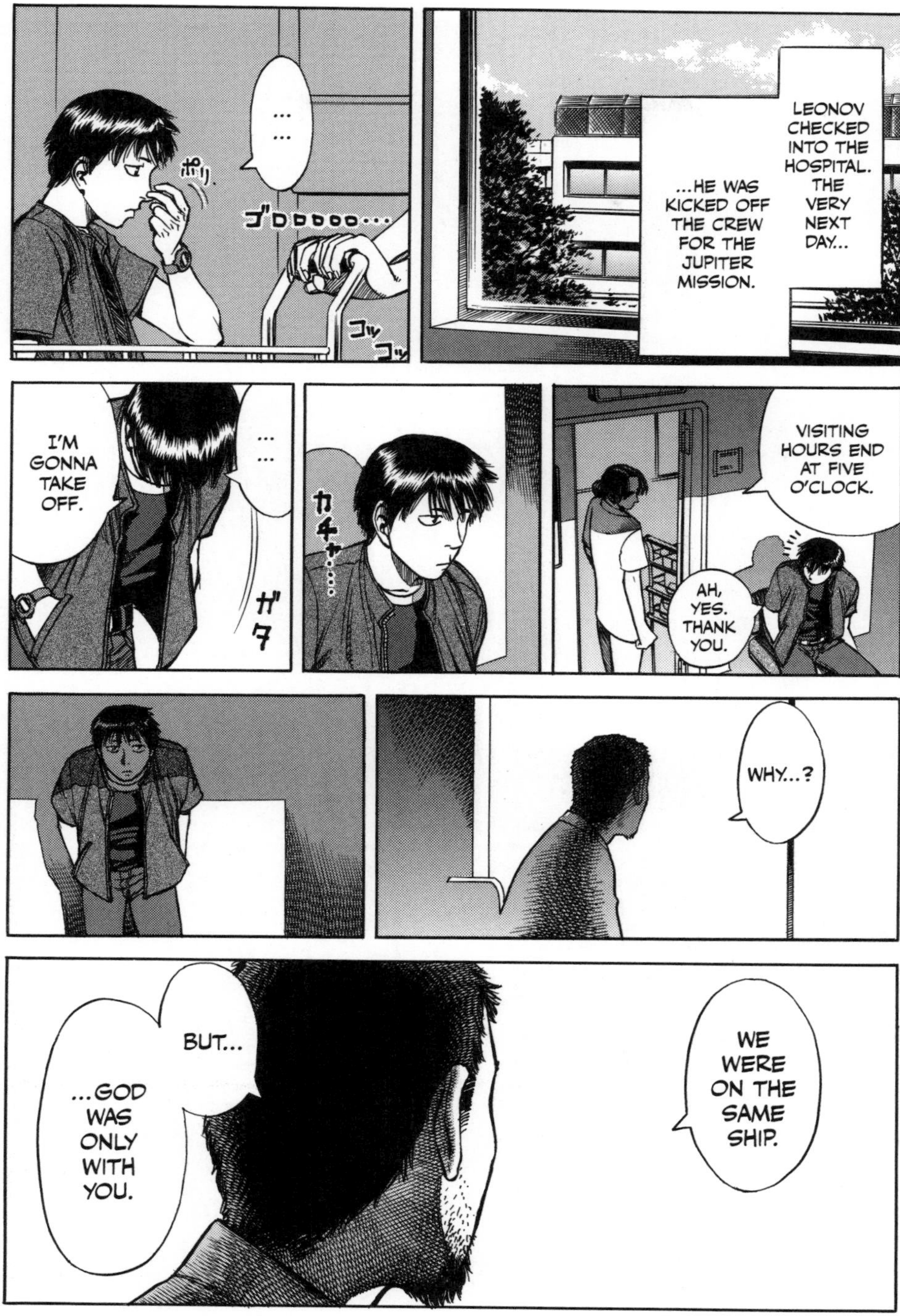
LEONOV CHECKED INTO THE HOSPITAL. THE VERY NEXT DAY...
...HE WAS KICKED OFF THE CREW FOR THE JUPITER MISSION.
......
ポリ
ゴロロロロロ...
コツコツ
VISITING HOURS END AT FIVE O'CLOCK.
AH, YES. THANK YOU.
カチャ....
......
I'M GONNA TAKE OFF.
ガタ
WHY...?
WE WERE ON THE SAME SHIP.
BUT...
...GOD WAS ONLY WITH YOU.

I MUST LEAVE.

UGH!

IT'S BORING HERE.

I WANTED TO CLIMB INTO THAT BRAND-NEW SHIP...

...TRAVEL TO A DISTANT PLANET...

...SOME-WHERE TOO FAR TO...

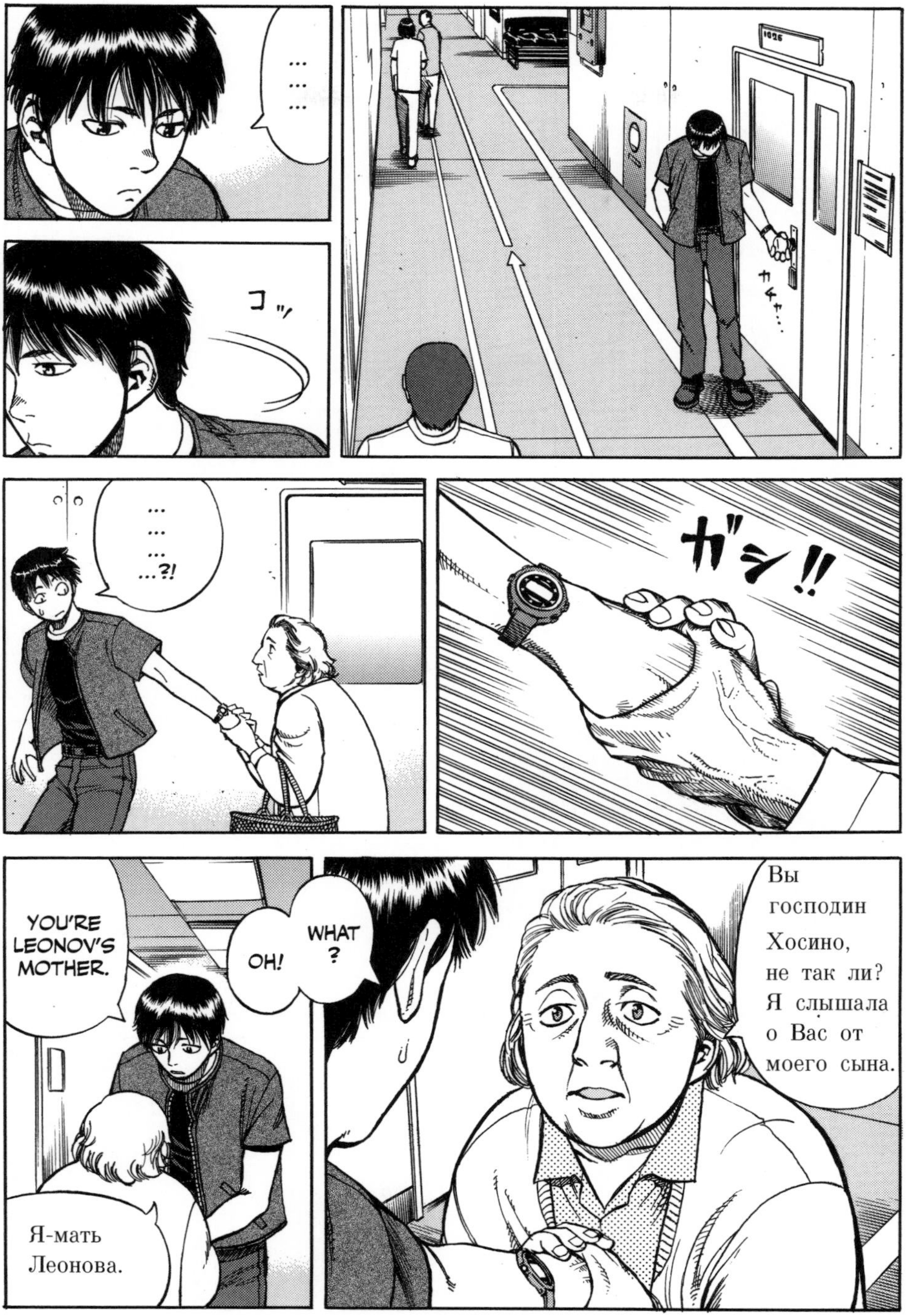
カチャ…
… … …
コッ
ガシ!!
… … … …?!
Вы господин Хосино, не так ли? Я слышала о Вас от моего сына.
OH! WHAT?
YOU'RE LEONOV'S MOTHER.
Я-мать Леонова.

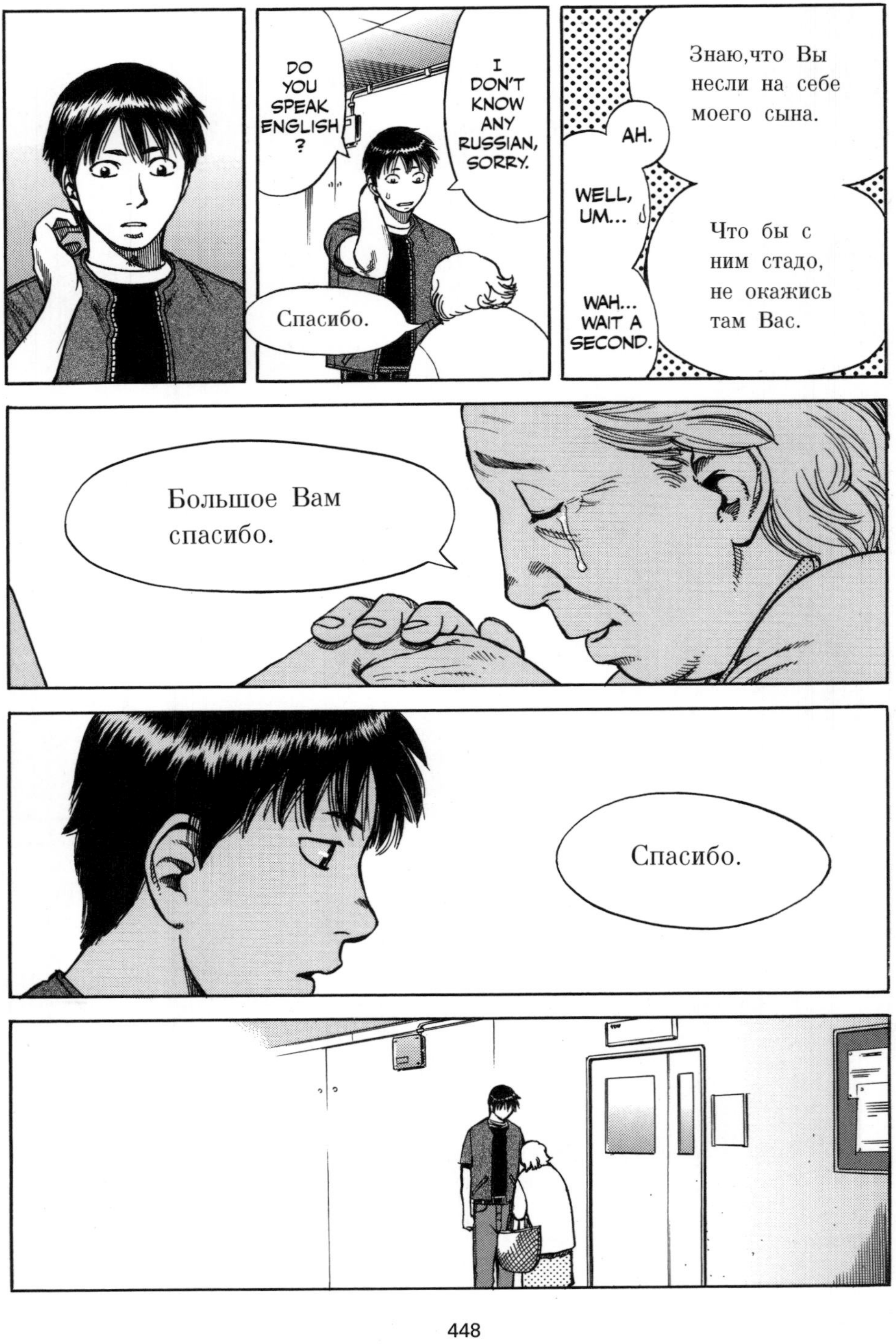
Знаю,что Вы несли на себе моего сына.
AH.
Что бы с ним стадо, не окажись там Вас.
WELL, UM...
WAH... WAIT A SECOND.
I DON'T KNOW ANY RUSSIAN, SORRY.
DO YOU SPEAK ENGLISH ?
Спасибо.
Большое Вам спасибо.
Спасибо.

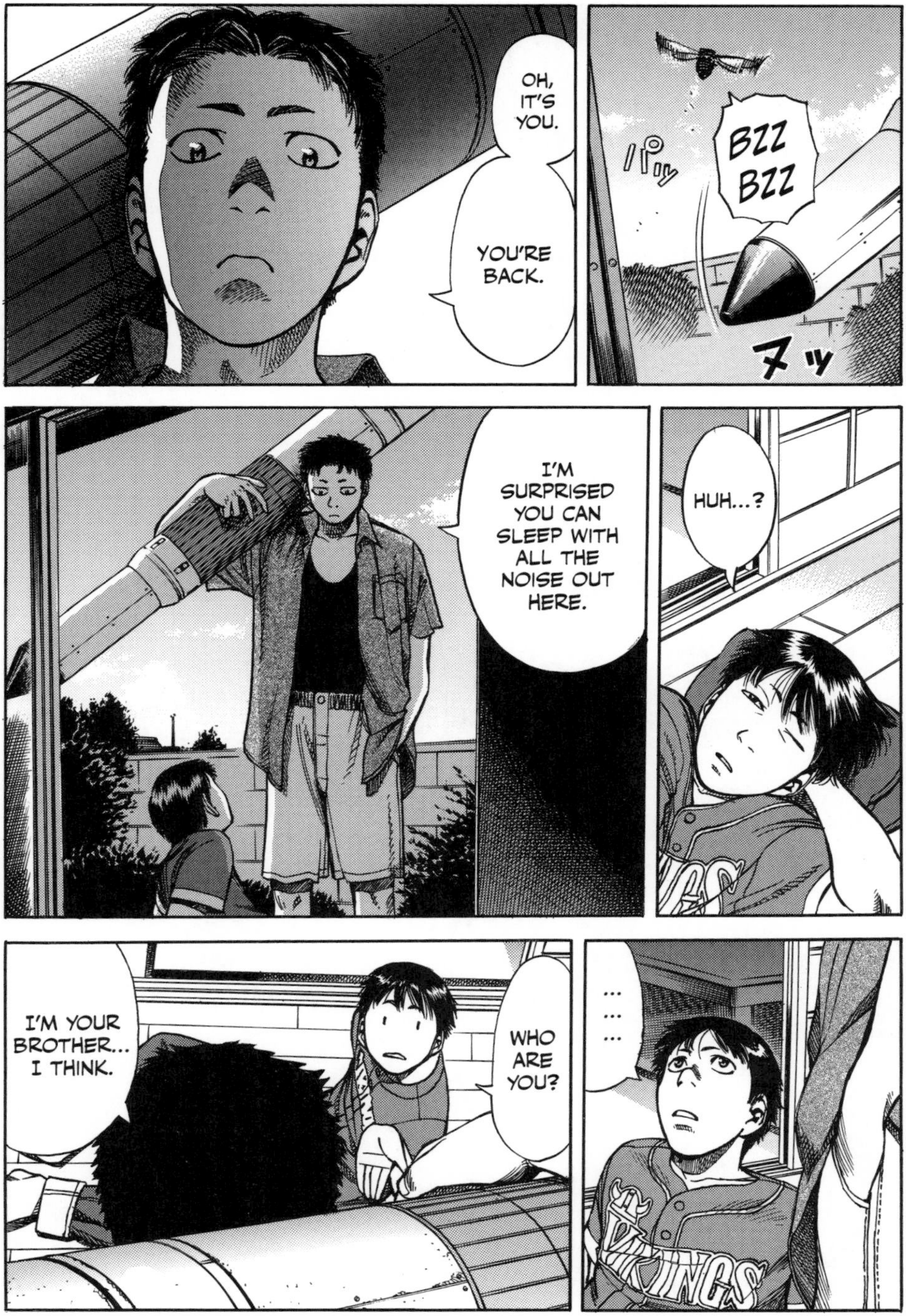
パッ
BZZ BZZ
OH, IT'S YOU.
YOU'RE BACK.
HUH...?
I'M SURPRISED YOU CAN SLEEP WITH ALL THE NOISE OUT HERE.
......
......
WHO ARE YOU?
I'M YOUR BROTHER... I THINK.

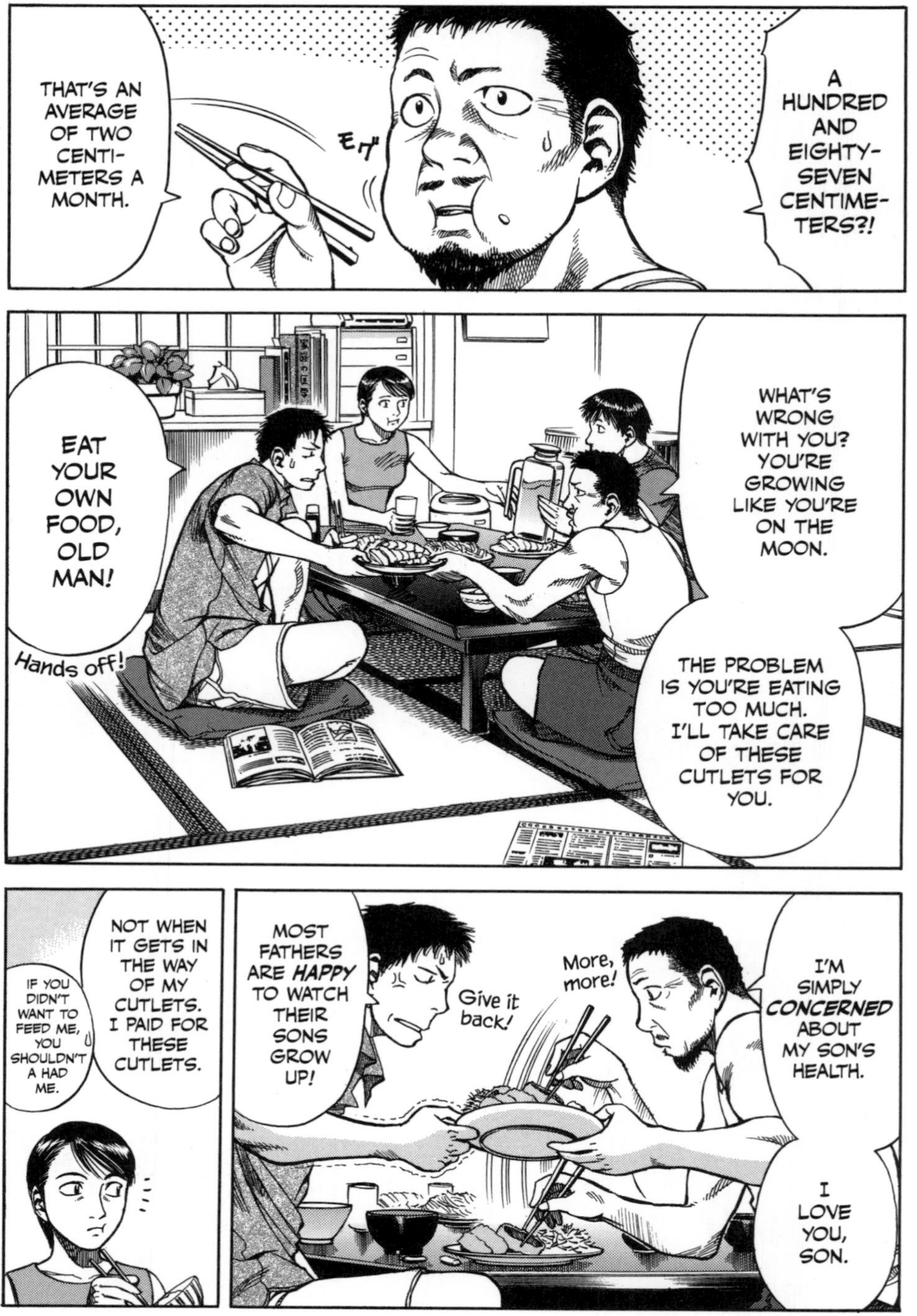
A HUNDRED AND EIGHTY-SEVEN CENTIMETERS?!
モグ
THAT'S AN AVERAGE OF TWO CENTIMETERS A MONTH.
WHAT'S WRONG WITH YOU? YOU'RE GROWING LIKE YOU'RE ON THE MOON.
THE PROBLEM IS YOU'RE EATING TOO MUCH. I'LL TAKE CARE OF THESE CUTLETS FOR YOU.
EAT YOUR OWN FOOD, OLD MAN!
Hands off!
I'M SIMPLY *CONCERNED* ABOUT MY SON'S HEALTH.
More, more!
MOST FATHERS ARE *HAPPY* TO WATCH THEIR SONS GROW UP!
Give it back!
I LOVE YOU, SON.
NOT WHEN IT GETS IN THE WAY OF MY CUTLETS. I PAID FOR THESE CUTLETS.
IF YOU DIDN'T WANT TO FEED ME, YOU SHOULDN'T A HAD ME.

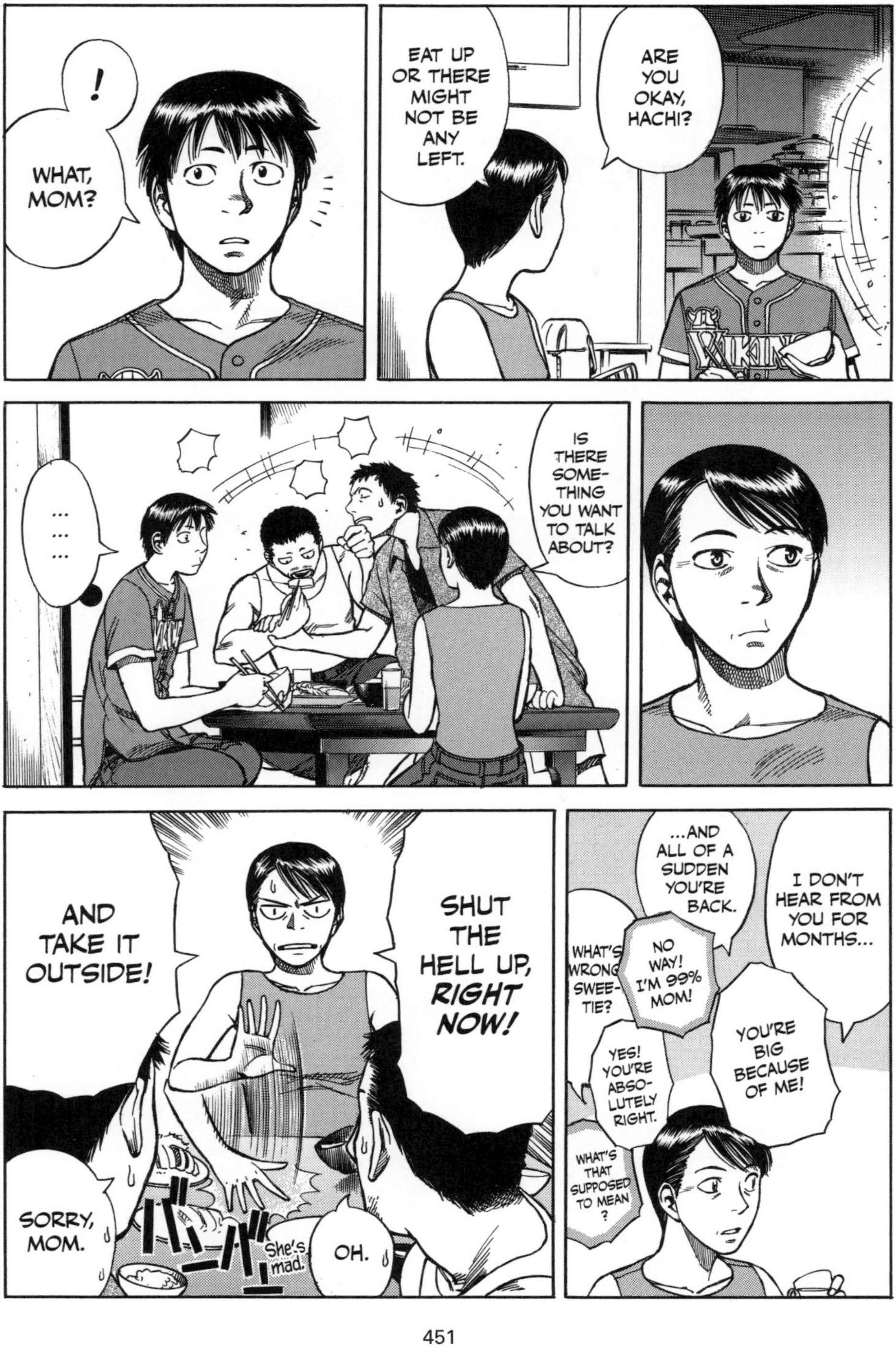
ARE YOU OKAY, HACHI?
EAT UP OR THERE MIGHT NOT BE ANY LEFT.
!
WHAT, MOM?
IS THERE SOME-THING YOU WANT TO TALK ABOUT?
... ...
I DON'T HEAR FROM YOU FOR MONTHS...
...AND ALL OF A SUDDEN YOU'RE BACK.
YOU'RE BIG BECAUSE OF ME!
NO WAY! I'M 99% MOM!
WHAT'S WRONG SWEE-TIE?
YES! YOU'RE ABSO-LUTELY RIGHT.
WHAT'S THAT SUPPOSED TO MEAN ?
SHUT THE HELL UP, RIGHT NOW!
AND TAKE IT OUTSIDE!
OH.
She's mad.
SORRY, MOM.

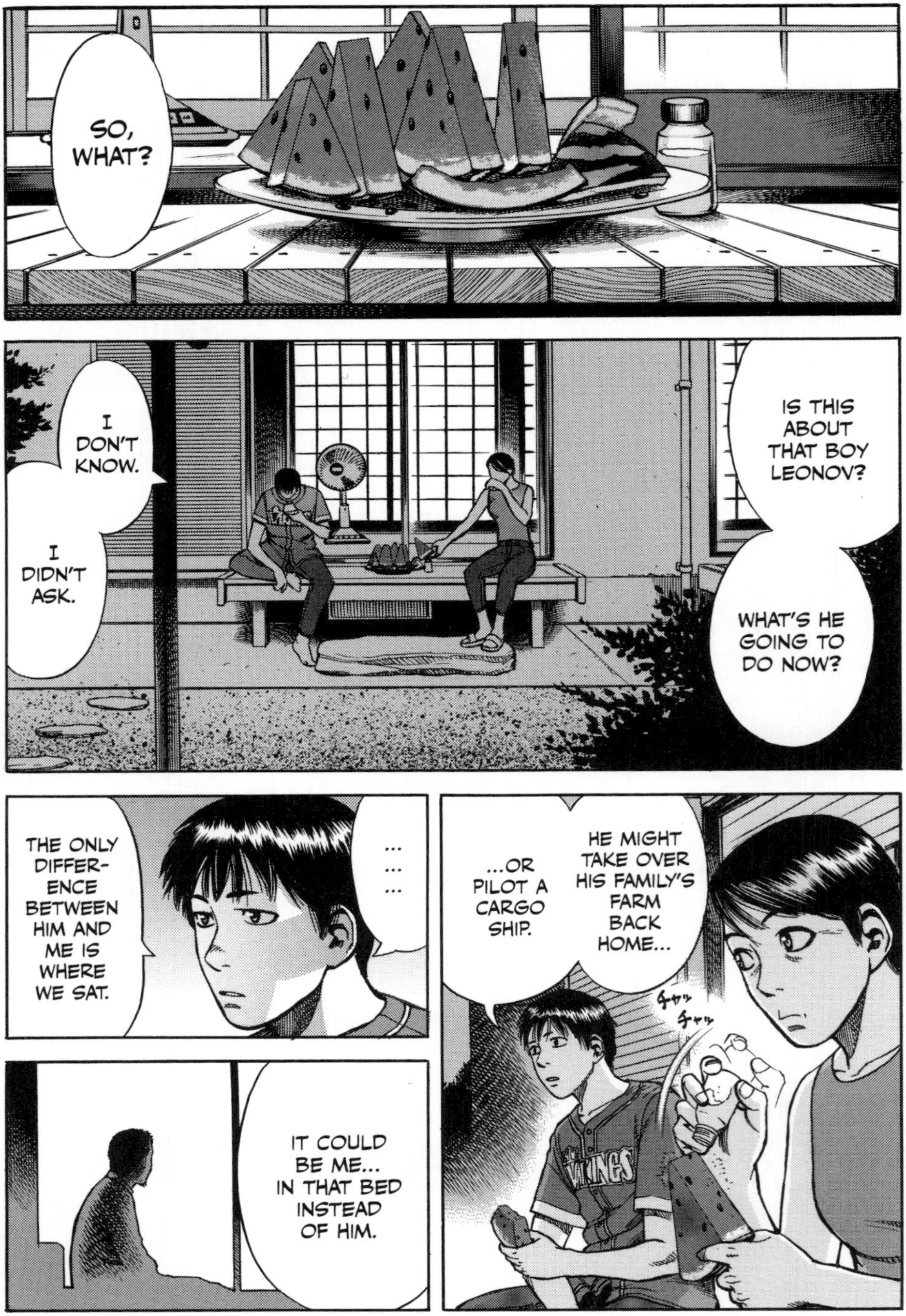
SO, WHAT?
IS THIS ABOUT THAT BOY LEONOV?
WHAT'S HE GOING TO DO NOW?
I DON'T KNOW.
I DIDN'T ASK.
HE MIGHT TAKE OVER HIS FAMILY'S FARM BACK HOME...
...OR PILOT A CARGO SHIP.
チャッ
チャッ
... ...
THE ONLY DIFFER-ENCE BETWEEN HIM AND ME IS WHERE WE SAT.
IT COULD BE ME... IN THAT BED INSTEAD OF HIM.

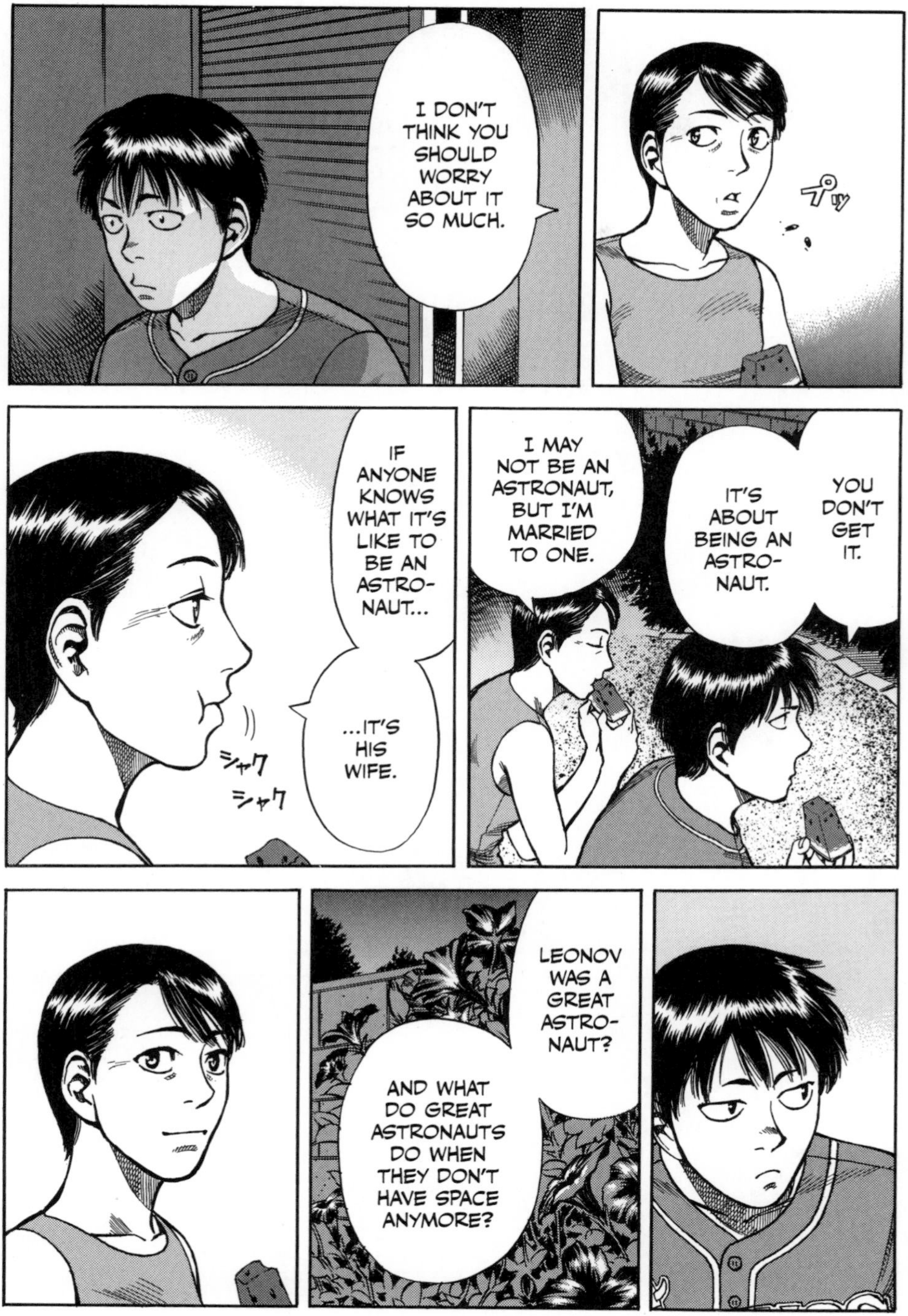
ピッ
I DON'T THINK YOU SHOULD WORRY ABOUT IT SO MUCH.
YOU DON'T GET IT.
IT'S ABOUT BEING AN ASTRONAUT.
I MAY NOT BE AN ASTRONAUT, BUT I'M MARRIED TO ONE.
IF ANYONE KNOWS WHAT IT'S LIKE TO BE AN ASTRONAUT...
...IT'S HIS WIFE.
シャク
シャク
LEONOV WAS A GREAT ASTRONAUT?
AND WHAT DO GREAT ASTRONAUTS DO WHEN THEY DON'T HAVE SPACE ANYMORE?

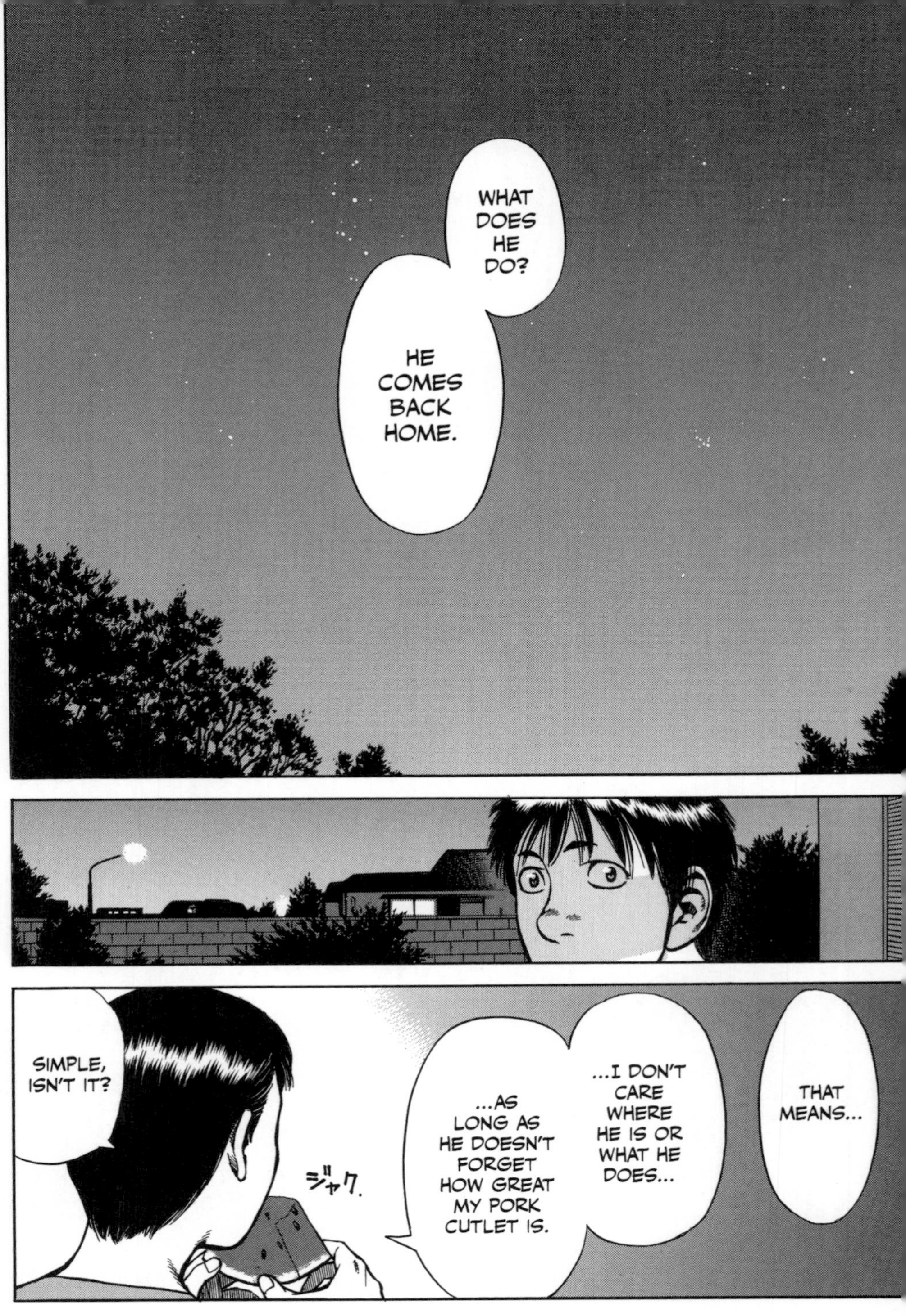
WHAT DOES HE DO?
HE COMES BACK HOME.
THAT MEANS...
...I DON'T CARE WHERE HE IS OR WHAT HE DOES...
...AS LONG AS HE DOESN'T FORGET HOW GREAT MY PORK CUTLET IS.
ジャク.
SIMPLE, ISN'T IT?

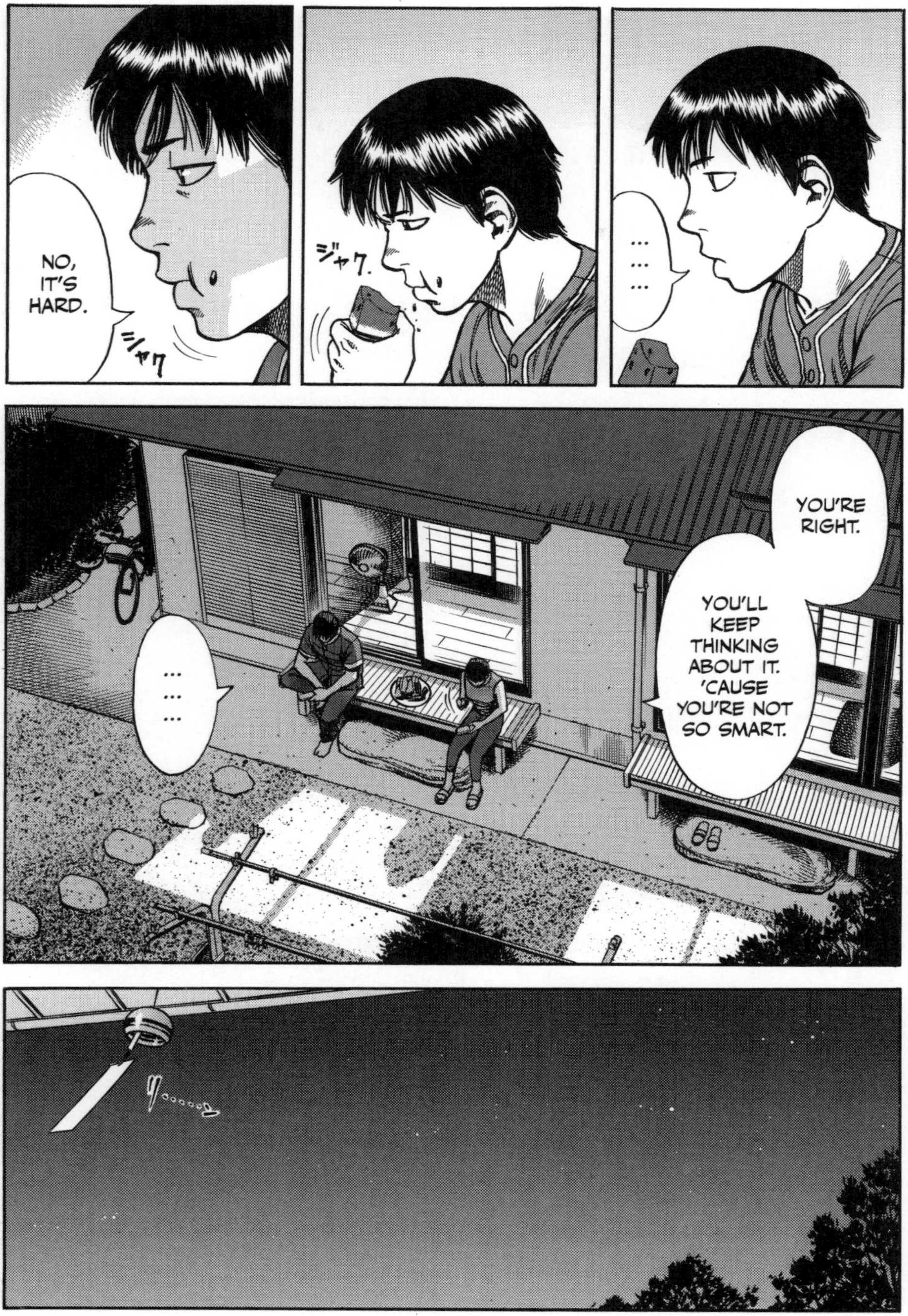
......
ジャク.
NO, IT'S HARD.
シャク
YOU'RE RIGHT.
YOU'LL KEEP THINKING ABOUT IT. 'CAUSE YOU'RE NOT SO SMART.
......

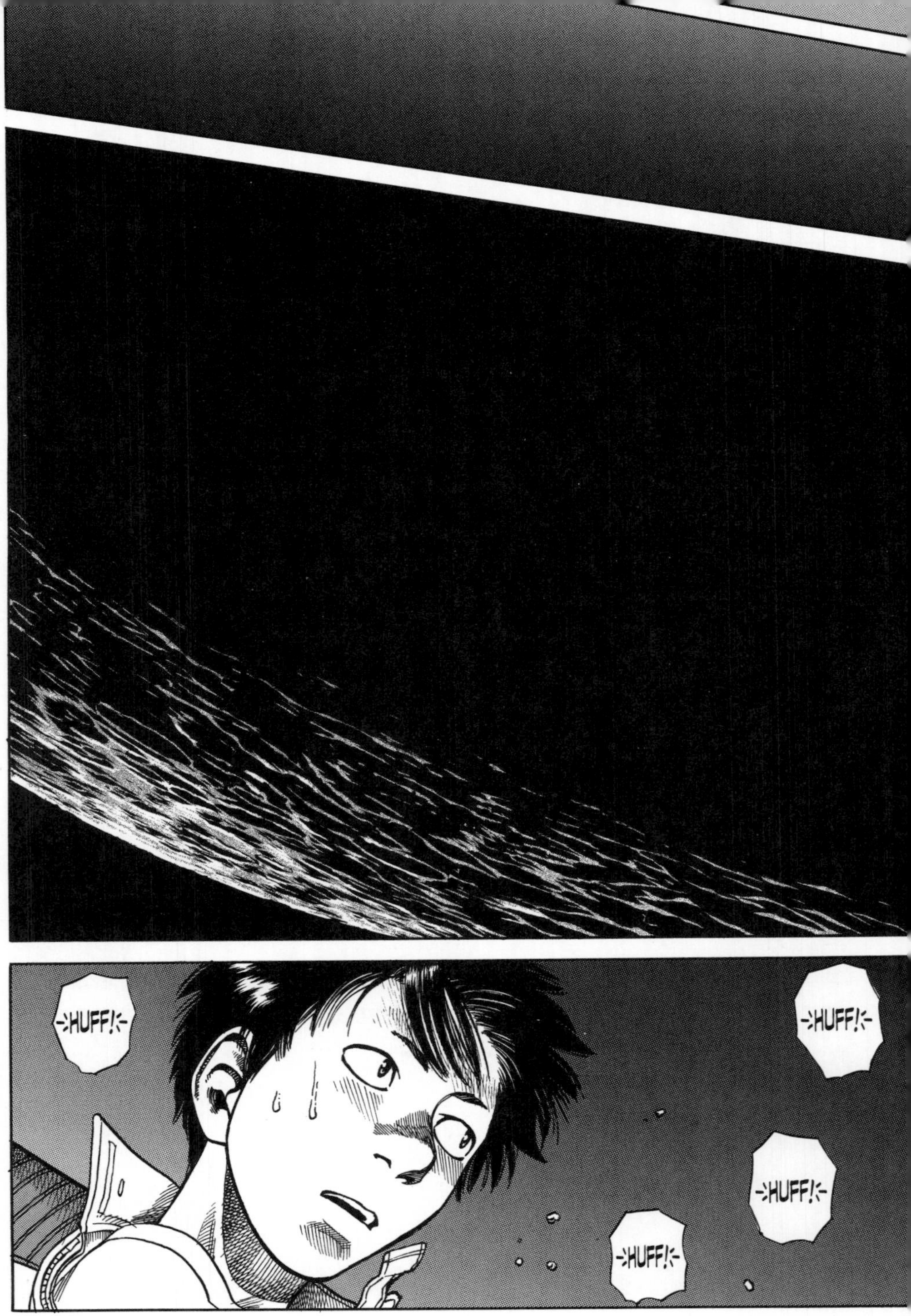
HUFF!
HUFF!
HUFF!
HUFF!

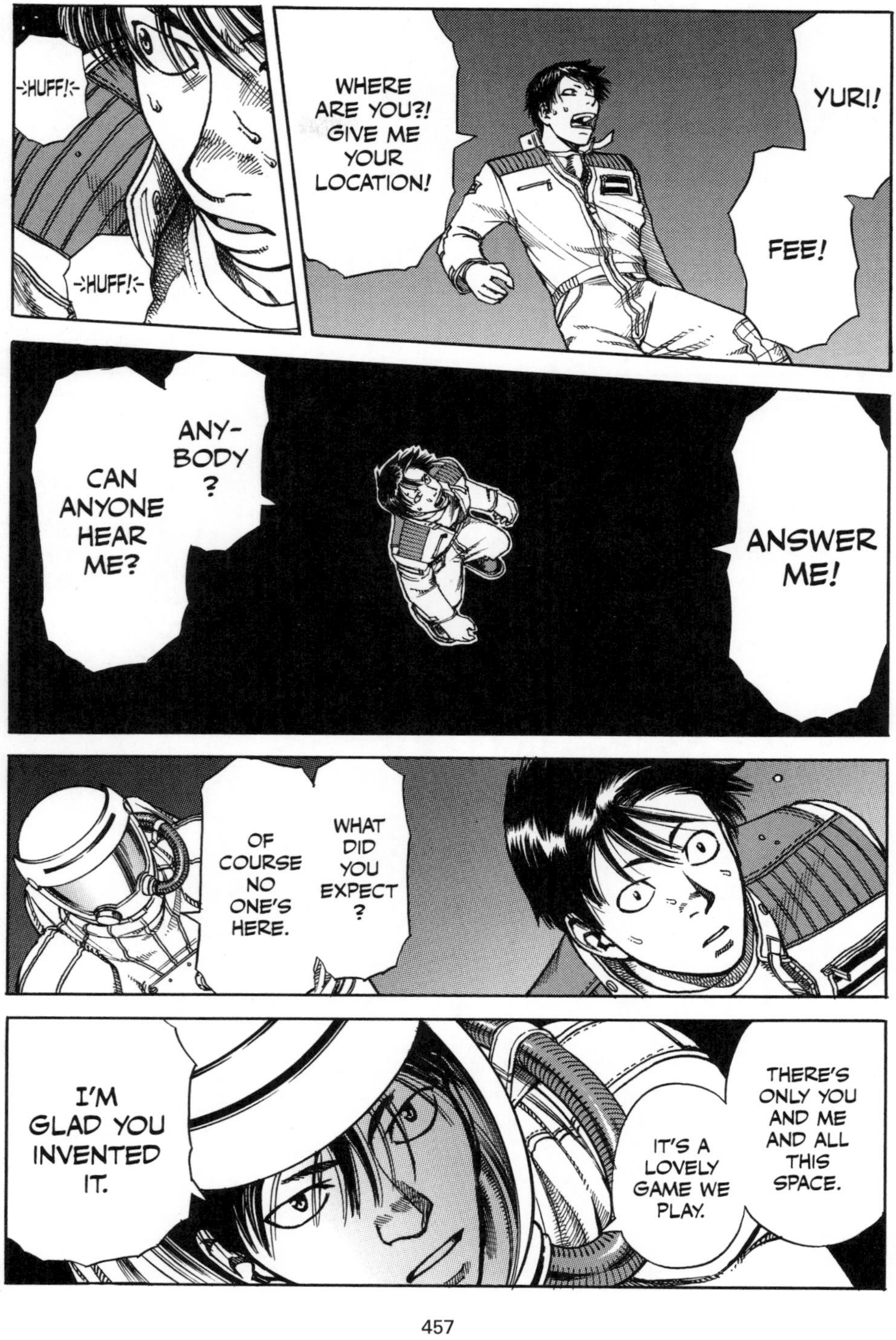
YURI!
FEE!
WHERE ARE YOU?! GIVE ME YOUR LOCATION!
HUFF!
HUFF!
ANSWER ME!
ANY-BODY?
CAN ANYONE HEAR ME?
WHAT DID YOU EXPECT?
OF COURSE NO ONE'S HERE.
THERE'S ONLY YOU AND ME AND ALL THIS SPACE.
IT'S A LOVELY GAME WE PLAY.
I'M GLAD YOU INVENTED IT.

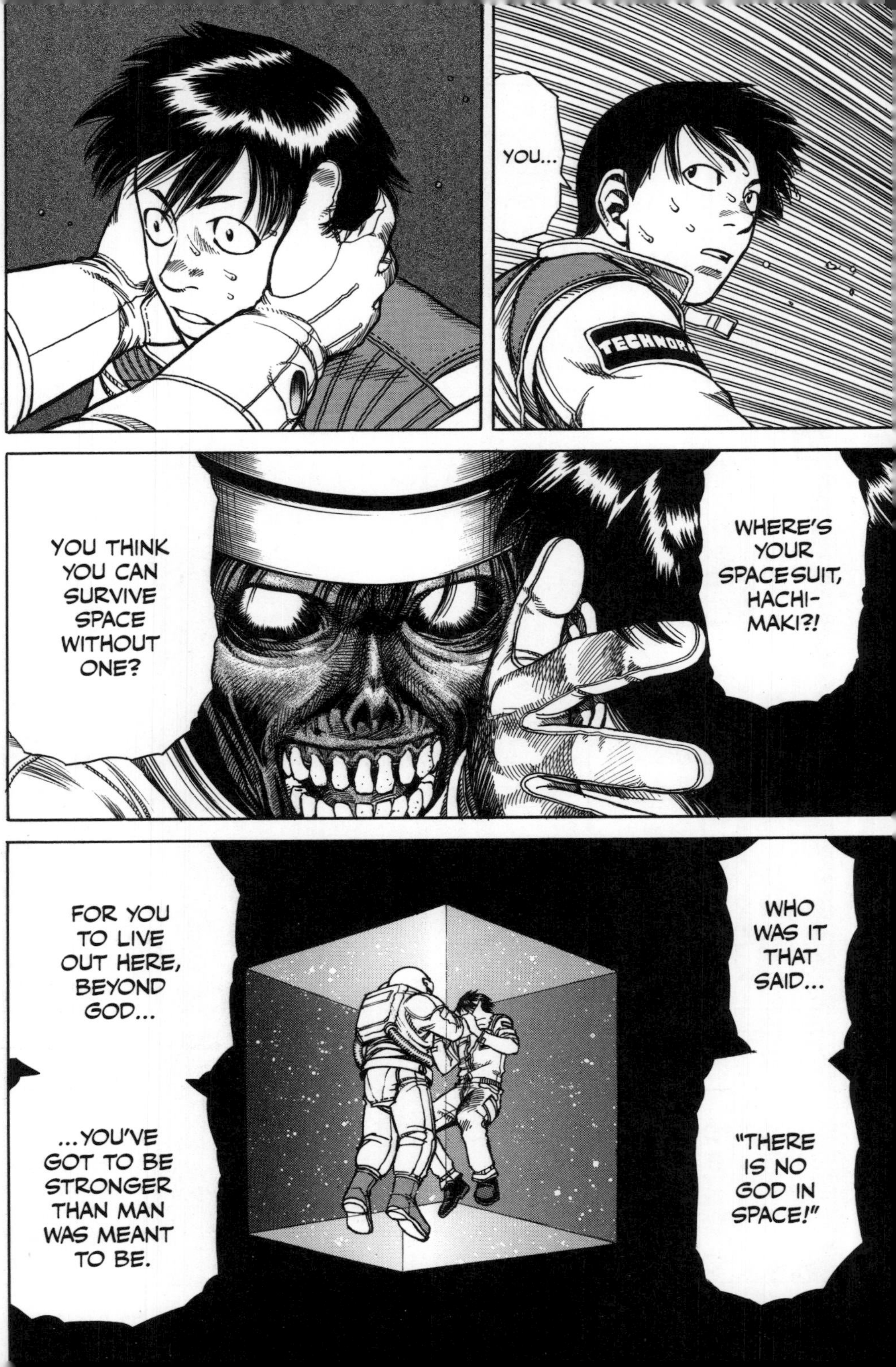
YOU...
WHERE'S YOUR SPACESUIT, HACHI-MAKI?!
YOU THINK YOU CAN SURVIVE SPACE WITHOUT ONE?
WHO WAS IT THAT SAID...
"THERE IS NO GOD IN SPACE!"
FOR YOU TO LIVE OUT HERE, BEYOND GOD...
...YOU'VE GOT TO BE STRONGER THAN MAN WAS MEANT TO BE.

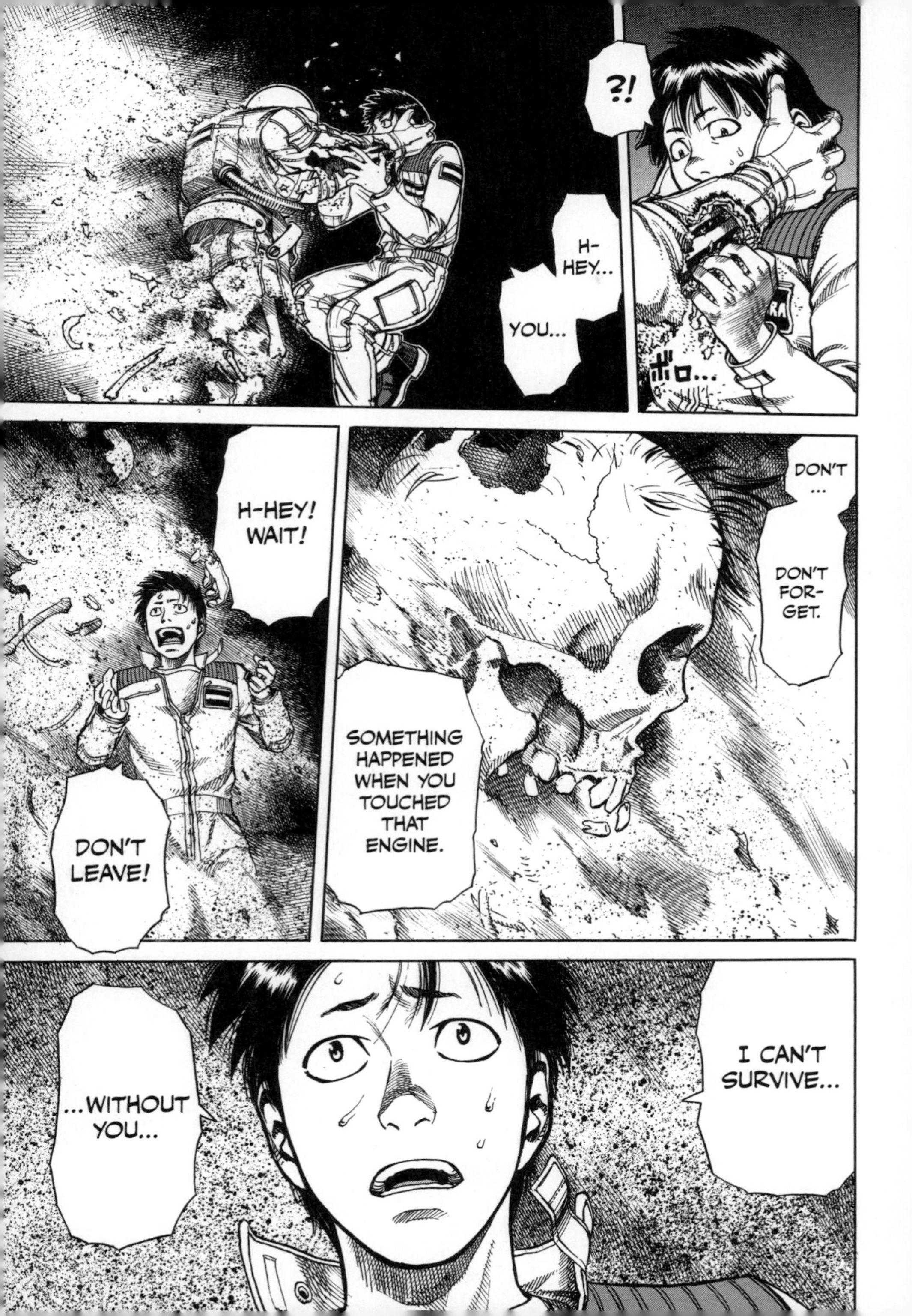
?!
ボロ...
H-HEY...
YOU...
DON'T ...
DON'T FOR-GET.
SOMETHING HAPPENED WHEN YOU TOUCHED THAT ENGINE.
H-HEY! WAIT!
DON'T LEAVE!
I CAN'T SURVIVE...
...WITHOUT YOU...

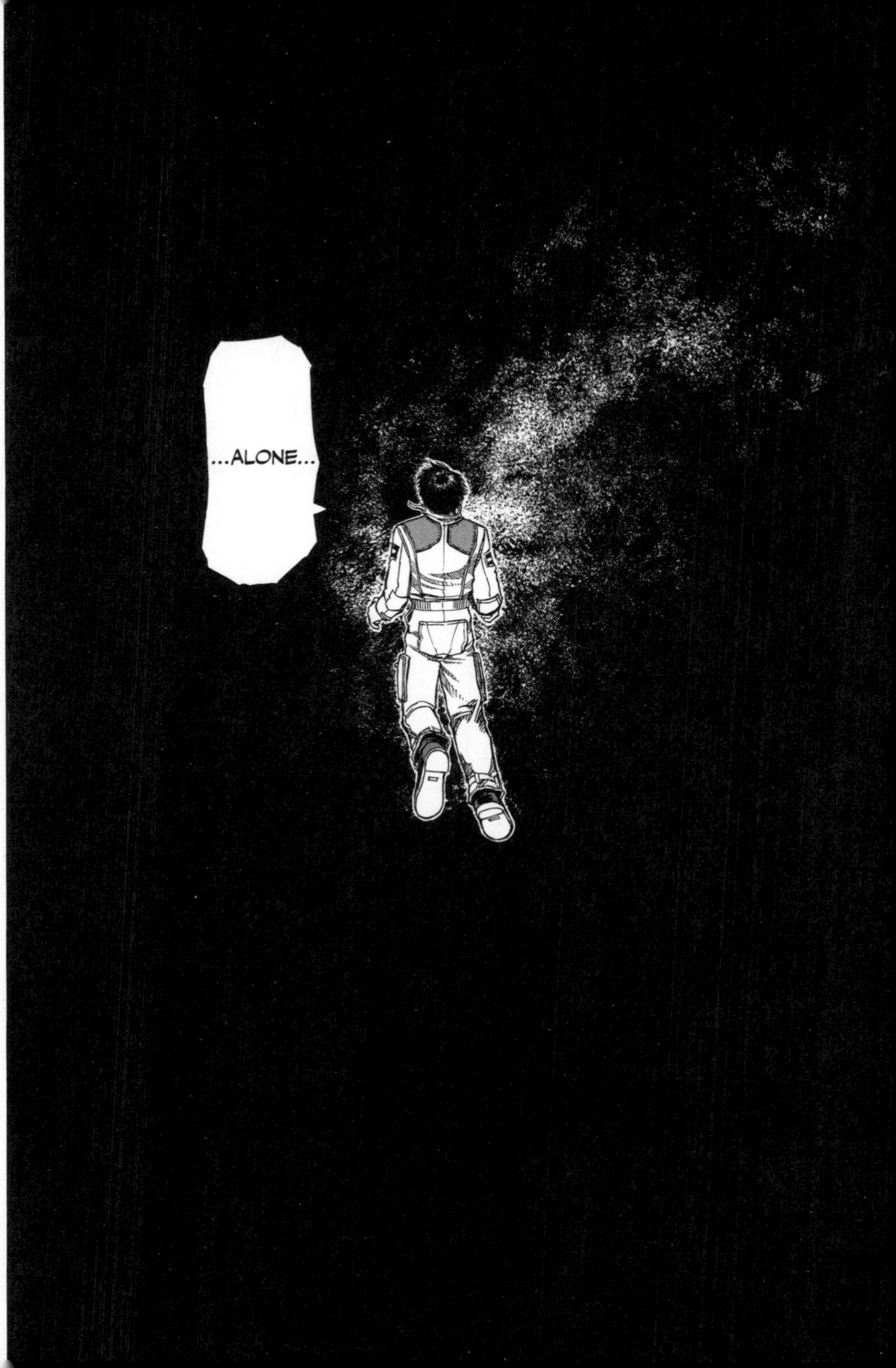
...ALONE...

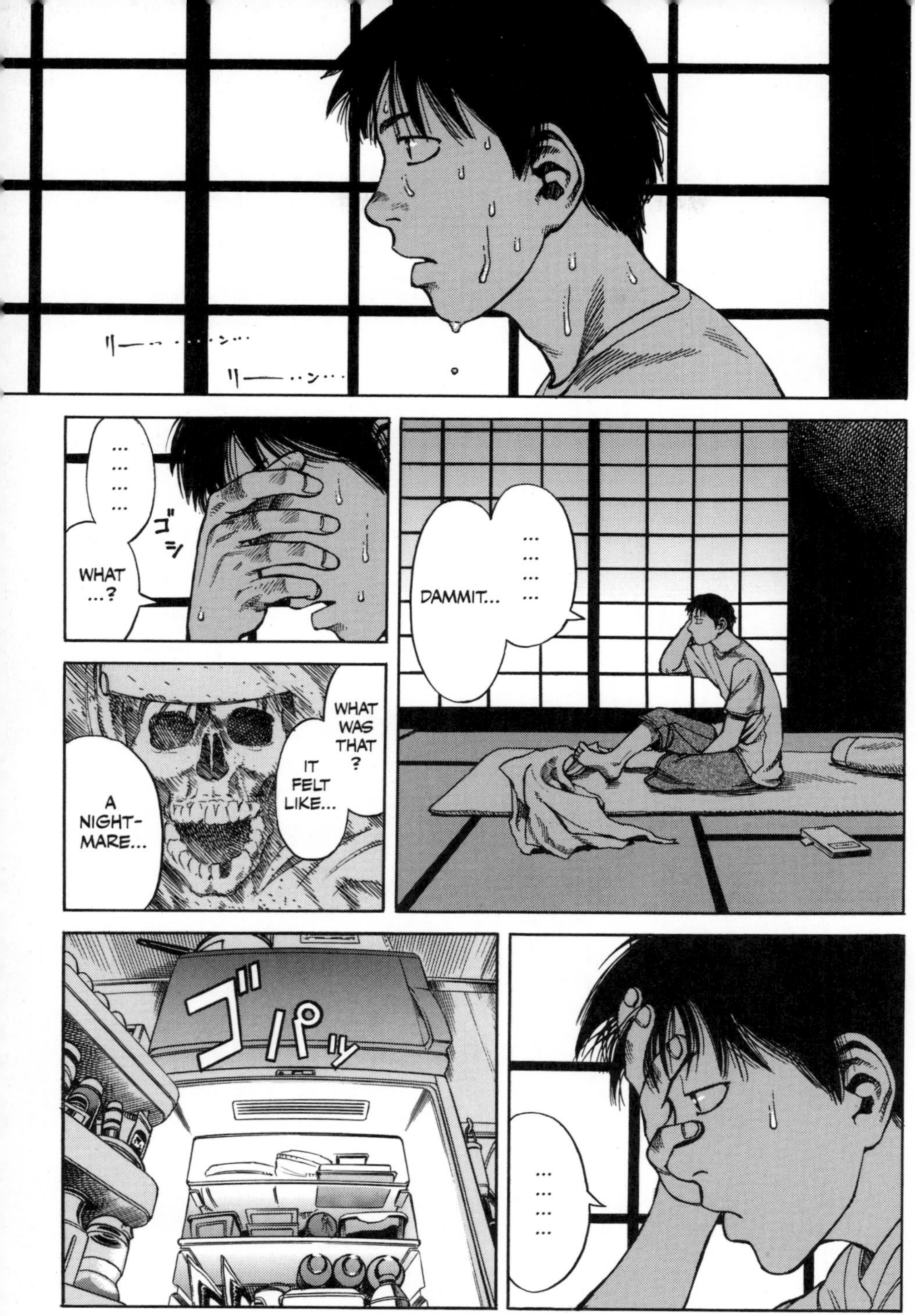

リ—ッ・・・・ン・・
リ——・・ン・・・
... ...
DAMMIT...
... ...
ゴシ
WHAT ...?
WHAT WAS THAT?
IT FELT LIKE...
A NIGHT-MARE...
... ...
ゴパッ

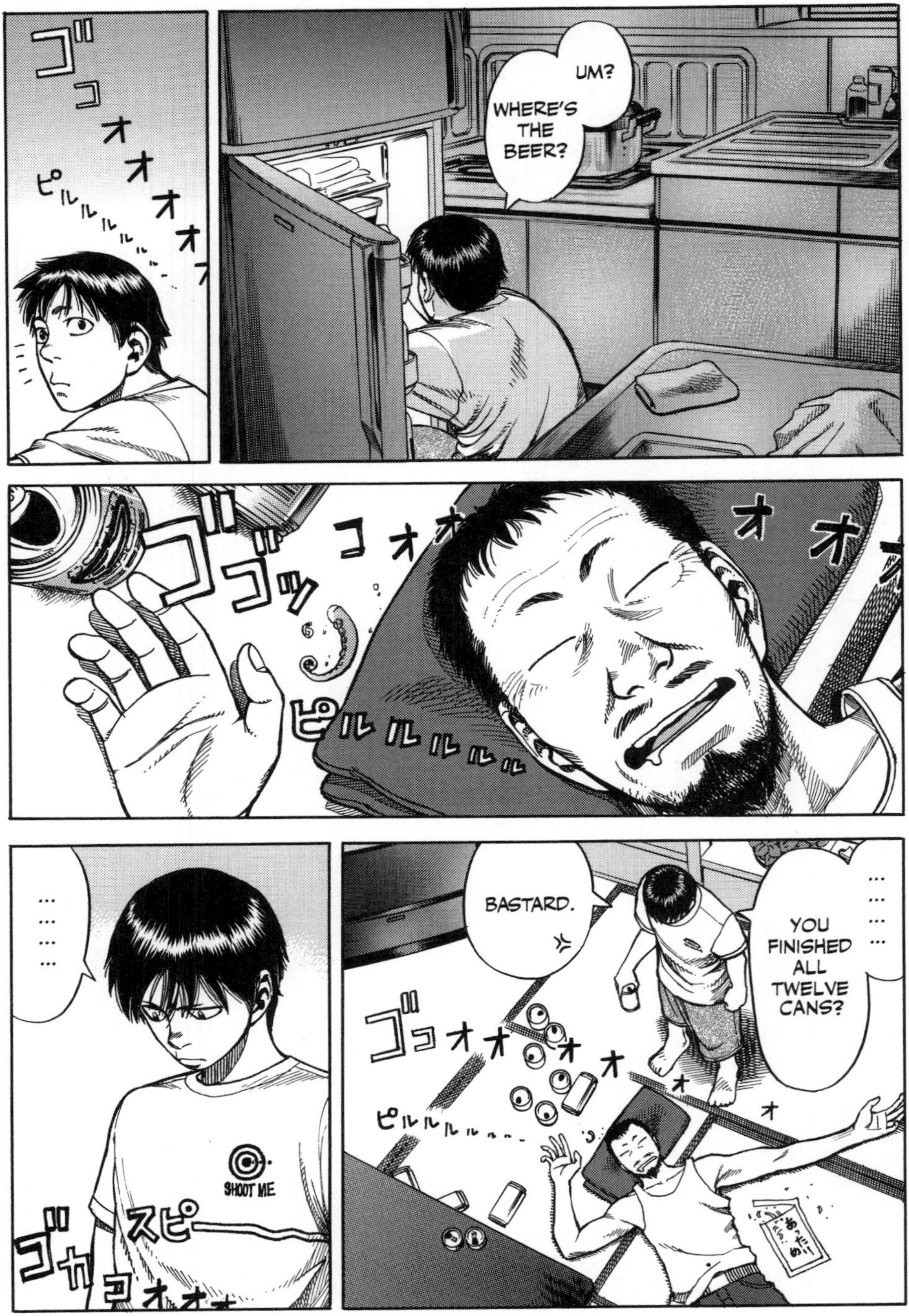
UM?
WHERE'S THE BEER?
ゴコオオオオオフ
ピルルルルル
ゴゴッ
コオオ
オオオ
ピルルルルルル
...
...
...
...
YOU FINISHED ALL TWELVE CANS?
BASTARD.
ゴコオオオオオ
ピルルルル
...
...
...
...
SHOOT ME
スピー
ゴカコオオ

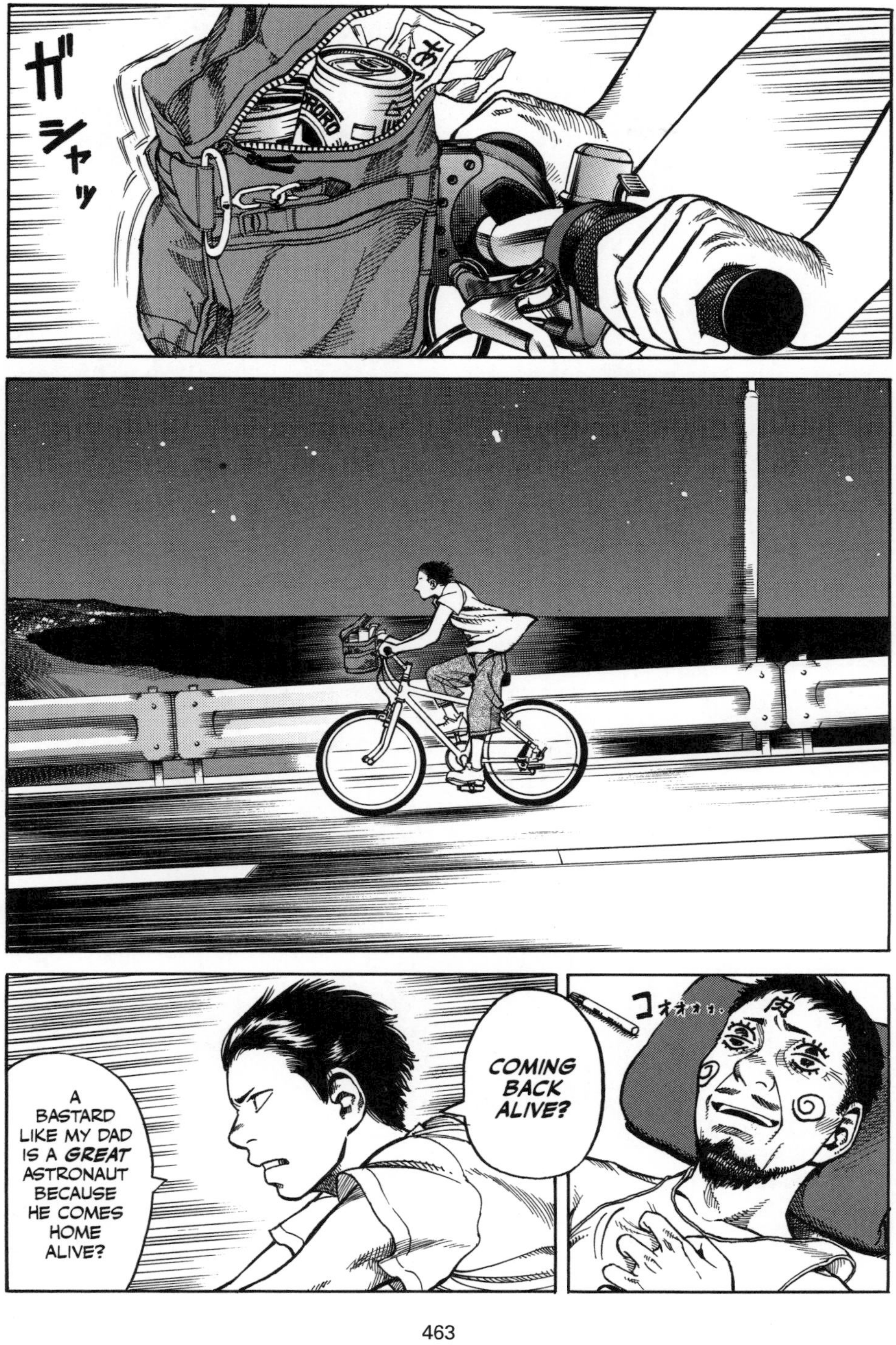
ガシャッ
あ
コォォォ
肉
COMING BACK ALIVE?
A BASTARD LIKE MY DAD IS A *GREAT* ASTRONAUT BECAUSE HE COMES HOME ALIVE?

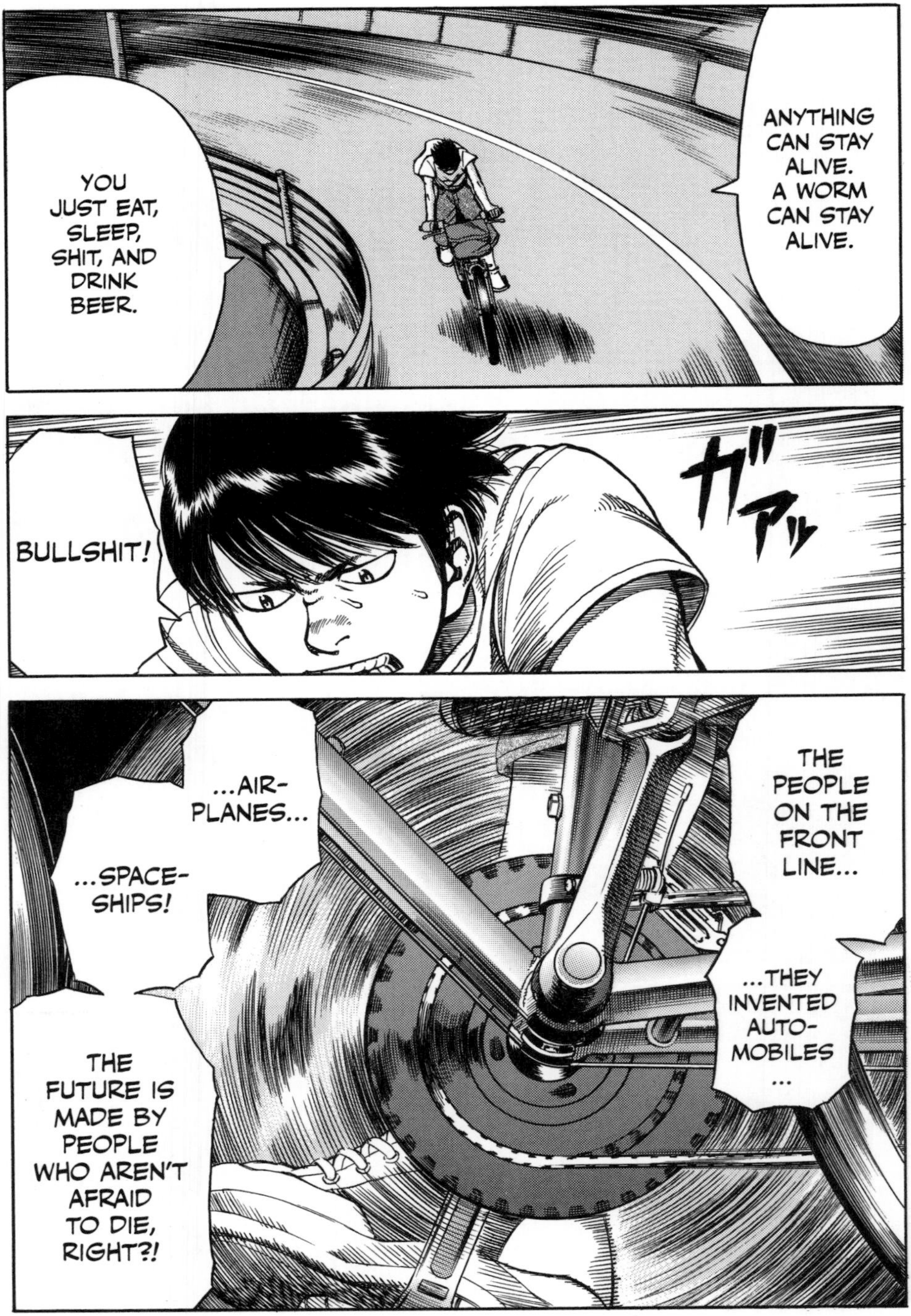
ANYTHING CAN STAY ALIVE. A WORM CAN STAY ALIVE.
YOU JUST EAT, SLEEP, SHIT, AND DRINK BEER.
ガアッ
BULLSHIT!
THE PEOPLE ON THE FRONT LINE...
...THEY INVENTED AUTO-MOBILES ...
...AIR-PLANES...
...SPACE-SHIPS!
THE FUTURE IS MADE BY PEOPLE WHO AREN'T AFRAID TO DIE, RIGHT?!

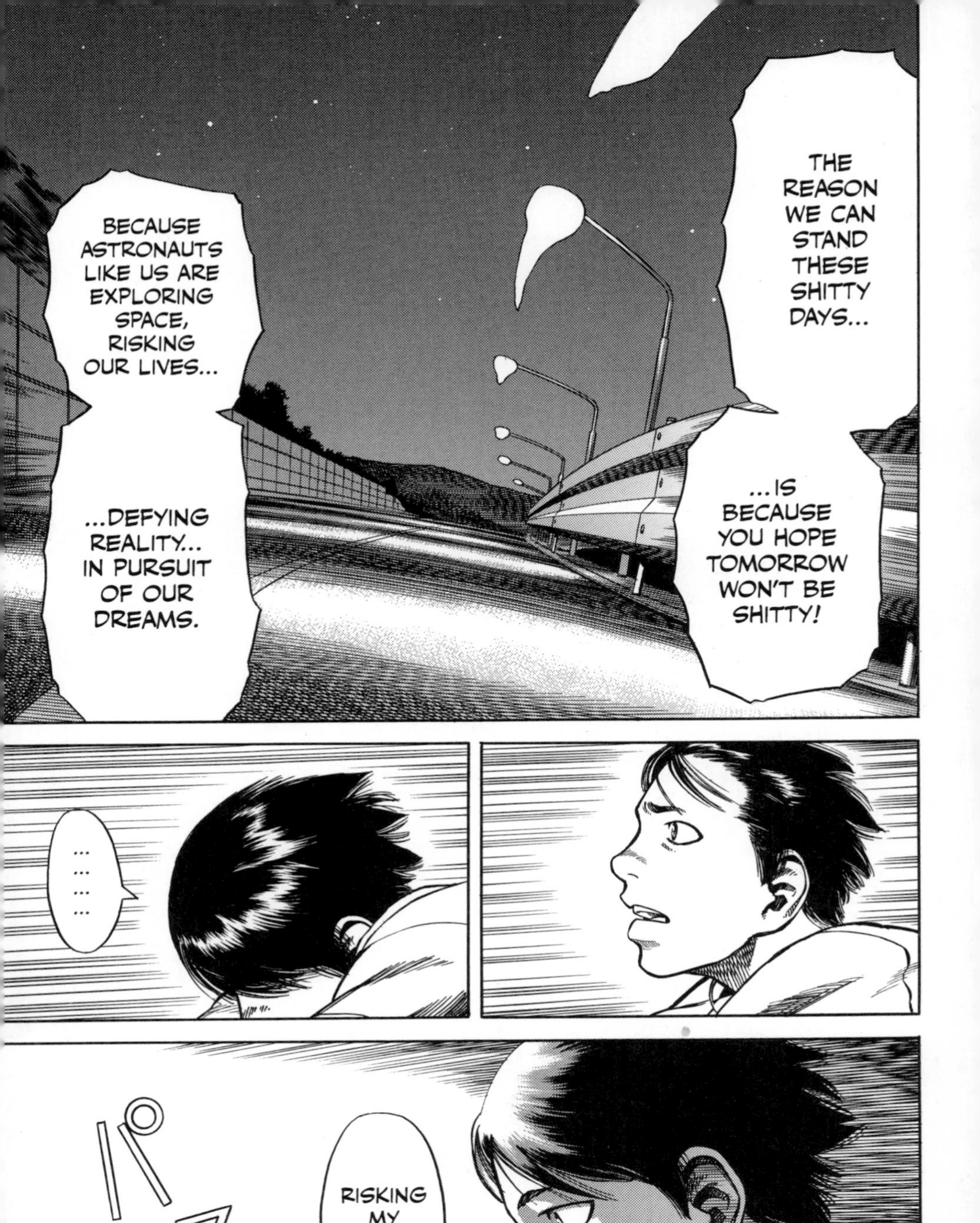
THE REASON WE CAN STAND THESE SHITTY DAYS...
...IS BECAUSE YOU HOPE TOMORROW WON'T BE SHITTY!
BECAUSE ASTRONAUTS LIKE US ARE EXPLORING SPACE, RISKING OUR LIVES...
...DEFYING REALITY... IN PURSUIT OF OUR DREAMS.
....
RISKING MY LIFE...
パァッ

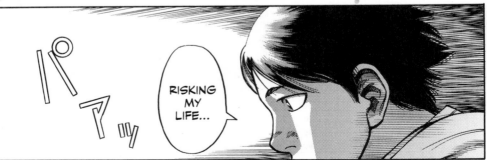

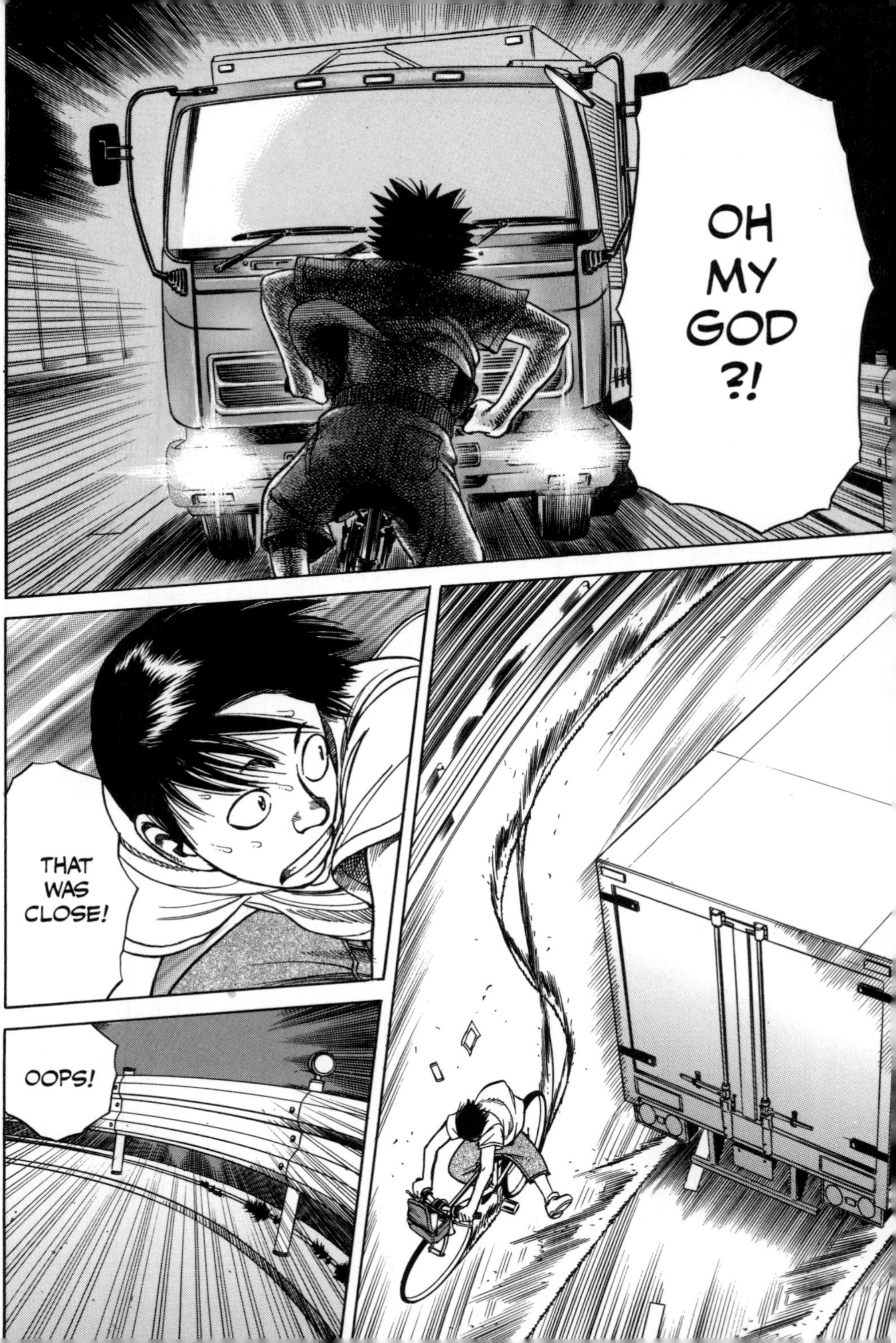
OH MY GOD ?!
THAT WAS CLOSE!
OOPS!

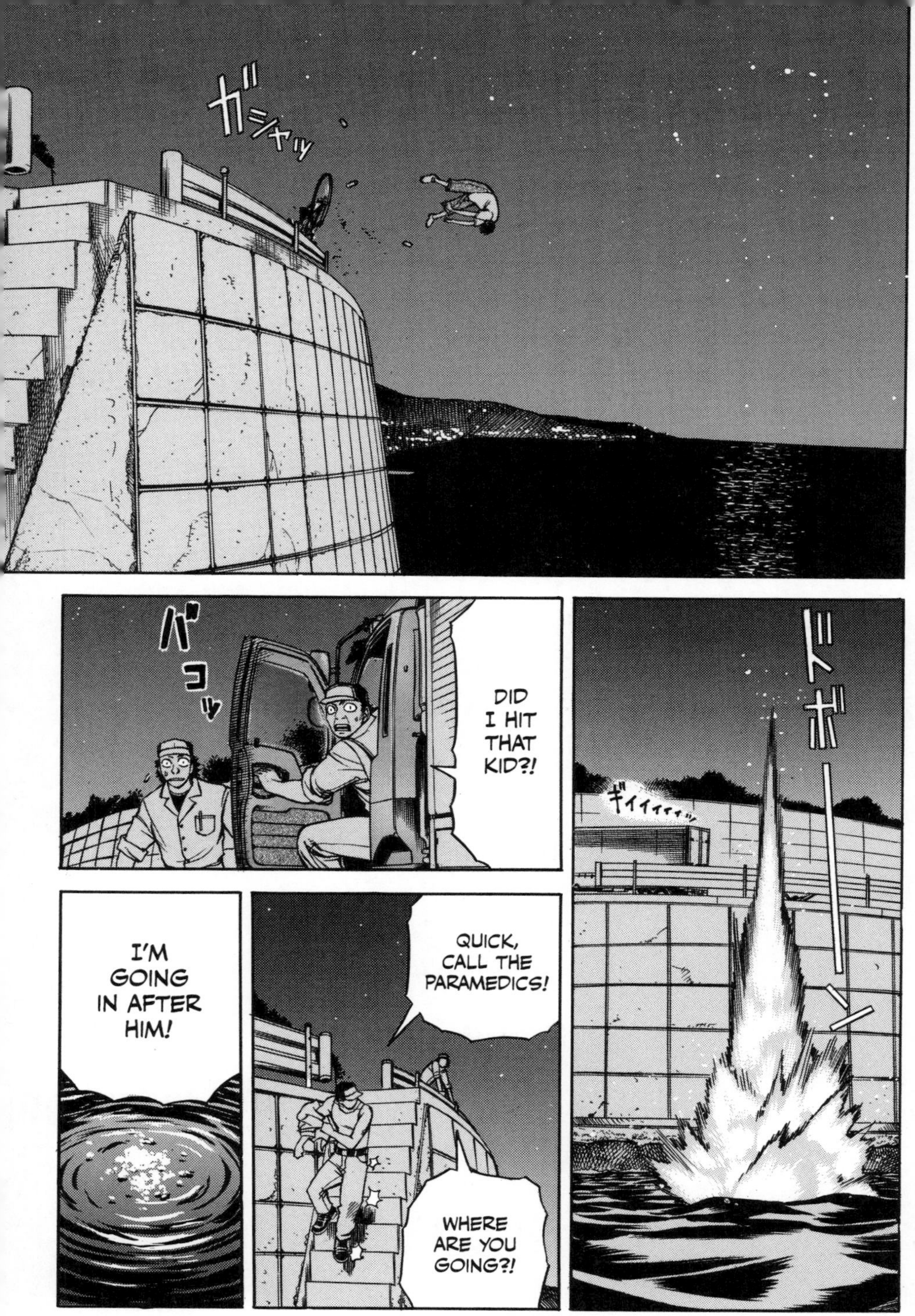
ガシャッ
ドボーーン
ギイイイイッ
バコッ
DID I HIT THAT KID?!
QUICK, CALL THE PARAMEDICS!
WHERE ARE YOU GOING?!
I'M GOING IN AFTER HIM!

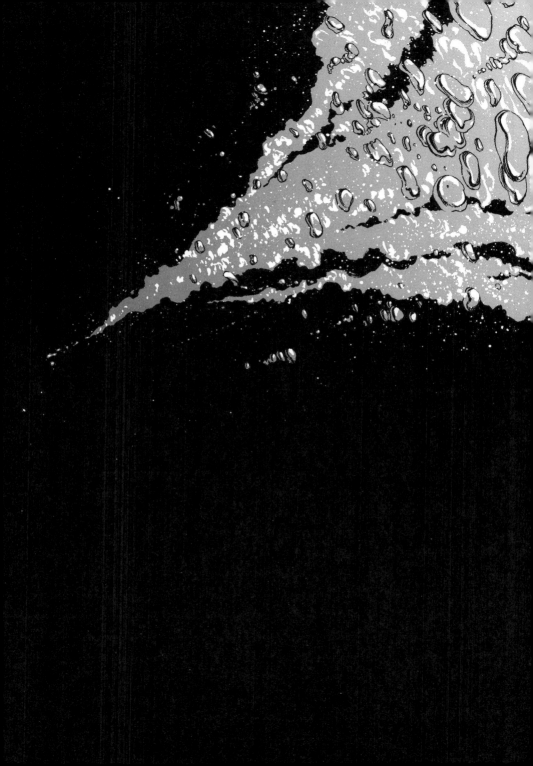

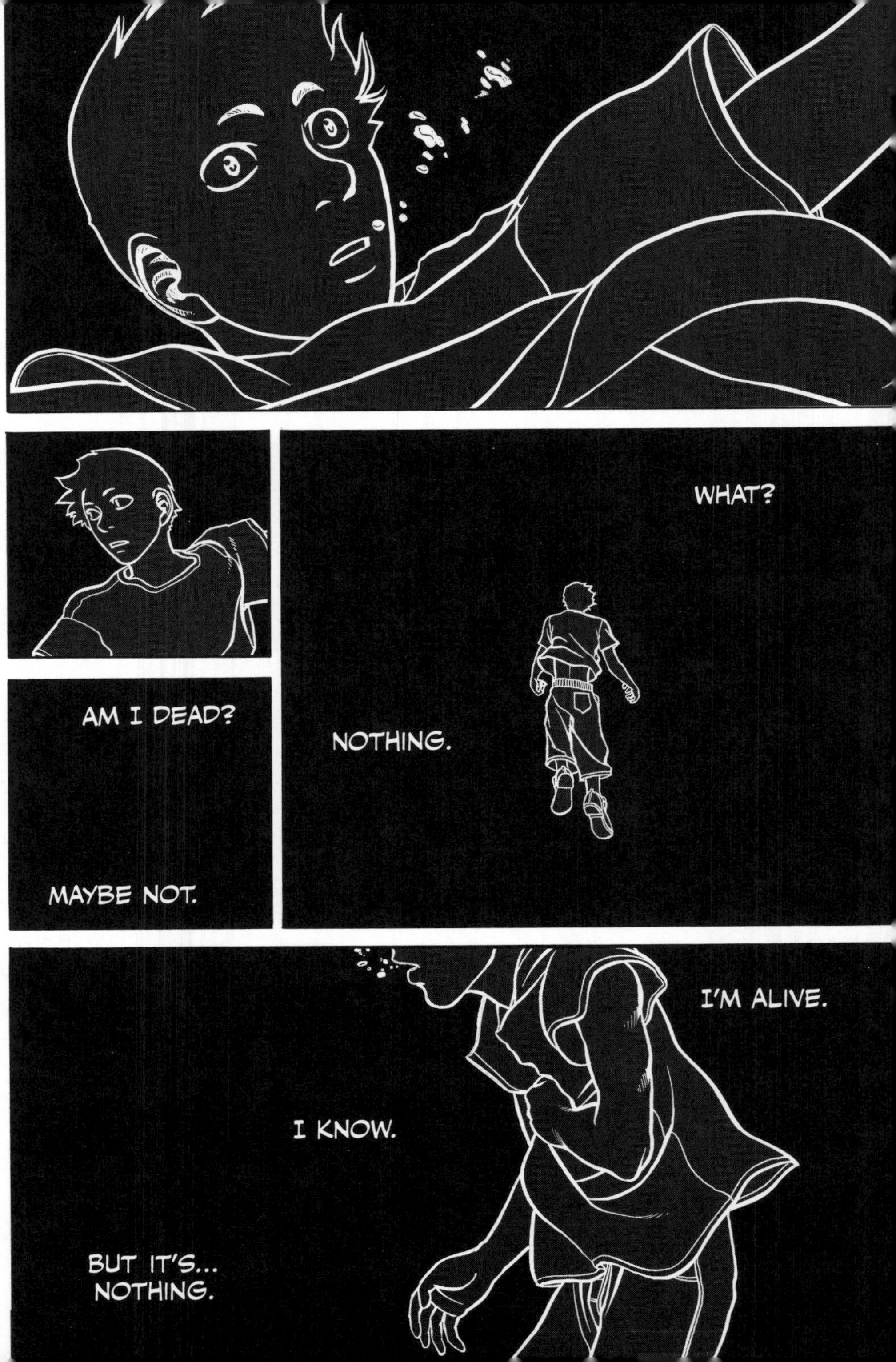
WHAT?
NOTHING.
AM I DEAD?
MAYBE NOT.
I'M ALIVE.
I KNOW.
BUT IT'S... NOTHING.

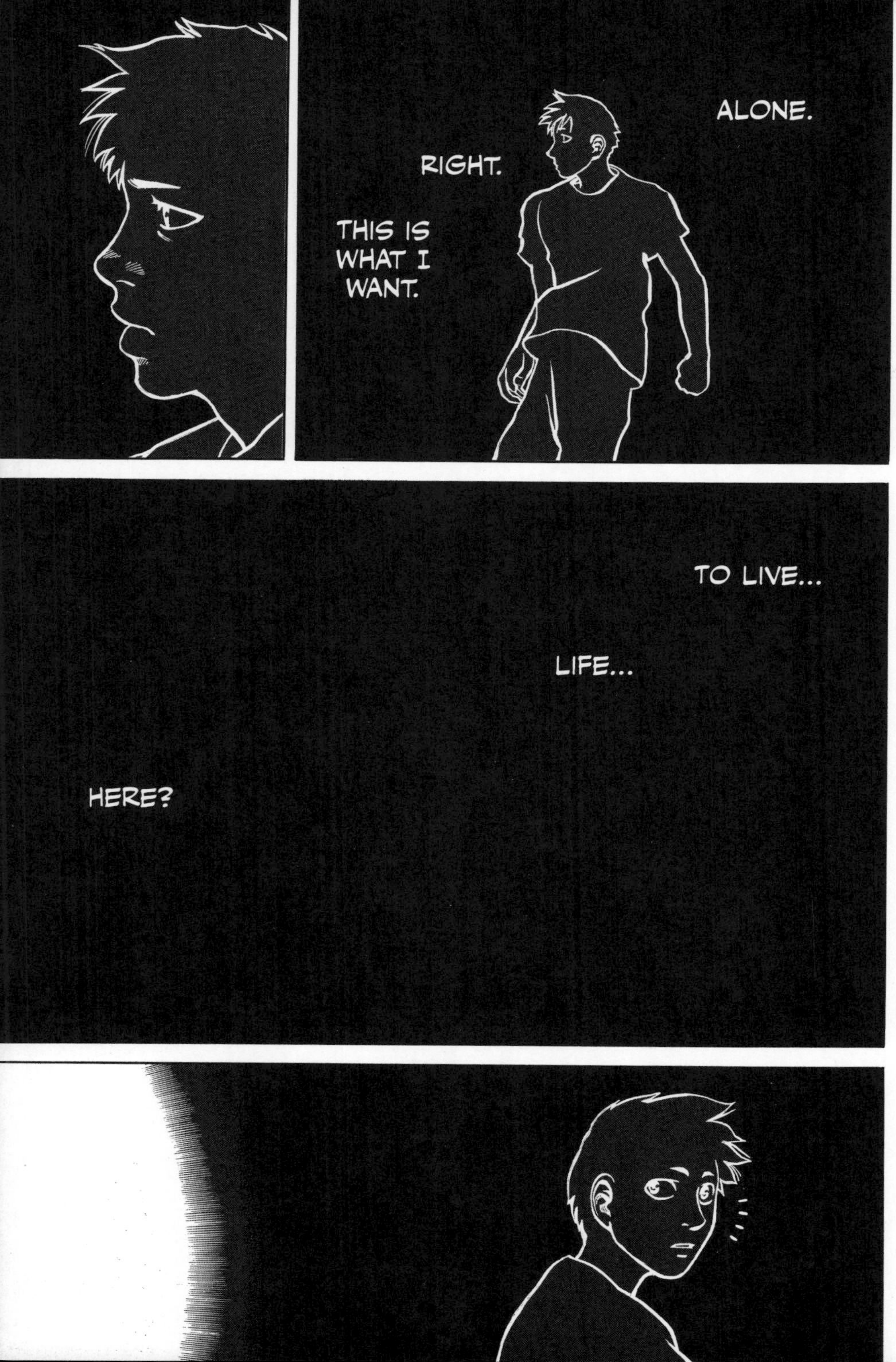
ALONE.
RIGHT.
THIS IS WHAT I WANT.
TO LIVE...
LIFE...
HERE?

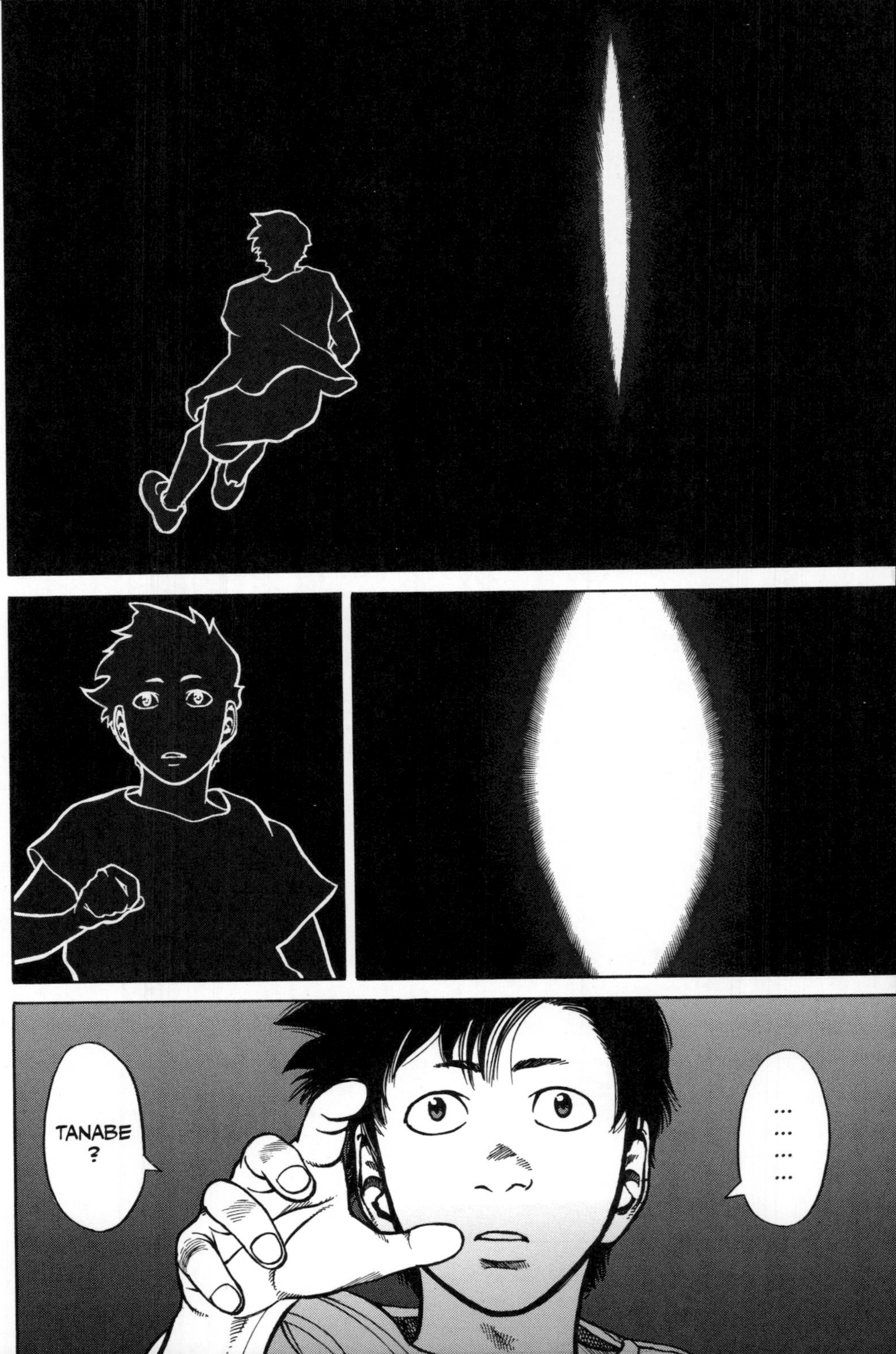
....
TANABE ?

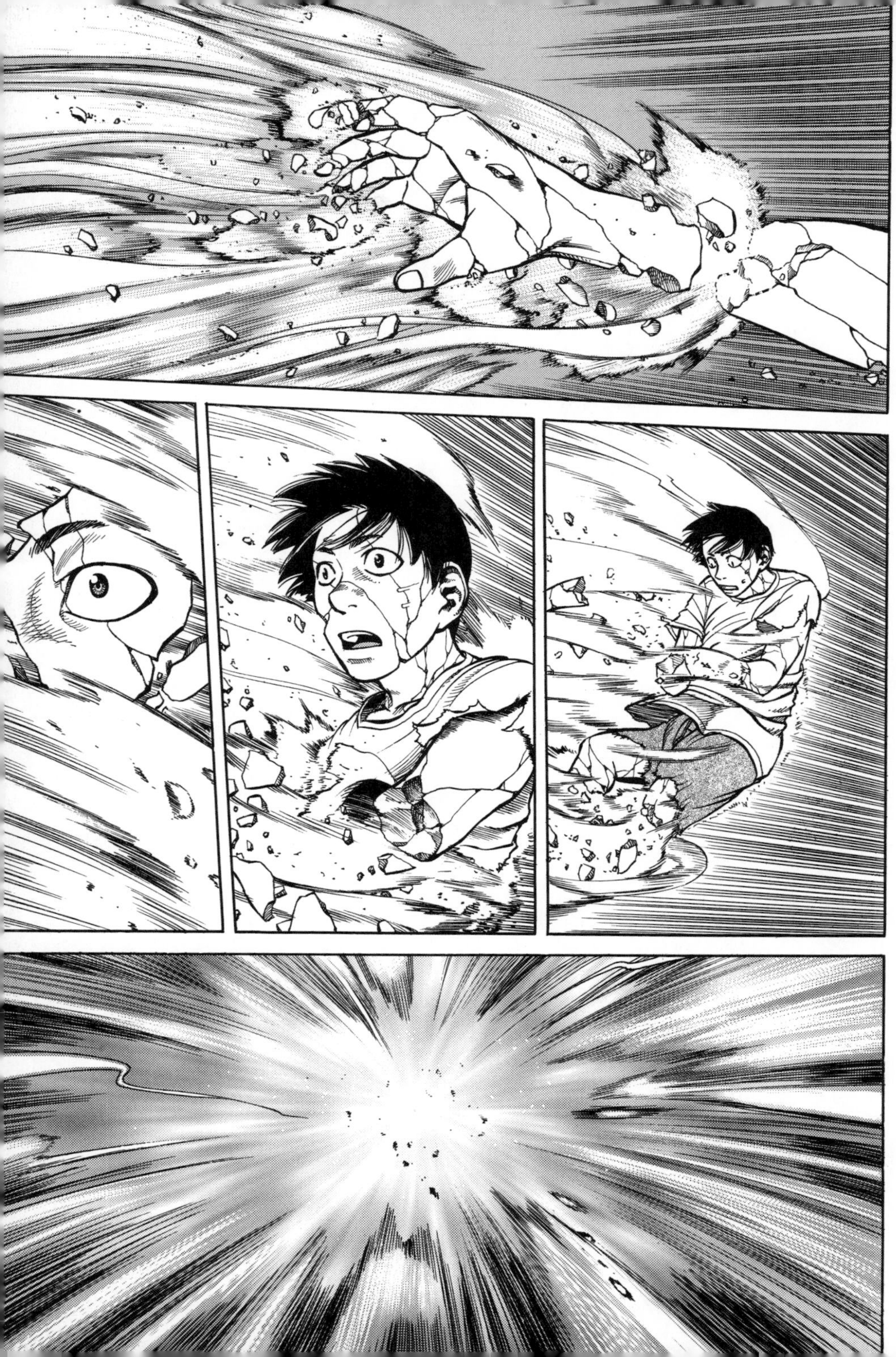

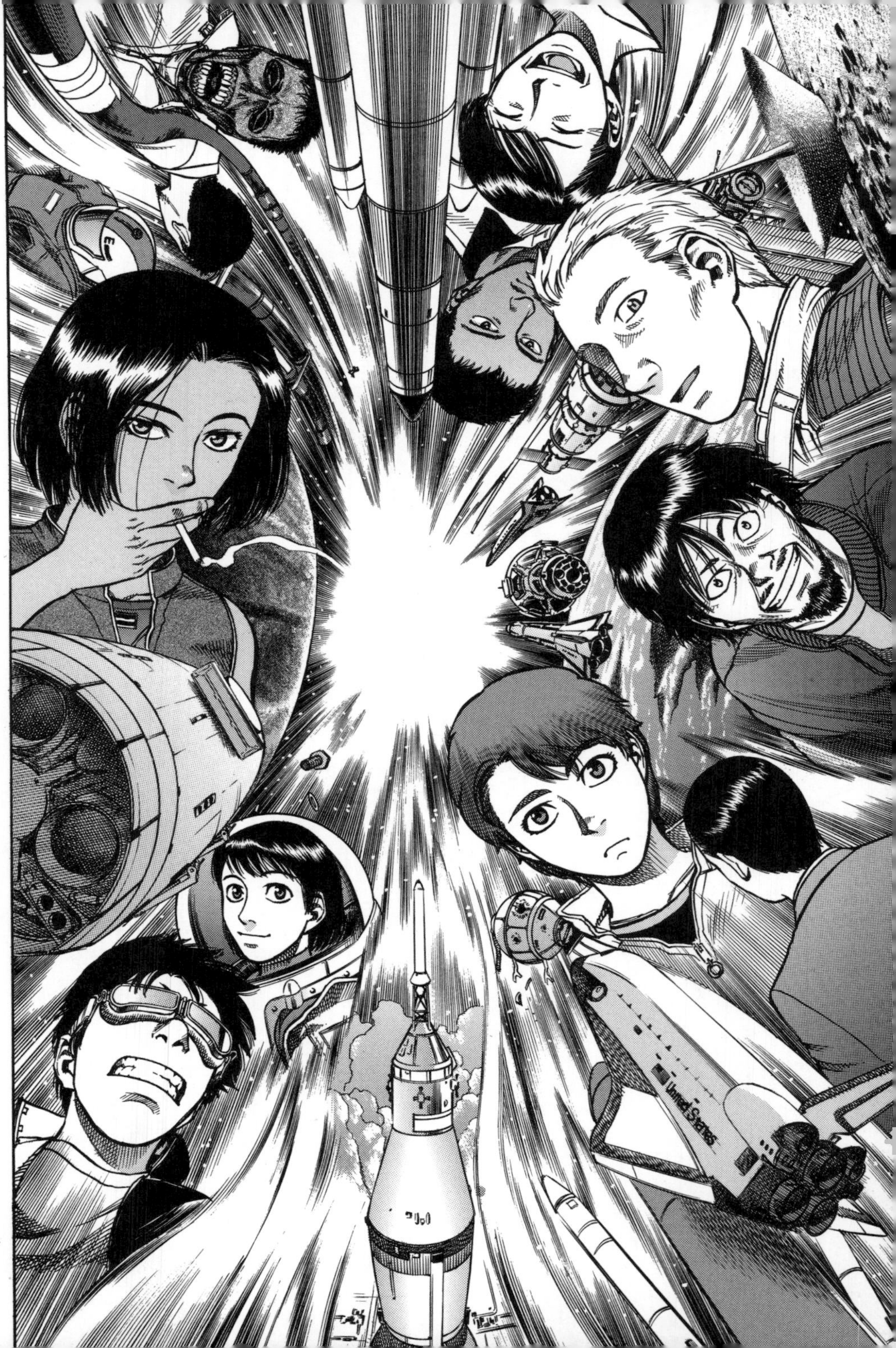
United States

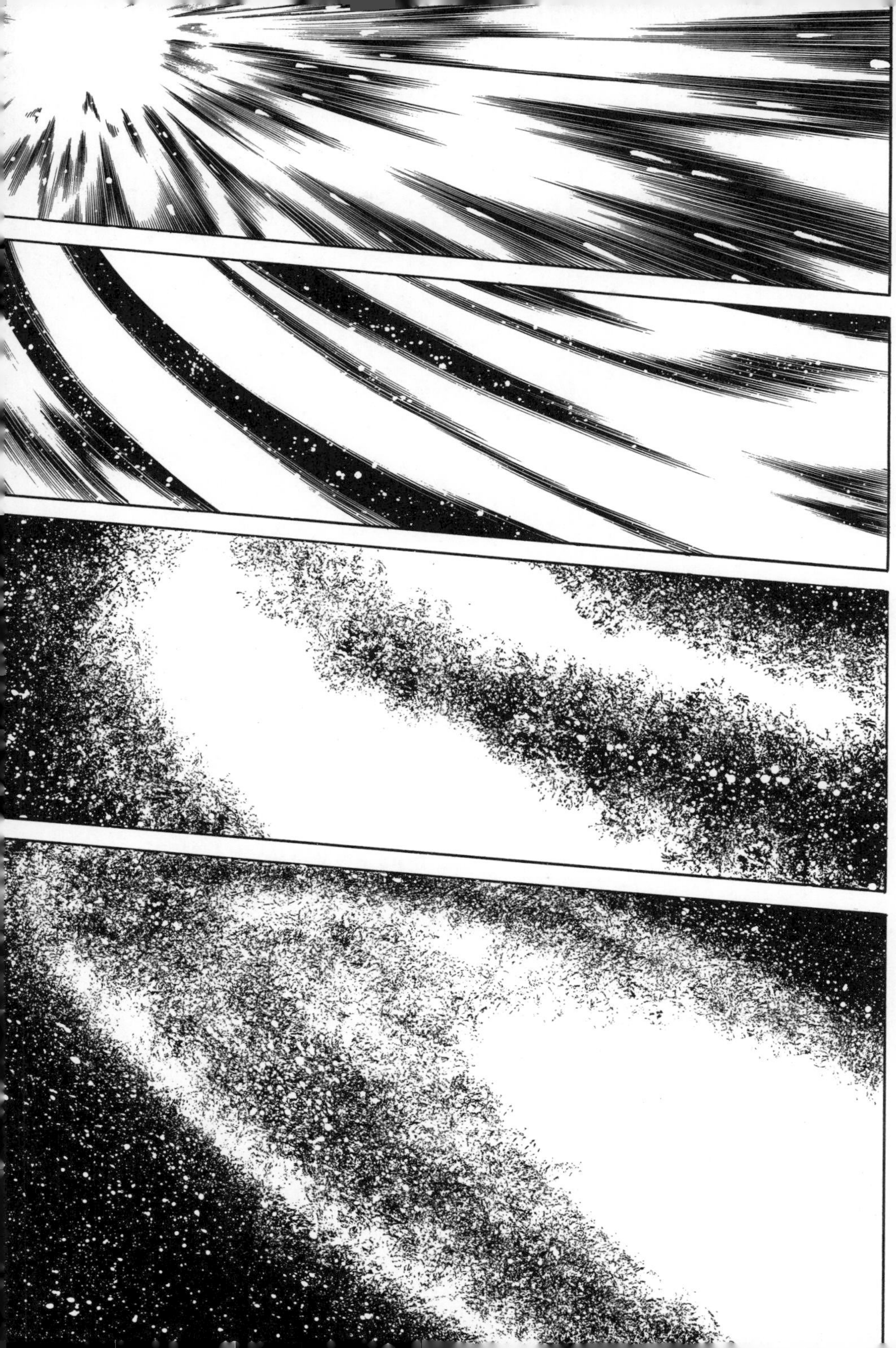

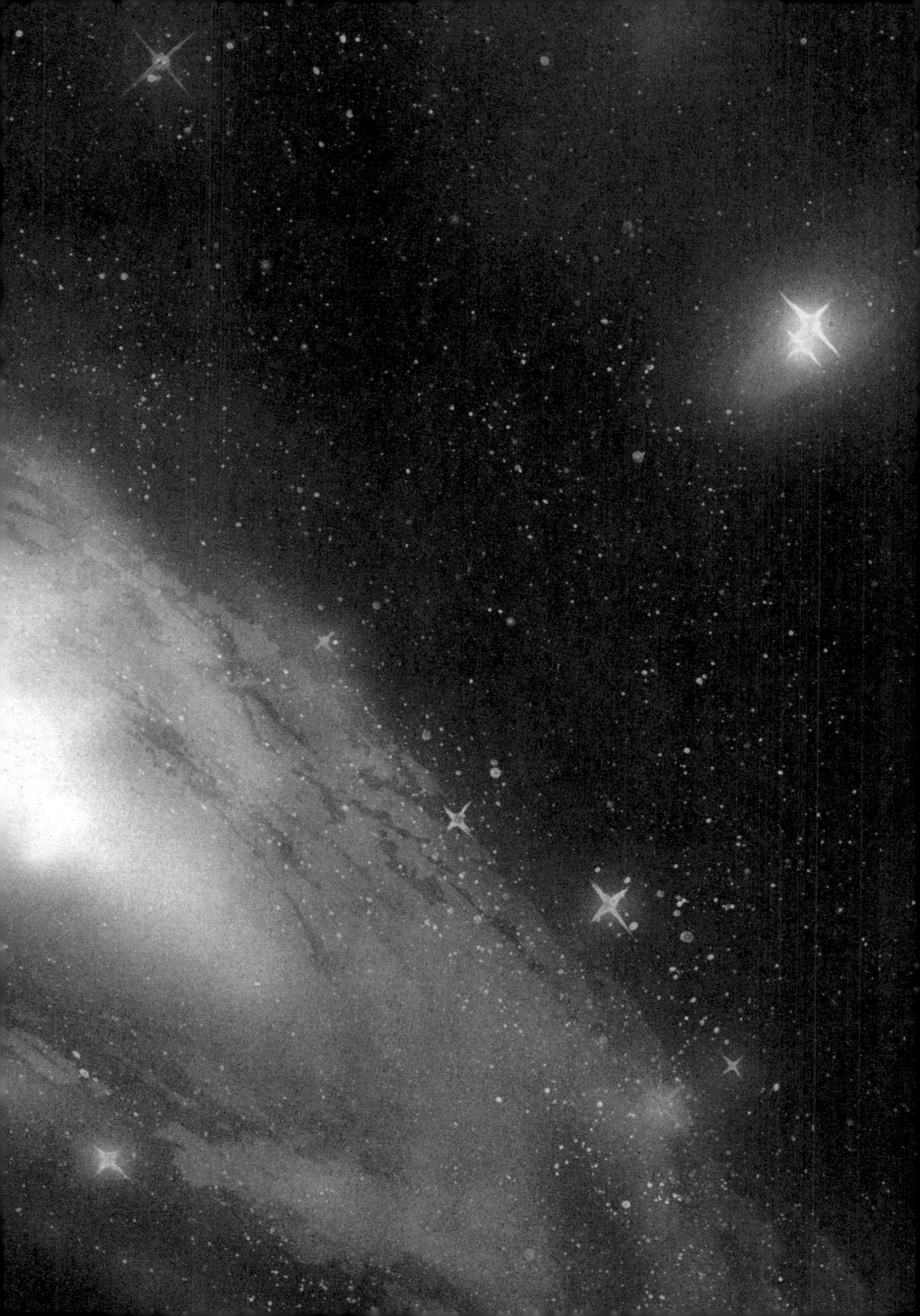

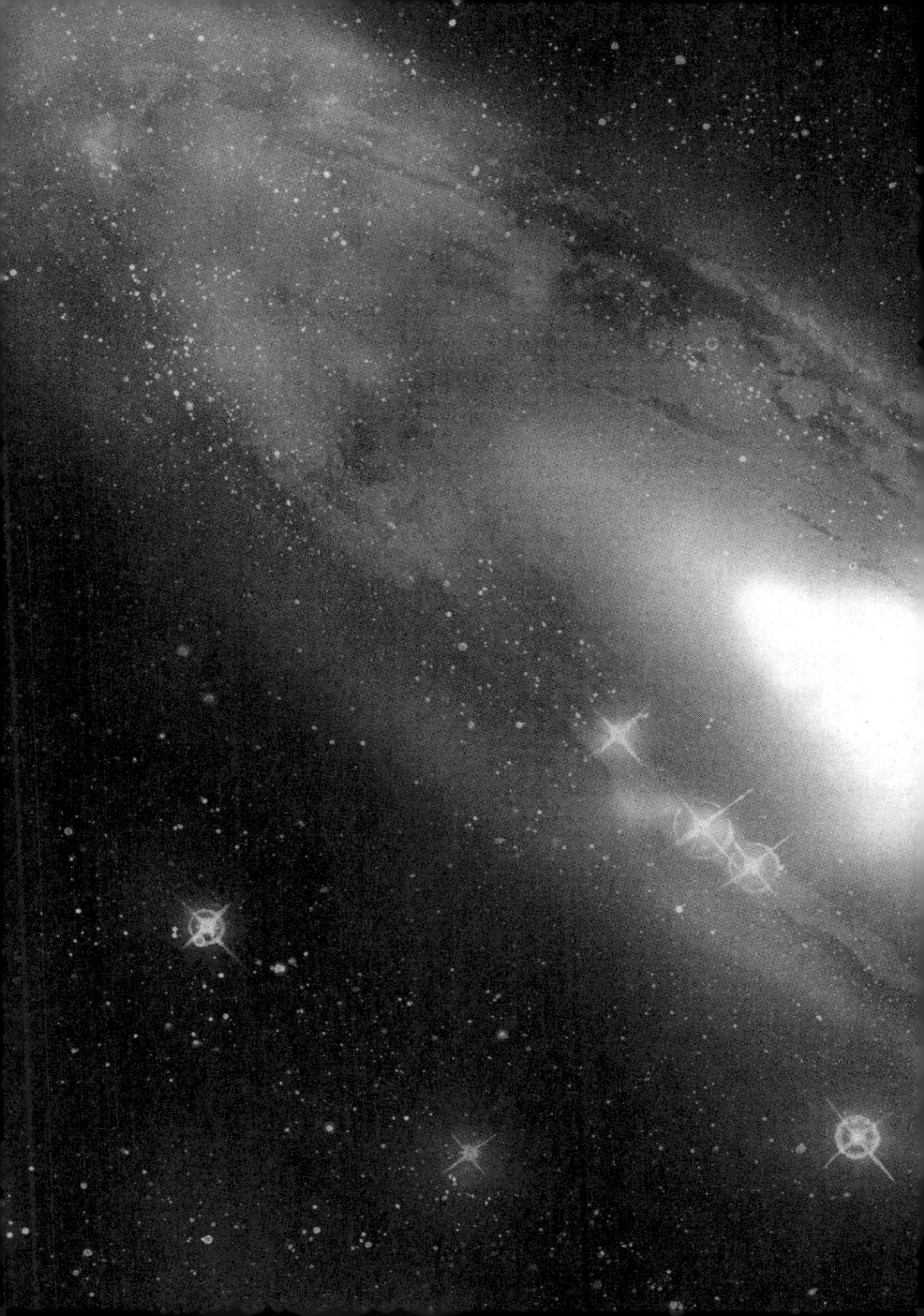

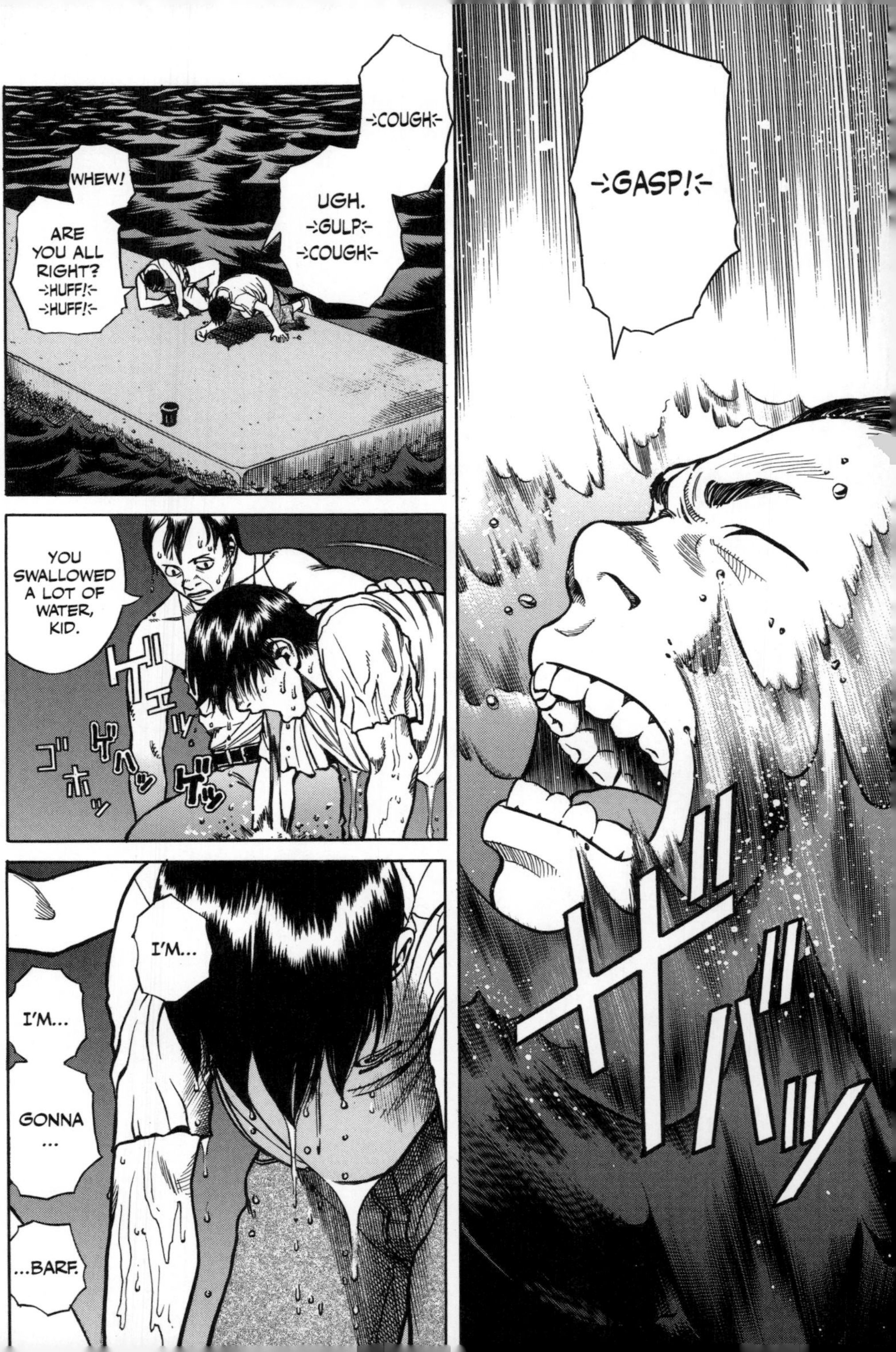
-:GASP!:-
ザバッ
-:COUGH:-
UGH. -:GULP:- -:COUGH:-
WHEW!
ARE YOU ALL RIGHT? -:HUFF!:- -:HUFF!:-
YOU SWALLOWED A LOT OF WATER, KID.
ゲェッ
ゲハッ
ゲッ
ゴホッ
I'M...
I'M...
GONNA ...
...BARF.

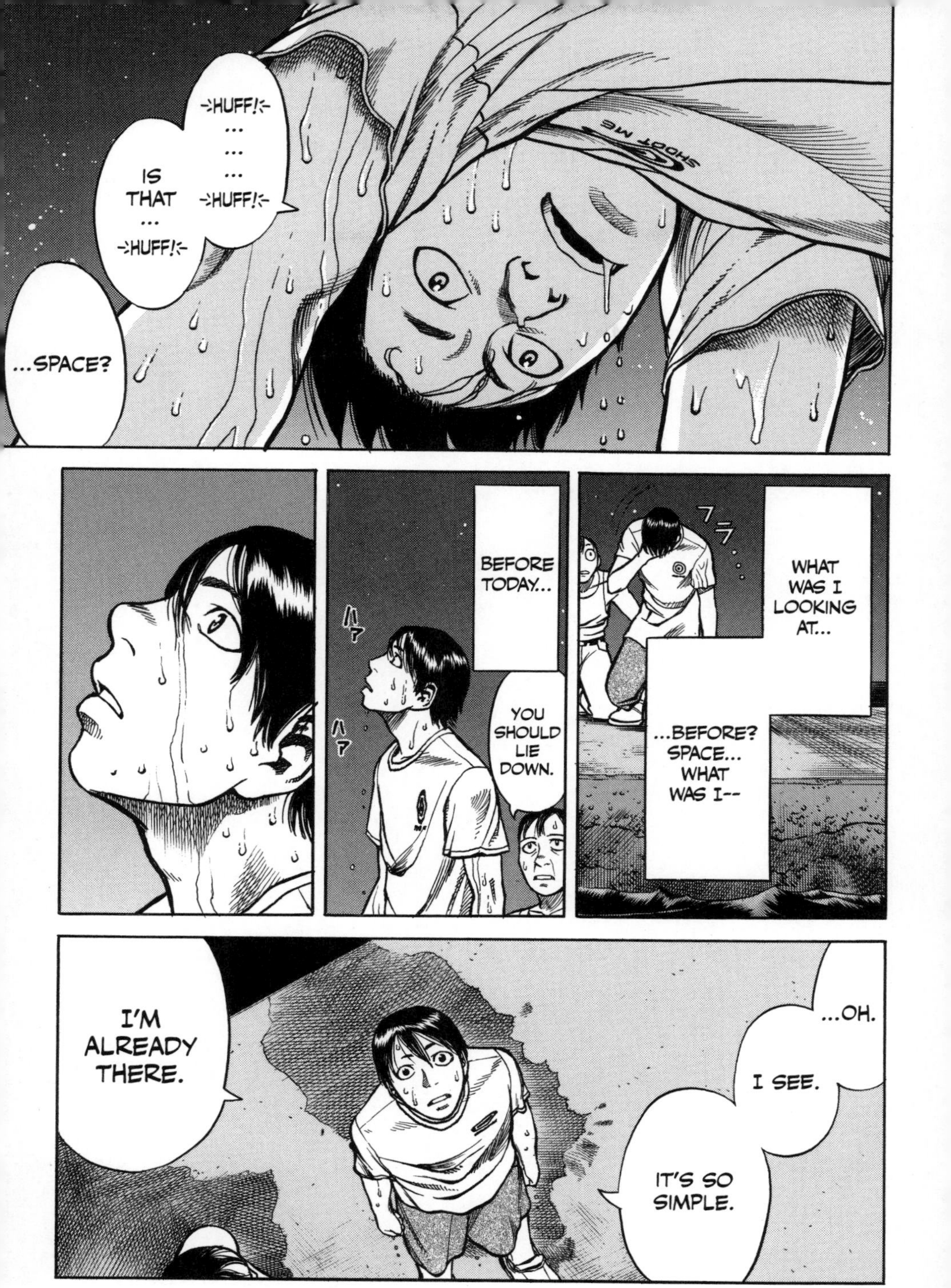
SHOOT ME
-HUFF!- ... ... -HUFF!-
IS THAT ... -HUFF!-
...SPACE?
WHAT WAS I LOOKING AT...
...BEFORE? SPACE... WHAT WAS I--
フラ
BEFORE TODAY...
ハァ
ハァ
YOU SHOULD LIE DOWN.
...OH.
I SEE.
IT'S SO SIMPLE.
I'M ALREADY THERE.

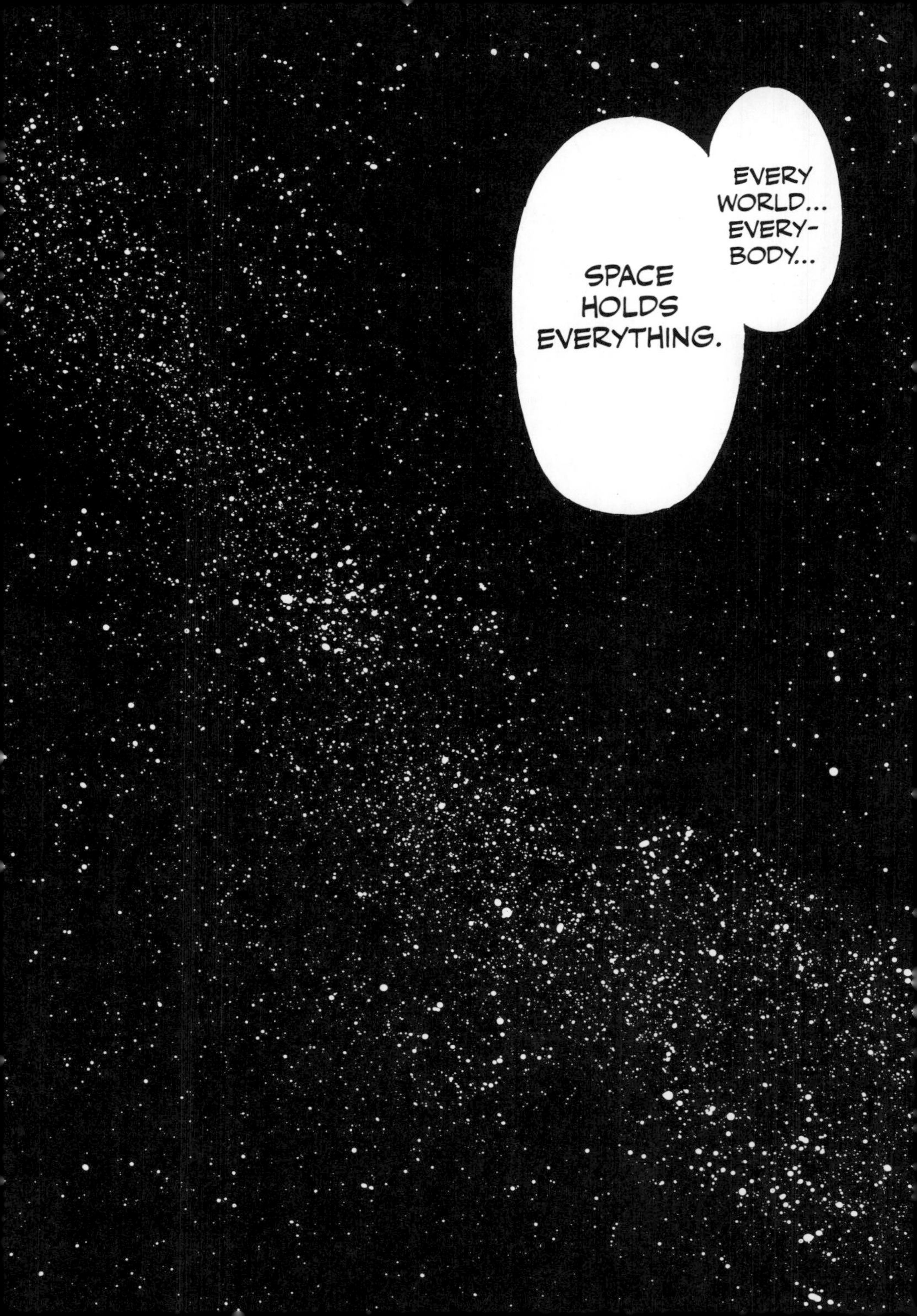
EVERY WORLD... EVERY-BODY...
SPACE HOLDS EVERYTHING.

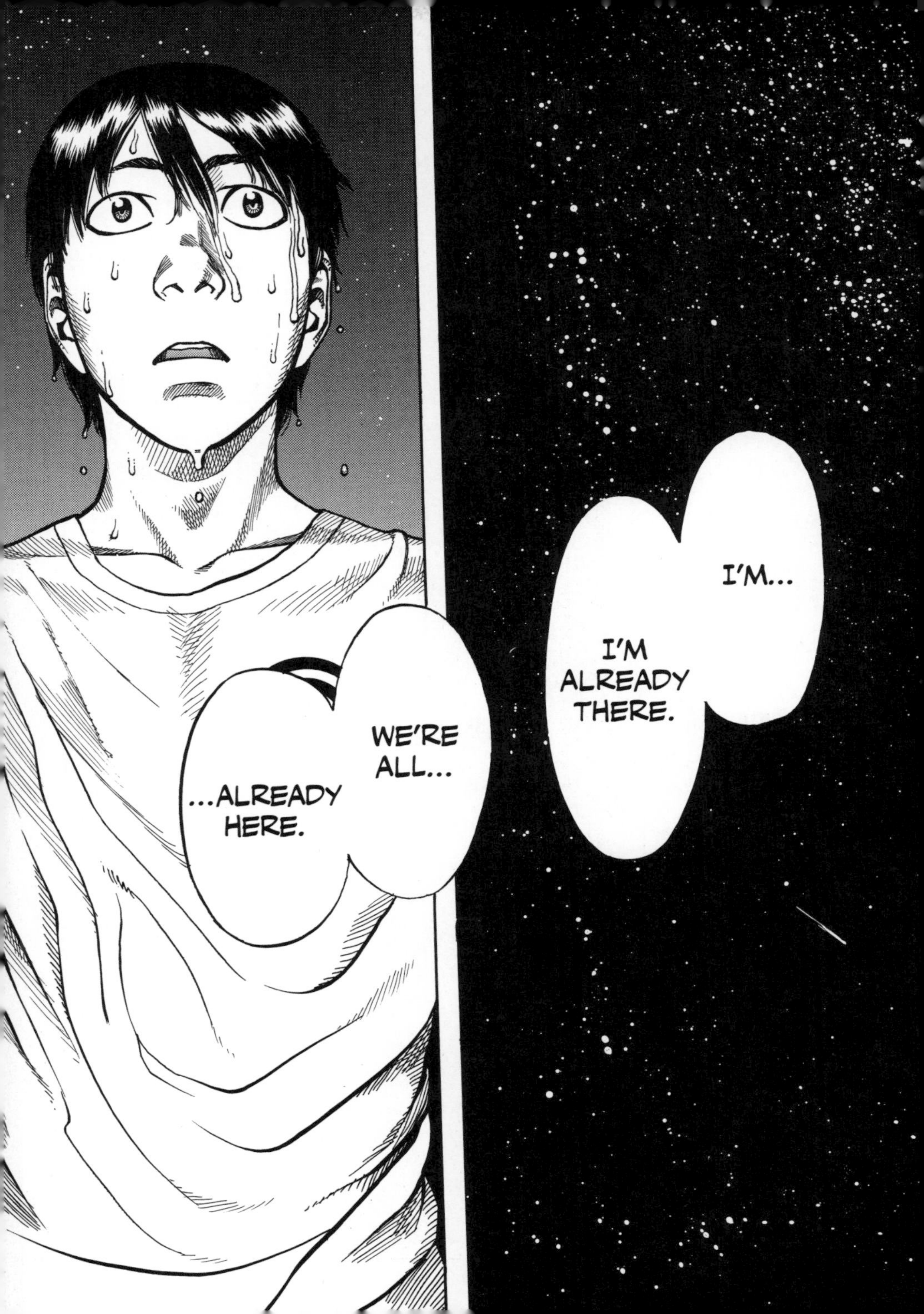
I'M...
I'M ALREADY THERE.
WE'RE ALL...
...ALREADY HERE.

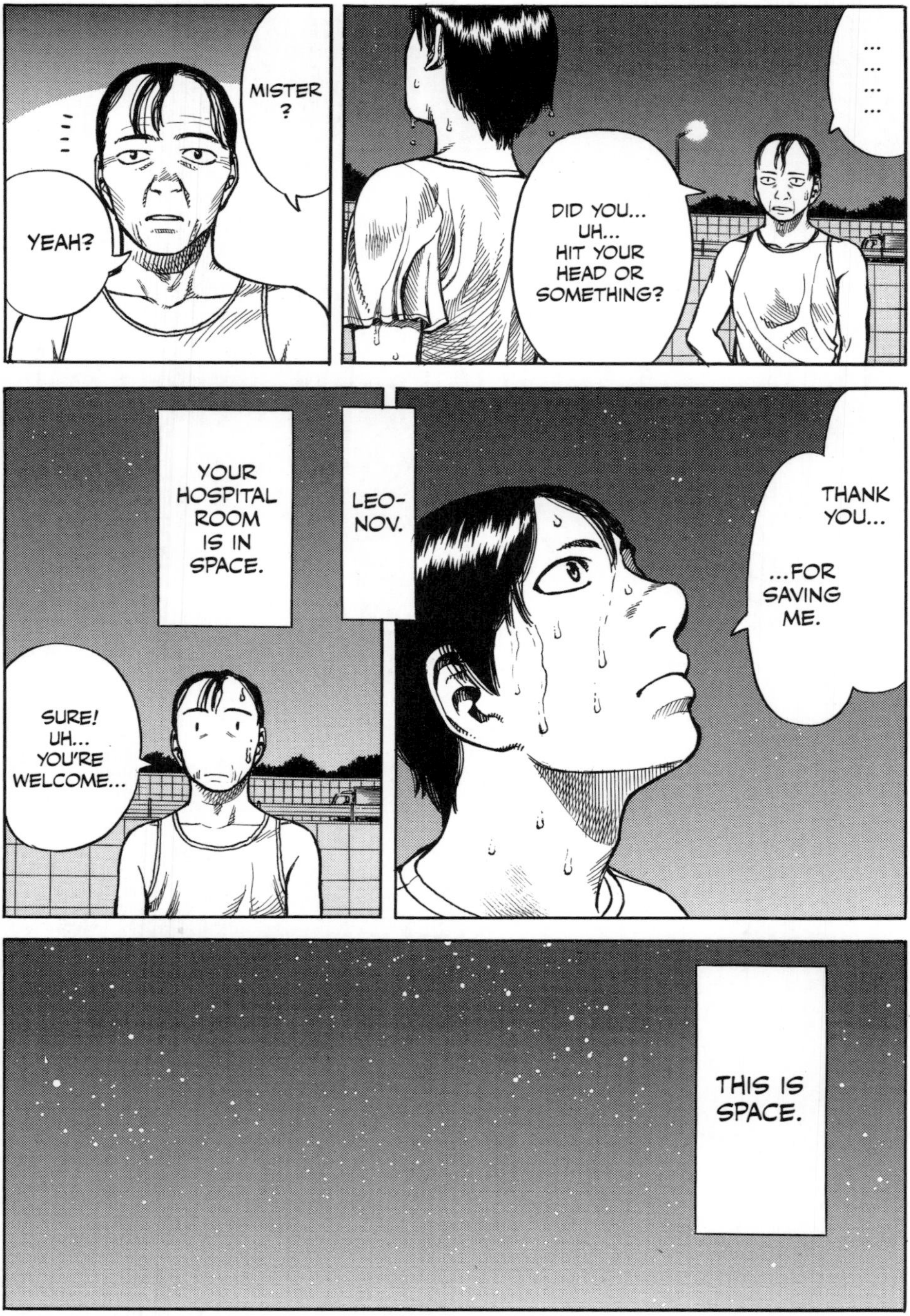
... ...
DID YOU... UH... HIT YOUR HEAD OR SOMETHING?
MISTER ?
...
YEAH?
THANK YOU...
...FOR SAVING ME.
LEO-NOV.
YOUR HOSPITAL ROOM IS IN SPACE.
SURE! UH... YOU'RE WELCOME...
THIS IS SPACE.

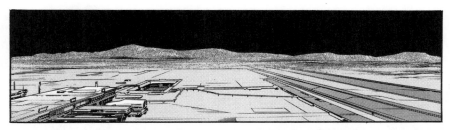

OUR VACATION TIME JUST GOT SHOT IN THE ASS.

Orientale Basin City.
Lunar surface, 2075.

YESTERDAY'S METEOR STREAMS HIT AN ORBIT OVER SIX KILOMETERS. DENSITY IS WAY OVER SAFETY LEVEL.

ALL DEBRIS-PICKUP SHIPS ARE WORKING OVERTIME.

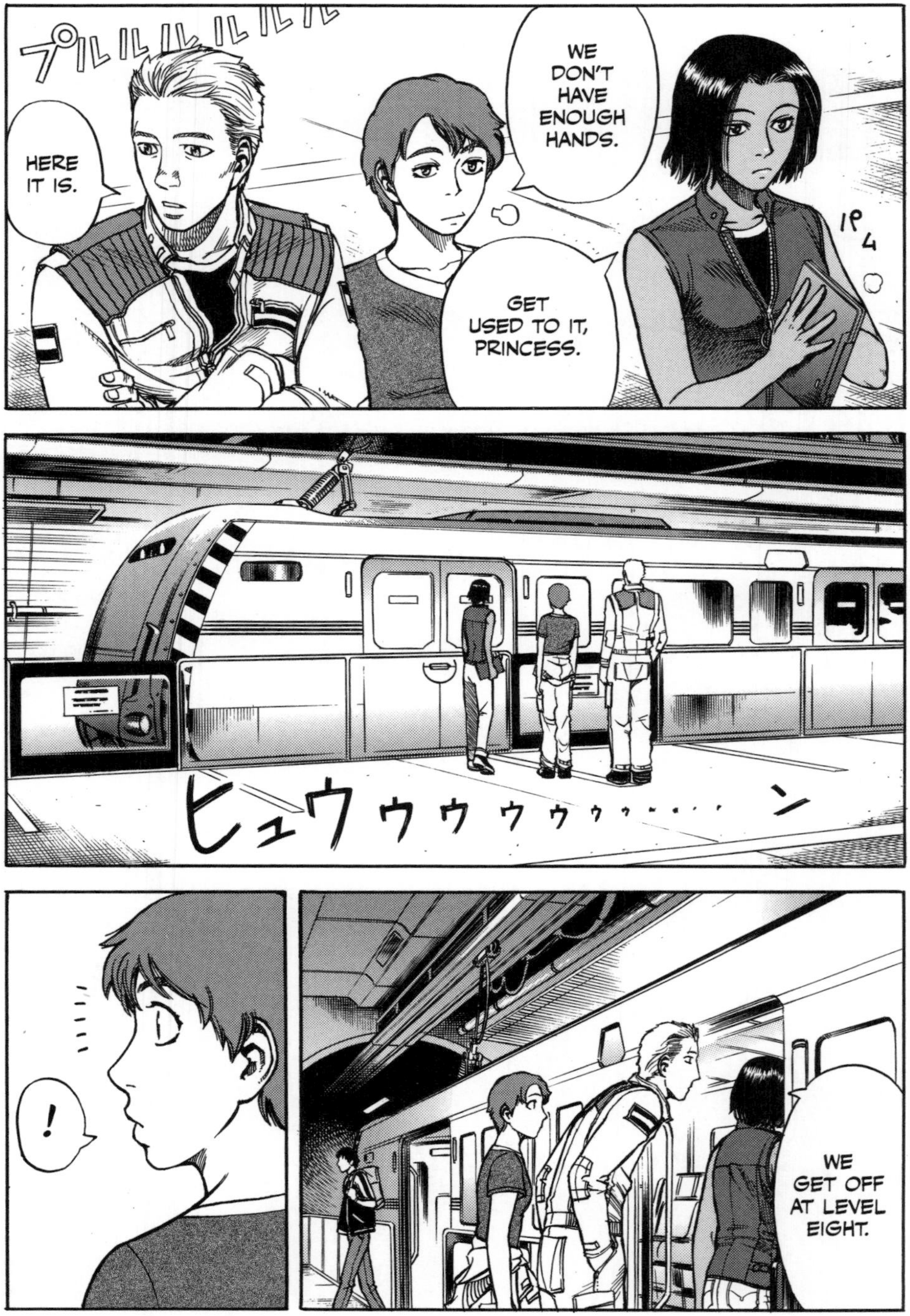
WE DON'T HAVE ENOUGH HANDS.
GET USED TO IT, PRINCESS.
HERE IT IS.
プルルルルル
WE GET OFF AT LEVEL EIGHT.
!

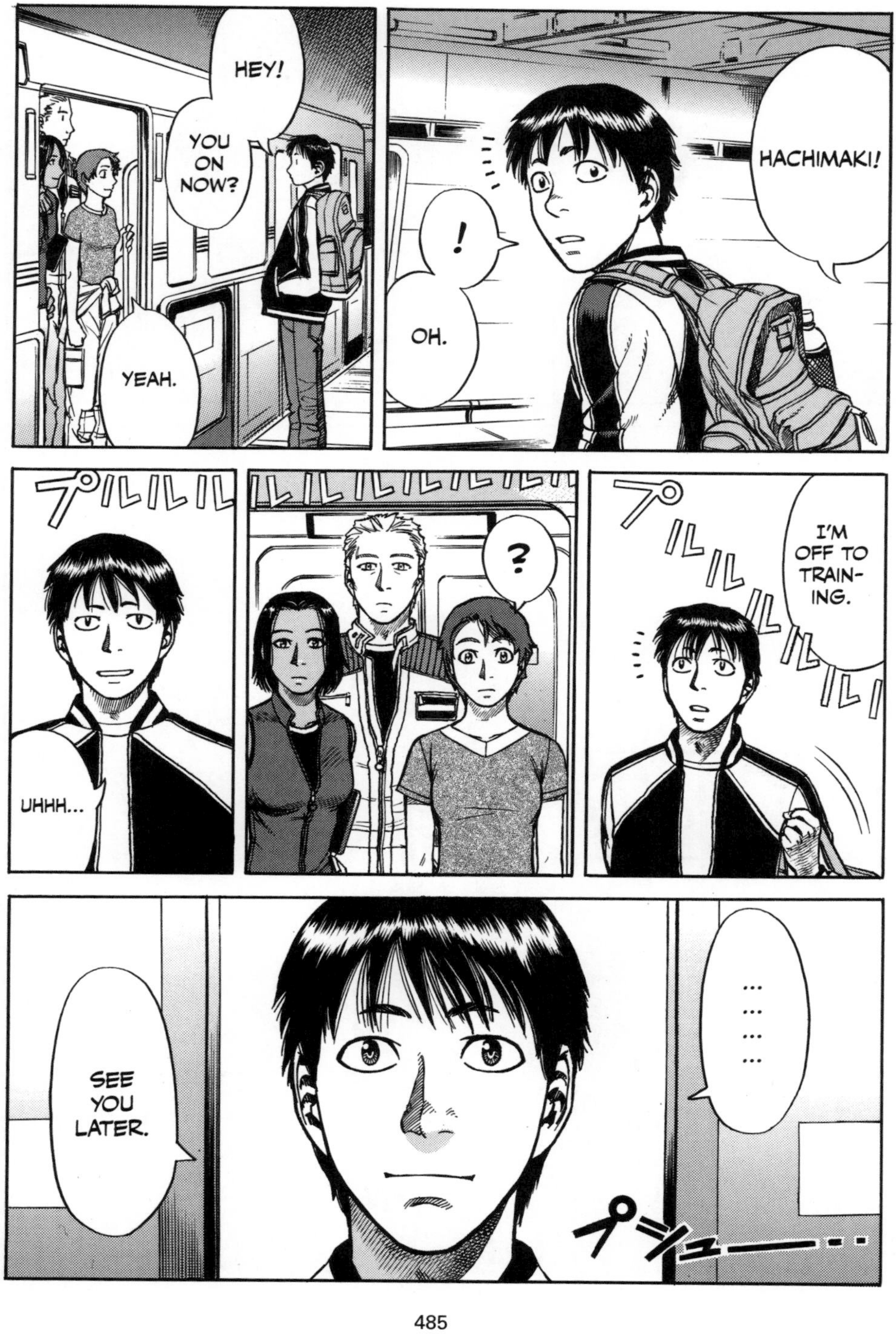
HACHIMAKI!
!
OH.
HEY!
YOU ON NOW?
YEAH.
I'M OFF TO TRAIN-ING.
プルルルルルル
?
プルルル
UHHH...
...
...
...
...
SEE YOU LATER.
プシュー…

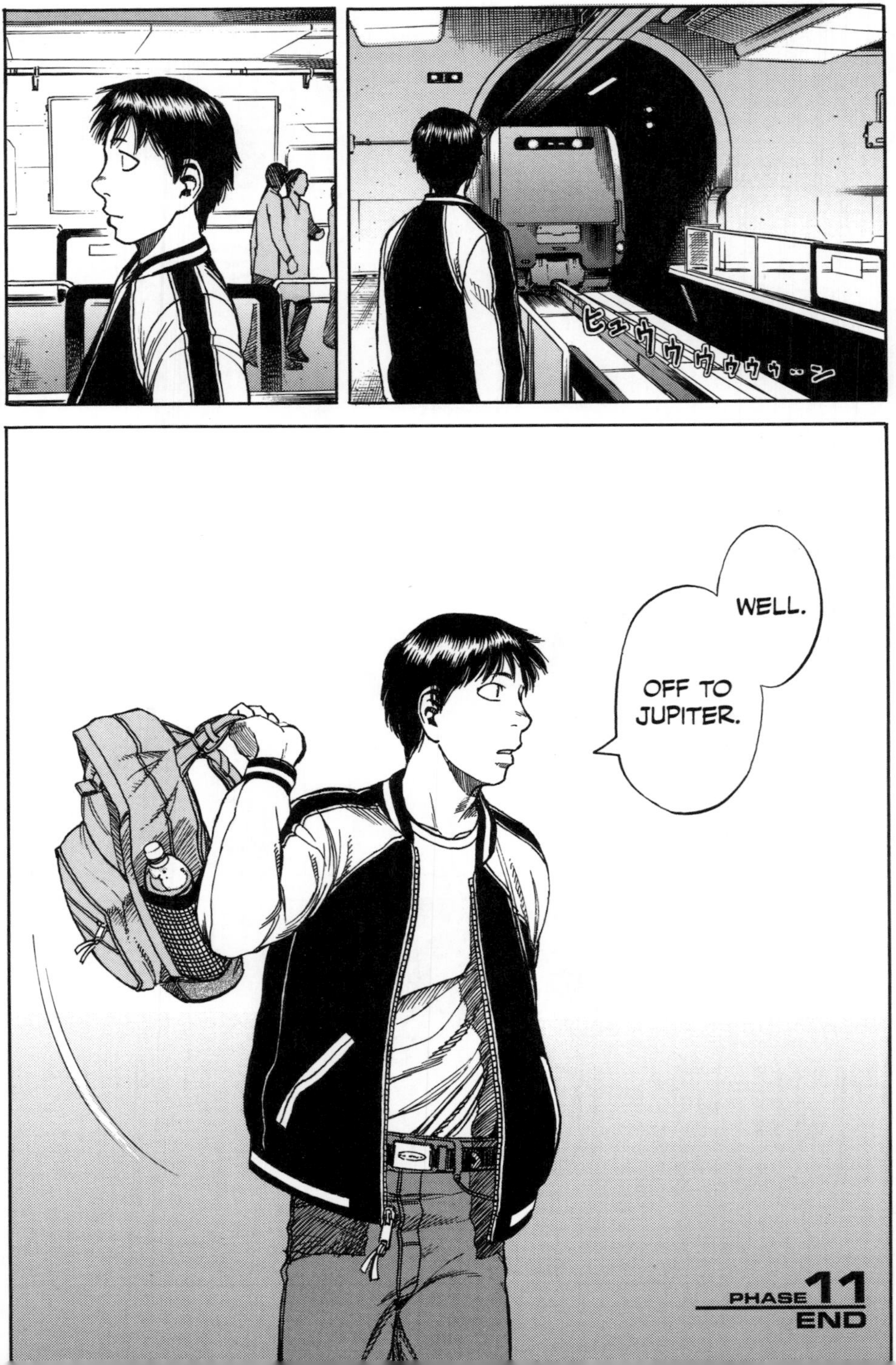
ヒュウウウウウゥ‥ン
WELL.
OFF TO JUPITER.

PHASE 11 END

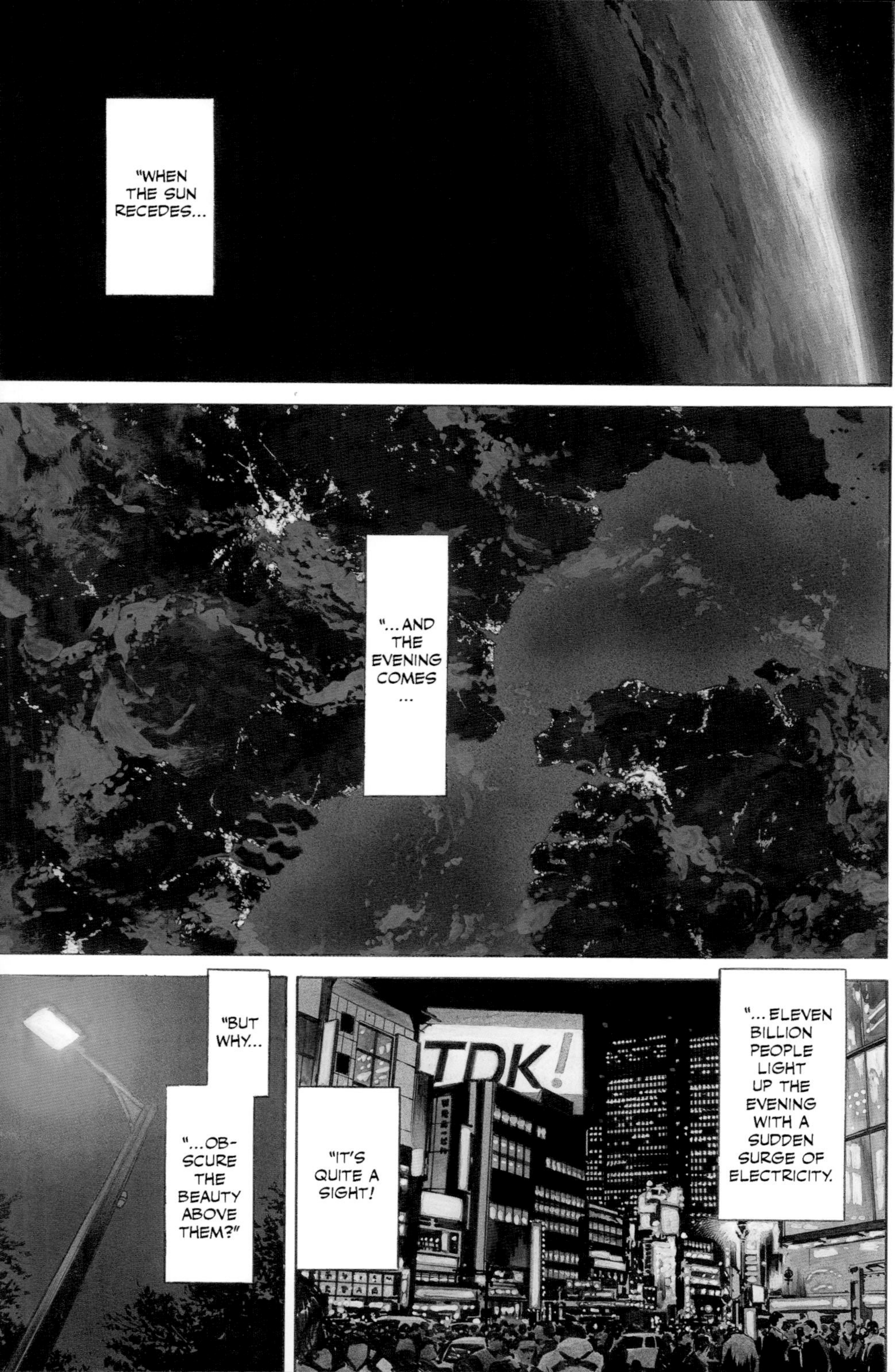
"WHEN THE SUN RECEDES...
"...AND THE EVENING COMES ...
"...ELEVEN BILLION PEOPLE LIGHT UP THE EVENING WITH A SUDDEN SURGE OF ELECTRICITY.
TDK!
"IT'S QUITE A SIGHT!
"BUT WHY...
"...OB-SCURE THE BEAUTY ABOVE THEM?"

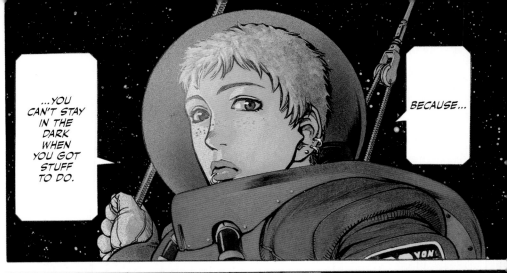

...YOU CAN'T STAY IN THE DARK WHEN YOU GOT STUFF TO DO.

BECAUSE...

...
...
...
...
...

WHY ARE YOU GIVING ME THAT LOOK?

AM I ANNOYING YOU, HACHIMAKI?

Jupiter mission training simulation. Earth's orbit. 2077.

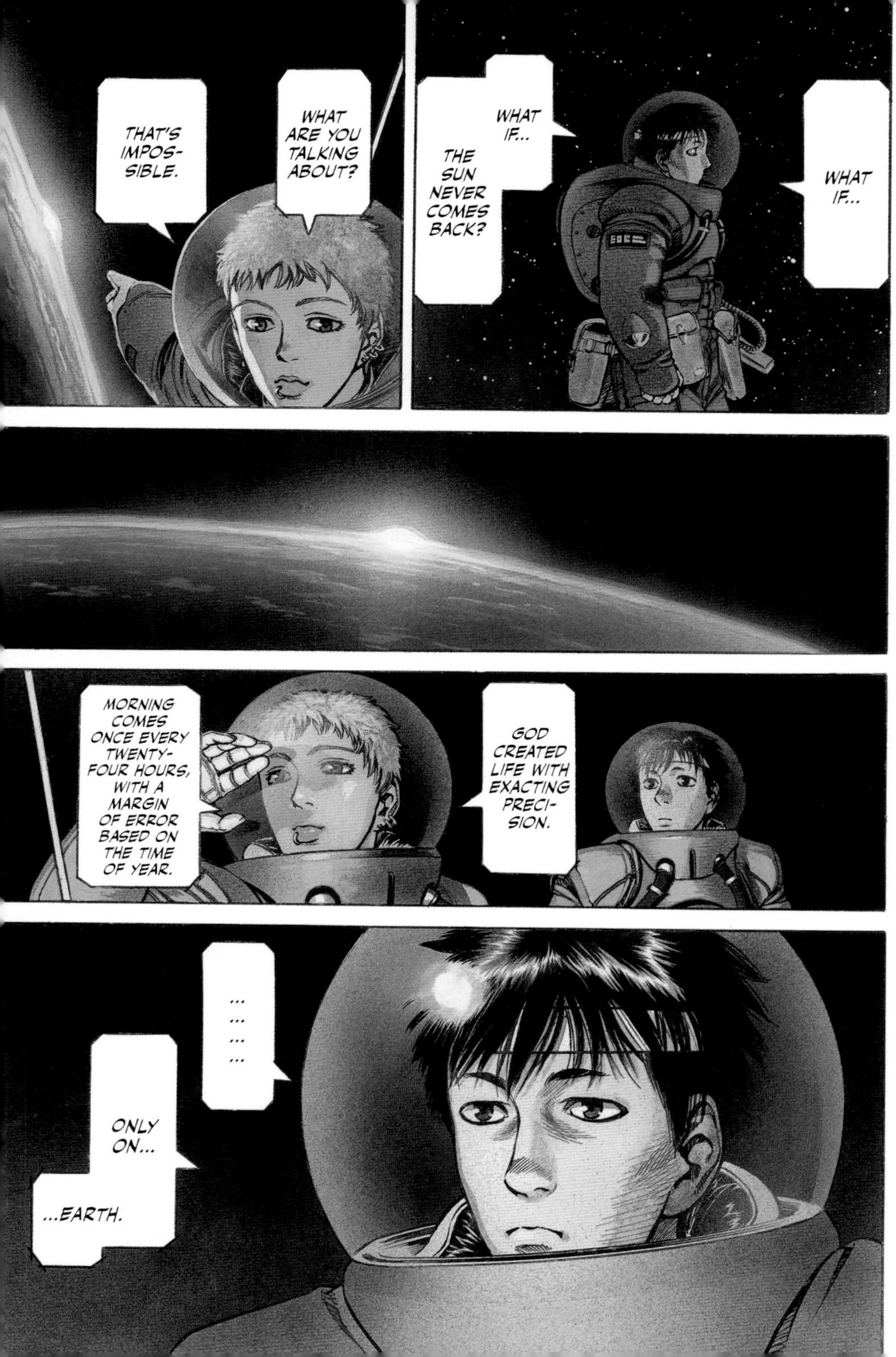
WHAT IF...
WHAT IF...
THE SUN NEVER COMES BACK?
WHAT ARE YOU TALKING ABOUT?
THAT'S IMPOSSIBLE.
GOD CREATED LIFE WITH EXACTING PRECISION.
MORNING COMES ONCE EVERY TWENTY-FOUR HOURS, WITH A MARGIN OF ERROR BASED ON THE TIME OF YEAR.
....
ONLY ON...
...EARTH.

PHASE 12
A CAT IN THE EVENING

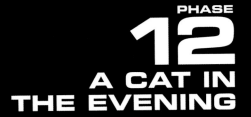

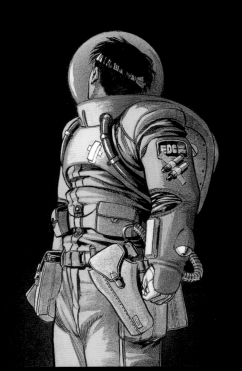

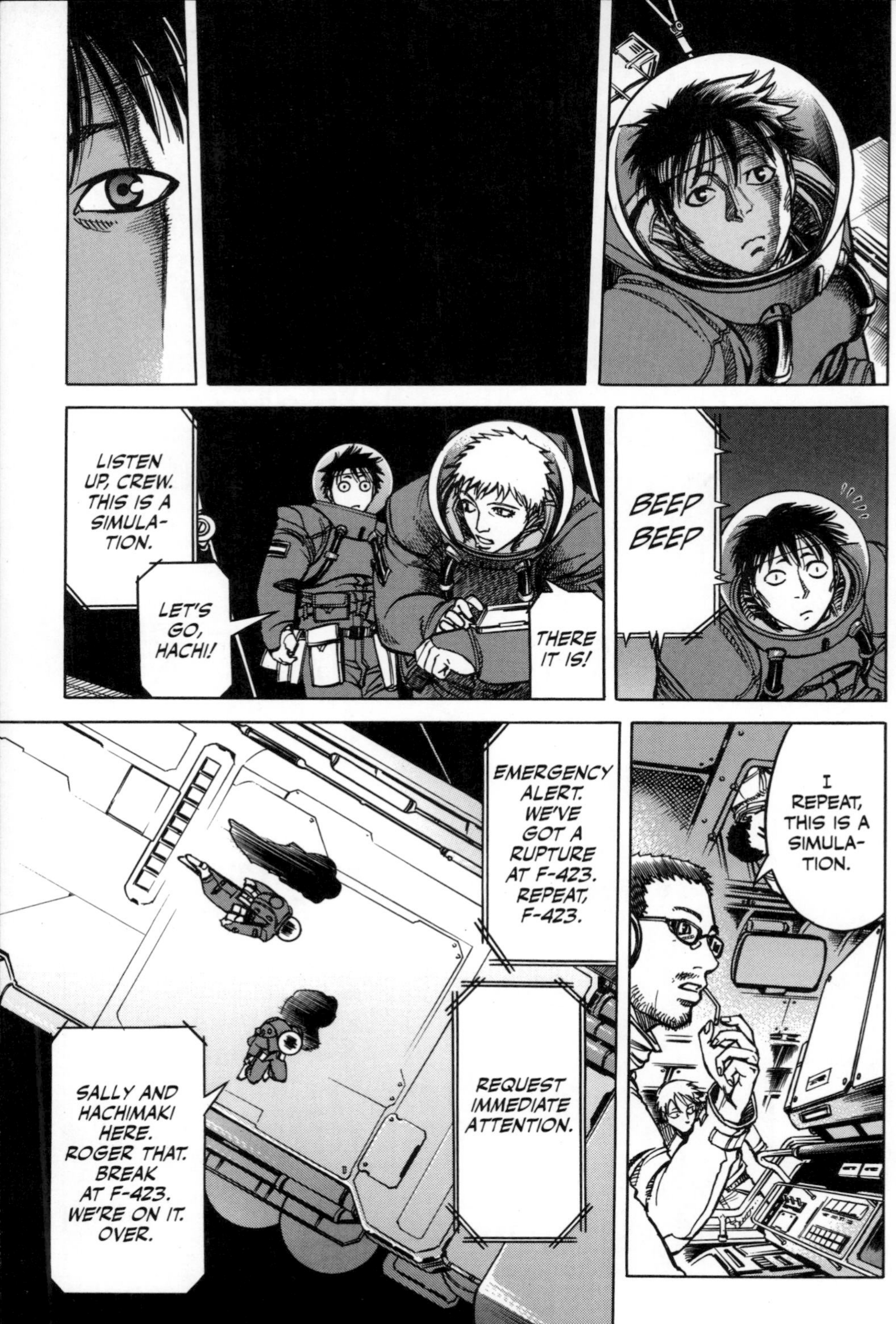
BEEP BEEP
LISTEN UP, CREW. THIS IS A SIMULATION.
THERE IT IS!
LET'S GO, HACHI!
I REPEAT, THIS IS A SIMULATION.
EMERGENCY ALERT. WE'VE GOT A RUPTURE AT F-423. REPEAT, F-423.
REQUEST IMMEDIATE ATTENTION.
SALLY AND HACHIMAKI HERE. ROGER THAT. BREAK AT F-423. WE'RE ON IT. OVER.

!
THERE IT IS!
WE'VE GOT A HOLE-- THAT'S SINGULAR-- ON THE FIFTH LEVEL. STARBOARD. LOOKS LIKE IT WAS CAUSED BY A MICROSCOPIC METEORITE. DIAMETER: APPROXIMATELY FIFTY CENTIMETERS.
WE ALSO GOT A BUSTED COOLER PIPE FROZEN OVER. BAD ENGINE OPS TO BLAME FOR THIS ONE.
AFTER WE GET THE HOLE SEALED, WE'LL DO A BYPASS FROM INSIDE THE SHIP FOR THE PIPE. YA READ ME?
LOUD AND CLEAR.
I WONDER WHY...

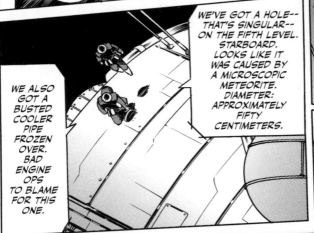

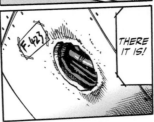

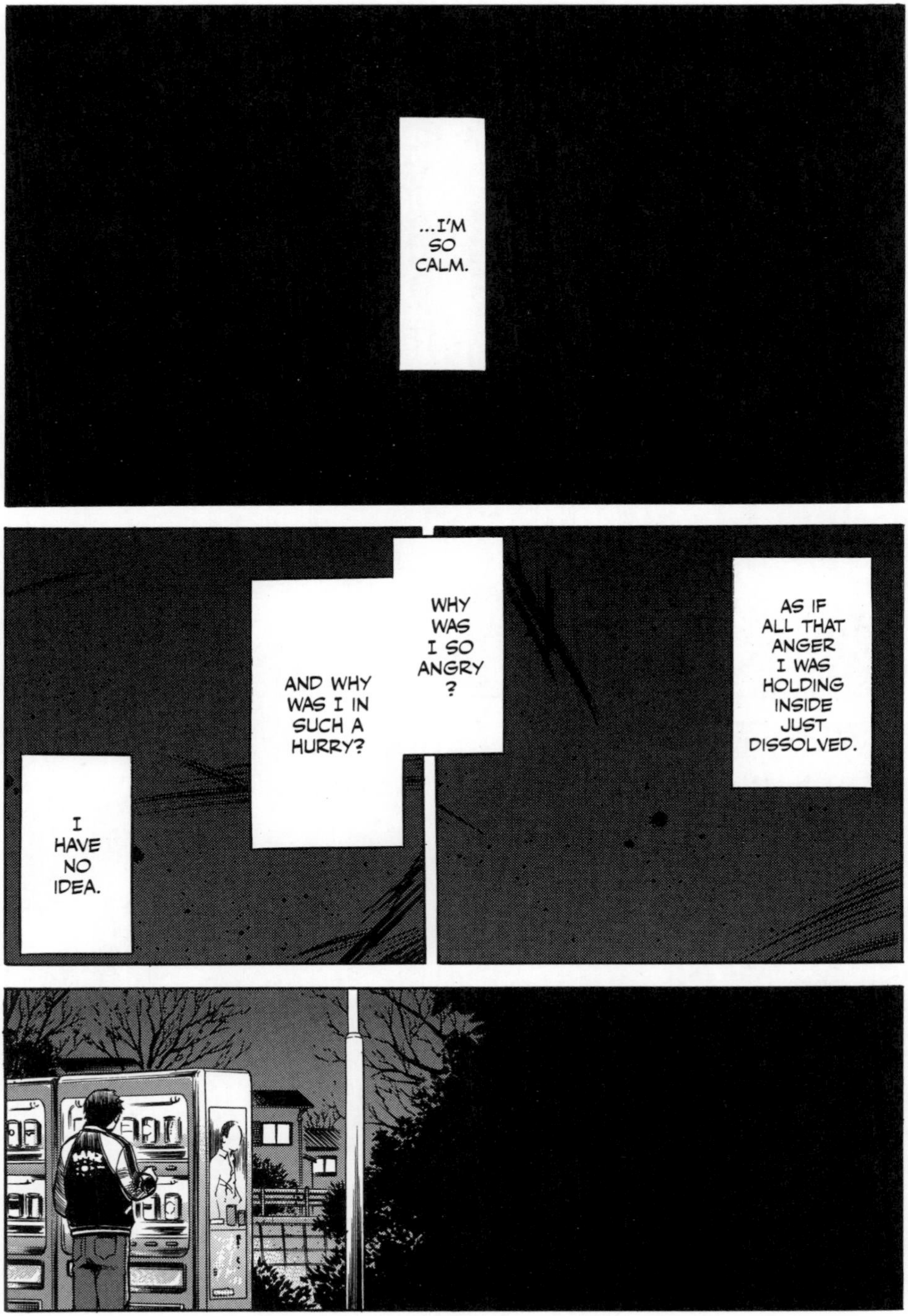
...I'M SO CALM.
AS IF ALL THAT ANGER I WAS HOLDING INSIDE JUST DISSOLVED.
WHY WAS I SO ANGRY ?
AND WHY WAS I IN SUCH A HURRY?
I HAVE NO IDEA.

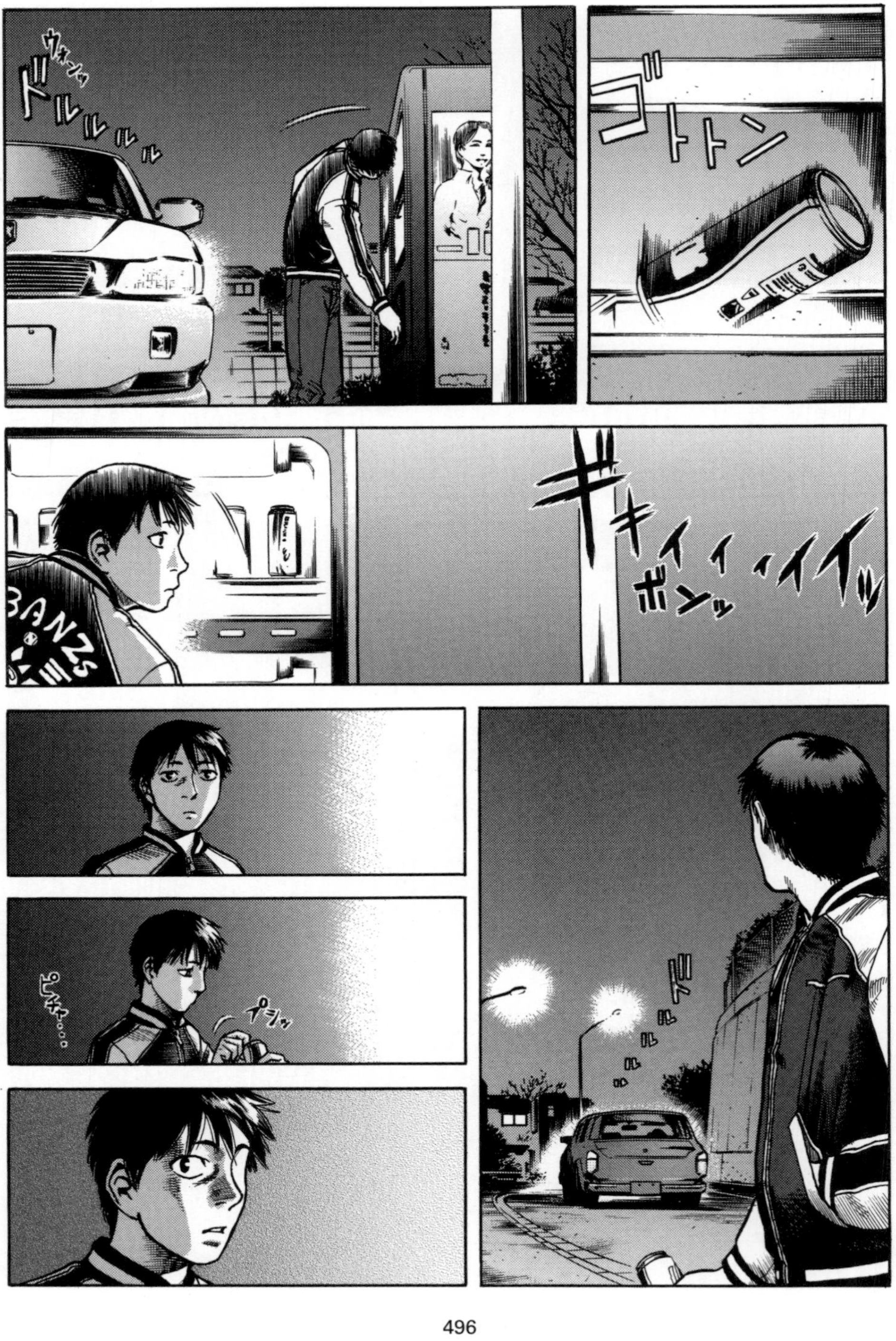
ゴトトン
ドルルルルル
ウォーンッ
ギキイイィイイッ
ボンッ
ドルルルル
ピチャ…
プシッ

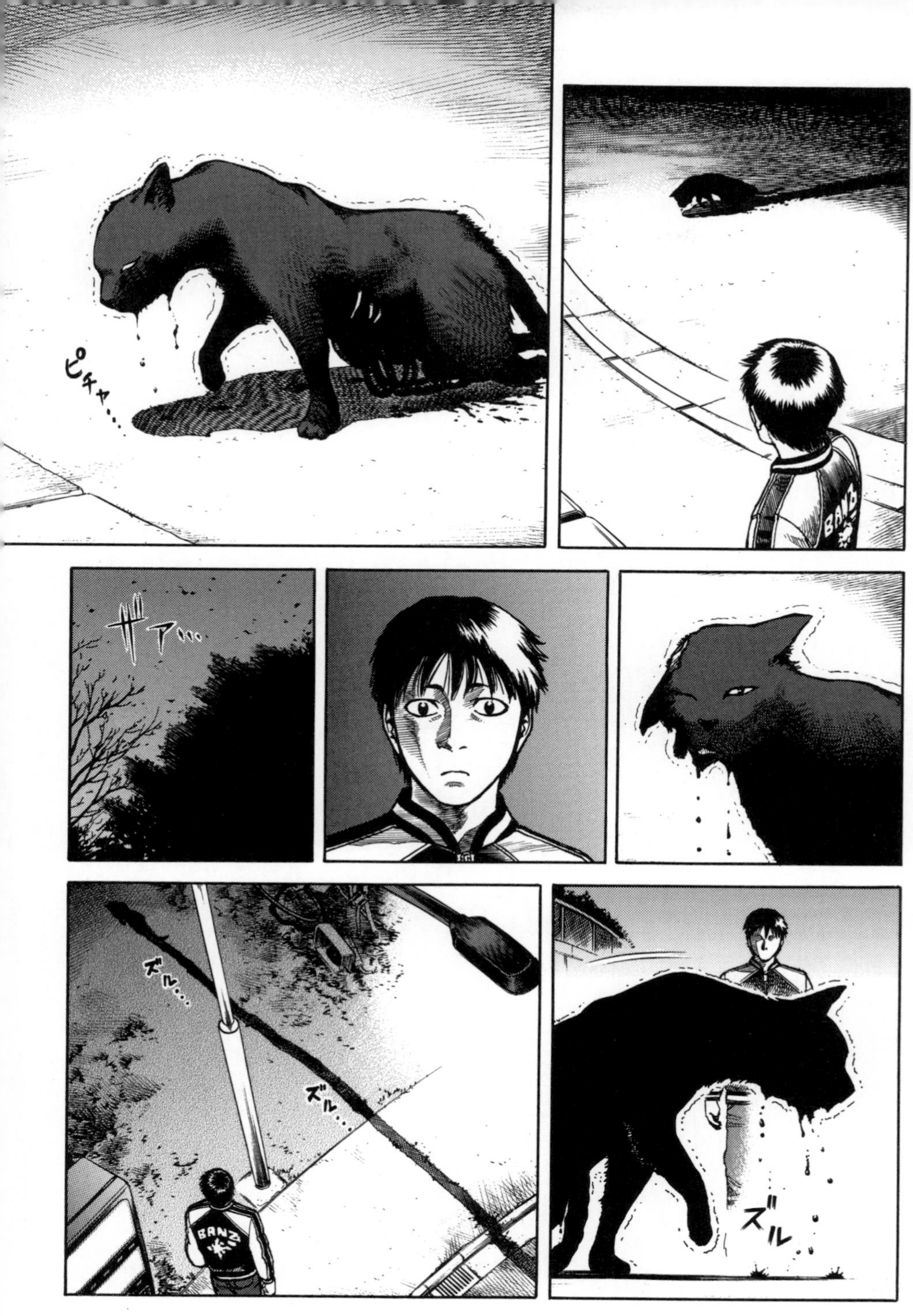
ピチャ…
ザァ…
ズル
ズル…
ズル…

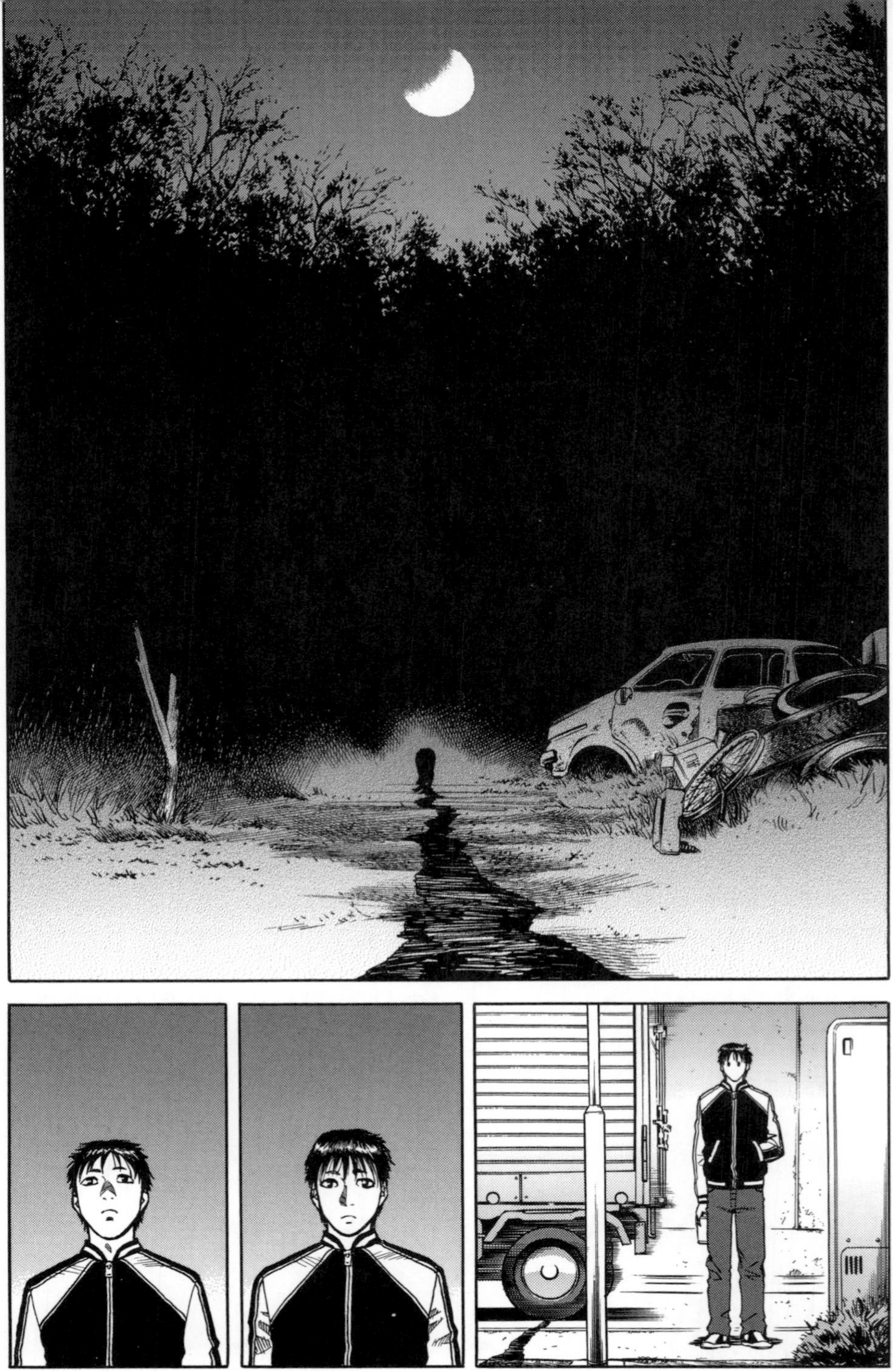

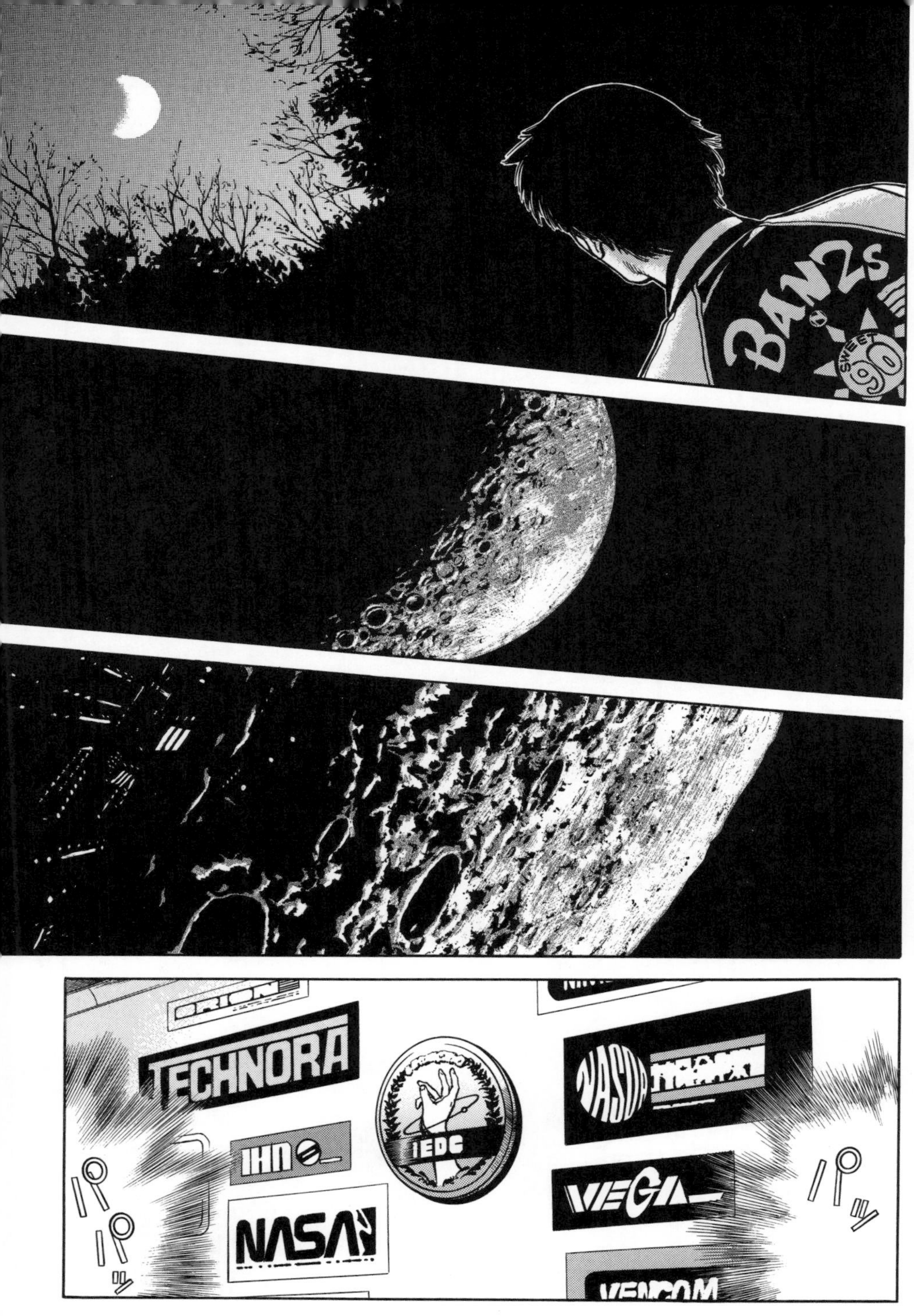
ORION
NASDA
TECHNORA
IEDC
VEGA
NASA

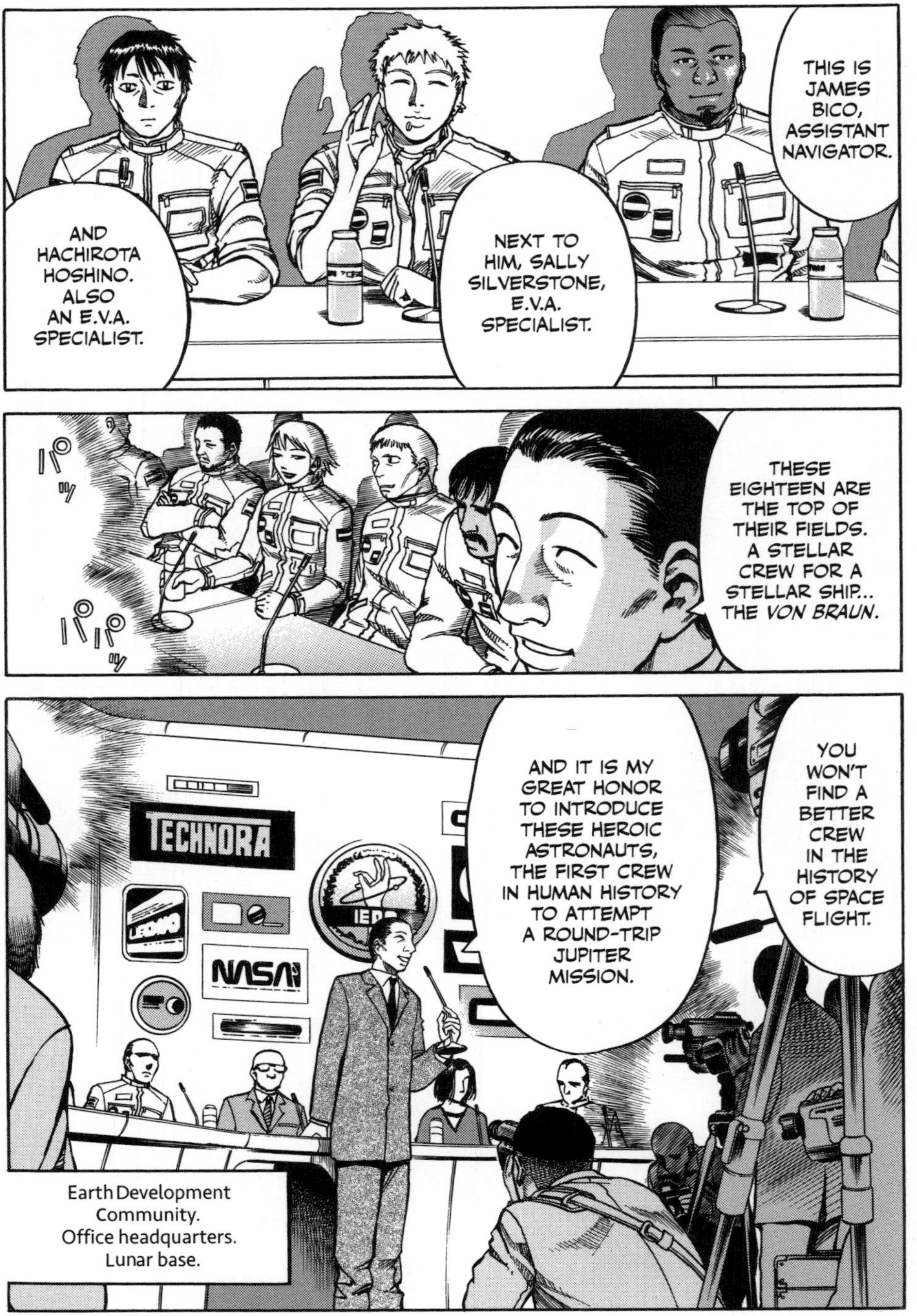
THIS IS JAMES BICO, ASSISTANT NAVIGATOR.
NEXT TO HIM, SALLY SILVERSTONE, E.V.A. SPECIALIST.
AND HACHIROTA HOSHINO. ALSO AN E.V.A. SPECIALIST.
THESE EIGHTEEN ARE THE TOP OF THEIR FIELDS. A STELLAR CREW FOR A STELLAR SHIP... THE *VON BRAUN*.
YOU WON'T FIND A BETTER CREW IN THE HISTORY OF SPACE FLIGHT.
AND IT IS MY GREAT HONOR TO INTRODUCE THESE HEROIC ASTRONAUTS, THE FIRST CREW IN HUMAN HISTORY TO ATTEMPT A ROUND-TRIP JUPITER MISSION.
TECHNORA
NASA
Earth Development Community. Office headquarters. Lunar base.

THE JUPITER PROJECT IS VITAL TO MAINTAINING LIFE AS WE KNOW IT AND ADVANCING HUMANKIND INTO A NEW AGE OF SCIENCE AND DISCOVERY...
THAT CAT LOOKED RIGHT AT ME.
THAT'S RIGHT.
IT WAS THAT CAT...
NO.
HE WAS JUST A CLUE.
THERE'S SOME-THING MORE OUT THERE THAN--
HACHI.
HACHI-MAKI!

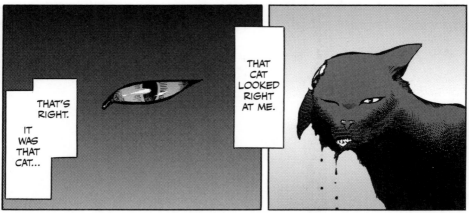

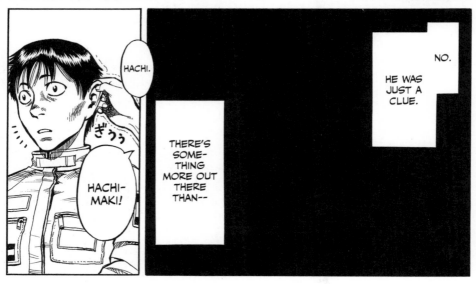

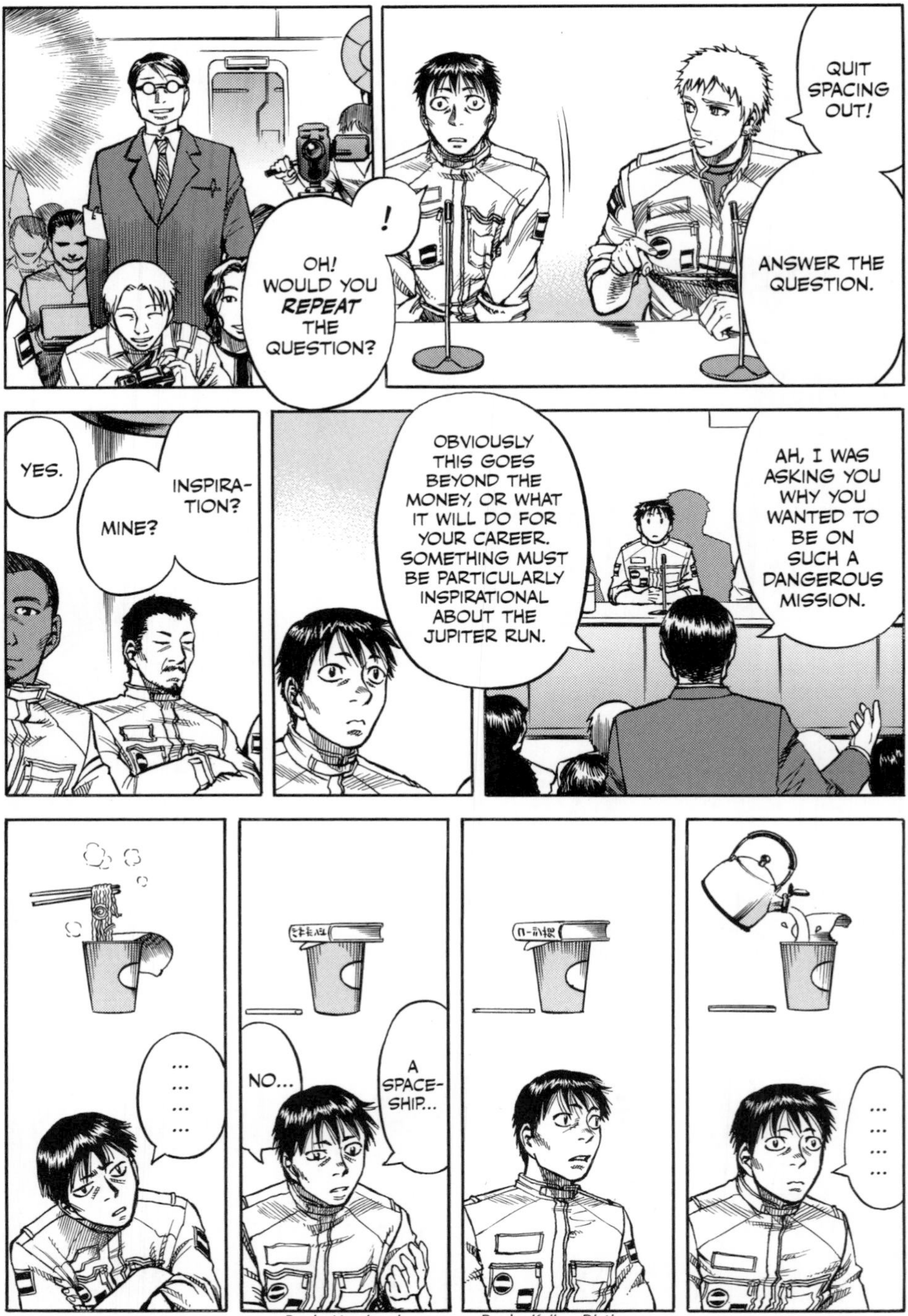
QUIT SPACING OUT!
ANSWER THE QUESTION.
!
OH! WOULD YOU *REPEAT* THE QUESTION?
AH, I WAS ASKING YOU WHY YOU WANTED TO BE ON SUCH A DANGEROUS MISSION.
OBVIOUSLY THIS GOES BEYOND THE MONEY, OR WHAT IT WILL DO FOR YOUR CAREER. SOMETHING MUST BE PARTICULARLY INSPIRATIONAL ABOUT THE JUPITER RUN.
INSPIRA-TION?
MINE?
YES.
... ...
A SPACE-SHIP...
NO...
... ...

Book: *Kojien Dictionary*.

Book: *Vagabond*.

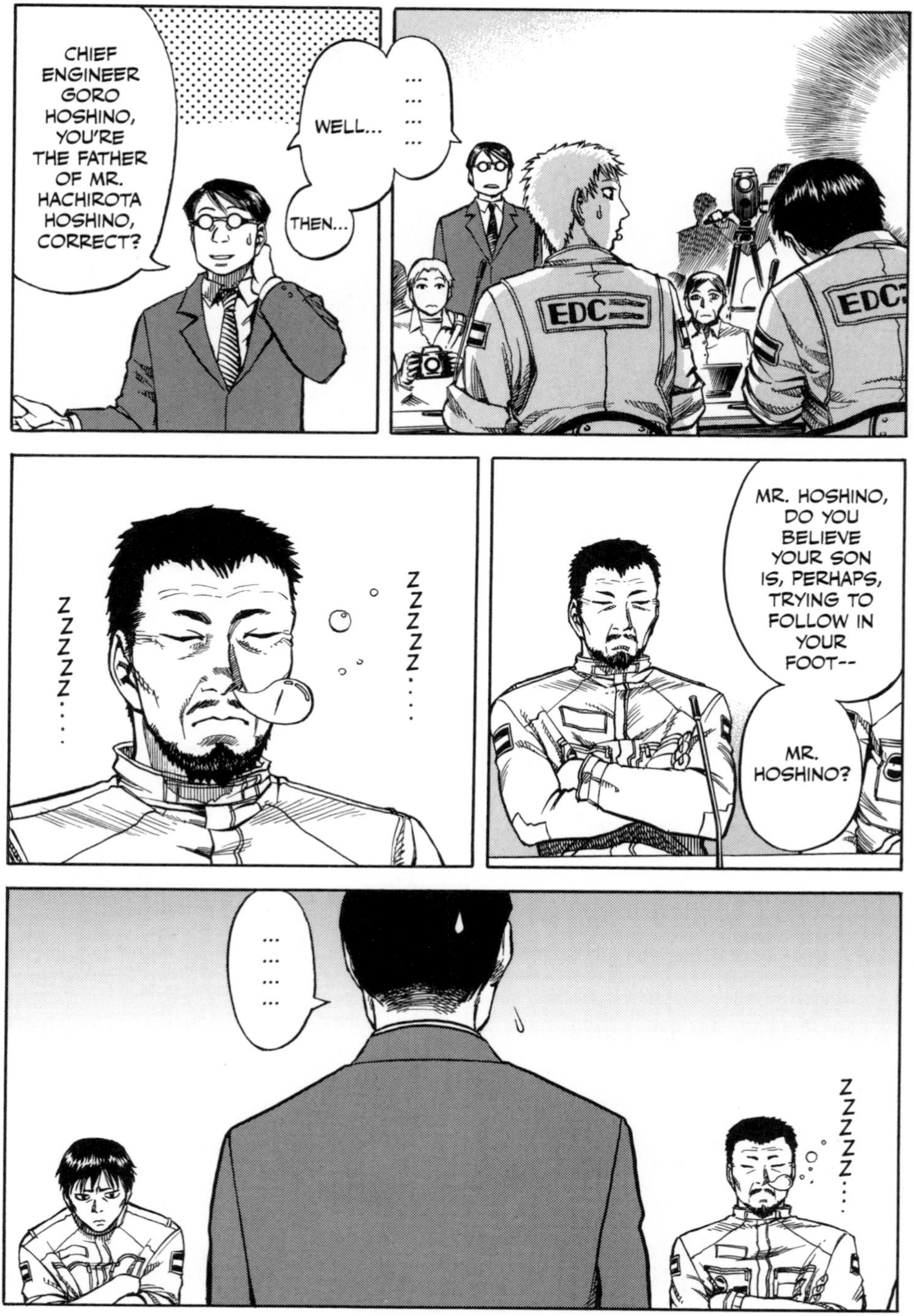
....
WELL...
THEN...
CHIEF ENGINEER GORO HOSHINO, YOU'RE THE FATHER OF MR. HACHIROTA HOSHINO, CORRECT?
EDC
EDC
MR. HOSHINO, DO YOU BELIEVE YOUR SON IS, PERHAPS, TRYING TO FOLLOW IN YOUR FOOT--
MR. HOSHINO?
ZZZZZ....
ZZZZZ....
....
ZZZZZ....

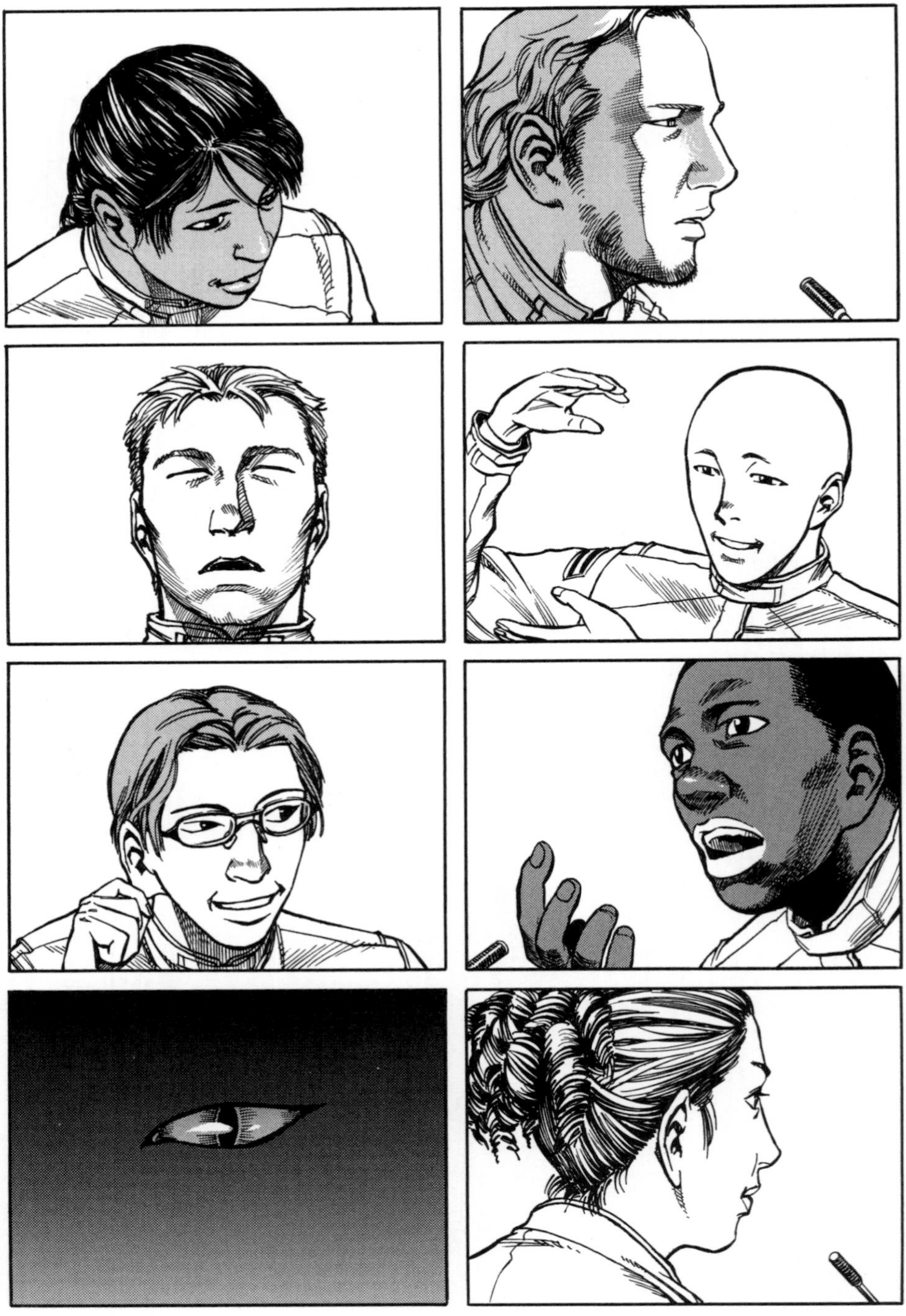

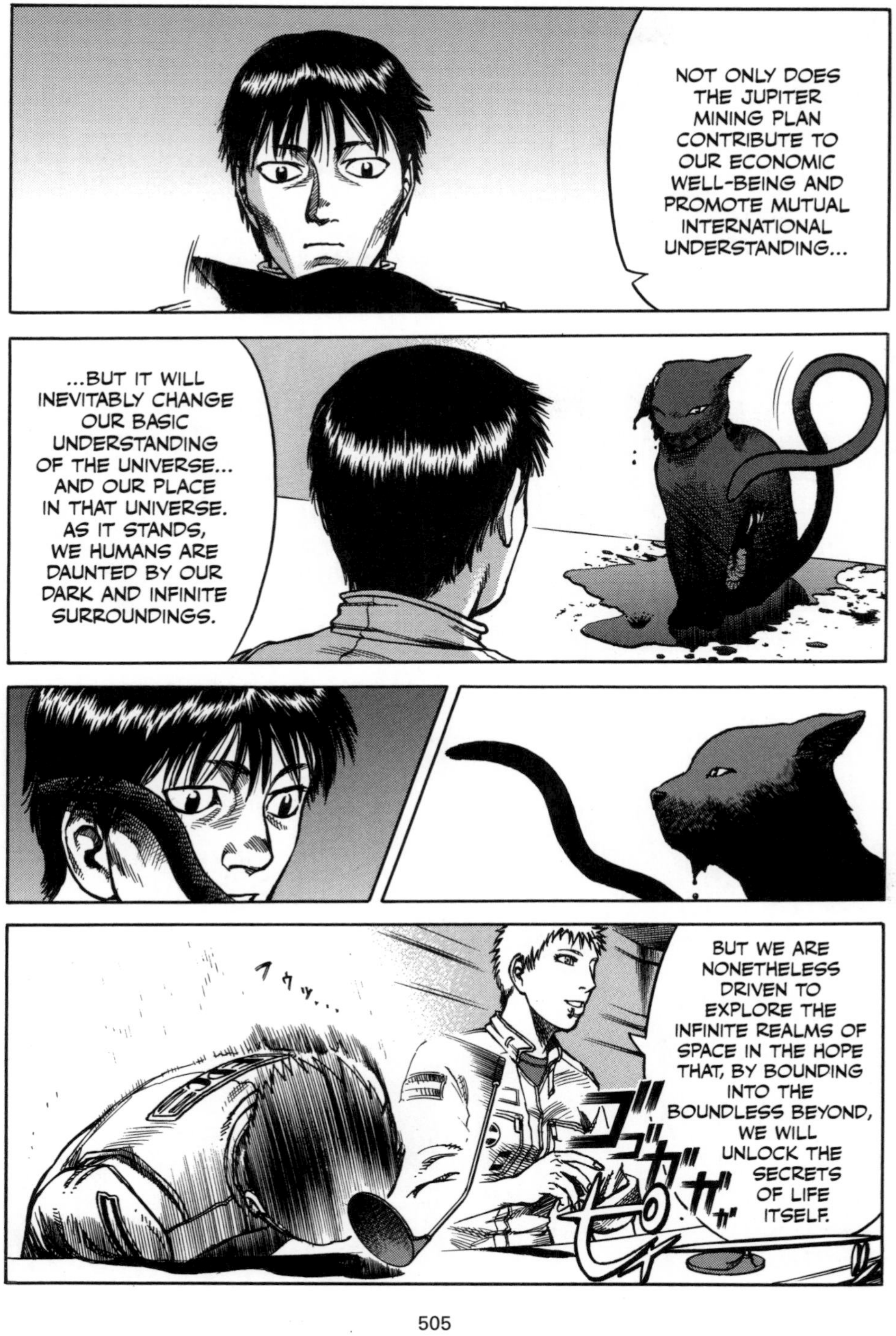
NOT ONLY DOES THE JUPITER MINING PLAN CONTRIBUTE TO OUR ECONOMIC WELL-BEING AND PROMOTE MUTUAL INTERNATIONAL UNDERSTANDING...
...BUT IT WILL INEVITABLY CHANGE OUR BASIC UNDERSTANDING OF THE UNIVERSE... AND OUR PLACE IN THAT UNIVERSE. AS IT STANDS, WE HUMANS ARE DAUNTED BY OUR DARK AND INFINITE SURROUNDINGS.
BUT WE ARE NONETHELESS DRIVEN TO EXPLORE THE INFINITE REALMS OF SPACE IN THE HOPE THAT, BY BOUNDING INTO THE BOUNDLESS BEYOND, WE WILL UNLOCK THE SECRETS OF LIFE ITSELF.

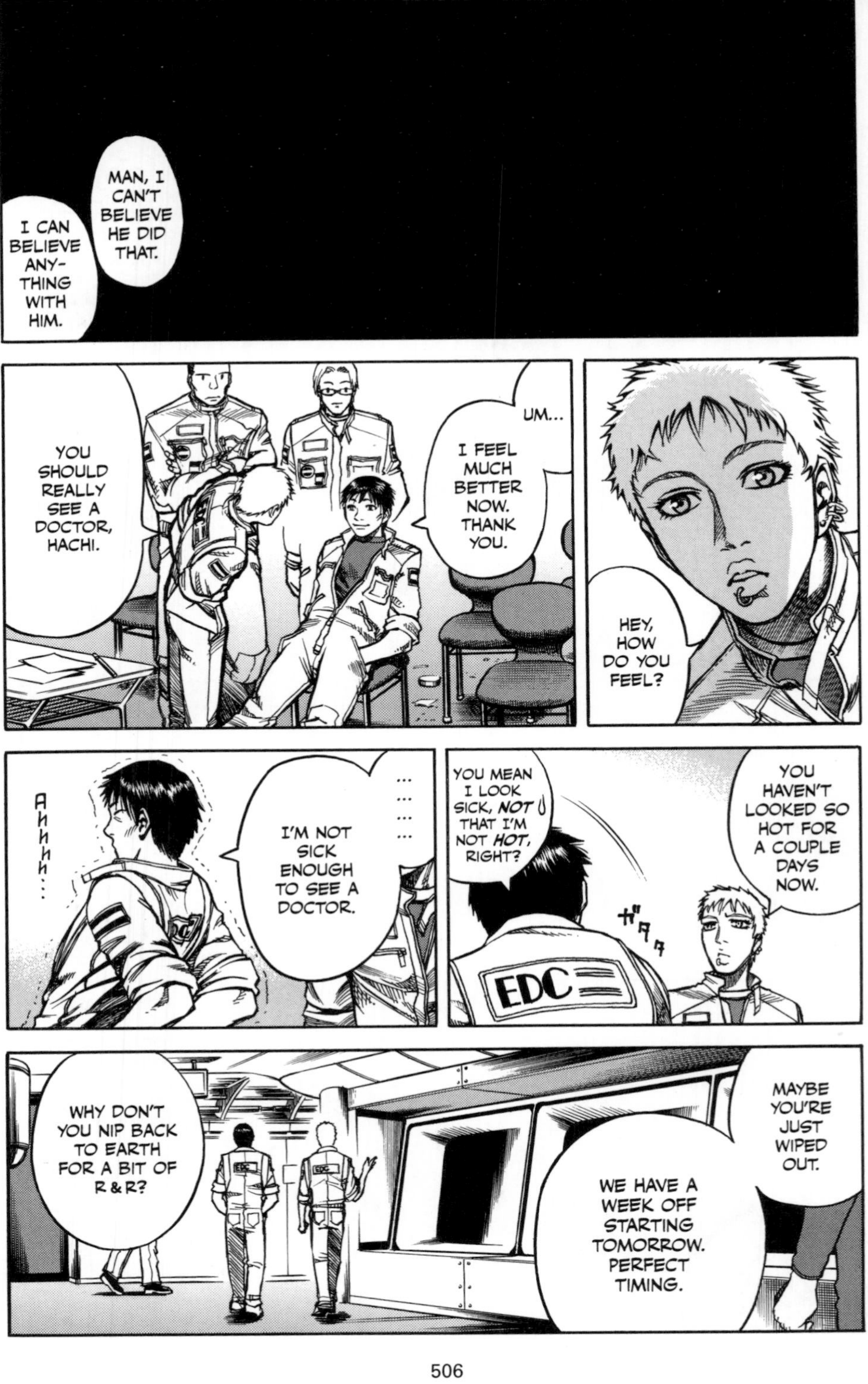
MAN, I CAN'T BELIEVE HE DID THAT.
I CAN BELIEVE ANYTHING WITH HIM.
HEY, HOW DO YOU FEEL?
UM...
I FEEL MUCH BETTER NOW. THANK YOU.
YOU SHOULD REALLY SEE A DOCTOR, HACHI.
YOU HAVEN'T LOOKED SO HOT FOR A COUPLE DAYS NOW.
YOU MEAN I LOOK SICK, *NOT* THAT I'M NOT *HOT*, RIGHT?
....
I'M NOT SICK ENOUGH TO SEE A DOCTOR.
Ahhhh...
MAYBE YOU'RE JUST WIPED OUT.
WE HAVE A WEEK OFF STARTING TOMORROW. PERFECT TIMING.
WHY DON'T YOU NIP BACK TO EARTH FOR A BIT OF R & R?

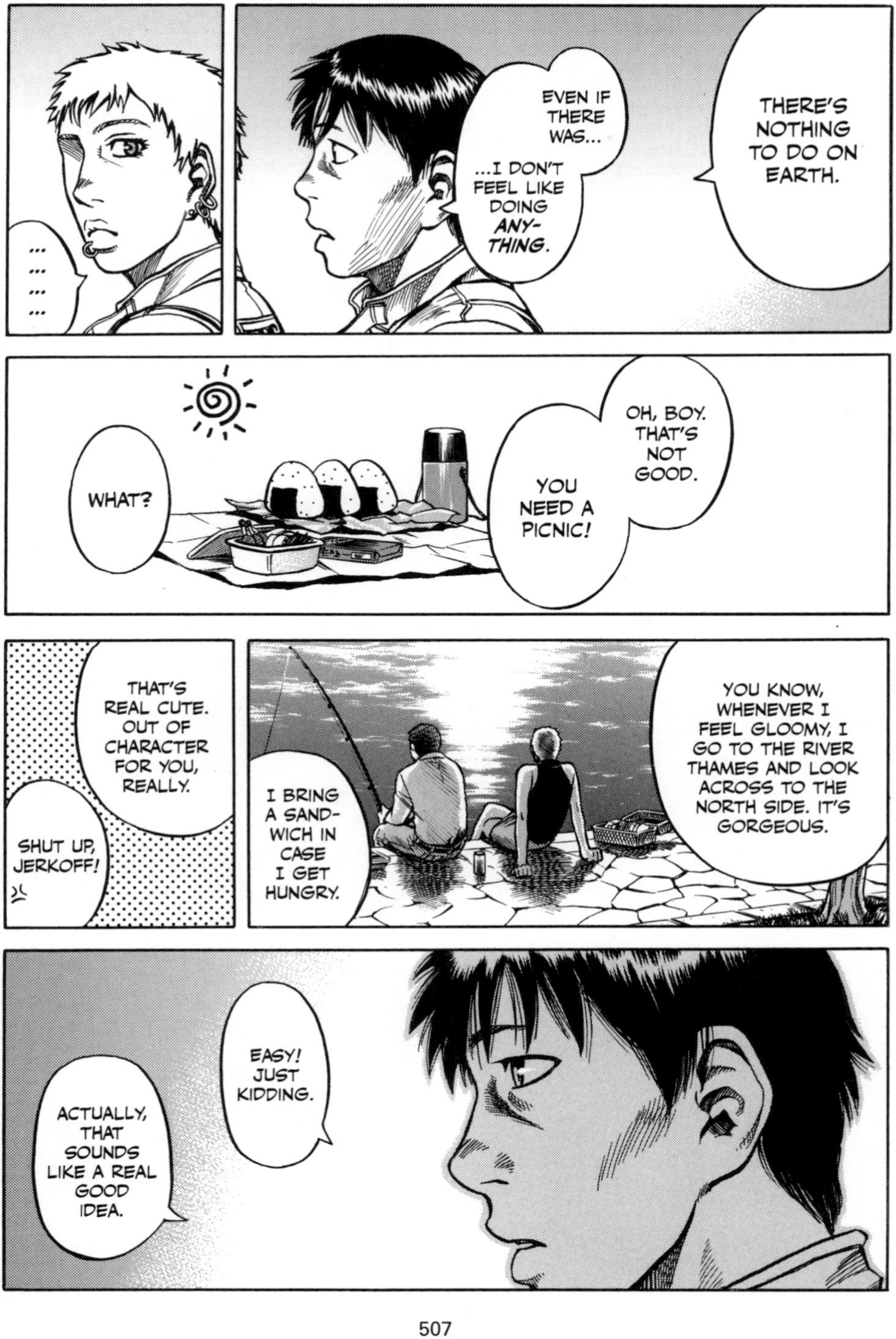
THERE'S NOTHING TO DO ON EARTH.
EVEN IF THERE WAS...
...I DON'T FEEL LIKE DOING *ANYTHING*.
... ...
OH, BOY. THAT'S NOT GOOD.
YOU NEED A PICNIC!
WHAT?
YOU KNOW, WHENEVER I FEEL GLOOMY, I GO TO THE RIVER THAMES AND LOOK ACROSS TO THE NORTH SIDE. IT'S GORGEOUS.
I BRING A SANDWICH IN CASE I GET HUNGRY.
THAT'S REAL CUTE. OUT OF CHARACTER FOR YOU, REALLY.
SHUT UP, JERKOFF!
EASY! JUST KIDDING.
ACTUALLY, THAT SOUNDS LIKE A REAL GOOD IDEA.

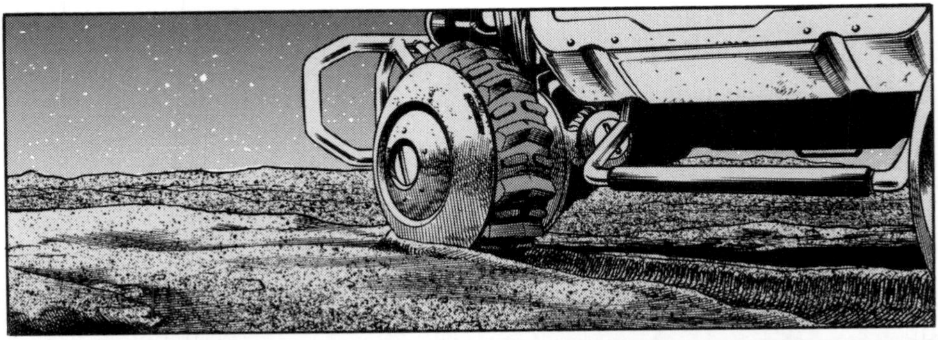
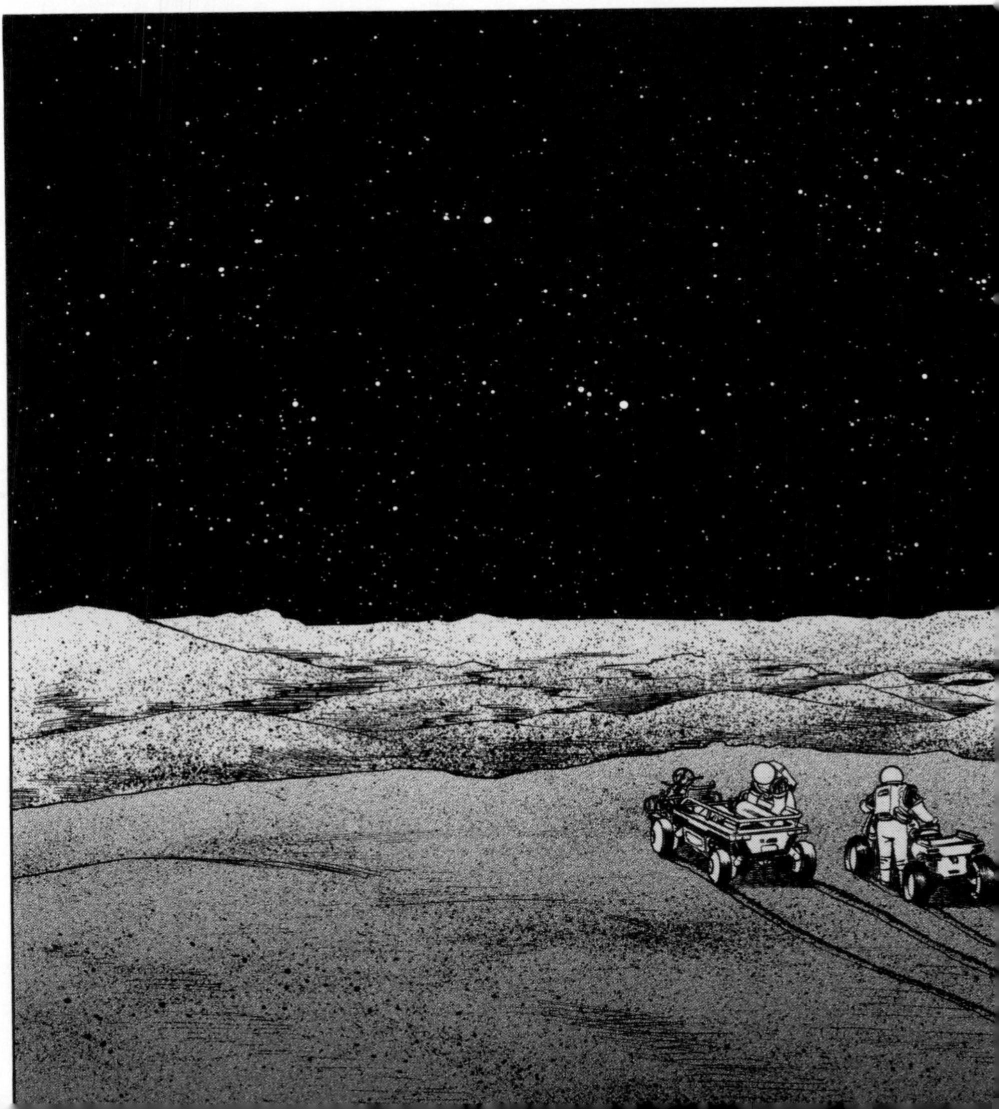

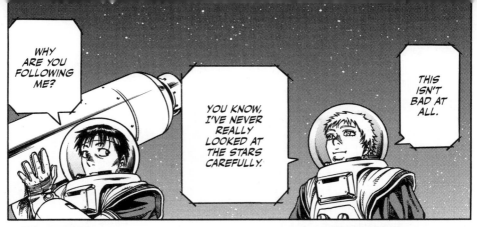

THIS ISN'T BAD AT ALL.
YOU KNOW, I'VE NEVER REALLY LOOKED AT THE STARS CAREFULLY.
WHY ARE YOU FOLLOWING ME?
BECAUSE YOU LOOK FRAGILE AND UNSTABLE.
IF SOMETHING HAPPENS TO YOU, IT'LL MEAN TROUBLE FOR ME TOO.
I MEAN-- I'D FEEL RESPONSIBLE FOR GIVING YOU THE IDEA.
DON'T WORRY ABOUT ME. IT'LL BE DARK FOR THE NEXT TEN DAYS.
イっこらせ.
IT'S NOT LIKE I'M GONNA GET A SUNBURN.
AND CHECK THIS OUT.
I ONLY HAVE ENOUGH FOOD AND WATER FOR A COUPLE DAYS, GUV. SO I'LL HAVE TO MAKE IT BACK BEFORE MY RATIONS RUN OUT.
BLIMEY.

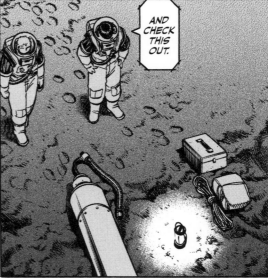

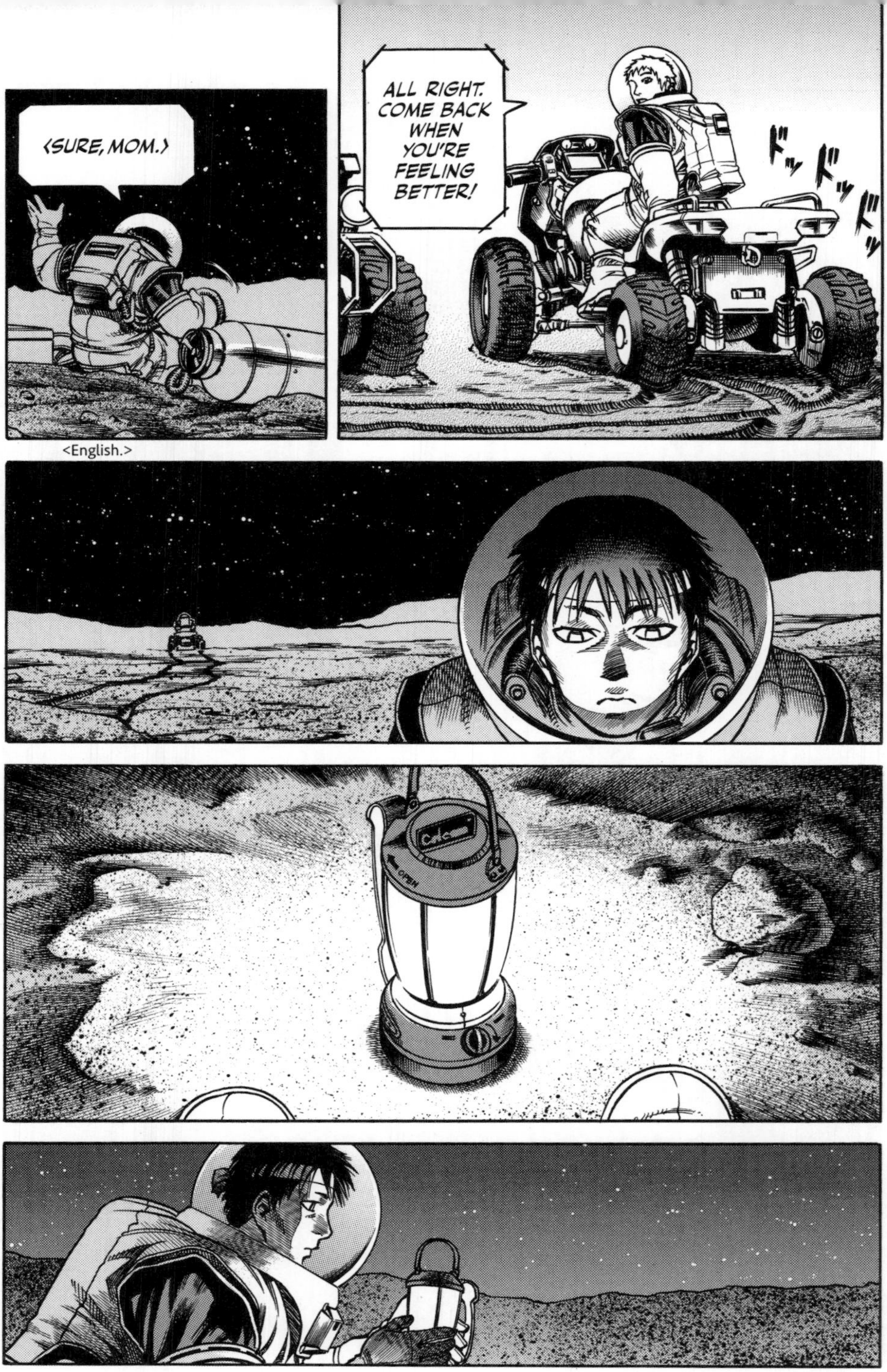
ALL RIGHT. COME BACK WHEN YOU'RE FEELING BETTER!
ドッドッドッ
<SURE, MOM.>
<English.>

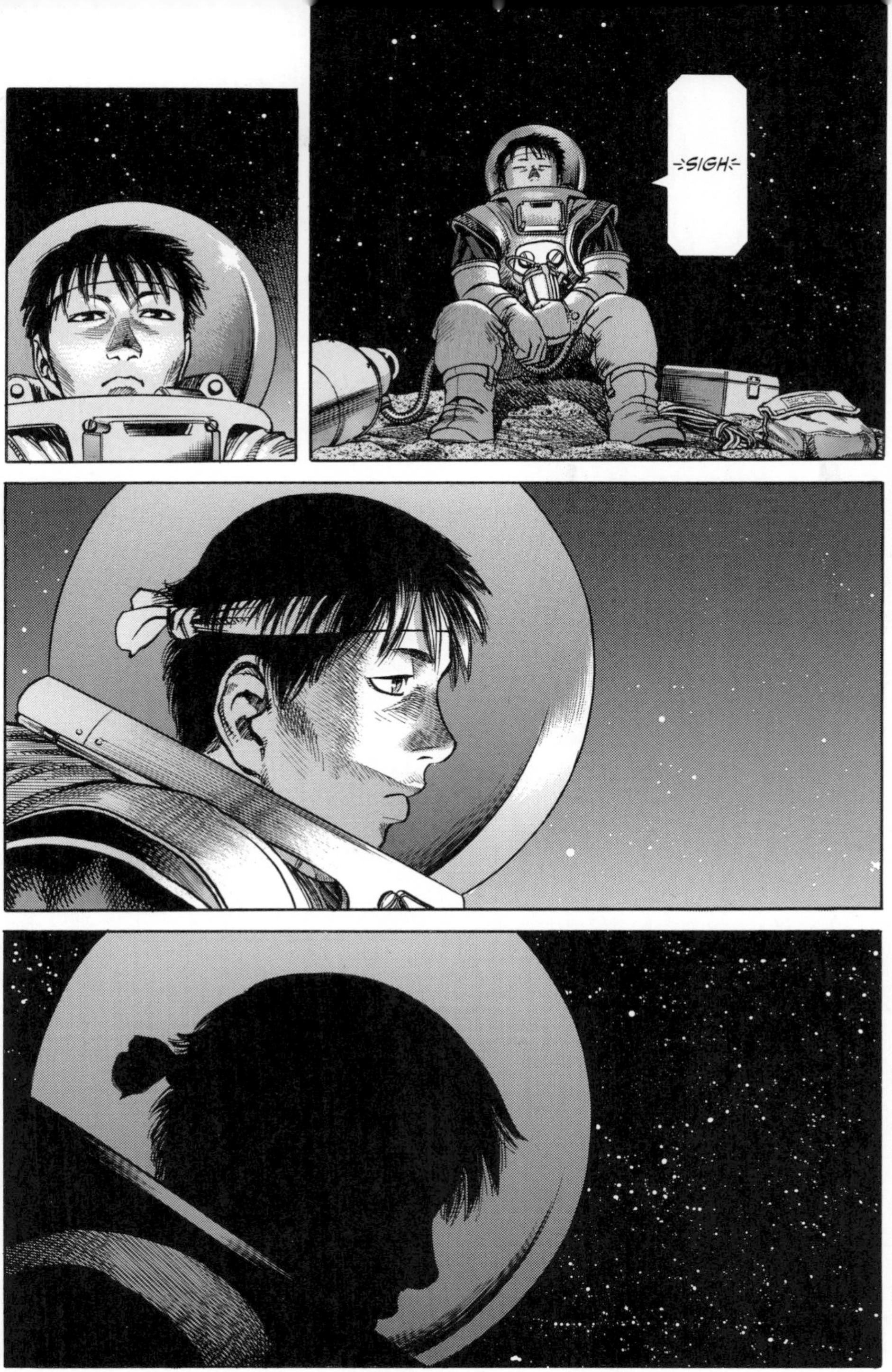
SIGH

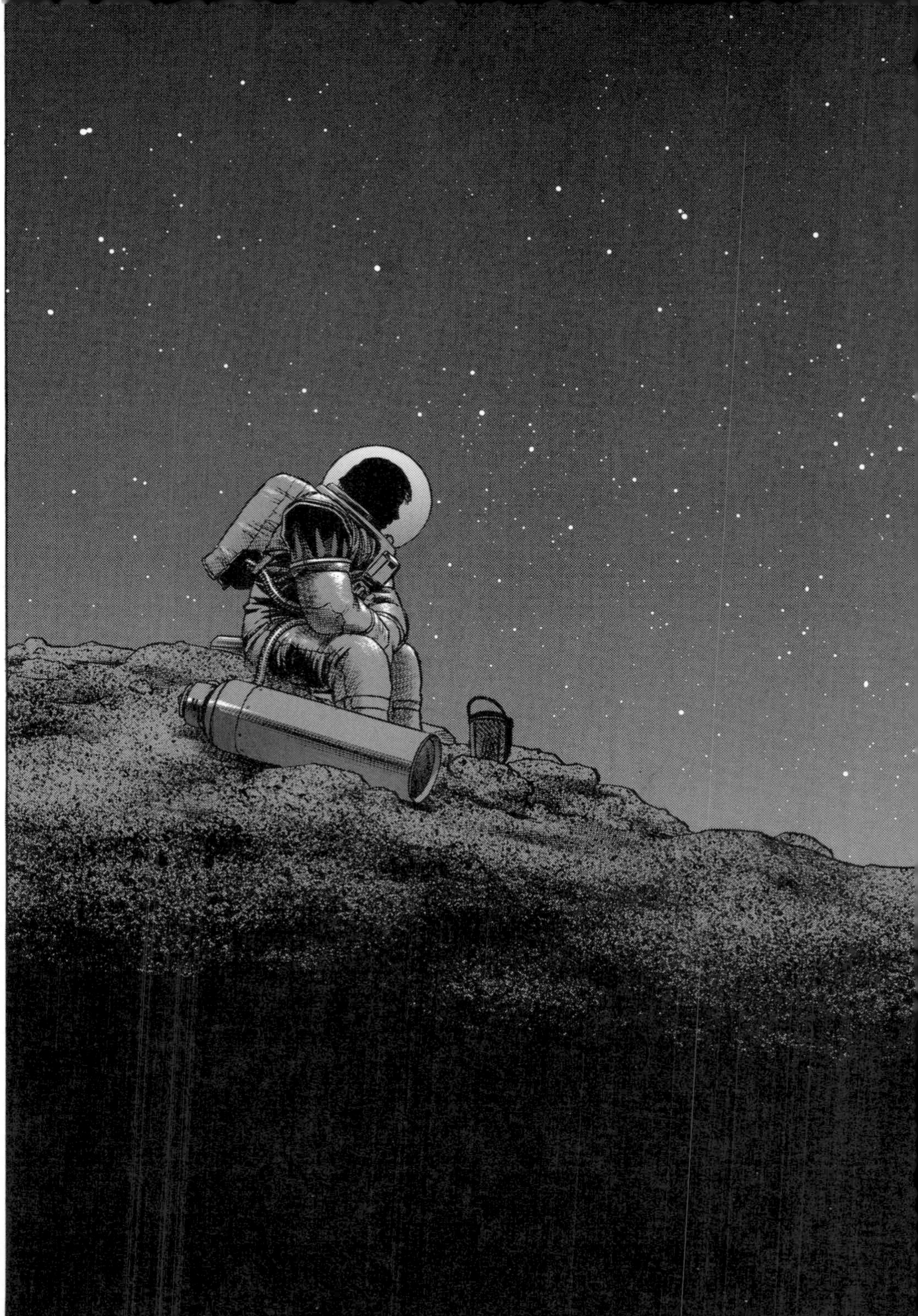

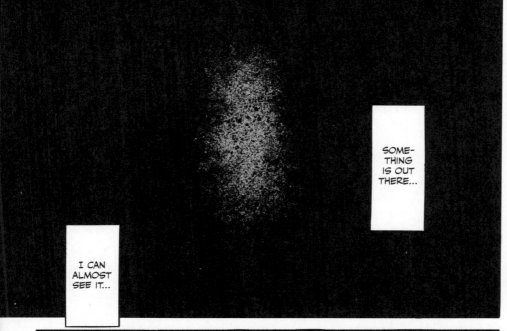

SOME-THING IS OUT THERE...
I CAN ALMOST SEE IT...
I'VE ALWAYS LOOKED OUT AT THE WORLD, SO I'VE NEVER SEEN *THIS* BEFORE...
BUT IN THE DARK-NESS...
...AT THE BOTTOM OF MY HEART...
...HE'S BEEN LURKING THIS WHOLE TIME...

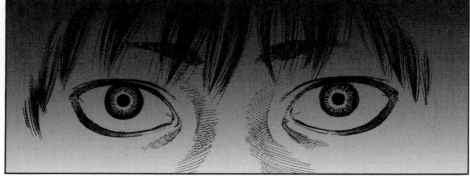

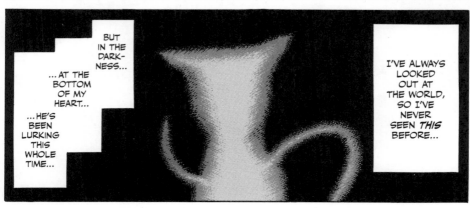

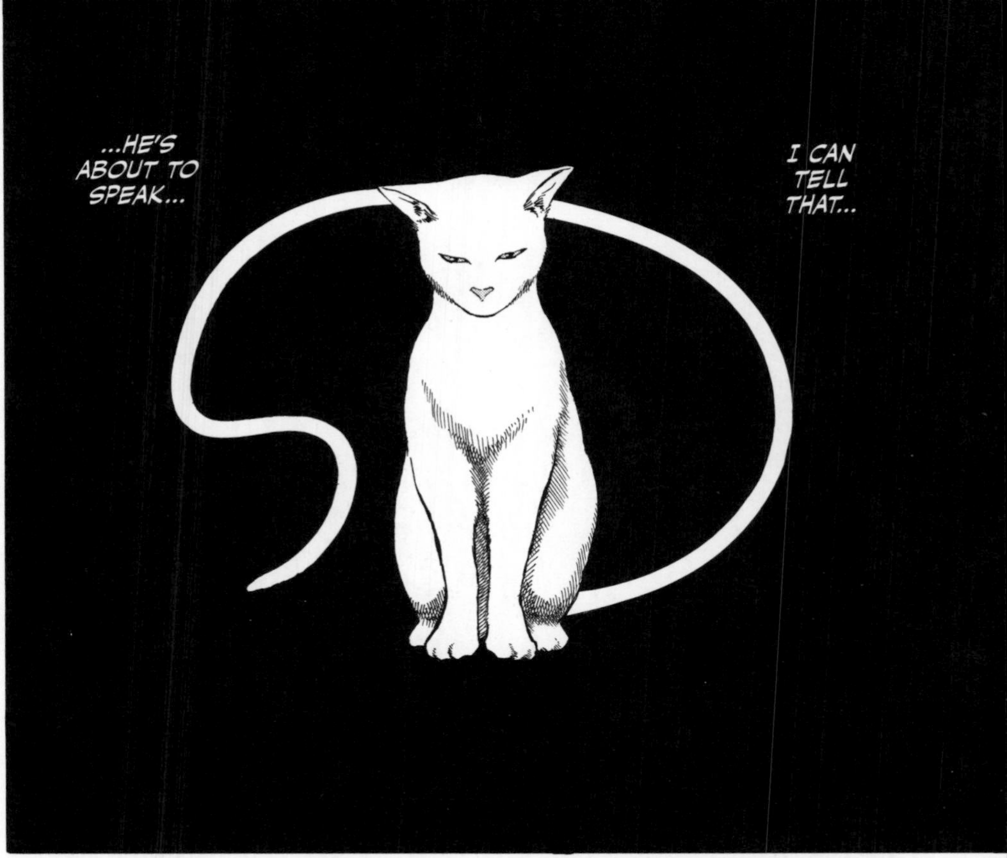
I CAN TELL THAT...
...HE'S ABOUT TO SPEAK...

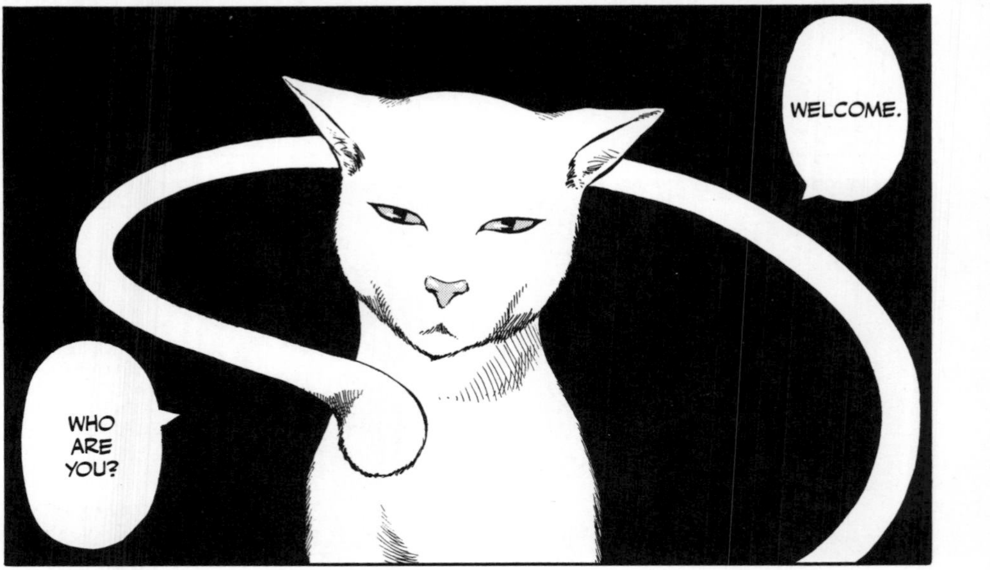
WELCOME.
WHO ARE YOU?

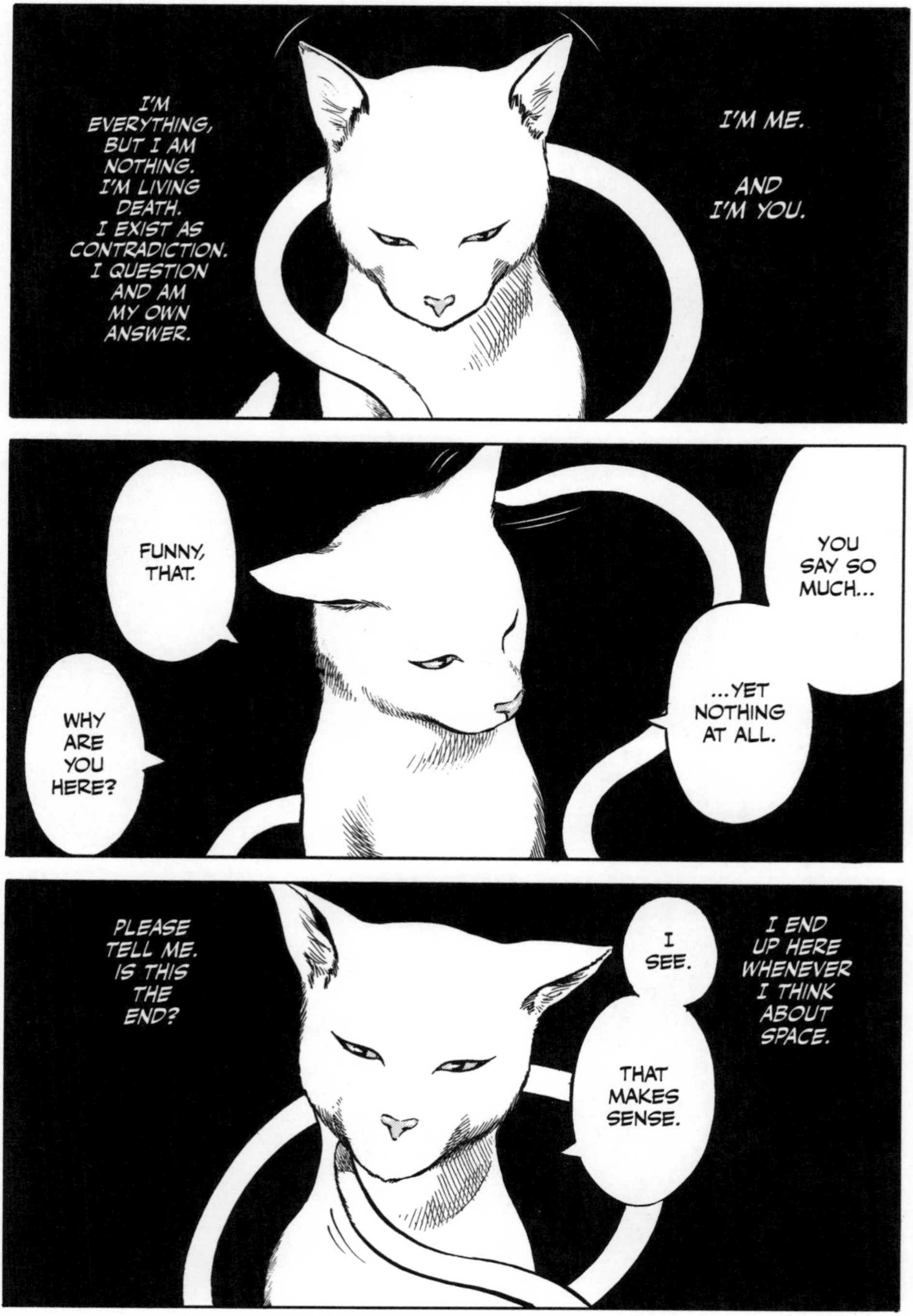
I'M ME.
AND I'M YOU.
I'M EVERYTHING, BUT I AM NOTHING. I'M LIVING DEATH. I EXIST AS CONTRADICTION. I QUESTION AND AM MY OWN ANSWER.
YOU SAY SO MUCH...
...YET NOTHING AT ALL.
FUNNY, THAT.
WHY ARE YOU HERE?
I END UP HERE WHENEVER I THINK ABOUT SPACE.
I SEE.
THAT MAKES SENSE.
PLEASE TELL ME. IS THIS THE END?

IT CAN BE.
YOU WANT IT TO END...
...BUT WHERE DID IT START?
I DON'T KNOW...
OKAY.
PERHAPS IT'S A CIRCLE.
NO BEGINNING... NO END.
SO I JUST HAVE TO GO ROUND AND ROUND...
FOREVER?
YOU DON'T *HAVE* TO DO ANYTHING.
WHY DON'T YOU GO HOME NOW?
IF YOU STAY HERE TOO LONG, YOU'LL NEVER MAKE IT BACK.

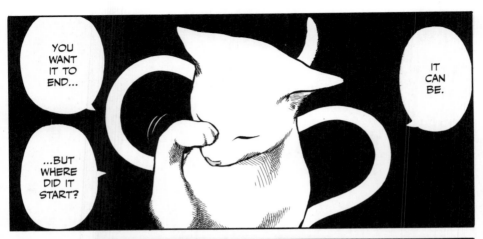

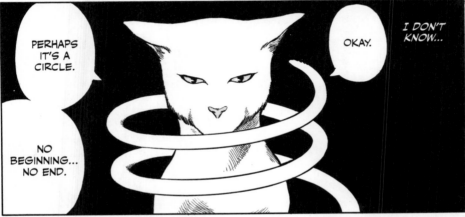

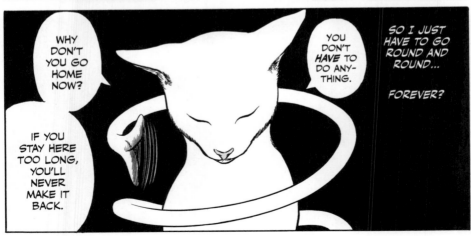

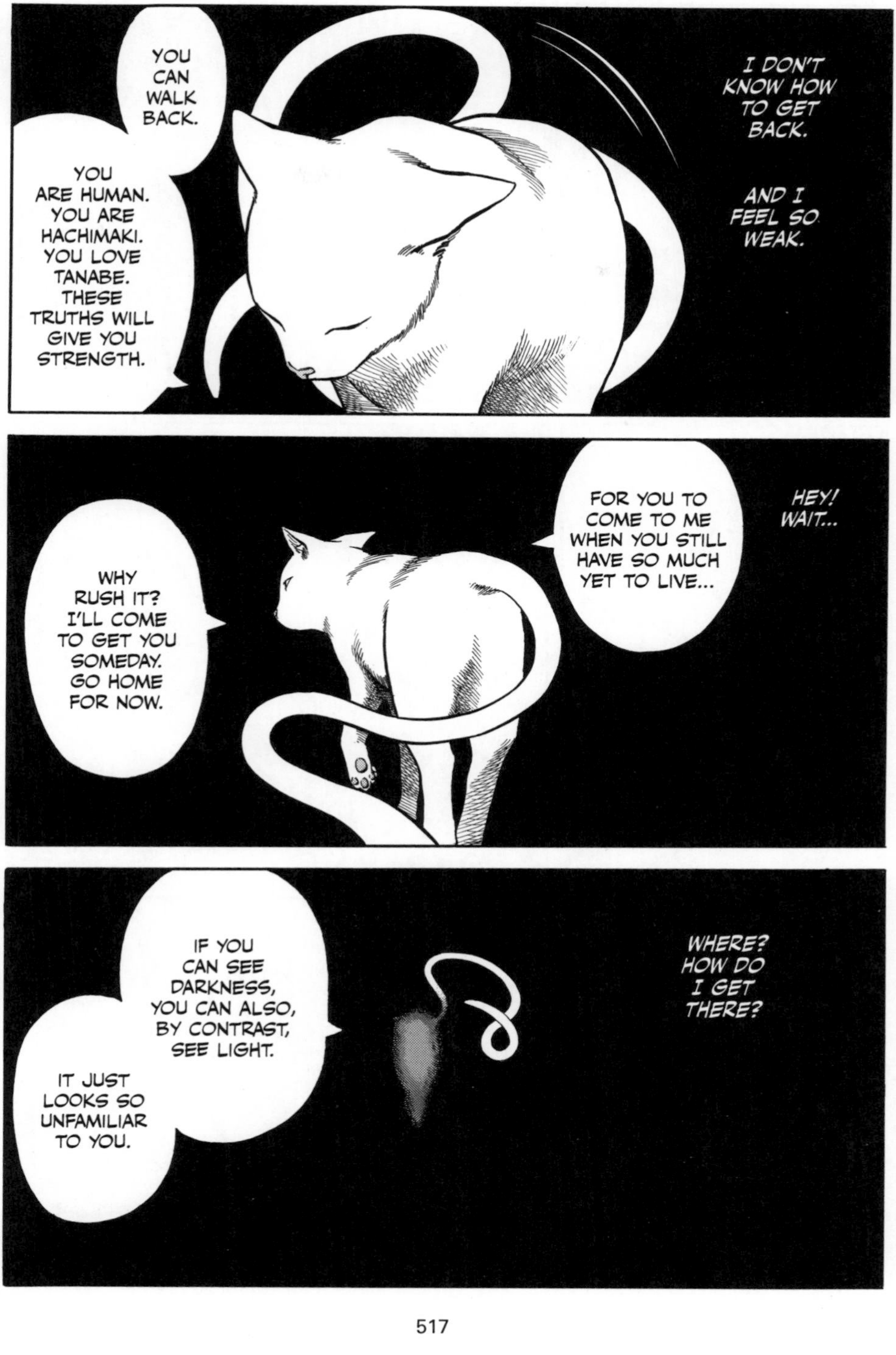
I DON'T KNOW HOW TO GET BACK.
AND I FEEL SO WEAK.
YOU CAN WALK BACK.
YOU ARE HUMAN. YOU ARE HACHIMAKI. YOU LOVE TANABE. THESE TRUTHS WILL GIVE YOU STRENGTH.
HEY! WAIT...
FOR YOU TO COME TO ME WHEN YOU STILL HAVE SO MUCH YET TO LIVE...
WHY RUSH IT? I'LL COME TO GET YOU SOMEDAY. GO HOME FOR NOW.
WHERE? HOW DO I GET THERE?
IF YOU CAN SEE DARKNESS, YOU CAN ALSO, BY CONTRAST, SEE LIGHT.
IT JUST LOOKS SO UNFAMILIAR TO YOU.

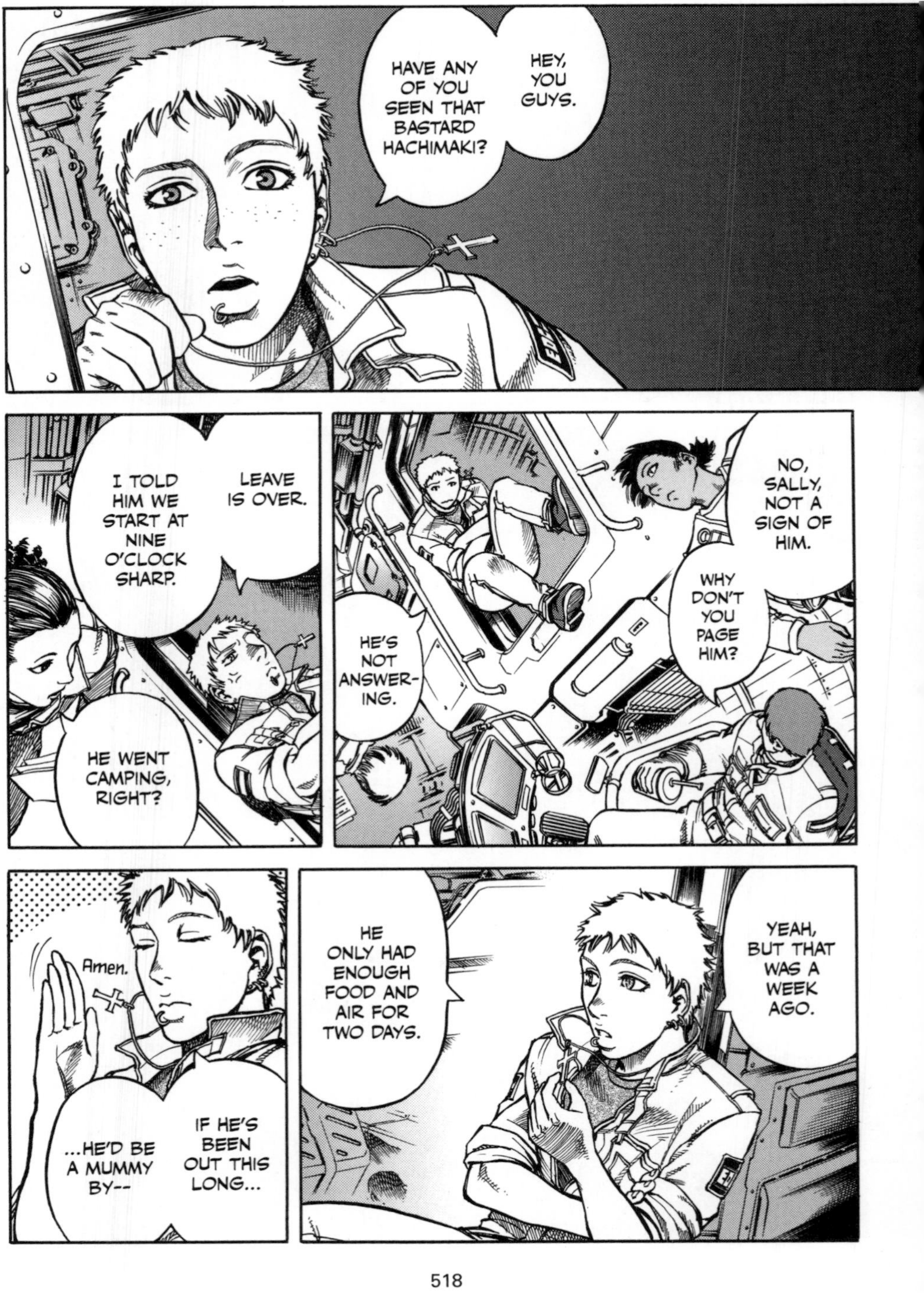
HEY, YOU GUYS.
HAVE ANY OF YOU SEEN THAT BASTARD HACHIMAKI?
NO, SALLY, NOT A SIGN OF HIM.
WHY DON'T YOU PAGE HIM?
HE'S NOT ANSWER-ING.
LEAVE IS OVER.
I TOLD HIM WE START AT NINE O'CLOCK SHARP.
HE WENT CAMPING, RIGHT?
YEAH, BUT THAT WAS A WEEK AGO.
HE ONLY HAD ENOUGH FOOD AND AIR FOR TWO DAYS.
IF HE'S BEEN OUT THIS LONG...
...HE'D BE A MUMMY BY--
Amen.

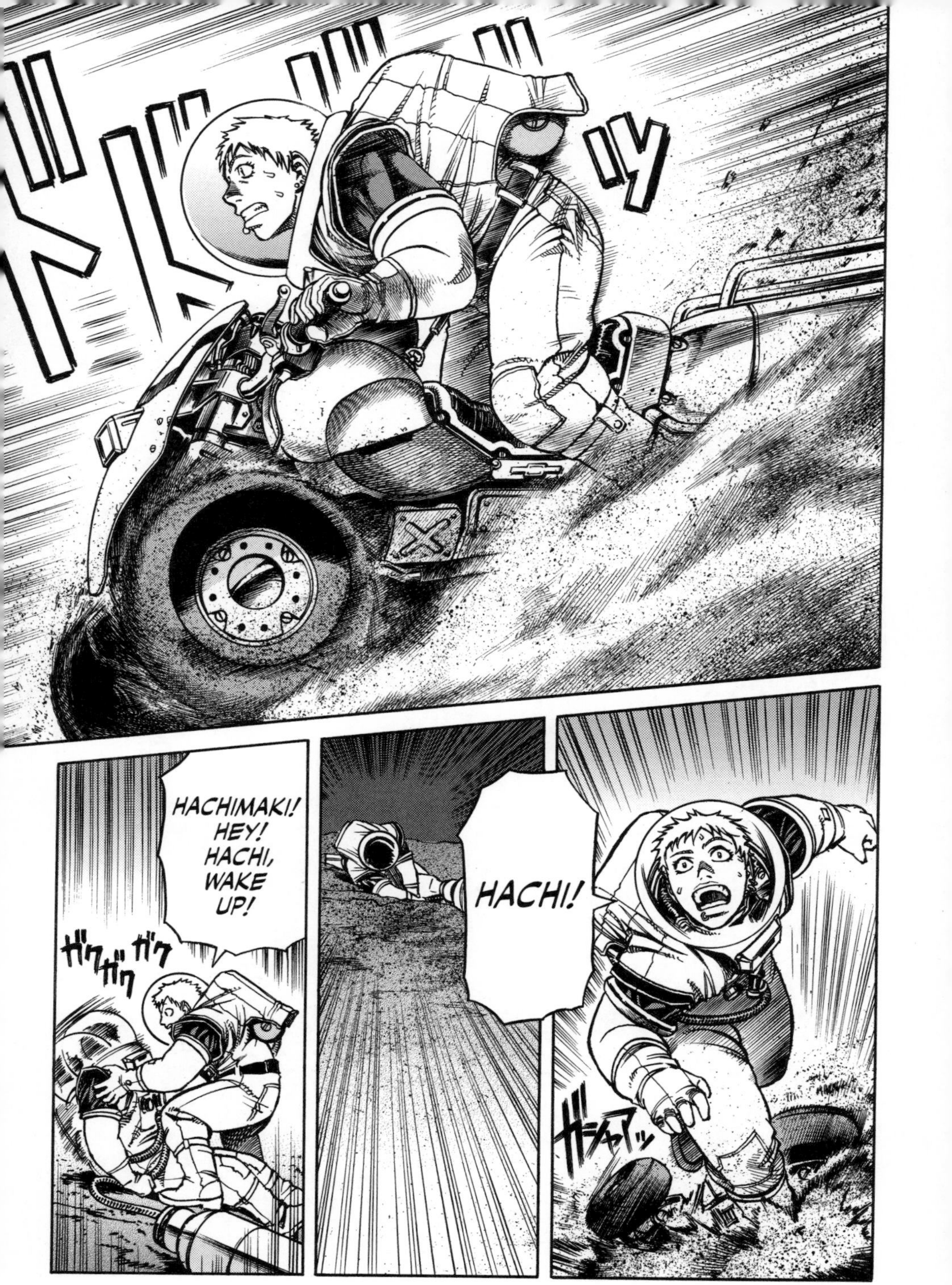
HACHI!
ガシャアッ
HACHIMAKI! HEY! HACHI, WAKE UP!
ガクガクガク

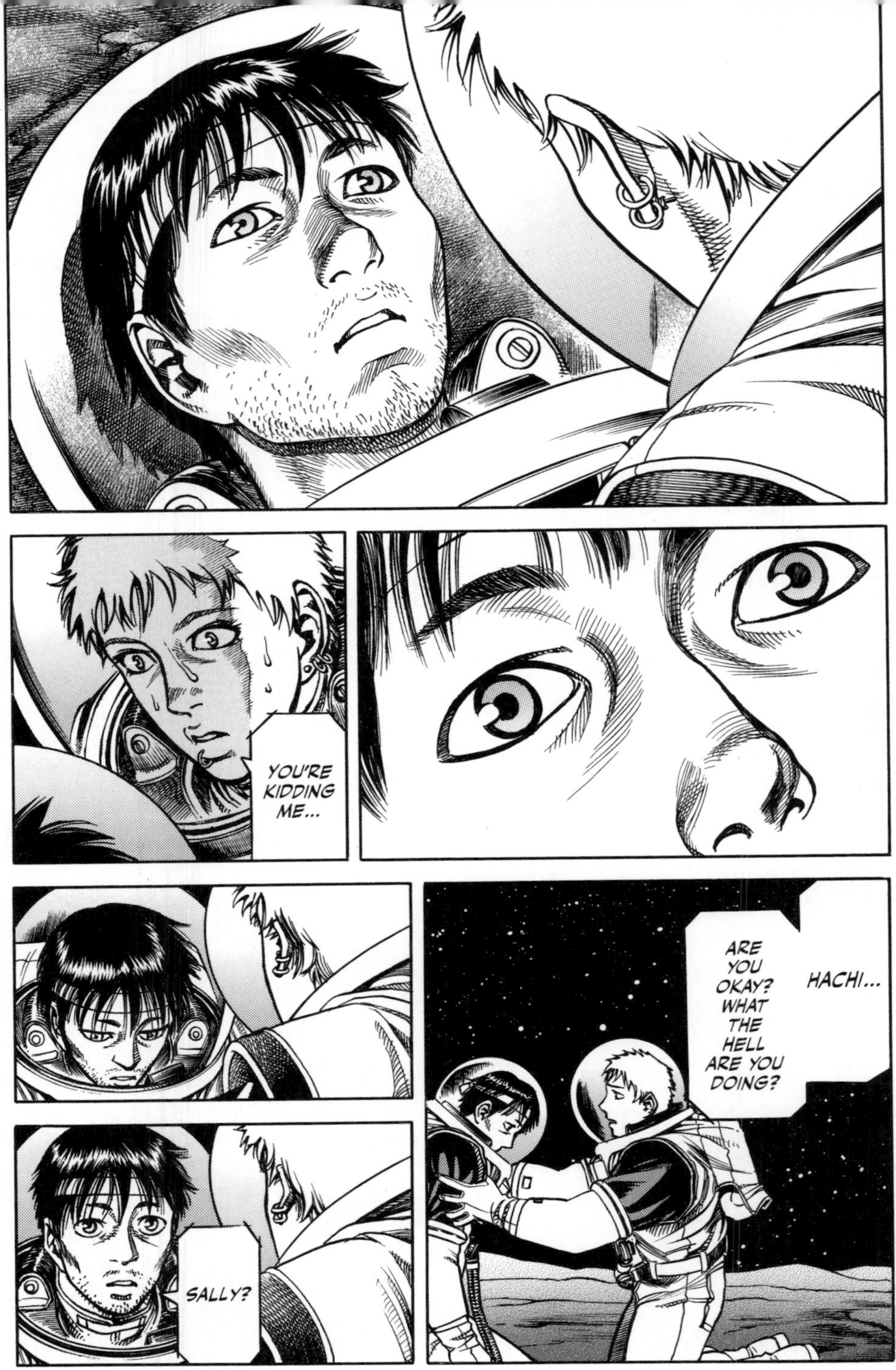
YOU'RE KIDDING ME...
HACHI...
ARE YOU OKAY? WHAT THE HELL ARE YOU DOING?
SALLY?

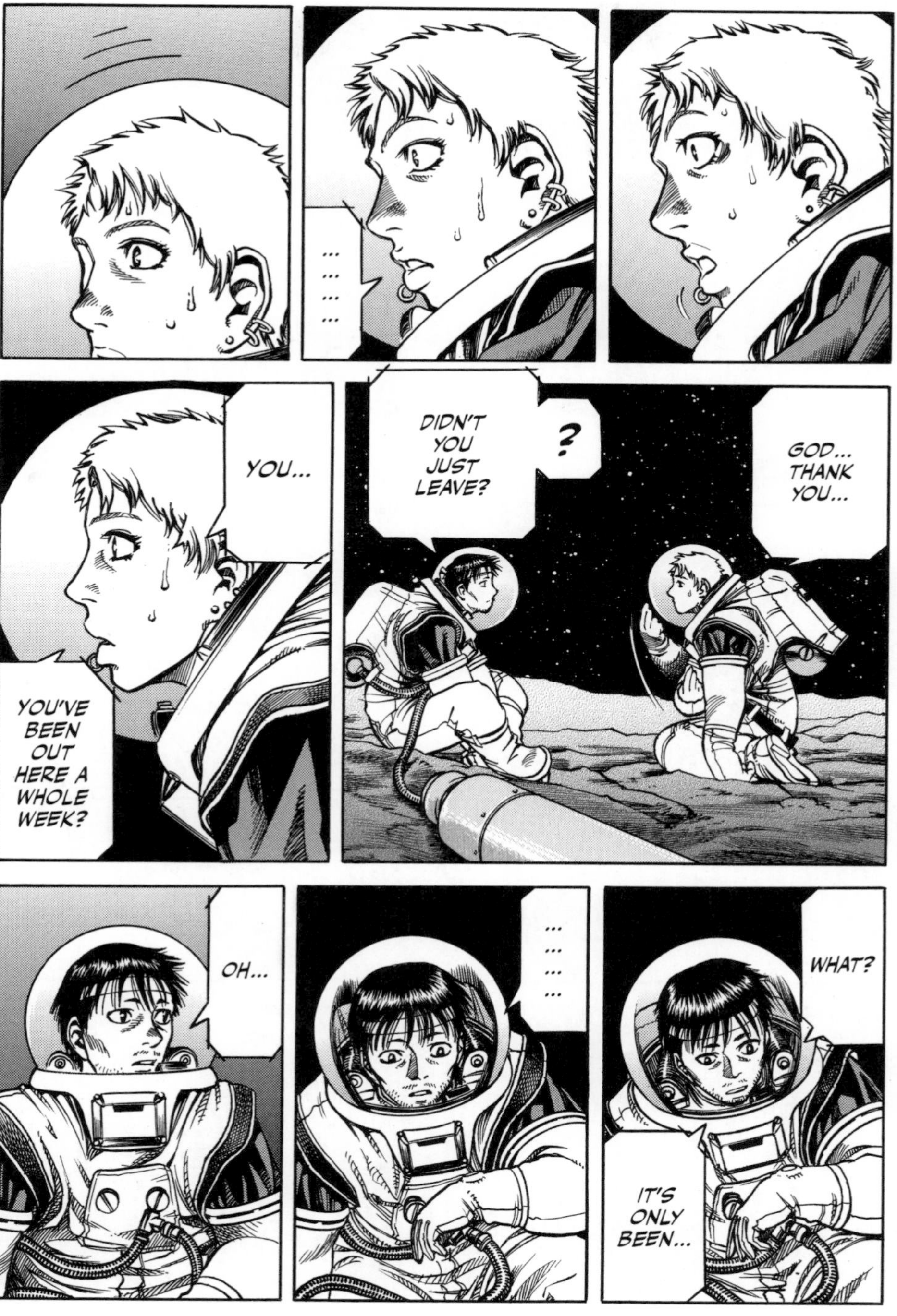
... ...
GOD... THANK YOU...
?
DIDN'T YOU JUST LEAVE?
YOU...
YOU'VE BEEN OUT HERE A WHOLE WEEK?
WHAT?
IT'S ONLY BEEN...
... ...
OH...

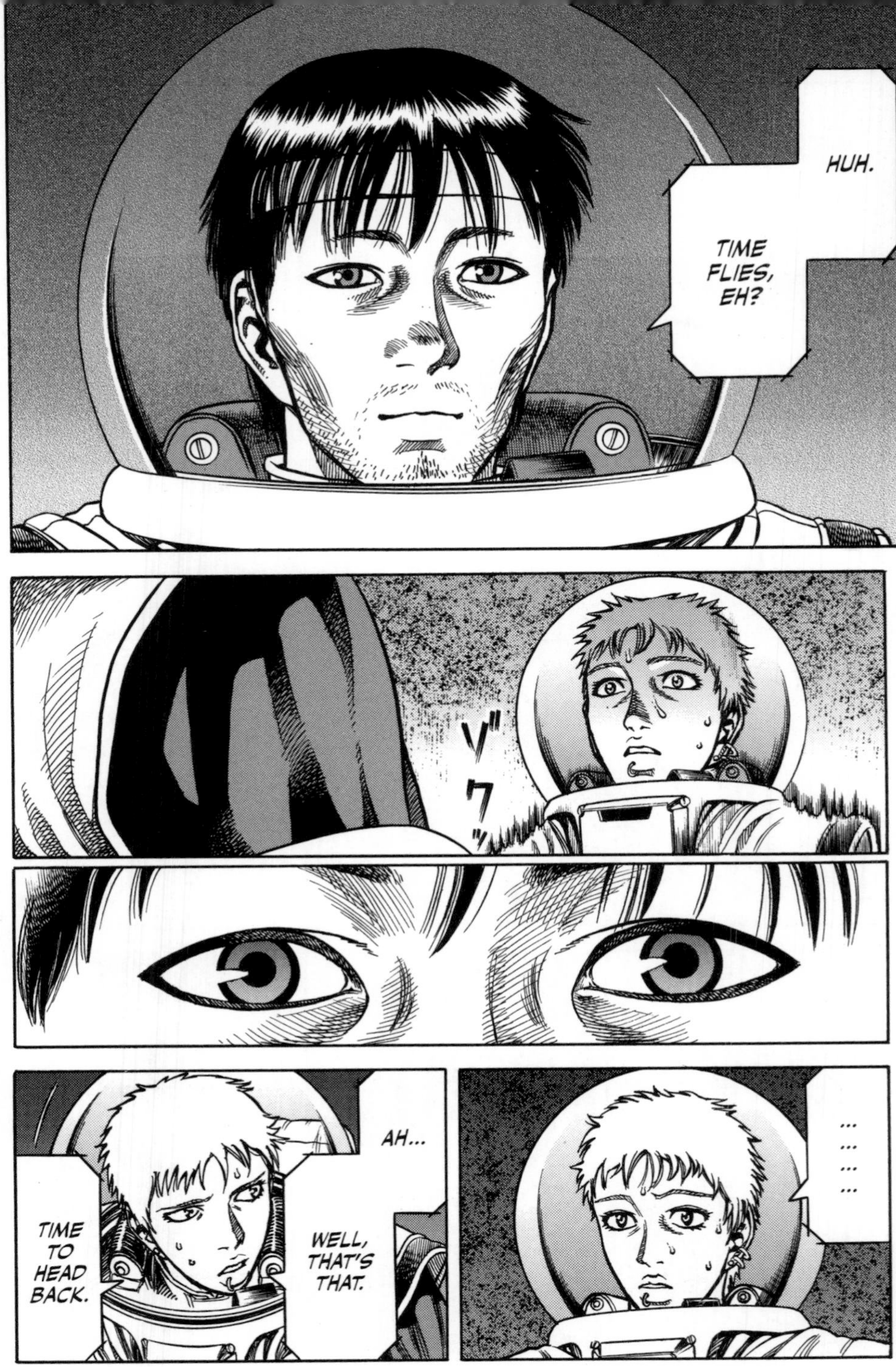
HUH.
TIME FLIES, EH?
ゾクッ
...
...
...
...
AH...
WELL, THAT'S THAT.
TIME TO HEAD BACK.

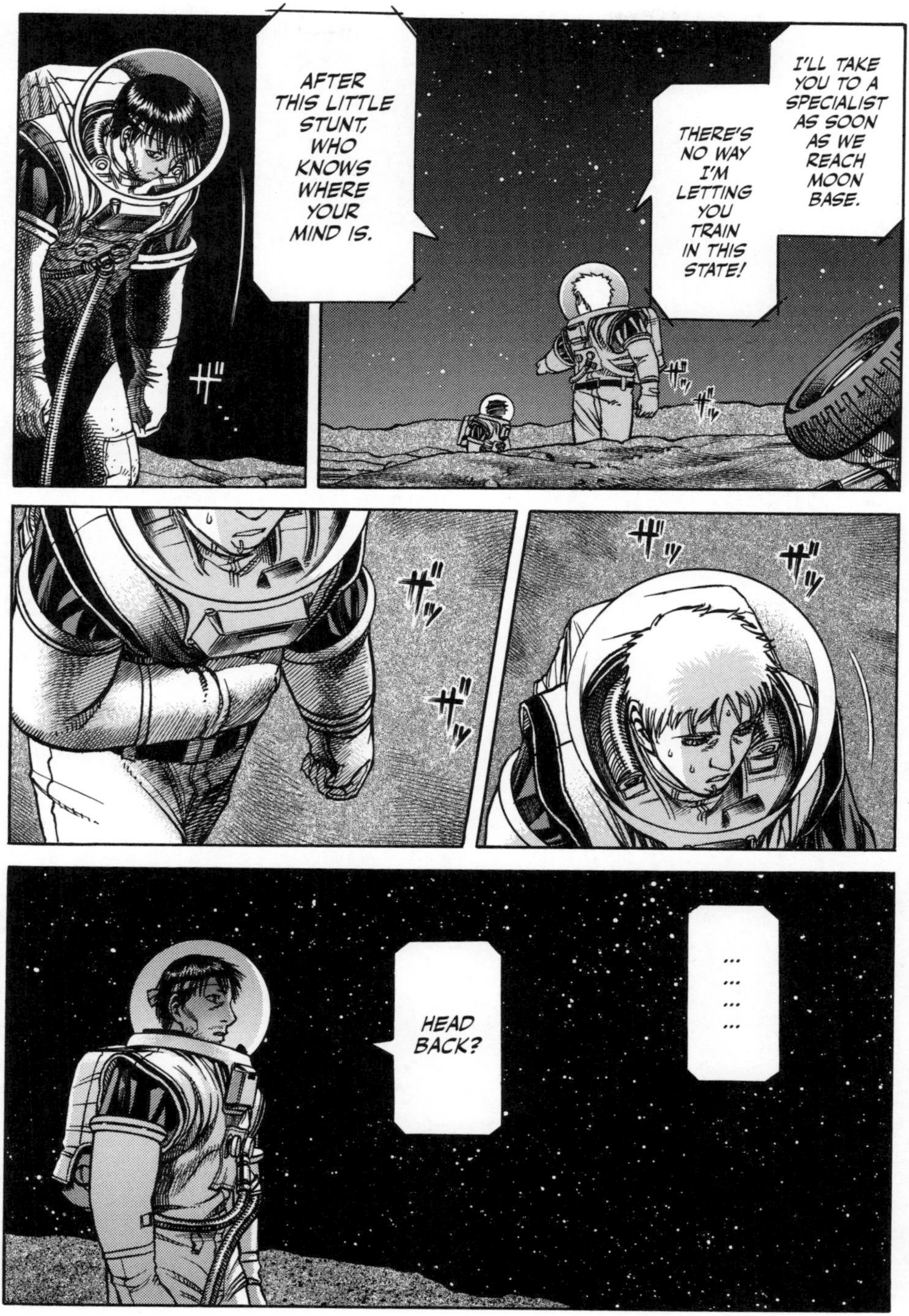
I'LL TAKE YOU TO A SPECIALIST AS SOON AS WE REACH MOON BASE.
THERE'S NO WAY I'M LETTING YOU TRAIN IN THIS STATE!
AFTER THIS LITTLE STUNT, WHO KNOWS WHERE YOUR MIND IS.
ザッ
ザッ
ザッ
ザッ
ザッ
ザッ
...
...
...
...
HEAD BACK?

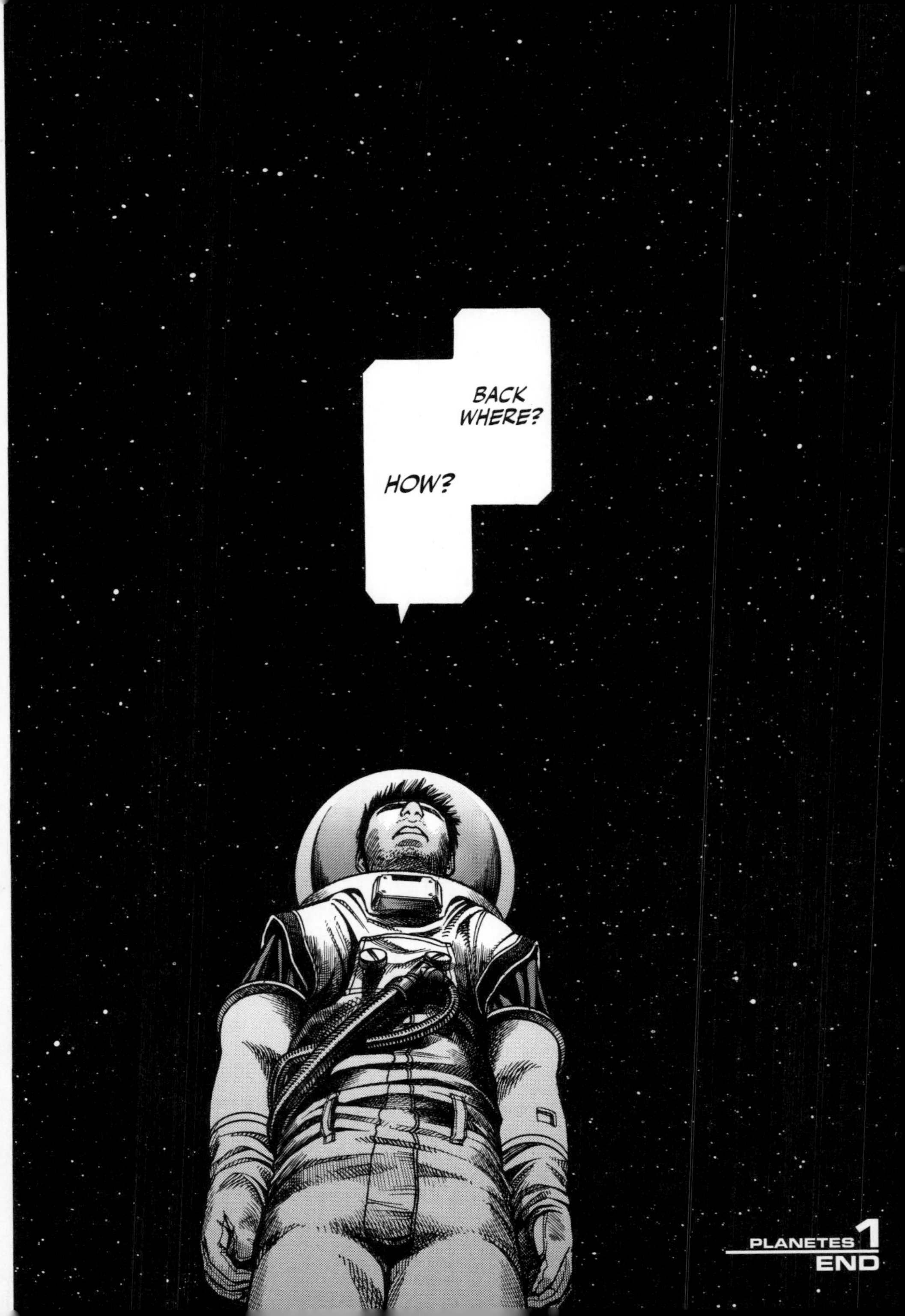
BACK WHERE?
HOW?

PLANETES 1
END